PIONEER OHIO NEWSPAPERS
1793 - 1810

Genealogical and Historical Abstracts

By Karen Mauer Green

The Frontier Press, Galveston, 1986

Copyright © 1986
Karen Mauer Green

All Rights Reserved

Second Printing 1989

Library of Congress Catalogue Card Number 86-80238
International Standard Book Number 0-932231-03-9

The Frontier Press
15 Quintana Drive
Galveston, Texas 77551

Dedicated to the memory of my grandmother,
Hazel Reay Webb Draper
1907-1985

PREFACE

These genealogical and historical abstracts of some of the earliest newspapers published in the newly settled Northwest Territory chronicle the development of the area from frontier settlement into statehood. The newspapers of a pioneer area were an extremely important part of everyday life since they tied the settlers to the world they left behind and provided a means of communication in the widely scattered settlements. For historians looking back on the period of 1793-1810, the first newspapers are a remarkable record of the people and events of the earliest beginnings of Ohio. For genealogists studying the period, they provide information on early Ohio families that simply can't be obtained in any other source. These abstracts are an attempt to make this information readily available to the many researchers studying early Ohio.

Contained within these pages are abstracts of five of the earliest Ohio newspapers. The "Centinel of the North-Western Territory" was the first newspaper published in the Territory, under the editorship of William Maxwell, from 1793 through 1796, at Cincinnati. Samuel and Edmund Freeman continued serving the area, by publishing their "Freeman's Journal", until 1800. The "Western Spy and Hamilton Gazette" was established in Cincinnati in May of 1799 by Joseph Carpenter who later took Jonathan S. Findlay as his partner. They published the paper until David L. Carney took over in July of 1806 and then George Williamson in 1809. The "Western Spy" was again published by Joseph Carpenter in September of 1810. Edmund Freeman moved his paper to Chillicothe in July of 1800 and called the new weekly "Freeman's Journal and Chillicothe Advertiser". Illness forced him to sell the paper in October of 1800, however, and the new owners, Winn Winship & Nathaniel Willis, renamed the paper the "Scioto Gazette and Chillicothe Advertiser". The paper was sold to Joseph S. Collins & Company in December of 1805, with Peter Parcels acting as editor from 1805 through 1809.

Every attempt has been made to locate missing issues of these newspapers, but unfortunately there are many odd issues missing. There is one long period of missing issues of the Western Spy that deserves mention. Issues from August of 1808 through April of 1809 could not be located and publication of the paper was suspended from April of 1809 through August of 1810.

These newspapers are all on microfilm and are held by the collections of many libraries throughout the nation. For a list of these sources, the reader should consult the book, "Newspapers in Microform: United States", which is available at the reference desk of most libraries. The microfilms can also be purchased from the Cincinnati Historical Society, the Ohio Historical Society and the Western Reserve Historical Society.

I would like to thank several people who were instrumental in the production of this book. Many thanks to Laura Chase at the Cincinnati Historical Society, Gary Arnold at the Ohio Historical Society, and John Grabowski at the Western Reserve Historical Society for patiently answering my questions and for their help in obtaining microfilmed copies of the newspapers. And a special thank you to my friend, Ann Hughes, whose instruction and suggestions were indispensable in the ultimate production of this book, and whose friendship and encouragement is always enjoyed and appreciated.

Finally, I thank my husband, Allan Green, who has now suffered through the production of my third book with greatly appreciated patience and encouragement. And thanks to our infant daughter, Sarah Denise Green, who managed to take just enough naps for her mother to complete this book.

Karen Mauer Green
Galveston, Texas
April, 1986

FOR YOUR INFORMATION:

In order to make the most effective use of this book, the reader is advised to take a few minutes to read these important notes.

As I abstracted these early Ohio newspapers, I used certain guidelines to determine what information to include. Every mention of a local person was abstracted, since the reference could be useful historically if not genealogically, but world and national news was only abstracted if it mentioned an Ohioan or former Ohioan. I did abstract articles from the newly formed settlements in Indiana, Illinois, Missouri, Mississippi, Louisiana and Michigan, however, since these news items so often pertained to Ohioans who had continued their migrations. I also included every mention of the Kentuckians right across the Ohio River in settlements such as Limestone and Newport. A frequent news item during this period was a report on the proceedings of the Ohio Legislature. I did not abstract the names of the legislators since that information can be easily obtained from the records of the Ohio House and Senate, but I did abstract any mention of other persons, societies and places in the proceedings. I also included whatever election returns were printed in the papers and you will find your legislators there.

I abstracted and noted only the first appearance of an ad or letter or article. Often it would be repeated several times in subsequent issues, but only the initial entry is indexed here.

The numbering of the issues has been left as it was in the original, and this can cause some confusion as the numbering was quite often incorrect and erratic. The dates of the paper are reliable, however, and you won't go wrong by referring to the abstract by the date of the newspaper.

I purposely kept the spelling as it was in the original. This has resulted in many variant spellings of even common names and care should be exercised in the use of the index. For example, the name "Farris" also appears as "Phares", "Adair" as "A'Dear" and "A. Dear", and "M'Henry as "Mackhenry". Placenames also suffer from this problem, and one should be careful to look, for example, under Bardstown as well as Beardstown. The editors spelled all "Mc" names with an apostrophe instead of the small "c", for example, M'Coy and M'Daniel. One should be careful to look under both "V" and "S" for a name such as Joseph Van Swearingen since it sometimes appears as Vanswearingen and sometimes as Swearingen. Where names are too faint to be read properly or where a typesetting error is suspected, I've tried to indicate it by using a slash between the possibilities, for example, Barnes/Barnet or Brafford/Bradford.

The names, placenames and subjects are all to be found in one combined index to ensure that the researcher will not miss, for example, the "Cunningham's mill" entries in a subject index by only looking for "Cunningham" in a name index. There will often be found, after the page number, a number in parentheses which indicates that the individual appears that many times on that page. I did not indicate how many times subjects and placenames appear on each page because it is very common for them to appear more than once. Thus, one should scan the entire page for subjects and placenames. I suggest that serious students of Ohio history do a quick scan of the entire index to become familiar with the type of categories indexed and the unusual names of organizations and societies that have been indexed just as they appeared in the original.

When I've listed a name after the word "mentions", I'm indicating that the entry doesn't contain genealogical or locational information. This does not mean that the descendent wouldn't find the entry interesting, however. In many cases the original ad or notice or article will contain more clues for further study. An effort was made to pull out the clues and include them in this book, but sometimes an important clue won't be recognized by someone who doesn't know the family. If at all possible, consult the original newspapers and use this book as an reference tool to help you locate the information in the original.

TABLE OF CONTENTS

The Centinel of the North-Western Territory, November 1793-June 1796	1
Freeman's Journal, July 1796-October 1799	23
The Western Spy and Hamilton Gazette, May 1799-December 1810	31
Freeman's Journal and Chillicothe Advertiser, July 1800-September 1800	178
Scioto Gazette and Chillicothe Advertiser, October 1800-December 1810	180
Index	320

THE CENTINEL OF THE NORTH-WESTERN TERRITORY

Volume I, Number 1, Saturday, 9 November 1793
William Maxwell, editor of the Centinel of the North-western Territory, writes a letter to the public introducing his newspaper.
An account of an Indian attack on 17 October 1793 on a convoy between Fort St. Clair and Fort Jefferson. Lieut. Lowrie and Ensign Boyd were killed.
An account is printed of an Indian attack on Saturday evening, 19 October 1793, on White's Station ten miles north of Cincinnati.
Army news mentions Gen. Scott.
W. Maxwell, at the printing office at the corner of Front and Sycamore Streets in Cincinnati, gives a list of persons taking subscriptions to the Centinel: John Armstrong in Columbia, Aaron Cadwell in North-Bend, Capt. John Dunlap in Colerain, and Capt. John Bartle in New-Port.
A. Adgate & Company have cards, dry goods and groceries for sale at their Card Manufactory in Pittsburg.
Job Gard lost his pocket book on the river above the North-Bend.

Volume I, Number 2, Saturday, 16 November 1793
The volunteers under Maj. Gen. Scott have crossed the Ohio River at Cincinnati to return home.
Lieut. Col. John Clarke arrived at Cincinnati on Tuesday last with eight boats of military supplies.
John Armstrong at Columbia asks those indebted to him to settle their accounts at his store. He has a new shipment of goods and groceries for sale.
Jacob Myers of Cincinnati writes regarding two boats going to Pittsburg.

Volume I, Number 3, Saturday, 23 November 1793
A note regarding the troops under Brig. Gen. Wilkinson is printed.
Gano & Company have dry goods and groceries at their store in Columbia.
Thomas Goudy of Cincinnati about a burglary at his house on November 20th.
A notice to John S. Gano (surveyor of the Miami Military Lands) from Hon. Jonathan Dayton (Superintendant of the Miami Military Lands) mentions Mr. Ludlow's survey.
Stewart Wilkins, Merchant of Cincinnati, has land for sale on Little Miami.
J. Pennington Smith of Cincinnati lost a packet of letters from Lieut. Reed.
John Ludlow of Cincinnati regarding a stolen horse.

Volume I, Number 4, Saturday, 30 November 1793
Obituary: David Strong, Jun., the seven-year-old son of Col. Strong, died Friday morning, 29 November 1793, of small pox.
Capt. Edw. Butler regarding some deserters: Corp. William Tucker (in Capt. Price's company, farmer, born in England, but late of Burlington, N.J., age 34); William Adair (born in N.J., but late of Wilmington, Del., farmer, 22 years old); John Stewart (born in Chester, Pa., 21 years old, miller); John Enesworth (private in Capt. Butler's Company, born in Washington County, Md., enlisted at Shepherd's Town, Va., 16 years old, mason); Daniel Hill (21 years old, born in Northumberland County, Pa.); Andrew Ware (born in Ireland, weaver); Patrick O'Hare (born in Ireland, mason); John Johnson (in Capt. DeButt's company).
Levi Woodward of Cincinnati found some saddle bags between Seth Cutter's Tavern and Samuel Thompson's house.
D.C. Orcutt of Cincinnati has land for sale on the Licking River.
A notice announcing a meeting of the merchants and the tavern keepers of Cincinnati to be held at John Grier's house.

Thomas Gibson has a new shipment of goods for sale at his store in Cincinnati across from John Ludlow's place.

Volume I, Number 5, Saturday, 7 December 1793

A. Hunt & Company of Cincinnati wants to buy pork and to hire a tanner.

A note about the sale of whiskey at the house of Levi Munsell in Cincinnati.

Daniel Duffey of Cincinnati asks those indebted to him to settle the bills.

W. Kelly of Cincinnati has a lot for sale in Cincinnati.

Volume I, Number 6, Saturday, 14 December 1793

A note regarding the army movements mentions Col. Hamtramck, Col. Strong and Mr. Wells.

John Dunlop of Cincinnati regarding the settlement at New Station on the Great Miami River three miles above Colerain on Capt. James Henry's land.

Obediah Scott at Bank Lick will board horses and cattle for the winter.

Volume I, Number 7, Saturday, 21 December 1793

C. Avery of Cincinnati asks those indebted to him to settle their accounts.

John Dealy of Cincinnati wants to hire coopers.

John Ludlow of Cincinnati regarding the settlement at Mount Pleasant, two miles from Ludlow's Station on the main road to Fort Hamilton.

W. Maxwell wants to hire an apprentice to the printing business.

Volume I, Number 8, Saturday, 28 December 1793

An account, reported by Capt. Faulkner, of the two spies who went to the Ogglaze with Mr. Wells.

A. Hunt & Company, of Cincinnati, have a new shipment of goods for sale.

Arthur St.Clair, Governor of the Northwest Territory, regarding the war in Europe. This item was entered by A.M. Dunn for Winthrop Sargent.

Volume I, Number 9, Saturday, 4 January 1794

A note regarding the blockhouses, under the command of Maj. Burbeck, on the "old Battle ground".

Wm. Tait, in Cincinnati, administrator of the estate of Robert Tait, deceased, late of Cincinnati, asks those indebted to the estate to settle their accounts with James Macconnel, merchant, in Cincinnati.

William Kelly, of Cincinnati, asks those indebted to him to settle their bills.

James Forguson, of Cincinnati, has a house and land for sale.

Mathew Winton, of Cincinnati, regarding a stolen horse.

Thos. Gibson and Robt. M'Crea, in Cincinnati, administrators of the estate of Robert Wilson, late of Cincinnati, deceased, regarding the estate settlement.

Volume I, Number 10, Saturday, 11 January 1794

John Galbraith is leaving Cincinnati and asks those indebted to him to pay their bills.

A note regarding a house for rent in Cincinnati, lately occupied by William M'Millen and presently occupied by the printing office.

Casper Sheets, at Greenville, regarding a note from Capt. John Armstrong that was lost. Deliver to Isaac Martin.

Volume I, Number 11, Saturday, 18 January 1794

A note regarding an Indian attack mentions Capt. Eaton and Capt. Collens.

An extract of a letter from Maj. Doyle at Fort Hamilton regarding an Indian attack mentions Mr. Demint of Cincinnati.

Capt. Uriah Springer at Greenville regarding two deserters: William Gibson (age 22) and William Newman (age 18).

John Dunlop, at Colerain, regarding the "donation lots" in Colerain.

Volume I, Number 12, Saturday, 25 January 1794

Capt. J. Guion, regarding a court martial at Greenville, mentions Maj.

Burbeck, Maj. Thomas H. Cushing and Capt. Edward Butler.
A letter from Maj. Gen. George R. Clark is printed.
William M'Millan has moved "to the country" and gives notice that his office of Judge of Common Pleas will be kept at the mansion house of Isaac Martin in Cincinnati.

Volume I, Number 13, Saturday, 1 February 1794
A. Hunt of Cincinnati wants an apprentice to the tanning and currying trade.
P.L. Willcox, of Cincinnati, regarding a stray cow.
Calvin Morrel, of Cincinnati, regarding fruit trees for sale at Point Pleasant.
Gano & Company have goods for sale at their store in Columbia.

Volume I, Number 14, Saturday, 8 February 1794
I.B. Miller of Cincinnati regarding some stolen mares.
Joseph Prince, of Cincinnati, wants to buy furs at his hatter's shop.

Volume I, Number 15, Saturday, 15 February 1794
Maj. John Mills at Greenville wants to buy produce for the army.
A note regarding an Indian attack on Mr. Serring of Columbia and three other men. Martin Vernor is missing and presumed a prisoner.
David Zeigler, of Cincinnati, lately arrived from Philadelphia, has dry goods for sale at his store in the house lately occupied by Robert Tait, dec'd.

Volume I, Number 16, Saturday, 22 February 1794
An account is given by Mr. Findley (a merchant of Cincinnati, lately arrived from Pittsburg) of an Indian attack on the Scioto River.
William Wilson has a new shipment of goods for sale at his store, kept by James Silver, on Front Street in Cincinnati, next door to Henry Reed, dec'd.
Daniel Duffey of Cincinnati asks those indebted to Mr. Acheson's store at Cincinnati to settle their accounts.
Samuel Thompson regarding a mare that strayed or was stolen.
Samuel Black, of Cincinnati, asks those indebted to him to settle their accounts with Thomas Goudy, attorney at law.
Richard Hall and Pheby Hall, at Columbia, administrators of the estate of John Fletcher, dec'd, regarding the estate settlement.

Volume I, Number 17, Saturday, 1 March 1794
G. Turner, of Cincinnati, wants to buy buffalo calves.
Capt. J. Guion, at Cincinnati, regarding a horse, formerly property of Maj. Adair in Kentucky, stolen from the stable of John Armstrong of Columbia. Deliver to John Belli in Cincinnati.
G. Wallace, of Cincinnati, regarding the settlement of the estate of Henry Reed, dec'd. Those indebted to Reed should pay their bills to Abner M. Dunn in Cincinnati.

Volume I, Number 18, Saturday, 8 March 1794
A note regarding an Indian attack on the wagons of Scott Traverse in which Traverse was killed. Also mentions Smith & Findley of Cincinnati.
John Meeker, of Columbia, says that his wife, Elizabeth Meeker, left him and he won't pay her bills anymore.
Capt. Ew. Butler regarding the deserter, John Johnson.

Volume I, Number 19, Saturday, 15 March 1794
A note regarding an Indian attack on Mr. Flin and Mrs. Prier on Gen. Harmer's old trace while they were on their way from White's Station to Cincinnati. They escaped.

Volume I, Number 20, Saturday, 22 March 1794
Obituary: Maj. Ballard Smith died Thursday morning, 20 March 1794, and was buried the next day, 21 March.

A note regarding an Indian attack mentions Mr. Litle (surveyor), Capt. Flinn and Gen. Scott (of Kentucky).

Sheriff John Ludlow, of Cincinnati, regarding courts in the Northwestern Territory, mentions Hon. George Turner.

Samuel Creigh, surviving partner of Alexander & Creigh, asks those indebted to the business to settle their accounts. He also has a new shipment of goods for sale at his stores in Cincinnati and Pittsburg.

Lieut. Bnd. Gains, at Greenville, regarding deserters: Isaac Kelsey (of Pratt's company, age 30, who lived with the Indians for 12 years), Amous Lewis (of Capt. Pastuer's company, born in R.I., enlisted in Cincinnati, age 27, blacksmith).

John Dunlop wants to hire a blacksmith at Colerain.

William Bryant, of Lincoln County, Kentucky, about a runaway slave, Sam.

Volume I, Number 21, Saturday, 5 April 1794

An extract from an unsigned letter, regarding the reward offered in Columbia for Indian scalps, mentions Capt. Ephraim Kibby and G. Turner.

W. Maxwell apologizes for not putting the paper out last week due to his illness.

James Macconnel, of Cincinnati, late Lieutenant in Capt. Bunton's militia of Hamilton County, regarding arms to be turned in to John Ward or D.C. Orcutt.

A. Andrews, of Cincinnati, regarding his heifer.

John Armstrong, of Columbia, asks those indebted to him to settle their bills.

John Miller regarding his new butcher shop in Cincinnati.

Volume I, Number 22, Saturday, 12 April 1794

The General Court has opened at Cincinnati before Hon. George Turner.

A letter from a man in Marietta to Maj. David Zeigler mentions Col. Lords.

John Armstrong, of Columbia, regarding a settlement near Fort Hamilton on the Great Miami River.

Wm. Tait, of Cincinnati, administrator of Robert Tait, dec'd, asks those indebted to the estate to settle their accounts to Abner M. Dunn of Cincinnati.

Abigail Brown, of North-Bend, administratrix of Carlisle Brown, dec'd, regarding the estate settlement.

Volume I, Number 23, Saturday, 19 April 1794

A speech by Hon. George Turner to the Grand Jury is printed.

The proceedings of the General Court of the Territory, with Judge Turner presiding, mentions James Dorsey (a free Negro) and Thomas Cochran (innkeeper).

A note regarding an "elegant entertainment" at the house of George Gordon in Cincinnati.

R. M'Clure, of Cincinnati, has bitters and salt for sale.

Gano & Company, in Columbia, asks those indebted to them to settle their accounts.

Volume I, Number 24, Saturday, 26 April 1794

A note regarding an Indian attack at Columbia mentions Capt. Kibbey.

An account of a party at the house of George Gordon for Hon. George Turner.

An elegy by Peter Pinder on the death of his wife is printed.

John Hole, of Cincinnati, asks those indebted to him to settle their accounts.

Anthony Smyth, of Cincinnati, executor of Maj. Ballard Smith, dec'd, regarding the estate settlement.

Peter Welsh, hairdresser and perfumer in Cincinnati, wants to hire an apprentice.

James Morrison asks those indebted to him to settle their accounts with Thomas Goudy, attorney at law in Cincinnati.

John Ward, of Cincinnati, for James Macconnel (merchant of Cincinnati), asks that those indebted to Macconnel settle accounts.

Volume I, Number 25, Saturday, 3 May 1794

An account of the court martial of Adam Caldwell, sutler of Cincinnati, mentions Capt. Ford, Capt. Porter, Capt. Cook, Capt. Greton, Capt. Thompson, Lieut. Ingersall, Lieut. Massey, Ensign Charles Hyde, Capt. Miller, Mr. Munsell's store, Lieut. Hasten Marks, Sarjent Colbath and Joseph Evilet.

An account of an Indian attack mentions White's Station and Capt. Kibbey.

Seth Cutter, innkeeper in Cincinnati, regarding a strayed or stolen mare.

Volume I, Number 26, Saturday, 10 May 1794

The text of Gen. Anthony Wayne's speech to the Indians at Greenville mentions Stephen Young and Robert Wilson.

G. Turner, at Cincinnati, lost a box containing two oil paintings. Deliver to Doctor Strong at Fort Washington.

Volume I, Number 27, Saturday, 17 May 1794

An account of an Indian attack on Maj. Winston's Company from Fort Washington mentions Lieut. Lee.

A letter to the public from a committee of Levi Woodward, Darius C. Orcutt and James Lyons (all of Cincinnati) and of Wm. Brown, Ignatius Ross and John Reily (all of Columbia) regarding rewards for Indian scalps.

Smith & Findlay, of Cincinnati, ask those indebted to them to pay their bills.

John & Charles Wilkins & Company have closed their business in Cincinnati and ask those indebted to them to settle their accounts to Thompson Ware.

Elizabeth Prier and William M'Millan, administrators of Moses Prier, dec'd, late of White's Station near Cincinnati, regarding the estate settlement.

Volume I, Number 28, Saturday, 24 May 1794

Account of an Indian attack mentions Columbia, Nelson's Station, A. Shipman, Mr. Nelson, Mr. Dunlap, S. Nutts, T. Nutts, Mr. Gordon and Lieut. Turner.

A note regarding the conduct of Lieut. Turner and Ensign Lee in Indian skirmishes mentions Corp. James Waters and Lieut. Clarke.

Capt. Zebu. Pike, at Greenville, regarding a deserter: Francis Waldron (age 26, born in N.J., blacksmith).

Robert Mitchel & John M'Leod have opened a rope making shop in Cincinnati.

Volume I, Number 29, Saturday, 31 May 1794

Charles Hyde writes a letter to the editor giving an account of the trial of Adam Caldwell and mentions Capt. M. Ford, Capt. Porter, Capt. Cook, Capt. Greaton, Capt. Thompson, Lieut. Ingersall, Lieut. Massey, Capt. Miller, Mr. Munsell's store, Lieut. William Marts, Lieut. Hastings Marks, Sergeant Colbraith, Joseph Evelet.

Capt. Thomas Lewis passed through Cincinnati on his way to Kentucky.

Geo. G. Taylor, living in Clark County on Boon's Creek, regarding a runaway slave named Aaron.

Lieut. Col. D. Strong regarding deserters named Casper Richcreek (age 24, of Capt. Bradley's company) and Eliakim Hull (age 20).

Volume I, Number 31, Saturday, 14 June 1794

Obituary: Monsieur Francis Solauder, an emigrant from France, died suddenly on 27 May 1794, at Fort Hamilton, as a result of a fall from his horse.

Peter Davis, of Cincinnati, says his wife, Elizabeth Davis, left him and he won't pay her bills anymore.

John Meeker, of Columbia, found a mare.

Thomas M'Cardell, of Cincinnati, asks those indebted to him to pay their bills.

Volume I, Number 32, Saturday, 21 June 1794

An account of an Indian attack on Maj. Stites and Nathaniel Reader of Columbia and of the capture and escape of Mr. Jones.

Obituary: Capt. Tarlton Fleming died on 17 June 1794 at Fort Hamilton.

A list of goods and books for sale at auction at the house of Samuel Freeman.

Lieut. John Whistler regarding a deserter named William Pilsworth, alias William Carrel, a weaver, age 25, born in Ireland.

Volume I, Number 33, Saturday, 28 June 1794
Abner M. Dunn is appointed Deputy Postmaster General at Cincinnati.
A. Hunt & Company, in Cincinnati, have a house and lot for sale.
R. M'Clure, of Cincinnati, says the horse he bought from William Barns has strayed.

Volume I, Number 34, Saturday, 5 July 1794
A note regarding Gen. Charles Scott's trip through Pittsburg is printed.
An account of an Indian attack mentions Maj. M'Machen (killed), Fort Recovery, Capt. Hartshorn (killed), Lieut. Craig (killed), Lieut. Torrey (killed). Capt. Taylor and Lieut. Drake were both wounded.
Capt. John Pierce at Fort Washington regarding deserters: William Mackelwaine (age 27, living near Carlisle) and James Brooks (age 25, resided at Misslenburgh).

Volume I, Number 35, Saturday, 12 July 1794
An account of the July 4th celebration mentions Capt. John Pierce, Mr. Gordon, Gen. Wayne, Maj. M'Machan, Mr. Hartshorn, Mr. Craig, Mr. Torry, Arthur St.Clair.
Gano & Company have a new shipment of goods at their store in Columbia.
Jas. Wilkinson, of Cincinnati, administrator of the estate of Francis Solander, dec'd, asks those indebted to the estate to settle their accounts with A.M. Dunn.
Rice Bullock, of Cincinnati, asks those indebted to William Tait, merchant, late of Cincinnati, to settle their accounts.
Thomas Thursbey, late of the U.S. Legion, has moved to North-Bend and opened a tailoring business.
A. Hunt & Company, of Cincinnati, has a new shipment of goods for sale. They also want to buy hides and deerskins.

Volume I, Number 36, Saturday, 19 July 1794
A note regarding the volunteers under the command of Gen. Todd.
John Houston, of Cincinnati, lost a pocket book that contained a note from Simon Kenton.

Volume I, Number 37, Saturday, 26 July 1794
An unsigned letter to the editor, about other letters in the paper, mentions Alexander Pope and Peter Pinder.
Winthrop Sargent, in Cincinnati, regarding printed copies of the laws of the Territory of the U.S. Northwest of the River Ohio.

Volume I, Number 38, Saturday, 2 August 1794
Gov. Winthrop Sargent, Northwestern Territory, writes a letter to the public.
Jacob Steward, of Cincinnati, regarding a purse said to be stolen by Edward Hart (age 25, late of Capt. Bradley's Company).

Volume I, Number 39, Saturday, 9 August 1794
William Jones has opened a dry goods and grocery store in Cincinnati in John Riddle's house, lately occupied by James Macconnel.
Bar. Carrel, in Cincinnati, found a horse near Fort Hamilton.
Francis Wilson, of Cincinnati, asks those indebted to him to pay their bills.
R. M'Clure, of Cincinnati, asks those who owe him money to settle their accounts so that he can send for a fresh supply of medicines.
I.B. Miller, of Columbia, asks those indebted to him to settle their accounts.

Volume I, Number 40, Saturday, 16 August 1794
Dan. Duffey, of Cincinnati, asks those indebted to D. Acheson & Company to settle their accounts as the store will soon move to Kentucky.
Samuel Seward, at White's Station, regarding a gun said to be stolen.

Volume I, Number 41, Saturday, 23 August 1794
Capt. John Pierce, at Fort Washington, regarding a deserter named Frederick Miller (a shoemaker, age 38, born in Germany).
Anthony Smyth will no longer handle the estate of the late Maj. Ballard Smith, dec'd.
Samuel Robinson, of Cincinnati, has land for sale on Harmer's trace four miles from Cincinnati and a lot for sale next door to Col. Gibson in Cincinnati.

Volume I, Number 42, Saturday, 30 August 1794
Notice to the Northwest Territory's militia from Winthrop Sargent is printed.
A letter to the editor from John Armstrong at Columbia states that he entered the army in 1776 and served until 1793. He also submits several letters from Anthony Wayne to Armstrong that mention Maj. Beatty and Gen. Wilkinson.
George Cullum, justice of the peace in Hamilton County, regarding William Wilson's deposition that mentions Ludlow's Station, Gen. St.Clair, John Churchill and Mr. Ewing. Wilson is late of Capt. Armstrong's company and enlisted at Philadelphia.
William M'Millan, justice of the peace in Hamilton County, regarding Wm. Schooly's deposition that mentions Lieut. Hartshorn. Schooly was a soldier in Capt. John Armstrong's company and enlisted at Philadelphia.
James Macconnel, of Cincinnati, asks those indebted to him to settle their accounts with Thomas Goudy. He has moved his store from Cincinnati.

Volume I, Number 43, Saturday, 6 September 1794
Winthrop Sargent writes a letter to the public regarding an old Indian grave opened at Cincinnati and mentions Capt. Jeffers, Mr. Goudy, Mr. Mitchell, Mr. Wait and Mr. Garrison.
Army news mentions Capt. Miss Campbell, Lieut. Henry B. Towles, Capt. Slough, Capt. Van Renssalar, Lieut. Campbell Smith, Gen. Wilkinson and Maj. Campbell.
James Robison, of Cincinnati, regarding a bond from Abraham Garrison.
James Kavenagh has opened a blacksmith and farrier's business in Cincinnati.
William Reed, of Cincinnati, says that he'll no longer pay the bills of his wife, Mary Reed.

Volume I, Number 44, Saturday, 13 September 1794
A letter from Winthrop Sargent regarding rioting in Cincinnati is printed.
John Dailey, of Cincinnati, wants to hire a cooper.

Volume I, Number 45, Saturday, 20 September 1794
John S. Gano and William Stanley, at Columbia, regarding the partnership of Gano & Stanley. They also have a new shipment of goods for sale at their store.
John Dunlap, at Colerain, regarding donation lots in Colerain.

Volume I, Number 46, Saturday, 27 September 1794
John Brown regarding his stable in Cincinnati.
Daniel Symmes, Sheriff of Hamilton County, regarding prisoners in the jail: William Courtnay (labourer) who broke out of jail in Mason County, Kentucky, and Ned, a slave who ran away from James Ward of Mason County, Kentucky.
Moses Teas lost a note from Gano & Company to Wm. M'Gowin.
W. Maxwell, of Cincinnati, asks those indebted to him to pay their bills so that he can buy paper for the winter.

Volume I, Number 47, Saturday, 4 October 1794
Daniel Symmes, Sheriff of Hamilton County, regarding prisoners that escaped from the jail: William Murfey (age 30), William Courtnay (age 35) and Ned (a Negro man).
Samuel Tomson, of Cincinnati, about a strayed or stolen horse, mentions William Gahagen.
Nancy Willcox about the estate sale of P.L. Willcox, late of Cincinnati, dec'd.

John Mercer, of Cincinnati, regarding a stolen horse.

John Finnyhon & Company regarding their shoemaking business in Cincinnati near Dr. M'Clure's and opposite Mr. M'Coy's blacksmith shop.

Volume I, Number 48, Saturday, 11 October 1794

Obituary: Robert Elliot, contractor for army supplies, was killed by the Indians on 6 October 1794 about four miles from Fort Hamilton.

Thomas Williams, of Cincinnati, asks those indebted to Nehemiah Hunt, Thomas Williams and Ely Curtis to settle their accounts.

Volume I, Number 49, Saturday, 18 October 1794

A charge delivered to the Grand Jury of the Northwest Territory by Hon. Rufus Putnam is printed and mentions Mr. Freeman.

A list of letters at the Post Office in Cincinnati mentions Maj. John Buell, Samuel Brewster, George Blackburn (soldier), James Bourns, William Campbell, Jacob Cox, Seth Carhart, George Clark (soldier), Silas Clark (soldier), Lieut. George F. Demler, William Dlashmutt, Zebulon Eynon, Elias Griffith, Lieut. William Harrison, Sergt. Krider, Capt. Thomas Lewis, John Lowman (soldier), Calvin Morrel, Sergt. M'Garvin, John M'Donald, Henry Mershal, Levi Munsell, Pat M'Naughton, Sylvenus Olney, William Powel, Stephen Perce, Ensign Robert Purdy, William Smith, Isaac Swearingen, Henry Stemble, Richard Stanton, Capt. D.E. Turner, Samuel Willard, Benjamin Whiteman, Sergt. John Wise, Lieut. Husband Young or Younghusband.

Nicholas Hawkins and William Robinson, living near Madison County Courthouse, regarding runaway slaves named Lewis and Harry.

Volume I, Number 50, Saturday, 25 October 1794

A note is printed regarding the Kentucky Volunteers under Maj. Gen. Scott.

A poem dedicated to the memory of Robert Elliot is printed.

Robert Kean, of Cincinnati, regarding a bond to Benjamin Brown.

Volume I, Number 51, Saturday, 1 November 1794

Obituary: Lieut. Isaac Pleasent Younghusband died the morning of 16 October 1794 at Fort Jefferson and was buried at Greenville that evening. Note mentions Maj. Buell.

Robert M'Clure, of Cincinnati, regarding a stray cow.

Francis Wilson has salt for sale at his store in Cincinnati.

Volume I, Number 52, Saturday, 8 November 1794

George Morfoot, of Cincinnati, found a rifle.

Volume II, Number 53, Saturday, 15 November 1794

Robert Benham, living on the Ohio River in Mason County, Kentucky, about a runaway slave named Will.

Will Turner about some stray horses. Deliver to Francis Jones in Cincinnati.

Luke Foster & James Seward, Jun., at Pleasent Valley Station, found some bar iron.

Jonathan Taylor, of Greenville, about a horse that strayed or was stolen. Deliver to Capt. Gordon in Cincinnati.

Volume II, Number 54, Saturday, 22 November 1794

Oliver Spencer, Probate Judge at Columbia, about administrations of estates.

John Miller, butcher, of Cincinnati, has candles for sale.

Volume II, Number 55, Saturday, 29 November 1794

A note regarding the arrival of Capt. Isreal Ludlow in Cincinnati mentions Gov. Arthur St.Clair.

A list of appointments made by Winthrop Sargent in Hamilton County includes Timothy Symmes, Stephen Woods, Aaron Cadwell, William M'Millan, John S. Gano, Isaac Danville, Isra F. Freeman, Lieut. William Rotenhouse, Robert Whealing,

Ensign Garret Vannice, Ensign Celadon Symmes, Samuel Seward, Lieut. James Lyon, Capt. Wallace, Ensign Uzuel Bates, Samuel Dick, Lieut. Darius C. Orcutt, Capt. Grier, John Schooly, John Riddle, Ensign Creigh, Seth Cutter, James Cox, John Brown, Ensign John Bowman.

Russel Farnum, of Cincinnati, regarding a horse that strayed or was stolen.

Volume II, Number 56, Saturday, 6 December 1794.

John Robertson, of Cincinnati, says he lost a mourning breast pin between Robertson's store and Charles Avery's.

Samuel Thompson, living in Fayette County, Kentucky, near Black's Station on Clear Creek, regarding a stray horse.

Volume II, Number 57, Saturday, 13 December 1794

The printing office has moved to the house lately occupied by Capt. Levi Woodward.

Thomas Gibson, of Cincinnati, has dry goods, hardware and groceries for sale.

Andrew Armstrong, of Round Bottom Station, regarding a stray horse. Deliver to John M'Cabe of Middletown or Jacob Reader of Mill Creek.

Volume II, Number 58, Saturday, 20 December 1794

Stuart Richey, of Cincinnati, is opening a school in the house lately occupied by David Williams, opposite James Forgason's store.

Stephen Reader has a house for sale. Apply to James Forguson in Cincinnati.

A letter to the editor from Winthrop Sargent about land surveying is printed.

A note from Oliver Ormsby regarding Gov. St.Clair at Marietta.

Winthrop Sargent writes a letter to the public regarding cutting down trees.

John S. Gano and William Stanley have goods for sale at their store in Columbia.

Oliver Ormsby has goods for sale at his store in Cincinnati.

John Wallere, at Fallsmouth at the Forks of Licking, has plank and scantling for sale.

Volume II, Number 59, Saturday, 27 December 1794

Winthrop Sargent writes a letter to the editor regarding the arrival of Gov. St.Clair and mentions Oliver Ormsby.

John Lee, living in Woodford County, Kentucky, about a runaway slave, John.

James Forguson has flour for sale at his store in Cincinnati.

Volume II, Number 60, Saturday, 3 January 1795

A note regarding the arrival of Hon. John Cleves Symmes, along with his wife and daughter, in Cincinnati.

An unsigned letter to the editor regarding the arrival of Gov. St.Clair at Marietta.

Matthew Winton, of Cincinnati, has iron for sale.

Aaron Cadwell regarding the proper licensing of taverns and stores.

Winthrop Sargent enters the proclamation of Ar. St.Clair regarding a meeting of the legislature of the Northwest Territory at Marietta.

Mathias Pierson, at Ludlow's Station, regarding a strayed or stolen mare.

Volume II, Number 61, Saturday, 10 January 1795

John Cleves Symmes, North Bend, about volunteer settlers in the Miami Purchase.

William Jones has a new shipment of goods for sale at his store in Cincinnati.

James Kamper, living at Walnut Hill near Cincinnati, regarding a stray steer.

B. Vanhook has a house and lot in Cincinnati for sale.

Volume II, Number 62, Saturday, 17 January 1795

Those indebted to Samuel Black, James Macconnel, Samuel Creigh and James G. Herron (all merchants) should settle their accounts.

T. Goudy, of Cincinnati, writes regarding his arrest of certain officers.

William Muir, of Cincinnati, has land for sale in the Miami Purchase near Fort Hamilton and one mile from Bruice's Station.

John C. Symmes, at Northbend, regarding lots in Northbend.

Elijah Craig, Jun., at the mouth of the Kentucky River, regarding the transport of goods up the River. He mentions Sluke's Warehouse.

Volume II, Number 63, Saturday, 24 January 1795

A list of letters at the Post Office in Cincinnati names Capt. Alexander Gibson, Alexander Davidson, Capt. Benjamin Price, Caleb Swan, Conrad Tague or Pogue, Dan. M'Ansay, David Leitch, Capt. Daniel Britt, Daniel Perine, Doctor David Davis, Lieut. Charles Hyde, Lieut. Benj. Lockwood, Francis Driver, George Ernst, Hezekiah Flint, Henry Hofner, Isaac Vanhook, Lieut. John Steele, James Johnston, Isaac N. Smith, Joseph Prince, Lieut. John Whisler, John Johnston, James Barnes, John Camphel, James Dement, James Handsbrough, Thomas Brown, Job Gard or Card, James Miller, John Miller, John Bush, Robert Kile, John Caldwell (merchant), Oveler Miller (drummer), Patrick Sulavan, Robert Culbert, Richard Allison, Thomas Fobes, Thomas Doyle, Mr. Vance, William Campbell, William Irvin, Lieut. William M'Rea, William Howthorn, William Dement, Lieut. William Clark, William Smith, Zebulon Eynon.

Daniel Duffey, of Cincinnati, asks those indebted to David Acheson to settle their accounts.

Timothy Scannell about his coopering shop at the stone landing in Cincinnati.

Robert M'Clure, of Cincinnati, asks those indebted to him to pay their bills.

Volume II, Number 64, Saturday, 31 January 1795

A. Hunt & Company want to buy oak bark at their tanyard in Cincinnati.

Timothy Scannel wants to hire coopers at his shop in Cincinnati.

Volume II, Number 65, Saturday, 7 February 1795

Isaac Mills arrived in Cincinnati with news of an Indian attack near the mouth of the Great Miami. They killed Benjamin Cox and Thomas Walter.

A public meeting is to be held at the house of Charles Avery in Cincinnati.

Jerimiah Salivan takes back what he said about John Baine. The notice is witnessed by J. Whisler, James Cox and I. Darneille.

A list of articles found by Nathaniel Stokes and David E. Wade under the root of a tree is printed.

Josiah Mott, of Cincinnati, administrator of the estate of Henry Moore, packhorseman, dec'd, regarding the estate settlement.

James Silver, for William Wilson, regarding a new shipment of goods at the store in Cincinnati.

Capt. John Pierce regarding deserters: John Johnston (age 30, born in Ireland) and Robert Hall/Ball (age 20).

Volume II, Number 66, Saturday, 14 February 1795

A notice regarding meetings to sign a petition to the legislature. The meetings will be held at Capt. Kibby's in Columbia, Francis Dunlavy's at Frazee's Station over the Little Miami, Robert Wheelen's in North Bend and Charles Avery's in Cincinnati.

James Ferguson, of Cincinnati, is leaving for the old settlement and asks those indebted to him to settle their accounts.

Volume II, Number 68, Saturday, 28 February 1795

An account of the celebration of the birthday of George Washington mentions Mr. Williams and Mr. Elliot.

Robert Mitchell, of Cincinnati, asks those indebted to him to pay their bills.

Capt. John Pierce about a deserter named Barnabas (alias Barney) Oldwine, a private, age 32, who was born in Germany.

John & Charles Wilkins and F. Jones, at Fort Washington, want to buy soap.

Volume II, Number 69, Saturday, 7 March 1795
James O'Hara, Quarter Master General, at Fort Washington, regarding freight charges for carrying public property.

Sheriff Dan. Symmes, of Hamilton County, regarding escaped prisoners: Isaac Williams (taylor), Patrick O'Hara (born in Ireland), Robert Frakes (age 17-18) and William Stewart. They stole Mr. Kennady's boat and went down the Ohio River.

Capt. John Pierce regarding a deserter from Fort Washington named John Carpenter (age 37, born in Germany).

Volume II, Number 70, Saturday, 14 March 1795
Note about an Indian attack at North Bend mentions Lieut. Celadon Symmes.

A notice regarding a lost note from James Fisher to Thomas Davis.

Volume II, Number 72, Saturday, 28 March 1795
Nackey Devaul, of Cincinnati, administratrix of Richard Devaul, dec'd, regarding the estate settlement.

John Machir, of Cincinnati, says that the partnership of Machir & Eynon in a tanyard in Cincinnati has expired. Those indebted to the partnership should settle their accounts.

Anderson Doniphan, living six miles from Washington in Mason County, Kentucky, regarding a burglary at his house that was committed by Thomas James (alias Moses Morgan and Moses John, the horsethief).

Daniel Symmes, Sheriff of Hamilton County, regarding escaped prisoners named Hugh O'Hara, Samuel Eidee and John Dillon.

John Galbraith is going "into the settlement" and asks those indebted to him to settle their accounts.

E. Sproat, inspector of the Ohio District, regarding the office in Cincinnati for collecting duties on spirits and wines.

John Pitman and Henry Weaver (both at Tucker's Station), executors of the estate of J. Limthecome, dec'd, about the estate settlement at Mr. Edwards' at Red Bank Station.

William Goforth, justice of the peace in Hamilton County, regarding a warrant for the arrest of Rheuben Whetstone of Hamilton County for the murder of his wife. Mentions Justice Cadwell.

Daniel Gano & Brother have whiskey and flour for sale at Mr. Bruice's Station near Fort Hamilton. Apply to Patrick Moore at the station.

Jas. Wilkinson, administrator, by his agent, A.M. Dunn, regarding the estate sale of Francis Solander, dec'd, at the house of John Brown in Cincinnati.

Volume II, Number 73, Saturday, 4 April 1795
James Taylor, at New Port, has land for sale on Clough Creek.

Francis Dunlavy, administrator of the estate of James Carpenter, late of Columbia, dec'd, asks those indebted to the estate to settle their accounts.

A.M. Dunn, postmaster at Cincinnati, regarding the receipt of mail at his office.

George Gordon regarding the sale of two boats and cargoes at the office of inspection at Cincinnati.

Volume II, Number 74, Saturday, 11 April 1795
A letter from Isaac Darneille to Hon. Winthrop Sargent is printed and mentions Arthur St.Clair.

Jacob Lowe about his ferry at Cincinnati across the Ohio River to Kentucky.

Volume II, Number 75, Saturday, 18 April 1795
Zekiel Fuller, of Cincinnati, says his wife, Elizabeth Fuller, left him and "has since taken up with another man", and he won't honor her debts anymore.

Robert Benham, at Newport at the mouth of the Licking River, regarding a runaway slave named Will.

William Hunt regarding a bond to Andrew Forsythe.

Volume II, Number 76, Saturday, 25 April 1795

Aaron Cadwell, of Cincinnati, about the licenses required to sell dry goods.

Lieut. Wm. Marts regarding a deserter named Patrick Melony (age 31, born in Ireland) from Capt. Turner's company.

Thomas Goudy and Seth Cutter, of Cincinnati, regarding the new courthouse to be built in Hamilton County.

David Zeigler has dry goods and groceries for sale at his store in Cincinnati.

Volume II, Number 77, Saturday, 2 May 1795

Nathaniel Stokes, living near Cincinnati, found some cows and calves.

Lieut. A. Gregg at Cincinnati regarding deserters: Alexander Terrel (in Capt. Bissell's Company, born in Ireland) and James Holland (born in England).

Volume II, Number 78, Saturday, 9 May 1795

William Kelly offers Kelly's Tavern, on Front Street in Cincinnati, for sale or for rent. Apply to Col. Gibson at his store.

Benj. VanHook, Constable of Cincinnati, regarding prisoners that escaped from the Hamilton County jail: George Gardner (in Lieut. John Whisler's company), John Tulley and William Ellery.

Charles Vitiar regarding a bill of sale from Thomas Irvin to William Moore for a town lot in Cincinnati that's now in the hands of John Bartle.

Thomas M'Intire, at Columbia, regarding stray horses.

Anthony Furney, says his wife, Elizabeth Furney, left him and he won't pay her bills.

Volume II, Number 79, Saturday, 16 May 1795

A note regarding the arrival of Gov. Arthur St.Clair in Cincinnati is printed.

Account of an Indian attack at Ludlow's Station five miles from Cincinnati.

Judge George Turner has arrived in Cincinnati.

A list of letters left at the Post Office in Cincinnati include Alexander Johnston, Benjamin Perlee, John Nailer (carpenter), Francis Driver, George Rowletter, Judge George Turner, George Dapenpower, Henley M'Farlane (sargent), Jotas King, Joseph N. Bennett, John Matthews, John Boyce (packhorsemaster), James Dement, Job Gard, Capt. Leonard Covington, Philip Butler (soldier), Mr. Skeating, Samuel Bridge, Lieut. William Marts, William Ready (sargent), William M'Can and William Evins (at Fort Recovery).

Oliver Ormsby of Cincinnati has goods for sale at the store of Ormsby & Bustard. He also asks those indebted to him to settle their accounts with John Bustard or Dan. Conner at Greenville.

Volume II, Number 80, Saturday, 23 May 1795

Jos. Rodgers regarding a runaway slave named Rachel.

W. Maxwell, of Cincinnati, reports a runaway apprentice to the printing business, Benjamin Stokes, age 19.

Volume II, Number 82, Saturday, 7 June 1795

A proclamation of Gov. Arthur St.Clair regarding a murder mentions Hon. George Turner.

M. Winton of Cincinnati regarding his stable in Cincinnati. He also has flour and whiskey for sale.

John Reily, of Cincinnati, writes a letter to Israel Ludlow, Samuel Freeman and Joel Williams regarding a lot in Cincinnati, the property of Capt. William Faulkner that was seized by a Court of Common Pleas of Hamilton County.

Charle Jaudin says his wife, Elizabeth, left him and he won't pay her bills.

Capt. James Taylor regarding deserters: Benjamin Spencer (age 24, born in Virginia, but lately lived in Kentucky) who is in the company of two boys, Samuel Straughter and Benjamin Stokes.

Volume II, Number 83, Saturday, 13 June 1795

The report of the proceedings of the legislature mentions Judge Symmes.

Peter Owns, living at North Bend, regarding a stray mare.

Wm. Jennings, living in Washington, Mason County, Kentucky, regarding the burglary at his jeweler's shop.

Ferdinand Brookaw, of Cincinnati, has a house and lot for sale.

Volume II, Number 84, Saturday, 27 June 1795

Maj. Thos. Doyle regarding the massacre of Col. Samuel Lloyd Chew (of Maryland) and 17 other persons.

W. Maxwell apologizes for the lack of a newspaper last week, but he was on business away from home.

Joseph Robison, of Campbell County, regarding a stud horse. Apply to William Martin living two miles from the mouth of the Licking on the road to Georgetown.

Mr. Ludlow, Mr. Freeman and Mr. Williams regarding lots in Cincinnati.

John M'Cullough, of Cincinnati, asks those indebted to him to pay their bills.

Philomon Thomas, of Mason Co., Kentucky, about a runaway slave, Quiller.

William Digbey says his wife, Catharine, left him and he won't pay her bills.

Volume II, Number 85, Saturday, 4 July 1795

The text of Gov. Arthur St.Clair's speech to the Legislature is printed.

John Finnehon & Company, in Cincinnati, ask those indebted to them to settle their accounts.

Daniel Symms about prisoners who escaped from the Hamilton County jail: John VanKamp, Daniel Sullivan, Joseph Kelly and James Dorsey (a Negro).

Smith & Findlay ask those indebted to them to settle their accounts.

Samuel Orsburn, of Cincinnati, says that he will no longer honor the debts contracted by his wife, Margaret Orsburn.

Volume II, Number 86, Saturday, 11 July 1795

The text of Gov. St.Clair's speech is continued.

Account of the July 4th celebration at Cincinnati mentions Gordon's Hotel.

Thomas Gibson, of Cincinnati, asks those indebted to him to pay their bills.

David Zeigler has a new shipment of goods for sale at his store in Cincinnati.

Thomas John regarding a stray cow at the tanyard of Mr. Eynon.

Robert Armstrong, at Fort St.Clair, says his wife, Elizabeth Armstrong (alias Elizabeth Buzzy), left him and he won't honor her debts.

Jerimiah Clark, of Cincinnati, regarding a note to James Glinn and John Mehony.

John Galbraith, of Cincinnati, says he's "leaving this country" and asks that those who are in debt to him settle their accounts.

Volume II, Number 87, Saturday, 18 July 1795

The text of Gov. St.Clair's speech is continued.

An account of the Fourth of July celebration at Columbia is printed.

John Whitstone asks that those indebted to him please settle their accounts.

Danial Duffey, of Cincinnati, asks those indebted to him to pay their bills.

Zachariah Dowty, of Cincinnati, regarding his butcher shop on the bank of the River below Kennedy's Ferry in Cincinnati.

Henry Pickle regarding the road from his ferry to William Matthew's on Bank Lick. It intersects with the road from Thomas Kennedy's ferry to Georgetown.

Volume II, Number 88, Saturday, 25 July 1795

Judge Symmes and Judge Turner reply to Gov. St.Clair's speech.

Obituary: Abner Martin Dunn, attorney at law and postmaster, died on Saturday, 17 July 1795 and was buried Sunday, 18 July.

Obituary: Armistead Churchill, attorney at law, died on Wednesday, 22 July 1795, and was buried on Thursday, 23 July 1795. He left a wife and an infant daughter.

A note about W. Maxwell's publication of the laws of the Territory. Subscriptions to the work are taken by William Goforth and John Armstrong in

Columbia; Francis Dunlavy at Frazes Station; Stephen Wood and R. Whealen at North Bend; Capt. John Shaw at Colerain; and Capt. D.C. Orcutt at Fort Hamilton.

David Telford, living in Georgetown, Kentucky, regarding a runaway slave.

Abijah and Jesse Hunt regarding the partnership of Abijah Hunt & Company. They ask those indebted to them to settle their accounts with William Wells at Fort Wayne or John Ash at Greenville. They have a new shipment of goods at the store in Cincinnati.

A note about a sale of horses at the house of James Kavenagh, blacksmith.

R. Hall, at the Little Miami River, found a runaway slave who belongs to Archibald Marshall of Kentucky.

Volume II, Number 89, Saturday, 1 August 1795

John Cleves Symmes and G. Turner's answer to Gov. St.Clair's speech is continued.

John Churchill, Jun., of Cincinnati, administrator of the estate of Armistead Churchill, dec'd, regarding the estate settlement.

Nackey Devaul, of Cincinnati, administratrix of the estate of Richard Devaul, dec'd, regarding the estate settlement to take place at the house of Charles Avery, innkeeper, in Cincinnati.

A. Thompson, at Fort Hamilton, reports a strayed or stolen horse. Deliver to Capt. Kibby at Columbia or Rawland Brown at Fort Hamilton.

W. Maxwell wants to hire an apprentice to the printing business.

Volume II, Number 91, Saturday, 15 August 1795

William Jones has a new shipment of goods for sale at his store in Cincinnati.

H. Taylor and James Taylor, attorneys in fact for James Taylor, Sen., at Newport, regarding the auction of lots in Newport.

Elisha Winters & Company want to hire ropemakers in Lexington, Kentucky.

A note regarding the Court of Oyer & Terminer at Lexington mentions Hugh Ross, Thomas Kennedy and Capt. Owen.

Silas Stansbury, for Abner Fagin, in Cincinnati, states that Fagin will not honor the debts contracted by Barbery Fagin.

John Hill, of Cincinnati, has steers and a wagon for sale.

James Brady, of Cincinnati, regarding a stray horse.

Lewis Laing regarding his saddler's business in Cincinnati in the house lately occupied by John Daily.

John Brown, of Cincinnati, asks those indebted to him to pay their bills.

James Flinn, at Columbia, regarding some borrowed muskets.

Capt. Wm. Marts, at Greenville, about a deserter named James Hall, age 35.

Archibald M'Donald, of Cincinnati, regarding a woman by the name of Rhodah M'Donnald (age 39) who ran away from him taking a male child, 18 months old, with her.

Volume II, Number 92, Saturday, 22 August 1795

The minutes of the meeting of the Legislature of the Northwest Territory mentions Gov. Arthur St.Clair, John Cleves Symmes, George Turner, Armistead Churchill, Joel Williams (regarding his ferry in Cincinnati), Rebecca Kennedy (regarding her ferry in Cincinnati), Patrick Simpson of Vincennes, Daniel Symmes (sheriff of Hamilton County), Wm. Lemond (for divorce) and the impeachment of Judge Henry Vanderburgh in Knox County.

John Hambleton, of Lincoln County, Kentucky, on the Dick's River, regarding a runaway slave named Henry.

Thomas Williams regarding his parchment making business in Cincinnati.

John Hunter regarding his tavern in Georgetown in the house formerly occupied by Josiah Pitts and lately by Littleton Robertson.

Charles Morgan (acting partner and agent for John Obannon & Company and Francis Ash & Company) regarding cutting down trees on their land. Mentions Jacob Fowler in Newport.

Volume II, Number 94, Saturday, 5 September 1795

The minutes of the Legislature are continued and mention Gov. St.Clair, Judge Turner and Judge Symmes.

G. Turner, of Cincinnati, about a settlement on the east banks of Mad River.

James Gillespie regarding his brew house on Dear Creek near Cincinnati. He wants to buy hops and barley.

Daniel Duffey says the partnership of Acheson & Duffey is dissolved. Please pay your bills to Thomas Acheson. Duffey continues his store in Cincinnati.

A proclamation of Gov. Arthur St.Clair regarding the Indians is printed.

Michael Lacassagne, of Louisville, regarding the settlement on his land in the Illinois Grant not far from Louisville. Apply to John Armstrong in Columbia.

John Armstrong, of Columbia, has whiskey for sale.

John Hole, of Cincinnati, has lots for sale in Cincinnati.

Notice of a meeting at John Brown's tavern about the bridge at Deer Creek.

Abraham Garrison, of Cincinnati, has lots for sale.

Sheriff Daniel Symmes regarding prisoners that escaped from Hamilton Prison: Rusell Farnum, William Reed, John Kidd, Frank M'Clain, David Beck and Mr. Lyndon.

George Kyler & Son, Potters, regarding their shop in Cincinnati.

Thomas Doyle, of Cincinnati, has land for sale.

Kimberly & Company have a new shipment of goods at their store in Cincinnati at Mr. Cochran's house.

Samuel Freeman, of Cincinnati, asks those indebted to him to pay their bills.

Volume II, Number 95, Saturday, 12 September 1795

The minutes of the legislature mention Gov. St.Clair and Judge Turner.

A list of letters left at the Post Office in Cincinnati includes Maj. John Armstrong, Thomas Alexander, John Bartell, Rev. Hejekiah Black, Maj. John Y. Buell, Thomas Bates, John Burk, John Ball, John Brown, Philo Beers, Aaron Cowling, Maj. Jonathan Cass, John Campble, Abraham Cuykendal, Armistead Churchill, William Ceureer, George Coad, John Demoss, Abraham Hoff, George Dresar, John DelaMater, Parvin Dunn, I. Darneille, Francis Delong, James Elliot, Ensign Finley, Ens. David Fero, William Ford, Lott French, George Gillaspie, Capt. Richard Grayton, Ens. Peter Grayson, Dr. Elias Griffith, Capt. Elijah Gates, Solomon Goss, John Gilkison, John Gailbraith, Rev. M. Henderson, Lieut. Charles Hyde, Wm. Hogland, Silvester Meek, John M. Hynamon, Geo. Hacket, Sergt. Hutson, Maj. J. Haskell, Gabriel Hutchings, Manerieffe Hill, Mr. Jowder, Wm. Cribbe, Col. Thomas Lewis, Lieut. Jesse Lewkins, Lieut. Lockwood, Arthur M'Gill, Capt. James Miller, P. Mayer, Patrick M'Kernan, Isaac Martin, James M'Clure, Dan M'Meead, Sam. M'Elhiney, Sergt. Ephraim Munson, John M'Cannon, David Nesbit, Simeon Nott, William Powers, Sam. Parson, Mathias Parson, Col. John Pryor, William Rittenhouse, William Ramsey, Stephen Russell, John Robarts, John Robertson, Ensign Henry P. Sterling, Capt. Benjamin Stites, Wm. Steedman, Lieut. Andrew Shanklin, Sergeant Sprig, Capt. Steveson, Hezekiah Stits, Peter D. Snyder, James Stoddard, Elisha Thacher, Samuel Turk, Harmanus Taleman, Elijah Tisdale (surgeon), T.J. Vandyke (surgeon), John Wilkins, Wm. Weathers and George Webb.

James Kavenagh lost a pocket book near the store of J. & A. Hunt. It included a note from John Ryland.

William Harris, of Cincinnati, has lots for sale in that town.

Capt. John Pierce, at Fort Washington, regarding deserters: Jacob Bruner (a cooper, age 36, born in Chester County, Maryland, but lived at Man's Lick, Kentucky), Benjamin Whittington (a carpenter, age 26, born in Queen Anne's County, Maryland, but lived in Cincinnati) and John Barry (coppersmith, age 30, lived in Boston and Philadelphia).

Campbell & Williams, of Cincinnati, want to hire cabinetmakers.

Capt. Andrew Marschalk, of Greenville, regarding a deserter named John Brown, age 37, who was born in France, but has no trace of accent remaining.

Gano & Stanley have a new shipment of goods at their store in Columbia.

Bates Dorsey, of Cincinnati, administrator of the estate of Benjamin Taylor, dec'd, regarding the estate settlement.

Sheriff Daniel Symmes regarding prisoners who escaped from the Hamilton prison: Thomas Hays, Josiah Ailsworth, Mark Lamar, Richard Workman and Theophilus Lindsey.

I. Darneille, of Cincinnati, will be absent from his business for a term.

Volume II, Number 96, Saturday, 19 September 1795

Minutes of the legislature mention Gov. St.Clair, Judge Turner, taverns, Martha Lemond (regarding abuses by her husband, Wm. Lemond) and Samuel Freeman regarding his ferry at Cincinnati.

Joel Williams regarding timber cutting on land he sold to Bigham & Irwin at Fort Hamilton.

Henry Pickel regarding his ferry across the Ohio River at Cincinnati.

Subscriptions for the paper are taken by John Armstrong in Columbia, Stephen Wood in North-Bend, Capt. John Shaw in Colerain and N. Kelley in New-Port.

Volume II, Number 97, Saturday, 26 September 1795

Minutes of the legislature mention Gov. St.Clair and Judge Symmes.

W. Maxwell is appointed postmaster in place of A.M. Dunn, dec'd.

Levi Sayre found some clothing near the Big Hill.

Israel Ludlow, of Cincinnati, has lots for sale in Cincinnati.

Daniel Symmes regarding an escaped prisoner named Timothy Haily (age 30).

Israel Ludlow, of Cincinnati, regarding a party returning to Pittsburg, mentions Darbey's Town, White Woman's Creek and Fort Lawrence.

Sheriff Daniel Symmes and Judge George Turner regarding the General Court of the Territory.

Volume II, Number 98, Saturday, 3 October 1795

An account of the robbery of Mr. Litle between Greenville and Cincinnati.

A notice regarding the mail carrier, John S. M'Dowel, on the route from Graham's Station to Cincinnati.

Minutes of the legislature mention Gov. St.Clair, John S. Gano & Company, Judge Symmes, Judge Turner and the petition of Eleanor Heth, the widow of Capt. Andrew Heth, dec'd, to keep a ferry at Clarkesville on the Ohio River in Knox County.

Volume II, Number 99, Saturday, 10 October 1795

Minutes of the legislature mentions Gov. St.Clair, Mary Starkey, William Maxwell, George Gordon (Coroner of Hamilton County), Judge Turner, Judge Symmes, Ezra Fitz Freeman, Darius Curtis Orcutt (regarding his ferry on the road from Cincinnati to Greenville across the Great Miami), Andrew Christie (regarding his ferry at the same place as Orcutt), Stephen Cisna, Stephen Wood and Wm. Maxwell.

John Humes, of Cincinnati, regarding his spinning wheel and chairmaking business in Cincinnati next door to Aaron Cadwell's.

Philip Buckner has lots for sale in Augusty, Mason County, Kentucky.

Volume II, Number 100, Saturday, 17 October 1795

Minutes of the legislature mention Gov. St.Clair, Judge Symmes and Judge Turner.

Smith & Findlay, of Cincinnati, ask those indebted to them to pay their bills to John Clarke (merchant), Thomas Goudy or Elias Wallen (late of Fort Hamilton).

There is a new shipment of goods at Col. Gibson's Yellow Store on the river.

Ezekial Sayre, of Cincinnati, has lots for sale near the town.

Volume II, Number 101, Saturday, 24 October 1795

William Goforth, living on the Ohio River a mile below the mouth of the Little Miami, has a plantation for sale.

Daniel Mayo has a new shipment of goods for sale at his grocery store.

David Zeigler, of Cincinnati, has a new shipment of goods at his store.

Daniel Symmes, sheriff of Hamilton County, regarding escaped prisoners Hugh Ross and Mr. Doherty.

Volume II, Number 102, Saturday, 31 October 1795

Griffin Yeatman, of Cincinnati, has opened a house of entertainment in the house lately occupied by Matthew Winton.

John Reed, in Georgetown, Kentucky, regarding stolen horses.

George Graham, at Preston, regarding some lost post notes.

Volume II, Number 103, Saturday, 7 November 1795

An account of Gov. St.Clair's visit to the Western Counties, in company with Judge Symmes, is printed.

Sheriff Danl. Symmes, of Cincinnati, regarding some escaped prisoners: Patrick Crayton, John Harden, Jun., and William Young.

James Kavenagh of Cincinnati asks that those indebted to him pay their bills.

Reuben Reynolds, deputy sheriff of Hamilton County, regarding an escaped prisoner named Thomas Brinton.

Aaron Abbot, at Gerrard's Station, says his wife, Mary Abbot, left him and he won't honor her debts from now on.

Volume II, Number 104, Saturday, 14 November 1795

John S. Gano regarding a lost watch.

A letter to the public from the editor regarding the end of the second year of publication of the Centinel.

Jas. Silver, for Wm. Wilson, of Cincinnati, asks that those indebted to Mr. Wilson please settle their accounts.

G. Turner says he is soon to leave the Territory and will hold a public auction of his personal property at the house of George Gordon in Cincinnati.

George Morfoot, of Cincinnati, says his wife, Catherine Morfoot, left him, and he won't honor her debts from now on.

Volume III, Number 105, Saturday, 21 November 1795

A note about the return of John C. Symmes to Hamilton County is printed.

The proclamation of Gov. Arthur St.Clair regarding the formation of Randolph County from St. Clair County is printed.

I. Felty found some money in Cincinnati.

John Prince, of Cincinnati, regarding his auctioneering business in Cincinnati in the house formerly occupied by James Caldwell, near Maj. Doyle's.

Volume III, Number 106, Saturday, 28 November 1795

A note regarding a meeting of the Court of Probate at Charles Avery's house.

Hugh M'Clure has a new shipment of goods at his store in Cincinnati next door to Doctor M'Clure's shop.

Michael Castner of Cincinnati regarding the gun stolen from his boat at Cincinnati. Deliver to Robert Mitchell or John Henderson.

John C. Symmes, at North-Bend, regarding a strayed mare.

A note asking those indebted to the late firms of Gano & Company and Gano & Stanley, at Columbia, to settle their accounts.

Volume III, Number 107, Saturday, 5 December 1795

Seth Cutter, of Cincinnati, administrator of the estates of John Cutter and Joseph Cutter, late of Cincinnati, dec'd, regarding the estate settlements.

Seth Cutter regarding a public sale to be held at his house.

Stuart Richy is opening a school in the house lately occupied by John Paul opposite Doctor M'Clure's.

John Prince, auctioneer, of Cincinnati, regarding goods for sale at auction.

Thomas Olliver, of Cincinnati, regarding a stray cow.

John Temple, of Cincinnati, says his wife, Sarah Temple, left him, and he won't honor her debts anymore.

T. Goudy, of Cincinnati, has land for sale.

David Reeder and Jedidiah Tingle, of Cincinnati, give notice to Israel Ludlow about payment for land.

Pullyman Merry, at Col. Robert Johnson's in Scott County, Kentucky, has land for sale in Kentucky.

Volume III, Number 108, Saturday, 12 December 1795

Samuel Mooney says that his wife, Mary Mooney, left him, and he won't honor her debts from now on.

Thomas Barroussel, of Cincinnati, regarding his French Store in James Hill's house in Cincinnati.

J. & A. Hunt, of Cincinnati, have a new shipment of goods at their store.

James Kavenagh, of Cincinnati, regarding a bond to Aaron Richardson.

Volume III, Number 109, Saturday, 19 December 1795

James Miller, Butcher, living in Cincinnati, regarding a stray cow.

Robert Mitchell, of Cincinnati, asks those indebted to him to pay their bills.

Benjamin Griffith regarding his business (deed and will writing and surveying) in the house lately occupied by Lawyer Dunn.

VanNyees & Smith, of Cincinnati, want to buy copper and brass.

Samuel Robinson, living on the road to Mad River about three miles from Cincinnati, has land for sale.

James Forguson, of Cincinnati, is leaving for Philadelphia soon.

Francis Hudson, of Cincinnati, has lots for sale in that town.

Volume III, Number 110, Saturday, 26 December 1795

A note is printed regarding the ball at Dr. Allison's on Christmas.

Hatch & Barns have medicines for sale at their store in Cincinnati.

J. & A. Hunt, of Cincinnati, have a new shipment of goods for sale. They also mention their saddlery business.

Thomas Gibson has a new shipment of goods at his store in Cincinnati.

Volume III, Number 111, Saturday, 2 January 1796

James Glenn, of Cincinnati, has land for sale in that town.

Robert Kean and Anthony Smyth ask those indebted to them to settle their accounts with Charles Avery.

Volume III, Number 112, Saturday, 9 January 1796

A list of letters left at the Post Office in Cincinnati include Thomas Altson, Thomas Alexander, Lieut. Daniel Bissell, William Browning, James Brady, Henry Brown, Zacheriah Burrel, Thomas Baty, Capt. Edward Butler, Samuel Bulmen, Hezekiah Balch, John Cain, Richard Clegg, John Campbell, Lt. Richard Chanler, William Coven, Lieut. Joseph Campbell, James Cunningham, Mr. Cuykindall, William Currier, Ambrose Clarke, Zepheniah Downs, Francis Delong, Paul Donaghy, John Donaran, John Dunlope, Samuel Davis, George Dryer, William Eaten, Ensign Peter Frothingham, Ensign Finly, Peter Florin, Aaron Gregg, James Gollahar, Capt. John Hearh, John Hunter, Andrew Hill, Wm. Hogland, Capt. Daniel Jinings, David Logan, Isreal Ludlow, Andrew Masters, Robert Moore, James Miller, William Mason, Mr. M'Micheal, Lieut. John Micheal, Ephram Munson, Patrick M'Kernan, Joseph Patterson, Daniel Prine, James Pollock, Rev. Mr. Henderson, John Robertson, Stephen Russel (soldier), Madame Serreau, James Stoddard, Samuel Spencer, Sergt. Sprigg, Price Thomson, Anthony Vancent, Benjamin Willis, William Weathers, David Yering.

Caleb Swan, at Greenville, regarding bills of exchange.

Nancy Alexander, of Cincinnati, has land for rent.

Francis Wilson has a new shipment of goods for sale at his store in the house lately occupied by Capt. Bullock in Cincinnati.

Ephm. Brown, at Keen's Station, found a horse near Ludlow's Station on St.Clair's old road.

Levi Sayre, administrator of Ezekiel Sayre, dec'd, who lately lived one mile south of Big Hill on the Great Road, regarding the estate sale.

Volume III, Number 113, Saturday, 16 January 1796
Henry Noble has liquor for sale in the house next door to Francis Wilson in Cincinnati. Also he has a boat for sale. Apply to John Armstrong in Columbia.
John Dunlop, Surveyor of Cincinnati, in an ad regarding Capt. Isreal Ludlow's settlement at Dayton.

Volume III, Number 115, Saturday, 30 January 1796
Daniel Symes, Sheriff in Cincinnati, regarding escaped prisoners: Archibald Diddip, Hugh O'Harra, Mr. Daugherty and Isaac Johnston.
Wm. Jones has a new shipment of goods for sale at his store in Cincinnati.
John Clark, of Cincinnati, has a new shipment of goods for sale at his store next door to James Silver and John Galbraith.
John Prince, Auctioneer in Cincinnati, regarding goods for sale at auction.
John Sayer & Company, of Cincinnati, regarding their baking business in the house next door to Mr. Duffey's store.
Joseph Lummis, living on Mill Creek two miles west of Tucker's Station, found a horse.
D.C. Orcutt gives notice to return borrowed guns to James Cox.
Uriah Gates, of Cincinnati, has apple trees for sale at the house next door to Jacob Stewart in Cincinnati.
John Cleves Symmes regarding deeds for settlement.
John S. Gano & Company regarding lots in the town of Deerfield.

Volume III, Number 116, Saturday, 6 February 1796
Samuel Highway and Evan Banes, in Columbia, regarding land they bought from Hon. John Cleves Symmes.
Matthew Winton about a stray cow. Deliver to Mr. Yeatman in Cincinnati.
Samuel Cresswell, at Colerain, regarding a bond to Hannah Current.
Thomas Williams regarding his breeches and glove making business in Cincinnati.

Volume III, Number 117, Saturday, 13 February 1796
Daniel Bryan has medicines for sale at Griffin Yeatman's house in Cincinnati.
Anthony Smyth, of Cincinnati, regarding his store in the house next door to George Gordon.
Thomas Frame, of Cincinnati, wants to hire a brick moulder.
Patrick Moore, of Hamilton County, found a stray steer.

Volume III, Number 118, Saturday, 20 February 1796
An account of a meeting of the inhabitants of Columbia at the house of William Stanley mentions Judge Goforth, William Brown, Daniel Lambert, Joseph Reader, Capt. Ephream Kibbey and Rev. John Smith.
A note regarding a letter from Philadelphia to John Billi of Cincinnati.
John M'Cullough, of Cincinnati, asks those indebted to him to pay their bills.
Elizabeth Morrow, of Cincinnati, administratrix of the estate of James Morrow, dec'd, regarding the estate settlement.
Jacob Steward, of Cincinnati, says that the partnership of Steward & Butler is dissolved and that those indebted to them should please settle their accounts.

Volume III, Number 119, Saturday, 27 February 1796
An account is printed of a fire at the Hamilton County jail during which William Lucas escaped.
An unsigned letter to the editor mentions Judge Symmes and Gov. St.Clair.
Marriage: Stephen Wood, of North-Bend to Miss Kitty Freeman, daughter of Abraham Freeman of Mill Creek, on Wednesday evening, 24 February 1796.
John Dunlop, at Dayton, regarding claims to donation lots in Dayton.
Wm. M'Cluny, of Cincinnati, has beef for sale at his store next door to Capt. Benham's tavern in Cincinnati.

Volume III, Number 120, Saturday, 5 March 1796
James Cox, of Cincinnati, asks that those indebted to him pay their bills.
Kimberly & Company have a shipment of goods at their store in Cincinnati.
John Galbraith has quit his business in Cincinnati and asks those indebted to him to settle their accounts to Robert Mitchell, merchant.
James Cox, of Cincinnati, warns the public not to deal with any member of his family unless he's present.
John Prince, Auctioneer of Cincinnati, regarding goods for sale at auction.

Volume III, Number 121, Saturday, 12 March 1796
An account of George Washington's birthday celebration in Greenville.
A note regarding roads to be built by the settlers of Post Vincennes to Louisville and to Pigeon Creek.
W. Maxwell regarding printing the laws of the Territory.
B. VanHook, of Cincinnati, asks those indebted to him to pay their bills.
Samuel Barns, of Hatch & Barns, asks those indebted to him to pay their bills.
A note is printed regarding the printing of Judge Symme's pamphlet on the first settlement of "this country".
John Prince, of Cincinnati, has moved his auction room in Cincinnati.
William Boner, at Licking, says that his wife, Katharine Boner, left him and he won't honor her debts anymore.

Volume III, Number 123, Saturday, 26 March 1796
A note regarding some trials in General Court mentions Benjamin Stites of Columbia (found not guilty of the rape of Mrs. Margaret Slown), Elizabeth Baker (acquitted of the charge of stealing a bag of flour), Daniel M'Kean (lately from New Jersey, found guilty of horse stealing). Divorces were granted between George Morfoot and Katherine Morfoot and William Lemond and Martha Lemond.
W. Maxwell asks those indebted to him to settle their accounts.
Robert Mitchel has opened a rope-making business in Cincinnati.
David Roas says his wife, Peggy, left him and he won't pay her bills anymore.
James Kavenagh, of Cincinnati, gives notice to the public not to deal with any member of his family unless he's present.
Elie Williams, surviving partner of Elliot & Williams, of Cincinnati, says that the partnership is dissolved due to the death of Mr. Elliot. Those indebted to the company should settle their accounts with Edward Day of Cincinnati.
James Kavenagh, Cincinnati, is leaving the Territory and has a house for sale.
J. Clarke, of Cincinnati, regarding the settlement of land on the Licking River in Kentucky. Apply to Edward Day.
Uriah Gates, on Lick Run three miles from Cincinnati, found a cow.
John M'Cormick, living near Tucker's Station on Mill Creek in Hamilton County, regarding a strayed or stolen horse.
John Gaston, of Cincinnati, has land for sale in that town.

Volume III, Number 124, Saturday, 2 April 1796
An account of the proceedings of the General Court regarding the trial of Isaac Darneille, attorney at law, late of Cincinnati, for malfeasance.
A note is printed regarding the settlement of Hamilton County and mentions Dayton, Chillicothe and Peyton Short.
A note is printed regarding a pamphlet published by M. Carey in Cincinnati about the sale of Western lands.
A list of letters at the Post Office in Cincinnati includes Samuel Agnew at North Bend, Sergeant James Anderson, Samuel Barnes in Cincinnati, John Brown (merchant), Sergt. Zachariah Burwell, David Burnet (soldier), Henry Brown in Greenville, Paul Butler in Cincinnati, Doct. Charles Brown in Greenville, John Baker at Fort Washington, Rice Bullock, Adam Caldwell in Cincinnati, John Clark (merchant), Mr. Claimorgan in care of George Gordon, Wm. Cowen, Ezra Chaman of Cincinnati, Maj. Thomas Doyle, Timothy Dimsey, Col. Andrew Donnally, Ben. Davis in Columbia, Isaac Darnielle, Marthy Demous on the Great Miami, Luther Dana in Cincinnati, Sergt. James Elliot, Hezekiah Flint, James Ferson, Wm.

Freligh, John Galbraith (merchant), James Giffin, Lieut. Aaron Gregg, Zechariah Gapen on the Little Miami, Squire Grant near the mouth of Licking, Lieut. Peter Grasson, Daniel Harrigan, Noah P. Hopkins at Fort Washington, Sergt. George Hacket, William Hamer, Lieut. Robert Hunter, Cumland Hamilton, Robert Johnston, John Kitchel, David Lowry, John Lipscom (soldier), Lieut. Ben. Lockwood, Angus M'Coy, Alexander M'Loughlin, Levi Munsell (merchant), Andrew Marster, Capt. Mercer on the Little Miami, James M'Loughlin, James Macky in care of George Gordon, Capt. Wm. Marts, Col. Return J. Meigs at Greenville, Capt. Wm. Mills, Maj. John Mills, Dan. M'Micael, Silvenius Olny, Lieut. Piercy Pope, Capt. Zebulon Pike, Joseph Prince, Capt. John Reed at Fort Wayne, Samuel Spencer, Lieut. James Sterret, Doct. John M. Scott, Mathias Spinning, Capt. Richard Sparks, Wm. Simonds, Ensign Thomas Swaine, James Shields, Hon. Winthrop Sargent, Revd. John Taylor, Robert Taylor (packhorseman), Maj. Wm. Winston, Robert Wyly, Cornelous Wared, John Wilson and James Wood.

David Zeigler has a new shipment of goods for sale at his store in Cincinnati.

Robert Benham, of Cincinnati, regarding land for sale in Turnerville and in Judge Turner's township on Mad River or Chillicothe River.

W. Maxwell asks those indebted to the Post Office to pay their bills.

Jeremiah Hunt, of Cincinnati, has land for sale including some mills.

Joseph Lummis, living on Mill Creek two miles west of Tucker's Station, found a horse.

Volume III, Number 125, Saturday, 9 April 1796

Nathaniel Stokes, near the mouth of Deer Creek in Cincinnati, found a cow.

John Prince, Auctioneer of Cincinnati, has lots, in Cincinnati, now occupied by Samuel Perkins, for sale at auction.

John Holland, of Cincinnati, has a lot for sale and mentions Abner Dunn and Edward Day.

J. & A. Hunt have land for sale. Apply to John S. Gano in Cincinnati.

Volume III, Number 126, Saturday, 16 April 1796

Marriage: Daniel Symmes married Miss Elizabeth Oliver, both of Cincinnati, on Sunday evening, 10 April 1796.

John Campbell, living at Taylor's Creek Station, found a horse.

David Kelly, living at the mouth of the Little Miami, found a horse.

Patrick Graham, living on Bold Face Run, found hogs.

J. Forguson has a new shipment of goods for sale at his store in Cincinnati.

Volume III, Number 127, Saturday, 23 April 1796

Isaac Bates reports that he has found a stray cow.

Volume III, Number 128, Saturday, 30 April 1796

W. Maxwell wants to hire a post rider and an apprentice to the printing trade.

Abraham Garrison, living at Big Hill, found some cows.

Kimberly & Company ask that those indebted to them please settle their accounts to John S. Wills.

Volume III, Number 129, Saturday, 7 May 1796

John S. Gano, living in Columbia, regarding a stray cow. Deliver to William Stanley at Columbia.

James Hill, of Cincinnati, regarding a note from John Shannon.

Gano & Stanley have a new shipment of goods for sale at their store in Columbia. Also those indebted to them should settle their accounts with John S. Gano or Daniel Gano. They also have land for sale near Columbia. Apply to John S. Gano in Cincinnati or William Stanley in Columbia.

Isaac Mills, on the Big Miami, found a horse.

Volume III, Number 130, Saturday, 14 May 1796

Robert Mitchel, of Cincinnati, asks those indebted to him to pay their bills.

James Demint, of Cincinnati, and his wife, Elizabeth Demint, have separated, and he won't honor her debts anymore.

James Taylor, at Newport, has land for sale near Garrard's Station on Little Miami.

John Holland, of Cincinnati, says his wife, Katharine Holland, left him, and he won't honor her debts. Also he wants to do masonry and bricklaying work.

John Dearmond, living near the Goose Pond Bottom on Great Miami, reports a stray horse.

Burt & Newman, saddlers and bridle cutters in Cincinnati, want to hire an apprentice at their shop next door to J. & A. Hunt's store.

Volume III, Number 131, Saturday, 21 May 1796 (this issue is badly torn)
A note is printed regarding the claims of William Sargeant, secretary of the Northwest Territory, for his services as governor and mentions the town of St.Clair and Judge Turner.

James Brown regarding the claim he makes against Robert Sproul.

John M'Clane regarding a note to James M'Cashen of Hamilton County.

Wm. Reid, of Cincinnati, asks those indebted to him to settle their accounts with George Fithian.

John Brown, of Cincinnati, asks those indebted to him to pay their bills.

Volume III, Number 132, Saturday, 28 May 1796 (this issue is badly torn)
Benjamin Wingate, living at Tucker's Station, regarding stray cattle.

Daniel Symmes, Sheriff in Cincinnati, regarding some escaped prisoners named James Sloan and James Ferrell.

Volume III, Number 133, Saturday, 4 June 1796 (this issue is badly torn)
A note is printed regarding the arrival of Winthrop Sargent, secretary of the Northwest Territory, in Cincinnati.

Archibald M'Cabe found a horse on the west side of the Great Miami.

John Smith regarding a meeting of the Commissioners of Hamilton County at the house of Mr. Avery in Cincinnati.

Joseph M'Henry, living on Mill Creek, found a horse.

Joseph Rogers, living at Bryan's Station five miles from Lexington, Kentucky, regarding a runaway slave named Harry.

John Prince, Auctioneer in Cincinnati, has a house and lot for sale at auction.

FREEMAN'S JOURNAL

Volume I, Number 4, Saturday, 9 July 1796

Daniel Duffy asks those indebted to Atchison & Duffy to pay their accounts.

John Hartley, of Cincinnati, regarding a stray heifer.

Robert Moore, of Cincinnati, regarding a bill of sale to Mercy Traverse for land between White's Station and Columbia.

Obadiah Scott, of Cincinnati, carries on the "Butcherin Business" in the shop formerly occupied by John Miller.

William Clarke, of Cincinnati, has land for sale.

Obituary: Major John Mills, a Revolutionary War soldier, died 8 July 1796, in Cincinnati.

A note that Anthony Wayne arrived in Cincinnati on Tuesday, 5 July 1796.

W. Maxwell, of Cincinnati, has quit printing the Centinel and thanks his former subscribers. (This letter dated 13 June 1796.)

William Goforth, living on the Ohio River about one mile below the mouth of the Little Miami River, has land for sale in Columbia between Maj. Benjamin Stites and Mr. Munroe. Apply to Anthony Smyth in Cincinnati.

Caleb Swan has bills of exchange for sale.

E. Sproat, Inspector of the Revenue, about licensing stills and distillers.

A list of letters at the post office in Cincinnati includes Robert Boyd, Captain Burd, William Bowland, Joseph Crane, John Campbell, James Caldwell, John Craig, Andrew Davidson, John Devor, Francis Driver, Robert Davidson, John Ely, Zebulon Eynon, George Ensley, David Ford, Lot French, Jonathan Focknor, John Focknor, Justice Gibbs, Lu Hoine, Ezekiel Hughes, Doct. John Hatch, Silas Howel, Joseph Innes, Rebecca Kennedy, Thomas Lindsay, Doct. William M'Coskry, Absalon Martin, Jeremiah Morrow, Hugh Meek, Ephraim Munson, William Mason, Ichabod Miller, James M'Clure, John Morris, Reuben Martin, William Owens, Samuel Peoples, Lieut. John Polhemes, Sergt. Thomas Rase/Rafe, Jacob Stewart, Robert Spriggs, Israel Smith, John Sunderland, Ann Taleman, George Webb, Richard Worth, John Wier, John Wilkinson, James Wood.

Henry Coleman, living in Harrison County, Kentucky, near Cynthiana, regarding a runaway slave named Jack.

Rebecca Kennedy, widow of Francis Kennedy, deceased, regarding her ferry at Cincinnati "at the Old Place long known by the name of Kennedy's Ferry".

John Hatch and S. Barnes have dissolved their partnership. Settle your accounts with John S. Wills.

Sheriff Daniel Symmes regarding the escaped prisoners, Richard Ferrill and Abraham Croxton.

John Smith, of Columbia, found a horse.

John Leathers, at Bank Lick, regarding a runaway slave named Daniel.

Charles Wickliff, living in Washington County on the waters of Beach Fork about sixteen miles from Beards Town, regarding a runaway slave, Jack. Mentions Beats. Dorcy of Cincinnati.

S. Freeman & Son regarding ads submitted to the printing office.

William Rice regarding his boating service on the Ohio River from the Falls to Cincinnati.

Thomas Goudy, attorney at law, for Benjamin Stites, Senr., regarding his suit of divorce, in the General Court in Hamilton County, against Rachel Stites, for adultery. They were married in New Jersey in 1768 and later lived in Washington County, Pa. It is followed by an ad summoning Rachel Stites to appear at the next General Court.

Subscriptions to the Freeman's Journal are available from John Armstrong, Maj. B. Stites and Capt. E. Kibby (all at Columbia); Francis Dunlavy at Freize's

Station; James Calwell at Calwell's Mill; Thomas M'Cullagh at Hamilton; James Barret at Colerain; Parvin Dun at North-Bend; Uzal Bates at South-Bend; Capt. B. Stites at Deerfield; Wm. Freeman at Newport; and William Smith at Bank Lick.

Volume I, Number 6, Saturday, 23 July 1796

A letter from Charles Lee, Attorney General, addressed to the House of Representatives, regarding land. Mentions John Cleves Symmes.

Winthrop Serjeant and Wm. Mills, of Cincinnati, executors of the estate of Maj. Mills, dec'd, ask those indebted to Maj. Mills to settle their accounts.

Samuel Freeman and Charles Avery, of Cincinnati, regarding Peter Green, a German born tallow chandler of Cincinnati, who escaped from jail.

A note regarding W. Maxwell's printing of the Laws of the Territory mentions Mr. Goudy.

Winthrop Sargent, Cincinnati, regarding the printing of the territorial laws, mentions Thomas Goudy.

Samuel Freeman, administrator of the estate of Wm. Miller, shoemaker, dec'd, regarding the estate settlement.

James Kavenagh, of Cincinnati, regarding a stray cow.

West Miller, of Cincinnati, regarding the ferry at his landing below the mouth of Deer Creek.

John Smith of Newport about a bond from James Taylor to Wm. Snodgrass.

Volume I, Number 7, Saturday, 30 July 1796

A letter from Col. England to Brigadier General Wilkinson mentions Capt. Short at Fort Miami, Capt. DeButts, Lieut. Col. Hamtramck.

Capt. T. Pasteur, at Fort Knox, regarding stolen horses.

Obed Denham, at Columbia, has land for sale. Apply to Francis Dunlavy near Newtown.

Edward Toner lost a pocket book between Hamilton and Ludlow's Station. Deliver to Mr. Kelly in Hamilton or Mr. Cox at Big Hill. Mentions Capt. Ford.

Volume I, Number 8, Saturday, 6 August 1796

James H. Stewart regarding his publication of the Kentucky Herald. Pay subscription bills to Thomas Gibson in Cincinnati.

E. Carpenter, of Cincinnati, has a house for sale. The house was formerly occupied by Josiah Mott.

Volume I, Number 9, Saturday, 13 August 1796

Daniel C. Cooper and W.C. Schenck have land for sale in the Miami Purchase. Apply to Thomas Gibson at Cincinnati. Mentions Ludlow's Station.

John Prince, Auctioneer in Cincinnati, has housewares for sale.

Daniel Mayo, of Cincinnati, wants to hire nailors.

John Prince, Auctioneer in Cincinnati, has land for sale. The land is presently occupied by Jacob Stuart.

Volume I, Number 10, Saturday, 20 August 1796

Robert M'Elheny, living on the west side of Mill Creek four miles from Cincinnati, regarding a public auction to be held at his house.

Volume I, Number 11, Saturday, 27 August 1796

Patrick Graham, living on Bold Face Run near Mill Creek, regarding a strayed horse that formerly belonged to Doctor M'Clure. Mentions Mr. Richardson.

Garrett Cavenagh says his wife, Nancy Cavenagh, formerly known as Nancy Rook, ran away with a soldier and he won't honor her debts.

Samuel Williams, living near Columbia, found a cow and calf.

Volume I, Number 12, Saturday, 3 September 1796

Gov. St.Clair arrived in Cincinnati on Sunday last.

Samuel Freeman, of Cincinnati, asks those indebted to him to pay their bills.

James Glenn, of Cincinnati, has a house and household furniture for sale.

Samuel Osburn, of Cincinnati, offers Kelly's Tavern in Cincinnati for sale.

Volume I, Number 14, Saturday, 17 September 1796

I.B. Miller is appointed justice of the peace in Hamilton County. J.S. Wills is appointed sheriff in Hamilton County. Arthur St.Clair is appointed Attorney General and John Armstrong is appointed treasurer for the Northwest Territory.

John Greer, at Hamilton, has a house for rent.

James Murdach reports a stray horse. Deliver to Mr. Cain's Tavern in Newtown on the upper side of the Little Miami.

Thomas Right, at Fairfield, reports that Cyrus Osborn found a horse.

John Armstrong, in Columbia, has land for sale.

Francis Wilson has goods for sale at auction at his house.

Abraham Freeman, at Freeman's Station, has wheat seed for sale.

Ezra Fitz Freeman, in Cincinnati, has land for sale.

John Prince, Auctioneer in Cincinnati, has a wagon for sale at auction.

John Mahany, of Cincinnati, regarding the house for sale by James Glenn.

Samuel Freeman, of Cincinnati, regarding a cow in the possession of Thomas Adams.

Volume I, Number 17, Saturday, 8 October 1796

Oliver Wolcott, Secretary of the Treasury, regarding the sale of lands in the Northwest Territory.

Jacob Burnet, Attorney for Rachel Stites, regarding her suit in the General Court of Hamilton County against Benjamin Stites for divorce. Signed by Daniel Symmes. They were married 22 September 1768 in New Jersey. She says he abused her and then left her to marry a woman called Mary. He then left Mary and married Hannah. This ad is followed by another ad summoning Benjamin Stites to appear in court.

Gano & Stanley have a new shipment of goods for sale at their store in Columbia. Also, those indebted to Dr. Stephen Wood of North-Bend should settle their bills.

Richard Morrow, for Francis Wilson, of Cincinnati, reports that his sale is postponed.

Stephen Lyon, at Newport, regarding a note due to D. Griffith.

Seth Field, at the Little Miami, found a cow.

A list of letters left at the post office in Cincinnati includes Sergeant Samuel Bliss, Sergeant Zacharias Burnell, Edmund Buxton, Deliverance Brown, George Cochran, Archibald Campbell (Clamorgan), Ensign Samuel Dold, Frederick Dudeg, Safford Dixon, John Edgar, Lot French, Leve Fletcher, M. Lanise Catelan, John Gilkison, Price Geddis, Henry Goble, Stephen Gillet, Cumberland Hamilton, Rev. David Jones, Capt. Kelly, Lieut. Jesse Luckins, John Lowrey, William Lawrence, Mr. Miller the interpreter, Andrew Murray, William Page, John Reynolds, Lieut. Richmond, Isaiah Sutton, George Shibeler, Israel Smith, Henry P. Sterling, John Tucker, Winthrop Sargent, Elisha Thatcher, Jonathan Tichnor, Enos Woodward, Thomas Wilkins, David Ward. Entered by Daniel Mayo, Post-Master.

Geo. Gordon, of Cincinnati, regarding licenses for distillers.

Daniel Symmes, of Cincinnati, regarding a stray cow.

Daniel Mayo, living in Cincinnati, has a house for rent at Fort Washington.

John Ludlow, at Ludlow's Farms, found some steers.

Thomas Trulock, living on Cluss Creek, found some steers.

Isaac Bates, of Cincinnati, warns the public not to give credit to any member of his family unless he's present.

Charles Conn, of Cincinnati, regarding a boat going to Pittsburg. Apply to John Prince, Auctioneer.

James Cox, of Cincinnati, has a house and lot for sale. Apply to Charles Avery in Cincinnati.

Ithamar White, at Springfield in Hamilton County, administrator of the estate of Andrew Masters, dec'd, regarding the estate settlement.

Isaac Anderson, living in Cincinnati, reports a stray cow.

Wm. H. Harrison, at Fort Washington, regarding some deserters.

Lt. Col. D. Strong, at Fort Wayne, regarding the following deserters: Robert Tharp (in Capt. Greatan's Company, born in Virginia, 24 years old, a carpenter by trade) and William Jones (in Capt. Kingsberry's Company, born in Mount Holly township, Burlington County, New Jersey, 22 years old).

Volume I, Number 19, Saturday, 22 October 1796

An account of an accident at North-Bend on Tuesday night last. The house of George Holland collapsed killing both him and his wife. They had been married only a few months. They were buried on Thursday. Mrs. Holland's little sister escaped. Mrs. Holland was a daughter of the Widow Kennedy of Cincinnati who lost another child the same day.

Abraham Hiley, at Gerrard's Station, found a blue boar.

Michael Brady, at Bank Lick, regarding land located four miles from Mr. Kennedy's in Campbell County, Kentucky, that Brady bought from John Dunnovan and Wm. Matthews.

John Smith and John Davis regarding land they bought from Judge John Cleves Symmes.

Volume I, Number 21, Saturday, 5 November 1796

Thomas Arral, living on Bull-Skin Creek opposite the mouth of Locus Creek, found a horse.

Francis Dunlavy, living near New-Town east of the Little Miami, found a horse.

Benjamin Archer, living in Campbell County, Kentucky, about seven miles from Newport, reports a stray horse. Deliver to John Dunkin near the Hamilton Road about fifteen miles from Cincinnati.

Thomas Acheson asks those indebted to David Acheson or Daniel Duffey to make payments on their accounts to Griffin Yeatman.

Andrew Christy has a field and cabin for rent in Fairfield.

James Blackburn, living on Mill Creek, found a steer.

John M'Cullagh is moving from Cincinnati and asks those indebted to him to settle their accounts with Thomas M'Cullagh at Fort Hamilton, William Freeman at Newport or Abner Wilkinson "at my store in Cincinnati".

Reuben Bood/Rood, at North-Bend, wants to hire stonemasons.

Volume I, Number 22, Saturday, 12 November 1796

Jacob Brown, living at Cochron's Tavern in Cincinnati, at the sign of the Red Lion, has land for sale.

Daniel C. Cooper, of Cincinnati, has land for sale near Cox's Tavern on the road to Hamilton.

Rachel Duffey, for Daniel Duffey, of Cincinnati, asks those indebted to settle their accounts with Thomas Acheson.

Volume I, Number 24, Saturday, 26 November 1796

James Smith is appointed sheriff in Hamilton County by the Governor.

George Gillaspie, on Mill Creek near James Cunningham's, found some steers.

Levi Munsell, of Cincinnati, regarding Winthrop Sargent's refusal to pay rent on his house.

William Kelly says that he won't pay the bills of his wife, Jane Kelly.

Volume I, Number 25, Saturday, 3 December 1796

A notice regarding the meeting of the fire company at the house of Griffin Yeatman in Cincinnati.

Thomas Williams, skin-dresser and breeches maker in Cincinnati, regarding his business.

James Barrett, of Colerain, found a heifer.

Thomas Acheson regarding the deed on the lot on which the store of Daniel J. Duffey and David Acheson now stands. Mentions Daniel Symmes and Griffin Yeatman.

Volume I, Number 26, Saturday, 10 December 1796
Samuel Williams, near Columbia, found a heifer.
Thomas Fream, living in Cincinnati, regarding some stray steers.
James Smith, of Newport, administrator of the estate of Samuel Pounds, late of Fairfield, dec'd, regarding the estate settlement.
Josiah Mott, living on Clear Creek 36 miles from Cincinnati on the route leading to the mouth of the Mad River, found a horse.
Jacob Reeder, living on Mill Creek, found some steers.

Volume I, Number 27, Saturday, 17 December 1796
Thomas Williams, of Cincinnati, administrator of the estate of Bartholomew Smith, late of Cincinnati, dec'd, regarding the estate settlement.
A notice regarding the singing school opening in Cincinnati.
John Ward, living in Cincinnati at Joel Williams' place, regarding a settlement on the Green River.
Mark Hardin, living in Washington County, Kentucky, regarding a runaway slave, Reuben.
James White, living at Isaac Anderson's in Cincinnati, regarding his evening school in Cincinnati.
Patrick Moore, living near Fort Hamilton, found some steers.
J. Bartle, living on the Licking River seven miles from New Port in Campbell County, has land for sale.

Volume I, Number 28, Saturday, 24 December 1796
John Brown, Saml. Dick and Griffin Yeatman, in Cincinnati, overseers of the poor, regarding a meeting to adjust their accounts. The meeting was held at Charles Avery's house in Cincinnati.
Levi Jennings, living on Duck Creek in Columbia township, found a cow.
A notice of a meeting at Cutter's Tavern regarding the support of the poor in Cincinnati township.
Thomas Banes, living at Middletown, found a bull.

Volume I, Number 29, Saturday, 31 December 1796
Jacob Kerr, of Cincinnati, regarding bounty lands located by John Dunlop, mentions Jonathan Dayton.
Daniel Symmes, of Cincinnati, regarding stray cows.
Ferdinand Brokaw, living near Big Hill, found a bull.
James Goudy, at South Bend, found some cows.

Volume I, Number 37, Saturday, 4 March 1797
A letter to the editor from Elisha Thatcher about a recent letter about him.
Smith & Findlay ask those indebted to them to settle their accounts.
William Wells, of Cincinnati, has land for sale.
Thomas Gibson, of Cincinnati, asks those indebted to him to pay their bills.
John Holland, of Cincinnati, has a house for rent next to Deer Creek and mentions Doctor M'Clure. Apply to Patrick Dickey.
Winthrop Sargent, of Cincinnati, asks those indebted to him to settle their accounts. Also he has a house for sale.
Aaron Cadwell, of Cincinnati, administrator of the estate of Nathan Barnes, dec'd, regarding the estate settlement.
George Fithian has opened a public house of entertainment in the house lately occupied by Capt. Robert Benham.
James Smith, Sheriff in Cincinnati, regarding a prisoner, Barnard Robert M'Ginnes (carpenter), who escaped from Fort Washington.
John M'Cullough, of Cincinnati, has a new shipment of goods for sale at his stores in Newport and Cincinnati. Also he has land for sale. Apply to Wm. Freeman in Newport.
Robert Edgar, at Mad River, lost a pocket book on the Mad River Road between Cunningham's Station and Josiah Mott's place. It contained a note from Aaron Richardson to John Dougharty and an invoice from Matthew Hueston.

Deliver to Samuel Dicks' in Cincinnati.

William Goforth, in Columbia, has land for sale.

William C. Scenk and Daniel C. Cooper, of Cincinnati, regarding donation lots in Franklin on the Great Miami River.

John Bustard, at Thomas Cochran's Tavern in Cincinnati, for Oliver Ormsby who has quit his business in Cincinnati. Those indebted to Ormsby should settle their accounts.

Patrick Moore, at Fort Hamilton, has land for rent.

Wm. Freeman, at Newport, has a new shipment of goods for sale at his store in Newport between Mr. Brasher and Sheriff Kelly.

Riddle & Woodson have purchased the entire stock of Ormsby & Bustard, Merchants, and now operate from the latter's former store.

Jacob Sorency, of Cincinnati, lost a pocket book. Deliver to Mr. Hunt.

Volume I, Number 38, Saturday, 11 March 1797

James Sutton, in Hamilton, regarding a stray cow.

William Goudy, living six miles below Cincinnati and one mile from the Ohio River, has land for sale.

Frederick Coonse found a cow.

William Kelly found a steer.

William H. Harrison, at Fort Washington, gives notice to those indebted to Judge Symmes.

Volume I, Number 39, Saturday, 18 March 1797

Robert M'Clure, of Cincinnati, asks those indebted to him to pay their bills.

J. Clarke, of Cincinnati, is leaving for Philadelphia and asks those indebted to him to settle their accounts with Smith & Findlay or with James Smith.

Patrick Lafferty, of Cincinnati, found a steer.

David Zeigler has a new shipment of goods for sale at his store in Cincinnati. Also he has a stud horse for sale.

Wm. Gowdy, in South-Bend township, regarding a horse that strayed or was stolen. Deliver to Thomas Gowdy, lawyer, in Cincinnati.

Daniel Symmes, of Cincinnati, regarding a house he bought from Nathan Barnes, late of Cincinnati, dec'd.

Wm. Hercules found a sow.

Volume I, Number 40, Saturday, 25 March 1797

A note regarding the publication of the poetical works of Peter Pindar. Apply to Wm. Freeman at Newport or to Thomas M'Cullagh at Hamilton.

George Gordon has opened a tavern in Cincinnati and wants to hire a bartender.

James Standiford, Thos. Saunders, Edward Rogers and Brackett Owen (all of Jefferson County, Kentucky) regarding runaway slaves named Joshua, Duke, Charles and James.

Thomas Fream, of Cincinnati, wants to hire brick makers.

Number 19, Volume III, Saturday, 17 October 1798, Whole Number 12

Gov. St.Clair returned to Cincinnati after his trip up the river to lay off the new county of Ross. The county seat is Chillicothe.

Married: Isaac Vanse (?) to Miss Betsy Broadrick, both of Cincinnati, were married "last week".

A note about the drowning of Daniel Bunnel who formerly lived at Columbia.

Sheriff James Smith regarding sheriff's sales of the various property at the suits of William Maxwell, James Riddle and William Chribbs. He mentions William M'Clellan of Hamilton.

Ralph W. Hunt regarding a bond he gave to Benjamin Jennings in 1788 for land in Judge Symmes' purchase.

John Dodson, living in Springfield township one mile from Caldwell's Mills, found a mare.

A. Whitlock, for the Quarter Master, at Fort Washington, reports that a Delaware Indian chief, Bohougedelass, brought in some stray horses.

Joel Williams, at Cincinnati, regarding a note passed to Rufus Elliot.

Joseph M'Mahan, living on Mill Creek about three and a half miles beyond Cunningham's Mill, found a mare.

Stephen Parker, living on Mill Creek, reports that he found a stray cow.

Aaron Ireland reports that a stray steer came to his plantation.

Levi M'Lean, Auctioneer for Hamilton County, regarding licenses required to sell goods at auction.

James Ferguson asks those indebted to him to settle their accounts. He also says the house and lot lately occupied by Woodward & Reeder are for sale or rent.

Joel Williams, in Cincinnati, gave Israel Shreves a store and goods to manage, but now Shreves won't settle the accounts with Williams.

John Speed has salt made at Man's Lick for sale at Charles Nabb's store in Louisville.

Jesse & Abijah Hunt have moved their store to the house formerly occupied by Mr. Daily and next door to Col. Gibson's place. Those indebted to the late firm of A. Hunt & Company or to Jeremiah and A. Hunt should make payments.

Lt. Col. John S. Gano gives orders for the First Battalion of Hamilton County Militia to meet at the public ground in Cincinnati.

John S. Gano has land for sale in the Miami Purchase near Sycamore Creek.

Ephm. Kibbey and Anne Tewillegar, administrators of Harmonious Talmon (?), late of Columbia, deceased, regarding the estate settlement.

Thomas Conn regarding horses for sale at Kibbey's Tavern in Columbia.

John R. Mills, living near Capt. Jacob White's Station, has land for sale.

John M'Cullagh asks those indebted to him to settle their accounts by delivering wheat to David Grummon's Mill. Also those indebted to Patrick Moore should make payment.

Wm. Freeman, on Beaver Creek, reports a work ox that broke out of the enclosure of S. Freeman. Deliver to Samuel Freeman in Cincinnati.

Wm. Terry reports a mare that strayed or was stolen from Mr. Reddingburgh's near Capt. White's place. Deliver to Mr. Grummon's Mill.

Ralph W. Hunt and William R. Phillips have land for sale in Hamilton County. Apply to Hunt and Phillips at Griffin Yeatman's Tavern in Cincinnati.

John Nancarrow at Columbia has military lands for sale. He also wants someone to build a saw mill on Five Mile Creek.

Freeman & Carpenter regarding the subscriptions to the Freeman's Journal available at Columbia by Timothy Kibby, Maj. B. Stites and Capt. E. Kibby; at Calwell's Mill by James Calwell; at Hamilton by Thos. M'Cullagh; at North Bend by Jas. Silvers; at S. Bend by G. Cullum; at Newport by J. M'Clure; and at Deerfield by Capt. B. Stites.

Number 38, Volume III, Tuesday, 5 March 1799, Whole Number 142

Francis M'Cormack, at Nettleville, has a stud horse for service.

Wm. H. Harrison, at Cincinnati, regarding a stud horse.

W.C. Schenck, living opposite Col. Gano in Cincinnati, has land for sale in Judge Symme's patent.

George Fithian, of Cincinnati, has moved to the house lately occupied by Seth Cutter in Cincinnati and continues operating his tavern there. He also speaks of his boot and shoemaking business.

Stephen Reeder, living two miles from Cincinnati, regarding a stud horse.

Thomas Fitzwater, living on the little Miami about four miles above the Round Bottom, found a horse.

John S. Gano, of Cincinnati, has land for sale in Judge Symmes' patent.

Martin Baum, of Cincinnati, asks those indebted to him to pay their bills.

Abia Martin, living on Mill Creek near Capt. Jacob White's place, regarding a stud horse at John Cummon's house near Cunningham's Mill.

The editor asks those indebted to the Freeman's Journal to pay their bills.

William Goforth, at Columbia, has land for sale.

Richard Hankens found a stray cow.

Andrew Lock, at Dayton, says that his wife, Sarah Lock, committed adultery with David Morris, and he won't pay her bills anymore.

F. M'Cormack wants to hire a school teacher in Nettleville.

Mary Felty, administratrix of the estate of Isaac Felty, tavern keeper at Cincinnati, deceased, regarding the estate settlement.

Miny Voorhees, at Mill Creek, regarding a stray mare.

Thomas Davis, living on the head waters of Clear Creek, about stray hogs.

Charles Jamison, living in Chillicothe, regarding a stray horse.

William Slone, living at Gerard's Station, found a steer.

Jac. Burnet and George W. Burnet, of Cincinnati, want to hire a person to manage the farm of Capt. Harrison.

Thomas Gibson, of Cincinnati, asks those indebted to him to pay their bills.

John R. Mills, living near Capt. Jacob White's Station, has land for sale.

Calvin Morrel writes regarding a stray horse.

Ezekiel Hughes, administrator of the estate of John Jones, late of Wales, dec'd, about the estate settlement. Hughes lives in Miami township near Colerain.

James Forguson asks those indebt to him to pay their bills. He also has salt for sale.

Hope Mills, living at Red Bank Station, found a heifer.

John Line says his wife, Sarah Line, left him and he won't pay her bills.

John W. Brown has salt for sale.

J. Whitworth, for Samuel Hildritch (owner of a store and tavern in Columbia), asks those indebted to Hildritch to settle their accounts.

W. & M. Jones regarding their bakery in the house opposite their store in Cincinnati.

Moses Leonard, living on the bank of the Ohio near Columbia, found a horse.

Barney M'Carran, of Cincinnati, asks those indebted to him to pay their bills.

John Nancarrow, at Columbia, has land for sale.

Wm. Mitchell, living on the Great Miami, found a mare below Hamilton.

John Hunter, at Georgetown, regarding his tavern and hotel in Georgetown.

A notice of a meeting of the Commissioners of Hamilton County at the house of Charles Avery in Cincinnati.

Number 19, Volume IV, Tuesday, 1 October 1799, Whole Number 172

Gov. Arthur St.Clair's speech to the House of Representatives is printed.

Mr. Sibley, representative from Detroit, arrived in Cincinnati last week.

Edm. Freeman asks those indebted to him for subscriptions to his "News-Paper" to settle their accounts. Deliver wheat to Mr. Gromin's Mill.

Thomas Gibson has a new shipment of goods at his store in Cincinnati.

Edward Tiffin and John S. Wills regarding a suit in Ross County Court of Common Pleas: Meeker, Cochran & Company vs. Bertrand Ewale and Jesse Ewale.

John Elliott, living at the mouth of Sycamore Creek, about eight miles from Columbia, reports some stray mare colts.

Thomas Morris, for Lydia Davis and James Davis, the administrators of the estate of Benjamin Davis, late of Columbia, dec'd, about the estate settlement.

Saml. Dick, in Cincinnati, asks those indebted to him to make payments in wheat to David Grummon's Mill.

Joshua Delaplane, at Fort Hamilton, regarding a stray steer. Deliver to Samuel Freeman in Cincinnati.

THE WESTERN SPY AND HAMILTON GAZETTE

Volume 1, Tuesday, 28 May 1799, Number 1
    A letter to the public from the editor, Joseph Carpenter, printer, mentions the post rider, Mr. Dorret.
    A note regarding Indian activities mentions Major Ludlow.
    Marriage: George Burnet of Cincinnati married Miss Sophia Greene of Marietta, in Cincinnati, Sunday evening of "last week", by Rev. Mr. Wilson.
    Marriage: John Daily married Mrs. Elizabeth Brown of Cincinnati on Monday evening.
    Lieut. Daniel Symmes gives battalion orders. He also reports that Francis Mennesiers is appointed quarter master of the First Battalion.
    Lieut. Col. John Armstrong and Adjutant Timothy Kibby give orders to the Second Battalion of Hamilton County Militia.
    J. Clarke and C. Killgore, of Cincinnati, have sold the rest of their stock and closed their business. Those indebted to them should settle their accounts.
    James Smith, Collector of Revenue, regarding duties on the still owners in Hamilton County.
    Griffin Yeatman regarding the expenses of operating his pump and the methods of payment for the use of it.
    Levi M'Clain, of Cincinnati, asks those indebted to him to pay their bills. He also wants to buy cattle.
    John Doyle, of Cincinnati, regarding his business of gun making and repairing.
    Wyllys Pierson, living on Duck Creek, found a heifer.
    Thomas Goudy, at Millcreek Farm, regarding Mr. Brownlee's operation of Goudy's mill, mentions Mr. Jessup.
    John Armstrong and William Wells, at Columbia in Hamilton County, regarding military warrants for land.
    George Gordon, of Cincinnati, regarding deeds in the Recorder's office, mentions James Smith. He also has a house for sale. Apply to Doctor Sellman.
    Wm. Jones, Merchant, has a house for rent in Cincinnati.

Volume 1, Tuesday, 4 June 1799, Number 2
    An unsigned letter to the editor mentions Mr. John Fowler's letter to the public of Kentucky.
    Bell & Bill regarding their blacksmithing business in Cincinnati in the shop formerly occupied by James Bell.
    Levi Woodward, for James Smith, in Cincinnati, regarding cattle for sale.
    John Crane, on the Miami River above the Big Passing, about a stray mare.

Volume 1, Tuesday, 11 June 1799, Number 3
    An unsigned letter to the editor mentions Gov. William Henry Harrison, the Second Battalion of Hamilton County Militia and Lieut. Fithean.
    A note regarding the trial of John Fries for treason.
    Marriage: Joseph Newman of Cincinnati married Miss Dolly Brooks of Augusta, Bracken County, Kentucky, on Sunday, 2 June 1799.
    John S. Gano, of Cincinnati, has land for sale in Judge Symmes' patent.
    John Lyon regarding his house of entertainment on the Hamilton Road eleven miles from Cincinnati.
    Justice Gibbs, at Southbend, found a horse.
    David Snodgrass, of Cincinnati, asks those indebted to the firm of William Snodgrass & Company to pay their bills to Col. Thomas Gibson, Jacob Burnet or Mr. H. M'Cullom.
    Petrus Ponta, living at the head of Turtle Creek near Taylor's mills, reports a strayed or stolen horse. Deliver to Isaac VanNuys in Cincinnati.

Volume 1, Tuesday, 18 June 1799, Number 4
   Notes regarding Indian activities mentions Capt. Hamilton.
   Charles Kilgore regarding a meeting of Masons in Cincinnati.
   Clemmenhouse Dowden, living two miles above the Little Miami on the Ohio River, found a horse.
   Lieut. Col. John S. Gano and Lieut. Daniel Symmes give Battalion orders to the First Battalion of Hamilton County Militia and mention Major Ludlow on Mill Creek.
   Burt & Newman have moved their saddler's shop to the house next door to Griffin Yeatman's Tavern on Front Street in Cincinnati.
   George Fithian, of Cincinnati, asks those indebted to him to settle their bills.
   Robert Park has opened a hatting business in Cincinnati.
   David Williams, living on Muddy Creek in Southbend township, found a horse.
   Wm. & Michael Jones have a new shipment of goods for sale at their store in Cincinnati. They also ask those indebted to their store or tavern to pay their bills.

Volume 1, Tuesday, 25 June 1799, Number 5
   A note is printed regarding Gov. St.Clair and his family arriving in Cincinnati.
   An account of a meeting of Masons mentions Gov. St.Clair and Mr. Austin.
   Stephen Wood, of Northbend, writes a letter to the public regarding his service as a justice of the peace in Hamilton County and mentions Parvin Dun.
   Mr. Mennesiers, of Cincinnati, regarding allum clay found in the district.

Volume 1, Tuesday, 2 July 1799, Number 6
   Abraham Southard, at Big Parara (?), regarding a stray horse.
   Marriage: Thomas Reddick married Miss Polly Carson, "both of this country", on Tuesday last.
   Obituary: Mrs. Jane Woodward, wife of William Woodward of Cincinnati, died on "Wednesday morning last".
   Aaron Cadwell, of Cincinnati, has land for sale.
   James Knight, living near the Round Bottom, found a horse.
   Levi M'Lean, of Cincinnati, offers a reward for the return of a stolen cane.
   Lieut. John R. Mills announces a meeting of the First Battalion of Hamilton County Militia near Maj. Ludlow's place.
   Wm. & M. Jones have a new shipment of goods for sale at their store in Cincinnati.
   A list of letters remaining at the Post Office in Cincinnati: James Armstrong of Colerain, Patrick Broadrick, John Bengannaw, Henry Brown of Loremiers, Capt. Daniel Bissell, Doctor D. Bryan, John Bomsill/Bomfill, Henry Cassidy at Vincennes, Frederick Conner on Licking River, John Cook at Falmouth in Campbell County, William Chamberlin in Northbend, Abraham Cary or Samuel Martin, Capt. James Dunn, Abner L. Duncan at Natchez, George Doxon, Amos Edgerton, Abraham Freeman, Thomas Goudy, Reese Gaddis of Campbell County, Ezekiel Hughes, John T. Hall in Deerfield, Luke Hudson, Doctor Thomas Hearley or Hearsey of Adams County, John Harris, Thomas Hutton at Pensacola, Ichabod Halsey at Newtown, Rebecca Johnston, Reuben Kemper, Ephraim Kibby, Isreal Ludlow, Francis Lennan at Natchez, Andrew and William Lyle, John Moutfort in care of Cornelius Vameyes, Jonathan Markland of Campbell County, Thomas M'Clelland, John Squire Marsh, Joseph M'Kean, Thomas M'Cormick, I.B. Miller at the mouth of the Little Miami, Doctor John Gilbert Pettet, John Roberts on Grassey Creek in Campbell County, James Riddle, Robert Reed in care of Joel Williams, James Smith at Natchez, Col. John Small in Vincennes, John Cleves Symmes, James E. Smith, William Steel (Hatter), Lieut. John Steel, James Swan at St. Louis, Solomon Sibley in Detroit, Thomas Truelark, Ensign David Thompson, Daniel Theu in care of Jacob Burnet, Isaac Vanmetre in care of Joel Williams, John Vanblarigan, Gen. James Wilkinson, Jonathan Williams, Nathaniel Williams, Moses Christ Westhing, Joseph Ward, Capt. Jacob White, Joseph Walker in Northbend, Samuel Welch. Entered by William Ruffin, Post-Master.
   Robert Harper reports that he found a stray heifer.
   Levi Woodward, for Sheriff James Smith, reports more sheriff's sales.

Volume 1, Tuesday, 9 July 1799, Number 7
An account of the Fourth of July celebration mentions the First Battalion of Hamilton County Militia, Capt. Miller, Capt. Smith and Mr. Yeatman's Tavern.

The governor issues orders for the militia and mentions Lieut. Col. Gano.

A note regarding Gen. Wilkinson and Col. Hamtramck is printed.

A note is printed regarding Maj. Ludlow's mission to lay out the "Indian boundary line".

Israel Ludlow about the lot presently occupied by Joel Williams in Cincinnati that is now offered for sale by Hon. John C. Symmes.

Martin Baum says the partnership of Martin Baum & Company is expired. Those indebted should pay their bills to Thomas Thompson.

John Dinsmore, living at James Snowden's near Cunningham's Mill on Mill Creek, reports a lost horse and mentions Capt. Goudy's Mill.

Volume 1, Tuesday, 16 July 1799, Number 8
An article is printed regarding the Fourth of July celebration at Columbia.

A letter to the editor from E. Langham and Samuel Finley at Chillicothe regarding an incident involving a Mr. Hedges of Wheeling and Benjamin Urmston, tavern keeper, mentions Capt. Nathan Reeves.

John Sellman, of Cincinnati, has medicines for sale at his store.

Thomas Gregg regarding his new tavern in Chillicothe.

Elias Langham, of Chillicothe, has land for sale. He mentions Lawrence Butler, Alexander Parker, Robert Beale, Mr. Quigly (living at the mouth of Indian Creek), Mr. Sargeant, Thomas Parker, Capt. Lamb and Mr. Young.

Robert M'Gennis, of Columbia, regarding a runaway apprentice named Philip Drum, age 17, who was born in Holland.

John VanNuys, of Cincinnati, regarding a runaway apprentice named William Flin, age 11 or 12.

Volume 1, Tuesday, 30 July 1799, Number 10
Obituary: Rev. Peter Wilson, age 45, died Wednesday morning, 24 July 1799. He will be buried Thursday at the meeting house with a sermon by Rev. Kemper.

Marriage: Edmund Freeman (printer) married Mrs. Elizabeth Rodman on "Thursday last" in Cincinnati.

Sheriff James Smith, in Cincinnati, regarding sheriff's sales of the property of Seth Cutter (at the suit of James Ferguson), Elmer Williams (at the suit of William Henry Harrison), Abraham & Garret Vorhese (at the suit of John Wilkins), Darius C. Orcutt (at the suit of James Morrison), James Brady (at the suit of E. Joice, executor of D. Joice, dec'd) and Charles & Amos Munroe.

Thomas Doyle, of Cincinnati, has houses and lots for sale. He mentions D.R. M'Clure, Mr. Paterson (saddler), J. Stewart, and Wm. Snodgrass & Company.

Jacob Williams regarding his blacksmithing business at his shop on Mill Creek near Cincinnati.

Seth Cutter, living a half mile west of the Courthouse, asks those indebted to him to settle their accounts with John Daily.

Thomas Gibson, of Cincinnati, has a new shipment of goods at his store.

Cyrus Sackett, living on the waters of Sugar Creek at Vance's Settlement six miles above Beansville, reports a stray horse.

Levi M'Lean, gaoler for Hamilton County, regarding the runaway servant boys, Joseph and John Gatz, who belong to John Bille.

James Silvers, in Northbend, reports that the partnership of Jones & Silvers is dissolved. Those indebted to them should settle their bills with W. & M. Jones, merchants in Cincinnati. Also W. & M. Jones would like to buy wheat at David Grummon's mill.

William Stuart has flour for sale. Apply to Isaac Anderson, merchant, in Cincinnati.

A note regarding deserters from Capt. John Whistler's Company mentions William O'Brian (born in Ireland, cooper, age 21) and John Bell (born in Ireland, carpenter, age 21).

Capt. Edward Miller reports a deserter, Thomas Caldwell (born in Virginia "of

Irish extraction", age 18), who is in company with a runaway apprentice of John M'Cullagh's.

John M'Cullagh, of Cincinnati, regarding a runaway servant boy named John Thompson, age 14.

Volume 1, Tuesday, 6 August 1799, Number 11

Obituary: Rev. Peter Wilson died Wednesday, 24 July 1799, leaving his small children orphaned.

Accounts of Indian attacks mention Maj. Ludlow and Capt. Hamilton.

A note regarding the post rider, Mr. Dorret, is printed.

A council for the Northwest Territory is announced: Jacob Burney and James Findlay of Hamilton County; Henry Vandeburg of Knox County; Robert Oliver of Washington County; and David Vance of Jefferson County.

William Austin, of Cincinnati, asks those indebted to him to pay their bills.

George Love, living on the dry fork of the White Water, found a mare.

John VanNuys, of Cincinnati, regarding a gun his apprentice stole.

Frederick Bondel, of Cincinnati, regarding his blue dying business near Mr. Carpenter's Printing office.

Elmore Williams, living on Hamilton Road, found a horse.

John Beckett, living near Cunningham's Mill on Mill Creek, about stray colts.

Benj. Walker, of Hamilton County, prints a letter of apology from Ephraim Morison.

A. Whitlock, at Fort Washington, found a horse.

Volume 1, Tuesday, 13 August 1799, Number 12

The text of a speech delivered by Chief Metholgy of the Creek Indians at the house of James Seagrove at Point Peter on St. Mary's River.

James Ferguson is leaving the Northwest Territory. Those indebted to him should settle accounts by making payments in wheat to David Grummen's mill.

A note regarding Indian actions mentions Maj. Ludlow.

Marriage: Benjamin M. Stokes married Miss Prudence Cadwell "on Thursday last" in Cincinnati.

Martin Baum and William C. Schenck, in Cincinnati, regarding military land warrants.

Caleb Hays, in Ohio township, asks those indebted to him to pay their bills.

James Smith, Collector of Revenue in Cincinnati, about the duty on distillers.

James Conn, of Cincinnati, reports that the partnership of James and Charles Conn is dissolved.

D.C. Cooper, at Dayton, wants to hire a distiller.

Volume 1, Tuesday, 20 August 1799, Number 13

A note regarding the Court of Common Pleas in Hamilton County mentions John Cleves Symmes and W.C. Schenk.

A letter to the editor from John Clarke mentions Mr. Freeman's paper and Maj. Ludlow.

Marriage: Robert Brasher married Miss Hannah Simone or Simons (no date).

A note about the drowning of John Bracaw near the mouth of Great Miami.

Mekinney Anthony, living at the mouth of the Great Miami, found a mare.

Paul Butler, of Dayton, lost a duebill on James Gillaspie.

Asa Harvey, living at Dunlap's Station at Colerain, regarding a stray mare.

Jacob or Geo. Burnet has land for sale. Mentions Mr. Dixon living on the big road to Hamilton.

Wm. & M. Jones have books and stationery for sale.

C. Avery, in Cincinnati, asks those indebted to him to settle their accounts.

Daily & Baxter regarding their coopering business.

Abraham Vorheas has lots in Cincinnati for sale.

Ross Crossley, on Duck Creek, found a cow.

Volume 1, Tuesday, 27 August 1799, Number 14

Simeon Kinton and William Ward print the speech of the Shawnee chiefs.

A note regarding Indian attacks mentions Maj. John M'Farlin.
A note is printed regarding Maj. Ludlow's boundary line.
Marriage: Peter Bell, of Columbia, married Miss Peggy Orr, of Cincinnati, at Cincinnati, on "Thursday last".
Obed Denham, at Hamilton County, regarding the scandalous remarks, in reference to Obed and William Denham, made by Samuel Westerfield. He submits a deposition signed by Harmon Parson, Jeremiah Beck, Sr., James South, Hauton Clarke, Kelly Burk, Jeremiah Beck, Jun., and Barcella Osborn.
John Becket, living near Cunningham's Mill on Mill Creek, about a stray mare.
Philip John Shingles, living on the Ohio River opposite Augusta, found some steers.

Volume 1, Tuesday, 3 September 1799, Number 15
Sheriff James Smith, at Cincinnati, regarding an election to be held at the house of Charles Avery in Cincinnati.
An unsigned letter to the editor mentions Judge Cadwell and Col. Sargent.
An unsigned letter regarding Aaron Cadwell and Mr. Dunlavy as candidates for the general assembly.
An unsigned letter to the editor regarding Dr. Alison and Thomas Gibson as candidates for the general assembly.
Obituary: Capt. Piercy Pope, of the Artillery, died at Natchez "sometime in June last", of a fever.
Lieut. Col. John Armstrong and Lieut. Timothy Kibby about battalion orders.
W.C. Schenck, at Cincinnati, regarding a stray horse.
B. Chambers, on Mill Creek, about a stray mare belonging to Joseph Vance.
Daniel Goble, of Ohio township, says that his wife, Margaret Goble, left him and he won't honor her debts from now on.
John Mahony asks those indebted to him to settle their accounts at Joel Williams' house.

Volume 1, Tuesday, 10 September 1799, Number 16
An unsigned letter to the editor is printed regarding Ichabod B. Miller and Richard Alison as candidates for the General Assembly.
An unsigned letter to the editor regarding Thomas Goudy as a candidate for the General Assembly.
Lieut. Daniel Symmes gives orders to the First Battalion of Hamilton County Militia to meet at the house of George Fithian in Cincinnati.
J. & A. Hunt have a new shipment of goods for sale at their store.
Sheriff James Smith regarding a sheriff's sale of the property of William M'Cann that was seized by suit of James Ardery, executor of John Smith, dec'd.
Leana Brokaw and John Cleves Symmes, administrators of the estate of John Brokaw, dec'd, regarding the estate sale to be held at his house near the mouth of the Great Miami River.
B. Leonard, of Cincinnati, found some hogs.
A notice regarding a blacksmith wanted in Dayton.

Volume 1, Tuesday, 17 September 1799, Number 17
A letter from John Cleves Symmes to John Smith, of Columbia, is printed regarding land in the Miami Purchase.
Samuel Westerfield writes a letter to the editor regarding the recent notice signed by Obed Denham, Harmon Pearson, Houton Clark, Jeremiah Beck, Sen., Jeremiah Beck, Jun., and Kelly Burk. He tells his side of the dispute and mentions Mr. Brackenridge, John Armstrong and William Brown.
Kelly Burk, J. Beck, Sen., J. Beck, Jun., and Harman Pearson (witnessed by Peter Light) state that they did not sign the letter regarding the Obed Denham and Samuel Westerfield dispute.
Houton Clarke says that he's sorry he signed the letter regarding Obed Denham because he now finds that he was misled.
Barzella Osborn says that he didn't sign the letter regarding Obed Denham.
James South says he didn't sign the letter regarding Obed Denham.

William Blair, John Evans, Nathaniel Donham, William Toph, Henry Donham, Joseph Frazier and John Webb regarding the character of Obed Denham.

Aaron Cadwell and Isaac Martin were chosen as representatives over Mr. Dunlavy, Mr. White and T. Brown.

Capt. E. Kibby has returned to Cincinnati after completing the road from Post Vincennes to the Great Miami.

A note regarding the meeting of the General Assembly of the Northwestern Territory mentions Mr. Darlington from Adams County.

A son of Mr. Lummis drowned trying to cross the Great Miami last week.

Marriage: William M'Farland married Miss Nancy Singer, both of Cincinnati, on "Sunday evening last".

Marriage: Silas Hurin married Miss Agnes Ludlow, daughter of John Ludlow, at Mill Creek. (no date listed)

Lieut. Daniel Symmes gives orders to the Hamilton County Militia to meet near Capt. Goudy's mill.

Francis Mennessiers has opened a coffee house in Cincinnati. He will also teach the French language.

Thomas Cochran has opened "private lodgings" at the house of Maj. Doyle in Cincinnati. He mentions Col. Gibson and Col. Gano.

A. Whitlock, of Cincinnati, reports that he found some horses.

Joseph Shaylor, living on the East fork of the Little Miami, says that he won't honor debts contracted by his wife, Mary Shaylor.

Volume 1, Tuesday, 24 September 1799, Number 18

An unsigned letter to John Smith of Columbia mentions John Cleves Symmes.

Leana Brocaw and John Cleves Symmes regarding the estate sale of John Brocaw, deceased.

C. Avery, of Cincinnati, asks those indebted to him to settle their accounts.

David Grummon, at his mill on Mill Creek, asks those indebted to him to settle their accounts.

Thomas Frazee, at the mouth of the Crawfish near Columbia, asks those indebted to him to settle their accounts.

Sqr. Grant, living in Campbell County, Kentucky, regarding a runaway slave.

Asa Kitchell, justice of the peace, says that Jonathan Stoker, of Ohio township, left the Territory without paying his debts. Mentions John Smith of Ohio township.

A note regarding the General Assembly mentions representatives: Mr. Tiffin, Mr. Langham, Mr. Worthington and Mr. Findley from Ross County; Mr. Darlington of Adams County; Mr. Small and Mr. Vanderberg from Knox County; Mr. Bond of Randolph County; Mr. Edgar of St. Clair County. Mentions Mr. Burnet, Mr. Vance.

Volume 1, Tuesday, 1 October 1799, Number 19

The text of a speech of Gov. Ar. St.Clair to the house of representatives.

The text of the speech of H. VanderBurgh, President of the Council, in answer to Gov. St.Clair is printed.

The speech of Edward Tiffin in answer to Gov. St.Clair is printed.

Thomas Gibson, of Cincinnati, has a new shipment of goods for sale.

Daniel Conner & Company, of Cincinnati, ask those indebted to them to settle their accounts.

Richard Jones & Company have a new shipment of groceries for sale at their store.

Jno. Machin/Macbin has a lot, including a tanyard, for sale in Cincinnati opposite Capt. Mercer's place. Apply to Col. N. Massie. The tanyard is now being operated by Zebulon Eynon.

Alexander Clements says his wife, Sarah Clements, left him, and he won't honor debts of her contracting from now on.

A note about the petition of Mr. Dunlavy about the election of Mr. Martin.

Marriage: John Bird of Cincinnati married Miss Martha Moore, of Southbend, on "Thursday last".

Volume 1, Tuesday, 8 October 1799, Number 20
　　Notes regarding the proceedings of the House of Representatives mention Edward Tiffin (elected as Speaker), Charles Killgore, John Reily, Abraham Cary, James Lowes, Mr. M'Millan, Mr. Small, Mr. Langham, Mr. Smith, Mr. Worthington, Mr. Edgar, Mr. Benham, Mr. Darlington, Mr. Findlay, Mr. Goforth, Mr. Massie.
　　A note regarding Francis Dunlavy's petition about Isaac Martin's election.
　　William Henry Harrison is appointed as representative to Congress.
　　A note regarding Rev. John Duff's sermon this Sunday.
　　Lieut. Col. John S. Gano and Lieut. Justice Gibbs regarding the meeting of the First Battalion of Hamilton County Militia at Capt. Goudy's Mill.
　　Asa Richardson, administrator of the estate of Darius Marsh, deceased, late of Cincinnati, regarding the estate settlement.
　　Daniel Conner & Company, of Cincinnati, wants to buy pork.
　　A list of letters remaining at the Post Office in Cincinnati mentions William Austin, Robert Armstrong in Natchez, Thomas Brown in Columbia, John Brown on the bank of the Ohio, Daniel Bradstreet, David Bradbery, John Brown, John Barber on the Detroit Riber, Burt & Newmen, Francis Butholomy, Daniel Clark on Duck Creek, Thomas Cory, Samuel Clark on the Great Miami, Sergeant Lemuel Church in Detroit, William Crofts (fife major), Moses Crist, Daniel Conner, Robert Cunningham Crawford (60 miles up the Great Miami), Daniel C. Cooper, James Cunningham, Augustin Chouteau in Cahokia, John Devor on the Mad River, John Death in care of John M'Cullough, Joshua Deleplane at Fort Hamilton, John Freeman, Luke Foster (?), James Guerdiner, Samuel Goloher, Daniel Guttrey at Old Chelicotha, Abraham Garrison, George Grege, Thomas Hunter, Cornelius Johnson at Hobsons Choice, Thomas Kenedy, James Lowe, John Squire Marsh, Mary Mages at Judge Symmes, William Mitchell, Jonathan Munger, Daniel Mayo, Col. John Mountjoy in Campbell County, Nathan Mayo, William M'Cullough, Robert M'Clure, Sergeant John Marshall in Natchez, William Morrison in care of D. Symmes, Michael M'Clury, Ephraim Morrison, John M'Cormick, Jacob Old, William Patton in care of John M'Cullough, James Patterson in care of Mr. Ramsey, Lidia Rhawle on Mill Creek, Ambrose Ranson in New Town, Jas. Riddle, Wm. Ramsey, Cornelius R. Sedam, William Snodgrass & Co., Maj. David Sutton in Deerfield, Thomas Stone, Bernard Stewart, Isaac Swearingin at Northbend, Hannah Seman in care of Samuel Dick, Lieut. Robert Semple, Benjamin Stites, Jun., Sarah Sayrs, Maj. Benjamin Stites, Sergeant John Seamers at Walnut hills, John Tharp, Ann Terwilleger at Columbia, Enoch Thompson, Robert Wilson in care of Robert Anderson, John Wallace in Columbia, J.B. Wilkinson, Griffin Yeatman and David Zeigler. Entered by William Ruffin, post master.
　　W. Wells, at Fort Wayne, regarding slaves that ran away from Dunn Lee and Mrs. Mosbey of Kentucky.
　　Poor & Washburn, of Cincinnati, want to buy good beef cattle.
　　David Broadbury, near Beedell's Station, reports a stray mare. Deliver to Andrew Prior near the Duck Creek Meeting House.
　　Henry Anderson, of Campbell County, Kentucky, regarding bonds to David E. Wade of Cincinnati.

Volume 1, Tuesday, 15 October 1799, Number 21
　　The proceedings of the House of Representatives mention Mr. Langham, John Harrison, William Sullivan, Mr. M'Millen, Mr. Worthington, Mr. Darlington, Mr. Massie, Mr. Small, Mr. Goforth, Mr. Smith, Mr. Findley, Mr. Benham, Mr. Cadwell, Mr. Pritchard, Mr. Bond, Mr. Schenk, Mr. Vance, Mr. Ludlow, Mr. Edgar and Solomon Sibley (of Detroit, Wayne County).
　　Michael Brokaw, of Cincinnati, is moving out of Cincinnati and asks those indebted to him to settle their accounts at David Grummon's Mill.
　　David E. Wade, shoemaker, writes a letter to the editor regarding the recent ad placed by Henry Anderson. He mentions John Anderson (Henry's son), Capt. Shamburgh, Aaron Cadwell and Robert M'Clure.
　　Abiah Martin regarding his stud horse, Celer Federal.
　　William Ludlow regarding a town established on his land on Mill Creek nine miles from Cincinnati, 7 miles from Columbia, 10 miles from Colerain and 11

miles from the Round Bottom. He's offering lots for sale.

John Cleves Symmes wants to buy wheat at his mill in Northbend. Deliver to the mill or to John Smith, Christian Wallsmith, David Grummon or Joel Williams.

James Smith, Sheriff in Cincinnati, has seized the blacksmith's tools of James Bell, of Cincinnati, at the suit of Hugh M'Collom and will sell them at auction.

Abraham Vorheese has town lots for sale in Redding.

Thomas Barlow, living near Georgetown in Scott County, Kentucky, regarding a runaway slave.

Bell & Bill have dissolved their partnership. Those indebted to them should settle their accounts.

Lebeus Marshall, on Mill Creek near White's Station, found a mare.

Wm. Ferguson regarding a bond to W. & M. Jones of Cincinnati, merchants, for wheat to be delivered to Mr. Grummon's mill.

John Quick, living at Hole's Station on the Big Miami, regarding stray cattle.

Volume 1, Tuesday, 22 October 1799, Number 22

The proceedings of the House of Representatives mentions Mr. Burnet, Mr. Worthington, Mr. Goforth, Mr. Cadwell, Mr. Ludlow, Mr. Langham, Mr. Small, Joseph Carpenter, Mr. Schenck, Abraham Carey, Mr. Massie, Mr. Smith, Mr. Benham, Francis Dunlavy, Mr. Sibley, Mr. Edgar, Mr. Pritchard, Mr. Darlington, Joshua Rowland, James Lowes, Mr. Findley, James Edwards of Adams County, Edwards' Ferry at the mouth of Fishinggut Creek, Mr. January on the road from Limestone to Chillicothe, Mr. M'Millan, Franklin township, Isaac Martin.

James Forguson, of Cincinnati, regarding wheat to be delivered to Mr. Grummon's Mill. He also has land for sale, lately occupied by Hugh M'Cullum, on Main Street in Cincinnati.

James White, of Cincinnati, has moved his school to the house next door to Thomas Williams, skindresser, on Main Street in Cincinnati.

Richard Jones & Company, of Cincinnati, wants to buy pork.

John Armstrong, of Columbia, offers his plantation for sale. He also wants to buy a horse "fit to perform a journey".

Wm. & M. Jones have a new shipment of goods for sale at their store.

Levi M'Lean asks those indebted to him to settle their accounts. He also mentions "my wife and family".

Levi Woodward, for Sheriff James Smith, announces a sheriff's sale that will be held at Timothy Kibbey's Tavern in Columbia to sell the household furniture of Charles and Amos Munrow.

Volume 1, Tuesday, 29 October 1799, Number 23

Silas Dumas, at Thomas Smith's place, regarding a slave, Frank, who ran away from Benjamin Craig's on the Ohio River. Frank's wife, Phillis, ran away from Elijah Hogan's (seven miles below Tanner's Station) at the same time. Deliver to William Houlet/Houler.

A communication is printed from Gov. Ar. St.Clair to the Representatives and mentions John Cleves Symmes and Mr. Boudinot.

A letter from Ar. St.Clair to Legislative Council mentions Mr. Cutler, Mr. Sargeant, Mr. Dayton, Mr. Marsh and John Cleves Symmes.

The proceedings of the House of Representatives mentions Mr. Goforth, Mr. Burnet, William H. Harrison, Mr. Massie, Mr. Sibley, Mr. Cadwell, Mr. Langham, Mr. M'Millan, the Presbyterian Church in Chillicothe, Mr. Worthington, Mr. Findlay, Mr. Smith, Mr. Bond, Mr. Small, Mr. Benham, Mr. Darlington, Mr. Edgar, Mr. Ludlow, Mr. Martin, Mr. Pritchard and Mr. Meigs.

A notice of a sermon to be preached by Rev. Mr. Duff.

John Kidd has opened a baking business in Cincinnati next door to Col. Thomas Gibson.

Those indebted to Dr. Homer/Homes/Humes should settle their accounts.

John Daily, in Cincinnati, wants to hire a cooper.

Wm. & M. Jones, of Cincinnati, regarding some wheat that they bought.

Martin Baum & Company, in Cincinnati, have a new shipment of goods.

James Smith, Sheriff in Cincinnati, regarding the sale of a house and lot in

Hamilton, the property of James Reed, at the suit of James Riddle.

John Armstrong, in Columbia, has 1000 bushels of corn for sale.

Levi M'Lean, of Cincinnati, regarding the Coroner's sale of blacksmith tools and other property of Miny & Abraham Vorhees.

George Gordon, of Cincinnati, about Doctor Sellman's cow and calf. Apply to James Smith for more information.

Volume 1, Tuesday, 5 November 1799, Number 24

The proceedings of the House of Representatives mention Mr. Massie, Mr. Sibley, Mr. M'Millan, Mr. Meigs, Mr. Visger, Mr. Cadwell, Mr. Ludlow, Mr. Findley, Mr. Langham, Mr. Goforth, Mr. Vance, Adams County, the town of Alexandria, the town of Manchester, Mr. Benham, Mr. Smith, Mr. Bond, Mr. Small, Mr. Darlington, Mr. Worthington, Mill Creek, William Ludlow, Jacob White, Denham's town, John Cleves Symmes.

John Cleves Symmes regarding the sale of the livestock of the late Rev. Mr. Wilson of Cincinnati. He implies that relatives will come "from Jersey" and mentions John Ludlow at Mill Creek.

Richard Alison, of Cincinnati, asks those indebted to him to pay their bills.

Timothy Kibby, of Columbia, asks those indebted to him to settle their bills.

Wm. M'Farland, of Cincinnati, makes and sells earthen ware.

David Poor and Tabor Washburn, of Cincinnati, announce that their partnership is dissolved. Those indebted to them should settle their accounts.

James Forguson regarding wheat to be delivered to Mr. Grummon's Mill. He also has Man's Lick salt for sale, and he has a house for sale, lately occupied by Hugh M'Cullum.

Volume 1, Tuesday, 12 November 1799, Number 25

Barton Leonard, living on Mill Creek, found a stray cow.

The proceedings of the House of Representatives mention Mr. Oliver, Mr. Cadwell, Mr. Massie, Mr. Goforth, Mr. Langham, Mr. Findley, Mr. Smith, Mr. Sibley, Mr. Edgar, Mr. Worthington, the Presbyterian Church in Chillicothe, Franklin township and Ross County.

A note regarding the trial of John Fries at Morris Town for treason.

An article regarding the trial of William Duane, editor of the Aurora.

Jacob Sly, living on the east fork of the Little Miami, found a mare.

Sergeant John Bently, at Fort Wayne, says his wife, Mary, left and took up with a man named Silvanus Reynolds. He won't honor her debts anymore.

A. Freeman, at the Great Miami, regarding his house of entertainment at Freemansburg on the road to the Mad River, 23 miles from Cincinnati and 11 miles from Cunningham's.

Volume 1, Tuesday, 19 November 1799, Number 26

The proceedings of the House of Representatives mention Mr. Langham, Mr. Meigs, Mr. Small, Mr. Massie, Mr. M'Millan, Mr. Sibley, Mr. Visgar, Mr. Ludlow, Mr. Worthington, Mr. Benham, William Maxwell, Mr. Cadwell, Mr. Smith, a letter from A. St.Clair, Mr. Goforth and the Illinois grant.

A note regarding Mr. Humes who just arrived in Cincinnati from Natchez.

A note is printed regarding Mr. Lyon and his family who left Vermont because he was on trial for sedition. They went to Kentucky by way of Cincinnati.

An article regarding a fire at Mr. Mennesier's Coffee House. It was burnt down, but Maj. Doyle's house next door was saved.

A letter to the public from F. Mennesier regarding the fire at his house.

Obituary: Mrs. Rhoda Kean, daughter of Aaron Cadwell of Cincinnati and wife of John Kean, formerly of Cincinnati, died at Natchez on 16 September 1799.

Peyton Short and William H. Harrison, in Cincinnati, want to hire an overseer and workers to cultivate lands at the mouth of the Big Miami. Apply to Judge Symmes. They also have a stud horse at "the late stables of Capt. Harrison at North Bend".

John Sellman, of Cincinnati, says that Doctor Sellman and Doctor Hall have formed a partnership.

R. Haughton regarding his dancing school in Cincinnati. He formerly taught in Pennsylvania and Virginia.

O.H. Spencer, in Cincinnati, will be here a short time to settle the accounts of Dr. Alison.

Christopher Sallmon, living three miles from Cincinnati on the Columbia road, found a stray cow.

Volume 1, Tuesday, 26 November 1799, Number 27

Benjamin Ives Gillman and Edwin Putnam (attorney), at Marietta, Washington County, regarding the suit of Perley Howe vs. Nathaniel Gardner Dabney.

The proceedings of the House of Representatives mention Mr. Langham, Mr. Smith, Mr. Darlington, Thomas Posey (of the Virginia line of the Revolutionary War), Mr. Fearing, Mr. Edgar, Mr. Massie, Mr. Meigs, Mr. Goforth, Mr. Cadwell.

Smith & Findlay, of Cincinnati, want to buy ten pack horses.

John R. Mills, living on Mill Creek, regarding a strayed or stolen horse.

The editor of the Western Spy says he's fired his post rider, Mr. Dorret, and hired Jonas Seamans in his place.

Obituary: Capt. Daniel Britt died at Fort Wayne. (no date listed)

Volume 1, Tuesday, 3 December 1799, Number 28

The proceedings of the House of Representatives mention Mr. Goforth, Thomas Posy, Mr. Massie, Mr. Langham, Mr. Smith, Mr. Worthington, Mr. Findlay.

Daniel Symmes, of Cincinnati, administrator of the estate of Rev. Peter Wilson regarding the estate settlement.

J. & A. Hunt, of Cincinnati, found a stray steer.

A note from the editor of the Western Spy asks those indebted to him to settle their bills by delivering grain to Cunningham's Mill, Wallice's Mill or Grummon's Mill.

O.H. Spencer asks those indebted to Doctor R. Allison to settle their bills.

Volume 1, Tuesday, 10 December 1799, Number 29

The proceedings of the House of Representatives mention Edmond Freeman (printer of Cincinnati), Mr. Fearing, Mr. Carey of Cincinnati and Mr. Smith.

A letter to the public from the editor of the Western Spy states that he's now in partnership with Jonathan S. Findlay under the name Carpenter & Findlay.

Israel Ludlow has land for sale in Judge Symmes' grant. Apply to John Smith.

Daniel Symmes reports that he found a stray steer.

J. Broadwell wants to hire a distiller at his distillery near New Town on the Little Miami.

Joshua Butler, living at the Big Priaria (?), found a stray steer.

William Brown, two miles above the mouth of the Little Miami, found a mare.

Volume 1, Tuesday, 17 December 1799, Number 30

A note about the looting that took place during the recent fires in Cincinnati at Mr. Baum's stable, Maj. Doyle's stable and Mr. Mennesier's house.

Smith & Findlay, of Cincinnati, ask those indebted to them to pay their bills.

Martin M'Cray, living above the Big Parairi on the Great Miami, reports a strayed or stolen horse.

Sheriff James Smith regarding a sheriff's sale in Cincinnati of some land, the property of John Clarke, dec'd, at the suit of John Jordan, Jun. The land was surveyed on George Holland's military warrant.

Cornelius R. Sedam, at Woodland Farms, three miles below Cincinnati, has land for sale. The land was first surveyed for David Nesbitt as a soldier in the Virginia line.

I.G. Wheeler, administrator of the estate of George N. Wheeler, dec'd, about the estate settlement. The deceased lived in Pendleton County on the Dry Ridge near Widow Arnold's, between Cincinnati and Georgetown.

A report of a committee on the allocation of college lands in Ohio mentions John C. Symmes, Manassah Cutler and Winthrop Sargent.

Volume 1, Tuesday, 24 December 1799, Number 31
   Edward Tiffin, H. VanderBurg, John Reily and W.C. Schenck submit a letter to the public from the Legislature of the Northwest Territory.
   The speech of Ar. St.Clair to the Legislature of the Northwest Territory.
   Charles Killgore about a meeting of the Nova Caesaria Lodge in Cincinnati.
   Edmund Munger, at Hole's Creek near Columbia, has lost four hogs.
   Daniel Symmes, in Cincinnati, reports some stray steers.
   Michael Ocheltree, living in Deerfield on Little Miami, found some heifers.
   Peter Kemper, at his plantation on Deer Creek, found a boar shoat.

Volume 1, Tuesday, 31 December 1799, Number 32
   A note regarding the resolution introduced to the Legislature by William H. Harrison mentions Mr. Craik, Mr. Bird and Mr. Harper.
   Sheriff James Smith in Cincinnati has land for sale in a sheriff's sale, the property of James Colwell, seized at the suit of James O'Hara. He mentions Jacob White, Isaac Martin and William Ludlow.
   A. Cary, in Cincinnati township, regarding lands on which the taxes have not been paid, mentions Michael Ayres, Lydia Ayres, Isaac Bunches, Calvin Ball, Luther Ball, C. Ball, William Hunter, David Leamon, Samuel Lee, Benjamin Perlu, Mar. Osborne, Edward Johnston, Ralph Schenck, Joseph Stewart, David Davis, Thomas King and Agnis Flinn.
   John Greer regarding the property of George Codd and Gorden Kelly, both of Hamilton County. The property is now under attachment.
   Carpenter & Findlay, of Cincinnati, regarding a strayed horse.
   James Smith, Collector of Revenue in Cincinnati, gives notice to distillers regarding their licenses.
   O.M. Spencer regarding deeds left in the Recorder's office.
   John Rice Jones, at Kaskaskia in Randolph County, regarding the suits of James Edgar vs. Robert Greer; Philip Rashblean vs. Andrew Fagot; John Edgar vs. John Marshall.

Volume 1, Tuesday, 7 January 1800, Number 33
   The governor has appointed Rice Bullock as Auditor of Public Accounts for the Northwest Territory.
   Edward Tiffin and H. VanderBurgh write a letter to President John Adams.
   James Forguson asks those indebted to him to settle their accounts.
   A list of letters left at the Post Office in Cincinnati includes Thomas Alstone, David Barber, Eli Balrommin at New Market in Ross County, Henry Brown, Otto V.T. Barberie in Natches, John Beaty at Dunlap's Station, Melyne Baker, Mary Brodrick, William Brodrick, Patrick Brodrick, John Chirry in care of Isaac Anderson, Christopher Carey, James Cunningham, Daniel Clark, Ariel Coy, Sally Davis, Jonathan Donnel, Thomas Doyle, Rev. John Duff, Mr. Enick in care of Joel Williams, Abraham Freeman, Thomas Goudy, Thomas Hardin, Dr. John Hole, Capt. Silas Howell, John T. Hall, Matthew Hedges (soldier), Peter Kemper, Asa Kitchel in North Bend, David and Phebe Loller, Thomas Lowry on Mad River, William Leard at Hunt's tanyard, Stephen Little, John Mansefild in care of John Luthers, Doctor Robert M'Clure, John Squire Marsh, Capt. Edmund Munger, John Miller, Isaac Willis, Dominicus M'Graw in care of Mr. Ludlow, William M'Laughlin at Walnut Hills, Jeremiah Morrow, Elizabeth Noble, Thomas Noble, John Necker near Columbia, Jacob Powers near Cox's tavern, John Reed on Clear Creek, Doctor John Rippey at Chickasaw Bluff, Nestern Strong, Rev. Peter Smith, Winthrop Sargent, Jared Scoffield at Deerfield, Robert Sagerson at Deerfield, Bernard Steward, Maj. Benjamin Stites, Abraham Townsend, James Tucker, Benjamin Tucker, Capt. Thompson, Benjamin Valentine in care of Benjamin Tucker, Thomas Vaughan at Little Miami, Carman Winans, Samuel and Charity Williams, Jacob White, Thomas Wilkinson at Natches, Jonathan Williams, Samuel Williams, Peter White at Big Miami, William Wells. Entered by William Ruffin.
   Ephraim Kibby, in Columbia, has land for sale.
   David Williams, living on Muddy Creek, reports that he found a horse.
   George Fithian has moved his public entertainment to the house of Charles

Avery in Cincinnati.
>Jacob Burnet, of Cincinnati, reports some stray steers.
>James Sutton, living on the Big Miami above the Great Prairia, found a steer.
>John C. Symmes, at North Bend, reports three stray oxen.
>Seth Cutter, tavern keeper in Cincinnati, has returned to his business.
>Thomas M'Farland, of Cincinnati, reports that he has found a stray heifer.
>John Lee, living about six miles above Deerfield on the Little Miami, about a strayed or stolen mare.
>Charles Smith, in Columbia, reports that he found seven stray hogs.
>David Nichols says that he found a stray heifer.

Volume 1, Wednesday, 15 January 1800, Number 34
>Thomas Thompson, agent for M. Baum & Company, in Cincinnati, asks those indebted to the company to settle their accounts.
>George Chesterson, living two miles from the Big Hill, found a stray horse.
>Thomas Williams, of Cincinnati, regarding his business of skin-dressing and breeches making.
>Abraham Lindley, living in Springfield township, found a heifer.
>John Ludlow, living at Ludlow Farms, found a stray heifer.
>Henry Ewing, of Cincinnati, wants to hire an apprentice to the tailor's trade.
>Thomas M'Farland found a stray heifer.
>George Hogan regarding a bond to Mr. Kunch.
>John Fisher, in Hamilton, regarding a stray cow and calf.
>Samuel Dunn, living near White's Station, reports some stray hogs.
>Moses Broadwell found a stray steer.

Volume 1, Wednesday, 22 January 1800, Number 35
>A note regarding memorial services for Gen. George Washington to be held at Fort Washington under the direction of Capt. Miller, commanding officer. They will also be held in Cincinnati at the Courthouse with Capt. James Findlay.
>Michael H. Johnson, living in Deerfield, found some hogs.
>Garret VanBlaricum, at North Bend, found a stray horse.
>Aaron Cadwell is moving into the country and has land for sale in Cincinnati.
>Cornelius R. Sedam, at Woodland Farms three miles below Cincinnati, reports some stray cows and hogs.
>John Brown found a horse on White Water near Mr. Simpson's.
>John S. Gano and Jacob Burnet (attorney) regarding a suit in the Hamilton County Court of Common Pleas: John M'Cullough vs. Abner Wilkinson.
>Peter Kemper, on Deer Creek, found a stray boar shoat and a heifer.
>Enos Hurin, on Mill Creek near Capt. Goudy's mill, regarding stray hogs.

Volume 1, Wednesday, 29 January 1800, Number 36
>A.J. Dallas, at Lancaster, regarding M'Kean's election.
>Notes regarding memorial services for Gen. George Washington mention Capt. Miller at Fort Washington, Lieut. Col. John S. Gano, the First Battalion of Hamilton County Militia, George W. Burnet of Nova Caesaria Harmony Lodge, and Mr. Yeatman.
>John S. Gano & William Stanley have land for sale and mention Rev. Kemper, Widow Stevens in Kentucky, Levi Jennings, and Spencer, Gano, Crane & Co.
>Levi Woodward, for Sheriff James Smith in Cincinnati, regarding a sheriff's sale of the property of Daniel Lambert.
>Isaac Vanmatre, living on the Little Miami about six miles above Deerfield, found some steers.
>Sheriff James Smith, in Cincinnati, regarding sheriff's sales of the property of Ezra F. Freeman at the suit of John Brown and Thomas Cochran and the property of William Woods (living on Little Miami near Deerfield).
>Rice Bullock wants to buy pork.
>James Davis, at New Town, regarding a stray cow.
>Thomas Edwards regarding the stray cow that came to the plantation of Maj. Joseph Shaylor on the East fork of the Little Miami.

Jacob Stroup and Adam Hoy regarding a bond to William Lytle and James Taylor, both of Kentucky.

Carpenter & Findlay, in Cincinnati, regarding the publication of the laws of the Northwest Territory.

Volume 1, Wednesday, 5 February 1800, Number 37

An account of a memorial service for Gen. George Washington, dec'd, mentions Maj. Gen. Hamilton, Capt. Miller, Fort Washington, Rev. Mr. Wallace, Dr. Sellman, Dr. Elliott, Capt. Prince, Maj. Zeigler, Col. Spencer, Maj. Goforth, Gov. St.Clair, Nova Caesaria Lodge and Geo. W. Burnet.

John Dodson, John Charles, Culbertson Park and Andrew Park regarding a meeting of the carpenters of Hamilton County.

Amos Smith, living in Williamsburg, found a stray mare.

Aaron Cherry says that his common law wife, Mary, left him and took his property. He won't honor her debts from now on.

James Cunningham found a stray cow.

Hezekiah Stites, of Columbia, found some stray steers.

E. Langham has land for rent, the property of Maj. Butler, Col. Parker and Maj. Beal. He mentions Mr. Light's plantation near the Ohio River. Apply to William Bohannon living near the land at the mouth of Big Indian Creek.

Silas Hurin, living on Turtle Creek near Taylor's Mill, found a sow.

Joseph Logsdon, living near the mouth of Bullskin Creek, found a stray bull.

John Lewis, living on the Ohio River six miles below the mouth of Bullskin Creek, found some stray heifers.

John St.John, living on Mill Creek six miles from Cincinnati, found a colt.

Henry Jennings, living on Duck Creek, found some stray heifers.

Elmore Williams, living on the Hamilton Road eleven miles from Cincinnati, reports a stray colt.

Christian Husong, living on Clough Creek, found five stray hogs.

Volume 1, Wednesday, 12 February 1800, Number 38

Pres. John Adams answers the letter from the Legislature of the Northwest Territory and mentions Edward Tiffin and Gov. St.Clair.

Thomas Gibson, regarding a meeting of the citizens of Cincinnati at the house of Seth Cutter, mentions the Congregation in Cincinnati and Rev. Mr. Wallace.

A note regarding a memorial service for Gen. George Washington mentions Capt. Brown's troop of horse from Columbia.

Rice Bullock, Auditor of Public Accounts in the Northwest Territory, submits laws to be printed regarding land taxes.

James Thompson, living on the Great Miami five miles below Dayton, wants to hire a school master.

Thomas Frazer asks those indebted to him to settle their accounts.

Volume 1, Wednesday, 19 February 1800, Number 39

Thomas Cohran has opened a tavern in Cincinnati in the house lately occupied by Mr. Austin.

John Hormell and Alexr. Porter, both living near White's Station, found a sow.

Benjamin Ives Gilman and Paul Fearing (attorney) about a suit in Washington County, Northwest Territory: Joseph Stewart (of Cambridge, Washington County, New York, yeoman) vs. Joseph Spencer (of Harrison County, Virginia, physician).

John Cleves Symmes has lots for sale at his settlement on his military lands.

Uzal Ward, at Indian Hill, found a stray heifer.

Joseph Williamson, living near Gerrard's Station on Little Miami, found a cow.

Volume 1, Wednesday, 26 February 1800, Number 40

Edward Tiffin, H. VanderBurgh and Ar. St.Clair print a legislative act.

Sheriff James Smith about the meeting of the General Court of the Territory at the house of Griffin Yeatman in Cincinnati.

Edward Tiffin, H. VanderBurgh and Ar. St.Clair print another act passed.

James Hill regarding land on Mill Creek that he bought from Isaac Wilson and the dispute over it with William Bills. He mentions Judge Symmes.

Daniel Symmes, administrator of the estate of Rev. Peter Wilson, regarding the estate sale at the house of Mr. Austin in Cincinnati.

Michael Brokaw asks those indebted to him to settle their accounts.

Volume I, Wednesday, 5 March 1800, Number 41

A note regarding the memorial presented by William H. Harrison from the inhabitants of the Little Miami mentions John Cleves Symmes.

Edmund Freeman asks those indebted to him to pay bills to Thomas Morris.

James Kamper, living on his farm near Cincinnati, has land for sale.

James Buchanan, living on the White Water in St. Clair township, found sows.

William Logan, living in St.Clair township on White Water, found a stray cow.

Elmore Williams, living on the Hamilton road eleven miles from Cincinnati, reports a stray colt.

Volume I, Wednesday, 12 March 1800, Number 42

John Cleves Symmes writes a note regarding the settlement of the village on his land on the Scioto and Whetstone Rivers.

The president has appointed Charles Willing Bird to be Secretary of the Northwest Territory.

Wm. Miller Flinn reports on a meeting of the inhabitants of Cincinnati at the house of G. Fithian with John M'Cullagh presiding. They voted not to inoculate for small pox.

Col. Samuel Finley and Alexander White regarding a memorial service for Gen. George Washington in Chillicothe. Rev. William Speer delivered the sermon and Isaac Cook, teacher of vocal music, led the singing.

Thomas Goudy, at the Mill Creek Farm, asks those indebted to him to settle their accounts.

Thomas Brown regarding a meeting of the Humane Society of the Northwest Territory at Columbus.

Elizabeth Chribbs, in Cincinnati, reports a stray cow and calf.

James Kain, at Williamsburg, found some stray cattle.

Rice Bullock and Charles Killgore, administrators of the estate of John Clarke, deceased, regarding the estate settlement.

James Dunseth, living in Newtown, found a stray steer.

Richard Allison, living at Belle Font on the east branch of the Little Miami, found a stray steer.

Alexander Gaston, living on Sycamore Creek, found a stray cow.

John Jenkinson, living on Mill Creek near White's Station, found a stray steer.

Joseph Walker, living in Colerain township, found a stray bull.

William M'Millan, Jesse Hunt and John S. Gano regarding a meeting of the Cincinnati Congregation.

Volume I, Wednesday, 19 March 1800, Number 43

Edward Tiffin, H. VanderBurgh and Ar. St.Clair regarding acts passed by the General Assembly.

A note regarding Mr. Harrison and Mr. Livingston at the U.S. Congress.

John Cleves Symmes wants wagons to transport settlers to his settlement on the Scioto and Whetstone Rivers. Meet at John Lyon's tavern on Mill Creek.

Sheriff James Smith, in Cincinnati, announces a sheriff's sale at the house of Griffin Yeatman to sell land, the property of Ezra F. Freeman, to satisfy the suits of John Brown and Thomas Cochran.

James Petecrow, living in Franklin township, found a stray heifer.

Jacob Fowler, living in Newport, reports a runaway slave named Nackey. Deliver to Isaac Anderson in Cincinnati.

Volume I, Wednesday, 26 March 1800, Number 44

Edward Tiffin, H. VanderBurgh and Ar. St.Clair print acts passed by the General Assembly.

Smith & Findlay ask those indebted to them to settle their accounts by bringing wheat to Goudy's Mill.

Nathaniel Massie and Thomas Carneal regarding a new town on their land on Caesar's Creek, the waters of Little Miami, ten miles from Waynesville.

Abraham Montanye regarding a stray mare that came to the plantation of Jacob and George W. Burnet on Mill Creek.

Benjamin Beall, living near the Stag Spring in Campbell County, reports a runaway slave named Edmund.

Washington Berry regarding the Academy at Newport. Rev. Robert Stubbs is the president and the trustees are Washington Berry, Charles Morgan, John Grant, Thomas Kennedy, Thomas Sanford, Thomas Carneal, Richard Southgate, Daniel Mayo, Robert Stubbs, James Taylor and Bernard Stuart.

Volume I, Wednesday, 2 April 1800, Number 45

More laws are printed by Edward Tiffin, H. VanderBurgh and Ar. St.Clair.

Michael Brokaw asks those indebted to him to settle their accounts.

James Clark and John M'Curdy, administrators of Daniel M'Curdy, regarding a note from Daniel M'Curdy, late of Franklin County, Pennsylvania, dec'd, to James M'Clelland, now living on the waters of Mill Creek, Northwest Territory, but formerly of Westmoreland County, Pennsylvania, near Hannah's Town.

Nicholas Jones, living one mile from James Cox's tavern on the Big Hill, found some stray hogs.

Volume I, Wednesday, 9 April 1800, Number 46

More acts are printed by Edward Tiffin, H. VanderBurgh and Ar. St.Clair.

Notes regarding the proceedings of Congress mention Mr. Nicholas, Gov. St.Clair and Mr. Harrison.

Obituary: Rice Bullock, Auditor of Public Accounts for the Northwest Territory, died Wednesday morning, 9 April 1800, at about 6 o'clock.

Benjamin Stites, living in Columbia, found a stray heifer.

A list of letters left at the Post Office in Cincinnati includes Caspar Abram at Detroit, Lorenzo Belcher at Hole's Station, Doctor Daniel Bryan, Francis Bartholemew, John Brown, Jonathan Bereman at New Market in Ross County, Ann Blagrove in Campbell County, Aaron Broadwell, Robert Bragley, Col. John Crane in Adams County, John Clark on Mad River in care of Simon Kenton, John Clark on the Miami, William Crain on Clear Creek, Peter Daniel in Campbell County, James Dunseth at New Town, Thomas Dill in Ross County, William Danford at Columbia, John Ewing in Dayton in care of William Jones, John Greer, Christian Goodhouse (joiner), Morgan Gwillin, Joseph Gabby, Hopkins & Henry, John Hall in Boon County, Thomas Hunter, Nathan Kelly in Deerfield, James Kennedy in Campbell County, John Kidd, Joseph Lee in care of John Abkrir, Gen. John Massie, Doctor Robert M'Clure, Thomas M'Clelland, Col. Thomas M'Gee in Detroit, John Pryer, Jonathan Pitmans on Mill Creek, Matthias Pierson, John Quigley in care of Doctor Bane/Bone, John Richardson near Fort Hamilton, Daniel Reider, William Snodgrass & Company, Rev. Peter Smith, Richard Smith (hatter), Enoch Thompson, William Tompkins on Bank Lick, Smith Thompson, Price Thompson, Ann Terwillager, Shobal Vail, Rev. William Wood, John Watson near the Big Hill, Peter White at Great Miami in care of Daniel Price, Susan R. Weaver, Mary White at Thomas White's, Francis Whitinger in care of Joel Williams, Rev. John Warwick, Henry Weaver. Entered by William Ruffin, post master.

Alexander Hamilton, living near Deerfield, lost a pocket book.

Bethuel Norris, living on the waters of Mill Creek about five miles northeast of Cunningham's Mill, reports a strayed or stolen mare. Deliver to Capt. John Tharp in Cincinnati.

John Cleves Symmes, of Cincinnati, regarding a wagon train to the settlement on the Whetstone River. They are meeting at the house of John Briney on the southern border of the military range on the road leading to Taylor's Mill.

John Wallace, living at his mill on Mill Creek, reports some stray colts.

Ezekiel Larned, living near Columbia, found a stray mare.

J. & A. Hunt want to buy bark. Deliver it to their tanyard.

Volume I, Wednesday, 28 May 1800, Number 47

A note regarding the Circuit Court of the U.S. mentions Conrad Marks.

Notes regarding the proceedings of the Grand Jury mentions Conrad Marks, Valentine Kuder, Jacob Eyreman, Michael Smyer, Henry Smith, Philip Rush, John Everhart, John Huber, Christ. Sox, John Klein, Jun., Daniel Klein, Jacob Klein, Adam Breich, G. Memberger, Geo. Gettman, Wm. Gettman, Abrm. Shantz, H. Memberger, Peter Hager, Abrm. Samsel, R. Huntsberger, Peter Gable, Daniel Gable, Jacob Gable, Anthony Stahler, Mr. Ross, Mr. Hopkinson.

An account of the proceedings of Congress on the question of the division of the Northwest Territory mentions C. Goodrich, Mr. Jackson, Mr. Harrison, Mr. Rutledge, Mr. Gallatin and the settlers of St. Vincents in the Illinois country.

A letter from Gov. St.Clair to Mr. Harrison at Congress is printed regarding the division of the Northwest Territory.

Appointments are made by the governor: Thomas Gibson is Auditor of Public Accounts in place of Rice Bullock, dec'd; John Armstrong is territorial treasurer; Cornelius R. Sedam is Adjutant General of the militia of the Territory.

John S. Gano regarding a stable for strays to be erected in Cincinnati. Levi M'Clean will be in charge of the stable.

Jesse & Abijah Hunt, in Cincinnati, have ceased their business of selling imported goods. They want to buy hides and calf skins at their tanyard.

William Stanley has a new shipment of goods for sale in the store formerly occupied by J. & A. Hunt. He wants to buy wheat at Grummon's or Smith's mills.

Ar. St.Clair, Jun., in Cincinnati, reports a strayed mare.

Lieut. Z.M. Pike, at Washington, Kentucky, regarding a deserter, Sergt. Jacob Messick, born in Rockingham County, Virginia, age 24.

Peter Audrain and E. Brush (attorney) about a suit in Wayne County Court: Israel Ruland (of Detroit, Wayne County, silversmith) vs. John Swift of N.Y.

James Cannon, living in Franklin, reports a stray horse.

Andrew Westfall says that he will not honor the debts of his wife, Susannah.

Richard Jones & Company are quitting business in Cincinnati. Those indebted to them should settle their accounts.

James Findlay and Wm. M'Cleland ask those indebted to the estate of Thomas Moore, dec'd, to settle their accounts.

Burt & Newman ask those indebted to them to settle their accounts.

Isaac Bates, living three miles from Cincinnati, reports a stray mare.

Thomas Doyle, of Cincinnati, reports a stray horse.

William Sweney, living on the headwaters of Turtle Creek four miles from Taylor's Mill, reports a stray mare.

Peter Willson reports that he found some stray mares.

John Bigger, in the Fourth Range, Hamilton County, regarding a stray horse.

James Galloway, living at Old Chillicothe on Little Miami, found a mare.

Volume I, Wednesday, 4 June 1800, Number 48

A note regarding the division of the Northwest Territory mentions John S. Wills, Gen. Gibson (of Pittsburg, appointed secretary of Indiana Territory), Mr. Harrison (appointed governor of Indiana Territory), H. VanderBurgh, Mr. Clark of Kentucky and Col. Pickering.

An account of the fatal stabbing of Alexander M'Fadon of Hamilton by an Indian mentions Mr. Scott.

John S. Gano about dividing Hamilton County into military districts.

Richard Jones & Company are moving their store from Cincinnati. Those indebted to them should settle their accounts as soon as possible.

William M'Millan and Jacob Burnet, in Cincinnati, regarding land they bought from Judge Symmes.

John Beaty, living on the Mad River Road at the headwaters of Gregorie's Creek, regarding a stray mare. Deliver to John Cummins near Cunningham's mill.

Robert M'Clure, living at Big Hill, reports a strayed mare.

Volume I, Wednesday, 11 June 1800, Number 49

A letter to the public from William Henry Harrison regarding the division of the Territory mentions Judge Symmes and Mr. Ludlow.

Daniel Conner & Company ask those indebted to them to pay their bills. They also have whiskey and Man's Lick salt for sale.

John S. Gano regarding the order of the Orphan's Court of Hamilton County to sell land owned by the estate of Thomas Moore, dec'd.

Levi Woodward reports sites for the collection of taxes in Hamilton County: at Henry Taylor's Mill on Turtle Creek, at the tavern in Dayton and at Thomas Frazer's house in Columbia.

Volume I, Wednesday, 18 June 1800, Number 50

Registers of the land offices are appointed: Israel Ludlow at Cincinnati, Thomas Worthington at Chillicothe, Perigrine Foster at Marietta and David Hoge of Pennsylvania at Steubenville. Receivers of public monies for land are also appointed: James Findlay at Cincinnati, Samuel Findlay at Chillicothe, Elijah Backus at Marietta, Zacheus Biggs at Steubenville.

William Stanley, in Cincinnati, about a meeting of the Nova Caesaria Lodge.

James Smith, Collector of the Revenue in Cincinnati, regarding the licensing of stills and distillers.

John R. Mills, Commissioner for the Western District, regarding taxes on property, mentions John Torrence (innkeeper in the town of Hamilton) and George Fithian in Cincinnati.

William Austin says he's leaving Cincinnati and asks those indebted to him to settle their accounts immediately.

A road is to be built from Jacob Frazee's Mill on Cluff Creek past John Van-Eaton's to New Market, intersecting the road from Newtown to Denham's Town.

A note about goods for sale on Mr. Mahoney's boat at the landing, Cincinnati.

Volume I, Wednesday, 25 June 1800, Number 51

R. Allison, at Belle-Font, regarding a letter from Lewis Bond in Detroit, mentions Carpenter & Findlay and Col. David Strong.

Nehemiah Hunt wants to buy beef cattle in Cincinnati. He has fresh meat for sale at his shop in Sycamore Street in Cincinnati.

Saml. Patterson, of Cincinnati, reports that he lost a black leather book.

Samuel Armstrong, Commissioner of the Eastern district of Hamilton County, regarding the collection of taxes at the house of James Kean, innkeeper, in Williamsburg and the house of Col. Thomas Paxton.

James Tatmen, in Hamilton County, regarding his ferry on the Ohio River.

William Fee about his ferry at the mouth of Bullskin Creek on the Ohio River.

Henry Jennings reports that he found several sheep.

Thomas Doyle reports a stray horse.

James Smith gives notice to the owners of stills in Hamilton County.

James Kamper reports some stray hogs.

Volume I, Wednesday, 2 July 1800, Number 52

W.H. Harrison reports on a bill in the House of Representatives about Judge John Cleves Symmes' grant.

A note regarding Lieut. Col. David Strong's arrival in Cincinnati with his family. Lieut. Climpson also arrived in Cincinnati on his way to Detroit.

A reminder that payments for subscriptions to the Western Spy can be made in wheat or rye delivered to Goudy's or Grummon's mill.

Martin Baum & Company are leaving Cincinnati by August 1st and ask those indebted to them to settle their accounts.

William Goforth, Jun., in Cincinnati, asks those indebted to him for "medicine and attendance for the year 1799" to settle their accounts. He is in the house formerly occupied by Doctor Richard Allison.

Smith & Findlay, in Cincinnati, ask those indebted to them to settle their accounts by delivering wheat to Thomas Goudy's or David Grummon's mills.

A list of letters left at the Post Office in Cincinnati includes Michael Ayres, Jonah Austin, Casper Brown near Detroit, Joseph Brown at the Great Miami, James Boyd, Samuel Boyd, Sydnor Baily in care of Thomas Sandford, Charles Baum near the mouth of Brackin, David Clark, Christian Christ, Joseph Cox, James Cunningham, Moses Crist, John Cassidy, Aaron Cadwell, Samuel Clark in care of Daniel Doty, John Craig, Sen., Thomas Travis Depriest, George Druard, Samuel Danford in Columbia, Lewis Davis, Capt. James Dunn, Walter Davis, Maj. Thomas Doyle, Timothy Davis on Tanners Creek, John Duff, Forsyth & Smith in Detroit, William Felter, Jacob Felter, Jeremiah French, Solomon Guess on Mill Creek, John Gustin on Little Miami, Smith Gregg near Dayton, Abraham Garrison, William Gwillym, Morgan Gwillym, Ralph W. Hunt, Charles Hunter, George Kelly in care of James M'Clure in Newport, Mr. Kavanah, Maj. James Lanier in Campbell County, Aaron Lane, Abraham Lukes on Turtle Creek, Isaac Martin, William M'Millan, Francis Meniceir, James Morrison in care of Isaac Morris at Round Bottom, James M'Cormick, James M'Garvin in Detroit, William M'Intosh, Thomas Noble, Sergeant Peter Nevious, Benjamin Nelly in Fort Wayne, Wyllis Pierson, James Peltier in Detroit, Thomas Paxton on Little Miami, John Robison, John Richardson, Mr. Roberts in Campbell County, William Rittenhouse at North Bend, Mr. Snodgrass, Daniel Sickels, John Schooley, William Simonds at Little Miami, James Silvers in North Bend, Capt. Obediah Scott at Bank Lick, James Smith at Fort Wayne, Peter Smith, John Cleves Symmes, Price Thompson, Daniel Vanvoorhis, Stephen Vail, John Winters, William Wells at Fort Wayne, Leonard Ware, Matthew Winton. Entered by Wm. Ruffin, post master.

Lieut. Eli B. Climson regarding deserters: Winget Pritchett (age 26, born in Delaware) and Peter Trexler (born in York County, Pennsylvania, age 24).

James F. Moore, of Jefferson County, Kentucky, about a runaway slave, Bob, who was formerly owned by John W. Hunt in Lexington, Kentucky.

Volume II, Wednesday, 9 July 1800, Number 53

An act to divide the Northwest Territory is printed.

An account of the 4th of July celebration at Mr. Frazer's tavern is printed.

William Ludlow has land for sale on Mill Creek in Springfield township.

Joseph P. Price, at Waynesville on the Little Miami, found a stray mare.

Israel Ludlow has land for sale at his settlement on the Scioto River.

Sheriff James Smith, in Cincinnati, has land for sale, at a sheriff's sale, the property of William Chribbs and Elizabeth Chribbs, his wife, at the suit of Charles Wilkins, agent for John Wilkins and Charles Wilkins.

Lyon & M'Ginnis have started a business of cabinet making on Hamilton road 11 miles from Cincinnati. Pay in wheat delivered to Grummon's or Goudy's mills.

Volume II, Wednesday, 16 July 1800, Number 54

An account of the Fourth of July celebration at Maj. Zeigler's house.

The editors of the Western Spy ask those indebted to them to settle their accounts in wheat delivered to Goudy's or Grummon's mills.

David J. Poor regarding his butchering business at Mr. Howard's slaughter house. He wants to buy beef cattle.

Francis M'Cormack and William Salter regarding a note to John Harper.

Thomas Williams, in Cincinnati, found a blacksmith's anvil.

Volume II, Wednesday, 23 July 1800, Number 55

Obituary: George W. Burnet, attorney, of Cincinnati, died Sunday, 14 July 1800, leaving a wife and children.

Henry Farry, of Cincinnati, has goods for sale at the house of Hugh O'Donnall.

Francis Mennessiers has reopened his Coffee House in Cincinnati.

John S. Gano, in Cincinnati, has land for sale in Judge Symmes' patent.

Thomas Davis, living three miles below Dayton, regarding a horse stolen from the stable of James Dement at the forks of the Mad River.

James Findlay and Wm. M'Cleland, in Cincinnati, have land for sale to satisfy the creditors of Thomas Moore, dec'd.

Robert Bullock, Lewis Bullock and James Findlay, administrators of the estate of Rice Bullock, dec'd, regarding the estate settlement.

Ar. St.Clair writes a letter to the public regarding the "Western Reserve of Connecticut" to be made into Trumbull County.

Volume II, Wednesday, 30 July 1800, Number 56

A note regarding a meeting at Mr. Yeatman's tavern for the formation of a Volunteer Light Infantry Company.

John Cleves Symmes asks those indebted to him to settle their accounts by delivering wheat to Thomas Goudy's mill for the use of John Lyon.

Sheriff James Smith, in Cincinnati, announces a sheriff sale at the house of William Wood near Deerfield with the property of William Wood for sale at the suits of Tibbs & Graham, Snodgrass & Doyle and Thomas Frazer. Also the property of Miney and Abraham Vorheese is for sale at the suit of John Wallace.

John Obannon regarding his ferry on the Ohio River at or near the mouth of Bullskin Creek on the road from Denham's Town, Hamilton County, to Salt's Ferry.

William Lytle, in Lexington, regarding lots he sold in Williamsburg.

Volume II, Wednesday, 6 August 1800, Number 57

An account of an accident six miles from Cincinnati on the Deerfield road in which William Stewart and Mash Williams, who had lately come down the river with their families, were caught in a storm and a branch fell on their wagon. It killed Mrs. Stewart and her child and a Williams child. Mrs. Williams was hurt badly and probably won't recover.

A note regarding Maj. Zeigler's celebration of the Fourth of July is printed.

James Forguson has a shipment of goods for sale at his store in Cincinnati.

W. & M. Jones, in Cincinnati, have a new shipment of goods for sale.

Alex. White, in Chillicothe, will also attend at the courts in Cincinnati.

James Conn, in Cincinnati, asks those indebted to him to settle their accounts by delivering wheat to Goudy's, Grummon's or Mason's Mills.

Joseph Frazee, living on Clear Creek Island on Little Miami about a mile from Meesty's Mill, reports that he found a stray mare.

Volume II, Wednesday, 13 August 1800, Number 58

A note regarding Maj. Zeigler's celebration of the Fourth of July mentions Mr. Rutter (saddler), Henry Smith (soldier) and Capt. Vance.

A note about Gen. Wilkinson's trip from Natchez to Philadelphia is printed.

Notice of a meeting of the Light Infantry Company at Mr. Yeatman's tavern.

E. Langham, in Chillicothe, regarding lots for sale in the town of Pinckney on the Little Miami, mentions George Clarke.

Volume II, Wednesday, 20 August 1800, Number 59

A notice to Philip Lice to pick up a message at the printer's from "a near relation, who has long been hunting for him".

A note regarding the letter about Maj. Zeigler's celebration of July Fourth.

A proclamation is printed from Gov. Ar. St.Clair, submitted by Charles Willing Byrd, secretary, regarding the division of the Northwest Territory.

Thomas Ramsey, at his shop in Cincinnati, has cast iron wheels for sale and carries on the wheat fan making business.

John Gaskins, living on the Ohio River a mile above the mouth of Bullskin Creek, reports that he found two steers.

Volume II, Wednesday, 27 August 1800, Number 60

Obituary: Mrs. Elizabeth Ewing, age 31, wife of James Ewing of Cincinnati, died "Saturday morning last" and was buried Sunday morning.

Obituary: John Lloyd, age 31, died "Wednesday morning last" about seven miles above Columbia, leaving a widow and two small children.

James Brownlee, living on Elkhorne above the Parara, offers a mill and land for sale.

John Charles, in Cincinnati, reports a runaway apprentice to the carpenter's business, Thomas Campbell, age 19.

J.J. & A. Wills, in Pittsburg, report runaway apprentices to the shoemaker's trade: Joseph Garvey (born in Ireland) and Andrew Shute (born near Lancaster of German parents).

William Forsyth, living near Detroit in Wayne County, reports a runaway slave named Jeffery Marsh.

James Parish, living on Boon Creek in Fayette County, reports runaway slaves named George and Jess.

Hez. Conn, in Cincinnati, has stills for sale. Apply to Roadham Morin, living at Conn's farm at the mouth of Twelve Mile Creek, 12 miles above Columbia.

Volume II, Wednesday, 3 September 1800, Number 61

An unsigned letter to the editor is printed regarding representatives in the General Assembly and mentions William M'Millan, Robert Benham, John Smith, Cor. R. Sedam, John Selman, Thomas Goudy and David E. Wade.

A. Whitlock, in Cincinnati, by order of Gov. St.Clair, reports a stray mare.

Obituary: Miss Eliza Brown, daughter of Rev. John W. Brown of Hamilton County, died Sunday morning, 24 August 1800.

Obituary: Mrs. Ruth Chambers, wife of Maj. Benjamin Chambers, died on Monday evening, 28 August 1800, near Dayton.

Capt. James Smith regarding a meeting of the Cincinnati Light Infantry Company at Fort Washington.

Sheriff James Smith, in Cincinnati, has land for sale, at a sheriff's sale, the property of John Brown at the suit of Alexander M'Laughlin and Oliver Ormsby. Also land for sale, property of Hezekiah Prick, administrator of William Harris, dec'd, at the suit of John Mercer.

James Smith, Collector of the Revenue, regarding duties on carriages.

David Sutton, at Deerfield, asks those indebted to him to pay their bills.

Volume II, Wednesday, 10 September 1800, Number 62

Unsigned letters to the editor about representatives in the General Assembly mentions John Cleve Symmes, Maj. B. Chambers and Moses Miller.

William Ruffin, in Cincinnati, asks those indebted to him to pay their bills.

John Lyon asks those indebted to him to settle their accounts by delivering wheat to Goudy's Mill.

W.C. Schenck, in Cincinnati, has land for sale and mentions Judge Symmes' patent, Gen. Cummings and Rev. Philip Stockton's heirs.

Volume II, Wednesday, 17 September 1800, Number 63

A note regarding the arrival, at Pittsburg, of the troops under Capt. Claiburn.

W.C. Schenck about a meeting of the citizens of Cincinnati at Mr. Yeatman's house to establish a company to build ships to export local produce to foreign markets. A committee was elected: John C. Symmes, James Findlay, William M'Millan, William Goforth, David Zeigler, Jacob Burnet and Jacob White.

Several unsigned letters nominate the following as representatives to the General Assembly: Wm. M'Millan, John Ludlow, John Smith, Moses Miller, Robert M'Clure, Daniel Reeder, F. Dunlevy, W. Goforth, R. Benham, I. Martin, B. Chambers, B. Stites, Sen., C.R. Sedam, I.B. Miller, T. Brown, W. Brown, W. Lytle, J. Gaskins, J. Morrow, J. White, D.E. Wade, T. Goudy, J. Sellman, D. Selder, W. Ludlow, J.W. Brown.

John M'Cullagh has a shipment of goods for sale at his store in Cincinnati.

James Findlay, agent for Lieut. Col. D. Strong, has lots for sale in Cincinnati.

James Findlay and William M'Clelland, in Cincinnati, have land for sale to satisfy the creditors of Thomas Moore, dec'd.

John S. Gano has land for sale, by order of the Orphan's Court of Hamilton County, to satisfy the creditors of the estate of Rev. Peter Wilson, dec'd.

Volume II, Wednesday, 24 September 1800, Number 64

W.C. Schenck announces a meeting, at Mr. Yeatman's, of a committee formed to encourage shipbuilding and export produce.

Several unsigned letters nominate representatives to the General Assembly: William M'Millan, Jeremiah Hunt, John Sellman, C.R. Sedam, James Barrett, William Ramsey, Benjamin Chambers, Joseph Prince, David Zeigler, Moses Miller, Isaac Anderson, John R. Mills, Jacob White, John Smith, Robert M'Clure, Francis Dunlevy, Thomas Goudy, Mr. Barrot (near the Big Parara), Mr. M'Henrey, Mr.

Salmon and Mr. Gibson.

An unsigned letter to the editor is printed regarding Judge Symmes.

Capt. James Smith about a meeting of Cincinnati Light Infantry Company.

Lemuel M'Donald regarding his school in Cincinnati. Apply to Col. John S. Gano or to M'Donald at Dr. William Goforth's place.

John Speed, at Louisville, has salt for sale.

Benjamin Flinn, living near White's Station, reports a stray mare. Deliver to Andrew Pryor on Mill Creek.

John Cleves Symmes, in Cincinnati, has land for rent.

Volume II, Wednesday, 1 October 1800, Number 65

A note from Maj. Zeigler declining the nomination to the General Assembly.

C. Killgore, regarding the formation of the Commercial Company, announces a meeting at Mr. Yeatman's and mentions John C. Symmes, John S. Gano, John Smith, John Armstrong and Jacob White.

A note says Col. Findlay declines the nomination to the General Assembly from Ross County.

The editors of the Western Spy ask those indebted to them to pay their bills in wheat delivered to Goudy's, Grummon's, Smith's or Lyon's mill.

Jacob Burnet, in Cincinnati, claims the land recently offered for rent by John C. Symmes.

A list of letters left at the Post Office in Cincinnati includes Mary Abraham at Detroit, Matthew Anderson in care of Samuel Moore, Charles Allen, Alexander Barns at Little Miami, James Bartett, Andrew Brown, Robert Brasher, Anne Bevis near Dunlapes Station, Ignatious Brown in Deerfield, Joseph Campau at Detroit, Doctor Evan Bane in Waynesville, Robert Buckles in Waynesville, Mr. Cadbury, Henry Cadbury, James Cane, James Cunningham on Little Miami, Christian Crist, John Campbell, James Caldwell at Mill Creek, Ebenezer Cooley near the mouth of the Big Miami, Oliver Calken in Colerain, Josiah Cadwell, William Darling at Little Miami, Walter Davis, John Dinsmore in care of Isaac Anderson, Elisha Davis, John Dodson, Sen., David Douglas, Samuel Davis in Colerain, Sarah Bloomfield Evans or Col. Oliver Spencer, William M. Flinn in care of Col. Gibson, Stephen Fox on Mill Creek, Edward Frame (soldier at Detroit), James Howard on the dry fork of White Water, John Hall, Ralph W. Hunt, Ezekiel Hughes, Stephen Hall (house carpenter), Ezra Harvey in Colerain, Thomas Hill, John T. Hall near Deerfield, John Holland, James Johnston in care of Samuel Baxter, Thomas Irvin, Samuel Johnston in care of Daniel Symmes, Mary Kirkpatrick at Mad River in care of Maj. Ludlow, Peter Kemper, Thomas Kemper, Henry Ker, David Layman, Aaron Lane, John Lyon, Capt. Edward Miller, Joseph M'Mahan at Fort Wayne, Ichabad B. Miller on Little Miami, Hugh M'Collum, John M'Chesney, Aaron Harlan, Jonathan Mundel at Little Miami, Jonathan Markland opposite the North Bend, William Owen at Big Parara, Amsa Owen, John Osenall, Josiah Post, Richard Parcell on Mill Creek, William Patton, William Robison (cabinet maker), Silvanus Reynolds, John Rea, William Reed, Jared Scofield, Thomas Sankey, David Snodgrass, Wm. Sanders (soldier in Detroit), James Sweney, Maj. David Sutton at Deerfield, Mary Steel on Miami, John Stewart near Columbia, Tobias Talbot in care of John Lyon, George Turner, John Naylor (tanner on the Ohio), John Vance, George Vannest in Fairfield township, Manuel Vantreece, Amos Valentine, George Weirick, Israel Willey in Colerain, Judah Willred, George Wallace in care of Smith & Findlay, David Williams, Sergeant William Watrs in Detroit, Rev. William Wood on Little Miami, A. White, John Wilson in Campbell Co., Ky. Entered by William Ruffin.

William Ruffin regarding the new post road to Frankfort, Kentucky.

Volume II, Wednesday, 8 October 1800, Number 66

John Cleves Symmes asks those indebted to him to pay their bills in wheat delivered to Grummon's Mill on Mill Creek for the use of William Jones of Cincinnati, or to Mason's Mill on the Little Miami for the use of James Conn, Charles Conn, and Joseph Conn, Jun., of Cincinnati.

An account of a fight between Charles Bruce and Benjamin Davis at Bruce's house near Hamilton. The latter was killed.

Several letters nominate representatives to the General Assembly: Thomas Gibson, John Smith, Isaac Anderson, Robert M'Clure, Francis Dunlavey, Jacob White, Thomas Goudy, Jeremiah Morrow, John Sellman, Daniel Reeder, Benjamin Chambers and James Barret.

Capt. James Smith regarding a Cincinnati Light Infantry Company meeting.

Daniel Connor & Company have a new shipment of goods for sale at their store in Cincinnati.

Sheriff James Smith regarding the election of representatives to the General Assembly mentions Aaron Cadwell.

James Smith, Collector of the Revenue, gives notice to distillers regarding the duty on stills.

John S. Gano, in Cincinnati, has land for sale, by order of the Orphan's Court of Hamilton County, to satisfy the creditors of the estate of William Miller, dec'd.

John Reily, Griffin Yeatman & William Ramsay about a suit in the Hamilton County Court of Common Pleas: James Demint and others vs. James Sloan and Peter Green. He mentions Yeatman's tavern.

Thomas Depriest is "going up the river" and offers his land on the Little Miami and all his household furniture for sale.

Volume II, Wednesday, 15 October 1800, Number 67

An account of a fight in Hamilton between Peter Killbuck and John Green (both Delaware Indians) in which Killbuck was killed. Green is the man who lately attempted to stab William M'Clelland of Hamilton.

Capt. James Smith regarding a Cincinnati Light Infantry Company meeting.

Carpenter & Findlay regarding their latest postrider, Timothy Boothby.

Archabald Steele, in Cincinnati, found some stray hogs.

John Cleves Symmes asks those indebted to him to settle their accounts by delivering wheat to Capt. Mason's Mill or Waldsmith's Mill, both on the Little Miami, for the use of Joseph Post of Ohio township.

John Finnie, in Woodford County, Kentucky, reports a runaway slave, Moses.

Anthoney Williams has opened a blue dying business in Cincinnati.

Wm. Stuart asks those indebted to him to settle their accounts with Isaac Anderson of Cincinnati.

Sophia Burnet, Jacob Burnet and David Zeigler, administrators of the estate of Geo. W. Burnet, dec'd, of Cincinnati, regarding the estate sale.

Volume II, Wednesday, 22 October 1800, Number 68

The following are elected to represent Hamilton County in the General Assembly: M. Miller, J. Smith, F. Dunlevy, J. Morrow, D. Reeder, J. Ludlow and J. White. W. Lytle is elected to replace A. Cadwell who left the territory.

Capt. James Smith regarding a Cincinnati Light Infantry Company meeting.

Lemuel M'Donald regarding his evening school in Cincinnati at Mr. Cutter's.

Samuel Biggart, living one mile from the Red Bank on Little Miami, reports a stray mare.

Michael Brokaw has sold his shop and intends moving to the country. Those indebted to him should settle their accounts.

Volume II, Wednesday, 29 October 1800, Number 69

Capt. James Smith regarding a Cincinnati Light Infantry Company meeting.

Sheriff James Smith regarding the sale of non-resident's lands.

Daniel Connor & Company want to buy pork at Fort Wayne.

Richard Haughton, dancing master, regarding his dancing school in the house lately occupied by Capt. Vance. Haughton lives at Mr. Yeatman's tavern.

Samuel Welch, living on White Water, found a mare. Apply to David J. Poor in Cincinnati.

John Hunter, living at the crossing of Main Eagle Creek, fifteen miles from Georgetown on the road to Cincinnati, has land for rent. Apply to Wm. Warren at Georgetown.

Volume II, Wednesday, 5 November 1800, Number 70

Obituary: Robert Orr, "an old and respectable citizen", died "Thursday morning last" at his house about two miles from Cincinnati.

Obituary: Edmund Freeman, printer, formerly of Cincinnati, died at his father's place on Bever Creek, Mad River settlement, on Saturday, 25 Oct. 1800.

Isaac Anderson has a shipment of goods for sale at his store in Cincinnati. He also wants to buy wheat at Grummon's Mill.

Robert M'Clure asks those indebt to him for medicines and medical assistance to settle their accounts by delivering wheat to Thomas Goudy's mill or David Grummon's Mill. He also has land for sale where he now lives, adjoining the Big Hill near the road to Fort Hamilton from Cincinnati. Apply to Smith & Findlay.

George Miller, living at John Lyons' about eleven miles from Cincinnati, reports a strayed mare.

Benjamin Flinn regarding a stray colt. Deliver to Flinn or Andrew Pryer on Mill Creek near White's Station.

Joseph Wilson, living on Dicks' Creek, has millstones for sale. Apply to Isaac Anderson in Cincinnati.

Joseph Parks, living on Dicks Creek, regarding a strayed or stolen mare.

Volume II, Wednesday, 12 November 1800, Number 71

William M'Millan is chosen delegate to Congress in place of W.H. Harrison. Paul Fearing of Marietta is chosen representative in Congress.

George Fithian asks those indebted to him to settle their accounts.

Thomas Morris has opened a tavern at Williamsburg.

Joseph Borough, living on Big Miami near the mouth of Silver Creek, reports some strayed horses.

Volume II, Wednesday, 19 November 1800, Number 72

The speech of Gov. St.Clair at the opening of the Territorial Legislature.

Robert Oliver and W.C. Schenck submit a letter to Gov. St.Clair from the Legislative Council and the governor's reply to that.

Andrew Dunseth, gunsmith, has opened his shop in the house lately occupied by Capt. Vance. He wants to hire an apprentice.

George Russel, living near the Big Hill, reports a stray horse.

Daniel Symmes and Jacob Burnet regarding suits in the General Court of the Northwest Territory: George Bickham and Jacob Reese vs. Alexander Scott and Joseph Kerr; Laurence Bazadon vs. George Rogers Clark.

Volume II, Wednesday, 26 November 1800, Number 73

Edward Tiffin and John Reily submit the address of the house of representatives to Gov. St.Clair and the latter's answer.

A note regarding the arrival of William Henry Harrison, Governor of the Indiana Territory, at Cincinnati, on Friday morning last.

John Doyle, gunsmith, has moved his gunsmithing business in Cincinnati.

David Daviss, living in Washington, Kentucky, about strayed or stolen horses.

John M'Cullagh and F. Mennessiers regarding a meeting of the Trustees of the Cincinnati School House at Mr. Fithian's Tavern.

John T. Hall, living near Deerfield, regarding some stray cows.

Volume II, Wednesday, 3 December 1800, Number 74

Rufus Putnam and R.J. Meigs, at Marietta, regarding the formation of the Society of the Cincinnati, mentions Col. Return Jonathan Meigs, Robert Oliver.

Burt & Newman have dissolved their partnership and ask those indebted to them to settle their accounts to A. Burt. J. Newman will carry on the business.

Daniel Symmes, in Cincinnati, regarding a stray horse.

Lieut. G.W. Stall regarding a pistol stolen from the house of Mr. Yeatman.

Volume II, Wednesday, 10 December 1800, Number 75

Proceedings of the House of Representatives mention Mr. Langham, Mr. Smith, Mr. Darlington, Mr. Meigs, Mr. Ludlow, Mr. Kimberly, Rev. William Spear of Chillicothe, Mr. Fearing, Mr. Worthington, Mr. Sibley, Rufus Putnam, the Ohio Company, Samuel Findlay, Solomon Sibley, Henry VanderBurgh, Mr. Massie and Mr. Goforth.

John C. Winans, lately arrived from Elizabeth Town, N.J., has opened his office as a physician and surgeon at Rev. Mr. Kemper's on Turtle Creek.

William Hammit, in North-Bend, regarding his ferry across the Ohio River.

James Conn gives the second notice to those indebted to him to settle their accounts by bringing wheat to Goudy's or Grummon's Mill.

Houton Clarke, justice of the peace, regarding the claims of William Nelson vs. John Harper, late of Hamilton County, Washington township. He mentions Samuel Nelson and Benjamin Frazee in Bethel (or Denham's Town).

James Caldwell, in Cincinnati, reports a stray horse.

George Miller, at John Lyons' on Mill Creek on the Hamilton Road, reports a stray mare.

Thomas Williams, in Cincinnati, wants to buy deer skins.

A note about goods for sale at Mr. Mahoney's boat at the landing, Cincinnati.

Volume II, Wednesday, 17 December 1800, Number 76

A note regarding acts passed by the Legislature mention Lucy Petet and Dr. William Burnet, the elder.

A notice is printed regarding a singing school in Cincinnati.

Daniel Conner & Company, in Cincinnati, want to buy soap and candles.

Wm. & M. Jones, in Cincinnati, moved to the shop, lately occupied by Samuel Patterson, saddler, opposite Thomas Williams' skindresser shop.

William Stanley, in Cincinnati, regarding a meeting of Nova Caesaria Lodge.

Sophia Burnet, David Zeigler and Jacob Burnet, administrators of the estate of George Burnet, dec'd, regarding the estate settlement.

Lieut. R. Webster, at Fort Washington, reports a deserter, John O'Brian (age 25, born in Ireland).

Archibald H. Reed, at the fork of the road from Georgetown to Cincinnati and the road from the mouth of Kentucky River to Washington, has land for sale. Apply to Thomas Kennedy living at the mouth of the Licking River.

Allen Simpson, living on White Water, found some steers.

Volume II, Wednesday, 24 December 1800, Number 77

A letter to Col. Robert Oliver and Edward Tiffin from Joseph Gilman and Return Jonathan Meigs, Jun.

The answer of Gov. Ar. St.Clair to the above letter is printed.

A letter to the public from Edward Tiffin is printed regarding the division of the territory.

Ar. St.Clair's speech to the Legislature of the Northwest Territory is printed.

Lieut. Col. David Strong and his troops passed by Cincinnati on Thursday morning on their way to the mouth of the Ohio River.

Uriah Gates says his wife, Rebecca, left him, and he won't pay her debts.

Libius Marshal, living on Mill Creek near Caldwell's Mill, found some cattle.

James Tucker, living on Hamilton road, reports a stray mare. Deliver to Jonathan Pitman, tavern keeper, on the Hamilton road.

Volume II, Wednesday, 31 December 1800, Number 78

John Smith writes a letter to the public regarding his actions in the House of Representatives.

A notice from Gov. Arthur St.Clair regarding establishing Clermont County.

Lieut. Peter Shiras, at Fort Washington, reports a deserter from Capt. Bird's Company, William Blackford, age 25, born in Massachusetts, district of Maine.

James Smith regarding bills for building the jail.

John Ferris, near Dayton, says that John Coulter robbed him.

Smith & Findlay have horses for sale.

A list of letters left at the Post Office in Cincinnati includes Mary Arnold, Samuel Arnold (in the U.S. Army), Zenas Ames (quarter master), Charles Bruce, Sergeant Benjamin Allen, Michael Brokaw, Zacharius Burwell in care of John

Smith, Daniel Broadstreet, John Clark, Thomas Carneal or Rice Bullock, William Curry in care of Jesse Hunt, Sarah Dewitt in Newport, John Dorrett, George Druyea in Detroit, Thomas Elliott, Amos Edgerton, William Frazee in care of Capt. Shomaker, Zebulon Foster in Springfield, Benajah Gustin at Little Miami, Samuel Hockings near Hamilton, Robert Higgins (15 miles below Limestone), Robert Hempstead, Jonathan Huntingdon on Little Miami, Jacob Hutchinson on Mill Creek, James Huston in Detroit, Isaac Hubble near Deerfield, Aaron Harlan (sergeant), Thadeus Hunbolt (U.S. Army), James Harris in care of Capt. Claiborne, Daniel Ingersoll on Big Miami, Ezekiel Julow near Columbia, William Johnson, Samuel Kirkpatrick on Mad River, Thomas Kompton, Asa Kitchell in Knox County, William Ludlow, John Ludlow, Joseph Laton, Isaac M'Calmont, Thomas Mason (soldier), Charles Moore, Capt. Edward Miller, Sergeant Thomas Maine, John Mills (8 miles from Cincinnati), Henry Myers on Little Miami, John M'Cune, Doctor Robert M'Clure, Patrick M'Carty, Doctor William M'Coskry, Capt. Thomas Pasture in Detroit, Lieut. Zebulon M. Pike, William Paxon in care of John M'Cullough, Isaac Parkson at Miami, William Rittenhouse in care of Daniel Woodward, Israel Ruling at Detroit, Nathaniel Ross on Duck Creek, Ezra Robertson near Deerfield, Lieut. Joshua S. Roog in Detroit, David Snodgrass, Jacob Snowden on Mill Creek, Abraham Skinner on Mill Creek, Isaac Stubeley on Little Miami, Thomas Shelldon, Simon Stockwell in care of Smith & Findlay, Lieut. Col. David Strong, William Smith, John Torrence, Abraham Townsend at Columbia, Amanuel Vantrees, Lieut. John Whipple, Massey White on Mill Creek, Rev. Robert Warwick in care of W. Ramsey, Andrew Wilson on Mill Creek, Frances Whitenger on Big Miami, George Weirick, Peter White on Big Miami. Entered by William Ruffin, post master.

Volume II, Wednesday, 7 January 1801, Number 79

An address of the General Assembly to Gov. St.Clair and the governor's reply.

An unsigned letter to Hon. John Smith in answer to his recent letter is printed and mentions Mr. M'Millan, Judge Symmes, Mr. Cadwell and Mr. Harrison.

An unsigned letter to the editor regarding the Rev. Mr. John Smith's recent letter mentions Mr. M'Millan, Mr. Harrison, Judge Symmes and Mr. Ludlow.

A note regarding Mr. M'Millan in Congress mentions John C. Symmes & Company and the establishment of schools in the Territory.

An account of the celebration of the Nova Caesaria Lodge mentions Mr. Yeatman and Gov. St.Clair.

David Kelly, living at Clough Creek, regarding a stray horse.

Martin Baum & Company stopped doing business in Cincinnati on 6 October 1800 and ask those indebted to them to settle their accounts.

Thomas Thompson & Company bought the remaining stock of Martin Baum & Company and offer it for sale at their shop in Cincinnati.

James Montgomery, Attorney, asks those indebted to John M'Cullagh, merchant, of Cincinnati, to settle their accounts.

Stephen Reeder, Cincinnati, about payments for the service of a stud horse.

Volume II, Wednesday, 14 January 1801, Number 80

An unsigned letter to John Smith mentions Judge Symmes and Mr. M'Millan.

A letter from John Sinclair in London to Gov. Arthur St.Clair is printed.

John Smith writes a letter to the editor.

Obituary: John Allen, of the Northwest Territory, member of Nova Caesaria Lodge in Cincinnati, was buried Saturday, 13 December 1800, at Georgetown, Ky.

Obituary: On Thursday last, Thomas Clarke, carpenter, living near Cincinnati, was found dead of exposure in the woods near his house. He left a large family.

A note regarding the death of Mr. A. Freeman's negro boy.

A note is printed regarding the recruitment of soldiers at Fort Washington under the direction of Capt. Vance.

Isaac Bush says "my wife Elizabeth Bush has refused to go with me" and he will no longer honor her debts.

The editors of the Western Spy ask those indebted to them to pay with wheat delivered to Grummon's, Goudy's, White's, Smith's, Lyon's or Williams' mills.

John Jackson, of Woodford County, Ky., regarding a runaway slave, Ephraim.

R. Allison, living at Bell Font on the east branch of the Little Miami, regarding the escape of an indented servant, Thomas Shannon, age 18.

Nathaniel Reeder has a new shipment of goods for sale at the house lately occupied by James Forguson in Cincinnati.

James Montgomery about collecting the debts owed to Francis Wilson, now of Pittsburg, late of Cincinnati, merchant.

John Sellman asks those indebted to him or to Sellman & Hall to settle their accounts with wheat delivered to Jacob White's Mill.

Levi M'Lean asks those indebted to him to settle their accounts.

Volume II, Wednesday, 21 January 1801, Number 81

John S. Gano and Jacob Burnet (attorney) about suits in the Court of Common Pleas, Northwest Territory: Abijah Hunt vs. Richard Throckmorton (mentions Joseph Lewis); Jacob D. Lowe vs. Robert Steveson; Barton Leonard and Mary his wife vs. William Travis and Silas Travis; George Carr vs. Andrew Edwards.

Joseph Logsdon, living on Bullskin Creek, found a stray horse.

John C. Winans, in Cincinnati, regarding his business as a physician.

Sheriff James Smith, in Cincinnati, has property of William Wood for sale at the suit of Thomas Frazer. Also the property of Thomas Carniel at the suit of John S. Gano and Benjamin Stites. Also the property of Israel Shreve at the suit of James Conn and Charles Conn.

Charles Vattier, in Cincinnati, administrator of the estate of Mary M'Night, deceased, regarding the estate settlement.

Libius Marshall found some stray cows.

Volume II, Wednesday, 28 January 1801, Number 82

Sheriff James Smith, in Cincinnati, regarding a sheriff's sale of the property of James Cox.

W. Hubbell, living at the forks of Elkhorn Creek, Franklin County, Kentucky, regarding a runaway slave named George.

Volume II, Wednesday, 4 February 1801, Number 83

A letter to the public from John Smith mentions Mr. Massie, Mr. M'Millan, Mr. Fearing, Mr. Tiffin, Gov. St.Clair, Judge Symmes, Mr. Ludlow, Mr. Martin, Mr. Benham and Edward Tiffin.

An unsigned letter to the public regarding Mr. Smith mentions Mr. M'Millan and Judge Symmes.

Solomon Sibley, of Detroit, is appointed to fill the seat of Henry VanderBurgh that is now vacant due to the division of the territory.

Marriage: Solomon Gottshalkson married Miss Eliza Nancarrow on Thursday, January 14, 1801.

David J. Poor says he's leaving Cincinnati and asks those indebted to him to settle their accounts as soon as possible.

Lucas Sullivant, at Franklinton, Northwest Territory, has land for sale.

Daniel Symmes and James Montgomery (attorney) regarding suits in the General Court of the Northwest Territory: George Turner vs. Charles Young; George Bickham and Jacob Reese vs. Edward Cook and Joanna Gorden (executors of William Bartlet, dec'd).

James and Robert Caldwell have just arrived from Kentucky and opened an earthen ware making shop at the house of William M'Farland in Cincinnati.

Rachel Innis, in Columbia, administratrix of the estate of Francis Innis, late of Columbia, dec'd, regarding the estate settlement.

Volume II, Wednesday, 11 February 1801, Number 84

An account of a meeting of the inhabitants of Marietta regarding statehood.

An unsigned letter to the editor regarding John Smith mentions Mr. Harrison.

Richard Downes takes back what he said about Mr. Smith of Columbia passing counterfeit notes. This is witnessed by James Matthews, Aaron Haugham, Philip Highsil/Highful and George Matthews.

John Dickson, living at Big Hill, regarding a stray mare.

Sheriff William Perry, at Williamsburg, regarding the justices of the peace for Clermont County: Richard Allison, Owen Todd, William Buchannon, Peter Light, Jasper Shotwell, William Hunter, Robert Higgins and Philip Gatch. Allison, Todd, Buchannon, Shotwell, Higgins and Gatch are also named justices of the Court of Common Pleas. The first court will be held at Thomas Morris' in Williamsburg.

Ralph Phillips has land for sale next door to Ralph W. Hunt. Apply to Jesse Hunt at Cincinnati.

Mr. Adams, the post rider, ran away and the editors of the Western Spy want to hire someone to take his place.

Volume II, Wednesday, 18 February 1801, Number 85

A note is printed regarding Mr. M'Millan in Congress.

A note regarding the boundary line of the Northwest Territory mentions Mr. Bird, Mr. M'Millan, Mr. Varnum, John C. Symmes, Mr. Pinckney, Mr. Imley, Mr. Morris and E. Goodrich.

An unsigned letter to the editor regarding Mr. Smith mentions Mr. M'Millan, Judge Symmes and Dr. Tiffin.

Col. Gano has supplied a list of appointed township officers that will be printed in the next paper.

Sheriff James Smith offers the stud horse that stood last season at Nathan Kelly's for sale at a sheriff's sale. He's the property of Robert Steveson, seized at the suit of Jacob D. Lowe. Smith also has land for sale in Hamilton, property of John Brown, seized at the suit of Oliver Ormsby and Daniel Conner.

Volume II, Wednesday, 25 February 1801, Number 86

An unsigned letter to Hon. John Smith mentions Mr. M'Millan, Judge Symmes, Maj. Langham, John Cleves Symmes, Mr. Ludlow and Mr. Fearing.

A letter from John Ludlow mentions Mr. Smith.

Sheriff Jacob Schnebly in Washington County, Maryland, regarding a debtor named Jacob Earhart who escaped from jail.

John Cleves Symmes wants to buy cows and whiskey. Deliver to John Smith in Columbia. He also wants wheat delivered to Capt. White's and Mr. Wallsmith's mills "for Mr. Baum's freight to Orleans".

John Sellman asks those indebted to Sellman & Hall to pay their bills by delivering wheat to Jacob White's Mill.

Charles Smith, at the Round Bottom Mills, regarding a stray mare.

Appointments of township officers are announced. In Columbia township, the supervisors of highways are Christian Waldsmith, James Pollock, Thomas Espy, Cheneniah Cavault, Mr. Armstrong, David Black, Erasmus Felter, John Wolverton, Edmund Buxton, John Cummins, Matthias Crow, Thomas Higgins, Andrew Prior, John Matthews, Joseph M'Gee, Joseph Patters, Wm. Drake, Isaac Ferras, Jun., Henry House. Overseers of the poor are Joseph Reeder and Willis Person. Viewers of enclosures and appraisers of damages are James Witham, Daniel Lambert and David Black. Auditors of supervisors accounts are Cornelius Snider, James Mason and Calvin Kuchell. Valuers of property are Thomas C. Wade, Garret Voorhese. David Black, lister.

Appointments made in Cincinnati Township: Supervisors of Highways are William Ruffin, John Harden, Patrick Dickey, Isaac Anderson, Cornelius R. Sedam, Joseph M'Henry, Marsh Williams, Stephen Reeder, Isaac Bates, Thomas Williams. Overseers of the Poor are Peter Kemper and Cornelius VanNuys. Viewers of enclosures are William Ramsey, Griffin Yeatman and John Riddle. Auditors of supervisors accounts are William Ramsey, Jesse Hunt and John Reily. Valuers of property are Cornelius R. Sedam, Samuel Dick. Abraham Cary, lister.

Appointments made in South Bend Township: Supervisors of highways are Samuel Moore, James Bennet and Isaac Sparks. Overseers of the poor are Thomas Spurrier and Isaac Wilson. Viewers of enclosures are Gershom Gard, William T. Cullum and Robert Terry. Auditors of supervisors accounts are James M'Kee, George Cullum and Justice Gibbs. Valuers of property are Samuel Martin, Jacob R. Compton. Robert Whelan, lister.

Appointments made in Miami Township: Supervisors of highways are John

Cassidy, William Rittenhouse and Andrew Hill. Overseers of the poor are John Matson and Brice Virgin. Viewers of enclosures are William Rittenhouse, Brice Virgin and Robert Collins. Auditors of supervisors accounts are Andrew Scott, Benjamin M'Clure and John Matson. Valuers of property are John Matson and John Campbell. John Matson, Jun., lister.

Appointments made in Anderson Township: Supervisors of highways are John Webb, Ignatius Ross, and Stephen Sutton. Overseers of the poor are Stephen Davis and John Corbly. Viewers of the enclosures are Jacob Frazee, Jonathan Gerrard, and Seth Fields. Auditors of supervisors accounts are John Corbly, Thomas Brown and James Clark. Valuers of property are Seth Fields and Moses Broadwell. David Kelly, lister.

Appointments made in Colerain Township: Supervisors of highways are John Walker and Samuel Bordine. Overseers of the poor are Alexander Martin and Thomas Allstone. Viewers of enclosures are John Clap, Albin Shaw and Daniel Davis. Auditors of supervisors accounts are John Davis, Joseph Walker and Knoles Shaw. Valuers of property are Isaac Gibson and Asa Harvey. Alban Shaw, lister.

Appointments made in Fairfield Township: Supervisors of highways are Darius C. Orcott, John Enyalt, Moses Veal and Benjamin Line. Overseers of the poor are John Dickson and John Humes. Viewers of enclosures are Celadon Symmes, Andrew Christy and John Torrence. Auditors of supervisors accounts are Joseph Kennedy, David Cummins and William Symmes. Valuers of property are William M'Clelland and Solomon Lyon. Darius C. Orcott, lister.

Appointments made in Springfield Township: Supervisors of highways are William Ludon, Jonathan Pittman, W. Snodgrass, James Lowes, Peter Kean and John Ludlow. Overseers of the poor are John Watson and John M'Cormack. Viewers of enclosures are John Jinkinson, Isaac Martin and Zibe Stibbins. Auditors of supervisors accounts are Henry Weaver, William Ludlow and John Jinkinson. Valuers of property are John Jinkinson and Henry Tucker. William Ludlow, lister.

Appointments made in Dayton Township: Supervisors of highways are William Gahagan, Thomas Davis, George Adams, Nathan Talbot, Amos Darrow, and Archibald Lowery. Overseers of the poor are William Westfall and John Devor. Viewers of enclosures are James Flinn, John Hole and Daniel Ferrel. Auditors of supervisors accounts are Samuel Freeman, William Maxwell and Benjamin Chambers. Valuers of property are James Flinn and John Ewing. Benjamin Vancleve, lister.

Appointments made in Franklin Township: Supervisors of highways are James Dearth, James Petticrew, Forgus M'Clain, Joseph Parks, Sen., Christian Null, John Wilson, John Vance, William Maxwell and Moses Potter. Overseers of the poor are William Crain and Asa Richardson, Sen. Viewers of the enclosures are Cyrus Osborn, Calvin Morrel and John Carson. Auditors of supervisors accounts are Joseph Parks, Sen., Joseph Crane and James Brady. Valuers of property are John Bennet and James Petticrew. John Kitchell, lister.

Appointments made in Deerfield Township: Supervisors of highways are David Fox, Jacob Lowe, John Miller, David Sutton, David Robertson, John Shaw, Sen., John Beaty, Thomas M'Intire, Daniel Baker, Moses Easton and Abraham Freeman. Overseers of the poor are Samuel Munen and Benjamin Stites, Jun. Viewers of enclosures are Jabish Philips, Andrew Lytle and Francis Beedle. Auditors of supervisors accounts are Nathan Kelley, Ephraim Kibby and Samuel Serring. Valuers of property are Alexander Hamilton and Henry Taylor. Ephraim Kibby, lister.

Appointments made in Ohio Township: Supervisors of highways are John Kitchell, John White, and William Cherry. Overseers of the poor are Joseph Hair and Harry Harden. Viewers of enclosures are Jonas Crane, Thomas Howe and George Criss. Auditors of accounts are Jonas Crane, Isaac Mills and Caleb Hays. Valuers of property are Thomas Miller and John White. Isaac Mills, lister.

Appointments made in St. Clair Township: Supervisors of highways are John Bennefield and Michael Wilkins. Overseers of the poor are William Parkeson and John Blackburn. Viewers of the enclosures are Joseph Brown, Conrod Vantresse and George M'Cleve. Auditors of supervisors accounts are Samuel Gamble, Robert Blackburn and Brison Blackburn. Valuers of property are Alban Simpson and David

Gibson. Hartman Vantresse, lister.

William Ruffin is commissioner in Hamilton County in place of Joseph Prince.

Volume II, Wednesday, 4 March 1801, Number 87

Two letters to the public from John Smith mention Capt. Harrison, Jacob Burnet, Charles Avery, Mr. St.Clair, Mr. M'Millan.

A note regarding acts of Congress pertaining to the lands of John Cleves Symmes mentions Mr. Bird and Mr. Otis.

Gov. Arthur St.Clair is reappointed governor of the Territory.

Sheriff James Smith about a meeting of the General Court of the Territory.

Henry Massey, Collector of taxes on lands in the Virginia Military Tract, regarding non-resident land taxes.

John Campbell, living in Newtown, found a steer.

Edward Tiffin, Robert Oliver and Arthur St.Clair regarding a law.

Volume II, Wednesday, 11 March 1801, Number 88

A letter to the public from John Smith mentions Judge Symmes, Mr. M'Millan and Maj. Langham.

A letter to John Ludlow from John Smith mentions Mr. M'Millan.

A note about a meeting at Mr. Yeatman's regarding steam boats.

Isabella Rodney, in Cincinnati, lately left Ireland to search for her brother, Patrick Rodney, shoemaker.

Sheriff James Smith regarding escaped prisoners, Enoch Drake (age 33) and George Russel. Drake's family lives 20 miles below the Great Miami.

David E. Wade, I.B. Miller and William Ruffin, at Cincinnati, about a meeting at Mr. Avery's regarding building a courthouse in Hamilton County.

Thomas Gibson, Auditor, in Chillicothe, about taxes on Virginia army lands.

W. Warfield, of Fayette County, Kentucky, has land for sale in the Virginia military lands. Apply to Col. Nathaniel Massie.

Robert Brasher, in Cincinnati, reports a stray cow.

Volume II, Wednesday, 18 March 1801, Number 89

Edward Tiffin, Robert Oliver and Ar. St.Clair regarding new laws.

Carpenter & Findlay, editors of the Western Spy, ask those indebted to them to settle their accounts as soon as possible.

A note about a meeting at Mr. M'Collom's about the education of the youth.

O.M. Spencer says he's leaving Cincinnati for Natchez and is turning over the Recorder's Office to G. Yeatman.

John Roll, on Mill Creek, reports that he found a stray horse.

Volume II, Wednesday, 25 March 1801, Number 90

Edward Tiffin, Robert Oliver and Ar. St.Clair regarding the laws.

A note regarding the trial of Charles Bruce for the murder of Benjamin Davis.

Two letters from Mr. M'Millan in Washington mention John Smith, Peyton Short and Judge Symmes.

A note regarding the celebration, at Mr. Mennessier's Hotel, of Jefferson's election as president mentions Hon. J.C. Symmes, Gen. Wolfe, Mr. LaFayette of Columbia and Gov. St.Clair.

A note regarding Judge Meigs' address to the Hamilton County Grand Jury.

Gov. Ar. St.Clair and Israel Ludlow have land for sale at Griffin Yeatman's.

Matthew Winton and James Charters, administrators of the estate of William Charters, late of Colerain township, dec'd, regarding the estate.

Samuel Heighway and John Pool regarding building steamboats at Cincinnati.

Hugh Hagan regarding a note to Alexander M'Hendrick for a town lot in Dayton mentions Daniel C. Cooper.

James Forguson has a new shipment of goods for sale at his store. Also those indebted to him should pay in wheat delivered to Cunningham's Mill.

Joseph Prince reports that his colt was stolen.

Volume II, Wednesday, 1 April 1801, Number 91
   The speech of Hon. Judge Meigs to the Grand Jury in Hamilton County.
   A letter from William M'Millan in Washington mentions Judge Symmes.
   Obituary: Ann Hutchinson, age 101, died 4 January 1801, at the house of Robt. Willis in East Windford township, Middlesex County. She was the mother of 13 children and grandmother to 375.
   Jacob Blasdel, living on Rev. John Smith's plantation below Columbia, found a stray heifer.
   Moses Jones, living one mile from Cincinnati towards Grummon's Mill, found a stray mare.
   Jacob D. Lowe and Ralph W. Hunt ask those indebted to them to settle their accounts at John Torrence's inn in Hamilton.
   A list of letters left at the Post Office in Cincinnati includes Thomas Ayers on Little Miami, John Askin, Jun., in Detroit, John Brant on Little Miami, Hugh Brownlee in care of Samuel Dick, John Bragdon at Columbia, Ephraim Blackford on Clear Creek, Barbara Bell, David Bradbery, Christian Blankard, Samuel Bennet, John Biggar, jun., in care of James Findlay, Benjamin Bradbury at Columbia, John Brown on the banks of the Ohio, John Bancratt (soldier in Capt. Shoemaker's company), James Cox, Sergeant Lemuel Church, James Clay (soldier), Maj. Benjamin Chambers, Capt. F. Leigh Claiborne, Joseph Colby at Columbia, David Douglas, Abraham Fordice on Big Miami, Daniel Gorden, Corporal James Gardner, Capt. John Gardner, Capt. Richard H. Greaton, John Gilman in Columbia, Leonard Harriman at Columbia, Richard Harris, Maj. Thomas Hunt, Joseph Hawley, Robert Houston, James Johnston (mill wright), James Irvin near Cunningham's mill, Joseph Jacobs, Joseph Jackson in care of Griffin Yeatman, Joseph Keppy on Clear Creek, John Reed on Clear Creek, Asa Kitchell, Adam Lilver near Columbia, John Larew in care of William Mason, Benjamin Megie on Mill Creek, Andrew May on Big Miami, John Squire Marsh, Capt. Edmund Munger, Ruthy M'Kee in care of Mr. Washburn, Doctor Robert M'Clure, James Marandy on Little Miami, James M'Kean (quarter master), Sergeant William Patton in care of John M'Cullough, James Patterson on Mill Creek, Samuel Perry, Corporal Seth Palmer, Capt. Abner Prior in Detroit, Henry Rockwell, Robert Reed, Nathaniel Reed near Beazley's Mill, Elizabeth Riggs, Ambrose Rastone on Little Miami, Lieut. Joshua S. Rogers care of Capt. Vance, Elijah Stebbins on Clear Creek, Lieut. G.W. Stall at Fort Wayne, William Sanders (soldier at Detroit), Rev. Peter Smith, William Sullivan (soldier), Augustus Strong, Elijah Sparks at Bank Lick, Thomas Sheldon, William Stewart, Solomon Sibbley, Cornelious Snider, Emanuel Vantrees, Curtis Vorris, Elder Maries Witham, A. Whitlock, Jonathan Williams, Capt. William Woulsey, Lieut. John Whipple, William Wells at Fort Wayne, Resin Webster, Doctor Joseph Wilkinson at Detroit in care of Capt. Vance, Christian Walsmith on Little Miami. William Ruffin, post master.

Volume II, Wednesday, 8 April 1801, Number 92
   An unsigned letter to the editor mentions Mr. M'Millan and Mr. Fearing.
   An unsigned letter regarding John Smith is printed and mentions Mr. M'Millan, Mr. Fearing and Judge Symmes.
   An act of Congress is printed regarding John C. Symmes' lands and mentions Israel Ludlow's survey.
   T. Gibson, in Chillicothe, regarding surveys of the Virginia military lands.
   Daniel Conner & Company have a new shipment of goods for sale at their store in Cincinnati.
   Emanuel Vantrees has land for sale.

Volume II, Wednesday, 15 April 1801, Number 93
   An act of Congress regarding Judge John C. Symmes' grant mentions Israel Ludlow's survey.
   Capt. Ferdinand L. Claiborne writes a letter to Lieut. Col. D. Strong about the tornado that came through the troops' camp and wounded these officers: Capt. Lukens, Lieut. Webster, Lieut. Leybourne, Lieut. Hook, Lieut. Shiras.
   An unsigned letter to the public regarding John Smith is printed.

Laurence Hilderbrand, in Clermont County, says his wife, Elizabeth, left him and took up with Jacob Crimm/Grimm, and he won't honor her debts anymore.

Sheriff James Smith about taxes on non-residents' lands in Hamilton County.

Carpenter & Findlay say that the new post-rider, Mr. Clark, will collect bills.

A list of patrons of the steam engine includes, in Cincinnati: Gov. Arthur St.Clair, Hon. John Cleves Symmes, Jesse Hunt, David Zeigler, Ar. St.Clair, Jun., Jacob Burnet, Smith & Findlay, James Montgomery, M. Baum, Jeremiah Hunt, Griffin Yeatman, P.P. Stuart, C. Killgore, Mr. Bush, H. Weaver, William Stanley, I. Loring, Benjamin Seamons, Peter Kemper, Dan. Symmes, William Goforth, Ephraim Kibby, John Baldwin, Thomas Goudy, Joel Williams, Mr. Conn, John Arthurs, Seth Cutter, Jno. M'Cullaugh, R. M'Collom, G. Fithian, G. Turner, C. Avery, J.S. Gano, C. Vattier. In Columbia: John Smith, W. Goforth, Sen., J. Wilson, Benjamin Stites. In Kentucky: Thomas Kennedy and Daniel Mayo.

Volume II, Wednesday, 22 April 1801, Number 94

Obituary: Maj. William Winston, cavalry, died at Detroit, Sunday, 29 March.

Capt. James Smith about a meeting of the Cincinnati Light Infantry.

Thomas Frazer moved his house of entertainment to the house formerly occupied by Capt. E. Kibby.

Capt. Samuel C. Vance, at Fort Washington, regarding deserters: William Davis (age 30, shoemaker, born in England) who was enlisted by Lieut. Arbuckle at Limestone, Kentucky, and has family living there, and John Reed (born in Chester County, Pennsylvania, age 25, shoemaker).

Andrew Shirk, living about nine miles from Cincinnati on Five Mile Run, reports a stray heifer.

David Beaty, living on Pleasant Run three miles below Fort Hamilton, has wool for sale.

Elizabeth Callahan, administratrix of the estate of Hugh Callahan, late of Detroit, deceased, regarding the estate settlement.

David Lanpher, at Fort Wayne, regarding the property belonging to George Rock who died on 28 March 1801 and is said to have relatives in Kentucky. The estate was inventoried by Lanpher, James Abbott and William Wells.

John S. Gano, in Hamilton County, has land for sale by order of the Orphan's Court in Hamilton County to satisfy the debts of Dr. William Burnet, Jun., dec'd.

Volume II, Wednesday, 29 April 1801, Number 95

Note about the brig St.Clair, from Marietta, sailed by Commodore Whipple.

Sheriff James Smith has land for sale at a sheriff's sale, property of Robert M'Clelland seized at the suit of Daniel Vantner. Also property of James Sloan and Peter Green seized at the suit of James Demint and others.

W.C. Schenck reports a strayed horse.

Abraham Freeman has land for rent at Freeman's Lick on the road from Deerfield to Cincinnati, five miles from Mr. Woods' grist mill on the Miami.

William Harper, living on Nine Mile Creek, reports a stray horse.

Volume II, Wednesday, 6 May 1801, Number 96

The results of the recent census of Hamilton County are listed.

Daniel Mayo, in Newport, wants to buy hemp.

John Reily, W.C. Schenck and J.S. Findlay about a suit in Court of Common Pleas in Hamilton County: Benjamin F. Randolph and others vs. George Codd.

Volume II, Wednesday, 13 May 1801, Number 97

William M'Millan, late delegate to Congress, returned to Cincinnati on the 5th of May and attended a dinner at Mr. Yeatman's. Gov. St.Clair is mentioned.

Daniel Symmes about forms for bail in the General Court of the Northwest Territory. Also reports that the following are appointed commissioners of bail: James Silvers, Robert Benham, Daniel Symmes, Daniel C. Cooper, John S. Gano.

Sophia Burnet, David Zeigler and Jacob Burnet, administrators of the estate of George W. Burnet, regarding the estate settlement.

Matthew Flournoy, living on the waters of Clear Creek near Shelbyville,

regarding a runaway slave named Sam.
James Bruff regarding his ferry across the Little Miami River at its mouth.
Geo. Carpenter, living on Capt. Cornelious R. Sedam's farm, found a heifer.

Volume II, Wednesday, 20 May 1801, Number 98
Patrick Dickey wants to hire apprentices to the tayloring business.
Griffin Yeatman, Daniel Conner and James Smith, trustees, about contracts for building a Market House in Cincinnati.
Sheriff James Smith regarding a sheriff's sale of the property of John Cleves Symmes taken in the suit of Daniel M'Clure and John R. Mills.

Volume II, Wednesday, 27 May 1801, Number 99
W. Wells, agent for Indian affairs at Fort Wayne, found a horse.
Griffin Yeatman, Daniel Conner and James Smith about building a Market House in Cincinnati.
Thomas White, living on the west side of the Great Miami three miles below Fort Hamilton, reports a stray horse.
Henry Furry, in Cincinnati, has whiskey and brandy for sale in the house lately occupied by Mr. Kidd near Mr. Ramsey's store.
George Newman, agent for Joseph Newman, asks those indebted to Burt & Newman to settle their accounts.
Joseph Newman, at Natchez, reports a runaway apprentice, Samuel Moore.
G. Yeatman, in Cincinnati, regarding the Recorder's Office.
Capt. Benham, two miles above Deerfield, wants to hire a school teacher.
John Cleves Symmes, Jun., at South Bend, found a stray mare.

Volume II, Wednesday, 3 June 1801, Number 100
An account of an incident in Chillicothe on Monday evening, 18 May 1801, in which John Bates and John Bowman fought at a tavern, and Bates was killed.
John Dunn, living at Little Prairie near Fort Hamilton, about a stray mare.
C. Avery & G. Fithian regarding water from their well.
Seth Cutter, in Cincinnati, is repairing his well and will sell water.
John S. Gano, of Cincinnati, has land for sale on Sycamore Creek adjoining Mr. Snyder and near Mr. Terwilleger's. He also has land for sale six miles above Deerfield on Little Miami near Levi Jennings.
Sellman & Hall, in Cincinnati, have a new shipment of drugs and medicines.

Volume II, Wednesday, 1 July 1801, Number 101
A note from the editors of the Western Spy apologizing for no newspapers for the past three weeks.
Charles Willing Byrd gives the results of the recent census of the territory.
Obituary: Frederick Augustus Muhlenberg, Receiver General of the Land Office, died at Lancaster, Thursday afternoon, 4 June 1801.
Sergt. Benjamin Seamans regarding the Fourth of July celebration mentions the Cincinnati Light Infantry Company.
John H. Williams and John Crain regarding their agreement with Andrew Hays, agent for John Fulton.
A list of letters left at the Post Office in Cincinnati includes Lieut. Arbuckle, Thomas Alston, James Armstrong in Deerfield, John Briney, James Buchanan in Deerfield, Robert Benham, David Black in Columbia township, David Beaty near Hamilton, John Beale at Franklin, Alexander Brannon on Little Miami, Patrick C. Mahan at North Bend, Henry Carson, William Coleman, Archibald Campbell at Alexander Campbell's, William Crooks on Miami, D.C. Cooper, John Carr in care of Daniel Reeder near Wallace's Mill, John Coliher, Sen., at Dunham's Town, Godfrey Corbus in Detroit, Thomas Cooch, Charles Cope in Colerain, Elisha Davis, Abner Denman at Springfield, James Dunn, Timothy Day, Samuel Dillon (cooper, care of Samuel Kenedy), Isaac Ferras on Little Miami, Jesse Fulton in care of Samuel Dick, Samuel Foot at Holes Creek, Justus Gerrard on Big Miami, John Gray in care of Rachel Innis, Jacob Helsler or John Gamo, Thomas Hill or John Beaty on Mad River Road, Samuel Highway in care of John Pool, Alexander

Hamilton, George Harlan on Big Miami, Aaron Hunt in care of Mr. Brasher, John Reed on Clear Creek, John Karr in care of Daniel Reeder, John Ludlow, Samuel Lane, Daniel Long near Tuckers Station, Shadrack Lane in Anderson township, James Lowes, Sampson M'Cullaugh, William Mongommery (tanner), Capt. Hugh M'Call, James M'Keene in care of John Scott on Great Miami, Mary Marsh in care of John Marsh, Charles Morgon, Peter Mickel, John M'Gilliard, F. Mitchell on Mill Creek, James M'Farland, Benjamin Megie on Turtle Creek, Joseph M'Mahan, Joel Williams, Samuel Patterson, Samuel Perry, John Pryer, Archelus Quinby, Doctor Reeder, Abraham Redlon in Columbia, Nathaniel Reeve near Beazley's Mill, Thomas Stone at Springfield, Thomas Sankey, William Smith (hatter) at Detroit, John Scot on Big Miami, William Sittle, George Smyth, Peter Smith on Duck Creek, John Shanklin in care of Jacob White, George Shook on Big Miami, John Thomas in Capt. Shoemaker's Company, Jacob Fingly on Big Miami, Joseph Thompson near Hamilton, Capt. E.D. Turner, Nathan Truesdall, John Todd in care of John Robertson, Charles Fulton, Enoch Thompson, Jemmy White at White Oak, Nancy White at White Oak, Carman Winans, John Watson at Springfield, Rev. Robert Warwick, Thomas Watson, Anthony Williams, Abner Wilkinson, Isaac Woods, William Whitaker in Anderson township, Jacob White at Fairfield, Doctor John C. Winans, William Watson, Peter White or Nancy White his wife, Ruffas Woodbridge, Isaac Ward, Thompson Wachop, Mary White in Fairfield. Entered by William Ruffin, post master.

John C. Symmes, Junr., at South Bend, reports that he found a mare.

Thomas Hill, living on headwaters of Gregories Creek, about a stray mare.

Israel Ludlow, Register of the Land Office, in Cincinnati, regarding payment owed for land.

Elihu Crain, living on the waters of Sycamore Creek near Wallace's Mill, reports a strayed mare.

Israel Ludlow about land for rent, in Judge Symmes' grant, by Rufus Putnam, surveyor general of the U.S.

John M'Clintock, in Dayton township, regarding a horse that strayed from Capt. John Ewing's farm.

Thomas Williams, in Cincinnati, wants to buy deerskins and to hire an apprentice to the skin-dressing business.

M. Nimmo, in Cincinnati, has dry goods for sale at Mr. Moore's house.

Edward Miller, on the east fork of Little Miami, reports a stray horse.

Moses Bladsoe and Thomas Jemison, living in Montgomery County, Kentucky, report two runaway slaves: Jim and Adam.

A. Cary, in Cincinnati, asks those persons indebted to William Austin or John M'Cullaugh to settle their accounts.

Charles Faran wants to buy barrel staves and heading at his cooper shop in Cincinnati.

Isaac Anderson, in Cincinnati, reports a stray horse and cow.

Charles Avery, of Cincinnati, asks those indebted to him to pay their bills.

David J. Poor, in Cincinnati, administrator of the estate of Samuel Welsh, dec'd, regarding the estate settlement.

N. Hunt about his butchering business in Cincinnati. He wants to buy beef.

Benjamin Bonum regarding notes to David Arreson.

Volume II, Wednesday, 8 July 1801, Number 102

Gov. St.Clair arrived in Cincinnati from touring the upper counties.

Accounts of several Fourth of July celebrations mention Capt. Smith's company of Light Infantry, Mr. Yeatman, John Cleves Symmes, Dr. Goforth, Mr. Frazer in Columbia, Maj. William Goforth, Maj. Benjamin Stites, Gov. St.Clair.

Henry Ewing, in Cincinnati, wants to hire an apprentice to the tailors' trade.

M. Hueston, administrator of the estate of George Rock, dec'd, about the estate settlement.

Col. James Smith, in Cincinnati, gives notice to distillers in Hamilton County regarding taxes due.

S. Hilditch has a new shipment of goods at his shop in Columbia.

Volume III, Wednesday, 15 July 1801, Number 103

Delzil Keasby, in Cincinnati, wants to hire apprentices to the hatting trade.

John Sellman says the partnership of Sellman & Hall is dissolved. Sellman continues the "Medicine Store" on Front Street in Cincinnati.

George Newman, agent for Joseph Newman, asks those indebted to Burt & Newman to settle their accounts in wheat to White's, Goudy's or Smith's Mills. The saddlery business is continued.

James Ferguson has a new shipment of goods for sale at his store.

Nathaniel Reeder says he has a new shipment of goods for sale at his store.

Volume III, Wednesday, 22 July 1801, Number 104

The editors of the Western Spy ask those indebted to them to pay their bills.

Brig. Gen. Wilkinson arrived at Fort Washington from Pittsburg.

The president has appointed James Findlay, of Cincinnati, to be Marshall of the District of Ohio.

Sheriff James Smith, in Cincinnati, regarding the following sheriff's sales: the property of George Fithian seized at the suit of Culbertson Park, William Stewart, John Hole and John Abrahams; the property of Thomas Doyle seized at the suit of James Conn and Charles Vattier; the property of Robert M'Clelland seized at the suit of Daniel Vartner and James Wilkens; the property of John Reed seized at the suit of James Henry; the property of William and Silas Travis seized at the suit of Barton Leonard and Mary his wife; the property of Richard Throckmorton (located by James Lewis) seized at the suit of Abijah Hunt.

Lieut. James B. Many, in Cincinnati, regarding a deserter, George Forrest (private in Capt. Memminger's Company, weaver, born in Ireland, age 31).

The land laws have been printed by the editors of the Western Spy.

Volume III, Wednesday, 29 July 1801, Number 105

The editors of the Western Spy ask those indebted to them to pay their bills.

The president has appointed William M'Millan U.S. Attorney for Ohio District.

An account of an accident near Franklin on Friday, 24 July 1801, in which three men drowned in the Miami River: John Potts (left a wife and four small children), Robert Buchannan (left a wife and three small children) and his brother, David Buchannan (single).

Sergt. Benjamin Seamans about a meeting of the Cincinnati Light Infantry Company at Mr. Avery's.

Daniel Conner & Company, in Cincinnati, ask those indebted to them to settle their accounts as soon as possible.

Benjamin Seamans, in Cincinnati, asks those indebted to Martin Baum & Company to settle their accounts.

Thomas Thompson & Company, in Cincinnati, have a new shipment of goods for sale. They also want to buy wheat at Waldsmith's Mill.

David E. Wade, J.B. Miller and William Ruffin, Commissioners of Hamilton County, regarding the county taxes.

Francis Andre, just arrived from Philadelphia, has a new shipment of goods for sale at Mr. Kidd's store in Cincinnati.

Jacob Williams, about four miles from Cincinnati, reports a stray mare.

Volume III, Wednesday, 5 August 1801, Number 106

John S. Gano, in Cincinnati, has land for sale, by order of the Orphan's Court of Hamilton Co., to satisfy the creditors of the estate of Rev. Peter Wilson, dec'd.

Daken Payn says his wife, Margret Payn, left him and he won't pay her bills.

William Mason, living on the northwest side of the Great Miami four miles from Dayton, reports a stray mare.

William Ruffin asks those indebted to him to settle their accounts.

John Doyle says he's "moving from this place" and asks those indebted to him to settle their accounts.

Samuel Pottenger, living near Hamilton, reports a stray horse and mentions William M'Clelland at Hamilton.

Volume III, Wednesday, 12 August 1801, Number 107

A note regarding the trial of John Bowman for the murder of John Betz mentions Judge Joseph Gilman and R.J. Megs. He was found guilty.

M. Nimmo, in Cincinnati, has a new shipment of goods for sale and mentions Jacob White's mill on Mill Creek and Mr. Waldsmith's Mill on Little Miami.

Benjamin Bundy, near Taylor's Mill on Turtle Creek, about a stray horse.

Ar. St.Clair, in Cincinnati, regarding two oxen that strayed from his farm.

Caleb Mulford, near Bedle's Station, reports a stray mare.

John Beezley, living on the Little Miami about five miles from Columbia, has land for sale.

William Stanley, in Cincinnati, offers for sale the stable lately occupied by George Burnet, dec'd, and presently by Mr. Newman. Apply to Robert Benham.

Conrad Teague, in Cincinnati, asks those indebted to him to settle their accounts by delivering wheat to Goudy's Mill.

Volume III, Wednesday, 19 August 1801, Number 108

A note regarding a meeting of the Congregation of Cincinnati.

Rev. Mr. Sarjent will preach a sermon at the Courthouse next Sunday.

Jesse Reeder regarding his wagon making business on Duck Creek seven miles from Cincinnati and three miles from Columbia.

James M'Cashen and Andrew Small, both living on Clear Creek near Franklin, have land for sale.

John Mercer opened a tavern at his house on Hamilton Road near Cincinnati.

Jacob Burnet, living near the mouth of Mill Creek, reports some stray cattle. Deliver to Abraham Montanye.

Volume III, Wednesday, 26 August 1801, Number 109

Mrs. Patrick Chesnut, living about ten miles from Chillicothe delivered four children on 4 August 1801, but all four died.

Ruben Twyman in Woodford County, Kentucky, regarding a runaway slave.

John Gibersleeve, late from Half-Moon, Saratoga County, N.Y., regarding land he bought on the Great Miami.

Volume III, Wednesday, 2 September 1801, Number 110

Sergt. B. Seamans about a meeting of the Cincinnati Light Infantry Company.

Barney M'Gehan says his wife, Tempy M'Gehan, left him, and he won't pay her bills from now on.

George Hoffman, living about three miles from the Big Hill, found a bull.

Edward Meeks, in Hamilton County, has land for sale. He mentions Mr. Hope Milis on Gregory's Creek, Mr. Irwin living fifteen miles from Cincinnati near Mad River Road, David Cox living near Mr. Irwin. Apply to Col. John S. Gano in Cincinnati or Col. John Armstrong in Columbia.

Francis Andre moved his dry goods store from Mr. Kid's to Mr. Mennessiere's house. He mentions White's Mill.

Jacob White reports that a horse strayed from Widow Mount's farm near Deerfield. Deliver to Capt. David Fox in Deerfield.

William Blieth has goods for sale at Mr. Moore's in Cincinnati.

Volume III, Wednesday, 9 September 1801, Number 111

Daniel Davis, administrator of the estate of Peter Stanley, dec'd, regarding the estate settlement.

W. & M. Jones have a new shipment of goods for sale at their store.

Henry Massie, Collector of taxes in the Virginia Military District, regarding delinquent taxes.

Oliver Spencer, in Cincinnati, regarding a horse that strayed or was stolen from Dr. William Goforth in Cincinnati.

Brice Virgin, living on the Ohio River at the mouth of Muddy Creek in North-Bend township, found a horse.

Caleb Mulford, near Bedle's Station, reports a stray mare.

Volume III, Wednesday, 16 September 1801, Number 112

The editors of the Western Spy ask those indebted to them to settle their accounts in wheat delivered to Waldsmith's Mill.

Daniel Conner & Company have a new shipment of goods for sale.

James Smith gives notice to the distillers of Hamilton County about duties.

Thomas Gibson, in Cincinnati, asks those indebted to him to pay their bills to John Mahard in Cincinnati or with wheat delivered to Jacob White's Mill.

A letter to the public from Gov. Arthur St.Clair regarding the division of Jefferson County to make Belmont County.

James Watson, near the Big Hill in Springfield township, about a stray mare.

Joseph Hancock, living on Sugar Creek, reports that he found some steers.

Volume III, Wednesday, 23 September 1801, Number 113

Note about a migration of squirrels from Kentucky mentions Capt. Claiborn.

P.P. Stuart, for W.C. Schenck, coroner in Hamilton County, regarding land for sale, at a coroner's sale, the property of Thomas Goudy seized at the suit of James Smith and James Findlay. He mentions neighbors John Tharp and Mr. Robertson.

W. Ruffin has pews at the Cincinnati Meeting House for sale.

Martin Hawkins regarding a robbery at the house of George Asher opposite the mouth of the Kentucky River, mentions Capt. Claibourne's troops.

Capt. Ferdinand L. Claibourne, regarding the accusation made by Martin Hawkins of Port William, Kentucky, mentions Mr. Craig of Port William.

Volume III, Wednesday, 30 September 1801, Number 114

A note regarding a meeting of the citizens of Cincinnati at Mr. Yeatman's tavern on the subject of having Cincinnati incorporated.

Charles Willing Byrd submits a proclamation from Gov. Arthur St.Clair about a meeting of the Legislature at Chillicothe.

A note regarding the Cincinnati Theatre says to apply to Mr. Killgore for tickets and Mr. Seamons for subscriptions.

A list of letters left at the Post Office in Cincinnati include Jacob Allen near Columbia, John Ankritt at Mr. Stitts, Doctor Richard Allison, the Widow Burgett at Dunlaps Station, James Burns in care of James Ferguson, Samuel Brewster, Dennis Billings, William O. Bowler, John or William Bustard, James Brady, Hannah Casto, Timothy Covolt on L. Miami, Moses Crane, Samuel Clark, Moses Christ, Henry Carson, James Chambers, Peter Davis in Columbia, John Doyle, James & Wm. Deniston near Hamilton, Elisha Davis at Columbia, Lewis Day (soldier at Detroit), William Duor, Thomas Espy on Little Miami, Stephen Fox in Springfield, Moses Farrell and John M'Hatton, Solomon Gotsholkson, John Gillman, Joseph Griffin in Detroit, E. Hughes, John Harrey on Pleasant Run, Robert Haston in care of James Wilson, Ezekiel Hutchinson, William Hunter, Daniel Johnson, Thomas Irwin living 30 miles west of Cincinnati, Innis & Grant in Detroit, James Long, John Ludlow, Daniel Lambert, Stephen Linsey, John Lyon, James Leesen in Springfield, Aaron Lane (wheelwright), Samuel Lee below the Big Miami, Joseph Layton, Dr. Robert M'Clure, John R. Mills, Capt. Edward Miller, James M'Hatton, John Squire Marsh, James Moore in Springfield, Moses Miller in Springfield, Joseph Morse near Tucker's Station, William M'Ginnis on Duck Creek, Benjamin Megie, Joseph Megie, Jacob Oliver, Abijah O'Neil in Waynesville, Robert Parks, John Poole in Columbia, John Reed on Blear Creek, John Roberson, John Reece at Joel Williams', Coonrod Snyder at Bailey's Station, John Steel on Great Miami, Andrew Stewart in care of John Tharp, Stephen Swelt, John Scott near the mouth of the Great Miami, William C. Schenck, Jacob Tingly at the mouth of Great Miami, Timothy Thompson, Edward Tupper, John Torrence, Stephen Vail, James White, Dr. John C. Winans, Lieut. William Whitley, Morris Witham, James Wilson at the mouth of Great Miami, Nancy Wilson on Big Miami, John Wallace, Revd. Wm. Wood, Joseph Wilson at Great Miami, Michael Wilkins on Great Miami, Henry Weaver, Lieut. John Wilson, Dr. John C. Wallace, Corporal John Ward in care of Capt. Vance, Capt. Rezin Webster, Robert M'Ginnis on Duck Creek, Wm. Ruffin.

G. Yeatman, James Smith and D. Conner, Trustees of the Market House in Cincinnati, mention Daniel Conner.

Levi Woodward, living near Deerfield, regarding a runaway bound boy, David Hardy, age 13. Deliver to William Woodward in Cincinnati.

John Humes, in Cincinnati, regarding a bond to John Cleves Symmes, mentions John Smith.

John M'Cullaugh has a shipment of goods for sale at his store in Cincinnati and at Thomas M'Cullaugh's store at Hamilton.

A notice regarding the Cincinnati horse races is printed.

Smith & Findlay want to buy hops.

Volume III, Saturday, 10 October 1801, Number 115

A note regarding the opening of the Cincinnati Theatre.

Obituary: Lieut. Col. David Strong died at Wilkinsonville on Wednesday, August 19, 1801.

Thomas Dugan, in Cincinnati, has dry goods for sale at James Conn's house.

Carpenter & Findlay, at the Western Spy office, ask those indebted to them to settle their accounts.

William Blieth has goods for sale at Mr. Moore's on Main Street.

Thomas Thompson & Company, in Cincinnati, ask those indebted to them to settle their accounts.

Lemuel M'Donald, in Cincinnati, is "going down the river about the first of December" and asks those indebted to him to settle their accounts.

William Lemond, living on the Ohio River near the mouth of Muddy Creek, in North Bend township, found a stray mare.

George Newman, agent for Joseph Newman, wants deerskins for saddlery. Also those indebted to Burt & Newman should settle their accounts.

Volume III, Saturday, 17 October 1801, Number 116

An account of the fight at Bardstown between Mr. Barry (teacher in the academy at Bardstown) and Mr. Gilpin (a silversmith) in which the latter died. They were fighting over the duel between Mr. Rowan and Doct. Chambers.

Henry Caldwell, living two miles from Woodford Courthouse, Kentucky, regarding a runaway slave named Ben.

David Dunseth, in Cincinnati, has Mann's Lick salt for sale at Thomas Doyle's red house on Main Street in Cincinnati.

M. Nimmo has winter clothing for sale.

Moses Millar, executor of the estate of Allen Oliver, dec'd, regarding the estate settlement.

Samuel Robb, two miles from Franklin on Big Miami, regarding a stray mare.

John C. Symmes asks those indebted to him to settle their accounts by delivering wheat to Jacob White's Mill on Mill Creek.

Volume III, Saturday, 24 October 1801, Number 117

The president has appointed William Goforth of Columbia and John Reily of Cincinnati to serve as commissioners of land. Note mentions John C. Symmes.

James Findlay, William Goforth and John Reily, in Cincinnati, regarding John Cleves Symmes' lands, mention Mr. Yeatman.

Sheriff James Smith, in Cincinnati regarding a sheriff's sale of land adjoining Thomas Brown and Henry Teabolt, property of Thomas Robertson seized in the suit of Moses Broadwell. Also the property of Shadrick Rice seized in the suit of Robert Armstrong and Betsey his wife. Also the property of Thomas Doyle seized at the suit of John Grass.

John Irwin regarding a bond to John Cleves Symmes for land mortgaged to John Smith.

Wm. Betts regarding a bond to John Cleves Symmes for land mortgaged to Mr. Highway.

Frederick Nuts says his wife, Elizabeth, left him and he won't pay her bills.

Carpenter & Findlay ask those indebted to them to settle their accounts in wheat delivered to Capt. White's Mill.

Volume III, Saturday, 31 October 1801, Number 118

Matthew G. Wallace, in Cincinnati, regarding his school teaching the Latin and Greek languages.

Daniel Conner wants to buy pork at Detroit.

Mary Mapes, living in North Bend, lost a coat between Mr. Vattier's and Mill Creek on the road to North Bend.

John Mahard, agent for Thomas Gibson, in Cincinnati, has goods for sale and wants wheat delivered to White's Mill or Waldsmith's Mill.

Thomas Gregg about his tavern in Chillicothe at the sign of the Green Tree.

D.C. Cooper, near Dayton, wants to hire a distiller.

Levi M'Lean regarding his singing school at Mr. Washburn's school house and at Mr. Avery's.

Volume III, Saturday, 7 November 1801, Number 119

A eulogy to Col. Strong delivered by Jonathan Williams at Strong's funeral at Wilkinsonville.

Abraham Freeman, living near Big Prairie, regarding a stolen mare.

James Ferguson is "preparing to go down the River" and asks those indebted to him to settle their accounts with wheat delivered to Jacob White's, David Grummon's or John Smith's Mills.

Solomon Gottsholkson has been "called to Europe by the death of his father" and has goods for sale. Apply to him at Widow Innis' in Columbia.

Nathan Nichols regarding his ferry on the Little Miami, about one mile from the mouth, at Gerrard's Station.

Charles Lynch, in Shelby County, Ky., regarding a runaway slave, Humphrey.

Volume III, Saturday, 14 November 1801, Number 120

Wm. Wells, Agent of Indian Affairs, at Fort Wayne, says that Polly Ford, age about 20, living at Fort Wayne, was taken prisoner by the Indians in the autumn of 1787 on her way to Kentucky with her father (Peter Ford), 5 brothers (John and Jacob Ford, the two eldest) and 2 sisters. Apply to Gen. Samuel Wells in Jefferson County, Kentucky.

Robert M'Clure, at Big Hill, is "preparing to go to Orleans" and asks those indebted to him to pay their bills in wheat delivered to Capt. Jacob White's Mill.

John Panton regarding a horse stolen from Hamilton by Thomas Smith.

Franky Graves, living in Fayette County, Kentucky, regarding a runaway slave named Daniel.

Michael Wilkins, living three miles below Colerain on the Great Miami, has stills for sale.

Volume III, Saturday, 21 November 1801, Number 121

William Ruffin, in Cincinnati, offers his land for sale in Cincinnati including the tavern and ferry.

A letter to the public from Gov. Arthur St.Clair regarding Belmont County.

Thomas Thompson & Company, in Cincinnati, are declining business in Cincinnati and ask those indebted to them and to Martin Baum & Company to settle their accounts to Abraham Cary.

Levi Moore, living near White's Station, regarding a stray horse. Deliver to Benjamin Bryant above Hamilton.

W.C. Schenck asks those indebted to him to settle their accounts.

Volume III, Saturday, 28 November 1801, Number 122

A note regarding a meeting, at Mr. Yeatman's place, of the commissioners to settle rights of pre-emption.

A letter from Rev. John Bailey of Kentucky regarding his religious pamphlet.

Lieut. Col. John S. Gano, of Cincinnati, announces officers in the First Regiment of Hamilton County Militia: Capt. James Smith, Capt. Stephen Reeder, Capt. Thomas Goudy, Capt. Daniel Symmes, Capt. John Riddle, Capt. Samuel Martin, Capt. Alexander Esau, Lieut. William Ruffin, Lieut. William Stanley, Lieut. William T. Cullum, Lieut. Isaac Bates, Lieut. James Caldwell, Lieut. John

Cummings, Lieut. Benjamin Perlieu and Maj. John Wallace.

James Baxter, living 2 miles from Capt. Jacob White's Station, found a mare.

Jacob Burnet, living near the mouth of Mill Creek, reports a strayed cow. Deliver to Abraham Montanye.

W. Stanley, in Cincinnati, wants to buy pork and beef.

Volume III, Saturday, 5 December 1801, Number 123

Gov. Ar. St.Clair's speech to the Legislature is printed.

A list of the members of the Legislature is printed and mentions Mr. Oliver, Mr. Burnett, Mr. Vance, Mr. Sibley, W.C. Schenck, John Reily. From Washington County: Eph. Cutler, W.R. Putnam. From Hamilton County: Moses Miller, F. Dunlavy, J. Morrow, John Ludlow, Daniel Reeder, Jacob White. From Jefferson County: Z. Kimberly, John Melligan, Thomas M'Cune. From Ross County: E. Tiffin, Elias Langham, T. Worthington. From Wayne County: C.F. Chobert de Joncaire, G. M'Dougall, J. Schiefflin. From Trumbull County: Edward Paine.

A note regarding the Cincinnati Theatre says that Mr. Killgore has tickets.

Smith & Findlay want to buy rye at their distillery or Grummon's Mill.

Volume III, Saturday, 12 December 1801, Number 124

The proceedings of the Legislature mention Edward Tiffin, John Reily, Mr. Cutler, Mr. Kimberly, Mr. Worthington, Mr. White, Mr. Dunlavy, Mr. Pain, Mr. Putnam, Mr. Morrow, Mr. Darlington, John Milligan of Jefferson County, Mr. M'Cune of Jefferson County, James May and Jacob Visgar (justices of the Court of Common Pleas at Wayne County), George M'Dougall, Jonathan Shiffelin, Mr. Schenck, Mr. Reeder, Mr. Ludlow, Mr. Miller, Nathaniel Massie of Adams County, Elias Langham of Ross County, Nathan Ellies (Collector of Revenue in Adams County), Mr. Schieffelin, Jehiel Gregory and John Hayner (regarding their mill on Hochoking), Oliver Rice, Earl Sproat, John Smith of Hamilton County, Jean Wilson (wife of William Wilson of Jefferson County) suing for divorce, Sally Mills of Washington County, Mr. Sibley, Mr. Burnet, Jonathan Zean, John M'Intire, Noah Zean, Arthur St.Clair.

A letter to Hon. Judge M'Clung from Joseph Prince, foreman of the Grand Jury, is printed.

Matthew Nimmo, in Cincinnati, writes a letter regarding silver mines.

William Goforth, Jun., in Cincinnati, regarding a meeting of the Nova Caesaria Lodge.

Matthew Nimmo has a new shipment of goods for sale at his Cincinnati store.

John Brownlee, Amus Darah and Thomas Lowery give notice to millwrights regarding a meeting at Joseph Crain's house in Franklin.

John Cleves Symmes regarding delivering wheat to Jacob White's Mill.

Sheriff James Smith regarding sheriff's sales of the property of John Cleves Symmes that has been seized in suits brought by the following: Daniel M'Clure, John R. Mills, John M'Lean (administrator of Allen M'Lean, dec'd), John M'Cabe, John Hole, Zachariah Hole, James Derth, William Stitt and Samuel Stitt, Mathias Peirson, Nathan Lamme, William Lamme, John Ewing, Daniel C. Cooper, Daniel Griffen and James M'Cashen, James Thompson, Elizabeth Lamme (administratrix of Robert Lamme, dec'd), Stephen Bunnel and Robert Ross, John M'Grew, Robert Maxwell. Mentions Samuel Irwin & John Mann, William Chribbs, Richard Allison.

Volume III, Saturday, 19 December 1801, Number 125

The proceedings of the Legislature mention Mr. Cutler, Mr. Schieffelin, John Rector, Mr. Langham, Mr. Reeder, Mr. White, Mr. Dunlavy, Mr. Kimberly, Oliver Rice and Earl Sproat.

Matthew Nimmo has a new shipment of goods for sale and he wants to buy wheat at Jacob White's, David Grummon's and C. Waldsmith's Mills.

John Smith, at the Round Bottom, reports some stray cows.

Wyllys Pierson regarding land he sold to Charles Roberts in Columbia township, Hamilton County. Roberts ran away owing him money. He mentions Judge Symmes and Alexander Miller.

Andrew Cox, regarding a bond to John Cleves Symmes, mentions John

M'Clean, administrator of Allin M'Clean, dec'd.
Benjamin VanHook regarding the sale of land and goods.
Aaron Goforth regarding claims against Hamilton County.
Daniel Symmes, in Cincinnati, offers land for sale.
Henry Weaver has a new shipment of goods at his store in Cincinnati opposite William Ramsey's place.
Joseph Newman, in Cincinnati, intends "to discontinue my business in this place in a few months" and asks those indebted to him to pay George Newman.
William Stanley, in Cincinnati, has a new shipment of winter goods for sale.

Volume III, Saturday, 26 December 1801, Number 126
A letter to the public from Gov. Arthur St.Clair is printed.
Clarke Bates found a stray steer.
A note regarding the Cincinnati Theatre mentions Mr. Kilgore.
George Fithian, in Cincinnati, asks those indebted to him to pay their bills.
John S. Gano, in Cincinnati, has land for sale by order of the Orphan's Court of Hamilton County to satisfy the creditors of Rev. Peter Wilson, dec'd.
Abm. & Minne Voorheese regarding land on Mill Creek they purchased from Col. Israel Shrieve.
John Tway reports that he found a stray steer.

Volume III, Saturday, 2 January 1802, Number 127
The proceedings of the House of Representatives regarding the lands of John Cleves Symmes mention Paul Fearing.
A letter to the House of Representatives regarding the division of the territory is signed by Edward Tiffin, T. Worthington and E. Langham of Ross County; J. Darlington and N. Massie of Adams County; Frances Dunlavy and Jeremiah Morrow of Hamilton County.
Sheriff James Smith about sheriff's sales of the property of John Reed (adjoining James M'Clure) at the suit of Joseph Henry; property of John Holland (now occupied by Mr. Wheeler in Cincinnati) at the suit of John Kidd; the property of Thomas Doyle (formerly owned by Jacob Stewart) at the suit of John Bishop; the property of John C. Symmes at the suits of John Ewing and James Thompson.
Joseph Carpenter has land for sale 3 miles below Hamilton on Pleasant Run.
A list of letters left at the Post Office in Cincinnati includes John Adams, Michael Ayres, Jotham Bragdon, Charles Brown in care of Samuel Dick, William Bridges (soldier at Fort Wayne), William Bolar, Alexander or James Barnes near the mouth of Mad River, John Bridge near Big Prairie, Samuel Baxter, Eliza Bond in Detroit, Joseph Bradford in Detroit, James Charter in care of Paul Hueston, Reuben Carter, James Cole at Big Miami, James Chittenden in Detroit, Chester Chittenden in Detroit, Lewis Day (soldier at Detroit), John Donald, James Gray, John Dinsmore, Jeremiah French, Samuel Frazy, John Gildersleeve, William Griffin, Patrick Graham on Gregories Creek, Levi Garrison, Adrian Hagarman in Columbia, Thomas Higgins, Francis Higgins in Detroit, Richd. Hannen, Stephen Hall, Ezekiel Hutchinson, William Jones, Nicholas Johnston, William Krozer in care of Cornelius VanNuys, Edward Lodor on Great Miami, Abraham Lakes at Deerfield, David Lee at Big Miami, John Lyon, Stephen Ludlow, David Lampier at Fort Wayne, Andrew Lytle, Hugh M'Clain at Williamsburg, Joseph M'Henry on Mill Creek, William Mahon at Dunlaps Station, Jesse Merrit at White Water, Thomas M'Cormack on Little Miami, James M'Clelland near Hamilton, James M'Cabe, Lt. Alexander Macomb in care of Gen. Wilkinson, Sarah Miller, Elizabeth May in Detroit, James Montgomery, John Oblinger, Joseph Philips at Detroit, Josiah Post on Big Miami, James Patterson at Deerfield, John Pryor, James Patterson on Mill Creek, Christopher Pratt, Leonard Petro, Robert Parks, John Rayburn in Detroit, John Richey (school master), Thomas Spencer, Thomas Sarky, Hendrick Seightes, Peter Smith, Andrew Simmons, Abel Stout, William Scott, John Cleves Symmes, Benjamin Tucker in Springfield, Geo. Turner, Price Thompson, Ephraim Tucker, William Thompson on Big Miami, John Templeton in Springfield, Rev. John Taylor in Kentucky, Abraham Vail on Little Miami, Mary Welsh in Detroit, Capt. John Whistler in Detroit, Sergeant W. Watts at Wilkinsonville, Capt. Resin Webster,

Rev. William Wood, John Warran, Capt. William Wells at Fort Wayne, William White on Great Miami, Cornelius Johnston. Entered by William Ruffin, P.M.

David J. Poor, in Cincinnati, says he caught Rachel, his wife, and William Griffin in the act of adultery and he will no longer honor her debts.

J. Banton, in Hamilton, reports a stray mare.

Volume III, Saturday, 9 January 1802, Number 128

The proceedings of the House of Representatives mention Mr. Kimberly, Paul Fearing, Zacheus Biggs and Zacheus A. Beatty (the latter two will erect a toll bridge across Will's Creek in Washington County), Mr. Todd, Michael Baldwin, Samuel M'Adow, Stephen Cissna, Reuben Abrams, Mr. Finley, Jeremiah M'Lene, John Reily, William Rutledge, Alexander Jenkins, Ar. St.Clair, Mr. Schenck, Mr. Darlington, Mr. Paine, Mr. Putnam, Mr. Ludlow, Mr. Langham.

James Forguson, in Cincinnati, says he's "going down the River shortly" and asks those indebted to him to settle their accounts.

Sophia Burnet, David Zeigler and Jacob Burnet, administrators of George W. Burnet, dec'd, regarding the estate settlement.

Gust. Reeves, living near Cincinnati, found a stray cow.

John Hunter regarding a due bill from Charles Murry.

Volume III, Saturday, 16 January 1802, Number 129

Alexander M'Laughlin, of Chillicothe, is appointed Collector of Revenue in the Virginia Military District in place of Henry Massie who resigned.

Account of an accident on Mill Creek in which Aaron Mash (?) of Sycamore, "an aged man", and his son (age 15-16) were drowned.

Carpenter & Findlay ask those indebted to them to settle their accounts.

Archelaus Alloway, living near Tanner's Station in Boon County, Kentucky, regarding a runaway slave named Bristow.

John Winters, living on Mill Creek, reports that he found a mare.

Volume III, Saturday, 23 January 1802, Number 130

An account of a fire at Mr. Forguson's on Sunday evening, 17 January 1802.

A note regarding a meeting of the citizens of Cincinnati at Mr. Yeatman's to procure a fire engine for the town.

Birth: Mrs. Eliza Gottshalkson gave birth to a son, Gottshalk Solomonson, at Columbia on Wednesday, 23 December 1801.

A. Carey, in Cincinnati, about a public auction of books at the Courthouse.

Shobal Vail has erected a fulling mill on Great Miami 1 mile from Big Prairie.

John Wilson, in Columbia, asks those indebted to him to settle their accounts since he "intends removing from the place where he now resides".

Volume III, Saturday, 30 January 1802, Number 131

William Goforth, in Columbia, has red clover seed for sale.

J. Carpenter has land for sale on Pleasant Run.

Volume III, Saturday, 6 February 1802, Number 132

Edward Tiffin, Robert Oliver, Ar. St.Clair and John Reily regarding the laws of the Territory.

Gov. St.Clair arrived in Cincinnati last Saturday from Chillicothe.

Joseph M'Henry is appointed inspector of pork and beef for Hamilton County.

The speech of Gov. Ar. St.Clair to the House of Representatives is printed.

The court has appointed John Reily as county commissioner.

George Fithian opened a house of public entertainment in Cincinnati in the house formerly occupied by Capt. George Gordon.

David Griffis regarding bonds to John C. Symmes.

Michael Teirnan, at Mr. Yeatman's Tavern, in Cincinnati, about a stray steer.

Samuel Harred, living on the west side of the Great Miami at the upper end of the Big Prarie, found a mare.

A list of acts passed by the Legislature mentions Sally Mills, Jane Wilson, Zacheus Biggs, Zacheus A. Beatty and Jonathan Zane.

Volume III, Saturday, 13 February 1802, Number 133

A note regarding the division of the territory mentions Mr. Fearing.

John S. Gano regarding a meeting of the Court of General Quarter Sessions in Hamilton County in order to divide Hamilton County into election districts. He mentions Isaac Mills, John Torrence in Hamilton, George Newcome in Dayton, David Sutton in Deerfield, Thomas Frazer in Columbia, Col. Higgins on the Ohio, James Kain in Williamsburgh, and Obed Denham in Plainfield.

A meeting at Mr. Yeatman's house regarding the Cincinnati Public Library.

The editors of the Western Spy ask those indebted to them to settle their accounts to Mr. Clarke, the post rider.

A note regarding the Cincinnati Theatre mentions Mr. Killgore.

Wm. & M. Jones, in Cincinnati, ask those indebted to them to pay their bills.

Smith Ludlam, living near Deerfield, reports a stray cow.

Joseph M'Hendry, Inspector, regarding the inspection of flour, beef & pork.

A note announcing the arrival of Gov. Claiborne in Natchez to take the place of Winthrop Sargent.

Volume III, Saturday, 20 February 1802, Number 134

An act to incorporate the town of Cincinnati is printed and mentions the following officers appointed: David Zeigler, Jacob Burnet, William Ramsey, David E. Wade, Charles Avery, John Reily, William Stanley, Samuel Dick, James Smith, William Ruffin, Joseph Prince, Abraham Cary.

Notes regarding the Mississippi Territory mention Winthrop Sargent, Edwin L. Harris and Nasworthy Hunter.

The proceedings of Congress mention Mr. Fearing, George Turner, John C. Symmes, Mr. Giles and Mr. Alstone.

Notes regarding Hon. W.B. Giles' resolution regarding the division of the territory mention Mr. Fearing.

Peter Audrain and Solomon Sibley (attorney) regarding a suit in the Court of Common Pleas in Wayne County at Detroit: the U.S. vs. Matthew Ernest (customs collector at Detroit).

John Eastin, at Louisville, regarding land entered by Richard Jones Waters on Cross Creek about twelve miles above the mouth of the Little Miami and claimed by William Harris or Harrison. He mentions Maj. George Wilson in Louisville.

William Jones says his wife, Elizabeth, left him and he won't pay her bills.

Thomas M'Cullough, in Hamilton, has a new shipment of goods for sale.

John Daily regarding a note to William Crossley. He also found a watch.

Volume III, Saturday, 27 February 1802, Number 135

A note regarding prisoners in the Hamilton County jail: Squire Brooks (suspected of the murder of Mr. Mefford at Man's Lick, Kentucky, last October, but he says it was his brother), Timothy L. White (arrested for concealing Brooks) and David Carson (arrested just for being with the other two).

Jacob Burnet, Recorder, regarding a meeting of the Select Council of the town of Cincinnati.

Sheriff James Smith, in Hamilton County, about the meeting of the General Court of the Territory.

Sheriff P. Light has land for sale at a sheriff's sale in Williamsburgh in Clermont County, the property of Charles Young, at the suit of George Turner.

Isaac Anderson asks those indebted to him to settle their accounts in wheat delivered to Grummon's, Williams' or White's mills.

John Bedford, living in Nelson County, Kentucky, on the waters of Ashers' Creek, regarding a runaway slave named Dick.

Volume III, Saturday, 6 March 1802, Number 136

Mr. Hueston, distiller, committed suicide at Franklin on Sunday, 21 February 1802. He's from Carlisle, Pennsylvania, where his uncle is a merchant.

John C. Symmes writes a letter from Washington about fruit trees.

Samuel C. Vance, at Fort Washington, regarding lots for sale in the town of Lawrenceburgh. Apply to W.C. Schenck at Franklin.

Lewis Kerr about a meeting at Mr. Yeatman's about the Cincinnati Library.
Daniel Conner & Company wants to buy beef at Fort Wayne.
Seth Cutter has commenced the butchering business in Cincinnati.
Joseph Blew says that his wife, Hannah, left him and he won't pay her bills.

Volume III, Saturday, 13 March 1802, Number 137
Jacob Burnet and John Reily regarding ordinances of Cincinnati.
William Macbean regarding the insurance company in Lexington, Kentucky.
Note about the loss of boats in a hurricane on the Mississippi River including Mr. Hilditch's of Columbia. He and Mr. M'Adams, a crew member, escaped.
Michael Krafft/Krasst, at Trenton, N.J., regarding his patented still.
Francis Langlois, in Cincinnati, "just arrived in this place", and has liquor for sale at the house formerly occupied by Dr. Prince.
Charles Avery, in Cincinnati, reports a mare that strayed or was stolen.
John S. Gano and Jacob Burnet (attorney) regarding suits in the Court of Common Pleas in Hamilton County: William Wood vs. William Coleman; Matthew Winton vs. James Neel; Joel Williams vs. Rufus Elliott; James Smith and James Findlay vs. Thomas Cochran; Ambrose Whitlock vs. Joseph Collins.
Abraham Geel/Ceel, for Conrad Tague, asks those indebted to Tague to settle their accounts.

Volume III, Saturday, 20 March 1802, Number 138
J. & A. Hunt, in Cincinnati, want to buy tan bark at their tanyard.
Calvin Morrel, living at Big Prairie, has land for sale and wants to hire a schoolmaster. He mentions Andrew Christy.

Volume III, Saturday, 27 March 1802, Number 139
A note about payments due from the Northwest Territory mentions George Todd (secretary to the governor), Nathaniel Willis (printer), Edward Tiffin, Elias Langham, Arthur St.Clair, Sheriff James Smith in Hamilton County, Paul Fearing, Sheriff Jeremiah M'Lene of Ross County, Thomas Worthington, John Reily, Daniel M'Allister, Ephraim Cutler, Alexander M'Laughlin, William Rutledge, Isaac VanNuise, Carpenter & Findlay (printers), James Phillips, Chrisman & Johnston, Winship & Willis (printers), John Hunter (printer).
T. Worthington writes a letter to the editor regarding statehood.
A notice regarding township meetings mentions William Perry in Columbia township; John Mercer in Cincinnati township; Alexander M'Kee in South Bend township; William Hammit in Miami township; Thomas Brown in Anderson township; Knowles Shaw in Colerain township; John Torrence in Fairfield township; Jonathan Pitman in Springfield township; George Newsome in Dayton township; Joseph Crane in Franklin township; David Sutton in Deerfield township; Isaac Mills in Ohio township; John Hamilton in St.Clair township.
Th. Gibson, Auditor, has moved his office to Cincinnati.

Volume III, Saturday, 3 April 1802, Number 140
Edward Tiffin, Robert Oliver and Gov. Ar. St.Clair regarding an act for collecting taxes in Clermont, Belmont and Fairfield Counties.
Jacob Burnet and John Reiley about a meeting of the citizens of Cincinnati.
A list of persons nominated as officers of the township and the town of Cincinnati includes Thomas M'Farland, David E. Wade, William Stanley, James Smith, Seth Cutter, James Findlay, Joseph Prince, Abraham Cary, William Woodward, Charles Vattier, Jonathan Williams, Asa Richardson, Joseph M'Henry, C.R. Sedam, Griffin Yeatman, William Ramsey, John Ridale, Levi M'Clean, David Zeigler, Jacob Burnet, William Ruffin, Jer. Hunt, John Reily, Charles Avery, James Smith.
Levi M'Lean regarding his candidacy for the constable's office.
Doctor Sellman has medicines, paints and dyes for sale at his "Medicine Store" in Cincinnati.
Wilson Crail/Grail about his baking business in the house formerly occupied by Mr. Mitchell in Cincinnati.
A list of letters left at the Post Office in Cincinnati includes Peter Audrain

in Detroit, John Bonsill, John Buchannon in care of Joseph Conn, Joseph Bolton, James Burnes, Joseph Brown at White Water, James Barrett, Hannah Bigger, Elizabeth Blair, Richard Burrows on Duck Creek, Lewis Bond in Detroit, Elizabeth Brownlee near the Big Praira, James Brackin at Detroit, Thomas Burnett at Niagara, John Bloom in Detroit, John Blackburn near Taylor's Station, Frederick Bates at Detroit, Bazill Clarke, James Chambers, Jacob Cooper at Big Miami, Benjamin Cross on Little Miami, William Concannon near Mad River, Hezekiah Clarke, Alexander Campbell, Joel Constock at Colerain, Lieut. William Carson at Detroit, Reuben Carter, Samuel Corwin, James Durn in care of James Findlay, Samuel Davis (soldier in Capt. Turner's Company), David Duncan at Detroit, James Dobbins, John Dodson, Maj. Thomas Doyle, Francis Dunlavy, Samuel Davis in Colerain, Doctor Cyrus Dart, Timothy Day at Columbia, Samuel Evans on Clear Creek, Eliphalet Faris, Phebe Freeman, Capt. R.H. Greaton at Wilkinsonville, Isaac Gildersleve, George Gillispie, John Gowble (surgeon of the Queens Rangers), Robert Guthrie, Levi Gregory, Smith Gregg in care of John Watson, Col. John F. Hamtramck, Maj. Thomas Hunt at Detroit, James Henry in Detroit, William Hunter in care of Isaac Anderson, Enos Heines at Waynesville, James Hall in care of Isaac Anderson, Ann Horsly in Boon County, William Harrison (fifer at Detroit), Thomas Hunt on Gregory Creek, William Hatfield on Sugar Creek, William Hoge in care of Joel Williams, Aaron Hougham on Duck Creek, Robert Hempstead in Franklin, Jacob Hoyde on Big Miami, Mrs. Joice, Edward Jackman on White Water, Simeon Jannings, Peter Keen, James Kenedy at Detroit, Nathaniel Knotts on Sugar Creek, James Lowes, Capt. Joseph Lamb, Rev. M. Levadoux in Detroit, Lieut. Peter Lampkin, Jacob Lang (soldier in Capt. M'Clary's company), Doctor Calvin Morrel, Jeremiah Morrow, Doctor Robert M'Clure, Edward M'Ginnes in Kentucky, David M'Clure near the Big Praira, William Markan at Dunlaps Station, William Middleton, Moses Martin at White Water, Maj. Thomas Martin at Detroit, James Morrison Senr. at Round Bottom, Lettice M'Clasky in care of William M'Millan, Robert M'Ginnes on Duck Creek, Robert M'Kay in Campbell County, Samuel M'Cray in care of Isaac Anderson, George Meldrum in Detroit, James Norris on Turtle Creek, Joel Nelson on Mill Creek, Ebenezer Orsborne at Deerfield, Samuel Perkins at Detroit, Charles Peltier in Detroit, Peter Perlee, Cournel Prentice (soldier in Capt. M'Clary's company), John Price in Springfield, Joseph Preston in Springfield, Jacob Powers, Lieut. Joshua S. Rogers at Detroit, Ambrose Ransome at Little Miami, John Roberts on Licking River in Kentucky, Doctor Edward Gantle Reynolds at Wilkinsonville, Richard Smith at Detroit, Samuel Sargent, Andrew Stewart, John Scott, Benjamin Sears on Little Miami, Conrod Snider at Beagles' Station, Peyton Short, Sargent Stewart, William Skinner, George C. Shreave, Hugh Shannon, Nathan Trowsdale in Kentucky, Noah Tryon at North Bend, Amos Volzetine, John Vaughan, Moses Vail at Big Hill, John Vance at Big Hill, John Wallace (schoolmaster at Turtle Creek), Lewis Washbourne near the mouth of the Miami River, Andrew Wilson on Mill Creek, Joseph Wilson in care of Isaac Anderson, William Wilson at the Illinois Grant, Rev. William Wood, Morris Witham, James Whallan on Mill Creek, William Wilson on White Water, Lieut. John Wilson, George Williams, Andrew or Sarah Young. William Ruffin, postmaster.

John H. Williams, living on Clear Creek, two miles above Franklin, reports a stray mare.

Volume III, Saturday, 10 April 1802, Number 141
A note is printed regarding Gov. St.Clair's arrival in Washington City.

Officers elected in Cincinnati: David Zeigler, Aaron Goforth, Samuel Stitt, Thomas M'Farland, George Fithian, David Grummon, Andrew Parks, James Smith, Joseph Prince, Isaac Anderson, William M'Farland, William Ruffin, Abraham Carey, William Stanley, Isaac VanNuys, Nehemiah Hunt, John Riddle, William Woodward, Alexander King, James Findlay, Joseph M'Henry, C.R. Sedam, James Jones, Abraham Montayne, Jonathan Williams, David J. Poor.

John Cook lost a due bill on George Fithian. Deliver to Andrew Dunseth in Cincinnati or Thomas Frazer in Columbia.

William Smith, for Loyd Ogg of Hamilton County, regarding land Ogg bought from John C. Symmes and a note from Knowles Shaw.

Daniel Reeder, administrator of the estate of Isaac Crain, dec'd, regarding the estate settlement.

Volume III, Saturday, 17 April 1802, Number 142
An account of the murder of an Indian below the Great Miami near the house of Isaac Mills.

A note regarding the statehood of the Northwest Territory mentions L.R. Morris, Mr. Hastings and Mr. Fearing.

Matthew Nimmo has a shipment of goods for sale at his store in Cincinnati.

Samuel C. Vance regarding his ferry across the Ohio River opposite the town of Lawrenceburg.

Israel Ludlow, on Mill Creek, wants to hire chain-carriers and axe men.

Sheriff James Smith, in Cincinnati, regarding sheriff's sales of the property of Thomas Doyle (land now occupied by James Conn) seized at the suit of John Graeff; the property of George Gregg seized at the suit of William Wood; the property of Aaron Cadwell seized at the suit of John Shaw; the property of John Hillier seized at the suit of John C. Symmes.

John VanNice, in Cincinnati, has land for sale. Apply to Peter Cassart on Turtle Creek.

Volume III, Saturday, 24 April 1802, Number 143
The house lately occupied by Joseph Newman, saddler, nearly opposite Griffin Yeatman is for rent.

John Greer, living near Hamilton, found a stray mare.

John H. Williams reports a stolen stud colt.

Volume III, Saturday, 1 May 1802, Number 144
Lewis Kerr and Aaron Goforth about a meeting of the Society of Cincinnati.

Notes regarding the division of Cincinnati township into districts mention Burnet's farm, Smith & Findlay's distillery, Alex. King, Jonathan Williams, John Mercer, James Jones, Grummon's Mill, James M'Hendry, Abrm. Montayne, Joseph M'Hendry, C.R. Sedam, James Smith, W. Stanley and Isaac VanNuys.

The proceedings of Congress regarding statehood for the Northwest Territory mention Mr. Morris, Mr. Fearing, Mr. Giles, Mr. Bayard, Mr. Goddard, Mr. Bacon.

Abraham Demott regarding notes to Peter Clawson.

Jonas Crane regarding Jefferson Town on White Water about one mile from Capt. Thomas Smith's Mill.

Elijah Strong, in Cincinnati, administrator of the estate of Col. David Strong, dec'd, regarding the estate settlement.

Thomas Cook, living on Clear Creek one mile from Newtown, reports a horse that strayed or was stolen.

Sutherland & Brown, in Hamilton, have William Goodwin's blacksmith tools for sale as a result of their suit.

Isaac VanNuys, in Cincinnati, reports a stray cow.

William Ruffin, William Ramsey and John Reily regarding the suit of William Wood vs. Wm. Coleman.

A list of officers at the various forts under Brig. Gen. James Wilkinson. At Detroit: Col. John F. Hamtramck, Maj. Zebulon Pike, Capt. R.H. Greaton, Capt. Merriwether Lewis, Capt. James Richmond, Capt. John M'Clary, Lieut. Moses Hook, Lieut. James Rhea, Lieut. John Whipple, Lieut. Elie B. Climson, Lieut. Wm. Whistler, Lieut. John W. Brownson, Lieut. Dan. Baker, Lieut. Alexander Macomb, Jun., Capt. John W. Livingston, Lieut. Phillip Rodrique, Lieut. Jesse Lull, Dr. David Davis (surgeon). At Fort Wayne: Capt. Tho. Pasteur, Lieut. George W. Stall, Lieut. Simon Owens, Nathaniel Bedford. At. Vincennes: Capt. Cors. Lyman, Lieut. Nathan Heald, Lieut. Ambrose Whitlock, Samuel M'Kee. At Kaskaskias: Capt. Russel Bissell, Lieut. Zebulon M. Pike, Lieut. Henry Hopkins, Francis Tuttle. At Fort Massac: Capt. Daniel Bissell, Lieut. William Swaine, Lieut. Daniel Hughes, Edward Reynolds.

Volume III, Saturday, 8 May 1802, Number 145

Edward Tiffin, Robert Oliver and Ar. St.Clair regarding new laws.

Samuel Kemper regarding a bond to John Cleves Symmes.

Henry Weaver, in Springfield township, administrator of the estate of William Weaver, leather dresser, late of Springfield township, dec'd, regarding the estate settlement.

Andrew Lock, near Dayton, regarding a horse that strayed or was stolen from Andrew Hill's below the mouth of Taylors' Creek.

Volume III, Saturday, 15 May 1802, Number 146

Mr. Daily arrived in Cincinnati on Thursday last from Natchez, and reports grain prices in Natchez.

Capt. James Smith regarding a meeting, at Mr. Avery's, of the Cincinnati Light Infantry Company.

Charles Willing Byrd regarding the establishment of the counties of Belmont, Clermont and Fairfield.

Edward Tiffin, Robert Oliver and Ar. St.Clair regarding a law pertaining to the killing of wolves and panthers.

Joseph Brown, living on White Water, reports a strayed mare. Deliver to William Drake in Columbia.

Volume III, Saturday, 22 May 1802, Number 147

Edward Tiffin, Robert Oliver and Ar. St.Clair regarding laws of the territory.

Daniel Conner wants to buy whiskey.

John Reily, William Ramsey and Jonathan S. Findlay, Auditors, regarding the suit of Ambrose Whitlock vs. Joseph Collins. They mention William Ruffin.

David J. Poor intends carrying on the butchering business and wants to buy beef, mutton and veal.

Hugh Brownlee regarding notes in the possession of James Johnston. He says that in 1799 he was at work at the Great Prairie.

David M'Cance/M'Gance reports a stray horse. Deliver to Seth Cutter, innkeeper in Cincinnati, or Robert Blackburn near Colerain.

Sheriff James Smith reports sheriff sales of the property of Robert Hempsted at the suit of John Cleves Symmes; the property of Charles Young (land entered by E. Clark) seized at the suit of George Turner; the property of Thomas Doyle seized at the suit of James Conn and Charles Vattier.

Volume III, Saturday, 29 May 1802, Number 148

A list of acts passed by Congress mentions Samuel Dexter, Lyon Lehman, Francis Duchonquer, Isaac Zane, Thomas K. Jones, Louis Tousard, Theodosius Fowler, J.C. Symmes, John James Dufour, Fulwar Skipwith.

Rev. John Smith will preach a sermon at the Meeting House in Cincinnati.

Samuel Gregory, on Gregories Creek, reports a stray mare.

Joseph Silvers, living on Clear Creek on the road leading from Deerfield and Taylor's Mill to Dayton, seven miles above Taylor's Mill, reports a stray mare.

Volume III, Saturday, 5 June 1802, Number 149

Edward Tiffin, Robert Oliver and Ar. St.Clair regarding laws of the territory.

James Wilson, at Erie, about treatment he got from Capt. Cornelius Lyman.

D. Keasbey, hatter, in Cincinnati, has wool hats for sale.

John M'Cullaugh asks those indebted to him to settle their accounts.

Volume III, Saturday, 12 June 1802, Number 150

The proceedings of Congress regarding the statehood of the Northwest Territory mentions L.R. Morris, Mr. Fearing, T. Worthington, Samuel Findlay, Mr. Davis, Mr. Griswold and R. Williams.

William M'Farland, in Cincinnati, about a meeting of Nova Caesaria Lodge.

Sheriff James Smith says the sheriff's sales are postponed.

Joseph Crane, in Franklin, has quit keeping a tavern in Franklin and asks those indebted to him to settle their accounts.

Robert Benham, on Turtle Creek two miles above Deerfield, wants to hire a schoolmaster.

Duncan M'Vicker reports a mare that strayed from the plantation of James Seward in Springfield township.

Samuel Dick, in Cincinnati, has a house for rent on Front Street. Apply to Isaac Anderson at the sign of the Green Tree.

Volume III, Saturday, 19 June 1802, Number 151

More debate on the statehood of the Northwest Territory mentions Mr. Macon, Mr. Goddard, Mr. Fearing, Mr. Giles, Mr. Bayard and Mr. Griswold.

Robert M'Clure opened a house of entertainment on the road from Cincinnati to Fort Hamilton adjoining the Big Hill where James Cox formerly kept a tavern.

Andrew Jackson, living on Cumberland River, regarding a runaway slave named George, mentions George Velvin and Thomas Hutchings.

Volume III, Saturday, 26 June 1802, Number 152

B. VanCleve and Capt. Isaac Spinning write a letter to the public from the Dayton Association.

A report on the Nova Caesaria Lodge meeting is submitted by Wm. M'Farland.

The body of Matthew Cunningham was found floating in the Ohio River two miles below Cincinnati on Monday last. Last seen at Jacob Lights' house.

Capt. James Smith about a meeting, at Mr. Ruffin's place, of the Cincinnati Light Infantry Company. The meeting is to prepare for the Fourth of July.

C. Avery has a wagon and harness for sale for wheat delivered to White's or Grummon's Mill.

John Brasher, living in Springfield township on the new road from Hamilton to Cincinnati, near Abraham Lindley's distillery, on the west branch of Mill Creek, wants to hire an apprentice to the hatting business.

James Smith, Collector of the Revenue, in Cincinnati, gives notice to the distillers regarding duties.

Charles Vattier regarding his ferry on the Ohio River in Cincinnati.

John Fisher, living five miles from Hamilton near Capt. Hamilton's, the administrator of James Fisher, dec'd, late of St. Clair township in Hamilton County, regarding the estate settlement.

Aaron Goforth regarding claims against Hamilton County.

William Barkley regarding a bond to Robert Higgin.

Volume III, Saturday, 3 July 1802, Number 153

Thomas Brown, Chairman of the Republican Corresponding Society, Township of Anderson, sends Moses Broadwell with Abbe Raynel's pamphlet on slavery.

A note regarding an act pertaining to John C. Symmes' land.

A note regarding a meeting of citizens of Cincinnati at David Grummon's.

Samuel Hilditch has a new shipment of goods at his store in Cincinnati lately occupied by Smith & Findlay. He also keeps a store at Columbia.

Robert Rowan regarding a bond to John Cleves Symmes.

Amos Harris, in Deerfield township, regarding a bond to John Cleves Symmes.

A U.S. law is printed regarding the lands of John Cleves Symmes. It also mentions Ludlow's survey.

Volume III, Saturday, 10 July 1802, Number 154

Accounts of various July Fourth celebrations in Cincinnati and Columbia mention Capt. Smith's Company of Light Infantry, Mr. Ruffin, Rev. Mr. Wallace, Gov. Arthur St.Clair, George Fithian, Thomas M'Farland, Society of Cincinnati, Aaron Goforth, Charles Avery, Doctor William Goforth, Daniel Symmes, Charles Willing Byrd, Maj. William Perry, Maj. William Goforth, Col. Oliver Spencer.

Aaron Goforth regarding a meeting, at George Fithian's house, of the Republican Corresponding Society of the Town of Cincinnati.

A list of letters left at the Post Office in Cincinnati includes Thomas Ayres on Little Miami, Thomas Anderson, John Brasher, Elijah Brush at Detroit, James Brackin at Detroit, Capt. Burnet (innkeeper), John & Andrew Baileys, Nathan A.

Brown, Charles W. Byrd, Hister Blackford on Clear Creek, Daniel Bradstreet, Doct. W. Brown at Detroit, Ensign Henry B. Brevort at Detroit, Valentine or Jacob Bone at Deerfield, Charles Bruce at Hamilton, Thomas Cowls in Detroit, Asa Kitchel at Miami, Abraham Crumb in care of Joel Williams, Samuel Culbertson, Richard Cunningham at Deerfield, James Calwell at Millcreek, John Casidy at North Bend, Robert & John Campbell in Deerfield, King Dearmond on White Water, Richard Dill, John Dill, Christopher Dickson, Thomas Dunn on White Water, Jonathan Davis at Beadles Station, Lebious Day on Little Miami, Christian Eversole, John Elliott, Matthew Ernest at Detroit, Eli Elstion, Isaac Ferris, Solomon Gottshalkson, Jonah Gilbert on Big Miami, Joseph Gest on Little Miami, Robert Hanna, Stephen Golden, W. Hammit at North Bend, James Henry at Detroit, Joseph Hewling at Waynesville, Margaret Hewlings at Waynesville, James Huston (soldier at Detroit or Natchez), Christopher Heartsough in Upper Canada, Elizabeth Henry in Upper Canada, Col. John F. Hamtramck at Detroit, Lemuel R. Hungerford at Big Miami, Nicholas Johnston, James Kennedy at Detroit, William Lytle, Aaron Lane, Stephen Linzy, Abraham Larue near Franklin, Samuel Latimore at Little Miami, Cornelius Little, Jacob Low, Charles Long (soldier in Capt. Reed's company), M. Langloir in care of M. Mennessiers, Andrew Lytle at Deerfield, William Maxwell, Reuben Morhouse, Jeremiah Morrow, John M'Clain, Ann Martin in Detroit, Geo. Meldrum at Detroit, Frazer Morris at Columbia, Richard Mayberry, Levi Moor & David Urmstone in care of Timothy Thompson, Thomas M'Adams on Mill Creek, Samuel Morrison near Mad River, Moses Miller, Hugh Meek in care of Col. Ludlow, Conklin Miller, W. Owen Franklin, James Patterson, Dav. Pugh in Waynesville, Daniel Parine at White Water, Jacob Piatt, Robert Piatt, Lieut. Joshua S. Rodgers in Detroit, William Reeder, James Russell in Columbia, Samuel or Susanna Reeve, Leonard Raper near Williamsburg in care of John Groom, George Riggle at Columbia, Samuel Robison, Sen., Isaac Reed, Michael Simmons in care of Capt. Strong, Doctor Wm. B. Scott in care of Col. Ludlow, Henry Stewer, Oliver M. Spencer in Columbia, Solomon Sibley, Gov. St.Clair or Charles Willing Byrd, Jacob Steward, John Templeton at Taylor's Station, Owen Todd, Geo. Todd (district attorney), Joseph Troxell (gunsmith), Francis Tinbrook (soldier at Detroit), John Taylor, George Turner, Joseph Vanmatre at Deerfield, Garret Vanblaricum, John Vaughan, Joseph Villars, Abraham Vail at Little Miami, William Wells at Fort Wayne, Capt. Jacob White, W. Woodworth, Francis White, John Wallace, Thomas White at Hamilton, John Wilson, Michael Wise on Little Miami. William Ruffin, postmaster.

Capt. William M'Farland regarding a meeting of the Artillery Company of Hamilton County at Mr. M'Cullom's place.

Gilbert M'Crea about a mare that strayed from the house of Thomas Alston near Colerain. Deliver to Joel Williams in Cincinnati.

Volume III, Saturday, 17 July 1802, Number 155

The editors of the Western Spy want to buy corn and oats.

Matthew Nimmo, in Cincinnati, has a new shipment of goods for sale.

Robert Brasher, Cincinnati, wants to hire an apprentice to the hatter's trade.

Wm. M'Millan, living near Cincinnati, reports a stolen horse.

Henry Cadbury about his town on the Ohio River next door to Maj. Chambers, midway between Great Miami River and the Indian boundary line. Apply to him at Mr. Avery's in Cincinnati.

Oliver Spencer, in Columbia, says the partnership of Spencer, Gano, Crane & Company is dissolved.

Samuel J. Dawson, living in Bourbon County, Kentucky, near Paris, reports a runaway slave named Charles Mumford.

Sheriff James Smith regarding sheriff's sales of the property of John Cleves Symmes at the suits of John M'Cabe, John M'Grew, John Hole, Elizabeth Lamme (executrix of Robert Lamme, dec'd), James Dearth, Robert Maxwell, Samuel & William Stitt, John M'Clane (administrator of Allen M'Clane, dec'd), Matthias Pierson, Stephen Bunnel & Robert Ross, John Ewing, Daniel C. Cooper, William Lamme. Also the property of James Neel at the suit of Matthew Winton.

Volume III, Saturday, 24 July 1802, Number 156

David Zeigler and William M'Farland regarding ordinances of Cincinnati.

The editors of the Western Spy ask those indebted to them to settle their accounts with Mr. Clark, the post rider.

The Cincinnati Congregation is to meet at the Meeting House.

J. Whitworth reports a meeting, at William Ruffin's house, of the Cincinnati Light Infantry Company.

Aaron Goforth regarding licenses for merchants.

John B. Townsend regarding a stray mare that Henry Jenkins found.

David Zeigler about money to be raised for the use of the town of Cincinnati at meetings at Charles Avery's and George Fithian's.

Lewis Kerr, at Louisville, writes a letter to the Republican Corresponding Society of the town of Cincinnati. Includes the answer from Thomas M'Farland and Aaron Goforth.

An ordinance of Cincinnati is submitted by David Zeigler, William M'Farlan and Aaron Goforth.

No. 1, Volume IV, Saturday, 31 July 1802, Whole No. 157

Gov. St.Clair arrived in Cincinnati on Thursday evening.

Mr. Williamson regarding his school for Young Ladies in the house lately occupied by Mr. Newman, saddler, in Cincinnati.

John Smith regarding his goldsmith and watch making business in Cincinnati in the house opposite Nathaniel Reeder's store on Main Street in Cincinnati.

No. 2, Volume IV, Saturday, 7 August 1802, Whole No. 158

David Zeigler and William M'Farland regarding town ordinances of Cincinnati.

Mr. M'Henry, inspector, reports amount of flour inspected in Hamilton Co.

Jacob White, C. Waldsmith, John Smith and Israel Ludlow & Company about their partnership in the milling of wheat to flour.

Jabez Percival has opened his practice of "Physick & Surgery" at Colerain.

Thomas Espy, Jer. Morrow and John Parkhill regarding land offered for sale.

Sheriff Peter Light regarding a sheriff's sale at Williamsburgh in Clermont County of the property of Robert Higgins seized at the suit of William Berkley. The land adjoins Abraham Buford and the heirs of John F. Mercer.

William Willis, living on Still Water near Dayton, reports a stray horse.

Lemmon & Wilson regarding a note to William Fuller.

No. 3, Volume IV, Saturday, 14 August 1802, Whole No. 159

A note asking those indebted to the editors of the Western Spy to settle their accounts at the houses of Jonathan Pitman, John Torrence in Hamilton, Joseph Parks in the Fourth Range, Mr. Campbell (innkeeper at Big Praiari), Smith's mill at Round Bottom, John M'Cashen at Franklin, George Newcome in Dayton, David Sutton in Deerfield, Thomas Brown in Newtown, William Perry in Columbia, Dr. Wood in North Bend, Mr. Fowler at Newport, Ky. Or pay Mr. Clark, postrider.

Rev. Mr. Sargent will preach tomorrow in Newport, Kentucky, and Cincinnati.

Obituary: Mrs. Nancy Kennedy, age 27, wife of Joseph Kennedy, died at the "Family Mansion on the bank of the Ohio opposite this town", on Thursday morning 7 August 1802.

A notice of a meeting at Hugh M'Cullom's house about Mr. Stubbs' school.

John S. Gano regarding the division of the county into election districts by the Court of General Quarter Sessions mentions William Perry in Columbia, Isaac Mills in Ohio Township, Jonathan Pitman (innkeeper in Springfield township), John Torrence in Hamilton, David Sutton (innkeeper in Deerfield), Samuel Heighway in Waynesville, John M'Cashen (innkeeper in Franklin), George Newcome in Dayton.

Daniel Conner & Company have a new shipment of goods for sale.

Isaac Anderson, in Cincinnati, executor of the estate of John Chapman, dec'd, regarding the estate settlement.

Samuel Hilditch, in Columbia, has land for sale in Judge Symmes' patent.

Bethuel Covalt regarding a bond to John C. Symmes for land adjoining Waldsmith's on Little Miami.

Jacob Burnet regarding land claimed by the heirs of George W. Burnet, dec'd, mentions Col. Thomas Gibson, a neighbor.

Andrew Dunseth wants to hire an apprentice to the gunsmith business.

No. 4, Volume IV, Saturday, 21 August 1802, Whole No. 160

Andrew Badgley, John Gossett and George Medsker in New Market township, Ross County, write a letter to the public regarding statehood for Ohio.

A note regarding a meeting of the citizens at Jonathan Pitman's house in Springfield township to nominate representatives.

Letters to the editor nominating the following as representatives: Jacob Burnet, John Smith, William C. Schenck, William Ward, Thomas Smith, William M'Millan, John Ludlow, John Paul, John Bigger, Junr., James Barret, Moses Miller, Jacob White, William James, W. Goforth, Senr., Jacob Reeder, Robert Benham, Isaac Anderson, Charles W. Byrd, Francis Dunlavy, Jeremiah Morrow, John W. Brown, John Kitchel, Stephen Wood, John Wilson, William Goforth, Michael Jones, Thomas Brown, David Enoch, E. Vantreese, Asa Kitchel, Ephraim Kibby, John Bigger, John Armstrong, B. Vancleve, David E. Wade, Stephen Reeder, Jonathan S. Findlay, W.C. Schenck, Colonel Ward, Israel Ludlow, John Reily, John Ludlow, Joseph Prince, Daniel C. Cooper.

Henry Cadbury, at Charles Avery's in Cincinnati, regarding his town on the Ohio River next door to Maj. Chambers' land.

George Bruharde, living about six miles from Hamilton, reports stray cows.

Thomas Dugan, "just arrived from Philadelphia", has a new shipment of goods for sale at his store in Cincinnati.

Amos Bartilow regarding a bond to Jesse Hunt of Cincinnati.

Andrew Brannon and his wife, Allice Brannon, have separated and he won't honor her debts anymore.

Daniel Conner, agent for Ormsbey & Wilson, Cincinnati, has whiskey for sale.

No. 5, Volume IV, Saturday, 28 August 1802, Whole No. 161

George Fithian, in Cincinnati, asks those indebted to him to pay their bills.

Jacob Burnet, in Cincinnati, has land for sale near Springfield Meeting House.

Allice Glen, in Cincinnati, about the note placed last week by her husband, Andrew Brannon. She says her "old age is fast approaching".

Sheriff James Smith regarding the upcoming election.

A note regarding the Cincinnati horse races.

No. 6, Volume IV, Saturday, 4 September 1802, Whole No. 162

Aaron Goforth regarding a meeting of the Republican Corresponding Society of the Town of Cincinnati at George Fithian's house.

John S. Gano and Jacob Burnet (attorney) regarding a suit in Hamilton County Court of Common Pleas: John R. Mills vs. John H. Craig.

Lieut. Col. John S. Gano and Adjutant Wm. Ruffin regarding orders for the First Regiment of Hamilton County Militia about a meeting at the house of David Grummon in Cincinnati.

Henry Wason reports that a Delaware Indian found a mare near Greenville.

Henry Loar regarding a note to John C. Symmes.

Abraham Iost regarding a note to J.C. Symmes.

John W. Brown reports that he found a stray cow.

Samuel C. Vance, in Cincinnati, has land for sale near Laughrey's Creek.

No. 7, Volume IV, Saturday, 11 September 1802, Whole No. 163

Unsigned letters to the editor nominate persons for the Convention and the Assembly: Jacob Burnet, Wm. M'Millan, James M'Clure, John Reily, John Paul, W.C. Schenck, David E. Wade, James Barrett, John Smith, John Ludlow, William Ward, Jer. Morrow, Francis Dunlavy, Thomas Smith, Wm. M'Clelland, Isaac Anderson, Isaac Spinning, William C. Schenck, William James, William M'Millan, Cornelius Snider, Daniel Reeder.

David Zeigler and William M'Farland on the use of public funds in Cincinnati.

William Lytle, assignee of Martin Varner who was assignee of Robert Todd, dec'd, regarding land surveyed in the name of Elisha King. He mentions the heirs of William Mounts, dec'd, and John Nealy.

Thomas Davis, for Col. John Finney, of Woodford County, Kentucky, about runaway slaves named Monday, Bill and Elau.

John Cherry, living on the Dry Fork of White Water, found a stray mare.

Sheriff James Smith, in Cincinnati, regarding a sheriff's sale of the property of Mary Reed seized at the suit of Abijah Hunt and Cornelius R. Sedam.

No. 8, Volume IV, Saturday, 18 September 1802, Whole No. 164

Rev. John Smith will preach in Cincinnati tomorrow.

Charles Willing Byrd writes a letter to the editor.

John Calhoon, living on South Elkhorn in Kentucky, regarding runaway slaves named Jacob and Sarah.

James Forguson, in Cincinnati, has a new shipment of goods for sale. He also "proposes moving from here, as soon as he can possibly get his business arranged."

Zenas Hill reports that he will no longer pay the bills of his wife, Lucy Hill.

Thomas Larison regarding a bond to John Cleves Symmes for land mortgaged to John Smith.

Joseph Roberson about land John C. Symmes mortgaged to John Smith.

Daniel Conner & Company, in Cincinnati, want to buy beef, pork and lard.

Isaac Martin reports a stray mare. Deliver to Abiah Martin on Mill Creek or to George Wilson at Wilson's Settlement.

No. 9, Volume IV, Saturday, 25 September 1802, Whole No. 165

John Smith, at Round Bottom Mill, writes a letter to Charles Willing Byrd regarding a letter from Robert Morris and mentions Maj. Zeigler and Mr. Stone.

The inhabitants at Mad River nominate the following for the Convention: J. Morrow, Charles W. Byrd, John Smith, W. Goforth, John Wilson, John Paul, John Corbly, Francis Dunlavy, William James and John Kitchel.

The editors of the Western Spy ask those indebted to them to settle their accounts by bringing wheat to Smith's, Wood's or Waldsmith's mills on Mill Creek or to White's, Ludlow's and Grummon's mills.

Lieut. Col. John S. Gano & Lieut. William Ruffin give orders to the First Regiment of Hamilton Co. Militia and mention Capt. Reeder, Capt. Symmes, the late Capt. Goudy, Capt. Riddle, Capt. Martain, the late Capt. Evans, the late Capt. Schooley, Capt. White, Capt. Smith, Maj. John Wallace and Capt. Stephen Reeder.

John Reily, William Ramsey and William Ruffin, Auditors in Cincinnati, about suits in Hamilton County Court of Common Pleas: Joel Williams vs. Ruffus Elliot and John R. Mills vs. John H. Craig.

John Smith, at Round Bottom, has land for sale in John C. Symmes' patent. He also asks those indebted to him to make payments in pork to Daniel Conner in Cincinnati. He also wants to hire a sawyer and a schoolmaster.

William Lowery, in Cincinnati, has started his saddlery business in the house opposite Nehemiah Hunt in Cincinnati.

William Stanley wants to buy rye at D. Grummon's Mill and J. Smith's Mill.

Daniel Badger, living on the east fork of Little Miami, about a stray horse.

Sheriff James Smith regarding a sheriff's sale of the property of John Briney seized at the suit of John C. Symmes. Also property of Benjamin Flinn seized at the suit of Samuel Caldwell.

No. 10, Volume IV, Saturday, 2 October 1802, Whole No. 166

John W. Browne writes a letter to the editor regarding nominees to the Convention and the election at Jonathan Pitman's house.

Stephen Wood regarding statehood and his candidacy for the Convention.

An unsigned letter to the editor regarding candidates to the Convention mentions Wm. Goforth and William M'Millan.

At a meeting of the inhabitants of Fairfield and St. Clair townships at Capt. John Hamilton's house, the following were nominated for the Convention and the Assembly: Jacob Burnet, Wm. M'Millan, John Reily, James M'Clure, Wm. C. Schenck, John Ludlow, Jacob White, James Barret, John Smith, William James,

William Ward, Daniel C. Cooper, Wm. M'Clelland, Thomas Smith, Isaac Anderson, William Brown and John Biggart.

An unsigned letter to the editor regarding candidates to the Convention mentions Mr. Byrd and Mr. Kerr.

Gov. Arthur St.Clair gives a proclamation regarding the militia and mentions Charles Willing Byrd, Capt. William M'Farland, Lieut. Tabor Washburn and Lieut. David Christy.

John Sellman, John Reily and James Findlay regarding lands in John Cleves Symmes' patent and a meeting at Griffin Yeatman's Inn in Cincinnati.

A list of letters left at the Post Office at Cincinnati includes Samuel Ayres at Deerfield, John Abraham in Clermont County, John Alexander at Big Parara, Thomas Alston, Peter Atherton below the Big Miami, Martin Baum, Samuel Brewster on Sugar Creek, Henry Byrd in Capt. M'Call's company), David Benson in care of Thomas Kenedy, Peter Ballow in North Bend, Abner Beuel or Joseph Lamb at Beagles Station, Mr. Bele, Thomas Boone at Round Bottom, Joseph Blue, Burt & Newman, David Beaty, Melvin Baker, Samuel Clark near the Big Parara, Joseph H. Clark at White River, James Charters at Springfield, William Carson at Columbia, Samuel Cooper on Little Miami, John or Benjamin Cross, Jesse Cooper near Columbia, Joseph Corier, Butrun Covert at Deerfield, Daniel C. Cooper, David Douglas, Isaac Debee, Robert Dun in care of James Forguson, Levi Estel, Edmund Freeman, Charles Farran, John Freeman, Samuel Frazee, Stephen Goble near North Bend, Joseph Gould at Little Miami, Allice Glenn, Adam Henthorn, David Handrix near Hamilton, Nathaniel Hinckley, Thomas Hunter, Jerom Holt at Dayton, John T. Hall, Elizabeth Hazel in care of William Hunter in Colerain, John Hamilton in care of Griffin Yeatman, Solomon Howard, Mr. Higgins, Peter Keen, Daniel Haragan, Asa Harvey, Daniel Jones at Begles Station, Effy Jennings, Asa Kitchel, Thomas Kenedy, Phillip Lamberson, Barton Leonard, Joseph B. Lerbert, Sally Lamb at Begles Station, Edward Lynch in care of William Amberson, James M'Closkey in care of Samuel Dick, Charles Morgan, George Markle in Campbell County, Benjamin & Nathaniel Moore, Samuel M'Cray in care of William Stanley, Richard Martin in care of Daniel C. Cooper, William Mason in Columbia, James Montgomery, Elizabeth M'Closkey in care of Samuel Dick, John R. Mills, Mary Mapes at North Bend, Rev. Richard M'Nemair, Michael M'Nemair, G. Moore, Joseph M'Mahan near Hamilton, William Patton, Capt. Thomas Pasture at Fort Wayne, John Phillips near Newtown, James Perine in care of Daniel Perine, Abraham Perley, Isaac Pierson, Samuel Parker, Garret Rittenhouse near Dayton, Nathaniel Ross, William Rittenhouse, James Riddle, Matthew Richardson, William Richardson, Patience Silvers, Henry Stewyer, Thomas Smith at White Water, Benjamin Stites, Jun., Isreal Smith, Robert Sagerson, John Stephen near Taylors Mill, Jesse Simpson in care of James Martin, George Turner, Noah Tryon at North Bend, William Thomas in care of Doctor Goforth, Azarres Thorn near Hamilton, John Tharp, Joseph Thompson on Little Miami, John Torrence at Hamilton, Joseph Vanmater near Deerfield, Amos Valentine or Joseph Scoffield, Rev. Matthew G. Wallace, Abraham Voorheese, Sen., Cornelius Voorheese, James White (school master), Col. Robert Worthington, William Wells at Fort Wayne, James Watson near Hamilton, Anthony Williams at Deerfield, John Wallace, Phillip Waggoner, Maj. Levi Woodward, Thomas & Moses Westfall at the mouth of Honey Creek, Frederick Weaver on Little Miami, John Wilkinson at Big Hill, Jonathan Waring, Junr., on Little Miami, John Watson in Springfield, Griffin Yeatman. William Ruffin, post master.

William Stanley, attorney in fact for Wm. Peters, has land for sale near Hamilton Road, adjoining James Cox on the Big Hill, property of Maj. Wm. Peters.

No. 11, Volume IV, Saturday, 9 October 1802, Whole No. 167

Officers of the First Battalion of Hamilton Militia are to meet at David Grummon's place.

Charles Willing Byrd regarding the new company of artillery he created in Hamilton County mentions Henry Dearborn and Arthur St.Clair, Sen.

Wallis & Ross, in Cincinnati, have commenced the tailoring business opposite James Martin's.

Charles Young, of Norfolk, Virginia, about his land that George Turner of the Northwest Territory has offered for sale in judgment against a Charles Young of Baltimore, Alexandria and Philadelphia. The land was entered by Edmund Clark.

Adam Stewart regarding a bond to John M'Dougle.

Andrew Hamilton, living near Beasley's Mill, reports a stray cow. Deliver to Samuel Muchmore living near said Hamilton.

No. 12, Volume IV, Wednesday, 20 October 1802, Whole No. 168

An unsigned letter to the editor from St. Vincennes mentions Gov. Harrison.

A note regarding the discovery of a method of kiln-drying grain by John James Dufour of Jessamine County, Kentucky.

Election returns mention F. Dunlavy, John Paul, J. Morrow, C.W. Byrd, John Wilson, J. Kitchell, W. Goforth, J.W. Brown, John Smith, John Reily, W. James, Thomas Smith, S. Wood, W.C. Schenck, W. M'Millan, Jacob Burnet, John Bigger, John Ludlow, James M'Clure, James Barret, W. Ward, Jacob White, B. Vancleve, David E. Wade, Abner Gerrard, J. Corbley, Michael Jones, T. Brown, D. Enoch, E. Kibby, Asa Kitchell, E. Vantreese, Isaac Anderson, J. Barret, D. Reeder, J. Wilson, William James, W. M'Clellan, John Corbley, D.C. Cooper, Isaac Spinning, William Brown, William Ward.

J.W. Russell is to deliver a lecture at the Courthouse in Cincinnati.

J.J. Dufour, at the First Vine-Yard, Ky., about his method of drying grain.

A note regarding land for sale. Apply to John Bucknell living one mile from North Bend or to George Williamson in Cincinnati.

George Williamson makes and repairs tin goods at his store in Cincinnati.

G. Turner, in Cincinnati, regarding the Mad River pre-emption rights.

Wilson Crail/Grail, in Cincinnati, found a hat at a cabin opposite Mr. Poor's.

William Lowery, in Cincinnati, is making fire buckets. He also wants to hire an apprentice to the saddling business.

Uriah Gates regarding a due bill to James Bill and his son, John Bill.

No. 13, Volume IV, Wednesday, 27 October 1802, Whole No. 169

An account of a meeting of the Republicans of Cincinnati mentions Charles W. Byrd, William Goforth and Lewis Kerr.

In an election in Ross County, Edward Tiffin, T. Worthington, James Grubb and Michael Baldwin are elected delegates to the Convention, and William Patton, David Shelby, Winn Winship, Joseph Kerr & Robert Culbertson are representatives.

Emanuel Carpenter and Henry Abrams are elected delegates to the Convention from Fairfield County.

Joseph M'Hendry, Inspector of Hamilton County, regarding the inspections.

Matthew Nimmo, in Cincinnati, asks those indebted to him to pay their bills.

Mercy Galloway, in Cincinnati, administratrix of James Farlin, dec'd, about the estate settlement.

Joel Woodruff regarding a bond to John C. Symmes.

James Gillaspie, living on Clear Creek about two miles from Franklin on the Big Miami, reports a strayed or stolen horse. Deliver to Dr. Reeder in Franklin or George Newcome in Dayton at the mouth of Mad River.

Carpenter & Findlay ask those indebted to them to make payments in wheat.

No. 14, Volume IV, Wednesday, 3 November 1802, Whole No. 170

A note regarding J. Burnet and Wm. M'Millan mention Mr. Brush and Mr. Sibley of Detroit.

David Zeigler and William M'Farland regarding an ordinance of Cincinnati.

Stephen Vail regarding his town, Middle-Town, on the east bank of Great Miami River about a mile above Big Prierie, where he has lots for sale.

Thomas Thompson & Company, in Cincinnati, have a new shipment of goods.

William Ruffin and William Ramsey regarding a suit in Hamilton County Court of Common Pleas mention Wm. Wood and Wm. Coleman.

No. 15, Volume IV, Wednesday, 10 November 1802, Whole No. 171

Notes regarding the Convention mention Edward Tiffin, William M'Farland of

Cincinnati and Thomas Scott of Chillicothe.

A letter to the public from Gov. Arthur St.Clair regarding statehood.

Robert Stubbs, in Cincinnati, about his school of science and language.

Daniel C. Cooper, in Dayton, has land for sale in Judge Symmes' patent. Apply to Charles Killgore in Cincinnati.

Daniel Conner, in Cincinnati, regarding pork he bought.

Thomas Williams, in Cincinnati, wants to buy deerskins.

James Barrett and John Brady, executors of James Brady, dec'd, regarding the estate settlement.

Mr. Mennessieres, in Cincinnati, has goods for sale for hemp and flax.

No. 16, Volume IV, Wednesday, 17 November 1802, Whole No. 172

The speech of Gov. Ar. St.Clair to the Convention is printed.

The proceedings of the Convention lists the members: Joseph Darlington, Thomas Kirker and Israel Donaldson of Adams County; Francis Dunlavy, John Paul, Jeremiah Morrow, John Wilson, Charles W. Byrd, William Goforth, John Smith and John Reily of Hamilton County; Edward Tiffin, Nathaniel Massie, Thomas Worthington, Michael Baldwin and James Grubb of Ross County; John Milligan, Rudolph Bear, and George Humphreys of Jefferson County; Samuel Huntingdon of Trumbull County; Phillip Gath and James Sargent of Clermont County; James Caldwell of Belmont County; Rufus Putnam, Ephraim Cutler, John M'Intire and Benjamin Ives Gilman from Washington County; John W. Browne of Hamilton County; Bazaleel Wells and Nathan Updegrast of Jefferson County; Elijah Wood of Belmont County; Emanuel Carpenter and Henry Abrams of Fairfield County. Also mentions William Goforth, William M'Farland, Adam Betz, Thomas Scott, William M'Farland, John Kitchel of Hamilton County and Arthur St.Clair.

Aaron Goforth, in Cincinnati, regarding a meeting of the Republican Corresponding Society of the Town of Cincinnati.

Matthew Nimmo, in Cincinnati, wants to buy flour, pork and cheese. He also wants to buy wheat at White's Mill on Mill Creek or Smith's Mill on Little Miami.

Elijah Craig, living at his paper mill near Georgetown, Kentucky, regarding a runaway slave named James.

John Hamilton, at Five Mile Spring, reports a strayed or stolen horse.

William Burtt and Jemimah Burtt, administrators of estate of John Kenneady, late of Hamilton County, dec'd, regarding the estate settlement at the house of William Brown in Columbia.

John Fisher, living on Dick's Creek, has land for sale. Apply to Archibald Steel living on Beaver Creek.

Roger Martin, living on the west side of Big Miami four miles above Franklin, reports that he found a stray cow.

No. 17, Volume IV, Wednesday, 24 November 1802, Whole No. 173

The proceedings of the Convention mention Mr. Putnam, Mr. Darlington, Mr. Massie, Mr. Baldwin, Mr. Reily, Mr. Goforth, Mr. Smith, Mr. Worthington, David Abbott or Trumbull County.

David Littell, living near Beedle's Station on the waters of Turtle Creek, reports a stray mare.

Steven Vail has lots for sale in Middletown on the Great Miami.

Francis Flournoy, living in Pendleton County, Kentucky, regarding a runaway slave named Billy.

Daniel C. Cooper, in Dayton, wants to hire a man to tend a grist mill.

No. 18, Volume IV, Wednesday, 1 December 1802, Number 174

The proceedings of the Convention mention Mr. Worthington, Mr. Morrow, Mr. Byrd, Mr. Kitchel, Mr. Goforth and Mr. Smith.

Samuel Bennett regarding land he claims that was entered by John Green, James Giles, David Lahaw, Benjamin Gray, Robert Blair, John Meed, William Cassel, John Demsey, John Halfpenny. The land is next to Bennet Tompkins.

Samuel Enyard and Jacob Lewis regarding their land claim.

C. Vattier has Orleans boats for sale.
Daniel Griffing regarding a note to Daniel Carey/Corey.
Carpenter & Findlay report a strayed horse.

No. 19, Volume IV, Wednesday, 8 December 1802, Whole No. 175
Mr. Reily, delegate to the Convention, submits a copy of the Constitution of the State of Ohio.
Ar. St.Clair declines the candidacy of Governor of the State of Ohio.
Sheriff James Smith says that Edward Tiffin has called for an election of a governor of Ohio.
M. Nimmo, in Cincinnati, regarding a meeting of the Nova Caesaria Lodge.
John M'Cullagh asks those indebted to him to settle their accounts.
G. Turner regarding pre-emption rights for sale.
Wm. Stanley found a piece of gold. He also wants to buy beef, rye and pork.
David Littell, living near Beedle's Station on the waters of Turtle Creek, reports a stray mare.

No. 20, Volume IV, Wednesday, 15 December 1802, Whole No. 176
John S. Gano, of the General Court of Quarter Sessions for Hamilton County, regarding election districts.
Magdalene Williams, administratrix of the estate of David Williams, late of Hamilton County, dec'd, about the estate sale at Isaac VanNuys' house, Cincinnati.
W.C. Schenck has land for sale on the waters of Dicks Creek adjoining Matthias Spinning, "the Mr. Morris's", Mr. Delse and Jonathan Crane.
David J. Poor, in Cincinnati, asks those indebted to him and to Dr. William Goforth to settle their accounts.
Thomas Williams wants to buy deerskins in Cincinnati.

No. 21, Volume IV, Wednesday, 22 December 1802, Whole No. 177
Obituary: William Clark, chief judge of the Indiana Territory, died December 11, 1802, at Vincennes.
A note regarding an election held at St. Vincennes in Indiana Territory to elect delegates to the Convention mentions J. Noble Wood and Mr. Baggs (both of Clark County).
A note from Shadrach Bond and Isaac Darneille regarding a meeting in St. Clair County, Indiana Territory, to choose delegates to the Convention mentions William Whitesides and George Atchison (both in St. Clair County); John Small and Luke Decker in Knox County; and William Clark in Clark County.
Obituary: Aaron Cadwell, formerly of the Northwest Territory, died in October of 1802 at Point Coupe.
A note regarding the camp of Gen. Wilkinson near the mouth of Yazou River.
A letter to Charles W. Byrd at Chillicothe from James Madison at Washington mentions Gov. St.Clair.
Thomas Brown and Jacob Broadwell regarding a meeting of the Republican Corresponding Society of New Town.
Elias Shoemaker, living at the Bark Stack, found a heifer and a bull.
Caleb German, living on Duck Creek, found a stray horse.
John Humes and Michael Brokaw regarding a bond to John Brown, merchant, late of Cincinnati, but now of "Bia Seria in the Spanish dominions", mentions Thomas Douny on Mad River.
Adam Dickey, living near the mouth of Mill Creek, found some stray cattle.
Daniel Griffing regarding a note to Daniel Corey.
The editors of the Western Spy have horses for sale. They also ask those indebted to them to settle their accounts.

No. 22, Volume IV, Wednesday, 29 December 1802, Whole No. 178
James Madison writes a letter to Gov. St.Clair dismissing him as governor.
Ar. St.Clair writes a letter to James Madison thanking him for the dismissal and mentions Mr. Byrd.
Unsigned letter to the editor nominate candidates for office: B.I. Gilman,

John Bigger, Jeremiah Morrow, F. Dunlavy, John Reily, William Ward, John Paul, Isaac Anderson, Wm. C. Schenck, Wm. James, Daniel Reeder, William M'Clure, James Smith, Michael Jones and William Brown.

A note regarding James Smith's candidacy for sheriff.

Nathaniel Massie, regarding statehood, mentions John Cleves Symmes and Thomas Worthington.

The editors of the Western Spy ask those indebted to them to pay their bills.

P. Dickey, in Cincinnati, wants to hire an apprentice to the tayloring trade.

Abner Ammidon wants to buy pork at Mr. Grommon's in Cincinnati.

Charles Beeler, living at Beech Spring near Man's Lick, regarding runaway slaves named Moses and Nat.

No. 23, Volume IV, Wednesday, 5 January 1803, Whole No. 179

Thomas Rusk, living on the Ohio River near Col. Sedam, found a stray cow.

An unsigned letter nominates candidates for office in Ohio: Mr. Christy, Edward Tiffin, John Paul, Jeremiah Morrow, Daniel Symmes, John Bigger, Francis Dunlavy, Thomas Brown, William James, Robert M'Clure, Ephraim Kibbey, Thomas M'Farland, William Maxwell, James Dunn, Michael Jones, Joseph Carpenter.

Daniel Symmes writes a letter to Hon. Charles Willing Byrd, acting governor, resigning his position as clerk to the General Court.

Marriage: Ichabod Benten Halsey married Miss Sally Watkins Smith, daughter of the late Rev. James Smith, dec'd, formerly of Powhatan County, Virginia, on January 1, 1803.

Matthew G. Wallace, in Cincinnati, regarding his school.

Daniel Conner & Company ask those indebted to settle their accounts.

Vance & Dill have opened a new store at Smith & Findlay's store room, lately occupied by Mr. Hilditch in Cincinnati.

A list of letters left at the Post Office in Cincinnati includes Peter or David Atherton at White Water, Charles W. Byrd, Joseph Ballew at North Bend, John Bigger, Jun., on Dick's Creek, Anthony Burns at Colerain, William Blieth, Patrick Broadrick on Clear Creek, John Bull at Deerfield, Joseph Brown at Whitewater, Daniel Bradstreet in Frankland, Jerimiah Butterfield, Capt. Bartholomy, Nathaniel Bond in Frankland, Edmund Buxton, William Francis Berealow at Frankland, John Clarke, Thomas Clarke, Daniel Clarke at Duck Creek, Michael Coppinger, Willian Chamberlin at Big Miami, Enos Daniel, John Doyle on Mad River, William Donnel on Little Miami, Leblue Day in Columbia, Joseph Ely in Frankland, Joseph Gest on Little Miami, John Fox, Samuel Ebernon at Clear Creek, John Ewing at Miami, Robert Eaton at Deerfield, Levi Gregory, William Grant, Sen., John Gillman, Thomas Hill on Gregories Creek, George Jarnison, Michael Hildebrand or Bazele Osborn at Dunham's Town, Samuel Hyndman on Mill Creek, Mr. Jinnius on Duck Creek, Jeremiah Johnston at Whitewater, Thomas John on Little Beaver, James Knight near Waldsmith's Mills, Moses Ketchel, Jacob D. Low in Deerfield, James Lewis in care of Jacob Wheeler, Alexander Ligget at Deerfield, Andrew Lytle at Deerfield, Jacob Light, John Marsh in Columbia, John Mears, William Major in care of Henry Rogers at Red Oak, Alexander Martin, Joseph M'Maken, James M'Clelland, Isaac Mullin in Frankland, Valentine Mixwell at Columbia, Serring Marsh in care of Jacob Wheeler, Joseph Nelson, John Nicholl on Little Miami, Adam Nutt in care of John Riddle, Abijah Oneal at Wanesville, Elias Porter on Little Miami, Thomas Paxton on Little Miami, William Patton in care of John M'Cullaugh, Susanna Pierce on Little Miami, Philip Porter on Little Miami, Matthew Richardson, Moses Rumery, John Ramsey at Fort Wayne, James Silvers at Northbend, Noah Strong in Columbia, James Sargent in Clermont County, Rev. Robert Stubbs, William Stone, Lieut. Aug't. Strong, Doctor Hubbard Sparkawk at Fort Wayne, George Smith at the mouth of Twelve Mile Creek, Rev. Peter Smith, Simeon Saunders on Little Miami, Robert Steel on Mill Creek, Michael Shock on Big Miami, Jesse Simpson, Daniel Skinner, John Thomas on Big Miami, Miss Margaret Todd, Henry Tice at Round Bottom, John Templeton near Capt. Smith's mills, David Vail, Arthur VanderVeer, Philip Waggoner, John Whetstone, Francis Whittinger at Big Miami, Josiah Wilson and Brown Wilson near Hamilton, Dennis Woodruff at Springfield, James Walker in care of Andrew Dunseth, James Wilson at the head of Dick's Creek, Henry Weaver at Big Miami, William Ruffin.

Elmor Williams asks those indebted to him to settle their accounts.

No. 24, Volume IV, Wednesday, 12 January 1803, Whole No. 180

Sheriff James Smith regarding sheriff's sales of the property of John Cleves Symmes at the suits of John R. Mills, Daniel Griffin, James M'Cashen, Nathan Lamme, Zacha. Hole, John Ewing, John M'Cabe, John M'Clain, J. Thompson. Also property of James Silvers and John Cleves Symmes at the suit of William and Michael Jones. Also property of James Cox at the suit of John Cleves Symmes. Also the property of Hezekiah Flint at the suit of Seth Cutter.

Election returns are printed and mention Edward Tiffin, B.I. Gilman, John Paul, Jeremiah Morrow, Francis Dunlavy, John Reily, Daniel Symmes, John Bigger, William James, Thomas Brown, James Dunn, William Maxville, Ephraim Kibby, William C. Schenck, William Ward, Thos. M'Farland, Robert M'Clure, James Smith, Michael Jones.

David Zeigler and William M'Farland regarding ordinances of Cincinnati.

William Lamb regarding his hotel at the sign of The Spread Eagle, Chillicothe.

John Gilman, living near Cincinnati, reports a stray mare.

Matthew Nimmo wants wheat at Jacob White's or David Grummon's mills.

No. 25, Volume IV, Wednesday, 19 January 1803, Whole No. 181

Election returns from Hamilton County are reported and mention Edward Tiffin, Benjamin Ives Gillman, John Paul, Jeremiah Morrow, Francis Dunlavy, Daniel Symmes, John Reily, William Ward, Thomas Brown, John Bigger, William James, James Dunn, Thomas M'Farland, Ephraim Kibby, Robert M'Clure, William Maxwell, William C. Schenck, John Wilson, John Kitchel, Edward Meeks, Daniel C. Cooper, Daniel Reeder, John W. Brown, David Sutton, James Silvers, George F. Tennery, Jacob White, James Smith, Michael Jones, Joseph Carpenter, William M'Farland.

The governor appointed William M'Farland to be Clerk of the General Court.

A note regarding a meeting at David Grummon's tavern in Cincinnati about the exportation of produce.

Matthew G. Wallace, G. Turner, John S. Gano, William M'Farland, David E. Wade, John Mercer, and John Stites, Junr., regarding students at Mr. Stubbs' academy in Cincinnati.

Robert Stubbs says he's recommencing his academy in Newport.

Henry Jenning, living on Duck Creek on the road from Cincinnati to Deerfield and from Columbia to White's Station, six miles from Cincinnati, has land for sale. Apply to John Reily in Cincinnati.

Stephen R. Wilson, in Wood County, Virginia, about notes to David Griffin.

Andrew Cox regarding a bond to John Cleves Symmes for land claimed by John M'Lean, administrator of the estate of Allin M'Lean, deceased.

Tanner's oil is for sale at Isaac Anderson's in Cincinnati.

William Lemmon, living eleven miles from Cincinnati on the Ohio River, has land for sale. Apply to John M'Cullagh in Cincinnati.

Daniel Hammitt has commenced the manufacture of nails in Cincinnati.

No. 26, Volume IV, Wednesday, 26 January 1803, Whole No. 182

Edward Tiffin writes letters to Congress and the president regarding the statehood of Ohio and mentions Thomas Scott and Mr. Randolph.

The proceedings of the House of Representatives mention Mr. Randolph, Mr. Gray, and Thomas Worthington.

Election returns from Ross County are printed and mention Edward Tiffin, Arthur St.Clair, Benjamin Ives Gillman, Return Jonathan Meigs, Nathaniel Massie, Abraham Claypool, James Dunlap, James Scott, James Grubb, Michael Baldwin, Thomas Worthington, William Patton, Robert Culbertson, David Shelby, Isaac Dawson, Jacob Smith, Thomas Stockdon, Reuben Abrams, John Blair, Walter Buel, William Robinson, Jeremiah M'Lene, Benjamin Urmston.

Election returns from Adams County are printed and mention Edward Tiffin, Arthur St.Clair, John Beasly, Joseph Darlington, Joseph Lucas, William Russel,

Thomas Kirker, Israel Donaldson, Andrew Ellison, Phil. Lewis, Mr. Parker, Mr. Eddie, Thomas Odle, Mr. Ledwick, Noble Grimes, N. Beasly, Mr. Denning, Mr. Carey, Mr. Washburn, Mr. Scott.

Election returns from Fairfield County mention Edward Tiffin, Bezaliel Wells, Robert F. Slaughter, Samuel Carpenter, David Rees, William Tremble, William Irwin, William Gass, Samuel Kratser, James Converse and Mr. Lynch.

An account of a fire at Clarke Bates' house three miles from Cincinnati.

Obituary: Mrs. Margaret Jones, wife of Wm. Jones, merchant of Cincinnati, died on Friday last, 21 January 1803.

Obituary: Mrs. Margaret Lowrey, wife of William Lowrey, lately from Kentucky, died on Friday, 21 January 1803.

William Lowrey, in Cincinnati, says that "on the fifth of February next I leave this place" and asks those indebted to him to settle their accounts.

Samuel Hilditch has a new shipment of goods at his store in Columbia.

William M'Farland and Lewis Kerr (attorney) regarding a suit in the General Court of the Northwest Territory: Christopher Case vs. William Helms, administrator of the estate of Edward Dunlop, deceased.

Catharine Martin, administratrix of the estate of Isaac Martin, late of Hamilton County, dec'd, regarding the estate settlement.

Alexander Weir, in Franklin, reports a stray mare.

No. 27, Volume IV, Wednesday, 2 February 1803, Whole No. 183

Election returns from Clermont County mention Edward Tiffin, Mr. Ellis, Mr. Buchannon, Rodger Warren. Election returns from Jefferson County mention Gov. Tiffin, James Pritchard, Bezaliel Wells, Mr. Humphrey, Mr. M'Cune, Mr. Bear, Mr. Meeks. Election returns from Belmont County mention Gov. Edward Tiffin, Elijah Woods, William Vance, Joseph Sharp.

A note regarding the fire at Mr. Bates' house.

Obituary: Mrs. Sarah Stark died on Thursday, 27 January 1803, in Cincinnati. She would have been 100 years old on April 1, 1803.

Obituary: Mrs. Nelly Gildersleve, widow of the late John Gildersleve, died on Sunday, 30 January 1803.

The editors of the Western Spy about payments made to Mr. Clark, postrider.

Charles Willing Byrd writes a letter to Mr. Arthur St.Clair.

William Goforth, in Columbia, has red clover seed for sale.

B. Chambers gives notice to people erecting fish dams on the Great Miami.

Joab Compstock regarding his ferry on the Great Miami River.

No. 28, Volume IV, Wednesday, 9 February 1803, Whole No. 184

An account of a meeting of the citizens of Hamilton County and Campbell County, Kentucky, at Mr. Grummon's Tavern regarding the export of produce mentions Dr. Robert M'Clure, Wm. C. Schenck, John Smith, Israel Ludlow, Martin Baum, James Taylor, Jesse Hunt, John Reily, Jacob White, James Findlay, Thomas Sanford, Daniel Mayo and William Stanley.

Carpenter & Findlay regarding the publication of the Weekly Messenger at Washington, Kentucky, mentions Daniel Vertner in Washington.

John Armstrong has fruit trees for sale at his nursery at Columbia.

Daniel Symmes, in Cincinnati, regarding land he owns in Hamilton County.

Joseph Charles, printer and bookseller, has moved his printing business from Philadelphia to Lexington.

Israel Ludlow, living on Mill Creek, reports that he found a stray mare.

Seth Cutter has beef for sale at his butchering business in Cincinnati.

Abraham Carey, Deputy Collector, regarding the collection of taxes in Cincinnati township, mentions John R. Mills.

Andrew Lock says his wife, Sally Lock, left him and he won't pay her bills.

The editors of the Spy want to hire an apprentice to the printing trade.

No. 29, Volume IV, Wednesday, 16 February 1803, Whole No. 185

James Forguson, in Cincinnati, has a new shipment of goods for sale.

Sheriff James Smith regarding sheriff's sales of the property of John Cleves

Symmes seized at the suits of John M'Clain, John M'Grew and Matthias Pierson.

David Little says his wife, Sarah Little, left him and he won't pay her bills.

Isaac Anderson has tanner's oil for sale.

Abner Green, in Natchez, reports a runaway slave that formerly belonged to Col. William Montgomery in Lincoln County, Kentucky. He mentions Henry Hall of Shelby County and Capt. Purdie.

James M'Clelland, in Cincinnati, regarding a bond to John Cleves Symmes, mentions John Smith.

David Zeigler asks those indebted to him to settle their accounts.

Daniel Mayo and William Ruffin, in Cincinnati, regarding a bond to Joseph Carico of Washington County, Maryland.

Hubbard Taylor, living on Boon Creek in Clark County, Kentucky, regarding runaway slaves named Pakosert and Joshua.

No. 32, Volume IV, Wednesday, 9 March 1803, Whole No. 188

An account of a meeting at Grummon's house regarding the Miami Exporting Company mentions William Ruffin, Samuel C. Vance, David Grummon, Jesse Hunt and Martin Baum.

John Armstrong, in Columbia, writes a letter to the editor regarding Judge Symmes' nephew, Daniel Symmes, and mentions Capt. Brackenridge in Kentucky.

John Armstrong, in Columbia, writes a letter regarding a letter in the Scioto Gazette regarding him and the Democratic Corresponding Society of Columbia. He mentions John Wilson, Benjamin Stites, Samuel Armstrong, William Perry, Robert Winslow, Francis M'Mahan, Fraze Morris, Thomas Shepherd, Philip Jones, Philip Dralinger, Jacob Griffis and John Young.

Edward Tiffin, H. Vanderburgh and Ar. St.Clair regarding a law.

J. Carpenter, town clerk of Cincinnati, regarding a meeting at Mr. Avery's.

James Barret, in Cincinnati, executor of the estate of James Bradey, dec'd, gives all responsibility for the estate to the other executor, John Bradey.

Jane Nelson, living five miles from Cincinnati on Colerain road, found a cow.

Abner Harris, living a bit below Beasley's Mill on Little Miami, found a cow.

Michael Grove and John Hall, living in Boon County, Kentucky, opposite North Bend, report runaway slaves named Lymas and Philip.

George Williamson moved his shop to the corner of Sycamore & Second in Cincinnati. He wants to hire an apprentice to the tin and coppersmith trade.

William Henry Harrison, Governor of the Indiana Territory, and John Gibson, secretary, write a letter to the public regarding the State of Ohio.

Matthew Nimmo, in Cincinnati, wants to buy wheat and rye delivered to David Grummon's Mill.

John S. Gano and Jacob Burnet (attorney) regarding a suit in the Court of Common Pleas for Hamilton County: Samuel Archer vs. Thomas Chovea.

Daniel Roudebush, living on Obanion Creek seven miles from Waldsmith's Mill, reports a stray mare.

Francis White, living at the mouth of Mill Creek, found a cow.

William Wallace reports that the partnership of Wallace & Ross is dissolved. Wallace continues the tayloring business in the house lately occupied by Alexander King in Cincinnati. He also wants to buy deerskins.

John S. Gano, David Grummon and Charles Avery, in Cincinnati, regarding the fire at Grummon's stable in Cincinnati on 1 March 1803.

John S. Gano offers a farm on Duck Creek for sale or for rent.

James Hill, near Ludlow's Mill, found a stray heifer.

Thomas Dugan, in Cincinnati, asks those indebted to him to pay their bills.

John Reily, Wm. Ruffin and J.S. Findlay, Auditors in Cincinnati, regarding the sale of the property of John H. Craig at the suit of John R. Mills. Also about the claims against Robert Park, late of Cincinnati.

Bryant Slone has commenced the saddlery business in Cincinnati in the house lately occupied by Wm. Lowry.

No. 33, Volume IV, Wednesday, 16 March 1803, Whole No. 189

The proceedings of the legislature of Ohio mention Nathaniel Massie, Wm. C.

Schenck, Michael Baldwin and William R. Dickenson.
David Grummon and Tabor Washburn regarding Judge Goforth.
David Zeigler and William M'Farland regarding an ordinance in Cincinnati.
Oliver Spenser, of Columbia, says the partnership of Spenser, Gano, Crane & Company is dissolved, and those indebted to them should settle their accounts.
George Need, living in Jessamine County, Kentucky, regarding a mare stolen by Job Davis, age 21.
John Barret, living on the west side of the Great Miami on the waters of Elk Creek, reports a stray mare.
Edmund H. Taylor, living in Jefferson Co., Ky., about a runaway slave, Jesse.
D. Keasbey regarding lending his horse.
Samuel Heighway regarding his recent loss by fire. He also asks those indebted to him to settle their accounts.

No. 34, Volume IV, Wednesday, 23 March 1803, Whole No. 190

David Zeigler and William M'Farland regarding ordinances of Cincinnati.
A note from Col. Armstrong of Chillicothe regarding acts of Congress.
William M'Farland is appointed treasurer and Thomas Gibson, Auditor, of Ohio. Thomas Scott is appointed clerk in place of W.C. Schenck, resigned.
Rev. Joseph Redding will preach in Newport on Monday, 28 March 1803.
Zenas Kimberly, Jeremiah Morrow, John Bigger, R. Safford and J. Quimby regarding the budget in Ohio.
Capt. James Smith regarding the meeting of the Cincinnati Light Infantry Company at William Ruffin's place.
Hugh M'Collom will keep a house of public entertainment at the house lately occupied by David Grummon in Cincinnati.
Sineas Pearson has apple trees for sale for wheat delivered to Ludlow's Mill on Mill Creek.
John Dill & Company, saddlers and harness makers, "just opened their shop in Mr. Dickey's room" in Cincinnati.
Paul Huston regarding a bond to John C. Symmes for land.
John Bigham, in Cincinnati, regarding a bond to J.C. Symmes for land.
J. Bucknall regarding the town of Shrewsbury on the bank of the Great Miami River about seven miles from the mouth. Apply to George Williamson, Cincinnati.

No. 36, Volume IV, Wednesday, 6 April 1803, Whole No. 192

Edward Tiffin, in Chillicothe, writes a letter to the legislature of Ohio.
T. Worthington writes a letter to the legislature of Ohio.
An act of Congress regarding the lands of J.C. Symmes.
Reports of fires set in Cincinnati mentions Mr. Grummon's stable, Mr. Reiley's stable and Mr. Avery's stable.
A list of township officers elected at Mr. Avery's: Joseph Prince, Charles Kilgore, William Ruffin, Culbertson Parks, Nathaniel Reeder, John Reily, John Sellman, Isaac Anderson, Thomas Ramsey, Joseph Carpenter, William Ramsey and Thomas Williams.
A list of letters in the Post Office at Cincinnati includes Michael Ayres in Deerfield, John Allen, James Bell on Four Miles Creek above Columbia, Ephraim Blackford, Daniel Bradstreet at Franklin, John Bridges on Little Miami, Jesse Beevis or James Wallace at Colerain, Robert Beaty, John Brown in Boon County, Michael Carver in care of James Matthews, James Clark and Samuel Johnston on Clough Creek, Joseph Cummins, Alexander Campbell, H. Cadbury, John Cummins at Fort Hamilton, William Coleman, John Campbell at Colerain, Edward Death at Franklin, John Daniel at Columbia, Samuel Dunn, Andrew Dillon at Fort Hamilton, Lebious Day on Little Miami, John Daily, Mary Elliott near Fort Hamilton, Samuel Enyart, Jonathan Garwood on Clear Creek, William Givylin at Colerain, Isaac Gregg, Josiah Gevaltney on Clough Creek, Daniel Gribe on Bear Creek, Alexander Hamilton at Deerfield, John Highlands, Robert Henderson at Fort Nelson, Thomas Heat on Gregorys Creek, Daniel Ingersol on Great Miami, Edward Johnston, James Jones on Great Miami, Joseph Jenkinson, Elizabeth John in Columbia, George Isham on Caesars Creek, Edward Jackson, Isaac John at Springfield, David Lawler

in Deerfield, Capt. Timothy Kibby, David Lampher, David Loudon at Fort Wayne, James M'Ginnis (currier), Barney M'Carran, Elizabeth Mellott, Joseph Mouney, William Maxwell or Baroti Hole, Ichabod Marshall at Sandusky, Daniel Moore in Springfield, Sampson M'Cullaugh, Matthew M'Dowell in Fairfield, James Marston, James M'Clelland, David M'Cord in Deerfield, Joseph Migic, James Martin on Big Parara in care of John M'Cullaugh, Thomas Newport on Mad River, John Oblinger, John Orbison, Isaac Polke on Miami, William Parkison in Colerain, Joseph Potter, Samuel Reese, Felix Rock, Abraham Inlow, Henry Runyon on Mill Creek, Arthur St.Clair, Jared Scofield in Deerfield, Collin Spencer on Little Miami, Daniel Stout in care of Jesse Hunt, John Cleves Symmes, Abraham Southard, Elijah Stibbons on Clear Creek, Jonathan H. Sparhawk at Fort Wayne, Isaac Pandine or Isaac Seward, Phillip Stoner in care of Col. Paxton, Capt. Thomas Smith on White water, William Thomas in care of Doctor Goforth, Margarat Todd in care of George Williams, Noah Tryon, John Tharp, Capt. John Templeton at White Water, James Thompson at Deerfield, Amos Travis, Abraham Vansickle at Big Parara, Arthur Vanderveere at Big Miami, John Warren, John Winters, Peter Weaver, Alexander Wilson living with John Blackburn, Mary Willis near Dayton, John Wood on Indian Creek in Clermont County, Francis Whitinger, James Wilson on Dicks Creek, Col. William Ward on Mad River, John Wallace. Entered by William Ruffin, post master.

Sheriff James Smith regarding a sheriff's sale of the property of John Gaston at the suit of Samuel Branin and the property of Thomas Hunter at the suit of Jacob Burnet.

John N. Cummins (of New Jersey, by William C. Schenck his attorney), Jacob Burnet, William M'Millan, James Findlay, Abraham Kinney and Hannah his wife (of New Jersey), John Burnet, Arthur St.Clair, Jun., and Stephen Wood (of North Bend) regarding their petition in the Court of Common Pleas of Hamilton County about land. They mention John Burnet, Isaac G. Burnet, Statis Burnet and David Burnet of N.J., John C. Budd of N.J., William Henry Harrison of Indiana Territory, Payton Short of Kentucky, and the heirs of Thomas Kenny (late of N.J., dec'd).

William Henry Harrison and John Gibson write a letter to the public of the Indiana Territory.

Wm. Wood, living on Little Miami below Deerfield, has mills for sale.

John Lemmon, living near Cunningham's Mill on Mill Creek, reports a stray mare. Deliver to Henry Runyon on Mill Creek.

Henry Ewing moved to the house lately occupied by Hugh M'Collom in Cincinnati and continues it as a house of public entertainment.

No. 37, Volume IV, Wednesday, 13 April 1803, Whole No. 193

The proceedings of the House of Representatives mention Mr. Maxwell, John Bigger and William James.

Senators chosen from Ohio to the U.S. Senate are Thomas Worthington and John Smith. Return Jna. Meiggs, William Spriggs and Samuel Huntington are to be supreme judges. W. Silliman, C. Pease and F. Dunlavy are chosen presiding judges.

Associate judges are chosen in the various counties: Michael Jones, James Silvers and Luke Foster in Hamilton County; John Green, James Dunn and John Kitchel in Butler County; William James, Jacob D. Lowe and Ignatius Brown in Warren County; Benjamin Archer, Isaac Spinning and John Ewing in Montgomery County; James Barret, Benjamin Whitman and William Maxwell in Green County; John Wood, Ambrose Ranson and Philip Garch in Clermont County; David Eddie, Joseph Darlington, and Hosea Moore in Adams County; Thomas Sweeney, John Collins and Joseph Lucas in Scioto County; Reuben Abrams, William Patton and Mr. Rennix in Ross County; John Dill, Joseph Foos and David Jamison in Franklin County; John Wallworth, Calvin Austin and Aaron Wheeler in Trumbull County; (Entries for Fairfield, Galia, Washington, Belmont, Columbia and Jefferson Counties are nearly illegible on the microfilm. The following can be made out, but is not complete: J.W. Putnam in Galia, David Vance in Belmont, William Smith and Robert Simpson in Columbia, and Philip Cable/Gable in Jefferson Co.)

The editors of the Western Spy say that payments for subscriptions are due to Mr. Clark the postrider.

William Clark regarding subscriptions due to the Western Spy. He says he will collect payments at Capt. White's, Duck Creek Settlement, Beasley's Mill, Pollox's Mill, Paxton's Settlement, Shaw's & Hathaway's on Turtle Creek, Willson's Settlement, Vance's Settlement, Davis' Mill on Beaver Creek, Capt. John Ewing's, Aaron Nutts', Munger's Settlement, Larance's Mill, Veal's Mill.

A note regarding lots for sale at an auction at Mr. M'Collom's Inn, Cincinnati.

James Smith, Collector, gives notice to distillers regarding duties.

Charles Avery, in Cincinnati, reports a stray mare.

John M'Cullagh asks those indebted to him to settle their accounts.

No. 38, Volume IV, Wednesday, 20 April 1803, Whole No. 194

Obituary: Mrs. Phebe Reeder, wife of Jesse Reeder living on Duck Creek, died on Saturday morning, 17 April 1803.

Robert Russell, in Belmont County, regarding land he bought from John M'Roberts in Donegal township, Washington County, Pennsylvania.

F. Mennessier, in Cincinnati, has goods for sale at his store in Cincinnati.

John Bouyer says he won't pay the bills of "my wife Margaret or her child".

Andrew Hill, living one mile below Taylor's Creek on the Great Miami, reports a stray horse.

D. Grummon has a farm for sale on Hamilton Road eleven miles from Cincinnati. The farm formerly belonged to Elmore Williams.

No. 39, Volume IV, Wednesday, 27 April 1803, Whole No. 195

A note about the proceedings of the legislature mentions Mr. Worthington.

A list of acts passed by the Ohio legislature mentions Isaac Helmich.

Errata: The associate judge for Butler County is John Geer, not John Green.

Hugh M'Collom, in Cincinnati, reports a stray mare.

John Gilman, in Cincinnati, reports that he found a stray cow.

Margaret Bouyer, in Cincinnati, regarding the ad placed by her husband, John Bouyer. She tells her side of the story.

Stephen Wheeler, in Cincinnati, reports a runaway apprentice, James Casto, age 18. He's probably gone to the Falls of Ohio where his brother-in-law lives.

Robert M'Clure, at the Big Hill, reports a stray mare.

Carpenter & Findlay ask those indebted to them to settle their accounts by delivering wheat to Waldsmith's Mill.

No. 40, Volume IV, Wednesday, 4 May 1803, Whole No. 196

A note regarding the robbery of Esther M'Dowell, age 18, on the way from Montreal to Kentucky to join her father, Dr. John M'Dowell. She was robbed by Benjamin Connet. She's now at the house of Rev. Isaac Green in Pennsylvania.

Michael Baldwin and Nath. Massie regarding laws of the state of Ohio.

Rev. John Smith, at Point Coupes, writes a letter to a friend in Cincinnati regarding the arrest, by Capt. M'Coy, of Sam Mason and sons near New Madrid.

More on the robbery of Esther M'Dowell.

Jesse Hunt, D. Grummon and M. Baum, in Cincinnati, regarding the Miami Exporting Company meeting at Jonathan Pitman's on the road to Hamilton.

William Jones and Michael Jones have dissolved their partnership. They offer their house and property for sale.

John Hubbard says his wife, Asenath, left him and he won't pay her debts.

No. 41, Volume IV, Wednesday, 11 May 1803, Whole No. 197

A note regarding candidates nominated to serve in the U.S. House of Representatives from Ohio mentions William Goforth, Sen.

Samuel Dillon regarding his candidacy for the sheriff's office.

Michael Jones, James Silvers, Luke Foster and John S. Gano, regarding the division of the county into townships, mention John Benefield, Joseph Colby, Samuel Muchmore, Thomas Brown in NewTown, John Ayres in Montgomery, John Harryman and Jonathan Pitman.

Maj. Zeigler has a box of medicines found floating in the Ohio River.

Benjamin Maltbie, living in the Morgan Settlement, reports a stray horse.

Robert Stubbs regarding tuition for his school.

Jacob White regarding a runaway slave named Jack.

Sutherland & Brown, in Hamilton, ask those indebted to them to settle their accounts as soon as possible.

John Dill & Company want to hire two apprentices to the saddling business.

J. Bucknell is opening a ferry across the Great Miami at Shrewsbury across the river from North Bend.

No. 42, Volume IV, Wednesday, 18 May 1803, Whole No. 198

Michael Baldwin and Nath. Massie regarding laws passed by the legislature.

Notes regarding ships on the river at Louisville mention James Merrill, John Clark of Wheeling, Edward W. Tupper of Marietta, John Instone, Capt. Samuel M'Cutcheon, and Capt. James M'Keever.

William Goforth, in Columbia, writes a letter to the editor regarding his candidacy for the U.S. house of representatives.

An unsigned letter to the editor nominates William M'Millan as candidate for the U.S. House of Representatives.

Unsigned letters to the editor mention William Goforth & Col. Elias Langham as candidates for representatives.

Selidon Symmes is appointed commissioner in Butler County for leasing the school lands.

Adj. Gen. Samuel Finley, Chillicothe, gives general orders to the Militia.

Joseph Prince regarding a meeting of the select council at Mr. Yeatman's.

Amos Derrough, near the mouth of Mad River, regarding a horse stolen by John Black, a 30-year-old Irishman.

No. 43, Volume IV, Wednesday, 25 May 1803, Whole No. 199

An unsigned letter to the editor nominates Jeremiah Morrow to Congress.

Mr. Mayo's rope-walk in Newport was blown down by wind on 20 May 1803.

Benj. VanHook regarding a meeting of the Infantry.

David Grummon & Jesse Hunt regarding the election of directors of the Miami Exporting Company. The election is to be held at Seth Cutter's house.

Lieut. Col. John S. Gano and Lieut. William Ruffin regarding a meeting of the militia officers at Charles Avery's place.

John Martin, in Cincinnati, "has just landed" and has nails for sale. Apply to Mr. Hutchinson, innkeeper, next door to Joel Williams.

No. 44, Volume IV, Wednesday, 1 June 1803, Whole No. 200

(part of this issue is missing)

Samuel Wilson, living on the waters of Dicks Creek about four miles from the Big Praire, reports a stray mare.

No. 46, Volume IV, Wednesday, 15 June 1803, Whole No. 202

Adj. Gen. Samuel Finley, in Chillicothe, regarding orders to the militia.

A note regarding the Indians' attack on Daniel Wall, Joseph White and Mr. Stapleton on their way from Natchez to Washington, Kentucky. Mentions Mr. Patterson living near Lexington.

An unsigned letter to a friend in Cincinnati mentions Capt. Nathan Lamme, Gov. & Mrs. Tiffin, Mr. Bagges of Green County, Mr. Lowry from Mad River.

An unsigned letter to the public mentions Mr. M'Millan, Judge Symmes, Mr. Morrow, William Goforth and William M'Millan.

Sheriff James Smith regarding the upcoming election lists the polling places: John Benefield's in White Water township, Joseph Colby's in Miami township, Samuel Muchmore's in Columbia township, Thomas Brown's in Anderson township, Mr. Ayrs' in the town of Montgomery, Jonathan Pitman's in Springfield township, and John Harryman's in Colerain township.

Lieut. Col. Cors. R. Sedam regarding meetings of the militia to be held at the houses of Joseph Colby in Miami township, John Benefield in Whitewater township, and John Harryman in Colerain township. Mentions Col. Gano and Col. Ludlow.

Jacob Sample lost a black leather pocket book including notes from John Smith of Round Bottom and from Cheniah Cavalt. Deliver to John Smith's Mill or

Col. Enoch's Mill on Great Miami.

Samuel Goudy says his wife, Elizabeth, left him and he won't pay her bills.

Samuel Hilditch has a new shipment of goods at his store in Columbia.

William M'Farland regarding a meeting of the Nova Caesaria Lodge.

B. Chambers has a farm for sale where he formerly lived on Mad River. He also has land for sale that includes Yellow Medical Springs. Apply to James Smith or Daniel C. Cooper (at Dayton).

E. Hutchinson, in Cincinnati, has opened a house of entertainment in the house formerly occupied by Mr. Felty next door to Joel Williams on Water Street.

Oliver Spencer, in Columbia, reports a runaway apprentice, William Crole.

James Gibson has commenced the reed making business in Cincinnati.

John & Matthew Nimmo have a shipment of goods at their Cincinnati store.

No. 47, Volume IV, Wednesday, 22 June 1803, Whole No. 203

Michael Baldwin and Nath. Massie regarding more laws of Ohio.

Ezra Spencer writes a letter to the editor in answer to a recent letter.

Election returns from Cincinnati and Columbia townships include William M'Millan, William Goforth, Jeremiah Morrow, Elias Langham, James Ewing, James Lyon, Isaac Bates, John Mahard and Enos Hurin.

Directors of the Miami Exporting Company are elected: Martin Baum, Daniel Symmes, Samuel C. Vance, Christian Waldsmith, William C. Schenck, John Bigger, William Lytle, Matthew Heuston, Jesse Hunt, Daniel Mayo, Israel Ludlow.

A notice is printed regarding the upcoming 4th of July celebration by the pupils of the Cincinnati Academy.

Joseph Prince and John Reily regarding ordinances of Cincinnati.

William Stanley, in Cincinnati, regarding a meeting of the militia at Hugh M'Collom's in Cincinnati.

Daniel Conner & Company ask those indebted to them to settle their bills.

Robert Brasher, in Cincinnati, has lead for sale and wants to buy furs.

Abraham Hosier says his wife, Polly, left him, and he won't pay her debts.

William Goforth, Commissioner, regarding land for rent.

Carpenter & Findley ask those indebted to them to settle their accounts in wheat to Waldsmith's Mill.

Isaac Zane, at the head of Mad River, writes a letter to Elias Langham and Duncan M'Arthur in Chillicothe. He includes a letter from the Wiandot chiefs that is witnessed by Sam. M'Collock and James Robitaile.

Gov. Edward Tiffin, by William Creighton, Jun., (Secretary of State), writes a letter to the Wiandot and Mingo nations. Mentions Capt. Herod, James M'Pherson.

No. 49, Volume IV, Wednesday, 6 July 1803, Whole No. 205

An unsigned letter to Mr. Willis, editor of the Scioto Gazette, regarding the murder of Polly Malony, age 9, by John Rowe, late of Kentucky and her uncle by marriage. Mentions Polly's step-father (William Thomas), Thomas Rowe and Amos Ellis & Alexander Martin (justices of the peace at Williamsburgh).

Leonard Wolff, living on Bear Creek about seven miles from Dayton on the west side of the Great Miami River, reports a strayed horse and mare.

John Hedger regarding a bond to John Cleves Symmes for land claimed by John R. Mills.

Reports on Fourth of July celebrations at Cincinnati and Columbia mention Hugh M'Collom, Mr. Ewing, Maj. David Zeigler, John Cleves Symmes, Edward Tiffin, Thos. Frazer, Col. Oliver Spencer, Jacob Blasdell, Col. John Armstrong, Gov. St.Clair, Col. John S. Gano, Doctor Stites, Mr. Seaman, Capt. James Smith, Light Infantry Company, Mr. Anderson, Mr. Ruffin.

Election returns in Ross County mention Elias Langham, Jeremiah Morrow, Michael Baldwin and William M'Millan.

Ezra Spencer, in Cincinnati, regarding "the concurrence between him and Revd. Matthew Wallace relative to the school in this town". Spencer is opening another school in Cincinnati.

Sutherland & Brown regarding a mare found by the Shawney Indians.

Vance & Dill has a new shipment of goods for sale at their store in the house formerly occupied by Smith & Findlay in Cincinnati.

Daniel Conner & Company, in Cincinnati, want to buy pork and corn.

Henry Ker, at Mr. Washburn's in Cincinnati, regarding his still erected in the still house belonging to J. & A. Hunt.

Thomas Harper, living on Mad River Road six miles from Cincinnati, reports a mare that strayed or was stolen.

Robert M'Clure, living at Big Hill about a half mile from Springfield Meeting House, 15 miles from Cincinnati on the road to Fort Hamilton, has a farm for sale.

Martin Baum and Daniel Mayo list the directors of the Miami Exporting Company: Jesse Hunt, Martin Baum, William Lytle, Daniel Symmes, Daniel Mayo, Matthew Huston and Christian Waldsmith. They mention William Stanley and Griffin Yeatman.

John S. Wills regarding the publication of the laws of Ohio.

James M. Bradford regarding the publication of "Notes on the Navigation of the Mississippi".

No. 50, Volume IV, Wednesday, 13 July 1803, Whole No. 206

Michael Baldwin and Nath. Massie print more of the laws of Ohio.

Election returns mention Jeremiah Morrow, William M'Millan, Elias Langham, Michael Baldwin, John Byland, and Philemon Beecher.

An account of the Fourth of July Celebration at Franklin on Big Miami.

William Stanley, in Cincinnati, regarding the meeting of directors of the Miami Exporting Company mentions Martin Baum, Israel Ludlow, Daniel Symmes, William Lytle, Samuel C. Vance, Daniel Mayo, Jesse Hunt & Christian Waldsmith.

A list of letters left at the Post Office in Cincinnati includes James Auld (taylor), Joseph Avery on Little Miami, Thomas Airs on the Ohio 15 miles from Cincinnati, S. Alsey, Archibald Armstrong 30 miles from Cincinnati, John Burger, James Bruff on Little Miami, James Bill, Joseph Blossom on Seven Mile Creek, Robert Ballentine in Franklin, Charles Barnes near Fort Hamilton, Thomas Boone at Round Bottom, John Briney on Little Miami, John Cherry, Noah Crane, Senr., Sarah Clifford, William Cooley at the mouth of the Great Miami, Peter Causel and Peter Cartrow in Franklin, William Dick, Maj. T. Doyle, Capt. Lewis Day at Franklin, John Day, Peter Davis in Springfield, Joseph Edwards, Robert Eaton at Deerfield, Col. John Gray at Great Miami Village, Abraham Garrison, Ann Horsley in Boon County, David Howe on the Geo.town Road, J. Hannah in care of Thomas Wilson, Capt. William Hays, Jacob Heuthorn at Beagles Station, John Jackson at Columbia, Moses Kitchel, Richard Kirby near Taylors Mill, William Legg, John Maxwell in Springfield, David M'Caw on the Georgetown road, Joseph Martin in care of B. Griffith, Moses Moorehead at Waynesville, Jonathan Mercer on Mad River, Richard Martin, Patrick M'Carty on White Water, James M'Ginnes, Peter Newcumber on White Water, Thomas Owry at Columbia, Matthias Ross, Andrew Rogers in care of Nath. Reeder, Robert Richey at Big Hill, John Robinson on Clear Creek, William Richardson, Usual Osborn on Big Prairie, John Richardson, Samuel Robison, Joseph Reeder on Little Miami, Jonathan Schofield at Deerfield, Moses Rumney near Williamsburgh, Simeon Sanders, John Smith on White Water, Samuel Stites at Miami, Francis Settle, John Sewell at Todds Fork, Samuel Trousdale on Dicks Creek, Luther Tilson, Senr., on Mill Creek, Henry Jice at Round Bottom, George Turner, David Vail near Columbia, William VanWinkle on Mill Creek, Samuel Walker on Miami, James Wilson on the South Branch of Great Miami, Leonard Wolff on Bear Creek, Dennas Woodruff in Springfield. Entered by William Ruffin, postmaster.

James Taylor, at Newport in Campbell County, Kentucky, about the arsenal for arms to be built at Newport.

John Armstrong, in Columbia, wants to buy corn.

John Beazley, on Little Miami 6 miles from the mouth, reports a stray mare.

There are scythes for sale at Weaver & Martin's store.

Isaac Hoff, living opposite the Prarie in Lemmon township, Butler County, reports a strayed mare.

Ross Crosley, living on the headwaters of Mill Creek five miles from Cincinnati, reports a strayed mare.

No. 51, Volume IV, Wednesday, 20 July 1803, Whole No. 207

Matthew Nimmo's speech to the Republicans of Cincinnati on July Fourth.

A proclamation is printed from Gov. Edward Tiffin regarding the Treaty of Greenville with the Indians.

Gov. Edward Tiffin's speech to the Indians is printed & mentions Capt. Herod.

A note regarding the murder, near Shelbyville, of Miss Bean by a slave belonging to Stephen Smith of Shelby County.

A letter to Mr. Reeder of Cincinnati about the U.S. purchase of Louisiana.

Election returns mention William M'Millan, Jeremiah Morrow, Elias Langham, William Goforth, Michael Baldwin, William M'Mullan, William M'Intire.

Carpenter & Findlay ask those indebted to them to settle their accounts by delivering wheat to Waldsmith's, White's, Ludlow's or Grummon's mills.

An unsigned letter to the editor regarding the Artillery Company mentions Capt. M'Farland and Tabor Washburn.

Marriage: Christian Hageman, of Hamilton County, to Miss Jane Harckless, of Warren County, on Thursday, 7 July 1803, by Rev. Mr. Kemper.

John S. Gano, in Cincinnati, regarding a meeting of the Associate Judges of Hamilton County.

Elijah Craig, at his paper mill in Georgetown, Kentucky, reports a runaway slave, a mulatto named James Adams.

Henry Ker, in Cincinnati, regarding patent rights for his still, mentions Tabor Washburn in Cincinnati.

William James writes a letter to the inhabitants of Warren County resigning as Associate Judge.

John Simpson lost a pocket book on the road between Esquire Deaths and Franklin. It includes notes on Robt. Williams and Samuel G. Martin to Anthony Arnold. He mentions Mr. Enock and Mr. Vannest.

John Brady regarding the land of James Brady, dec'd, now claimed by Doctor Calvin Morrell.

Samuel Wilson, living on the waters of Dicks Creek about four miles from Big Prarie, reports a strayed mare.

No. 52, Volume IV, Wednesday, 27 July 1803, Whole No. 208

Michael Baldwin and Nath. Massie print more of the laws of Ohio.

William M'Farland regarding the letter in the last paper about him.

T. Washburn & D. Christy regarding the letter about Capt. M'Farland mention Capt. Symmes.

An account of the Fourth of July celebration at Dicks' Creek.

Officers of the Artillery Company are elected: Capt. William M'Farland, Lieut. David Christy and Lieut. Aquila Wheeler.

An account of an accident in which William and Thomas Bermagem, brothers, drowned in Massie's Creek.

A list of letters left at the Post Office in Williamsburgh includes Samuel Boyd at Williamsburgh, William Crossley of Clermont Co., John Stewart at Williamsburgh, William Walker at Waynesville on Little Miami, Anthony Williams on Little Miami near Deerfield. William Lytle is postmaster.

Carpenter & Findlay say the Western Spy will now be published by Joseph Carpenter & Company. Those indebted to them should settle their accounts.

Capt. James Smith regarding a Cincinnati Light Infantry Company meeting.

James Finnie, living in Woodford County, Kentucky, regarding a runaway slave named Billey.

John C. Winans, physician and surgeon, "has returned from New York" and has medicines for sale at his office near Beedle's Station.

David J. Poor regarding his butchering business in Cincinnati. He wants to buy beef and sheep.

Archibald Armstrong, living in Butler County near Seven Mile Creek about nine miles above Fort Hamilton, reports a stray mare.

No. 1, Volume V, Wednesday, 3 August 1803, Whole No. 209

Michael Baldwin and Sam. Huntington regarding the laws of Ohio.

A letter from Pres. Tho. Jefferson to Gov. Tiffin is printed.

A note regarding seats of justice for the new counties mentions Mr. Hathaway on Turtle Creek about five miles from Deerfield.

Jeremiah Morrow is elected representative to Congress over David Abbott, William M'Millan, Michael Baldwin, Elias Langham, William Goforth, Bazaleel Wells, and William M'Mullan.

Tabor Washburn regarding a meeting of the Republicans of Cincinnati at George Fithian's house in Cincinnati.

John & Matthew Nimmo want to buy wheat at Ludlow's and Grummon's mills.

Patrick Dicky wants to hire an apprentice to the tayloring business.

Sarah Shaw and Judah Willey, administrators of the estate of John Shaw, late of Colerain, dec'd, regarding the estate settlement.

Thomas Williams regarding a bond to Ephraim Doughty of Rockbridge Co., Va.

Catherine M'Clean regarding claims against Levi M'Clean.

No. 2, Volume V, Wednesday, 10 August 1803, Whole No. 210

Michael Baldwin and Sam. Huntington regarding more new laws of Ohio.

D. Keasbey has returned from Detroit with furs for his hatting business. He also wants to hire an apprentice to the hatting business.

Squire Little, M.D., in Springfield, physician and surgeon, has moved from Cincinnati to John Lyon's, one mile from Pitman's Tavern on the road to Hamilton.

Aaron Jenkins, living on the headwaters of Clear Creek, reports a stray horse.

No. 3, Volume V, Wednesday, 17 August 1803, Whole No. 211

Lieut. Col. John S. Gano and Lieut. William Ruffin regarding a meeting of the First Regiment of Hamilton County Militia at Charles Avery's place.

James Smith, Collector of the Revenue, regarding duties on stills.

Nathan Lamme regarding his plans to erect a mill dam on Little Miami. He mentions John Cleves Symmes' patent.

James Long, living about five miles below Fort Hamilton on the west side of Big Miami, reports a strayed horse.

W.C. Schenck, at Franklin, wants to hire a schoolmaster.

Robert Benham wants to hire a schoolmaster at the new school house on his farm on Turtle Creek two miles above Deerfield in Warren County.

John Mansfield, taylor, regarding his shop in Cincinnati.

Isaiah Orr, in Springfield, reports a stray horse and mentions David Walker.

No. 5, Volume V, Wednesday, 31 August 1803, Whole No. 213

Daniel Kain, Deputy Sheriff of Clermont County, regarding a prisoner who escaped from the jail: John Rowe, age 27. Rowe's parents live in the Lexington Valley, Pa. He lived near Washington, Kentucky, but lately lived in Clermont County, Pleasant township. He raped and murdered his wife's niece.

Lieut. Col. John S. Gano and Lieut. William Ruffin give orders for the First Regiment of Hamilton Militia.

Thomas Ramsey, Cincinnati, says he will no longer lend his horse to anyone.

Benjamin Green, living in Fayette County, Kentucky, near Bryan's Station, reports runaway slaves, John and a woman belonging to Benjamin Howard.

Israel Marsh says his wife, Sarah Marsh, is insane and has left him. He warns everyone that he will not honor any debts she might contract.

Jacob Wheeler, Cincinnati, reports runaway apprentice, James Lewis, age 18.

No. 6, Volume V, Wednesday, 7 September 1803, Whole No. 214

F. Dunlavy and A. Wallace about a meeting of the Republican Corresponding Society at the house of John Beaty. They nominated the following as representatives to the Legislature: Daniel Symmes and John W. Browne of Hamilton County; John Bigger of Warren County; Isaac S. Swearingin of Butler Co.; Stephen Wood and Adrian Hagerman of Hamilton County; Ezekiel Ball of Butler County; Ephraim Kibby of Warren County; John Sterritt and James Snowden of Green Co.; Abner Gerrard and James Thompson of Montgomery County.

A note that the Western Spy office has moved into a new building on Main

Street opposite the Meeting House.

An organizational meeting for the Cincinnati Fair will be at Isaac Anderson's.

Capt. James Smith about meetings of the Cincinnati Light Infantry Company at Mr. Yeatman's and Isaac Anderson's.

Sheriff James Smith regarding a sheriff's sale of the property of Mary Reed at the suit of Abijah Hunt and Cornelius R. Sedam.

James Denning, living in St. Clair township, Butler County, reports a stray horse. It formerly belonged to Mr. Wheaton who now lives near Chillicothe.

J. & M. Nimmo, in Cincinnati, wants to buy wheat at Ludlow's or Grummon's.

John Carlisle, Collector of Virginia Army Lands, at Chillicothe, regarding taxes due on non-residents' lands.

John Lyttle, at Williamsburgh in Clermont County, about a stolen mare.

No. 9, Volume V, Wednesday, 28 September 1803, Whole No. 217

A note regarding nominations for the legislature mentions Mr. Beaty, John Ludlow, I.B. Miller, William Schenck, John Bigger, Ephraim Kibby, Samuel Dick, William Ward, John Wallace, William Snodgrass, Thomas Smith, William Dodds, and John Armstrong.

A list of persons nominated to public office includes Daniel Symmes, John W. Brown, John Bigger, Isaac Swearingin, Stephen Wood, Ephraim Kibby, Ichabod B. Miller, Abner Gerrard, John Sterret, Adrian Hagerman, Ezekiel Ball, James Thompson, John Wallace, James Snowden, John Ludlow, William Ludlow. Samuel Dick and William M'Clure in Butler County. Wm. C. Schenck, John Bigger and Ephraim Kibby in Warren County. William Ward and Andrew Reed in Green Co. William Dodds in Montgomery County. William M'Clure, Isaac Reed, William M'Clelland, Samuel Kennedy and Samuel Dick in Lemmon township, Butler County.

Joseph C. Vance has lots for sale in Xenia. Apply to John Paul.

Moses Hutchins regarding a bond to John Cleves Symmes.

James Mapes, at North Bend, regarding a stray mare.

Thomas Ramsey makes wheat fans, also known as windmills.

John S. Gano regarding the election to be held at the house of James Harden in Colerain township.

Gov. William Henry Harrison and Secretary John Gibson about an ordinance of the Indiana Territory.

Christian Waldsmith about his fulling mill operated by Wm. Campbell, fuller.

William Clark about payments due for the Western Spy. Pay Thomas Clark, the present post rider.

D. Murray, at Waynesville, has land for sale on Todd's Fork.

J. Carpenter & Company ask those indebted to them to settle their accounts with wheat delivered to Mr. Waldsmith's, John Smith's, Mr. Ludlow's, Mr. White's and Mr. Grummon's Mills.

Sheriff James Smith regarding the upcoming elections to replace Francis Dunlavy and Jeremiah Morrow who both resigned.

No. 10, Volume V, Wednesday, 5 October 1803, Whole No. 218

Capt. Daniel Symmes regarding meetings of his company of militia at Mr. Avery's and at Ludlow's Mill.

John Wilson and John M'Knight are nominated to the legislature from Green County.

James Maranda, of Warren County, regarding the erroneous report circulated by James Armstrong who lives near Deerfield. It includes depositions of Joseph Case, Joseph Halfield and Samuel Tarrants.

No. 11, Volume V, Wednesday, 12 October 1803, Whole No. 219

Results of the election in Cincinnati township mention John Ludlow, William Ward, Daniel Symmes, Mr. Swearingin, W.C. Schenck, John Bigger, John W. Brown, E. Kibby, Sam. Dick, John Wallace, A. Reed, Wm. M'Clure, Wm. Ludlow, E. Ball, I.B. Miller, Stephen Wood, Mr. Snowden, James Thompson, A. Hagerman, John Sterrett, A. Gerrard.

A list of letters left at the Post Office in Cincinnati includes John Allen in

Hamilton, Hugh Brownlee in Butler County, James Brownlee, Sen., James Barnes, Samuel Boyle, James Bell 38 miles up the Little Miami, James Bruce in care of Joshua Carmon, Rev. Elisha Bowman, Anthony Burne at Colerain, Ezekiel Bell 35 miles up the Little Miami, Stephen Bollingar in care of William Buckner at Brackin, William Brand, Capt. James Colwell, Ebenezer Case at Deerfield, Joshua Carmon, Hezekiah Clark, James Cole in White Water, Joseph Carson in Deerfield, Daniel Cunningham and James Adaire, John Cotcher, Oliver Crawford, Sarah Clifford in care of Michael Harness, Walter Cox near Franklin, Aaron Cherry at White Water, John Cherry, jun., at White Water, John Day near Franklin, Jesse Dodd on Mill Creek, Amos Ellis in Clermont County, William Ellis in Clermont County, Capt. Reece Gaddis, Joseph Gould, Ezekial Hughes, John Harriman, Isreal Harris, Ebenezer Heaton in Franklin, Lowrence Hoover in Waynesville, Joseph Hanna, Aaron Jenkins on Caesars Creek, Henry Jennings on Duck Creek, Joseph Jones on Little Miami, Nathaniel Knotts in Montgomery County, Peter Kettro in Franklin, Peter Keene, Nathan Kelly in Warren County, Stephen Linsay at Miami, Henry Ludlow at Round Bottom, Doctor David at Lootborough at Dunham's Town, Jonathan Mercer at Mad River, Francis M'Cormac at Little Miami, James Milligan near Dayton, William Martindale in Warren County, Robert Moorehead, Jonathan M'Carty in Dearborn County, Samuel Martin, Mary Martin in Warren County, James M'Clelland 25 miles from Cincinnati, Alexander Martin at Colerain, Thomas Matthews, Robert M'Ginnis on Clear Creek, William M'Cain, Aaron Nutt, Joseph Potter, James Perine in Lawrenceburg, Richard Parsel in Deerfield, John Patton at Deer Creek, Isaac Perkins in Waynesville, Isabel Pike, Abner and Elizabeth Rude, Robert Robison in care of Isaac Anderson, Samuel Robb at Big Prarie, Nathan Rumsey at Big Prarie, Andrew Rogers on Mill Creek, Capt. Ziba Stibbins, Capt. John Shaw, Joseph Shaylor, John Stout, Elias Shomaker, Jonas Seaman in care of John Seaman in Columbia, Amelia Sullivan, Samuel Stewart in Deerfield, William Slaget in care of William Hunter, John Horner Smith, Elder John Smith, Jesse Simpson on Seven Mile Creek, Peter Smith, John Toomy, Christopher Troy on Cluff Creek, James Throckmorton, Samuel Tibbals in Franklin, John Templeton at White Water, Abraham Voorheese, John Wilson on the South west branch of the Great Miami, Joseph Wilson, Doctor Joseph Walker near Fort Hamilton, Anthony Williams in Warren County, Adam Woods in care of Sutherland & Brown. Entered by William Ruffin, postmaster.

Malcom Worley regarding a horse that strayed from Taylor's Creek. Deliver to Aaron Tullis on Turtle Creek.

Oliver Spencer says the partnership of Spencer, Gano, Crane & Company is dissolved. Those indebted to the firm should settle their accounts.

Ar. St.Clair, in Cincinnati, has given his black servants, Tony and his wife, Winney, permission to find employment for themselves.

No. 12, Volume V, Wednesday, 19 October 1803, Whole No. 220

John Cleves Symmes, regarding College township, mentions Mr. Boudinot.

Election results mention W.C. Schenck, Daniel Symmes, John Ludlow, John W. Brown, John Bigger, William Ward, Isaac Swearingin, William C. Schenck, Ephraim Kibby, William Dodds, Abner Gerrard, Samuel Dick, William M'Clure, Andrew Reed, John Wallace, Mr. Miller, Stephen Wood, Ezekiel Ball, John Sterrett, James Snowden, William Ludlow, Adrian Hagerman and James Thompson.

William M'Farland, Clerk of the Sup. Courts, regarding the petition filed by Jacob Burnet about the division of a tract of land into 8 parts. The parts are to be assigned to said Jacob Burnet, John Burnet, Hannah Kinney, Eliza Thew, Isaac G. Burnet, States Burnet, David Burnet, and the remaining part to be split by Abigail J. Riggs, Mary Hornblower, Joseph Burnet, William Burnet, Ichabod Burnet, Hannah Burnet and Caroline Burnet.

Matthew G. Wallace, in Cincinnati, regarding his school's upcoming term.

James Forguson has salt and lead for sale. He also has dry goods & groceries.

Hannah Willis, in Cincinnati, regarding her petition of divorce from her husband, Isaac Willis.

A note announces a meeting, at Mr. Anderson's, about the Cincinnati Horse Races. Enter horses with Henry Weaver.

No. 15, Volume V, Saturday, 5 November 1803, Whole No. 223, The Spy Extra

Thomas Dugan just arrived in town from Philadelphia with goods for sale.

Jacob Richeson, living on Twin Creek six miles from Franklin on the west side of the Great Miami River, reports a stray horse.

Fredrick Nutts, living near Franklin at Big Miami, reports he found a mare.

John Acreman, regarding Andrew Small's hogs, mentions Daniel M'Donnal.

John Sellman, in Cincinnati, asks those indebted to him to settle their bills by delivering wheat to Jacob White's Mill.

Jacob Reeder reports a runaway bound boy named John Clark, age 15.

Benjamin Bridge, in Lemmon Township, Butler County, about a stray horse.

James Smith, Sheriff, about the suit of Gershom Gard vs. John C. Symmes.

John Benefiel, living on the Dry Fork of White Water, reports a stray mare.

Daniel Kain, for Sheriff John Boude, in Williamsburgh, regarding horses stolen by William M'Kinnis, late of Williamsburgh in Clermont County.

Ichabod Corwin, Silas Hurin and Ephraim Hathaway, in Warren County, about a sale of lots in the town of Lebanon. The sale to be held at Hathaway's Tavern.

No. 18, Volume V, Wednesday, 30 November 1803, Whole No. 226

Joseph Prince and Daniel Symmes regarding an ordinance of Cincinnati.

J. & M. Nimmo, in Cincinnati, have a new shipment of goods for sale.

John Townesley about a bond to James Lemmon of Georgetown, Kentucky, for land on Massie's Creek in the Northwest Territory.

Zenas Hill lost a green morocco pocket book between Columbia & Cincinnati. It includes a note for wheat payable to Christian Waldsmith's Mill. Deliver to William Ruffin in Cincinnati.

Francis Luke, living at the headwaters of Clear Creek three miles from Waynesville, reports a stray mare.

John Ludlow asks those indebted to him to settle their accounts with wheat delivered to Ludlow's Mill on Mill Creek or pork delivered to Joel Williams in Cincinnati or John Mahard.

Andrew Glass and Jacob Cotts have chairs, settees, and cradles for sale at their shop in Cincinnati.

Robert M'Clure reports a stray mare. Deliver to James M'Cormack in Springfield.

Cor. R. Sedam has a farm for sale. Apply to Wm. M'Clelland at Hamilton.

Vance & Dill want to buy pork, flour and deerskins.

No. 19, Volume V, Wednesday, 7 December 1803, Whole No. 227

John W. Browne is appointed Recorder for Hamilton County.

Marriage: William Woodward to Miss Abigail Cutter, both of Cincinnati, on Tuesday, 29 November 1803, in Warren County.

A note regarding the robbery of Elisha Winters on his way to Natchez.

Ebenezer Fisher regarding a bond to John C. Symmes for land.

Benjamin VanHook, in Cincinnati, has a house for sale. He also has household goods and furniture for sale.

Joab Comstock about town lots in Crosby, about 3 miles from Mr. Williams' Mill, adjoining Comstock's Ferry on the Great Miami opposite Colerain, on the road from White Water & Thomas Smith's Mill to Hamilton and Cincinnati. Apply to Capt. M'Farland in Cincinnati.

Hugh M'Cullom, in Cincinnati, reports a strayed mare.

Weaver & Martin wants to buy fur and bear skins at their store in Cincinnati.

Levi M'Clean regarding a power of attorney to Catharine M'Clean.

J. Carpenter & Co. ask those indebted to them to pay their bills in wheat.

Samuel Moore says his wife, Hannah, left him and he won't pay her bills.

No. 20, Volume V, Wednesday, 14 December 1803, Whole No. 228

Capt. James Smith regarding a meeting of the Cincinnati Infantry.

Oliver Spencer regarding the appointment of John W. Brown as Recorder of Hamilton County. The records are kept at the house of Griffin Yeatman.

No. 21, Volume V, Wednesday, 21 December 1803, Whole No. 229

Nath. Massie is chosen Speaker of the Senate and Thomas Scott, clerk. Elias Langham is Speaker of the House and James Mason, clerk.

John Whetstone, living on the Ohio River near the mouth of Little Miami, reports that he found a stray mare.

Ezra Spencer regarding persons stealing wood from Maj. Peyton Short's land.

Weaver & Martin moved to the new brick building opposite their former store.

Thomas M'Cullough has a new shipment of goods for sale at his store in Mount Pleasant two miles from Fort Hamilton.

Edward Robinson, living near the mouth of Beaver Creek on Little Miami, reports a stray horse. Deliver to Philip Turpin in Middletown or Isaac Anderson in Cincinnati.

Samuel Arbuckle, living on Hammon's Creek in Franklin County, Kentucky, reports a runaway slave named Morris. He has a pass signed by Charles Allin, Robert Blackwell, William Payne and Stephen Arnold.

John S. Gano asks those indebted to Gano & Stanley to settle their accounts. He also has land for sale near Parson Kemper's on the hill 2 miles from Cincinnati.

Edward Tiffin's address to the legislature of Ohio is printed.

No. 22, Volume V, Wednesday, 28 December 1803, Whole No. 230

Daniel Conner & Company moved their store to the house formerly occupied by Thomas Gibson in Cincinnati. They have a new shipment of goods for sale.

J. & M. Nimmo, in Cincinnati, have a new shipment of goods for sale.

Samuel Hilditch has a shipment of goods for sale at his store in Columbia.

E.W. Finney, living on Mill Creek two miles from Ludlow's Mill, found a mare.

Sheriff James Smith regarding sheriff's sales, at the house of Charles Avery, of the property of the following: Mary Reed at the suit of Hunt & Sedam; Samuel French at the suit of Daniel Conner and Oliver Ormsby; Jesse Grant (adjoining James White and James Moor) at the suit of Mary John; James Thruston at the suit of John M'Cullagh; John Parcel at the suit of Ferdinand Brokaw; James Cox at the suit of John C. Symmes; Michael Brokaw at the suits of William Woodward, Azariah Ayres and Cornelius Vorheese; Thomas Goudy at the suit of Robert Wilson; Michael and Ferdinand Brokaw at the suit of William Ryon; Cornelius and Minny Vorheese at the suit of Daniel Hammit; Joseph Totton at the suit of Charles Patterson; James Davis at the suit of Jacob Allen; David Bay and William M'Cann at the suit of Samuel Robb.

No. 23, Volume V, Wednesday, 4 January 1804, Whole No. 231

A note regarding a resolution in the legislature is signed by Ephraim Kibbey, James Smith, Abner Garrard, William M'Clure, Daniel Feagans, David Abbot, Josiah Dillon, Samuel Dick, Jesse Fulton, Philemon Beecher, John Wallace, J.B. Miller and Jonathan Taylor.

William M'Farland regarding a meeting of the Nova Caesaria Lodge.

John Cleves Symmes writes a letter to the public regarding the land between the Great and Little Miami Rivers.

William Stanley, Clerk and Agent at Cincinnati, regarding a meeting of the Miami Exporting Company at Griffin Yeatman's. He mentions Martin Baum, Israel Ludlow, Daniel Mayo, Jesse Hunt, Matthew Huston and Christian Waldsmith.

Wm. Stanley has a new shipment of goods for sale at his store in Cincinnati.

C. Avery has a lot for sale on Main Street in Cincinnati.

A list of letters at the Post Office in Cincinnati includes Edmond Buxton, John Bridges, Archibald Armstrong, Ebenezer Ayer, Frederick Bouner, Elijah P. Barrous, Sally Broadwell, Arthur Buchanon, Jonathan Bragdon, Francis Dunlavy, Robert Benham, William Broderick, Mary Carter, Samuel Cory, Noah Crane, Maj. Benjamin Chambers, Ruth Crane, David Davis, James Dunn, John Donald, Stephen Davis, Isaac Dexter, Jeremiah French, Francis H. Gaines, Jesse Geoung, Richard Heirs, Nicholas Holner, Jacob Highday, John Howard, Jeremiah Hall, Alexander Hamilton, Samuel Hindman, Huhey Hagan, Thadeus Handford, John Hagerman, Margaret Hagerman, Thomas John, Joseph Jenkinson, Henry Jennings, Rachal Johnson, Christian King, Andrew Lewis, Elisha Landon, David Lewis, Robert Luse,

Daniel Landon, William Moore, Jacob Miller, William Mahon, Samuel M'Cray, Rev. Robert Marshall, Hans Morrison, Richard Martin, Samuel Martin, James Matthews, James Miller, Mary M'Ginnes, Robert M'Kay, Daniel Mulford, David Myers, John M'Cane, John Mullin, John Nelson, William Nevil, John Nichols, John Nancarrow, Senr., Jabish Phillips, Isaac Patton, Isabela Pike, Emanuel Felter Rees, Elizabeth Reed, John Runyon, Philip Rowan, Jacob Robison, Samuel Riker, Mary Rodgers, Isaac Swearingen, Thomas Stone, Joseph Silver, James Silver, Abigail Seward, Andrew Stewart, Samuel Shepherd, M'Kegah Simonds, William Shannon, Thomas Smith, Charles Smith, Capt. John Smith, Jesse Simpson, Isaac Seward, Michael Shots, Isaac Sparks, Col. C.R. Sedam, Isaac Thomas, Rev. John Thompson, Garet Vanest, Peter Wilcox, W. Wilson, Isaac Wilson, James White, Major W. Wells, Andrew Wakefield, Joseph Wilson, Junr., Peter Weaver, Cornelius Westfall, Brown Wilson, Robert Wilson, Josiah Wilson, Jacob Zeller, Jun., William Ruffin.

No. 25, Volume V, Wednesday, 25 January 1804, Whole No. 234

Obituary: Israel Ludlow, age 38, Register of the Land Office and Colonel Commandant of the Third Regiment of Hamilton County Militia, died on Saturday morning, 20 January 1804, at his farm near Cincinnati, leaving a wife and children. He was buried on Monday, 23 January, with a eulogy delivered by John Cleves Symmes. A memorial sermon will be delivered by Rev. Mr. Wallace.

An unsigned letter to the editor regarding Judge Symmes and the Miami Purchase mentions College Township.

Abraham Cary, living on Mill Creek, reports a stray mare.

Obituary: John Patton, of Ross County, committed suicide by hanging himself on "Thursday morning last". He left a wife and ten children.

Edward Miller, in Columbia, lost a pocket book on the road from Deerfield to Columbia between Maj. David Sutton's and Mr. Ayres' tavern. It includes a note to Jacob Teal signed by Ezekiel Dimett and signed over to Ed. Miller. Also a note from Return Jonathan Meigs and papers signed by Joseph Shaylor.

Edward H. Stall, Druggist & Apothecary, "just arrived from Baltimore" and opened a store in the house formerly occupied by Mr. Ramsey, in Cincinnati, under the sign of John Stall & Son.

John W. Browne, Recorder for Hamilton County, regarding the Recorder's Office in the house of Capt. William M'Farland.

Samuel Smith, in Cincinnati, regarding a certificate for land granted to Samuel Smith of Kentucky.

William Clark asks those indebted for subscriptions to the Spy to pay him.

Vance & Dill asks those indebted to them to settle their accounts. They also have a new shipment of goods for sale at their store.

Thomas Dugan, in Cincinnati, has a farm for sale.

No. 45, Volume V, Thursday, 7 June 1804, Whole No. 253

The governor appointed Lewis Bell/Belt presiding judge in the Court of Common Pleas in the place of Wyllis Silliman who resigned.

Joseph Coleby found a mare five miles below Cincinnati on the Ohio River.

John Armstrong, in Columbia, administrator of Hamilton Armstrong, late of Fort Wayne, dec'd, regarding the estate.

Robert M'Cullah & Son, in Cincinnati, regarding their new store in the house formerly occupied by Smith & Findlay and lately by Vance & Dill.

John Armstrong, in Columbia, about trespassing on the lands of the following: Jonathan Clarke on the Ohio River about two miles above the mouth of the Little Miami; Hite & Robertson below Eight Mile Creek, adjoining Nevil & Nancarrow; Richard C. Anderson on Clough Creek adjoining Widow Hawkins; the heirs of John Anderson on the east side of the Little Miami opposite Armstrong's Mill.

William Ruffin has land for sale on the Ohio River next to Maj. Chambers.

Sheriff James Smith, in Cincinnati, regarding a sheriff's sale of the property of William Wood at the suit of Wm. Goudy, John Bigger and John Sterret, executors of John Lowry, dec'd, and at the suit of Daniel Conner and Oliver Ormsby.

William Goforth, Jun., in Cincinnati, asks those indebted to him to settle their accounts to Alexander King, Constable of Cincinnati township.

John S. Gano regarding a meeting of the commissioners of Hamilton County.

James Russell regarding a mare that strayed or was stolen.

Wm. Stanley lists the directors elected for the Miami Exporting Company: M. Baum, Daniel Mayo, John N.C. Schenck, Jesse Hunt, G. Yeatman, John Riddle, Matthew Huston, Christian Waldsmith, David E. Wade, Charles Kilgore and Samuel C. Vance.

John S. Gano has land for sale to satisfy the creditors of the estate of John Davis, deceased.

Benjamin Stites regarding his ferry across the Ohio River at Columbia.

Thomas Dugan, in Cincinnati, asks those indebted to him to pay their bills.

Seth Cutter, in Cincinnati, reports that he found a stray horse.

The administrators of the estate of Col. Israel Ludlow, dec'd, regarding the estate settlement to be held at William M'Clellan's house in Hamilton and James Conn's house in Cincinnati.

David Shobe, living on the North fork of Paint Creek fifteen miles from Chillicothe, reports a stolen horse.

John Luce regarding his claim of land in Cincinnati district.

Joseph Black regarding a horse that strayed from Waldsmith's Mill.

Seth Cutter reports that he found a mare.

No. 1, Volume VI, Wednesday, 1 August 1804, Whole No. 261

Elias Langham and Nath. Massie print more of the laws of Ohio.

A letter to the governor of Ohio, signed by William Ward, Robert Renick, William Moore, Jesse Brackin, Daniel Robertson, Able Crawford, Joel Newland and Archibald Dowden, regarding Jas. M'Pherson's account of the Indian who killed Capt. Herod.

Unsigned letters to the editor regarding nominations for office mention Wm. M'Farland, Mr. Pritchard, Mr. Massie, Mr. Bigger, William Goforth, Mr. Smith, Mr. Carpenter, Sheriff Smith and Capt. Smith.

John W. Browne regarding a meeting of the Republican Corresponding Society at Williams' Tavern, Matthew Nimmo presiding. They nominate Jeremiah Morrow to Congress and William Goforth, Nathaniel Massie and James Pritchard to be electors. They mention Daniel Symmes and William M'Farland.

Sheriff James Smith regarding sheriff's sales of the following property: that of John Cleves Symmes at the suit of James M'Cashen and Daniel Griffin; that of Benjamin Stites at the suit of Evan Banes and Joseph Meeker; that of Samuel Berry at the suit of George Rich; that of George Fithian at the suit of Martin Noll; that of John Briney at the suit of Edward Ralston; that of Thomas Goudy at the suit of Joel Williams; that of James Moran at the suit of John M'Intire.

Joseph Sawyers, living on Clear Creek near Mad River Road in Franklin township, Warren County, reports a stray horse.

Charles Vattier, in Cincinnati, regarding the property of Robert Montgomery.

Robert Benham has two stills for sale.

Sutherland & Brown, at Hamilton in Butler County, reports a stray horse. Deliver to William Ruffin in Cincinnati.

Benjamin VanHook has household furniture for sale at auction.

Peter Audrain regarding suits in Wayne County, Indiana Territory: Alexander Grant vs. William Robertson; Hugh Jameson & William Shepherd (surviving partners of their late partnership with George Leith and George Shepherd, late merchants in Montreal, Canada, operating as the firm Leith, Jameson & Company) vs. Elias Wallen, late of Detroit.

Bladen Ashby about land he bought with Alexander Chambers in Butler Co.

R. Patterson, living near Dayton, reports a stray mare.

Ralph French, living near Dayton in Montgomery County, about a stray mare.

Samuel Seward, living four miles from Ludlow's Mill on the new Hamilton Road, found a cow.

James Goudy found a heifer.

Mr. Mennessier about a bond to Charles Vattier for land for a Market House.

Daniel Conner & Company, Cincinnati, have a new shipment of goods for sale.

Charles Killgore (Register of the Land Office) and James Findlay (Receiver of Public Monie) regarding land for sale in the Indiana Territory and mention John Cleves Symmes' patent and Ludlow's line.

Samuel Frazey is erecting a Tan Yard in the town of Redding where he'll carry on the tanning and shoemaking businesses.

John & Matthew Nimmo, in Cincinnati, want to buy wheat and pork.

James Forguson wants to buy wheat at White's, Ludlow's, VanHorne's, Smith's and Waldsmith's Mills.

Joseph Prince and Matthew Nimmo regarding the destroyed fence at the public pound.

Levi Woodward has lots near Cincinnati for sale at public auction.

Jacob Williams, in Cincinnati, has nails for sale. He continues making nails in the shop formerly occupied by Cornelius Voorheese opposite Gen. Gano's office.

No. 2, Volume VI, Wednesday, 8 August 1804, Whole No. 262

Elias Langham and Nath. Massie print more of the laws of Ohio.

Samuel Foster, in Cincinnati, wants to hire two apprentices to the tanner and currier's business.

John Crum, living on Great Miami six miles below Hamilton in Butler County, reports a stray horse.

Daniel Conner & Company want to buy pork at their store in Cincinnati.

William Smith, living on the waters of Seven Mile Creek, west of the Great Miami, about a stray horse. Deliver to John Bigger on Dick's Creek.

Samuel Thompson, at Dayton, says that his wife, Catharine Thompson, left him, and he won't honor her debts from now on.

Macbean & Poyzer, in Lexington, Kentucky, regarding a horse stolen from the pasture of Pat. M'Cullough by Obadiah Williams. He took the road from Lexington to Cincinnati past Ewing's Tavern.

Thomas Dugan, in Cincinnati, has sherry wine and mustard for sale. Apply to Isaac Anderson.

Maj. Gen. John S. Gano, by William Ruffin, gives orders to the Militia and mentions Capt. John Hamilton of Warren County and Calvin Ball/Bell.

John S. Gano regarding a meeting of the Commissioners of Hamilton County.

Margaret Ewing, administratrix of the estate of Samuel Ewing, late of Butler County, deceased, regarding the estate settlement.

Thomas Dugan, in Cincinnati, asks those indebted to him to pay their bills.

John S. Gano and Daniel Symmes (attorney) regarding a suit in the Court of Common Pleas, Hamilton County: William Inglish vs. Jacob Green. They mention a note in the hands of Ezekiel Huthison.

No. 3, Volume VI, Wednesday, 15 August 1804, Whole No. 263

An unsigned letter to the editor nominates electors: Bazaleel Wells, John Reily and Benjamin I. Gillman.

A note regarding the carriage tire stolen from between Capt. White's and Charles Moor's. Deliver to Jacob Williams.

John Smith, in Cincinnati, has a new shipment of goods for sale at the house lately occupied by Baum & Thompson. He also says that John Brownson has taken over Smith's business in the country.

Stephen Reeder and Ogden Ross, in Colerain township, Hamilton County, executors of the estate of Robert Hanes, dec'd, regarding the estate sale.

Robert Stubbs about the examinations of the students at Newport Academy.

Daniel Hammitt has moved his nail factory to Wainsville on Little Miami.

James Smith, living on Seven Mile Creek about eight miles above Winton's Mills, Butler County, regarding a strayed mare.

Samuel Hilditch, James Matthews, William Brown, Benjamin Stites and Edward Meeks regarding a meeting, at Samuel Armstrong's Inn in Columbia, about building the Columbia school house.

Rosewell Bartlett, living near Ludlow's Mill, has household furniture, livestock and other goods for sale.

Thomas Williams, in Cincinnati, wants to buy deerskins.

Maxfield Ludlow, living on Mill Creek, reports a strayed horse.

Jacob Burnet has lots for sale.

Christian Myer, living on Bear Creek in German township in Montgomery County, reports a strayed mare.

M. Nimmo's speech to the Masonic Society is printed.

No. 4, Volume VI, Wednesday, 22 August 1804, Whole No. 264

Elias Langham and Nath. Massie print more laws of the State of Ohio.

A note regarding a duel fought at Kaskaskias between William Lowrey (formerly of Lexington, son of Nathaniel Lowrey) and a Mr. Hurd from Georgia in which Lowrey was killed.

A letter to the editor from John Bigger in Warren County regarding his candidacy for elector mentions Mr. Goforth and John W. Browne of Cincinnati.

A letter to the editor from John W. Browne regarding his intention to publish the paper, Liberty Hall, in Cincinnati. He mentions Mr. Carpenter, Mr. Findlay.

A letter to the public from the editors of the Western Spy regarding Browne's accusations mentions Squire Pugh of Waynesville, Sam. Browne (John W. Browne's son) and Mr. Crane.

The deposition of Gersham Gard regarding J.W. Browne's accusations with respect to Mr. Carpenter and Mr. Findlay.

Capt. James Smith regarding a meeting of the Cincinnati Light Infantry.

Vance & Dill, in Cincinnati, ask those indebted to them to pay their bills.

Seth Cutter is "about removing from town" and offers town lots and household furniture for sale.

Rufus Putnam and Saml. Carpenter have lots for sale at Doctor Perkins' house in Athens.

No. 5, Volume VI, Wednesday, 29 August 1804, Whole No. 265

Obituary: Revd. John Gano, age 79, died Thursday evening last, 23 August 1804, at his house near Cincinnati. He served as Chaplain to the army in the Revolutionary War. He was pastor of the Baptist Church in New York City for 30 years until 1788 when he moved to Kentucky. In 1802 he wrote a narrative of his life which will soon be published.

Letters to the editor from John W. Browne mention Mr. Bigger, Maj. Goforth, Thomas Jefferson, and Mr. Clinton.

A letter to John W. Browne from John Bigger mentions Thomas Jefferson, Mr. Clinton and Mr. Livingston.

A letter to the editor from John W. Browne mentions Mr. Findlay.

The editors of the Western Spy answer John W. Browne's letter and include depositions from John & Matthew Nimmo. They mention Squire Pugh of Waynesville, Mr. Browne, Mr. Findlay, Mr. Dill, Jonathan Findlay, Mr. Carpenter.

An unsigned letter to the editor regarding John W. Browne mentions his many occupations: recorder of Hamilton County, trustee of the school section, school master, preacher, taylor and intended editor of the Liberty Hall.

Gov. Harrison's proclamation about elections in Indiana Territory is printed.

John W. Browne about a meeting of the Cincinnati Republican Corresponding Society at Mr. Elmore Williams' house.

Maj. Gen. John S. Gano and Charles Killgore give orders to the Militia. They say that James Findlay is elected brigadier general of the First Brigade. The Third Brigade is to meet at Capt. John Hamilton's house in Butler County and the Fourth Brigade at Calvin Ball's house in Warren County.

David J. Poor, in Cincinnati, has his house, lot & household furniture for sale.

James Richey, in Cincinnati, has commenced the blue dying business in the house lately occupied by James Ewing in Cincinnati. He's also opening a school.

Benjamin Ross and John Ross, in Warren County, administrators of the estate of Robert Ross, late of Warren County, dec'd, regarding the estate settlement.

No. 6, Volume VI, Wednesday, 5 September 1804, Whole No. 266

Elias Langham and Nath. Massie print more of the laws of the State of Ohio.

Christian Cooper, in Kentucky, says his wife, Rachel Cooper, left him, and he won't honor any debts of her contracting.

Patrick Rock, living in Mad River township, reports a stray horse.
Daniel Conner & Company want to buy pork in Cincinnati.
D. Keasbey, in Cincinnati, asks those indebted to him to pay their bills.
Asa Richardson has oxen and miscellaneous farming tools and goods for sale.
David Grummons, in Cincinnati, reports a strayed or stolen horse. Deliver to Jacob Williams in Cincinnati or to Jonathan Pittman.

No. 7, Volume VI, Wednesday, 12 September 1804, Whole No. 267

Various letters to the editor nominate persons for public office and mention Elmore Williams of Cincinnati, Bazella Wells, Nathaniel Massie, John Reily, Elias Langham, Jacob White, Icha. B. Miller, John Wallace, John R. Gaston, David E. Wade, James Smith, Thomas M'Farland, James Pritchard, William Goforth, Henry Ewing, William M'Farland, Jeremiah Morrow, Cornelius Snider, Stephen Wood, Hezekiah Price, Judah Willey, Zebulon Foster, Mr. Carpenter, Daniel Symmes.
Samuel Dick and Solomon Lyons are nominated to represent Butler County.
A note regarding Mr. Goforth's voting record regarding pay for legislators.
An unsigned letter to the editor regarding John W. Browne.
John S. Gano prints a note regarding selling estray animals.
Ebenezer Griffin, living on Twin Creek, four miles from Franklin on the east side of Great Miami, reports a stray cow.
Thomas Shepherd, living in Columbia, reports a runaway apprentice, Thomas Stackhouse, age 19.
Bryson Blackburn, on the Dry fork of White water, reports a stray cow.
P. Dickey reports a stray heifer and cow.
Benjamin Stites, James Maranda and Ephraim Kibby, at Columbia, regarding the estate sale at the house of Benjamin Stites, late of Columbia, dec'd. Also those indebted to the estate should pay their accounts to Samuel Armstrong, innkeeper at Columbia.
Daniel Conner asks those indebted to him to settle their accounts.
Rachel Cooper regarding the ad placed by her husband, Christian Cooper. She says he left her and took all her property.
Thomas C. Wade, near Middletown in Butler County, has land for sale in Duck Creek Settlement 2 miles from Columbia. Apply to John Ferris near the land.
James H. Audrain, at Detroit, declares that Lieut. N. Pinkney of the First U.S. Regiment is "not only a Rascal, but a Coward and an infamous Scoundrel".
Armistead Thompson Mason, of Virginia, has land for sale at Todd's fork.

No. 8, Volume VI, Wednesday, 19 September 1804, Whole No. 268

Elias Langham and Nath. Massie print more laws of Ohio.
Levi M'Clean, in Cincinnati, says he's a candidate for sheriff.
Maj. Gen. John S. Gano and William Ruffin give orders to the Militia.
Culbertson Parks wants to hire an apprentice to the carpenter's business.
Jacob Burnet regarding the publication of Doctor R. M'Whorter's sermons.
Constance M'Millan and William Corry, executors of the estate of William M'Millan, dec'd, regarding the estate settlement.
William Lynes, in Cincinnati, has "just arrived from the city of Baltimore" and opened his taylor's shop in the house lately occupied by Vance & Dill between Doctor Selman and Maj. Zeigler's on Front Street.
Alexander Simpson regarding his divorce from his wife, Rebecca. He says she doesn't get any of his property since he caught her in the act of adultery with two different men: Reuben Doty and John Doty, brothers.

No. 9, Volume VI, Wednesday, 26 September 1804, Whole No. 269

Elias Langham and Nath. Massie print more of the laws of Ohio.
Election returns are printed and mention Ephraim Kibby, Abner Garrard, John Sterret, Ezekiel Ball, Stephen Wood, James Snowden, James Thompson, William Dodds, William Ludlow, Samuel Dick, William M'Clure, Ichabod B. Miller, John Wallace, Abraham Reed.
Results of an election held at Elmore Williams' in Cincinnati mention Bazella Wells, Nathaniel Massie, John Reily, Elias Langham, Jacob White, Icha. B. Miller,

John Wallace, John R. Gaston, James Smith, Thomas M'Farland, David E. Wade.

An unsigned letter to the editor regarding the County Jail mentions David E. Wade and David Grummons.

A notice of a meeting at Ezekiel Hutchison's Tavern to organize the Cincinnati Horse Races.

Brig. Gen. James Findlay gives orders to the Brigade and mentions Samuel Armstrong in Columbia, Vantrees' mill, Col. Wallace, Col. Brown, Col. Lytle and John R. Mills.

Sheriff James Smith regarding the elections.

No. 10, Volume VI, Wednesday, 3 October 1804, Whole No. 270

David E. Wade writes a letter to the editor regarding the recent letter about him. He mentions David Grummon and includes the deposition of John S. Gano who mentions Charles Avery and Robert Benham.

H. Craig writes a letter to the editor regarding David E. Wade.

Jacob Sallady, living in Harrison County near the Rocky Spring, reports a mare that strayed from Widow Gregories' place. Deliver to George Riggs near Columbia or Daniel Thatcher in Kentucky on the road to Grant's Lick.

Thomas Burk says that his wife, Hannah Burk, left him and he won't honor her debts anymore.

Capt. James Smith regarding a meeting of the Cincinnati Light Infantry.

Maj. Gen. John S. Gano and Charles Killgore give orders to the Militia and mention Thomas Fream at the Medical Springs in Green County.

James Ferguson wants to buy wheat and whiskey.

Lieut. Col. John Wallace gives orders for the First Regiment.

A note regarding the rules of the Cincinnati Horse Races.

A list of letters left at the Post Office in Cincinnati mentions Daniel Antrim in Warren County, John Allen, Doctor Silas Allen, Rebecca Allen in Columbia, Everard Beatle in care of Stephen Davis, William Barcalow in Franklin, Samuel Bassett in Lawrenceburgh, Moses Bradley in Franklin, Ethan Baldwin, Roswell Bartlett, Charles Brown in Franklin, Nathan Barns on the Miami circuit, Daniel Bradstreet in Franklin, Frederick Bonner, Melyn Baker, John Clark in Mercer County, Reuben Carter, James Charters in Colerain, Thomas Cissna, William Cox twelve miles from Cincinnati, William Cornit at Mr. Anderson's, Doctor John Collins, William Crouch at Miami, William Cunningham, Jesse Cleavenger, Maj. Benjamin Chambers, Peter Cossel in Franklin, Cornett & Pratts, John Davenport, David and Loes Davis on Little Miami, John S. Dailey, Philip Dennis, Yunice Dexter, Beracha Dunn, James Davis, Parvin Dunn, Jesse Dodd, Joseph Draper at Waynesville, John Dennis, Benjamin Dancels, Samuel Davis, David Enyart, Martin Eartost on Turtle Creek, Joseph Edwards, Andrew Endsley, John Ewin on Miami, Bartholomew Fleming in care of Mr. Conner, Thos. Frazer, Ebenezer Fisher at Columbia, Joseph Gest at Little Miami, Philip Gordon, John Gillman, Stephanas Hoggatt in Green County, David Griffith, Daniel Haynes, Thos. Hopkins, Richard Haskins in Franklin, John Hart, John Huston, Doctor John Hammill, William Hunter in Warren County, John T. Hall, Thomas Hunter, Alexander Hamilton, William Harrison at Franklin, John Irwin on Sugar Creek, John Johnston at Fort Wayne, Samuel Jameson, Baldwin Jenkins in Green County, James Joice, John Jardon in Warren County, Alexander Jameson, George Kylor, Joseph Kelly in care of James M'Clure, Francis Knott, James Kelly, William Legg, Robert Lydle, Robert Luce on Clear Creek, Benjamin Lewis at Miles Ferry, James M'Kane or John M'Ewin, Samuel G. Martin in Warren County, Henry Misneer at Miami, John Moore, Patrick M'Carty, M'Cullaugh & Son, Jeremiah Morrow, John Miller, Chauncy Morse, Jacob Minton in Green County, Robert Martion, Capt. John Manson, Robert M'Mullen at the mouth of the Little Miami, Nancy Miller, James M'Ginnes, Henry W. Miller, Jean Ogle, Thomas Oliver, Abijah O'Neal, Lindsay Piatt, Rebecca Perlee, Joseph Potter, Michael Pierce, Daniel Potter at Franklin, John Piatt, Andrew Rogers in care of Nathaniel Reeder, John Radley on Mill Creek, Augus Ross, John Robinson, Andrew Robb in Middle-town, S. Robb in Middle-town, Simeon Rogers, Mary Rogers, Samuel Ricker, John Smith (chairmaker in Waynesville), Eacy Smith, David Stinchcomb in Fort Wayne, Collin

Spence, William Smith, Isaac Sparks, Col. Cornelius R. Sedam, William C. Schenck, James Stanes on Shade River, William Sawyers at Franklin, Mary Stout, James Shields, Thomas Shepherd at Columbia, Major Jonathan Silley, Gideon Sears, Samuel Stuart, Samuel Tamset, Amos Tullis, Christopher Tray, George W. Tucker, John Taulman in care of Col. Armstrong, Philip Titus in Warren County, Thomas Towsey, Moses Towsey, David Toot, Mary Tetrick, Henry Tucker, Capt. Saml. Tebbals, Noah Tryon in North Bend, John Vantilburg in Franklin, Alexander Wilson, Andrew Vanclerveer in Franklin, Andrew Wilson, George Wallace, John Williams at Sycamore, Nathaniel Williams, Robert Wilson, Nehemiah Ward, George Williams at Sycamore, James Walker, Moses B. Young at Chillicothe. William Ruffin, Post Master.

James Baxter, living in Dayton township on James Thompson's farm five miles below Dayton on the Great Miami, reports a stray horse.

Long & Price have commenced the clock and watchmaking business in Cincinnati. Harman Long also carries on the tinning business.

No. 11, Volume VI, Wednesday, 10 October 1804, Whole No. 271

An unsigned letter to the editor regarding the conflict over David E. Wade and the courthouse in Hamilton County mentions David Grummon.

David E. Wade writes a letter to the public regarding the letter from Hugh Craig and mentions Mr. Hunt's tan yard and Matthew Nimmo.

Several depositions are printed regarding David E. Wade. They are signed by Charles Avery, James Ewing, Robert Benham, Aaron Goforth, John Mahard, John S. Gano, and Arthur St.Clair, Jun.

Asa Harvey and Judah Willy (living in Colerain), administrators of the estate of Asa Harvey, late of Hamilton County, dec'd, regarding the estate.

Joseph C. Vance regarding the sale of an inn and lots in Xenia.

James Findlay, in Cincinnati, for William Wills, has land for sale.

Francis Settle regarding a bond to Daniel Hollis.

William Stanley regarding a meeting of the Miami Exporting Company.

J. Carpenter & Company ask those indebted to them to settle their accounts in wheat delivered to John Smith's, Jacob White's or VanHorn's Mills.

Samuel Caldwell is closing his business in Cincinnati and "moving a great distance". Those indebted to him should settle their accounts with wheat delivered to Vanhorn's mill on Mill Creek.

No. 12, Volume VI, Wednesday, 17 October 1804, Whole No. 272

John Nimmo writes a letter to the editor about David E. Wade and mentions H. Craig, Henry Ewing, Thomas Rawlins, Joseph Carpenter, Matthew Nimmo, A. St.Clair, Judge Foster, Judge Silvers and David Grummon.

Hamilton County election returns mention Mr. Morrow, Mr. Langham, Mr. White, Mr. Snieder, Stephen Wood, H. Price, J. Willey, I.B. Miller, J. Wallace, J. Gaston, William M'Farland, James Smith, H. Ewing, T. M'Farland, Z. Foster, and D.E. Wade.

Samuel Cary opened his tayloring business at Elmore Williams' tavern.

John Watton, living near Washington, Mason County, Kentucky, regarding a runaway slave named Bolar.

Isaac Stanley regarding a runaway apprentice, John M'Cormack, age 18.

Jacob Broadwell, for John Smith, at Round Bottom, wants to hire workers for digging a Mill dam. He also wants to hire apprentices to the cooper's trade.

Daniel Searles, living at Fort Hamilton in Butler County, about a stray mare.

No. 13, Volume VI, Wednesday, 24 October 1804, Whole No. 273

An unsigned letter to the editor nominates William Goforth, Sen., Nathaniel Massie and James Pritchard as electors.

Sheriff James Smith, in Hamilton County, regarding election districts.

Benjamin Stites, James Maranday and Ephraim Kibby, in Columbia, administrators of the estate of Benjamin Stites, dec'd, ask those indebted to the estate to settle their accounts with William Sump of Columbia.

Timothy W. Parker "intends settling in the town of Cincinnati and intends carrying on the business of Arch and Geometry Bridge building, and the Millwright business".

Jacob Williams, in Cincinnati, asks those indebted to him to pay their bills.

Edmon Buxton, living near Redding town, Hamilton Co., about a stray mare.

E. Stone, living in Cincinnati, regarding a stray horse.

William M'Farland, Sheriff of Hamilton County, regarding election districts.

Asa S. Richardson, in Cincinnati, regarding wheat delivered to Vanhorn's Mill, mentions William Gannon (living on Richardson's place), James Ewing and Jacob Burnet (attorney).

John Tice, living near Hamilton in Butler County, reports a stray horse. Deliver to Isaac Anderson in Cincinnati or John Torrence in Hamilton.

Thomas Carter, in Cincinnati, found a small chain.

No. 14, Volume VI, Wednesday, 31 October 1804, Whole No. 274

Capt. James Richmond, Capt. Jn. M'Clary, Lieut. Eb. Climson, Jno. Roney and D. Davis, at Detroit, write a letter to the editor regarding the ad placed by J.H. Audrain about Lieut. Ninian Pinkney.

A letter to the editor from Lieut. N. Pinkney regarding the ad placed by James H. Audrain. He speaks of the family of P. Audrain and the "lascivious conduct" of the Audrain daughter which led to the illegitimate child she had with N. Pinkney.

Obituary: Col. William Brown, of Columbia, died Monday evening, 23 October 1804, and was buried Tuesday afternoon. He left a wife and nine children.

Obituary: Abner Amidon died in Cincinnati on Wednesday, 24 October 1804.

Jeremiah Morrow has been elected to Congress over Mr. Langham.

J. & M. Nimmo want to buy wheat at Ludlow's, Vanhorne's, Waldsmith's and Armstrong's mills. They also have winter goods for sale.

I. Gildersleve, in Cincinnati, has land for sale on the west side of Great Miami five miles above Hamilton. Apply to William Broadrick living near the land.

Samuel Hilditch has a new shipment of goods at his store in Columbia.

John Armstrong, in Columbia, about goods left at his store by Isaac Sittler, junr. He mentions N. Perkins in Columbia and Mr. Davis of Pittsbury.

David Dunseth, of Cincinnati, asks those indebted to him to pay their bills.

Esther Gardner & John Sinkey, administrators of James Gardner, dec'd, about the estate sale at Esther Gardner's house in Colerain township.

Maj. Gen. John S. Gano and William Ruffin give orders to the Militia. William C. Schenck is elected Brigadier General of the Second Brigade and Simon Kenton is elected for the Third Brigade.

No. 15, Volume VI, Wednesday, 7 November 1804, Whole No. 275

Some appointments are made by the president: Philip Green (collector of revenue at Marietta), John Gibson (secretary of the Indiana Territory), George Hoffman (register of the land office in Detroit), Return J. Meigs and Daniel Smith (commissioners for holding a treaty with the Cherokees), John Badollet (register of the land office at Vincennes), Michael Jones (register of the land office at Kaskaskia), Ephraim Kirby (judge of the Mississippi Territory), Frederick Bates (receiver of the public monies at Detroit), Elijah Backus (receiver of the public monies at Kaskaskia).

Election returns from Hamilton County mention Mr. Goforth, Mr. Massie, Mr. Reily, Mr. Pritchard, Mr. Wells, Mr. Bigger, Mr. Gillman. Returns from Belmont County mention Jeremiah Morrow, Elias Langham, Thomas Wilson, John Stewart, Josiah Hedges, John Duncan. Returns from Butler County mention Jeremiah Morrow, Elias Langham, Ezekiel Ball, Mathew Richardson. Returns from "Columbiana, attached to Jefferson" mention Jeremiah Morrow, Elias Langham, James Pritchard, Mr. Kemberly, Rudolph Bear, John M'Connel. Returns from Trumbull County mention George Tod, Mr. Kirtland, Benjamin Tappan, Amos Stafford, Thomas Kine, Ephraim Quimby, Martin Smith.

Joseph Prince and M. Nimmo print an ordinance of the town of Cincinnati.

Charles Killgore, in Cincinnati, reports a stolen horse.

James Cowan and Mary Cowan, administrators of the estate of John Cowan, late of Warren County, dec'd, regarding the estate settlement.

James Ewing, administrator of the estate of Abner Amidon, deceased, late of Cincinnati, regarding the estate sale at the house of Hezekiah Flint.

George Kelly, living on Elk Creek in Butler County in St. Clair township, reports a stray horse.

Wm. Wallace, in Cincinnati, reports a stray horse.

Joseph Prince, Henry Weaver and William Ruffin, Auditors, regarding the suit of John Roll vs. Isaac Winans.

Matthew Steaurt, living in Green County on King's Creek about four miles from the mouth, reports that he found a stray mare.

Charles Conn, who "lives at the sign of the White Horse in Cincinnati", has tables for sale. He wants to buy beef, pork and whiskey.

No. 16, Volume VI, Wednesday, 14 November 1804, Whole No. 276

Obituary: Pierre Gilman, first judge of the Court of Common Pleas, died at Vincennes. (no date listed)

William Clark asks those indebted to him to settle their accounts in wheat delivered to Waldsmith's, Armstrong's, White's, Ludlow's, VanHorne's, Joel Williams', Dr. Wood's or Thomas Smith's mills. Or deliver pork and whiskey to J. Carpenter & Company in Cincinnati.

Thomas Frazer, in Columbia, reports that he found a stray horse.

John T. Chunn regarding his store in Columbia in the house lately occupied by Maj. Benjamin Stites, dec'd. He also has a keel-boat for sale.

Ruth Brown and Thaddeus Hanford, administrators of the estate of William Brown, dec'd, regarding the estate settlement.

No. 17, Volume VI, Wednesday, 21 November 1804, Whole No. 277

Marriage: Martin Baum, merchant in Cincinnati, to Ann Wallace, daughter of William Wallace of Marietta, on Wednesday evening, 14 November 1804, by Revd. Dr. Wallace.

A letter to Maj. Gen. John S. Gano from Gov. Edward Tiffin, by Samuel Finly, regarding the militia.

Griffin & Hatfield report a horse that strayed or was stolen from the stable of John Torrence in Hamilton. Deliver to George Hatfield at the Big Prairie or to Daniel Griffin at Brownlee's Mill.

David Walker, living in Springfield township, administrator, offers for sale the personal property of James Reddick who is "in a state of insanity".

Andrew Brannon offers stalls at the Market House in Cincinnati for sale.

No. 18, Volume VI, Wednesday, 28 November 1804, Whole No. 278

Nathaniel Massie, William Goforth, sen., and James Pritchard are elected to serve as electors.

Sheriff James Smith regarding sheriff's sales to be held at the house of Isaac Anderson in Cincinnati: the property of Samuel James seized at the suit of Thomas Thompson, Martin Baum and Matthew Nimmo; the property of George Fithian at the suit of Martin Null; the property of John Briney at the suit of Edward Ralston; the property of Josephus Waters at the suit of the U.S.; the property of Calvin Bonnel at the suit of Har. Toulman; the property of Cornelieus Voorheise at the suits of Daniel Hammit and David Killgore.

Hugh Moore has a new shipment of goods for sale at his store in Cincinnati.

Wm. Jay and James Moon, executors of the estate of John Vestal, late of Warren County, dec'd, regarding the estate settlement to be held at the house of Thomas Goodwin in Wainsville.

James Moore, living at the mouth of Muddy Creek on the Ohio River two miles above North Bend, reports a stray horse.

Daniel Symmes, agent for William Henry Harrison, has land for sale on Mill Creek. Apply to Judge Symmes, John M'Mahan and Joseph M'Mahan.

Merrie & M'Nicoll, cabinet and chairmakers from Philadelphia, regarding their business in Cincinnati in the house lately occupied by Mr. M'Ginnis.

Jonathan Morgan, Jun., has opened a school in Cincinnati.

No. 19, Volume VI, Wednesday, 5 December 1804, Whole No. 279
Pallas P. Stuart, in Cincinnati, regarding a horse that strayed or was stolen.
Christian Moier and Elizabeth Moier, administrators of the estate of Henry Moier, dec'd, regarding the estate settlement.
Wisler & Wells have a blacksmith shop in Cincinnati opposite David J. Poor's.
Matthias Roll reports some stray oxen.
Benjamin and John Piatt, in Lawrenceburgh, about a note to John Holstead.

No. 20, Volume VI, Thursday, 13 December 1804, Whole No. 280
Thomas Rawlins regarding a meeting of the citizens of Cincinnati at Griffin Yeatman's. Matthew Nimmo presided over the debate on inoculations of cowpox.
Joseph Prince and Matthew Nimmo regarding an ordinance of the town of Cincinnati with respect to small pox.
A note about inoculations with small pox mentions Dr. Sellman, Yeatman's tavern, and Doctor Cranmore.
William M'Farland about a meeting of the Nova Caesaria Lodge in Cincinnati.
Joseph Charles regarding books published at his store in Lexington, Kentucky.
Samuel James, in Cincinnati, has lots and household furniture for sale.
John Mercer, in Cincinnati, reports a stray mare.
John & Matthew Nimmo ask those indebted to them to settle their accounts. Also John Nimmo is retiring from the partnership on December 25th.
William Sawyer, living on Clear Creek, about a horse that strayed or was stolen from the pasture of James Seeman in Lebanon, Warren County.

No. 21, Volume VI, Wednesday, 19 December 1804, Whole No. 281
A list of legislators in Ohio includes, in the Senate, Thomas Kirker for Adams & Scioto Counties; William Vance for Belmont; James Sargent for Clermont; John Milligan and James Pritchard for Columbiana and Jefferson; Abraham Claypool and Joseph Kerr for Ross and Franklin; Joseph Buel for Washington, Gallia and Muskingum; Cornelius Snider for Hamilton; John Bigger for Warren, Butler, Green and Montgomery. Thomas Kirker is speaker of the Senate and Thomas Scott is clerk. In the House of Representatives: Abraham Shepherd, Thomas Waller and Philip Lewis, Jr., for Adams; Mich. Baldwin, James Dunlap, Duncan M'Arthur, and William Patton for Ross; Elijah Hatch, Seckel Marvin and Seth Carhart for Washington; Mathias Corwin and Peter Burr for Warren; Daniel C. Cooper for Montgomery; David Rees and William Gass for Fairfield; Ezekiel Ball and Mathew Richardson for Butler; Stephen Wood, Hez. Price and Judah Willey for Hamilton; Thomas Wilson and John Stewart for Belmont; John Sterritt for Green; Thomas M'Cune, John Sloan and John M'Luaghlin for Jefferson; Rudolph Blair for Columbiana; Amos Spafford and Homer Hine for Trumbull; Robert Higgins for Clermont. Michael Baldwin is elected speaker of the House and John M'Dugal is clerk.
A note regarding contested elections mentions Maj. M'Arthur, Capt Shelby, D.C. Cooper and Mr. Thompson.
Daniel Symmes is Speaker of the Senate and Michael Baldwin is Speaker of the House.
John Babbs reports that he found a stray horse.
Adam Swinehart and Sally Swinehart, administrators of the estate of Gabriel Swinehart, late of Montgomery County, dec'd, regarding the estate settlement.
Thomas Ramsey, in Cincinnati, has a horse for sale.

No. 22, Volume VI, Wednesday, 26 December 1804, Whole No. 282
An unsigned letter to the editor regarding the Debating Society mentions Rev. John W. Browne.
Isaac Anderson, in Cincinnati, has a house and lots for sale in Cincinnati and Newport, the property of Francis Wilson.
The plantation belonging to the heirs of James John, dec'd, including the Grist Mill, is for rent.
G. Turner, at Mad River, regarding a certificate for land signed by James Findlay and Charles Killgore.
William Gannon, in Cincinnati, about a stray horse. Deliver to David J. Poor.

No. 23, Volume VI, Wednesday, 2 January 1805, Whole No. 283
A note regarding a meeting of the Nova Caesaria Lodge.
Jacob Broadwell offers horses and mares for sale at the Round Bottom mills.
John Robinson, living near Beagle's Station in Deerfield Township of Warren County, regarding a stray mare.
Stephen Reeder & Ogdon Ross, administrators of the estate of Robert Hains, dec'd, late of Hamilton County, Colerain Township, regarding the estate settlement at the house of Ogdon Ross, near the deceased's house.
John Mercer, in Cincinnati, reports a stray mare.

No. 24, Volume VI, Wednesday, 9 January 1805, Whole No. 284
J. Carpenter has land for sale in Kentucky. He mentions Samuel Woodson of Kentucky and Thomas Dugan.
William Clark asks those indebted to him to settle their accounts. Payments can be made in wheat delivered to Van-Horn's, White's, Waldsmith's, Armstrong's or Holly's Mills.
Jacob Broadwell, administrator of the estate of Nathaniel Broadwell, late of Hamilton County, deceased, regarding the estate settlement.
Abraham Van-Sickle, living 4 miles from Vail's Mill on Great Miami in Lemon township, Butler County, reports stray oxen bearing Israel Ludlow's mark.
A list of letters left at the Post Office in Cincinnati includes Anthony Burns at Colerain, Tobias Bretney, John D. Brown, Nathan Barns on the Miami Circuit, Richard Benham, Paul Brown, James Baxter or Samuel Caldwell, Philip Crichfield, Thomas Cook, John Cogwill in care of John Misner, Joseph Cook, Thomas Carter, James Clark, John Caldwell on White Water, Joseph Compton, Enoch Danford, Elizabeth Dillow, Henry Davis on Little Miami, Charles Dawson, John Ewing, Richard Frazy, Laura Fairchild, Samuel Fairchild, Absolum Gray, Charles and Edward Humphreys, Jonathan Ganison, William Grant, Robert & Delila Goudy, Doctor John Hammil, James Heaton, Jacob Harding, Thomas Hill on Mad River Road, Andrew Jolly, James Johnson on Clear Creek, John Clark Irish in care of Jesse Hunt, David Kinnan, Doctor Squire Little, Jonathan Lyon, Anthony Logan, William Legg, John Lee, Sally Lyons, Thomas M'Farland on Little Miami, Peter Mills, Abner Moore, William M'Intosh, James Martin in Columbia, Jacob Minthon, John Magrew, Archibald M'Cray on Mill Creek, Alexander Meek, Issachar Muhum, Benjamin Mulford, Robert M'Mullen in Columbia, Henry May on Dick's Creek, Peter Newcommer, Allen Nixon, Thomas Patterson, Thomas Perkins, Matthias Painter in care of W. Sailor, James Patterson at Sycamore, Nicholas Perkins at Columbia, Matthias Pierson, William Patton, Rees Pritchard in Columbia, Joseph Robinson, Henry Runion on Mill Creek, William Saltors, Isaac Sparks on Mill Creek, John Seward, Aaron Street, Zadoc Steward, Stephen Smith, George Stothard on Duck Creek, John Shuppert (cooper), Jacob Shuppert, Jun., Archibald Shields on Dick's Creek, Joseph Sawyer in Franklin, Daniel Stout in care of Capt. Crichfield, Aaron Scogin, Aaron Sacket at Redding, John Street, John Templeton, Joseph Toulman at Columbia, Noah Tryon, John Thompson, Isaac Van-Ness in Franklin township, Benjamin Van-Hook, Joseph Wingate at Springfield, Isaac Ward for Jesse Wilson, David Walker in care of Samuel Caldwell, James Whalon on Mill Creek. Entered by William Ruffin, postmaster.
James Ferguson asks those indebted to him to settle their accounts by delivering wheat to White's, Ludlow's, VanHorn's, Waldsmith's and Armstrong's Mills.

No. 25, Volume VI, Wednesday, 16 January 1805, Whole No. 285
A letter to the editor of the Palladium in Frankfort, Kentucky, from Harry Toulmin regarding the settlement of the Ohio Valley by ancient Welshmen is printed and mentions John Childes of Jessamine County, Kentucky. He tells the story of Maurice Griffith, a Welshman, who was taken prisoner by the Shawnee Indians when he was sixteen and found a colony of Welsh speaking people.
A list of bills before the Ohio Legislature mentions Jehiel Gregory and John Havner (for building a mill dam over the Hockhocking River), Humphrey Fullerton (for erecting a toll bridge over the Scioto at Chillicothe).
Marriage: Oliver Spencer, merchant, of Columbia, to Miss Electa Oliver, of Cincinnati, on Sunday evening, 13 January 1805, by Rev. Mr. Kamper.

G. Turner, in Cincinnati, regarding land, on Mad River in Green County, in dispute with Alexander King of Cincinnati.

Jacob Whisler says that the partnership of Whisler & Wells is dissolved. Whisler will continue the blacksmith business in Cincinnati.

T. Washburn, in Cincinnati, about an auction of household goods. He "intends to leave this place immediately after" the sale.

Isaac VanNuys, at Cincinnati, regarding the sale of the personal estate of John Gildersleve, deceased.

Robert M'Elhenny regarding a power of attorney he gave to William Terry, of Hamilton County, to sell some land in Virginia.

No. 26, Volume VI, Wednesday, 23 January 1805, Whole No. 286

J. & M. Nimmo ask those indebted to them to settle their accounts.

Thomas Dugan "is now winding up his business" and asks those indebted to him to settle their accounts. He has just returned from the Atlantic States.

William Byrd has goods for sale at Mrs. M'Cullaugh's store in Cincinnati.

Sheriff James Smith regarding the sheriff's sale of property of John Cleves Symmes, including land known as Pollock's Mill tract, at the suit of John M'Cashing and Daniel Griffing.

H. Craig, in Cincinnati, has land for sale between the Miamies.

Thomas Williams, in Cincinnati, wants to buy deerskins and country sugar.

No. 27, Volume VI, Wednesday, 30 January 1805, Whole No. 287

C.R. Sedam, living four miles below Cincinnati, reports he found stray cattle.

Alexander King answers the recent ad placed by G. Turner.

Frederick Coonse, Sen., living near Ludlow's Mill, regarding his sale of livestock, farming utensils and household furniture.

Isaac Wilson, living in Cincinnati township, found some stray cattle.

The plantation belonging to the heirs of James John, dec'd, including the grist mill, is for rent. It is on Nine Mile Creek, Ohio Township, Clermont County.

No. 28, Volume VI, Wednesday, 6 February 1805, Whole No. 288

Aaron Goforth regarding land for sale. He also warns persons not to cut wood on the property of Rev. William Van-Horne.

Christian Waldsmith has land for sale in Warren County adjoining on the west the town of Deerfield, on the east on Mr. Kelly's plantation and on the north by Mr. Seward's lands. Apply to Waldsmith at his mills.

Jacob Williams is going "up the river after a stock of nail-iron" and asks those indebted to him to settle their accounts. He also has land for sale. Apply to Jacob or Elmore Williams of Cincinnati.

No. 29, Volume VI, Wednesday, 13 February 1805, Whole No. 289

Gov. William C.C. Claiborne's speech to the legislative council is printed. The answer from J. Poydras is also printed.

A note regarding the formation of the Ohio Canal Company to open a canal around the Falls of the Ohio.

Daniel Symmes is appointed judge of the Supreme Court of Ohio. Matthew Nimmo is appointed as associate judge for Hamilton County.

J. & M. Nimmo regarding goods for sale at their store in Cincinnati. They also will dissolve their partnership in the summer.

John Sellman, in Cincinnati, asks those indebted to him to pay their accounts.

Samuel Best, clock and watchmaker and silversmith, regarding his business next door to Mr. Anderson's tavern on Front Street in Cincinnati.

Mrs. Williamson about her school at Mr. Nimmo's on Main Street, Cincinnati.

D. Keasby, in Cincinnati, asks those indebted to him to pay their bills.

Thomas Couch has land for sale on Mill Creek next door to John Becket, James Cunningham and Thomas Higgins. Apply to James Findlay of Cincinnati.

Sineas Pierson, living on Mill Creek five miles from Cincinnati on the Great road leading to Detroit, has land for sale, including his mills.

Seth Cutter, in Cincinnati, offers his land for sale, including the public house, as he is "about quitting public business".

No. 30, Volume VI, Wednesday, 20 February 1805, Whole No. 290

Thomas Dugan has a number of books, slates, pencils and sealing wax for sale.

Obituary: Maj. Thomas Doyle, of Cincinnati, aged about 45, was buried on Sunday, 17 February 1805, with military honors. Mentions Capt. Smith's Light Infantry, Maj. Gen. Gano, Maj. Zeigler and Maj. Doyle's widow.

Obituary: Mr. John Nancarrow died at Cincinnati on 14 February 1805.

W.C. Schenck of the Second brigade, first division, Ohio Militia, says that John Greer, of Hamilton, is appointed Inspector and John Whiteworth, of Franklin, is appointed quarter master of the brigade.

John Carlisle, Collector of the Virginia Army Lands, at Chillicothe, regarding the sale of lands in the Virginia Military Tract.

John S. Gano and Jacob Burnet (attorney) regarding the suits in Hamilton County Court of Common Pleas of Charles Vattier vs. Asa S. Richardson; and Isaac Dexter vs. James Turner and Asa S. Richardson. Mentions James Snieder.

Joseph Kibby, at Deerfield, regarding a horse that strayed from the house of Charles Vattier in Cincinnati. Deliver to William Ruffin.

The editor of the Western Spy wants to hire a post rider to replace Mr. Clark.

Moses Ferral reports that he found a stray steer.

John Grant, of Campbell County, Kentucky, informs those to whom he is indebted that they may apply for payment to Samuel Bryan at Grant's salt works. He says he is about to move his family to Tanner's Station in Boon County six miles below the mouth of the Great Miami where he will keep a supply of salt.

No. 31, Volume VI, Wednesday, 27 February 1805, Whole No. 291

Henry Weaver is appointed associate judge for Butler County in place of Judge Kitchell, deceased.

Obituary: Daniel Conner, merchant, of Cincinnati, died on Saturday night, February 23, 1805, leaving a young widow.

The editor of the Western Spy regarding the terms of payment for the paper.

Ezra Spencer announces that he is opening a store in the town of Crosby on the Great Miami River opposite Colerain.

Timothy W. Parker, in Cincinnati, wants to hire an apprentice to the "Millwright and Bridge building business".

A notice to Robert Boyes and James Boyes, children of Robert Boyes who was the son of the "late esq. Boyes of Londonderry in the county of Rockingham and state of New Hampshire, deceased". Robert the elder left Londonderry over 30 years ago, married in Baltimore, Maryland, and moved to Virginia where he died. His sons should apply to Silas Retton of Salem, New Hampshire, or to Alexander Boyes of Londonderry to hear of some property due them.

No. 32, Volume VI, Wednesday, 6 March 1805, Whole No. 292

A note regarding the legislature of Ohio mentions John Bigger, Daniel Symmes, Jehiel Gregory, William Jackson and Sylvester Ames.

General Massie's mills at the falls of Paint Creek were consumed by fire.

A note regarding an act to form Michigan Territory from Indiana Territory.

Notes regarding the editor of the Liberty Hall mentions Mr. Browne.

A list of acts passed by the Ohio General Assembly mentions Israel Putnam (agent for the heirs of Doctor Jedediah Ensworth, dec'd), the Dayton Library Society, Jehiel Gregory and John Havner.

E. Reeder, of Franklin, says Dr. Bradford, of Hamilton, inoculated Mrs. Reeder and a grandchild with small pox vaccine. It has gone wrong and the two are very ill with the disease. He warns the public against Dr. Bradford. He mentions General Schenck.

John M'Mechan has just commenced the weaving business in Cincinnati at the Stone House formerly occupied by J. & A. Hunt. He has weavers reeds for sale.

D.C. Cooper, at Dayton, regarding the stud horse, Miami Chief, who "will stand the ensuing season at the town of Lebanon, under the care of Mr. Earheart".

David Pugh, in Waynesville, wants to hire a tanner and currier.

No. 33, Volume VI, Wednesday, 13 March 1805, Whole No. 293

William Creighton, Jun., Secretary of State, regarding laws of Ohio.

A note regarding flood waters states that Mr. Armstrong's saw mill on the Little Miami was washed away.

A letter to the editor nominates the following persons for office: Samuel Patterson, Martin Baum, Isaac Anderson, Thomas Ramsey, Francis Mennessier, David E. Wade, Henry Weaver, John Bowyer, Matthew Nimmo, William Stanley, Joshua Williams, John Ludlow, Joseph Prince, Aquilla Wheeler, Andrew Branon, Jacob Stewart, Alexander King, Joseph Conn, Jun., William Ramsey, John Stall, James Ferguson, Thomas Rawlins, John Humes, Thomas Thompson, John Cranmer, Elmore Williams, Ezekiel Hutchinson, John Mahard, John W. Browne.

A note regarding the impeachment trial of William Irwin, associate judge of the Court of Common Pleas for Fairfield County.

Charles Conn, in Cincinnati, asks those indebted to him to pay their bills.

Ichabod B. Miller, Thomas Brown and Aaron Goforth, administrators of the estate of John Nancarrow, dec'd, regarding the estate sale at the house of Mrs. Willis in Cincinnati. Those indebted to the estate should pay Elmore Williams.

James Ewing, administrator of the estate of Maj. Thomas Doyle, dec'd, about the estate settlement.

James Smith, late sheriff, regarding a sheriff's sale of the tract of land known as Pollox's mill tract, the property of John Cleves Symmes, at the suit of James M'Cashen and Daniel Griffing.

Richard A. Oden regarding his school in the public schoolhouse that was formerly occupied by Mr. E. Spencer in Cincinnati. A meeting of the trustees of the school will be held at Henry Ewing's house.

Proposals for work done on the Hamilton County courthouse can be left with John S. Gano.

Rev. David Rice will preach at several places in the area. Mentioned are John Ludlow, Joseph Parks on Dicks Creek, Francis Dill at Bethany, William Lamme on Hole's Creek, Mr. Richardson on Clear Creek and Daniel Skinner.

No. 34, Volume VI, Wednesday, 20 March 1805, Whole No. 294

Michael Baldwin, James Pritchard & Daniel Symmes print some laws of Ohio.

Road Commissioners are appointed by the Legislature: John Blair, Thomas Irwin, Jehiel Gregory, Simon Kenton and Lewis Kenny.

The Trustees of the Ohio University are Joseph Buell, Benjamin Tupper, Jacob Linley, Michael Baldwin and William Creighton, Jun.

Appraisers of the College townships are James Denny, Emanuel Carpenter, Jun., Isaac Dawson, Pelatial White and Ezekiel Demming.

Associate judges for Highland County are John Davidson, Richard Evans and Jonathan Berriman.

Associate judges for Champaign County are John Reynolds, John Runyan and Samuel M'Cullough.

A note regarding the report in Taylor Browne's paper that Mr. M'Cullough had lost his mills in the floods. That report is false.

James Ewing, Charles Moore and James Lyon will take bids, at a meeting at Henry Ewing's place, for constructing a fence around the graveyard.

Robert Stubbs regarding his Academy at his farm two miles from the Ohio opposite Cincinnati in Campbell County, Kentucky.

John Armstrong wants to sell or rent his land in Columbia.

Notice about land for sale mentions Crawford's place four miles from Springfield and Rock's farm in the forks of Mad River within two miles from Springfield.

George Larrison asks those persons indebted to the estate of Rachel Bidgley, late of Hamilton County, deceased, to settle their accounts.

George Larrison, living near Ludlow's Mill, reports that he found a mare.

Notice of land for sale on Wolf Creek. Apply to Dr. James Welsh in Dayton.

Benjamin Stites, James Maranda and Ephraim Kibby, administrators of the estate of Benjamin Stites, late of Columbia, deceased, regarding the settlement of the estate. Those indebted to Timothy Kibby should make payments to Col. J.

Armstrong in Columbia or to Ephraim Kibby near Deerfield.

John Mahard, justice of the peace, says that Delzil Keasby is now in the Cincinnati jail for debt. Keasby told Aquilla Wheeler, jailor, that he will apply to the Court of Common Pleas for relief.

Delzil Keasby asks those to whom he owes money to place their claims.

No. 35, Volume VI, Wednesday, 27 March 1805, Whole No. 295

Appointments made by the Senate include General Hull as governor of the Michigan Territory.

The ticket for the Corporation of Cincinnati is announced and mentions James Findlay, Matthew Nimmo, John Stall, Thomas Williams, James Forguson, Ethan Stone, Samuel Stitt, Aaron Goforth, Thomas Thompson, Hezekiah Flint, John Mahard and Alexander King.

Judge Huntington, a judge in the Supreme Court of Ohio, has been appointed judge for the Michigan Territory.

Dr. John Bradford, M.D., writes a letter to the public regarding the recent letter about him from Mr. E. Reeder of Franklin. He says the cow pox vaccine was obtained from David Thompson's cow at Hamilton in the presence of Mrs. Thompson. He also inoculated 2 of John Tucker's children near Jonathan Pitman's place, and they aren't sick.

Thomas Cooch regarding a note he gave to John Irwin.

A notice regarding a cow that strayed from Widow Myers' one mile above Bear Creek on the west side of the Great Miami.

Nancy Post and Saml. C. Vance, administrators of the estate of Josiah Post, late of Dearborn County, Indiana Territory, dec'd, about the estate settlement.

Harry Toulmin, in Frankfort, Kentucky, reports a runaway slave named Silas. Deliver to James Cole near Frankfort.

Christopher Cary and William Cary, administrators of the estate of Samuel Cary, late of Cincinnati, dec'd, regarding the estate settlement.

Josiah Holly, living in Anderson township on the Little Miami, regarding a runaway bound servant girl, Matilda Burns, age 15.

John R. Mills has land for sale on Mill Creek nine miles from Cincinnati.

No. 36, Volume VI, Wednesday, 3 April 1805, Whole No. 296

A note regarding the recent floods says that a Mr. Bell drowned in the mud fork of Salt Creek on his way from the Saltworks. "He lately removed to this country, and has left a large family."

An account of an election of officers of the Corporation mentions James Findlay, Aaron Goforth, Ethan Stone, Nathaniel Reeder, Thomas Williams, Samuel Stitt, Griffin Yeatman, Nehemiah Hunt, John Stall, John Mahard, Alexander King and Thomas Carter.

An anonymous poem is printed obviously referring to the dispute between Dr. Bradford and Mr. Reeder.

Capt. James Smith about a meeting of the Cincinnati Light Infantry.

William Ruffin, in Cincinnati, has several tracts of land for sale.

A list of letters left at the Post Office in Cincinnati includes Matthew Adams, Isaiah Briant, David Bowman in Dearborn County, Hamilton Blackburn in care of Mr. Ramsey, William Burton or Philip Hill, Abner Bolton, John Babb, Abraham Bush, Paul Brown, David Bowman, David Black, David Burnet, Thomas Carneal, John Clark, Philip Crag, Jesse Clark, John or Bazil Clark, David Close, Samuel Crane at Springfield, John Compton, Jun., Cephas Dodd or David Morris, John Dixon on Great Miami, John Day on Little Miami, George Dixon, David Douglas, Maj. Thomas Doyle, Amos Embree, Andrew Endsley, David Faris, John Frazer, Susannah Gohren, William Green in New Port, James Gilliland on Great Miami, David Griffith, Elizabeth Gilman, Gray Gary, Absolom Gray, James Gray on Mill Creek, John Gillman, Anthony Highlands on Mill Creek, John Horner, Robert Hudson at Columbia, Thomas Hill on Mad River Road, Sally Hanes, Robert Hanna, Joseph Hunter, Abraham Harry in Warren County, Enox Hurin, James Hughes, John Hand, George Howard, Philip Highfield, Edward Jackman on White water, Joseph Jenkinson, Elisha Inman on Little Miami, Andrew Jolly, Joseph

Jones, Joseph Kitchel, George Kiler, Edward Kinnan, William Legg, Abigail Long, Isaac Lindlay on Duck Creek, Abraham Lindlay, John Lorey in care of John Beaty, Jacob Light, John Lyon, Dr. David Morris, Sarah Marsters on Mill Creek, Isaac Martin on Great Miami, Doctor Morril, Thomas Miller in Indiana Territory, William M'Millan, Chauncey Marsh, James Montgomery in care of Mr. Browne, Christopher M'Gill, David M'Cance, Sirran Mash, Henry Misner, Jacob Miller in care of Maj. Zeigler, James Nickels on White water, James Nisbet in care of Gen. Findlay, Joseph Nelson on Mill Creek, Isaiah Orr, Watson Orr, Caleb Osborn, Daniel Pierson, William Patterson in Springfield, Thomas Phillips, Aaron C. Page, Aaron Powers, Daniel Reeder, Adam Richey, Matthias Ross, Abraham Rawle or Elias Miller, John Roll, Daniel Rhinehart, Israel Smith, John Schovley in Springfield, Simon Stockdell, David Sprong, Aaron Sacket, Benjamin Sayre, Lieut. James Swearingen, Adam Swadner, Henry Sullivan, Stephen Smith, Samuel Smith on Duck Creek, Lawrence Sanford, John Schetler, Timothy Titus, George Turner, Smith Thompson, Edmond Thompson, Charles Tustin, Isaac Trimble, James Wilkinson, Dennes Woodruff, Thomas Williams on White water, Stephen Wood, Isaac Willis, Joseph Wingate in Springfield, Andrew Wallace in Springfield, William Ruffin.

J. Delaplaine, in Cincinnati, wants to buy hemp.

Enos Hurin and Elizabeth Bartlett, executors of the estate of Roswell Bartlett, deceased, regarding the estate sale at the house of Jacob Steward near Ludlow's Mill.

William Salter, at Nettleville, reports a runaway apprentice boy named Joshua Meryman, age 18. He has called himself Billy Arther.

John R. Gaston, in Colerain Township, Hamilton County, about a stray mare.

A note regarding building a courthouse in Lebanon, Warren County. Apply to Ephraim Hathaway in Lebanon.

J. Delaplane, agent for John Smith, asks those indebted to Smith to settle their accounts.

No. 37, Volume VI, Wednesday, 10 April 1805, Whole No. 297

E. Reeder writes a letter to the editor regarding Dr. Bradford's letter. He mentions Gen. Schenck, Mr. Caldwell's store, Samuel James of Cincinnati, Elmore Williams.

W.C. Schenck, in Franklin, gives a deposition regarding his conversation with Dr. Bradford about the inoculation of Mrs. Reeder. He mentions Dr. Reeder.

Gen. James Wilkinson is appointed Governor of Upper Louisiana.

Officers chosen for the township of Cincinnati are listed: Samuel Patterson, Thomas M'Farland, Isaac Anderson, Stephen Wheeler, Matthew Nimmo, Nehemiah Hunt, John Harding, Joseph Vanhorn, C.R. Sedam, Joshua Williams, John Humes, Thomas Dugan, Jacob Williams, Elmore Williams, David E. Wade, Alexander King, Andrew Brannon, Elisha Landon, Jacob Stuart, Joseph Conn.

William Legg regarding his bond to John Cleves Symmes for land in Butler Co.

W.C. Schenck gives orders to his Brigade of Ohio Militia.

Abraham Freeman, in Butler County, reports a stray colt.

John Wingate, Isaac Stanley and Joseph Hunter, in Hamilton, regarding the estate settlement of John Gordon, deceased, late of Hamilton, to be held at the house of John Torrence in Hamilton.

John Daily, in Cincinnati, offers the Market House for sale.

T. Washburn, "being obliged to leave Cincinnati immediately", asks those indebted to him to settle with James Ewing or Aaron Goforth.

John S. Gano offers grist and saw mills for sale in addition to 100 acres of land. Apply to Capt. Nathan Kelley.

No. 38, Volume VI, Wednesday, 17 April 1805, Whole No. 298

Michael Baldwin, Daniel Symmes, Joseph Kerr and William Creighton, Jun., print some laws of Ohio.

Brig. Gen. James Findlay gives orders to the Troop of Light Horse Brigade.

William Corry, executor of the estate of William M'Millan, deceased, about the estate settlement.

Silas Hurin wants to hire a tanner and currier and a shoemaker at Lebanon.

John Dill & Company have moved their saddlery shop to the house formerly occupied by Lewis Lang on Columbia Street in Cincinnati.

John Reily and William Corry (attorney) regarding a suit in the Butler County Court of Common Pleas: Peyton Short, of Kentucky, vs. Gen. James Wilkinson.

Martin Baum, D.E. Wade, D. Mayo, Jesse Hunt and C. Killgore regarding goods for sale by the Miami Exporting Company. Apply to William Stanley or to Griffin Yeatman in Cincinnati.

John S. Gano has property of Israel Ludlow, dec'd, for sale by order of the Hamilton County Orphans' Court.

No. 39, Volume VI, Wednesday, 24 April 1805, Whole No. 299

Michael Baldwin, James Pritchard and William Creighton, Jun., print laws.

Marriage: Aaron Goforth, of Cincinnati, married Miss Debby Winters, of Frankfort, Kentucky, on 8 April 1805.

John B.C. Lucas is appointed Chief Justice of the Courts of Upper Louisiana. Dr. Joseph Brown, of Philadelphia, is appointed Secretary.

John Stall & Son have dissolved their partnership.

Edward H. Stall, druggist and apothecary, has moved his store across the street to the house formerly occupied by John Mahard.

Mr. Davenport regarding his display of wax figures at Mr. Yeatman's tavern.

J.T. Chunn, at Columbia, has corn for sale.

Alexander Smith, Baker, in Cincinnati, has lime and gunpowder for sale.

John Griffin, in Cincinnati, has goods for sale at Henry Ewing's house.

John S. Gano offers land for sale, property of the estate of George W. Burnet, deceased, by order of the Orphans' Court of Hamilton County.

No. 40, Volume VI, Wednesday, 1 May 1805, Whole No. 300

Michael Baldwin and Daniel Symmes print another law of Ohio.

Officers for the Troop of Horse are elected: Capt. James Forguson, Lieut. Elmore Williams, Lieut. Isaac Mills and Cornet Stephen Ludlow.

Wm. C. Schenck, at Franklin, has land for sale. He mentions Griffing's Mill, Gunkle's Mills, James Dearth, George Gillespie, Joseph Crain, M'Donald's Mill on the Miami.

John W. Miles, in Cincinnati, reports a runaway apprentice, Ignatius Gattin.

Jacob Wheeler, of Cincinnati, regarding a runaway apprentice, James Lewis.

Robert Brasher has hats for sale at his shop in Cincinnati.

John N. Cumming (living in Newark, New Jersey) and Wm. C. Schenck have land for sale. They mention Symmes' patent, Judge Lowe's farm, Mr. Hineman, Reuben Carter.

Isaac Anderson, in Cincinnati, offers a house for rent, formerly occupied by Samuel Dick and next door to Isaac Anderson.

James Smith, late Sheriff, regarding land for sale, the property of Benjamin Stites, dec'd, at the suit of Evan Bane. Also the property of Levi Woodward (part of James Henry's section) at the suit of Robert Wilson.

No. 41, Volume VI, Wednesday, 8 May 1805, Whole No. 301

Michael Baldwin, Daniel Symmes and William Creighton, Jun., print laws.

Gen. Gano is appointed clerk of the Supreme Court for Hamilton County.

Marriage: Charles Farran married Miss Pheby Kotts, both of Cincinnati, on Thursday evening, 2 May 1805.

William Orr, living in Waynsville, reports a stray horse.

Thaddeus Hanford, in Columbia, wants an apprentice to the cooper's trade.

Benjamin and John Piatt, at Lawrenceburgh, regarding a runaway slave, Rose.

O. Ormsby, in Cincinnati, says the partnership of Daniel Conner and Oliver Ormsby is dissolved due to the death of Mr. Conner. Please settle your accounts with William Stanley.

No. 42, Volume VI, Wednesday, 15 May 1805, Whole No. 302

Michael Baldwin, Daniel Symmes and William Creighton, Jun., print laws.

Notes from the Court of Common Pleas of Hamilton County mention Jacob

Gray, Benjamin Williams, Aaron Cherry, Nicholas Walters, James Richardson, the heirs of Asa Harvey, Mr. Long, Mr. Joyce, Charles Willey, Barton Lovelace.

Matthew Nimmo, in Cincinnati, lost a gold watch engraved with his name and the date of 20 August 1777.

David M'Clure, of Montgomery County, regarding a note to Doctor M'Clellan of Greene County.

Jacob White has several horses for sale.

Samuel Bennet, of Anderson Township, Hamilton County, administrator of the estate of Thomas Jewel, dec'd, regarding the estate settlement.

No. 43, Volume VI, Wednesday, 22 May 1805, Whole No. 303

Gideon Grainger, Postmaster General of the U.S., arrived in Cincinnati.

John S. Gano regarding appraisements and inventories due in the Court of Common Pleas, Hamilton County.

James Ferguson, in Cincinnati, is going to Philadelphia and asks those indebted to him to settle their accounts before he leaves.

Mrs. Hannah Willis is opening a boarding house in the house lately occupied by Daniel Conner in Cincinnati.

William Stanley, agent for O. Ormsby, has goods for sale, formerly the property of the late Daniel Conner & Company.

William Love, living on Clear Creek near Squire Ball's place, regarding a strayed mare.

No. 44, Volume VI, Wednesday, 29 May 1805, Whole No. 304

Capt. James Smith regarding a meeting of the Cincinnati Light Infantry.

Gen. Wilkinson arrived in Cincinnati on Wednesday on his way to St. Louis.

The following were elected Directors of the Exporting Company: Martin Baum, Daniel Mayo, John N.C. Schenck, Jesse Hunt, G. Yeatman, John Riddle, Samuel Heighway, Christian Waldsmith, David E. Wade, Charles Killgore and Samuel C. Vance. The meeting was held at Mr. Yeatman's place.

Robert Robison, living on the S.W. branch of the Big Miami, four miles from Dayton, reports a stray horse. Deliver to Isaac Anderson in Cincinnati or to Joseph Parks on Dicks Creek.

John S. Gano reports that the Court of Common Pleas of Hamilton County have appointed John Matson, of Miami Township, as County Commissioner in the place of William Ludlow who resigned.

Ralph Hunt, living on the Little Miami in Warren County, at the place known as Woods' Mills, has land for sale.

Brownson & M'Farland have opened a hatting business in Cincinnati.

Elias Crane, living near the Big Hill, reports a mare that strayed from Nathan Kelly's place. Deliver to Ephraim Kibby in Deerfield.

No. 45, Volume VI, Wednesday, 5 June 1805, Whole No. 305

A notice regarding an election for the president of the Miami Exporting Company to be held at Griffin Yeatman's.

Michael Baldwin has been appointed U.S. Marshal for Ohio in place of David Zeigler who resigned.

Capt. James Ferguson regarding a meeting of the Troop of Light Dragoons.

John Lemon, Jun., of Georgetown, Kentucky, regarding a bond to Tobias Butler of Hamilton County for land on White Oak Creek in Ohio.

Samuel James, in Cincinnati, reports a stray horse.

Mary Wallen, William M'Clellan & James Smith, in Hamilton, administrators of the estate of Elias Wallen, of Butler County, deceased, about the estate sale.

Mary Wallen, administratrix of the estate of John Kiser, deceased, regarding the estate sale to be held at Elias Wallen's late residence in Butler County.

Isaiah Bryant has taken over Christian Waldsmith's fulling mill on the Little Miami where he intends carrying on the Clothier's business. He mentions Ezekiel Hutchinson's Inn in Cincinnati in the house formerly occupied by Joel Williams.

No. 46, Volume VI, Wednesday, 12 June 1805, Whole No. 306

Michael Baldwin and Daniel Symmes print a new law of the state of Ohio.

A note regarding a meeting of the Republican Society of Cincinnati to be held at Elmore Williams' house.

An account of the shooting death, in Champaign County, of Major Jesse Braken, by Asa Roberts. Daniel Roberson offers a reward for his arrest.

Aaron Goforth and Griffin Yeatman regarding an ordinance of Cincinnati.

No. 47, Volume VI, Wednesday, 19 June 1805, Whole No. 307

Michael Baldwin and James Pritchard regarding the budget of the State of Ohio mentions Nathaniel Willis (printer), George Renick, Robert Smith, Anthony Smith, John Carlisle, Adam Betz, William Creighton, Jr., James Davenport, Robert Steele, William Goforth, Nathaniel Massie, John Blanchard, Thomas Steele, William Betz, Edward Sherlock, Thomas G. Bradford, Dix & Cutler. Also about the repeal of certain laws mentions Doctor William Burnet, the elder, Sally Mills, Jane Mitchson, Lucy Petit.

Michael Baldwin & Daniel Symmes print a law and mention George Fithian.

Aaron Goforth and Griffin Yeatman about ordinances of Cincinnati mention Charles Vattier and Richard Harris' ferry house.

Jacob Grey, horse thief, has escaped from the Cincinnati jail.

William Fuller, suspected of having killed an Indian on the Miami River, was killed on Monday last by a fall from his horse.

Thomas Williams, in Cincinnati, wants to buy good deer skins.

Ray & Schillenger, at the Round Bottom, want to buy hogshead hoop poles.

John & Matthew Nimmo, in Cincinnati, ask those indebted to them to settle their accounts.

Weaver & Martin, in Cincinnati, ask those indebted to them to settle their accounts with John Mahard.

James Smith, living near Winton's Mill, reports a stray mare. Deliver to John Torence or William M'Clelland in Hamilton.

Daniel Reeder, Jonathan Williams, John R. Mills, Daniel Schenck and Mars Williams, Trustees of the Presbyterian Meeting House on Duck Creek, want to hire brickmakers.

John Orbison, living on Seven Mile Creek, three miles above Winton's Mill, reports a stray mare. Deliver to John Torrence in Hamilton.

William Goforth, Jr., about a Nova Caesaria Lodge meeting in Cincinnati.

Samuel Heighway, at Waynesville, about pre-emption land, mentions Samuel Tamsett, John Tamsett, Richard Lackie, Solomon Stanbury, William Vineyard.

Apply to Doctor James Welsh, of Dayton, about land for sale on Wolf Creek.

Daniel Roberson, at Mad River in Champaign County, offers a reward for the arrest of Asa Roberts for the murder of Jesse Braken.

Thomas Dugan, of Cincinnati, asks those indebted to him to pay their bills.

Isaac VanNuys wants to hire an apprentice to the clock and watchmaking and tinning businesses.

Samuel James, in Cincinnati, regarding a stray horse.

No. 48, Volume VI, Wednesday, 26 June 1805, Whole No. 308

John Cranmere regarding the meeting of the Nova Caesaria Lodge.

A note about the robbery of Thomas Nelson, merchant, of Brackin County.

William Stake, taylor, has "lately removed from the state of Maryland", and has opened his shop at Mrs. Doyle's house on Main Street.

Peter Love has started his rope making business in Cincinnati.

Brig. Gen. W.C. Schenck, at Franklin, says that Maj. Ephraim Kibbey is appointed Inspector of the Brigade in place of John Greer, absent from the state.

William Ferguson has dry goods for sale at his store in Lebanon.

Enoch Ingersull, administrator of the estate of John Hereman, dec'd, late of White Water township, Hamilton County, regarding the estate settlement.

William Clark, post rider, asks those indebted to him to settle their bills, including those holding J. Carpenter's or Thomas Clark's receipts.

John Riely, at Hamilton, is taking bids for building a jail in Butler County.

John Franklin, living in Gallatin, Sumner County, Tennessee, reports a runaway slave named John, a wagon maker.

Elijah Embree and Jesse Dunkin, living at Old Chillicothe on the Little Miami, report a stray mare.

William M'Farland, Sheriff, Hamilton County, regarding Jacob Grey's escape.

Carmack & Smith have commenced the cabinet and house carpenter's business in Cincinnati in the house belonging to Jeremiah Hunt.

George Hughes wants to buy starch at his shop in the Artificer's Yard in Cincinnati.

No. 49, Volume VI, Wednesday, 3 July 1805, Whole No. 309

John Sloane, Daniel Symmes, Michael Baldwin and James Pritchard print some laws of Ohio.

A letter to the editor from Jacob Burnet is printed and mentions Mr. Symmes. Aaron Goforth and Griffin Yeatman regarding an ordinance of Cincinnati.

Marriage: Doctor Abraham Edwards, Surgeon's mate in the Army, to Miss Ruth Hunt, daughter of Col. Thomas Hunt, Commandant of the 1st U.S. Regiment, at Fort Wayne on 4 June 1805.

Mr. Brown, who lately returned from Fort Wayne, gives a report of the great fire in Detroit.

The following are appointed members of the legislative council of Indiana Territory: Benjamin Chambers of Dearborn, Samuel Gwathmey of Clarke, John Rice Jones of Knox, Pierre Menard of Randolph and John Hay of St. Clair County.

Capt. James Smith announces a meeting, for July Fourth, of the Cincinnati Light Infantry Company at William Ruffin's house. Mentions A. King.

Capt. Stanley's and Capt. Carpenter's companies of Militia will meet at the Courthouse in Cincinnati for the July Fourth celebration.

David Zeigler is closing out his store and will rent the building.

Jacob White and Joseph Delaplaine, in Cincinnati, regarding their dry goods business and partnership under the name of White & Delaplaine.

Martha Bird, daughter of Samuel Moore of South bend and wife of John Bird, formerly of South bend, regarding her suit, in the Ohio Supreme Court, for divorce from her husband. She says he left her and married Abigal Atter.

William Wells, Agent of Indian Affairs, at Fort Wayne, regarding some stray mares found by the Delaware Indians. Apply to Henry Brown at Fort Hamilton.

A list of letters at the Post Office in Cincinnati includes Capt. Dudley Avery, Henry Allen, Joseph Avaicest, Thomas Arthers, David Atherton at White water, William Buchanan in care of Joseph Conn, James Badgley, John Blackburn in Columbia, Armiger Bell in Dearborn County, Issachar Bevis at Colerain, Capt. Charles Britain, William Brown at Columbia, Jacob Blasdel, Frederick Blew, James Baxter, Jona Buffonton, Joshua Carter, James Cunningham, Daniel Clark on Duck Creek, Samuel Carpenter, Ezra Clark, Joseph Carberry in Dearborn County, Able Casto in care of Mr. Fox, Noys Canfield, Barnerd Cross, Thomas Cammel, Jacob R. Comton, Isaac Connor, King Dearmond, Daniel Doty on Big Prairie, Enoch Danford, Zina Doty, Samuel Doris on Little Miami, Eli Elstun in Columbia, David Eaton, John Ferguson, John Fryer in Columbia, Stephen Fox on Mill Creek, Andrew Gill, Francis Griffee, James Gallahar on Turtle Creek, John Groom in Columbia, Daniel Gillman, James Green in care of Mr. Kamper, Philip Gatch on Little Miami, Mary Hanna, John Hancock, Elisha Hopkins on Little Miami, Christian Hilderbrand on Little Miami, Thadeus Handford in Columbia, Jones Harris, David Harris, Rubert Hewit, Zenis Hill, Joseph Hart, Jose Heulings on Little Miami, Asa Harvey on Great Miami, Barbary Howard, Walter Johnston or John Bridges, Elijah Inman at Columbia, Cornelius Johnson, John Kinny, William Killen on Duck Creek, George Kelly, Alexander Kirkpatrick, Daniel Lambert, John Little, Sally Lusk, Richard M'Clure in Columbia, John M'Allester in care of Joseph Conn, Capt. Jonathan M'Carty in Dearborn County, Isaac Mullin on Little Miami, John Miller, Conkling Miller, Joshua M'Dowell, John Melick, Robert M'Elhany, Ezra Miller in Springfield, Serren Marsh, John Machesney, Jr., Rebecca M'Call, Thomas Neal, Joel Nelson, Ezekial Oliver, Andrew Prier, Thomas Philips on Little Miami, Margret Patterson, Daniel Perine at North Bend, Geo. Rittenhouse or

Doctor Loosborough, David Riddle, Robert Richey, George Roach, Henry Reese, John Richardson on Great Miami in care of Joseph Conn, Stephen Robinson in Boon County, Jean Stuart, George Swingle, Rev. Peter Smith, Abraham Smith on Duck Creek, Oliver Stutson, Litishi Smith, Elijah Sparks, Mahlon Smith, Timothy Suel, James Stevenson, Nathan or Thomas Smith on Great Miami, Calvin Sayrs in Springfield, Andrew Tharp, William S. Tump or Jump, John Trim in Springfield, Noah Tryon at North Bend, Cornelius Vanorsdall at Peter Banta's, David Vail on Little Miami, James Whallon on Mill Creek, Robert Warwick on Mill Creek, Anthony Williams, John Wrigley, Maj. Woodward, Wm. Wilson, Lewis Wilie at White Water, Samuel Wilson at Colerain, Lodewick Weller, David Walker in care of Enoch Buckson, Joseph Wingate, Jacob Wilson, John Ward on Little Miami, Peter Youtzer. Entered by William Ruffin, post master.

Edward Roll says his wife, Sally Roll, left him and he won't pay her bills.

Ezekiel Hutchinson, in Cincinnati, regarding a horse stolen by David Gleen of Washington, Kentucky.

Jacob Skellman, living on the Hamilton Road about twelve miles from Cincinnati in Springfield township, reports some stray horses.

No. 50, Volume VI, Wednesday, 10 July 1805, Whole No. 310

The contract between John Cleves Symmes and Elias Boudinot is printed. Signed by Isaac Woodruff, judge in Essex County, N.J., and Griffin Yeatman.

A letter from John Cleves Symmes, witnessed by Abraham Kinney and Jacob Losey, mentions Mr. Boudinot and William Burnet of Newark.

Accounts of Fourth of July celebrations mention Thomas Rawlins' oration, John Cleves Symmes, Matthew Nimmo, Governor Tiffin, Capt. Smith's Infantry Company, James Smith, Judge Turner, T. Williams, I. Anderson, S. M'Farland.

A note regarding Judge Symmes' answer to Mr. Burnet's observations about the College Township.

Lieut. Elmor Williams about a meeting of the Troop of Light Dragoons.

Joseph Prince and William Ruffin about the suits of Charles Vattier vs. Asa S. Richardson and Isaac Dexter vs. James Turner and Asa S. Richardson.

John S. Gano regarding rates of taxes in Hamilton County.

George Larison, administrator of the estate of Rachel Badgley, dec'd, about the estate sale.

Patrick Maniville has opened a skin dressing, breeches and glove making business in the house lately occupied by Mr. Dill, saddler, on Main Street.

Elmor Williams, in Cincinnati, regarding the well owned by Williams & Moore.

John Whetstone, living on the Ohio, one mile above the mouth of the Little Miami, reports that he found two horses.

No. 51, Volume VI, Wednesday, 17 July 1805, Whole No. 311

The text of the court case of Elias Boudinot vs. John C. Symmes is printed and mentions John Smith, Davis Keelin, James Humphreys, George Sickle, Mr. Findlay, Mr. M'Millan, Mr. Smith, Mr. Massie, Mr. Langham, Mr. Cadwell, Mr. Meigs, Mr. Goforth.

John Cleves Symmes writes a letter to the public and mentions Mr. Burnet.

A letter to the public from A. Wheeler mentions Mr. Fuller, "my friend John W. Browne, in Liberty Hall", Mr. How of Whitewater, Daniel Piatt.

Mr. & Mrs. Smith say that Mrs. Smith has recovered from her illness and they will perform a play at the Theater.

More accounts of the Fourth of July celebrations mention Thomas Hinkson in Columbia, Maj. Gen. Gano, Col. Oliver Spencer, Col. John Armstrong, Maj. Ruffin, Mr. Peck, Col. Spencer, Col. Thomas Sanford.

John Whitworth & Company have goods for sale at their store in Cincinnati.

John Stall, N. Hunt and T. Williams regarding the addition to be made to the Market House in Cincinnati.

John Nimmo, in Cincinnati, has his house and buildings for sale.

Peter Banta, living near Holes' Station above Franklin on the Great Miami, reports a stray horse.

Ezekiel Hutchinson regarding two notes in David Glenn's coat, one from

Richard Allen and the other from Jno. M'Clean.

No. 52, Volume VI, Wednesday, 24 July 1805, Whole No. 312
An excerpt from the journals of the House of Representatives mentions John Cleves Symmes, William H. Harrison. A deed is printed from James Smith, sheriff of Hamilton County to Jacob Burnet, William M'Millan and James Findlay. It mentions Nathan Lamme, John Cleves Symmes, Daniel Symmes. A letter from Jacob Burnet is printed regarding Mr. Symmes.

An unsigned letter to the editors mentions Mr. Smith, Judge Symmes, Mr. M'Farland, Mr. Grey, Mr. Walters.

Henry Montfort, in Warren County, found a horse within two miles of Beaty's tavern in Butler County.

John S. Gano regarding Sarah Barker's suit for divorce from Stephen Allison Barker, her husband. She says they married about 11 years ago and he left her in January 1804. They had six children, two who died and four who are bound out.

John S. Gano and Trypheny Rogers regarding her suit of divorce from Philip Rogers, her husband. They married about six years ago near Wheeling, Virginia. He left her and their one child after three years and took all the household furniture with him. He is said to reside in Georgia where he works as a sailor.

William Byrd wants to buy wheat.

Alexander Stinson and William Nesbit, living on Twin Creek near Squire Gunkle's mill, in German township, Montgomery County, reports a stray horse.

Capt. James Smith regarding a meeting of the Cincinnati Light Infantry Company at William Ruffin's house.

James Smith, late sheriff, regarding a sheriff's sale of the property of Benjamin Stites, dec'd, at the suit of Even Bane.

No. 1, Volume VII, Wednesday, 31 July 1805, Whole No. 313
Michael Baldwin, Daniel Symmes and Joseph Kerr print laws of Ohio.

The president has appointed Thomas Doyle, age 11, a son of the late Major Thomas Doyle of Cincinnati, a midshipman in the U.S. Navy. Included is a letter from Gen. Henry Carbery to young Mr. Doyle. He mentions Maj. Zeigler (who was with Maj. Thomas Doyle during the Revolutionary War). Carbery says the young Doyle was "born in war - in a Garrison while your father commanded it".

A note regarding the drowning of Carman Parce on the 19th of July. He had a paper from John Nimmo on his person. Mr. Daulton, postmaster at Limestone, says he left some property there. He was buried at Limestone.

John S. Gano and Jacob Burnet regarding the suit of James Hinds vs. William Gregg, a non-resident, in the Court of Common Pleas of Hamilton County.

Thomas Davis, in Cincinnati, has had a lot of sickness in his family for the past year and informs his creditors that he will pay them soon.

Samuel Foster, in Cincinnati, regarding a runaway apprentice boy, Joseph Walling, nearly 12 years of age.

No. 2, Volume VII, Wednesday, 7 August 1805, Whole No. 314
Michael Baldwin, Daniel Symmes and Joseph Kerr print some laws of Ohio.

The Republican Society will meet next Monday at the Courthouse.

Two boys by the name of Davis, age 14 and 8, drowned in the Little Miami on Monday, 29 July 1805, while at Waldsmith's Mill.

Caleb German and Ezra Ferris, at Duck Creek, write a letter to the Miami Baptist Association and the church at Pleasant Run regarding their meeting.

Thomas Williams and Samuel Stitt regarding an ordinance of Cincinnati.

Brig. Gen. James Findlay and John R. Mills regarding meetings of the brigade regiments. They mention Mr. Ferris on Little Miami and Emanuel Vantreese.

A note regarding a meeting of the coopers of Hamilton County to be held at the house of Mr. Hinkston in Columbia.

An unsigned letter to the editor mentions the Liberty Hall, Mr. Browne, John W. Browne, Taylor Browne, Maj. Gen. Gano.

A letter to the inhabitants of the Miami Purchase mentions Mr. Burnet, Elias Boudinot, John Cleves Symmes, Gen. Ogden, Doctor William Burnet, Judge Marsh, Gen. Cummins, Gershom Gard, Daniel Marsh.

A note regarding the spinning records made by Mrs. Hause and Miss Betsy Chinoweth, both of Jefferson County, Kentucky, on 18 July 1805.

A note regarding the death of Basil Beckwith, merchant of Shepherdsville, who was killed by lightning in Livingston County on Thursday, 11 July 1805.

Thomas Gibson and John S. Gano regarding a recent unsigned letter in the Spy, mention Adrian Hagerman and William M'Farland.

Wm. M'Farland regarding a meeting of the Republicans of Cincinnati at the house of Elmor Williams.

Allan B. Magruder is appointed an advocate of the U.S. in Lower Louisiana.

Obituary: Capt. Daniel M'Lane, died Monday evening, 30 June 1805, (at Natchez?). He was an officer during the Revolutionary War.

David Zeigler and Wm. M'Farland regarding an ordinance of Cincinnati.

Charlotte C. Ludlow, John Ludlow, James Findlay and Sineas Pearson, administrators of the estate of Israel Ludlow, deceased, regarding the estate sale.

John Nimmo and Matthew Nimmo have dissolved their partnership. The store is now operated by John Nimmo. Witnessed by Hezekiah Flint.

Samuel C. Vance, at Lawrenceburgh, has land for sale on Tanner's Creek.

An auction of books will be held at the late store of Mr. M'Cullough.

Samuel Hilditch, James Matthews, William Brown, Benjamin Stites and Edward Meeks, at Columbia, regarding a meeting, at Samuel Armstrong's Inn in Columbia, about building a School House.

Samuel C. Vance, at Lawrenceburgh in Indiana Territory, has land for sale.

Samuel C. Vance and Sineas Pearson have land for sale. Apply to John Reily of Hamilton.

John Nimmo has a new shipment of goods for sale at his store in Cincinnati.

John Huston, in Hamilton, says his wife, Mary Huston, left him on the 29th of January 1802, and he will not honor debts of her contracting.

Mahlon Baker has land for sale on Gregory's Creek, 1 mile from Great Miami.

Peter Bell, at Sycamore near Waldsmith's Mill, reports that he found a mare.

No. 4, Volume VII, Wednesday, 21 August 1805, Whole No. 316

More of a letter to the inhabitants of the Miami Purchase from John Cleves Symmes mentions Mr. Boudinot, Elias Boudinot, Mr. Burnet, William Burnet, Capt. Thomas Kinney, Jacob Burnet.

Michael Baldwin and Daniel Symmes print another law of Ohio.

A letter to the editors from John W. Browne, of Cincinnati.

William M'Farland says the Republican Society of Cincinnati has elected Matthew Nimmo as chairman. John Riddle and John Nimmo are appointed delegates to the meeting at Pitman's Tavern.

An account of the shooting death of John Marshal, son of a farmer living near Cincinnati, on Monday night, 19 August 1805, by Mordaica Thruston.

Jockey John Long and Long John Long have been convicted of horse stealing.

A note regarding nominees for offices mentions Dr. Stephen Wood, Thomas M'Farland, Hezekiah Price, Adrian Hagerman, Col. John Jones and John Matson.

Hugh Moore "has just arrived in this place" with dry goods for sale.

Walter L. Robertson, at Anderson in Hamilton County, says he will not pay the bills his wife, Patty Robertson, might contract.

John Lyon and Cornelius Voorheese regarding the Cincinnati and Yellow Spring stage coach. It leaves from Mr. Yeatman's tavern.

John Stall, Thomas Williams and N. Hunt, in Cincinnati, regarding an addition to the Market House now being built by Thomas Clark.

Isaac VanNuys, administrator of the estate of Isaac Gildersleve, deceased, regarding the estate sale.

John Dill & Company regarding a runaway apprentice to the saddling business, Edward Miller, about 18 years old.

No. 5, Volume VII, Wednesday, 28 August 1805, Whole No. 317

Michael Baldwin and Daniel Symmes print a law of the State of Ohio.

A reply to John W. Browne's recent letter is printed.

Jonathan S. Findlay, one of the partners in the firm of Joseph Carpenter & Company, has sold out his interest in the Western Spy to Joseph Carpenter who will now act as sole editor.

A note regarding the County Collector, Adrian Hagerman, mentions Mr. Browne and the Liberty Hall.

An account of the death of Seth Cutter, of Cincinnati, on Saturday, August 24, 1805. He was buried when the well he was digging collapsed. He "left a widow and a numerous offspring".

A note regarding the shooting of Mr. Marshal by Mr. Thruston.

Notice of a meeting of the Republican Society delegates at Pitman's Tavern.

Hugh Moore has just returned from Philadelphia and Baltimore with goods for sale. He wants to buy wheat at his mill on Mill Creek, lately known by the name of Ludlow's Mill.

Joseph F. LaCroix and Alexis Dubois, in Springfield, have dissolved their partnership as LaCroix & Dubois, and ask those indebted to them to pay their bills.

Thomas Dugan has a new shipment of goods for sale at his store in Cincinnati.

John Whetston, living on the Ohio River one mile above the mouth of the Little Miami, reports that he found some horses.

White & Delaplaine have moved their store to the house lately occupied by John & Matthew Nimmo in Cincinnati.

Maj. Gen. John S. Gano, Charles Killgore and William Ruffin regarding the meeting of the Brigade at Aaron Nutts' house.

Thomas Moore, living at Mr. Hunt's tanyard, says he carries on the pump making business there.

William Walker, living near Yellow Springs, lost a note from Jacob Fowler.

Isaac Parker, living in Butler County, on Elk Creek about six miles from the Big Prairie, reports a stray horse.

No. 6, Volume VII, Wednesday, 4 September 1805, Whole No. 318

More of the letter to John W. Browne is printed.

Michael Baldwin and Daniel Symmes print another law of Ohio.

Hon. Wm. Sprigg, a judge of the Supreme Court of Ohio, has been appointed a judge in the Michigan Territory in place of Hon. Samuel Huntington.

A note regarding the arrival of Gen. James Wilkinson at St. Louis.

Joseph Carpenter, editor of the Western Spy, says he has changed the name of the paper to "The Western Spy and Miami Gazette".

A note regarding the meeting of the Hamilton County delegates at Pittman's Tavern mention Jacob Skillman, Othniel Looker, Edward Tiffin, Stephen Wood, Adrian Hegeman, Hezekiah Price, Col. John Jones, James Ewing and John Matson.

Thomas Dugan has a supply of books for sale at his store in Cincinnati.

William Woodward, Samuel Foster and Seth Cutter, administrators of the estate of Seth Cutter, late of Cincinnati, deceased, about the estate settlement.

John Smith has moved his store to the house lately occupied by John Dill & Company on Main Street in Cincinnati.

Zachariah Holland, in Cincinnati, reports that he found a horse.

George Paine, of Smith County, Tennessee, reports a runaway slave, Bill, who calls himself Tom Gibbs and crossed the Ohio at Kenady's Ferry in March of 1805.

Joel Williams has found a horse. He also is buying wheat.

William Wyatt, at Redding in Hamilton County, has lots for sale in Redding.

Hugh Moore lost a green umbrella on the road from Deerfield to Chillicothe.

No. 7, Volume VII, Wednesday, 11 September 1805, Whole No. 319

Michael Baldwin and Daniel Symmes print another law of the State of Ohio.

The administrators of the estate of Israel Ludlow, deceased, have land near the Big Hill, now occupied by George Wallace, for sale.

Letters to the public nominate persons for offices and mention Col. John Jones, Jonathan Pittman, Jacob Broadwell, Ogden Ross, Joseph Kitchel, John

Ludlow, Stephen Wood, John Wallace, Ichabod B. Millar, John Matson, Wm. Ruffin.

Obituary: Asa Brownson, "lately settled in this place", died on Monday night, 9 September 1805, in Cincinnati.

Benjamin Park is elected a member of Congress from Indiana Territory.

Anna Bowser and Daniel Bowser regarding their petition as heirs of the estate of Henry Moyer, deceased. They mention the widow of the deceased.

Jesse Reeder, living on Duck Creek in Columbia Township, found saddle bags.

John Smith wants to buy hogs and wheat at his store in Cincinnati, his mill, and his warehouse in Columbia.

Sidney Field, executrix, and John Smith, executor, of the estate of Seth Field, deceased, late of Anderson Township, regarding the estate sale.

A notice regarding the Cincinnati Horse Races is printed.

William Woodward, Samuel Foster and Seth Cutter, administrators of the estate of Seth Cutter, deceased, regarding the estate sale.

Jacob Williams, of Cincinnati, asks those indebted to him to settle their accounts by delivering wheat to Joseph Vanhorn's mill.

John Nimmo & Matthew Nimmo ask those indebted to them to pay their bills.

A notice that Mr. Brannon will soon inspect each house for their fire buckets.

No. 8, Volume VII, Wednesday, 18 September 1805, Whole No. 320

Michael Baldwin and James Pritchard print another law of Ohio.

Benjamin Anderson has land for sale in Hamilton County on the east side of the Little Miami on the state road to Chillicothe now occupied by Mr. Harness. Apply to Col. John Armstrong of Columbia.

John Armstrong, in Columbia, has land for sale or rent.

Jonathan Williams, Daniel Reeder, John R. Mills, Daniel Schenck and Marsh Williams, trustees of the Duck Creek Presbyterian Congregation, about building a meeting house in Columbia township.

A letter to the editor mentions Colonel Jones, Mr. Broadwell and Mr. Smith.

Capt. James Smith regarding a meeting of the Cincinnati Light Infantry Company at Major Ruffin's place.

A Cincinnati school trustees' meeting is to be held at Yeatman's house.

The Ohio Almanac for 1806, by Robert Stubbs, will be printed.

William M'Clelland, at Hamilton, Butler County, says a negro man named William Hawkins is in the jail there. He says he belongs to William Ross, living six miles from Limestone, and has indentures signed by Hamilton Clark of the court of Greensburgh, Pennsylvania.

Alexander Chambers about the ad placed by Bladen Ashby concerning their interest in a section of land. He mentions Edward Gee.

John Nain, living on Bear Creek about 8 miles from Dayton, reports a stray horse. Deliver to George Koons, living near Dayton.

Robert Benham, living in Warren County, near Lebanon, has land for sale.

No. 9, Volume VII, Wednesday, 25 September 1805, Whole No. 321

Michael Baldwin, Joseph Kerr and James Pritchard print laws of Ohio.

Marriage: Daniel C. Cooper, of Dayton, to Mrs. Sophia Burnet, of Cincinnati, on Sunday evening, 22 September 1805.

A letter to the editor nominates men for office and mentions Joseph Kitchel, John Armstrong, Aaron Goforth, John Jones, I.B. Miller, Joseph Vanhorn.

Jacob Broadwell says that he is not eligible to serve as representative.

An account of the death of Gen. Wm. Lucas on Tuesday, 17 September 1805, in Scioto County. He was killed by a falling tree. He leaves a wife and 2 children.

John S. Gano says that Col. Benjamin Whiteman is elected Brigadier General of the Third Brigade of Ohio Militia.

William M'Farland, Sheriff, regarding the sites of elections mentions Thomas Brown in Anderson township, Ebenezar Ayres in Sycamore, Samuel Muchmore in Columbia, Ebenezer Cooly in White water, Jonathan Pitman in Springfield, James Harding in Colerain, Jacob Mogan in Miami, Col. John Benefield in Crosby.

Brig. Gen. W.C. Schenck, at Franklin, regarding meetings of the regiments of Ohio Militia. He mentions Calvin Ball, Capt. Clark, Dr. Benjamin DuBois.

John Daily wants to hire a cooper. He also lost notes from Jacob Williams and Seth Cutter.

John M'Quady and Samuel Berry, living in Woodford County, Kentucky, report several runaway slaves: Selah, John, Peter, Bill, Jacob, Charles, Jack, Cyrus.

No. 10, Volume VII, Wednesday, 2 October 1805, Whole No. 322

John Slone, Daniel Symmes, Joseph Kerr and Michael Baldwin print Ohio laws.

William Allger, living on Dick's Creek at David Logan's, reports a stray horse. Deliver to Dr. Reeder in Franklin.

A list of letters at the Post Office in Cincinnati includes John Arnall at Big Miami, Thomas Armstrong, Rosswell Bartlett, Thomas Bradsh, George Bickham, Jr., in care of Maj. Zeigler, Joseph Billings in Columbia, Jonathan Baker, John Broadwell, William Bugh, John Baldwin, Reuben Carter at Big Hill, John Clark, John Cotton on Big Miami, George Cooper, Peter Camp, James Crooks, John Cummins, Edward Covington, William Cunningham in Dearborn County, Conrod Cook, Jacob R. Compton, Wm. Callwell in care of Capt Jamison, George Cullom, Stephen Clark in Butler County, James Charters, John Clark, James Crane on White water, William Cox, Joseph Catterline, Jesse Dodd, James Dill in care of John Ludlow, Thomas Depriest, Joseph Davis, David Enyart, James Eliot, Joshua Edwards at White water, Andrew Endsley at White water, Arthur Elliot, Richard Frazy, Jeremiah French, David Felter, Elizabeth Gard in care of Moses Veal, Robert Goudy, Elizabeth Gilman, Andrew Gill, John Hart, David Harris, Richard Harris, Henry Hennen in care of Capt. Fox, Cornelius Harley, William Hunter in care of Charles Conn, Robert Hanna, Enos Hurin, Sarah Hinsey in care of Sampson M'Cullough, John Harris, Archibald Hood in care of Mr. Dugan, Capt. John T. Hall, Ezekiel Hutchinson, Thomas Hunt on Gregory's Creek, William Irvin, Edward W. Miller, Joseph Jenkinson, Alexander Kirkpatrick, Benajah Kitchell at White water, Joshua Knowlton, Paul Lewis, James M'Nealy on Mill Creek, Samuel B. Miller, Alexander M'Nutt, Francis Molston, Nicholas Molston, James Martin, Henry W. Miller, Benjamin Morris in Columbia, John Oblinger, Jeremiah Orsborn, James Porter, Jane Pottman, Bethier Potter, David Pierson in Springfield, Michael Parse, Hezekiah Phelps, Robert Piatt, John Radlay, George Reno in North Bend, Mary Rogers on Duck Creek, Benjamin Ross, Nathaniel Ross in Columbia, Reuben Stout, Thomas Skinner, William Spencer in Dearborn County, Reuben Staton in Coldrain, Jacob Stewart, Henry Sullivant, John Smith and William Anthony, Samuel Shumar, Joseph T. Smith, John Stockton, John Smalley, Daniel Symmes, Isaac Sparks, Adam Stewart, George Sly on Little Miami, Robert Steel, Cornelius R. Sedam, Oliver Stutson, Aaron Stout in Colderain, Jacob Taylor, Christopher Troy on Little Miami, James Thomas in care of Joseph Brown at White water, Robert Townsley, Isaac Vanmeter, Abraham Vansickle or Henry Weaver, Amos Valentine, Stephen Vorhees, William Vanwinkle, Clark Valentine, Andrew Wilson, Clayton Webb, Major Waltars, Aaron Wesson, Nathaniel Whitaker, Elihu Woodruff, Ashbel Waller, Loudewick Weller, Francinah Wilson, Abraham York. William Ruffin, postmaster.

A letter to the editor mentions Mr. Broadwell, Mr. Smith and Mr. Bilbren.

Adrian Hegeman, Jr., writes to Mr. Carpenter about the recent reports about him. He says he is leaving soon for New Jersey where he'll stay until spring.

Aaron Goforth writes a letter to the editor about his nomination to the senate by John Armstrong. He says he's not eligible since he's not yet 30 years old.

An unsigned letter to the editor regarding Adrian Hegeman mentions Thomas Gibson, John S. Gano.

Capt. James Smith announces a meeting of the Cincinnati Light Infantry Company at Isaac Anderson's house.

A note about a meeting of the Dragoons commanded by James Ferguson.

Daniel F. Reeder has a new shipment of goods at his store in Lebanon.

James Ferguson has just returned from Philadelphia with a supply of goods.

A note regarding land for sale at Red Bank Station.

Wm. Stanley, for O. Ormsby, has a new shipment of goods for sale at the store in Cincinnati. Those indebted to Daniel Conner & Company should settle their accounts.

William M'Farland, Sheriff, regarding sheriff's sales, at Elmore Williams' house, of the property of George Fithian at the suit of Martin Nall; that of Roswell Bartlet, dec'd, at the suit of William Toph; that of Henry Long at the suit of John Smith; that of Andrew Wilson at the suit of John and Mathew Nimmo; that of Seth Cutter, dec'd, at the suit of David J. Poor; that of William Stump at the suit of Jacob Allen.

Pallus P. Stuart, in Cincinnati, reports a stray horse. Deliver to James Smith at Hamilton.

Jesse Cravens, agent for Nehemiah Cravens, at the Christian County court house, Kentucky, regarding the robbery committed by Richard Thomas, lately from Georgia, who kept a school in Christian County and worked for Nehemiah Cravens as a store keeper. Thomas is about 26 years old. They also note that a person called Thomas Gains who lately stayed at Capt. William Lamb's place in Chillicothe is probably the same as the above Richard Thomas.

A note regarding the horse races to be held at Hamilton.

No. 11, Volume VII, Wednesday, 9 October 1805, Whole No. 323

John Slone and Daniel Symmes print more laws of the State of Ohio.

A note regarding a meeting of the militia companies commanded by Capt. Stanley and Capt. Carpenter.

A letter to the editor mentions Adrian Hegeman, Mr. Gibson, Mr. Gano.

Marriage: Thomas Elder married Miss Jane Scott at Colerain on 1 October 1805, by Judah Willy.

David L. Carney will soon publish a paper in Franklin called "The Whig".

Election returns in Cincinnati township mention Edward Tiffin, Stephen Wood, Hezekiah Price, John Jones, I.B. Miller, John Matson and James Ewing.

Edward B. Hannegan, in Cincinnati, will open a school in that town.

Sheriff William M'Farland regarding the meeting of the Ohio Supreme Court.

Ephraim Caterlin, living within two miles of Hamilton, reports a stolen horse.

William Noble regarding wheat to be delivered to Thomas M'Cullough's Mill and Joel Williams' Mill.

No. 12, Volume VII, Wednesday, 16 October 1805, Whole No. 324

Michael Baldwin and Joseph Kerr print another law of Ohio.

Election returns in Hamilton County mention Edward Tiffin, Stephen Wood, Hezekiah Price, John Jones, Adrian Hegerman, John Matson and James Ewing. Returns in Butler County mention Edward Tiffin, William Ward, Jacob Smith, Richard S. Thomas, Matthew Richardson, James M'Clure, William M'Clelland, and Joshua Delaplane.

An unsigned letter to the editor regarding Mr. Hagerman mentions Gen. Gano and Mr. Gibson.

A note from the Quakers of Ohio regarding military requisitions.

John S. Gano, living on Duck Creek three miles from Columbia, offers his farm for sale or rent.

Wm. M'Farland, Sheriff, regarding sheriff's sales at Elmore Williams' house of property seized at the suit of David Grummon; that of Tabor Washburn at the suit of Charles Vattier; of property of Robert M'Mullen at the suit of Benjamin Fisher.

Alexander King, Collector, in Cincinnati, regarding the collection of taxes.

Jacob Williams and Caleb Amidon, in Cincinnati, have dissolved their partnership and ask those indebted to them to settle their accounts.

Conrad Webb, of Petersburgh, Virginia, regarding land in Ohio for sale by Robert Watkins, of Notoway County, Virginia. The land was already sold by Watkins to Abner Osborne, of whom Webb is the sole executor and devisee.

Joseph Beazley, living on the Little Miami near to John Beazley's house, reports a strayed or stolen horse.

No. 13, Volume VII, Wednesday, 23 October 1805, Whole No. 325

A notice regarding a theater production is printed.

Joseph Crane, Enos Cutler, Ethan A. Brown and Thomas Rawlins have been certified as attorneys by the Supreme Court of Ohio.

An unsigned letter to the editor regarding Mr. Hegeman mentions Mr. Gibson.

William Woodward, Abigail Woodward, Samuel Foster, Hepziba Foster, and Samuel Foster, attorney for Mary Cutter, in Cincinnati, regarding land belonging to John Cutter, late of Cincinnati, dec'd. Among those entitled to land are Seth Cutter of Cincinnati, and Abigail Pitsby and Mary Cutter, both of Massachusetts.

Isaiah Bryant has commenced the fulling and dying businesses on the Little Miami at Waldsmith's Mill. He mentions "his long experience therein in the Atlantic States". He will receive cloth at Mr. Hutchinson's tavern, Mr. Ruffin's, and the house formerly occupied by Joel Williams.

Mary Davis, administratrix of the estate of Thomas Davis, dec'd, who lately lived 3 miles below Dayton, regarding the estate settlement.

Emmanuel Vantrees, living on the Miami River nine miles above North Bend, offers his farm and mills for sale.

No. 14, Volume VII, Wednesday, 30 October 1805, Whole No. 326

John Cleves Symmes writes a letter to the inhabitants of the Miami Purchase and mentions Mr. Burnet and Mr. Boudinot.

A note regarding the proceedings of the Supreme Court mention Mordecai Thuston's indictment for the murder of John Marshal.

Obituary: Thomas Brown died at Newtown on Wednesday, 23 October 1805.

A note regarding the burning of the School house in Cincinnati.

A note regarding the recent Fair and Races in Cincinnati.

James Forguson, in Cincinnati, has a new shipment of goods for sale.

John W. Miles "intends leaving this place as soon as he can get his business settled" and offers his house, lot, furniture and cabinet maker's tools for sale.

The administrators of the estate of Col. Ludlow, dec'd, regarding a sale of his land at Griffin Yeatman's house in Cincinnati. The land is next door to David E. Wade, Patrick Moore, Hezekiah Flint and Maj. John Riddle.

Hugh Moore wants to hire a distiller in Cincinnati.

Mills & Dunn regarding a note to William Cherry, late of the state of Ohio.

A notice that Hannah Burk, wife of Thomas Burk, will apply for a divorce.

John M'Adams, on King's Creek in Green County, reports a stray mare. Deliver to John M'Adams living at Columbia town in Hamilton County.

No. 15, Volume VII, Wednesday, 6 November 1805, Whole No. 327

More of John Cleves Symmes' letter mentions Mr. Boudinot and Mr. Burnet.

Subscriptions to the Whig should to be forwarded to Gen. Schenck in Franklin.

A note regarding the Supreme Court proceedings mentions Mr. Thurston.

James Findlay and Griffin Yeatman regarding an ordinance of Cincinnati.

A note regarding the duel at the settlement of Bel-pre, Ohio, between Mr. Stephen R. Wilson and Alexander Henderson, both of Wood County, Virginia.

The editor of the Western Spy asks those indebted to him to pay their bills.

James Findlay announces a meeting of the citizens of Cincinnati.

Daniel Miller and Catharine Gaphart, of German township in Montgomery County, administrators of the estate of Peter Gaphart, deceased, regarding the estate settlement.

Daniel Miller, in German township, Montgomery County, about a stray horse.

Notice that Sarah Barker, wife of Stephen Alison Barker, will sue for divorce.

Peter Love, Ropemaker, on Sycamore Street, Cincinnati, has rope for sale.

Alexander King, Collector, regarding the payment of taxes at the following houses: Samuel Muchmore's in Columbia township, Mr. Ares' in Sycamore, Mr. Harden's at Coldrain, Jonathan Pitman's in Springfield, Col. Benefield's at White water, Jacob Morgan's at Miami.

Patrick M'Meker, in the district of St. Genevieve, Louisiana Territory, says he lately married Polly Chriest who had moved from Ohio in the family of Tobius Butler. She has left him. He revokes a power of attorney to John Gaston, of Hamilton County, to sell land "to which I am owner by said marriage."

No. 16, Volume VII, Wednesday, 13 November 1805, Whole No. 328

An extract of a letter from Pascal Paoli Peck, son of Col. Wm. Peck, an officer in the U.S. Navy.

Obituary: Maj. Mathew Newcom, age 26, of Dayton, died 27 October 1805. He was buried the next day attended by Capt. James Brown and his company.

An account of an accident in which William Beard was killed.

Obituary: Hon. William Patton, a member of the Senate, died at Chillicothe on 15 October 1805.

Aquilla Wheler, living in Cincinnati, regarding a stray mare.

James Findlay, in Cincinnati, has land for sale. He mentions Col. Chambers who lived near Dayton, Benjamin VanCleve in Dayton, Cassel & Loy in Franklin, Gen. Schenck at Franklin, Martin Verner on Little Miami River.

Capt. James Ferguson regarding a meeting of the Troop of Dragoons.

John Crail, in Cincinnati, wants an apprentice to the saddle tree business.

No. 17, Volume VII, Wednesday, 20 November 1805, Whole No. 329

Obituary: Mrs. Hepziba Foster, wife of Samuel Foster, died in Cincinnati on Tuesday, 19 November 1805, of an apparent overdose of medicine.

James Findlay and Griffin Yeatman regarding an ordinance of Cincinnati.

A note regarding a meeting of booksellers and printers of Ohio and Kentucky mentions John Bradford, T. Anderson, William Hunter, Joseph Carpenter, N. Willis and Daniel Bradford.

A note regarding the Thespian Society's performance at the Theater.

Matthew Nimmo, at Spring Farm near Cincinnati, offers for sale his buildings on Main Street in Cincinnati.

Hugh Moore, in Cincinnati, wants to buy good Orleans boats.

David Squire, Collector, at Dayton, regarding the collection of taxes.

Abraham Miller, living on Obannon's Creek about five miles above Christian Waldsmith's Mill, reports a stray horse.

John Eastwood, living on Twin Creek near the town of Franklin, regarding some strayed or stolen mares.

Benjamin Stites, James Maranda and Ephraim Kibby, administrators of the estate of Benjamin Stites, dec'd, regarding the order by John S. Gano of the Court of Common Pleas of Hamilton County to sell lands of the deceased.

No. 18, Volume VII, Wednesday, 27 November 1805, Whole No. 330

William Robinson is elected representative and George Newcome, Sheriff, of Montgomery County. In Belmont County, Joseph Sharp is elected senator and John Stewart and James Smith, representatives.

Obituary: Cornelius Voorheese, formerly of Cincinnati, died very suddenly on Saturday, 23 November 1805.

White & Delaplaine have a new shipment of goods for sale at their store.

Maxfield Ludlow regarding certificates for surveyed land.

Ephraim Hathaway, Sheriff in Warren County, reports that a prisoner escaped from the jail in Lebanon. He is Martin Colwell, arrested for debt.

Ignatius Ross, administrator of the estate of John Culberson, late of Montgomery County, dec'd, regarding the settlement of the estate to be held at Hugh M'Collom's inn in Dayton.

Alexander King, Collector, in Cincinnati, regarding taxes due.

John Rabb won't honor any debts his wife, Elizabeth Rabb, may contract.

Aaron Rochenfield, on Beaver Creek in Green County, reports a stray mare.

Zachariah Holland, in Cincinnati, reports that he found a stray mare and colt.

Richard Dicken, of Boon County, Kentucky, reports a runaway slave named June. Deliver to Joseph Kennedy at the mouth of the Licking River.

Thomas Dugan offers a good saddle horse for sale.

The sale of John W. Miles' house has been postponed.

Israel Brown, living in Springfield township, Hamilton County, over three miles west of Caldwell's Mill, reports a stray horse.

No. 19, Volume VII, Wednesday, 4 December 1805, Whole No. 331

Marriage: Hugh Moore, merchant, to Miss Polly Symmes, both of Cincinnati, on Sunday evening, 1 December 1805, by Rev. Mr. James Kemper.

A note regarding the imprisonment of Long John Long.

A biographical sketch of Col. Thomas Butler says he was a student of law with Judge Wilson in Philadelphia in 1776, but quit and joined the army. There were five Butler brothers in the Revolutionary War: Col. Richard Butler, Col. William Butler, Capt. Thomas Butler, Lieut. Pierce Butler and Lieut. Edward Butler. Pierce Butler is the only one still living.

John Smith, at his mill at Round Bottom, asks those indebted to him to settle their accounts.

Capt. James Forguson regarding a meeting of the Troop of Dragoons.

George Hughs, in Cincinnati, reports a strayed horse.

Ezra Spencer asks those indebted to him to pay in wheat delivered to Joel Williams' grist mill.

Joseph B. Leibert has just received a new shipment of goods at his new store in Cincinnati.

Capt. James Smith regarding a meeting of the Cincinnati Light Infantry Company at Alexander King's house.

Griffin Yeatman, William Stanley and Thomas Dugan, auditors, regarding the suit of James Smith and James Findlay vs. Thomas Cochran.

Smith Thompson says his wife, Sally Thompson, left him and he won't honor debts of her contracting from now on.

No. 20, Volume VII, Wednesday, 11 December 1805, Whole No. 332

Jared Brooks writes a letter to the managers of the Ohio Canal Company.

An extract of a letter from Dr. Wood, state senator, the the editor of the Spy mentions James Prichard, Thomas Scott, John Sloan, Joseph Darlinton, Thomas Worthington, Mr. Todd, Edward Tiffin, Thomas G. Bradford and Nathaniel Willis.

Jacob Williams & Jacob Voorheese, administrators of the estate of Cornelius Voorheese, dec'd, regarding the estate sale. Another ad is entered regarding the estate settlement.

Charles Faran, in Cincinnati, wants to hire a journeyman cooper.

Mary Henderson, late Mary Post, and Samuel C. Vance, at Lawrenceburgh, administrators of the estate of Josiah Post, late of Dearborn County, dec'd, about the sale of his land by order of the Orphans' Court. Mentions the bond of Joseph Hays, jun.

No. 21, Volume VII, Wednesday, 18 December 1805, Whole No. 333

Gov. Edward Tiffin's address to the legislature is printed.

A list of the members of the Senate is printed and includes Thomas Kirker of Adams and Scioto Counties, Joseph Sharp of Belmont, James Sargent of Clermont, Cornelius Snieder and Stephen Wood of Hamilton, Jacob Burton of Fairfield, James Pritchard and Benjamin Hough of Jefferson and Columbiana, Joseph Kerr and D. M'Arthur for Ross/Franklinton/Highland, George Tod for Trumbull, John Bigger and Jacob Smith for Warren/Butler/Montgomery/Green, Joseph Buell and Hallam Hamstead of Washington/Gallia/Muskingum/Athens. James Pritchard is elected speaker, Thomas Scott is clerk and Edward Sherluck is doorkeeper. Also mentions Col. Worthington, Edward Tiffin, Thomas G. Bradford, N. Willis, Hon. S. Huntington, Benjamin White, William Irwin, the Quakers, James Denny, Wm. Irwin, William Creighton.

The proceedings of the House of Representatives mention John Sloane, Stephen R. Dickinson, Mr. Langham, Mr. Kingsbury, Mr. M'Laughlin, Mr. Beecher, Mr. Shepherd, Mr. Burr, Mr. Elliott, Mr. Dunlap, Mr. Price, Mr. Hine, Mr. Sterrett, Mr. Williams, Mr. Lewis, Mr. Cloud, Mr. M'Connell, Mr. Corwin, Mr. Hatch, Mr. Robinson, Mr. Jones, Mr. M'Clure, Mr. Kingsbury, Mr. Shelby, Mr. Clark, William Irvine of Fairfield County, Mr. Phelps.

A letter from T. Worthington to the House of Representatives is printed.

James Kemper, Jun., says he lost a saddle, bridle and loose coat.

William Hunter, in Colerain township, Hamilton County, reports a stray mare.

Sheriff James Hamilton, at Lawrenceburgh, says that William Johnston escaped from the jail of Dearborn County, Indiana Territory. He was there for the murder of Daniel M'Elvey.

Thomas Hamel, living within about four miles of Cincinnati on the Deerfield

Road, at James Lyons' place, reports a stray mare.

Samuel C. Vance has land for sale near Lawrenceburgh.

William Byrd, in Cincinnati, wants to buy wheat at Van-Horn's mill.

Abraham Freeman, living in Lemon Township, Butler County, found a mare.

Christian Waldsmith reports that he found a stray cow.

Joseph Carpenter, in Cincinnati, reports that he found a stray cow and calf.

John Parker says his wife, Nancy Parker, left him and he won't pay her bills.

No. 22, Volume VII, Wednesday, 25 December 1805, Whole No. 334

A notice regarding the Cincinnati Theater is printed.

Frederic Haifligh & Son, in Cincinnati, have groceries for sale at their store opposite the court house and next door to Henry Ewing's tavern.

Thomas Dugan, in Cincinnati, asks those indebted to him to pay their bills.

Joseph Conn asks those indebted to him to settle their accounts by delivering wheat to Mr. VanHorn's Mill.

Matthew Nimmo announces a meeting of the Cincinnati Lodge.

Hugh Moore, in Cincinnati, has a house for rent that was lately occupied by John Humes. It includes a stable and a smoke-house.

Charles J. Nourse, at Washington City, regarding buying land in Cincinnati.

Burrows Smith, in Cincinnati, has note books for sale.

Thomas Dugan has a good saddle horse for sale.

No. 23, Volume VII, Wednesday, 1 January 1806, Whole No. 335

Frederick Nutts, living on the Great Miami in Montgomery County, reports a stray mare.

An account of the meeting of the Cincinnati Lodge of Masons is printed.

Obituary: Mrs. Margaret Humes, wife of John Humes, late of Cincinnati, died on Saturday, 28 December 1805, in Springfield Township. She was buried in Cincinnati on Tuesday, 31 December 1805.

Edward B. Hanagan announces an examination of the pupils of his school.

William Ward, at Mad River, reports some stolen horses.

John Misner, living in Hamilton County, reports that he found a mare.

John S. Gano announces a meeting of the Commissioners of Cincinnati.

R. Brasher has a lot for sale in Cincinnati.

A list of letters left at the Post Office in Cincinnati includes Thomas Auter, Jackson Ayres, Caleb Amidon, Abner Amidon, John Allen at White water, David Brown 12 miles from Lawrenceburgh, Joseph Bolten, Samuel Bonnel on Mill Creek, Dr. Henry W. Blachly in care of Col. Spencer, Sarah Bigham, John Boyer, Abigail Bigger, Ezekial or Martha Cleaver, John H. Crawford, Jesse Cravens, Abraham Crum, John Carlen at Sycamore, Joseph Carpenter on Mill Creek, Charles Cox, Charles Cone at White water, Nancy Christy, Elias Crane, Andrew Carrigue, Rachel Chandler, Cornete & Piat, Joel Craig, Peter Demoss at Big Indian, Elizabeth Daily, Jacob Deterly, Alexander Eson, Jacob Felter, Joel Ferree, Judah Foulke in care of John Stall, Nathen Frakes on Lochery Creek, Garret Guest, Charles H. Gordon, Ruben Garrison at Colerain, Jacob Garrison at Sycamore, Josiah Gevaltney, Philip Gatch, Edward Humphreys, William Hall, Samuel Hall, Noah Hart, James Hill, Levi Hardisty, Thomas Havans, William Harris, Thomas Holinsworth, George Hand, David Harris, James Jones, Jeremiah Johnston in Dearborn County, James Irwine, Kastner Jones, David Keneday on Mill Creek, Calvin Kitchell, Moses Kitchell, Asa Kitchell, Robert Lyttle, Amos Lampson on White water, Eleazer Lamson, Amos Lamson, Solomon Loree, George Larrison, Sarah Little, William Logan in care of Matthew Brown, David Lowler, Robert M'Neely, Jacob Miller at White water, Cavliea Morris, John M'Hatton, Stephen Miller, Robert Morris, John R. Mills, Henry Marshal, Robert Moorhead, John Morrow, Chancy Moss, Samuel M'Cullough, Samuel M'Millan at White water, Lydie Moore, Ezra Miller, Stephen Minor, Levi Neal and Christopher Nosteller (hatters), Peter Newcomer, Pollard Newby, Daniel Nihell, Andrew Overter, Sineus Pierson, Issabella Pike, Robert Piatt, William Pack, Nathaniel Porter at North Bend, Benjamin and John Piatt, Henry Rockwell, Daniel Repblogel, Abner Rude, Jacob Roll, Samuel Rockenfeller, John Rockenfeller, James Riddle, John B. Hymer,

James Scott, Hezekiah Stout on Little Miami, Major Cealy, William Smith, Noah Strong, William Snoock, Joel Spencer, Pollus P. Stewart, Samuel Shepherd at Columbia, Joseph Shepherd at Redding, Henry Siftin at White Water, Aaron Sackett at Redding, John Salyear at White Water; Turner, Wadsworth & Gilkisson; Thomas Taylor, John Templeton on Mill Creek, William Thompson at Columbia, James Todd, Isaac Voorhis, Eli Wood at South Bend, James Walker, Israel Willey at Colerain, Jonathan Williams, John Wert, Mary Westend at New-town, Jude Warner, James Watkins, Samuel Wilson, Joshua Woodward, Jonathan Wallace.

A note regarding a Theater production in Cincinnati.

William Ruffin, Joseph Prince and Henry Weaver, regarding property to be sold at the house of Henry Ewing in Cincinnati as a result of the suit of Charles Vattier vs. Asa S. Richardson.

T. Ridgley, in Woodford County, Kentucky, has land for sale on the Little Miami 12 miles from Wm. Lytle's place. Apply to Dr. Sellman in Cincinnati.

A note regarding a sale of Cincinnati town lots at the house of A. King.

Samuel Best wants to hire an apprentice to the clock and watchmaking trade.

John Schooly, in Springfield township, has four milk cows for sale.

No. 24, Volume VII, Wednesday, 8 January 1806, Whole No. 336

Mr. Kennedy who keeps a ferry opposite Cincinnati submits a list of the number of immigrants from each state who've crossed into Ohio on his ferry.

Obituary: Mary Winton, age 17, on Friday evening, 3 January 1806.

An unsigned letter regarding the performance by Mr. Hanagan's pupils.

Thomas Dugan, in Cincinnati, again asks those indebted to him to pay now.

George Collom, Jun., in Cincinnati township, reports that he found a mare.

Jacob Broadwell, living near the Round Bottom mills, agent for John Smith, has land for sale on the Little Miami just below Armstrong's Mill, known by the name of Smith's section.

William M'Farland, Sheriff, regarding the sheriff's sale of the house and lot in Columbia, "occupied by Maj. Stites at his death", seized at the suit of Richard S. Thomas. Also the property of Tabor Washburn, at the suit of Charles Vattier.

Samual Foster reports a runaway apprentice to the tanner's trade named Thomas Garner, about 17 years old.

No. 25, Volume VII, Wednesday, 15 January 1806, Whole No. 337

Note about the impeachment of William Irvin, associate judge in Fairfield Co.

Henry Weaver, in Cincinnati, has a new shipment of goods for sale.

Dixon Greer has moved his store to the house next door to O. Ormsby's new store where he has dry goods and groceries for sale.

Aquilla Wheeler, in Cincinnati, reports a stray mare.

B. VanCleve and Jacob Burnet, in Dayton, regarding a suit in the Montgomery County Court of Common Pleas: Nicholas Horner vs. William Brookie.

B. VanCleve and George F. Tennery, in Dayton, regarding a suit in the Montgomery County Court of Common Pleas: Job Westfall vs. Jacob Brown.

Uriah Gates, in Cincinnati township, Hamilton County, says that his wife, Rebecca Gates, has left him, and he won't pay her debts anymore, and "any person who brings her home must pay me one hundred dollars".

Elizabeth Baird and Abraham Barnet, in Montgomery County, administrators of the estate of John Barnet, dec'd, regarding the estate settlement.

Henry Taylor, in Butler County on Four Mile Creek, about a stray horse.

Geo. Williamson, in Cincinnati, reports a stray mare. He also speaks of his book binding business in the house opposite Mr. Reeder's store in Main Street.

George F. Miller, administrator of the estate of William Beard, late of Cincinnati, dec'd, asks those indebted to the estate to make payments to William Ruffin in Cincinnati or Miller at Limestone, Mason County, Kentucky.

Robert Robinson, living on the south west branch of the Great Miami, four miles from Dayton in Montgomery County, reports a stray mare. Deliver to Isaac Anderson in Cincinnati or Joseph Park on Dick's Creek.

William M'Farland, Sheriff, regarding sheriff's sales of the property of Asa S. Richardson at the suits of Charles Conn, Joseph Conn and Charles Vattier.

No. 26, Volume VII, Wednesday, 22 January 1806, Whole No. 338
   A note regarding the impeachment trial of William Irvin is printed.
   Thomas Gibson's letter to the Ohio representatives is printed and mentions Francis Douglass and Oliver Jennings.
   Gov. Edward Tiffin's letter to the Ohio representatives regarding the appointment of Joseph Tatman to fill the vacancy of associate judge in Green County.
   Hugh Moore announces that he's now in partnership with Hugh M'Clelland in the dry goods and grocery business as the firm Moore & M'Clelland.
   Joseph Michel, in Cincinnati, says that his wife, Kisiah Michel, has left him and he won't honor her debts.
   Daniel Roe, in Cincinnati, asks the person who borrowed his saddle bags to return them.
   Burrows Smith, in Cincinnati, has notebooks and a compass for sale.
   Cornelius R. Sedam reports two strayed colts.
   Alexander King, Collector, regarding the sale of lots belonging to John Sharp, Darius Marsh, Asa Richardson, Winthrop Sargeant, Henry Keer, William Freeman, David Sutton, Samuel Richardson.
   John Smith & Co., Cincinnati, want to hire men to cut timber on Duck Creek.
   Joseph Nelson, in Cincinnati township, reports that he found a cow.
   Francis White, at the mouth of Mill Creek in Cincinnati township, reports that he found a stray mare.

No. 27, Volume VII, Wednesday, 29 January 1806, Whole No. 339
   William M'Farland, Sheriff, regarding sheriff's sales of the property of Seth Cutter, dec'd, at the suits of James Cummins, Henry Kerr, Jane Matson, John Matson, administrators of J. Matson, dec'd, Charlotte Ludlow, James Findlay and Senias Pierson, administrators of Israel Ludlow, dec'd, and Oliver Spencer, late judge of probate. Also the property of John Cleves Symmes, adjoining James White and William Grant, taken at the suit of Gersham Gard.
   Thomas Thompson, Cincinnati, has a farm for sale or rent on the Ohio River.
   John Goble, in Cincinnati, has for sale the uniform of the Light Infantry.
   Fox & Adams, in Cincinnati, ask those indebted to them to settle their bills.
   John Torrence, in Hamilton, has established a ferry across the Miami River.
   Maxfield Ludlow has land for sale near the mills formerly owned by Ludlow & Co. on Mill Creek. Apply to John Ludlow, Mill Creek, or Jesse Hunt, Cincinnati.
   Isaac Anderson, Cincinnati, asks those indebted to him to pay their bills.
   David Zeigler has a new shipment of goods for sale at his Cincinnati store.

No. 28, Volume VII, Wednesday, 5 February 1806, Whole No. 340
   William Creighton, Jun., is appointed Secretary of State, Thomas Gibson is Auditor of Public Accounts and Wm. M'Farland is Treasurer of State.
   The following are appointed associate judges: John Wellsworth, Jesse Phelps, and Abraham Wheeler in Geuaga County; Henry James and Jacob Burton in Fairfield County; Celadon Symmes in Butler County; Alexander Skidmore & Abraham Miller in Athens County; John Kingsman and Turhand Kirtland in Trumbull County.
   James Taylor, in Newport, Kentucky, has land for sale in Clermont County. He mentions William B. Wallace, Squire Buckhannon, Benjamin Moseley.
   Thomas Dugan "is now closing his business in this place with an intention of leaving the country" and asks those indebted to him to settle their accounts.
   Dixon Greer, in Cincinnati, asks those indebted to him to pay their bills.
   Alexander King, Collector, regarding taxes due in Cincinnati township.
   John Hagerman about lots for sale in the town of Milford, at John Hagerman's mill on the Little Miami.
   John Irwin, living on Four Mile Creek, nine miles from Fort Hamilton in Butler County, reports that he found two stray mare colts.
   John S. Gano, in Cincinnati, about a meeting of the county commissioners.

No. 29, Volume VII, Tuesday, 11 February 1806, Whole No. 341
   Samuel Stitt, in Cincinnati, reports two runaway apprentices to the shoemaking business, William Stansbury (age about 19) and Francis Berry (age 17).

A note regarding the drowning of Mr. Marks.

An unsigned letter to the editor mentions Parson Browne.

James M'Ginnes, in Cincinnati, reports a runaway apprentice to the cabinet making business, Walter Moules, about 18 years old.

William M'Farland, Sheriff, regarding the sheriff's sale of the property of Maj. Stites at the suit of Richard S. Thomas and the property of Tabor Washburn at the suit of Charles Vattier.

H. Cadbury and Wm. Ruffin, in Cincinnati, has land for sale adjoining Col. Chambers and Mr. Davis on the Ohio River.

John Lyon and Samuel Lyon have dissolved their partnership. Samuel Lyon will carry on the cabinet making business at Hamilton. They also have land for sale. Apply to Gen. Gano in Cincinnati or John Lyon 11 miles from Cincinnati.

No. 30, Volume VII, Tuesday, 18 February 1806, Whole No. 342

Thomas Gibson, Auditor, regarding an act levying taxes mentions A. Goforth in Cincinnati, Thomas Scott in Chillicothe, William Skinner in Marietta, James Herron in Steubenville and James Hillman in Warren.

An unsigned letter to the editor regarding Parson Browne mentions Mr. Browne and the Liberty Hall.

There will be a meeting about a Circulating Library at Griffin Yeatman's.

Jacob Williams, in Cincinnati, wants to hire a blacksmith.

John S. Gano regarding a meeting to select Grand Jurors.

Enos Williams, in Lebanon, wants to hire carpenters to work on the Warren County courthouse.

John Jackson, in Cincinnati, about a stray colt. Deliver to Thomas Williams.

Joseph Tatmen and Elizabeth Lowrey, administrators of the estate of Thomas Lowrey, dec'd, regarding the estate settlement.

Samuel C. Vance, at Lawrenceburgh in Indiana Territory, have land for sale.

John Dill & Company announce that their partnership is dissolved.

No. 31, Volume VII, Tuesday, 25 February 1806, Whole No. 343

A note regarding Indian alarms in Ohio mentions Maj. Moore, Judge M'Cullock in Champaign County.

Marriage: Thomas Thompson, merchant, married Miss Polly Nancarrow, both of Cincinnati, on Sunday evening, 23 February 1806, by Rev. Mr. Wallace.

Peter Bell, at Mount Vernon, writes a letter to the citizens of Hamilton Co.

William Bruce regarding lots for sale in the town of Eaton in Montgomery Co.

Henry Weaver has Scotch snuff for sale at his store in Cincinnati.

Stephen Vail, at Middletown on the Great Miami in Lebanon township, Butler County, reports a stray horse.

No. 32, Volume VII, Tuesday, 4 March 1806, Whole No. 344

William M'Farland declines a nomination to sheriff in the next election.

J. Carpenter asks those indebted for the Western Spy to make payments to Henry Taylor or Thomas Clark, the post rider.

A note about Mr. M'Cullom's publication of the Patriotic Farmer in Dayton.

William M'Farland, Sheriff, regarding sheriff's sales of the property of Robert M'Mullen at the suit of Benjamin Fisher; that of Henry Jenkinson at the suit of William Ludlow; that of Timothy Kibby at the suit of the state of Ohio; that of Abraham Voorheese, jun., at the suit of Hugh Meek.

Capt. James Ferguson about a meeting of the Troop of Light Dragoons.

James Ferguson wants to buy a saddle horse and red clover feed.

Thomas Ramsey reports a runaway apprentice boy named Absalom Runyan.

Hugh Moore, in Cincinnati, wants to hire someone to cut wood.

William M'Farland, Sheriff, regarding sheriff's sales of the property of Ruliff Peterson at the suit of C. Lowes; that of T. Goudy at the suit of John Lyon; that of Miny and Abm. Voorheese at the suit of James Witherow; that of John Becket at the suits of Matthew Winton and Wm. Stanley.

No. 33, Volume VII, Tuesday, 11 March 1806, Whole No. 345

John S. Gano regarding the letter from Peter Bell at Mount Vernon.

Certificates are printed from Samuel Martin and Stephen Reeder regarding the charges made against Rev. Matthew G. Wallace. They mention Maj. Riddle, Abraham Montayne and William Betts.

Alexander King says he's a candidate for sheriff of Hamilton County.

A note regarding a meeting of the Cincinnati Presbyterian Church.

Stephen Benton, near Newport in Campbell County, Kentucky, regarding the horse said to belong to Levi Barber, of Ohio, surveyor, that was delivered to Gov. Harrison at Vincennes. He mentions Archibald Brown, Jacob Barrickman, Daniel Lewis and James Smith of Campbell County, Kentucky.

John Smith, in Cincinnati, has land for lease. Apply to Jacob Broadwell living near Round Bottom on the Little Miami.

Phebe King and Henry Thompson, administrators of the estate of John King, dec'd, late of Campbell County, Kentucky, about the estate settlement.

Charles Bruce, Henry Brown and John Torrence, at Hamilton, trustees of the estate of Elias Wallen, dec'd, regarding the estate settlement.

James Gallaher, in Warren County, administrator of the estate of Wm. Jackson, dec'd, regarding the estate settlement.

No. 34, Volume VII, Tuesday, 18 March 1806, Whole No. 346

Obituary: Jas. M. Holmes, of Georgia, died very suddenly on Monday, 17 March 1806, at Isaac Anderson's house.

James Findlay and Griffin Yeatman regarding ordinances of Cincinnati.

Letters regarding nominations mention Mr. Morrow, Elmore Williams, William M'Farland, Matthew Nimmo, John Mahard, James Lyon, Wm. Collum, James Ewing, Enos Hurin, Andrew Brannon, Jacob Stewart, Joseph Colby, jun., Aquilla Wheeler, Elisha Landon, Alexander M'Nutt, Nathan Reeder, Samuel Patterson, John Riddle, George Williamson, Isaac Bates, David Zeigler, Abraham Chase, Sen., Thomas Dugan, Cornelius Johnson, jun., Cornelius R. Sedam, Alexander King, Joseph Conn, jun.

Abraham Montanye about charges made against Rev. Matthew G. Wallace. He mentions Maj. Riddle. The letter is witnessed by Joseph VanHorne, James Ewing, and Stephen Wheeler.

David E. Wade, William Ramsay and William Ruffin, in Cincinnati about a suit in Hamilton County Court of Common Pleas: James Hinds vs. William Gregg.

Moore & M'Clelland, in Cincinnati, have whiskey for sale.

No. 35, Volume VII, Tuesday, 25 March 1806, Whole No. 347

The speech of Mr. Smith of Ohio to the Senate of the U.S.

Maj. Zeigler declines all nominations for public office.

Charles Faran, in Cincinnati, wants to hire three coopers.

Edward B. Hannegan, in Cincinnati, regarding his school in Cincinnati.

No. 36, Volume VII, Tuesday, 1 April 1806, Whole No. 348

Marriage: William G. Goodwin, hatter, of Cincinnati, to Miss Eliza Tucker, of Springfield township, Hamilton County, on Thursday, 27 March 1806, by Rev. Matthew G. Wallace.

The route of Thomas Clark, post rider, will be discontinued.

An error appeared in the ad from the Trustees of Elias Wallen, deceased.

Edward B. Hannegan, Cincinnati, will have a public examination of his pupils.

A note regarding some cash lost on the road between Gen. Mansfield's and Capt. Joshua Williams' house. It mentions the Miami Exporting Company.

Thomas M'Cullough, at Mount Pleasant, has goods for sale.

George Williamson, in Cincinnati, reports a strayed or stolen mare.

John Hart regarding a note to Jonathan Gilly/Cilly of Colerain.

Henry Disbrow, in Cincinnati, has taken over the public entertainment lately occupied by Elmore Williams in Cincinnati.

Moore & M'Clelland, in Cincinnati, ask those indebted to them to settle their accounts before H. M'Clelland goes east to buy goods in May.

Charles Killgore, in Cincinnati, regarding the Register of the Land Office.

John Lyon and Samuel Lyon, living 11 miles from Cincinnati on the Hamilton road, have land for sale. Apply to Gen. John S. Gano in Cincinnati.

William Woodward, Samuel Foster and Seth Cutter, Cincinnati, administrators of the estate of Seth Cutter, dec'd, regarding the estate settlement.

Isaac Herrell, on Twin Creek in Montgomery County, reports a stray mare.

John Fuller makes tombstones, head and foot stones at his shop in Cincinnati.

No. 37, Volume VII, Tuesday, 8 April 1806, Whole No. 349

A note from Mr. Morrow in Congress says he will serve again if elected.

Matthew Nimmo, at Spring Farm near Cincinnati, declines the nomination of Sheriff.

Rev. David Rice will preach at David M'Ance's house on the Dry Fork of White water, at Joel Williams' on Indian Creek, at Robert Lytle's on Seven Mile Creek, at Joseph Parks' on Dick's Creek, at Col. William Ward's at Mad River, and at Mr. Runyan's on Buck Creek.

A meeting will be held at Griffin Yeatman's regarding building a bridge at the mouth of Mill Creek.

Capt. James Ferguson regarding a meeting of the Troop of Light Dragoons to elect a cornet in place of Stephen Ludlow who resigned.

Flora Jackson, in Cincinnati, regarding the ad placed by her husband, Thomas Jackson. She says she left him because he abused her.

James Ferguson, Joseph VanHorn & James Ewing, Trustees of the Cincinnati Presbyterian Congregation, regarding land for rent.

Archibald Talbott has town lots in Rossville for sale, including the ferry.

A list of letters left at the Post Office in Cincinnati includes John Adams, Abraham Augustus, John Ayres, Samuel Arnet at Whitewater, Thomas ARville, John Andrews in Crosby, David Bryant, Jeremiah Blackford, John Broadwell, Phinehas Bower on Duck Creek, Zebulon Brown in Springfield, Samuel Borden in Colerain, Charles Briton, John Blackburn in Columbia, Thoams Boone, John Bradway, Jacob Bruner, Joshua Bell, Lewis Baker, Samuel Clannen, James Coleman, Edward Coen, James Cole, Enock Carson, John Coleman in care of Enock Ingersul, Fisher Conner, Joseph Connover, Jonathan Clark in Columbia, Robert Compton, Samuel Crane in Springfield, Uriah Craig, Robert Campbell in Colerain, John Caldwell at Whitewater, John T. Chunn, John Clark at Mill Creek, Agness Cogan in care of Andrew Dunseth, Charles Dawn, David and Daniel Debott in Newtown, Isaac Dubois, John Dennes in care of Benjamin Stewart, James Dill in care of John Ludlow, Daniel Dykman, George Daugherty, William Denny, George Denny, David Enyart, Benjamin Enyart, Kendel Emerson, Samuel Elliott, Christian Eversole, Adam Fisher, Evans Feckleton, Ziba Foot, Samuel Grimes, Stephen Gard, William Grant, William Golden, Louis Gex at the Swiss Settlement, Josiah Gwaltney, Seth Gard, Francis Hiltzaroad, Martha Henley in care of Robert Hill, Zenas Hill, Martin Harrell, Anthony Haden, Jacob Houch in care of Joel Williams, Isaac Hutchinson at Mill Creek, John Halstead, David Harris, Arthur Henrie, James Hinds in care of Hugh Moore, Jones Harris, Robert Hudson, John Hand, William Hand, Robert Hill, Richard Hankins at Colerain, John Hubbert, Ralph W. Hunt, Noah Hart, Robert Jackson in care of Rev. M. Warwick, Aron Ireland, Casner Jones, Joseph Jenkinson, Jonathan Jones, Joseph Long, Calvin Lawrence, William Landon, Henry Leasner in Campbell County, John M'Chesney, Cornelius Moore in Columbia, Isaac Martin, Thomas Manson, Lawrence Moore, John Meeker, Chancy Morse, Jethro Nevill, Joseph Orsborn, Thomas O'Brian in Lawrenceburgh, William Peterson, David Pierson, Polly Peters, Joshua Pigman, Rebecca Pigget on Duck Creek, John Picket in Springfield, Stephen Reeder, Jacob Ross, Daniel Ross, Asa S. Richardson, Jacob Roman, John Smiley, General Arthur St.Clair, William Sebree & Company, James Scott, Thomas Spurrier, Abraham Simpson, Michael Scott, Jonathan Spinning (hatter), Charles Sipes, C.R. Sedam, Henry Sulivan, Ephraim Tucker, John Tuff, Abigall Tower, William Thompson in care of Col. Joseph Lamb, Nathan Taylor, William Thompson in Lawrenceburgh, Sally Taylor in care of Isaac Anderson, Daniel Trimbly, Jacob Taylor, Moses Tousey, Samuel Wheeler or Richard Minner, Tolomin Wilkins, John Wilkinson, James Walker,

Joshua Wilson, Jonethan Williams, Charles Weakland, Jacob White, Thomas Young.

No. 38, Volume VII, Tuesday, 15 April 1806, Whole No. 350
A letter to the editor regarding the performance of Mr. Hannegan's pupils.
A note regarding Mr. Smith of Ohio in Congress.
Thomas Dugan, in Cincinnati, has land for sale near Cincinnati and near Springfield. Apply to George Fithian in Springfield.
Richard Averson, in Cincinnati, has started his hatting business.
The companies of militia commanded by Capt. Stanley and Capt. Carpenter are to meet at the house of William Ruffin.
Capt. James Smith regarding a meeting of the Cincinnati Light Infantry Company at the house of Isaac Anderson.
Capt. James Ferguson regarding a meeting of the Troop of Light Dragoons.
Samuel Moore, Bustard Moore, and Charles Moore, administrators of the estate of Patrick Moore, dec'd, regarding the estate settlement.
James Ferguson, Joseph VanHorn and James Ewing, Trustees of the Cincinnati Presbyterian Congregation, have land for sale.

No. 39, Volume VII, Tuesday, 22 April 1806, Whole No. 351
A note nominating William Ludlow as candidate for Sheriff. Also a note nominating Aaron Goforth as Sheriff.
Elmor Williams "has declined the business of keeping tavern" and wishes to settle all of his accounts.
John F. Kamper lost a log chain on Deer Creek near where John M'Fall lived.
Andrew Boden, in Cincinnati, about a note to Andrew M'Farran for whiskey.
Moore & M'Clelland want to buy 1000 bushels of Indian corn at their mill.
Thomas West, living in Boon County, Kentucky, regarding a runaway slave named Ben. Deliver to West near Lawrenceburgh.
John T. Chunn about two runaway slaves, the property of Samuel M'Cormick of Virginia, now in the jail at Cincinnati.
Martin Baum, in Cincinnati, regarding a meeting of the citizens of Cincinnati.

No. 40, Volume VII, Tuesday, 29 April 1806, Whole No. 352
Jacob Cozad, in Beaver township of Green County, regarding a note he gave to Alexander Hughey.
Aaron Goforth, trustee of Delzil Keasby (an insolvent debtor), has property of Keasby for sale including his stone house and a collection of mammoth bones.
Wm. M'Farland, Sheriff, regarding sheriff's sales of the property of James Smith at the suit of Thomas Gibson, Auditor of the State of Ohio; also land on the road from Col. Armstrong's to Turkey Bottom, property of Benjamin Stites, dec'd, at the suit of Washington Berry; also that of Philip Gordon at the suit of Mary John and Thomas John, administrators of Mr. John's estate; also that of Asa S. Richardson at the suit of Charles Vattier.
Adam Hurdus has dry goods for sale in the house in Cincinnati lately occupied by Henry Ewing as a tavern.
John Mercier, in Cincinnati, reports a stray horse. Deliver to him at the French Tavern where he has store goods for sale.
An extract of a letter from Thomas Worthington in Congress.
William M'Farland declines a nomination to Congress as long as Mr. Morrow continues holding that post.
Martin Baum and Tho. Thompson have dissolved their partnership. Martin Baum continues the mercantile business in Cincinnati opposite Mr. Yeatman's.
John Welch, postrider, lost a purse containing money and silk gloves.

No. 41, Volume VII, Tuesday, 6 May 1806, Whole No. 353
A note about the beating death of Wm. Orr in Green County on 12 December 1805. Robert Frakes (Orr's son-in-law) and a Mr. M'Cloud argued with Orr and beat him up. After 20 days he died. M'Cloud has absconded.
Marriage: Elisha Tabor married Miss Ellenor Britton, both of Lebanon in Warren County, married on Thursday, 1 May 1806, by Matthias Corwin.

James Richey regarding a meeting of the Republican Corresponding Society at the house of Henry Disbrow in Cincinnati.

William Ludlow wants to buy corn in exchange for apple trees.

Robert Blair has started a school in Cincinnati in the shop of Mr. James near James Ewing's house.

Frederick Haifligh & Son have a shipment of goods at their store, Cincinnati.

John Miller, on Wolf Creek, about the renewal of his certificate of land.

James Ferguson regarding a meeting of the Troop of Light Dragoons.

No. 42, Volume VII, Tuesday, 13 May 1806, Whole No. 354

John Martin, "Gentlemen's Hair Dresser", has just arrived from Baltimore and has opened his shop in Cincinnati in the east end of Samuel Stitt's house.

Jacob Williams has just arrived from Pittsburgh with nail iron and will make nails in Cincinnati.

A note regarding electing directors of the Miami Exporting Company.

No. 43, Volume VII, Tuesday, 20 May 1806, Whole No. 355

Marriage: John Andrew married Miss Eliza Ewing, both of Cincinnati, on Sunday evening, 18 May 1806, by Rev. Matthew G. Wallace.

Edward B. Hannegan regarding his school in Cincinnati.

Daniel Roe has just returned from Baltimore and has a new shipment of goods at his store in Lebanon in the house formerly occupied by Daniel F. Reeder.

William Ramsay, David E. Wade and William Ruffin, Auditors, regarding the suit of James Hinds vs. William Gregg.

Peter Brewer, living about four miles from Cincinnati on the Mad River Road, reports that he found a stray horse.

Brig. Gen. W.C. Schenck gives militia orders and mentions Calvin Ball.

Lieut. Patrick Dickey regarding a meeting of the Cincinnati Light Infantry.

Lieut. David Christy regarding a meeting of the Artillery Company in Cincinnati to elect a captain in place of William M'Farland, resigned.

John Mountjoy, living near the forks of the Licking in Pendleton County, Kentucky, reports a runaway slave named Bill.

No. 44, Volume VII, Tuesday, 27 May 1806, Whole No. 356

Jacob Broadwell, agent for John Smith, has lots for sale at Germantown, on a branch of Honey Creek east of Staunton and three miles north of John Paul's house. He will also sell lots in Staunton at Mr. Phelix's house.

Marriage: Obadiah Schenck married Miss Abigail Freeman on Thursday, 22nd May 1806, in Butler County, by Rev. Mr. Gard.

Obituary: Joseph Conn, Sen., age 61, died in Cincinnati on Thursday, 22 May 1806. He was "an old and respectable citizen of this place".

John Reily and William Corry, attorney, regarding the suit in Butler County Court of Common Pleas of John Hamilton vs. Joseph W. Lloyd, a non-resident. Also regarding the petition of James M'Clelland.

Frederick Alter & Co. has a shipment of goods at their store in Cincinnati.

Aaron Goforth has land for sale.

Cornelius R. Sedam, Martin Baum, Charles Fox and John Matson are taking bids for building a bridge across Mill Creek.

No. 45, Volume VII, Tuesday, 3 June 1806, Whole No. 357

Marriage: Samuel Foster married Miss Susannah Cutter, both of Cincinnati, on Thursday evening, 29 May 1806, by James Ewing.

Obituary: Joseph Gilman, age 68, late judge of the Supreme Court of the Northwestern Territory, died at Marietta on 14 May 1806.

The Directors of the Miami Exporting Company are Martin Baum, Jesse Hunt, Daniel Mayo, Samuel C. Vance, David E. Wade, Charles Killgore, John Riddle, Griffin Yeatman, Christian Waldsmith, John Schenck and Samuel Highway.

An unsigned letter to the editor mentions Mr. Hannegan's school and Rev. Jacob Gregg of Warren County.

B. VanCleve, at Dayton, regarding the petition of George W. Smith to the

Court of Common Pleas of Montgomery County.

James Campbell regarding a mare that strayed from Robert Taylor's place about eight miles below Dayton in Montgomery County.

Edward H. Stall, druggist and apothecary, has a new shipment of medicines for sale at his shop in Cincinnati.

James Chambers, of Cincinnati, has castings and iron along with whiskey and flour for sale at his shop in the house formerly occupied by Seth Cutter.

No. 46, Volume VII, Tuesday, 10 June 1806, Whole No. 358

Capt. David Christy regarding a meeting of the Cincinnati Artillery.

David Sutton regarding the petition in the Warren County Court of Common Pleas from Robert Whitacre asking that a partition be made of land entered by John Peyton Harrison and patented to Barr Powel at the mouth of Todd's Fork of Little Miami. William Ellzey of Louden County, Virginia, owns a part of it.

Harman Long & Phillip Price say the partnership of Long & Price is dissolved.

Phillip Price carries on the clock, watchmaking and jewelry business in the house of Thomas Williams on Main Street in Cincinnati.

John Whitworth announces a meeting of the Cincinnati Lodge. An oration will be delivered at the court house by Brother Corry.

Brackin & Hargraves have commenced the butchering business in Cincinnati.

No. 47, Volume VII, Tuesday, 17 June 1806, Whole No. 359

A note regarding the Indian attack, at St. Louis, on Judge Meigs mentions Col. Meggs and Mr. Hammond.

Note of a Republican Corresponding Society meeting at Mr. Disbrow's Tavern.

Ezekiel Cretors, in Cincinnati, reports a strayed or stolen horse.

Doctor Sellman has a fresh supply of medicines for sale in Cincinnati.

Burt & Dill, in Cincinnati, have a carriage for sale. Also those indebted to the late firm of John Dill & Company should settle their accounts.

Norton & Gibbs have erected wool carding machines at Capt. Thomas Smith's Mill on White water.

Charles Ketrow & Peter Ketrow about a renewal of their certificate for land.

Charles Farran, in Cincinnati, says David M'Cash is his agent to prevent the cutting of timber on Farran's land.

The militia companies of Capt. Stanley and Capt. Carpenter are to meet.

Peter Youtsey, living near Col. John Benefiel's on the Dry Fork of White water, reports a strayed mare.

Jonathan Gilly regarding bonds payable to Henry Wasson.

Ignatius Brown and Ann Brown, at Newtown in Hamilton County, administrators of the estate of Thomas Brown, dec'd, about the estate settlement.

R.W. Waring, Clerk of the Supreme Court of Clermont County, regarding the petition of William Lytle for partition of lands on Clover Lick Creek. The lands are held with the heirs of James Morrison, late of Kentucky, by Morrison's agent, William M'Clung. Also in question is land patented to William Payne of Virginia, assignee of Robert Todd, by his agent John Payne.

James Ferguson, in Cincinnati, reports a stray horse.

Capt. James Ferguson regarding a meeting of the Cincinnati Light Dragoons.

David Sutton regarding the suit in the Warren County Court of Common Pleas of Mary Wade and David Wade (heirs and representatives of Jotham Wade, dec'd) minors, by Francis Dunlavy, their next friend vs. Benjamin Stites, James Miranda, Phebe Miranda, Richard Stites, Timothy Kibby and Rachel Kibby, heirs and representatives of Benjamin Stites, dec'd. States that Richard Stites and Timothy and Rachel Kibby are not residents of Ohio.

No. 48, Volume VII, Tuesday, 24 June 1806, Whole No. 360

John Bradburn, Secretary of the Cincinnati Lyceum, submits an address of the president to the membership.

Thomas Rawlins, regarding the meeting of the Republican Corresponding

Society at Henry Disbrow's house, mentions Jonathan Pittman's tavern, E.A. Brown and John Riddle.

Elias Glover will deliver an oration to the Republican Corresponding Society.

John Nimmo submits a letter written to the Republican Society of Cincinnati stating why he can no longer be a member. He mentions Judge Daniel Symmes and Ethan A. Brown.

William Carty will preach a sermon at the courthouse on Sunday evening.

A note about an accident at Natchez involving Mr. Lucket's boat from Ohio.

Hugh Moore, in Cincinnati, about the fence at the grazing lot, late Patrick Moore's lot, within the Race course.

Thomas J. Warman has a wagon, horse and furniture for sale at the house of Jesse Dodd, one mile from Hugh Moore's Mill.

The Market House will be sold at a meeting at Joseph Conn's house.

James Gallaway, living in Cincinnati, reports a stray mare.

Ichabod Spinning, in Cincinnati, reports a horse that strayed from the plantation of Joseph Reeder at Duck Creek. Deliver to Judge Spinning at Dayton.

Lieut. Patrick Dickey regarding a meeting of the Infantry Company to elect a captain in place of Capt. James Smith, resigned.

Stephen Law about a note from him and Nathaniel Saunders, late of Anderson township, dec'd, to Jonah Frazee of Anderson township.

William Ferguson, at Lebanon, has just returned from Philadelphia and has a new shipment of goods for sale at his store in Lebanon.

Peter Lefever, of Warren County, says that his wife, Rachel Lefever, has left him, and he won't honor her debts.

Andrew Lewis, living in Butler County in St. Clair township, found a mare.

Edward B. Hannegan, in Cincinnati, announces a public exam of his pupils.

Doctor Sellman has lemmon juice for sale.

No. 49, Volume VII, Tuesday, 1 July 1806, Whole No. 361

William Wells, Indian agent at Fort Wayne, regarding Indian attacks.

A meeting of the Cincinnati Lyceum is to be held.

The select council of Cincinnati will dine together at G. Yeatman's on the Fourth of July. Apply to John S. Gano, George Gordon or Andrew Burt.

A note about a Fourth of July celebration dinner catered by Henry Disbrow.

Robert Martin regarding a horse stolen from Samuel Moore's house six miles below Cincinnati. It was taken by Samuel Shelcut, age 13 or 14.

Abraham Leet offers for sale his house in Rossville, Butler County.

David Sutton, Richard S. Thomas and Joshua Collet regarding suits in the Warren County Court of Common Pleas: Stephen Julien vs. John Thompson; and John Shaw vs. Isaac M'Cluchy. Mentions M'Cluchy's blacksmith tools.

William Ludlow, on Mill Creek, offers his farm for sale.

Joseph Henry, ten miles above Fort Hamilton at the Big Praire in Butler County, reports two stray mares. Deliver to Thomas Ramsey in Cincinnati.

Thomas Dugan asks those indebted to him to settle their accounts.

Samuel Dick, living on Indian Creek west of the Miami in Butler County, reports a stray horse.

Jno. O'Ferrall has opened a new store in Cincinnati in the store lately occupied by Mr. Dugan.

Jacob Williams, administrator of the estate of Cornelius Voorheese, dec'd, late of Springfield township in Hamilton County, about the estate settlement.

William Ludlow, on Mill Creek, says he has apple trees for sale.

Aaron Flowlers, living at his mills (formerly Davis' mills) at Middletown on the Great Miami in Butler County, reports some stray animals.

No. 50, Volume VII, Tuesday, 8 July 1806, Whole No. 362

John Reily, at Hamilton, agent for Jonathan Dayton of Elizabethtown, N.J., offers his half of the mills and distillery on Mill Creek for sale.

Reeder & Marcell about their coach and chairmaking business in Cincinnati.

Long & Carr regarding their cut nail manufactory in Cincinnati.

Long & Conrad continue the coppersmith's business in Cincinnati.

Long & Bretney have commenced the coppersmith's buiness in Lebanon.

Samuel Vail, living in Cincinnati township on the Ohio River, found a horse.

Griffin Yeatman, Wm. Stanley and Thomas Dugan, in Cincinnati, about the suit of James Smith and James Findlay vs. Thomas Cochran, late of Cincinnati.

A list of letters at the Post Office in Cincinnati includes Nancy Adams in Columbia, Benjamin Ashby, Richard Ayers, James Adair in White water, John Boos, Ashy Brown in Columbia, Alexander Bowers, Jonathan Burdge, Alexander Bigham, Daniel Brant, John Backman at White water, Hugh Carson, Henry Clark, Andrew Carrigue in care of Capt. Vance, Thomas Cox on Great Miami, Duncan Cameron, Joseph Case, Robert Crawford in care of Mr. Yeatman, John Carpenter, Samuel Crane, Isaac Cooper, Rhoda Corington, Francis Coursolle on White water, Col. Benjamin Chambers, Samuel Clark in care of Isaac Reed, WAlter Cox, Edward Covington, James Chalmers in care of Wm. Lynes, John T. Chunn, James Caldwell on Mill Creek, Ansly Cogan in care of Mr. Dunseth, Nehemiah Charles, James Charters, Mathias Crow near Cunningham's mill, Daniel Clark on Duck Creek, John Counsellor, David Carl and Lambert Blue, Isaac Dunn, Hugh and William Davis, James Dunlap, Abraham Day, John Decoursey, Sary Dickson, George Dost, George Enos, David Ford, Thomas Fitzwater, William Foster, Ziba Foot, John Grubb, John Guthrie, John Gordin, John Garrard, John Gaston, William Gledwell, John K. Graham, William Goff, Samuel Garrison, William Grant, George Gillaspie, Thomas Hinkson at Columbia, Richard Hogaland, John Holden, Elanear Harding at Colerain, James Harn, Joseph or Thomas Hart, Thomas Havens on Little Miami, David Harris, Levy Hardisty, Christopher Harden, Thomas Harper on Mill Creek, Michael Harness, William Hicks, Martin Herold, Giles Harlow, Andrew Jelly, James Jordan, William Jones on Duck Creek, David Jones, Henry Kendel, William Kinkade, Thomas Larison in Colerain, Robert Lockart, Lewis Laing, Mary Lyon, John Lum, Doct. Josleph Lane, Solomon Line, William Logan near Columbia, Isaac Lemasters, John M'Farland, Archibald M'Crary, John Morris, Alexander Moore, James Miller, Nathaniel M'Intire, Patrick M'Carty at White Water, Moses Musgrave, Joseph M'Dugal, Chancy Morse, Andrew Miers, William Medearies, James M'Cormack for John Campbell, Robert M'Millan, Mrs. John Nimmo, John Newel, Austin Nicholl, Henry Natches, Rebecca Piggot on Duck Creek, Matthew Nicol in care of Rev. Mr. Warwick, John Nash at Columbia, Nancy Parker, William Patterson, Benjamin Pears, Josleph Pierce, David Pooterpaugh on Great Miami, William Pickens, Abraham Pearson, Benjamin Piatt, James Reed, Thomas Roberts on Little Miami, William Rideles in Springfield, John Redenbauch near Redding, Abner Rude in Springfield, Henry Reese, David Riner in care of Capt. Vance, Wm. Rector in care of Griffin Yeatman, Daniel Schenck, Joseph Scudder, Jeremiah Smith, Solomon Smith, Aaron Scogan on Great Miami, Mary Smith, Willaughby Staton at Lawrenceburgh, Abraham Stout, Jacob Salor or Talor, Phebe Skelton, Michael Scott, Rev. John Thompson, John Tibbs in Columbia, Andrew Tharpe, David Vangilder, David VanBlarracom, Joseph Wood, Joseph Wingate, James Williams (cordwainer), Benjamin Webb, Daniel Woodward, Mr. Wormuch or John Crane, Peter Wolrick in care of Squire Light, Nathaniel Whitaker, Michael Wilkins, Elijah Whipple, Mary Winans at John Winans', Thomas White from New Jersey, Isaac Wilson, Peter Youtsey, Polly Zellor in care of James Bills, Wm. Ruffin.

Accounts of the Fourth of July celebrations mention G. Yeatman, Gen. Gano, Doctor Stall, Cincinnati Light Infantry.

No. 51, Volume VII, Tuesday, 15 July 1806, Whole No. 363

A Mr. Lee, from Mason County, Kentucky, was killed Tuesday, 15 July 1806, at Mr. Bracken's stone house when the scaffold gave way. He was a mason.

Jacob Williams, in Cincinnati, reports two stray horses.

Jacob White and Joseph Delaplaine have dissolved their partnership. Joseph Delaplaine will carry on the mercantile business in the brick house on Main St.

Brownlow Fisher, in Cincinnati, wants to buy honey.

Thomas Mounts, living in Dearborn County at the mouth of Grant's Creek, reports that he found a stray mare.

Hugh Moore wants to hire a man to drive a team.

A note regarding the examinations of Mr. Hannegan's pupils.

Accounts of the Fourth of July celebrations mention Doctor Lanier, Thomas Hough, and John Torrence of Hamilton, Maj. William Perry of Columbia, Gen. St.Clair, Jeremiah Morrow, John Smith.

A note regarding the fire at Kirby Hubbert's house near North Bend.

Mathias Rigel, living in German township of Montgomery County on the bank of the Great Miami near Holes Station, regarding three stray horses.

John Arthurs, in Cincinnati, reports that he found a mare.

Thomas Dugan has Man's Lick salt for sale at his store in Cincinnati.

No. 52, Volume VII, Tuesday, 22 July 1806, Whole No. 364

More accounts of the Fourth of July celebrations mention Capt. Clark, Capt. Sawyers, Gen. W.C. Schenck, Maj. John Whitworth, Capt. Robert Benham, Judge Low, Daniel Roe, Capt. D.F. Reeder.

William Stanley, for the Miami Exporting Company, wants to buy produce.

Robert Hunt, living at the first cabin above Deer Creek bridge, regarding his business of paper hanging.

Elizabeth Gallaway regarding a rumor she had circulated about Capt. Christy and a young woman. It is witnessed by Elmore Williams and J. Daily.

Joseph Carpenter has sold the Western Spy to David L. Carney.

Othaniel Looker and E.A. Brown report that the Republican Corresponding Society of Hamilton County held a meeting at Jonathan Pittman's house and nominated the following as candidates in the upcoming election: Jeremiah Morrow, William M'Farland, Col. John Jones, Hezekiah Price, Joseph Kitchell, Aaron Goforth, Jacob Felter, William Woodward.

Joseph Buel about the Republican Society of Washington County meeting. He mentions Joseph Buell, Edward W. Tupper, Return Jonathan Meigs, Junr.

William Stanley, agent for Oliver Ormsby, regarding a new shipment of goods for sale at Ormsby's store. Also those indebted to D. Conner & Company or to Oliver Ormsby should settle their accounts.

Hugh Moore, in Cincinnati, has plank for sale at his Lumber Yard.

Samuel Best wants to hire an apprentice to the clock and watchmaking trade.

Joseph Wingate, living on Mill Creek near Jonathan Pittman's house, reports that he found a stray horse.

No. 1, Volume VIII, Tuesday, 29 July 1806, Whole No. 365

A list of those who will receive subscriptions for the Western Spy includes John Reily in Hamilton, Gen. Schenck and Maj. Whitworth in Franklin, Daniel Roe in Lebanon, Joseph Peirce in Dayton, Samuel Heighway in Waynesville, Maj. Kibby in Deerfield, John Paul in Zenia, Capt. Vance in Lawrenceburgh, Col. Lytle at Williamsburgh and Mr. Brian at Grant's Lick, Kentucky.

Alex. A. Meek submits the speech made by the Cincinnati Lyceum's president.

More accounts of the Fourth of July celebrations mention the Mechanics of Cincinnati, Capt. Holt, Joseph Crane, Hugh M'Cullum, Judge Archer, Caleb Hunt, Maj. Gen. Gano, Dayton Library Society, Doctor I. Welsh, Doctor Elliot, Mr. Nolan, Thomas Wardell's oration, Jonathan W. Lyon, Benjamin Walker, Isaac Mills, T. Wardell, Col. Grant.

A note regarding a meeting at Mr. Disbrow's regarding building a new building to house the Academy of Cincinnati.

Obituary: Joseph B. Leibert, merchant, of Cincinnati, died on Friday last, July 25, 1806.

Thomas Thompson, in Franklin, regarding his new shipment of goods for sale at his store in the house lately occupied by John Jourdon next door to Doctor Reeder's tavern in Franklin.

Anthony Woolley, living near Springfield meeting house, reports a stray mare.

James Dover wants to buy hops, barley and honey at his "Brew & Bake-House" in Cincinnati opposite the market house.

Jesse Herran, living at Moses Ferral's near Cincinnati, regarding a stray mare. Deliver to Alexander King in Cincinnati.

No. 5, Volume VIII, Tuesday, 26 August 1806, Whole No. 369

Isaac Spinning, living near Dayton, reports a stray mare. Deliver to Ichabod Spinning in Cincinnati.

Ichabod Spinning and J. Delaplaine regarding a meeting held at Mr. Disbrow's tavern in Cincinnati to erect a building for the Academy. A committee is elected: William M'Farland, Rev. Matthew G. Wallace, Thomas Stansbury, William Stratten and James Ferguson.

Aaron Goforth, collector of taxes, regarding taxes due in Symmes' purchase.

James Cannon regarding a certificate to Maj. John M'Cashen for land.

Sidney Leibert, executrix, and James W. Sloan, executor, of the estate of Joseph B. Leibert, late of Cincinnati, dec'd, regarding the estate settlement.

William Wilson, in Lawranceburgh, has land for sale adjoining Ralph W. Hunt. Apply to Martin Baum in Cincinnati or Isaac Wilson in South Bend.

Benjamin Lambert says his wife, Mary Lambert, left him, and he won't honor her debts anymore.

David Sutton, Clerk of the Supreme Court of Warren County, regarding the suit of Catharine Boothby for divorce from her husband, Timothy Boothby. They married in Hamilton County in February 1798 and he left her in September 1800.

Benjamin K. Cozier, in Cincinnati, about a stray steer. Deliver to Isaac Dexter.

A note regarding the meeting at Mr. Disbrow's about building an Academy.

An unsigned letter to the editor mentions the Liberty Hall and Mr. Browne.

Several certificates concerning Henry Cadbury are printed. Cadbury stabbed Griffin Yeatman on 23 April 1802. Mentioned are Maj. Killgore, Jonathan Findlay, George Newman, Doctor Sellman, Charles Avery, Henry Weaver, Thomas Dugan.

Sergt. James Reed regarding a meeting of the Cincinnati Light Infantry.

A note regarding the publication of biographical sketches of the late Rev. John Gano. Subscriptions are received by John Reiley in Hamilton, David Sutton in Lebanon, Thomas Thompson in Franklin, Benjamin VanCleve in Dayton, John Paul in Xenia, George Fithian in Springfield, Col. William Lytle in Williamsburgh.

Garrett Lane has opened a dancing school at Mrs. Willis' house in Cincinnati.

Alexander Smith, in Cincinnati, has household goods for sale and offers his house on Columbia Street for lease.

Joseph Conkling, at the headwaters of Duck Creek near Ezra Ferris' still house, in Butler County, reports a stray horse.

John S. Gano, in Cincinnati, has lots for sale next to Jesse Reeder.

E. Hutchinson, in Cincinnati, is erecting a fulling mill on Mill Creek.

Those wishing to receive the Patriotic Farmer should pay Benjamin VanCleve, postmaster, in Dayton.

Samuel Marsh, living near Cincinnati, reports a stray mare. Deliver to William Squire at Middletown.

Henry Weaver, in Cincinnati, has a supply of school books for sale.

Ezekiel Hutchinson has land for sale on Mad River road adjoining Adrian Hegeman and James Greer.

Hugh Moore, in Cincinnati, has a house for rent next door to Gen. Findlay.

John S. Gano, Clerk of Hamilton County Court of Common Pleas, regarding the petitions filed by John Lambert and John Tway about their debts.

J. Carpenter regarding the sale of lots in Sycamore Street in Cincinnati.

Jacob Ball, on the Dry Fork of White Water near Col. Benefiel, about a horse.

Agnes Alexander, in Cincinnati, has a house and lot for sale.

Bryson Blackburn and Sarah Armstrong, administrators of the estate of James Armstrong, dec'd, late of Hamilton County, regarding the estate settlement.

John Wall has moved his saddlers' shop to Mrs. M'Cullough's.

Laurance Cavanaugh, taylor and ladies habit maker in Hamilton, has moved his shop to the house formerly occupied by George Snider.

Moore & M'Clelland, in Cincinnati, want to buy live hogs.

Joseph Carpenter has lots for sale in Cincinnati.

John O'Ferral, Cincinnati, has a stock of merchandize for sale.

No. 9, Volume VIII, Tuesday, 23 September 1806, Whole No. 373

William Ludlow declines the nomination of sheriff.

Thomas Ramsey, in Cincinnati, wants to hire apprentices to the house joiner's and carpenter's business.

Ephraim Carmack and Christopher Smith, in Cincinnati, have dissolved their partnership and ask those indebted to them to settle their accounts.

Those indebted to Doctor William Goforth should settle their accounts.

The Ohio Almanack for 1807, by Robert Stubbs, is for sale.

Thomas Henderson, late teacher of the school at Paterson, N.J., has opened a Seminary in Cincinnati. Mrs. Henderson will make mantuas.

John Binjamann, living near John Beaty's, reports some stray cows. Deliver to Henry Weaver in Cincinnati.

James Wilson or Andrew Wilson have land for sale on the west branch of Mill Creek near Springfield Meeting house.

Henry Hafer regarding his baking business in Cincinnati between Alter's and Philipson's stores on Main Street.

John O'Ferrall, in Cincinnati, wants to buy wheat at Moor's or White's mill.

A note regarding a performance by the Cincinnati Theater.

Marriage: John Adams, merchant, married Miss Christian Fox, both of Cincinnati, on Thursday evening, 18 September 1806, by Rev. Matthew G. Wallace.

Alexander King says he is a candidate for Sheriff at the upcoming election.

Brig. Gen. William C. Schenck gives orders to the Brigade and mentions Berry's Ford and Calvin Ball.

Capt. James Ferguson regarding a meeting of the Troop of Dragoons at Joseph M'Henry's house.

William M'Farland, Sheriff, regarding a sheriff's sale of the property of Luther Kitchel, dec'd, at the suit of Calvin Kitchel.

VanNuys & Best want to hire an apprentice to the clock and watchmaking, silversmith and jewelry business.

Philip Price, in Cincinnati, wants to hire an apprentice to the watch and clock making business.

George Gordon, in Cincinnati, has a store room, lately occupied by John Smith, contractor, for rent.

Charles Collins, living on the Dry Ridge in Campbell County, Kentucky, found a stray horse. He adds that the horse was stolen near Cincinnati by a free negro man, Isaac Davis, who was arrested for the crime.

John Dill, Cincinnati, saddle and harness maker, wants to hire an apprentice.

Peter Love, rope manufacturer, has rope for sale at his factory.

George Williamson has good pasture for rent near Col. Sedam's place.

Henry Wason, in Butler County, writes about the character of Major Jonathan Cilley of Colerain. He mentions Samuel Patterson of Cincinnati, Judah Willey.

Nathan C. Findlay has for sale a large quantity of lead.

Alexander King, for James Smith, late sheriff of Hamilton County, regarding a sheriff's sale of the property of Thomas Goudy at the suit of Joel Williams.

Joshua Sled, near Lawrenceburgh, Dearborn County, says Elisha Chism, late of Warren County, Kentucky, took away Sled's wife, Winny Sled, age 36, and much of his property. Winny Sled left a family of seven children behind.

Gustavus Reeves and Manassah Brown regarding a meeting of the militia companies of Capt. Stanley and Capt. Carpenter of Cincinnati.

No. 11, Volume VIII, Tuesday, 7 October 1806, Whole No. 375

Unsigned letters to the editor mention James Pritchard, Jeremiah Morrow, James Miller, Mr. Gallatin, Thomas Worthington and Mr. Pritchard.

An unsigned letter nominates men for office and mentions Jeremiah Morrow, William M'Farland, John Jones, Hezekiah Price, Joseph Kitchell, Aaron Goforth, James Ewing, Mr. Pittman and William Woodward.

Marriage: Joseph Delaplaine to Miss Jane Ann Levingston, daughter of William Levingston of N.Y., on Monday evening, 6 Oct 1806, by Rev. Matthew G. Wallace.

Ethan Stone is a candidate for the state legislature.

An unsigned letter to the editor mentions James Miller, Jeremiah Morrow, Mr. Gallatin, John C. Symmes, Jonathan Donnald.

John Paully, living on Twin Creek, reports a stray mare.

Ephraim Carter, living in Cincinnati, reports a strayed mare.

James Bill, in Cincinnati, has a lot for sale opposite the Liberty Hall.

A notice regarding the Horse Races at Newport, Kentucky.

Thomas M'Cullough, at Mount Pleasant, asks those indebted to him to settle their accounts immediately.

Peter Love, in Cincinnati, regarding a strayed cow.

Thomas Dugan asks those borrowing books to return them.

J. & A. Hunt, Cincinnati, want to buy hogs at their stillhouse on Deer Creek.

A notice regarding two farms for sale. Apply to Benjamin Mason on Sycamore Street in Cincinnati or George Williamson at Beech Grove on the Ohio.

Wm. M'Farland, Sheriff, regarding the upcoming elections mentions James Clark in Anderson township, Samuel Muchmore in Columbia township, Jonathan Pitman in

Springfield township, Jacob Morgan in Miami township, James Harding in Colerain township, Col. John Benefiel in Crosby township, and Ebenezer Cooley in White water township.

Andrew Burt and John Dill say that the partnership of Burt & Dill, Saddlers, is dissolved. Those indebted to them should settle their accounts.

Wm. M'Farland, Sheriff, regarding sheriff's sales of the property of John M'Cullough at the suit of Jonas Crane; that of James Lowes at the suit of James Morrison; that of James Smith at the suits of Charles Bruce, Samuel Utter, James Demint and J. Morrison.

A copy of a letter from Joseph Thompson of Butler County to David Davice at the Scioto Salt Works regarding a runaway horse.

Those indebted to Doctor William Goforth should settle their accounts.

James Ferguson wants to sell his entire stock of goods and rent the store.

G. Turner, in Cincinnati, has a farm for sale, in the forks of Mad River near Springfield, now occupied by Mr. Lewis. Apply to Mr. Doughty at Springfield.

Grizel Little asks those indebted to the estate of Ephraim Little, late of Deerfield township, Warren County, dec'd, to pay their bills.

J. Carpenter asks those indebted to him to pay their bills to William Clark.

John Torrence, in Hamilton, has good breeding mares and colts for sale.

No. 12, Volume VIII, Tuesday, 14 October 1806, Whole No. 376

Obituary: Mrs. Eleanor Moore, age 80, died in Hamilton on 4 October 1806 and was buried on 5 October 1806.

Jacob Philipson has opened a new dry goods and grocery store in Cincinnati.

Peter Yawger, in Lebanon, has town lots for sale in Lebanon.

Robert Blair, in Cincinnati, is opening a singing school soon.

W. Stanley announces a meeting of the Miami Exporting Company.

John Nimmo has a store for rent in Cincinnati. It was lately occupied by Mr. Delaplaine who has sold out.

John C. Winans, in Lebanon, offers his house and lot for sale.

A list of letters at the Post Office in Cincinnati includes Henry Anderson, Richard Allison, John Brumfield, John Bell (carpenter), Robert Badgley on Mill Creek, Uzal Bates in care of Jeremiah Hunt, Jonathan Burdge, Peter Borders, Matthias Crow, Stephen Campbell in Crosby, Lewis Coon, Henry Cossart, Collumby Crossen near Waldsmith's mill, Edward Covington, Amsty Cogan in care of Andrew Dunseth, Edward Cowins, Elias Crain, Andrew Campbell, Abraham Christ, John Cochran, Robert Campbell in Colerain, Peter Davis or Jonathan William, Rev. Daniel Duffy, Joseph Denman in Sycamore, Azariah Dunn, George Ely, Alexander Eson in care of Colin Miles, David Engart, William Fleckner, Rosswell Fenton, Jeremiah French, Alexander Fowler, Elizabeth Fredrick, Samuel Fairchild, Hugh Gaston, Samuel Goodwin, Timothy Green on Little Miami, Samuel Gray in Columbia, John Goble, Samuel Grimes, Samuel Hilditch, James Hines, Thomas How, John Howard in care of Harmong Long, Thomas Hurford, Daniel Horton, Robert Hamill in care of John Becket, Robert Hewit, John Harris, Archibald Hood, Alexander Holanes, James Heath, William Hillmane, John Hart, Thomas Holland, Jones Harris, David Harris, Joseph Jones, Abraham Jones, Joab Jeffers, Jonathan Jones in Columbia, Gary Johnston, John Johnson, Samuel Irwin, Jaen Kelly on Little Miami, Thoams Kinner at Columbia, Moses Knap, Hoffman Keen, George Larrison, John Larue in Springfield, Paul Lewis, William Leman, Israel Longfelt, Benjamin Lakin, David Long on Great Miami, William Ludlow, John Laurance in care of Ezekiel Creatures, Benjamin Loder, Joseph Lane or Alexander Robb, William Lend, Mary M'Kee, John M'Donnel, Jacob Miller, Moses Martindale, Joseph M'Henry, John M'Cormick, Samuel Mow in care of Thomas King, Jese Nolelon, John Nash in Columbia, John Nief on Little Miami, Nathaniel Nicholas, Letty Nash, James Patterson at Sycamore, Enoch Parvin, Edward Phelps, Daniel Pierce, Mark Patten, Joseph Porter on Beever Creek, James Piper, Thomas Phleming, Amos Quick in care of Isaac Anderson, Ezekiel Ross, John Robb, William Rector, John Ross, Abraham C. Roll, Ignatius Ross, James Roseman (reed maker), Jordon Reams, Assa Richardson, Abraham Roads in Columbia, Hugh Sprowl, Joseph Stockwell in Boon County, William Squires, Jacob Skillman, Walter Smith, William Stillwagon, Israel Smith, James Stockhouse in Columbia, Andrew Shirk at Great Miami, James Smiley, Stephen Shearwook, Isaac Sparks, Vincen Shinn, Aaron Stout in Colerain, Joseph Scuder, John or Joel Sanders, David Snider, George Turner,

Joseph Tetrick, Teakle Taylor, William Thompson on Mill Creek, Lewis Usard, John Vernor in care of Thomas M'Farland, Henry Vantrees in care of James Bills, David Vangelder, Andrew Wakefield in care of Isaac Anderson, Peter Weill, Losen Wells, Benjamin Weeks, James Weir, William Whitacre, Isaac Wilson, Hatfield Williams, Col. John Wallace, Judah Willey, Lewis Ward. Entered by William Ruffin, post master.

No. 13, Volume VIII, Tuesday, 21 October 1806, Whole No. 377

An unsigned letter to the editor mentions the Ohio Gazette, Judge Meigs, Mr. Blannerhassat (living a few miles below Marietta, "a foreigner who has resided but a few years in our country").

A letter from Elias Glover mentions Abraham Bishop of Connecticut.

Mr. M'Donald, living about twenty miles up the east branch of the Little Miami, has found a lead mine.

Isaac G. Burnet and Nicholas Longworth are admitted to the practice of law by the Supreme Court in Cincinnati.

A note about the Troop of Dragoons commanded by Capt. James Ferguson.

Election returns in Hamilton County mention Jeremiah Morrow, Jacob Felter, James Pritchard, William M'Farland, John Jones, Hezekiah Price, Ethan Stone, Jacob Broadwell, I.B. Miller, Othniel Looker, Aaron Goforth, Alexander King, William Woodward, James Ewing and Jonathan Pitman.

John Martin, gentlemen's hair-dresser, lately from Baltimore, has moved his shop to the house lately occupied by Mr. Dunseth in Cincinnati.

A notice regarding the Cincinnati Horse Races.

M. Ellis & Company regarding their plane making business in Pittsburgh.

Matthew G. Wallace, in Cincinnati, is "designing to leave this place" and offers for sale his house and lots next door to the new Academy in Cincinnati.

James M'Neely, in Springfield township, Hamilton County, says that his wife, Sarah M'Neely, left him and he won't pay her bills.

James M'Neely reports a stolen mare.

William Sutton, in Scott County, Kentucky, reports a runaway slave, Phill.

Samuel Beeler, Jr., on Four Mile Creek, Butler County, has horses for sale.

Moore & M'Clelland has Man's Lick salt for sale.

No. 15, Volume VIII, Tuesday, 4 November 1806, Whole No. 379

Hannah Burk, wife of Thomas Burk, will apply for a divorce from her husband.

Burrowes Smith, in Cincinnati, reports three stray horses.

The Western Spy office has moved to the house next to Mr. Disbrow's tavern.

A note regarding the Supreme Court's sentence of Mordecai Thruston for the murder of John Marshall.

A note regarding the trial of Joshua Edwards mentions Mr. St.Clair, Mr. Rawlins, Mr. Glover, Mr. Burnet. Edwards is nearly 60 years old and has a wife and a large family.

Capt. James Ferguson regarding a meeting of the Troop of Light Dragoons.

John M'Dugal regarding the map of Ohio made by John F. Mansfield.

Charles Killgore, Register of the Land Office, has land for sale and mentions William Cooper, David Beaty, James Smith, Arthur St.Clair, Jr., John James Dufour, Daniel Conner, Isaac Reed, James B. Wilkinson, Israel Loring, James Hamilton, Sam. C. Vance, Joseph Wilkinson, Andrew Scott, Cave Johnson, Bayless Ashby, Zebulon Pike, Daniel Ingersoll, Alexander Scott.

A note regarding building a public road from Greenfield on Paint Creek to John Haine's mill at Waynesville.

John Smith, in Cincinnati, wants to buy wheat at his mill on Little Miami.

No. 17, Volume VIII, Tuesday, 18 November 1806, Whole No. 381

Ezekiel Cretors, in Cincinnati, has household furniture for sale at his house.

Andrew Boden, in Cincinnati, reports a stray mare.

John Hart, in Northbend, regarding produce he bought.

Aquila Wheeler, late deputy sheriff, regarding sheriff's sales of the property of James Caldwell at the suit of Joseph Thornton; that of Nathaniel Whitaker (next door to Christopher Hardon) at the suits of Isaac Mills and James Ferguson; that of James Smith at the suits of Charles Bruce, Samuel Utter and James Demint; also that of Abraham Voorheese at the suit of Hugh Meek.

Obituary: Capt. John Mercer, of Cincinnati, an officer in the Revolutionary War, died on Saturday, 15 November 1806. He was buried on Sunday.

G. Turner, in Cincinnati, reports a theft of papers from Mr. Disbrow's tavern.

William Byrd "has just arrived from the eastward" and has goods for sale at his former store in Cincinnati.

J.W. Albright, Ensign, at Newport, Kentucky, is recruiting men for the army.

A note regarding the publication of Robert Frazer's journal of the Lewis and Clark expedition. Available at John Armstrong's in Columbia.

Joseph Prince, in Cincinnati, reports a stray horse.

James Ferguson has a new shipment of goods for sale in Cincinnati.

Day Wood has opened a new dry goods store in Cincinnati in the house owned by John Nimmo and lately occupied by Mr. J. Delaplaine.

Richard Steele, at Shelbyville, Kentucky, reports two stolen horses.

The Ohio Almanack for 1807 is for sale at the Western Spy office.

Isaac Dexter, living in Cincinnati, reports that he found a stray horse.

Hamilton Reed, in Boon County, Kentucky, regarding a bond to Benjamin Duncan of Ross County, Ohio.

No. 18, Volume VIII, Tuesday, 25 November 1806, Whole No. 382

James T. Martin, living in Clark County, Kentucky, has land for sale in Ohio.

Col. Aaron Burr arrived in Cincinnati on Friday evening, 21 November 1806.

Henry Ewing, Coroner, regarding a coroner's sale of the property of William Perry at the suit of Nathan Nicholas.

John Martin, in Cincinnati, "intends to leave this place, early in the spring, for Baltimore" and wishes to sell his present stock of goods.

No. 19, Volume VIII, Tuesday, 2 December 1806, Whole No. 383

A notice of a theater production in Cincinnati.

There will be a meeting of the Cincinnati Lyceum.

John O'Ferrall has a new shipment of goods for sale at his store in Cincinnati.

John Dill, saddle and harness maker, has moved his shop to the house lately occupied by Moore & M'Clelland, merchants, in Cincinnati.

Samuel Simonton, of Springfield, or Henry Cadbury, of Cincinnati, say that Simeon Sears (about 35 years old) and Amos Hutchison (about 25 years old) stole three horses. The thiefs spent the night at Border's Tavern at Smith's mills.

No. 20, Volume VIII, Tuesday, 9 December 1806, Whole No. 384

Gov. Edward Tiffin's speech to the General Assembly is printed.

A note regarding the proceedings of the legislature mentions Thomas Kerker, Thomas Scott, Mr. Hough, Mr. Wood, Mr. Sargeant, Mr. M'Arther, Mr. Hampstard, Mr. Thomas, Mr. M'Farland, Mr. Cane, Mr. Jewit, Mr. Bane, Mr. Sharp.

William Stanley, in Cincinnati, has land for sale that formerly belonged to Maj. W. Peters and lately occupied by J. Cox. Mr. Symmes, Mr. Porter, Mr. Jones, Mr. Walker and Mr. Dickson live adjoining the land.

William M'Clelland, sheriff of Butler County, reports that John Welch, age 20 or 21, broke out of jail. He was there on suspicion of mail theft.

Alexander King, in Cincinnati, has a house and lot for sale.

No. 21, Volume VIII, Tuesday, 16 December 1806, Whole No. 385

John Watson, painter and glazier, lately from the city of Baltimore, regarding his business in Cincinnati.

Aquila Wheeler, Deputy Sheriff, regarding the sheriff's sale of the property of James Smith at the suits of Samuel Utter and James Demint.

An unsigned letter mentions Matthew Nimmo, Lamb's tavern in Chillicothe and Mr. Casset from Wheeling.

The militia commanded by Capt. Stanley and Capt. Carpenter are to meet.

Those indebted for the Western Spy can make payments to Mr. House.

Jacob Fowble & Company "have just arrived from Baltimore" and have goods for sale at their store in Cincinnati. Payments may be made in wheat delivered at Fowble's mill, on Mill Creek, formerly owned by Mr. Van-Horn.

W. Stanley, in Cincinnati, about a meeting of the Miami Exporting Company.

Benjamin Leavel, living on the Great Miami in Montgomery County, found a silver watch on Langham's trace between Thomas Townsley's and Deer Creek. Apply to James Brown in Dayton.

James Ellis, in Cincinnati, regarding a bond to William M'Farland, Cincinnati.

Daniel Searles, in Cincinnati, has started his gun and whitesmith's business.

No. 22, Volume VIII, Tuesday, 23 December 1806, Whole No. 386

David L. Carney, in Cincinnati, about a meeting of the Cincinnati Lodge. A speech will be delivered by Brother Henderson.

John O'Ferrall, in Cincinnati, regarding teas and wines for sale at his store.

Stephen Shepherd, Thomas Kirker and Edward Tiffin print a new law of Ohio.

John H. Piatt & Company, in Cincinnati, have goods for sale at their store at the house of Joseph Carpenter, lately occupied by the Western Spy office.

Peter Love, in Cincinnati, reports a strayed or stolen mare.

John Goldtrap, in Reading, lost a pocket book that includes notes on John Parci and John Hunter.

The workshop and stable of Mr. Kauz in Cincinnati burned down on Thursday.

Gov. Edward Tiffin's speech to the General Assembly is printed.

Gideon Granger, Post Master General, offers a reward for the arrest of John Welch who escaped from the Butler County jail.

Aquila Wheeler, late deputy sheriff, regarding the sheriff's sale of the property of Nathaniel Whitaker at the suits of Isaac Mills and James Ferguson. The land adjoins that where Christopher Haydon now lives.

Charles Brittain has apples and cider for sale in Cincinnati.

Jacob Malson, in Cincinnati, reports a strayed or stolen mare.

Isaac Bates, near Cincinnati, regarding a steer that broke into the inclosure of Matthew Nimmo.

No. 23, Volume VIII, Tuesday, 30 December 1806, Whole No. 387

E. Hutchinson, in Cincinnati, has completed his fulling mill. Cloth should be delivered to Isaiah Brient, at the mill on Mill Creek, who will operate the mill.

A note regarding the proceedings of the legislature mentions the resolution requesting John Smith's resignation from Congress.

Obituary: Charles Avery, age 57, died on Thursday, 25 December 1806.

Thos. Gibson, Auditor, reports on his audit of the state of the revenue.

Several letters are printed between Henry Dearborn, Capt. James Ferguson of Cincinnati, Matthew Nimmo and Th. Jefferson.

Daniel Roe, in Cincinnati, has a new shipment of goods for sale at his store in the house lately occupied by Joseph B. Leibert in Cincinnati.

James Ferguson, in Cincinnati, regarding the Troop of Dragoons.

John O'Ferrall, in Cincinnati, "being desirous of returning to the Eastward as soon as possible", offers all his stock and goods for sale.

Thomas Dugan, in Cincinnati, asks those indebted to him to settle their bills.

Thomas Scott or Wm. Ruffin want to hire a mail carrier to Chillicothe.

No. 24, Volume VIII, Tuesday, 6 January 1807, Whole No. 388

Gov. Edward Tiffin's address to the legislature is printed. He mentions Judge Meigs of Marietta, Maj. Gen. Buell, Mr. Blannerhasset, Comfort Tyler, Gen. Gano, Gen. Nimmo, Gen. Findlay, Jacob Wilson of Steubenville, Col. Phelps of Virginia.

A list of letters at the Post Office in Cincinnati includes David Adams, Robert Buntin, Labin Bramble, Mary Barbary, Stephen Benton, Fielding Belt, Edmund Bacon, John Cliver, Enos Cutler, Joseph Cassin, Nehemiah Charles, John Craft, John Crary, Arm Cook, Aaron Caldwell, Margaret Clark in care of James Patterson, Maj. Jonathan Cilly, Hugh Davis in care of John Elliott, John Day, John Davis, Maj. King Dearmond in care of John W. Browne, Col. William Ellzey, Richard Fairman, Charles Fariss, Thomas Foster, Ezra Ferras, John Gordon in Boon County, Charles Griner, William Goff, Samuel Grimes, Isaac Goble, Joseph Gillispie at Sycamore, John Hynd at Sycamore, William Hinton in care of Joseph Conn, Richard Hankins in Colerain, James Harvey in Crosby, Philimon Harvey in Colerain, John Hos or Ros, Edward Hunt, Wm. Hanby, Thomas Hill, James Heath, David Jones near Columbia, David Inyard in care of John Ludlow, Thomas Jones in care of Mr. Anderson, Joshua Isguig, Stuffel Karm at Columbia, Samuel Moss, Joseph Kirkbridge, Philip Kirker, John List in Springfield, Thomas Lanaway, John Manson, Samuel Mow, Capt. Edward Miller,

Rowland T. M'Daniel, Peter M'Clane, William Merry, Barnabas Newkirk, Leazen Newell in New-Town, John Newell, Patrick O'Neal, Andrew Pryer, Capt. John Pollock, Daniel Pierce, Chatfield Parsons, Joseph Personett, James Patterson at Sycamore, John Powner, Lewis Rees, William Robinson, Abraham Swatselby, Samuel Stibings, Lemuel Stephenson in care of Isaac Sturgus, Jacob Stephans, James Shamrock, John Shaw, Hezekiah Shaw, Aaron Sackett, Isaac Swallow at Springfield, Hannah Stevens, Joseph Smith, Joseph Scudder, Augustus Stone, Benjamin F. Stone, Nathan Stubbs in care of the editor of the Liberty Hall, John Tharp, Isaac Tegarden, Tekel Taylor, Ephraim Tucker, Frederick Uncel, David Vangilder, David Vail in Anderson township, John Wooly, Aaron Wagoner in Springfield, John Willey, Jacob Warwick, John Wilson, George Wall, John Woods, John Williamson, Robert Warwick, John Woodward, John Watson in Springfield, John Ware in Columbia township, Jacob White, Wm. Ruffin.

Rev. Hiram Miram Curry will preach at the courthouse on Wednesday.

A note regarding the proceedings of Congress mention Robert F. Slaughter and Seth Pease.

Gov. Edward Tiffin writes a letter to the legislature.

John H. Crawford, living in Elizabeth township, near Honey Creek, reports some strayed cattle.

Uriah Gates says his wife, Rebecca Gates, left him and he won't pay her bills.

Those indebted for the Western Spy should pay David Sutton in Lebanon.

No. 25, Volume VIII, Monday, 12 January 1807, Whole No. 389

A note regarding the meeting of the Cincinnati Lyceum.

George Tod is elected, over Richard S. Thomas, to replace William Sprigg, judge of the Supreme Court, who resigned. Gov. Tiffin is elected, over Philemon Beecher, as senator to Congress in place of Col. Worthington whose term had expired. Joseph Buell is elected an associate judge of the Court of Common Pleas for Washington County, and Peter Burr is elected for Warren County.

Obituary: Allen Halley, age 18, son of Capt. Samuel Halley of Anderson Township, Hamilton County, died Sunday morning, 4 January 1807. He had just returned from nearly eight months in the West Indies.

John S. Gano regarding an ordinance of the town of Cincinnati.

Fielding Loury, agent for John Smith, has land for sale.

John Reily regarding a suit in Butler County Court of Common Pleas: Stephen Vail vs. George Bridges. He mentions Ezekiel Ball, a justice of the peace in Lemon township, and Joseph Henry, a constable in Lemon township. Also about the suit of Stephen Vail vs. Edward Steen.

Aquila Wheeler, late deputy sheriff, regarding the sheriff's sales of the pro-perty of Alexander Rowan at the suit of John Huston; that of John Lyon at the suit of David Grummon; that of Cornelius Voorheese at the suit of Edward Meeks.

Joseph Vanhorn, Thomas Dugan and Joseph Carpenter about the estate settle-ment of Cornelius Voorheese, dec'd, at the house of Joseph Conn in Cincinnati.

A note about the publication of the journals of Robert Frazer. It's available at Henry Weaver's store or Sutherland & Brown's stores in Hamilton and Dayton.

No. 26, Volume VIII, Monday, 19 January 1807, Whole No. 390

E.W. Finney reports that he found a stray horse.

James Ewing regarding the publication of Doctor W. Whorter's sermons.

Obituary: Gershum Gard, age 70, died on 28 December 1807.

A note regarding a meeting of the citizens of Cincinnati at Yeatman's Hotel mentions David Zeigler, Isaac G. Burnet, Doctor John Sellman, Andrew Burt, Dr. Edward H. Stall, Griffin Yeatman.

John S. Gano prints an ordinance of the town of Cincinnati.

William Lytle, intending to move to Cincinnati, offers his farm for lease. It is located near Williamsburgh, Clermont County.

John S. Gano, in Cincinnati, regarding the settlement of estates.

No. 28, Volume VIII, Monday, 2 February 1807, Whole No. 392

John Arthars, Collector, in Cincinnati, regarding payment of the road tax.

An unsigned letter to the editor mentions Mr. Anderson, Mr. Yeatman, Daniel Symmes, Elias Glover, Mr. Smith, Mr. Disbrow, Judge Daniel Symmes.

A note regarding the governor requesting Gen. Gano to accept a major's pay.

An account of the meeting at Mr. Disbrow's mentions Mr. Conn, Daniel Symmes, Elias Glover, Mr. Anderson, Mr. Symmes, John Sellman, John Bradburn, Stephen M'Farland, Andrew Burt, Thomas Ramsey, John Smith, G. Yeatman, Isaac Anderson, Thomas Rawlins.

Thomas Smith has land on Whitewater River for sale including his mills seven miles from the Ohio River and twelve from Lawrenceburgh. Apply to Joseph Kitchell living next door.

A note states that Aaron Scudder is now in Cincinnati jail for debt.

Thomas Ramsay, in Cincinnati, reports a runaway apprentice named Samuel Runyan, about 16 years old.

Capt. Amos Stoddart, at Newport, Kentucky, reports some deserters: John Davison (age 32, joiner, born in Holland), Philip Rogers (age 33, carpenter, born in New York), Nahum Spring (age 28, born in Massachusetts), James Rains (age 18, born in North Carolina), Benjamin Madearys (age 28, saddler, born in Virginia), John Thompson (age 26, born in Germany), Robert Johnson (age 19, born in Mary-land), Bogardus Lyons (age 24, tailor, born in Massachusetts), Abraham Loukes (age 26, carpenter, born in New York).

Jacob Wheeler & Rhoda Wheeler, executors of the estate of Stephen Wheeler, late of Hamilton County, dec'd, regarding the estate settlement.

Wm. M'Clellan, Sheriff of Butler County, regarding sheriff's sales of the property of Thomas Powers at the suit of Jonathan Dayton; that of James Hamilton at the suit of Samuel Dillon; that of the heirs of Patrick Graham, dec'd, in order to divide the inheritance.

John S. Gano regarding the election of grand jurors and petit jurors.

No. 29, Volume VIII, Monday, 9 February 1807, Whole No. 393

Elizabeth Oden regarding her divorce from Richard A. Oden who left her.

Notes regarding the Ohio legislature mention William M'Farland, Thomas Tudor Tucker, Samuel Findlay.

Marriage: Andrew Burt to Miss Sarah Gano, daughter of John S. Gano, both of Cincinnati, on Wednesday evening, 4 February 1807, by Rev. James Kemper.

A note regarding the performance of Mr. Henderson's pupils at the Theater.

An account of the meeting of the Democratic Republicans of Cincinnati mentions Henry Disbrow, Daniel Symmes, Elias Glover, D. Zeigler, I.G. Burnet, Mr. Yeatman, John Smith and his son Ambrose Smith, Mr. Blannerhasset, Mr. Tyler, Mr. Conn. Included are various depositions that mention Col. Burr, A.D. Smith, Matthew Nimmo, A. Burr, Judge Symmes, Mr. Anderson.

John Nimmo writes a letter to the public regarding Elias Glover's slander. He mentions Capt. Ferguson's store, Matthew Nimmo. Witnessed by Andrew Burt, Edward H. Stall and James Ferguson.

A letter to the public from Elias Glover regarding last week's letter about him mentions Mr. Anderson, Mr. Brown, Mr. Rawlins, Mr. Disbrow.

An unsigned letter to the editor mentions Democratic Republican Society, Judge Symmes, John Smith, Judge Nimmo, Matthew Nimmo, Mr. Conn, Mr. Burr, Mr. Yeatman, Isaac Anderson, Elias Glover, Mr. Disbrow, Doctor John Sellman, Doctor John Bradburn.

Jeremiah Morrow reports that Doctor Eric Bollman and Mr. Swartwout are prisoners in the marine barracks in Washington City.

Robert F. Slaughter has been found guilty of the charges against him. He is removed from the Court of Common Pleas. Levin Belt will succeed him.

Charles Farran, in Cincinnati, regarding trespassing on his land. David M'Cash is appointed his agent to prevent injury to his land.

William Ludlow, at Mill Creek, offers his land for sale.

Peter Imlay has dry goods for sale at Spring Farm near Cincinnati.

Eden Burrows, administrator of the estate of David Adams, dec'd, late of the township of Franklin, Warren County, regarding the estate settlement.

John Armstrong and Andrew Burt, administrators of the estate of Charles Avery, late of Cincinnati, dec'd, regarding the estate settlement.

Rachel Armstrong and John Armstrong, administrators of the estate of Samuel Armstrong, late of Columbia, dec'd, regarding the estate settlement.

Samuel James, in Lebanon, regarding a bond he gave to William Walton.

No. 30, Volume VIII, Monday, 16 February 1807, Whole No. 394
A list of laws passed by the Ohio Legislature mentions Cincinnati University, Daniel Evans and Joseph Swearingen (agents for the heirs of James Trimble, dec'd), Hannah Burk, St. John's Church at Worthington, Granville Library Society, Athens University, James Innes Clark, Marietta, John Smith.
    E. Glover regarding the accusations of John Nimmo mentions M. Nimmo.
    Andrew Burt regarding the "scoundrel", Elias Glover.
    Unsigned letters to the editor mention Judge Daniel Symmes, Isaac Anderson, William M'Farland, Stephen Wood, Matthew Nimmo.
    Charles Killgore, Register of the Land Office, regarding land for sale, mentions David M'Cance, W. Allensworth, Wm. Remey, James Wilson, Peyton Short, James Irwin Nesbit, Tho. R. Smith, John Vanasdol, N. Talbot.
    Adam Hurdus "intends shortly to remove out of town" and offers his stock for sale at his store in Cincinnati.
    Andrew Brannon, constable, regarding guard duty in Cincinnati.
    Fox & Adams ask those indebted to them to settle their accounts.
    Henry Marshall, living on Isaac Bates' place near Cincinnati, reports that he found a stray heifer.

No. 31, Volume VIII, Monday, 23 February 1807, Whole No. 395
Unsigned letters to the editor mention Mr. Conn, Mr. Carney, Judge Symmes, Mr. Nimmo, Mr. Anderson.
    John Sellman, Andrew Burt, Stephen M'Farland and Thomas Ramsey write a letter regarding Elias Glover.

No. 32, Volume VIII, Monday, 2 March 1807, Whole No. 396
John Nimmo writes a letter to the public about Elias Glover. He mentions Mr. Burt, Mr. Stall and Mr. Ferguson.
    A letter to the public from Elias Glover regarding the letters about him. He mentions Andrew Burt.
    Stephen M'Farland writes regarding the letter from himself, John Sellman, Andrew Burt and Thomas Ramsey. He says the others have lived in Cincinnati "upwards of 10 years", but he's only been there for a little over two years.
    Thomas Dugan regarding the settlement of his debts.
    William Ludlow, at Mill Creek, has apple trees for sale.
    John O'Ferrall "intends moving from Cincinnati by the first of April" and asks those indebted to him to settle their accounts.
    Rev. Matthew G. Wallace will preach at the Meeting House in Cincinnati.
    John Sellman writes a letter to the editors of the Scioto Gazette, J.S. Collins & Company, regarding the slander they printed about him. Mentions John Smith.
    Henry Weaver, in Cincinnati, has a new shipment of goods at his store.
    John Cleves Symmes, agent for Peyton Short, has land for sale. Apply to Hugh Moore's store to see the plat map.
    Elias Glover, administrator of the estate of Ziba Foot, late of Cincinnati township, dec'd, regarding the estate settlement.
    Robert Renick, for Elizabeth Lowrey, administrator of Archibald Lowrey, dec'd, regarding the sale of Lowrey's house and lot in Springfield.
    Levi M'Clean, Auctioneer, has books for sale at auction in Cincinnati.
    James Sisson, Jr., has garden seeds and medicines for sale at the brick house on Ludlow's Station.

No. 33, Volume VIII, Monday, 9 March 1807, Whole No. 397
James Ewing, justice of the peace for Hamilton County, submits a deposition of Ephraim Kibby about Burr's Conspiracy. He mentions Gen. Eaton, Col. Aaron Burr.
    Obituary: Joshua Delaplaine, age 68, died at his farm about two miles from Hamilton on Thursday, 26 January 1807. He was buried the next day.
    William Ludlow is offering his farm for sale.
    Jesse Hunt, in Cincinnati, offers town lots for sale at Dickey's tavern in Sycamore Street, Cincinnati.
    B. Chambers has land for sale in the Ohio bottom. Apply to Gen. Findlay.
    John Lyon about a stud horse at the stable of Henry Disbrow in Cincinnati.
    A meeting regarding the lottery for the Cincinnati University mentions Mr.

Disbrow's Inn, Mr. Riddle, Mr. Van-Horn, Mr. Symmes, Mr. Stratton, Mr. Nimmo, Mr. Wood, Luke Foster, Mr. Hilditch and Mr. Stone.

James Gray and Mary Sayres, administrators of the estate of Sarah James, dec'd, late of Cincinnati, Hamilton County, regarding the estate settlement.

A note states that Frank Lawrence is now in the Cincinnati jail for debt.

Moore & M'Clelland ask those indebted to them to settle their accounts.

No. 34, Volume VIII, Monday, 16 March 1807, Whole No. 398

Samuel & J. Halley, in Cincinnati, have salt for sale at their store.

Ann Hay, executrix of the estate of William Hay, dec'd, late of Montgomery County, regarding the estate settlement.

Levi M'Clean or Elias Glover have a lot for sale in Cincinnati.

George Folk, in Beaver township, Green County, about the theft of watches.

Aquila Wheeler, late deputy sheriff, regarding sheriff's sales of the property of John Becket at the suits of James Dunn and Matthew Winton; that of John Humes at the suit of the executors of John M'Cullough, dec'd; that of Levi Pigg at the suit of Isaac Hubble; that of Josiah Decker and Frederick Coons at the suit of the administrators of Israel Ludlow, dec'd.

William Byrd, in Cincinnati, asks those indebted to him to pay their bills.

Henry Disbrow, in Cincinnati, has "declined my former business" and asks those indebted to him to settle their accounts.

No. 35, Volume VIII, Monday, 23 March 1807, Whole No. 399

An account of the robbery of James Findlay, Receiver of Public Monies. It was said to be committed by Charles Brittain, a mulatto, formerly Findlay's servant, Charles Vattier of Cincinnati, and Thomas Matthews.

Garret Lane regarding his dancing school in Mrs. Willis' house.

John Nimmo offers a store for rent, lately occupied by Day Wood, Cincinnati.

John Stitt, living on Dick's Creek, reports a stray horse. Deliver to Samuel Stitt in Cincinnati.

John Riddle, Joseph VanHorn, Luke Foster, Stephen Wood, Wm. Stratten, Daniel Symmes and Ethan Stone regarding the Cincinnati University lottery.

Mrs. H. Willis has opened a house of public entertainment in the house lately occupied by Henry Disbrow in Cincinnati.

John O'Ferrall, in Cincinnati, offers Rock Farm for sale.

Hugh Moore has boards for sale at his lumber yard in Cincinnati.

Ezekiel Hutchinson, Cincinnati, offers his farm on Mill Creek for rent. It was formerly owned by Capt. Samuel Martin.

No. 36, Volume VIII, Monday, 30 March 1807, Whole No. 400

Andrew Brannon, Constable, regarding an election in Cincinnati township.

Providence White, living on the Dry Fork of White water, reports a horse that strayed from Henry Tucker's on Mill Creek. Deliver to Jacob White on Mill Creek.

Joseph Evans, at Milton, about the new town of Still water on Great Miami.

Poor & Kershner, in Cincinnati, regarding their wagon making business.

Susanah Mercer, administratrix of the estate of John Mercer, dec'd, late of Cincinnati, regarding the estate settlement.

Marriage: Robert Caldwell to Miss Ann Avery, daughter of the late Charles Avery, of Cincinnati, on Wednesday, 25 March 1807, by Rev. James Kemper.

Marriage: Dudley Avery to Miss Mary Ann Browne, daughter of Rev. John W. Browne, on Thursday, 26 March 1807, by Rev. John W. Browne.

Obituary: The infant daughter of Hugh Moore, merchant, of Cincinnati, died on Sunday evening, 29 March 1807.

John H. Piatt regarding notes in possession of the Miami Exporting Company.

Henry Weaver has a new shipment of goods for sale at his store in Cincinnati.

Aquila Wheeler, deputy sheriff, regarding a sheriff's sale of the property of James Smith at the suits of Charles Bruce, Samuel Utter and James Demint.

John Ludlow and Isaac Bates about the settlement of the estate of Roswell Bartlett, dec'd, at the house of Alexander King in Cincinnati.

Isaac Anderson is "about to quit the public business, to close the business of eleven years standing" and has beds, bedding, furniture, and more for sale. He has rented his house to Ezekiel Hutchinson.

Elmore Williams and Samuel Littell regarding their business of making and laying brick in Cincinnati.

No. 37, Volume VIII, Monday, 6 April 1807, Whole No. 401

Henry Kerr says he's operating Ruffin's ferry across the Ohio. It's located nearly opposite Ruffin's tavern.

Marriage: John M'Clean, editor of the Western Star, married Miss Rebecca Edwards, of Newport, Kentucky, Sunday, 29 March 1807, by Rev. Robert Stubbs.

Lewis Cass is appointed marshal for the district of Ohio.

The house occupied by Ross & Green in Marietta was burned recently.

A list of letters at the Post Office in Cincinnati includes Bridget Adams in care of John M'Cullom, Richard Allen, Thomas Brown, Lisman Basey, Daniel Brown, Thomas Billingsly near White's Mill, Jacob Bender, H. Bradley, John Bradway, Peter Cowel, David Carle in Springfield, Samuel Clannin, Swithin Chandler, Abel Cosen in Boon County, Samuel Craigs, Charles Cannon, Eli Carson, Lucy Coleman, Joshua Cox, Lewis Cass, Jonathan Davis, Joseph Davis, Thomas Depriese, John Davis, Jonathan or Sarah Dunn, James Donnel, Thomas W. Evans, Mary Ennis, Joseph Felty, Thomas Gray, Samuel Grimes, John Guthrie, Daniel Gillman, John Green, Christopher Girton on Mill Creek, John Garrison, William Green, Robert Headon, William Harris, Ezra Harris in Colerain, Thomas Hubbell, Charles Hutchinson, Thomas Hutchinson, Sampson Hubbell, William Hand, James Hutchinson, Jones Harris, William Hall, James Hall in care of Samuel Patterson, Joshua Isgrig, Michael Isgrig, Thomas Johns in care of Mr. Anderson, David Jones, Samuel Jones, John and Peter Kisling, Henry Kase in Springfield, John Kiernan, William Kenedy, Joseph Linnel, Joseph Larwill, Gabriel Liming, Allen Leeper in care of Thomas Ewing, Nathaniel Lyon in care of Mr. Dexter, Charity Lawrence, John Murdock, Peter M'Arthers, James M'Neely in care of Andrew Dunseth, John and James Matthews, William Mills and James Stephenson near the mouth of Eagle Creek, William M'Gee, Richard Morgan, Jonathan M'Guire, Sampson M'Cullough, Jane Moore, Robert M'Millan, James M'Ginnes, William Mills, Jonathan Melvin, Isaac Morrison, John Morris, Samuel Mount, Adam Nutt, Moses Nap, Petrick O'Neal, Caleb Orsborn, John Piatt, Joseph Reling, Samuel Rolins, William Reeve, Elijah Richardson, Stephen Reeder, Aaron Ross, James Richardson, Jane Rowland in care of Ezekiel Hughes, Johnathan Shepherd, Solomon Smith, William Smith, Zadock Stephenson, John Smiley, Daniel Stineman, Samuel Smith living at John Mills' house, Samuel Shannon, Isaac Sparks, Abner Smith, Thomas Skinner, Daniel Skinner, Mathias Steel, Noah Sayres in Springfield, Christopher C. Stone, Augustus Stone, Abraham Stout, Aaron Scudder in care of Joseph Scudder, Thomas Stacy in Columbia, George Stoddard, Hezekiah Shaw, Zedoc Stewart, David Foot, Teagle Taylor, Smith Thompson, John Vaughan, William Vanwinkle, Dominieus VanDyke in Colerain, Thomas White or Jonathan Scott, Demas Woodruff in Springfield, Isaac Whitaker, Michael Wilkins on Great Miami, Matthias Woodruff, John Whitcomb on Duck Creek, John Wilson, William Wentzell, Jacob Warwick, Duvern Whitlecey.

Arthur Stewart, living near Stauton on the Big Miami, reports a stray mare.

Cornelius R. Sedam has horses for sale at his farm.

Ezekiel Hutchinson regarding his new public house lately occupied by Isaac Anderson. He also has imported liquors for sale.

Green Clay, in Madison County, Kentucky, regarding a runaway slave, Joe.

No. 38, Volume VIII, Monday, 13 April 1807, Whole No. 402

Results of an election held for officers of the corporation of Cincinnati and the township mention Martin Baum, Thomas Dugan, Griffin Yeatman, Hugh Moore, George Gordon, James Ewing, Jesse Hunt, Thomas Ramsay, Jacob Fowble, Jacob Hardin, George Williamson, Joseph Carpenter, James Ferguson, William Ramsay, Hugh Bracken, Thomas M'Farland, Culberson Parks, Ezekiel Miexer, John Riddle, Peter Kamper, Corn. Johnson, Robert Kempton, Robert Orr, Joseph VanHorn, Andrew Brannon, James Chambers, Jacob Stewart, Jedediah Ayers, Robert Terry.

Results of an election of township officers for Anderson township mention James Clark, William Webb, Nathaniel Abbet, Josiah Crossey, Jacob Frazee, John Corbley, Josiah Crosley, Philip Critchfield, James Dunseth, Nathan Hatfield, John Bocover, Josiah Gwatney, John Whetstone, George Vail, Jacob Broadwell.

John O'Ferrall will "leave here the 25th" of April and asks those indebted to settle their accounts. He mentions the debt owed by Peter Felix.

Henry Ewing reports a runaway apprentice to the tayloring business named John Murphey, age about 14 or 15.

No. 39, Volume VIII, Monday, 20 April 1807, Whole No. 403

Daniel C. Cooper, in Dayton, has lots for sale in Dayton.

A note regarding the trial of Alexander Prodis for the theft of 100 yards of woolen cloth from Ezekiel Hutchinson of Cincinnati.

John Riddle, Joseph Vanhorn, Luke Foster, Stephen Wood, Wm. Stratten and Daniel Symmes regarding the Cincinnati University lottery.

Burrows Smith, in Cincinnati, has land for sale. Apply to Stephen Smith in Williamsburgh. He also carries on the Windsor chair making business.

John Miller, of Ohio County on Rough Creek, says his daughter, age 6, disappeared on 23 February 1807. Any person returning her will be rewarded even "if it should take every thing I possess".

No. 40, Volume VIII, Monday, 27 April 1807, Whole No. 404

A note regarding the trial of Charles Vattier for stealing from Gen. James Findlay. He was found guilty.

A note regarding the trial of Lucy Lightner, alias Ruth Ann Liganier.

Obituary: James Smith, of Newport, Kentucky, died on Thursday, 23 April 1807, and left a wife and a young family.

An article regarding Charles Vattier says he's a native of France, but has lived in Cincinnati "for many years". He was found guilty of robbing Gen. James Findlay. The testimony of Charles Britton, mulatto, is discussed.

Almanacs for 1808 by Robert Stubbs are for sale at Campbell County, Kentucky.

Baum & Perry, in Cincinnati, have received a new shipment of goods.

Wm. Stanley says the store of Ormsby & Stanley, in Cincinnati, has received a new shipment of goods. Those indebted to the late Daniel Conner & Company and to Oliver Ormsby should settle their accounts.

No. 41, Volume VIII, Monday, 4 May 1807, Whole No. 405

A note regarding a meeting of the Masons at Brother Menissier's house.

An article regarding Charles Vattier's theft of Gen. James Findlay. It says Vattier was a private soldier in the Western army and came to Cincinnati right after his discharge. Some of the proceedings of his trial are printed and mention James Ewing, John Heighway, Mr. Wheeler, John Adams.

Sutherland & Brown, in Dayton and Hamilton, have dissolved their partner-ship and ask those indebted to them to settle their accounts.

Nathaniel Reeder, in Cincinnati, asks those indebted to his store on Main Street to settle their accounts.

Jacob Fowble, in Cincinnati, has land for sale, including his grist and saw mills. Apply to Frederick Haifleigh or John Sholly at the mills.

John Becket, living next door to James Cunningham on Mill Creek about 12 miles from Cincinnati, has land for sale. Apply to Jeremiah Morrow, William Stanley in Cincinnati, or Thomas Espy between the Miami Rivers.

Ezekiel Hall, in Cincinnati, regarding his boot and shoe manufactory in his shop next door to John Nimmo's brick house on the hill in Main Street.

No. 42, Volume VIII, Monday, 11 May 1807, Whole No. 406

A note regarding Judge Toulmin's sentence of Mr. Blannerhasset, an Irish gentleman, to take his trial in Virginia, where he formerly resided. It says that his wife and children are in Natchez. Mr. Floyd and Mr. Rolston wish to be tried in Kentucky and Indiana, where they live.

A note about the boats of Mr. Lard and Mr. Gilman, both built at Marietta. Also Mr. Clarke and Mr. Jones' boats were wrecked at the falls. Col. Lard's ship was stranded on Sandy Island. It mentions Mr. Gallagher's ship.

Nathaniel Reeder, in Cincinnati, has land for sale near Redding.

John Wall has moved his saddlery manufactory to his new house opposite Mr. Reeder's store on Main Street in Cincinnati.

Richard W. Ray, in Liberty township of Butler County, reports a stray horse.

Baum & Perry, in Cincinnati, have received a new shipment of goods.

No. 43, Volume VIII, Monday, 18 May 1807, Whole No. 407

An article regarding ship wrecks at the Falls of Ohio mentions Col. Lord.

A list of appointments made includes William Hull (governor of Michigan), William Henry Harrison (governor of Indiana), John Coburn of Kentucky as a judge in Michigan Territory, Frederick Bates of Michigan Territory to be secretary for Louisiana Territory.

Thomas Kirker, acting governor of Ohio, says that Col. Thomas Worthington is appointed Adjutant General of the Ohio Militia in place of Maj. David Zeigler. He also gives general orders to the militia.

The Cincinnati Light Infantry will meet in front of the Old Garrison.

Marriage: Abraham Chase, Jun., to Miss Harriet Wheeler, of Cincinnati, on Thursday evening, 14 May 1807, by Rev. William Lynes.

Marriage: Jesse Reeder, carriage maker, to Miss Mary Kennedy, on Thursday, 14 May 1807, by James Ewing.

Obituary: Daniel Conrod, of Cincinnati, died on Thursday evening, 14 May 1807, and was buried on Friday.

A note regarding the whipping due to Charles Vattier for robbing Gen. Findlay mentions Mr. Kirker, acting governor.

A note regarding Col. Burr mentions Blannerhasset's island near Marietta.

An article about the fire in Detroit in June of 1805 mentions the Delaware Indians, Maj. Campbell, Fort Malden, Samuel Andrew Shultz.

The proceedings of the trial of Charles Vattier are to be printed along with particulars of his life.

Thomas Rawlins says the office of the Hamilton County Commissioners is now kept at James Ewing's house.

William M'Clelland, Sheriff of Butler County, regarding sheriff's sales of the property of George Harlan at the suit of Joshua Delaplane; that of Henry Toxell at the suit of Hugh Moore; that of Samuel M'Cullough and William Patton at the suit of Charlotte C. Ludlow and others; that of Wm. Symmes at the suit of J. Burnet, J. Smith and others; that of Daniel Griffin at the suit of Isaac Reed.

Thomas Barker, near North Bend, regarding a strayed or stolen horse.

John S. Gano regarding notes given to John Lyon of Springfield township.

Jacob Fisher, in Clermont, about the report that he is indebted to Mordecai S. Ford. He says he's not in his debt.

Thomas Best, Jun., in Cincinnati, reports a stray mare.

Jacob Philipson regarding the note for the barrel of coffee he sold to Samuel Simonton, merchant, in Springfield, that was endorsed by Henry Weaver.

No. 44, Volume VIII, Monday, 25 May 1807, Whole No. 408

A note regarding tickets for the Cincinnati University lottery.

Those indebted for the Western Spy may make payments to Mr. House.

An article regarding the punishment of Charles Vattier and his pardon by Thomas Kirker, acting governor. Mentions Gen. Findlay, Mrs. Vattier. Also a story, in biblical style, of the robbery and trial mentions Pamela Vattier.

John Reily regarding a suit in Butler County Court of Common Pleas: Thomas M'Cullough vs. James Hamilton, an absconding debtor.

John Mahard, in Cincinnati, asks those persons indebted to Doctor Goforth to settle their accounts.

W.C. Schenck, in Franklin, has land for sale in Butler County near Enoch's mill. Apply to his brother at the Post Office in Franklin.

Brig. Gen. W.C. Schenck, in Franklin, gives brigade orders and mentions Calvin Ball and Col. Mills.

Peyton Short regarding town lots in Cincinnati sold by John Cleves Symmes. Hugh Moore will receive payments. Also Judge Silvers, Benjamin Vancleve, of Dayton, and Jonathan Donnel will act as his agents to sell land.

Samuel James, in Lebanon, has a farm for sale adjoining Lebanon, formerly occupied by John Shaw on Turtle Creek. Apply to Thomas Dugan in Cincinnati.

No. 45, Volume VIII, Monday, 1 June 1807, Whole No. 409

Obituary: Capt. Robert Kenney died on Saturday, 30 May 1807, at Newport, Kentucky. He was buried on Sunday in Cincinnati attended by the brethren of the Cincinnati Lodge.

More regarding the trial and punishment of Charles Vattier.
A note regarding Col. Lord's boat at the falls of Ohio.
Simon M. Stockdell has opened a tavern in Cincinnati.
John O'Ferrall has a new shipment of goods for sale at his store.
Lieut. Aquila Wheeler, in Cincinnati, regarding a meeting of the Artillery.
James Ferguson has a house and lot for sale in Cincinnati.
William Stake, in Cincinnati, reports a runaway apprentice to the taylor's trade, John Sherman, nearly 17 years old.

No. 46, Volume VIII, Monday, 8 June 1807, Whole No. 410

Joseph Vanhorn regarding a meeting of the commissioners of the lottery at William Stratton's house in Cincinnati.

A note about an Indian attack on Obanion above Stanton. Mentions Mr. Price and Mr. M'Intire (a half-blood who was educated at Pittsburgh).

Thomas Rawlins regarding a meeting of the Hamilton County commissioners.

Samuel Best, in Cincinnati, wants to hire an apprentice to the clock and watchmaking and silversmith's business.

David Zeiglar, in Cincinnati, submits a humorous ad regarding money owed him and his militia school. He also has goods for sale at his store.

Edward H. Stall, druggist and apothecary, in Cincinnati, has just returned from Baltimore with a new supply of medicine for sale.

John Bercount reports that a stray mare was found in Cincinnati at the shop of Jacob Williams.

Capt. James Ferguson regarding a meeting of the Troop of Dragoons.

Thomas Best says he and Isaac VanNuys have dissolved their partnership in the clock and watchmaker's, silversmith and jewelers' business. Thomas Best will carry on the business in the same shop in Sycamore Street, Cincinnati.

William Patton, administrator of the estate of John M'Nabb, late of Rossville, deceased, regarding the estate settlement.

Joseph VanHorne about a Cincinnati University shareholder's meeting.

Mr. Mennessier wants to hire well diggers to dig a well between Stephen M'Farland's and Mr. Dunseth's in Cincinnati.

Jerom Holt, in Dayton, lost a pocket book between Joshua Williams' tavern and the first ford of Mill Creek. It includes a note from H.G. Philips.

No. 47, Volume VIII, Monday, 15 June 1807, Whole No. 411

David L. Carney regarding a meeting of the Cincinnati Lodge.

C. Killgore regarding a meeting of the Cincinnati Light Infantry Company.

William Stanley says that Ormsby & Stanley have received a new shipment of goods at their store in Cincinnati. They also have land for sale.

A note regarding Mr. Vattier mentions Gen. Findlay.

Capt. R. Bissell, at Newport, Kentucky, reports deserters: Corp. James Clarke (age 28, born in Massachusetts, laborer), Samuel Luke (age 20, born in York County, Penn., laborer), Samuel Cope (age 26, born in Virginia, laborer), John Dougherty (age 28, born in County Donegal, Ireland, laborer), Edward Smith (age 28, born in Penn., laborer, has a wife and two children at the Falls of Ohio), Levi Pearce (29-30 years old, born in Connecticut, laborer).

John S. Gano regarding a suit in Hamilton County Court of Common Pleas: Samuel Foster vs. Seth Cutter. Mentions the "widow of the said Seth", Joseph Carpenter, and the administrators of Seth Cutter.

Jos. VanHorne regarding a meeting of the Presbyterian Society in Cincinnati.

No. 48, Volume VIII, Monday, 22 June 1807, Whole No. 412

Rev. Hiram Miram Curry will preach a sermon after the Masonic oration.

An extract of the trial of Charles Vattier mentions Charles Britton, Tom Matthews, Mr. Findlay.

John Armstrong & Company have a new shipment of goods at their store.

Caldwell & Jenkinson have a new shipment of goods at their store in Franklin.

Jacob Grow, living in Montgomery County near the head of Wolf's Creek and 14 miles from the mouth, reports two stray mares.

No. 2, Volume IX, Monday, 3 August 1807, Whole No. 418
An account of the Fourth of July celebration by the apprentices of Cincinnati mentions Mrs. Mercer's Inn.

A note from the jurors of Charles Vattier's trial is signed by Samuel Best, Peter M'Nicoll, Tho. Frazee, Wm. Betts, Tho. Ramsey, Hugh Brackin, Joshua Williams, John Seamer, E.Y. Kamper, Wm. T. Cullom, Benjamin Mason and Jonah Vandevert. They mention Thomas Kirker, Francis Dunlavy, Gen. Findlay, and Mr. Britton.

John S. Gano regarding the suit in the Hamilton County Chancery Court of Abraham Freeman vs. Ralph W. Hunt and Ralph Phillips.

John Brasher, at Crosby, wants to hire apprentices to the hatting business.

William Goforth will serve as governor if elected.

An unsigned letter to the editor mentions the Light Infantry Company, Mr. Waps, Gen. Benningsen.

John Martin, in Clarke County, Kentucky, reports a runaway slave, Trent.

Aaron Scudder, in Rossville, regarding his brick making business there.

William Moss, at Mr. Wade's farm 1 mile from Cincinnati, about stray mares.

Hugh Moore, in Cincinnati, has four houses for rent.

Joseph VanHorn has land for sale near Cincinnati.

C. Vattier, in Cincinnati, regarding land for sale by Nicholas Longworth.

Hugh Moore, for the trustees of Cincinnati University, about the accounts.

John S. Gano has land for sale adjoining Thomas Williams' farm near Parson Kamper's place. Also a lot on Main Street adjoining Jesse Reeder's.

Ensign J.W. Albright, at Newport, about deserters: John Christian Gall (age 22, born in Saxony, Germany, carpenter and glazier), Joseph O'Neal (age 37 or 38, born in Ireland, a papermaker), and James Adams (age 21, born in Delaware, a shoemaker).

Peter Love regarding his rope and sein manufactory in Cincinnati.

James Russell, in Cincinnati reports a mare found dead near the Seminary.

Henry Disbrow, at the sign of the Indian King in Cincinnati, has moved his tavern to the large white house at the corner of Market and Main Streets.

James Sloan, in Cincinnati, has dry goods and groceries for sale at his new store opposite Capt. Ferguson's on Main Street.

Elias Shoemaker, living on Four Mile Creek above Hamilton, reports a stray mare. Deliver to Thomas Ramsey in Cincinnati.

Jacob Fowble, in Cincinnati, has land for sale in that town.

No. 3, Volume IX, Monday, 10 August 1807, Whole No. 419
The text of Thomas Henderson's speech on the Fourth of July is printed.

C. Killgore regarding a meeting of the Cincinnati Light Infantry Company.

A note about the parade of the companies of Capts. Stanley and Carpenter.

A note regarding a meeting of the citizens of Cincinnati mentions Luke Foster, Aaron Goforth, Hon. James Silvers, Jacob Burnet, Joseph Vanhorn.

Tho. Kirker, T. Worthington and Gen. James Findlay give orders to the militia.

A note regarding a meeting of the citizens of Chillicothe mentions Forrest Meeker's tavern, Edward Tiffin, William Creighton, jun., Samuel Finley, Henry Brush and Charles A. Stewart.

Thomas Henderson regarding the opening of his school in Cincinnati.

William Corrothers & Richard Fanchard say Thomas Langley found a mare.

John Lakin, William Fee and Silas Sargent say that Aaron Wells found a mare.

O.M. Spencer, in Cincinnati, regarding a Miami Exporting Company meeting.

Andrew Sinks, living 12 miles above Dayton on the southwest branch of the Great Miami, reports a stray mare.

Jacob Kautz, living in Cincinnati, reports a stray mare.

James W. Sloan, in Cincinnati, reports two runaway slaves, Perry Johnson and Henny, his wife.

Ensign J.W. Albright, at Newport, about deserters: Patrick Branagan (age 24, born in Ireland, a taylor) and James Campbell (age 25, born in Frederic Co., Va.).

David Hayes, at Newmarket, has lots for sale in the town of Hillsborough.

Hugh Brackin says someone threw a stone at his wife on Tuesday, 28 July 1807, injuring her.

Richard Oliver, in Cincinnati, reports a horse that strayed from the pasture of Samuel James in Lebanon.

No. 4, Volume IX, Monday, 17 August 1807, Whole No. 420

Thomas Henderson is appointed surveyor for Hamilton County.

Joseph VanHorne, John W. Browne, John Matson and Thomas Henderson submit an address from the Republican Corresponding Society of Cincinnati and mention Jonathan Robbins and Return Jonathan Meigs, jun.

Francis Dunlavy writes a letter to the public in answer to the letter about him. He mentions Charles Vattier, Mr. Brittain, Gen. Findlay.

A note regarding the meeting of the Cincinnati Light Infantry Company.

C. Killgore regarding another meeting of the Cincinnati Light Infantry.

Susan Symmes will sign deeds conveying the property of John Cleves Symmes at the house of Mr. Joseph Delaplaine, near the Academy.

Jacob Sagersa, living at David's Fork of Elkhorn, Kentucky, about a runaway slave named Nick. He's in company with a white woman and mulatto child.

James Campbell, living near Cunningham's mill on Mill Creek, reports a stray mare and colt.

Joseph VanHorne regarding tickets for the Cincinnati University lottery. He mentions the Miami Exporting Company.

George Williamson has moved his book binding business to the house on Main Street next door to Ezekiel Hall, shoemaker.

O.M. Spencer regarding payments due to the Miami Exporting Company.

Jesse Herrin, living within five miles of Cincinnati, found a colt.

John Mahard says that Isaac Anderson found a mare.

No. 5, Volume IX, Monday, 24 August 1807, Whole No. 421

An unsigned letter to the editor regarding Gen. Mansfield.

Burrowes Smith, in Cincinnati, wants to hire an apprentice to the Windsor chair making business.

James Ferguson has sold all his stock and "being determined to close all his business" asks those indebted to him to settle their accounts.

Joseph Delaplaine, living near the Academy in Cincinnati, says he's "intending to leave this country" and offers his property in Cincinnati for sale. He also has a lot in Lawrenceburgh near Capt. S. Vance's house. He will also have a sale of all his household and kitchen furniture.

No. 6, Volume IX, Monday, 31 August 1807, Whole No. 422

An account of a meeting of the citizens of Montgomery and Miami Counties at Dayton mentions Col. William Dodds, Daniel C. Cooper.

An account of a meeting of the citizens of Clermont County mentions Ambrose Ransone, David C. Bryan, R.W. Waring, Jacob Huber, Levi Rogers, Robert Towsley, Thomas Morris, Samuel W. Davis, Richard Taliaferro, William Fee, Alexander Martin and Daniel Kain.

An account of a meeting of the Republican Corresponding Society of Hamilton County mentions Jonathan Pitman, Return J. Meigs, Jun., Stephen Wood, Hezekiah Price, Othniel Looker, Zebulon Foster, John C. Symmes, John Riddle, James Ewing and Cornelius Snider.

James Ferguson regarding a meeting of the Light Dragoons.

David Zeiglar, in Cincinnati, again asks those indebted to him to settle their accounts. He also wants to form a military school.

Aquila Wheeler, for William M'Farland, late sheriff, regarding a sheriff's sale of the property of Alexander Rowen at the suit of John Huston.

John S. Gano regarding Sarah Miller's suit of divorce from her husband, John Miller, in the Supreme Court of Hamilton County.

William Shettrick, living four miles above the mouth of the Little Miami, reports a stray mare.

No. 7, Volume IX, Monday, 7 September 1807, Whole No. 423

An account of the drowning death of James M'Clure on Wednesday, 26 August 1807, in the Great Miami within twenty feet of the shore.

An unsigned letter to the Republican Corresponding Society of Cincinnati mentions Return Jonathan Meigs, jun.

Harrison & Striker, taylor and ladies' habit maker, have opened their shop in Cincinnati next to the Indian King Tavern. They were formerly of Philadelphia.

A pocket book was lost containing notes to Hans Lacky and Andrew Lacky. Deliver to Wm. Ruffin, post master.

No. 8, Volume IX, Monday, 14 September 1807, Whole No. 424

Robert M'Clellan, at York, reports a runaway apprentice to the printing business, Thomas A. Wilson, and a negro boy called Isaac Williams, age 18. Wilson is 17-18 years old and went off with a man called Mr. Kelly, a farrier.

Hugh Moore, in Cincinnati, has a house for sale in Hamilton.

Hugh Moore, clerk to the trustees of Cincinnati University, about the lottery.

C. Killgore gives notice to the Cincinnati Light Infantry of a meeting.

Marriage: Dr. James W. Lanier to Miss Helana Barcalow, of Butler County, on Thursday, 20 August 1807.

J. Fowble regarding a meeting of the Republican Corresponding Society of Cincinnati at the house of James Conn.

Dixon Greer says his partnership with John Greer is dissolved. The business will be carried on as Greer & Baymiller, by Dixon Greer and Jacob Baymiller.

Stephen M'Farland, in Cincinnati, wants an apprentice to the hatting trade.

Samuel M'Cormack, at the mouth of the Kentucky River, reports a runaway slave named Daniel. Deliver to Jesse Hunt in Cincinnati.

No. 9, Volume IX, Monday, 21 September 1807, Whole No. 425

A deposition of Col. Timothy Kibby, formerly of the Cincinnati area, about Gen. James Wilkinson mentions Col. Burr, Lieut. Pike. Otho Shroder, judge of the Territory of Louisiana, witnesses the deposition.

The Almanac for 1808, by Rev. Robert Stubbs, is for sale at the Spy office.

Jonathan Rollins, at Staunton, administrator of the estate of John Campbell, late of Elizabeth township, Miami County, regarding the estate settlement.

A note regarding the publication of the trial of Charles Vattier.

A letter about the election mentions Mr. Pittman, John C. Symmes, Joseph Prince, Republican Society, Judge Symmes, Col. Jones, Nathaniel Massie, Ethan Store, John S. Wallace, John Jones, Othniel Looker, Joseph Kitchel.

Thomas Kirker & Samuel Finley give orders to the Ohio militia and mention Gen. Whiteman, Gen. Darlinton, Gen. M'Lene.

Martin Baum and John Mahard about an ordinance regulating the butter market.

John H. Piatt has a new shipment of goods for sale at his store in Cincinnati.

Benjamin & John H. Piatt have dissolved their partnership. Those indebted to them should pay Benjamin Piatt in Lawrenceburgh or John H. Piatt in Cincinnati.

Isaac Dunn has a new shipment of dry goods at his store in Lawrenceburgh.

John Armstrong, at Columbia, has arrested a black man named Sam who says he's the property of Michael Cable of Kentucky, near Bairdstown.

No. 10, Volume IX, Monday, 28 September 1807, Whole No. 426

Josiah Crosley, of Anderson township, is candidate for county commissioner.

A note regarding publication of the trial of Charles Vattier.

Capt. A. Wheeler regarding a meeting of the Artillery Company.

Capt. James Ferguson about a meeting of the Dragoons at Widow M'Henry's.

John Armstrong, justice of the peace, Columbia township, says William Perry, of Columbia, found a horse appraised by John T. Chunn and Silvester Ralston.

Joseph Carpenter, Thomas Dugan and William Ruffin regarding the suit of Samuel Foster vs. Seth Cutter.

John Buchanon, living in Washington township, Clermont County, regarding a stolen mare.

Samuel Bray and James Brown, in Jefferson County, Kentucky, reports two runaway slaves, Fountain and Bill.

Walker Baylor, of Bourbon County, Kentucky, about a runaway slave, Walker.

No. 11, Volume IX, Monday, 5 October 1807, Whole No. 427

A note regarding the Cincinnati Horse Races is printed.

Letters to the editor about the election mentions John C. Symmes, John Jones, Mr. Massie, Col. Meigs, Judge Symmes, Mr. Stone, Mr. Wood, Mr. Wallace, Mr. Price, Nathaniel Massie, Ethan Stone, John Wallace, Mr. Pittman, Mr. Kitchell.

John Armstrong, of Columbia, regarding a stray cow.

John S. Gano, Clerk of the Hamilton County Court of Common Pleas, about Evi Martin petition regarding his debt.

John T. Chunn, Silvester Rowlson and John Armstrong report that John Seaman, of Columbia, has found some stray sheep.

William Ludlow, at Mill Creek, has apple trees for sale.

John Stiver, living on Little Twin Creek in German township, Montgomery County, reports a strayed or stolen horse.

Obituary: Charles Killgore, Register of the Land Office for the District of Cincinnati and Captain of the Cincinnati Light Infantry, died on Friday morning, October 2, 1807. He was buried on Saturday.

A note from Othniel Looker and James Ewing regarding land purchased for a road includes a deposition from Jesse Jones. Mentions John Jacob (living at the mouth of Taylor's Creek in Colerain township), Big John Cherrey, Joseph Kitchell of White water township.

David Reid and James Steel, of Dayton, regarding Indian hostilities mention Hugh M'Cullom.

A note regarding nominations for public office mentions John Hart of Miami township, Jonathan Pittman, Garah Markland, John C. Symmes, Col. John Jones.

A list of letters left at the Post Office in Cincinnati includes Skilman Alger, Ebenezer Ayers in care of Col. Armstrong, Thomas Auter at Mill Creek, Benjamin Abbot, John Beal, Joseph Bolton or Jeremiah Butterfield at Colerain, Thomas Bishop, John Becket on Mill Creek, Thomas Black, Joseph Byrns, Polly Brown, Samuel Bachelor in care of Mr. Bills, Zebulon Brown at Colerain, Catharine Bennet, Joshua B. Brewer, Charles Cannon, James Caskey, John Clark in care of Isaac Anderson, Jonathan Carmack in Kentucky, James Colnwell, John Carpenter, Enoch Carson, Elias Cownovor in Warren County, Azariah Casto, Frederick Coons, Col. Matthew Culley in Springfield, Nemiah Charles, James Colwell, Andrew Conrod in care of J. & B. Piatt, Lewis J. Curtiss, Mary Carr, Eli Corson, John Councellor, Reuben Douty, David Ford, Lot French, Luke Foster, Jane Hare, John Harrison, Romenous Hanick at Sycamore, Maj. Joseph Harris, Andrew Forepaugh, James Fletcher (shipwright), Jacob Groh, George Ginnans, Elijah Garrison, Jacob Gay, Samuel Griffin, Rhoda Galena, Phillip Gatch, Hiram Hanchet, Daniel Isgrig, Daniel Hosbrook, Adam Hurdus, James Jones on Colerain road, Thomas Johns in care of Isaac Anderson, Daniel Jessup, George Igeming (22 miles from Cincinnati), Mrs. Judeth Kamper, William Kirkwood, James Logan, Thomas Ketchen or Dennes Clark, Gerhana Lee or John Haden at Columbia, William Logan in care of John Whetstone, Isaac Lemasters at Great Miami, Maxfield Ludlow, Samuel Lyon, Ami Musard in care of Mr. Mennesier, Thomas Moseley, Daniel Mitchel, Thomas Mason, Joseph Murphy, Nathaniel M'Intire, William M'Dermett, Jonathan Myers on Mill Creek, John Miller, Eli Miller, Peter Moudy, Alexander Mackey, James Mordock, Robert Martin in care of Newton Spinning, Alexander M'Nutt, Charles Nichelson, Joel Nelson in Colerain, Hugh Nisbett (saddler), Simon Nicholson in care of Mr. Ramsay, Charlotte Porter, Col. Thomas Paxton in Clermont County, George Peck in Indiana Territory, Thomas Phillips, James Parcel, William Pringle in care of Thomas M'Farland, William Patterson, Mr. Pigman, Jun., John Peak on Little Miami, Wyllis Pierson, Solomon Pelly, Zachariah Parash, John Mellheny and Joseph Perrin, Lewis F. Randolph, Nathaniel Reeve, Capt. Ramsay, Alexander Rowan, Jacob Roman, Abraham C. Roll, Matthias Ross, Adam Rittenhouse, S.H. Smith, Zadock Stewart, Constantine Smith, Erreminah Swallow at Springfield, Thomas Skinner at Columbia, Gurdeon F. Saltonstall (rope-maker), Edward Smith, Jacob Smith, John Single and Jacob C. Cook, James Starkey, Mrs. Ann Smith, Henry Scudder, Aaron Scogan, Mary Skillman, Jean Street in care of Peter Love, Joseph Stephenson at Columbia, Thomas Sherwood at Columbia, Ezra Spencer, George Storck, Peter T. Schenck, John Sheerman in care of Wm. Stake, Michael Shautz, Christopher C. Stone, Ephraim Tucker in Springfield, Henry Tucker, James Turner, David Vangilder in Colerain, Garret Vansont, Stephen Woodruff near Columbia, Maj. Isreal Willey in Colerain, Thomas Wade, Lewis Ward at Little Miami, Demas Woodruff, Benjamin Wilson, Jr., Jonathan Warring in Columbia, Francis Wilds, Elijah Whipple, Widow Lois Willis at Sycamore, Benjamin Wallace in care of John Misner, Ludwick Willer in Sycamore, William Ruffin (postmaster).

James Young, Daniel Mitchell and John F. Robinson, in Shelby County, Ky., regarding runaway slaves named Dick, Jude, Moses, Will and Charles.

Spy Extra, Saturday, 8 October 1807
Unsigned letters regarding the election mention Judge Huntington, Philemon Beecher, Lawyer Stone, Levi M'Clean, Mrs. Willis' Hotel, William Ludlow, Arthur St.Clair, Mr. Burnet, Thomas Henderson, the Liberty Hall, Mr. Stone, Samuel M'Henry, Ezekiel Hughes, Joseph Kitchell, Mr. Patterson.

No. 12, Volume IX, Monday, 12 October 1807, Whole No. 428
A note regarding the publication of the trial of Charles Vattier. Apply to George Williamson, book binder, in Cincinnati, for copies.
A gentleman in Clark County, Indiana Territory, writes about Davis Floyd.
A note regarding the Newport Horse Races is printed.
A letter regarding the siting of a comet mentions Cincinnati University.
Thomas Henderson's funeral address for Charles Killgore is printed. He mentions Killgore's aging mother.

No. 14, Volume IX, Monday, 26 October 1807, Whole No. 430
Hugh Moore and Hugh M'Clelland, in Cincinnati, have dissolved their partnership, and ask those indebted to them to settle their accounts.
Jesse Reeder and Mr. Marcell have dissolved their partnership. Jesse Reeder will continue the business of chair and wagon making.
George Robinson and Washington Allen, in Shelby County, Kentucky, report runaway slaves named Timothy and Flora.
James Gallaway, in Cincinnati, reports a strayed mare.
John Sample, living on Big Miami in Butler County near Middletown, lost a pocket book between Middletown and House's Tavern. It contained notes from Tobias Barcalow, David Williams, John M'Cashin, Samuel French, Michael Tullas, James Noble, Abraham Vansickle, John Torrence of Hamilton.
James M'Ginnis, in Cincinnati, reports a runaway cow.
Henry Weaver has a new shipment of goods for sale at his store in Cincinnati.
William Steel, Robert Ogle and Alexander Ogle report that Henry Taylor, of Milford township, Butler County, found a horse.
David M'Cord and Samuel Hagan say that Abraham Barnett, living four miles from Dayton on the Miami River, found a stray colt.
Anderson Spensor, Abner Wilson and Joseph Hunter say that David Beaty, in Fairfield township, found a strayed horse.
A notice regarding a mare that strayed or was stolen out of the pasture of Zachariah Holland, living on Mill Creek one mile from Cincinnati.
Zachariah Archer, Stephen M'Farland and Arthur St.Clair, Jun., administra-tors of the estate of Charles Killgore, dec'd, regarding the estate settlement.
James Findlay and Wm. Ruffin have horses for sale.
John O'Ferrall has a new shipment of goods for sale at his store in Cincinnati.
Baum & Perry have a new shipment of goods for sale at their store.
Uriah Gates informs "the public for the 8th time, that my wife, Rebecca, has robbed me of my money, meal, flour, meat etc. and taken up her residence at the house of a man, by the name of Winters." He will not honor her debts.
John Musgrove reports that he found a horse.
T. Worthington and Duncan M'Arthur's letter to Gov. Kirker is concluded and mentions Mr. Wells. Includes a letter from Stephen Ruddell about the Indians.

No. 15, Volume IX, Monday, 2 November 1807, Whole No. 431
Election results mention Mr. Massie and Mr. Meigs.
James Ferguson wants to buy 3000 bushels of wheat delivered to Armstrong's and Fowble's mills.
Joel Williams has moved to Cincinnati and keeps the ferry on Main Street.
Jacob Wheeler has dry goods and groceries for sale at his new store near Hunt's tanyard. He also wants an apprentice to the tanning & currying trade.

No. 16, Volume IX, Monday, 9 November 1807, Whole No. 432
A letter to the editor from Lieut. Z.M. Pike regarding Philip Nolan, dec'd.
(part of this issue is missing)

No. 17, Volume IX, Monday, 16 November 1807, Whole No. 433

Day Wood has a new shipment of goods for sale at his store in Cincinnati.

James Smith, justice of the peace in St. Clair township, says that William Mitchell, of St. Clair township, found a stray mare. It was appraised by Darius C. Orcott and Benjamin Randel.

William Robb, John White & John Hunter say that Samuel B. Kyle found a mare.

Maxfield Ludlow, on Mill Creek, reports two strayed milk cows.

Elmore Williams' house burnt down on Friday morning, 13 November. Mr. King, a mechanic, had just rented it and lost all his tools.

James Richey & Company, in Cincinnati, have a new shipment of goods for sale at their store opposite Capt. Stanley's store.

John Armstrong, justice of the peace, reports that Jonah Vandevert, of Columbia, found a stray cow. It was appraised by John Craige & James Mathews.

James Kemper, "intending to leave the western world", has a farm for sale.

Baum & Perry have writing paper for sale at their store.

James Chambers, collector for Cincinnati township, regarding taxes due.

Jacob Williams asks all those indebted to him to settle their accounts by delivering wheat to Hugh Moore's mill.

Brown Wilson, living near Fort Hamilton, reports a stolen horse.

Samuel Harding, James Johnson and Maxwell Parkinson report that Emanuel Vantreese, of Ross township in Butler County, found a mare.

J.W. Sloan wants to buy good corn fed pork. He also has salt for sale.

William Moss reports two strayed or stolen mares.

John Whetston asks those indebted to him to settle their accounts as "he is going to move away".

No. 19, Volume IX, Monday, 30 November 1807, Whole No. 435

John O'Ferrall, in Cincinnati, has lead and shot for sale.

William Pack, in Cincinnati, regarding a bond he gave to Robert Caldwell.

Marriage: Alexander A. Meeks to Miss Patty M'Cullough, both of Cincinnati, on Friday evening, 27 November 1807, by James Ewing.

Obituary: Elias Stratton died on Wednesday evening, 25 November 1807.

Obituary: Rev. Davis died of dropsey on Tuesday, 24 November 1807, and was buried the same day in the Presbyterian church yard.

Moses Musgrove, in Clermont County, attorney in fact for the heirs of John Hamilton, dec'd, gives notice to George Clark regarding land in dispute. He lists the heirs of John Hamilton: Thomas Hamilton, Sarah Leggett, Nancy Musgrove, Elizabeth Jones, Catharine Simmermon and George Hamilton.

E. Hutchinson, in Cincinnati, has land for sale twelve miles from Cincinnati.

S. & J. Halley have land for sale including Clough mill and a distillery. Apply at their Miami Mill or at their store in Cincinnati.

John Mahard, Isaac Anderson and William Dennison say that Benjamin Little, in Cincinnati, found a stray horse.

Thomas Wilson, Nathaniel Stewart and Mary Wilson, executors of the estate of Francis Wilson, dec'd, late of Cincinnati, regarding the estate sale.

No. 20, Volume IX, Monday, 7 December 1807, Whole No. 436

The editor of the Western Spy asks those indebted to him to pay their bills.

Marriage: Daniel Searles to Jean M'Farland, daughter of Thomas M'Farland, all of Cincinnati, on Wednesday, 2 December 1807, by Rev. James Kamper.

Obituary: Miss Ann Lewis Howell, age 17, died Tuesday, 1 December 1807.

David L. Carney regarding a meeting of the Cincinnati Lodge.

Miss Abby Harris has commenced the mantua making business at the house of John Mahard in Cincinnati.

David Lowry & Benjamin Simonton, administrators of the estate of Elizabeth Lowry, late of Champaign County, dec'd, regarding the estate settlement.

James M'Cashen lost a watch between South bend and Mr. Hart's tavern at North Bend. Deliver to Mr. Hutchinson in Cincinnati.

Isaac Stanley, William Riddle and David Smith report that Wm. Catterline found a stray mare.

John Reily, at Hamilton, agent for J. Dayton in Cincinnati, has land for sale. He mentions Hutchinson's Fulling and Grist mills.

No. 23, Volume IX, Monday, 28 December 1807, Whole No. 439

John O'Ferrall offers for sale the Rock Farm in the forks of Mad River. He says he wants to sell out in a few months and has goods for sale.

William Stanley, for Ormsby & Stanley, has a new shipment of goods for sale at their store. They also have land for sale and mention Maj. William Peters, John Carmichael, Coxe's old place and D. Conner & Company.

Marriage: Nicholas Longworth married Mrs. Susan Conner on Thursday evening, 24 December 1807, by Rev. Matthew G. Wallace.

Marriage: John Armstrong, merchant, married Miss Susan Willis, both of Cincinnati, on Thursday evening, 24 December 1807.

Marriage: Daniel Roe, merchant, of Lebanon, married Miss Patty Longly, of Kentucky, on Thursday evening, 24 December 1807.

An unsigned letter to the editor mentions Col. Meigs, Gen. Massie, Thomas Kirker, Judge Symmes, Gov. Kirker, Gov. Hull of Michigan Territory, John Smith.

A list of the state senators includes Stephen Wood and Hezekiah Price of Hamilton County; David C. Brian for Clermont; Richard S. Thomas and John Bigger for Warren, Butler, Montgomery, Greene, Champaign, Miami; Thomas Kirker for Adams and Scioto; Abram Claypool and Duncan M'Arthur for Ross, Franklin and Highland; Elnathan Scofield for Fairfield; Leonard Jewett and John Sharp for Washington, Gallia, Muskingum and Athens; Josiah Dillon for Belmont; John M'Laughlin and John M'Connell for Jefferson and Columbiana; Calvin Cove for Trumbull and Geauga.

A list of representatives includes John W. Seeley & James Montgomery for Trumbull and Geauga; John Sloan for Columbiana; Benjamin Hough, Thomas Elliot, and Thomas M'Cune for Jefferson; William Vance and John Paterson for Belmont; John Roman, P. Bureau, Joseph Palmer and John Matthews for Athens, Washington, Gallia and Muskingum; Philemon Beecher and William W. Irwin for Fairfield; Thomas Worthington, Elias Langham, Jeremiah M'Lene and William Lewis for Ross, Franklin and Highland; Philip Lewis, Jun., Andrew Allison and Alexander Campbell for Adams and Scioto; Othniel Looker, Zebulon Foster and John Jones for Hamilton; George Harlan and Mathias Corwin for Warren; Daniel C. Cooper for Montgomery; William Cory and James M'Clure for Butler; Joseph Tatman for Green and Champaign; John Pollock for Clermont.

Alexander M'Callester, William Hartman & William Hunter, in Clermont County, Williamsburgh township, report that Christopher Hartman found a mare.

Wm. Hunter, Isaac Hartman & Robert Dickey, in Clermont County, Williamsburgh township, say that William Fletcher found a mare.

Wm. Hunter, Ezekiel Hutchinson and Joseph Wood, in Clermont County, in Williamsburgh township, report that John Trout found a stray mare.

Isaac Anderson, in Cincinnati, has lots for sale in Cincinnati.

Hugh Moore, in Cincinnati, intends "to move out to his mills, early in the spring" and will sell or rent his house in Cincinnati.

John Armstrong & Company have dry goods, groceries, salt and lead for sale.

Archelus Alloway, living on the Ohio River about three miles below the mouth of the Big Miami, in Kentucky, report runaway slaves named Bristol and Matt.

Evan Price has a new shipment of goods for sale at his store in Cincinnati. He just returned from Baltimore.

Joseph Edwards, near Columbia, reports that he found a stray horse.

James Richey & Company have teas, coffee, sugar, & Spanish segars for sale.

O.M. Spencer, clerk, regarding bills due the Miami Exporting Company.

Peter Mills, inspector of provisions for Hamilton County, says he will inspect goods at Moore's mill on Mill Creek.

Hugh Brackin, William Pack & James Ewing, in Cincinnati township, Hamilton County, report that James Richardson found a stray mare.

D. Vertner, living in Washington, Kentucky, reports a runaway slave named Brooks. Deliver to Sanford Carrell at Limestone.

Isaac Stanley, Daniel Milikin and John Torrence, in Butler County, report that David Line, of Fairfield township, found a stray mare.

A note regarding the proceedings of the legislature mentions Thomas Kirker, Thomas Scott, Mr. Jewett, Mr. Thomas, Mr. Cone, Mr. Scofield, Mr. Wood, Mr. Price, Mr. Claypool, Mr. Bigger, Mr. Sharp, Mr. M'Arthur, Joseph S. Collins & Company, Thomas Worthington, Philemon Beecher. A tally of the votes for governor shows Return Jonathan Meigs winner over Nathaniel Massie.

William Barbee, at Staunton, administrator of William Hendricks, late of Concord township, Miami County, dec'd, regarding the estate settlement.

John H. Piatt, in Cincinnati, has a new shipment of goods for sale.

William Ludlow, at Mill Creek, regarding payments for his apple trees.

William Ludlow & Ludlow Pierson, executors of the estate of Sineus Pierson, dec'd, regarding the estate sale at Ezekiel Hutchinson's in Cincinnati.

Cornl. R. Sedam, at Woodland Farm four miles below Cincinnati, and Wm. T. Cullom report that Sedam found a mare and colt. They were appraised by Stephen Dexter and Joseph Pugh.

William Pack, Zachariah Holland and James Ewing, in Cincinnati township, report that Thomas Holland found a stray mare.

George Dawson has Scioto Lick salt for sale at Mr. Greer's store, Cincinnati.

Ezekiel Hutchinson, in Cincinnati, has repaired his fulling mill and hired Mr. Bryant and Mr. Sweet to operate it.

Peter Love has moved his rope making shop to his new house on Main Street near to Mrs. Mercer's house.

James Ferguson asks those indebted to him to settle their accounts.

Jacob Fouble, in Cincinnati, asks those indebted to him to pay their bills.

No. 24, Volume IX, Monday, 4 January 1808, Whole No. 440

A list of appointments made includes William Barbee appointed associate judge in the Miami Court of Common Pleas in place of David Hoover. William M'Farland is associate judge in Hamilton County in place of Matthew Nimmo who resigned. Moses Bixley is associate judge in Franklin County in place of John Dill who resigned. Elijah Hatch, jun., is appointed associate judge in Athens County in place of Sylvanus Ames, resigned. There is also a vacancy for associate judge in Ross County to take the place of Reuben Abrams, dec'd.

Marriage: Capt. James Ball married Miss Sarah Stittwell, both of Crosby township, on Thursday evening, 24 December 1807, by John Benefiel.

Marriage: Frederick Acres to Miss Margery Colby on 24 December 1807.

John O'Ferrall, in Cincinnati, regarding an auction of the property of Pierre Felix to pay his debt to O'Ferrall.

Wm. T. Cullom, Adam Henthorn and James Nicholson, in Cincinnati township, report that Isaac Wilson found a stray horse.

A list of letters left at the Post Office in Cincinnati includes James Allen, Alexander Ayres, Ziba Arnold at Colerain, Matilah Burns in care of Josiah Hally, John Bowyer in Crosby township, Henry Bomhart in Columbia, Patrick Bryson, Col. John Benefiel, Isaiah Bryant, Benjamin Chambers, Samuel Campbell (taylor), Thomas Cox, Levi Crosby, Col. Matthew Culley in Springfield, John Clark, Robert Campbell, Polly Clark, Peter Creegar in Springfield, Aaron Cadwell, Andrew Carrigen in care of Mr. Mansfield, Achsha Carson, Ezra Darby, Samuel Davis, Isaac Doraw, Reuben Dowty, David Debolt near Newtown, Robert S. Denny, Abraham Eversole, John Evatt (care of Wm. Lynes), Zacharias Ernst, Ezra Ferris on Duck Creek, John French, John Felty, Daniel M. Fleming, Isaac Fares, Christopher Girton at Mill Creek, George or John Gordon at Miami, John Gordon, Barney Greenwell in care of Wm. Peck, John M. Gray, Whitehead Geurin at Colerain, Charles Hassley/Haffley on Great Miami, Wm. W. Howard, Elizabeth Hollond, Michael Harness, Adrian Hagerman on Mill Creek, Wm. Hand, Jones Harris, Thomas Harper, Joseph Harris, Jonathan Jones at Columbia, John Jenkenson at Mill Creek, Enoch Jones, Sarah Jones, Kastner Jones, Jacob Kinser (12 miles from Cincinnati), Thomas Kennedy, John Kennedy, Jonathan Kirby, George Kinzer, John Kennard, Wm. Kirk in care of Wm. Stake, David Loofbourow near Reding, James Lyon, jr., Sally Lyon, Maxfield Ludlow, William Lyttle, Joseph Lord, Robert Laws, Timothy Lyons, Henry Lape, David Morrison, William M'Clave near Colerain, John Myers at Sycamore, Samuel M'Kee at Columbia, John R. Mills, Adam Nutt, James Nicholson, Jonathan Oston in care of Benjamin Chambers, Russel Prentes, Capt. Z.M. Pike, Phillip Pearce, Daniel Prine, Thomas Phillips, Lanson Rutten, Thomas Runnian, Phillip Ruddenbough, Reuben Reed in care of George Reed, Samuel Reading, Henry Reese, Joseph Ridenour in care of Martin Baum, Robert Rogers, Paul Sanders, William Squire, Aaron Sackett at Voorhees Town, Samuel Seward, Benjamin Skillman, Henry Sullivant, Ludiwick Sharer, Michael Sharer, Daniel Skinner, Lydia Smith, David Stille, Ephraim Tucker, Ziba Wingate, John and Anthony Whitecomb, Sarah or Robert Wilson, Christian Waldsmith, Wm. Ruffin.

John Sellman asks those indebted to him to settle their accounts since "he intends shortly to leave the country".

Edward Meeks and Jonah Vandervort, in Columbia, report that Thaddeus Hardford of Columbia found a stray barrow.

Stephen Benton regarding his school of Science (surveying, geometry and trigonometry) in Elmore Williams' new house on Main Street.

Wm. Swisher, Samuel Feel and Isaac Herrel report that George Kelly found a stray mare.

No. 25, Volume IX, Monday, 11 January 1808, Whole No. 441

P. Beecher, Thomas Kirker and Wm. Creighton, Jun., print a new law of Ohio.

Notes on the proceedings of the legislature mention Mr. Worthington, Mr. Jewett, Nathaniel Massie, Return Jonathan Meigs, Mr. Kirker, Mr. Thomas.

A letter from Nathaniel Massie to Return Jonathan Meigs, Jun., says that he will contest their recent election for governor on the grounds that Meigs has not lived in Ohio for the 4 years previous, but lived in Upper Louisiana.

A note regarding the trial of Mr. Blannerhassett and Mr. Burr.

Daniel Symmes is appointed Register of the Land Office.

A note regarding a meeting of the Republican Mechanics of Cincinnati to be held at the house of Simon M. Stockdell on Main Street.

Obituary: Charles Conn died on Wednesday, 6 Jan 1808, leaving a small family.

Robert Renick, Robert Boyle and Conrad Crites, in Springfield township of Champaign County, report that Jacob Wagoner found a stray horse.

Simon M. Stockdell regarding a note against Benjamin Stites and James Miranda, administrators of the estate of Benjamin Stites, dec'd. The note was given to Joel Craig and by him to Henry Disbrow.

John Loring, living in the forks of the roads from Cincinnati to Hamilton or Dayton, reports a stray horse.

Tho. Rawlins about the accounts of the tax collectors in Hamilton County.

No. 26, Volume IX, Monday, 18 January 1808, Whole No. 442

The proceedings of the legislature regarding the election between Return J. Meigs and Nathaniel Massie for governor. Mentions P. Lewis, Thomas Kirker, T. Scott, Mr. Irwin, Mr. Brush.

Daniel Symmes and James Findlay print a federal law signed by Nathl. Macon, Geo. Clinton and Th. Jefferson regarding land sales in Cincinnati.

James Clark, Joseph Hawkins and Ebenezer Ayer report that Samuel Bennett, jun'r, in Anderson township, Hamilton County, found a stray mare.

Samuel & Josiah Halley want to buy 2000 bushels of wheat at their mill.

Jacob Fowble regarding a meeting of the Republican Corresponding Society at Brownlow Fisher's house.

Samuel & J. Halley, in Cincinnati, have received a new shipment of goods in the store formerly occupied by Frederick Alter at Main and Columbia Streets.

Jacob Fowble offers for sale his grist and saw mills on Mill Creek. Apply to John Shalley at the mill or to Fowble in Cincinnati.

No. 27, Volume IX, Monday, 25 January 1808, Whole No. 443

The proceedings of the U.S. Circuit Court at Chillicothe mentions judges Thomas Todd & Charles Willing Byrd, Mr. Cass, Return Jonathan Meigs, jun., Levi Barber, William Skinner, William Reynolds, Isaac Humphreys, Abel Lewis, Levi Whipple, Samuel Wallace, Isaac Cook, James Armstrong, Thomas Hicks, Ezekiel Denning, Hugh Boyle, Joseph Buell, David Vance, John S. Gano, Ethan Stone, Isaac Vanhorne, Mathew Ferguson, James M'Donald, John Armstrong, Mr. M'Dougal.

William Creighton presents a recognizance from John Marshall, chief justice of the U.S., regarding the U.S. vs. Herman Blannerhassett, Israel Smith and John Cummins. Mentions William Marshall, Lyne Starling.

Maj. David Zeigler is appointed surveyor of the port of Cincinnati.

An extract of a letter from Hon. Edward Tiffin is printed.

A letter from John Smith, in Washington, to a friend in Ohio.

Elmore Williams reports a runaway apprentice to the masons and bricklayers trade, Jacob Grose, age 17.

James Findlay, agent for William Wells, of Zanesville, has land for sale.

David J. Poor, in Cincinnati, has for rent the house where he keeps a tavern.

Horatio G. Philips, in Dayton, Montgomery County, reports a stray horse.

Richard Barry, boot and shoe maker, at his shop near to Wilson's Inn in Lexington, Kentucky, regarding his business. He mentions Jeremiah Neave.

More proceedings of the legislature regarding Nathaniel Massie vs. Return J. Meigs, Jun. Mentions Charles Hammond and Mr. Brush. The decision is that Return J. Meigs is not eligible for governor.

No. 28, Volume IX, Monday, 1 February 1808, Whole No. 444

A letter from Thomas Power regarding Gen. James Wilkinson's trial mentions Philip Nolan, Montgomery Brown, Abijah Hunt of Cincinnati.

A note regarding the proceedings of the U.S. Circuit Court at Chillicothe mentions Aaron Burr, Herman Blannerhassett, Charles Duval, Joseph Barker, Pallas P. Stewart, Peter Taylor, David C. Wallace, Robert Wallace, Junr., Simeon Pool, Elias Glover, Edmund B. Dana, Return Jonathan Meigs, jun., Joseph Buell, Isaac Humphries, Luther Martin, John Cummins.

Obituary: Mrs. Mary Reeder, wife of Jesse Reeder, of Cincinnati, died on Saturday, 16 January 1808.

A note regarding Senator Smith's defense in the Congress.

An account of the meeting of the Mechanics of Cincinnati at Mr. Stockdell's tavern mentions Robert Brasher and Robert Blair.

John M'Dougal is appointed clerk of the U.S. District Court for Ohio in place of Richard E. Meade who resigned.

A note from Mr. Tiffin regarding the purchase of arms and artillery.

John S. Gano regarding grand and petit jurors in Hamilton County.

A note regarding the Hamilton horse races is printed.

Isaac Stanley, James Heaton and Joshua Rowland report that George Harlan of Fairfield township in Butler County, found a stray horse.

Christopher Curtna, David Riffle/Rissle and Aaron Vanseyte report that John Small, living in Dayton township, Montgomery County, found a stray horse.

No. 29, Volume IX, Monday, 8 February 1808, Whole No. 445

Obituary: John Torrence, died on the morning of 29 January 1808, at his house in Hamilton. He left a wife and five small children.

The defense of John Smith of Ohio is printed and mentions Mr. Hay, Peter Taylor, Elias Glover, Washington Boyd, Aaron Burr, Morris B. Bellknap, Lieut. Jackson, his son A.D. Smith, Matthew Nimmo, Col. Taylor of Newport. A note about Elias Glover says he is a native of Connecticut, but lately practiced law in Delaware County, N.Y., where he was indicted by a grand jury for forgery. Elias Glover's affadavit is reproduced. Also Col. James Taylor, of Newport, Kentucky, gives a statement and mentions Gen. Carbury, Gen. Findlay, Ambrose Dudley Smith (John Smith's son).

Daniel Reeder, John Clark and Issac Fares, in Sycamore township of Hamilton County, report that John Fares found a stray mare.

William Swisher, in Harden township of Montgomery County, reports that William Cannutt found a stray mare.

Rebecca M'Gill and William Powell, in Salem township, administrators of the estate of Christopher M'Gill, late of Champaign County, dec'd, ask those indebted to the estate to make immediate payments.

Benjamin Chambers, living on the Ohio River 13 miles below Lawrenceburgh, reports a runaway slave, Harry. He was formerly the property of Davis Floyd at the Falls of Ohio.

George Brown says Moses Musgrove, living in Washington township, Clermont County, found two stray horses, appraised by Thomas Owens & Philip Means. Also Elijah Fee, living in Washington township, found a stray appraised by David Brown, James Simmons and Zachariah Stanley.

No. 30, Volume IX, Monday, 15 February 1808, Whole No. 446

More documents regarding John Smith's defense includes the rest of Elias Glover's affidavit which mentions Col. Burr, Maj. Ephraim Kibby, Judge Nimmo, Wm. Richardson. Washington Boyd's affidavit mentions A. Burr, Morris B. Belnap, Mr. Blannerhassett, Mr. Tyler, Mr. Belknap, Sen. John Smith. Jacob Jackson's affidavit.

Also a letter from John Smith to Pres. Thomas Jefferson mentions Gov. Tiffin, Tyler and Blannerhassett, Gen. Gano, Gen. Findlay, Maj. Thomas Martin at Newport, Adjutant Stall, Elias Glover, Mr. Nimmo, Judge Symmes, Allan Brown, Daniel Symmes, John C. Symmes, Wm. Berry. Ambrose D. Smith's affidavit, John Randolph's statement, Pallus P. Stuart's deposition (sworn to by John Mahard, he mentions Jonathan Pittman), John S. Gano's letter to Hon. John Smith (mentions Judge Nimmo, Maj. Ruffin, Dugan's store, Conn's tavern).

A note from Mr. Anderson regarding the committee to hear the defense of Senator John Smith.

Thomas Dugan reports that he found a stray cow.

William Byrd asks those indebted to him to make payments to Ethan Stone or Job Truesdell.

Jacob Romane, William Bruce and Matthias Dawson, of Eaton township in Montgomery County, report that Joseph Caldwell found a stray mare.

C.R. Sedam, at Woodland Farms, reports that he found a stray heifer that was appraised by George Carpenter and Joseph Pugh. Sworn by John Mahard.

No. 31, Volume IX, Monday, 22 February 1808, Whole No. 447

A letter from Gen. James Wilkinson to Hon. John Smith is printed.

A Mr. Lyons, of Lebanon, was thrown from his horse on 18 February 1808 while trying to cross Mill Creek at Mr. Fowble's mill. He was drowned. He was buried at the Presbyterian burial ground in Cincinnati the next day.

A note regarding a bill to establish a bank at Chillicothe.

A letter from Edward Tiffin and Jeremiah Morrow to the speaker of the U.S. Senate is printed regarding arms purchases for Ohio.

Emmy Torrence, Robert Benham and John Wingate, administrators of the estate of John Torrence, dec'd, regarding the estate sale at his house.

Isaac Stanley, in Butler County, reports that Abraham Piatt, of Fairfield township, found a stray horse, appraised by James Heaton and Charles Bruce.

H. Theall, "intending shortly to leave this place", has Mann's Lick salt for sale. Apply to Ezekiel Hutchinson's tavern in Cincinnati.

No. 33, Volume IX, Monday, 7 March 1808, Whole No. 449

Geo. Williamson, Cincinnati township clerk, regarding a meeting of the trustees at the house of Joseph Carpenter, in Cincinnati.

Joel Williams regarding land he claims from John Cleves Symmes through Matthias Denman of New Jersey.

Appointments made by the legislature: Benjamin Hough, Auditor, in place of Wm. W. Irwin, resigned; Wm. Vance, major general of the 2nd division; P. Beecher of the 6th division; Wm. Lytle of the 7th division; W. Dodds of the 8th division; Duncan M'Arthur of the 2nd; John Timmons is quarter-master general of the 2nd division; Leonard Jewett for the 3rd division; Wm. Harbaugh for the 4th; George Newcom for the 8th; Timothy Buell is elected trustee of the religious land in Washington County in place of Matthew Backus, dec'd.

Capt. James Ferguson regarding a meeting of the Troop of Light Dragoons.

John O'Ferrall says he'll leave Cincinnati "for the eastward" in about 12 days and asks those indebted to him to settle their accounts.

John H. Piatt has stills, groceries and hardware for sale at his store.

Robert Ogle, in Millford township, Butler County, reports that George Markelin, living on Four Mile Creek in Millford township, found a mare. It was appraised by John Irwin and Thomas Sankey.

John Siegmond, in Cincinnati, reports that he has opened a tavern next door to the Western Spy office in Cincinnati.

John Wall, saddler and harness maker, regarding his business in Cincinnati.

Samuel Vail reports that he found a stray mare at the mouth of Mill Creek.

Capt. John Gardner lost a packet of letters from John Sutherland. Deliver to Capt. Gardner near Lexington or to William Ruffin in Cincinnati.

John Armstrong, at Columbia, reports that Jonah Vandivert found a stray mare that was appraised by Jonathan Seaman and John Seaman.

Robert Ogle reports that Zachariah P. Dewitt, living in Butler County, Mill-ford township, on Four Mile Creek, found a stray mare. It was appraised by Conrad Darr and William Ogle. Edward Lytle, living on Four Mile Creek, also found a stray mare, appraised by Conrod Darr and Thomas White.

James Clark reports that Daniel Gilman, of Anderson township, Hamilton County, found a stray horse that was appraised by John Day and Josiah Gwaltney.

William Hutchin regarding the stud horse, Bonaparte, at the stables of Piper and Hunt, at Middletown and Franklin, in Warren County.

David Dunseth has Monongahela whiskey for sale at his store.

Mrs. Henderson and Miss S. Caldwell about their Academy for young ladies.

No. 34, Volume IX, Saturday, 12 March 1808, Whole No. 450

Daniel Symmes, Register of the Land Office, regarding land for sale mentions William Carter, Wm. Cheek, Barnet Hulic, Jeremiah Hunt, Samuel Vance, John Mast, John Brownson and Samuel Beeler.

A list of acts passed by the Ohio Legislature mentions the heirs of John Francis Hamtramick, dec'd, Nathaniel Beasly (agent for the heirs of John Beasly, dec'd), Marietta, Presbyterian Society on Red Oak, Newtown Library company, Dayton Academy, Worthington Academy, Henry Barrow, Bank of Chillicothe, Daniel Stewart (agent for the heirs of Judediah Ensworth, dec'd), Harris Parsons and John Sweat, Athens University.

Doctor Sellman was robbed of $1,100 last Sunday evening.

Simon Natten, Dentist, lately from Germany, regarding his practice at Mr. Yeatman's Inn in Cincinnati.

Thomas Dugan, Cincinnati, offers for rent the store house formerly occupied by John O'Ferrall.

Jeremiah Hunt has land for sale. Apply to Mr. Carpenter's tavern, Cincinnati.

George W. Stall, at Newtown, has a wagon and horses for sale.

Abraham Freeman, in Butler County on Pleasant Run next door to Capt. Blackburn, has land for sale.

Geo. Williamson, township clerk, regarding a meeting to elect officers for Cincinnati township.

No. 35, Volume IX, Saturday, 19 March 1808, Whole No. 451

William DeHart, living in Pendleton County, Kentucky, reports a runaway slave named Peter.

Those who receive the Western Spy from Mr. Vanness should pay him.

An account of a hunting accident, on 5 March 1808, which resulted in the death of Col. John Armstrong's son. Mentions Capt. Gray.

John O'Ferrall has moved to the house lately occupied by John Wall next door to James W. Sloan's. He has goods for sale and will leave Cincinnati in 8 days.

Thomas Moore, in Cincinnati, reports that he found a silver watch.

John S. Gano has several lots for sale in Cincinnati.

Capt. James Ferguson regarding a meeting of the Troop of Light Dragoons to elect a second lieutenant in place of Henry Disbrow who resigned.

Michael Debolt, in Anderson township, Hamilton County, reports that William Shattrick found a mare. It was appraised by Daniel Carter & Vincent Goldsmith.

William Shattrick, in Anderson township, reports that John Lin sold him a mare, but William Shepherd and James Clark sued him because it was a stray.

Samuel Murfy, at Crosby, says his wife, Levina Murfy, has left him, and he won't honor debts of her contracting.

Tho. Stansbury, in Cincinnati, wants to hire an apprentice to the house carpenter and joiner's business.

George Gorden, Dixon Greer and Samuel Youart have purchased the patent rights for a boring machine from Christopher Hoxie, the inventor. The auger is for sale at the store of Greer & Baymiller in Cincinnati.

No. 36, Volume IX, Saturday, 26 March 1808, Whole No. 452

Doctor E. Tiffin submitted a letter and documents from Pres. Th. Jefferson regarding the possibility of war and the preparation of the militia.

John Armstrong & Company, in Cincinnati, ask those indebted to them to pay their accounts. J. Armstrong will start for Philadelphia in April.

J. Carpenter, in Cincinnati, asks those indebted to him to pay their bills.

Benjamin Beall, in Campbell County, Kentucky, has land for sale on Well's Creek and the Ohio in Kentucky, about 18 miles above Cincinnati. Rev. B. Riggs is the present occupant. Apply to David L. Carney in Cincinnati.

Joseph Brown, at Staunton, administrator of the estate of Francis Martin, dec'd, late of Greenville, Miami County, should pay any debts to the estate to Peter Felix in Staunton.

Thomas Higgins says that William Ludlow, of Springfield township, Hamilton County, found a stray mare, appraised by Anthony Highlands and Thomas Clayton.

John H. Piatt asks those indebted to him to settle their accounts.

Tho. Dugan, Wm. Ruffin and J. Carpenter regarding land for sale, the pro-perty of Seth Cutter, seized at the suit of Samuel Foster.

No. 38, Volume IX, Saturday, 16 April 1808, Whole No. 454

A list of letters left at the Post Office in Cincinnati includes Hugh A. Anderson, Ebenezer Ayres, Elizabeth Brierly, Lilly Burch, Jacob Brunher, Amos Butler, William Byrd, Jonas Beason, Deacon Joseph Billings, Joseph Black, James Beard, Robert Brown, John Buck, Polly Bevelin, James Beck, Doctor John Collins, James Coen, Elias Cowenhoven, Samuel Corwin, Joseph Compton, Col. Matthew Culley, Josiah Crosley, Andrew Cox, Joseph Cilley, Joseph Clark, Archibald Davis, Robert Davidson, John Donham, George Dick, Daniel Duvall, John S. Daily, John Delany, Elizabeth Daily, Joseph Denman, Eli Elston, John Ensworth, Eli Elder, Josiah Elwell or John Brick, Jacob Eron, Doctor Edwards, Richard Fairman, Prudy Foreson, Josiah French, Chambers Foster, Daniel M. Fleming, William Glidwell, Elias Glover, Samuel Gooding, James Gutry, John Griffith, Isaac Goble, James M. Griffin, William Grant, sen., William Humes, Thomas Holland, James Harrison, John Hendison, Daniel Hosebrook, Margrate Heaton, Ronemas Hane, George Hinkson, James Hearne, Lydia Jones, Cornelius or William Hindsey, Nathan Hatfield, Edward Johnston, Jonathan Jones, Samuel Jimison, Samuel Johnson, Daniel Jones, Joseph Jones, Thomas Kerr, Henry Kerr, Henry Lower, Thomas Larrison, John C. Lourens, Capt. John Leathers, Samuel Lees, Joseph M'Beath, Isaac Murphy, Capt. Richard Morgan, Ezekiel Mixer, James M'Kinsey, Joseph Miles, Charles Moore, John M'Cary, Jacob Miller, Robert Martin, John Myers, Matthias Miller, Daniel M'Kinnor and Joseph Stockwell, James M'Cormack, Matthew Nicol, Joseph Nelson, Joel Nelson, Andrew Noe, Samuel Newell, James Patterson, Ralph Phillips, John Padget, Richard Phillips, John Penwell, John Page, Hezekiah Price, James Parsonet, George Price, John Pacier, George Riggle, John Radley, Jacob Roman, Reve. Redden, Charles Reily, Charles Robison, John Roll, sen., Joseph Ronck, Jackson Rambo, Elizabeth Ramsey, George Russell, James Russel, Aaron Stout, Charles Smith, jun., Thomas Steer, Adam Stewart, Thomas Stone, Thomas Stenson, Jeremiah Smith, Paul Sanders, Samuel D. Stout, Robert Swan, Daniel S. Skillinger, Warkam Stacy, Joseph Shepherd, Hachalia Theall, Alexander Thomas, William Thomas, Demas Woodruff, Rev. Mr. Warwick, Benjamin Wilson, Matthias or Mahala Woodruff, John Webster, Francis H. Wilson, John Willey, Thomas Williams, Elmore Williams, Jacob Warwick, John White, Samuel Wilson, William Wallsworth, Thomas Wilson, Judah Willey. Entered by William Ruffin.

M'Guffin & Hittle, in Wayne township, have land for sale or rent. Apply to Ezekiel Hutchinson in Cincinnati.

James Reed, living in Wayne township on the road from Chillicothe to the college township, has land for sale. Apply to Capt. William Stanley, Cincinnati.

John Godfrey, living on the road from Williamsburgh to Newmarket, reports a stolen mare. Supposed to be stolen by Mr. Caldwell, the horse thief.

Isaac Stanley, in Butler County, reports that Christopher Hannaman, of Fairfield township, found a filley appraised by Solomon Line and Tho. M'Cullough.

Wm. Stanley and J. Carpenter, Captains, regarding a meeting of the militia at Mrs. S. Mercer's house.

Lieut. N.C. Findlay regarding a meeting of Capt. James Ferguson's dragoons.

Joseph Hough, at Hamilton, reports a stray mare.

James Moore, living four miles below Hamilton on the west side of the Great Miami, reports a strayed mare.

No. 39, Volume IX, Saturday, 23 April 1808, Whole No. 455

Jacob Miller, at Williamsburg, Clermont County, regarding the perjury of Mr. Sommers/Summers that Miller had beat him up.

Township and corporation officers are elected: Samuel Foster, John W. Miles, Samuel Swing, O.M. Spencer, D.L. Carney, Benjamin Mason, Jacob Fowble, David J.

Poore, Ezekiel Hall, Th. M'Farland, James Chambers, Jacob Stewart, Jedidiah Ayres, Robert Terry, Andrew Brannon, William T. Cullum, Robert Richardson, Joshua Williams, Wm. Woodard, Th. Dugan, Christopher Cary, Isaac Anderson, Clarke Bates, Daniel Symmes, Aaron Goforth, Jacob Harden, John Mahard, Samuel Patterson, N. Hunt, J. Pancoast, R. Brasher, T. Dugan, F. Karr, J. Ewing.

Lieut. P. Dickey regarding a meeting of the Cincinnati Light Infantry Com-pany at Mrs. Mercer's house.

Lieut. N.C. Findlay regarding the meeting of Capt. James Ferguson's troop of dragoons at the house of Mrs. Mercer.

John Sellman, in Cincinnati, says that Charles Brady and his wife had nothing to do with the robbery at his house.

John W. Miles, S. Swing and S. Foster regarding a meeting of the electors of the Cincinnati township to vote money for the support of the poor.

Thomas M'Farland and Ezekiel Hall, overseers of the poor, about a meeting at Joseph Carpenter's house, to find support for William Skevington, Mr. Horner and Frederick Dewese for the present year.

Jacob Williams and Patty Conn, adminstrators of the estate of Charles Conn, dec'd, late of Cincinnati, regarding the estate sale and settlement.

John S. Gano about payments of court costs in the Court of Common Pleas.

Richard Eaverson, in Cincinnati, reports a strayed or stolen horse.

William Fee, in Washington township, Clermont County, says that John Cook and James Muin appraised a horse found by Harry Young. Also William Watson and John Aldrige appraised a horse found by James Fee, in Washington township.

No. 40, Volume IX, Saturday, 30 April 1808, Whole No. 456

Daniel Symmes and James Ewing submit an ordinance of Cincinnati.

The editors of the Western Spy say that the rumour that Joseph Delaplaine has bought the Spy is incorrect.

Obituary: Mrs. Sarah Prince, daughter of Joseph Conn, of Cincinnati, died on Thursday, 28 April 1808.

Obituary: Miss Sally Silvester died on Thursday, 28 April 1808.

An account of the death of Archibald M'Donald while he was cleaning out a well in Cincinnati.

A rumour is about that John Smith has been acquitted by the senate.

James Welsh, in Dayton, regarding lots for sale in Dayton.

John Parker, in Lexington, Kentucky, reports a stray mare. Deliver to Gen. Lytle at Williamsburgh or Peter Krumbaugh at the Round Bottom.

Francis Baldwin, living in Waynesville township, four miles from Lebanon, reports a stray horse.

Garut VanNest, living near Enox's mill on Great Miami, reports a stray mare.

John Burns is carrying on the buckle making business at Waldsmith's mill on the Little Miami.

Emmy Torrence, Robert Benham & John Wingate, in Hamilton, administrators of the estate of John Torrence, late of Hamilton, dec'd, regarding the estate settlement at the house of Mrs. Torrence in Hamilton.

No. 41, Volume IX, Saturday, 7 May 1808, Whole No. 457

More on the case of John Smith's defense mentions Elias Glover. The decision was to expel Smith from the Senate.

Jesse Camp, in Cincinnati, regarding his boot and shoe making business.

Susan Mercer, administratrix of the estate of John Mercer, dec'd, regarding lots for sale at Mr. Stockdell's tavern.

Jesse Hunt, in Cincinnati, regarding the sale of lots at Stockdell's tavern.

Those indebted for last year's Western Spy should pay by delivering rye to Mr. Mennessier's still house on Deer Creek.

John Hick reports a stray mare. Deliver to Mr. Redenbough in Reding or John Rim on Twin Creek or Jacob Camp on the Miami River.

John M. Gray, living at Hunt's tan yard near Cincinnati, reports a stray mare.

O.M. Spencer about stockholders' payments to the Miami Exporting Company.

Clark Bates, living on Mill Creek near Cincinnati, reports he found a cow.

Robert Moore, in Cincinnati, reports a stray cow. Deliver to James Ewing in Cincinnati.

No. 42, Volume IX, Saturday, 14 May 1808, Whole No. 458

M. Huston, in Fairfield township, Butler County, reports that Thomas Hueston found a stray horse. It was appraised by Thomas Hunter and Martin Waggoner.

A note regarding a meeting, at Mr. Swing's, of the Cincinnati Republican Corresponding Society.

Obituary: John Roll, sen., age 76, died on 23 April 1808.

Officers of the Revolutionary War are meet at Mr. Yeatman's in Cincinnati.

Letters to the editor regarding the acquittal of John Smith.

Sutherland & Brown, at Hamilton & Dayton, have a new shipment of goods.

Samuel Hilditch, at Columbia, asks those indebted to him to pay their bills.

W.T. Cullom reports that Francis Cullom, living in Cincinnati township, found a mare. It was appraised by Wm. Mills and James Nicholson.

Jacob Williams, living in Cincinnati, has cut and hammered nails for sale.

Hugh Moore regarding a meeting of the shareholders of Cincinnati University.

No. 43, Volume IX, Saturday, 21 May 1808, Whole No. 459

Benjamin Idding and Ruth Neal, administrators of the estate of William Neal, late of Union township, Miami County, dec'd, about the estate settlement.

The Trustees of Cincinnati University are David E. Wade, Joel Williams, Jacob Williams, Jesse Reeder, Ezekiel Hall, Wm. Ruffin, Jacob Burnet, Nehemiah Hunt, W. M'Farland, James Chambers.

A note regarding a meeting of the Miami Exporting Company.

Mr. Coleman has just arrived at Cincinnati and will open his dancing school.

Edward H. Stall, apothecary and druggist, has a new shipment of medicines.

Benjamin Hough, Auditor, at Chillicothe, regarding land taxes.

Samuel & Josiah Halley have nails and hardware for sale at their store.

William Smith reports that Jonathan Greagry found a stray mare. It was appraised by John Morris and John Richardson.

No. 44, Volume IX, Saturday, 28 May 1808, Whole No. 460

John Mansfield, taylor and ladies habit maker, regarding his shop in the house next door to Isaac Anderson in Front Street, Cincinnati.

An unsigned letter to the editor mentions Dr. Tiffin, R.J. Meigs, John Smith.

Matthew Caldwell reports that Obediah Priest found a mare. It was appraised by Joseph Hiderd and Charles Hillard.

William Ludlow and Matthias Roll, executors of the estate of John Roll, dec'd, will sell his late residence on the west fork of Mill Creek.

Joseph Delaplaine intends to "abandon this country" and go to his mother. He will not publish "The Friend of Liberty" as he'd planned.

Capt. P. Dickey regarding a meeting of the Cincinnati Light Infantry.

Mr. Coleman regarding his dancing school at Mr. Williams' new building next door to Mrs. Willis' Inn.

Emmy Torrence, in Hamilton, reports a runaway apprentice, James Morrow.

Susan Mercer, administratrix of the estate of John Mercer, dec'd, about lots for sale at Mr. Stockdell's tavern.

John Hunter says that Zachariah Chapman, living in Ohio township, Clermont County, found a mare that was appraised by Daniel Bailiff and Daniel Husong.

Isaac Stanley offers his tavern in Hamilton for sale.

James Clark reports that Andrew Ketchum, in Anderson township, Hamilton County, found a mare, appraised by Samuel Bennet, sen., and Samuel Bennet, jun.

John Wingate, sheriff of Butler County, reports a runaway prisoner, James Dougherty, about age 30, a native of Ireland.

No. 45, Volume IX, Saturday, 11 June 1808, Whole No. 461

The publication of the trial of Charles Vattier is available at the book binding shop of Mr. Williamson on Main Street.

David L. Carney regarding a meeting of the Cincinnati Lodge.

John F. Mansfield has maps of the state of Ohio for sale.

Samuel Kirkpatrick regarding a certificate of land to replace the one that burned when his house burned down.

Daniel Searles has moved his gunsmith shop to the corner of Water and Elm Streets in Cincinnati next door to Thomas M'Farland.

Levi M'Lean, collector, regarding the hogs running loose in Cincinnati.

Wm. Perry reports that John Seamon, of Columbia township, found a mare that was appraised by Jonah Vandivont and Jonathan Seamon.

James Ewing regarding a meeting of the Corporation of Cincinnati.

Moses Ferral, living near Cincinnati, reports that he found a stray cow.

James Coldwell, living on Mill Creek, near Cincinnati, reports a stolen mare.

No. 48, Volume IX, Saturday, 2 July 1808, Whole No. 464

Sen. John Smith's letter to acting Gov. Thomas Kirker is printed and mentions Elias Glover, Col. Taylor, Matthew Nimmo.

A note regarding an ordinance of the Corporation of Cincinnati.

J. O'Ferrall has received a new shipment of goods at his store.

Walter Hole regarding his son, James Hole, formerly an apprentice to John Maxwell, blacksmith.

Samuel Pogue says he lost a warrant for land in Cincinnati.

James M'Whorter, in Cincinnati, regarding a bond to George W. Fenton.

John Riely and Jacob Burnet regarding a suit in the Butler County Court of Common Pleas: Jonathan Dayton vs. Thomas Cohoon.

Daniel Symmes, Register of the Land Office, regarding land for sale. He mentions George Gillespie, Thomas Elliott and William M'Clelland.

James Ferguson has a new shipment of goods for sale at his store, Cincinnati.

A coat was lost between Jacob Wheeler's and Christopher Carey's. Deliver to Gen. Gano's office.

Stephen Wood, Caleb Osburn and William Zyph, in Miami township, Hamilton County, report that Michael Rybolt found a horse.

Luddow Pierson, in Hamilton, regarding two notes to David Smith.

Joseph Delaplaine, in Cincinnati, regarding a note to John W. Browne.

Thomas Godfrey found a mare on Masses Creek, Zenia township, Green County.

George Vail, administrator of the estate of David Vail, dec'd, regarding the estate sale and estate settlement.

No. 2, Volume X, Saturday, 13 August 1808, Whole No. 470

An unsigned letter to the editor mentions Mr. Burr, Mr. Smith.

Nashee & Denny, in Chillicothe, intend to publish a newspaper there called "The Supporter".

An article about the trial, in the Court of Common Pleas, Hamilton County, of John Miller for the assault of his wife, Sarah Miller. Mentions Judge Mahard.

Thomas Kirker will serve as governor if he's elected.

George Williamson, editor of the Western Spy, regarding the paper.

Daniel Symmes about the meeting of the Republican Corresponding Society of Cincinnati at Samuel Swing's house. Jeremiah Morrow and Dr. Stephen Wood are nominated to offices.

Obituary: Mrs. Elizabeth Barnet, of Cincinnati, died Thursday, 11 August.

James Ewing regarding a meeting of the Corporation of Cincinnati.

Jesse B. Thomas, at Lawrenceburgh, has lots for sale in Brookeville in Dearborn County.

Hannah Willis, in Cincinnati, wants to rent her tavern and stable.

Lt. Enos Cutler, at Cincinnati, about a deserter, Daniel Payne, of Kentucky.

William Stake, taylor and ladies habit maker, about his shop on Main Street, in Cincinnati, adjoining Adam Moore's store.

Maj. John S. Gano, William Ruffin and Edward Meeks give militia orders.

John Frazer, living on Seven Mile Creek near Hamilton in Milford township, Butler County, reports a stray mare.

Long & Mears, in Cincinnati, regarding their coppersmith business.

Samuel & Josiah Halley, in Cincinnati, want to buy wheat at their mill.

Thomas Rawlins regarding the collection of taxes in Hamilton County.

John C. Winans, in Lebanon, has for rent the farm where John VanNuys now lives on the road leading from Cincinnati to Lebanon.

Daniel Symmes, Register of the Land Office, regarding the request from Andrew Fouts and James Ewing to issue George Leslie a new certificate of land.

Jno. O'Ferrall has a new shipment of goods for sale in Cincinnati.

George Studdert, on Duck Creek, has land for sale.

Col. John Armstrong, in Columbia, wants to hire a teacher.

(The papers from August 20, 1808 through April 9, 1809 are missing. The paper was not printed from April 1809 through August 1810.)

Volume 1, Saturday, 1 September 1810, No. 1
A letter to the public from the editors of the Western Spy, Joseph Carpenter & Company, stating their philosophies. They have changed the name to "The Western Spy". They ask those indebted for subscriptions to settle their accounts.

A note regarding the Shaker settlement on Turtle Creek in Warren County. Many citizens assembled there to take away three of the grandchildren of Col. James Smith of Kentucky.

Obituary: Noah Crane, age 28, one of the editors of the "Western Star", died at Lebanon on 21 August 1810.

Obituary: Adeline Moore, the daughter of Adam Moore, died in Cincinnati, August 25, 1810.

Obituary: Prentis Wyeth, son of Joshua Wyeth, died 27 August 1810.

Joseph Carpenter & Company have books for sale at their office, Cincinnati.

Garret Vorris, in Cincinnati, reports two runaway apprentices to the blacksmith's business, William Clark and Joseph Southward.

Robert Patterson, of Pittsburgh, and Benjamin K. Hopkins, of Philadelphia, have formed a partnership in the bookselling business in Pittsburgh.

W. & J. Allison have taken over E. Hutchinson's fulling mill on Mill Creek.

Wm. Stake, in Cincinnati, wants to hire three good taylors.

Volume 1, Saturday, 15 September 1810, No. 2
An article regarding Indian affairs mentions Gov. Harrison, Mr. Barron, Gen. Gibson, Lieut. Jennings, Tecumseh.

The Wasington Presbytery will meet at the Presbyterian Meeting House in Cincinnati on Wednesday, 3 October 1810.

A note about the ceremony at Newport, Kentucky, naming Fort Eustis.

An account of the robbery of Maj. Halley, Mr. Hamilton and Mr. Enness (John H. Piatt's partner), all of Cincinnati, while they were on their way to Philadelphia. They were possibly robbed by L. Browne of Philadelphia.

Clayton Webb and John Hart about a meeting of the Republican Delegates of Hamilton County at J. Williams' house in Mill Creek township nominated the following for offices: Return J. Meigs, jun., Jeremiah Morrow, Othniel Looker, Aaron Goforth, Peter Bell, John Jones, Samuel M'Henry, Joseph Kitchell, Ezekiel Hall and William Butler. Another meeting will be held at James Patterson's in Springfield township.

Edward Meeks, at Columbia, is a candidate for sheriff in Hamilton County.

Obituary: Mrs. M'Mullen, age 38, wife of Rev. Samuel M'Mullen, died near Mill Creek in Hamilton County, on 5 September 1810.

Obituary: Mrs. Nancy Riddle, age 28, wife of Maj. John Riddle, of Mill Creek township, died on 7 September 1810.

Wm. Woodward, coroner, and J. Carpenter, deputy coroner, regarding the upcoming election. Mentions Stephen Wood who resigned as state senator.

John Armstrong, at the Columbian Inn, regarding his storage and commission business and his warehouses.

Daniel Drake & Company have medicines, spices and school books for sale at their store in Cincinnati.

Jacob Fowble has opened a tavern in Main Street in Cincinnati.

Judah Willey reports that Samuel Dillon, of Colerain township, Hamilton County, found a mare, appraised by Abner Johnson and David Gibson.

Uriah Gates and John W. Langdon regarding a due bill they gave to Philip Highfill now in the hands of Stephen Weston.

Alex. A. Meeks has for rent the house lately occupied by Joseph Carpenter.

Philip P. Price, in Cincinnati, has a brick house for sale.

John O'Ferrall wants to buy pork, hemp, tobacco, bees-wax and tallow.

Adam Martin has just commenced the baking business in Front Street one door east of Christopher Walker's tavern in Cincinnati.

Volume 1, Saturday, 22 September 1810, No. 3

A note regarding a meeting of the delegates at Williams' place is printed. It includes an account of a meeting of the Republican Corresponding Society of Cincinnati at Mr. Fowble's Tavern and mentions Thomas Worthington, Jeremiah Morrow, Hezekiah Price, Aaron Goforth, James Clark, John Jones, John Wright, Samuel M'Henry, Joseph Jenkinson, Ezekiel Hall, William Butler, Robert Brasher.

Volume 1, Saturday, 29 September 1810, No. 4

An unsigned letter to the editor mentions Col. Meigs, Gen. Massie, Return Jonathan Meigs.

(Most of this issue is torn and missing.)

Volume 1, Saturday, 6 October 1810, No. 5

Aaron Goforth has resigned his office of associate judge of the Court of Common Pleas for Hamilton County.

A note nominates Wm. Woodward for coroner, Adam Moore as commissioner.

An unsigned letter to the editors mentions Baum & Company's cotton factory, Ohio Exporting Company, Bank of Cincinnati.

A letter to the public regarding the election mentions Mr. Kitchell, John Hart, Jesse Jones, Mr. Brown, Mr. Golding, Joseph Kitchell, Othniel Looker, James Ewing, Mr. Carson, Hugh Carson.

A letter to Francis M'Cormic from Joseph Kitchell mentions Ezekiel Hughs, David Carson (and his brother Hugh Carson), Wm. Carson.

Seth M. Levenworth regarding a meeting of the Republican Association at the Union Inn.

Daniel Drake & Company received a new shipment of goods at their store.

Daniel Cost, in Cincinnati, lost a pocket book between the house of Garret Vanness near Franklin and Thomas Flemming's on the road to Cincinnati. It includes bonds on William M'Clure, Zadock Sexton, Hugh M'Cullom, Abner Enox. Deliver to Sutherland & Brown in Hamilton or Thomas Flemming near the Big Hill.

Isaac M'Cammon, tailor and ladies habit maker, regarding his business at the house of Charles Fox in Front Street, Cincinnati.

Wm. Cary and Roswell Fenton, administrators of the estate of Roswell Fenton, dec'd, regarding the estate settlement.

Judah Willey reports that John M'Nutt and Samuel Torrence, both of Colerain township, have found stray animals. The appraisers were Samuel Torrence, Alex. M'Nutt, Alexander M'Nutt and John M'Nutt.

Peter Love regarding his rope and seine factory in Cincinnati.

Wm. Woodward and J. Carpenter regarding a coroner's sale of land in the Miami Purchase at the suit of Mathias Denman.

Volume 1, Saturday, 13 October 1810, No. 6

A note about Wm. Green's steam mill at Marietta. Mentions Benj. I. Gilman.

A note about the Farmers' and Mechanics' Exporting Company of Hamilton in Butler County.

Hamilton County election notes mention Mr. Meigs, Mr. Goforth, Mr. Looker, Mr. M'Henry, Mr. Jones, Mr. Bell, Mr. Hall, Mr. Jenkinson, Mr. Butler, and Mr. Morrow.

Obituary: Samuel Hilditch, age 52, merchant, died at Columbia on Saturday, 6 October 1810. He was buried at the Baptist burial ground the next day. A sermon was preached by Rev. Wm. Jones, minister of the Baptist church, Columbia.

A note regarding books for sale at the Spy office.

Volume 1, Saturday, 27 October 1810, No. 8

An unsigned letter to the editor mentions Dr. Goforth.

Obituary: Calvin Percival, second son of Doctor Percival of Lawrenceburgh, and Sampson Smith, a carpenter, formerly a resident of Cincinnati, drowned on Saturday, 20 October 1810, as they were crossing the Ohio River.

Obituary: John M'Clelland Dickey, the young and only son of Capt. Patrick Dickey, of Cincinnati, died on Tuesday, 23 October 1810. He was buried the next day in the Presbyterian burial ground.

G. Turner, in Cincinnati, has a farm for sale.

Robert Blair, collector, regarding the payment of taxes in Cincinnati.

Wm. M'Kee says his wife, Sarah M'Kee, left him, and he won't pay her bills.

John S. Gano has lots for sale in Cincinnati at the house of Capt. Carpenter.

John Wright, in Cincinnati, has moved his school from the White House on the Hill to the new house on Main Street nearly opposite Gen. Gano's.

Hezekiah Flint, in Cincinnati, reports a stray mare.

Abraham Voorheese, at Reading, about a mare left with him by Mr. Bradbury, son of Benjamin Bradbury, until Abraham Byres came for her.

Abraham Voorheese, at Reading, regarding due bills he gave to Elijah Sexton, of Springfield township.

Ann Martin and Matthew Richardson, of Milford township in Butler County, administrators of the estate of James Martin, dec'd, about the estate settlement.

Matthew Richardson reports that Elias Shoemaker, of Milford township, in Butler County, found a mare, appraised by William Robeson and Joseph Hains.

Andrew Young, in Butler County, Milford township, reports a stray mare.

James Andrew, in Clermont County, reports that Joseph Love, living on the road between Williamsburg and Deerfield, on the waters of Obannon, found a horse. He was appraised by Michael Banghart in Miami township.

Robert Gillespie, taylor and ladies' habit maker, regarding his taylor's shop in Columbia Street, Cincinnati. He also wants to hire an apprentice.

Volume 1, Saturday, 3 November 1810, No. 9

Note about the election for governor between Mr. Meigs and Mr. Worthington.

Marriage: Martin Miller married Miss Nancy Long, daughter of Harmon Long, all of Cincinnati, on Tuesday evening, 23 October 1810, by Ethan Stone.

Obituary: Newton Spinning, son of Ichabod Spinning, of Cincinnati, died at Natchez on 27 September 1810.

Thomas Rawlins about a meeting of the Republican Corresponding Society.

Wm. Hendricks has opened a school in the house lately occupied by James Ewing in Sycamore Street, Cincinnati.

Joseph Jenkinson has a new shipment of goods at his store in Cincinnati.

John Kerr, living in Mr. Carter's house in Cincinnati, regarding the gun stolen by Thomas Wilson who says he's a Tuckahoe and lives south of Ohio in Kentucky.

John Kerr wants to buy land near Cincinnati.

Volume 1, Saturday, 17 November 1810, No. 11

More election returns for governor mentions Mr. Meigs and Mr. Worthington.

Obituary: David Elby, of Cincinnati, died Monday, 12 November 1810.

James Kirby wants to buy wheat at Walker's mill on Mill Creek.

John Whetstone, living two and a half miles above Cincinnati, offers for sale or rent the house he lately occupied in Sycamore Street, Cincinnati.

Peter Mills, inspector, at Mill Creek, regarding the inspection of produce.

Ethan Stone, Ezekiel Hall and John Wilson report that Danforth Wetherby, in Cincinnati, found a stray mare and colt.

Volume 1, Saturday, 1 December 1810, No. 12

The editors of the Western Spy apologize for the lack of a newspaper last Saturday, but they had no paper on which to print.

Marriage: John R. Riddle married Miss Jane Marshall, both of Mill Creek township, on Tuesday evening, 27 December 1810, by Rev. Joshua Wilson.

There are many books for sale at the Western Spy office.

J. Carpenter regarding the coroner's sale of the property of Andrew Lamen seized at the suit of Robert Johnson.

Thomas Rawlins regarding a meeting of the Hamilton County commissioners.

Henry Hafer regarding a promissary note to Robert Baily, of Cincinnati. He also continues his baking business on Main Street, Cincinnati.

Wm. Perry wants to hire a shoemaker in Franklin.

A notice regarding the sale of the Cincinnati University.

Thomas Bishop lost a receipt book in Cincinnati.

Volume 1, Saturday, 8 December 1810, No. 13

Paul Saunders, in St. Clairs township, Butler County, wants to exchange good

potter's ware for clean cotton and linen rags.
Ezekiel Hutchinson, on Mill Creek, regarding a fox chase.
John Johnston, Indian Agent at Fort Wayne, about trespassers on Indian land.
Jeptha Garnigus, living in Fairfield township, reports a stray mare.
Frederic Miller reports that Benedic Stoner, in Twin township, Preble County, found a mare that was appraised by Martin Russel and Peter Star.
Archelaus Alloway, in Boone County, Kentucky, reports a stray horse.
Isaac Mills reports that John Kenyon, living in Hamilton County on the plantation of Edward Hunt, found a mare, appraised by Caleb Asberry & Lewis Dunn.

Volume 1, Saturday, 15 December 1810, No. 14
The state legislature met at Zanesville. Mentions Thomas Kirker, Edward Tiffin, Carlos A. Norton, Ralph Osborn, Edward Sherlock, Adam Betz.
Luke Foster, in Springfield township, wants to buy wheat delivered to the mill belonging to Christopher Walker on Mill Creek.
John S. Gano and William Ruffin give militia orders regarding a court martial.

Volume 1, Saturday, 22 December 1810, No. 15
Proceedings of the legislature mention Mr. Corwin, Mr. Heaton, Mr. Marple, Mr. Putnam, Mr. Woods, Mr. Hitchcock, Mr. Clark, Mr. Imlay, Mr. Morrow, Mr. Campbell, Mr. M'Lene, Thomas Morris, Mr. Pritchard, Mr. Pollock, Mr. Coulter, Mr. Faulks, Mr. Buel, Mr. Ford, Return J. Meigs, jun.
A note regarding the election of a senator mentions Mr. Worthington, Mr. Pritchard and Mr. Huntington.
Governor Samuel Huntington's address to the Senate and House is printed.
The inaugural speech of Gov. Return Jonathan Meigs, jun., is printed.
A note regarding the boat belonging to Col. Chambers of Lawrenceburg.
J. Carpenter has offered his tavern for rent in Cincinnati.
Hannah Hilditch, executrix of the estate of Samuel Hilditch, dec'd, late of Columbia township, Hamilton County, regarding the estate sale.
James Matson, Ezekiel Hall, Thomas Rawlins and Geo. Williamson submit the annual statement of the Hamilton County commissioners.

Volume 1, Saturday, 29 December 1810, No. 16
Mr. M'Cormic gives the results of the Hamilton County census of 1810.
Proceedings of the Ohio Legislature mention John and Peter Sells (living on the Scioto River almost five miles from Worthington, Franklin County), James Findlay, Joseph Darlingnon, Wm. M'Farland, W. Silliman, Reasin Beall, Thomas Elliott of Jefferson County, George Todd, Alexander M'Beth of Champaign County, Farmers' Manufacturing Company of Little Miami, Return Jonathan Meigs, Mr. Pritchard, Thomas Worthington, Mr. Huntington, Mr. Todd, Mr. Bigger, Mr. Morris, Mr. Kirker.
J. Carpenter & Company want to hire a post rider to carry the Western Spy.
A report on the case of the State of Ohio vs. Ebenezer Case, alias Ebenezer Eldridge, for counterfeiting. The attorneys were Elias Glover and Jacob Burnet for the state and Col. J. Munroe and Thos. Rawlins for the defendent.
Obituary: James Lowes died in Springfield township on 15 December 1810.
Robert Gillaspey, in Cincinnati, wants to hire taylors.
Daniel Symmes, in Cincinnati, reports a stray horse.
Dix & Farrar, in Cincinnati, want to buy tallow at the Columbian Inn.

FREEMAN'S JOURNAL AND CHILLICOTHE ADVERTISER

Volume 1, Friday, 11 July 1800, No. 12

Walter Buell received a new shipment of medicines at his Chillicothe store.

Joseph Tiffin, post master, enters a list of letters left at the Post Office at Chillicothe that includes William Austen at Chillicothe, Samuel Armstrong at Columbia, Thomas Barr near the Picuway Plain at Scioto, Catharine Britton near Chillicothe, John Blare at Chillicothe Scioto, Joseph Buck at PeePee Scioto, Isaac Cook at Chillicothe, Abraham Claypoole near Chillicothe, George Disebauck near Chillicothe Town, Emd. Freeman (editor at Chillicothe), John Fremore at Chillicothe Scioto, Richard Haughton (dancing master at Chillicothe), Adam Hosuck on the Scioto above Chillicothe, E. Johnston on the Hockhocking to the care of Mr. Laremer, James Kelgore at Chillicothe, Elizha Kelly at Chillicothe on the Scioto River, William Laughlin on the Ohio near the mouth of Scioto, Alexander Laverly in care of Uriah Barber near Chillicothe, Archibald M'Donald near Chillicothe, Adam M'Murdie at Chillicothe, John Robbins living near the Scioto River, William Tremble (3 miles from the Hockhocking), Mary Ward on Little Scioto, David Watson (two miles from Chillicothe, living with Jos. Camble).

Thomas M'Donald, near Chillicothe, has a yoke of oxen for sale.

M'Landburgh & Candlish, in Chillicothe, want to buy cattle and sheep.

John Rutherford wants to establish a ferry across the Scioto at his house.

Samuel Howard wants to establish a ferry at his house.

John Brown has military land on the Little Miami and Paint Creek for sale. Apply to Thomas Worthington near Chillicothe.

John Brown has opened a house of entertainment on the road from Chillicothe to Limestone near the Falls of Paint Creek.

Solomon Cox, living on Salt Lick Creek at the ford on the old Indian Trace, reports two stray horses.

A note regarding the Fourth of July celebration in Alexandria, at the mouth of the Scioto, mentions Thomas Hart.

Edward Tiffin regarding taxes owed on lands in Ross County.

Daken Payne, for Aaron Cherry, regarding a horse in possession of Daniel M'Farland. It was stolen from Aaron Cherry by Big John Cherry.

John Galbraith has opened a store in Chillicothe in the house lately occupied by Maj. Langham. He will take ginseng, deerskins and furs as payment.

Reuben Abrams, at Chillicothe, regarding claims against Ross County.

Volume 1, Friday, 22 August 1800, No. 18

Edm. Freeman regarding payment due for the Freeman's Journal.

Joseph Kerr, at Manchester in the North-western Territory, has military land for sale and mentions William Fowler, John Wilkins, jun., Hardon's Creek, Rattle Snake Fork of Paint Creek, Eli Williams on Buckskin Creek, John Phillips, and the heirs of William Giles. Apply to Henry Massie at Chillicothe.

John M'Dougal, at Chillicothe, has land for sale on Paint Creek.

Sam. Finley, at Chillicothe, reports a stray cow.

John M'Dougal says he has recommenced the mercantile business at his former store in Chillicothe.

James Denny, collector at the Office of Inspection, regarding taxes due on stills and distilleries.

Jer. M'Lean, Collector for Ross County, regarding land taxes due.

John M'Dougall says that during his absence from Chillicothe his accounts were handled by William Creighton, Jun. He expects to go to Philadelphia soon or to send Mr. Vertner for him.

A. Stewart says he has sold his goods to John M'Dougall and "expect shortly to leave the Territory and shall be gone for some time."

John M'Dougal regarding a note he gave to Walter Buell of Chillicothe.

Thomas Gregg asks those indebted to him to settle their accounts.

William Cooper regarding his baking business in Chillicothe.
Obituary: Mrs. Elizabeth Collins, wife of Wm. Collins, in Alexandria, on Monday evening, August 11, 1800, of child bed fever. She was buried on Tuesday and a sermon was delivered by Rev. Mr. Jackson.
John M'Dougal, in Chillicothe, wants to buy butter and beef cattle.
Michael Baldwin wants two men to settle on the Whetstone River at the Old Delaware Town, 25 miles from Franklington.
Benj. Urmston wants to establish a ferry across the Scioto at Chillicothe.
James Parish, at Lexington, Ky., about runaway slaves, George & Phillis.

Volume 1, Friday, 5 September 1800, No. 20
Lucas Sullivant regarding the establishment of roads in Ross County.
T. Worthington, at Walnut Grove, has land for sale on the Scioto near Maj. Dunlap's house. Apply to Thos. V. Swearingen "who resides at my house".
John M'Dougal wants to buy beef cattle and butter. He will soon establish a distillery and brewery in Ross County.
John M'Dougal asks those indebted to him to settle their accounts at his store in Chillicothe or to Wm. Creighton, Sen.
E. Langham, at Chillicothe, is a candidate for the General Assembly.
Wm. Creighton, attorney, regarding the suit in Ross County Court of Common Pleas, of Bazil Abrams vs. Charles Brotherlin.
Jacob Smith, at Falls of Paint Creek, is a candidate for General Assembly.
E. Freeman says "having disposed of my right and title to this office, request those in arrears to make immediate payment".
John M'Dougal regarding a lot he exchanged with Walter Buell.
Valentine Bishong asks those indebted to him to settle their accounts.

Volume 1, Friday, 12 September 1800, No. 21
M'Landburg & Candlish, at Chillicothe, want to buy beef cattle.
D. Duncan, at Franklinton, wants to hire a cooper to make barrels at the Sandusky Bay. Apply to Thos. F. Blair.
Lucas Sullivant has military land for sale on Darby's Creek.
Saml. Finley will not be a candidate in the next election.
James Denny, Collector, regarding taxes due on carriages in Chillicothe.

Volume 1, Friday, 19 September 1800, No. 22
Andrew Noteman, opposite the mouth of Derby Creek, reports that his wife, Catharine Noteman, left him, and he won't honor her debts.
E. Langham, at Chillicothe, asks those indebted to him to pay their bills.
John M'Dougal will take hides, furs and deerskins in exchange for goods.

Volume 1, Friday, 26 September 1800, No. 23
Thomas Morris has opened a house of public entertainment in Williamsburgh on the road from Cincinnati to Chillicothe.
Obituary: Jacob Saylor, Sen., died on 21 September 1800, near Pickaway, leaving a widow and a large family of children.
Jer. M'Lene, Sheriff of Ross County, regarding the upcoming elections.
James Crawford, at Indian Creek, is a candidate for the General Assembly.
John M'Dougal wants to buy corn fed pork in Chillicothe.
John Clarke regarding a bond he gave to Isaac Eaton.
John M'Dougal wants to hire a cooper at his store in Chillicothe.

SCIOTO GAZETTE AND CHILLICOTHE ADVERTISER

Volume 1, Friday, 10 October 1800, No. 25
Col. Thomas Worthington "stands a poll" at the ensuing election. If he is absent, Col. Finley will represent him.
Obituary: William Port, Sen., and William Port, Jun., died near Chillicothe "a few days since".
John M'Dougal asks those indebted to him to settle their accounts with William Creighton in Chillicothe.
The printing office has moved to Col. Worthington's house on second street.
Winship & Willis have purchased the Freeman's Journal from Edmund Freeman and renamed the paper the Scioto Gazette & Chillicothe Advertiser.
Walter Buell asks those indebted to him to settle their accounts.
A list of letters at the Post Office in Chillicothe includes John Anderson, Frederick Braucher, Alexander Crawford, Bennett Cook, John Chenoweth, Robert Carson, Jacob Decamps, John Dunkill, Nehemiah Davis, David Dawson, George Emery, John Daman, Robert Findley, Nathan Gregg, David Gregory, John Imble, Thomas Herey, Joseph Hopkins, Robert Huston, Daniel Hayway, Robert Justice, Samuel Johnson, Daniel Lambant, John Lund, John M'Lane, Jacob Medsker, Josiah M'Kennie, John M'Coy, Susanna Mitchell, Robert Patrick, John Pusley, George Porter, John Rutherford, Henry Smith, Daniel Stookey, John Shields, Peter Sturgeon, John Thompson, Levi Woodward, Joseph Wilson, Hugh Woods, Isaiah White. Entered by Joseph Tiffin, assistant post master.
John M'Dougal has a new shipment of goods for sale in Chillicothe.
Aaron Stephenson, in Chillicothe, wants an apprentice to the cooper's trade.
Anthony Franklin, at the Falls of Paint Creek, lost notes from Wm. Mitchel, of Nicholas County, Kentucky, and John Stokesbury.
Thomas Gregg writes a letter to the public regarding his contract with James Crawford mentions Mr. Keys, Mr. Komer, Mr. Baldwin. He includes depositions from Samuel Smith and John G. Macan.

Volume 1, Thursday, 16 October 1800, No. 26
Results of an election for representatives from Ross County to serve in the General Assembly show that Edward Tiffin, Maj. Elias Langham and Col. Thomas Worthington are the winners over Capt. Thomas Gregg, William Patton, Jacob Smith and James Crawford.
John M'Dougal has a new shipment of goods from New Orleans at his store.
Lucas Sullivant has military lands for sale.

Volume 1, Thursday, 23 October 1800, No. 27
A note regarding a fight on Saturday, 18 October, between Charles Bruce and Benjamin Davis, at Bruce's house near Hamilton, in which Davis was killed.
Col. Nathaniel Massie and Joseph Darlington are elected from Adams County.
John Smith, Francis Dunlavy, Jeremiah Morrow, Daniel Reader, John Ludlow, Moses Miller and Jacob White are elected representatives from Hamilton County.
William Lytle is elected to replace Aaron Cadwell, resigned.
Winship & Willis about payments for the newspaper, mention Mr. Freeman.
Thomas Worthington, at Walnut Grove, has land for sale near Maj. Dunlap's.
John G. Macan, at Chillicothe, regarding locations of military land.
M'Landburgh & Candlish ask those indebted to them to settle their accounts.
George Haines asks those indebted to him to settle their accounts.

Volume 1, Thursday, 6 November 1800, No. 29
Election returns from Cincinnati mention M. Miller, J. Smith, P. Dunlevy, J. Morrow, D. Reeder, J. Ludlow, J. White, Wm. Lytle, A. Cadwell.
Benjamin Urmston asks those indebted to him to settle their accounts.

John Shannon and Jarret Mennefee report two runaway slaves, Roger & Ben. Deliver to William Brooks near Limestone.

A list of the legislature mentions Gov. Arthur St.Clair, Mr. Olivar, Mr. Burnett, Mr. Vance, Mr. Finlay, Mr. W.C. Schenck, John Riley. Representatives from Ross County are Mr. Tiffin, Mr. Worthington, Mr. Langham, Mr. S. Finly; for Hamilton: Mr. Smith, Mr. Ludlow, Mr. Benham, Mr. Goforth, Mr. M'Mellon, Mr. Lytle, Mr. Martin; for Adams: Mr. Massie and Mr. Darlinton; for Washington: Mr. Meigs and Mr. Fearin; for Jefferson: Mr. Pritchard and Mr. Kimberly; for Wayne: Mr. Sibley, Mr. Visgar, C.F. Chebert de Joncaire. Also mentions William M'Mellon, W.H. Harrison, Paul Fearin of Washington County.

Obituary: Edmund Freeman, late editor and proprietor of the Freeman's Journal, died last week at Beaver Creek on Mad River.

N. & R. Gregg, at Chillicothe, ask those indebted to them to pay their bills.

N. & J. Zane, attorneys for E. Zane, regarding the sale of lots at his town at the crossing of the Hockhocking River.

Volume 1, Thursday, 13 November 1800, No. 30

The speech of Gov. St.Clair to the Legislature is printed.

Robert Oliver and W.C. Schenck give the legislature's answer to the governor.

Ar. St.Clair's reply to the legislature is printed.

A note about the Society of the Cincinnati meeting at Marietta. Mentions Gen. Rufus Putnam, Col. R.J. Meigs, Robert Oliver.

Volume 1, Thursday, 20 November 1800, No. 31

The proceedings of the General Assembly mention Hon. Henry Harrison, Mr. Meigs, Mr. Lytle, Mr. Sibley, Mr. Fearing, Mr. Langham, Mr. Darlington, Mr. Benham, Mr. Kimberley, Mr. Findlay, Mr. Worthington, Mr. Smith, Mr. Goforth, Mr. M'Millan, Mr. Martin, Mr. Edgar, Mr. Ludlow, Mr. Visger, Rufus Putnam, Benjamin Ives Gilman, Jonathan Stone, Mr. Schenck, William M'Millan, William Henry Harrison, Paul Fearing, Mr. Chobert, Mr. Pritchard.

Volume 1, Thursday, 27 November 1800, No. 32

The proceedings of the General Assembly mention Rev. William Speer, Rufus Putnam, Benjamin Ives Gilman, Jonathan Stone, Henry VanderBurgh.

John M'Dougal wants to hire a cooper at his store in Chillicothe.

Joseph M'Coy, administrator of the estate of Rachael Brown, late of Chillicothe in Ross County, dec'd, regarding the estate sale at John Jackson's house.

Nathaniel Massie has land for sale.

Robert W. Finly has land for sale adjoining Chillicothe.

Samuel Freeman, administrator of the estate of Edmund Freeman, late of Chillicothe, printer, dec'd, regarding the estate settlement. Make payments to Winship & Willis in Chillicothe.

C. Platter reports a mare that strayed or was stolen from his house between the Falls and the Crossings of Paint Creek.

John Buzzard reports a stray horse. Deliver to Maj. James Dunlap on Scioto.

Reubren Abrams regarding the meeting of the commissioners of Ross County at the house of Wm. Keys.

John M'Dougal has just received a shipment of winter goods at his store.

James Phillips wants to hire a Windsor chair maker.

Volume 1, Thursday, 4 December 1800, No. 33

A letter from Return Jonathan Meigs, Jun., and Joseph Gilman to Col. Robert Oliver and Edward Tiffin is printed.

A letter to Gov. Arthur St.Clair from the inhabitants of Gallipolis.

Marriage: Wm. M'Farland married Miss Peggy Ferguson on Tuesday evening last, 2 December 1800.

A letter to Winship & Willis from E. Langham is printed.

John M'Dougal asks those indebted to him to settle their accounts.

Volume 1, Thursday, 11 December 1800, No. 34

A letter from Ar. St.Clair to Hon. Joseph Gilman and Return Jonathan Meigs.

Edward Tiffin and John Reily write a letter to the public.

The speech of Ar. St.Clair to the legislature is printed.
James Denny, collector of the revenue, regarding taxes on distillers.
Samuel Carpenter, justice of the peace in Ross County, regarding an attachment against the goods of Isaac Heaton. Mentions John Keens, tavern keeper at Hockhocking.
John M'Dougal regarding the delivery of the pork he purchased.
Hugh Rankins asks those indebted to him to settle their accounts at the house of Wm. Lamb in Chillicothe.

Volume 1, Thursday, 18 December 1800, No. 35
Edward Tiffin, Robert Oliver and Ar. St.Clair regarding a new law.
A list of laws passed by the first General Assembly of the North-west Territory mentions Doctor William Burnet, the elder, the town of Athens, Lucy Petit.
William Speer, in Chillicothe, asks for the return of a borrowed book.
J. Crocker & N. Kennedy ask those indebted to them to pay their bills.

Volume 1, Thursday, 25 December 1800, No. 36
The proceedings of the legislature mentions William M'Millan, Joseph Gilman, Return Jonathan Meigs, jun.
D. Duncan, at Franklinton, wants to hire workers to manufacture salt. He also encourages 4 to 5 families to settle at Duncan's Lick.
Abner Meeker and Ephraim Bates, overseers of the poor, at Chillicothe, about the payment of poor taxes.
James Kelly, at Salt Lick, regarding notes he gave to John Mays.

Volume 1, Thursday, 8 January 1801, No. 38
Notes from the legislature mention Lucy Petet's divorce.
E. Langham will act for the Territorial Treasurer in the latter's absence.
John Carlisle & Company have a shipment of goods at their store in Chillicothe.
William Irwin, for Alexander M'Laughlin & Company, regarding their new store in Chillicothe opposite John Carlisle & Company.
A list of letters left at the Post Office in Chillicothe includes Isaac Brodley, John and Hugh Boyle, John Baird or Samuel Hamill, John Bedeford, Jonathan Bereman, John Beasley, Abraham Holmes Beyfield, James Connel in care of Philip Woolf, John M'Climmons in care of Capt. Claypole, John Calloway at the mouth of Scioto, Samuel Davison near Chillicothe, Joseph Dickson at Franklinton, Samuel Gates, Joseph Husam near Chillicothe, Samuel Hyer, Francis Hollinshead, William Johnston at Franklinton, John Leeth, Alexander Latta, William Lamb, William Oliver, John Mooney, Samuel M'Farland in care of John Beasley, William M'Cluney at Chillicothe, John M'Donald near Chillicothe, William Parker in care of Mr. Carlisle, Jonathan Rinicks, John Rollins, John Rodgers (16 miles from Chillicothe in care of John Sharp), Barney Restine on Walnut Creek, Esquire Stoops, Hezekiah Smith at Chillicothe, Edward Shadons, Robert Smith at Chillicothe, George Turner at Chillicothe, Robert Templeton at Old Chillicothe, John Vanhorn, Philip Woolf, Robert Worthington, Samuel Willett at Hocken, Uni Welton at Chillicothe, Youell Williams at Chillicothe, Alexander White at Chillicothe, Joseph Tiffin.
M'Landburg & Candlish, at Chillicothe, ask those indebted to pay their bills.
Thomas Worthington, E. Langham, John Collet, William Chandler and Evorard Harr will meet at Joseph Tiffin's house in Chillicothe to take bids from persons willing to build a Courthouse in Ross County.
John Watts warns people not to cut timber on his land adjoining Mr. Massie and Mr. M'Arthur near Chillicothe.

Volume 1, Thursday, 29 January 1801, No. 41
Edward Tiffin, Robert Oliver and Ar. St.Clair print laws of the Territory.
A letter from the citizens of Marietta regarding statehood.
John M'Dougal asks those indebted to him to pay William Niblack.
Wm. Niblack, for John M'Dougal, wants to buy rye and corn.
A note regarding the appointment of a governor of the Northwest Territory mentions Gov. St.Clair and Mr. Tracy.
James Johnston, at Chillicothe, asks those indebted to him to pay their bills.
George Haines, at Chillicothe, asks those indebted to him to pay their bills.

John Hubbard has a lot for sale next door to William Creighton's office.

Everard Harr has cane for sale at his shop in Chillicothe next door to Colonel Finley on Water Street. He speaks of the "thirty years experience that he has had of the Weaving Business and Reed Making, in different parts of Pennsylvania."

The citizens of Franklinton want to hire a school teacher.

Thomas Duff, Jun., living at Benjamin Urmston's at the sign of the Black Horse in Chillicothe, has land for sale.

Benjamin Ives Gilman, at Marietta, regarding the suit in Washington County Court of Common Pleas of Adamson Tannahill vs. Anselm Tupper.

Gov. Arthur St.Clair gives a message to the citizens of the Territory.

Volume 1, Thursday, 5 February 1801, No. 42

John M'Coy, Jun., Collector of the Revenue, who was appointed in place of James Denny, resigned, regarding the Office of Inspection at Chillicothe.

William Clark is appointed chief justice of Indiana Territory. Also Henry VanderBurgh is second judge and John Griffin is third judge of Indiana Territory.

Thomas Davidson, of Wayne Township, regarding land he sold to John S. Wills.

J. Reed regarding a stud horse at the stables of Capt. Thomas Gregg, Chillicothe, and at "Mr. Crouse's mill, Kinnickanic, 8 miles from Chillicothe".

Volume 1, Thursday, 12 February 1801, No. 43

Daniel Symmes, in Cincinnati, reports a stray horse that he bought from John S. Wills of Chillicothe. Deliver to William Austin, Chillicothe, or Mr. Kain at Williamsburg in Clermont County.

Duncan M'Arthur has land for rent at "Col. Anderson's cat tail priari".

Volume 1, Thursday, 19 February 1801, No. 44

A letter from Winthrop Sargent, in Mississippi Territory, in answer to the accusations of Mr. Davis. Mentions Gov. St.Clair, Judge Parsons, Judge Symmes, Judge Varnum, Cato West, Narsworthy Hunter, Hugh Davis, Col. Clark, D. Clark, Mr. C.C. Claiborne, Robert Ashley, Gen. Wilkinson, Hon. T.T. Davis of Kentucky.

E. Langham regarding the stud horse, Gimcrack, at William Keys' stable in Chillicothe. Includes a pedigree from Warner Lewis in Woodford County.

John Vanmetre, constable of Pickaway township, Ross County, near the Hockhocking River, about a suit of Samuel Carpenter against Isaac Eaton. Mentions Mrs. Eaton, Lawyer Creighton in Chillicothe, Samuel Burk, John Kuntz, Mr. Hunter, Mr. Harlin, Mr. Convers, Mr. Orr, Mr. Edge, James Convers, Mr. Miller.

Henry Huston wants to establish a road from his house, past Rev. William Speer's meeting house, to Thomas Crowse's mill on Kennekanic.

Alexander Fowler, in Aleghaney township, regarding a power of attorney to John Barnett of Manchester, Adams County. Since Barnett is "about removing from this country to the Mezzura" (Missouri?) he revokes the power of attorney.

The partnership of John Crocker and Nathan Kennedy is dissolved.

Volume 1, Thursday, 12 March 1801, No. 47

Walter Buell has medicine and furniture for sale at his shop in Chillicothe.

Philip Wolffe wants to establish a road from John Crows's mill to the head of the Pickaway Plains.

Lucas Sullivant, at Franklinton, has military land for sale.

Jer. M'Lean, Sheriff of Ross County, in Chillicothe, about sheriff's sales at the house of Wm. Keys of the property of Joseph Wilson at the suit of Wm. Keys; that of James Mitchell at the suit of Kennedy and others; that of Samuel Shaw at the suit of John Montgomery; and that of William Cooper at the suit of William Guthrey.

John Brown lost a pocket book between Zanesville and Samuel Chinno's, 25 miles from Muskingum, containing papers mentioning John Gantz, David Gardner, Andrew Gantz, David Enoch, Abner Broadway, Samuel Hendric, George Carn, Daniel Marsh, Jonathan Jaquess, Alexander Kerr, William Edgar, James Parker, Joseph Tiffin in Chillicothe, Mr. M'Intire at Zanesville.

Henry Massie, Collector, regarding taxes on the Virginia military lands.

Duncan M'Arthur, Frederick Bray, Thomas M'Donnald, John M'Dougal, Charles Mackin, Benjamin Urmston, Samuel Parris, William Keys, Joseph Potter, Furgu Moor, John Beswell, William M'Donnald, William Rogers and James Sibbet about a road from Chillicothe. Mentions Mr. N. Willis, printer in Chillicothe.

J. Crocker & N. Kennedy, at Chillicothe, say the debts of their business are in the hands of John Carlisle for collection.

Doctor John Crocker may be found at Benjamin Urmston's.

Thomas Gibson, Auditor, regarding the collection of the taxes.

James Ferguson, at Chillicothe, asks those indebted to pay their bills.

John Carlisle & Company ask those in debt to John Collerick for the Western Telegraphe to make payments to them.

Ruben Abrams, at Chillicothe, asks those persons indebted to Doctor M'Adow to settle their accounts.

R.W. Findlay asks that his books be returned to Joseph Potter in Chillicothe.

Volume 1, Thursday, 26 March 1801, No. 49

An account of the drowning death of Mr. Fairburn, of Rockingham County, Virginia, at the crossings of Paint Creek.

William West, in Lexington, Kentucky, has land for sale on Deer Creek next door to the surveys of Jack Brown and Richard Call. Apply to Winn Winship, Chillicothe.

Jos. Convers, for D. Woodbridge, Jun., & Company, regarding the robbery at Woodbridge's store at the crossings of Hockhocking on Zane's road on March 7th.

Sheshbazzan Bentley, in Washington County, Penn., regarding a horse stolen from Joseph Tiffin's lot in Chillicothe.

Volume 1, Thursday, 16 April 1801, No. 52

Jer. M'Lene reports on the recent census taken in Ross County.

An account of an accident on Paint Creek on Tuesday, 14 April 1801, in which Mr. Downs, an "unfortunate old man", lost almost all of his property.

Nathan Kennedy regarding an arbitration bond between John Crocker and himself, with John Carlisle as umpire.

Adam Rice regarding a note he gave to Dr. Nathan Kennedy for rent on the house he now occupies. He now finds that Kennedy doesn't own the house.

Phielding Hubbard regarding a note from Joseph Sheerer for property he bought from Hubbard and William Rector.

A list of letters at the Post Office in Chillicothe includes Jonathan Anderson in care of J. Tiffin, Ele Bereman in Chillicothe, Mr. Beard at Hocken, J. & H. Boyle, David Bankard near Chillicothe, Robert Boggess, John Britten, David Bonner, Walter Bewell, John Collett in Chillicothe, William Cochran, Samuel Cissna, Stephen Clark at PeePee, John Conn at Chillicothe, Robert Chewshwell, John Car, Joseph Clark, Jonathan Clark, James Denny, James Dorian, David Duncan, Joseph Eker at Hocken, James Frances for Alexander M'Harry, David Gates, Robert Greer on Scioto, Thomas Gregg, James Hays, Johnston Hamphell, Joseph Hoffman at Chillicothe, Doct. Thomas Harsey, Joseph Hunter, Alexander Harper in care of J. Denny, Cornelius Johnston, Samuel Knox, Frances M'Clelland in care of J. Beazley, Capt. Edward Meeks, Jun., James Mitchell in care of J. Clark, John Moots, Robert M'Hary in care of Mr. M'Collister in Chillicothe, Joseph M'Clelland, John M'Clenaugh in care of J. January, Robert M'Mahen in care of Hugh Coehran, William M'Farland, Robt. Patton, Thomas Noland near Chillicothe, John Philips in care of J. Carlisle, Jacob Powers, William Rogers, John Richardson near Deer Creek, John Reed (care of Robt. Rolston living 12 miles from the Three Islands), David Reed at Darby's Creek, Hamilton Rogers at North Fork, Jacob Smith (merchant in Chillicothe), Lucas Sullivant, Samuel Thomas, Andrew Thompson at High Bank, Aram Vansicle on Mill Creek, Robert Vance, William Warren, William Wells. Joseph Tiffin, assistant post master.

Rueben Abrams, at Chillicothe, regarding the order by Edward Tiffin, clerk of the Court of Quarter Sessions for Ross County, about taxes.

John Crocker enters the statement of the accounts of Dr. Crocker and Dr. Nathan Kennedy. The accounts were arbitrated by Col. Samuel Finley and John G. Macan. Mentions W. Porter, J. M'Dougal.

John M'Candlish, living on Big Belly, up the Scioto, regarding a mare that strayed or was stolen from the stable of William Keys in Chillicothe.

Joseph Sheerer regarding his note to Phielding Hubbard.

John Carlisle asks those indebted to Doctors Crocker and Kennedy to settle their accounts.

Robert Worthington has a good riding horse for sale.

Volume II, Thursday, 30 April 1801, No. 54
N. Willis, editor of the Scioto Gazette, asks those indebted to him to pay their bills to Maj. Belie at Alexandria.

John Crocker asks those indebted to himself or Dr. Kennedy to make their payments to John Carlisle.

Jeremiah M'Lene, Sheriff of Ross County, regarding sheriff's sales at the house of William Keys in Chillicothe of the property of Charles Brothulu at the suit of Bazil Abrams; that of Samuel Shaw at the suit of John Montgomery; that of John and Samuel Jackson at the suit of Samuel Smith and others.

Benjamin Urmston regarding a road from the ferry opposite his house in Chillicothe to the road leading to Crowse's mill.

T. Worthington, Register of the Land Office, regarding land for sale.

John Beasley, of Manchester, lost a pocket book between John Draber's and Jesse Worthington's on Zane's road in Adams County. Including papers mentioning Mr. Burke on Paint Creek, John Ellison of Manchester. Deliver to William Keys in Chillicothe, Maj. Brown at Limestone or John Draber on Zane's Road.

Nathan Kennedy, residing at Thomas Gregg's, regarding his business. Also regarding his accounts with John Crocker now in the hands of John Carlisle.

W. Winship and N. Willis have dissolved their partnership. N. Willis will keep the books and continue to print the Scioto Gazette.

Volume II, Thursday, 7 May 1801, No. 55
Marriage: John Carlisle, merchant, married Miss Eliza Mann on Thursday evening, 30 April 1801.

John Lile, living at Franklinton in Ross County, regarding a stray mare. Deliver to Moses Brown at Kinnickanic.

M'Landburgh & Candlish, at Chillicothe, have a new shipment of goods.

N. Kennedy about the dispute with Dr. John Crocker over their accounts. He mentions Mr. John Carlisle, Samuel Finley, J.G. Macan.

Volume II, Thursday, 14 May 1801, No. 56
Marriage: Walter Buell, of Chillicothe, married Miss Cogswell, daughter of Doct. Cogswell, at Paris, Kentucky. (no date given)

J. Crocker writes a letter to Dr. N. Kennedy regarding their dispute and mentions Mr. Carlisle, Col. Finley, Mr. Macan.

Mark Causland, at the Falls of Ohio, reports a runaway slave named Sam who calls himself Samuel Galloway, age 25-30. Deliver to Andrew Boyd of Manchester or Peter B. Almsbury at Washington.

Volume II, Thursday, 21 May 1801, No. 57
An account of a fight on Monday evening, 18 May 1801, in Chillicothe, between John Bates/Betz and John Bowman in which Bates was stabbed to death. Bowman was arrested for murder. "This rash and unreflecting man was late from Berkeley County, Virginia, has a wife and family." Bates was buried Tuesday.

Doct. John Edmiston has opened a "medical shop" adjoining Elias Langham's.

Wm. Lamb regarding working on the streets in Chillicothe.

N. Kennedy writes more on his dispute with John Crocker. He says Crocker abandoned his wife. He mentions James Phillips.

Volume II, Thursday, 28 May 1801, No. 58
More about the fight between Mr. Bates and Mr. Bowman.

Thomas Gregg asks those indebted to him to settle their accounts.

John M'Mullon, living on Scioto, 3 miles below Salt Lick Creek, found a mare.

Volume II, Thursday, 4 June 1801, No. 59
John M'Dougal has a new shipment of goods for sale at his store, Chillicothe.

John Nolind wants to establish a ferry at his house on the Scioto River.

Robert Beale regarding his power of attorney to Col. Elias Langham of Ross County. Also a note from Elias Langham about this.

Col. Elias Langham & Col. James Dunlap give notice to the following officers of a meeting in Chillicothe: Maj. William Patton, Maj. Jeremiah M'Lene, Maj. Duncan M'Arthur, Maj. James Manary, Capt. Isaac Dawson, Capt. Thomas Gregg, Capt.

William Lamb, Capt. Samuel Davis, Capt. John Chenoweth, Capt. David Shelby, Capt. Ebenezer Petty and Capt. John Barns.

John Mathews, at Zanesville, has military lands for sale.

Benjamin Welch, living near Chillicothe, regarding a stray mare.

Reuben Abrams, administrator of the estate of William Port, dec'd, regarding the estate settlement.

Joseph Potter, administrator of the estate of George Steel, dec'd, regarding the estate settlement.

Volume II, Thursday, 17 June 1801, No. 61

Daniel Symmes regarding a General Court of the Territory at Cincinnati held before Hon. John Cleves Symmes, Hon. Joseph Gilman and Hon. Return Jonathan Meigs. The following are appointed Commissioners of Bail: Benjamin Ives Gilman, Dr. Matthews, Isaac Pierce, Alban Bingham and Robert Oliver for Washington County; James Silvers, Robert Benham, Daniel Symmes, Daniel C. Cooper and John L. Gano for Hamilton County; James Henry and James May for Wayne County; John Billi, Geo. Gordon and Joseph Darlington for Adams County; Edward Tiffin and Samuel Finley for Ross County; John Ward for Jefferson County; Calvin Pease and Benjamin Tappin for Trumbull County.

John M'Dougal regarding his accounts which were in the hands of William Creighton, Jun. Those indebted to him should settle their accounts.

Thomas Dick lost a great coat between Mr. Urmston's and Mr. Massie's field.

Dr. Samuel M'Adow has returned from Baltimore with a supply of medicines.

Peachy Harrison, living with Dr. Tiffin's family, about his medical practice.

Thomas Scott regarding his business of attorney at law.

Thomas Worthington, justice of the peace for Ross County, about the petition of John Brown against Bazil Abrams, mentions Joseph Tiffin. Also a note from Joseph Potter, constable of Scioto township, about the property of Bazil Abrams.

Orasha Strong, justice of the peace in Ross County, regarding the suit of William Griswold vs. Abner B. Ackley.

John Hopkins regarding the town at the place called Miller's Bank, below the Pe Pee on the Scioto River. Col. Guthry is starting a saw mill there.

Thomas Smith regarding a stray horse. Deliver to J. Sharp in Chillicothe.

A note about property, left at Limestone with Mr. Brown, of a Mr. Pancake who came down the Ohio from Wheeling to settle on the Hockhocking.

Thomas Gregg, at Chillicothe, has land for sale.

William Creighton, Sen., wants to hire laborers to work in Chillicothe.

Volume II, Thursday, 25 June 1801, No. 62

A letter from Charles Willing Byrd regarding the recent census.

John Carlisle asks those indebted to the late firm of Crocker & Kennedy to settle their accounts.

N. Kennedy writes another letter about his dispute with John Crocker. He says Crocker has left town and may be known by the name Doct. Hart or Doct. Hartshorn. He had been living at William Austin's in Chillicothe. He also owns a house and lot in Washington City. Kennedy gives a complete description of him.

Col. Elias Langham, Col. James Dunlap, Maj. Jeremiah M'Lene, Maj. Duncan M'Arthur, Capt. David Shelby, Capt. John Chenoweth, Capt. William Lamb, Capt. Thomas Gregg, Capt. John Barnes and Capt. Ebenezer Petty about the military districts of Ross County. John M'Coy is appointed clerk to the First Regiment. They mention Patton's run, James Furguson, Henry Abrams, Henry Massie's farm adjoining Chillicothe, William Darke, the settlement on Darby Creek, Michael Fisher, John Clouser, Doctor Huff's survey, Hoddy's mill, Heller's Bottom, Campbell's mill.

John M'Coy reports that Capt. Thomas Gregg was arrested by Col. Elias Langham for unofficer-like behavior.

William Nolin about the estate sale of Richard Nolin, of Ross County, dec'd.

Volume II, Thursday, 23 July 1801, No. 66

Doctor Scott has just commenced the practice of medicine in Chillicothe in the house lately occupied by Doctor Buell as an apothecary's shop.

James Martin regarding his practice of medicine in Chillicothe. He has just been to the mouth of the Scioto to get medicine.

Alexander M'Laughlin has a new shipment of goods for sale at his store nearly opposite John Carlisle & Company, in Chillicothe.

John Carlisle & Company want to buy pork at their store in Chillicothe.

Thomas Hinton, of Ross County, regarding the rumors of Moses Dawson, of Ross County, being guilty of felony in Kentucky. Witnessed by Reuben Abrams, Henry Abrams, William Devall, William Hinton and Isaac Dawson.

William Boyce, in Surry County, Virginia, has military land for sale on Todd's Fork of the Little Miami. Apply to David Sewell near the premises.

John Nolind wants to keep a ferry at his house on the Scioto River.

A note regarding the trial of John Bowman for the murder of John Betez. It is postponed due to the "indisposition of Judge Meigs".

Doctors Martin & Irvine regarding their practice of medicine in the house next door to Capt. Thomas Gregg's tavern in Chillicothe.

Nathan & Robert Gregg, in Chillicothe, ask those indebted to them to settle their accounts.

Humphrey Montgomery about the estate sale of Humphry Montgomery, dec'd.

Joseph Wilson says that he and his wife, Sarah Wilson, and four children were brought to Ross County from Berkeley County, Virginia, two years ago by the Widow Mary Hall. Though they were entitled to freedom then, they voluntarily indented themselves for another 5 years. Now Mrs. Hall is marrying Mr. Cox and wishes to sell Wilson's indenture. He says they will not serve anyone else.

J. Blair has a lot for sale in Chillicothe where Mr. Wherley lives next to Mr. Hubbard's store. Apply to Mr. Willis, printer.

Moses Bledsoe, near Mount Sterling, Kentucky, about a runaway slave named James. He went to Ohio with Adam, the property of Thomas Lamison.

Lucas Hawkins lost a pocket book between Chillocothe and Falls of Paint Cr.

John Hubbard, in Chillicothe, reports a stray mare. He bought the mare from Col. Elias Langham.

Michael Mullen reports a mare that strayed from him on Indian Creek. Deliver to Joseph Tiffin in Chillicothe.

D. Duncan, Jun., writes a letter to Mr. Willis regarding the ad placed by the partnership of James Abbott & Sons. He mentions his partnership with Ichabud Marshall. Mentions R. & J. Abbott.

John Carlisle & Company, at Chillicothe, ask those indebted to pay their bills.

R. & J. Abbott, surviving partners to the late firm of James Abbott & Sons, at Franklinton, request payment of debts. Pay to Ichabad Marshall, but not to David Duncan, Jun.

Ferguson & M'Farland have a new shipment of goods for sale at their store in Chillicothe, opposite the sign of the Red Lion.

John M'Dougall wants to buy corn.

A list of letters left at the Post Office in Chillicothe includes Samuel Allen in care of Mr. Lamb at Chillicothe, Francis Alexander, John & Hugh Boyle, Lewis Bible near Manchester, Robert Boggess, Eli Bereman, Samuel Clifton, Robert Coane, Maj. Jonathan Cass at Muskingum, Andrew Cherry at Chillicothe, Reuben Baxter at Franklinton, David Cowin or Zabud Rundle at Scioto, Coonrod Chrisman, Miss Lydia Champlin at Belville, John Collett, Jane Campbell in care of Joseph Vanhorn, Dr. John Corman at Chillicothe, Robert Chenewell near Chillicothe, Mrs. Dean in care of Abm. Dean, William Dumegan, George Emrick nine miles from Chillicothe, John Ewing on the road to Deerfield, Robert Ewing in care of Maj. Finley, Margaret Edgar at Mad River, Thomas Fanstee near Chillicothe, Jesse Fulton in care of Thomas Gregg, John Galloway near Pee Pee, Joseph Gifford, Mrs. Marean Gossert at Deer Creek, John Gilman at Chillicothe, Daniel Grubb, William Gessell in care of E. Carpenter, Samuel Hutchinson in care of Mr. Keys, Aaron Hedge in Chillicothe, Beltze Hess, Margaret Hemphill in care of John M'Connell, Mary Higgins, Samuel Henry, Harzava Horsington at Waterford, Thomas Hersy at Adams, Andrew Johnston at Chillicothe, Henry Kirkindall, John Lusk, John Loveless on Paint Creek near Chillicothe, Ellis Marshall near Chillicothe, Daniel M'Farland, Reuben Manneg near Chillicothe, John Matthews, John M'Cafferty, John Miller in care of Joseph Clark, Robert M'Mehan, John M'Clenehan in care of John Ellison, John Mitchell at Chillicothe, John M'Lene, John M'Mahan at Chillicothe, William Nicholson near Chillicothe, James Orr near Chillicothe, Simon Pool at Newport in Washington County, William Robison, Matthew Ritchey in care of Mr. Keys, John Rager, John

Mestine, Alex. Scott at Chillicothe, John Smith (printer at Chillicothe), Lucas Sullivant, Rev. Mr. Spear, David Shadd near the old Chillicothe, Isaac Shadden on Licking Creek, Andrew Simmermon, Robert Simpson at Chillicothe, Israel Stone up the Muskingum, John Thompson, William Turner at Chillicothe, Isaac Vanmeter at Chillicothe, Isaac Williams, senr., in care of D. Duncan, Bailey Washington at Chillicothe, Isaac Willits at Chillicothe, Winn Winship, George Williams (25 miles from Chillicothe), Isaac Warner, William Willson at Chillicothe, John Wallace at the Falls of Paint Creek, John Work at Chillicothe. Joseph Tiffin, assistant post master.

John S. Wills has houses and lots in Chillicothe for sale. They are presently occupied by Joseph Tiffin and John Carlisle.

John S. Wills requests the return of borrowed books.

Volume II, Thursday, 30 July 1801, No. 67

A note regarding the trial of John Bowman for the murder of John Betz.

Wm. C.C. Claiborne is appointed Governor of the Mississippi Territory.

John M'Dougal has land for sale on Paint Creek.

Z. Dawson reports the theft of a saddle from Reuben Abrams' stable.

Volume II, Thursday, 6 August 1801, No. 68

Account of the trial of John Bowman for the murder of John Betz mentions Judge Gilman, Judge Meigs, A. White, Michael Baldwin, William Creighton.

Doctor Buell has moved his shop to his new house in Chillicothe.

James & M'Coy want to buy pork at their store in Chillicothe.

Jeremiah M'Lene, sheriff, reports that territorial taxes are due.

Jacob Hubbard reports the escape of a bound black woman named Dolly.

Tilman Lewis, in Ross County, reports that his wife, Mary Lewis, has been disposing of his property and he won't honor her debts.

Joseph Willson and wife regarding the indenture they signed with Mrs. Hall in Berkely County, Virginia. They signed because Mrs. Hall threatened to sell them and take their four children with her to Ohio.

Volume II, Thursday, 13 August 1801, No. 69

Mrs. Patrick Chesnut, living about ten miles from Chillicothe, delivered quadruplets on Tuesday, 4 August 1801, but they all died.

Obituary: Rev. John Kennedy, at an advanced age, died Thursday, 6 August, and was buried on Friday.

N. Willis has land for sale in Nelson County, Kentucky. Apply to Col. Henry Crist living near the land.

John M'Dougal regarding his purchase of beef cattle.

Jacob Hubbard has brought three black children to this Territory to serve him until they are twenty-one years old.

R.F. Finley asks for the return of some borrowed books.

Volume II, Thursday, 20 August 1801, No. 70

William M'Millan is appointed U.S. Attorney for the District of Ohio.

Obituary: Doctor James Irwin, lately from the vicinity of Carlisle, Cumberland County, Pennsylvania, died Wednesday morning, 19 August 1801, at about nine o'clock. He was buried at 6 o'clock the same day.

Obituary: Capt. Caleb Stockton, age 28, son of David Stockton, died on Friday evening, 14 August 1801. He was buried on Sunday in Chillicothe.

John S. Wills has land for sale.

Amasa Delano has opened a house of entertainment at New Lancaster.

E. Langham regarding the suit of Philip Cherry vs. John Star mentions Jacob Stingley as garnashee for John Star.

William Cooper regarding a deed he received from William M'Donald for land adjoining Duncan M'Arthur and Joseph Tiffin, mentions John M'Donald.

Volume II, Thursday, 27 August 1801, No. 71

Elias Langham, justice of the peace in Ross County, regarding a bond from William Cross to Elias Rector for land adjoining George Porter on Darby Creek.

Furguson & M'Farland ask those indebted to them to settle their accounts.

Isaac Dawson regarding a road from Mr. Rutherford's ferry to the Big Praira.

John Carlisle wants to buy some pork barrels.

Volume II, Thursday, 3 September 1801, No. 72
John G. Macan regarding a meeting at William Keys' in Chillicothe for the purpose of locating military lands.
John M'Dougal will accept territorial bills for debts due.

Volume II, Thursday, 10 September 1801, No. 73
Jer. M'Lene reports that the land taxes for this year are due.
Henry Massie, Collector of the taxes in the Virginia Military district, about the collection of taxes.
John G. Macan is appointed collector of revenue in place of John M'Coy who resigned. He asks those who owe taxes to pay immediately.

Volume II, Thursday, 17 September 1801, No. 74
A reward is offered for the arrest of Jason Fairbanks who escaped from the Dedham jail, Norfolk County, and is thought to be heading for Chillicothe. He was to have been executed for murder.
A notice of a meeting at the house of Capt. Thomas Gregg regarding the incorporation of Chillicothe.
John S. Wills, at Chillicothe, has land for sale on Pe Pee Creek.
T. Gregg asks those indebted to him to settle their accounts.

Volume II, Thursday, 24 September 1801, No. 75
John Carlisle asks those indebted to him to make payments to John Waddle.
A proclamation from Gov. Arthur St.Clair is printed.
John M'Dougal wants to buy pork at his store in Chillicothe.
John Nickols, living south of the Ohio River, reports two runaway slaves named David and Abraham.
Noah Zane wants to keep a ferry on the Scioto River, below Chillicothe, where John Rutherford now lives.

Volume II, Thursday, 10 October 1801, No. 77
An account of the court martial of Capt. Thomas Gregg, of Ross County, is signed by Gov. Ar. St.Clair and mentions Lieut. Col. Dunlap, Col. Langham, Capt. Chenoweth.
Lieut. Col. E. Langham and Lieut. Col. James Dunlap give regimental orders and mention Capt. John Entriken, Capt. Mathew Kilgore, Capt. Parnick George, Capt. Joseph Conklin, Capt. George Emry, Lieut. John M'Lene, Lieut. Benjamin Holton, Lieut. George Frederick, Lieut. Andrew Davidson, Lt. Zedekiah Dawson, Lt. John Nolin, Lieut. John Pancake, Lieut. Uriah Pauling, Lieut. John M'Lanburg, Lieut. Benjamin Urmston, Michael Crider, John Odle, David Crouse, Nathaniel Wyatt, John Guthrie, George Johnston, Timothy Green, Henry Sheley, William Wallace, Capt. David Henderson, Capt. Joseph M'Coy, Capt. Moses Brown, Capt. Andrew Badgeley, Capt. Joseph Clarke, Capt. James Hawkins, Lieut. Jacob Hair, Capt. Thomas Herrod, Capt. John Robinson, Lieut. Francis Alexander, Lieut. Ignatious Sollers, Lieut. James Armstrong, Lieut. Stephen Warren, Lieut. George Mitzker, Lieut. Joshua Baxter, Lieut. Andrew Dill, Lieut. Jonathan Holmes, Lieut. Charles Briggs, James Curry, Daniel Robins, John Phibus, Thomas M'Clish, David Stockdon, George Skidmore, George Hill, William Cochran, Enoch Smith, William Williamson, Samuel Briggs, Isaac Dawson, John Chenoweth, John Barnes, William Lamb, Thomas Gregg, Ebenezer Petty, Samuel Davis, David Shelby.
A list of letters left at the Post Office in Chillicothe includes Thomas Antram at Chillicothe, John Barrett in care of Noble Grimes, James Adair at the mouth of the Scioto, John Biggart in Chillicothe, John Bogs, jun., in care of James Furgeson, Ezekiel Bogs, Samuel Conner in Chillicothe, William Cummins, Seth Carhartt at Scioto, Samuel Clark at or near Chillicothe, Col. John Carnahan near Chillicothe, Jacob Gundy near Chillicothe, James Curry, Robert Gregg at Chilli-cothe, Samuel Evans near Chillicothe, Joseph VanGrundy in Chillicothe, George Givins, Mary Gossard at Deer Creek, William Guthrie, Thomas Gregg, Capt. Lucas Hawkins, Miss Mary Hoglin, Johnston Hemphill, Andrew Huston at Scioto, Doctor James Irvine at Chillicothe, William Johnston in care of John Rutherford, Andrew Johnston at

Chillicothe, Samuel Jinkins at Chillicothe, Mr. Genatt at Chillicothe, Robert Kerr near Chillicothe, James Kilgore in Chillicothe, William Lenton, Frederick Lewis at Chillicothe, Maj. Israel Ludlow at Chillicothe, John Lindsey at the mouth of Little Scioto, Richard Mills, William Middleton in Adams County, John M'Donald, John M'Lain, James M'Donald, William Morgan at Chillicothe, Isaac Pierse at Belpre, William Philips in care of David Stockman near Chillicothe, Benjamin Reily (saddler at Scioto), Adam Rice, Robert and Ezekiel Rolston in Adams County, William Robinson, Robert Renick in care of Mr. Urmston, John Stall in care of William Lytle in Chillicothe, Col. Robert Saunders at Scioto, John Sargent near Bulskin, David Shadd at Old Chillicothe, James Short in care of Mr. Smith at Chillicothe, Isaac Stadden on Licking Creek in Muskingum in care of Mr. M'Cullock, Margret Smith in care of Doctor Bewel in Chillicothe, George Tong in Chillicothe, Thomas Truitt on Deer Creek, Isaac Warren, James Wilson on the road from Chillicothe to Limestone, Thomas White, John Wright in care of Robert M'Clelland at West Lancaster, George Williams near Chillicothe, John Young in care of John Carlisle at Chillicothe. Entered by Joseph Tiffin.

    Wm. Creighton has land for sale, the property of Gen. J. Swan of Baltimore.

    Gov. Ar. St.Clair and Charles Willing Byrd regarding the General Assembly.

    Obituary: Dr. Joseph Cogswell, late of Bourbon County, Kentucky, died in Chillicothe on Saturday, 5 October 1801.

    Gov. St.Clair passed through Chillicothe on 3 October on his way to Marietta.

    Obituary: Col. David Strong died at Wilkinsonville, Thursday, 20 Sept. 1801.

    Evangelist Jones says that his wife, Isabella Jones, left him, and he won't honor her debts anymore.

    John Hubbard, at Chillicothe, asks those indebted to him to pay their bills.

    Joseph Tiffin has moved into the hotel, lately occupied by Mr. Wm. Keys, at the sign of the Red Lion in Chillicothe. He will operate the tavern and stables.

    William Hoddy, living on the North Fork of Paint Creek about eight miles from Chillicothe, has land for sale including his grist and saw mills.

    Celadon Symmes and William Symmes, at Cincinnati, about land they bought from Hon. John Cleves Symmes. The deed was witnessed by James Silvers.

    Arthur Stewart asks those indebted to him to settle their accounts.

    Reuben Abrams regarding a meeting of the Ross County commissioners.

    Sebastian Foust, in Chillicothe, reports a stray mare.

Volume II, Thursday, 17 October 1801, No. 78

    A note about two prisoners who escaped from the jail in Frankfort, Kentucky: Robert Robinson (age 20-25) and Alexander Bowen (about age 20).

    Hon. John Cleves Symmes passed through Chillicothe on his way to Marietta on Thursday morning, 10 October 1801.

    William Hoddy regarding the public sale of his land and mills.

    Anthony S. Davenport, at the mouth of Willow Bottom, reports a stray mare.

    Francis Alexander, Collector for Ross County, reports that taxes are due.

    A. M'Laughlin, in Chillicothe, wants to buy a late-calved cow.

Volume II, Thursday, 24 October 1801, No. 79

    George Haynes, in Chillicothe, asks those indebted to him to pay their bills.

    E. Langham and James Dunlap, in Chillicothe, regarding regimental musters.

Volume II, Thursday, 7 November 1801, No. 81

    Robert Ballentine, near Franklinton, reports a stolen horse.

    John M'Dougal requests those indebted to him to settle their accounts.

    Simon M. Stockdell, at the Forks of Mad River, reports a stray mare.

Volume II, Thursday, 14 November 1801, No. 82

    Gov. Arthur St.Clair's speech to the General Assembly is printed.

    A notice regarding a road from the large spring on Darby's Creek, near Paul Huston's place, to Franklinton.

    Isaac Brink, at Chillicothe, lost a pocket book containing papers from John M'Dougal, Wm. Keys, Peter Dunnin, Daniel Swigard, Geo. Keller, John Brown.

    James M'Kelvy, living opposite the Big Bottom about fifteen miles from Chillicothe, reports that he found a stray horse.

Volume II, Thursday, 21 November 1801, No. 83

Thomas Kirker, at Eagle Creek in Adams County, regarding the suit of James Dunken vs. Armstead Adams.

Walter Buell, at Chillicothe, has land for sale in Kentucky.

M'Landbugh and Candlish asks those indebted to them to pay their bills.

Thomas Brown, in Fairfield County, regarding the children he had with Polly Iams. He married her in Frederick County, Maryland. She was taken to Ohio by her master, James Croecheney. Brown came to find her and found her living with a man named Richard Noker.

James January says he has paid taxes on the land surveyed in the name of Ambrose Buchanan or David Jackson.

Volume II, Thursday, 28 November 1801, No. 84

The proceedings of the legislature mentions Edward Tiffin, John Reily, John Milligan, Thomas M'Cune, James May, Jacob Visger, George M'Dougall, Jonathan Shieffelin, Nathan Ellis, the Quakers. A speech by Arthur St.Clair is printed.

Election returns at Detroit, Wayne County, mention Francois Joncaire Chabert, Jonathan Schieffelin, George M'Dougall, James May, Jacob Visgar, Elijah Brush, J.M. Beaubien, Louis Buffet, Lewis Bond.

Martin Landes, living at Clear Creek near the Muddy Praira in Fairfield County, reports a stray horse.

Benjamin VanCleve, surveyor of Hamilton County, about land in the Virginia Military district in Hamilton County.

James Carnohan, near Riddle's Mill in Bourbon County, Kentucky, reports a mare that strayed from W. Wilson's pasture on Kinnickanick. Deliver to Col. Samuel Findley in Chillicothe or William M'Entire's horse mill on Eagle Creek.

James Reed asks those indebted to him to make payment to James & M'Coy. They will accept pork as payment.

Volume II, Thursday, 5 December 1801, No. 85

Notes from Gov. Arthur St.Clair to the legislature and vice versa.

Marriage: William Creighton, Sen., of Chillicothe, married Miss Ann Stockton on Thursday evening, 28 November 1801.

Rev. Thomas Steel Cavander will preach next Sunday in Chillicothe.

John Carlisle & Company regarding the purchase of pork in Chillicothe.

The printer gives notice to James M'Cormick, Wm. Singelves, Jacob Harper and John M'Kinney, jun., to contact him at the printing office.

John M'Dougall regarding the delivery of pork at his store.

Volume II, Thursday, 12 December 1801, No. 86

Rev. Thomas Steel Cavender will preach tomorrow week at the courthouse.

Joseph Hopkins, living at High Bank, three miles below PePee, has spinning wheels for sale.

Jeremiah M'Lene, sheriff of Ross County, regarding sheriff's sales of the property of Elias Langham at the suit of Daniel Gregg; that of John and Samuel Jackson at the suit of John and Hugh Boyle; that of Samuel Wilson at the suit of Archibald Head.

Volume II, Thursday, 19 December 1801, No. 87

Proceedings of the legislature mention John Cleves Symmes, Paul Fearing.

A proclamation from Gov. Arthur St.Clair is printed.

Daniel Swigard, in Chillicothe, wants to buy beef cattle.

Ferguson & M'Farland have a shipment of goods at their store, Chillicothe.

Volume II, Saturday, 26 December 1801, No. 88

John Carlisle & Company have received a new shipment of goods.

John Leach and Jean Smith, executors of the estate of Henry Smith, late of Iron Ridge township, Adams County, dec'd, regarding the estate settlement.

Jacob Kirtz, living in Lancaster, Fairfield County, reports a runaway apprentice to the cabinet maker's trade named Johnson Wolcot, age 13. He is the son of John Wolcot of Fairfield County.

Robert W. Finly about the deeds for lots in Chillicothe held by Joseph Kerr.

A letter of protest against dividing the territory is signed by Edward Tiffin, T. Worthington, E. Langham, Joseph Darlinton, Nath. Massie, Francis Dunlavy and Jeremiah Morrow.

Volume II, Saturday, 2 January 1802, No. 89

Thomas M'Donald has a house and lot for sale in Chillicothe.

Samuel Finley writes a letter to the editor and mentions Gov. St.Clair, Dr. Samuel M'Adow, Mr. Schieffelin, Tiffin's tavern. He includes correspondence between himself and Gov. A. St.Clair. They mention Mr. Potter. He also includes depositions signed by John Reily, J. M'Lene, William Rutledge and A. Jenkins who mention M. Baldwin, Reuben Abrams, Samuel M'Adow, Stephen Cissna, Jeremiah M'Lene, Col. Worthington, Mr. Lamb's tavern, Mr. Baldwin, Mr. Gregg's tavern.

Volume II, Saturday, 9 January 1802, No. 90

A note regarding the divorce of Jean Wilson includes the testimony of James M'Connel and David Vance. They say that in July of 1798 William Wilson, an heir to William Wilson the Indian trader, married Jean Cochran. He left for Pittsburgh to settle the estate and never returned. Mentions David Barr of Belmont County.

The governor appoints Robert Gregg as a justice of the peace to replace Samuel Finley who resigned, and Alexander M'Laughlin, collector of the taxes in the Virginia Military District in place of Henry Massie who resigned.

R. Abrams regarding taxes due.

Robert Safford, executor of the estate of Maria Josephine Dallier, late of Gallipolis, dec'd, has land for sale, granted to Stephen Mounot, by order of the orphans' court of Adams County. Mr. Young lives on the premises.

A list of letters left at the Post Office in Chillicothe includes Thomas Antrim in Chillicothe, Charles Willing Byrd at Chillicothe, Jacob Burnet at Chillicothe, Solomon Boderick at Chillicothe, Elijah Brush at Chillicothe, William Bowdle, Walter Buel, Henry Bellenger, Ebenezer Buckingham at Tuskerora, T. Brownlee in care of Mr. Dick, William Cooper in care of Mr. Willis at Chillicothe, William Cummons, Conrod Crisman, Andrew Coins in Chillicothe, William Craig near Chillicothe, John Collit, Joseph Clark in care of John Carlisle, John Craigmiles in care of Mr. Keys, Hugh Cochran, Charles Cisney, Joseph Craine (innkeeper at Franklintown on Big Miami), Nathaniel Collins in Adams County, James Denny, Silas Dexter at Chillicothe, John Dill, John Davis in care of Mr. Hardy near New Lancaster, Thomas Gregg in Chillicothe, Benjamin Gooding at Manchester, John Graham near Franklinton, Daniel Hamilton, Lucas Hawkins, Charles Hunter in care of John Collit, Paul Huston, James Hardie at Chillicothe, John Hopkins (24 miles below Chillicothe), Samuel D. Jackson, John Johnston, Joseph Carir, Isaac Kook, John Kinkade, Stephen Kendall in Chillicothe, Samuel King, John Willey in Chillicothe, William Lenton, Robert Long, Frederick Lewis at Chillicothe, Moses Latta, David Looborough at New Lancaster, Jacob Moyer in Chillicothe, Duncan M'Arthur, William Marsh, James M'Donald, Col. Jonathan Meigs at Chillicothe, Thomas M'Donald, James M'Michel in care of Mr. Walten at Brush Creek, James M'Conall at Chillicothe, Soloman Munrow at Brush Creek, John Myers, Hamilton Maxwell, Joseph Martin at Fall Muskingum, William Patton, Col. James O'Hara at Chillicothe, Thomas Proviance at Chillicothe, William Russel at the mouth of Scioto, John Rollins in care of Squire Sharp, Oliver Ross, Isaac Ruby, Robert Ross, sen., above Chillicothe, Adam Rice at Chillicothe, Charles Rosebrough near the mouth of Scioto, James Reede at Darby Creek, Lucas Sullivant, David Stockdon, Abraham Slipp, Mrs. Jane Stockdan at Chillicothe, Benjamin Sells, Able Smith at Chillicothe, John Strickberry on Paint Creek near Chillicothe, Robert Smith at Chillicothe, William Sidener, Rev. William Speer at Chillicothe, Mrs. Sally Speer at Chillicothe, James Taylor at Chillicothe, William Stockmorton in care of Mr. Winship in Chillicothe, Benjamin Urmston, Joseph Vanmeter, Isaac Warner, Mr. C. Westen Haver in Chillicothe, Joseph Wilson, Stephen Warren at forks of Scioto, Matthew Woods in care of Hugh Cochran at Chillicothe, Winn Winship in Chilli-cothe, Hugh Woods at Chillicothe, Robert Young in care of Mr. M'Dougall in Chil-licothe. Joseph Tiffin, assistant post master.

N. Willis has out lots for sale.

Volume II, Saturday, 16 January 1802, No. 91

A note about petitions against dividing the territory mentions Joseph Kerr.

Volume II, Saturday, 23 January 1802, No. 92
The proceedings of the legislature mention Winship & Willis, Daniel Symmes, William Austin, Jeremiah M'Lene, John Blanchard, Jonathan Zane, Dudley Woodbridge (manufacturer of stone ware in the Territory).
Peter Porter, on the North Fork of Paint Creek, executor of the estate of George Porter, late of Ross County, dec'd, regarding the estate sale.
James Norrell, at Natchez, regarding runaway slaves, Jim, George & Jerry. Deliver to Mr. Martin, inspector at Limestone.
Walter Buell asks those indebted to him to pay Alexander M'Laughlin.

Volume II, Saturday, 30 January 1802, No. 93
A speech of Gov. Ar. St.Clair to the legislature is printed.
A list of laws passed by the legislature mentions Sally Mills, Marietta, Athens University, Jane Wilson, Zacheus Biggs and Zacheus A. Beatty, Jonathan Zane.
Benjamin Smith reports a stolen horse. Deliver to William M'Cullick at the mouth of the Licking, on the Muskingum River.
Francis Alexander, Collector, says pay your taxes to R. Abrams, Chillicothe.
John M'Dougall, agent for Richard Gernon, merchant of Philadelphia, has land for sale that was surveyed for R.C. Waters in Hamilton County, Mr. Eggleston in Hamilton County, Everard Mede and Peter Field Archer in Ross County.
Joseph Kerr, below Chillicothe, wants to hire workers.

Volume II, Saturday, 6 February 1802, No. 94
Samuel M'Adow asks those indebted to him to settle their accounts.
W. Creighton, attorney, regarding the suit of Anthony Symmes Davenport vs. William Hewitt in Ross County Court of Common Pleas.
Arthur Stuart, "intending to remove from this Territory, by the first day of April next", asks those indebted to him to settle their accounts.
Thomas M'Coy, living 3 miles above Chillicothe, has a house for rent lately occupied by Capt. Thomas Gregg. Apply to John M'Coy, merchant in Chillicothe.
Benjamin Bundy, living on Turtle Creek near Taylor's Mill, Hamilton County, reports a stray horse.

Volume II, Saturday, 13 February 1802, No. 95
Edward Tiffin, Robert Oliver and Ar. St.Clair print a law of the Territory.
A bill for the relief of Isaac Zane is printed.
A note regarding the debate over the division of the Territory.
John M'Dougall has cotton for sale at his store in Chillicothe.

Volume II, Saturday, 20 February 1802, No. 96
Mr. Fearing presented the petition from George Turner regarding land in the Northwest Territory. Mentions the petition of J.C. Symms.
Everard Harr about the stud horse, Young Salem, at his stable in Chillicothe.
M'Landburg and Candlish, at Chillicothe, "being determined to resign business in this place", have all their stock for sale at their store.
John Murphey regarding his town, called Fairfield, on the road from Wheeling to Limestone, 8 miles east of Hockhocking.
Thomas W. Twinney, administrator of the estate of Dennis Murphy, dec'd, late of Adams County, about the estate settlement at Wm. Campbell's house on the Scioto River in Union township, Adams County.
Caristian Yengundy regarding a road from Lancaster, past Yengundy's mill, to Chillicothe in Ross County.

Volume II, Saturday, 27 February 1802, No. 97
A note regarding Mr. Fearing in Congress.
An account of the petition of Mr. M'Cashen regarding lands granted to John C. Symmes mentions Mr. Davis and Mr. Nicholson.
Thomas Dick, trustee, announces a meeting at Joseph Tiffin's, regarding the school house building near the graveyard in Chillicothe.
A note regarding the case of Jason Fairbanks of Dedham.

Volume II, Saturday, 6 March 1802, No. 98

Michael Baldwin writes to the editor and mentions that he just arrived in the Territory from the City of Washington. He also mentions Col. Worthington.

Doctor Scott has moved his medical shop to the house lately occupied by Joseph Tiffin as a tavern.

T.V. Swearingen, at Walnut Grove, regarding his stud horse, Forgason Grey, half a mile from his mill on the North Fork of Paint Creek.

William Kimmell has carpenters' tools for sale at Maj. M'Arthur's brewhouse. He also asks those indebted to the firm of Bowman & Company to pay their bills.

Ann Rogers and Lucas Sullivant, at Franklinton, administrators of the estate of James Rogers, dec'd, regarding the estate settlement.

Volume II, Saturday, 13 March 1802, No. 99

Appropriation of funds for the payment of debts in the Northwest Territory mentions George Tod, Nathaniel Willis, Edward Tiffin, Elias Langham, Arthur St.Clair, James Smith (sheriff of Hamilton County), Jeremiah M'Lene, Paul Fearing, Thomas Worthington, John Reily, Ephraim Cutler, Alexander M'Laughlin, Daniel M'Allister, William Rutledge, Isaac VanNuiss, Carpenter & Findlay, James Phillips, Chrisman & Johnson, Winship & Willis, John Hunter.

A note about a meeting of the select council of Chillicothe at Joseph Tiffin's.

John Hutt regarding his school for young ladies in the house now occupied by M'Landburgh & Candlish. Mrs. Hutt will teach morals. Apply to him at Wm. S. Hutt's in Chillicothe.

Duncan M'Arthur regarding the stud horse, Young Granby. Mentions J. Reed and B. Urmston's ferry.

E. Langham regarding his stud horse, Gimcrack, at Benjamin Urmston's stable in Chillicothe. Includes the deposition of Warner Lewis in Woodford County, Ky.

Alexander M'Laughlin, in Chillicothe, has a lot for sale in Cincinnati. Apply to Daniel Cooner, merchant in Cincinnati.

Volume II, Saturday, 20 March 1802, No. 100

The report of the Congressional committee studying the statehood of Ohio.

An account of the meeting of the Select Council of Chillicothe mentions Edward Tiffin, Samuel Finlay, Thomas Scott, Wm. S. Hutt and Caleb Armentage.

The Light Infantry Company should meet at Abner Meeker's on Saturday.

R.W. Finlay has several negroes to bind out.

Volume II, Saturday, 27 March 1802, No. 101

Obituary: Mrs. Mary Delano, age 24, wife of Dr. Amasa Delano, died at Lancaster on 13 March 1802.

Peter Rever, at New Lancaster, has a house for lease.

Volume II, Saturday, 3 April 1802, No. 102

A list of letters left at the Post Office in Chillicothe includes Benjamin Brackney in care of William Rogers on the north fork of Paint Creek, William Bowdle, Ebenezer Buckingham at Tuskarawa, John Beggart, Eli Bereman, John Blair, Solomon Brodrick at Chillicothe, Benjamin Bradbury on Clover Creek Fork in Clermont County, William Brown at Chillicothe, Samuel Badley or Levi Hurst, John Collet, Edward Crabb in Chillicothe, Robert Crane at the mouth of Scioto in care of James Gray in Chillicothe, James Connel in care of Mr. Wolff on Wheeling road, Joseph Campbell, Samuel Clark near Chillicothe, Asa Dunn in Chillicothe, Benjamin Duncan on Picaway Plains, Abraham Dean, David Davis (a Welshman, carpenter and joiner by trade, at Chillicothe), Capt. John Dill, Dr. Joseph Eaker near Chillicothe, Thomas Earle, Lemuel Evans in Chillicothe, George Emery, John Eakins at New Market, Anthony Franklin, John Gorrel near Franklinton, James Grubb, John Gay, jr., at Chillicothe in care of Mr. Wolff, Hopkins & D. Henry, Silas Atcheson, Robert Hume, John Humpson in care of Thomas Sturgon at New Lancaster, Alexander Jenkins, Dr. David Jameson, Robert Jones near Chillicothe, Benjamin Kerns at High Bank, William Kimmel, Elisha Kelly at Paint Creek, Robert Lucas at Chillicothe, William Lytle at Williamsburg, John M'Lene, Graney Mitchell, James M'Mickle near Chillicothe, John Maxwell (printer at Chillicothe), William M'Cabe at Hockhocking in Fairfield County, William M'Gowen at Chilli-cothe, Stephen Mates at Chillicothe,

Peter Mickle at Chillicothe, Robert or Levi Patrick, Peter Parcels, Uriah Pawling in or near Chillicothe, William R. Dickinson, Widow Riddle near Dunan's salt works, Henry Rush near the Pickaway Plains, Samuel Smith, Jonathan Schieffelin at Chillicothe, Miss Nancy Sellers living on Deer Creek, John Short near Chillicothe, James Stuart at the Muddy Praira in care of Alexander Denison at Pickaway Plains, John S. Wills, Benjamin Tappan at Ravenna, William Thompson in care of John Rutherford, James Taylor living in Newport in Campbell County, Solomon Templain, George Turner in Ross County, Thomas Thomson for Mark Morris (from William Badley near Chillicothe), Frederick Unsel six miles below Pe Pee, Nathaniel Wilson near New Lancaster, Taylor Webster near Chillicothe, George Wood (of Philadelphia, at Chillicothe), William Williams at Chillicothe, John Davis Weby at Scioto, Joseph Yates in Ross County. Entered by Joseph Tiffin, assistant post master.

Nathaniel Johnson has moved his school to the house lately occupied by Rev. William Speer in Chillicothe.

Thomas Gregg wants to buy a good saddle horse.

Volume II, Saturday, 10 April 1802, No. 103

Ferguson & M'Farland, in Chillicothe, ask those indebted to pay their bills.

M'Landburg & Candlish have household furniture, books, stock for sale. They "intend leaving this Territory immediately after the vendue".

Arthur Stewart has moved to Kentucky and asks those indebted to him to pay their accounts by paying William Creighton, John M'Dougall or John Carlisle.

Benjamin Urmston wants to hire a hostler.

Volume II, Saturday, 17 April 1802, No. 104

Gideon Granger regarding land for sale in Trumbull County. Apply to Calvin Pease in Young's-Town in Trumbull County.

Thomas Reed has whiskey for sale at Mr. Hubbard's store in Chillicothe.

Margaret Walker gives an account of an incident involving Mr. Inglish in which he accused her of taking his property. She mentions her husband, "an old acquaintance from Mad River", Mr. Pierce and Mr. James.

Volume II, Saturday, 24 April 1802, No. 105

James Patten, at Louisville, reports that Aaron Boman, living in the Indiana Territory, has been piloting boats through the rapids, but damages many boats.

John Fowler regarding the statehood of Ohio.

Edward Tiffin and Thomas Scott about ordinances of the town of Chillicothe.

N. Willis asks those owing money for the Scioto Gazette to pay their bills. He will discontinue publication of the paper until he has collected his accounts.

Volume III, Saturday, 22 May 1802, No. 106

The debate of the U.S. Congress regarding Ohio's statehood is printed.

Charles Willing Byrd regarding the erection of new counties in the Territory.

N. Willis writes to the public regarding subscriptions to the paper.

John Carlisle & Company have dissolved their partnership. Accounts should be settled with Creighton & Baldwin, attorneys.

Those wishing to record their brands or marks should call on William Niblick at John M'Dougal's store.

John M'Dougal asks those indebted to Arthur Stewart, late of Chillicothe, to settle their accounts immediately.

The text of the act to allow statehood for Ohio is printed.

Alexander Hawthorn has nails for sale, made at his manufactory, and sold by him at Morgantown.

Andrew Young, living on Dick's Creek between Big Miami and Little Miami, reports several stray horses.

John M'Cale, living on Great Miami in Payton township, reports stray colts.

John M'Dougal has a new shipment of goods for sale at his store, Chillicothe.

Volume III, Saturday, 29 May 1802, No. 107

More of the debate regarding the statehood of Ohio.

Unsigned letters to the editor regarding the statehood of Ohio.

Jacob Cox has horses, cows, farming tools and a wagon for sale at public vendue at Mr. Beever's plantation on Deer Creek near Oswald Thompson's house.

W. Creighton regarding the suit of Conrod Moois vs. Alexander M'Cartney in the Ross County Court of Common Pleas.

Benj. Miller, Collector, about building the new Market House in Chillicothe.

Thomas Parker says that Maj. John Belli is authorized to transact the business of Thomas and Alexander Parker in the Territory. John Paul, of Hamilton County, is authorized to lease out Parker's lands on the Little Miami.

Doctor Crane, lodging at Capt. William Lamb's in Chillicothe, regarding his practice of medicine.

Volume III, Saturday, 5 June 1802, No. 108

More of the Congressional debate regarding statehood for Ohio.

M'Landburg & Candlish have left their accounts in the hands of John Carlisle and William Creighton for settlement.

Volume III, Saturday, 12 June 1802, No. 109

Dennis Brogan, living in Chillicothe, reports a strayed or stolen horse. Deli-ver to Brogan at Abner Meeker's house.

Francis Alexander about the recording of brands or marks in Wayne township.

A notice regarding a road to be constructed from the Hockhocking road to the Pickaway road between Risdau Beauchamp's and Philip Wolf's tavern.

Joseph Gardner wants to keep a ferry over the Scioto River at his house.

Volume III, Saturday, 19 June 1802, No. 110

Unsigned letters to the editor regarding Ohio's statehood are printed.

Samuel Smith wants to sell his farm on the road to Deer Creek three miles from Chillicothe, on the Scioto River. Also land on the Scioto River about two miles below Col. Worthington's mill and his horses, cows, farming tools, furniture.

Phielden Hubbard & Company, in Chillicothe, have received a new shipment of goods at their store in the house lately occupied by John Hubbard, opposite Capt. William Lamb's tavern.

Edmund Frayatt, at Alexandria at the mouth of Scioto, will store goods.

Volume III, Saturday, 26 June 1802, No. 111

A note regarding the Northwest Territory is printed.

N. Willis regarding the theft of some white lead from his house.

W.R. Dickinson says the recorder's office has moved to Joseph Tiffin's tavern.

Duncan M'Arthur reports a stray mare colt.

Jacob Hubbard forbids a negro named Michael (who formerly belonged to Col. Massie) from entering his property.

Edward Tiffin and William Creighton, attorney, regarding the suit of Nathan Kennedy vs. John Crocker in the Ross County Court of Common Pleas. Also the suit of Reuben Abrams vs. Bazil Abrams.

Volume III, Saturday, 3 July 1802, No. 112

An unsigned letter to the editor regarding the statehood of Ohio.

A note regarding Francis Cramer's attempt at arson in Chillicothe mentions his wife and children, Ruben Abrams, Mr. Miller, Robert Gregg.

Robert Lucas, living on the north fork of Paint Creek opposite Old Chillicothe adjoining the lands of Mr. Pollard and Mr. Preston, has land for sale.

T. Worthington, Secretary of the Treasury, regarding the internal taxes.

Thomas Gregg has land and a quantity of household furniture for sale.

Nicholas Devolt reports a stray mare. Deliver to Capt. Lamb.

Phielden Hubbard & Company have dissolved their partnership. Phielden Hubbard will continue the business in the same place.

Volume III, Saturday, 10 July 1802, No. 113

Accounts of Fourth of July celebrations mention the Light Infantry, Lieut. Niblack, Ensign Miller, Capt. Wills, Col. Langham, Pickaway Plains.

John Odle about his butchers' business in Chillicothe. Apply for meat at John Mantle's cellar door. He mentions Daniel Brina, the former butcher, Chillicothe.

William Creighton, Sen., in Chillicothe, reports a stray mare.

A list of letters left at the Post Office in Chillicothe includes Hannah Adams in care of Thomas Gregg in Chillicothe, Bartholomew Anderson at Brush Creek, Benjamin Brackney, John Clark in care of Mr. Gregg in Chillicothe, Sarah Bails on Paint Creek, Robert Ballentine, William Blair, Solomon Brodrick at Chillicothe, Rudolf Buzzard in Chillicothe, John Beakeman, John Buck in Chillicothe, Eli Bereman, Adam Bingiman, John Cissna, Henry Carter at Pe Pee, Jonathan Clark at Pe Pee, William Creigan (ten miles from Chillicothe), James Crawford, Andrew Carnell in Chillicothe, Andrew Cummerman, Francis Dill on Tortle Creek, Hannah Davis at Pe Pee, Amos Derrough, Hamilton Dougherty, Thomas Davidson, Silas Dun on the Scioto River, Alexander Dow at Chillicothe, Benjamin Duncan (20 miles from Lancaster), David English at Chillicothe, James Finley, Enoch Fenrick at Chillicothe, Joseph Flemmond near Big Belly at Chillicothe, William Gabriel, Anthony S. Gadburg at Chillicothe, George Givens, James Gaskill, John Gutman (8 miles from Chillicothe), Noker Holt (living with Mr. Armstrong), Nicholas Hall, G. Hoshawe, Thomas Hill near Mad River, Thomas Kelly, John Loveless (12 miles from Chillicothe), Samuel Langdale at Chillicothe, William Lytle at Williamsburg, William Laughlin at the mouth of the Scioto River, James Miligan at Greenfield on Paint Creek, William M'Clintock near Chillicothe, Sally Maholam in care of B. Urmston, Alexander M'Mullin, James Mitchell (5 miles from Chillicothe), John M'Naman at Chillicothe, Humphrey Montgomery, jun., Benjamin Nevell at Salt Creek, William Reed on Twin Creek, Nathan Reeves, John or Joseph Rucub near Chillicothe, Mathew Richey, Rev. William Spear at Chillicothe, James Steward at Muddy Priari in care of A. Denison, David Simons at Salt Creek, Joshua Stephens at the mouth of Deer Creek, Lucas Sullivant, Mathew Taylor, John Starks Edwards at Masapotamia, Solomon Templin, Michael Thomas, Benjamin Tappan (attorney at law, at Ravenore), James Webster, David Wolff (living at Old Chillicothe), Morgan Williams at Chillicothe, George Whetstone in care of Philip Wolff, James Williams at Brush Creek, David Wolcott, George Williams, Isaac Warner, Joseph Tiffin.

E. Tiffin and W. Creighton regarding the suit of Daniel Hamilton vs. the estate of John Underwood in the Ross County Court of Common Pleas.

A notice regarding a road from Swearingen's mill on the north fork of Paint Creek running to intersect the Limestone road near Andrew Pontious' house.

Volume III, Saturday, 17 July 1802, No. 114

Andrew Badgley, John Gossett and George Medsker, of New Market township, write a letter to the public regarding the statehood of Ohio.

Obediah Williams was arrested for horse stealing on the road from Chillicothe to Lancaster. He is suspected of being the same Obediah Williams, alias John W. Ball, alias John Logan Williams, who escaped from the Frederiksburg jail.

An account of the Fourth of July celebration at St. Clairville mentions Capt. Martin, Col. David Vance, James M'Donald.

William Keys has opened a new tavern in Chillicothe in the house lately occupied by Capt. Thomas Gregg.

Thomas Reed has whiskey and crockery for sale at Pheilden Hubbard's store.

Thomas Gregg says the sale of his household goods is postponed.

Samuel Dawson, living near Paris in Bourbon County, Kentucky, reports a runaway slave named Charles Mumford.

Benjamin Miller, Collector, about donations for building the Market House.

Volume III, Saturday, 24 July 1802, No. 115

Obediah Williams escaped from jail on Wednesday evening.

James & M'Coy have moved their store to the house formerly occupied by John M'Dougal in Chillicothe.

John M'Dougal says that William Niblack will travel to Philadelphia in August to purchase goods for the store. He asks those indebted to him to pay their bills.

Thomas Gregg regarding the sale of his household furniture at the house now occupied by William Keys.

Lewis Rodgers wants to keep a ferry over the Scioto River at his house.

Joseph Potter, living seven miles from Chillicothe, has his house and lot for sale opposite Col. Worthington's place. Apply to John Carlisle.

An account of the Fourth of July celebration at Marietta mentions the Muskingum Academy, Judge Meigs' oration, Mr. Brough's hall.

A letter to Mr. Silliman, editor of the Ohio Gazette, regarding the election of delegates to the convention mentions Benjamin I. Gilman, William R. Putnam, Return J. Meigs, jun., G. Greene, P. Fearing.

Volume III, Saturday, 7 August 1802, No. 117

An unsigned letter to the editor regarding James Caldwell of Belmont County mentions James Ross, Judge Addison, Gov. St.Clair.

Nathan Ellis writes a letter to the public.

John M'Dougall wants to buy pork at his store in Chillicothe.

Lt. Col. E. Langham and Lt. Col. James Dunlap regarding a meeting of the officers of the Ross County militia at Capt. William Lamb's tavern.

Benjamin Urmston regarding his tavern and ferry in Chillicothe.

Volume III, Saturday, 14 August 1802, No. 118

Henry Massie and Joseph Kerr about lots in the town of New Market.

Charles Mullin, at Spring Hill town in Adams County, says that his wife, Jane Mullin, left him, and he won't honor her debts.

Volume III, Saturday, 21 August 1802, No. 118

David Shepherd, in Chillicothe, reports the theft of a horse. Deliver to his brother, Thomas Shepherd, living in Shepherds-Town, Berkely County, Virginia.

Jer. M'Lene, sheriff, regarding the collection of the land taxes.

John M'Coy regarding a meeting of the militia officers in Chillicothe.

Volume III, Saturday, 28 August 1802, No. 119

Duncan M'Arthur, William Keran, William Robinson, David Stockton, William Rodgers, John Crouse and James Dean write a letter to the electors of Ross County regarding the statehood of Ohio.

Edward Tiffin, Michael Baldwin and T. Worthington all write letters to the public regarding statehood for Ohio.

Charles Brown, living on the Great Miami near Franklin in Franklin township of Hamilton County, reports a stray mare. Deliver to John Brown near the Falls of Paint Creek or Thomas Sturgeon, innkeeper at New Lancaster.

T.V. Swearingen, treasurer of Ross County, will be absent on business in Virginia and Mr. Winn Winship, of Walnut Grove, will handle his office.

Volume III, Saturday, 4 September 1802, No. 120

Letters to the public are printed from James Dunlap, Jacob Smith, James Crawford, E. Langham, Samuel Finley regarding statehood and slavery. They include an address from Edward Tiffin and H. VanderBurgh.

John S. Wills says that he will serve in the Convention if elected.

Volume III, Saturday, 11 September 1802, No. 122

A letter to the public is printed from James Caldwell in Belmont County and, at St. Clairville, Elijah Martin, John Thompson, Andrew Marshall, William Congleton, Moses Morehead, and David Kirkpatrick. They mention Gov. St.Clair, Maj. Campbell, Charles Hammond.

Letters to the public from James Grubb and William Craig about statehood for Ohio are printed.

T. Gregg and John G. Macan are candidates for the Convention.

An unsigned letter to the editor regarding the letter from Mr. Langham mentions Mr. Goforth, Thomas Posey, Mr. Smith, Mr. Fearing.

A letter to the public from John S. Wills regarding his views on slavery.

A letter from Duncan M'Arthur to the public regarding Mr. E. Langham mentions Mr. Spencer, Mr. M'Millan, Mr. Sibley, Mr. Massie, Mr. Worthington, Mr. Tiffin, Samuel Finley.

T. Gregg has household furniture for sale at the house of William Keys.

John Carlisle, Collector of the Virginia Army lands regarding taxes due.

Charles Mullin, in Chillicothe, reports a stray horse. Deliver to Col. James Dunlap, four miles above Chillicothe.

Volume III, Saturday, 18 September 1802, No. 123

An unsigned letter regarding slavery mentions Mr. Wills and Mr. Macan.

A letter to the public from Nath. Massie regarding slavery.

A letter from Samuel Finley is printed regarding Elias Langham and mentions Reuben Abrams.

An unsigned letter to the editor mentions Elias Langham, Mr. Willis, Col. Worthington, W. Patton, Col. Finley, Mr. Fearing, Mr. Baldwin, Mr. Tiffin, Simon Cray M'Mahon (dancing master), Col. Samuel Finley, Maj. Vanderburgh, Mr. Sibley, Col. Oliver, Col. Massie, Col. Vance, Mr. Burnett, Mr. Reeder, John M'Donald (Elias Langham's brother-in-law).

Abraham Claypool is a candidate for the convention and gives his views.

E. Langham regarding the letters written about him.

Moses Latta asks those indebted to him to pay at Capt. Joseph M'Coy's house.

Volume III, Saturday, 25 September 1802, No. 124

An unsigned letter regarding the accusations made against Col. Worthington mentions Henry Massie.

A letter from Samuel Finley regarding land he bought from Henry Massie.

Joseph Kerr is a candidate for the convention and the Assembly.

James Scott, at Franklinton, is a candidate and is opposed to slavery.

Dan. Vanmeter reports a stray cow. Deliver to Wm. Patton on Paint Creek.

John M'Dougal, administrator of the estate of Joseph Potter, dec'd, about the settlement of Mr. Steel's estate. Potter was administrator of the estate.

Benj. Miller regarding the debts of E. Langham.

A note regarding a meeting at Big Hill in Hamilton County to nominate candidates for the Convention. It mentions Francis Dunlavy, Charles W. Byrd, John Wilson, William Goforth, Jeremiah Morrow, John W. Browne, John Kitchel, John Paul, Thomas Smith, Stephen Wood, Jonathan Pitman's tavern, James Findlay, John Ludlow, Moses Miller, Daniel Reeder, Jacob White, William M'Millen, Henry Weaver, John Reily, Dr. Salmon, Dr. Reeder, Maj. Ludlow, Capt. Reeder, John Smith, John Ludlow, W.C. Schenck, Jacob Burnet, Isaac Anderson, John Bigger, jun., Robert Benham, Daniel C. Cooper, James Barret.

Note from Jeremiah M'Lene, sheriff of Ross County, about elections mentions Solomon Cox (on Salt Lick Creek), Philip Woolf, James Scott in Franklinton, Richard Chenoweth in Pe Pee township, Fergus Moore in Wayne township, Arthur St.Clair, Christian Platte in Paxton township, Oliver Ross in New-Market.

John G. Macan regarding a letter written by John Hut.

N. Kennedy reports a strayed or stolen horse. He mentions Mr. Jones on the Ohio and Peter Nicewanges on the Ohio River.

Volume III, Saturday, 2 October 1802, No. 125

John Hopkins is a candidate for the convention and against slavery.

Noble Crawford is a candidate for the convention and opposes slavery.

William Craig is a candidate for the convention and opposes slavery.

A letter from Thomas White to D. M'Arthur mentions Thos. Worthington, Edward Tiffin, Nathaniel Massie, Michael Baldwin and James Grubb.

Charles Willing Byrd writes a letter to the editor.

A note from David Bradford of Adams County mentions Nathan Ellis, sheriff of Adams County.

A note from the editor regarding the dispute over Col. Elias Langham.

Robert W. Finley, author of the New Market address, is a candidate. Also William Patton, Reuben Abrams and Winn Winship are candidates.

A list of letters left at the Post Office in Chillicothe includes James Brown near Chillicothe, Joseph Ballew at North Bend, John Biggeit in Chillicothe, Joseph Boggs eight miles below Chillicothe, John Blair at Franklinton, William Bready, Uriah Blue at Chillicothe, Risdon Beauchamp at Chillicothe, Levi Cotter in Chillicothe, Joseph Campbell, Charles Coulter near Chillicothe, Joseph Colleau on Brush Creek, Thomas Dick, Rev. John Dunlavy, Jacob Eigelberner in Chillicothe, Charles Ewen at Franklinton, James Ellis at Franklinton, Enoch Fenyer at Chillicothe, William Featherstone at Wood Courthouse, Thomas Gamble, James Gaskill, Col. John Guthrie, David Gerge at Alexandria at the mouth of Scioto, Capt. Thomas Gregg, John Hoop on Scioto, Thomas Hill at the head of Gregory's Creek on new Mad River road, Robert Humes,

William Harrison (hatter in Chillicothe), David Hamilton, Johnston Hemphill, Thomas Heady at Chillicothe, James Hays at Paint Creek near Chillicothe, Philip Hobough four miles from Chillicothe, Philip Hoback, David Hays, Thomas I. Janis on Brush Creek, Henry Jones near Chillicothe, Nicholas Kelley, Moses Lata, Joseph Lane in Chillicothe, Joseph M'Clennan in Chillicothe, Richard Malone at Chillicothe, George Mackey on Brush Creek below Chillicothe in care of Doctor Edmiston, Joseph Mone by the Grassy Praira five miles from Chillicothe, Samuel Myers, Ephraim M'Kenney at Mad River, John M'Kenny at Columbia, Joseph M'Coy near Chillicothe, William Marcus on Darby Creek, William Mustard on Pe Pee, Archibald M'Donald at Chillicothe, Rev. Jesse Mounts seven miles above Pe Pee, Bartle Maybee at the salt works in Chillicothe, James M'Donald in Chillicothe, Henry M'Casland on Paint Creek, James M'Ginnis in care of Noble Crawford, George Nelson at Chillicothe, Easter Price, Seth Purl in care of John Crouze at Chillicothe, George Parkinson in care of Michael Cryder in Chillicothe, Joshua Parish at Adams County, Isaac S. Patten at Great Praira, Robert Ross or Andrew or William Noutman living at Dorbe in Ross County, Miss Elizabeth Silvers at North Bend, Elijah Rinker, Thomas F. Reddick at Chillicothe, Anthony Roades at Chillicothe, Mr. Reed near the forks of Scioto in care of Mr. Ballentine, Isaac Reily, Jacob Strouse at Chillicothe, John Shields (tailor in care of Mr. Clemens in Chillicothe), James Spurgeon near the crossings of Brush Creek in care of Isaac Tygoard (living on the Pickaway Plains near Chillicothe), Edward Southwourth, Salmon Templin at Old Town, Benjamin Turwan at Chillicothe, James Toner or Hugh M'Clain near Williamsburgh in care of William Lytle, Thoams Tootte near Chillicothe, John Thompson near Chillicothe in care of James Ferguson, James Templen in Chillicothe, Maj. William Wills at Fort Wayne, Samuel Wilson in Chillicothe, Benjamin White at Franklinton, Mrs. Drusilla Welsh, Thomas Wilkins near Chillicothe, John Wallis (18 miles from Chillicothe), James Wallis at Chillicothe, James Williams at Brush Creek, George Young, David Yates in Ross County. Joseph Tiffin, assistant post master.

Samuel Evans regarding a road from New Market to Manchester.
John Brown and Jonathan Rees regarding the horse races at Maysville.
Joseph M'Coy wants to hire a distiller.

Volume III, Saturday, 9 October 1802, No. 126

William Mathers, William M'Williams, James M'Connell, Jeremiah Martin and Andrew Marshall regarding the meeting at the house of Elijah Martin in Belmont County mention Allen Stewart, Richard M'Gibbons, John M'Williams, Benjamin Acy, James Alexander, Benjamin Masters, John Harris, Caleb Russell, Alexander Bogs, Joshua Hatcher, Daniel Merrit, William Develine, Moses Meritt, Duncan Morrison, John Boyd, John M'Donald, Joseph Parish, Alexander Gaston, David Enloe, John Dougherty, Peter Wyrick, Jacob Lash, Robert Giffin, Jacob Nagle, Thomas Richards, Joseph Sharp, James Caldwell, Joseph Dillon, Daniel Harris, Jacob Coleman, Thomas Mitchell, Elijah Woods, David Vance.

A letter from C. Hammond to James Caldwell of Belmont County.
An unsigned letter to James Caldwell mentions John Thompson, Sterling Johnson, Robert Johnson, Gov. St.Clair, Lieut. Cook, Sergt. Simeons, Caleb Wells. It implies that James Caldwell lived at Wheeling.
Robert W. Finley writes a letter to the public of Ross County.
Edward Tiffin and William Creighton regarding the suit of Nathan Kennedy vs. John Derush in the Ross County Court of Common Pleas.
John Mantle, at his tan yard in Chillicothe, is a candidate for the Assembly.
A list of candidates for the Assembly and the Convention is printed: Edward Tiffin, Thomas Worthington, Abraham Claypool, James Grubb, Nathaniel Massie, Michael Baldwin, Elias Langham, Samuel Finley, Robert W. Finley, Jacob Smith, Noble Crawford, James Dunlap, William Craig, I. M'Coy, John Hopkins, Reuben Abrams, John Guthrie, James Scott, John G. Macan, John S. Wills, Thomas Gregg, James Crawford, Winn Winship, David Shelby, Joseph Kerr, William Patton, Isaac Dawson, Robert Culbertson, Hugh Cochran, Lucas Sullivant, John Turner, David Bonner, James Armstrong and John Mantle.

Volume III, Saturday, 16 October 1802, No. 127

Edward Tiffin, Col. Nathaniel Massie, Col. Thomas Worthington, Michael Baldwin and James Grubb are elected delegates to the Convention from Ross

County. They won over Abraham Claypool, Elias Langham, Samuel Finley, Jacob Smith, James Dunlap, James Scott, Noble Crawford, John Guthery, Robert W. Finley, John G. Macan, William M'Coy, John Hopkins, James Crawford, John S. Wills, Thomas Gregg, William Craig and Stephen Timmons.

William Patton, David Shelby, Winn Winship, Joseph Kerr, Robert Culbertson are elected representatives in the territorial legislature.

Other election results: Emanuel Carpenter and Henry Abrams are elected in Fairfield County. Joseph Darlington, Mr. Beasley, Israel Donaldson and Thomas Kirker are elected in Adams County.

Charles Willing Byrd writes a letter of protest to the public and mentions Henry Dearborn and Arthur St.Clair, sen.

John M'Dougal, administrator of the estate of Joseph Potter, dec'd, regarding the estate sale and settlement.

N. & R. Gregg ask those indebted to them to settle their accounts.

Reuben Abrams regarding a meeting of the commissioners at Joseph Tiffin's.

William Creighton, Sen., regarding building a Bank in Chillicothe.

William Lamb regarding his new tavern in Chillicothe.

Duncan M'Arthur reports a stray mare at Mr. How's near the Muddy Praira.

Volume III, Saturday, 23 October 1802, No. 128

William Mathers writes a letter to the public.

John Edwards, Sen., has land for sale at the mouth of the Little Scioto.

Arthur St.Clair writes a letter to the public and mentions Charles Willing Byrd, Hamilton Artillery Company, Capt. William M'Farland, Lieut. Tabor Washburn, Lieut. David Christy.

Volume III, Saturday, 30 October 1802, No. 129

Obituary: Mrs. Mary Tiffin, wife of Joseph Tiffin of Chillicothe, died on Wednesday evening, 27 October 1802.

James Peairs regarding the estate sale at the house of Isaac Peairs, dec'd.

Volume III, Saturday, 6 November 1802, No. 130

The address of Ar. St.Clair to the Convention is printed.

A note from Gov. Arthur St.Clair regarding the legislature of the territory.

Jethro Nevill, Parnish George and Joseph Bogart about the High Bank races.

James January has lots for sale in Williamsburgh.

Joseph Tiffin says the rumor that he's quit tavern keeping is false.

John Martin, of Baltimore, appoints John Lee, of Whelen, to sell his land.

Volume III, Saturday, 13 November 1802, No. 131

Some proceedings of the Convention are printed.

Alexander M'Laughlin asks those indebted to him to make payments to John Kerr in Chillicothe.

T.V. Swearingen wants to buy pork at James & M'Coy's store.

W. Creighton asks those indebted to M'Landburgh & Candlish, late of Chillicothe, to make payments immediately.

George Gordon and William Creighton regarding the suit of John S. Wills, assignee of Jessee Seinnes, vs. the estate of William Hickman, one of the late partners of John Hickman & Company, in Adams County Court of Common Pleas.

Peter Sunderland, Sen., wants to sell his tavern on the road from Wheeling to Chillicothe near St. Clair's Ville.

Volume III, Saturday, 18 December 1802, No. 133

Jeremiah M'Lene, sheriff of Ross County, regarding the upcoming elections mentions Solomon Cox on Salt Lick Creek, Philip Wolf, Richard Chenoweth in Pe Pee township, James Scott at Franklinton, Fergus Moore in Wayne township, Christian Platto in Paxton township, Oliver Ross in New Market.

M'Landburg & Candlish, at Capt. William Lamb's house, ask those indebted to them to settle their accounts immediately.

John M'Dougal, in Chillicothe, regarding pork and salt he purchased.

Andrew Galbreath has commenced the blue-dying business near Mr. Mantle's in Water Street, Chillicothe.

John Carlisle "has again commenced business in Chillicothe" in the house opposite Mr. Lamb's tavern where he has a new shipment of goods for sale.

William Rutledge, living one mile from Col. Dunlap, has land for sale.

William Keys has a farm for sale on Deer Creek road.

Belshazer Dragoul, living on Eagle Creek, says do not purchase his land from Neal Lasserly or any of Alexander M'Intire's heirs.

David Hansel says his wife, Rachael, left him and he won't pay her bills.

Samuel Smith says to deliver the pork he bought to James & M'Coy's store in Chillicothe and the grain he bought to Col. Worthington's mill.

Arthur St.Clair, sen., declines the nomination for Governor.

Dr. Buell is a candidate for the legislature and W.S. Hutt for coroner.

Jacob Smith is a candidate for the Assembly from Ross County.

Edward Tiffin is nominated to run for governor of Ohio.

The editor of the Scioto Gazette apologizes for the lack of newspapers for the past two weeks, but he couldn't obtain paper on which to print.

John Brandy, near Chillicothe, reports a runaway black man, Henry Williams.

W. Moore, living at the head of Pickaway Plains, about a stray horse. Deliver to William Keys, tavern keeper in Chillicothe, or Samuel Hill near the Plains.

Volume III, Saturday, 1 January 1803, No. 135

James Scott, of Franklinton, is a candidate for the Senate. A list of candi-dates is given: Edward Tiffin, Nathaniel Massie, James Grubb, James Dunlap, John Blair, Abraham Claypool, Thomas Worthington, Michael Baldwin, David Shelby, Thomas Stockton, Walter Buel, Reuben Abrams, Isaac Dawson, William Patton, Robert Culbertson, William Robertson, Jacob Smith, Francis Alexander, Joseph Tiffin, Jeremiah M'Lene, Benjamin Urmston, William S. Hutt, William Rutledge.

William Patton writes a letter to the public regarding the election.

Duncan M'Arthur will not be a candidate for the Assembly.

Jeremiah M'Lene writes a letter about his candidacy for sheriff.

M. Baldwin says he is a candidate for the Assembly.

Joseph Tiffin writes a letter to the public about his candidacy for sheriff.

Francis Alexander also writes a letter about his candidacy for sheriff.

John Thomas, at the Pickaway Plains, administrator of the estate of Samuel Thomas, dec'd, late of Ross County, regarding the estate settlement.

Volume III, Saturday, 8 January 1803, No. 136

Election returns at Columbia mention Edward Tiffin, Daniel Symms, Jeremiah Morrow, John Paul, Francis Dunlavy, Thomas Brown, William James, William Maxwell, John Bezzars, James Dunn, Thomas M'Farland, Robert M'Clure, Ephraim Kibby, Michael Jones, Joseph Carpenter.

Marriage: George Gibson married Miss Nelson (no date or place listed).

John M'Dougal regarding the delivery of pork.

A blue coat was lost between Thomas Swearingen's mill and Chillicothe.

James & M'Coy have dissolved their partnership. Lemuel James will carry on the business in the same house.

Frederick Brays, living about two miles from Old Chillicothe on the Westfall road, reports that he found a stray colt.

A list of letters at the Post Office in Chillicothe mentions Thomas Armstrong at Salt Lick in care of J. M'Dougal, Reuben Abrams, Eli Bereman at New Market, John Beggart, Dr. Walter Buell, Jacob Button at Chillicothe, William Bready, Joshua Ballenger, Michael Brown at Kinnicinic in care of J. Lamb, Moses Brown in care of William Lamb, Benjamin Bradbury at Clermont, William Craig, Joseph Clark, John Clark, Elizabeth Cook at Buckskin, Joseph Campbell, William Cockran, Joseph Conklin near Chillicothe, James Cummings in care of Col. Finley, David Dawson on the head waters of Salt Creek, Asa Dunn in Franklinton, Hamilton Dougherty, John Entreken, James Edmiston, William Edmiston at Chillicothe, Charles Ewing in care of John Blair at Franklinton, Thomas Earle near Chillicothe, Hezekiah Farnum at Salt Lick, Peter Fuller, Samuel Finley, Sarah Burton Frame at Chillicothe, Enoch Fenwick, Robert Grunby at Buckskin, Thomas Hardy, Geo. Hurlem, jun., John Huet at Scioto, Richard Harrison at Chillicothe, Mr. Hamilton at Westfall, John Gutman at Scioto, William Gabriel on Deer Creek, William Holdenby at the mouth of Guyan, Capt. Robert Higgins in care of Joseph Harness, Francis Herran at Scioto Salt Works,

John Henthom, Samuel Jackson, David Lewis near Chillicothe, David Latin at Scioto, James Morrison (21 miles below the mouth of the Scioto), James M'Gill (taylor in Chillicothe), John M'Lean (tanner), Robert M'Mahon on Paint Creek in Ross County, James Mitchel near Chillicothe, Thomas Morris near Franklinton, David Suth Meade at Chillicothe, Benjamin M'Clure in care of John Brown in Chillicothe, Samuel Moyers at Chillicothe, Isaac Penniston at Ross County in care of Mr. Pellers at Sunfish, Peter Paugh at Pe Pee, William Reed near Chillicothe, William Robinson, Oliver Ross, Joseph Reynolds in Adams County, John Rhods near Chillicothe, Samuel Rabb, jun., William Russell at the mouth of the Scioto, Dr. Joseph Scott, Charles Cisnor, Thompson Smith & Samuel Huey at Pe Pee, William Sturgeon, Joseph Shoutts, Stephen Smith, Roger Selden at the Salt Works, Jacob Singer at falls of Paint Creek, Henry Shees, Samuel Smith, Henry Sheely, Stephen Timmons, George Turner in care of Adam Turner, Harden C. Webb at Chillicothe, Michael Thomas, Henry Warlick at Chillicothe, Thomas Thompson (merchant), Isaac Williams, jun., near Franklinton in care of David Duncan, jun., Thomas White at Westfall, James Wilson at Chillicothe, Peter White (20 miles above Chillicothe), Isaac Warner, George Zimmer, John Walker (care of John Carlisle), Edward Wilcocks (care of Joseph Tiffin).

James Ferguson "intends leaving this town next spring" and has land for sale.

Reuben Abrams writes regarding his candidacy for the legislature.

Volume III, Saturday, 15 January 1803, No. 137

Charles Willing Byrd writes a letter to Gov. Arthur St.Clair, sen.

Edward Tiffin's letter to the Congress is printed. Also a letter from Thomas Worthington.

Ross County election results mention Edward Tiffin, Arthur St.Clair, Return Jonathan Meigs, Benjamin Ives Gilman, Nathaniel Massie, Abraham Claypoole, James Dunlap, James Scott, James Grubb, Thomas Worthington, Michael Baldwin, William Patton, Robert Culbertson, John Clair, David Shelby, Isaac Dawson, Jacob Smith, Reuben Abrams, Thomas Stockdon, William Robinson, Walter Buell, Jeremiah M'Lene, Benjamin Urmston. Adams County results mention Joseph Lucas, Joseph Darlinton, John Beasley, William Russell, Thomas Kirker, Israel Donalson, Andrew Ellison, Phil Lewis, Mr. Parker, Mr. Eddie, Thomas Odle, Mr. Ledwick, Noble Grimes, N. Beasley, Mr. Denning, Mr. Carey, Mr. Washburn, Mr. Scott. In Fairfield County: Bazaliel Wells, Robert F. Slaughter, Samuel Carpenter, David Rees, William Trimble, William Irwin, William Gass, Samuel Kratser, James Converse, Mr. Lynch.

Winn Winship, Duncan M'Arthur and Samuel Finley regarding property taken by Reuben Abrams in his suit against the estate of Bazil Abrams.

Volume III, Saturday, 22 January 1803, No. 138

Election returns from Clermont County mention Edward Tiffin, Mr. Ellis, Rodger Warren, Mr. Buchanan. In Jefferson County: John Milligan, James Pritchard, Bazaliel Wells, Zenas Kimberly, Mr. Humphrey, Mr. M'Cune, Mr. Bear, Mr. Meeks, Mr. Beal, Mr. Ellicott, Mr. Beaty, Mr. Boughman. Belmont County returns mention William Vance, James Alexander, James Smith, Elijah Woods, Joseph Sharp, Josiah Hatcher, Andrew Marshall, Daniel M'Elheran, Jacob Coleman and Moses Moorhead.

John M'Dougal has a new shipment of goods for sale at his store.

Volume III, Saturday, 29 January 1803, No. 139

A note regarding Fairfield County elections mentions William Irwin.

Isaac Claypool wants to establish a ferry on the Scioto River on his land opposite the Praira just below the mouth of Deer Creek, Ross County.

Ferguson & M'Farland have dissolved their partnership in Chillicothe.

Volume III, Saturday, 5 February 1803, No. 140

A note regarding a meeting of the Republican Society of Columbia at which Col. John Armstrong presided.

Hubbard Tayler, living in Clark County on Boon's Creek, reports two runaway slaves named Packolett and Joshua.

Thomas Davidson, in Chillicothe, reports a stray horse.

Volume III, Saturday, 12 February 1803, No. 141

A note regarding Washington County election returns mentions William Wells,

Joseph Buel, W. Silliman, Robert Safford, William Jackson and Edward Tiffin. Reuben Abrams regarding taxes paid in 1802.

Adam Betz, jailor, Ross County reports an escaped prisoner, George Fridley, a German, who was arrested by order of the Virginia governor.

James Denny has opened a house of entertainment in the house in Chillicothe formerly occupied as a tavern by Mr. Gregg and lately by Mr. Keys.

Volume III, Saturday, 19 February 1803, No. 142

T. Worthington sends a report of the Congressional committee on the business of Ohio. He mentions Edward Tiffin, Thomas Worthington, John Cleves Symmes.

Samuel Brown has just commenced business in Chillicothe and has goods for sale in the house formerly occupied as a tavern by Thomas Gregg.

William Irwin asks those indebted to Alexander M'Laughlin & Company to pay their bills. Mr. Carlisle will be buying spring goods for them.

John Carlisle wants to buy racoon, fox and wild cat skins.

John Clemons says he had nothing to do with the escape of George Fridley and prints a deposition from George Forker who lodged with Clemons and his family in Chillicothe. Sworn by Reuben Abrams, justice of the peace.

Volume III, Saturday, 25 February 1803, No. 143

Washington County election returns mention Edward Tiffin, W. Wells, J. Buel, R. Safford, W. Silliman, W. Jackson, W. Skinner, J. Brown, D. Woodbridge, O. Rice, G. Devol, W.R. Putnam, Ebenezer Sproat, C. Green.

A note regarding the Orleans boat belonging to James & M'Coy of Chillicothe.

Volume III, Saturday, 5 March 1803, No. 144

The proceedings of the legislature mention William R. Dickinson, Noble Grimes, Israel Donalson, George Humphreys, Thomas M'Cune, Zacheus A. Beatty, Thomas Elliot, Edward Tiffin, Judge Meigs.

Charles Willing Byrd regarding his assistants in taking the census.

Charles Anderson, for Richard C. Anderson, has land for sale in the names of Thomas Hill, William Parsons, John Harvie, Seymore Powell. Apply to Duncan M'Arthur, Col. Massie, Henry Massie, or John Beasley.

Thomas Scott regarding the suit of Jacob Shepherd vs. John Templane in the Ross County Court of Common Pleas.

Jacob Richart about a petition in the Ross County Court to divide a tract of land and a mill amongst the heirs of Richard Nolin, dec'd, late of Ross County.

Volume III, Saturday, 12 March 1803, No. 145

Gov. Edward Tiffin's speech to the General Assembly is printed.

Wm. Campbell and Joseph Campbell regarding a meeting of the Republican Society in Pleasant township mentions Mr. Willis.

Proceedings of the Legislature mention Joseph Darlinton, Aaron Wheeler of Trumbull County, George Humphreys, Thomas M'Cune, William Creighton, jun., Israel Donalson, Zacheus A. Beatty, Thomas Elliot, Noble Grimes, John M'Dougal, James & M'Coy, Joseph Campbell's mill dam on the Scioto River.

Henry Vanmeter, at Chillicothe, regarding his stud horse.

Volume III, Saturday, 19 March 1803, No. 146

A message to Gov. Edward Tiffin from the legislature is printed.

The proceedings of the legislature mention John M'Dougal, James & M'Coy, Rice Bullock, Anna Rickabough's divorce from Peter Rickabough, Sally Woolcot's divorce from John Woolcott, John Armstrong.

A note regarding the robbery of Mr. Kraizer, sheriff of Fairfield County.

Appointments made by the President include Joseph Wood (Register of the Land Office at Marietta in place of Peregrine Foster, resigned), John Lelman (Commissioner of John Cleves Symmes' lands vice W. Goforth, resigned), Daniel Bissell (of the Indiana Territory, collector for the district of Massac vice William Chritles, who has moved from the area), Jesse Spencer (Register of the Land Office at Chillicothe, vice Thomas Worthington, resigned), Charles William Byrd (judge of the District of Ohio), Michael Baldwin (District Attorney for Ohio), David Zeigler (Marshal of the District of Ohio).

Tho. Gibson, Auditor of Ohio accounts, regarding the payment of taxes.

Charles Daily, at New Lancaster, Fairfield County, wants to hire carpenters.

Volume III, Saturday, 26 March 1803, No. 147

Edward Tiffin and T. Worthington regarding acts of the U.S. Congress which pertain to the government of Ohio.

Henry Musselman about the estate sale of John Immel, dec'd, at his house in Ross County about three miles from Chillicothe on the Wheeling road.

Joseph Kerr, near Chillicothe, wants to hire workers.

Sam. Kratzer, sheriff of Fairfield County, regarding the men who robbed him.

Proceedings of the Assembly mention Joseph Campbell, Thomas Worthington, N. Willis, Athens University, William James, John Bigger, Anna Rickabough, Sally Woolcot, Nathaniel Willis.

J. Maxwell lost a pocket book between Zanesville and Wills' Creek crossing.

John Chenoweth wants to establish a ferry on the Scioto River on the road from Kentucky to the Scioto Salt Works.

Volume III, Saturday, 2 April 1803, No. 148

The proceedings of the legislature mention Edward Tiffin, Sally Woolcot, Anna Rickabough, Joseph Campbell, Darby Creek, Isaac Helmick.

John Smith and Thomas Worthington are chosen U.S. Senators. Return Jna. Meiggs, William Spriggs and Samuel Huntington are chosen supreme judges. W. Silliman, C. Pease and F. Dunlavy are chosen presiding judges.

Samuel Finley says that Rev. William Speer left his accounts in Finley's hands when he left Chillicothe.

John M'Dougal, "wishing to decline the mercantile business", offers the rest of his stock for sale at his store in Chillicothe.

Thomas Scott and Wm. Creighton regarding the suit of Lucas Hawkins vs. Emanuel Viner in the Ross County Court of Common Pleas.

Joseph Cookes, at Zanesville, says that his wife, Mary Cookes, has left him, and he won't pay her debts.

Volume III, Saturday, 9 April 1803, No. 149

Proceedings of the legislature mention Joseph Campbell, William C. Schenck, Athens University, Paint Creek, New Market, Rice Bullock.

A list of associate judges in the various counties includes John Walworth, Calvin Austin and Aaron Wheeler in Trumbull; William Smith, Henry Backman and Robert Simmison in Columbiana; James Pritchard, Philip Cabell and Jacob Martin in Jefferson; David Vance, David Lockwood and James Alexander in Belmont; Griffin Green, Ducley Woodbridge and Joseph Buell in Washington; Robert Safford, Bruster Heigley and G.W. Putnam in Gallia; John Collins, Joseph Lucas and Thomas Leviney in Scioto; Joseph Darlinton, David Eddy and Hosea Moore in Adams; John Wood, Ambrose Ranson and Philip Gatch in Clermont; Michael Jones, Luke Foster and James Silver in Hamilton; Jacob D. Lowe, William James and Ignatius Brown in Warren; John Greer, James Dunn and John Kitchel in Butler; Benjamin Archer, Isaac Spinning and John Ewing in Montgomery; James Barrot, Benjamin Whiteman, and William Maxwell in Green; John Dill, David Jameson and Jos. Foos in Franklin; Reuben Abrams, William Patton and Felix Renix in Ross; William Irvin, Samuel Carpenter and Daniel Vanmeter in Fairfield.

John Sherer, in Chillicothe, has whiskey for sale at William Keys' place.

Henry Massie has laid out a town on the Ohio and Scioto Rivers.

Henry Huston says Samuel Kratzer has accused him of robbing him, but Huston produces depositions from Jared Jones, George Coffenberry of Lancaster, Elizabeth Coffenberry and Mary Coffenberry (sworn before Hugh Boyle, justice of the peace in Fairfield County) that prove he couldn't have. He mentions Mr. Pitzer's store.

J. Gibbons wants to hire taylors at his shop in Water Street, Chillicothe.

A list of letters left at the Post Office in Chillicothe includes John Alexander in care of James Ferguson, Thomas Armstrong near Chillicothe, Job Broughton, Solomon Broderick, William & Biggerhead (5 miles from the Falls of Paint Creek), John Blair, Conrad Bitzer in Chillicothe, John Brown, Frederick Bray, John Croskey at the mouth of Deer Creek, Samuel Clifton, Thomas Cellar, Patrick Cunningham at Newark, Samuel Coover, Michael Creamer, William Cook, John Sharp, John Comens near Chillicothe, Daniel C. Cooper, John Clark, Thomas C. Dowden (printer), Aaron Dawley near Chillicothe, John Dill, James Dungan, David Davis, John Dunlap near Chillicothe, Edward Dawson, Josiah Doddridge at the crossings of Paint Creek, James Ewing, Joseph Eakins at New Market, Ambrose Everits near Chillicothe, Widow Hezekiah Furnam, Robert Greenlee at Buckskin settlement, George Givins, John Gillum at Chillicothe, Thomas Gibson, Jacob Groninger at the mouth of the Scioto River, Francis Heron, Samuel Hopkins, Charles Hammond (attorney), Daniel Hamilton, John Hawkins (drummer in Capt. Cooper's company), Samuel Henry at Pe Pee, Elizabeth Haslip, John Hampsher in care of John Carlisle, John Hunt on the Chillicothe road, Richard Harrison, Alexander Jinkins, John James in Chillicothe, John Johnston in Ross County, Samuel Jordan in care of Col. Massie, Robert Jones, Doctor Leonard Jewett at Belprie, James Killgore, Simon Kenton on Mad River, Elijah Lockard, Elias Langham, Samuel Lukis in care of Doctor Tiffin, William Lukis, James M'Gill (taylor), Jacob M'Dill, Obid Macy, John M'Cleary in care of Matthew Taylor, John May (16 miles from Chillicothe), John M'Connel, James Mills in Chillicothe, William M'Landish in care of John Carlisle, Daniel M'Axter, Francis or Samuel Malone near Chillicothe, John M'Lain, Alexander M'Mullen, Charles Moore in care of Joseph Thompson, James Milligan, John M'Afferty, Benjamin Newell at Salt Creek, Ichabod Marthau in Chillicothe, Hugh Montgomery or Montgomery Sherry, George or Mathew Newhum at Dayton or Franklinton, Robert and Levi Patrick, Robert Patton, John Peppers near Chillicothe, Sarah M. Holland in care of Nathan Reeves, Mrs. Roberts at Chillicothe, Andrew Rolston, William Reed, John Rush in Ross County, Nathan Rawling near Franklinton, John Scott, Samuel Smith (surveyor in Franklinton), Capt. Thomas Stockdon near Chillicothe, Anthony Strout at New Market, David Seelize at Franklinton, Alexander Scroggs in care of Samuel Findley, Oliver Strong, Thomas Smith, Maj. Uriah Springer, George Smith at Deer Creek, David Shepherd, Joseph Swearingen at New Market, Lemuel Sayers at Chillicothe, Jacob Smith, Adam Turner, William Thornton at Chillicothe, George Trautner, jun., Samuel Thomas near Chillicothe, William Underwood at Chillicothe, William Vazy, Henry Vanmetre, Henry Ballentine at Ross County, John Terrel, John S. Wills, Isaac Williams, sen., in care of David Duncan at Franklinton, Capt. James Waugh, Thomas White, Noah Willey, John Wilson, Isaac Warner, James Wallace near Chillicothe, William Wallace, Thomas Wilkins, John Walker (blacksmith near Chillicothe), Jacob Widner, George Zimmer on Pickaway Plain, William Wilson near Chillicothe, David Yates. Joseph Tiffin.

Volume III, Saturday, 16 April 1803, No. 150

Proceedings of the legislature mention Rice Bullock, Athens University, William Goforth, sen., William Sprigg, Samuel Huntington, Return Jonathan Meigs, Calvin Pease, Wyllys Williman, Francis Dunlavy.

George W. Selby has opened a house of entertainment in New Lancaster in the house formerly occupied by Doctor Delano and lately by Mr. Austin.

John Stidger has hats for sale at James Denny's house in Chillicothe.

Volume III, Saturday, 23 April 1803, No. 151

Proceedings of the legislature mention Samuel Huntington, Moses Thompson, Thomas Gibson, Return J. Meigs, jun., Samuel Kratzer (sheriff of Fairfield County), Winthrop Sargent, Charles W. Byrd.

Michael Baldwin and Nathaniel Massie print several laws of Ohio.

William M'Farland asks all those indebted to the late firm of Ferguson & M'Farland to settle their accounts.

John Beasley, at Manchester, asks those indebted to him to pay their bills.

William Walker, living at Wayne's-ville on the Little Miami River, reports a stray horse.

Volume IV, Saturday, 30 April 1803, No. 153

Michael Baldwin and Nath. Massie print a law of the state of Ohio.

Gov. Edward Tiffin says that Col. Samuel Finley, of Chillicothe, is appointed Adjutant General of the Ohio Militia.

John M'Dougal is the clerk of the Ross County Court of Common Pleas.

A note regarding a meeting of the Chillicothe Debating Society.

Thomas Reed has returned to Chillicothe with whiskey to sell at Phielden

Hubbard's store opposite Capt. Wm. Lamb's.

Stephen Carey, at the mouth of the Scioto, wants to hire a shoemaker.

Proceedings of the legislature mention Winthrop Sargent, Miami Exporting Company, N. Willis. Commissioners are named: David Shelby, John Chenoweth and Reuben Abrams in Scioto County; Samuel S. Spencer, Robert Patrick and Timothy Green in Gallia County; James Ferguson, Jeremiah M'Lene and William Creighton, sen., in Franklin; John Leavitt, Calvin Austin and John H. Adgate in Columbiana; James Barret, John Brownlee and Cornelius Snider in Warren; John Silvers, Benjamin Stiles and David Sutton in Butler; Ichabod B. Halsey, Bladin Ashbey and William M'Clelland in Montgomery and Green.

Volume IV, Saturday, 7 May 1803, No. 154

Proceedings of the legislature mention Winthrop Sargent, Thomas Gibson, N. Willis, Erie Literary Society.

Edward Tiffin regarding a letter he received regarding New Orleans.

A note about Benjamin Connet who robbed Miss Esther M'Dowell. Connet's parents live near Redstone.

Adj. Gen. Samuel Finley gives general orders to the Ohio militia.

James Denny, agent for the salt works, regarding his office at the Salt Works.

John M'Dougal regarding the grand and petit jurors mentions Wyllys Silliman, Reuben Abrams, William Patton and Felix Renix.

John G. Macan has land for sale near Franklinton and in Chillicothe.

Volume IV, Saturday, 14 May 1803, No. 155

Proceedings of the legislature mention Samuel Carpenter, James Wells, Henry Abrams, Nathan Ellis, Erie Literary Society.

An unsigned letter to the editor mentions Jeremiah Morrow.

Daniel Vanmeter, living near the Muddy Praire in Fairfield County, has livestock for sale at auction. He bought them from Col. Worthington & Col. Sproat.

Amos Derrough, near the mouth of Mad River, reports a stolen horse. The thief is John Black, an Irishman and a distiller, who came from Clarksburg.

David Worley, of Belmont, says he won't honor the debts of his wife, Sarah.

John M'Dougall regarding the township boundaries decided on by Reuben Abrams, William Patton and Felix Renix, associate judges. He mentions Ezekiel Driver in Pickaway township, John Crouse in Green township, William Lewis in Jefferson township, Arthur Chenoweth in Pe Pee township, Samuel S. Spencer at the salt works in Lick township, Vincent Hollers in Scioto township, Swearingen's mill in Scioto township, Henry Massie in Scioto township, Joseph Clark in Union township, Lemuel Sayers in Concord township, Christian Plato in Paxton township, Oliver Ross in New Market, Fergus Moore in Wayne township.

Volume IV, Saturday, 21 May 1803, No. 156

A letter to the public from Michael Baldwin mentions Col. Huntington, Col. Worthington, Mr. Humphrey, Mr. M'Cune.

A note regarding the Indian attack on Capt. Herod near Old Chillicothe.

Commissioners for leasing school lands have been appointed by the governor: John Levit in Trumbull County, Robert Simmison in Columbiana, Reason Bell in Jefferson, John M'Williams in Belmont, Samuel Carpenter in Fairfield, Winn Winship in Ross, Joseph Vance in Franklin, Joseph Lucas in Scioto, Robert Safford in Gallia, William Goforth, jun., in Hamilton, Celadon Symmes in Butler, Robert Boggess in Green, John Kitchel in Montgomery, Ignatious Brown in Warren.

Thomas Reed has goods for sale in Fielding Hubbard's late store.

James & M'Coy ask those indebted to them to pay Lemuel James.

William Goforth is a candidate for the U.S. Congress.

J. Smith, watch maker, gold & silver smith, has opened a shop in Chillicothe.

Volume IV, Saturday, 28 May 1803, No. 157

A note regarding the murder of Polly Malony, age 9, by her uncle, John Rowe, late from Kentucky. Mentions her step-father, William Thomas, in Pleasant township. Also Alexander Martin and Amos Ellis in Williamsburg.

A note regarding the murder of Capt. Herod. Mentions Mr. Ferguson, Mr. Williams, and Mr. Wolff, living a short distance from Old Chillicothe.

John Porter reports clothes and papers stolen from his saddle bags on his horse outside of Thos. Reed's store.

Ephraim Bates found a horse near Chillicothe.

John Brumley says his wife, Elizabeth, left him and he won't pay her debts.

Volume IV, Saturday, 4 June 1803, No. 158

A letter from Isaac Zane, interpretor, at the head of Mad River to Elias Langham and Duncan M'Arthur in Chillicothe about the Wiandot nation of Indians includes a letter from the Wiandot chiefs. It's witnessed by Sam. M'Collock and Jas. Robitaille. Another letter from the Indians is taken to Gov. Edward Tiffin by James M'Pherson, and a letter in answer mentions Capt. Herod.

Joshua Parish is elected sheriff in Scioto County and James Munn, coroner.

John M'Dougall offers his house for sale in Water street adjoining Mr. Keys' tavern in Chillicothe.

Reuben Abrams, Wm. Creighton, sen., and James Ferguson regarding the suits of Nathan Kennedy vs. John Crocker and Nathan Kennedy vs. John Derush in Ross County Court of Common Pleas. Mentions James Denny in Chillicothe.

Walter Buell, in Chillicothe, says he is "about to remove to Bourbon, Kentucky" and will sell his household, kitchen and medicinal shop furniture, live-stock and land. Those indebted to him should pay William Creighton.

Volume IV, Saturday, 18 June 1803, No. 160

A note regarding the arrest of Benjamin Connet who robbed Miss M'Dowell.

Jeremiah Gustin, on Clear Creek in Franklin township of Warren County, reports a strayed or stolen horse.

Thomas Scott, of the Select Council of Chillicothe, regarding the incorpora-tion of Chillicothe.

Paul Streeby regarding people killing his hogs and chickens and trespassing on his land just outside of Chillicothe.

John S. Wills will print a digest of the laws of the State of Ohio.

Jacob Smith, at the Falls of Paint, regarding lots in the town of Amsterdam.

Volume IV, Saturday, 25 June 1803, No. 161

A proclamation from Gov. Edward Tiffin regarding the Indians.

A speech from the Shawnee and Wyandott nations to Gov. Edward Tiffin mentions Gov. Harrison, Capt. Herod. Also Tiffin's answer to them.

Election returns in Ross County mention Elias Langham, Jeremiah Morrow, Michael Baldwin, Wm. M'Millen, John G. Macan, Thomas Scott, W. Creighton, sen., Robert Adams, G. Vincenheller, W. Robinson, Isaac Cook, David Shelby, Sam. Edwards, Jos. Gardner, John Odle, G. Williams, Sam. Wilson, Sam. Evans, John Davidson, John Johnston, John Barns, John Guthrey, John Robins, John Hoddy, Noble Crawford, William Davis, Joseph Tayler.

Adam Hollar, Baker, has moved from the house next to Capt. Lamb's tavern to the new frame house south of the Courthouse.

Adj. Gen. Samuel Finley says that Lieut. Col. James Dunlap will preside over the court martial, at John Crouse's house at Kinnickinic, of Capt. William Roberts. The court will consist of Maj. M'Lene, Capt. Dawson, Capt. Lamb, Capt. Lewis, Capt. Barns, Capt. Chesnut, Capt. Entriken, Maj. Manara, Maj. M'Arthur, Capt. Petty, Capt. Henderson, Capt. M'Coy, Capt. Hawkins, Capt. John S. Wills.

Peter Fuller, post rider, regarding his route mentions Mr. Houghland.

James Denny, in Chillicothe, wants the return of his borrowed saddle.

Volume IV, Saturday, 2 July 1803, No. 162

Election returns mention Jeremiah Morrow, William M'Millan, William Goforth, John Byland, Michael Baldwin, Elias Langham, Samuel Shepherd, Philemon Beecher.

John G. Macan says he is "shortly about to leave the country for some time" and has much of his land and property for sale.

Samuel Teeter, Jun., living near Twinn Creek, reports a stray mare. Deliver to Maj. Duncan M'Arthur near Chillicothe.

Adj. Gen. Samuel Finley about the court martial of Capt. William Roberts.

Volume IV, Saturday, 9 July 1803, No. 163

Accounts of the Fourth of July celebration mention Gov. Edward Tiffin, Henry Abrams, John Rowland, Emanuel Carpenter, Alexander White, Col. Saml. Carpenter.

More election returns mention William Goforth, Jeremiah Morrow, Michael Baldwin, William M'Millan, Elias Langham, William M'Intire.

Samuel Brown has goods for sale in the house formerly occupied by Thomas Gregg as a tavern in Chillicothe.

Those in Scioto township needing their brands and marks recorded should apply to Nathaniel Johnson on Main Street in Chillicothe.

A list of letters left at the Post Office in Chillicothe includes Doctor Silas Allen, Priscella Angel, Henry Ballenger, Lewis Bible, Robert Beaty, Risdon Beachamp, Soveren Brown at Chillicothe, Robert Blare, Widow Boyde, Samuel Brown, Robert Breeden, Eli Bereman, Edward Busick, Doct. Walter Buell, James Bonner, William Bowler, Thomas Bullett, John Clemmons (jailor), James Caldwell (son of Samuel Caldwell), Judge Byrd, Joshua Bogart, Isaac Brink, Mr. Collins at the mouth of the Scioto, William Craig, John Clark in care of E. Tiffin, Joseph Catterlin, Henry Coons, William Croll, Joseph Campbell, Th. Cellars, John Dill, Tho. Duggen, Daniel Drolener, Hugh Flyn at Pee Pee, Michael Fisher, William Fulkner in care of Wm. Creighton, James B. Findley, John Grovner, John Graham at the forks of Scioto, James Galaway near Old Chillicothe, James Gordon, William Gabriel, John Higgans at Scioto salt lick, Daniel Hamilton, John Hamble near M'Coy's mill, Thomas Housewright, Hugh Gaston, John Hixson, Thomas Hicks, Asher Harbert, Nicholas Hall, Lieut. Nathan Heald at Chillicothe, David Jones, James Johnston at Indian Creek, John Klowser, David Kirkpartrick, Barnabas Lambert, James Lambert, Joseph Lane, William Lewis, John M'Donald, Nelchor Meyers in care of John Mantle, John M'Nemar (ten miles above Chillicothe), John M'Ginnis, Samuel M'Dowll near the mouth of Scioto, Francis Mallon, William Martin at Scioto, Bill Miller at Darby, Daniel M'Arther, John M'Coy, Samuel Mitchel on Darby Creek, Thomas M'Donald, Harmond Ness at Franklin on Scioto, Orgmond Cradle in Chillicothe, Doct. Anthony Potts at Pee Pee, John Pancake, William Pittinger, jun., nine miles below Chillicothe, Thomas Pilman on Darby Creek, Joshua Parnish, Robert and Levee Patrick, James Robinson, Horatio Strong, George Ligner near Alexandria, John N.C. Schenck at Franklin, James Safrington at Chillicothe, John Searle at Toby-town, David Latin on Deer Creek, Catharine Seels near Franklinton, Oliver and Daniel Strong, Anthony Swinehart (millwright near Gundy's mill), Richard Sparrow at the salt works, Hon. William Sprigg, Ethan Stone at Chillicothe, John Saylor, Oliver Smith, Andrew Sukey in care of Wm. Lamb, Isaac Sayman in care of Henry Massie, George Ruble, Abijah Rinker near Chillicothe, Mary Robinson, Wolsey Robinson, Jacob Richart, James Reed in care of William Keys, Jacob Reeder at Franklinton, Daniel Ross on Pickaway Plain, George Turner in Franklinton, Samuel Thomas near Chillicothe, Robert Townsley near Chillicothe, Jacob Teal, Emanuel Trexler in care of Wm. Lamb, Frederick Unsell living on the Ohio, John Wilson (living 25 miles from Chillicothe), George Vashen or Pashen in Chillicothe, Moses Wright, George Williams, John Walter on Lee's Creek, Rachael Wilkins at New Market, Lenhort Wolf (innkeeper near Chillicothe), Henry Wohrley, James George Whetstone at Scioto, Philip Wolff (innkeeper), Josiah Wilson near Chillicothe, Noah Zane at Chillicothe, Martin Zimmerman at Chillicothe, David Yatts near Chillicothe, Col. James Dunlap, Abraham Jones, William Rainey. Entered by Joseph Tiffin.

Oliver & Buchanan have a new shipment of goods for sale in the house lately occupied by Doctor Buell on Water Street in Chillicothe.

John Brown, of Franklin County, about a note to Samuel Smith, of Kentucky, signed over to Nathaniel Barker of Lexington, Kentucky.

Volume IV, Saturday, 16 July 1803, No. 164

Election returns mention Jeremiah Morrow, William M'Millan, Michael Baldwin, Elias Langham, William Goforth, Bazaleel Wells, David Abbott.

Obituary: John Barnes, formerly of Berkeley County, Virginia, died at Pe Pee on 7 July 1803. "He was a respectable citizen and an honest man."

William Rogers, on the north fork of Paint Creek, 4 miles from Chillicothe, reports a stray mare.

Christian Moura, living near Maj. M'Arthur's, reports a stray cow.

Volume IV, Saturday, 23 July 1803, No. 165

A letter from Pres. Th. Jefferson to Gov. Edward Tiffin is printed.

Lt. Col. E. Langham says the following are appointed officers in the Ross County militia: Adj. Joseph Campbell, John Edmiston (surgeon), Ephraim Johnston (surgeon's mate), George Hoffman (clerk), Jonathan Redick (pay master), William S. Hutt (quarter master).

N. Willis asks those indebted to him to settle their accounts so that he can buy new printing type.

Samuel Brown has just received a new shipment of goods in Chillicothe.

John Carlisle, collector of the Virginia Army Lands, regarding taxes due.

Robert M'Mahon, at Paint Creek, reports that he found a cow.

John Brown, at the Falls of Paint, regarding a note to Jacob Myers.

Volume III, Saturday, 30 July 1803, No. 166

A note regarding the supposed robbery of Esther M'Dowell suspecting her story. Mentions her father in Kentucky, Benjamin Connet, John Armstrong, Mr. Con (taylor at Watsonburgh) and Rev. Mr. Grier.

John M'Dougal wants to buy pork in Chillicothe.

Jer. M'Lene, sheriff in Ross County, regarding the land taxes.

William Dusinbery, living 22 miles from New Lancaster on the road to Muskingum, on the waters of Jonathan's Creek at Pleasant Point, found a mare.

Volume III, Saturday, 6 August 1803, No. 167

N. Willis wants to hire two printers at the office in Chillicothe.

Volume III, Saturday, 13 August 1803, No. 168

Solomon Cox, living on Salt Lick Creek, has land for sale including the mill.

William M'Garrah, on Beesley's fork in Adams County, reports a stolen mare.

John Carlisle, Collector of the Virginia Army Lands, has land for sale.

Elias Rector, at Chillicothe, has land for sale adjoining Maj. D. M'Arthur and Col. Thomas Worthington near Chillicothe. He also has land on Deer Creek next to Buskirks' place. And land on Paint Creek surveyed by John M'Donald.

Isaac Davis, John Evans & James Menary, in Adams County, about a meeting of the Commissioners at John Megate's tavern in Manchester.

Volume III, Saturday, 20 August 1803, No. 169

A note regarding the death of a man believed to be Isaac Miller on the road from Wheeling to Chillicothe.

Michael Feely, at Philadelphia, son and heir to Timothy Feely who served as a lieutenant in the Virginia line, under Gen. Morgan, during the Revolutionary War, says that Michael Feely, a nephew to Timothy Feely, and Wm. Daly are trying to sell lands on Paint Creek near Chillicothe belonging to the deceased.

David Hudson, in Trumbull County, regarding taxes in the county.

Charles Thompson and Edward Stall say that they are not partners in the blacksmithing business. Charles Thompson carries on that business.

Dr. Johnston, living at the Pickaway Plains, reports a strayed or stolen mare. Deliver to Wm. Carnehand on Darby Creek.

Volume III, Saturday, 27 August 1803, No. 170

Samuel Beeler, Sen., living on Cane Run near Lexington, Kentucky, reports a runaway slave named Daniel.

James Corbat, living in Union Township, reports a strayed or stolen mare. Deliver to Wm. Creighton in Chillicothe.

Volume III, Saturday, 3 September 1803, No. 171

Joseph Reed reports a mare that strayed from the forks of Mad River.

Volume III, Saturday, 10 September 1803, No. 172

A proclamation from Gov. Edward Tiffin is entered by Wm. Creighton, jun., regarding John Row's escape from the jail at Williamsburgh, Clermont County.

Joseph Tiffin, in Chillicothe, has opened a house of entertainment in the house lately occupied by James Denny in Chillicothe.

More on the case of Easter M'Dowell mentions Judge Harris on Loyal Stock Creek, Robert Robb, Rev. Mr. Grier, Benjamin Connet.

Capt. Thomas Gregg is a candidate for representative to the legislature.

Obituary: Mrs. Eliza. Steele, wife of Mr. James Steele, died in Chillicothe on Thursday morning, 8 September 1803.

Reuben Abrams regarding a meeting of the associate judges of Ross County.

Doctor Edmiston has a new shipment of medicines for sale at his Apothecary's shop in Chillicothe.

William Irvine, for Alexander M'Laughlin & Company, says the partnership of Alexander M'Laughlin and John Carlisle is dissolved.

John Lytle reports a mare stolen from Williamsburgh in Clermont County.

Christian Bottleman has completed his cellars and store house at the mouth of the Scioto River.

Charles Brown regarding a mare that strayed from him on Clear Creek about two and a half miles from Franklinton.

Volume III, Saturday, 17 September 1803, No. 173

An article regarding federal appointments mentions Ar. St.Clair.

John G. Macan says he's not leaving Ohio and will be a candidate for office.

Hannah Webster & John Webster, administrators, have land for sale lying five miles from Chillicothe on the Wheeling road and the main road to Hockhocking.

W. Silliman is moving to Chillicothe and will practice law there.

Apply to Wm. Keys regarding a farm for sale on the road to Deer Creek.

James Grubb, at Westfall, Executor of the estate of Francis Alexander, dec'd, late of Ross County, regarding the estate settlement.

Volume III, Saturday, 24 September 1803, No. 174

Rev. Francis Asbury, Bishop of the Methodist Episcopal Church, will preach at the Courthouse in Chillicothe on Sunday, 25 September.

Wm. Niblack has goods for sale in John M'Dougal's former house.

John M'Dougal asks those indebted to him to settle their accounts.

John Machir, in Washington, Kentucky, warns the public not to buy land from John S. Wills that was entered in the name of William Hickman on Isaac's Creek.

E. Langham, William Irvine and James Denny regarding the dispute between Adin Webb and Asa Lake.

Jer. M'Lene and Isaac Dawson about the court of inquiry that met at Gundy's mill to examine charges against Capt. Roberts and Lieut. Crow regarding their conduct during the Indian alarm. Capt. Isaac Brink was unable to attend. E. Langham considers the two honorably acquitted from the charges.

Volume III, Saturday, 1 October 1803, No. 175

G. Hoffman, Commissioner, regarding the leasing of lands for schools.

Henry Musselman says he is a candidate for public office.

Andrew Hawke, living on Little Beaver near Owen Davis' mill in Greene County, reports a stray mare.

Frederick Burgett, at the mouth of Darby, says that his wife, Phebe Burgett, has left him and he won't honor her debts.

Michael Feely, Jun., at Philadelphia, regarding the advertisement placed by Michael Feely, lately from Ireland, that he's the only heir of Timothy Feely. Michael Feely, jun., says that Timothy Feely was unmarried and bequethed the land, in his will recorded at Winchester, to his brother, Michael Feely, Sen., who is now deceased. He says he has sold the land to William Daly.

Volume III, Saturday, 8 October 1803, No. 176

John S. Wills offers his house and lot and furniture for sale.

Joseph C. Vance and John Paul about lots for sale in Xenia in Green County.

Solomon Bower, living on the north fork of Paint about four miles above Old Chillicothe, in Concord township of Ross County, reports a strayed or stolen mare.

G. Hoffman about suits in the Ohio District Court of John Stephenson, Marcus Stephenson, Hugh Stephenson, John Massie & Ann Massie his wife, William Massie and Betsey Massie his wife, devisees of Hugh Stephenson, dec'd, vs. Abraham Shepherd. Also John S. Wills vs. Peter Lionbuger. Also Uriah Springer and Sally

Springer his wife, William M'Cormack and Effe/Esse M'Cormack his wife, devisees of William Crawford, dec'd, vs. Thomas Armat. Also Philemon Thomas vs. William George for land on Paint Creek and Rattlesnake fork.

Joseph Foos, living in Franklinton, wants to hire house carpenters.

Samuel Evans regarding a road from New Market to Manchester.

A list of letters left at the Post Office in Chillicothe includes Henry Alstred at the mouth of Brush Creek, John Beatty in Butler County, Peter Bunn, William Boid, Ely Bereman, Amour Bales near Chillicothe, Michael Bradley at Chillicothe, Buckley Blasongane at the salt works, Isaac Brink, William Bitver near Chillicothe, Mr. Beaty, Edward Bustick, Joseph Boggs, Lewis Foster in care of Nathan Gregg, Augustus Friend in care of Judge Abrams, Thomas Bowen, John Clemens, David Colbertson, John W. Campbell in Ross County, Robt. Cunningham in care of Noble Crawford, Isaac Cook, David Curran at Westfall, John Coffey, John Conklen, John Cilliman, James Doulin, Robert Duglass, David Dillin, Adam Desabaug, Aaron Dawley, Hamilton Dougherty, Benj. Duncan, John Dougherty, John Deured, Dr. John Gassaway in Chillicothe, Stourton Edwards in care of O. Thomson, John Gundy, James Gaskell, Jacob Grubb, Lieut. Nathan Heald, John Higgans, Adam Hosack at Franklinton, Philip Hobaugh, Andrew Hobaugh at Barron courthouse, Colial Haynes, Samuel Henry at Pe Pee, Maj. John Hays, Johnston Hemphill, Alexander Hamilton near Old Chillicothe, Francis Herron, Robert Humes, Isabelle Jones (12 miles below Chillicothe), Samuel Jordan, Ja. Johnston, Abraham Jones, Saml. Kilpatrick, James Kilgore, Lemuel Kilbourn, John Linsey, Abraham or Chs. Leonard near Westfall, Patrick Lusk, Asa Luke at Salt Lick, Samuel Linton at Wainsville, Elias Langham, James Munn six miles above Big Scioto, David Munn on Salt Creek, John M'Ginnis in care of Jos. Thompson, John Mantle, Polly Mantle, Dan. Mullin in care of Capt. Greg, James Morris, Joshua M'Farling, William M'Bride, James M'Ginnis, Thomas Morris near Franklinton, Henry M'Dannel near Chillicothe, Rbt. M'Mahan, William Millar at Walnut Creek, John M'Clain (hatter), John M'Laughlin in care of Alex. M'Laughlin, Benj. M'Clure on Paint Creek, Humphry Montgomery, James Mitchell, Henry Northup at Greensburg, Philip D. Peyster at Chillicothe, John Paul, Nathan Peddycord, John Pursell, Avery Powers, Samuel Paturr six miles from Scioto, Robert Robinson, William Rodgers, John Rush, Mathew Richardson on Seven Mile Creek, Alex. Robertson, Ananis Randal, Mary Robinson, Thomas Reed, Geo. Ramsey, Thomas Spilman on Darby Creek, Richard Speer in care of Jos. Karr, Oliver Smith near Hamilton, James Sterfar in care of N. Gregg, Samuel Smith near Old Chillicothe, Alexander Screggs in care of Col. Finley, Oliver Strong, John Sillik at Greenfield, Henry Snider in care of John M'Dougal, Zachariah Stephens at Franklinton, Lucas Sullivant, Jos. Silvers, John Thomas, John Thompson in care of James Ferguson, Walter Tiley at Wheatstone, James Tapscott at Franklinton, Joseph Thompson at Athens, Stephen Timmans, Anthony Weaver near Chillicothe, George Vinsonhaylor, Isaac Warner, George Williams, Thos. White, John Williams, Robt. Worthington, John D. Wiley, Jno. Worley, Henry Worley, Samuel Wilson, John Welch at Franklinton, Jno. Walker (blacksmith), William Waddle, Moses Week, Lieut. Aaron Welch at Whetstone in care of Esq. Powers. Entered by Joseph Tiffin.

Volume III, Saturday, 15 October 1803, No. 177

William Smith, at Westfall, regarding a note to Charles Thomas of Virginia.

Volume III, Saturday, 22 October 1803, No. 178

Abraham Claypool is elected senator and Elias Langham, James Dunlap, John Evans and William Creighton, representatives, for Ross & Franklin Counties. Election returns in Ross and Franklin Counties mention Wm. Askew, Jos. Kerr, John G. Macan, James Grubb, John Blair, Isaac Cook, William Seymour, David Shelby, Isaac Dawson, James Crawford, John Crouse, Jon Perrell, James Beard, Henry Musselman. In Washington County: Elijah Backus, Joseph Buell, Jesse Fuller, Charles Mills, William Jackson. In Fairfield County: Philemon Beecher and Mr. Guess. In Clermont County: James Sargent, Jonathan Taylor and Daniel Figgans, sen. In Adams County: Thomas Kirker, Daniel Collier, Mr. Wright, Mr. Shepherd.

A note regarding the horse races at the Deer Creek Praira near Oswell Thompson's house.

Joseph Campbell regarding a note he gave to John Clark, of Mason County, Kentucky, for mill wright work.

Joseph Cleverston, in Green township of Ross County, found a stray horse.

James January regarding a bond to Benjamin Wood, now of Adams County.

Volume III, Saturday, 29 October 1803, No. 178

A meeting of the Scioto County commissioners will be held at the house of William Lucas, sen.

John Kerr regarding Mr. Richardson's invention of a new type of still.

Celadon Symmes, John Cleves Symmes, jun., & Daniel Symmes, at Lancaster, regarding land they bought from John Cleves Symmes, mention Benjamin Murphy.

Volume III, Saturday, 5 November 1803, No. 179

An account of the celebration of the Louisiana Treaty ratification at the Red Lion in Chillicothe.

Election returns mention John Milligan, Richard Beeson, John Sloane, Samuel Dunlap, Joseph M'Kee, Zenas Kimberly, Thomas Elliott, Isaac Meeks, and Zach. A. Beatty of Columbiana and Jefferson counties. And Benjamin Tappan, Ephraim Quimby and David Abbott in Trumbull County.

Moses Leonard, near Williamsburg, reports a stolen mare.

James Buchannan asks those indebted to the late firm of Oliver & Buchannan to settle their accounts. He says he will continue the store as usual.

Volume III, Saturday, 12 November 1803, No. 180

A letter to Gov. Edward Tiffin from H. Dearbourn at the Department of War.

Samuel Kratzer, Sheriff, regarding the robbery last March.

James Denny, at Chillicothe, asks those indebted to him to pay their bills.

Nathan Ellis, for William Hathaway, regarding surveying Hathaway's land, mentions Foster's warrant.

Robert W. Finley regarding his school in New Market.

John M'Clean, tanner, at Chillicothe, wants to buy hides or skins. He also wants to hire two apprentices to the tanning business.

Volume III, Saturday, 19 November 1803, No. 181

Benjamin Wood, on Eagle Creek, writes a letter to Nathaniel Willis, printer of the Scioto Gazette, regarding the note from James January, mentions Mr. Hunter of Clermont County and William Lytle of Williamsburg.

Duncan M'Arthur writes a letter to the public about the Louisiana Purchase and the recent letter from the War Department to Gov. Tiffin. He mentions Maj. Manary, John M'Donald, James Manary and Joseph Thompson.

James Dunlap about a meeting of the First Battalion of the Second Regiment of Ross County Militia at Christian Platter's near the Falls of Paint.

Benj. Urmston, George Yocken and Jethr. Nevil about the Chillicothe horse races mentions Joseph Kerr.

Duncan M'Arthur is "about to leave home on the Louisiana expedition" and asks those indebted to him to settle their accounts.

Volume III, Saturday, 26 November 1803, No. 182

John Sherer has barrels of Menongahala whiskey for sale at the Red Lion.

Joseph Tiffin, James Ferguson and John M'Lene regarding the sale of the property of John Underwood at the suit of Daniel Hamilton in the Ross County Court of Common Pleas.

Henry Nevell and Henry Rush regarding lots for sale in the town of Jefferson on the Pickaway Plains, adjoining Mr. Gay and Mr. Hetler.

Edward Tiffin has land for sale adjoining John Odle a mile below Walnut Creek. Also adjoining Joseph Gardner on the Scioto, 4 miles from Chillicothe.

R.J. Meigs, jun., and Wm. Sprigg, at Lancaster, regarding the Supreme Court.

A public notice to Jacob Bierle, a German, by trade a carpenter, who left Pennsylvania about 9-10 years ago, to write to John Beckley in Washington City.

Volume III, Saturday, 3 December 1803, No. 183

Joseph Tiffin has moved his tavern to the large brick building lately occupied by James Denny, at the sign of the Seventeen Stars.

William Keys, at the sign of the Red Lion in Chillicothe, has made an addition to his tavern and hotel.

Andrew Noteman, in Concord township of Ross County, says that his wife, Catharine Noteman, has left him, and he won't honor her debts.

William Niblack regarding his purchase of pork.

Volume III, Saturday, 10 December 1803, No. 184

Notes from the journal of the legislature mentions Nathaniel Massie, Thomas Scott, Elias Langham, James Mason, Adam Betz, Daniel Symmes, William Wood, Andrew Marshall, Jesse Fulton of Washington County, Geo. Hoffman. Includes the speech of Gov. Edward Tiffin.

John Carlisle has a new shipment of goods for sale at his store.

Thomas Gregg, at Pleasant Farm, has a sugar camp for rent.

William Johnston, living on Hockhocking, six miles above New Lancaster, reports a stray mare.

Volume III, Monday, 19 December 1803, No. 185

Proceedings of the legislature mention Abraham Shepherd, Daniel Collier, Samuel Dunlap, William Creighton, sen., Richard Beeson, Josiah Dillon, William Dodds, Samuel Dick, Abner Garard, Ichabod B. Miller, Ephraim Kibby, Philemon Beecher, William Gass, William M'Clure, John Wallace, Stephen Wood, Elias Langham, James Dunlap, David Abbot, John Sloane, Jonathan Taylor, Daniel Feagans, sen., Ephraim Quimby, John Wright, John Evans, Jesse Fulton, Charles Mills, William Jackson and James Smith.

Robert M'Connel has liquor and groceries for sale at Joseph Tiffin's.

John Ludwig has cattle for sale at Mr. F. Feathers' house, Fairfield County.

Jeremiah Johnson regarding cattle that strayed from him at Toby-town in Amanda township of Fairfield County. Deliver to Dr. Silas Allen at Toby-Town, George M. Selby at Lancaster or Esq. Edwards at Pickaway Plains.

Joseph Kerr has land for sale near the Sinking Spring.

Volume III, Monday, 26 December 1803, No. 186

More proceedings of the legislature mention Andrew Marshall, James Dunlap, Nathaniel Willis, Charles F. Chobert de Joncaire, John Schieffelin, George M'Dougall, Joseph Carpenter, Josiah Dillon, St. Clair's Ville.

A letter to the House of Representatives is signed by Ephraim Kibbey, David Abbot, Philemon Beecher, James Smith, Josiah Dillon, John Wallace, Abner Garard, Samuel Dick, J.B. Miller, William M'Clure, Jesse Fulton, Jonathan Taylor, and Daniel Feagans.

John Elliot, at Dayton, reports a stray horse.

Abraham Bitcher, at Lancaster, reports a strayed horse. Deliver to Jacob Grubb in Franklinton.

William Green and John Clemons have opened a blue dying and weaving shop.

Volume III, Monday, 2 January 1804, No. 187

More proceedings of the legislature mentions St. Clairsville, Josiah Dillon, William Wood, Israel Ludlow, James Smith, James Dunlap.

Edward Stalcup, of Ross County, was arrested on Thursday evening, Dec. 29, 1803, for the murder of Asa Mounts the night before. He confessed to Thomas Scott. The circumstances are printed.

An account of the dispute between the Indians and David Wolf mentions Maj. James Manary and Capt. M'Coy.

Elias Langham and Nath. Massie print a law of the State of Ohio.

John James, of Wood County, Virginia, about a statement made by Philemon Beecher, of New Lancaster, Fairfield County. Witnessed by Wyllys Silliman.

John Odle has opened a house of entertainment on the new Salt Lick Road, ten miles from Chillicothe.

William Hall regarding two bonds to John Beaver for land in Ross County.

Volume III, Monday, 9 January 1804, No. 188

Proceedings of the legislature mention Samuel Finley, John Armstrong, James January, William Crawford of Adams County, James Magovney of Adams County, James Dunlap, Pe Pee settlement, Salt Lick settlement.

A note about the militia of Ohio mentions Maj. Gen. John S. Gano, Qr. Master Gen. Daniel Symmes, Maj. Gen. Nath. Massie, Qr. Master Gen. David Bradford, Maj. Gen. Joseph Buell, Qr. Master Gen. Sam. Carpenter, Maj. Gen. Elijah Wadsworth, Qr. Master Gen. Brice Viers.

John Patton, of Ross County, committed suicide on Thursday morning, 5 January 1804, by hanging himself in his cellar. He left a wife and ten children.

Duncan M'Arthur, near Chillicothe, regarding a strayed or stolen mare.

Henry Musselman, administrator of the estate of John Immel, dec'd, late of Ross County, regarding the estate settlement.

Volume III, Monday, 16 January 1804, No. 189

The proceedings of the legislature print the letter of Gov. Edward Tiffin to Pres. Tho. Jefferson.

David Shelby, living in Sumner County, Tenn., reports a runaway slave, Josh.

Levi Sedwell, living in Chillicothe, wants to hire workers.

A list of letters left at the Post Office in Chillicothe includes Isaac Austin near Chillicothe, Thomas Brown, Wm. Brown at Franklinton, Samuel Bare, Richard Brown, Joshua Bradford, Ezekiel Brown, James Blair, John Biggert in care of James May, P. Bureau of Galliapolis, Sovereign Brown at Scioto, John Blaty, Benjamin Blair, Job Broughton, Benjamin Brackney, George Bunnix, William Champ near Chillicothe, Israel P. Case, William Crull at Salt Lick, Easter Cook, Emmon Cox, Ira Carpenter, James Compton, John Cartley, John Clowser, John Comstock at White Water, Samuel Conner, Isaac Cook, David Colbertson, Joseph Concklin, William C. Blackmore, Thomas Collins, F. Carfort at the Salt works, John Conner, Jacle Colvin in care of A. Jenkins, Asa Dunn, John Doyle at the forks of Mad River, James Denny, Patrick Donnan, Mary Dill, Thomas Davis, Eli Fuller, Joshua Ewing at Darby, John Francis, James Gordon, James Grubb, J. Goff in Pelmira, Timothy Green, J. Green at Newport, Samuel S. Hall, Alexander Hamilton, Everard Harr, Lawrence Hover, Jesse Haines, John Hawkins, Isaac Husler, George Hanshaw, William Hill, Joseph Hunter near Franklinton, Lucas Hawkins, Robert Holliday, Jacob Hubbart, Jna. Holmes, Levi Hurst, David Jones, Elizabeth Jamison, John Johnston, Mrs. Abram Jones, Thomas Kemplin in care of James Johnston, David Kehr, William King, Samuel M'Farland, Samuel Mallon, John M'Landburgh, James Mun, James M'Clure at Blackwater, Dr. M'Dowe, John M'Clary, William M'Donald, William M'Clasky, Gen. George Mathews, David Nelson, Arthur O'Harrow & Company at the forks of Scioto River, Robert Patrick, Ro. Parks, Elisha Perkins, Joshua Parler, Andrew Ponshes, Alexander Robinson, Hamilton Rodgers, William Reed at Twin Creek, Samuel and James Ramsey, Mat. Richey, Elihu Scott, Samuel Shaw, Henry Sullavent, Reuben Strong, George Smith, James Shaw, J. Smith, J. Templin, James White in care of James M'Dougal, John S. Wills, Samuel Wyckoff, Thomas White, Jos. Woolsey at Scioto River, Samuel Wakely, Anthony Wheaver at P. Plains. Entered by Joseph Tiffin.

Volume III, Monday, 23 January 1804, No. 190

Proceedings of the legislature mention Return J. Meigs, Jr.

Thomas Reed intends "to leave the neighborhood the 1st day of February" and has dry goods and groceries for sale at his house.

Jacob Shelby regarding his stud horses in New Lancaster, Fairfield County.

James Johnston, in Chillicothe, wants to hire tailors. Apply to him next door to Mr. Buchannon's Store on Water Street.

John Mantle says he "has again commenced the tanning business at his yard in Chillicothe". He recently sold the Tan Yard, but the purchaser backed out.

William Dodd, living in Montgomery County about eight miles below Dayton, reports a strayed mare.

James Ferguson, in Chillicothe, reports a strayed mare.

John M'Connell, living on Buckskin Creek, reports a stray filly.

Volume III, Monday, 30 January 1804, No. 191

A letter from William C.C. Claiborne to Gov. Edward Tiffin is printed.

John Baker, at Deer Creek, regarding his bond to John Kerkendall.

David Jones, Gideon C. Forsyth and Wm. Ewing Patterson, physicians, swear that they believe John M'Clernand, of Newell's Town and formerly of Grave Creek, is not a qualified physician. Witnessed by J. Wilson and Benj. M'Vay before Levin Okey or Oaky, justice of the peace.

Robert Clindenen, living on the head of Laurel Creek in Fairfield County, reports that he found a stray horse.

Proceedings of the legislature mention Return J. Meigs, jun., Joseph M'Kee of Jefferson County, William Creighton.

Volume III, Monday, 13 February 1804, No. 192

Hugh Rankin regarding a stud horse at William Rankin's place at the head of Buckskin one mile from Samuel Davis' smith shop. He mentions Col. Massie's mills at the Falls of Paint. The following have used the horse's services and were pleased: John Boman, Thomas Brabston, Michael Fraker, John Oren, Abraham Smith, Ellis Ellis, Mordica Ellis, John Crist, Seth Smith, Enoch Smith, Moremon Balled, James Kilworth, William Hamon, Peter Dillen, Samuel Standfield, Jonah Standfield, John Rogers, Ephraim Brabston, William Rees, James Right.

Proceedings of the legislature mention Hannah Willis, Jonathan Schieffelin, Charles F. Chobert de Joncaire, George M'Dougal, Wm. Ludlow, John Armstrong.

Elias Langham and Nath. Massie print a law of the State of Ohio.

W.C. Schenck, living in Franklin on the Great Miami in Warren County, has land for sale on Whetstone Creek, Allum Creek, Licking, Owl Creek, Tuscarawa Creek. Apply to Samuel Smith living in New Ark at the forks of Licking.

Samuel Reed, living on Brush Creek near the mouth, in Scioto County, reports a runaway apprentice, Charles Lanester, about 19 years old.

Edward Campwell says he's traveled 400 miles to find the "celebrated Doctor, of the name of John M'Clelland...on the Pickaway Plains".

A public notice to Nicholas Bierle, a German and a carpenter by trade, who left Pennsylvania 9-10 years ago. Apply to John Beckley in Washington City.

John Davidson says his wife, Isabella Davidson, has left him and he won't honor her debts anymore.

John S. Wills regarding his petition for the partition of land in Adams County entered by Wm. Holliday, asse. of William Hickman, mentions Joseph Darlinton.

Volume III, Monday, 20 February 1804, No. 193

A note regarding appointments made by the legislature mentions Silas Bent, jun., and Joseph Barker, associate judges in Washington County in place of Joseph Buell and Dudley Woodbridge, resigned. David Harvey and William Wells are associate judges in Muskingum County. Needham Perry is associate judge for Adams County in place of Joseph Darlinton, resigned. Joseph Tatman is associate judge in Green County in place of William Maxwell, resigned. John Kitchell in Butler County in place of William James, resigned. James M'Donald is agent for the Scioto salt works, and Ebenezer Buckingham for the Muskingum salt works.

Road commissioners are appointed: Benjamin Hough, David Reece, John Matthews, James M'Clure, James Denny, Israel Donaldson, Jehiel Gregory, Homer Hine, Isaac Anderson, John Clarke, Daniel Cooper, Samuel S. Spencer, Duncan Morrison, Robert Carrithers, Simon Kenton, Lewis Kenny, Jere. Martin.

Gov. Edward Tiffin, by Samuel Finley, addresses John S. Gano, Nathaniel Massie, Joseph Buell and Jesse Wadsworth, commanders of the Militia.

Walker Baylor, at Lexington, Kentucky, has land for sale on Paint and Deer Creeks that was entered by Col. George Baylor.

Joshua Porter, living on the north fork of Paint Creek within three miles of Chillicothe, regarding his stud horse.

N. Willis has lots for rent.

Ennis Duncan regarding his note to Samuel Brown of Nelson County.

Dr. John Dunn, Dr. Alex. Brown and Dr. J. M'Clernand regarding the recent ad placed by Dr. Forsyth and Dr. Patterson about John M'Clernand of Newell's town and Grave Creek. They state that he's very well qualified and mention Edinburgh College. Includes depositions from Alex. Amory, Will. Alexander, John Mathies, George Ireland and George Vance.

Volume III, Monday, 27 February 1804, No. 194

Proceedings of the legislature mention Hannah Willis, John S. Gano, Daniel Symmes, David Bradford, Nathaniel Massie, Elias Langham, Joseph Buell, Samuel Carpenter, Elijah Wadsworth, Brice Viers.

N. Willis has a house and lot for sale, presently occupied by John Kerron Water Street. He also has for sale, an out lot, opposite Mr. Kirkpatrick's.

Joseph Brown has a new shipment of goods for sale at his store, Chillicothe.

Thomas Whiting regarding his stud horse who will be at Mr. Welsh's at Deer Creek near Mr. Thompson's and at R. Worthington's five miles from Chillicothe near the road leading to the Old Town.

Frederick Bray (on the Westfall road near the Old Town) and Joshua Baxter (five miles from Chillicothe near Capt. Clark's) about their stud horse.

Volume III, Monday, 5 March 1804, No. 194

Elias Langham and Nath. Massie print another law of the State of Ohio.

Proceedings of the legislature mention Return Jonathan Meigs, jun., George Renick, William Wallace, William M. Miller.

Jacob Wider regarding his stud horse at John Hutt's stable in Chillicothe across from William Lamb's stable.

Jacob Weider regarding his stud horse at John Neel's stable in New Lancaster.

Adam Ervin about his stud horse, formerly the property of Mr. Samplers, at Samuel Wilson's mill in the Big Bottom and at John Odle's on Walnut Creek.

Thomas Gregg has goods for sale at Joseph Tiffin's house.

Philemon Thomas informs William George that he will take depositions of Garland Chiles, James Lounsdil, Benjamin Thomas, John Morford, John T. Henry, William Ward, Robert Smith and Jesse Barber at the house of Stephen Hiette in Mason County, Kentucky, before Jesse Peper and Thomas Weatherington, to be used in their suit in the District Court of Ohio.

Uriah Wheaton regarding his note to James Hutton for ten bushels of salt.

Geo. Huffman, Michael Baldwin and William Creighton regarding the suit of William Robinson and James Baird vs. Samuel M'Cullock (a non-resident of Ohio) in Ohio District Court. The land in question is described by Jer. M'Lene and D. Zugler and mentions Nathan Lammer and Reuben Taylor on Brush Creek.

Volume III, Monday, 12 March 1804, No. 195

John & Joseph Creviston ask those persons indebted to the estate of Nicholas Creviston, dec'd, to settle their accounts.

William Chandler, of Jefferson Township, is a candidate for commissioner in Ross County. Also running for commissioner are William Niblack of Chillicothe, Thomas Stockton of Union township and John Collet of Green township.

Officers of the town of Chillicothe are Samuel Finley, William M'Farland, John Carlisle, Michael Baldwin, William Niblack, George Haines, William Hutt, Thomas Steel, Henry Johnston, William Keys, Michael Byerley, John M'Cullough.

John Edmiston, John G. Macan and John Hutt, at Chillicothe, about the case of Lucas Hawkins vs. Emanuel Viner, in Ross County Court of Common Pleas. They have land for sale at William Keys' house in Chillicothe that Henry Massie sold to Viner. It's part of Thomas Dick and Bigger Head's survey on Rocky Fork.

Joseph Fawcett gives notice to Thomas Carneal that he will take depositions from Robert M'Kay, Asle/Aste Cain, Gen. Daniel Symmes and Griffin Yeatman in Cincinnati to be used in his suit against Carneal and John Craig.

Volume III, Monday, 19 March 1804, No. 196

Proceedings of the legislature mention John Bonde, sheriff of Clermont Co.

Thomas Dick, living on the Newmarket road, reports a stray horse.

Sam. Finley and Winn Winship regarding the suit of Reuben Abrams vs. Bazil Abrams in the Ross County Court of Common Pleas.

John M'Clean, tanner, wants to hire apprentices to the tanning business.

Joshua Porter, living on the North Fork of Paint, has land for sale.

Volume III, Monday, 2 April 1804, No. 198

An account of the drowning death, on Saturday, 31 March 1804, of Henry Young, bachelor and taylor by trade, who moved from Europe to Marietta in the spring of 1803. Benjamin Urmston, coroner, has his belongings.

William Patton, executor of M. Patton, dec'd, has a lot for sale opposite Reuben Abrams' place in Chillicothe.

Christian Richharts, on Deer Creek, regarding his stud horse.

Walter Baylor regarding the sale of the military lands of Col. George Baylor.

James Demens has lots for sale in Springfield. The sale will be held at the house of Griffith Foose.

John Enterkin regarding the stud horse at Capt. John Entrickin's house near Mr. Crouse's mill.

James Denny asks those indebted to him to settle their accounts.

Lieut. N. Heald, at Chillicothe, is recruiting for the Ohio Militia.

James Denny lost two new saddles.

Henry Olner, living between the two Miami Rivers on Clear Creek, regarding a stray horse.

Military divisions in Ohio are outlined and mention Robert Morris, jun., Logan's Gap, Benjamin Beasley, Adam Pennywitt, Donaldson Creek, Edwards road, Manchester, Holmes' old mill, Holmes' mill road, Benjamin Sutton, Hill's fork, William Hannah, Hempehill's road, David Young, Kellin's town, Beasley's fork, John Clark, Lewis Bible, Joseph Williams, Soldier's run, Mr. Driver, Mr. Chapman, Caedar run, Benjamin Pyatt, and Peter Wickerham in Adams County. In Scioto County: Alexandria, Thomas Waller, Cox's run, Bear Creek, Henry Phillips, Peter Noel, sen., Darlington's run, Peter Rusher, Henry Hales. In Ross County: Salt Lick Creek, Sunfish Creek, Brush Creek, Crooked Creek, Downing's ford, Beaver Creek, Snowden Sargent, Wilson's Mill, Indian Creek, Pea Pea Road, Patton's run, John England on Paint Creek, James Ferguson, Thomas James in Chillicothe, William Lamb in Chillicothe, Henry Massie's farm, Westfall road, William Dark, Joseph M'Coy, Yellowbud Creek, Abraham Shanton, Scippo Creek, Pickaway Plain, Fergus Moore, Samual S. Shenar at Salt Lick, Campbell's mill on Scioto, Walnut Creek, William Lewis, Kinnickinic Creek, Martin Myers, Thomas Gregg, Capt. Dawson, Mr. Emrick, Mr. Driver at the head of Pickaway, Oliver Ross at New Market, Evans' settlement on Clear Creek, Anthony Franklin, Nathaniel Pope, Samuel Erwin on Buckskin Creek, Coar's mills on Lower Twin Creek, Christian Platter, William Pilars on Sunfish Creek, John Clouser on waters of Buckskin Creek, Jacob Davis on Buckskin Creek, Devalt's mill on north fork of Paint Creek, Lemuel Sayers, William Rogers on the north fork of Paint Creek. In Franklin County: Robert Culbertson, Barnabas Lambert, James Kilburn, North Liberty, Darby Creek settlements. Entered by Maj. Gen. Nath. Massie.

Volume III, Monday, 9 April 1804, No. 199

T. Worthington, in Washington, writes a letter to N. Willis in Chillicothe.

William Niblack (of Scioto township), Thomas Barr (of Pickaway township), and John Collet (of Green township) are elected county commissioners.

Morel Geuramand has groceries for sale at Joseph Tiffin's in Chillicothe.

Benjamin Newell has lots for sale in the town of Terlton.

Volume III, Monday, 16 April 1804, No. 200

The President makes the following appointments: Benjamin Tupper (receiver of public monies at Marietta), Wyllys Silliman (register of the land office at Zanesville), Thomas VanSwearingen (receiver of public monies at Zanesville), Charles Kilgore (register of the land office at Cincinnati).

Nathaniel Beasly, Benjamin Wood, Selathel Sparks, William Collings, John Briggs, William Marshall and Aaron Moore regarding lots for sale in West Union.

A list of letters left at the Post Office in Chillicothe includes James Armstrong near Chillicothe, Caleb Armitage, H. Abrahams, John Adair on Slat Creek, Job Broughton, Peter Barreck on waters of Licking Creek, William Bennett (30 miles above Chillicothe), Frederick Brown in Paxton township, William Bready, Robert Bennet near Salt Lick, White Brown, Jacob Cutler, James Bollton, James Brown, Rebecca Brown, Benjamin Brackney, Samuel Cavender near Chillicothe, William Corns at the mouth of Scioto, Colin Campbell, Jacob Cox, John Crocket, James Crawford, Lawyer Clinton, Obediah Clark, William Caldwell at Franklinton, Thomas Carneal, Robert Culbertson, David Davis (Wale's Man), John Dill, William Dunban, Aaron Dawley, Enons Davis, Samuel Davis, Thomas Dugin, John Eversole in care of William Lamb, Joseph Eakins, John Fulton at New Port, Bartholamew Fryatt, Michael Fisher, David Gerke at the mouth of Scioto, Jacob Grubb at Franklinton, Timothy Green in care of John Carlisle, Francis Herron in care of J. Tiffin, Edward Holmes in care of J. Carlisle, Hugh and A. Oharra at Franklinton, John Householder,

Jesse Hains, John Hubbard, James Hall, Richard Harrison, Robert Harvey, Oliver Hortwell, Robert Holleday at Buckskin settlement, Colial Haynes, John Hawkins at Chillicothe Bluffs, John Johnston at Pickaway, James Johnston at Pe Pee, Jacob King, George King, Rachel Lupton, John M'Lernand, Jesse Mounts in care of Mr. Gregg, Robert Means, John W. Miller near Pe Pee, Elias Langham, Jashua M'Farling on the north fork of Paint, Peter Millington, John Murphy (13 miles from Chillicothe), J. Meigs, Barthotlomew Mabee at Scioto salt lick, John Miller, Thomas Morris at the forks of Scioto, Josias M'Kinnie in care of James Scott at Franklin Town, John M. Ginnis, Christopher M'Conico, William M'Mum on Buckskin, William M'Coy in care of John Crous, Thomas Moore at the forks of Scioto, Lewis Luttrell at Greenfield town, John Paul in care of H. Massie, Joseph Petty, sen., in care of Joseph Petty, jun., John Peppers at Salt Lick, Robt. Patrick, William Rose near Brush Creek, William Reed in care of James Johnston, Daniel Ross on Pickaway Plains, James Reed, John Ross, Leonard Reasner, Aaron Strong at Franklinton, Thomas F. Reddick, Nehemiah Reed, Augustus Richards, John Rush, William Sprig, Lucas Sullivant, John Smith in care of Robert Gregg, Thomas Sellars, Orasha Strong at Salt Lick, Elijah Rinker, John N.C. Schenck at Chillicothe, John Swan, James Sapington, James Smith, Jacob Sheeley in care of Jacob Weider, Samuel S. Spencer, Joseph Swayne on Paint Creek, W.S.T. Strother, Mr. Strother (attorney), Reuben Strong, John Shoemaker, Thomas Smith at Deer Creek, William Stanley (merchant), Philip Sidenor at the forks of Scioto, John Simpson, Uriah Springer, Isaac Wetzel (9 miles from Chillicothe), James Taylor, Thompson Smith, Benjamin Thompson, Jacob VanCounty, George Whitestone, John Warden on Licking. Entered by Joseph Tiffin.

Volume III, Monday, 23 April 1804, No. 201

Hon. Thomas Worthington and his family returned to his home near Chilli-cothe on Sunday, 22 April, from the city of Washington.

Seth Thompson has opened his watch repairing and silver smithing business in the shop next door to Key's tavern in Chillicothe.

John Sherer has just returned from Brownsville and has whiskey for sale at the sign of the Red Lion in Chillicothe.

Richard Orsborn, living on Kinnickanic near John Crouse's in Ross County, reports that he found a strayed mare.

White Brown, at Deer Creek, reports a strayed or stolen horse.

Volume V, Monday, 30 April 1804, No. 202

Elias Langham and Nath. Massie print a law of Ohio pertaining to roads.

A note says that the ships commanded by S. M'Cutcheon and James M'Keever have arrived at Limestone. Charles Gallager launched a ship at Limestone on April 2nd. Mentions a ship owned by Tarascon, Brothers, Berthoud & Company.

A note regarding a meeting of the trustees of the Ohio University.

Jesse Spencer and Sam. Finley regarding land for sale in Indiana Territory.

John Carlisle has a new shipment of goods for sale at his store, Chillicothe.

Wm. R. Dickinson intends "to leave this part of the state for several months" and asks those indebted to him to settle their accounts.

Charles Cissna, at Chillicothe, reports a stray mare.

Adam Yearian carries on the gunsmith business in his shop in back of Capt. Lamb's Tavern. Edward Stall does smith work in the same shop.

John M'Coy has goods for sale in the house lately occupied by Elias Langham.

Francis Brohers regarding his stud horse. He will be at Frederick Lether's tavern at Clear Creek at the sign of the Plough and Harrow and at Benjamin Dunkin's farm at the Pickaway Plain.

Volume V, Monday, 7 May 1804, No. 203

Jack Brandy, a negro man, was arrested in Chillicothe on Wednesday, 2 May 1804, for the murder of Joseph Fitzgerald, a labourer at the salt works.

Obituary: Mrs. Sarah Reed, wife of Thomas Reed, died in Chillicothe.

Henry Massie has land for sale near Chillicothe, adjoining Zane's tract.

N. Willis asks those persons in Springfield, Medical Springs, Exenia, Caesar's Mill, Deerfield and Mad River subscribing to the Scioto Gazette to make payments for the paper to Joseph Price, the post rider.

Volume V, Monday, 14 May 1804, No. 204

A note regarding the celebration, at Chillicothe, of the Louisiana Purchase mentions Adam Hollar's house on the public square.

Wm. Niblack, at Chillicothe, "intends moving from this state some time this summer" and asks those indebted to him to settle their accounts.

Thomas Hardy, at Chillicothe, wants to hire an apprentice taylor.

Alexander Calderhead and Matthew Henderson report some stray horses. Deliver to William Lamb, innkeeper at Chillicothe.

George Williams, living in the upper end of Ross County, two miles from Marquis' mill on Darby Creek, reports a stray mare.

James Robitaille, at the head of Mad River, reports a stray mare. It was brought from Kentucky by Col. Langham who sold it to Mr. Studeybaker, who sold to James Kent, who sold to Robitaille. Deliver to James Denny in Chillicothe.

Volume V, Monday, 21 May 1804, No. 205

Absolem Brown, living on the north fork of Paint Creek, about five miles from Chillicothe, reports a stray mare.

A note about the trial of Edward Stalcup, in the Supreme Court, for the murder of Asa Mounts. Also the trial of John Brandy for the murder of Joseph Fitzgerald at the salt works. Also of Joseph Barton for theft. Also of James Heffernan for theft.

A note regarding the celebration of the Louisiana Purchase at Lancaster mentions Jacob Burton's house, Emanuel Carpenter, Henry Abrams.

W. Silliman, at Zanesville, has resigned his position as judge of the Courts of Common Pleas and resumed his practice of law.

Volume V, Monday, 28 May 1804, No. 206

Levin Belt is appointed presiding judge of the Court of Common Pleas in place of Wyllys Silliman, resigned.

Edward Stalcup has been sentenced to death for the murder of Asa Mounts. He will be executed on Friday, 3 August 1804.

Nathan Muzzy, at Chillicothe, says his wife, Anna Muzzy, "has, by adultery, misconduct and obstinacy, in which she still persists, rendered herself unworthy of that character." He won't honor her debts anymore.

James May, sen., at Chillicothe, offers his house in Second Street, opposite Col. Worthington's lots in Chillicothe, for sale.

Volume V, Monday, 4 June 1804, No. 207

William Bull, living on Massie's Creek in Green County, reports a stray mare.

Reuben Abrams, at Chillicothe, has lots for sale in the town of Adelphi. The town was laid out by Henry and Reuben Abrams on Salt Lick Creek. The sale will be held at Moses Dawson's house at Adam Deavabaugh's mills.

Volume V, Monday, 11 June 1804, No. 208

An account of the celebration of the Louisiana Purchase at St. Clairsville mentions Joseph Sharp and Capt. Wm. Riddle and includes the text of the speech delivered by Doctor William B. Herren.

Samuel Holton lost some money in Chillicothe.

Volume V, Monday, 18 June 1804, No. 209

James Buchanan asks those indebted to the late firm of Oliver & Buchanan to settle their accounts.

Thomas Reed has whiskey for sale at Elias Langham's old house in Chillicothe.

Jacob Bowman, living in Chillicothe, reports a stray horse.

Samuel Brown has a new shipment of goods for sale at his store in Chillicothe.

John M'Landburgh has a new shipment of goods for sale at his store next to John Carlisle, lately occupied by Fielding Hubbard, in Chillicothe, nearly opposite Capt. Wm. Lamb's tavern.

John Mathews says the partnership of Matthews & Scofield is dissolved, and those indebted to the firm should settle their accounts with Elnathan Scofield or John Creed. John Creed continues the business at the old store in Lancaster.

Wm. Niblack, at Chillicothe, regarding claims against the county.

Thomas Thompson, living on Indian Wheeling Creek, reports a stray horse.

Volume V, Monday, 25 June 1804, No. 210

John Edmiston has a new shipment of medicines at his store in Chillicothe.

Robert Allen, justice of the peace in Green County, regarding the escape of Peter Patterson from jail in Green County. Patterson was arrested for counterfeiting. Mentions David Wilcock (sheriff in Green County) and Thomas Logwood (the counterfeiter from Virginia).

William Lamb has flour, whiskey, gin and brandy for sale at John Carlisle's.

Kilcan Rousz lost a pocket book containing a note from Benjamin Urmston.

William M'Farland has a new shipment of goods for sale at his store in the house formerly occupied by N. & R. Gregg.

Hugh Litle, living near Crouse's mill on Kinnickinic, reports a strayed horse.

Maj. Gen. Nath. Massie regarding the Ohio Militia mentions Alexander Mullin, Tilman Lewis, Richard Action and John Brown.

Volume V, Monday, 2 July 1804, No. 211

Gen. Nath. Massie of Ross County, James Pritchard of Jefferson County and John Bigger of Hamilton County are nominated as electors.

Jer. M'Lene, sheriff, regarding the sale of the property of George Porter, dec'd, seized at the suits of George Matthew and Paul Huston.

Volume V, Monday, 9 July 1804, No. 212

Jesse Spencer, register of the land office, regarding road improvements. Mentions Mr. Denny, surveyor.

John Edmiston has "family medicines" for sale at his shop in Chillicothe.

Ebenezer Petty, living on Darby, near the road leading from Franklinton to Chillicothe, reports that he found several stray horses.

A list of letters left at the Post Office in Chillicothe includes Alathia Asa living on Scioto Brush Creek, Caleb Armetage, Rosanna Boggs, David Banhard, Jacob Braughton, John Bouton, William Brown, M. Burcaus at Chillicothe, Robert Buckles, George Brown on Buckskin, Frederick Bray in care of Mr. Gregg, Henry Brevoot, Isaac Bradley, Titus Brockway, Jacob Coven, Thomas Cissna at Salt Lick, John Clark at Deer Creek, Margaret Cooper, Jacob or Benjamin Colven, William Crull at Salt Lick, Jacob Caldun at Clear Creek, James Denny, David Dollon, John Dever, Thinsey Davis, John Dison, Samuel Dougherty, Adam Deffenbaugh, Peter Ditsler, Abner Essery at the mouth of Salt Lick, Jn. Edwards at the salt works, Lanart Floobur, Jacob Fisher, Abraham Funkhouser, Patrick or Timothy G. Ford, Adam Gillolian, William Green at Salt Lick, James Gordon, Isaac Husser, James Hamlet, Wilas Hotchison, Dr. P. Harrison, Thos. M. Johnson, Samuel Jordan, William Justice, John Kingery, John Koouts, Lathan Lundy, Wm. Lockard at High Bank, Charles Leonard at Westfall, J.W. Loofbourrow, Barnard Lambert, Elias Langham, Benjamin Miller, Edward M'Deed, Christopher M'Connico, Dr. James Martin, Jacob Miller on Paint Creek, Robert or Simon M'Mustrie, James M'Clure, Daniel Musselman, James Morris, Robert M'Mahon, Robert Means, Maj. James Munn, John Mitchell, James Milligan on Paint Creek, Pallace Morgan, Jacob Mostker, John Meigs, Wm. Millar in Franklin County, John Maise, Wm. Pickrell at Paint Creek, Uriah Poullin on Paint Creek, John Jackson, John Poolley, Wm. Pickerell, Elizabeth Phillips, Joshua Parrish at the mouth of Scioto, John Peppers, Robert Patrick at Salt Lick, Thomas F. Riddick, David Reed at Darby Creek, James Reed, Christian Richard, Joseph Reed, Rezin Redman, Thomas Rogers at Gallipolis, Wm. Rankin in Franklin County, Sarah Rhodes at Deer Creek, George Reid, William Sprigg, John Sterete on Caesar's Creek, Robert Strother in care of Mr. Rennick, Job Sharp, Daniel Storms in Franklin, Roger Selden, Ann Stokes of Franklinton, Mathew Stokes, James Sisk, Thomas Selby, Enock Limpus, Cornelius Shelpman, Nicholas Smith, Joseph Suppan on Bull Creek, Nicholas Stutzman, Thomas Smith on Deer Creek, James Tapscott, John Tootte on Deer Creek, Baslitt Timmins, James Templin, Benjamin Terman on Mad River, Henry Vanmeter at Darby, John Vanmeter in care of John Kerr, John Walker (blacksmith), John Zane, Edward Willcocks in Union Township, Jesse Weatherinton, Jos. Waugh on Buckskin, James Woldon, J. Wright, James Whitecotton, James or John Williams, Ebenezer Zanes, Patrick Young, Rev. John Wright, John Right, William Wilson, Rebecca Wolff, George Wilson, John S. Wills. Entered by Joseph Tiffin, post master.

Volume V, Monday, 16 July 1804, No. 213
Elijah Backus, Benjamin Tappan, John Milligan, James Sargent and Thomas Kirker regarding an act pertaining to roads in Ohio. W.C. Schenck, Daniel Symmes, Wm. Ward, Wm. Vance and John Bigger answer their letter.

An account of the celebration of the Fourth of July by the Republicans of Marietta mentions Mr. Brough's hall, Muskingum Academy, Rev. Daniel Story's oration, Gov. Tiffin.

Daniel Mallott, in Williamsburg, Clermont County, reports a stray horse.

Volume V, Monday, 23 July 1804, No. 214
Edward Cole, at the office of the Western Star, at Lewistown, Pennsylvania, reports a runaway printer's apprentice, William Johnston, age 18-19.

Stephen Carey, living in Union township, near Alexandria in Scioto County, reports that he found a stray mare.

John M'Dougal and Michael Baldwin regarding the suit of Uriah Springer vs. Daniel Stull in Ross County Court of Common Pleas.

Volume V, Monday, 30 July 1804, No. 215
An account of the Fourth of July celebration at Worthington in Franklin County mentions E. Griswold's house, James Kilbourn, William Thompson, Ensign P. Pinney, A. Morrison, jun. It says, "Fourteen months ago, this town was an unbroken forest."

George Phelps, Clerk in Trumbull County, regarding the Salt Spring Tract originally sold by Connecticut to Samuel H. Parsons in 1788. Elijah Wadsworth of Canfield has petitioned the Court of Common Pleas in Trumbull County for his share of this land. Witnessed by Calvin Pease at Warren County Court.

P. Bureau regarding the suit of John Badot vs. John Frison's heirs in the Gallia County Court of Common Pleas. Also the suit of John Peter Romaine Bureau vs. Stephen Chandivert's heirs.

William Marshall regarding land known as the "Irish Land". He says don't purchase land from Nathan and Robert Gregg in Samuel M'Craw's survey.

Volume V, Monday, 6 August 1804, No. 216
Edward Stalcup was executed in Chillicothe on Friday, 3 August 1804, for the murder of Asa Mounts.

A note regarding the Indian who murdered Capt. Herrod.

John M'Coy has moved his store and has a new shipment of goods for sale.

Thomas Dick, living in New Market township, Ross County, found a horse.

J. Harvey about the appointment of a county surveyor in Muskingum County at Zanesville mentions L. Wiple and William Wells.

Volume V, Monday, 13 August 1804, No. 217
A letter to Gov. Edward Tiffin from William Ward, Robert Renick, William Moore, Jesse Brackin, Daniel Robertson, Abel Crawford, Joel Newland, Archibald Dowden, in Springfield, is printed regarding the Indians. Mentions Capt. Herod.

Jas. M'Pherson writes a letter to Col. Ward regarding the Indian named Kenawa Tuckaw who killed Capt. Herod.

Michael Baldwin writes a letter to the editor regarding the confession of Edward Stalcup of the murder of Asa Mounts. Stallcup gave Baldwin letters to his brother and wife just before the execution.

Wm. Niblack, John Collett and Thomas Barr say that the 1804 tax is now due and payable to John Mathews, the tax collector.

James Phillips, in Chillicothe, reports a stray mare.

David Harvey, at the Eagle and Ball Tavern in Zanesville, has returned from Philadelphia with assorted liquors for sale. Mr. Spangler carries on the black-smith's business on the opposite corner in Zanesville.

William Patton and Mary Patton, administrators of the estate of John Patton, dec'd, regarding the estate sale and settlement.

Frederick Braucher, living near the Sinking Spring on the road from Chilli-cothe to Limestone, reports that he found a mare.

William L. Foster, near Deerfield in Warren County, about two stolen mares.

Volume V, Monday, 20 August 1804, No. 218

Lemuel James has a new shipment of goods at his store opposite Mr. Gregg's.

Henry Massie has several tracts of land for sale and mentions Rev. James Kilburn, Justice Miller (living on the west fork of Scioto about nine miles from Franklinton), Job Sharp on the head waters of Darby, Roger Warren living in Williamsburg, John Winder (living on the waters of Dry Run).

Thomas Scott, in Chillicothe, reports a horse stolen from the pasture of Mrs. Sarah Scott, living on Bracken Creek in Mason County, Kentucky. He was stolen by Robert Barker, alias Robert Freeport, alias Robert Freeheart, age 33.

Sarah Applegate, George Applegate and Jarnied Irwin, in Paxton township of Ross County, executors of the estate of John Applegate, dec'd, about the estate.

Rufus Putnam and Samuel Carpenter have land for sale to benefit the Athens University. The sale is at the house of Doctor Perkins in Athens.

Thomas Reed has goods for sale at the house formerly occupied by Elias Langham in Water Street, Chillicothe.

Hugh Boyle and Elnathan Scofield, in Lancaster, Fairfield County, administrators of the estate of Alexander White, 3rd, dec'd, regarding the estate.

Christian Myer, living in German township on Bear Creek, 10 miles below Dayton, in Montgomery County, regarding a stray mare.

Volume V, Monday, 27 August 1804, No. 219

Marriage: James Mountain, age 25, married Mrs. Sarah Cammell, age 73, at New Market "a short time past".

Samuel Brown has a new shipment of goods for sale at his store in Chillicothe.

Volume V, Monday, 3 September 1804, No. 220

Capt. Robert Linzee, of Middletown, has contracted with Maj. Jehiel Gregory for opening the state road from Marietta to Chillicothe.

David Shepherd says he is a candidate for sheriff in Ross County.

William Craigg is a candidate for the Assembly.

James Thompson has started his blue dying business in Chillicothe.

A note regarding the petition of Jehiel Gregory and John Havner to erect a mill dam over the Hockhocking River opposite the town of Athens.

John Noland, at Pee Pee, wants to keep a ferry over the Scioto River at his house on the road leading from Sunfish to the Salt Lick.

Volume V, Monday, 10 September 1804, No. 221

A note regarding Gov. Harrison's note about elections in Indiana Territory.

Michael Baldwin says that he is a candidate for the legislature.

Reuben Abrams has lots for sale in the town of Adelphi at the house of James S. Webster.

Jer. M'Lane, sheriff, regarding the sale of land near Westfall, the property of Daniel Hamilton seized at the suit of Benj. Brooks, Lucas Nibuchar and others.

Philip Green, at Merrietta, administrator of the estate of Griffin Green, late of Merrietta, dec'd, regarding the estate settlement.

Volume V, Monday, 24 September 1804, No. 223

Lorenzo Dow will deliver a sermon at the courthouse in Chillicothe tomorrow.

John Evans is a candidate for representative in the Assembly.

Samuel Evans says he is a candidate for representative from Ross County.

John G. Macan is a candidate for representative in the General Assembly.

Jer. M'Lane says that he is a candidate for sheriff from Ross County.

Wm. Craig and Joseph Kerr about a meeting of the Republicans at William Keys' house in Chillicothe. They recommend the following for public office: William Goforth, sen., Nathaniel Massie, James Prichard, William M'Farland, Henry Massie, Abram J. Williams, Michael Baldwin.

John M'Dougal regarding the upcoming elections.

John Collett and Wm. Niblack regarding a meeting about taxation.

Joseph Parks, Joseph Vance and Benjamin Sells regarding the horse races at Franklinton.

Patrick Rock, sen., living at the forks of Mad River, reports a stray horse.

William Keys says, "I shall decline business in a few days", and asks those indebted to him to settle their accounts.

Wm. Irwin and E. Stewart, in Belmont County, administrators of the estate of Isaac Irwin, dec'd, late of St. Clairsville, regarding the estate settlement.

Volume V, Monday, 1 October 1804, No. 224

James Ferguson & John G. Macan, in Chillicothe, about a meeting of the Republicans at Capt. Wm. Lamb's tavern to nominate candidates mention John Riley, John Carlisle, Baz. Wells, Elias Langham, John M'Landburgh, John S. Wills and John Kerr.

Jack Brandy, a negro convicted of man-slaughter, escaped from jail.

Col. James Dunlap, Maj. Duncan M'Arthur and William Patton are candidates for the house of representatives of Ohio.

Benjamin White, Collector in Franklin County, regarding lands for sale for failure to pay taxes.

W. Silliman, attorney for Alex. Struthers, gives notice to Jonas Stanberry about a petition presented to the Court of Common Pleas in Muskingum County.

Abel Westfall will convey deeds for lots in the town of Westfall at the house of Benjamin Urmston in Chillicothe.

Obituary: James Crawford, of Indian Creek, died. (no date listed)

Thomas Needham has purchased the tavern of William Keys, known by the name of Lyon Tavern, in Water Street, Chillicothe.

John Carlisle has a new shipment of goods for sale at his store, Chillicothe.

Benjamin Urmston has land for sale on Deer Creek, adjoining the lands of James M'Nutt who will show the land.

Volume V, Monday, 8 October 1804, No. 225

William Keys has "declined public business and intending shortly to leave Chillicothe", asks those indebted to him to settle their accounts. He has sold the tavern, at the sign of the Red Lyon, to Thomas Needham.

N. Willis asks all persons to stop cutting timber on his out-lots.

Obituary: Edward Holmes, age 20, died Thursday evening, 4 October 1804. He'd been "but a short time a resident here". He was buried on Friday.

Obituary: John Hubbard, sen., of Dry Run, died (no date given). He was "an aged and respectable citizen".

A note regarding a meeting of the Republicans at Capt. Lamb's on Sept. 21st.

John Boggs, of the Pickaway, will serve in the Senate, if elected.

Jacob Hubbard, in Chillicothe, says he will not honor the debts of his wife, Elizabeth Hubbard, late Elizabeth Stacker.

John M'Dougal regarding tavern licenses in Ross County.

Felix and Jonathan Renick, administrators of the estate of Thomas Renick, dec'd, regarding the estate sale.

N. & R. Gregg asks those indebted to them to settle their accounts.

Jacob Crider reports that he found a stray horse.

Lucas Sullivant and Ep. Bonham regarding the suit of John Graham vs. Peter Heath in Franklin County, Court of Common Pleas.

Volume V, Monday, 15 October 1804, No. 226

Election results in Ross County mention Elias Langham, Joseph Kerr, Benj. Urmston, M. Baldwin, Wm. Patton, J. Dunlap, D. M'Arthur, Jeremiah M'Lene, Wm. Niblack, Mr. Morrow, Mr. Boggs, Mr. Armstrong. In Adams County: Mr. Lewis, Mr. Sweney and Mr. Shepherd. In Fairfield County: Mr. Slaughter, Mr. Guess, Mr. Rees.

Obituary: Mrs. Mary Stockton, age 60, died near Chillicothe, on Tuesday, October 9, 1804, and Thomas Stockton, age 61, died the following day. They had been married for 38 years. They were buried in one grave on Thursday.

Jeremiah M'Lene, sheriff, regarding the choice of electors for Ross County.

Aeneas Foulk has a mare for sale at Benjamin Urmston's stable in Chillicothe.

William M'Farland has a new shipment of goods for sale at his store.

A note regarding a stud horse at Benjamin Urmston's stable in Chillicothe.

Lydia Case and Mills Case, administrators of the estate of Joseph Case, late of Richfield in Trumbull County, dec'd, regarding the estate settlement.

John A. Harper and James A. Harper, administrators of the estate of John Miner, late of Middlefield, in Trumbull County, dec'd, regarding the estate.

Jonathan Clark has laid out a town on Miller's bank on the Scioto River.

Volume V, Monday, 29 October 1804, No. 228
 The editor of the Scioto Gazette asks those indebted to pay their bills.
 John Dever, living on the Scioto River, Scioto County, about stray horses.
 Duncan M'Arthur says he declines his seat in the General Assembly because he believes that David Shelby, of Pickaway County, is entitled to it.
 Jeremiah M'Lene regarding the election called by Gov. Edward Tiffin to replace Duncan M'Arthur who resigned as representative.
 Winn Winship, James Ferguson and Joseph Tiffin about the suit of Philemon Thomas vs. William George in the District Court of Ohio.
 John Stockton and Thomas Stockton, in Union township, administrators of the estate of Thomas Stockton, dec'd, regarding the estate sale and settlement.
 James Winder and Erasmus Jones, on Dry Run, executors of the estate of John Hubbard, dec'd, late of Union township, regarding the estate settlement.
 Wm. Rufus Putnam, at Marietta, executor of the estate of Peregrine Foster, late of Bellepre in Washington County, dec'd, regarding the estate settlement.
 Benjamin White, collector, about the suit against Benjamin White & Company in the Franklin County Court of Common Pleas.
 Witteker & Willard want to buy all types of furs at the Scioto Salt Works.
 Samuel Taylor, living in Chillicothe, reports a stray horse.
 Robert Slaughter was found guilty of murder at Vincennes, Indiana Territory, and sentenced to be executed on 25 October 1804.
 Election returns in Belmont County mention Jeremiah Morrow, James Smith, Elias Langham, Thomas Wilson, John Stewart, Josiah Dillon, Josiah Hedges, John Duncan. In Butler County: Ezekiel Ball and Mathew Richardson. In Columbiana County: James Pritchard and Zenas Kimberly, Rudolph Bear, John M'Connel. In Trumbull County: George Tod, Jurhard Kirtland, Benjamin Tappan, Amos Stafford, Thomas Kine, Ephraim Quimby and Martin Smith. In Adams & Scioto Counties: Abraham Shepherd, Philip Lewis, Thomas Waller, John Lodwick, John Guttridge.
 Nathaniel Massie, William Goforth, sen., and James Pritchard regarding the election of electors in Ohio.
 A note regarding the resignation of Duncan M'Arthur.
 E. Langham writes a letter to the public regarding the election to replace Maj. Duncan M'Arthur mentions Capt. Shelby.
 Abraham Niceley reports a horse that strayed from Mr. Wallace's place about two miles from Chillicothe.
 Jesse Eastburn, in Adams County, regarding his mill dam on Cedar Run.
 Samuel Smith, executor of the estate of James Crawford, dec'd, regarding the estate sale at Crawford's house on Indian Creek.
 Adam Turner, administrator of the estate of William Holland, dec'd, regarding the estate sale and settlement.
 John Collett, Thomas Barr & William Niblack write a letter to John Mathews regarding the collection of taxes.
 William Niblack has a new shipment of goods for sale at his store.
 J. Savary, at Millersburg, Bourbon County, Kentucky, has land for sale in Ohio. He mentions Rich. C. Waters, Edward Meade, Joseph Egleston, Peter Archer, William Lytle (surveyor of Williamsburg), Mr. O'Neal near Waynesville, Gen. Nathaniel Massie near the Falls of Paint Creek, Francis LeClerg (surveyor at Gallipolis), Go. Mercer.
 Isaac Washburn, administrator of the estate of Walker Tyler, dec'd, late of Scioto Salt Lick, regarding the estate settlement.
 Joseph Lane and Margaret M'Cune, executors of the estate of Joseph M'Cune, dec'd, regarding the estate sale and settlement.
 Samuel Smith, administrator of the estate of William Smith, dec'd, who lately lived on the Scioto two miles above Westfall, regarding the estate sale.

Volume V, Monday, 5 November 1804, No. 229
 Election returns mention Nathaniel Massie, William Goforth, Bazaleel Wells, James Pritchard, John Carlisle, John Riley, Elias Langham, Duncan M'Arthur.
 Simon Kenton regarding William George's land offered for sale recently.
 John Gay and John Barr, at the Pickaway Plains, about the Pickaway races.
 Joseph Campbell wants to build a dam at his mill on the Scioto River.

Volume V, Monday, 12 November 1804, No. 230

Election returns in Ross County mention Jeremiah Morrow, Elias Langham and Duncan M'Arthur.

John Dever regarding the calf Abraham Dean left with him.

William Hull, in Chillicothe, reports a horse that strayed out of Mr. Urmston's pasture in Chillicothe.

Volume V, Monday, 19 November 1804, No. 231

Robert Slaughter was executed at the American burying ground in Vincennes, Indiana Territory, on Thursday, 25 October 1804.

Election returns mention Nathaniel Massie, William Goforth, sen., James Pritchard, John Bigger, Bazaleel Wells, John Reily, Benjamin Ives Gilman, John Carlisle, Mr. Langham, Mr. Shelby.

Gov. Edward Tiffin, by W. Creighton, jun., says that William Goforth, sen., Nathaniel Massie and James Pritchard are elected as electors of Ohio.

John M'Dougal and Jno. S. Wills regarding the suit of Duncan M'Arthur vs. Thomas Holt in the Ross County Court of Common Pleas.

Samuel Clark regarding notes for land that he gave to Philip Piper.

Dix & Cutler have a new shipment of goods for sale at their store opposite Maj. Urmston's Tavern in Chillicothe. They also operate a tin manufactory.

Sarah Olney, Ebenezer Nye and Daniel Davis, at Marietta, executors of the estate of Maj. Coggershel Olney, late of Marietta, dec'd, about the settlement.

George Kile, administrator of the estate of Jacob Miller, dec'd, late of Concord township, Ross County, regarding the estate sale and settlement (2 ads).

Volume V, Monday, 26 November 1804, No. 252

John M'Coy has a new shipment of goods for sale at his store in Chillicothe.

John Hemphill, living on the head of Buckskin Creek, reports a stray horse.

Alexander M'Clintick, living on the North Fork of Paint Creek, 3 miles from Chillicothe, reports a stray mare that was brought from Pennsylvania last spring.

Joseph Darlinton and Wm. Creighton, jun., regarding the suits of John Barret vs. George Gordon and Neal Lafferty vs. Simeon Sumners in Adams County.

Volume V, Monday, 3 December 1804, No. 253

Samuel G. Jones and Henry Brush (attorney) regarding the suit of Robert Johnston vs. Elias Barker in the Scioto County Court. Also the suit of Samuel Vesser vs. Elias Barker and William Walton Boush vs. Elias Barker and William Gumb.

Abel Lewis and William Ervin (attorney) about the suit of William Richardson vs. Richard Dickeson in the Muskingum County Court of Common Pleas.

Isaac Starrett regarding a mare that strayed from the Great Miami near Franklin. Deliver to James Robinson living near Chillicothe.

Daniel Mickey regarding a horse that strayed from Indian Creek.

John M'Dougal and John S. Wills regarding four suits in the Ross County Court of Common Pleas: James Denny vs. Uriah Springer; Oliver & Buckhanon vs. Uriah Springer; James Buckhanon, one of the late partners of the firm of Oliver & Buckhanon, vs. Uriah Springer; and Jacob Shepherd vs. John Templane.

John M'Dougal regarding a meeting of the Associate Judges mentions John Hutt and Isaac Cook.

Wm. Niblack lists the payments of Ross County to John M'Dougal, George Hoffman, Phil. Beecher, William Rutledge, John Edmiston, Thomas Reed, William Holland, William Chandler, Levin Belt, Thomas Scott, Benjamin Urmston, Felix Renicks, Jeremiah M'Lene, William Patton, Reuben Abrams, Thomas Gregg, Adam Betz, Winn Winship, James Denny, William Craigg, Thomas Barr, Robert Robinson, John Kerr, Thomas Chenoweth, James Grubb, Samuel A. Hall, Thomas Scott, William Niblack, John Collett, Henry Brush, N. Willis.

James Johnston, at Chillicothe, wants to hire tailors.

John M'Dougal and William Creighton, jun., regarding the suit of Nathan and Robert Gregg, merchants, trading as Nathan & Robert Gregg, vs. Augustus Richards.

Volume V, Monday, 10 December 1804, No. 256

A note about the contested election between Maj. M'Arthur and Capt. Shelby. Also a note about the election between D.C. Cooper and Mr. Thomson.

Fuller Elliot, administrator of the estate of Andrew Mealman, late of Gallia County, dec'd, regarding the estate settlement.

James Buchannon, at Chillicothe, reports a stray horse.

Gov. Edward Tiffin's message to the General Assembly is printed.

Volume V, Monday, 24 December 1804, No. 257

Stephen Smith, deputy sheriff of Scioto County, reports an escaped prisoner named Asa Tubbs.

Proceedings of the legislature mention Daniel Symmes, William C. Schenck, Martha Byrd of Hamilton County (for divorce from John Byrd), Elizabeth Gould of Washington County (for divorce from James Gould), Oliver Grosvenor & Lucy Ensworth (petition for the sale of certain lands).

Benjamin Urmston regarding the return of his log chain.

Abraham Nellson, in Trumbull County, administrator of the estate of James Nellson, dec'd, regarding the estate settlement.

John Mathews, collector, regarding the taxes due.

John M'Dougal regarding a meeting to distribute tavern licenses.

Jacobas Hines, living on the tract of land known as Round Praire, lying on Deer Creek, offers his land for sale.

David Denny has lots for sale in the town of Bloomfield.

Joseph Beard, living on the road from Zanesville to New Lancaster, reports a stray mare that he purchased from Mr. M'Ginnes.

Mark Morris, in Chillicothe, reports a strayed heifer.

John S. Edwards regarding a petition in Trumbull and Warren Counties from Oliver Elsworth, Thomas Bull, William Hillhouse, Stephen Clay, Arthur Magill and Moses Cleareland of Connecticut and Samuel Tylee of Trumbull County, Ohio, for shares in land patented to Samuel Holden Parsons in Trumbull County.

John M'Landburgh asks those indebted to him to settle their accounts.

John Reily regarding the petition, in Butler County, of John Shaw, an heir to John Shaw, late of Colerain, dec'd, for the partition of his lands. The other heirs of John Shaw, dec'd, are Knowles Shaw, Albin Shaw, Sally Shaw, Reuben Rood and Huldah his wife, and the heirs of Sina Newton, late of Granby, Conn., dec'd.

Volume V, Monday, 7 January 1805, No. 238

Maj. Gen. Elijah Wadsworth, Lieut. Col. Wm. Niblack, Lieut. Col. P. Lewis and Maj. Benj. Urmston, for Gov. Edward Tiffin, give general orders to the militia regarding the court martial of Maj. Gen. Joseph Buell and mention Joseph Barker, Ichabod Nye, Philip Lewis. Buell was acquitted.

David Reddick, of Washington County, Pennsylvania, and W. Creighton, jun., (attorney) about his petition in Ross County, Ohio, for land in Ohio, mentions John Mercer, the heirs of John Hardin, dec'd (said to live in Kentucky), David Gray, John Schenck of Lancaster County, Penn., Moses Hoge of Jefferson County, Va.

Frederick Overly, in Green township of Ross County, administrator of the estate of Martin Overly, dec'd, regarding the estate settlement.

An unsigned letter about the General Assembly mentions Michael Baldwin.

An account of a duel in Louisville, Kentucky, between Dr. John M. Luckett, of Louisville, and George Strother on Friday, 24 December 1804. Luckett died leaving a mother and two sisters, "only a few days landed in this country" and several brothers.

Levi Whipple, administrator, and Gisley Oliver, administratrix, of the estate of David Oliver, late of Muskingum County, dec'd, regarding the settlement.

Joseph Campbell regarding the state of his mill.

Volume V, Monday, 14 January 1805, No. 259

Proceedings of the legislature mention Humphrey Fullerton.

Thomas Needham, at the Red Lion in Chillicothe, reports a stray horse.

A list of letters left at the Post Office in Chillicothe includes William Askue, jun., Thomas Anderson, John Brown at Pe Pee, Thos. Briel, David Banker, Levi Buttles, Jesse Brakin, David Bradford on Bush Creek, Charles Bown near Franklin, William Brown at Chs. Brown's near Franklin, Robt. Bennet near Salt Lick, Isaac Bradley, Benj. Brackney, Jesse Cook, Robt. Corken, George Coonrod, Israel Clark, William Cory at Old Chillicothe, Jesse Conner on Salt Creek, Samuel Clark, William Crull at the Salt Works, David Conklin, Joseph Conklin, Joel Caey, Emmor Cox,

Samuel Cambell, Will Cambell, Thos. Cissna, George Clarke at Chillicothe, Aaron Danly on Dry Run, Levy Distiller six miles from Chillicothe, James Dunlap, Neal Daugherty, John Dill at Franklinton, Benj. Duncan in care of J. Tiffin, John Dunlap, Mr. Ebinowen at Keys' tavern, Benjamin Foster, Thomas Green in care of William Lamb, James Grubb, James Gordon, William Hewitt, James How, John Hixson, George Holloway, Joseph How, John Hunt, Benjamin Haines, Frances Harrow, Samuel Huntington and William Sprigg, George Haines, William Johnston, Thomas James, jun., James Johnston at Chillicothe or Franklinton, John Kight at Salt Lick, Adam Knowles, Elisha Lindsay, Charles Leonard at Westfall, Samuel Leppenneott, John Kreddlebough, E. Langham, Solomon Lupton, William Leather at Pe Pee, Nancy Moore in care of Levy Hurst, Jas. M'Cish, John M'Lernard, Wm. Brown in care of Samuel M'Lone, Alex. M'Ay, James M'Farland, John Moffitt, John M'Mullin in care of Cochran Amistead, John Mason, James Mouser, William Miller near Worthington's mill, John M'Lean, Henry M'Aully, Benjamin M'Meeker, Ezekiel Morris, William M'Meerice, Pecket Morvin, John Miller at Musselman's mill, James Martin, Peter Michel, Polly Miller, David Owen, George Penister in care of Mr. Platter, Thomas Phelps at Worthington, Sam. Phebus, Doc. Anthony Potts, Wm. Pope in care of John Carlisle, James Reed at Brush Creek, Jonathan Reddick, Mary Rogers on Clearfield Creek, William Reed, Ths. F. Reddick, Joseph Shoots and William Thompson, John Kingorre, Noah Strong, Wm. Sillman, William Smith, Ellender Sorden in care of Mich. Crydor, Ruben Strong, Cornelius Snyder in care of Mr. Bedast, Rev. John Steel, Samuel Smith, Enoch Smith in care of C. Platter, Aaron Sullivan, Alexander Scroggs in care of John M'Lanburgh, John Schofield in the town of Lebanon, Charles Stunbergin, William Sprigg, Soloman and Arthanial Tuttle, Robt. Tate, Ezra Travis on Scioto branch, Henry Turney, Henry Tell, William Whitthor, Malcom Wright, Jonathan Write on Paint Creek, Isaac Williams, John Waller on Lee's Creek, John Walter in care of Duncan M'Arthur, Valentine Welch, Obed Wyer on Miller's Bottom, Joshua Willington, John Walker (blacksmith near Chillicothe), Henry Williams, David Yerkia at Alexandria. Joseph Tiffin.

Volume V, Monday, 21 January 1805, No. 240

Proceedings of the legislature mention Humphrey Fullerton's bridge over the Scioto River and Gov. Edward Tiffin.

Obituary: Daniel Story, age about 40, died at Marietta on 30 December 1804.

William Russel is appointed post master at Alexandria and Adam Hosack is appointed at Franklinton.

Nicholas Devault, living on the North fork of Paint Creek about eight miles from Chillicothe on the road from Springfield, offers his farm and mills for sale.

William Kerst, of Paxton township, administrator of the estate of Mesheck Baker, late of Ross County, dec'd, regarding the estate settlement.

Catharine Eyre, living near the Falls of Paint Creek, reports a stray mare.

Richard Hoskins, administrator of the estate of David Willian, dec'd, late of Franklinton in Franklin County, regarding the estate settlement.

Absolem Vanmatre & Elizabeth Vanmatre, in Meiggs township, administrators of the estate of Joseph VanMatre, late of Adams County, dec'd, about the estate.

Lucas Sullivant and W. Creighton, jun., regarding the suit of Justice Miller vs. John M'Worter in the Franklin County Court of Common Pleas.

Volume V, Monday, 28 January 1805, No. 241

Proceedings of the legislature mention the University at Athens and James White's petition.

Henry Sheeley, in Chillicothe, regarding John and William Perry (blacksmith and carpenter) who "clandestinely eloped from this town".

Benj. Jones regarding due bills he gave to Wm. Evans for salt.

Volume V, Monday, 4 February 1805, No. 242

J. M'Lene, sheriff, regarding the sale of the property of Joshua Porter at the suits of Lemuel James, John M'Dougal and others.

Abraham Skinner, Edward Paine, jun., and Aurel Paine (administratrix), administrators of the estate of Elea zer Paine, late of Zanesville, Trumbull County, dec'd, regarding the estate settlement.

Amos Spafford and James Hamilton, administrators of the estate of Samuel

Hamilton, late of Cleveland, Trumbull County, dec'd, regarding the settlement.

Joseph Lemun has moved a few miles from Chillicothe, but continues to make spinning wheels. He sells them at John M'Lanburgh's store in Chillicothe and at the house of Matthew Taylor at the foot of Second Street.

Adam P. Browne has rented the warehouse in Alexandria, at the mouth of the Scioto, formerly kept by Christian Bottelman, dec'd.

Marriage: Dr. Joseph Scott to Miss Patty Finley (no date or place given).

Henry Sheeley regarding John and William Perry and their behavior.

John Brown, in Paxton township, Ross County, about the sale of his property.

James Carson and Agnes Dillon, in Tiffin township of Adams County, administrators of the estate of John Dillon, dec'd, regarding the estate settlement.

Volume V, Monday, 11 February 1805, No. 243

A list of judges appointed includes Daniel Symmes, Robert F. Slaughter, Isaac Cook, James Armstrong, Matthew Nimmo, Seth Carhart, Jesse Fulton, Richard M'Bride, Thomas Patton, Ezekiel Demming and Samuel Reed.

T.G. Bradford, book-binder, has opened his business in Chillicothe.

Nathaniel Massie regarding his stud horse at Chillicothe.

Benjamin Urmston, "having declined public business", asks those indebted to him to settle their accounts.

William Kent, in Paxton township, administrator of the estate of Mesheck Baker, late of Ross County, dec'd, regarding the estate settlement.

John Carlisle, collector for the Virginia Military Lands, regarding taxes.

Christian Endrick, living at Springfield on Mad River, reports a stray mare.

David C. Wallace, druggist in Marietta, has medicines for sale at his shop.

Volume V, Monday, 25 February 1805, No. 244

William Creighton, Jun., regarding the laws of Ohio.

A list of laws passed by the General Assembly mention Letart's Falls in Gallia County, Dayton, Steubenville, Israel Putnam (agent for the heirs of Dr. Jedidiah Ensworth, dec'd), Athens, Dayton library society, Jehiel Gregory, John Havner.

A note regarding the land Gov. W.H. Harrison acquired from the Indians.

Proceedings of the legislature mention Daniel Symmes, John Bigger, Jehiel Gregory, William Jackson and Sylvester Ames.

Gen. Massie's mills at the Falls of Paint Creek were burnt down last week.

A note about the impeachment of William Irwin, judge in Fairfield County.

John Hoddy, by Abm. J. Williams, regarding his petition in Ross County Court of Common Pleas about land located in 1787 for James Fitzpatrick, William Bryan, Alben Gorden, Charles Gunter and John Green.

George Fryback, living on the lower end of the Pickaway, found a mare.

Michael Baldwin and Daniel Symmes print two laws of the state of Ohio.

Jacob Burnet regarding his claim to the lands, in Fairfield County, of William M'Cabe and Jacob Harman.

Thomas Reed has a house for sale at Portsmouth at the mouth of Scioto.

Volume V, Monday, 4 March 1805, No. 245

Th. Gibson, Auditor of Public Accounts, regarding a contingency fund.

Henry Musselman has a stud horse at Musselman's mill, two and a half miles from Chillicothe. His ad is witnessed by E. Baxter and J. Armstrong.

William Burnham, at Marietta, administrator of the estate of Rev. Daniel Story, late of Marietta, dec'd, regarding the estate settlement.

Joseph Kerr regarding his stud horse at Gen. Massie's mill and at Frederick Brougher's house. He mentions Record's mill.

Nath. Massie about his stud horse at Benjamin Urmston's stable in Chillicothe.

Gibson & Armstrong have opened the Black Horse Tavern in Chillicothe in the tavern lately occupied by Major Urmston, opposite the upper ferry.

Wm. Niblack asks those indebted to him to settle their accounts.

John Carlisle, agent for Bickham & Rees, has a house for sale. It was lately occupied by Reuben Abrams.

N. Willis has a lot for sale in Chillicothe opposite Gen. Finley.

Isaac Vanmeter, living in Pleasant township, Highland County, on the waters of the east fork of Miami, reports a strayed mare.

Volume V, Monday, 11 March 1805, No. 246
William M'Coy, in Green township of Ross County, executor of Jane Mitchell, late of Ross County, dec'd, has land for sale, a part of the estate.

Obituary: James Buchanon died in Chillicothe on Tuesday, 5 March 1805.

Winn Winship, James Dunlap and William Rogers regarding the suit of James Baird and William Robinson vs. James M'Cullock in the Ohio District Court. They mention Samuel M'Cullock and Nathan Lammer's survey.

Joseph Tiffin offers his house for sale. He will also sell household furniture such as beds and bedding and several town lots.

Volume V, Monday, 18 March 1805, No. 247
Jacob Minturn about land on Mad River that he bought from William Ward. He says that Ward has since entered the land in his brother's name, James Ward, and refuses to admit that it was sold to Minturn.

Marriage: John Pickens married Miss Nancy Carlisle in Chillicothe (no date).

Wm. M'Farland asks those indebted to him to settle their accounts.

Wm. Jackson and Isabella Harmon, administrators of the estate of Middleton Harmon, late of Scioto County, dec'd, regarding the estate settlement.

P. Bureau regarding the suit of John Peter Romain Bureau vs. Hannah Mion Thevenin, Nicholas Thevenin, and Stephen Willermy in the Gallia County Court.

Matthias Ridingout, on Jonathan's Creek, about a note to William Lancaster.

Volume V, Monday, 25 March 1805, No. 248
Phielden Hubbard regarding his stud horse at the stables of Bartholomew Fryatt in Chillicothe and Thomas Hicks on Dry Run (eight miles from Chillicothe on the road from there to Old Town).

Mr. Vail and Mr. M'Collough have left their mills on the Great Miami due to the flooding of the river.

William Seymore, Joseph M'Coy and James Grubb regarding the establishment of a seat of justice in Highland County.

Volume V, Monday, 1 April 1805, No. 249
Mary Willoughby has purchased the tavern lately occupied by Jos. Tiffin at the sign of the Green Tree at the corner of Paint and Water Streets, Chillicothe.

Robert Oliver, administrator of the estate of John Quigley, late of Waterford, Washington County, dec'd, regarding the estate settlement.

Benjamin Kearns regarding notes payable to Thomas Cox.

Volume V, Monday, 8 April 1805, No. 250
T. Worthington, near Chillicothe, has several tracts of land for sale and mentions Devenbaugh's mill, Smith & Loveland's mill, Jonathan's Creek.

William Ruffin, in Cincinnati, has land for sale, adjoining Col. Chambers, near Lawrenceburg and on the Ohio River.

Tushland Kirtland, agent for the petitioners, at Poland, regarding the petition of Isaac Cowles, Noadiah Hooker, William Wadsworth and Lemuel Whitman (all of Farmington, Hartford County, Conn.) and Elias Evelin Hart (of Chatham, Conn.) regarding their shares in the land of Samuel Holden Parsons in Trumbull County.

Phielden Hubbard gives a description of his stud horse. It's signed by Andrew Mickinson, John Williams, James Kinslair, Thomas Mickinson, Robert House and John Kinslair, all of Harrison County, Kentucky.

Volume V, Monday, 15 April 1805, No. 251
A list of letters left at the Post Office in Chillicothe includes William Anderson near Chillicothe, Rebecca Brown, John J. Brice at New Ark, Robert Ballentine, William Blacksom, Thomas Britton, Joseph Boggs, Stephen Barton, White Brown, Joshua Baxtor, Peter Burr, John Barrett on Brush Creek, Job Broughton, Elisha Cowgell, George Clark, John Cottrell, Richard Clark at the Falls of Paint, Thomas Carneal, Jacob Culp, John Dever, Benjamin Duncan, James Davis on Paint Creek, William Dickson, Peter Dunen, Thomas Davidson, Enock Danvigan, Mary Dill, John Dill, Eli Elder, James Eredin, Mahlon Farguhar in care of W. Lamb, Jonah Farguhar, Aron Fredman at Singing Spring, John Florunce, George Field in care of W. Niblack, Joseph Fliming, Adam Getz, Luis Gibler near Chillicothe, Daniel Gurley, James

Hilmam, Joseph Horn, John Hunt, Jacob Heir, Samuel Henry on Sunfish Creek, Joseph Harness, Thomas Hollinback, Frencas Herron, Abram Jones, David Jones in care of John Brown, Mr. Jones, James Johnston, John Johnston, George Johnston, William King, Elias Langham, John W. Loosberry at Pickaway Plains, William Lewis, Thomas Long, Jacob Lutz, Joseph Miller, James Mouser on the north fork of Paint Creek, Peter Mouser, Daniel M'Farland, Josiah M'Kenny, James M'Farland, Robert M'Guire, Isaac Micks, John M'Connel, Abner Micker, James Mahin, James Murrander, Richard Morrass (22 miles from Lancaster, Henry Northup, G. Meann, Philip Moomaw (house joiner), William Macdoniel, John M'Meal, Peleg Potter on Salt Lick, William Pillars, Ralph Pillips, John Proud, Shelea Russel on Pickaway Plains, John Rush, James Robinson, Job Reed, William Reed on Twin Creek, Samuel Hopkins, Jerod Strong, Gen. Wm. C. Schenck, Joseph Swayne, Charles Steenbergen, Michael Shagley, Elizabeth Saylor, George Smith, Ruben Strong, George Smith (printer), Abraham Shepherd, Walter Smallwood, John Sherradan in care of Benjamin Duncan, James Smith, Jesse Tomlinson, Louther Taylor, Joseph Tipton, William Uselton, John Webstor, Edward Williams, Samuel Wilson, Robert Wallace, Jesse Worthington, David Wolcott, Jacob Widner, John Watson in care of D. M'Arthur, George Zemmer, Andrew Zimmerman, Michael Zimmerman. Entered by Joseph Tiffin.

Volume V, Monday, 22 April 1805, No. 252

W. Ward writes a letter to Mr. Willis regarding the ad placed by Jacob Minturn about their dispute over land. Mentions Mr. Runyan, S. Kenton.

Wm. Gibson and Robert Armstrong say that their partnership in the tavern-keeping business is dissolved. Armstrong will continue the business.

The Rosian Society in Chillicothe regarding a performance at the theater. Tickets are available at Mr. Meeker's next to the Theater.

Wm. Rogers lost a bundle of papers including a note from Wm. Keys and a receipt to Philemon Thomas from John Carlisle.

Azariah Pinney, administrator of the estate of Abner Pinney, late of the town of Worthington in Franklinton County, dec'd, regarding the estate settlement.

Volume V, Monday, 29 April 1805, No. 253

Samuel Stover reports that Abraham Brubaker, from Woodstock town in the county of Shenadoah, Virginia, died on Wednesday, 27 April 1805, at John Odle's house in Jefferson township, Ross County, on the road to the salt works.

James Pullen has opened a tavern at the Lower Blue Licks in Kentucky.

Thomas Reed, at the sign of the Mermaid, at the corner of Mulberry and Water Streets, regarding his house of entertainment.

A note regarding a stray horse says to deliver it to William Russell of Alexandria or Capt. William Lucas at the ferry.

Volume V, Monday, 6 May 1805, No. 253

Robert Lucas, in Chillicothe, has land for sale on Paint Creek.

Abraham Stipp, in Westfall, has land for sale in Wayne township, Ross County, presently occupied by William King. It includes a distillery.

James Denny says John G. Macan will handle the business of county surveyor.

John Collins, at Alexandria, has corn for sale at Lucas' ferry, eight miles above the mouth of Scioto.

Volume VI, Monday, 13 May 1805, No. 254

Robert Means and Nath. Massie have military lands for sale and mention John Clemons on Brush Creek, Temple Elliott, Joseph Horn on Brush Creek, John Graham, William Fowler, Pettie's run, White Oak Creek, Matthew Clay, Leven Powell, C. Minnis, T. Gaskins, Falvory Frazer, Boke's Creek, Henry Shackleford, Wm. Reynolds, Thomas Sears, James Holt, Justis Miller, Robert Campbell, Lucas Sullivant, Payton Powell, Robert C. Jacobs, Richard K. Meade, J. Heron, Ebenezer Scrogg, John Arrenote, James Taylor, jun. (executor of J. Heron), Chas. Lewis, Dan. Clark, James Broadus, William Reynolds, Edward Casington, Ballard Smith, Robert Powel, Cadwallader Jones. John Carlisle certifies them free of taxes.

John M'Dougal, living in Chillicothe, reports a stray horse.

Mary Hedges, in Franklinton County, Harrison township, administratrix of the estate of Joshua Hedges, dec'd, regarding the estate settlement.

Thomas Scott, justice of the peace in Ross County, about the deposition of Thomas Graves (or Issaac Grave) of Jefferson township in which he states that his certificate for land was burned along with his house.

Volume VI, Monday, 20 May 1805, No. 255

An account is printed of two drownings. John Dougherty, of Green township, Ross County, was found drowned in the Scioto River on Sunday, 12 May 1805. Mr. Nevel, late living at the Miami River, drowned on Monday, 13 May, while trying to cross the Scioto River opposite the High Bank.

John M'Coy has a new shipment of goods for sale at his store.

John Markel, living on Black Water in Green township of Ross County, reports a strayed horse.

Volume VI, Monday, 27 May 1805, No. 256

Michael Baldwin is appointed marshal for the state of Ohio in place of David Zeigler who resigned.

John Sherer has Menongahala Whiskey for sale in Chillicothe.

Dr. Sam. M. Venable "will practice physic and surgery" at his shop on Water Street in Chillicothe adjoining Mr. Needham's public house.

Henry Nevill has opened a store in Jefferson on the Pickaway Plains.

Thomas Jones, living near Romney on the south branch of Potomack River, reports a runaway slave, Tom, now known as Daniel, who lived with Mr. Lamb in Chillicothe last winter.

Isaac Stanley, at Scioto salt lick, says his wife, Elizabeth Stanley, has left him and he won't honor her debts.

Tickets for the theater performance of the Rosian Society can be had at Mr. Meeker's tavern, next door to the Theater.

Volume VI, Monday, 10 June 1805, No. 257

Paul Streby reports that he took up a stray horse. A second ad is entered regarding a note he gave to George Vincenthiller for land.

Eli Baldwin and Cook Fitch (commissioners) and Archibald Johnston and Tryal Tanner, at Canfield, administrators of the estate of Mathew Steele, late of Canfield, Trumbull County, dec'd, regarding the estate settlement.

Daniel Harbaugh and John Cumbacker, at New Lisbon, executors of the estate of Jacob Rudisyll, late of New Lisbon, Columbiana County, about the estate.

Jonathan Taylor and Joseph Vanlard, executors of the estate of William Salterthwaite, late of Belmont County, dec'd, regarding the estate settlement.

George Bowers about a horse he got from Jacob Huff/Hough of Scioto Salt Lick.

D. Harvey regarding his Eagle and Ball Tavern on Zane's Road in Zanesville in Muskingum County.

Wm. Niblack asks those indebted to him to settle their accounts.

Abner Meeker, administrator of the estate of James Buchanan, late of Ross County, dec'd, regarding the estate settlement.

Joseph Myer says his wife, Nancy Myers, has left him, and he won't pay any of her debts from this day.

Andrew M'Collock, living in Jefferson County, Steubenville township, reports a stray mare.

Samuel Lafferty, in Springfield, reports a stray horse.

Isaac Pierce, in Jefferson County, says that his wife, Sarah Pierce, left him and he won't honor her debts from this date.

Ariss Throckmorton reports two mares that strayed from the waters of Scippo. Deliver to Maj. Brown in Limestone.

John Brown, living near Washington in Mason County, Kentucky, reports a runaway slave named George who was raised in Fauquier County, Virginia.

George Givans, on Indian Creek near Chillicothe, reports a stray mare.

William F. Campbell, in Chillicothe, reports a stray mare. Deliver to Samuel Finley's place in Chillicothe.

Volume VI, Monday, 17 June 1805, No. 258

An account of a family disagreement at the mouth of Big Sandy in Kanhawa County between Dr. Hampton's son and Col. Sortridge. Hampton had recently married Col. Sortridge's daughter and gone to live at his father's house.

Wm. Hunter, at Frankfort, Kentucky, reports a horse stolen from John Waller's stable in Millersburg, Bourbon County, Kentucky.

John Oliver, surviving partner of Oliver & Buchanan, says do not pay debts owed the firm to Abner Meeker, administrator of the estate of James Buchanan, dec'd. Pay them to Oliver or to John G. Macan.

Volume VI, Monday, 24 June 1805, No. 259

John M'Dougal wants to buy 150 head of beef cattle in Chillicothe.

John M'Dougal, clerk of Ross County, regarding the payment of taxes.

Jacob Cox says that he will not pay the debts of his wife or anyone else.

Jesse George reports a horse that strayed from Lee's Creek, Highland County.

Jacob Crull, living in Jesemon township of Montgomery County, regarding a stray mare.

Reuben Perkins about a promissary note from John Dunkle to Elijah Perkins.

Volume VI, Monday, 1 July 1805, No. 260

Abel Lewis regarding two suits in the Muskingum County Court of Common Pleas: Martin Stull vs. Levi Wentworth; and George Beymer vs. Ezekiel Tophand.

Note about a meeting at Ephraim Hathaway's tavern, Lebanon, to discuss college township in Symmes' purchase mentions the Liberty Hall, Robert Renick, Mr. White, J.C. Symmes, Jacob White, Matthew Nimmo, Thomas Rawlins, Richard Thomas.

Samuel Hays, age 20, was thrown from his horse while crossing the Scioto on Saturday evening, 29 June 1805, and drowned. He'd been working at Mr. Brown's store. He was buried on Sunday.

Jean Brown and William Lee, in Adams County, administrators of the estate of James Brown, dec'd, regarding the estate settlement.

Isaac Bennet, living four miles west of Bedson, Penn., reports a stray horse. Deliver to Philip Wolff (three miles west of the Pickaway Plains) or to Adam Yerion, gunsmith, in Chillicothe.

William Morrison and James Morrison, in Adams County, administrators of the estate of Joseph Morrison, dec'd, regarding the estate settlement.

Abel Lewis about the suit of George Beymer vs. John Welch in the Muskingum County Court of Common Pleas.

James Chambers, justice of the peace in Mason County, Kentucky, regarding the deposition of Francis Boyd, on his way from Cynthiana, Kentucky, through Maysville, to Presquelisle, regarding the robbery of Thomas Neilson.

Michael Schaag, in Lexington, regarding the cure of mad dog bites.

Volume VI, Monday, 8 July 1805, No. 261

Lewis Davis, in Green County, reports a stolen mare.

A list of letters at the Post Office in Chillicothe includes John Armstrong at the Falls of Paint, John Askew, Samuel Brown at Buckskin, Jos. Brown on the waters of Paint Creek, Joshua Baxter, Nathan Britton, Benjamin Baker on Paint Creek, Isaac Bonney in care of J. Tiffin, Christian Blocker, Isaac Brink, Nancy Bell and Rosanna Boggs, Mr. Byrd in care of Jos. Tiffin, Andrew Badgley, David Bristol, Robert Cunningham on Buckskin, David Conklin, Jos. Conklin in care of J. Carlisle, James Creathers at High Bank, Nicholas Cunningham, Elisha Cowgill, Noble Crawford, William Carns, Wm. Cozard, Nicolas Clopper, James Compton, John Cochran, Daniel Curtright, Philip Cherry near Walnut Creek, Jeremiah Curtis, William Clark, Alexander Dunlap, Thomas Duff, Thomas Davidson, John Dawson, John Deuckson on Walnut Creek, Robt. B. Dobbins, James Dungan in care of J. Carlisle, Hannah Ewing, William Ewing in care of W. Lamb, William Favers, John Francee, Hugh Flyn near Pe Pee, John Fleming at Westfall, Joseph French, Timothy Gissert, Alexander Griffin, Wm. Gray in care of B. Urmston, John Gray in care of B. Urmston, Alexander Hamilton, Samuel Hayes in care of D. Hayes, Nathan Hayes, George Hayner, Lucas Hawkins, James Hughey in care of J. Kerr, Phineas Hunt in care of J. Tiffin, John Dickson, Jacob Hamer in care of G. Wilds, Bigger Head, Jarid Hill, David Irons in care of James Wilson, Benjamin Kirkpatrick on Deer Creek, Gen. Simon Kenton, Elias Langham, Robert Lucas, Martha Little or James Little, Edward Long, Martha Logan, Benjamin V. Lakin, Ad. Merchant, Philip M'Namar at Yellow Bud, Hugh Montgomery, William M'Munn, James M'Dowell, John M'Neal, Robert Mitchell,

Timothy Mershon in care of B. Urmston, John Middleton, Elias Matten, Hugh M'Clean, William Kent, Nathaniel Nichols, Thomas Nowlin in care of J. Tiffin, Daniel Nichols on Twin Creek, Moses Norton in care of J. Brown, Philip Pipper in care of W. Lamb, James Powels in care of James Grimes, Abraham Peters on Sun fish, Robert Parks, William Patton, N. Pope, Daniel Peters, Shelah Russell or Samuel Hoptkins, Will. Read on Twin Creek, Jacob Robertson, Alexander Rowen on Deer Creek, Thomas Reed, Jas. Reed, John Ross at High Bank, Joseph Swayne (carpenter), Obadiah Schenck, Andrew Simmerman, John Stretchbery near Paint Creek, Stephen Smith or Israel Smith, Thomas Smith, Eliza Smith, Thomas Smith, Jacob Smith, Samuel Spangler (18 miles from Chillicothe), John Savary, Jacob Saltgarver in care of Isaac Witsel, Job Sharp, William Sprigg, Jacob Scrager, John Todhunter, Michael Thomas, William Taylor, sen., on Paint Creek, Jonathan Saylor, Lowther Taylor, Isaac Thomas, Henry Utt, Benjamin Vail, John S. Wills, Rev. Robert Wilson, James Wyche, Willian Wilson, Christopher Wever, Obed Were near John Gutery on Pe Pee, Aden Webb on Pe Pee, Samuel Wilson on Pickaway Plains, John Whitoath, James Wilson at Brown's crossroads, Thomas White on Dry Run. Joseph Tiffin.

Adam Neff, living in Moorefield, Hardy County, Virginia, reports 3 runaway slaves named Mingo, Ama and Zack. Deliver to Henry Neff living on the Ohio near the mouth of Big Guiandot.

Volume VI, Monday, 15 July 1805, No. 262

A letter from Robert Munro at Detroit to Gov. Harrison is printed regarding the fire at Detroit. Mentions Col. Hamtramock, Mr. Dodemead (living in a corner of the public store house at the ship yard in Detroit), Mr. Donovan and family (on their way to Sandwich), Mr. Ondrian, Mr. May, Mr. M'Intosh.

Marriage: John Dix, merchant, married Miss Betsy Byers on Sunday evening, 14 July 1805.

Daniel Musselman says that on his journey from Natchez to Chillicothe, on the 28th of June, he was riding in company with Felix Boil and Mr. Cavet when they were detained at Lexington on suspicion of horse stealing.

Benjamin Doolittle, at Chillicothe, wants to buy ginsang at Ephraim Doolittle & Company's store.

Dani. Benjamin and Joseph Cougell, four miles from Franklinton on Whetstone in Franklin County, regarding stray horses found by the Indians.

Reasin Beall and W.C. Larwell (attorney) regarding the suit of David Spears and David Dickinson in the Columbiana County Court of Common Pleas over land entered by Jacob Gaunt.

Volume VI, Monday, 22 July 1805, No. 263

An account of the Fourth of July celebration at Adelphi is printed.

Volume VI, Monday, 29 July 1805, No. 264

T. Worthington, near Chillicothe, reports a stray horse. Deliver to Mr. Winn Winship in Chillicothe.

Volume VI, Monday, 5 August 1805, No. 265

Maj. Gen. Nathl. Massie about meetings of the militia at Thomson's tavern on Deer Creek and Christian Platter's house.

Thomas Barrus, living on Two Mile Creek, Clarke County, Kentucky, reports a runaway slave named Frank.

Joshua Baxter, in Ross County, administrator of the estate of William Dunbarr, dec'd, regarding the estate settlement.

Joshua Porter, jun., has land for sale in Chillicothe now occupied by John M'Dougal and George Renick.

Samuel Smith, executor of the estates of James Crawford and William Smith, dec'd, late of Ross County, regarding the estate settlement.

Lucas Sullivant and James Davenport (attorney) about the petition of George M'Alpine, an insolvent debtor, in the Franklin County Court of Common Pleas.

Charter M'Clung and Wm. Martin, at Pleasant township, executors of the estate of David Martin, late of Pleasant township, Fairfield County, dec'd, regarding the estate settlement.

Hannah Howard and Joseph Howard, executors of the estate of Samuel Howard, dec'd, regarding the estate settlement.

Elizabeth Stinson, administratrix of the estate of Robert Stinson, late of Concord township, Ross County, dec'd, regarding the estate settlement.

James Blincoe, in Chillicothe, regarding a bond to George Emery of Ross County for land on the Rocky fork of Paint Creek.

Thomas Peebles, living near Lexington, Kentucky, reports a runaway slave named Charles (who was raised near Manchester, Virginia).

Samuel Holton, near the crossing of Paint Creek, found a bundle of clothes.

Anthy. Williams reports a horse that strayed from Col. Dunlap's plantation. Deliver to Wm. Patton's on Paint Creek.

Volume VI, Monday, 12 August 1805, No. 266

Doctor Ramus Davis & Company have opened a new apothecary store on Water Street next door to Mr. Lamb's Tavern in Chillicothe.

Joseph Kerr reports a horse that strayed from the pasture of Jas. Wilson at Brown's Crossroads. Deliver the horse to Frederick Brougher.

Adam Turner, administrator of the estate of William Holland, dec'd, regarding the estate settlement.

Jesse Cravens, agent for Nehemiah Cravens, at Christian County Court House in Kentucky, regarding Richard Thomas, lately from Georgia, schoolmaster in Christian County, who robbed Nathaniel Cravens, storekeeper.

An unsigned letter nominating Col. Thomas Worthington as brigadier general.

James W. Johnson, in Chillicothe, reports a stray horse.

Fred. Elerenman has hats for sale at Capt. Lamb's tavern in Chillicothe.

Wm. Craig says he is a candidate for the Assembly.

A note regarding Ge. Emery's reply to James Blincoe's advertisement.

Volume VI, Monday, 19 August 1805, No. 267

George Emrey writes a letter regarding James Blincoe's ad and mentions Alexander Gorden (of Manchester, Virginia), Maj. M'Arthur, Perregan Fitchew.

S. Thompson, watchmaker, jeweller and silversmith, regarding his shop in Water Street in Chillicothe. He also repairs watches.

Augustine Davis, in Richmond, Virginia, has land for sale on Paint Creek.

Wm. M'Intyre, living three miles from West Union, has his farm for sale.

Martin Carr regarding a mare that strayed from him in Concord Township.

P. Bureau and Wm. Sterret (attorney) regarding the suit of John Miller vs. Francis Valton in the Gallia County Court of Common Pleas. Also regarding the suit of John Bing vs. James Wilson and Wm. M'Kinley, executors of the estate of Richard Speers, also in the Gallia Court.

Peter Wolf and Elizabeth Wolf, in Letart's township, Gallia County, executors of the estate of Adam Wolf, dec'd, regarding the estate settlement.

Robert M'Cutchen, at the public prison in Staunton, regarding the accusation that he committed a murder with Samuel Meeks in Ohio. He says he lived in Ohio from 3 October 1803 through 15 July 1804. He mentions Matthias Whiteman in Tyger's Valley and the testimony of David Cail. He was hired by four Dutch families, that of Samuel Landers and three families named Shobe, to drive cattle to the North Fork of Paint Creek, Concord township, Ross County, in September of 1803. He mentions his friend Capt. Francis Wells in Concord township.

John Steauthus and John P. Bissell (commissioners) and Mary Fitch and Joseph Fitch (administrators), for the estate of Andrew Fitch, late of Youngstown township, Trumbull County, dec'd, an insolvent, regarding the estate settlement to be held at the tavern of David Stewart in Youngstown.

Maj. Jeremiah M'Lene is elected Brigadier General of Ross County militia.

A. Marshall, at St. Clarville, and N. Willis, at Chillicothe, regarding the mail stage from Chillicothe to Frankfort, Kentucky.

A note from the editor of the Scioto Gazette that he will sell one half interest in the printing office and business.

Doctor Ramus Davis regarding his practice of medicine in Chillicothe.

Hugh Boyle and Wm. W. Irvine (attorney) regarding a suit of Christian King vs. Robert King in the Fairfield County Court of Common Pleas.

Volume VI, Monday, 26 August 1805, No. 268
Obituary: Mr. O. Little died in Chillicothe on Friday, 23 August 1805.

Stephen Smith, in Chillicothe, about a prisoner, Jacob Harness, who escaped between Wilson and Brougher's taverns on the Limestone Road.

Volume VI, Monday, 2 September 1805, No. 269
Capt. David Shelby is a candidate for the legislature. Wm. Askew, sen., and Stephen Timons are also candidates.

Stephen Smith regarding the horse Jacob Harness was arrested for stealing.

Rebecca Kerkendall, administratrix of the estate of John Kerkendall, late of Ross County, dec'd, regarding the estate settlement.

Joseph Kerr, near Chillicothe, regarding people killing and eating his hogs.

Volume VI, Monday, 9 September 1805, No. 269
Marriage: Wm. Creighton, jun., Secretary of the state of Ohio, married Miss Betsy Mead, of Kentucky, on Thursday, 5 September 1805.

The Brigadier General appoints Col. James Curry to be inspector and David Crous to be quarter master.

Thomas Reed, in Chillicothe, about the charges made by John Page in an ad in the Ohio Herald. He mentions Hugh Wood (bar-keeper at Reed's tavern), Mr. Emery (Page's father-in-law), Mr. Lownes (Page's brother-in-law), Mr. Thomson, Mr. Hall.

Joseph Jeffers says that his wife, Catharine Jeffers, has left him and he will no longer honor her debts.

N. Willis regarding books he will soon publish.

Volume VI, Monday, 16 September 1805, No. 270
Wm. Askew, sen., writes a letter to the public regarding the elections.

An account of the death of Gen. Wm. Lucas, on Tues., 10 Sept. 1805, in Scioto County, from being struck by a falling tree. He leaves a wife and two children.

Notes regarding candidates for public office mention John Evans, John M'Lene, John Mathews, John Hutt, Thomas Scott.

Jeremiah M'Lene regarding the location of polling places for the upcoming election mentions Arthur Chenoweth in Pee Pee township, Samuel S. Spencer in Lick township, William Lewis in Jefferson township, John Crouse in Green town-ship, James S. Webster in Colerain township, John Barr in Pickaway township, Fergus Moore in Wayne township, Jarred Davis in Deerfield township, Joseph Elliott in Twin township, Christian Platter in Paxton township, Joseph Clarke in Union township and John Gossurre in Concord township.

John Ward, in Jefferson County, regarding the petition of Samuel Graham, an insolvent debtor, in the Court of Common Pleas at Steubenville. Also regarding the petition of John Wolf, an insolvent debtor.

John Dunlap says his wife, Mary Dunlap, "for a considerable time past, has behaved in an unbecoming manner, by neglecting her business and involving me in debt", and he will no longer honor her debts.

John Waddle & Company have a new shipment of goods for sale at their store in Chillicothe next door to Capt. Lamb's tavern in Water Street.

J.P. Minguy, at Gallipolis, administrator of the estate of Henry Minguy, late of Gallipolis, Gallia County, dec'd, regarding the estate settlement.

Michael Chanterlle, at Gallipolis, administrator of the estate of Michael Cransar, late of Gallipolis, Gallia County, dec'd, regarding the settlement.

Jeremiah M'Lene says to pay land taxes to John Shearer in Chillicothe.

John R. Gaston, in Colerain township, Hamilton County, reports a stray mare.

The books and papers belonging to Ross County that were kept by William Niblack are now in the possession of John M'Lene, in Chillicothe.

Thomas Reed writes another letter regarding John Page. He mentions Mr. Lownes and Mr. Meeker.

Volume VI, Monday, 23 September 1805, No. 271
A note regarding the re-election of Gov. Tiffin.

Abraham J. Williams, of Chillicothe, says he is a candidate for Assembly. Also Col. James Dunlap and Maj. Duncan M'Arthur are candidates.

Joseph Kerr, agent for Henry Massie, has land for sale, lately owned by Mr.

Zane, opposite Chillicothe.

John Waddle & Company have a new shipment of goods for sale in the store lately occupied by John Kerr & Company next door to Capt. Lamb's tavern.

Duncan M'Arthur, near Chillicothe, regarding military land grants in Ohio.

Jonathan Talbert, living in Chillicothe, reports a stray mare.

John Trebar, in Adams County, found a horse five miles from West Union on the Lick fork of Brush Creek.

Jesse Cravens, agent for Nehemiah Cravens, at Christian County Courthouse, Kentucky, about Richard Thomas. It is thought that Thomas Gains who recently lived at Capt. Wm. Lamb's house in Chillicothe is the same as Richard Thomas.

Volume VI, Monday, 30 September 1805, No. 272

Marriage: Jacob Hinkle, printer, married Miss Nancy Kennedy, both of Chillicothe, on Tuesday evening, 24 September 1805.

Notes regarding candidates for office mention Edward Tiffin, William Askew, Duncan M'Arthur, James Dunlap, Abraham Williams, David Shelby, Peter Jackson of Deerfield township, John Evans, William Lewis.

A letter from Duncan M'Arthur regarding his candidacy.

John Carlisle has a new shipment of goods for sale at his store.

Daniel Camron, living six and a half miles from Chillicothe on the Limestone road, reports a stolen mare. She was taken by William Marshall, age 24.

Michael Shoppell about an agreement with James Philips and Wm. Creighton.

Joel Smith, at Gallipolis, regarding a stolen mare left in his custody.

Public notice to William Ellery and Elias Ellery, brothers, natives of Charlestown, Mass., printers, "who have for some years past resided in the South Western parts of the U.S.", to contact John Somes in Boston for valuable information.

Lemuel James asks those indebted to him to make payments by delivering wheat to Col. Thomas Worthington's mill.

Doctor Ramus Davis & Company have a new shipment of medicines for sale at their apothecary shop in Chillicothe.

Volume VI, Monday, 7 October 1805, No. 273

Unsigned letters to the editor regarding the elections mention Mr. Askew, Mr. Patton, Joseph Kerr, Wm. Patton, John M'Dougal, Mr. Bradford, Wm. Askew, John Bowman, John Betz, Benjamin Rolston's brother Robert Rolston, Michael Baldwin.

Joseph Tiffin prints the mail schedule in full.

A list of letters left at the Post Office in Chillicothe includes John Ayres, George Alen, Elijah Anderson on Clear Creek, Dr. Silas Allen at Amanda Village, John Allen in care of J. Evans, William Blackmore at Pee Pee, Nath. Blackmore, Samuel Barr near the Falls of Paint, Jacob Bartley, Amos Barr, Isaac Brink, Risdon Beauchamp, Charles Coulter at Pickaway, Joseph Boggs, Robert Clarke in care of W. Seymores, William Bloxom at Pickway, Benjamin Brackney, Joseph Briggs at High Bank, Wm. P. Bennett, John Bryan at Buckskin, Abraham Claypool, William F. Campbell, John Cradlepaugh on Salt Creek, John Craig, David Cobbs, Isaac Cook, William Clark in care of J. Tiffin, Hugh Cockrane, Henderson Crabb in care of J. Furguson, Gen. Jonathan Dayton in Chillicothe, James Dodd, Precila Donoughe at Yellow Bud, Michael Dougherty at Squire Smith's at Salt Creek, Lemuel Evins, Jacob Earkart on Scippo Creek, George Emery, Capt. Fortiner on Brush Creek, Ann Foster at Pee Pee, John P. Finley, James Fosbiner, Moses H. Grigg at the Falls of Paint, Alexander Gincon, James Hughes, James Hughey in care of J. Kerr, Hugh Huston, Horton Howard at Concord, Hugh Husk, Samuel Hopkins, Joseph Hopkins on the north fork of Paint, John Higgins, Nathaniel Hunt, Thomas and Nathaniel Hill, Mr. Horn (tavernkeeper), Mrs. Hargis in care of Johnston Hemphell, Abraham Holderman, William Hamilton on Pickaway, David Irons, Aramus Jones or John M'Kefferty, Robin Joans near White Brown, David Kennedy of Aurora, James Kight, William King at Westfall, Aaron Kendall, Tilgman Lewis at Pickaway, Thomas Lock at Westfall, Samuel Lybrand, Thomas Lee, John Lusk, Martha Little, Philip Lyassert in Concord township, James Martin near Paint Creek, William M'Munn, Peter Millington, jun., at Liberty Town, Ichabod Marshall, Dossie Mason, James M'Cartney near Chillicothe, Abraham Monnett at Salt Creek, John Medford, James Moore, William M'Coy near Crouse's mill, Daniel Musselman, Miss Kezea M'Cune, Alexander M'Clentock at High Bank, Archibald M'Donald, Thomas M'Donald, John M'Donald (12 miles from

Chillicothe), Capt. Peter Marks, Ellis Menshall at High Bank, Bolace Nichols, John P. Neal, William Patton, John Proud on Little Twin Creek, John Perkins, Col. Francues Payton, William Rector, Elias Rector, Alexander Reed on Darby Creek, John Richards, George Reed on Deer Creek, William Reed in care of James Johnson (carpenter), Woolsey Robinson on Pickaway Plain, James Renicks, John Renicks, Nathan Reeves, Alexander Rowan, Dickey Shephard, Peter Stilley, Timothy Spelman of Granville, Robert Sebring at Old Station, John Stedgar, Job Smith in Liberty township, Jonathan Simpson on the north fork of Paint, Gabriel Steley in care of John Mitchell, Samuel Smith, Samuel Arrow Smith, Samuel Scott, Isaac Spinney, John Shields at the Falls of Paint, Thomson Smith, Noah Strong and Ruben Strong at Cessorsville, Areal Strong at Liberty, Joseph Tipton, Zachariah Taylor, Matthew Thomson at the mouth of Scioto, Alexander Vance in care of William Lamb, Jacob Wedner, Geo. Yellott, Issac Werden, Nathaniel Wyalt or Thomas Brundige, Samuel Wilson on Zane's road on the salt fork of Wells Creek, Thomas Whiting, Keziah Walrond at J. Miller's house, Luthar Willard, Thomas White, George West, George Zimmers. Entered by Joseph Tiffin.

John Mathews and Wm. Creighton, sen., about Mathews' collection of the taxes.

John S. Wills, in Chillicothe, has land for sale near Maj. Anthony Franklin's and the Falls of Paint Creek.

Samuel Canby, in Washington, Kentucky, has rented Daniel Vertner's oil mill.

Henry Dreshbac and John Thomas have lots for sale in the town of Livingston on the Pickaway Plains, Ross County.

John Devour, living on the Scioto River, twelve miles above the mouth, reports a stray mare.

Volume VI, Monday, 14 October 1805, No. 274

John Clemens' six-year-old daughter was burned when her clothes caught on fire on Wednesday, 9 October 1805, and she died the next day.

Election returns mention Edward Tiffin, William Patton, James Dunlap, A.J. Williams, David Shelby, John M'Lene and John Mathews.

Jesse Spencer and Samuel Finley regarding land for sale in Ohio.

James Ferguson, Winn Winship and Thomas James regarding the suit of James Denny vs. Uriah Springer in Ross County Court of Common Pleas. Mentions the house of Thomas Needham in Chillicothe.

Election returns in Warren County mention Edward Tiffin, Richard S. Thomas, Mathias Corwin, Peter Burr, Ephraim Hathaway, Andrew Lytle.

Samuel Brown & Company ask those indebted to them to settle their bills.

Andrew Ellison, living near Manchester in Adams County, found a stray mare.

Samuel Wallace says his wife, Nelly Wallace, "persists in conducting herself in a very unbecoming manner, by taking away and secreting my property", and he won't honor her debts anymore.

Volume VI, Monday, 24 October 1805, No. 275

Election returns in Ross County mention William Patton, William Askew, James Dunlap, A.J. Williams, David Shelby, Elias Langham, Duncan M'Arthur, William Lewis, John Evans, J.G. Macan, William Craig, Stephen Timmons, John M'Lene, John Mathews, Thomas Scott, John Hutt, Ebenr. Finnemore, Daniel Chesnut. In Adams County: Thomas Kirker, Abraham Shepherd, Daniel Cather, Philip Lewis, Alexander Campbell, Thomas Waller, Daniel M'Kenney. In Scioto County: John Simpson. In Butler County: William Ward, Jacob Smith, Richard S. Thomas, Matthew Richardson, James M'Curr, William M'Clelland, and Joshua Delaplane. In Clermont County: James Sargent, Jonathan Taylor, Levi Rodgers. In Columbiana County: Benjamin Haugh, John Milligan, John M'Connel, Isaac Pearce, William Staler. In Warren County: Richard S. Thomas, William Ward, Jacob Smith, Abner Garrard, James Smith, Mathias Corwin, Peter Burr, George Harlan, John Haynes, James Long, Calvin Ball, Ichabod Corwin, John Reed, Ephraim Hathaway, Andrew Lytle.

William H. Puthuffs, at Gallipolis, has taken over the tavern lately occupied by Joel Smith at the sign of the Spread Eagle in Gallipolis.

John Meek, at Hocking, says he's hopelessly in debt and will petition the court as an insolvent debtor.

James Poage, living in Mason County, Kentucky, near May's Lick, reports a runaway slave named Ben, age 28.

John Dively, hatter, in Alexandria, Scioto County, reports a stray horse.

Volume VI, Monday, 31 October 1805, No. 276
Gov. Tiffin has called an election to fill the seat of Wm. Patton, dec'd, in the senate of Ohio.
Gov. Tiffin has called a meeting of the trustees of Ohio University at Athens.
Obituary: Hon. Wm. Patton died on Friday morning, 28 October 1805.
Duncan M'Arthur is a candidate to fill the vacancy left by Wm. Patton, dec'd.
William Askew writes a letter saying he is also a candidate to fill this seat.
Jeremiah M'Lene regarding the election to fill William Patton's vacancy.
A note regarding the state road laid out by Mr. Gregory from Chillicothe to New Lancaster in Fairfield and Ross Counties.
John Kenton, in Mason County, Kentucky, reports a runaway slave, Wilson.
A note regarding the Chillicothe horse races at Joseph Kerr's farm.
Wm. Creighton, sen., has lots for sale in Chillicothe.
A note regarding Charles Friend's petition to the legislature regarding his water and grist mill on Clear Creek in Fairfield County.

Volume VI, Monday, 7 November 1805, No. 277
Gov. Hull's address to the Territory of Michigan is printed. It includes the answer to Gov. William Hull from James Henry, Elijah Brush, Geo. M'Dougall, C. Joncaire and G. Meldrum.
James Denny is a candidate to fill the vacancy left by William Patton, dec'd.
A note regarding Gov. Hull's inaugural speech.
Obituary: William Craig died in Ross County on Sunday night, 6 Nov. 1805.
John M'Coy has a new shipment of goods for sale at his store.
John M'Clean and John Mathews regarding a meeting of the commissioners.
Elizabeth Lucas and Joseph Lucas, in Scioto County, administrators of the estate of William Lucas, jun., late of Scioto County, dec'd, about the estate.
Kraft Shelkey about opening the state road from Lancaster to Chillicothe.
Thomas Reed, "having declined tavern keeping", is erecting a smith shop.

Volume VI, Thursday, 14 November 1805, No. 278
Unsigned letters to the editor about the upcoming election mention Duncan M'Arthur, James Denny, Mr. Claypool, Mr. Lewis, Mr. Cook, Mr. Creighton, Mr. Edmiston, Worthington's road, Mr. M'Dougal.
James Denny writes a letter about his candidacy and mentions Mr. Patton.
Wm. Askew says he declines the candidacy to fill Wm. Patton's seat.
Election returns in Montgomery County mention Edward Tiffin, William Robinson, George Newcomb, James Miller. In Belmont County: Joseph Sharp, John Stewart and James Smith.
Catharine Patton, Wm. M'Farland and Wm. Creighton, jun., administrators of the estate of William Patton, dec'd, regarding the estate sale.
Michael Cryder will petition the Assembly for permission to build a dam across the Scioto opposite to where Jacob Wedener formerly lived.
Samuel Brown & Company ask those indebted to them to make payments in wheat delivered to John Crous' mill on Kinnickonic.

Volume VI, Thursday, 21 November 1805, No. 279
Unsigned letters to the editor mention Wm. Patton, dec'd, Maj. M'Arthur, James Denny, Mr. Rector, Mr. Denny.
Benjamin Urmston has again opened his tavern in Chillicothe.
James Finley, at the Brush Creek Settlement, living near Squire Wright's mill on Cherry fork, reports a stray mare.
Joseph Darlinton regarding the petition of William D. Thorp, an insolvent debtor, in the Adams County Court of Common Pleas.
John Lowman and Jacob Foster, living on Sunfish Creek, report stray horses.

Volume VI, Thursday, 28 November 1805, No. 280
Election returns to fill the seat of Wm. Patton, dec'd, mention Mr. M'Arthur and Mr. Denny.
Wm. Creighton, sen., John Carlisle, Wm. M'Farland, John M'Lene and Sam.

Finley, trustees of the Congregation of New Hope in Chillicothe, about erecting a new meeting house.

Volume VI, Thursday, 5 December 1805, No. 282
An act to incorporate the Indiana Canal Company is printed and mentions Benjamin Hovey, Josiah Stephens. Signed by Jesse B. Thomas, Benjamin Chambers and Gov. William H. Harrison in Indiana Territory.

A note regarding the election of Edward Tiffin as governor.

Proceedings of the legislature mention James Pritchard, Thomas Scott, Edward Sherlock, John Sloane, Jos. Darlinton, Adam Betz, Wm. R. Dickenson.

An account of the fire on Sunday morning last at Mr. Fullerton's house, now occupied by Mr. S. Smith, cabinet maker and painter.

William Keyes, living about four miles from Chillicothe, has land for sale.

John L. Tabb, cabinet maker, has opened his business in Chillicothe in his shop opposite John Mantle's tanyard on Water Street.

Sarah Buttles, Joel Buttles and Levi Hays, at Worthington, Liberty township, administrators of the estate of Levi Buttles, late of Worthington, dec'd, about the estate settlement.

John M'Lanburgh asks those indebted to him to settle their accounts.

Peter Lee, living in Washington, Kentucky, reports a horse that strayed from the pasture of Jacob Vincenheller on Paint Creek, eight miles from Chillicothe.

Andrew Moore & James Moore, administrators of the estate of Robert Moore, late of Adams County, dec'd, about the estate settlement.

Volume VI, Thursday, 12 December 1805, No. 282
The address of Gov. Edward Tiffin to the legislature is printed.

Proceedings of the legislature mention James Pritchard, Thomas Scott, Robert Cloud, John Sloane, Joseph Darlinton, Adrian Heggerman of Hamilton County, Thomas Worthington, Thomas G. Bradford, Nathaniel Willis.

A note regarding a meeting, at Mrs. Willouby's tavern, to discuss fire alarms.

James Galloway, jun., on Little Miami in Green County, will locate lands in the Virginia Military District.

Abel Casto reports a mare that strayed from the pasture of Jacob Broadwell near the Round Bottom, Little Miami.

Ebenezer Dean, formerly of Farmington and East Haven in Connecticut, lately of Milbury and now of Chillicothe, gives public notice to his mother, Anna Dean, who is now on the way to Ohio from Braintree, Vermont.

Benjamin Kerns, living near Chillicothe, reports a stolen horse.

Volume VI, Thursday, 26 December 1805, No. 284
Proceedings of the legislature mention William Irwin, Lancaster, Henry Brush.

J.S. Collins & Company, printers, have purchased the Scioto Gazette.

Lemuel James and Thos. James have dissolved their partnership and Thomas James will continue the business.

William Ward, at Mad River, reports some stolen horses.

Humphrey Fullerton asks those indebted to him to settle their accounts.

Thomas James gives notice to those who promised to deliver wheat to Col. Worthington's mill for the benefit of Lemuel James.

Duncan M'Arthur regarding the ear mark in his cattle and hogs.

An unsigned letter to James Galloway, jun., about locating lands, mentions Mr. M'Arthur's surveys and Springer's camp.

William Gibson says the partnership of Gibson & Armstrong is dissolved and the accounts are with C.A. Stuart, attorney, at Mr. Needham's in Chillicothe.

Capt. Joseph Cambell regarding a meeting of the Chillicothe Light Infantry.

Hector Sanford has opened a chair manufactory in Water Street, Chillicothe.

P. Bureau regarding the suit of Jether Bailey vs. Jether Bailey, jun., in the Gallia County Court of Common Pleas.

Thos. Reed will do smith's work at his shop in Chillicothe.

Volume VI, Thursday, 2 January 1806, No. 285
Proceedings of the legislature mention Marietta, Francis Douglass (late sheriff of Jefferson County), Oliver Jennings, Thomas Gibson, Benjamin Whiteman (judge in

Green County), Joseph Tatman (judge in Green County).

Marriage: Thos. James, merchant of Chillicothe, married Miss Charlotte Massie, of Ross County, on 1 January 1806, by Rev. Mr. Dobbin.

Mr. Crouse's boats passed Chillicothe on Jan. 1st headed for New Orleans.

John Martin, at Chillicothe, lately from the Federal City, has commenced the baking business in Water Street. He served his apprenticeship in "one of the largest towns in England".

Wm. W. Evans regarding a horse that strayed from Jesse Spencer's plantation one mile from Chillicothe.

John Bainter, administrator of the estate of Godfrey Bainter, dec'd, late of Muskingum County, regarding the estate settlement.

Jacob Houch, at Marietta, reports some horses that strayed from the pasture of Wm. Newel in the town of Springfield, opposite Zanesville. Deliver to Paul Halin in Zanesville, Isaac Mixer, jun., in Marietta or John Collins in Alexandria.

Levi Sidwell, in Chillicothe, wants to hire workers to clear land.

Volume VI, Thursday, 9 January 1806, No. 286

Proceedings of the legislature mention Marietta and Thomas Worthington.

A note regarding the trial of Wm. Irwin, associate judge in Fairfield County, mentions Mr. Couch, his attorney.

W. Raynolds has opened a house of entertainment in Zanesville.

Richard Bibb, sen., has military lands for sale and mentions William Parsons, Col. Wm. Lytle of Williamsburgh, Z. Tatum and Henry Massie of Chillicothe.

William Niblack asks those indebted to him to make payments to Samuel Niblack at Benjamin Urmston's tavern.

Samuel M'Adow asks those indebted to him to settle their accounts.

N. Willis, late editor of the Scioto Gazette, asks those indebted to him to make payments to Thos. Scott.

Joseph Boman, stone cutter, living at William Hoddy's house on the north fork of Paint Creek, seven miles from Chillicothe, regarding his business.

Robert Lucas, James M'Dowel, Isaac Bonser and Thos. Patton, trustees of the Farmer's Academy on the Ohio River, one mile above the mouth of Little Scioto, in Scioto County, regarding the school. Rev. Robt. W. Finley, member of the Independent Church is the president of the academy.

J.A. Fulton, in Chillicothe, has "an excellent new waggon and geers" for sale.

A list of letters left at the Post Office in Chillicothe includes James Atkinson at Woodstown, Francis Adams, Jonathan Arnett, Jacob Bartley, Abelard Bradford, Mr. Biggarhead at the Falls of Paint, Robert Boyle, Daniel Brining, John Buck, Mary Carter, Clement Brown, Frederick Braucher, White Brown, John Boggs, Sally Clemans, Thomas Carneal, David Cobler, Abraham Claypool, Jacob Croes, Wm. Badley, Jesse Cockrull, Samuel Cissna, Sanford Carder, Noah Clifton on Deer Creek, Londer Cannon, Amer Cox, Joseph Cory on Paint Creek, William Douglass, Conner Doud at Salt Creek near Samuel Cox's, James Douglass (printer), Peter Drace, James Doulin, William Elder, Jame Dungan on North Paint Creek, John Dix, Sanders Darby, John Deever, John Defenbaugh, Daniel Dieffenbach, John Derickson in care of Maj. Ferguson, John Flaurence, Moses H. Grigg at Falls of Paint, Alexander Griffith, Daniel Cambril, John Gossom, John Givens, Joseph Hill, Jared Hill, Eleazer Hickcox, Burton Henry, Hester Jacob, Hoss Heintz, Hugh Huston, Mr. Higgins on the Little waters of Scioto, John Harper at the head of Paint Creek, Henry Hister, William Hamilton near Chillicothe, Abraham Jones, James Jenkins on Salt Creek, Miss Elizabeth Jones, John Erwin, Vallentine Kisser, William Kennedy on Deer Creek, Caty Kight, Francis Lefiuvr on Little Prairie, John Leavells on Deer Creek, Moses Latta, Elias Layton on Sunfish Creek, Peter Moore near New Market in care of James Mayes in Chillicothe, Coonrod Mood, Marama Miller, John M'Connel in care of Dr. Edmiston, Isaac Mullen, James Marks, John M'Donald, John M'Cuiel in Pickaway township, Leonard Neff at High Bank, Doctor John Nicholas, William Powers, James Phiplips in Green township, Balace Nichols, Richard Osborn, John Peppers, Nathaniel Pendleton, David Reed, Job Reed on Pickaway, John Rector, George Ritchey, Thomas Roberts, Nehemiah Royr on Pickaway, Robert Ritchey, William Renick the third, Margaret Ritchey, Christian Richards on Deer Creek, Samuel Rittenhouse, Michaell Senss in Colerain township, Charles Steenburgan, Job Sharp on the head waters of Darby, James Sisk, David Sayers, John Swain in care of James Furguson,

James Smith on the forks of Paint, Stephen Smith, John Sherrer, Hon. Daniel Symmes, Samuel H. Smith at New Ark, Elias Turner, James Futhell (5 miles from the Falls of Paint), Daniel Thunn, James Tomlinson, John Timmons, Ebenezer Tuttle in care of William Lamb, Barnet Vankerk, James Vasbender in care of J. Tiffin, Hugh Woods (hatter), Littleberry Weaver in care of Col. Langham, John S. Wills, Phipps Waldo, Thomas White, George Williams, Ann Worthington, Nathaniel Wyatt or Thomas Breendige, Adam Westerberger, John Willcocks on Twin Creek, Tully Ward, Jacob Wickton, George Wildbrand, James Wilson. Entered by Joseph Tiffin.

Wm. Chandler, living at the High Bank Prairie, Ross County, reports a horse that strayed from him on Rattle Snake fork. Deliver to Wm. Lamb in Chillicothe.

Volume VI, Thursday, 23 January 1806, No. 288

A note regarding an election in the legislature mentions Col. Thos. Gibson, Wm. M'Farland, and Wm. Creighton, jun. The following were elected associate judges: Aaron Wheeler, Jesse Phelps and John Wolworth in Geauga County; John Kingsman and Turhand Kirtland for Trumbull County; Henry Abrams and Jacob Burton for Fairfield County; Celedon Symmes for Butler County; Abel Miller and Alex. Stedman for Athens County.

Charles J. Nourse, living in Washington City, regarding payments for land in the Chillicothe district, mentions Samuel Finley in Chillicothe.

Volume VI, Thursday, 30 January 1806, No. 289

Proceedings of the legislature mention the Virginia Army Lands, David Putnam (agent for the heirs of Doctor Jedediah Ensworth, late of Conn., dec'd).

A note regarding the collection of taxes in John Cleves Symmes' purchase. Aaron Goforth, Thomas Scott, William Skinner, James Heron, Charles Maxwell and James Killman are appointed collectors of the taxes.

Obituary: James Grubb, of Westfall, died Wednesday evening, 29 January 1806, in Chillicothe, "after a short, but severe illness".

Daniel Davis, in Chillicothe, wants to buy hops.

John G. Macan, administrator of the estates of Samuel Conner or Thomas Gregg, dec'd, regarding the estate settlements.

Volume VI, Thursday, 6 February 1806, No. 290

Proceedings of the legislature mention Wills' Creek, William Blunt, John M'Intire, Joseph F. Morris, David Harvey, Samuel Kratzer (sheriff of Fairfield County), Kraft Falkey, John Rector (insolvent debtor in Chillicothe).

An account of a boating accident, on Monday, 23 December 1805, opposite Connelstown, near Marietta. Daniel Johnston, Hugh Cunningham (of Fayette County, Penn.) and Gilbert Strong (of Washington, Kentucky) were descending the Yoghigany River when they hit a bridge and all drowned. William Williamson drowned in the same place about the same time.

William Sprigg has been appointed judge in the territory of Orleans.

An extract of a letter from Col. Worthington is printed.

Thomas Gibson regarding the state taxes due. The collectors are A. Goforth, Thomas Scott in Chillicothe, William Skinner in Marietta, James Herron in Zanesville, Charles Maxwell in Stubenville, James Hilman in Warren.

Thomas Crow, living on Col. Thomas Worthington's plantation near Jesse Spenser's, on the Scioto, reports two stray mares.

Volume VI, Thursday, 13 February 1806, No. 291

A dinner was held to celebrate the appointment of William Sprigg as judge in the territory of Orleans. Mentions Mr. Needham, Joseph Kerr, Gen. M'Lene, Mr. Couch, Mr. Creighton, jun., Jos. Kerr, Mr. Baldwin.

Mr. Parks, of Ross County, died suddenly at the Salt Works on Friday last.

Henry Hews, living on the road from Pe Pee Creek to the mouth of Scioto, reports a robbery that took place at his house on Friday, 31 January 1806. He says the robbers were Mr. Bryan and Mr. Hall.

John Carlisle, collector of the Virginia Army lands, regarding taxes due.

Volume VI, Thursday, 20 February 1806, No. 292

The governor received a note regarding Indian activities from Maj. Moore, Capt.

Moore and Capt. M'Pherson. Also mention Greenville, Gen. Kenton, Mr. M'Ilvain, Brig. Gen. Whiteman of Green County.

Mr. Marks, of Beardstown, Kentucky, is thought to have drowned in the Miami River on Tuesday, 11 February 1806. He was making a settlement on the Miami.

Roger Selden and Samuel S. Spencer, at the Scioto salt-works in Licking township, have dissolved their partnership.

Samuel Nicols, in Scioto County, reports a stray horse. Deliver to Capt. Wm. Lamb in Chillicothe.

David Hoge, register of the land office at Steubenville regarding land grants mentions Jacob Sadler, Michael Carrol, Josiah Dillon and John M'Connell.

Volume VI, Thursday, 27 February 1806, No. 293

William Sprigg has left Chillicothe.

Peter Jones, living on the road leading from Chillicothe to Marietta, about five miles from Chillicothe, reports a stray mare.

Volume VI, Thursday, 6 March 1806, No. 294

The act incorporating the Ohio Canal Company is printed and mentions James Berthoud, Thomas Prather, George Wilson, Peter B. Ormsby, James Hunter, John Bradford, Alexander Parker, John Jordan, jr., Adam Steele, Wingfield Bullock and Worden Pope, the directors of the Company.

James Galloway, Jun., in Green County, regarding the recent unsigned letter about him. He mentions Col. Anderson, Soney Creek, Mingo Village, Springers' Camp, Maj. M'Arthur, Arbuckle's survey, Stony Creek.

Levi Springer regarding land he obtained from Uriah Springer who served as a captain for three years in the Virginia Continental line.

Hugh Whitlow says his wife, Susan, has left him and he won't pay her bills.

John M'Clean regarding a meeting of the commissioners of Ross County.

Elizabeth Moor and Abner Foster, in Adams County, administrators of the estate of John Moore, dec'd, regarding the estate settlement.

Emanuel Carpenter, jun. and Henry Shellenberger, in Fairfield County, administrators of the estate of David Shellenberger, dec'd, about the estate.

Wm. M'Farland, in Chillicothe, asks those indebted to him to pay their bills.

Volume VI, Thursday, 13 March 1806, No. 295

More of the act incorporating the Ohio Canal Company is signed by William Logan, Thomas Posey, Christo. Greenup and John Rowan.

Reports on the treaty with the Indians mention Maj. Moore of Champaign County, Charles M'Lean, Capt. Snake, Capt. Lewis.

Marriage: Mr. J.E. Nesbit married Elizabeth Patterson, daughter of Col. R. Patterson, all of Montgomery County, on 20 February 1806, by Rev. Dr. J. Welch.

Joseph Campbell writes a letter to the editor regarding the recent Indian alarm and mentions the Ohio Herald and the Chillicothe Light Infantry Company.

David Irwin & Company about their nail manufactory in the town of Wheeling next door to Joseph Caldwell's store.

Jonathan Renick regarding his stud horse at his stable on Darby Creek five miles from the mouth and two miles above Hall's mill.

Volume VI, Thursday, 20 March 1806, No. 296

More about the Ohio Canal Company is submitted by the managers in Louisville: Thomas Prather, Geo. Wilson, James Hunter, Alxr. Parker, John Bradford, James Crawford, Nicholas Clark, Adam Steele, and Wingfield Bullock.

Nathan Ellis wants to rent his ferry and his house opposite Limestone at the state road from Chilliocothe.

Joseph Kerr regarding his stud horse at his farm near Chillicothe.

Thomas Needham has sold the Lion tavern in Chillicothe to Forrest Meeker, but continues to operate his house of entertainment.

Isham Talbot, living in Frankfort, Kentucky, reports a runaway slave, Lewis.

Thomas Hunter, living in Beaver township, Green County, about a stray mare.

John Morgan, in Chillicothe, regarding his blue dying business.

Volume VI, Thursday, 27 March 1806, No. 297
Notes about the Ohio Canal Company mentions Benjamin Hovey, Mr. Floyd, Samuel Gwathney, Daniel Hudson, Josiah Stephens, William Craghan, Davis Floyd, Gen. John Patterson, James Glover, James Wilkinson, Dr. Stephens, Jared Mansfield, Albert Gallatin.
Nathl. Massie regarding his stud horse at his mills at the Falls of Paint.
G. Renick regarding his stud horse at his stable in Chillicothe and at Wm. Nicholson's place four miles from Chillicothe on the Deer Creek road.
Jer. M'Lene gives brigade orders to the militia.
Richard Baley, living on the Limestone road about two and a half miles from Chillicothe, reports three stray mares.
John Morgan, living in Green County near Jacob Smith's mill, found a watch.

Supplement to the Scioto Gazette, Saturday, 29 March 1806
More documents pertaining to the Ohio Canal Company are printed and mention James Wilkinson, Gen. Benj. Hovey, Jonathan Dayton, John Smith, Mr. Brown, Samuel A. Otis, Jared Brooks in Louisville, Dr. Stevens, Indiana Canal Company, John Bradford, Alexr. Parker, Adam Steele, John Jordan, Jr., William Trigg, M.D. Hardin, John Rowan.

Volume VI, Thursday, 3 April 1806, No. 298
John Riddle and Alex. M'Nutt state that the Republican Society recommends Wm. M'Farland as a candidate for representative.
A list of letters left at the Post Office in Chillicothe includes David Abbot, John Anno, Susanah A. Dear, George A. Dear, Elijah Abbot and Nathan Mesteck, Joseph Bowdle, William Baley, David Beaver at Deer Creek, William Blaer in care of James Nanary, Jacob Burnett, Miss Elizabeth Boggs on Pickaway Planes, William Boyle on Darby Creek, Joel Bacon at Adelphia, Joseph Briggs and Jacob Miller on the north fork of Paint, Maj. Abraham Baldwin, Samuel Barr at the falls of Paint, John Boggs, Sen., Edward Condon in care of James Fredin, Ephraim Carmack, Nathaniel Cox, Thomas & Elijah Chenoweth, Robert Clark on Walnut Creek, Lettia Clarke, John Creel, James Crawford near Chillicothe, James Curry, Nathan Cory, Nicholas Cunningham, Thomas Cunningham, William Crawford at Pee Pee, Isaac Cockren, Rev'd. John Cridlebough, Israel Clark on Whetstone River, Carvill Combess in care of Joseph Kerr, Donner Doud, Martin Duncan, Joseph Doerab on the Chillicothe road, Lewis Demols, Robert B. Dobbins, Peter Ditchlow, John England, Ely Elder, George Fry, Coonrod Flesher in care of W. Patton, Fisher Conwell and David Conwell near Scioto, Joseph Franklin on Salt Creek, Edmond Fryatt, Anthony Franklin, James Famulener in Green township, John Gosson on Paint Creek, Richard Glaze on Darby Creek, John Garrett Nelson, William Gray in care of Benjamin Urmston, Thomas Gray, Jacob Green, Paris Griffeth or William Donovan at Pickaway, James Hays, John Hoff at Bigbelly, John Hand (attorney), Lucas Hockins, Caleb Huff, Jesse Hughes, John Hauer (blacksmith), Jonathan Hains at the head of Darby, Stephen Hoggatt on the waters of Paint, Mr. Hohns, Abraham Holderman, David Henderson, Amos Jones, William R. Jonston, David Irons, George Johnston, John Johnston in care of W. Lamb, Isaac Jones, Joshua Inskep, Gavin Johnston in care of Gen. Findley, Abraham Jones, Valentine Kesser, Frderick Krantz in care of Mr. Cutler, Peter Kear, Samuel Kratzer, John Kuter on Pickaway, Samuel Killgore, John Kight on Paint Creek, Thomas Kan, Edward C. Livingston, Elisha Littler on Darby Creek, Uriah Lowther on Walnut Creek, Maj. Lingard, Abraham Love, Peter Mills, Peter Mickle, John M'Laughlin, William Montgomery, John M'Cafferty in Union township, James Murphy in care of John Boggs on Pickaway, Samuel M'Munn on Buckskin, George Markham, Thomas Mouser, James Mouser, William Mason, John M'Kenney, William Myer, John Miller, James Morris in care of George Morris, Daniel M'Farland, Mathew Mitchel in Green township, Alexander M'Clintock, James Medill, Nathan Mefseck, Joseph Moore on Grassy Prairie, James Marks, John Mecutchen, Mebeker Mayer, David M'Elwain on Sunfish, Samuel M'Cormack, Thomas Morris on Bigbelly, Christian Neff, Daniel Nichlas, Jetho Nevill, John Olinger in Green township, Isaac Owins, William Oldfield, John Odle, Richard Pennell in care of Eaneas Davis, Ann Popejoy, Mary Popejoy at Old Chillicothe, Robert Parks, James Powel at Salt Creek, Michael Pearce, John Port, William Peppers, George and Lukes Nebeker, Widow Patton, James Phillips, Ephraim Quinby, Owin Quality and Isaac Harris, John Right, George

Reed, Andrew Roseboom, Joseph Rocksold, Adam Rider at the mouth of Paint Creek, Mr. Reed (blacksmith), Abraham Rhodes, Eli Sargent, Snowden Sargent, William Seamore, Samuel Smith, Jacob Shob, Jun., north fork of Paint Creek, Jacob Streve in Coal Rain township, John Sinclair, Boawter Sumner, Solomon Smith in Franklin, William Stump, John Sherer, Jesse Stroud on Salt Creek, Rev'd. John Sale, Francis Smith in care of Isaac George, Isaac Stewart at the Falls of Paint, Nicholas Snidner, Henry Twrney, Mibeah Tomlinson or Nancy Heath at Big Bottom, Lenard Tught in care of Mr. Stumb, James Trege, Mr. R. Taylor, James Taylor, Jonathan Taylor, Barnet Vankirk, James Vince near George Comton, Henry Vanmeter, Nathaniel Wyatt or Thomas Brundgee, Spence Wilson, John White on Darby Creek, Col. John Watts, Isaac Warner, John S. Wills, Sireno Wolcomb in Granville, Daniel Weimar (taylor), Joseph Wickton, Jesse Watson, Eli Willes, William Williamson, George Wildbahn, Thomas White, Edward Williams, Cornelius Westfall. Entered by Joseph Tiffin.

Geo. Phelps regarding the petition of John Cummins, of Canfield, an insolvent debtor, in the Court of Common Pleas of Trumbull County.

William Lamb, in Chillicothe, asks those indebted to him to pay their bills.

Jer. M'Lene has land for sale, the property of Jacob Foster, sen., seized at the suit of Charles Hughey.

John Odle, living on Salt Lick Road, ten miles from Chillicothe, found a mare.

Volume VI, Thursday, 10 April 1806, No. 299

Obituary: Miss Polly Cross died in Muskingum County on 29 March 1806.

William Smith, at Amherstburgh in Upper Canada, found a stray horse.

John M'Dougal about the publication of "The Ohio Justice or New Conductor Generalis" by Francis M'Henry.

George Phelps regarding his petition as an insolvent debtor to the Trumbull County Court of Common Pleas.

John Riddle and Alex. M'Nutt regarding the nomination of Wm. M'Farland by the Republican Society to be candidate for representative.

Volume VI, Thursday, 17 April 1806, No. 300

Obituary: Maj. John Beasley, "an early adventurer to the western country", died on 5 April 1806, at Manchester, Adams County.

Obituary: Miss Elizabeth Williamson, a sister-in-law to Robert Steele, of Chillicothe, died on Sunday, 13 April 1806.

A letter from Edward Tiffin to the Shawney Indians is printed and mentions the settlements on Mad River. A reply mentions Maj. Moore.

A note regarding a dispute on 12 December 1805 between Robert Frakes (son-in-law to Wm. Orr), Mr. M'Cloud and Wm. Orr in which Orr was killed.

Thomas Crow, living at the head of Kinnickinic about six miles from Crouse's mill in Ross County, reports a stray mare.

Wm. Drury and John Lutz, administrators of the estate of Henry Myres, late of Clear Creek township, Fairfield County, dec'd, regarding the estate settlement.

Volume VI, Thursday, 24 April 1806, No. 301

A meeting of the Democratic Republicans of Ross County is announced.

Gillian Ruse regarding his stud horse at his stable in Adelphi and at George Richey's tavern near Crouse's mill.

John Miller & Company regarding their nail manufactory in Water Street, next door to Doct. John Edminston's, in Chillicothe.

Sarah Beasley and Nathl. Beasley, at Manchester, administrators of the estate of John Beasley, late of Manchester, dec'd, regarding the estate settlement.

John Cutlar, at Chillicothe, reports a stray horse.

John M'Clanburgh has a new shipment of goods for sale at his store.

Volume VI, Thursday, 1 May 1806, No. 302

A letter from Col. Worthington in Washington is printed. Includes his speech.

A note regarding a meeting of the citizens of Ross County mentions James Pritchard, Maj. James Menary and Gen. Jeremiah M'Lene.

Wm. Cochran, living near the Old Town in Concord township, Ross County, reports a stray mare.

Jacob Eckleberner, in Chillicothe, reports a stray horse.

James Cummins reports a horse that strayed from James Criswell's house on Mr. Crider's plantation about 3 miles from Chillicothe. Deliver to John Scott, living in Milford township, Butler County.

George Brown, in Chillicothe, asks those indebted to the firm of Samuel Brown & Company to settle their accounts.

Volume VI, Thursday, 8 May 1806, No. 303

Obituary: Robert Gregg, of Chillicothe, died Friday, 2 May 1806.

John M'Coy has a new shipment of goods for sale at his store in Chillicothe.

Levin Belt, at Chillicothe, has land for sale on Little Miami River near the mouth of Massie Creek, mentions Wm. Fitzhugh of Maryland and Gen. Massie.

Dr. Ramus Davis & Company have a new shipment of medicines for sale.

William Hoddy, living on the north fork of Paint Creek about seven miles from Chillicothe, on the road to Springfield and Mad River, has land for sale. It includes the house he now occupies as a tavern.

Volume VI, Thursday, 15 May 1806, No. 304

A note regarding a meeting of the Republicans of Chillicothe.

A letter to the public from Thomas Scott regarding his dismissal from the office of prosecuting attorney in Ross County, mentions Mr. Couch and includes depositions from John M'Clean, Isaac Cook and James Armstrong.

John Hutt enters an ordinance of Chillicothe that mentions Daniel Briney.

Forrest Meeker has purchased the Red Lion Tavern from Thomas Needham.

John Waddle & Company, next door to William Lamb's tavern, have a new shipment of goods for sale at their store in Chillicothe.

John Sherer has goods for sale at his shop next door to the Red Lion Tavern.

Volume VI, Thursday, 22 May 1806, No. 305

Obituary: David Morgan, stone-mason, lately from Virginia, died "yesterday morning", 21 May 1806.

George Tod, of Trumbull County, is appointed judge of the Supreme Court in place of Wm. Sprigg, resigned.

Jeremiah M'Lene and James Menary regarding a meeting of the citizens of Ross County in which James Pritchard is nominated to Congress.

A meeting of the Republicans of Chillicothe is announced.

Humphrey Fullerton asks those indebted to him to settle their accounts.

Nicholas Spicker, living at William Cox's on the middle fork of Salt Lick Creek, reports that he found a stray horse.

Volume VI, Thursday, 29 May 1806, No. 306

Obituary: John Graham died on Monday evening, 26 May 1806, in Lancaster, Fairfield County, leaving a wife and children.

John Carlisle has a new shipment of goods for sale at his store in Chillicothe. He has also established a store in Livingston on Pickaway Plains.

John Mitchel, living one mile below Chillicothe, reports a stray mare.

Mathew Creed, living on the Rocky fork of Paint Creek, about a stray colt.

George Smith, at Springfield in Muskingum County, says do not buy land from Abraham Snider who lately moved from Georgetown in the District of Columbia.

Volume VI, Thursday, 5 June 1806, No. 307

An unsigned letter to the editor mentions Mr. Morrow.

Abel Lewis, clerk of the Muskingum County Court of Common Pleas, about a motion of Lewis Cass to grant the petition of James Johnston, of Pittsburgh, for the partition of land owned by Johnston and Jonas Stanberry of New York City.

Thomas Steele, in Chillicothe, regarding the "assignment of an order given by me upon Thomas James, in favor of William R. Dickenson" for a lot in Chillicothe.

Volume VI, Thursday, 26 June 1806, No. 310

Unsigned letters to the editor regarding the election mentions Mr. Pritchard and Mr. Morrow.

John Odle, living near the Salt Lick Road, 10 miles from Chillicothe, reports that he found a stray horse.

Stephen Horsey, in Chillicothe, has a house and lot for sale.

Sarah Wright and Nathan Cory, in Ross County, administrators of the estate of Jonathan Wright, late of Concord township, dec'd, about the estate settlement.

Abraham Tanquary, living in Ross County about 6 miles above Chillicothe near Ebenezer Finamore's place, reports a stray horse.

Samuel Achason & John Briney have opened a Butcher's shop in Chillicothe.

Whaland Gootee, living on Paint Creek near Adam's mill, in Ross County, reports a stray horse.

John Hoddy, living near Old Chillicothe, reports a stray mare.

Jesse Spencer, Register of the land office at Chillicothe, regarding a new road from Dayton to the Western Indian boundary line.

G. Renick, in Chillicothe, has a new shipment of goods for sale.

Joseph Liming, living on White Oak Creek, Tate township, Clermont County, reports a stray mare.

Isaac Swanger, living near Lebanon, Warren County, on the Little Miami, reports two stray mares. Deliver to John Tucker in Chillicothe.

Volume VI, Thursday, 3 July 1806, No. 311

Robert Wilcox has a "waggon and geers" for sale at Walter Turner's house in Water Street, Chillicothe.

Thomas James asks those indebted to Lemuel & Thomas James to settle their accounts before he leaves for Baltimore on August 20th.

William Craft, living near Waynesville on the Little Miami, Warren County, reports a stray horse and mare.

Wm. M'Farland has a new shipment of goods for sale at his store, Chillicothe.

T. Worthington, living 2 miles from Chillicothe, reports a stray mare.

Joseph Kerr, in Chillicothe, has several tracts of land for sale and mentions the Sinking Spring, New Market, Manchester, Bullskin Creek, Williamsburgh, Mr. Walsmith's mill, Lucy's River, Darby's Creek next to Elijah Chenoweth.

A list of letters left at the Post Office in Chillicothe includes Nancy Boyd in care of Mr. Cryder, James Anderson, Fanny Armstrong in care of William Brown, Robert Armstrong, John Beggart, Rosanna Boggs, William Beaty in care of William Mason, Thomas Armstrong, William Anderson, Daniel Butler on Licking Creek, John Brombley, Alexander Berry, Joseph Bennett, William Boyce, Charles Burgher, Jacob Boltenberger, Louder Cannon, Rev. Henry Chy at Randolph, Joseph Chisas, George Currothers, James Chalmers in care of Gov. Tiffin, Israel Clark, Jacob Cox, Thomas Cook at Milford, Elizabeth Connelly in care of Joshua Hobbs, Gabriel Coil, Capt. Adam Calderwood, Jonathan Craig, John Coffee, John Core, James Dinnil, Priscilla Donoughe, John Dodd, Benjamin Duncan, Luke Dicker, Amew Duke, John Dix, Rev. Robert Dobbins, Catharine Dobbins, John Downing, Martin Duncan, Richard Dickerson, Peter Early, John Evans, Col. William Ellzey, Joseph Evans, George Fry, John Foley in care of Mr. Brown, David Faris in care of William Harper, Aaron Freeman, William Flowrance, James Fenner, Alexander Ginkins, Thomas Green, John Guthrie, Joseph Gifford, Alexander Gillespie, Richard Gabriel in care of J. Furguson, Thomas Goulds near Old Chillicothe, Thomas Glaze on Darby Creek, William Gibson, John F. Gabriel, Daniel Garwood in care of H. Massie, Levi Garwood in care of H. Massie, William Harrison, George Hays, George Hormston living with F. Fisher, Thomas Hanks, Nathan Hays, Henry Hughes, Andrew Heaverlom at Pickaway, Benjamin Haff at Northumberland in Ohio, Daniel Hollinger on the north fork of Paint, John Huff, Gavin Johnston, Isaac Jones, Jacob Jumulear, Samuel Keyes, John Keener, Joseph Kiene (brewer), James Killgore, Peter Kear on Deer Creek, William Leiven in care of Stephen Short, David List, Robert Longworth on Shade River in Ohio, William Lewis, Wm. Lot, Gabriel Murphy, Philip M'Nenar, Peter Moore in care of James May, Patrick M'Manus, Robert Maxwell (printer), Polly M'Connel, John M'Atthur on Salt Creek, Miss Margarat M'Clure, Thomas Morgan, William M'Mahen, John M'Cutchen, Jacob Millar at Sinking Spring, Alex'r. M'Clintock in care of J. Carlisle, Samuel Nicholas, Andrew Nicholas, Leonard Neff, Patrick Neal in Ross township, Ross Nelson, Uriah Paullen, William Pool, Robert Parish, William Pierson, Robert Patton in care of J. Furguson, James Parrell, William Poorkins, John Port, James Pettigrew, Peter Porter, Rev. James Quinn, James Ross, John Reynolds in care of William M'Coy, John P. Ransome, Stephen Ross, Job Reed, William Sharp, Job Smith in Liberty township, William Stalnaker at Darby, Charles Smith at

Pickaway, Andrew Smawly, jun., George Smith, Benjamin Salman on Paint Creek, William Snook (mill wright), James Sealls at Pickaway, Mr. Stockton in care of John M'Dougal, John Stockton, William Smith in Lick township, Joseph Swearringame in Chillicothe, Anthony Swineheart (mill wright), Jeremiah Smith, James Stone at Richfield, Ezra Tubbs on Paint Creek, Henry Twiney, Abraham Voorhees, John Thomas, Jonathan Taylor, John Trimble, Asa Truesdell at Nelson in Ohio, Rev. Robert Wilson, Elizabeth Wilson, Rev. William Williamson, James Walker (book binder), Abraham Warrington at Salem in Ohio, Miss Elizabeth Woolcutt in care of Charles Scissna, Joel Walker, David Wolff, John Wilson, James Wilson, James Wilson, Joseph Waugh, Spencer Wilson, John S. Wills, Samuel Yarnell in Union town.

Volume VI, Thursday, 10 July 1806, No. 312

An unsigned letter to the editor mentions Mr. Morrow and James Pritchard.

Joseph Buel regarding a meeting of the Republicans of Washington County mentions Edward W. Tupper, Return Jonathan Meigs, Junr.

Peter Sentz reports a mare that strayed from Benjamin Saldmon's plantation on the Chillicothe road. Deliver to Griffeth Foos in Springfield.

Hubbard Jones, living 14 miles above Portsmouth, regarding a robbery at his house. Stolen was a rifle engraved with "H. Harden" on the barrel. He suspects a Mr. Brown and a Mr. Carter of the robbery.

William Hoddy, living on the north fork of Paint Creek, seven miles from Chillicothe on the road to Mad River and Springfield, has land for sale.

Hugh Boyle regarding the petition of John Meeks, insolvent debtor, in the Fairfield County Court of Common Pleas.

Volume VII, Thursday, 7 August 1806, No. 315

S. Thompson, watch-maker, jeweller and silversmith, has moved to a new shop opposite Capt. Lamb's Tavern in Chillicothe.

John Cellars, clock and watchmaker, silversmith and jeweller, has just opened his business next door to the Red Lion Tavern in Chillicothe.

P. Bureau, in the Supreme Court of Gallia County, regarding the divorce of Samuel Logue from his wife, Sarah Logue, otherwise known as Sarah Helvinstin.

Robert Fleming, living on Paint Creek about six miles above Chillicothe, reports a stray mare.

John Petit John, administrator of the estate of William Petet John, late of Gallipolis township, Gallia County, dec'd, regarding the estate settlement.

More regarding the Ohio Canal Company mentions James Berthoud, Thomas Prather, George Wilson, Peter B. Ormsby, Adam Steele, Worden Pope, James Hunter, John Bradford, Alexander Parker, John Jordon, jr., Wingfield Ballock.

Abraham Claypool is a candidate for the Ohio Senate.

Letters from David Shepherd, Wm. Creighton, sen., and Wm. Niblack are printed in which they offer themselves for public office.

Jacob Beyerly regarding a note he gave to Col. E. Langham.

Doctor Wilcox, from Martinsburg, Va., has moved to Mr. John Neel's Tavern in Lancaster where he will "attend to the practice of Physic and Surgery".

Benjamin Jonas regarding a bond to William Evans.

John Collet offers himself as a candidate for Sheriff of Ross County.

John L. Tabb, cabinetmaker, regarding his shop northeast of Capt. Lamb's tavern opposite George Hanes' smith shop in Chillicothe.

James Jonston wants to hire a taylor in Chillicothe.

John M'Clean, John Mathews and Ebenezer Fenimore regarding a meeting of the Ross County Commissioners to discuss building a new jail.

James Ross, "of Thomas", living about four miles above Chillicothe, in Ross County, reports a stray horse.

Jon. Lynch and Fanny Morres, in Lancaster, Fairfield County, administrators of the estate of Ralph Morres, late of Fairfield County, dec'd, about the estate.

Samuel Foster, at Westfall, regarding a note he gave to Daniel Johnston for whiskey. It was witnessed by Robert Potts.

William Lockard, living on Walnut Creek, "including the forks", in Jefferson township, has land for sale.

Balace Nichols, in Chillicothe, reports a stray horse.

Abel Lewis regarding the suit of John Chandler vs. Jesse Cook in Muskingum

County Court of Common Pleas.

Abraham Stewart, in Chillicothe, reports the theft of a pocket book taken from a bureau in the house of Stephen Smith in Chillicothe. It contained papers that mentioned Joseph Winlock on Mill Creek, John M'Lene (of Ohio County, Va.), and Wm. Goldsberry.

John Burke, in Chillicothe, reports a strayed horse.

John Briney and Samuel Atchison, in Chillicothe, have dissolved their partnership in the Butcher's business.

A notice regarding Doctor Lee's "patent New London bilious pills" for sale by Dr. John Edmiston in Chillicothe, Mr. Nevill (merchant at Pickaway), and James Kilbourn at Worthington.

Ephraim Doolittle & Company, in Chillicothe, have a new shipment of goods for sale at their store.

Catharine Patton, Wm. Creighton, junr., and Wm. M'Farland, administrators of the estate of William Patton, dec'd, regarding the estate settlement at the house of Mrs. Catharine Patton near Chillicothe.

Volume VII, Thursday, 28 August 1806, No. 318

Notes regarding the Ohio Canal Company mention Goose Island, Corn Island, James Berthoud, James Glover, Gen. Benjamin Hovey, Mr. Floyd, Mr. Gwathney, Gen. John Patterson, James Wilkinson, Daniel Hudson, Joseph Stephens, William Craghan, David Floyd, Samuel Gwathney, Jared Mansfield, Jared Brooks, Mill Creek, Indiana Canal Company, J. Brooks, John Bradford, Alexr. Parker, Adam Steele, John Jordan, junr., William Trigg, M.D. Hardin, John Rowan, Samuel A. Otis, Cane Run, Jeffersonville, Clarkesville, Silver Creek.

The citizens of Fairfield County nominate Robert F. Slaughter to Congress.

John A. Fulton says that he's a candidate for the house of representatives.

Isaac M. Reily, in Chillicothe, regarding a stray horse. Deliver to Dr. Edmiston in Chillicothe.

Robert Hume, at the Red Lion in Chillicothe, reports a horse that strayed or was stolen from the pasture of John Townsley on the Little Miami, Green County.

John M'Donald, in Twin township, Ross County, reports a stray horse.

John Casey about the horse he bought from James Erow Chanay for 7 hats.

Hyatt Lownes, in Chillicothe, says he is a candidate for coroner.

Philip Ott, in Chillicothe, regarding a note he gave to Johnston Phares.

Joseph C. Vance has lots for sale in Urbana, Champaign County.

Volume VII, Thursday, 4 September 1806, No. 319

Henery Massie, in Chillicothe, has land for sale and mentions Mr. Lawson on the Ohio River, Winn Winship of Chillicothe, Jos. Vanmeters, David Hays of New Market, Zachariah Stephens at the mouth of Boaks Creek, John Elleson, jun., near Manchester, Mr. Wright near the forks of Eagle and Cherry Creeks.

John A. Fulton says he is a candidate for the house of representatives.

An unsigned letter to the editor mentions Mr. Pritchard, Maj. M'Arthur, Thomas Worthington, Col. James Pritchard, Mr. Morrow.

Aaron Burr passed through Chillicothe on Sunday on his way to Cincinnati.

Return J. Meigs, jun., is not a candidate for Congress. William Hutt and Thomas M. Donovan are candidates for coroner.

A letter from W. Silliman, in Zanesville, is printed and mentions Mr. Morrow.

An unsigned letter is printed that mentions Mr. Pritchard, Thomas Elliot, Mr. Boyd, Thomas Scott, Obediah Jennings, Robert M'Creary, Benjamin Hough.

Stephen Horsey, in Chillicothe, offers his livestock and furniture for sale.

M. Baldwin regarding trespassing on his land near Chillicothe.

George Phelps regarding the suit of John Stodard (of Northampton, Mass.), vs. Daniel Wright (non-resident of Ohio) in Trumbull County Court of Common Pleas.

Abraham Stipp, at Westfall, has land for sale near Westfall.

John Grubb, at Chillicothe, executor of the estate of James Grubb, late of Ross County, dec'd, regarding the estate settlement to be held at Maj. Urmston's.

Hugh Boyle and W.W. Irwin (attorney), at Lancaster, regarding the suit of Margaret Fairchild vs. John Fairchield, Jun., her husband, for divorce, in the Supreme Court of Fairfield County.

John M'Cart, in Richand township, administrator of the estate of Andrew

M'Cart, late of Richand township, Fairfield County, dec'd, about the settlement.

Joshua Baxter, trustee of Thomas M'Donald, insolvent debtor, about his debts.

E. Langham about the recent ad placed by Jacob Beyerly. He says that Peter Helphinstine, who now lives at Thomas M'Coy's, was to make the title for Beyerly.

Nathan Ellis regarding his power of attorney to John Barrett, of Adams County to sell lands on Booke's Creek in Franklin County, mentions Joseph Vance.

Volume VII, Thursday, 18 September 1806, No. 321

Robert F. Slaughter declines the nomination to Congress.

Hugh Boyle and W.W. Irvin (attorney) regarding the suit of John Schoonhover vs. John Fairchild, jun., in the Fairfield County Court of Common Pleas.

John M'Lene about a meeting of the Ross County Commissioners.

Abraham Shain, at John Treber's, says William M'Grig ran away from him.

Christopher Etienne, at Gallipolis, administrator of the estate of William Clayton, late of Gallipolis, Gallia County, dec'd, regarding the settlement.

Thomas Hodges, at Indian Creek in Ross County, tells the store keepers of the Chillicothe area not to credit any of his children.

Peter Eyster, in Columbiana County, regarding his land in Fairfield County, mentions James Herron, collector of taxes at Zanesville.

Peter Mickles asks those indebted to the singing school to pay their bills.

Volume VII, Thursday, 9 October 1806, No. 325

An unsigned letter mentions Gov. Tiffin, the Ohio Herald, Thomas Scott, Col. Niblack, Thomas Stockton, Judge Cook, Mr. Askew, Mr. Claypool, Mr. Carlisle.

A letter to the public from Duncan M'Arthur mentions Mr. Baldwin, Mr. M'Dougal, Mr. Bradford, Mr. Norton, Mr. Morrow.

Unsigned letters to the editor mention Nathaniel Massie, James Dunlap, David Shelby, John A. Fulton, Lawyer Williams, Lawyer Brush, Mr. Pritchard, Mr. Morrow, Mr. Creighton, Mr. Shepherd, Mr. Miller, Mr. Creighton, sen.

A list of letters left at the Post Office in Chillicothe mentions Peggy A'Dear, George A'Dear, Rosanah A'Dear, John A'Dear, Philip A'Dear, Elijah Abbott, James Anderson, Isaac Adams at Danston, Amos Abrams near the Plains, Eliza About, David Augustus, William Askew, sen., Benjamin Baker near the crossings of Paint, John Burr, Joel Bacon, Christian Brotherline, John Buck, Samuel Bancroft at Greenville, Richard Berry, William Burnett, Michael Bylery, John Ritzer, Isaac Brink, Ammor Beale, Abelard Bradford, Patrick Boyle near Chillicothe, Solomon Boner, Thomas Cruw, Joseph Cambell, Eden Clevenger, Joseph Cantwell, Robert Cross on the waters of Sunfish, James Carathers, Thomas Carpenter in care of T. Worthington, David Conklin, Charles Coulter, Charles Cade, James Cain, Moses Clauson near D. Henderson, Ander Correll, John Cambell on Sunfish, Barnabas Cockran in care of Seth Smith, William Crawford on Pee Pee, James Crochancy, Jesse Cook, Sanford Corder at Old Chillicothe, Solomon Campbell on Salt Creek, Daniel Carrol, Daniel Coss, Clament Carrell, Alexander Cunningham, Michael Creamer, Person Cremer, John Dolohan, Aaron Donaldson at Worthington's mill, Benjamin Dunvan, Francis Dougherty, Charles Deford, Robert C. Davison, Samuel Daniel, Polly Dunlap, Jesse Dulton, Ben. Elliott, Mordicah Ellis near Greenfield, Aaron Freeman at Sinking Spring, Robert Fleming in care of Mr. Carlisle, Jacob Foz, George Givens, Alexander Goyer, Samuel Goff, William Gibson, Thomas Green in care of W. Lamb, Allen Gaylord, Hudson Titus Knox at Granville near the Scioto River, James Hall, Thomas S. Hinde, Elizabeth Hubbard in care of James Winder, William Harvey, Lucas Hawkins, Caleb Hester on Paint Creek, George Hitchens, William Huston, Samuel Hayes at Worthington's Mill, Michael Hanke, Johnston Hemphell, Pertheney Hodges, William Hewvitt, William Hamilton, James Hamilton in care of Rev'd. Wilson, Daniel Hollinshead, Elizabeth Harvey near Chillicothe, William Jamison, Levi Johnston (living in Viana, 190 miles below Pittsburgh), Alexander Karr, Rachel Kerswell in care of Joseph M'Dill, James Inskeep, Nicholas Jacks on Paint Creek, Robert Jones, Velentine Heffer, William Kiddy in care of Gen. Massie, John Kilburn on Paint Creek, John Laurence near Pe Pee, Francis E. Lawrence near Pe Pee, Denis Lane, Samuel Lybrand, William Lott, James Larkins in Paxton township, James Mooney, James M'Creary, John Miller in care of James Hughy, William Lawson, Henry Lundbeck, Nicholas Lues in care of Samuel M'Cord, Mahlon Longshore, Conrod Mutes or Thomas Wilkison, Joseph Moore on Grassy Prairie, Elizabeth M'Neonar on Yellow Bud Creek,

John Morean, John M'Neal, Thomas Morgan, Revd. John Mathews, James M'Cluer, Samuel Miller in Pickaway township, John M'Kinzey, James Masters at Chillicothe, Peter Marks, James Malone, John M'Cutchen, Edward Mace, Daniel Mickles, Robert M'Cullok in care of H. Fullerton, Henry Moore in care of Nathan Updigraff, Margaret M'Kim in care of Mathew Mitchel, William Mobray, Alexander M'Clane, James M'Creary and Joseph Clark, Alexander M'Clintock, John Mickneal, John M'Mullin, Robert M'Neill, John Miller in care of Cryder's Mill, Samuel Miller in Pickaway township, Charles Millbank (pedler at Old Chillicothe), James Murphey near the Wheeling Road, Lucas Nebecker, Prentes Park, John Phillips, Purnel Parmer, Rossil Beach, Rewben Pursell on Paint Creek, Willys Pierson, Major Phillips, David Potts on Paint Creek, John Parks, Owen Quality or Isaac Harris, Samuel Rittenhouse, Mrs. Kerrh, William Rector, Job Roberts, Thomas Russell, Samuel Ravenscraft (at Mr. Parker's, the mill wright), James Ross, John Reiley, Jacob Reed at Roots town, Mathew Ridenour, John Swan, Jacob Stingley on Pickaway Plain, John Howard on Pe Pee, Alexander Shaw, William Spotswood, Abraham Stewart, Zadock Street & Son, Salem Harden Summers (house carpenter), David Shelby for John Evans, jun., George Shiepy, George Signer, Adam Strayer, John Strickler, Mr. Shannon, William Sutherland, Mr. Malon, Gideon Tyson in Jefferson township, Arch'd. Thompson, John Thomas, Samuel Tœs, Isaac Vanmeter, Isaac Verdue, Cornelius Vellee, Richard Williby, Jeremiah White on Darby Creek, William Willoughby, John W. Millar, Jacob Weyer (hatter, to the care of Mr. Hot, a baker by trade, living in Chillicothe), Henry Williams (8 miles above Chillicothe in Ross County), Cornelius Westfall at Salt Creek, Titus Wood (merchant in Chillicothe), Henry Wisler (12 miles from Chillicothe), David Watson, Jesse Watson, James Webster, William Weker and Mathias Speese on the Pickaway Plains, Thomas Wilkins, John Ward in care of George Yocas, Thomas White, James Wilson on Buckskin, Jacob Welsh, Z. Welsh, Isaac Warmsley, Edward Williams, Eias Wright, Stephen Warum, Parker Warren on Pickaway Plain, White Brown, Robert Wallace on Buckskin, Jon. Wallace on Buckskin, Benjamin Yats, Michœl Zineaurman or George Anght.

Samuel Jones has placed money in the hands of William M'Farland for the redemption of a tract of land purchased by William Barlow, of Kentucky, from Henry Massie, tax collector. The land, on the waters of the Little Miami, was entered by Samuel Jones, and was sold for delinquent taxes in 1800 and 1801. He says he was a minor at the time of its sale and thus is entitled to redemption.

N. Willis enters the arrivals and departures of the mail by stage and horse.

William Belsland, at Daniel M'Farland's on the south side of Paint Creek near Chillicothe, reports a stray horse. Deliver to Abner Meeker in Chillicothe.

E. Woods regarding the petition of Jesse Huntsman, insolvent debtor, in the Court of Common Pleas, Belmont County.

John M'Coy has castings, iron and salt for sale at his store in Chillicothe.

John Waddle & Company has one thousand barrels of salt for sale.

Michael Stroup, at New Market, reports a runaway apprentice to the hatter's trade named John Ward, age 15.

John M'Lœn regarding a meeting of the tax commissioners.

Daniel Harr, tin-plate worker, has opened his business in Water Street.

James Ferguson, jun., John Ferguson and Creighead Ferguson, administrators of the estate of James Ferguson, late of Chillicothe, dec'd, about the estate.

John Barr, Richard Morris and Samuel Edwards, at Levingston, managers of a horse race to be held near Levington on Pickaway Plains.

Forrest Meeker wants an apprentice to the brickmaking and laying trade.

John Mahin, living on upper Twin Creek, Ross County, reports a stray mare. Deliver to George Kilgore.

Jacob Widar, living on Kinickinic, Green township, Ross County, wants to hire an English schoolmaster.

Volume VII, Thursday, 23 October 1806, No. 327

Benjamin Urmston offers his tavern and other property for sale.

David Hoge, Register of the Land Office, regarding land for sale, mentions Dav. Vance, Jonathan Jassoft, Joseph Dorsey, Robert M'Clerry, Mordecai Yarnall, Thomas Hayne and Nathan Shepherd.

William Askew, sen., reports that he lost a log chain between his house and Col. Worthington's mill.

J. Woodbridge & Company, Chillicothe, have opened a store in the house on Paint Street formerly occupied by Collins & Company as a printing office.

Election returns for Ross County mention James Pritchard, Jeremiah Morrow, Abraham Claypool, Elias Langham, Nathaniel Massie, James Dunlap, David Shelby, A.J. Williams, J.A. Fulton, Henry Brush, David Shepherd, William Creighton, John Collet, William Niblack, E. Finnemore, David Boner. For Highland County: J. Jonston. In Clermont County: David C. Bryare and Thomas Morris.

A letter to White Brown from a friend in Cambridge, Md., is printed and mentions Charles Harrison.

Extracts from a Lancaster paper mentions Jeremiah Morrow, William W. Irvin, Elnathan Scofield, Philemon Beecher, Emanuel Carpenter, jun., and Jonathan Lynch.

The partnership of John Kerr & Company will expire in a few months.

R. Whiteside, clock and watch maker, silversmith and jeweller, has purchased Seth Thompson's store opposite the Eagle Tavern, adjoining Mr. Carlisle's store.

John Martin, living in Chillicothe, reports a stray horse.

Bakewell & Company, at Charlestown, on the Ohio River, 15 miles above Wheeling, have stone ware for sale.

John Iams and Abraham Welch regarding the Salt Lick horse races.

A barkeeper is wanted at the Red Lion Tavern in Chillicothe.

Benjamin Welsh, living in Jefferson township near Joseph Gardner's ferry, reports a stray horse.

Volume VII, Thursday, 30 October 1806, No. 328

Marriage: William Wallace married Miss Nelly Dill, daughter of Capt. Thomas Dill, of Ross County, on Thursday, 23 October 1806.

Election returns in Greene and Champaign Counties mention Richard S. Thomas, George Harlin, William Ward, Joseph Tatman, John Steritt.

Mr. M'Donald, living about twenty miles up the east branch of the Little Miami, has found a lead mine.

A note regarding Capt. James Ferguson's troop of Dragoons.

Christian VanGundy, at Kinickinic, wants to erect a mill dam at his house.

Geo. Phelps regarding the suit of Jesse Hollada vs. Josiah Cleaveland, an absconding debtor, in the Trumbull County Court of Common Pleas.

T.S. Hinde, in Chillicothe, has land for sale in Adams County, on Brush Creek, about three miles from Brougher's tavern on the road to Limestone.

E. Pentland, in Pittsburgh, reports a runaway apprentice to the printing business, Robert Cisna, age 17, who has relatives living in Chillicothe.

Volume VII, Thursday, 6 November 1806, No. 329

Obituary: Rev. Samuel Welch, "for several years past a respectable preacher of the Methodist Church", died on Wednesday evening last, at High Bank.

Obituary: William Ewin died in Chillicothe on Tuesday evening last.

A note regarding a meeting of the Chillicothe Polemic Society.

Election returns from Muskingum County mention Jeremiah Morrow, Leonard Juette, Levi Barber, Ephraim Clarke, Zekiel Greggery, Lewis Cass, William H. Puthuff, Elijah Hatch, James Clark, James E. Phelps, George Beemer.

John Robinson, at Chillicothe, has opened his weaving and blue dying business.

Jesse Spencer regarding land for sale by the Chillicothe Land Office mentions Thomas Rees, Noah Zane, Robert F. Slaughter, Richard Morris, Philip Wolf, Joseph Loveland, Hezekiah Smith, David & Henry Shellenberger, Martin Landes, Frederick Leather, John Edgar, Elias Langham, Samuel Kratzar, Joseph Nicholson, William Sturgeon, Henry & Reuben Newkirk, Lewis Rodgers, Henry Brown, Henry Massie, Ebenezar Larimer, John Murphey, Reuben Abrams.

Volume VII, Thursday, 13 November 1806, No. 330

Obituary: William Fullerton died in Chillicothe on Tuesday evening last.

Jeremiah Morrow is elected representative to Congress. Mr. Pritchard was defeated. Election returns from Jefferson and Columbiana Counties mention John Tagart; in Jefferson County: Thomas Elliot, Samuel Boyd, John M'Laughlin. In Belmont County: John Stewart and Josiah Dillon. In Washington, Gallia, Athens and Muskingum Counties: Leonard Jewett, Lewis Cass, Levi Barber, William H. Puthuff. In Fairfield County: Elnathan Scofield, William W. Irvin, Philemon

Beecher. In Ross, Franklin and Highland Counties: Abraham Claypool, Nathaniel Massie, James Dunlap, David Shelby, A.J. Williams. In Adams & Scioto Counties: Abraham Shepherd, Philip Lewis and James Scott. In Clermont County: David C. Bryan. In Hamilton County: William M'Farland, John Jones, Hezekiah Price and Ethan Stone. In Warren, Butler, Montgomery, Green and Champaign Counties: Richard S. Thomas. In Butler County: James Shields and Solomon Line. In Warren County: Matthias Corwin and Peter Burr. In Montgomery County: Philip Gunchel. In Green & Champaign Counties: Joseph Tatman. In Columbiana County: John M'Connel.

Thomas Martin, of New Port, Kentucky, regarding Col. Burr.

Thomas James has a new shipment of goods at his store in Chillicothe.

Joseph Darlington regarding the suit of Belteshazer Drogoo vs. Cornelius Lafferty, dec'd, and Lydia his wife, dec'd, John M'Kentire, Benjamin M'Kentire, Alexander M'Kentire and William Hamilton. Benjamin and Alexander M'Kentire are not inhabitants of Ohio.

John M'Coy has a new shipment of goods for sale at his store in Chillicothe.

John M'Landburgh has a new shipment of goods for sale at his store in Chillicothe. He also has Joseph Lemun's spinning wheels for sale.

Thomas M'Donald, living on the north fork of Paint Creek, reports a horse that strayed from Col. Duncan M'Arthur's Mills.

William S. Hutt, tax collector for Scioto township, has land for sale.

Volume VII, Thursday, 20 November 1806, No. 331

Marriage: John Waddle, merchant, married Miss Nancy Mann, both of Chillicothe, on Tuesday evening, 18 November 1806.

Samuel Davis, living on Buckskin Creek, Ross County, reports a strayed mare.

John Brown, in Chillicothe, says that his wife, Priscilla Brown, has left him, and he will no longer honor her debts.

Daniel Ludwig, at Pickaway, about land he bought from John Thomas.

Thomas Scott, tax collector, regarding the payment of taxes due.

Wm. M'Dowell, in Chillicothe, has a new shipment of goods for sale at his store in Chillicothe between Maj. Urmston's and Lawyer Scott's.

John Cellars says his shop was broken into on 15 November 1806 and much jewellry was stolen. He mentions Mr. Brown at Cincinnati, Mr. Hunter at Frankfort, Kentucky, and Mr. Ritchards at Washington, Kentucky.

Volume VII, Thursday, 27 November 1806, No. 332

Peter Spurck, clock and watchmaker, silversmith and jeweller, has moved his business to the house in Water Street next door to the Red Lion Tavern in Chillicothe. He says he had 16 years experience in Philadelphia.

John Carlisle, in Chillicothe, asks those indebted to him to pay their bills.

John Thomas, at Livingston, regarding the ad placed by Daniel Ludwig.

Joseph Darlinton regarding the suit of James Lawson vs. Nathaniel Fox and Claibourne Fox (not inhabitants of Ohio) in the Adams County Supreme Court.

Volume VII, Thursday, 25 December 1806, No. 336

John Sherer has a new shipment of goods for sale at his store next door to the Red Lion Tavern in Chillicothe.

Josiah Jinkins, in Belmont County, says that his wife, Ann Jinkins, has left him, and he will no longer honor her debts.

Charles Buck and Charles Mills, at Gallipolis, executors of the estate of John Nisewonger, jun., late of Gallipolis, Gallia County, dec'd, about the estate.

James Kilgore, in Ross County, lost a pocket book that included a bond from Col. Duncan M'Arthur to Samuel Kilgore.

E. Scott, taylor & habit maker, from London, has opened his shop opposite the Red Lion Tavern in Chillicothe.

William Sterret, in Chillicothe, has a wagon and team for sale.

John M'Clean about a meeting of the commissioners at Benjamin Urmston's.

Jer. M'Lene regarding a meeting of the Scioto Lodge of Masons.

John Creek, living on the waters of Clear Creek, Liberty township, Highland County, found a pocket book near the Scioto Salt Works. It contains papers from George M'Cullock, John Barritt, John Murday, Arnie Mussard in Gallipolis.

Doctor Monett has opened his medical practice in Chillicothe.

William MacKenzie, in Richmond, Virginia, has land for sale on the waters of Little Miami. The land was entered by Baylor Hill.

A note regarding the resignation of John Smith from Congress.

A letter from Joseph Kerr to the editors is printed regarding a road to Ohio.

Col. Worthington's letter to Gen. Massie is printed.

A notice of a meeting of the citizens of Chillicothe at Forrest Meeker's.

M. Baldwin, Marshal of the Ohio District, regarding Marshal's sales, in Zanesville, of the property of Samuel C. Vance at the suit of the United States. He mentions Mr. Sibley and John Bradshaw.

W.R. Dickinson, at the Red Lion Tavern, regarding the person who borrowed the volume of Shakespeare that he had borrowed from Charles A. Stewart.

Joseph Kerr, living near Chillicothe, reports a stray horse. Deliver to Leonard Reed at Kerr's farm.

T.S. Hinde, at the Red Lion Tavern, has a carriage and horses for sale.

John Hall, living in Boon County, Kentucky, reports a runaway slave, Limus.

Nathan G. Thomas, living in Boon County, Kentucky, but formerly living at Lexington, Kentucky, reports a runaway slave named York.

Edward Phelps and Isaac Griswold, at Sharon, give public notice to Jonas Stanbery, Thomas Salter, Jonathan Noble and Francis Olmsted that they will petition for the partition of their land.

Burrowes Smith, in Cincinnati, reports three stray horses.

Wm. Wallace, at Chillicothe, reports a stray cow.

Wm. Buckner reports a slave named "Dick" who ran away from David L. Ward on Man's Lick. Deliver to Capt. James Johnson near Georgetown, Scott Co., Ky.

Volume VII, Thursday, 8 January 1807, No. 338

Proceedings of the Legislature mention James Heaton (commissioner of the state road from Lebanon), Thomas Irwin (commissioner of the road from Chilli-cothe to College Township), Erie Literary Society, Benjamin Wood, John Gutbery, New Market, Virginia Military lands.

A list of letters left at the Post Office in Chillicothe includes Calib Armitage, Jonathan Anderson, Rhoda Abrams, Prizey Angel, John Anderick, Amos Barr, Joseph Boyiler at Pee Pee, Solomon Boner, William Barlow, William Brown, H. Burton in care of F. Meeker, William Brown in care of Samuel M'Lone, William Beaty near Westfall, John Begget in care of James Matt, Charles Burgher, John Brown near Chillicothe, Ephraim Buits, Robert Carson, Elizabeth Crawford on Indian Creek, Isaac Connely, jun., at Bush Mills, Adam Coulderwood, John Curlet, Elijah Carson (hatter), John Cuthright, Jonathan Craig, Noble Crafford, Mary Clevenger, Sary Cleavenger, Samuel Clark, Micheal Anders, Joseph Conklin, Redmond Condon in care of James Irvin, Isaac Clowes, Jonathan Crabel on Deer Creek, Aaron Donaldson at Worthington mill, Col. J. Depestre, Thomas Donevan, Doct. John Doddridge in care of N. Reeves, Mr. Deffbough, George DeWald, Doct. Andrew Dixon, Arthur Dickey, Priscilla Donoughe, Nela Delahay at Old Town, John Elliott, Evens Evens, Benjn. Elliott, Lemuel Evans, Joshua Ewing at Darby, John Fulton, Coonrod Flesher on Westfall road, James Farrell in care of David Henderson, Alexander Fleming, Richard Gregory in care of W. Lamb, Andrew Glaze (16 miles from the mouth of Scioto), James Gilkison, Peter Goodman, James Graham, Faris Griffith or William Donovan, Richard Gale, George Gubanks in Paxton township, William Green or George Green, John Gabrell on Darby Creek, Zachariah Griffis, James Hughs in care of H. Fullerton, Randolph Hughes, Zehial Hurlbunt, jun., Peter Helphinstine, Jacob Hubbard, Doct. John Hamill, William Hamilton, Andrew Heaverlo in Pickaway township, Gavin Johnston, Moses Jones, Joseph Jones, John Kore, Lemuel Kilburne, George Koil, John Kellor, William King, John Kuter, Samuel Kerr, James Kerr (attorney), John King near the Falls of Paint, Sarah Lewis in care of G. Renick, Frederick Leininger, John Long in care of Mr. Petlers, William Linton, Elias Lovett, Samuel Langdale in care of John Carlisle, Abraham Millar, John M'Lain, James M'Nutt, Elizabeth Millar in care of W. Lamb, Charles Millbank, William Myer, Abraham Miller, James Martin, William M'Munn, jr., Robert Michel, James May, Henry Moore on Scipo Creek, Alexander M'Clintick in care of D. M'Arthur, John Morris on Pee Pee road, Joseph Moore on Gressy Prairie, James M'Connell, Henry Meliorn, Thomas M'Clintock, Thomas Napp, Henry Nicholson, William Odle, William

Oldfield, Peter Porter, John Port, Doct. Anthony Potts at Westfall, Capt. William Peirson in Highland County, William Recton, Cyrus Reaves near Westfall, John Robins, John P. Ransone, Mary Rogers at Bever town, Ohio, Felix Renick, Whorton Rector, Polly Renick, James or Thomas Ross, Joseph Robinson, John Raldiff, jun., on Salt Creek, Michael Shoppel, Aaron Sullivan, Thomas Smith, James Smith, Henry Slith, Thompson Smith at Pee Pee, Jeremiah Stode, James Stewart, Harden Summers, John Snook at Adelphia, Daniel Smith, Charity Shelby, Abraham Sheridan, John Shevrin, J.J. Shaw & Company, Joseph Tompson, Thomas Ting, John Tucker, Emanuel Trexler in care of Adam Hollar, Ezra Tubbs, Titus Wood, Joel Walker, James Wall in care of John M'Cafferty, John Yeakey. Entered by Joseph Tiffin.

Capt. James Denny gives orders to the Militia.

Jacob Smith and Philip Gunckle regarding lands they purchased.

Samuel Hopkins, on the Pickaway Plains, reports a stray horse.

Anthony S. Davanport and Isaac Cade, executors of the estate of John Rush, of Pickaway township, Ross County, dec'd, regarding the estate sale.

Mary Marshall and James Campbell, in Adams County, administrators of the estate of William Marshall, dec'd, regarding the estate settlement.

Anthony S. Davenport and Isaac Cade, executors of the estate of John Rush, of Pickaway township, dec'd, regarding the estate settlement.

Catharine Patton, William M'Farland and William Creighton, Jr., administra-tors of the estate of William Patton, dec'd, regarding the estate settlement.

Isaac Redman, living in Green township, reports that he found stray horses.

Benjamin Sells, Tavernkeeper in Franklinton, regarding his house of entertainment and stable in Franklinton.

Edward Paine, jun., clerk of the Court of Common Pleas in Geauga County, regarding the petition of Joshua Hall, jun., an insolvent debtor.

William Cogan, from Pittsburgh, has opened a baking business on Water Street nearly opposite the Scioto Gazette office in Chillicothe. He says he's been a baker for twenty years.

William Wilson, living on Yellow Bud Creek in Deerfield township, Ross County, reports that he found a stray mare.

Volume VII, Thursday, 5 February 1807, No. 342

George Parsons, Clerk of the Court in Trumbull County, says he has attached the property of Josiah Cleavland, an absconding debtor, at the suit of Jesse Holerder.

John Woodbridge & Company have sugar for sale at their store in Chillicothe.

Moses Latta, in Twin Township of Ross County, reports a stray mare.

A list of grand jurors appointed includes James Finley of Cincinnati, John Armstrong, Isaac Cook, James Menary, William Robinson, David Vance, Thomas Hicks, William Rodgers, Zacheus A. Beaty, Jeremiah A. Munson, John Thompson, Thomas M'Coy, Samuel Hill, John Crouse, William Justice, Adam Turner, Jacob Burnett, Lincoln Goodal, James Armstrong, Levin Belt, John Belli, John M'Coy, Thomas Rodgers, Henry Brush. They also mention Nathaniel Massie.

A report of a meeting of the Democratic Republicans of Cincinnati at the house of Henry Disbrow mentions Hon. Daniel Symmes, Elias Glover, David Zeigler, Isaac G. Burnet, Mr. Yeatman, John Smith, Ambrose Smith, Col. Burr.

David Conger, in Butler County on the Old Deerfield Road, Liberty township, reports a stray horse.

Anthony Smith reports a lost or stolen saddle and saddle bags.

William Seymour has land for sale in Union township of Ross County.

George Coder, in Paxton township of Ross County, reports a stray horse.

S. Dryden, Jun., & Company have a new store in the house formerly occupied by H. Fullerton at the corner of Water and Walnut streets in Chillicothe.

N. Willis has lots for sale in Chillicothe.

Capt. James Denny gives orders to the Dragoons in Chillicothe.

Joseph Dickson and William Brown, jun., executors of the estate of Hugh Grant, late of Franklin County, dec'd, regarding the estate settlement.

Samuel Merrill, in Chillicothe, reports a stray mare.

A committee is appointed to supervise a lottery to repair the bank of the Scioto River at Chillicothe. The Committee is Samuel Finley, Isaac Cook, John Kerr, Duncan M'Arthur, William Creighton, sen., John Carlisle, Nathaniel Massie, George Renick, and Nathaniel Willis. It mentions Abraham Shepherd and Thomas Kirker.

Volume VII, Thursday, 12 February 1807, No. 342
Marriage: Robert Nicholson married Miss Polly Dungan, both of Ross County, on Thursday last, 5 February 1807.

Marriage: John Cutler married Miss Mary Willbourn in Chillicothe on Sunday last, 8 February 1807.

An extract from the Journal of the Senate mentions Levin Belt, John Worth, Aaron Gaforth, Return J. Meigs, jun., Abraham J. Williams, Wm. Skinner, Wm. Wells, William Phillips, James Hillman, Hallam Hempstead, David Hoover, John Garrard and John A. Crawford.

Proceedings of the Legislature mentions Marietta, Portsmouth, Erie Literary Society, St. Clairsville, James Innes Clarke, Ohio Company, Presbyterian Society in Cincinnati, George Tod, Athens, Daniel Evans and Joseph Swearingen (agents for the heirs of James Trimble, dec'd), Fanny White, Library Society in Granville, Hannah Burke, Cincinnati University, St. John's Church at Worthington, John Smith.

John T. Evans regarding a meeting of the Chillicothe Polemic Society.

J. Woodbridge & Company have moved to the store lately occupied by Nathan Gregg near the Red Lion Tavern.

Edward Phelps and Isaac Griswold, at Sharon, give notice to Jonas Stanbery, Thomas Salter, Jonathan Noble and Francis Olmsted regarding the partition of the land they own together.

James French, living near Col. Payne near Mount Sterling in Montgomery County, Kentucky, has a stud horse for sale.

John Chipman, at Mr. Stipp's still house near Westfall, lost a note from William Rector to Israel Thompson, and a receipt from George Renick to Abraham Stipp.

Mary Burbridge, at Patterson's Creek in Hampshire County, Virginia, reports a runaway slave named Lewis.

Levi Sidwell lost an ax between his house and James M'Dougal's in Chillicothe.

Jacobas Hines asks Gen. George Mathews to make him a deed to the land called the Round Prairie, lying on Deer Creek in Deerfield township, Ross County.

Volume VII, Thursday, 5 March 1807, No. 346
Edward Tiffin has resigned as governor in order to take his seat as Senator to Congress. Thomas Kirker took his place as governor.

John M'Dougal about flour he's sending to New Orleans mentions Col. Burr, James M'Dougal (his brother), Levin Belt.

Angus L. Langham, secretary of the Chillicothe Polemic Society, regarding their last meeting, mentions John T. Evans, John Kerr, Patrick M'Lene, Thomas Steel, Daniel Turney, John Woodbridge, Ephraim Doolittle, Robert Hume, Richard E. Meade, William M'Donald, jun., John M'Dougal, Winn Winship, jun.

E. Langham & Thomas James about property of Thomas Reed, dec'd, that the sheriff of Ross County has advertised for sale. They mention Francis M'Henry.

Samuel Finley, Nathaniel Willis, Duncan M'Arthur, Isaac Cook, Nathaniel Massie, George Renick, William Creighton, sen., John Carlisle and John Kerr regarding the Scioto Bank Lottery.

John M'Clean, tanner, asks those indebted to him to settle their accounts.

Joseph Hopkins, at the Bluegrass Prairie on the north fork of Paint Creek in Concord township, Ross County, regarding a stud horse at Mr. Brady's on Hay Run.

Henry Nevill, at Jefferson on the Pickaway Plains in Ross County, has just received a new shipment of goods at his store.

Humphrey Fullerton asks those indebted to him to settle their accounts.

John S. Wills and Joseph Tiffin regarding land sold to Jesup N. Couch.

Sergt. Thomas Steel regarding a meeting of the Light Dragoons in Chillicothe.

Volume VII, Thursday, 12 March 1807, No. 347
Marriage: Noah Andrews married Miss Ruth Griswold, both of Worthington, on Sunday, 22 February 1807, in the church by Rev. James Kilbourn.

T. Worthington sends letters from Washington about Virginia Military land.

John M'Dougal regarding the petition of William Hoddy, an insolvent debtor, in the Ross County Court of Common Pleas.

Elizabeth Rowbuck and Aaron Rowbuck, in Adams County, administrators of the estate of Benjamin Rowbuck, dec'd, regarding the estate settlement.

Jesse Spencer, Register of the Land Office in Chillicothe, has land for sale and mentions R. Pitcher, Abraham Stipp, D. Rees and G. Cline.

Thomas Gholson, Tandy Bush (both of Bushe's settlement in Clark County, Kentucky) and Clabourn Boblette (of Flat Creek, Montgomery County, Kentucky) report a runaway mulatto slave named Nimrod.

John Parker regarding the actions of a deranged man named Mr. Moore from Kentucky mentions Isaac Peniston in the neighborhood of Morgan's fork of Sunfish.

Volume VII, Thursday, 19 March 1807, No. 348

Obituary: Mrs. Lucy Kilbourn, wife of Rev'd. James Kilbourn, age 38, died in child bed seventeen hours after delivering a stillborn child, on 8 March 1807, at Worthington. She left her husband and six children.

Zecheriah Welch, living on Dry Run near Squire Gardner's Ferry, regarding his stud horse named Sportsman.

Daniel Hare, in Ross County, reports that he found a stray mare.

Isaac Evans, in Chillicothe, wants to lease his land on Walnut Creek.

Volume VII, Thursday, 9 April 1807, No. 351

Robert Means, at the Red Lion Tavern, agent of John Graham, of Richmond, Virginia, has land for sale. Apply to Thomas Gibson.

Daniel Ludwig, at the Pickaway Plains, warns against trespassing on his land.

A list of letters left at the Post Office in Chillicothe includes John Anderick, Rebecca Armitage, Isaac Anstill at Big Bottom, Mary Atres, Thomas Armstrong, Susana Anderson, John Arthur, John Archer in Centerville, Thomas Andrew, John Armstrong, Rev'd. Joseph Bennett, Joseph Blossom at Milford, John Berryhill, Jacob Bartley, Benjamin Brown, John Baker on Walnut Creek, William Barnes, Levin Belt, Daniel Bowyer, William Barlow, Nicholas C. Boales, Frederick Bray, Bradford & Company, Benjamin Brackney, John Bearns in care of Wm. Carlisle, Lampkin Brown, Jacob Baldy, Joseph Burk, White Brown, Lewis Cass, John Core, Theis Currine or Gen. John Macklain, Charles Crull, Redmond Condon in care of James Irwin, Moses Colvin in Deerfield township, David Conklin, Francis Clark, Thomas Cunningham, Lowder Cannon, Woollery Conrod, Henry Cungim, Nathaniel Cartmill in care of Mr. Renick, Daniel Carroll, Edward or John Crab on Deer Creek, Andrew Carrell, John Clingham, Micheal Conn in care of W. M'Dowell, Isaac Cook, Lemuel Conly, William Caldwell, Col. Moses Chapline, George Cogle on North Paint, Neal Dougherty, Joseph Davis or James Cadwell, David W. Davis, Rev. Robert B. Dobbins, Chapman Denslow on Deercreek, Daniel Delania, Samuel Davison, Lewis Deraoss, William Denny, James Dunlap, Aron Dowley, Evan Evans, John T. Evans, Miceal and Peter Elshite, Jacob Eckleberner, Betsey Engle, Robert Fleming in care of H. Bishop, Mary Finimore, Philip Fellons, Hugh Forsman, Conrod Fry, Elias Glover, Nathan Gale, Joseph Gillespie on Deercreek, Joseph Griffeth at Smithfield, William Gibson, Richard Glaze at Westfall, John Goodman, James Hamilton, Thomas Holloway in care of Isaac Warner, James Hays at Big belly, Tevault Hickle, Caleb Huff, Henry Haller, John Huller, Jacob Hestend on Brush creek, Frederick Hauk, Abraham Holderman, Joshua Hall, Thomas Hinde, Daniel Hollinger, William Johnston, Samuel Harvey, Jonathand Hand, Benjamin Haines, Peter Helpenstine, John Johnston, Samuel Jones, Elizabeth Jones, Isaac Jones, James Irwin, Joseph Kerr, Thomas B. King, John Kuter, John King, Samuel Kirkpatrick, John Kinesly, John Kenney, L. Kilburn, William Keran on Twin Creek, Daniel Ludwig, George Ludwig, Joseph Linnel, Thomas Lettleton, Joseph Loveless at Adelphia, Elisha Littler, John Lewvell on Deer Creek, Samuel Lemmons in care of Aron Busson on Brush Creek, William Littlejohn, Benjamin Lakin, Jesie Mountz, Richard Morris, Thomas M'Millin, William M'Farland, Micheal Miles, Phelix Millar, John G. Macan, Thomas Mouser, John M'Cullough, John Millar, Joseph Moore at Old Town, Cornelous Moreford, James Murphy, William Morial, John M'Kim in care of J. Carlisle, ##om, Jacob Nyel on Deercreek, Lott Odle, Jonathan Orsea, John Olinger, John Oldkre, Sebulon Orr, Robert Patton, Thomas Pye, Nathaniel Pope, Reuben Pursel, Doct. Anthony Potts, Richard Reed, John P. Ransom, Mary Reynolds in care of Col. Findley, John Robinson, William Rankin, John Runkle, William Ross, John Rush or Peter Rush, John and Jacob Reyley, William Rector, Stephen Ross in care of Joseph Harness, Daniel Ross on Deer Creek, Thomas Strane, John Scott, James Sish, John Steily, William Scott, John Stars, William Shaw in care of G. Richey, Martha Shepherd, John Salters, Henry Strawster at Adelphia, James Sulivance, Samuel Smith, Archibald Shockley, William C.

Schenck, Robert Steel, Mary Smith, Christian Shearer, Henry Shelley, Mathew T. Scott, Marshall Stone, Thomas Steward in care of S. Thompson, Ezra Tubbs, Richard S. Thomas, Stephen Terry, Charles Thompson, Nimrod Thompson, John Trimble, John Timmons, John Tucker, George Taylor, John Vanmatre in care of J. Tiffin, Henry Valentine, John Valentine, George Vinsonhealter, Thomas White at Westfall, Samuel Wilson, George West, Leve Warner, John S. Wills, William Wilson at Highbank, James Withrow, John Wallace, Thomas Wilson, John Webster at Kinnickinic, Samuel Willman, Miss Mary Wood, John Whaley, John Woodruff.

Benjamin Urmston asks those indebted to him to settle their accounts.

Brown & M'Cort have opened a store in the house on Paint Street formerly occupied by James Johnston, taylor, where they will sell dry goods and groceries.

Jesse Spencer, Register of the Land Office at Chillicothe, prints the depo-sition of George Johns, signed by John Hutt, regarding a certificate of land.

A note from John Stafford to William Hook was found.

Ships owned by Col. Lord and Marshal S. Jones, both built at Marietta, landed safely at Alexandria.

David Yeats, administrator of the estate of Benjamin Yeats, dec'd, late of Union township, Ross County, regarding the estate settlement.

J. Meigs' letter to Doct. Samuel H.P. Lee is printed regarding Lee's pills. The pills are on sale by Rev. James Kilbourn in Worthington.

Isaac Evans & Company have opened their store in the brick house formerly occupied by John M'Coy at the corner of Water and Mulberry Streets.

John M'Coy has moved his store to the house formerly occupied by Thomas James and opposite N. & R. Gregg's store in Chillicothe.

George Parsons and John S. Edwards (attorney) regarding the suit in Trumbull County Supreme Court of William W. Morsman, of Warren in Trumbull County, vs. Susanna Morsman, his present wife, for divorce.

Andrew Zeller, living in German township on Twin Creek in Montgomery County, reports two stray mares.

Joseph Kerr regarding David Shepherd's advertisement of a sheriff's sale of the property of Joseph Kerr at the suit of N. & R. Gregg. Kerr says he was a security for John Ludwig who failed to pay his debts.

Abraham Stipp, at Westfall, has land for sale including a distillery.

Volume VII, Thursday, 28 May 1807, No. 358

Benjamin Urmston, living in Chillicothe, reports two stray horses and mentions the Whiteoak settlement.

Archelaus Alloway, living in Boone County, near Tanner's Station, on the Ohio River, three miles below the Great Miami, reports a runaway negro named Limus.

George Parsons regarding the petition of George Mull, of Trumbull County, an insolvent debtor, in the Trumbull County Court of Common Pleas.

J.P.R. Bureau regarding the suit, in the Gallia County Supreme Court, of Samuel Logue, of Gallipolis, vs. Sarah Logue, his wife, for divorce. He says that Sarah Logue committed adultery with Zibbin Owens.

Geo. Wolfley, living at Jacob Shoemaker's, fifteen miles from Chillicothe, near Hobbs' tavern in Fairfield County, reports a stray horse. Deliver to John Waddle & Company in Chillicothe.

William Skeed, in Chillicothe, reports a strayed or stolen horse.

Obituary: Mrs. Mary Wood, wife of Zachariah Wood, died in Chillicothe, last evening, 27 May 1807.

James & M'Coy have goods for sale at their store in Chillicothe.

William Evans, in Buckingham, Virginia, regarding his land on Deer Creek.

Moses Hewitt, at Athens, reports a horse that strayed from Scioto Salt Lick.

John Carlisle has a new shipment of goods at his store in Chillicothe.

Duncan M'Arthur, near Chillicothe, is authorized to sell Col. Richard C. Anderson's Spring Prairie Survey.

David Sullivan, living in Highland County near New Market, reports several strayed head of cattle.

G. Renick has a new shipment of goods for sale at his store in Chillicothe.

Philip Griffith has started his hatting business in Chillicothe in the house formerly occupied as a printing office by Bradford & Company. He supplies "the neatest fashions, at Pittsburg prices".

John Sherer has a new shipment of goods for sale next to the Red Lion.

David Hays about the suit of George Emery vs. James Blinco in the Highland County Court of Common Pleas mentions Jesup N. Couch, attorney for Emery. They appoint Geo. W. Barrere, Samuel M'Quitty and Moses Patterson, auditors.

George Parsons and J. Noyes (attorney) about a petition of James Thompson, an insolvent debtor, in the Trumbull County Court of Common Pleas.

George Parsons & John S. Edwards about the divorce of William W. Morsman from his wife, Susanna Morsman, in Trumbull County.

Michael Cryder, Jur., has pasturage for lease.

Martha Mitchel, administratrix of the estate of James Mitchell, late of Green township, Ross County, dec'd, regarding the estate settlement.

W. Raynolds, in Zanesville, has a supply of goods for sale at his store.

Joshua Bogart and Michael Fisher, in Harrison township, Franklin County, executors of the estate of Ezekiel Bogart, dec'd, about the estate sale.

Zacheriah Gillaspie regarding the five notes he gate to Francis M'Henry of Chillicothe for land lying at Pe Pee.

John Woodbridge and Company have a new shipment of goods at their store.

Benjamin Urmston regarding the title bond he gave to David Shepherd.

Volume VII, Thursday, 4 June 1807, No. 359

An account of the Indians' murder of Mr. Boyer in Champaign County. Mr. Boyer's brother-in-law burned an Indian camp last spring.

James & M'Coy and Isaac Evans have dissolved their partnership in the firm known as Isaac Evans & Company.

Isaac Evans has a new shipment of goods for sale at his store in Chillicothe.

John M'Landburgh has arrived from Baltimore with a new shipment of goods.

John M'Farland about his school in Chillicothe. Rev. R. Wilson is overseer.

William H. Puthuff wants to hire a cook at the Eagle Tavern.

Geo. Parsons, at Ravenna, Trumbull County, about the petition of "Benjamin and Benjamin Tuppan" for the partition of land. John Kinsman, David King, Fidelio King, Ebenezer King, and Ephraim Starr are also owners of the land.

Thomas Scott, in Chillicothe, regarding the payment of taxes.

Volume VII, Thursday, 11 June 1807, No. 360

Peter Spurck has purchased the Black Horse Tavern in Chillicothe. He also continues his clock and watch making business.

William Lamb has sold his tavern in Chillicothe to William H. Puthuff.

Thomas Moore, administrator of the estate of James Criswell, dec'd, late of Adams County, regarding the estate settlement.

George Ritchey found some strays horses east of Chillicothe.

Moses Nickins, living on Benjamin Kerns' plantation at the High Bank about five miles from Chillicothe, reports a stray mare.

John M'Dougal regarding the printing of the laws of Ohio.

Volume VII, Thursday, 30 July 1807, No. 367

William M'Farland has returned from Philadelphia with a new supply of goods to sell in his store in Chillicothe.

Abraham J. Williams, Tax Collector, regarding the taxes due on Ohio lands.

William L. Foster, living in Warren County, Deerfield township, about a horse.

Brown & M'Cort asks those indebted to them to settle their accounts.

John M'Dougal, Supreme Court, Ross County, about the divorce of Catharine Hargus from her husband, John Hargus, on the grounds that said John had a former wife living in Kentucky and deserted Catharine for the past five years.

Peter Lalance, in Gallipolis, administrator of the estate of Jether Hailey or Bailey, late of Letart's township, Gallia County, dec'd, regarding the estate settlement. Those indebted to the estate should pay J.P.R. Bureau in Gallipolis.

Amzi Atwater and Charlotte Blair, in Hiram township, administrators of the estate of Jacob Blair, late of Trumbull County, dec'd, about the estate.

J.B. Ferard and J.P.R. Bureau, at Gallipolis, administrators of the estate of Marin Duport, late of Gallipolis, dec'd, regarding the estate settlement.

Peter Jackson, in Deerfield township, Ross County, reports that Stephen Timmons found a stray mare.

The publication of the conversations of Nehemiah Duncan is announced.

Thomas Beavers and John Davis, appraisers, say that David Smathy, of Brush Creek on the west fork of Scioto, Meigs township, Adams County, found a mare.

John Timmens reports a stray mare and colt.

John Evans, in Wayne township of Ross County, reports that Abraham Shanton found a stray mare.

John A. Fulton is a candidate for the house of representatives.

An unsigned letter to the editor nominates the following for public office: Nathaniel Massie, Duncan M'Arthur, Thomas Worthington, John A. Fulton, Joseph Kerr, Elias Langham and John M'Lane.

Philip Griffeth, at Chillicothe, wants to buy lamb and skin wool.

John Judy, in Ross County, regarding a note he gave to Gillian Ruse for land.

D. Shepherd, Sheriff of Ross County, regarding a sheriff's sale of the property of Prentis Park, heir to the estate of Fergus Moore, dec'd, at the suit of Mary Lenard. The land, adjoining Westfall, was entered by Abraham Stipp.

David Hayes, at New Market, regarding lots in the town of Hillsborough.

John Guthery, in Pe Pee township of Ross County, reports that Charles Steenberger found a mare that was appraised by Arch. Guthery and Wm. Guthery. Also Uriah Wheaton found a mare appraised by Arch. Guthery and Geo. Guthery.

Daniel M'Kenney, in Scioto County, Nile township, says that James Applegate found a mare that was appraised by John West and William Corn, sen.

Humphrey Fullerton has opened a store in Bainbridge at Maj. Cutler's house.

William Gunnel, jun., in Fairfax County, Virginia, reports a runaway mulatto man named Tom Poston.

James Moore reports that William Divine, living in Tiffin township of Adams County, found a mare. It was appraised by Arthur Ellison and James M'Comas.

Henry Nevill has a new shipment of goods for sale at his store in the town of Jefferson on the Pickaway Plains.

Samuel H. Smith has land for sale in the town of Clinton on Owl Creek.

William Wilson, living in Chillicothe, reports a stray horse.

J.P.R. Bureau, at Gallipolis, administrator of the estate of Margueritte Violette Ferard, late of Gallipolis, Gallia County, dec'd, about the estate.

John Evans, in Wayne township, Ross County, reports that Ozwell Thompson found a stray horse.

Joseph Miller & Company have nails for sale at their nail factory, Chillicothe.

John Kerr regarding the Scioto Bank Lottery.

John Scott, living in Pickaway township, Ross County, reports a stray horse.

Samuel R. Holcomb, in Raccoon township of Gallia County, reports that Stephen Holcomb found a stray horse.

William Stubbs, lately from Philadelphia, regarding his painting, glazing and gilding business in Chillicothe.

William Williams regarding his hatting business in the house in Chillicothe formerly occupied by Daniel Harr next door to Maj. Urmston's. He says he "served a seven year apprenticeship in a principal shop in Europe, and carried on the trade upwards of twenty years in America".

Thomas Hicks, in Union township of Ross County, says that William Robinson found a stray horse.

Robert Spear, administrator of the estate of Elijah Hart, dec'd, late of the county of Muskingum, regarding the estate settlement.

Volume VIII, Thursday, 20 August 1807, No. 370

Peter Jackson, in Deerfield township of Ross County, reports that George Ater has found a stray horse.

John Greave, in Jefferson township, reports that Benjamin Cox found a stray mare. She was appraised by John Miller and Amos Brewer.

Peter Jackson, in Deerfield township of Ross County, reports that John Timmons, sen., found a stray horse that was appraised by Henry Hines, sen., and William Nolin.

A note regarding the meeting of the militia under Col. Niblack is printed.

An unsigned letter to the editor nominates candidates for public office and mentions Nathaniel Massie, Duncan M'Arthur, Thomas Worthington, John M'Lane, John A. Fulton, David Shelby, Elias Langham.

An account of a meeting of the citizens of Warren and Trumbull Counties mentions John Leavitt, Calvin Austin, John S. Wards, Ephraim Quinby.

White Brown and Samuel Langdale regarding a meeting of the citizens of Deerfield township mention John Timmons, sen., Stephen Timmons, Peter Jackson.

Brown & M'Court have moved their store to Livingston on Pickaway Plains.

David Bonner, at Chillicothe, has land for sale on the Wheeling road, next door to Humphrey Fullerton.

John Wallace, in Buckskin township, reports that Abraham Stooky, in Ross County on Buckskin Creek, found a horse.

John Greave, in Jefferson township, Ross County, reports that John Gregg, living on Salt Creek eight miles from Moffit's mills, found a stray mare. She was appraised by Alexander Greave and Amos Brewer.

Nathan Ellis reports that Hugh Power found a stray mare at Ellis' ferry opposite Limestone.

Amzi Atwater, in Trumbull County, Hiram township, reports that Delaun Mills and Thomas Kennedy have appraised a stray mare found by Isaac Mills.

E. Meeker has flour and fruit for sale at the Red Lion Tavern in Chillicothe.

John Baker, in Chillicothe, reports a stray horse.

John Guthery, in Seal township, Scioto County, reports that D. Boultinghouse and George Davis appraised a stray mare found by Henery Huse.

Wm. Robinson, in Union township, Ross County, reports that John Johnson and John Ferrel appraised a stray horse found by Adam Yerion.

Wm. Davis, in Mifflin township, Ross County, reports that John Campbell has found a stray mare.

Joseph Hopkins, in Concord township, says that John Paterson found a mare. Also Patrick Pendergrass found a stray horse.

David Yates, living six miles from Chillicothe on the waters of the North fork of Paint Creek, has land for sale on Dry Run above the Pickaway Plains. It was entered by Benjamin Yates, late of Ross County, dec'd.

Samuel Longsvite regarding two notes he gave to John Wood.

Peter Spurck, clock and watchmaker, silversmith and jeweller, has moved his shop to the Black Horse Tavern.

Volume VIII, Thursday, 27 August 1807, No. 371

T. Worthington writes a letter to the public declining public office.

Unsigned letters to the editor mention Return Jonathan Meigs, jun., the Cincinnati Republican Society, Gen. Massie, Gen. Worthington, Gov. St.Clair.

An account of a meeting of the citizens of Pee Pee township, Ross County, mentions John Guthery, Joseph J. Martin, Maj. John Parrell, John Chenoweth, Henry Brown, Arthur Chenoweth, Jonathan Clark, Aaron Burr, R.J. Meigs, jun., Jeremiah M'Lene, Elias Langham, Joseph Kerr, William Lewis, John A. Fulton, John M'Lane.

An account of a meeting of the citizens of Athens County mentions Leonard Jewett, Alexander Stedman, Ebenezer Currier, Return J. Meigs, jur., Gen. Massie, Ph. Martimer Starr, Judge Huntington, Gen. Worthington.

An account of a meeting of the Ohio Militia mentions Old Town, Mr. Platter, Col. Langham, Gen. Worthington, Maj. Cutler, Capt. M'Donald, Col. M'Arthur. Capt. M'Donald's speech is printed and mentions Col. M'Arthur, Capt. David Yates, Lieut. Robert Smith, Ensign William Stocton, Capt. John M'Donald, Lieut. Samuel Davis, Ensign John Jones.

Robert Smith, living on the Deercreek road two miles from Chillicothe, offers all his livestock, household furniture and farming utensils for sale.

Joseph Hopkins, in Concord township, reports that Joseph Perrety and Joseph Briggs have appraised a mare found by Joseph Perret, sen.

Samuel Hindman, in New Market township, Highland County, reports that James M'Onnell found a mare.

Elizabeth Buck, Moses Donaldson and Jacob Grubb, in Walnut township of Franklin County, administrators of the estate of Joseph Buck, late of Walnut township, dec'd, regarding the estate settlement.

John Brown reports that Adam Shewmaker and William Tucker have appraised a stray mare found by William Lawsin.

James Daily, in Chillicothe, regarding the land of William Daily that the sheriff has advertized for sale at the suit of Nathaniel Massie.

John M'Dougal and Jesup N. Couch (attorney) regarding the suit of House Bentley, George Bentley, Sashbozzor Bentley and Hannah Bentley vs. R. Lott Mathews and Samuel Jacobs in the Ross County Court of Common Pleas. John Hutt and Joseph Tiffin are appointed commissioners to sell the land.

Volume VIII, Thursday, 3 September 1807, No. 372

Unsigned letters to the editor mention Samuel Huntington, Return J. Meigs, jun., N. Massie, Nathaniel Massie, S. Huntington, T. Worthington, Mr. M'Arthur.

Obituary: Gustavus Spencer, attorney, age 24, died Saturday last, 29 August 1807, between the hours of three and four in the morning. He was buried on Saturday evening in Chillicothe.

A note regarding Indian activities mentions William Wells at Fort Wayne, J. Gerrard at Staunton on the Big Miami, Major Moore, Greenville.

An unsigned letter to the editor about candidates for the election mentions Joseph Kerr and Gen. J. M'Lene.

Another letter to the editor about the election mentions Nathaniel Massie, Duncan M'Arthur, Thomas Worthington, Joseph Kerr, Elias Langham, Jeremiah M'Lene and John M'Lane.

Account of a meeting of the citizens of the Cleveland area mentions Samuel Huntington, Amos Spafford, Samuel Baldwin, John Walworth, and Lorenzo Carter.

A meeting of Green township citizens mentions George Ritchey, Nual Brown, Christian Levey, James Stanly, John Collet, Col. Worthington, Duncan M'Arthur, Henry Brush, John Crouse, Jeremiah M'Lene, William Lewis, John M'Lene.

William Lee regarding a note he gave to Alexander Carr of Franklin.

Jesse Spencer, Register of the Land Office, regarding land for sale, mentions J. Robinson, N. Massie, T. Barr and E. Traxler.

Jacob Lutz, in Colerain township, Ross County, reports that Jacob Bausher and Christopher Teats have appraised a mare found by John Drum who lives on Salt Creek near Deffabaugh's mill.

D. M'Kenney, in Nile township, Scioto County, reports that Samuel Nanhook and Truster Woller have appraised a mare found by Barney Dewit.

Stephen M'Dougal regarding the petition of Benjamin Jones, an insolvent debtor, in Ross County Court of Common Pleas.

Joseph Tiffin and James Brown regarding notes and orders that Brown lost near Carr's mill on Paint Creek. The notes mention D. Scott, Francis Nicholas, Mary Patton, Charles Chesnut, John Nicholas.

Adam Hollar has quit tavern keeping in Chillicothe, but will continue his bakery. Those indebted to him should settle their accounts.

Nathaniel Pope, administrator of the estate of William Barlow, late of Highland County, dec'd, regarding the estate settlement.

Hugh Boyle, W.W. Irwin (attorney), and P. Beecher (attorney), at Lancaster, regarding the suit of divorce of Jacob Runckle from his wife, Catherine Runckle, in Fairfield County Supreme Court. Catherine eloped with a Mr. Kirk. Also about the suit of divorce of Catharine Eckert or Ecker from her husband, Abraham Eckert or Ecker. Also the divorce of Margaret Fairchild from John Fairchild, jun., because of his adultery with Margaret Pane.

Volume VIII, Thursday, 10 September 1807, No. 373

Thomas Kirker and Samuel Finley give general orders to the Ohio Militia. The mention Gen. Schenk, Gen. Whiteman, Gen. Darlinton, Gen. M'Lene.

Obituary: Mrs. Cloe Palmer, age 31, wife of Thomas Palmer, died on the 12th August, 1807, at Worthington. She died in child bed and left seven small children, the oldest is age 12.

Obituary: Jedediah H. Lewis, age 32, died on 14 August 1807, leaving a wife and six small children (the eldest is age 11).

An unsigned letter regarding the election mentions Gen. Worthington, Mr. M'Arthur, Leonard Jewett, Alexander Stedman, Ebenezer Currier, Gen. Massie, Judge Huntington, Judge Meigs.

T.S. Hinde regarding a meeting of the Chillicothe Polemic Society.

A note regarding a meeting of the Humane Society of Deerfield.

An unsigned letter to the editor regarding the election mentions Nathaniel Massie, Duncan M'Arthur, Thomas Worthington, Joseph Kerr, Elias Langham, John

M'Lane and Jeremiah M'Lene.

John Waddle & Company have a new shipment of goods at their store.

Samuel M'Cormick reports a runaway slave named Daniel. Deliver to Jessey Hunt in Cincinnati.

James Kilgore, in Jefferson township, reports that Samuel Kilgore and Benj. Holton have appraised a horse found by James Carter.

Robert Lucas, in Union township, Scioto County, reports that John White and John Dever have appraised a horse found by David Pollock who lives at the mouth of Scioto, Brush Creek.

Elijah Holliday, by Th. S. Hinde, regarding land entered by William Hickman and William Holliday on Isaac's Creek in Adams County. William Holliday, dec'd, late of Frederick County, Virginia, paid tax on the land, but it was sold by Thomas Scott, to John Machir, for failure to pay taxes. Elijah Holliday is the heir of the said William Holliday and has entered his right of redemption in Adams County.

Volume VIII, Thursday, 17 September 1807, No. 374

An unsigned letter to the editor mentions Judge Meigs.

Samuel Huntington declines the nomination to governor.

Obituary: David Stockton, sen., age 60, died at his farm near Chillicothe on Saturday evening, 12 September 1807. He left a widow and nine children.

An unsigned letter to the editor regarding the election mentions Nathaniel Massie, Duncan M'Arthur, Jeremiah M'Lene, John A. Fulton, Elias Langham, Henry Brush, John M'Lane and Twin township.

William Gibbons, at Chillicothe, regarding the wife of Dr. William Gibbons, age 31, late of the state of New York.

Hugh Boyle and P. Beecher, in Fairfield County Supreme Court at Lancaster, regarding Robert Willcox's suit of divorce from his wife, Mary Willcox.

William M'Dowell asks those indebted to him to settle their accounts.

Daniel Chesnut reports that Thomas Hodges & Robert Ritchey have appraised a horse found by Thomas Mitchel on Indian Creek in Ross County.

James Potts, at Paint Creek, regarding land he bought from Alexander Kerr.

Volume VIII, Thursday, 1 October 1807, No. 376

Richard Springer reports that Thomas Casey, about age 22, robbed him.

F. Meeker regarding the "swindler", H.G. Bradford.

Unsigned letters to the editor regarding the election mention Return J. Meigs of Marietta, Gen. Massie, Judge Huntington.

A note regarding a muster of Capt. David Yates' volunteer company of militia mentions Thomas Worthington, Henry Brush, William Lewis and James Dunlap.

An unsigned letter to the editor regarding the election mentions Nathaniel Massie, Thomas Worthington, Duncan M'Arthur, James Dunlap, Henry Brush, William Lewis and John M'Lane.

A list of letters at the Post Office in Chillicothe includes Martin Armstrong, Thomas Armstrong in Colerain township, James Armstrong, John Alexander, Elijah Alexander, Thomas Andrews, Abraham Bilsland, William Beans, Philip Both at Sinking Spring, William Bradley, William Bready, Joseph Burk (saddler), Adam Buckenon in care of N. Crawford, William B. Beckets in care of Joseph Collins, Henry Brown, John Bacus, David Bristol, John Baker, William Barns, Josiah Brown, Elizabeth Brown, Benjamin Brackney, John Burke, Barton Blizard, Robert Breden in care of N. Crawford, Chauncey Baker, Henry Beaty in care of S. Gundey, William Boss, Edward Crabb, John Cummins, Mr. Cellers, Walter Crew, Charles Coulter, Israel Clark, Rev'd. Robert M. Cunningham, Isaac Davis, Neal Daugherty, Henry Davis, Chapman Denslow, Capt. John Davis, Jesse Dodd, Peter Donnan, Patrick Donly, Francis Duffey, John Daniel and Thomas Daniel, Daniel Devorse, Edward Dosch or Joseph Mather, William Dickey, William Erwin, Benjamin Evans, John Endler, Samuel Evans, Jacob Eckelberner, John Edwards at Buckskin, William Flowrance, Christopher Earnest, Alexander Fleming, Barthy Fryatt, John Ferreal, David Flint, Adam Funk, John Glosson, Frederick Gibler, Richard John and Adam Glaze, Andrew Glaze, Joseph Gellespie, John Galloway, Charles Green, John Goings, Andrew Gilmore, Robert Gamble in care of N. Crawford, Jacob Gunde, Jacob Gregg at Salt Creek, David or James Henderson, Caleb Huff, John Hall, Samuel Harvey near Crouse's mill, Hon. Samuel Huntington, Jacob Helm, James Hughey, John Hunter, Jacob Jackson,

John Jackson, James Jameson, John Jobe, Thomas Jones, John Jenkins, Isaac Jones, Rev'd. William Johnston, John Jones, Benjamin Kirns, John Kreysure at Adelphia, William Keyes (carpenter), John Kuder, John Kight, John Lane, Jacob E. Lehre, Joseph Lane and Mrs. M. M'Cune, William Lot, Jonathan Lesslie, John Leavell, John Ludwig, Joseph Lannel, William Lacey, Dorsey Mason, Samuel M'Munn, William Mills, James M'Donald, Charles Medford, Soloman Moffitt, Archibald M'Donald, Abraham Massie (a black man), Jonathan M'Clure, Joseph Mcafee, Joshua Milin, Micheal Miller in care of Felix Renick, William More, Willi Osstill or Gardner Jacks, Dennis O'Lackey, Ralph Osbourn (attorney), John Odle, William Ogden, Isaac Penneston, John Parress, William H. Pleasants, William Pickings, William Parker, George Phebus, David Peirson, James Potts, Jonathan Purcell or George Yoakum, William Perrins, Jacob Pitman, William Pursell, Thomas Roberts, Alexander Reed, Dudley E. Richards, Henry Ritler in care of John Ritler, William Reed, Andrew Rush, Joseph Ramsey, John Ratcliff, John Rollans, Samuel Writtenhouse, Samuel Ravencraft, Joseph Rockhold, Stephen Ross, Jobe Reed, David Shepherd, Jonathan Simpson, John Swan in care of James Furgeson, Jacob Saltzgarver, Jacob Shetz, Aaron Sullavan, Micheal Snaveley, George Smith (printer), Micheal Slegge, John Stocton, William Sprigg, John Stipp, John Smith, John Sherraden in care of Benj. Duncan, Lemuel Sayers, Richard Steel, William Tracy, Ebenezar Tuttle, Oswell Thompson, Thomas Tomlinson near Moffit's mill, Hon. Thomas Todd, James Taylor, Nimrod Thompson, William Vezey, Joel Ward at Salt Creek, James Wallace, Henry Warnstorf, Samuel Waron, William Wyrin, John Wolf, Rev'd. Robert Warwick in care of Gen. Finley, James Withrow, William Walker, Charles Willing Byrd, Tubman or Elias Wright, Robert Wallace on Buckskin in care of Doct. Edmison, Malcom Wright, John S. Wills, John Crouse, Samuel Coover, Frederick Helm, James Marks, John M'Keen, William Robinson, John Snider, Peter Snider, Anthony Potts, Felix Renick, Samuel Wallace, James Wallace. Joseph Tiffin also says the post office has moved to the house next door to Mr. Sparks' tavern in Chillicothe.

David M'Cune and William M'Cune regarding notes to James T. Ross.

James S. Webster, in Adelphia, Colerain township, says that Henry Strouser and Bastion Foust have appraised a horse found by Frederick Hanes.

John Evans, in Wayne township, Ross County, reports that George Emery and William Hall have appraised a horse found by James Whitesides.

Frederick Lineninger regarding his note to Thomas Wheeler.

Joseph Parrit, living on the waters of Paint Creek in Ross County, reports a stray horse.

William Buckner, jun., about a slave named Dick who ran away from David L. Ward on Man's Lick, by saying he was freed by Rev. James Suggett of Scott Co., Kentucky. Deliver to Gen. Thomas Sanford, of Kentucky, near Cincinnati.

Van Brady says the heirs of Samuel Brady, dec'd, have exercised their rights of redemption for land in Adams County that was sold to Mary and Sarah Oneel, and James Moore.

E. Woods and O. Jennings (attorney), at St. Clairsville, regarding the petition of John Nawles, an insolvent debtor, in Belmont County Court of Common Pleas. Also about the suit of James Murphy vs. Burris Vanwy, mentions Isaac Montony.

Samuel S. Spencer, at Salt Lick in Ross County, reports a stolen horse.

John Evans, Jun., has a new shipment of goods for sale at his store in the house formerly occupied by H. Fullerton on Water Street in Chillicothe.

James Atkinson, in Salem township, Belmont County, reports that Robert Hardesty and Alex. Kirkpatrick have appraised a horse found by Jacob Ollim.

Volume VIII, Thursday, 8 October 1807, No. 377

A note regarding the court case of Daniel M'Faddon vs. Benjamin Rutherford in Jefferson County Court of Common Pleas.

Several anonymous notes to the editor regarding the election mention Duncan M'Arthur, Nathaniel Massie, Thomas Worthington, J.A. Fulton, E. Langham, Henry Brush, James Dunlap, William Lewis, John M'Lane.

Thomas James regarding an ordinance of Chillicothe.

E. Mason has land for sale at Mr. Meeker's tavern. He mentions Samuel Eddins, Ambrose Gordon, Colin Cocke, Tarpley White, William Washington.

Volume VIII, Thursday, 15 October 1807, No. 378

John M'Clean regarding a meeting of the Ross County commissioners.

Prentes Park, in Wayne township, about the lease Phinchos Corwin obtained from Furgus Moore, dec'd.

H. Fullerton and Thomas James about an ordinance of Chillicothe mentions G. Renick, William Wallace, John Hutt, James Furguson and James & M'Coy.

Marriage: Thomas Evans married Miss Jane Stein, both of Ross County, on Tuesday evening last, 13 October 1807.

Election returns mention Nathaniel Massie, R.J. Meigs, Duncan M'Arthur, Elias Langham, John A. Fulton, David Shelby, Jeremiah M'Lene, Henry Brush, Thomas Worthington, James Dunlap, John M'Claen.

David Hoge, Register of the Land Office at Steubenville, has land for sale and mentions R. Gilson, Thomas M'Causlin and Joseph Berry.

Joseph Lamun, living near Chillicothe on the Westfall road, reports two runaway wheelwright's apprentices, John Calander (age 17) and Clem Hurt (age about 14).

Samuel Heath, in Scioto township, living on Paint Creek one mile from Wm. Kerr's Mill, will hold a public sale of his possessions.

James Matthews and William M'Kinley have appraised a colt found by William Moore of Liberty township in Trumbull County and entered it in the estray book of Nehemiah Scott in Trumbull County.

Volume VIII, Thursday, 29 October 1807, No. 380

Marriage: Thomas Steel married Miss Elizabeth Philips, both of Chillicothe, on Monday evening last, 26 October 1807.

Obituary: Reuben Abrams, an associate judge for Ross County, died on Wednesday, 28 October 1807, at Adelphi.

A note regarding election returns mentions Mr. Massie, Mr. Meigs, John Bigger, Mathias Corwin, George Harlen. In Belmont County: Josiah Dillon, John Patterson, William Vance, R.J. Meigs.

John Sharp and Henry Chapman, administrators of the estate of Benjamin Sharp, late of Plesant township, Clermont County, about the estate settlement.

John Carlisle has opened a new store a mile and a half from Hillsborough in Highland County. He still keeps his store at the Pickaway Plains.

Joseph Kirkpatrick regarding fences erected on his land.

Samuel R. Holcomb, in Rackoon township, Gallia County, reports that William Glann and Jobez Alfred have appraised a mare found by Samuel M'Murtry.

George Hays says that James M'Clure and George Wilbourn appraised a horse found by Joshua Hodes of Pickaway township, Ross County. Also Robert Miller and George Sidenbender appraised a horse found by John Scott of Pickaway township.

Eli Reeves, in Byrd township, Adams County, reports that Nevill Redman and Micah Woods have appraised a mare found by Alexander Jolly. Also Elijah Redman and John Glendening appraised a horse found by John Lyons.

Samuel Atchison, living two miles below Chillicothe, has animals for sale.

D. Duncan, jun., agent for Mary Grimes, John Brown and James Brown, the administrators of the estate of Thomas Grimes, dec'd, late of Tiffin Township, Adams County, regarding the estate settlement.

Rachel Allisson and Daniel Allisson, at Gallipolis, administrators of the estate of Benjamin Allison, late of Gallipolis, Gallia township, about the estate.

John Ellison reports that Allen Lee and Thomas Greenlee have appraised a mare found by Elijah Kimble of Sprigg township, Adams County. William Jinnin and Henry M'Greary appraised a mare found by Joseph Beam of Sprigg township. And Daniel Brown and Elisha Whiting a mare found by William Grimes.

Lewis Day, at Deerfield, reports that Ezekiel Nott and Stephen Mason have appraised a mare found by Alva Day, living in Deerfield, Trumbull County.

John Brown, in Ames township, Athens County, reports that Capt. Benjamin Brown found a stray mare.

Volume VIII, Thursday, 19 November 1807, No. 383

Doctor Wilcox, in Lancaster, regarding his practice of "Physic and Surgery" in Lancaster. He speaks of patients he cured 16 years ago in Virginia.

Robert Miller regarding a note he gave to John Libey.

Peter Jackson, in Deerfield township, Ross County, reports that Alexr. Gillaspie and Josiah Baker appraised a mare found by Baynard White.

The students of the Chillicothe Grammar School will deliver speeches.

Adam Hosack, Sheriff of Franklin County, has land for sale, late the property of Samuel Breckinridge, dec'd. The land is in Mathew's survey.

William S. Hutt, in Scioto township, has land for sale in Chillicothe.

Elizabeth Gilkison, at Portsmouth, administratrix of the estate of James Gilkison, late of Scioto County, dec'd, regarding the estate settlement.

James Freeman, at the Red Lion Tavern in Chillicothe, reports a horse that strayed from the house of Mr. Dunnings on Big Belly.

Noble Crawford, in Ross County, living on Buckskin Creek, Paxton township, reports that he found a stray mare.

John Wallace reports that Matthew Kelly and Daniel Robins have appraised a mare found by Jesse Wiley on Buckskin.

James & M'Coy have a new shipment of goods for sale at their store.

Andrew Glaze, in Seal township of Scioto County, has land for sale.

Thomas Rodgers, in Gallipolis, Gallia County, administrator of the estate of Patrick G. Fords, late of Gallipolis, dec'd, regarding the estate settlement.

Thomas Scott, attorney in fact for Edward Harris, sen., has land for sale.

Volume VIII, Monday, 21 December 1807, No. 387

Jesse Hitchcock and Caleb Hitchcock, at Portsmouth, administrators of the estate of Caleb Hitchcock, late of Scioto County, dec'd, about the estate.

John M'Landburgh asks those indebted to him to settle their accounts. He also has Joseph Lamun's spinning wheels for sale.

E.B. Merwin and J. Wilson ask those indebted for subscriptions to the Western Oracle to make payments to Peter Parcels at the office of the Scioto Gazette.

R.E. Post regarding a meeting of the Scioto Lodge of Masons.

John M'Clean regarding a meeting of the Ross County Commissioners.

John Sherer has goods for sale at his shop next to the Red Lion Tavern.

Brown & M'Court have moved their store to the house formerly occupied by S. Brown in Chillicothe. They also have a store at the Pickaway Plains.

Thomas Elliot, executor of the estate of Joseph Dunlavy, dec'd, has land for sale on Pee Pee Creek in Ross County, part of Samuel M'Cullough's survey, and land belonging to Morris Dunlavy. Apply to William Robertson on Paint Creek.

David Shepherd, sheriff of Ross County, about a sheriff's sale of the land of William Beard, Robert J. Beard, Joseph Beard and Charles M'Gowan and Elizabeth his wife, at the suit of John A. Fulton, John G. M'Can and Jeremiah M'Lene.

Amzi Atwater and John Cochran, in Trumbull County, administrators of the estate of Solomon Cochran, late of Hudson township, dec'd, regarding the estate.

Philip Griffeth, at Chillicothe, won't pay the debts of his wife, Elizabeth.

James Bonner, at Chillicothe, reports a stray horse.

Gilbert Evans, at Scippo, asks those indebted to him to settle their accounts.

Eli Reeves, in Byrd township, Adams County, reports that Isaac Hughey and Micah Woods have appraised a colt found by Noble Melvin.

George Frederick reports that Andrew Crouch and Nicholas Bunn appraised a horse found by William Caldwell, of Ross County, Green township.

George Richards reports that David Evans and Terah Templin have appraised a horse found by David Jolly, of Highland County, Liberty township.

James Parker, in Huntington township, Adams County, reports that Charles O'Connar and Stephen Sams have appraised a mare found by James Sams.

John Parker, in Mifflin township, reports that George Peneston and George Grove have appraised a mare found by Isaac Peneston.

John Wallace, in Buckskin township, Ross County, reports that John Robins and Mathew Kelly have appraised a mare found by Jaret Wiley.

John Ellison, in Adams County, reports that Nathl. Collins and Joseph Carl have appraised a horse found by John Stephens of Spring township.

David Kinkead & Company have opened their store in the house formerly occupied by Ephraim Doolittle in Chillicothe.

Calib Evins, living on the Pickaway Plains, Ross County, about a stray mare.

W. M'Dowell, in Chillicothe, has a new shipment of goods at his store near the Market House and opposite Mr. Ferguson's house.

James Scott, in Adams County, Tiffin township, reports that Jacob Shultz and

Robert Smith have appraised a mare found by James Allen.

Edward Harris, sen., in Washington, Kentucky, about his power of attorney to Thomas Scott to sell his land in Ohio.

Robert M'Ferson, administrator of the estate of William Stephenson, late of Adams County, dec'd, regarding the estate settlement.

Joseph Hopkins, in Concord township, Ross County, reports that Adam Mallon and William Harpole appraised a horse found by Michael Hyne, living on the waters of the north fork of Paint Creek, 15 miles from Chillicothe.

Samuel Dryden, in Chillicothe, asks those indebted to him, and to Humphrey Fullerton, to make payments to Jobe Thompson, attorney, in Chillicothe.

Robert Wilson, in Washington, Kentucky, has land for sale on Leading Creek, Gallia County. Apply to Rev. Robt. Wilson in Chillicothe.

John Combs has "just moved to Bainbridge, into the house formerly occupied by Major Cutler as a store-house" where he will keep entertainment for travellers.

John Guthery, in Seal Township, Scioto County, reports that Thos. Dugan and John Leath have appraised a mare found by William Graves.

Volume VIII, Monday, 4 January 1808, No. 389

A note regarding the U.S. Circuit Court mentions Judge Tod, Col. Burr and Mr. Blannerhassett.

Daniel Symmes is appointed Register of the Land Office in Cincinnati in place of Charles Kilgore, dec'd. Col. Gibson is appointed Register and John Sloane, Receiver, of the new land office at Canton, Ohio.

A list of letters left at the Post Office in Chillicothe includes Abraham Alter, John Alkier, John Arthur, Robert Adams, Felty Angel, Peter Apple, William Anderson, White Brown, William Bateman for John Campbell, Moses Bierd, Jacob Bawsier, Francies Baldwin, Robert Buckles in care of Joseph Lucas, Isaac Brink, Samuel Barr, John Britain, Edward Bennett, Joseph Barton, Christopher Baker, William Bradley, jun., William Bass, James Beck, Abraham Bonnet, John Baker on Walnut Creek, Joseph Burke, John Brigs, Timothy Beach, Barnabas Cockrian, Col. James Currey, Joseph Chew, Mr. Close, Alexander Cowgill, John & David Crouse, Isaac Cook, William Chidester, Thomas Cunningham, James Carter, Rev. Robert Cunningham, William Campbell, Elazar Cowgill, Rachel Cursevell in care of J. M'Dill, James Clark, Abraham Craig, George Clifton, Andrew Coffinbery, John Chenoweth, Joseph Conklin, Sanford Cardor, Moses Cook, John Dolly, Michael Duffy, Edward Dailey, Samuel Davidson, Thomas Davidson, Anthony Dennis, jun., Rev. Robert Dobbins, John Derickson, George Dawson in care of W. Puthuff, Isaac Darneille, Gen. Jonathan Dayton, Hugh Dolehan, Joshua Davis, Benjamin Elliot, Abner Essery, Aggress Fleming, Elisha Fitch, Jacob Gundy, Elizabeth Gorden, James K. George, Andrew Glaze, John Gone, Robert B. Gaines, Joseph Gillaspy, Daniel Green, Elizabeth Hendricks, John Hurley in care of J. Crouse, Moses Hopkins, Simpson Hatchinson, Mary Coover, Jonathan Hand, William Hunis, Joseph Hendricks, Levay Hays on Deer Creek, James Hoge, William Harper, Heath Heart, Elias Hedges, Rev. Joseph Hays, Benjamin Hill, Samuel Hinkson, Hugh Leves, Gaven Johnston, Peter Jackson, John Johnston in care of J. Hoge, Peter Jones, Margaret Johnston, Richard Jones or Samuel Driver, James Johnston, Absolam Kirkpatrick, John Keener, Aaron Kendall, Samuel N. Lucket, Samuel Langdale, James Little, John Lebey, Milton Ladd, David London, James Marks, John M'Kim, Samuel Mosley, James Mooney, Robert M'Mahan, Joshua Milton, John Miller, John Morton, George or Nathan Messack, Enoch Mason, Peter Mills, George M. Mullen, Polly M'Kim, Charles Medford, David M'Clellan, Andrew Machey in care of Dr. Duffin, George M'Cormack, John Mathews, John Nowland, William Nicol, Martin Overly, John Oldaker, William Oldfield, Jacob Orears, Mrs. Potts, Dr. Ptts at Westfall, Uriah Poullen, John Peshon, Sela Pain, William Parker on Sunfish, John Parks, Andrew Rush, A. Rice, Sandrige Rowe, William Robinson, Mary Raynold, John Ross, James T. Ross, Samuel Rittenhouse, Jacob Riley, John Read, John Sherar, John Shyreigh, Jacob Stingley, Michael Stockwell, Marshal Storee, John Steel, Philip Stout in care of James Hoge, C. Sumption, William Sprigg, William Stockwell, Peter Songe, William Stewart, Jacob Shireck, Abraham Simors, James Sainders, George and John Snapp, James Taylor, James Tomason, John Vanmetre, Cuthbert Vinson, Valentine Weaver, Robert Wasson, William Wilson at High Bank, Thomas Wright, Benjamin Williams, Col. Thomas Williams, Samuel Wilson, Joseph and William Wilson, James Walace, Samuel Warren,

James Wilson, George Yokum, Nicholas Zimmerman. Entered by Joseph Tiffin.

Benjamin Welch, living in Ross County on Lick Run a mile above Gardner's Ferry, has land for sale.

Thomas James, in Chillicothe, asks those indebted to Thomas and Lemuel James to settle their accounts.

John Russel reports that William M'Clarin, of Green township, Adams County, found a stray mare.

John Scott reports that Peter Shultz and John Rodgers have appraised a mare found by Samuel Kincaid of Tiffin township, Adams County.

Adam Yearian says that his wife, Barbary Yearian, left him on January 4th and he will no longer honor her debts.

Jesse Spencer, Register of the Land Office, has land for sale and mentions John Edwards and Adam Young.

William Niblack regarding a meeting of the militia at John Pancake's house.

James Kilgore says that Benjamin Kerns and Robert Corkin have appraised a horse found by Henry Hinshaw of Jefferson township.

John Cellars, clock and watchmaker, silversmith and jeweller, has moved his shop to the house next door to M'Landburgh's store in Chillicothe.

Jesup N. Couch, administrator of the estate of Gustavus Spencer, dec'd, regarding the estate settlement.

Noah Clark, at Chillicothe, says that his wife, Ann Clark, left him on the 6th of March, 1807, and he will no longer honor her debts.

David Bonner, in Chillicothe, has a house for sale.

James Bonner, in Chillicothe, reports a strayed or stolen horse.

Curtis Cannon reports that Joseph Carson and Jacob Bratten have appraised a mare found by William Williams of Adams County, Meigs township.

John Wallace, Adams County, says that Alexander Younds and James M'Gines, sen., have appraised a mare found by Elisha Jones, living in Buckskin township.

George Hays reports that John Scott and James Dowlen have appraised a mare found by George Ross of Pickaway township, Ross County.

Volume VIII, Monday, 11 January 1808, No. 390

Part of a letter from Hon. Edward Tiffin is printed.

A note from John Smith regarding his vindication.

The speech of Judge Todd is printed.

A note from the editor regarding the publication of the German newspaper, the German Virginia Eagle, at Staunton.

Samuel Hindman, in Highland County, New Market township, says that John Strain and Adam Bengerman have appraised a horse found by James B. Finley.

Sabra Lewis and Stephen Maynard, administrators of the estate of Jedediah H. Lewis, late of Worthington in Franklin County, dec'd, about the estate.

Jonathan Anderson, in Chillicothe, reports three stray steers.

Abel Lewis, Samuel Herrick (attorney) and W. Sillyman (attorney) about the suit of Silas Durkee vs. Truman Peet in the Muskingum County Court of Common Pleas. Also regarding the suit of Andrew Alexander vs. Valentine Schmelzer.

Robert Willcox, at Lancaster, has a house and lot for sale. He continues his practice of medicine in Lancaster.

G. Renick asks those indebted to him to settle their accounts.

Thomas Hicks, in Union township, Ross County, reports that Yewel Williams found a stray mare colt on Dry Run.

James Wright, in Wayne township of Adams County, says that James Smiley and Thomas Williamson have appraised a mare found by William Glasgow.

Moor & Kanedy have Onondago Lake salt for sale in Chillicothe and Pickaway Plains at the stores of Brown & M'Court.

David Munn, in Union township, regarding lots for sale in Portsmouth.

Henry May has started his wheel-wright business opposite Mr. Winship's office on Second Street in Chillicothe.

Volume VIII, Monday, 8 February 1808, No. 393

W.H. Puthuff, in Chillicothe, has land for sale and mentions Kerr's mill on Little Darby and Dr. Cornelius Baldwin of Virginia.

James Brown, administrator of the estate of Lowder Cannon, dec'd, late of

Deerfield township, asks those indebted to the estate to pay John M'Dougal.

John Greave, in Jefferson township, Ross County, reports that Nicholas Cox and Alexander Greave have appraised a horse found by Daniel Dixson.

Job Dinning, in Tiffin township, Adams County, says that David Weacamp and John Boxlas have appraised a horse found by Henry Moor of Jefferson township.

James Parker says that Jonathan Rees and Alexander Parker have appraised a horse found by Joseph Douglass, of Adams County, Huntington township.

James Scott, in Adams County, Tiffin township, says that Andrew Woodrow and Samuel Young have appraised a horse found by Lewis Coryell.

George Frederick reports that Abraham Miller and Alexander Finley have appraised a horse found by William Chetterson of Ross County, Green township.

James Kilgore, in Jefferson township, Ross County, reports that John Davis and Joseph Hendricks have appraised a stray mare.

John Hutt, in Ross County, reports that James K. George and William Groves have appraised a horse found by David Dye.

Daniel Chesnut reports that Samuel Richey and Daniel Hodges have appraised a horse found by James Stinson, living on Indian Creek, 5 miles from Chillicothe.

John Mathews reports that David Downs and Daniel Dulency have appraised a heifer found by William Park of Scioto township, Ross County. Also David Murphy and Amos Jones appraised a cow found by William Keys of Scioto township.

W.H. Puthuff regarding his Eagle Tavern in Chillicothe.

Bigger Head, of Highland County, Brush Creek township, reports that Jacob Wiger and Archibald Smith have appraised a mare found by Antony Franklin.

Allan Killogh reports that John Bercus and Donald Camoron have appraised a horse found by David Poats, living in Twin township, Ross County.

Curtiss Cannon, of Adams County, Meigs township, says that Jesse Shimer & Thomas Rodgers have appraised a mare found by Robert Adams on Brush Creek.

James Atkinson, in Belmont County, reports that Charles Crairaft and John Watson have appraised a stray horse.

Eli Reeves, in Bird township, Adams County, reports that Thomas Moore and James Miller have appraised a horse found by Robert Moore.

E. Woods and Alexander Caldwell (attorney) about the suit of James Caldwell vs. Reese Branson in the Belmont County Court of Common Pleas.

Mr. Sloan's speech to the House of Representatives is printed.

Volume VIII, Monday, 21 March 1808, No. 399

Daniel Symmes, Register of the Land Office, has land for sale and mentions Wm. Carter, Wm. Cheek, Barnet Hulic, J. Hunt, S.C. Vance, John Mast, John Brownson and Samuel Beeler.

John Mantle regarding land he bought from John Kent, living on Darby Creek in Franklin County.

John Johnston reports that Solomon Tivebough and Alexander M'Mullen have appraised a mare found by Thomas Stewart of Ross County, Franklin township.

James Martin reports that John M'Neal and James Keeler have appraised a mare found by Peter Bosher, living in Washington township, Ross County.

Samuel Hindman, in Highland County, New Market township, reports that Joseph Davidson and David Chapman have appraised a mare found by John Hair. Also John Keyt and John Hair have appraised a mare found by John P. Finley.

John Wright, in Adams County, Wayne township, reports that James Clark and Samuel Williams have appraised a mare found by Thomas Williamson.

William Leedham reports that Amos Duncan and Alexander M'Cutchen have appraised a colt found by Basset Gorden.

Joseph M'Cune, in Muskingum County, Union township, reports that Joseph Wilson and Wm. M'Donnald have appraised a horse found by Hugh Martin.

Obituary: Mrs. Maria M'Mullin, age 24, wife of French M'Mullin, of Chilli-cothe, died on Friday evening last, 18 March 1808. She left a one week old baby.

John Lieby, in Chillicothe, has Monongahala whiskey for sale in the house on Water Street formerly occupied by Doctors Scott and Davis.

George Richards has lots for sale in Hillsborough, Highland County.

David Mitchell, living at Salt Lick, Ross County, reports a strayed horse.

Samuel R. Holcomb, in Rowan township, Gallia County, reports that Jabez Alford and Benj. Mills have appraised a horse found by Stephen Holcomb.

Samuel Finely, Wm. M'Farland and John Carlisle, in Chillicothe, regarding the Bank of Chillicothe.

G. & W. Renick, guardians of Ann Renick, have land for rent.

George Wildbahn, in Pickaway township, Ross County, says that his partner-ship with Mr. Brotherlin is dissolved. He also wants furs in exchange for hats.

Michael Fisher and Joshua Bogart, in Franklin County, administrators of the estate of Ezekiel Bogart, dec'd, regarding the estate settlement.

Robert Whiteside wants to hire a clock and watch maker.

Wm. M'Farland asks those indebted to him to settle their accounts.

Maj. Gen. Duncan M'Arthur regarding orders for the Ross County Militia.

Edward Long, living in Chillicothe, has land for sale in Green township, one mile from Chillicothe. Apply to William Long living on the land.

Samuel Finley and Winn Winship have land for sale on the Pickaway Plains adjoining Henry Bowman, Daniel Ludwig, Livingston, Samuel Hill, Henry Seamore, and Henry Valintine.

Winn Winship, in Chillicothe, has land for sale in Worthington's survey.

Capt. John Rodgers, in Guiandot, Kenhawa County, Virginia, reports three runaway slaves: Nace and Mill and an eleven-year-old boy.

Samuel Finley, Nathaniel Willis, Duncan M'Arthur, Isaac Cook, Nathaniel Massie, George Renick, Wm. Creighton, sen., John Carlisle and John Kerr about the Scioto Bank Lottery.

Volume VIII, Monday, 4 April 1808, No. 401

Gen. Jeremiah M'Lene gives Brigade orders for the Militia and mentions Col. Duncan M'Arthur and John Gossom.

A.K. Marshall, near Washington, Kentucky, regarding a runaway slave, Tom.

Lewis Cass regarding a sheriff's sale in Lebanon, Warren County, of the land of Samuel C. Vance (entered by John Bradshaw) at the suit of the U.S.

Benjamin Urmston regarding his stud horse at his stable in Chillicothe.

James Parker, in Huntington township, Adams County, says that Robert West and James Hayman have appraised a horse found by John Perry.

James Kilgore, in Jefferson township, reports that Joseph Alexander and Neal Nest have appraised a horse found by Edward Conner.

Wm. Creighton, jun., regarding the Chillicothe Academy under the operation of Rev. Robert Wilson. Apply to Samuel Finley and William M'Farland.

Marriage: Joseph Bentley to Miss Sally Price, daughter of William Price, all of Ross County, on Monday evening last.

Marriage: Michael Baldwin, attorney at law, married Miss Catharine Braden, both of Chillicothe, on Sunday evening last.

A list of letters left at the Post Office in Chillicothe includes William Askew, Mary Aters, Samuel Anderson, John Apling, John Betzer, Daniel Baum, Philip Barnet, Edward Bennett, Samuel Barr, Joseph Bowdel, Christopher Bartly, Amos Barr, Henry Brown near Pe Pee, John Baynon, Henry Beaty, Mr. Birerly, William Badley, Adam Betz, Isaac Cook, Elijah Bowcock on Paint Creek, James Bramble, Soloman Boeding, Benjamin F. Cockran, Thomas Cook at Dear Creek, John Coor, Beel Cullum, John Compton, John Cissna, Sarah Clifford, William Carson, William Chapman, Mosses Cook, Levi Connell, Alexander Cummins, Thomas Cunningham, John Crabb (hatter), Eleazer Cowgell, Micheal Corpman, John Collet, Easther Cook, Francis Duffy, Joshua Davis in care of B. Urmston, James Dean, Mrs. C. Dean, Isaac Dawson, Jesse Dungan, Benjamin Dear, William Dicky, Johnson Elliot, James Dowlien, Doct. John Edmison, George Emery, John T. Evans, Abner Eusry, Ignatious Edwards, Runnel Fielders, Elisha Fitch, Conrod Fultz, John Fulton, Peter Frans, Ebenezer Finemore, Joseph Foster, George Fry, Thomas Gilkeson in care of J. Carlisle, Hugh Garmiley, Levi Goodwin, Joseph Gillaspie, James Gregery, George Green, Daniel Henderson, Mosses Henderson, Mary Hewes, Daniel Hodges, Samuel Harvey, Evared Harr, Eli Harrison, Elisha Harrison, Thomas Holladay in care of J. Warner, Robert Hudson, James Hillman, Thomas Hentor, Samuel Heath, Jonathan Henderson, William Hill, Jacob Hotsenpillen, John Hixson, Benjamin Hill, John Holloway, Christopher Husey, jun., Abraham Holderman, Sophia Harrison, Charles Hessley, James Hughs, Randolph Hughes, Nicholas Jacks, Garner Jacks, Amos Jones, John Juder, Thomas Johnston, Isaac Johnston near Pe Pee, Samuel Jacson, Edward Johnston, Zacariah Jaens, Thomas B. Johnston, John Johnston in care of Joseph Kerr, Peter Jones, William

Justices, William Johnston, Mr. Kerr at Darby, Fielding Knight, William Kerr at Paint Creek, Alexander Linn, William Lamb, Elias Lovett, James M'Leise, Francis Lawrence at Pe Pee, Hugh Milligen, Cornelius Mannan, John M'Kim, James Milligan, Abraham Millar, Jane M'Kim, John Mathews, William Moore, Jacob Mace, Samuel M'Farland, Joseph Myers, John M'Neal, Pritchett Mills, Joseph Mounts, Lewis M'Near, Joshua Milton, George and Nathan Messicks, John Mirega, Ezekiel Morris, Frederick Minack, Samuel M'Kee, George M'Cormick, James M'Mahan, Samuel H. Oram, Jacob Ott, Stephen Ozier, Lucas Nebeker, Isaac Noggle, Jacob Nebergal, Henry Nickelson, John Patterson, Thomas Patton, William Peirson, Henry Pratter, John Peeble, William Parker, Nehemiah Philips, Zabul Randle, Jeremiah Riley, Benjamin Rea, Nathan Reeves, Samuel Rittenhouse, John Reed, James Redman, William Roberts, Benjamin Reed, Elizabeth Rodgers at Pe Pee, Abraham Reed, William Ross, Jane Reed at Darby, George Reed at Darby, Amos Reeder, Stephen Ross at High Bank, John Scott in Franklin township, Lyne Sterling, Jacob Steely, Mary Satts in care of Philip Ross, John and George Snapp, Ariel Strong, Thomas Strane, Elizabeth Strane, Hugh Steward, Thomas Smith, William Shaw, Robert Steel, John Sheren, Robert R. Smith, George Sigler, William Scott, Washington Sterrat in care of W. Winship, Thomas Sterret, Nimrod Thompson, George Teeters, Jeremiah Thomas, Jacob Thomas, Andrew Thompson in care of W. Kear, Seth Thompson, John Thompson at Pe Pee, John Vandement, Isaac Vanmater at Darby, Thomas Wilkins, Abraham J. Williams, Eli Vanderford, John Vanmatre, Edward Vernon, Parker Warren, Thomas White, Thomas Weewn, Wm. Walker, Daniel Waggoner, Jacob Wagner, Benjamin Williams, Henry Wisler, Samuel Watt, Jabez Wright, Mr. Walker, Thomas Williams (attorney), Philip Woolf, Eblet Wilson, Hugh Woods, Levin Wright, Maj. Wagoner, George Yoakam. Entered by Joseph Tiffin.

Nathaniel Johnston has a barrel of French Brandy for sale in Chillicothe.

Wm. H. Puthuff offers several tracts of land for sale.

Tounsand Nichols about a lease he bought from Wm. Sibrael. Sibrael bought it from Henry Muselman, Nicholas Sibrael & Frederick Overly, trustees of Township Eight. Nichols heard that Sibrael is "about to leave these parts".

John Hutt, justice of the peace in Ross County, say that Abraham Black and George Unseht swear they have known Michael Zimmerman for about 11 years and that he has never had a wife. Someone gossiped that he had a wife in Virginia.

George Vinsonhaler, in Twin township, Ross County, reports that John Timmons and Abijah Floro have appraised a colt found by Pressley Johnston.

Andrew Lindsay reports a pair of spurs stolen from the Theater in Chillicothe.

Volume VIII, Monday, 11 April 1808, No. 402

Marriage: William Carlisle married Miss Susannah Dresbach, both of Ross County, at the Pickaway Plains on Thursday last, 7 April 1808.

Part of a letter from Hon. Edward Tiffin in Washington is printed.

Peter Spurck offers the Black Horse Tavern in Chillicothe for rent.

Joseph Kerr wants to hire workers to make rails on his farm.

Joseph Miller & Company have moved their Nail factory to the house next door to the Lion Tavern in Chillicothe.

Daniel Sayre, at Gallipolis, administrator of Elizabeth Alexander, late of Gallia County, dec'd, regarding the estate settlement.

Massie & Sterret, at Chillicothe, regarding their stud horse at the stable lately occupied by Stephen Horsey. James Paul at Stuart's Crossings lists his pedigree and mentions Thomas Gregg in Pennsylvania.

Henry Dresbach, at the Pickaway Plains, lost a purse. Deliver to John Carlisle in Chillicothe.

John Hutt regarding the deposition of George W. Williams in Ross County stating that his house burned down on 30 March 1808 and he needs replacement land certificates. Jesse Spencer, Register, will issue the replacements.

James Wright, in Wayne township, Adams County, says Cornelius Williamson and William Williamson have appraised a mare found by James Smiley.

Volume VIII, Monday, 18 April 1808, No. 403

John Leiby has goods for sale at his shop in Water Street, Chillicothe.

Marriage: Robert Evans married Miss Sally Stein, both of Chillicothe, on Sunday evening last in Chillicothe.

A note regarding the fire at Mr. Brown's tavern in St. Clairsville.

John Carlisle has a new shipment of goods for sale at his store. He also "carries on the tin ware and saddle manufactory".

Michael Beyerly and Joseph Miller, administrators of the estate of Benjamin Miller, dec'd, regarding the estate settlement.

Joseph S. Collins and Clemt. Brown, administrators of the estate of Rebecca Brown, dec'd, regarding the estate settlement.

James S. Webster, in Colerain township, reports that Solaman Moffet and Nathan Landy have appraised two steers found by Enoch Cox.

John Hutt, in Ross County, reports that John Nichols and David Woolcott have appraised a mare found by Alexander Bilsland.

Volume VIII, Monday, 16 May 1808, No. 406

John M'Landburgh has a new shipment of goods for sale at his store.

James & M'Coy have received a new shipment of goods at their store.

Isaac Evans has a new shipment of goods for sale at his store, Chillicothe.

Martha Gelston, in Gallipolis township, Gallia County, administratrix of the estate of Samuel Gelston, late of Gallia County, dec'd, about the settlement.

James Moore, living 4 miles below Hamilton, reports a stray mare.

Joseph Hopkins, in Concord township, Ross County, reports that David Sayers and Robert Hoddy have appraised a horse found by John Hopkins on Paint Creek.

An account of a meeting of the citizens of Muskingum County mentions Judge Wm. Mitchell, William Reynolds and Zanesville.

Henry Nevil has goods for sale at his store at Jefferson, Pickaway Plains.

Benjamin Hough, Auditor, at Chillicothe, regarding taxes due.

G. Renick, at Chillicothe, asks those indebted to him to make their payments to Abraham J. Williams who has his books during his absence.

Elizabeth Waldon, administratrix of the estate of Cornelius Waldon, dec'd, late of Licking County, regarding the estate settlement.

D. M'Kenney reports that Samuel Vanhook and John Logan have appraised a mare found by James Logan, of Nile township, Scioto County.

David Kreble, in York township, Belmont County, reports that David Hart and William Atkinson have appraised a colt found by Levin Okey.

Edward Miller reports that William Miller and John Davidson have appraised a mare found by Thomas Johnston of Ohio township, Gallia County.

Jacob Miller, in Ohio township, Gallia County, reports that Joseph Miller and Thomas Singer have appraised a mare found by Israel Haighut.

Capt. John L. Tabb regarding a meeting of the Chillicothe Light Dragoons.

Thomas M. Donovan, in Urbanna, Ohio, has commenced keeping a tavern in the house lately occupied by George Fithian.

Robert M'Dill, on the North fork of Paint Creek, near Chillicothe, reports a strayed mare.

John Greave, in Jefferson township, Ross County, reports that John Redfeam and Robert Wilkinson have appraised a horse found by Isaac Greave.

Samuel Evans reports that Henry Alt and Benjamin Blumer have appraised a mare found by Joseph Bleimen in Liberty township, Highland County.

James Bishop, in Springfield township, Champaign County, says that Richard Robinson and Abraham Snider have appraised a horse found by Thomas Robinson. Also they appraised a filley found by Andrew Hodge.

Curtiss Cannon reports that Jacob Cox and Henry Franklin have appraised a mare found by Jacob Newland, of Meigs township, Adams County.

Brown & M'Court have a new shipment of books for sale at their store.

Wm. Creighton, sen., in Scioto township, Ross County, reports that Wm. M. Miller and Forrest Meeker have appraised a mare found by Henry Massie.

Volume VIII, Monday, 23 May 1808, No. 407

Marriage: Samuel Todd married Miss Polly Ballard, both of Chillicothe, on Sunday evening last.

An unsigned letter to the editor regarding the elections mentions Mr. Morrow, John Bigger, Nathaniel Massie, Gen. Wadsworth.

Stephen M'Dougal and Wm. W. Irwin (attorney) regarding the petition of Elias Stanberry, Erkurious Beaty and Samuel H. Smith in the Licking County Court of

Common Pleas. They own land with Jonas Stanberry, of New York, and the heirs of Nathaniel Leonard, of New Jersey, dec'd, and want to divide it.

Abel Lewis and Samuel Herrick (attorney) regarding the suit, in Muskingum County Court of Common Pleas, of Moses VanWinkle vs. Thomas Romans to attach his possessions in the hands of Edward Tanner, David Parks and George Jackson. Also regarding the petition of John Philbee, an insolvent debtor. Also regarding the suit of George Jackson vs. Benjamin Robinson and Job Robinson, executors of the estate of John Robinson, dec'd.

The farm occupied by Robert Boyce on Mad River, Champaign County, near Springfield, is for sale. Apply to Henry Cadbury; to Wm. Ruffin or Daniel Symes in Cincinnati; or to John G. Macan in Chillicothe.

Charles Cade reports that Isaac Cade and Nimrod Thompson have appraised a mare found by John Timmons, living in Deerfield township, Ross County.

John Hutt reports that Peter Long and Geo. Shane have appraised a horse found by Abraham Shane.

Davis & Scott ask those indebted to Doctors Davis & Scott to make payments.

Volume VIII, Monday, 30 May 1808, No. 408

Marriage: William C. Berry married Miss Nancy S. Musgrove, both of Mason County, Kentucky, on Tuesday last.

Gen. Jeremiah M'Lene is a candidate for sheriff in Ross County.

Col. W.H. Puthuff regarding regimental appointments mentions Bartholomew Fryatt, Abraham J. Williams, Jesup N. Couch, William S. Hutt, Dr. Ramus Davis, Samuel B. Kincart, and E. Pritchard.

Henry Porter, in Ross County near Chillicothe, reports a runaway indented servant boy, Bosman Clifton, age 18, who is probably heading for Delaware.

John Sherer has a new shipment of goods for sale at his store.

Samuel Hindman, in Highland County, New Market township, reports that John Davidson and Jesse Bryan have appraised a horse found by John Hair.

Samuel Finley & John Carlisle about stockholders of the Bank of Chillicothe.

John Hutt is collecting money due to John Kerr & Company in their absence.

Enos Prather, in Pe Pee township, Ross County, reports that George Sargent and Arthur Chinowith have appraised a horse found by William Barns.

Andrew Erwin, in Kiger township, Gallia County, reports that James Gray and Edward M'Mullin have appraised a mare found by Joseph Rife.

Volume VIII, Monday, 6 June 1808, No. 409

John Smith has resigned his seat in the Senate of the United States.

John Russel, in Green township, Adams County, reports that Robert Ralston and William Murphy have appraised a mare found by Abner Ewing.

An act incorporating the Bank of Chillicothe is printed.

John Woodbridge, in Chillicothe, regarding a meeting of the Scioto Lodge.

Joseph Tiffin, in Scioto township, Ross County, reports that John Anderson and Jonathan Anderson have appraised a horse found by Edward Tiffin.

Samuel Finley and John Carlisle, commissioners of the Bank of Chillicothe, have stock for sale.

Samuel Finley, in Chillicothe, regarding the Scioto Bank Lottery.

Isaac Evans has moved his store to his new brick building next to the Eagle Tavern and nearly opposite M'Landburg and Carlisle's stores.

Samuel Evans, in Liberty township, Highland County, reports that Heth Hart and George M'Dannel have appraised horses found by Thomas Hart and John Hart on the Rocky Fork of Paint Creek. Also Daniel Weyer and David Reese appraised a horse found by Benjamin Blumer on Paint Creek.

Martin Landes, living in Clear Creek township, Fairfield County, near Friend's mill, reports a strayed mare.

James Kilgore, in Jefferson township, Ross County, reports that William Wilson and Joseph Hendricks have appraised a mare found by William Lewis. Also James Widnor and James Davis appraised a horse found by William Dickey.

John Smith reports that Cotency Tanner and John Martin have appraised a mare found by Elijah Chenoweth, living on Great Darby Creek, in Pleasant town-ship, Franklin County.

Brown & M'Cort, in Ross County, have moved their store from Livingston to

Jefferson, at the Pickaway Plains, where they have a new shipment of goods.

John Ellison reports that Edward Scott and Samuel Santee have appraised a horse found by Daniel Brown of Manchester, Sprigg township, Adams County.

Curtis Cannon reports that William Pemberson, sen., and Thomas Ogle have appraised a horse found by William Pemberson, jun., of Meigs township, Adams Co.

Isaac Hent, in Newton township, Muskingum County, reports that Benjamin Beckworth and Daniel Chanler have appraised a horse found by Jesse Simerl.

John Russel, in Green township, Adams County, reports that William Russel and Josiah Stout have appraised a horse found by Peter Walker. Also Robert Ralston and Abner Ewing appraised a mare found by William Murphy.

John Greave, in Jefferson township, Ross County, reports that William Greave and Thomas Pierce have appraised a mare found by Joseph Wyatt.

Daniel Chesnut, in Scioto township, Ross County, reports that Levi Hodges and Isaac Thomas have appraised a mare found by Worrick Miller, living on Indian Creek, about three and a half miles from Chillicothe.

Volume VIII, Monday, 20 June 1808, No. 411

Samuel Henry reports that William Mustard and Richard Cartar appraised a horse found by Cornelius Shilpman in Scioto County, Seal township.

Samuel Finley, in Chillicothe, regarding the Scioto Bank Lottery.

John Walters and Catharine Livingood, administrators of the estate of Jacob Livingood, late of Muskingum County, dec'd, regarding the estate settlement.

George Ruth, living at Mr. Fitche's Inn, regarding his painting business.

James Kilgore, in Jefferson township, Ross County, reports that William Wilson and Joseph Hendricks have appraised horses found by James Kilgore and Jesse How.

John Timmons, living in Twin township, Ross County, reports a stray horse.

William Lacock, in Eagle township, Adams County, reports that William Davison and Andrew Dragoo have appraised a mare found by James Kindle.

Thomas Steel is a candidate for sheriff.

Joseph Darlinton, in Adams County, regarding the petition of Darby Sullivan, an insolvent debtor, in the Court of Common Pleas.

James Wright, in Wayne township, Adams County, reports that John Miller and R. Brackenridge have appraised a mare found by Elias Boatman. Also James Noland and Geo. Campbell appraised a mare found by William Paris.

James Atkinson, in Salem township, Belmont County, reports that Elijah Johnston and Thomas Tribel have appraised a mare found by James Tribel. Also James Scott and Thomas Tribel appraised a mare found by Elijah Johnston. Also Andrew Gitts and George Hupp appraised a mare found by Christopher Dayne.

Joseph Martin, in York township, Belmont County, reports that Benjamin Shepherd and Martin Baker have appraised a horse found by John Shepherd.

Robert Smith, in Chillicothe, asks those indebted to him to pay their bills.

Duncan M'Arthur gives brigade orders to the militia. He mentions Isreal Donaldson, Thomas Lewis, Charles A. Stewart, Jesup N. Couch.

H. Fullerton asks those indebted to him to pay their bills to John T. Evans.

Peter Jackson, in Deerfield township, Ross County, reports that Wm. Bready and Joseph Timmons have appraised a horse found by John Clark. Also Nimrod Lister and Alex. Watson have appraised a mare found by Stephen Timmons.

John Parker, in Mifflin township, Ross County, reports that John Brumley and Benjamin Brumley appraised a mare found by William Beckman, living on Morgan's fork of Sunfish. Also Isaac Penisten and Joseph Moore appraised a mare found by Gabriel Beckman, also living on Morgan's fork of Sunfish.

Joseph Kerr, in Chillicothe, wants to buy cattle to drive east to market.

Abel Lewis regarding the suit of Henry Carbeny vs. Thomas Boudea nd Abraham Wasser in the Muskingum County Court of Common Pleas.

W.H. Puthuff, in Chillicothe, asks those indebted to him to pay their bills.

William Whitten, in Muskingum County, Tuskarawa township, reports that Henry Core and Andrew Libargar appraised a mare found by Charles Williams.

Volume VIII, Monday, 11 July 1808, No. 414

Matthias Hoofnougle, living in Chillicothe, reports strayed steers.

Robert H. Johnston, in Chillicothe, reports a stray horse.

George Richards, in Liberty township, Highland County, reports that William

Scott and Matthew Creed have appraised a mare found by Augustus Richards. Also Ezekiel Kelly and Lewis Summers appraised a mare found by George Hobson.

James Galloway, Jr., at Ramblers retreat, attorney for the heirs of Severn Teagle, dec'd, says that redemption money has been paid on land sold to Joseph Kerr, John Waddle, Nathaniel Pope, Humphrey Fullerton and James Taylor.

A list of letters left at the Post Office in Chillicothe includes Robert Adams, Joseph Anderson, Isaac Adamson, Gershom Anderson, Bennet Armsworthy, Reben Abrams, John Anderick, Barnet Blue, Benjamin Brown, William Bears, Edward Busack, Joshua Ballinger, Joseph Bell, Frederick Bishop, Job Broughton, Peter Busenbark, Joshua Baxter, James Blue, John Bush, Isaac Bartley, John Berry, Nathen Brown, Purnal H. Baker, Elias Barcroft, William Baley, Frederick Bray, William Brown, Daniel Bower, Solomon Bonner, Amer Burnett, John Baker at Walnut Creek, John Core, Andrew Correll, John Corkrin, John Coffey, George Cramer, John Clark, Bozman Clifton, Nicholas Cunningham, John Cummons, John Cellers, Henry Clover, Jasper Chery, William Chandler, Daniel Crabb, Adam Cayler, Beel Cullum, John Chinnowoth, Jonathan Craig, John Cockran, Benjamin F. Cockran, Joseph Campbell, John Crain, Mary Camilin, John Collinsworth, Robert Corken, Nicholas Devolt, Moses Dimmitt, Catrin Dean, Aron Dawley, James Dannel, Valintine Donaldson, Jesse Dungan, Thomas Dickings, John Dixson, James Evans or Hugh Steward, Evan Evans, Doctor Edmison, Thomas Emmorson, Thomas Eddenfield, William Elsey, Alexander Enos, Benjamin Evans, George Emery, John Evans, Lemuel Evans, John Ford, John Flin, Jacob Fording, Thomas Farrell, Thomas Gillfillan, Thomas and William Goldsberry, Lewis Goodwin, Moses Gutery, James Garwood, Gudrich Giskin, William Gardner, Samuel Garrer, John Gamble, John Hanes, Samuel Hopkins, John Hays, George Hays, Daniel Handerson, Jacob Holderman, George Hayens, William Hall, James Harper, Benjamin Haines, Henry Hoshawr, James Hamilton, Moses Hutchings, Sarrah Hughs, Wm. Hason, William Holaday, Harness & Penick, Christian Hoffman, Robert Hoddy, Charles Hanger, Samuel Hargrave, Outy Hosey, William Huston, John Howard, Elizabeth Hendricks, John Harrod, Isaac Hollingsworth, Sarah Hanks in care of John Timmons, Samuel Hinksman, Robert Jones, William Johnston on Walnut Creek, William Jenkins, William Johnston in care of H. Massie, William Johnston in care of N. Pope, John Johnston in care of J. Hoge, Moses Jones, Mathias Ingle, Wider Johnson on Twin Creek, Thomas John, Jourdan Parker, Samuel Johnston, Robert Kerr in care of J. Tiffin, Paul Kingston, John Kight, Christian Krum, John Kent, Elizabeth King on Buckskin, James Higans, Jeremiah Kirkindall in care of Joseph Waugh, Aron Kindal, Valentine Knight, William Kent, Jacob Kishler or Daniel Baum, William Kerr, Joseph Koontz, David Kitterle, Tilman Lewis, Margret Lunbeck, Joseph Ladd, John Love, James Long, William Long, William or Charles Lott, Miss Catharine Leer, John Lewell, William Ligget in care of H. Brown on Pee Pee, Zachariah Linton, John Miller in care of L. Warner, Miss Jeny Murray, George Miers, Joseph Meeker, Miss Jane M'Kiman, James Moore in care of Capt. J. M'Donald, John M'Lain on Hay Run, William M'Bride, John Martin, Daniel Miller, Charles Millbanks, Francis M'Henry, Thomas M'Crackin, Andrew M'Beath, George or James Milligan, William Mobray, John Montgomery, John Mathews, Robert M'Mahan, Andrew Mickey in care of Doct. Duteing, Edmund Mare, William M'Nuttey, Pesse M'Kingle at Hellard's Bottom, George M'Can, Samuel M'Munn, Robert M'Apherson, Eli Nichols, Carlos A. Norton, Micheal Nunnamacker, Thomas Noland, William Nicol, Richard Osborn, William Odle, Sela Paine, Andrew Parkins, John Patterson, Samuel Patton in care of B. Urmston, John Parrill, Robert Pitt, John Picken, Uriah Pawlin in care of J. Carlisle, William Parks, Johnston Phares, William Robison, George Renick, Richard Reed, Polly Ramy, William Ritchey, William Reed, John Roberts, George Roback, Robert Sharp, Thompson Smith, John Sergent, Mary Smith, Esquire Sharp, Abraham Swarts, Samuel Swearingan, Thomas Sillik, Peter Sheaner in care of Col. D. M'Arthur, Frederick Steen, Henry Sharp, Curtis Smith, James Stanley, John Sotherland, Adam Stewart, Eli Sargent, John Smith, James Skigenes, John Scott (ten miles from Chillicothe), Revd. John Seward, Nicholas Sipperel, Charles Snyder, John Shippard, Thomas Smiley, Anne Stockton, Thomas Steward, John Sellers, Samuel Strane, Mary Scott in care of Doct. M'Adow, Edward Salts, William Shaw, Ezra Tubbs, Thomas Thompson in care of John Kerr, John Thompson in care of John Kerr, Warnel Tracy, William Tracy, Elizabeth Timmons, James Timmons, Heth Thomas and Joseph Heart, John Thomas, John Timmons in care of J. Collins, Stephen Taylor, Ebenezer Tuttle, John Todd, John Thompson, Edward Vernon, William Wilson, Samuel

Wallace, David Wilson, John Wright, Thomas White, William Warner, John Wast, Asal Wert, Peter West, Thomas Wilson at Foster Bottom, William P. Watson, Anthony Williams, George Williams, John Williams, George Willihn, Henry Whitley.

Jesse Spencer, Register of the Land Office at Chillicothe, has land for sale and mentions G. Green, S. Bingham, Ezekiel Bogart, William Young.

David Shepherd, sheriff, regarding the sheriff's sale of the property of Benjamin Miller at the suit of the commissioners of Ross County.

John Ernhard, in Livingston, regarding his blacksmith's business there.

William Daly, in Chillicothe, is a candidate for sheriff.

Gen. Samuel Finley is president, William Sterrett, cashier, and John Waddle, clerk, of the Bank of Chillicothe.

A note regarding the Scioto Bank Lottery mentions Mr. M'Coy, Mr. Irwin, Mr. Waddle, Mr. Woodbridge, Mr. Kinkead and Mr. Fullerton.

David Shepherd is a candidate for sheriff.

Ephraim Baits asks those indebted to him to pay William Creighton, sen.

H. Cassill, in Alexander township, Athens County, reports that John Halso and Isaac Pearson have appraised a horse found by Moses Sidim.

James Wright, in Wayne township, Adams County, reports that Benjamin Vanpelt and Thomas M'Coy have appraised a horse found by Stephen Clark.

George Frederick, in Green township, Ross County, reports that Peter Bunn and Nicholas Bunn have appraised a horse found by Andrew Crouch.

Joseph Tiffin, in Scioto township, Ross County, reports that Peter Spurck and Sam. Williams have appraised a horse found by Samuel Wallace.

Gen. Jer. M'Lene has orders for the Militia and mentions Thomas Lewis, Peter Porter, Edward Duff, Isaac Templin, Capt. Krider, Capt. Chesnut, Capt. Hall, Capt. Kilgore, Capt. Wilkinson, Capt. Raidliff, Capt. M'Clure, Capt. Taylor, Capt. Isaac Dawson, Capt. Ingle, Capt. Maracle, Capt. Thomas, Capt. Roberts, Capt. Weaver, Capt. Hopkins, Capt. Tomling, Capt. Stalcup, Capt. Lavett.

Ezekiel Brown, in Berkshire township, Delaware County, reports that David Welsh and John Patterson have appraised a mare found by James Harper.

James Wright, in Wayne township, Adams County, says that William Jackson and Samuel Williamson have appraised a mare found by Jacob Birtcher. Also Samuel Wright, jr., and Robert Wright have appraised a mare found by John M'Intire. Also James Odell and Robert Wright have appraised a horse found by William Morelan.

Wm. Rutledge, in Chillicothe, reports a stray horse.

Joseph Keana, of Chillicothe, has a land for sale including his brewery.

Wm. M'Farland, in Chillicothe, has a new shipment of goods for sale.

Wm. M'Dowell, in Chillicothe, reports a stray horse.

Wm. & James Irwin, in Chillicothe, have a new shipment of goods for sale.

Lewis Cass regarding a marshal's sale of the property of Samuel C. Vance.

Curtis Cannon, in Meigs township, Adams County, said that Thomas Thompson and Wm. Pemturton, Jur., have appraised a horse found by Andrew Smalley, sen.

Doctors Davis & Scott have a new shipment of goods for sale at their shop.

John Waddle & Company have land for sale, entered by Patrick Donalley.

William Loveless, administrator of the estate of John Loveless, late of Twin township, Ross County, dec'd, regarding the estate settlement.

Amzi Atwater reports that Phineas Perkins and John Blair have appraised a mare found by Ebenezer Sheldon of Aurora township, Portage County.

Samuel Evans, in Paint township, Highland County, reports that Joseph Knox and Jacob Easter have appraised a horse found by John Jessop.

Daniel Chesnut, in Scioto township, Ross County, reports that James Stinson and Levi Hodges have appraised a mare found by David Ogden, sen.

Benjamin Feurt, in Union township, Scioto County, reports that John Wright and George Feurt have appraised a mare found by Samuel Nicholas.

Volume VIII, Tuesday, 19 July 1808, No. 415

An unsigned letter regarding Gen. Worthington's candidacy for governor.

An account of the Fourth of July celebration at Worthington mentions Maj. James Kilbourn, Dr. Stephen Maynard, Capt. Abner P. Pinney, Capt. Joseph Sage, Dr. James H. Hills.

Duncan Morrison, of Union township, Belmont County, reports that Jacob Dovanbergar and Samuel Halloway have appraised a horse found by William Pindle.

William Whitten, of Tuskarawa township, Muskingum County, reports that Abel Cain and Andrew Libarger have appraised a horse found by John Hanson who lives about ten miles from the forks of Muskingum on White Woman Creek.

Polly Johnson, administratrix of the estate of Michael Johnson, late of Jefferson township, Franklin County, dec'd, regarding the estate settlement.

Alex. Holdin, of Licking township, Licking County, reports that Archibald Wilson and Patrick Cuningham have appraised a horse found by Ephraim Harriss of New Ark.

Henry Smith, of Hanover township in Licking County, reports that John Channel and John Hook have appraised horses found by William Barrick, junr., and Philip Barrick. Also John Radiliff and Samuel Varner appraised a mare found by Jonathan Simpson.

Volume VIII, Tuesday, 26 July 1808, No. 416

Thomas Kirker is a candidate for governor of Ohio. Henry Brush and Jessup N. Couch are candidates for representatives.

An unsigned letter to the editor regarding the upcoming election mentions Jer. Morrow, Thomas Worthington, Winn Winship, sen., Jessup N. Couch, James Dunlap, Samuel Monett, Abraham Claypool, John Crouse, Jer. M'Lene, Nathaniel Massie, Stephen Wood and Thomas M'Cune.

Charles Cissna, at Chillicothe, offers all his household furniture for sale as well as his house and lot.

Moses Byxbe, jur., regarding the petition of John Scribner, an insolvent debtor, in the Delaware County Court of Common Pleas.

Peter Jackson, of Deerfield township, Ross County, reports that Zacheriah Gillaspie and Edward Ulm have appraised a horse found by George Jameson.

Winney Webb, of Bourbon County, Kentucky, reports a slave named John who ran away from John Fisher in Lexington. He was last seen living with Thomas Knowles (or Noels) at Wills Creek in Ohio where he called himself Bob Knight. He also lived with Thomas Warren between Zanesville and Wills Creek.

Isaac Vore and Samuel Sharp, at St. Clairsville, administrators of the estate of Nicholas Bowers, dec'd, late of Belmont County, about the estate settlement.

Benjamin Urmston, at Chillicothe, has a house for sale, formerly occupied by Charles Thompson.

John Wallace reports that Jacob Davis and Robert Wallace have appraised a horse found by John Hampton who lives in Buckskin township, Ross County.

John Mathews, of Scioto township, reports that Michael Kingary and Alex'r. Scantlin have appraised a horse found by Robert M'Can who lives on the new Limestone Road, seven miles from Chillicothe.

Jacob Noel, in Union township of Scioto County, reports that James Black and Henry Spangle have appraised a horse found by Mechee Plowman.

Maps of Ohio by John F. Mansfield are for sale at the printing office.

David Shepherd, sheriff, regarding a sheriff's sale of the property of Benjamin Miller at the suit of the commissioners of Ross County.

Volume VIII, Tuesday, 9 August 1808, No. 418

James Wright, of Wayne township in Adams County, reports that Nathan Odell and Thomas Maxwell have appraised a horse found by Michael Moore.

John Pickett, of Mason County, Kentucky, reports a runaway slave, Nathan.

John Crouse, of Green township of Ross County, says that Samuel Jones and Isaac Whitser have appraised a horse found by Samuel Campbell, on Kinikinick.

Curtiss Cannon, of Meigs township in Adams County, reports that Timothy Mershon and Benjamin Mershon have appraised a mare found by Solomon Mershon.

Lewis Cass regarding the postponement of the marshall's sale of the lands of Samuel C. Vance.

Marriage: John L. Tabb married Miss Hannah Betz, both of Chillicothe, on Wednesday evening last.

Abraham Claypool declines the nomination for the legislature.

A note regarding the road from Cumberland to the Ohio River mentions Maj. Shepherd's and Mr. Champline's mills.

An unsigned letter to the editor mentions Dr. John Van Grout Skemmelpenick of Chillicothe, Gen. Worthington, Judge Huntington, Gen. Beecher.

An unsigned letter to the editor nominates persons for office: S. Huntington, P.

Beecher, Henry Massie, H. Brush, J.N. Couch, S. Monett, J. Dunlap, J. Collet, J. M'Lene, T. Steele, J. Mathews, N. Massie, J. Bigger and Gen. Wadsworth.

Bartholomew Fryat, at Chillicothe, is a candidate for representative.

William S. Hutt, collector for Ross County, regarding taxes due.

Duncan M'Arthur wants to rent his distillery. Also he wants to rent his saw mill and grist mill on the north fork of Paint Creek.

George Richards, in Highland County, reports that Ezekiel Kelly and Robert Branson have appraised a horse found by James Frame.

Conrod Fultz, living in Chillicothe, reports a stray horse.

Alexander Blair, in Jefferson township of Franklin County, reports that John Dyer and William Dyer have appraised a mare found by James Logan.

Peter Jackson, of Deerfield township in Ross County, reports that William Kenedy and John Timmons have appraised a mare found by Clement Brown.

Capt. James M'Donald, at Chillicothe, reports a deserter named John Warren, alias John Lawrel, age 29, a native of Ireland.

William Daly, of Chillicothe, is a candidate for sheriff.

Wm. M'Farland has a new shipment of goods for sale at his store.

David Shepherd is a candidate for sheriff in Ross County.

Volume VIII, Tuesday, 23 August 1808, No. 420

John M'Donald reports that he is a candidate for representative.

George Hays reports that William Williamson and William Denny have appraised a mare found by William Bearse of Ross County, Pickaway township. Also Samuel Denny and Matthew Ferguson have appraised mares found by George Sidenbender and Gabrial Stealy, both of Pickaway township.

John Ellison reports that Samuel Larimore and Nathaniel Collins have appraised a mare found by Alexander Rachford, of Adams County, Sprigg township. Thomas Burnet and Samuel Larimore appraised a horse found by James Lawson of Sprigg township.

Jesse Spencer and James Armstrong regarding the land certificate that Robert F. Slaughter lost. A duplicate has been issued.

John A. Fulton will survey land in the Virginia Military District.

John Contryman says that Martin Contryman and Henry Contryman appraised a horse found by Frederick Braucher of Highland County, Brush Creek township.

Jacob Newman, Joseph H. Larwill and James Hedges regarding lots for sale in the town of Mansfield in Richland County.

A note regarding the publication of the newspaper, "The Supporter", at Chillicothe, by George Nashee and George Denny.

Marriage: John M'Coy, merchant, married Miss Jane M'Crackin, both of Chillicothe, "on Tuesday evening the 23rd inst.", by Rev. Robert Willson.

Henry Massie is a candidate for senator, and Thomas White is a candidate for county commissioner.

Gen. T. Worthington gives general orders to the militia.

John Horner, at Salem in Trumbull County, reports that his wife, Nancy Horner, left him on July 6th, and he won't honor her debts.

D. Mitchel reports that Samuel Mitchel and Christian Sager have appraised a horse found by David Mitchel.

Bigger Head, in Brush Creek township of Highland County, says that William M'Laughlin and William Head have appraised a horse found by Parker Kelough.

Samuel Henry, in Seal township of Scioto County, reports that William Mustard and Jesse Williams have appraised a horse found by Samuel Star.

Samuel Huntington, George Tod, William Sprigg and R.J. Meigs, jun., at Marietta, regarding the Circuit Courts of Ohio.

Jer. M'Lene, in Chillicothe, is a candidate for sheriff. Wm. Creighton, senr., is a candidate for sheriff. M. Baldwin is a candidate for representative.

John Thompson has land for sale on Dry Run, nine miles from Chillicothe.

Charles Cade reports that George Reid and Robert Godfrey appraised a mare found by John Tevebaugh, living on Deer Creek, Deerfield township, Ross County.

Volume VIII, Tuesday, 6 September 1808, No. 422

Thomas Steel is a candidate for coroner, and John A. Fulton, representative.

Thomas White, in Union township, Ross County, reports that William Robinson found a stray mare.

Brown & M'Cort, in Chillicothe, regarding a note to John Enick, with George Bobts as security.

P. Lewis, Jun., in Jefferson township, Adams County, says that Jacob Sample and James Williams appraised a mare found by John Welsh on Scioto Brush Creek.

John Guthery, in Seal township of Scioto County, reports that David Murphey and John Hannaman have appraised a horse found by Hezekiah Merret.

Alexander Jolly, in Byrd township of Adams County, reports that Isaac Hughey and Peter Parker have appraised a horse found by John Philips.

An unsigned letter to the editor regarding the election mentions Jeremiah Morrow, Philemon Beecher.

An unsigned letter nominates Thomas Worthington, Jeremiah Morrow, Henry Massie, John A. Fulton, Henry Brush, Michael Baldwin, Samuel Monett, William Lewis, Jeremiah M'Lene and Thomas Steele for public office.

Capt. James M'Donald regarding the deserter, Benjamin Codinton, age 34, born in Essex County, New Jersey.

Humphrey Fullerton, in Chillicothe, asks those indebted to him to pay their bills as soon as possible.

Abel Lewis regarding the petition of Henry Carbeny vs. Thomas Boude and Abraham Mosser in the Muskingum County Court of Common Pleas. William Wells is appointed commissioner to transfer land to Carberry.

Joseph Darlinton and J.N. Couch regarding the suit of Philip Lewis, sen., vs. Benjamin Goodin in the Adams County Court of Common Pleas.

Alex'r. Curran & J.N. Couch about the suit, Elijah Glover vs. William Points.

Jacob Miller, in Gallia County, reports that Josiah Doddridge and Abraham Miller have appraised a horse found by William Holley.

John Cummings is a candidate for representative in the House.

James Parker reports that Richard Balison and James Jones have appraised a mare found by William Foosythe, living near the mouth of Red Oak Creek in Adams County, Huntington township.

Jacob Willenmyre, near the Pickaway Plains, regarding a horse that strayed or was stolen from Mr. Bowman's on Pickaway Plains.

Benjamin Beasley regarding land on Three Mile Creek entered by Timothy Peyton.

John Nichols, in Chillicothe, wants to hire a distiller.

Volume VIII, Friday, 23 September 1808, No. 424

Thomas White, on Dry Run, Union township, is a candidate for commissioner.

Seth Adams, at Jefferson on Wackatomaka Creek, has sheep for sale. Apply to Isaac Cook at Dry Run near Chillicothe.

John Karr, at Great Darby in Franklin County, reports two horses that strayed from White Brown's place on Deer Creek.

Cadwallader Wallace, in Chillicothe, has land for rent on Rattlesnake Creek.

Walter Dun, in Chillicothe, at W.H. Puthuff's tavern, administrator of the estate of Robert Means, dec'd, has land for sale. He also has the land of John Grayham and James Heron, dec'd, for sale.

E. Woods regarding the petition of Absolom Dille, an insolvent debtor, in the Belmont County Court of Common Pleas.

Peter Spurck, in Chillicothe, regarding the mare someone left with him.

Anthony Barnard, in Chillicothe, at Mr. Puthuff's tavern, about a stray horse.

Joseph Miller & Company ask those indebted to them to settle their accounts.

Benjamin Urmston, in Chillicothe, wants to hire apprentices to the tanning and currying business.

E. Woods regarding the petition of James Beard, an insolvent debtor, in the Belmont County Court of Common Pleas.

James Egan, saddle tree maker, from Winchester, Virginia, will make saddle trees at John Carlisle's store in Chillicothe.

Henry Chapman, in Clermont County, reports that Wm. Campbell and Fielden Martin have appraised a horse found by Edward Hall in Pleasant township and a mare found by William White in Pleasant township.

J. Russel, in Green township of Adams County, reports that Joseph Westbrook and Wm. Russel have appraised a horse found by Moses Beard.

Thomas Nisbet reports that Hugh Beard and George Olinger have appraised a mare found by Joseph Beard, living in Madison township, Muskingum County, about 12 miles from Zanesville on the road to Lancaster.

William Whitton reports that Robert Darling and Robert Giffin have appraised a mare found by John Concle, living in Tuskarawa township, Muskingum County.

An unsigned letter mentions Jeremiah Morrow & Philemon Beecher. Another letter mentions Gen. Worthington, Judge Huntington, Mr. Morrow, Mr. Tiffin.

Adam Kirkpatrick, in Wayne township of Adams County, reports that Samuel Milligen and John M'Neel have appraised a mare found by Thomas Quinn.

H. Cassill, in Alexander township, Athens County, reports that John Philips and Jacob Shry have appraised a horse found by Levi Johnson.

John Robins says he is a candidate for commissioner.

Zachariah Welsh reports that William Dickey and John Ross appraised a horse found by Jeremiah Asher, living on Walnut Creek, Springfield township, Ross Co.

David Boner is a candidate for coroner in the upcoming election.

David Boner, acting sheriff of Ross County, reports the polling places of the upcoming election and mentions A. Chinoweth in Pee Pee township, William Pillar in Mifflin township, Christian Plater in Paxton township, John Robins in Buckskin township, Mrs. Elliott in Twin township, Jerard Davis in Deerfield township, Mrs. Moor in Wayne township, John Popejoy in Concord township, the Presbyterian Meeting House in Union township, West Miller in Washington township, Jacob Stingley in Pickaway township, James S. Webster in Colerain township, John Crouse in Greene township, Capt. James Taylor in Jefferson township, William Niblack in Lick township, William Walace in Springfield township, Benjamin Foster in Franklin township, Sanford Carder in Paint township.

Nashee & Denny, in Chillicothe, regarding subscriptions to the Supporter.

Volume VIII, Monday, 12 December 1808, No. 429

Samuel Finley, Duncan M'Arthur, Nathaniel Willis, Isaac Cook, Nathaniel Massie, George Renick, Wm. Creighton, sen., John Carlisle and John Kerr regarding tickets for the Scioto Bank Lottery for sale by Thomas James.

William S. Hutt, collector of Ross County, has lots for sale.

David Kinkead & Company, in Chillicothe, ask those indebted to them to settle their accounts.

Martin Bartholomew, in Franklinton, administrator of the estate of Seth Noble, late of Franklin County, dec'd, regarding the estate settlement.

Lewis Cass regarding a marshal's sale of the property of Wm. M'Culloch, at the suit of Beckham and Reese. The land includes mills on the Big Miami in Butler County near Fort Hamilton. And the property of Samuel C. Vance.

Zacheriah Welsh reports that Samuel Hanson and John Russel have appraised some hogs found by Larry Rusell, living on Walnut Creek, Springfield township, Ross County.

Samuel Finley about a meeting of the stockholders of the Bank of Chillicothe.

Daniel Chesnut, of Scioto township, Ross County, reports that Joseph Kirkpatrick and Isaac Heaton have appraised a horse found by Hugh Cochran, sen.

Jacob Larrick, in Colerain township, Ross County, says that Gillian Ruse and Elisha Hornet appraised a horse found by John Dunkel on Salt Creek near Adelphi.

Joseph Miller says his partnership with William Porter is dissolved due to the death of Porter. The business is continued by Joseph Miller.

Hon. Samuel Huntington was sworn in as governor on the evening of December 12th. Hon. Return J. Meigs, jun., is appointed senator to replace John Smith. Jeremiah M'Clene is appointed secretary of state.

Election returns mention Samuel Huntinton, Thos. Worthington, Thos. Kirker.

A letter from Marietta regarding the election mentions Mr. Huntington, Mr. Morrow, Mr. Beecher, Mr. Woodbridge, Mr. Cutler, Doct. Jewett, Seth Fuller, J. Clark, E. Sproat.

John Woodbridge, in Chillicothe, regarding a meeting of the Scioto Lodge.

John Wallace reports that William M'Munn, jun., and Samuel Dean appraised a horse found by Samuel M'Munn, living in Buckskin township of Ross County.

Lewis Cass regarding a marshal's sale of the property of Lucas Sullivant, of Franklinton, at the suit of Samuel Meeker.

John M'Lanburgh, in Chillicothe, has a new shipment of goods for sale.

John Mathews, in Scioto township of Ross County, reports that Daniel Daleny and Adam Knowles have appraised a horse found by Ezekiel Knowles.

Eli Reeves, in Byrd township of Adams County, reports that Reuben Waits and Elijah Redman have appraised a mare found by David Lawwell.

Samuel Laramore says that because of "her extravagant conduct", he will not pay the bills of his wife, Catherine Laramore, out of debts due to him or to the estate of John Meggitts, dec'd.

John Woodbridge has just received a new shipment of goods at his store.

William Kilgore, in Buckskin township, Ross County, reports that Josiah R. Finch and James Harper have appraised a mare found by William Harper.

Benj. Urmston has land for sale, entered by Gen. Duncan M'Arthur, on Deer Creek adjoining James M'Nut. Also a house formerly owned by Charles Thompson.

Thomas Hardy, in Union township of Ross County, reports a stolen horse.

Isaac Evans, in Chillicothe, has lost several bank notes.

Davis & Scott ask those indebted to them to settle their accounts.

Nathaniel Reeves wants to buy cow's hides or calf skins at the shop of John Cutler, shoemaker, in Chillicothe.

Henry Musselman, in Springfield township, Ross County, reports that John Crider and Frederick Houck have appraised a horse found by Henry Crider who lives on the New Lancaster Road.

William Daly has land for sale on Hardin's Creek in Highland County.

Elnathan Scofield says that Richard Poland swears that his cabin burned down and a certificate of land, co-owned with Jacob Jackson, was lost.

Jesse Spencer, Register of the Land Office at Chillicothe, regarding a certificate to replace the one Richard Poland and Jacob Jackson lost.

John Sherer, in Chillicothe, has goods for sale.

Isaac Evans has sold his stock to John S. Snead who will continue the business.

Isaac Evans, in Chillicothe, regarding his lost bank notes.

George Haynes reports a runaway apprentice boy named Jacob Basteon.

Th. S. Hind and Ch. A. Stuart, in Chillicothe, have land for sale.

George Gibson has a house and lot for sale in Chillicothe. Apply to Humphrey Fullerton or to Peter Parcels at the Scioto Gazette office.

John Waddle & Company have a new shipment of goods for sale at their store.

James Crockwell regarding his new gunsmith business in Chillicothe.

James & M'Coy have a new shipment of goods for sale at their store.

David Kinkead & Company, in Chillicothe, have Burr's Trial for sale.

James Wright, in Wayne township of Adams County, reports that Thomas Maxwell and William Wright have appraised a horse found by Elias Boatman.

Volume VIII, Monday, 26 December 1808, No. 421

William Whitten says that Thomas L. Kerr and Andrew Lebergar appraised a mare found by Charles Williams, living in Tuskarawas township, Muskingum Co.

Samuel M'Colloch about a horse stolen from Thomas Barr's stable, Ross Co.

Peter Porter, administrator of George Porter, dec'd, who lately lived on the north fork of Paint Creek, 3 miles from Chillicothe, regarding the estate sale.

Jesse Lucas reports that Jonathan Boyd and Bosel Lucas have appraised a mare found by Daniel M'Ckaaihn, living on the waters of the rocky fork of Paint Creek, Paint township, Highland County.

John S. Snead has purchased the goods of Isaac Evans and has opened a store in the store room of Mr. Evans near the Eagle tavern.

Davis & Scott ask those indebted to them to settle their accounts.

Obed Denham, in Tate township of Clermont County, reports a horse stolen from his stable at Dunham's town by James Black, a deserter from Capt. Cutler's company at New Port, Kentucky.

Capt. E. Scott regarding a meeting of the Chillicothe Republican Blues at Mr. Irwin's tavern at the sign of the Green Tree in Chillicothe.

Notes regarding the impeachment trial of Calvin Pease mention the suit of E. Wadsworth vs. Sol. Braynard.

An unsigned letter to the editor regarding the appointment of Return J. Meigs, Jr., to the seat vacated by John Smith, resigned. Mentions Mr. Tiffin.

Samuel Finley, at Chillicothe, regarding the printing press Mr. Waddle bought in Philadelphia for the Bank of Chillicothe.

James Davenport, in Chillicothe, regarding his "conveyancing business". He can be found at the office of John M'Dougal.

Enoch B. Smith, in Liberty township of Highland County, reports that Robert Carson and James Fenner have appraised a horse found by Daniel Inskip.

Volume VIII, Monday, 16 January 1809, No. 424

Elie Williams and Thomas Moore, the commissioners of the road from Cumberland to Ohio, regarding the construction of the road, mention Joseph Kerr.

Notes about the impeachment of Judge George Tod and a statement by Alex. Campbell and Thomas S. Hinde of the House of Representatives are printed.

W. Woodbridge, in Chillicothe, is acting as agent for Elijah Backus, late of Washington County, Ohio, but now of Kaskaskia, to sell Backus' land.

Alexr. Curran and Saml. S. Crawford regarding the suit, in Scioto County, of Naomi Rector vs. Frederick Rector, her husband, for divorce on the grounds of cruelty.

Duncan M'Arthur regarding land Peter Porter is offering for sale as part of the estate of George Porter, dec'd.

James M'Dougal, in Chillicothe, offers his house and lot for sale.

The partnership of Ramus Davis and Joseph Scott is dissolved.

L. Cass regarding the sale of land, conveyed by John Guthry to his sons, at the suit of Edward Hart M'Donough vs. William Kelso and John Guthry.

John D. Wiley regarding people removing timber from the land on Paint Creek adjoining Adam Knoles' land.

Thos. Elliot, executor of the estate of James Dunlevy, dec'd, has land for sale, originally entered in the name of Samuel M'Cullough on Pee Pee Creek.

George Corwine reports that Eli Ragon and Gardner Jacks have appraised a horse found by James Longshore, of Franklin township, Ross County.

A list of letters left at the Post Office in Chillicothe includes John Anderick, Daniel Archer, Richard Acton, sen., Andrew Allison, Isaac Austin, David Augustis, William Armsted, Martin Armstrong, Isaac Austell, John Apling, William Bars, John Blair, Joshua Bahinger, Sidle Bender, William Billings, Micheal Beyerly, Richard Berry, Rev. Joseph Bennett, Augustus Brown, Jeremiah Brown, Mary Brown, Peter Brown, Saml. J. Brown, Benjamin Bocssean, Mr. Bata, Andrew Brunn, White Brown, David Bonner, Henry Bowell, David Baird, Christain Blocher, Frederick Bishop, George Benagh, Robert Breden, Joseph Bell, William Kent, Elizabeth Bowen, Charles Cade, Henry Clover, George Chapell, Barnabus Cochran, Joseph Chew, John Crouse, Alexander Caldwell, Thomas Carneal, Mary Camlin, Richard Cavet, James Curry, John Coffee, John Clouzer, Adam Caylor, William Carson, junr., Jacob Cox on Deer Creek, Racheal Culver, John Cellars, Alexander Cummin, Hugh Cochran, Capt. Edmund Clark, Elias Chestrester, William Connel, Doct. Daniel Drake, Thomas Dugan, William Daughson in care of James Phillips, Nicholas Devault, Doctr. Delano, Valentine Donaldson, Aaron Dawley, John Dawley, John Dickson, Mosses Dimmit, Henry Downs, Anthony Donnis, Joseph Elsso, junr., John Exline, John Evans, Samuel Ervine, Doctr. Edmison, Mrs. Echart, Joseph Essix, junr., Samuel Evans, James Ewings, John France, David Ford, Christopher Fry, David Feiks, Elisha Fitch, Conrod Flush, John Fulton, Charles Franklin, Hugh Forsman, John Gillisbie, Mrs. Clander Green, Robert Graham, Thomas Gray, Andrew Glaze, John Greer, Alexander Geague, Peter Hacket, Daniel Hoffman, William How, Frederick Houck, Thomas Hurst, Samuel Harrey, Joseph Hays, William Hudson, John Harison, James Hamilton, George Hown, Ashel Heath, Rev. James Hoge, Henry Hester, Elisha Harrison, Everard Harr, James Hughey, Heth Hart, Joseph Honducks, Thomas Jones, Lawrence James, Alexander Irwin, John Johnston, William Johnston, Cornelius Johnston, James Johnston, Abraham Jones, John Joabe, Isaac Johnston, Gabriel Kyle, Samuel B. Kincart, Daniel Kolly, Micheal Kingrey, John Knight, David Kniseley, Ths. & Benj. Kue, Mosses Latta, Genl. W. Lytle, Edward Long, Joseph Lightfoot, Betsey E. Lawnes, Andrew Linzes, Elias Lovett, John G. Macan, David M'Ilvain, Doct. Thomas Massie, Robert Mackey, Hon. Samuel M'Kee, John E. Morgan, Barbara Millar, Cornelius Mannan, David Mawthews, John M'Dougal, Joseph M'Clintock, Elizabeth Mastin at Greenfield, David Mitchel, E. Middleton, Jesse Mounts, Elizabeth Mineos, Jesse M'Kinsey, Elisha Maning, Samuel M'Munn, William M'Intosh, Mandwelle Moren, John Massete, Peter M'Mickle, Joshua M'Farling, William Nichols, Christain Nicholas, John Newman on Brush Creek, Isaac Oyston, Jacob Ott, Sally Points, Absolom

Parker, William Pierson, William Price, Catherine Patton, Hugh Poore, Nathan Popejoy, John Pikens, Prentes Park, John Peppers, James Port or John Port, Benjamin Radliff, Felix Reneck, James Runix, Margaret Ritchey, William Rogers, Daniel Ross, Thomas Rankin, Lewis R. Rogers, Micheal Rore, Samuel Reeves, George Ramsey, William Snodgrass, George Sargent, George Segler, William Shannon, John Snapp, Lawrence Shirley, Micheal Senff, Henry Snider, Nicholas Stickle, Thomas Stothard, Nicholas Shultate, Ruben Strong at Sessor's-vill in Ohio, John Sherrer, David Sears, Andrew Simermon, Stephen Timmons, John Thompson, Micheal Thomas, John Timmons, Samuel Teters, Thomas Todd, Mrs. Fanny Thompson, Israel Thompson, Seth Thompson, Isaac Tindle, John VanGundy, John Vandement, John Williams, Joseph Woodrow, Isaac Warner, John Watson, William Wilson, Drussella Welsh, Andrew Wilson, Daniel Weyer, James Webster, John Walker (blacksmith), John Whaley, Samuel Wyokoff, James Widner, William Worthington, Joseph William, Joseph Tiffin.

John Martin regarding his baking business in Chillicothe. He says he started his baking business in Chillicothe three years ago.

Samuel Monett, in Chillicothe, asks those indebted to him to pay their bills.

Robert Kerr, living on the northwest fork of Paint, two miles from Chillicothe, reports a stray mare.

Jane M'Quality and John Ireland, administrators of the estate of Owen M'Quality, dec'd, asks those indebted to the estate to make payment at Mr. Keys'.

Joseph Kerr, near Chillicothe, wants to buy staves for pork barrels.

P. Lewis, jun., in Jefferson township, Adams County, says that William Baker & David Thomas appraised a horse found by William Womsley on Scioto Brush Creek.

Volume VIII, Monday, 23 January 1809, No. 425

Alexr. Curran regarding several suits in the Scioto County Court of Common Pleas: Owen Davis vs. John Wood; Mr. Henderson & Mr. Calhoun vs. Patrick Donnally; and Stephen Simmons vs. Peleg Canady. Mentions the attorneys William Creighton, junr., John Tompson, and Saml. S. Crawford.

A note regarding the acquittal of Judge Tod. Also extracts from the trial of impeachment against George Tod are printed and mention Mr. Creighton, Mr. Cass, Mr. Brush, Mr. Morris, Mr. Campbell, Mr. Hough, the case of M'Faddon vs. Rutherford, Justice Hough, Mr. Pritchard, Mr. Looker, Mr. Monett.

John Gillfillan and Samuel M'Quilkin, in Chillicothe, have dissolved their partnership in the shoemaking business. Gillfillan will continue the business.

A list of the winning tickets in the Scioto Bank Lottery.

Daniel Frally, in Liberty township of Highland County, reports that William C. Scott and Tho. Fitzpatrick have appraised a horse found by Matthew Creed.

Wm. Keys, living on Main Paint Creek, 3 miles from Chillicothe, offers his land for sale.

Enos Prathers, in Pe Pee township of Ross County, reports that Eli Sargent and William Sargent have appraised a mare found by David Lewis.

Volume VIII, Monday, 30 January 1809, No. 426

A note regarding allegations made by the editor of the Supporter regarding the answer of Judge Tod to the impeachment trial. Includes Judge Tod's plea and mentions Benjamin Rutherford, Daniel M'Faddon, Justice Hough of Steubenville.

A note regarding the impeachment trial of Judge Pease.

A letter from Hon. John Bigger about the impeachment trial of George Tod.

George Caley, in New Market township of Highland County, reports that Moses Patterson found a stray mare.

Ezekiel Brown reports that Enoch Dunagin and Clark Beeby have appraised a mare found by Oliver Still, living in Sunbury township of Delaware County.

Nehemiah Gates reports that Jacob Johnston and John Johnston have appraised a horse found by Calvin Cary, living on Big Darby Creek in Jefferson township of Franklin County.

Adam Kirkpatrick, in Adams County, reports that Nathaniel Reed and Thomas Young have appraised a mare found by Andrew M'Intire, living in Wayne township.

Wm. Davis reports that Elias Layton, sen., and Wm. Thornsburgh have appraised a mare found by Asher Layton, living on Morgan fork of Sunfish in Mifflin township of Ross County.

Volume VIII, Monday, 6 February 1809, No. 427
The conclusion of Judge Tod's plea in his impeachment trial.
Marriage: Wm. Saddler married Miss Nancy Porter, both of Ross County, on Thursday last, by Rev. John Collins.
A note regarding Hon. John Bigger's vote in Judge Tod's impeachment.
A note regarding the impeachment of Calvin Pease mentions Judge Tod.
James Moore reports that Larence Ramsey and Adam Selman have appraised a horse found by John Glendening, living in Byrd township of Adams County. Also George Beard and Abraham Shepherd have appraised a horse found by Joseph M'Kinley, living in Byrd township of Adams County.
James Martin, in Washington township of Ross County, reports that Thomas Waddle and John Morris have appraised a mare found by Jacob Shoup, junr.
Jesse Spencer, Register of the Land Office, has land for sale and mentions Danl. M'Kinney, Jacob Strouse, Abm. Peters, Samuel Landes, John Stalda, John Sharp, Robert Cloud, Jonathan Holmes, Jesse Hedges, Edmund Ingman, Jacob Marks, Jno. Marks and William Kennel.
Samuel Rittenhouse, living on the north fork of Paint Creek, reports a runaway apprentice to the tanning business, Samuel Ruff, age 16.
John Harrs, in Jefferson County, Kentucky, wants to hire a teacher.
Bigger Head, in Brush Creek township of Highland County, says that Thomas Edingfield and William Backen have appraised a mare found by Peter Moore.
Samuel Finley about the election of Directors of the Bank of Chillicothe.
Daniel Fraley, in Liberty township of Highland County, reports that William C. Scott and Tho. Fitzpatrick have appraised a horse found by Matthew Creed.

Volume VIII, Monday, 13 February 1809, No. 427
Obituary: Hon. Jesse Phelps, an associate judge for Geauga County, age 47, died very suddenly "of the apoplexy", on 10 January 1809 at Painsville.
Obituary: Maj. George Painter, age 59, died on 5 February 1809 at Zanesville. "He was for many years past an inhabitant of Burlington, ... New Jersey, and about seven months ago, moved with a small family of hopeful children to this place, in order to carry on his former business, that of brewing." He served in the Revolutionary War.
A letter from C. Hammond, Lew. Cass, Jesup N. Couch, Wm. Woodbride, Henry Brush and Wm. Creighton, junr., regarding the acquittal of Judge Tod.
An unsigned letter to the editor regarding the recent letter by Hon. John Bigger mentions Judge Tod.
Robert Whiteside, at Chillicothe, reports a strayed or stolen horse.
John Greere, in Warren township of Belmont County, reports that Harman Davis and Demsey Balden have appraised a horse found by Richard English.
George Darrow, junr., of Hudson in Portage County, administrator of John Ross, late of Hudson township, dec'd, regarding the estate settlement.
John R. Connell reports that Seth Foster and Abner Foster have appraised a mare found by Alexander M'Nutt, of Sprigg township, Adams County.
Jacob Shoemaker, in Clear Creek township, Fairfield County, says that John Zehring and Jacob Helm, sen., have appraised a cow found by Henry Matthias.
Frederick Linseninger, in Chillicothe, wants to sell his house and lot on Second Street, opposite Mr. Betz's tavern and near the Presbyterian Meeting House.
Stephen M'Dougal and Edward Herrick regarding the petition of Jonathan Simpson, an insolvent debtor, heard in Licking County Court of Common Pleas by Hon. William Wilson, Timothy Rose, Alexander Holmes and James Taylor, associate judges.
Jonathan Menshal reports that Andrew Cyssherd and Elias Barcraft appraised a mare found by Elias Langham, living in Union township of Franklin County.
Henry Porter reports that John Parks and George Santee have appraised a mare found by Hugh Finley of Twin township in Ross County.
Archibald Guthery, Aron Guthery, Moses Guthery and Joseph Guthery regarding the ad placed by Lewis Cass to sell land taken in the suit of Edward Hunt M'Donough vs. William Kelso and John Guthery.
Enoch B. Smith, in Liberty township of Highland County, reports that George Richards and Ezekiel Kelley have appraised a horse found by Robert Branson.
John Partimore, living about a mile from Chillicothe, reports a stray mare.

Jacob Shoemaker, in Clear Creek township of Fairfield County, reports that John Marks and Jacob Marks have appraised a cow found by Henry Mare. Also John Parcels and Nicholas Thomas have appraised a steer found by Thomas North.

Volume VIII, Monday, 27 February 1809, No. 429

Samuel Huntington, commander in chief of the militia of Ohio, writes a letter of general militia orders to Gen. Thomas Worthington. Gen. T. Worthington writes a letter to the militia regarding the orders.

Alexr. Campbell and Thomas Kirker print a new law of the state of Ohio.

A note about "Thomas Miller, son of John Miller, of Lancaster County, Va., a young man who has been long absent, and supposed to be in the state of Ohio."

Obituary: Andrew M'Kee, merchant of St. Clairsville, age 21, died on 9 February 1809, after an illness of 24 days. "This young gentleman was a native of Pittsburgh, and had only been a few months established in business..."

John M'Dougal is now a Notary Public for the town of Chillicothe.

George Corwine reports that Michael Robinson and Andrew M'Curdey have appraised a mare found by Richard Foster of Franklin township in Ross County.

William Williamson, living in Pickaway township near the road to Lancaster, 12 miles from Chillicothe, in Ross County, reports a stray mare.

John Evans, in Wayne township of Ross County, says that Jonathan Craybell and William Beaty have appraised a mare found by Philip Hoofman. Also Daniel Bender and Ebenezer Betherds appraised a horse found by Enos Knight.

Daniel Chesnutt reports that James Stinson and Charles Mitchel appraised a horse found by Charles Chesnutt, on Indian Creek, four miles from Chillicothe.

Arthur O'Harra, in Franklin township of Franklin County, reports that Thomas Thomas and Nicholas Houghn have appraised a horse found by Jonathan Morgan, about two miles from Franklinton.

Henry Chapman, in Clermont County, Pleasant township, says that Abraham Sells and William Ellis have appraised a mare found by Alexander Hill. Also James Melone and Cain M'Kiney, jun., appraised a mare found by Cain M'Kiney.

Curtiss Cannon reports that Nicholas Fry and George Rodgers appraised a mare found by James Hemphill on Brush Creek in Meigs township, Adams County.

John Stump, of Jefferson township in Scioto County, has land for sale.

Michael Beyerly, at Chillicothe, offers his house, furniture and lot for sale.

Samuel Lucas, in Scioto County, administrator of the estate of John Brewer, late of Scioto County, dec'd, regarding the estate settlement.

Charles Cade, in Deerfield township of Ross County, reports that John Page and James M'Cafferty have appraised a horse found by Samuel Myns. Also Samuel Myers and John Page appraised a horse found by Stephen Barton.

Zachariah Welch, in Springfield township of Ross County, reports that Jonathan M'Clure and William Linton have appraised a mare found by Zachariah Linton. Also Philip Waldren and George Engle have appraised a heifer found by John Argubright. Also Zachariah Linton and Benjamin M'Neale have appraised a mare found by Jonathan M'Clure. Also Benjamin Smith and John Suck have appraised a steer found by Adam Cates, living on Dry Run.

John Millikan, in Colraine township of Ross County, reports that George Will and Reuben Zerkins have appraised a mare found by John Bunn, living in Adelphi.

John Ferguson, in Chillicothe, regarding a strayed or stolen mare.

Volume VIII, Monday, 6 March 1809, No. 430

A letter from Edward Tiffin in Washington is printed.

An account of a meeting of the citizens of Muskingum County at Zanesville mentions George Jackson and Samuel Herrick.

Maj. Gen. Duncan M'Arthur gives division orders for the militia.

John Russel, in Green township, Adams County, reports that William Webb and John Eakins have appraised a mare found by William Cole.

John Greaves, in Jefferson township, Ross County, reports that James M'Call and John Redfearn have appraised a horse found by John Coon on the state road two miles from Moffitt's Mills.

Volume VIII, Monday, 20 March 1809, No. 431

William Wallace reports a runaway apprentice to the saddler's business named

James Baker, age 18.

Henry Musselman, in Springfield township of Ross County, says that William Carson and Jonathan Rothrauf have appraised a cow found by James Thompson.

John Smith reports that Robert Alhine and Joseph Powel appraised a mare found by John Oxford, living on Possom Run, Franklin County, Pleasant township.

William Whitten, in Muskingum County, Tuscarawas township, says Abel Cain and Charles Williams appraised a horse found by Hugh Eddy, living on Wills' Creek.

Henry Culp and Abraham Miller, at Lancaster, executors of Christian Miller, late of Pleasant township, Fairfield County, dec'd, about the estate.

William M'Farland has a new shipment of goods for sale at his store.

A note regarding Hon. Edward Tiffin in Congress.

Adam Betz wants to lease the Indian King Tavern in Chillicothe.

Moses Byxbe, jun., regarding the petition of Ebenezer Welch, an insolvent debtor, in the Delaware County Court of Common Pleas.

Daniel Symmes, Register of the Land Office, Cincinnati, regarding land for sale, mentions James Welsh, David Reed, Lawson M'Cullough, Robt. Patterson, Win. Blackburn, John J. Dufour, David Long, John VanNuys, Isaac Gildersleve.

William Raynolds, at Zanesville, Muskingum County, innkeeper, regarding a letter he received accusing Richard M'Bride, Andr. M'Bride and James Fleehort of robbery. The letter is signed by J.R. Johnson in West Union, Ohio.

Benjamin Tupper, at Zanesville, clerk of the commissioners of Muskingum County, regarding building a new county court house.

Ramus Davis says his partnership with Joseph Scott is dissolved. Joseph Scott has purchased the stock of medicines and will continue the business.

John A. Fulton, Chillicothe, will survey land in the Virginia Military District.

Asaph Stebbons about his dancing school in Mr. Meeker's Hall in Chillicothe.

Isaac Vanmeter, in Ross County, reports a runaway apprentice to the farming business, Joseph Scott, age 17-18.

David Rees, at Gallipolis, Gallia County, administrator of the estate of John Henry Entsminger, late of Gallipolis township, dec'd, about the estate settlement.

Brown & M'Court, at Jefferson, at the Pickaway Plains, about a stud horse.

Volume VIII, Monday, 27 March 1809, No. 432

Marriage: Rev. William Monett married Mrs. Mary Ann Smith, both of Chillicothe, on Saturday evening last, 25 March 1809, by Rev. Thomas Scott.

Samuel Finley, at Chillicothe, regarding the Academy.

Jeremiah M'Lene, Secretary of State, at Chillicothe, regarding new districts.

Thomas Dick, living on the main road from Chillicothe to Cincinnati, 14 miles east of New Market, offers his land for sale.

Thomas White, in Wayne township, Ross County, about land he bought from Abel Westfall, adjoining Westfall's land.

Moses Byxbe, Jun., regarding the petition of Elam Vining, an insolvent debtor, in the Delaware County Court of Common Pleas.

Robert Smith, in Union township, administrator of the estate of Martha Smith, late of Union township, Ross County, dec'd, about the estate settlement.

Isaac Pavey, in Highland County, lost a pocket book on the road between Jos. M'Coy's and Chillicothe.

Enos Prather, in Peepee township, Ross County, reports that Thomas Wiley and Samuel Ridgeway have appraised a mare found by David Lewis.

William Spencer, in Reding township, Fairfield County, reports that James Dean and Samuel Ramsey have appraised a cow found by John Ramsey.

John Parker, in Mifflin township, Ross County, reports that Joseph Moore and George Grove have appraised a mare found by Gabriel Beckman, living on Morgan's fork of Sunfish, Mifflin township. Also Isaac Peniston and Michael Grove have appraised a horse found by Frederick Grove, living on Morgan's fork of Sunfish Creek. Also Joseph Moore and George Grove appraised a horse found by William Beckman, living on Morgan's fork of Sunfish.

George Caley, in New Market township, Highland County, reports that Samuel Hindman found a stray horse.

Henry Waugh, in Ohio township of Gallia County, reports that John Sloane and Wm. Ross have appraised a horse found by George Waugh.

John Russel reports that Nathaniel Foster and Morgan Young have appraised a mare found by William Russel of Green township in Adams County.

John Julin, in Clear Creek township of Fairfield County, reports that Windel Bonner and Martin Lauders have appraised a horse found by Jacob Ditzler.

Wm. Byers, in Nile township of Scioto County, reports that John Asa and Charles Burton have appraised a mare found by Joseph Horner and Stephen Lewis.

Volume VIII, Monday, 24 April 1809, No. 434

Curtiss Cannon reports that James Boyd and Peter Platter have appraised a horse found by Joseph Horn, in Meigs township, Adams County.

David Mitchell, William Gabriel and John Taylor, auditors of the suit of James Galloway, jr., vs. Alexander Karr, will meet at David Mitchell's on Darby.

Wm. Creighton, sheriff, regarding sheriff's sales of the property of George Emrey, sen., at the suit of George Renick. Also the property of Elias Langham at the suits of James Speed and Nathaniel Anderson.

Marriage: Dr. Edward Tiffin married Miss Polly Porter, formerly of Delaware, on Sunday, 17 April 1809.

A note regarding Judge Pease's trial.

Gen. Th. Worthington reports that William Creighton and Henry Brush are appointed aids-de-camp to the Governor.

An unsigned letter to the editor mentions Mr. Carlisle, the Quakers, the Presbyterian Church, Mr. Wilson.

A list of letters left at the Post Office in Chillicothe includes Manna Aliail, John Aberna, David Augustas, Joseph Adamson, John Arthars, Vallentine Angel, Pleasent Arthers, Gersham Anderson, John Andericks, Richard Acton, White Brown, Clement Brown, Joseph Bell, William Kent, John Borris, John Baum, Mary Baum, Alexander Billsland, William Brown, William Badley, John Berry, Rasanah Bogs, William B. Bailay, Alexander S. Bartley, Samuel Ballenger, Jackson Brown, Job Broughton, Nichols P. Carr, Gidion Coover, Daniel Crabb, Beel Colem, David Clark, George Clark, Andrew Cummins, James Colwell, Jonathan Craig, Shederick Cole, Robert Cunningham, Noah Clark, Rev. John Collins, Joseph Campbell, William Caldwell, John Chenoweth, Lydia Cox, John Campbell, George Chapple, Mary Curtes, John Cissna, John Clark, Israel Crow, Nichols Devault, Mrs. Dyson, Chapman Denslaw, Amasa Delana, Jesse Dungan, Valentine Donaldson, John Day (Williamson County, Ohio), Alexander Enos, Evan Evans, Richard Evens, Samuel Evans, John T. Evans, John Emmit, Lemuel Evins, James Evans, John Fraley, George Fry, William Forst, Hugh Forseman, Christly Fry, Thomas Fawcett, James Fliming, Henry Forman, Robert Gamble, Philip Griffith, John Gunday, John Gossom, Reubin Gore, Jacob Grim, John Hutton, William Hutt, John Hamilton, Joseph Hendricks, Elisabeth Hendricks, Robert Holladay, Ashel Heath, Samuel Hurford, James Hains, Henry Hains, Jared Hill, Heny Henson, John Hall, James Henderson, Thomas Hicks, Anthony Hall, Mr. Heth, Thomas Hart, Thomas Irwin, Benjamin Jones, George Johnston, John Jackson, Zachariah Jeanes, James L. Johnston, Charles Johnston, William Johnston, Micajah Johnston, John Justices, Gabril Kyle, Ephraim Klimper, Ezekiel Knowles, John Kees, Valentine Keffer, Wm. Kinan, George Lees, Elias Lovete, Benjamin W. Ladd, James Larkins, John Lane, Andrew Little, Elisha Letler, Widow Lafferty, Samuel Myers, Peter Marks, John Millone, Dudley Millenee, Anthony Miller, Susannah Madden, Thomas M'Neal, Thomas Massie, Michael Miler, John M'Lain, Robert Martin, Abraham Miller, Capt. Robert M'Farland, John M'Connell, John M'Cullough, Joseph M'Coy, Thomas M'Coy, Rees M'Neal, Dennis M'Connel, John Mielimans, Henry Niceleson, Jacob Nivergall, Henry Nelzle, John P. Neal, John Newman, William Oldfield, John Peppers, William Pittenger, William Pattin, Isaac Pancake, James Potts, Reuben Parceil, Casper Piyley, Nathaniel Parker, Nehemiah Phillips, Joel Riely, Mary Robinson, Thomas Rogers, William Rutledge, William Rankins, Samuel Rittenhouse, George Richey, John Rodgers, Daniel Radcliff, James or John Ruck, James Roberts, William Records, Benjamin Severen, Curtis Smith, David Sayrs, Lloyd Selby, William Sprigh, John Sharp, Thomas Stockton, Robert Steel, George Sidenbender, Michael Sniff, Serice Smith, Lemuel Sayers, Isaac Snyder, Robert Shields, George Smith, William Townsand, Townsand Taylor, Stephen Timmons, John Timberlake, Ezra Tubbs, John Trego, James Trego, Orms Thomas, Martin True, Samuel Taylor, John Thomas, John Timmons, Joseph Taylor, J. Thompson, Alexander Underwood, Barnet Vankirk, Benjamin Williams, John Watson, Thomas Walker, Samuel Watt, John White, William Wilson, Leven Willaughbay, Walter Watson, George

Wood, Joseph Wilson, John Queen, Samuel or Ephraim Quinby, George Ziglar or Barnet Foreman, Peter Yeakey. Entered by Joseph Tiffin.

John M'Dougal and Abraham J. Williams about a writ of attachment obtained by Burgess Elliott for the property of John Williams in the Ross County Court of Common Pleas. Includes a list of Williams' property taken by William Creighton.

Caleb Hitchcock, in Wayne township, Scioto County, reports that John Brown and William Huston have appraised a colt found by Uriah Barber.

John Martin offers his house on Water Street, Chillicothe, for sale.

Lucas Sullivant, in Franklin County, regarding the petitions of Ephraim Bonham, Joshua Burton, John G. Dewitt and Christopher Marquis, insolvent debtors, in the Court of Common Pleas of Franklin County.

Thomas Arnold, Tax collector for Union township, Scioto County, has land for sale at Elijah Glover's house in Portsmouth, Scioto County.

John T. Barr & Company, Chillicothe, regarding their store in the house formerly occupied by J. & C. Furguson.

William Jordan, in Harrison township, Franklin County, about a stray mare.

Benjamin Urmston regarding a stud horse at the stable of Thomas Craycraft in Union township.

John Robinson, in Union township, weaver, asks those indebted to him to settle their accounts.

Joseph Miller, Chillicothe, reports two stray horses.

Volume VIII, Monday, 8 May 1809, No. 436

Obituary: William Saddler, age 62, died on Sunday last.

Ann Towns, the sole heir of John Towns, dec'd, by her agent Peter Mills, has paid redemption money for land in Franklin County that was sold to Duncan M'Arthur, James M'Donald and George Corwin.

Abel Lewis and S. Herrick (attorney) regarding the petition of John M'Donald, an insolvent debtor, in the Muskingum County Court of Common Pleas.

Joseph Jefferies, in Ross County, asks those indebted to pay their bills.

William Wells and Christian Spangler (of Zanesville) about the suit of Moses VanWinkel vs. Thomas Romans in the Muskingum County Court of Common Pleas.

David Boggs, in Gallipolis, administrator of the estate of James Boggs, late of Gallia County, dec'd, regarding the estate settlement.

John Hubbard says his wife, Mary Hubbard, left him at the advice of "some of her connections by marriage", and he will no longer honor her debts.

Preslay Morris, at Mr. Fitch's tavern, regarding a horse that strayed or was stolen from the plantation of Zadock Pursel.

Job Dinning, in Adams County, reports that John Barrill and David Duncan have appraised a horse found by James Brown of Tiffin Township.

Arthur Oharra, in Franklin township, Franklin County, reports that John Rodgers and John Ashbough have appraised a horse found by James M'Ilvain.

William Robinson reports that James Menary and James Cochran have appraised a horse found by William Rogers, of Union township, Ross County.

Joseph S. Collins & Company will print cards, hand-bills and pamphlets.

Frederick Overly, administrator of the estate of Eve Overly, widow, dec'd, regarding the estate settlement.

John Evans reports that Robert Shurly and Jacob Tittle have appraised a horse found by Anthony S. Devenport, of Wayne township. Also White Brown and Robert Shurly have appraised a horse found by Thomas Rains.

Samuel Monett, William S. Hutt and John Martin, trustees of the estate of Lowder Cannon, dec'd, regarding the estate settlement.

Isaac VanHorn, at Zanesville, administrator of the estate of Maj. George Painter, dec'd, of Zanesville, Muskingum County, regarding the estate sale.

Lewis Cass regarding the marshal's sale of the property of Samuel C. Vance.

Volume VIII, Monday, 29 May 1809, No. 439

A letter to the public regarding the bank of the Scioto River at Chillicothe mentions Mr. Day's blacksmith shop on Water Street.

Enos Prather, in PeePee township, Ross County, reports that Eli Sargent and William Ward have appraised a horse found by George Sargent.

John Sherer has a new shipment of goods for sale at his store in Chillicothe.

Peter Jackson, in Deerfield township of Ross County, reports that James Smith and Charles Shockley have appraised a mare found by Thomas Nolin, sen.

William Henry Harrison, at Vincennes, Indiana Territory, revokes his power of attorney to Jesse B. Thomas that authorized him to sell land in Ohio belonging to the estate of John F. Hamtramack, dec'd.

John M'Dougal, in Chillicothe, has the laws and journals of the late General Assembly ready for distribution.

Samuel Henry reports that William Mustard and Richard Cartar have appraised a mare found by Jacob Elsworth of Seal township, Scioto County.

George Teter, administrator of the estate of Daniel Teter, late of Ross County, dec'd, regarding the estate settlement.

John Johnston, in Franklin township, Ross County, reports that Thomas Foster and George Johnston have appraised a mare found by Yose Ragon.

John L. Tabb wants to hire an apprentice to the cabinet making business.

John Edmiston wants to close his business and asks those indebted to him to settle their accounts. He also has whiskey for sale.

James Foster has started a book binding business in Chillicothe in the house lately occupied as a store by James Ferguson.

John Parker reports that Isaac Peniston and Joseph Moore appraised a mare found by George Peniston, living on Morgan's fork of Sunfish, Mifflin township.

John Lodwick, in Adams County, administrator of the estate of Samuel Larimore, dec'd, regarding the estate settlement.

John T. Barr & Company have a new shipment of goods for sale at their store.

William Creighton regarding a sheriff's sale of the property of Daniel Hollinger at the suit of John Mathews.

Sandy Smith & Caleb Lewis dissolved their partnership in the sawing business.

George Smith, in Franklin township, Ross County, near the Big Bottom, reports a strayed horse.

Enos Prather, in PeePee township, Ross County, reports that William Word and William Acton have appraised a mare found by Snowden Sargent.

John Greave, in Jefferson township, Ross County, reports that William Odle and William Darby have appraised a mare found by John Odle, living on the state road, three miles from Moffit's mills.

John M'Dougal has land for sale near Chillicothe.

W. Byers, in Scioto County, reports that John Moore and Solomon M'Coll have appraised a horse found by John Moor, living on the Ohio River, twelve miles below the mouth of the Scioto River.

Volume VIII, Monday, 5 June 1809, No. 442

Peter Jackson, in Deerfield township, Ross County, reports that James Smith and Charles Shockley have appraised a mare found by Thomas Nolin, sen.

A note regarding the case of an alleged rape of Mary Ireland.

Dudley Woodbridge, Jesup N. Couch, John P.R. Bureau, Benjamin Tupper and Rufus Putnam, trustees of the Ohio University, say the building is now ready at Athens and students will be admitted. Rev. Jacob Linley, the instructor, was educated at Princeton.

Thos. James and John M'Coy have dissolved their partnership. John M'Coy will continue the business at the same store.

John M'Dougal, Chillicothe, reports a strayed or stolen horse.

Robert Culbertson, in Franklinton, wants to rent the public house, now occupied by Thomas M'Collum, at the sign of the Green Tree.

John Chapman, in Meigs township, Adams County, reports that Jacob Bratton and William Davis have appraised a mare found by John Morris.

Adam Turner, in Chillicothe, reports a stray horse.

Joseph Tiffin, in Scioto township, Ross County, reports that Charles Cissna and William Groves have appraised a mare found by William Chandler.

Thomas Orr & Company have started a copper and tin plate working business at the corner of Water and Mulberry Streets in Chillicothe, in the house formerly occupied by Isaac Evans, merchant. They have copper stills and boilers for sale.

John Grave, in Ross County, reports that John Cox and John Redfearn have appraised a mare found by Jesse Redick.

John Guthery, in Pee Pee township, Ross County, reports that Archd. Guthery and Joseph Guthery have appraised a horse found by Caleb Huff.

Volume VIII, Monday, 12 June 1809, No. 443

Obituary: Maj. John Belli died at his home in Scioto County on 10 June 1809.

A letter to the editor regarding Gov. Huntington's appointment of Stanley Griswold as senator in Congress to replace Hon. Edward Tiffin who resigned. Mr. Griswold is originally of New Hampshire and late of Connecticut and has lived in Ohio less than a year.

An account of an accident in Millford township, Butler County, on Sunday morning, 28 May 1809, in which Isaac Simpson was killed in his well. His wife's father, Matthias Richardson, and her two brothers came to help rescue Simpson and the two brothers were also killed.

John Woodbridge regarding a meeting of the Scioto Lodge.

John Waddle and John Carlisle say that their partnership will expire soon and ask those indebted to settle their accounts. They also have a new shipment of goods for sale at the store of John Waddle & Company in Chillicothe.

Wm. Creighton, sheriff of Ross County, regarding a sheriff's sale of the property of Jervis Cutler at the suit of Martin Blake and Alexander Dix.

Thomas Steel regarding a marshal's sale of the property of Tunis Newkirk at the suit of John Myles.

John Evans, in Wayne township, Ross County, reports that Robert Sherly and Philip Hoofman have appraised a mare found by White Brown, jun.

William Trimble, in Pleasant township, Fairfield County, reports that Jacob Horsman, junr., has found a stray horse. Also Robert Sturgeon found a mare.

Dr. John Hamm has a new shipment of medicines for sale at his shop in Water Street, Chillicothe, near the Eagle Tavern.

John M'Landburgh has a new shipment of goods for sale at his store.

Charles Willing Byrd, in Adams County, living at Buckeye Station, on the Ohio River, 12 miles from Limestone, offers his land for sale. Apply to Gen. Massie, Lawyer Creighton, Henry Massie and Joseph Kerr, all in Chillicothe, or to Gen. Darlington of West Union.

Job Dinning reports that Darby Sulivin has found a stray horse.

Peter Jackson, in Deerfield township, Ross County, reports that John Baker and Joseph Timmons have appraised a mare found by John M'Lean.

Jno. Russel, in Green township, Adams County, reports that George H. Puntany and William M'Laren have appraised a mare found by Josiah Stout.

Henry Carberry gives notice to Thomas Boude and Abraham Mosser that he will apply to the court for a partition of their land in the Military Tract.

Gen. Jeremiah M'Lene regarding a meeting, at Maj. James Kilgore's house, of the Militia in order to replace Col. Wm. H. Puthuff who moved out of the district.

John Turner, in Pleasant township, Franklin County, reports that Samuel Kerr and James Johnston have appraised a mare found by John Kerr on Darby Creek.

David Shelby, in Pickaway township, Ross County, reports that William B. Gould and William Young have appraised a horse found by Thomas Emmerson.

Samuel Niblack, Constable of Lick township, Ross County, reports that Aaron Friend, arrested for horse stealing, escaped from him at James Kilgore's house. He was about 35 years old and formerly lived on Racoon Waters.

Thomas Nisbet reports that John Baird and James Baird have appraised a horse found by William Kaufman in Madison township, Muskingum County.

Volume VIII, Monday, 26 June 1809, No. 445

David Kinkead & Company have a shipment of goods for sale at their store.

An artist is at Forrest Meeker's tavern, at the sign of the Red Lion, Chillicothe, and will paint portraits and do profiles.

Peter Spurck offers for sale the Green Tree Tavern in Chillicothe.

William Robinson carries on the cabinet making business in the shop formerly occupied by Wm. Wallace on Paint Street, Chillicothe.

William Duval, administrator of William Price, dec'd, has 3 tracts of land for sale by order of the Franklin County Court of Common Pleas. One tract adjoins Seymore Powel and Saml. Seldon; another adjoins John Nelson; and the third was located for Thomas Frazer on Boke's Creek.

The Scioto Gazette wants to hire an apprentice to the printing business.

Aeneas Foulk, in Bainbridge, wants to rent a hatter's shop and tools.

Amos Evans and George Wilson, living on Clear Creek in Highland County, agents for the heirs of John Wilson, dec'd, have land for sale in Chillicothe.

Thomas Nisbet reports that Thomas Beard and James Wimp have appraised a mare found by Joseph Beard in Madison township of Muskingum County.

Thos. White, in Union township, Ross County, reports that William Robinson has found a stray mare. Also, Thomas Withgott found a horse.

James M'Cluer, in Pickaway township, Ross County, reports that Robert Miller and Talmage Ross have appraised a horse found by John M'Cutchan.

Zechariah Welsh reports that Abraham Doll and Charles Asher have appraised a mare found by Richard Melone, Jr., living in Springfield township, Ross County.

Joseph Heistand, in Liberty township, Fairfield County, reports that George John and Martin Cofman have appraised a mare found by George Longbrake.

D.M. Kenney reports that Samuel VanHook and John Corn have appraised a mare found by James St.Clear of Nile township, Scioto County.

An unsigned letter regarding Stanley Griswold's appointment to fill Edward Tiffin's office. It says Griswold was editor of a paper in Walpole, N.H., and "his native state" of Connecticut. He also served as secretary of Michigan Territory. He now lives on a farm at Cleveland with his family.

Samuel Huntington, Henry Brush and Wm. Creighton, jun., say that Joseph Kerr, of Chillicothe, is appointed adjutant and inspector-general of the Militia.

Bigger Head, in Brush Creek township, Highland County, reports that William Head and Kendel Bradford have appraised a mare found by David Irons.

Robert Grayham, in Franklin township, Ross County, reports that Samuel Corwine and William M'Conkle have appraised a horse found by Thomas Grayham. Also William Russel and John Traughmon have appraised a mare found by Jacob Hoover.

John Perkins, in Colerain township, Ross County, reports that Nathan Merchant and George Reid have appraised a horse found by Tevault Hickle.

Peter Jackson, in Deerfield township, Ross County, reports that William Bready and David Hardy have appraised a mare found by Canaley Vass.

Henry Musselman, in Springfield township, Ross County, reports that John Gryder and Jacob Byerly have appraised a horse found by James Wallace.

M. Dickey, in Jefferson township, Franklin County, reports that William Johnson and Philip Sidenor have appraised a horse found by Nicholas Moore. Also George Jones and Wm. Jones have appraised a horse found by Vestall Blair.

John Cutler, boot and shoemaker, in Chillicothe, has calf skins for sale.

William Trimble, in Pleasant township, Fairfield County, reports that Jacob Horsman, junr., has found a stray mare.

John O'Ferrall, in Cincinnati, offers a reward for information on William Geo. Bray, a native of Great Britain, a tanner and currier, who came to Ohio or Kentucky last spring from Pittsburg.

James Clark, in Jefferson township, Scioto County, reports that John Clark and Jesse Vincent have appraised a horse found by Samuel Henry, living on Sun-fish Creek in Seal township.

John Chapman, in Meigs township, Adams County, reports that Jacob Bratton and William Davis have appraised a mare found by John Morris.

Volume VIII, Monday, 10 July 1809, No. 447

John Hutt and Saml. Williams print a copy of John Hamm's speech, delivered on the Fourth of July.

An account of the Fourth of July celebration at Col. James Dunlap's house in Union township, Ross County, mentions William Robinson, Thomas M'Coy, Gen. Worthington, Gen. Duncan M'Arthur, Gen. James Manary, Maj. John Willett, Richard Stanton, Mr. Jenkins, Gen. Thomas Worthington.

Daniel Symmes, Register of the Land Office at Cincinnati, has land for sale that had been applied for by Robert Willson and Dennis Pottinger.

Wm. M'Farland, in Chillicothe, has stock of the Miami Exporting Company for sale at Nathan Gregg's house on Water Street in Chillicothe.

A list of letters left at the Post Office at Chillicothe includes David Archer, William Askew, Jacob Armitage, Jacob Adams, William Anderson, William Ankrom, Leonard Armstrong, John Brittain, Capt. John Bennett, Allen S. Bartley, William

Butler, Philip Beal, David Baggs, Sarah Blane, Joshua Baxter, Joseph Burk, John Bryan, Jeremiah Bush or D. Comstock, Christopher Baker, Michael Bush, sen., David Baird, Mary Baum, Peter Van Boskirk, James Blain, Henry Bunn, Joshua B. Brewer, Jonathan Blanden, Thomas Bartley, Thomas Barrit, Mr. Bradley (attorney), Benjamin Brackney, Henry Baker, James Bryant, John Burns or James Long, Sarah Burt, Solomon Beeding, Samuel Cochran, Joseph Clemens, Hugh Cochran, Beel Colem, John Cunningham, John Combs, Joseph Chizem, William Coutch, Henry A. Christian, Gidion Coover, Christopher Cox, William Chandler, Cornelius Conrod, Michael Conger, Joseph Dix, Joseph Davidson, Moses Dimmitt, John Drennan, John Doddridge, Randolph Darth, Thomas Darslinger, Isaac Dawson, David Dawson, Luke Decker, William Dickey, Thomas Dugan, Thomas Davidson, James Devanport, Richard Diline, William Dixson, Col. John Evans, Montgomery Evan, Joseph Essex, Benjamin Ermsten, Conrod Foltz, David Fairlow, Peter Frederick, David Ford, John Flinn, John Free, William Fliming, Agness Fleming, James Ford, Thomas Goldsberry, James Gibbs, Zacheriah Griffey, John Grimes, John Gundy, jun., John Gabraith in care of Gen. Findley, Jesse German, John Gossom, Daniel Green or Daniel Davoss, Levi Godwin, Jacob Gundy, John Gardner, John Holyergrass, Henry Huffman, Jacob Weston Harden, Wm. Hudson, William Hanaman, James Hanies, John Hamson, Levi Hays, Elizabeth Hill, William Highland, George Hays, Benjamin Hill, Andrew Haines, Jacob Holderman, William Holloway, Elizabeth Holloway, Henry Hester, Mary Hoover, Lieut. Michael C. Hays, William Hampton, John Haines, Samuel Huston, Henry Hosletter, Samuel Hall, John Johnston, Joseph Jones, George Ish, Abraham Inskeep, Joshua Inskeep, James Inskeep, John Jobe, Jacob Keefer, Capt. John Beach, Ezekel Kelly, Samuel Kerr, Henry Kirkendall, Thomas Kerney, Ben. Kendrick, Josiah Kilbourn, Jacob Ladd, Robert Long, Henry Long, John S. Langham, Wood Loyd, Frances Lawrence, Uriah Lowther, Frederick Lininger, Thomas Leyrand, John M'Neil, Richard E. Mead, Martha M'Clintick, James Moore, Francis M'Henry, Archibald M'Donald, Joseph John Martin, Thomas Mitchel, Joseph A. Morton, Samuel M'Cormick, Joseph M'Coy, Joseph Morris, Ezekial Morris, Joshua Mitten, William Millar, Robert M'Ginnes, John M'Donald, William Mason, Martha Michel, William M'Machen, William M'Bride, Alexander M'Clean, Joseph Moore, Otho Norriss, Jacob Newman, Jacob Nebergal, John Nickans, Peter Noel, Prentis Park, John Perrell, Philip Putman, John Pricker, James Philips, Silas Prior, Henry Turney, Ebenezer Petty, Joseph Petty, Joel Ryley, Joseph Russell, Anthony Ridenour, Mathias Ritenour, Richard Rowe, Joseph Reynolds, Daniel Radcliff, George Reed, William Rodgers, John Rodgers, Rev. James Robinson, John Reeker, Alpheus Rowley, Jean Reed, Elizabeth Reams, Catea Riller, Barey Robinson, Thomas Reynolds, Alexander Robinson, Felix Renick, Benjamin Reed, Thomas Roberts, John Stockton, Nichols Simmerman, Permenius Smallwood, Jacob Shepherd, Peter Snyder, John Sargent, Jacob Strouse, Samuel Smith, Benjamin Sanders, George Snyder, Samuel Starks, Benjamin Shockley, Nicholas Stickell, Asaah Stevenson, Peter Shaner, Robert Smith, Henry Smith, Nichols Siberell, John Rippy Strane, Capt. Philip Mortemer Stars, John Sherer, John Sillick, John Scott, White B. Smith, George Squires, John Snap, Michael Thomas, James Thompson, David Thompson, Jacob Thomas, Ezra Tubbs, Samuel Tod, Hannally Vass, Isaac Virdin, John West, Thomas Wright, James Wright, Samuel Watt, Sally Watts, Andrew Willson, Richard Willits, Samuel Wilson, James Withrow, Jacob Wagner, John Work, Thomas Wiggins, Alexander White, James Widner, Jacob Widner, William Watson, John White, Thomas White, James Wallace, Ann Worthington, Isaac Warner, Benjamin Williams, Thomas Ward. Entered by Joseph Tiffin.

    Levin Belt, at Chillicothe, offers Mr. Sprigg's house on Main Street for sale.
    Duncan M'Arthur gives the division orders to the Militia.
    Jesse Spencer, Register of the Land Office, Chillicothe, has land for sale entered by Peter Hush, Ebenezar Larimer, John Roads, Henry Culp, Anthony Weaver, William Lucas, sen., Joseph Babb, John Elder, Philemon Beecher, Edward Irwin, Benjamin Waddle, Jacob Dittoe, M. Baldwin, E. Rector, Frederick Leather, Richard Harper.
    Nathl. Massie, in Chillicothe, regarding the ad placed by William Creighton, sheriff, about the sheriff's sale of the property of Jervis Cutler in Bainbridge at the suit of Martin Blake and Alexander Dix.
    Thos. Steel has postponed the sale of the property of Tunis Newkirk.
    Saml. Finley, in Chillicothe, regarding the Bank of Chillicothe.
    J. Douglass reports that James Welch and William M'Ilvain have appraised a

horse found by David Walgmot, living in Tuscarawas County, Oxford township.

John Turner, in Pleasant township, Franklin County, reports that Samuel Kerr and James Johnston have appraised a horse found by John Kerr on Darby Creek.

Eli Reeves, in Byrd township, Adams County, reports that Wm. Cuttraugh and Jonas Shreaves have appraised a horse found by Andrew Foot.

Jesse Lucas, in Paint township, Highland County, reports that Joshua Lucas and Henry F. Mires have appraised a mare found by Bowten Summer, living on the waters of Rocky fork of Paint Creek, eight miles from Hillsborough.

James Williams, in Adams County, reports that Jacob Sample and Michael Freeman have appraised a mare found by James Sandeson.

John Ellison, in Sprigg township, Adams County, reports that Abraham Watson and Van Brady have appraised a horse found by Philip Cole and Charles Larsh.

Capt. E. Scott regarding a meeting of the Chillicothe Republican Blues.

Volume VIII, Monday, 17 July 1809, No. 448

James Moore reports that James Moore, jun., and John Brown have appraised a horse found by Lewis Beble, in Tiffin township, Adams County.

Joseph Hopkins reports that Jacob Shobe and John Miller have appraised a horse found by Andrew Rice on the North fork of Paint, 18 miles from Chillicothe.

Nathan Ellis, in Huntington township, Adams County, reports that Math. Campbell and Hugh Power have appraised a mare found by James Bonner, opposite Limestone.

An account of the Fourth of July celebration at Worthington mentions Lieut. Col. J. Kilbourn, Doctor Stephen Maynard, Capt. Joseph Sage, Lieut. Levi Pinney, James Russel, Judge Thompson.

An account of the Fourth of July celebration at Zanesville mentions Capt. Samuel Thompson, Samuel Herrick, Maj. William Reynolds, Richard Reeve, Col. Isaac VanHorn, John Matthews.

An unsigned letter to the editor mentions Mr. Griswold and Gov. Huntington.

Isaac Evans, in Chillicothe, has a new shipment of goods for sale at his store.

John M'Dougal has a new shipment of goods for sale at his store in the house lately occupied by Brown & M'Cort, on Water Street, near the Market House.

Duncan M'Arthur, near Chillicothe, reports a strayed mare. Deliver to John Ross near the head of Deer Creek.

Volume VIII, Monday, 7 August 1809, No. 451

Th. S. Hinde has military lands for sale and mentions Dr. Wm. Brown, George Gilpin, John Stokes, Benjamin Boisseau, W. Carter, A. Forbornes, Holland Hand, Richard Kennon, Philip Slaughter, John Pride, James Jenkins, Edward Dorose, James Galloway, jun., Benjamin Biggs, Jno. Holmes, Benjamin Beisseau, Henry Massie, Mr. Spain, Lewis Booker, Miles King, John Biggart, L. Booker, Thomas Lemming, Henry Bowyer, Abraham Buord, James Sargeant, Gideon Minor, Wm. Payne, Thomas Martin, Wm. Brownlee, Capt. Joseph Parret, John Edwards, George Friskett, Smith Snead, John Marks, John Countryman, Henry Gaines, George Hethe, James Coleman, Charles Symmes, Lucas Sullivant, Benjamin Telliaferro, Quaker settlement, Thomas Martin, Mr. M'Kibbon, John and James M'Allister, Matthew Rhea, John Barbee, Wm. Mountjoy, Robert Green, Mallory's survey, Daniel Duval, Peter Mulenburgh, Thomas Posey, Robert Patterson, Andrew Dunscomb, James Merewether, John Belfield, Isaac Webb, Wm. Parson, Thomas Shelton, John Peyton, F. Frazier's heirs, William Price, Seymour Powell, Samuel Seldon, John Nelson, John Roberts, Achilles Perkins, Samuel Haw, Thomas Really, Thomas Fenn, Obediah Smith, Mr. M'Konkey (living on Langham's Trace from Chillicothe to Urbanna), Alex. Peters, John Campbell's heirs, Wm. Waters, John Kean, Lawrence Butler, Robert Armstrong, Samuel Smith, Wm. Washington, Col. Guthridge, Wm. B. Wallace, Dr. Geo. Monroe, Levin Joyns, James Curries, A. Murray, Wm. Brownlee, Capt. Parret, Gen. Morgan, John Marshall, E. Mead, Alex. Belmain, Theo. Bland, John Tench, George Baylor, Edward Dowse, Wm. Quarles, George Franciscos, John Ritchie, Robert Nourse, Bixbee's Settlement.

A letter to the editor nominates Duncan M'Arthur, Edward Tiffin, Thomas Worthington, James Dunlap, Isaac Dawson and Samuel Monett for public office.

John Haines, living in Chillicothe, reports a stolen horse.

John Julien, in Clear Creek township, Fairfield County, reports that Henry More and Stephen Julien have appraised a horse found by Christian Souglar.

John Green, in Morgan township, Knox County, administrator of the estate of Isaac M'Clary, dec'd, regarding the estate settlement.

John Contryman says that Martin Contryman and John Rhoad have appraised a horse found by Frederick Braugher in Highland County, Brush Creek township.

James Johnston reports that Henry Thurman and Caleb Reese have appraised a horse found by Jonas Stafford in Fairfield township, Highland County.

William Whitten, at Tuscarawa, says that Thomas L. Keer and Elijah Newcom appraised a mare found by Charles Williams in Tuscarawa, Muskingum County.

Thomas Evans, living five miles west of New Lancaster, about a stray mare.

A notice regarding the Scioto Bank Lottery.

Volume VIII, Monday, 11 September 1809, No. 456

Wooly Coonrod, in Washington township of Ross County, has land for sale near the mouth of Walnut Creek on the road from Chillicothe.

James D. Shelton, agent for the heirs of Lawrence Trant, dec'd, have put up redemption money for the land bought by Nathan and Robert Gregg, William Buchannon, John Obannon, James Buchannon, George Brown, Robert M'Knight, Duncan M'Arthur, Nathaniel Willis, Jacob Wheeler, John S. Wills, Thomas Needham, James Ferguson.

Elijah Spurgeon reports that Samuel Spurgeon and Dorsey Mayson have appraised a mare found in Bloom township, Fairfield County.

Blackall Stephens, "saddle, cap and harness maker, lately from New York", has opened his shop in Cincinnati near the Columbian Inn.

Samuel Marshall, in Franklin township, Scioto County, reports that Adam Shunkwiler and Daniel Shunkwiler have appraised a horse found by Jesse Marshall.

John Julien, in Clear Creek township, Fairfield County, reports that Rene Julien and Henry More have appraised a horse found by James M'Clelland.

John Overdear, in Franklinton, has opened a house of public entertainment.

Jos. S. Collins, in Chillicothe, executor of Clemt. Brown, dec'd, who lately lived on Limestone road near Samuel Turner's tavern, about the estate sale.

James Foster has moved his book binding business to a new house.

Abel Lewis and W. Silliman (attorney) regarding the petition of Elijah Brall, an insolvent debtor, in the Muskingum County Court of Common Pleas.

John Greave, in Jefferson township, Ross County, reports that Benjamin Cox and Joseph Moffitt have appraised a horse found by Robert Wilkinson.

Francis Nichols asks those indebted to him to settle their accounts.

Justice Millar and James Marshall, auditors of the case of Joseph Foos vs. Michael Spanglar in the Franklin County Court of Common Pleas, will meet at the house of David Breathington in Franklinton.

A letter about the election mentions Duncan M'Arthur, Edward Tiffin, Samuel Monett, James Dunlap, Joseph Gardner, John Thompson and John Matthews.

Daniel Wilson and James Bain, at Xenia, Ohio, write a letter to the editor.

William M'Farland has a new shipment of goods for sale at his store.

Edward Miller, in Union township, Gallia County, reports that Edward Simmons and John Johnson have appraised a mare found by James Wilson.

James Moore reports that James Brown and Edward Hemphill have appraised a mare found by Daniel Con, living in Tiffin township, Adams County.

Thomas Lloyd, taylor and habit maker, has opened his shop in Mr. Miller's building, lately owned by James Johnston, taylor. Lloyd mentions his long practice of his profession both in England and America.

John Cummins, Union township, Ross Co., is a candidate for representative.

Thomas Steel offers the land of Thomas M'Cullough for sale in a marshal's sale, the result of the suit of Beckham & Reese.

Peter Jackson, in Deerfield township, Ross County, reports that Lewis Messick and Alexr. Gillaspie have appraised a mare found by Baynard White.

More nominations for office mention Duncan M'Arthur, Edward Tiffin, Nathaniel Massie, Samuel Monett, James Dunlap, Isaac Dawson, Joseph Gardner.

Volume VIII, Monday, 25 September 1809, No. 458

Wm. Creighton, sen., sheriff of Ross County, reports the polling places for the upcoming election and mentions A. Chinwith in Pee Pee township, Wm. Pillars in Mifflin township, Widow Combs in Bainbridge in Paxton township, John Robbins in

Buckskin township, Mrs. Elliott in Twin township, David Yates in Deerfield township, Mrs. Moore in Wayne township, John Popejoy in Concord township, David Corbett in Union township, West Miller in Washington township, Jacob Stingley in Pickaway township, Peter Goodman in Adelphia in Colerain township, John Crouse in Green township, Capt. James Taylor in Jefferson township, William Niblack in Lick township, Benjamin Foster in Franklin township, Daniel Boyer in Springfield township, Sandford Carder in Paint township, George Jamison in Madison township.

John T. Barr & Company have books for sale.

John Millar, in Jefferson township, Ross County, says he will no longer honor the debts of his wife, Elizabeth Millar, because of her adultery.

An unsigned letter to the editor mentions Joseph Kerr and Gen. Massie.

Marriage: James G. Gray, late of Huntington County, Penn., married Mrs. Eleanor Middleton, of Ross County, on Monday evening last, 18 September 1809, by Joseph Tiffin.

Marriage: John Hunter married Miss Margaret Moore, daughter of William Moore, all of Chillicothe, "on Sunday evening the 19th inst."

Marriage: James Bonner married Miss Ann Stubbs, both of Chillicothe, on Friday evening last by Rev. Mr. Wilson.

Maj. Joseph Campbell is a candidate for representative. John A. Fulton is also a candidate for representative. More nominations include Gen. Duncan M'Arthur, Doctor Edward Tiffin, Col. James Dunlap, Joseph Gardner, Doctor Samuel Monett, John Thompson (clerk of the Chillicothe bank), John Hutt.

Wm. Clancy, stone cutter, has opened his business in Chillicothe. Apply to Jacob Paisals, shoemaker, now living in the house formerly occupied by Doctor Edmiston on Water Street in Chillicothe.

Benj. Urmston, in Chillicothe, reports a horse that strayed from near White Brown's house. He was formerly owned by William Read (living 4 miles northeast of Franklinton) and John G. Macan (of Chillicothe).

Michael Fisher, in Montgomery township, Franklin County, says that Thomas Johnston and Joseph Shrom have appraised a horse found by Michael Beard.

W.H. Puthuff, at Jefferson, regarding the horse races at Pickaway Plains.

David Mitchel, in Darby township, Franklin County, reports that Samuel Mitchel, sen., and Samuel Robinson appraised a mare found by James Robinson.

Charles Cade reports that Simon Hornback and William Abit have appraised a horse found by John Redden in Deerfield township, Ross County.

Jno. W. Millar, for Seal and Jefferson townships, Scioto County, reports that Dennis Murphy and Jacob Groniger have appraised a horse found by David Murphy.

John Perkins, in Colerain township, Ross County, reports that Peter Bunn and William Thompson have appraised a horse found by Ross Nelson.

John G. Macan, in Ross County, reports that someone stole a certificate for land, grants to Matthew Ritchey, from the house of James Ritchey.

John Cummings, in Union township, is a candidate for representative.

Volume VIII, Monday, 2 October 1809, No. 459

A letter to the editor gives nominations for public office and mentions Gen. Massie, Gen. Kerr, Judge Sprigg, Duncan M'Arthur, Edward Tiffin, Samuel Monett, James Dunlap, John Thompson, Joseph Gardner. Another letter mentions Duncan M'Arthur and Joseph Kerr. Another letter mentions Gen. M'Arthur. Another letter mentions John Thompson. More letters mention James Dunlap, Edward Tiffin, Gen. Duncan M'Arthur, Samuel Monett, John Thompson, Joseph Gardner, Maj. Joseph Campbell, Nathaniel Massie, John A. Fulton, Isaac Dawson.

Col. John M'Donald is a candidate for representative.

David Bonner, Tax collector for Chillicothe, regarding taxes due.

Zachariah Welsh reports that Zachariah Linton and Abraham Doll appraised a mare found by James Redman, living in Springfield township, Ross County.

Christian Benner reports that Talbott Ward and James Tuthill have appraised a horse found by Christian Platter in Paxton township, Ross County.

Jacob L. Eckett reports that Samuel Shellenberger and Frederick Duncurg appraised a horse found by John Roads living in Beaver township, Fairfield County.

Volume VIII, Monday, 9 October 1809, No. 460

Marriage: George M'Cormick married Miss Fanny Armstrong, both of Ross

County, on Thursday evening last, by Rev. James Davisson.

Joseph Kerr writes a letter to the editor regarding the letters about him.

An unsigned letter to the editor mentions Nathaniel Massie and Joseph Kerr. Another letter mentions Gen. Worthington. Another letter mentions Dr. Hamm.

Jesse Spencer, Register of the Land Office in Chillicothe, has land for sale and mentions Peter Aller, Joel Kendall, Matthew Campbell, Winn Winship, Frederick Zimmerman, John Crist, Caleb Hitchcock, Elnathan Scofield, John Graham, Christian Hoover.

Jacob Newman, James Hedges and Joseph H. Larwill have lots for sale in Mansfield at the house of Samuel Martins.

Joseph S. Collins, executor of the estate of Clement Brown, dec'd, regarding the estate settlement.

Jesup N. Couch, in Chillicothe, is not a candidate for public office.

Joseph Kerr reports that the horse races at Pickaway Plains are cancelled.

A list of letters left at the Post Office in Chillicothe includes Charles Adensen, Joseph and Isaac Adamson, William Alhire, William Arksom, Michael Byerley, John Bushong, George Bender, Eliza Blain, James Blain, Purnal H. Baker, David Berry, James Bramble, Joseph Bell, Adam Bowers, Capt. Henry Brown, John Briney, Miss Elizabeth Butler, Daniel Bailey, Moses Blann, Curtis Berry, Elijah Bartley, Hugh Commons, Alexander Cummen, Hugh Cockran, Phineas Curwin, Abraham Claypool, Isaac Claypool, John Clingman, Solomon Campbell, Hugh Carson, Mary Camlin, William G. Cantrell, Jeffery Cox, James Cissna, Stephen Cissna, Henry A. Christian, Samuel Coal, James M'Cartney, Joseph Crouch, Levy Clark, Charles Clifton, John Crouse, Thomas Davidson, Jesse Dodd, John Dovenberger, Henry Due, William Dixson, J. Downing, Samuel Denny, James Daniel, James Dunlap, William Dutton, George Davis, Nicholas Devalt, Hezekiah Davis, Samuel Daniel, Col. John Evans, John Exline, Abner, Esrey, George and Adam Engle, George Emrey, Thomas Edmanson, John A. Fulton, Alexander Fleming, Andrew Featherchild, Alexander Fulton, George Fry, Eneas Foulk, Jacob Foy, William Gordon, sen., James G. Gray, Hugh Ghormley, John Gordy, Mr. Golds, Robert Gordon, Andrew Galer, Marcus Heylin, John How, William Holloway, Peter Harper, William Hopkins, William Adams, Thomas Hinton, sen., Levi Hays, Thomas Hardy, William Hiett, James Huston, James Hendrix, Christian Hartes, Sally Hardy (wife of Samuel Hardy), Thomas C. Henry, Joseph How, John Holmes, William Hanaman, Robert Hudson, William Hill, Moses Jones, Jared Irwin, Samuel Johnston, John Johnston, John James, Lemuel John, John Knigh, William Karns, Elison Ladd, Joseph Lane, Andrew Leist, Zachariah Linton, Francis Lindsey, John M'Mullen, Eleanor Middleton, John G. Macan, Robert M'Farland, William Morgan, John Morgan, Thomas Martin, Jesse Millikan, William M'Bride, William Moore, John M'Cullough, Jesse Miller, Robert M'Mahan, Hannah Minshal, Samuel M'Connel, Charles Miller, John E. Morgan, Thomas C. Nutter, David Maddus, Robert Morrison, William Ogden, Mordecai Odel, Peter Moore, James and Alexander M'Kown, Peter Nichols, Henry Nickelson, Miss Isabella O'Faukne, Henry Porter and B. Turner, James Potts, Doctor Printes Parks, John Priddy, Stephen Price, George S. Parker, James Proud, Jesse Pigman, William Parcels, William Price, Joshua Porter, Nehemiah Phillip, William Polen, Felix Renick, James Readman, Thomas Ross, Magdalain Ross, William Rogers, Mathias Ridenour, Alexander Robinson, Jane Reed, James Rogers, James Robinson, Alpheus Rowley, Margaret Ritchey, William Ross, Charles Roberts, John Reiley, John Rush, Conrod Reety, John Ryley, John Roads, Joseph Rion, John Robins, Robert Shirley, John Stockton, Jonathan Spyker, Simon Shover, Lawrence Shirley, Hugh Scott, Jacob Shepherd, Abraham Stooky, James Seeds, Joseph Sweringen, Charles Snider, John Shearer, Jacob Snider, William Shew, George Santer, John Scott, John Stow, Aleander Stow, Samuel Smith, Thomas Smith, Peter Sturm, Joshua Speak, John Shoub, John Sharp, William Spriggs, John Salyers, Abraham Swarts, John Tolbert, William Turner, Jacob Thomas, Isaac Taylor, Henry Taylor, Judge Todd, Samuel Todd, William Townsend, Henry Torn, George Vance, John Vandermont, Edward Willcox, James Watt, Andrew Wilson, Moses Wilk, George W. Weight, Ezra Walker, Joseph Williams, Thomas Williams, Leven Wroughtor, James Wallas, Parker Warren, Isaac White, Jonathan Watkins, Robert Whitesides, Rev. Jacob Young, John Zent. Entered by Joseph Tiffin.

Volume VIII, Monday, 16 October 1809, No. 461

Marriage: Samuel Williams to Miss Eliza Armstrong, both of Chillicothe, on

Monday, 16 October 1809, by Rev. John Collins.

Election returns mention Duncan M'Arthur, Joseph Kerr, John M'Donald, John Matthews, James Dunlap, Edward Tiffin, Joseph Gardner, David Shelby, Nathaniel Massie, John Hutt, Samuel Monett, Isaac Dawson, James Renick, John Guthrie, John Thompson, John A. Fulton, Joseph Campbell, John Cummings, Peter Apple, Hugh Fordsman, L. Finimore, John Blair.

Stephen M'Dougal, Edward Herrick and Jeremiah R. Munson regarding several suits in the Licking County Court of Common Pleas. In all of them, the following are listed as plaintiffs: "Timothy Spelman, Samuel Thrall, Job Case, Hiram Rose, David Messenger, Samuel Waters, Israel Wells, Ezekiel Wells, Hugh Kelly, Silas Winchel, Rosewell Graves, John Philps, Job W. Case, Amos Carpenter, Enoch Graves, William Jones, Worthy Pratt, Levi Rose, Jun., Timothy Rose, Levi Hays, Ethen Bancroft, Eleazor C. Clemmans, James Sinet, Lemuel Rose, Joseph Lennell, Wm. Gariet, Spencer Spelman, Jesse Munson, Jesse Munson, jun., Elkanah Lennell, Sylvanus Mitchell, Nathan Allen, Augustus Munson, Justin Hillyer, Jeremiah R. Munson, Elias Gilman, Martin Root, John Johnston, and Wm. Cooley, together with George Areery and Gideon Cornwell, deceased, and David Butler, declared a lunatic." The defendents in the various suits are Daniel Goddard, Cornelius Stocum, Spencer Wright, Zadock Cooley, and Seth Hays. (Note that there are several more of these suits in the next issue of the paper, 6 Nov 1809. The defendents of those are Ezra Holcomb, Moses Goddard, Daniel Wodsworth.)

John Waddle, in Chillicothe, has chewing tobacco for sale, made by James H. Overstreet in Lexington, Kentucky.

David Kinkead & Company, Chillicothe, have moved their store to the stand formerly occupied by George Renick.

James M'Calla and Wm. Gariet, in Licking County, executors of the estate of William M'Calla, dec'd, regarding the estate settlement.

John Irwin, in Chillicothe, has taken over the tavern lately occupied by Elisha Fitch on Paint Street.

Reuben Perkins, collector in Colerain township, has lots for sale.

Samuel Niblack, constable of Lick township, says he arrested a black man called David at the Scioto Salt Works. David says he belongs to Obediah Dooley, of Clarke County, Kentucky.

Eli Manvil reports that Benjamin Carpenter and Cephas Cone have appraised a mare found by Cumfort Blets, living in Sunberry township, Delaware County.

J.P.R. Bureau reports that John Miller and Edward W. Tupper have appraised a mare found by George Cortrell and given to Joel Smith, in Gallipolis township, Gallia County.

A. Buford regarding a sale of land at Jonathan Bereman's tavern in New-Market, Highland County. The land was entered by Abraham Buford, located by Peter M'Arthur, and will be shown by Maj. A. Trimble of Hillsborough. He mentions Gen. Geo. Matthews.

Silas Winchil reports that Ethen Bancraft and Sylvenus Mitchel have appraised a mare found by John Heron of Granville township, Licking County.

Samuel Wiseman reports that Jacob Culp and James Miller have appraised a horse found by James Maxon, living in Walnut township, Fairfield County.

Samuel Young, in West Union, Tiffin township, Adams County, reports that Leonard Cole and David Bradford have appraised a mare found by Peter Shultz.

Geo. Will, in Colerain township, Ross County, reports that James S. Webster and James Creain have appraised a horse found by John Purtee.

Volume VIII, Monday, 6 November 1809, No. 463

Lucas Sullivant regarding the sale of the land of Jedediah H. Lewis, dec'd, in Worthington, in order to pay his debts. Stephen Maynard and Sabra Lewis are the administrators of his estate.

John Ellison says that Samuel Daugherty and Hugh R. M'Clellon appraised a mare found by Samuel Davidson, of Sprigg township, Adams County. Also Thomas Morford and Henry M'Geary appraised a mare found by Peter Cooley.

Michael Shackley, in Chillicothe, regarding a robbery at his house.

John D. Wiley, in Chillicothe, has land for sale. He also wants to hire two or three apprentices to the carpenter's trade.

Joseph S. Collins, executor of the estate of Clement Brown, dec'd, has corn for sale in Heller's Bottom on the south side of Paint Creek, at Brown's house.

Elizabeth Lucas, administratrix of the estate of William Lucas, dec'd, has land for sale at Peter Noills' house in Union township, Scioto County.

Henry Chapman, in Clermont County, says that Grafton Baker and Abraham Sells have appraised a mare found by Alexander Hill in Pleasant township.

John Ellison reports that Saml. Daugherty and Saml. Davidson have appraised a mare found by Charles Larsh of Adams County, Sprigg township.

James Williams says that James Sanderson and John Prather have appraised a mare found by Derbey Solavan, living in Adams County, Jefferson township.

Isaac Meason, in Fairfield County, reports that Hezekiah Hubbell and William Drake have appraised a mare found by Abraham VanCourtright of Bloom township.

James Parker, in Huntington township, Adams County, reports that Jonathan Rees and Thomas Evans have appraised a horse found by James Bonner.

John Ludwig, in Washington township, Ross County, reports that Joseph Lane and Anthony Weaver have appraised a mare found by John Williams.

Henry Chapman, in Clermont County, says that John Ross and James Calvin have appraised a mare found by Moses Hiks in Pleasant township.

Zabud Kendall, administrator of the estate of Moses Corwin, late of Franklin County, dec'd, regarding the estate settlement.

Volume VIII, Monday, 13 November 1809, No. 465

Joseph S. Collins regarding Gen. M'Arthur and General Kerr.

A note about Judge Scott mentions Judges Huntington, Sprigg and Tod.

An article regarding the suit of David Reid vs. Samuel Moore in the Court of Common Pleas in Montgomery County. It is signed by Thomas Scott.

Thomas James and John Wood regarding their new store, James & Wood, in the house formerly the property of H. Fullerton and lately occupied by Samuel Taggart as a store in Chillicothe.

John M'Coy has a new shipment of goods for sale at his store.

Joseph Miller, boot and shoemaker, Chillicothe, regarding his business.

William Spencer reports that Isaac Reynolds, of Fairfield County, Reading township, found a stray mare.

Robert Russell has moved his store into the house opposite Henry Neville's store in Jefferson, Pickaway Plains, and he has a new shipment of goods.

W. Silliman, Register of the Land Office at Zanesville, has land for sale and mentions Henry Beemer, John Zane, and Christian Buckman.

Volume VIII, Monday, 20 November 1809, No. 466

George Hoffman about the trial in the Supreme Court of Michigan Territory of Gov. William Hull, mentions Augustus B. Woodward, James Witherall, John Whipple, William M.D. Scott, James M'Closkey. The grand jury was composed of Jacob Visgar, George Hoffman, Robert Abbott, George M'Dougall, James Henry, James May, Richard Smyth, Christian Clemens, Jean Marie Beaubien, George Cotterall, Francois Lasselle, Francois Lafontaine, David Hull, Joseph Jobin, Jean Baptiste Couture, Antoine Dequindre, Hugh R. Martin.

David Bonner, tax collector for Chillicothe, has lots for sale.

John M'Mullin and William Crosan, administrators of the estate of James Crosan, late of Fairfield County, dec'd, regarding the estate settlement.

John Hunter and Thomas Lloyd, tailors and habit makers, regarding their shop at Hunter's house six doors east of the Eagle Tavern, Chillicothe.

John Martin, in Chillicothe, offers his house, lot, household furniture and a complete set of baking utensils for sale.

John M'Dougal, Chillicothe, regarding pork that he bought.

Abner Meeker has two houses and lots for sale in Chillicothe.

Joseph M'Mullen, in Thorn township, Fairfield County, reports that Henry Bowman and John Graves have appraised a mare found by Jacob Addison.

Volume VIII, Wednesday, 29 November 1809, No. 467

An account of a hunting accident in which Mr. Boots shot and killed Mr. Hoshaw, "a young man of this county".

Several unsigned letters mentions Gov. Huntington, Stanley Griswold, and Gov. Samuel Huntington.

Elisha Kelly says that Warford Bonhorn and Hudson Southard have appraised a mare found by James Gaskill, in Paxton township, Ross County.

Christian Benner says that John Swan and Jacob Tornapseed have appraised a horse found by George Eubank, in Paxton township, Ross County.

Joseph Tiffin has horses for sale. Make notes payable to Gideon Granger.

Joseph Kerr, in Chillicothe, wants to buy 500 hogs.

John Woodbridge, at the Bank of Chillicothe, about a stockholders' meeting.

Jn. W. Millar, in Seal township, Scioto County, reports that Cornelius Miller and Jessee Cockrell have appraised a mare found by Samuel Dannil.

Burgess Elliott says that William Parker and Laurence Foster have appraised a horse found by Mary Ann Peeters, living in Mifflin township, on Sunfish Creek.

Jeptha Beasley, in Byrd township, Adams County, reports that Isaac Hughy and William Vance have appraised a horse found by Micah Woods.

Volume VIII, Wednesday, 6 December 1809, No. 468

Several letters to the editor regarding Gov. Huntington and Stanley Griswold mentions Gov. Hull, Peter Parcels (printer).

Samuel Swearingen & Company, Chillicothe, have a new shipment of goods.

James Parker, in Huntington township, Adams County, reports that Neal Lafferty and William Dickson have appraised a horse found by Samuel Ellis. Also Robert Meek and Samuel Ellis have appraised a horse found by Hugh Power.

Hugh Andrews reports that Fredirick Harmin and Jacob Macklin appraised a horse found by Josiah Beall, living in Pleasant township, Fairfield County.

John T. Barr & Company have a new shipment of goods for sale at their store.

Grantham Earle, living in Union township, Ross County, says he found a mare.

Volume VIII, Wednesday, 13 December 1809, No. 469

Dr. Alexander Campbell is elected to replace E. Tiffin, resigned. Dr. Edward Tiffin is elected speaker of the house in place of Hon. Alexander Campbell. Carlos A. Norton is elected clerk of the senate.

A letter to the editor regarding Gov. Huntington and Mr. Griswold.

Gov. Samuel Huntington's address to the legislature is printed and mentions Hon. Edward Tiffin, David Eddy (of Adams County), William Wetmore (of Portage County), Nehemiah King (of Geauga County), William Gass (of Knox County), David Shepherd (surveyor), Stanley Griswold, Lewis Day (of Portage County), Eleazer Hickox (of Geauga County), Jehiel Gregory (a trustee of Ohio University), Scioto Salt Works.

David Kinkead regarding a meeting of the Scioto Lodge of Masons.

William & J. Irwin have a new shipment of goods for sale at their store in Chillicothe nearly opposite the Spread Eagle Tavern.

Benjamin Urmston, Chillicothe, has land and property for sale.

Daniel Fraley, in Highland County, reports that Fred. Fraley and James Fitzpatrick have appraised a horse found by Robert Fitzpatrick, living on the waters of the Rocky Fork of Paint Creek.

Volume VIII, Wednesday, 20 December 1809, No. 470

The election of Mr. Hughes in Trumbull County is contested.

Gen. Duncan M'Arthur is elected speaker of the Senate.

An unsigned letter to the editor mentions Peter Parcels, editor of the Independent Republican.

Cadwallader Wallace, in Chillicothe, has land for sale, entered in the name of William Washington, adjoining Uriah Paullin, in Green County, on Paint Creek.

Joseph Darlinton and John W. Campbell (attorney) about the suit of William Armstrong and Jacob Shaffer in Adams County Court of Common Pleas.

Joseph Miller, in Chillicothe, says David Thompson, a shoemaker, was working in Miller's shop, but Thompson left and stole his property. Thompson, age 34-35, lived in Pittsburgh before coming to Chillicothe.

John Johnston, in Franklin township, Ross County, reports that Daniel Bower and John Boman have appraised a mare found by Enos Moore.

Volume VIII, Wednesday, 3 January 1810, No. 472

Directors of the Chillicothe Bank are Samuel Finley, William M'Dowell, John M'Landburgh, Humphrey Fullerton, George Renick, John Carlisle, Thomas James,

Thomas Worthington, and John Waddle.

A note regarding the right of Mr. Livingston and Mr. Fulton to navigate the waters of Ohio with boats propelled by fire and steam.

Marriage: James Bramble married Miss Eliza Poe on Thursday evening last by John Ferguson.

Marriage: George Scott married Miss Ann Thompson, both of Chillicothe, on Thursday evening last by John Ferguson.

Proceedings of the legislature mention the petition of James Millar of Adams County. He has 6 crippled children, aged 8 to 25, who have never walked or talked. Mentions Mr. Darlington, James Clark, George Clark, Mr. Murray and Mr. Shepherd and Mr. Bradford.

An unsigned letter to the editor mentions Stanley Griswold, Gov. Huntington, Mr. Morrow, Mr. Campbell.

John M'Landburgh asks those indebted to him to settle their accounts.

Thomas G. Prentiss, in Marietta, has land for sale in Worthington's survey. Apply to Gen. Finley in Chillicothe.

A list of letters left at the Post Office in Chillicothe includes William Askew, sen., Samuel Alexander, Peter Apple, Abraham Ater, Samuel Atchison, Andrew Alexander, William Allan near Brandy Camp, Dumah Bartlett, Hugh Black, White Brown, William Bears, Francis Boldwin, Isaac Brink, David Bowin, John Biggert in care of James May, Henry Baker, Isaac Bowen, John Bratton, Isaac Bradley, Isaac Bonner, Lismund Basye, Isaac Bonnet, Thomas Brown, Joshua B. Brewer, Elijah B. Bartley, Absalom Brown, William Barr, Samuel Byers, John Beach, Rosanah Boggs or Nancy Bell, John Berry, William Buttler Becket, Thomas Cooper, James Cross, Rev. John Collins, John Cryder, William Colwell, Thomas Crow, Jeffery Cox, Andrew Correll, John Clouzar, William Clark, George Chapple, Gilbert Carpenter, James Cumings, John Clark, William Chandler, Thomas Comer, John H. Cannon, Peter Clark, James Coldwell, Thomas Chineth, George Conrod, Barnaba Cochren, William Cochran, Amasa Delano, John Davis, Samuel Duffield, James Denney, John Dovenberger, Charles Davis, Benjamin Duncan, George Dawson, Jesse Dodd, David Dye, James Devanport, Benjamin Davis, Samuel Denny, William Donwooddy, Col. John Evans, Grantham Earle, John Emmit, Dr. George Evans, Jacob Echman, John Exline, John Etty, Mr. Fry, Christian Fry, David Foard, William Foster, Hugh Flin, John Free, Elisha Fitch, Richard Goslee, Thomas Graham, Robert Galbraith, William Garrett, William Gorden, James Globs, Dr. William B. Gould, Alexander Gillaspe, William Glancy, Joseph Gaston, Andrew Galbreath, Henry Hesher, John Hyde, John Hall, William Harper, Thomas Hust, Sarah Headly, Hugh Huston, John Hutton, James Howard, Alexander Hamilton, Jacob Hoover, William Hannaman, Joseph Hopkins, Gen. Benjamin Howey, John Hoffman, Mrs. Huston, Phielden Hubbard, James Hughey, Nathan Hanchet, Philip Hewit, James Huy, Benjamin Haines, William Hampton, Geo. Heath, Henry Hains, Henry Hester, Marcus Heyfin, James B. Henly, Robert Holms, John Huffman, John Hampson, Job Inskeep, John Jackson, John Johnston, Mathias James, Jonathan Johnston, Jacob Johnston, Isaac Johnston, John Jenkins, Samuel Jones, Abner Kerns, Cornelius Kating, Andrew Kinniar, Thomas Kerney, Andrew Long, John Knight, Samuel Kerr, Ephrim Knoles, Thos. Kearney, BarnetLauman, Thomas Lyons, John Long, Robert Long, William Lacey, Samuel Langdale, Widow Lafferty, Samuel M'Klewer, William Moore, Hugh Millegan, John Millar, William Mowbray, John M'Whorton, John Morrison, William M'Gibben, George M'Cormack, Joseph M'Clain, Thomas M'Donald, Wm. M'Donald, James M'Mahen, Henry May, William Martin or Joseph Gould, Archibald M'Clain, Donald M'Arthur, John Nowland, Robert M'Ginnis, Henry Milleasey, Wm. Mason, James M'Certney, Joab Norton, William Nicol, Thomas North, Ralph Philips, William Peirson, Charles Parker, William Pool, Aaron Parker, Maj. Puthuff, Gersham M. Petters, Edward Phelps, William Perrineence, James Phillips, David Pratt, Andrew Pontious, Mathias Redenour, Miss Jane Ross, William Rodgers, James Robinson, James Rogers, Lewis R. Rogers, William Raines, Jesse Rowe, sen., Anthony Ridenour, William Robinson, William Russell, Elizabeth Rogers on Pee Pee, Aaron Reuck, William C. Schenck, Rev. Hector Sandford, Samuel Spugg, William Slaughter, George Scot, Andrew Saxon, John Shever, Elizabeth Stewart, Miss Margaret Stewart, Hugh Stewart, James Somerville, Archibald Snider, Peter Smith, James Sloan, Lewis Summers, Jacob Shirick, David Smith, Miss Ann Scott, Abraham Stump, James Shargent at Pee Pee, John Stuthard, John Stockton, Jonathan Spyker, William Shaw, James J. Stokely,

Robert Southard, Abraham Timmons, John Trimble, James Thompson, John Trigo, David Thompson, George Teditner, Richard Tomlinson, Samuel Tod, Simon Thald, Asa Truerdale, Jonathan Thopson, John Talbot, Henry Thurman, Mary Thomas, John Tootle, John Vouht, David Vanwinkle, Jacob Vinconhaler, William Wilson, John Warner, Benjamin Williams, Peter Wickerham, Wm. Wynn, Thomas White, Thomas Wilkins, Ure Welton, John Wright, David Worley, John White, Gammage Williams, Isaac Whetsail, William S. Winn, James Whetnow, Winn Winship, Sarah Williams, John Wells, John Welshaunce or Abraham Welshaunce, Isaac Zorder, Joseph Tiffin.

Saml. Evans, in Highland County, reports that Thomas Green and George M'Daniel have appraised a horse found by John Hines of Liberty township.

Mills Stephenson, in Huntington township, Adams County, reports that John Redman and Forgus M'Clain have appraised a horse found by George Simmons, near the mouth of Eagle Creek.

Jos. Kerr wants to hire two or three coopers to make pork barrels.

Zophan Topping, administrator of the estate of John Topping, dec'd, regarding the estate settlement at Ezra Griswold's house in Worthington.

Abraham Millar, in Jefferson township, Scioto County, reports a runaway bound boy named James How, age 19-20.

Js. Foos wants to sell his tavern in Franklinton. Apply to Elias N. Delashmutt in Franklinton or Foos at the Red Lion in Chillicothe.

Jacob Miller, in Lancaster, has found a negro boy named Harry who belongs to Charles Jinens who is moving from Farquer, Virginia, to Kentucky.

Enos Prather, in Pee Pee township, Ross County, reports that Henderson Crab and Patrick Johnson have appraised a mare found by John F. Davis.

Boaz Walton, in Salem township, Tuscarawas County, reports that James Watson and Thomas Carr have appraised a mare found by Mathew Williams.

John Chapman, in Meigs township, Adams County, reports that Peter Platter and William Walling have appraised a mare found by William Pemberton.

John Smith says that George Hornbeck and Coteney Tanner appraised a mare found by Joseph Powel, living on Deer Creek, Pleasant township, Franklin County.

John Parker, in Mifflin township, Ross County, reports that Isaac Penniston and Joseph Moore have appraised a mare found by Geo. Pennisten.

Peter Jackson, in Deerfield township, Ross County, reports that Jeremiah Brown and Lewis Messick have appraised a horse found by Alexander Gillaspie.

Charles M'Clung, in Kurkereck township, Fairfield County, reports that Moses Woods and William Shaw have appraised a horse found by Isaac Larimer.

Samuel Smith, living 3 miles from Chillicothe, wants to exchange land.

Volume VIII, Wednesday, 10 January 1810, No. 473

William Robinson reports that William Rodgers and William Cohran have appraised a horse found by Gen. James Menary, of Union Township, Ross County.

John Waddle has a new shipment of goods for sale at his store in Chillicothe.

Saml. Finley has stock for sale in the Bank of Chillicothe.

J. Woodbridge regarding a dividend on the stock of the Bank of Chillicothe.

Michael Cryder, living three miles from Chillicothe, has land for sale.

Nathan Cory, administrator of the estate of Simeon Cory, dec'd, late of Union township, Ross County, regarding the estate settlement.

John M'Dougal wants to buy corn fed pork.

Enoch B. Smith, George Richards and Morgan Vanmetre, Commissioners for Highland County, will accept bids, at Levi Warren's house in Hillsborough, to build a stone jail.

John Ellison reports that John Thompson and Thomas Mofford have appraised a horse found by William Robinson, of Sprigg township, Adams County.

Henry Mussleman, in Springfield township, Ross County, reports that Jacob Haynes and Philip Haynes have appraised a mare found by Frederick Overly.

Zechariah Welsh reports that Francis Cramer and John Boblit have appraised a mare found by Philip Waldren, of Springfield township, Ross County.

Bigger Head, in Brushcreek township, Highland County, reports that Peter Heter and Felix Hufman have appraised a mare found by Anthony Franklin.

Volume VIII, Wednesday, 17 January 1810, No. 474

Proceedings of the legislature mention Lebanon, Episcopal Church, United

Brethren, Pickaway County, William Russel, Alexander Campbell, Steubenville, James Clark, Samuel Dunlap, Reeves' Crossing on Paint Creek.

John Parker, in Mifflin township, Ross County, reports that Elias Layton and Joseph Moore have appraised a horse found by Asher Layton.

Richard Hickman, living in Clark County, Kentucky, reports a runaway slave named Aaron, age 36.

David Spangler reports that John Dickson and Wm. Goldwell have appraised a mare found by George Kizinger of Hamilton township, Franklin County.

Saml. Evans, in Liberty township, Highland County, reports that Thomas Green and George M'Daniel have appraised a horse found by John Hines. Also Joseph Knox and Thomas Green appraised a mare found by Eli Blunt.

John Ellison reports that Israel Donalson and Samuel Santee have appraised a horse found by Perminus Washburn, of Sprigg township, Adams County. And John Thompson and Joseph Beam appraised a horse found by Peter Connor.

Volume VIII, Wednesday, 24 January 1810, No. 475

Marriage: Robert Russell, merchant at the Pickaway Plains, married Miss Polly Cain, of Franklin County, on Tuesday evening, 16 January, at Franklinton.

Obituary: Dr. Richard Brown, died in Chillicothe on Saturday, 21 January 1810. He was lately of Louisville, Kentucky, and was the son of the late Doct. Wm. Brown of Alexandria, Virginia.

Benjamin Hough is elected auditor and Jeremiah M'Lene is Secretary of State.

Proceedings of the legislature mention James Millar, John Ellison, junr., William Russel, Alexander Campbel, Zanesville.

Epraim Doolittle & Company have a new shipment of goods for sale.

John Ellison reports that Alexander Vernor and William Laughridge have appraised a mare found by William Nixon, of Adams County, Sprigg township.

William Williams, living across from the Green Tree tavern, has salt for sale.

Samuel Tagart has a new shipment of goods for sale at his store.

Geo. Will and Thos. Armstrong, administrators of the estate of Christian Hains, late of Colerain township, Ross County, dec'd, about the settlement.

Edward Paine, Jun., clerk of the Geauga County Court of Common Pleas, about the petition of David Abbot for partition of land in Avery township.

George Caley, in New Market township, Highland County, reports that Henry Pence and Frederick Saum have appraised a horse found by Abraham H. Byfield. Frederick Saum and Adam Shaefer have appraised a horse found by Isaiah Ross.

Enoch B. Smith, in Liberty township, Highland County, reports that Joseph M'Carty and Richard Ibiff have appraised a mare found by Richard Wilkins.

Volume VIII, Wednesday, 31 January 1810, No. 476

A letter from Hon. Alexander Campbell in Washington is printed.

Proceedings of the legislature mention James Hillman, Coshocton County, Guernsey County, Edward Tiffin, Th. S. Hinde, Abraham Shepherd, James Clark.

Jesse Spencer, Register of the Land Office at Chillicothe, has land for sale and mentions John and Hugh M'Mullin, James and William Friend, William Gay, John Kerr, John Graham, E. Friend, Jacob Bouse, Michael Baldwin, Thomas Needham, Jacob Pickle, Nicholas Earhart, John Parr, David Shalenberger, Moses Boggs, Christian Wisenhaver, Henry Moore, Isaac Thompson.

John Cutler reports a runaway apprentice boy named Drury Hicks.

Volume VIII, Wednesday, 7 February 1810, No. 477

Marriage: Richard Snider married Miss Polly Johnston, both of Chillicothe, on Thursday evening last.

Proceedings of the legislature mention Nathan Ellis (and his ferry on the Ohio River), James Millar, James Dunlap, Miami University, Humphrey Fullerton, Nathaniel Massie, Gov. Samuel Huntington, Hon. Edward Tiffin.

Jesse Spencer, Register of the Land Office in Chillicothe, has more land for sale and mentions Nath. Wyatt, Isaac Greave, and Thos. M'Neal.

Frederick Pontus, living nine miles from Chillicothe, reports a stray mare. Deliver to John Goodman's tavern in Green township or to Charles Rairy, living in Madison township, upper Walnut Creek, 15 miles from Franklinton.

Charles Brandell says his wife, Polly, has left him, and he won't pay her bills.

Daniel Kain reports that Jacob Barstler and Oliver Lindsey have appraised a mare found by Jacob Sly, in Williamsburgh township.

William Robinson reports that Alexander Robertson and Joseph Pearce have appraised a mare found by John Jefferson of Union township, Ross County.

Job Dinning reports that John Brown and John Capas have appraised a horse found by Armstrong Davidson in Adams County.

Enos Prather, in Pe Pee township, Ross County, reports that Soloman Beeding and David Lewis have appraised a mare found by James Burk.

Jessee Lucas, in Paint township, Highland County, reports that Jacob Easter and Samuel Evans have appraised a mare found by Jacob Wyre.

Volume VIII, Wednesday, 14 February 1810, No. 478

Proceedings of the legislature mention Zanesville, Western Library Associ-ation, Humphrey Fullerton, Nathaniel Massie, Clinton County, Thomas Scott, William W. Irwin, Benjamin Tappan, Ethan Allen Brown, Thomas Morris, Richard S. Thomas, Samuel Herrick, W. Sprigg, C. Pease, John Thompson, John M'Lean, Francis Dunlavy, Levin Belt, Isaac Cook, Mr. Griswold, Mr. M'Kinney, George Tod, Benjamin Ruggles, Ben. Tappan, Mr. Hitchcock, L. Belt.

Curtiss Cannon reports that Henry Franklin and Jacob Cox have appraised a mare found by Solomon Mershon, in Meigs township, Adams County.

Thomas Orr & Company have stills, wash kettles and tea kettles for sale.

Thomas Ward, in Cabell County, Virginia, reports a runaway slave named Ben.

William Kilgore, in Buckskin township, reports that Josiah R. Finch and Anderson Bryant appraised a mare found by Benjamin Rodgers.

Job Dinning reports that Duncan M'Kinsey and Samuel Black have appraised a mare found by Thomas Egal, in Tiffin township, Adams County.

Volume VIII, Wednesday, 21 February 1810, No. 479

Marriage: Col. James Pritchard, representative from Jefferson County, married Mrs. Sally Huston, of Chillicothe, on Sunday evening last.

A list of acts passed by the legislature mentions Hamilton, Lebanon, New Lisbon Academy, Steubenville, Cuyahoga County, Episcopal Church, United Brethren, Stanton, Moravian Indians, James Hillman, Tuscarawas County, Guernsey County, Coshocton County, Miami University, John Chiventon, Richland County, Troy, Madison County, Virginia military tract, Western Library Associ-ation, Zanesville, Muskingum Salt Works, Erie Literary Society, Washington Social Library Company, Poland Library Society, John S. Reide, Black River, Scioto Salt Works, Cuyahoga County, Presbyterian Society, Clinton, Humphrey Fullerton, Nathaniel Massie, James Millar, Christian King, James Hampson, Asahel Cooley, Joseph Guthrie, Stephen Buckingham, Michael Thomas.

The commissioners for fixing the seat of government are James Finley, Joseph Darlinton, William M'Farland, Wyllys Silliman, Reasin Beall.

John Warth is re-elected agent for the Scioto Salt Works.

The legislature appointed the following associate judges: Moses Baird, Needham Perry and Andrew Livingston in Adams County; John Patterson, James Alexander and John Wiley in Belmont; Philip Gatch, Alexander Barr and Joseph Campbell in Clermont; Ezekial Ball, Daniel Milikin and Robert Lytle in Butler; George Aterholt, Geo. Brown, and Wm. Smith in Columbiana; Wm. Read, Robert Shannon and Alexander Morison, jun., in Franklin; Samuel Carpenter, James Quinn and Henry Abrams in Fairfield; Robert Safford, Joseph Fletcher and Fuller Elliott in Gallia; Thomas Patton, Joseph M'Kee and Andrew Anderson in Jefferson; Isaac Cook, James Armstrong and Thomas Hicks in Ross; David Huston, James Snowden and Samuel Hyle in Green; Robert Hughes, Ephraim Quimby and Herman Canfield in Trumbull; Stephen Wood, James Silvers and Aaron Goforth in Hamilton; Abner Gerard, Wm. George and Isaac Spinning in Montgomery; Charles F. Mastin, John Collins and Wm. Russell in Scioto; Paul Fearing, Thomas Lord and Ezekiel Denning in Washington; Ignatius Brown, Jacob D. Low and George Harlan in Warren; Jesse Hughs, Peter Bure and Thomas Hickston in Clinton; Augustus Gilbert, Nathan Perry and Timothy Doane in Cuyahoga; James Mooney, Anthony Potts and Wm. Blackmore in Fayette; Robert Speer, Tho. B. Kirkpatrick and Jacob Gomber in Guernsey; Isaac Minor, Samuel Baskerville and David Mitchel in Madison; Wm. Seymour, Thomas Barr and Jacob Shoemaker in Pickaway; Ebenezer Merry in place of Nehemiah King, resigned, in

Geauga; James Colvin in place of Wm. Gass, resigned, in Knox. Samuel Forward, associate for Portage County, is appointed to replace Wm. Wetmore, resigned. Collectors appointed are William Murray, A.J. Williams, William Skinner, Samuel Herick, Robert Carrel, Reuben S. Clark.

A notice of a meeting of the Black Oak Club in Chillicothe.

C. Hammond, in Belmont County, writes a letter to the public regarding the letter about him in Peter Parcels' paper, the Independent Republican. He mentions his friend, Mr. Scofield.

Emmanuel Carpenter, in Gettysburgh, has applied to the Adams County, Penn., courts as an insolvent debtor.

Frederick Braucher and Peter Garman, living in Highland County, Brush Creek township, near the Sinking Spring, reports a stray horse.

Volume VIII, Wednesday, 28 February 1810, No. 480

Obituary: Mrs. Mary Davis, wife of Daniel E. Davis, of Chillicothe, died on Friday evening last.

Capt. J. Whistler, at Fort Dearborn, regarding the conduct of Matthew Irwin, United States Factor, at Chikago.

William Lacock, in Eagle township, Adams County, reports that James Kendal and James Willson have appraised a mare found by William Davidson. Also Mathew Tomb and William Martin have appraised a mare found by James Wilson.

James Parker, in Adams County, reports that Alexander Harrover and Joseph Hall have appraised a mare found by Moses Race.

Volume VIII, Wednesday, 7 March 1810, No. 481

An account of a meeting of the citizens of Chillicothe for the purpose of "establishing Manufactures in this place" and mentions Thomas Worthington, Henry Massie, Samuel Finley, William Creighton, jun., George Renick, A.J. Williams, Henry Buchannon, Henry Brush, Joseph S. Collins, Jesup N. Couch, Isaac Evans, Humphrey Fullerton.

A note regarding Dr. Campbell in Congress.

James Renick says he is a candidate for sheriff of Pickaway County.

Hugh Boyle and W.W. Irvin (attorney), in Lancaster, regarding the suit of Ludwick Wolfley vs. James Easton in Fairfield County Court of Common Pleas.

Jesse Spencer, Register of the Land Office, regarding the sale of lands.

Joseph Miller asks those indebted to him to settle their accounts. He also wants to hire two apprentices to the nailing business.

Joseph S. Collins, executor of the estate of Clement Brown, dec'd, has land for sale near Chillicothe.

Wyllys Silliman, Register of the Land Office in Zanesville, has land for sale and mentions Thomas Spear, Geo. Beviner, Wm. Thompson, John Briggs, James Brown, jr., and Thomas Dyson.

Daniel Symmes, Register of the Land Office in Cincinnati, has land for sale and mentions John Gerrard, Wm. C. Schenck, Obediah Schenck, Adam Swinehart, Martin Baum, John Brownson, Peter Swinehart, Jacob White, Isaac Bonta, George Medsker, John M'Maken and Henry Akenberry, Joseph Williamson, John Brill, Frederick Miller, John Kennedy, John Thompson, Lawrence Grewel, Edward Mitchell, Jonas Hatfield, Peter Bonta, Peter Demoss.

Hugh Boyle and Wm. W. Irvin about the suit of William Kittsenfiller vs. Jacob Hoover in Fairfield County Court of Common Pleas.

George Shane, at the ferry opposite Chillicothe, offers his house, livestock, household furniture and farming utensils for sale.

Volume VIII, Wednesday, 14 March 1810, No. 482

Obituary: Michael Baldwin died in Chillicothe on Friday evening last.

Jeremiah M'Lene, Secretary of State, reports that Hon. Thomas Scott is appointed judge of the Supreme Court.

Samuel Lybrand is a candidate for sheriff of Pickaway County.

Benj. Hough, Auditor of Ohio, regarding the taxes on land.

Samuel Smith reports that Ezekiel VanHorn and William Boyd have appraised a horse found by Daniel Strong, of Radner township, Delaware County.

John Spenser reports that Joseph Evans and William Evans have appraised a mare found by William Morrison, of Newton township, Licking County.

Wm. Rutledge, Adjutant of the Second Regiment, Ohio Militia, about a meeting of the regiment.

George Caley reports that Andrew Shaefer and Phillip Willkin have appraised a mare found by Thomas Colven.

James Moore says that Lewis Bible and John Markland have appraised a mare found by Gerret VanHorn, living on the Ohio River, Tiffin township, Adams Co.

David Gharky, in Union township, Scioto County, reports that John Collins and Stephen Smith have appraised a horse found by Phillis Moore.

John M'Donald, in Twin township, Ross County, reports that John M'Lane and Aaron Foster have appraised a horse found by William M'Bride.

David Grant reports that Samuel Boggs and Thomas Mathews have appraised a horse found by Joseph Fletcher, of Saline township, Gallia County.

Elisha Kelly reports that Charles Reeder and Soloman Chaffin have appraised a horse found by John Torbet, in Paxton township, Ross County.

Job Dinning reports that Joseph Oiler and David Decamps have appraised a mare found by Leazelyear Swim.

Volume VIII, Wednesday, 21 March 1810, No. 483

Tobias Ruffner, in Chillicothe, has Kenawha salt for sale at the house of Wm. Williams, opposite the sign of the Green Tree.

Volume X, Wednesday, 11 April 1810, No. 487

Rudolph Pitcher and Abraham Pitcher, at Lancaster, have erected a paper mill and will buy linen and cotton rags delivered to the stores of Rudolph Pitcher and Andrew Crocket at Lancaster; at the potter shop of Joseph Bond in Lancaster; the potter shop of Jacob Her on Little Walnut Creek; to Abraham Pitcher's mill on Hockhocking; to Thomas Hanna at Washington; to H. Neville, Wm. Carlisle and R. Russell at Pickaway Plains; to J. Carlisle, J. M'Coy and G. Brown in Chillicothe; to John Overdear in Franklinton; and to Samuel Lybrand in Tarlton.

Marriage: Col. John Ferguson, of Chillicothe, married Miss Jane Denny of Wheeling, Virginia, on 27 March 1810, by Rev. John Brice.

Marriage: Col. Robert Lucas married Miss Betsey Brown, daughter of John Brown, on Thursday evening last, at Portsmouth.

Carlos A. Norton regarding a meeting of the Tammany Society.

A list of letters left at the Post Office in Chillicothe includes Larkins Adams, Francis Ayers, Benjamin Adear, Peggy Adear, George Adear, George Anshultz, James Argo, Richard Acton, Aaron Ashbrook, Peter Aiman, Philip Argenbright, John Argenbright, Isaac Black, Capt. James Budge, Dinah Bartlett, Barnet Blue, William Betzer, Sam. H. Browne, Joel Bacon, John Brush, William Bradshaw, Jacob Baum, Samuel Brown, James Bramble, Thomas Brown, Nancy Beakets, Joseph Boggs, Henry Brown at Pee Pee, Joseph or John Brians, White Brown, Benjamin Brock, George Brown at Irwin Creek, Job Broughton, Michael Baldwin, Thomas Brown in Deerfield township, Jas. Blaine, William Barr, Joseph Brians, William Bathard, Joseph Blackney, Benjamin Cox, Jonathan Craig, George Creamer, James Carter, James Clifford, Andrew Carrel, William Crawford, Samuel Clark, Nicholas Cuninham, Edward Creaton, David Croll, John Clendeneen, Andrew Cooper, Joseph Czar, Daniel Chesnut, James Conduke, Solomon Coles, John H. Cannon, Thomas Crew, Moses Cox, Peter Clark, Joseph Campbell, Rubin S. Clark, William Conwell, Thomas Cunningham, Woolery Conrad, Enoch Cockerill, Nancy Dunbar, Enock Doddridge, Sam. Duffield, James Dunlap, Benjamin Davis, Clarend Dix, Joseph Dix, Randolph Dart, Grantham Earle, Isaac East, Joseph Evans, jun., Jesse Edgington, George Fry, Anthony Franklin, Samuel Francis, Richard Foster, Elisha Fitch, Joseph Flinte, John Fernow, John Franklin, George Golle, George Florey, Elizabeth Gosslee, Philip Griffith, William Gordon, sen., Edward Goldsberry, Robert Greghon in care of Felix Rinick, James K. George, Priscilla Golds, Hugh Ghormley, Jacob Gundy, James Howard, Daniel Hear, Jonathan Hand, Joseph Hufman, Obed Harrison, Charles Hays, Thomas Harman, William Harper, Nancy Hust, Edward Hobbs, Wm. Howsman, William Hampton, Frederick Houch, James Hughs, Levi Hodges, Elizabeth Hendrick, Daniel Haggard, Thomas Harman, Joseph Hays, Isaac Hartman, Mrs. Joanna Hughs, William Hall, Philip Hewit, Jacob Hickle, Robert Huston, George Hamilton, George Horey, John Hall, James Hedges, Philip Hedges, Andrew Harter, Charles Hangerer,

Samuel Jones, Isaac Jones, Henry Jones, Cornelius Johnston, John Erwin, Alexander Irwin, John James, Peter Jones, Garnder Jacks, John Johnston, Abner Kerns, Andrew Kissinger, John Kight, Ephraim Knoles, Andrew Knox, Adam Knoles, William King, Daniel Kelly, William Keran, Barnet Lowman, Andrew Lindsey, Thos. Lilly, Samuel Little, John Lewis, E.N. Lashmutt, Mrs. Jane Linch, Lewis Luttrell, Morris Loyns, Abraham Lucas, Jane Lafferty, Martha Little, James M'Chord, Reese M'Neill, William Moore, George Myers in care of A. Turner, Robert M'Mahon, David Meredth, George M'Kinness, John Manly, John M'Neille, Joseph M'Lain, Jenny M'Illeree in care of Daniel Kelly, Mary Moringo, Daniel M'Hory, George M'Cormick, Wm. Morral, John L. Mansfield, Alfred Meaden, Henry May, John Millar, John Maddison in care of T.S. Hinde, Robert Mackey, Archibald M'Clean, Peter Mark, Martha Mitchell, Jesse Mann, John Maccgee, Jesse Miller, Isaac Mackhenry, John Morrison, George Miers, David Murphey, Baly Nicels, Daniel Nicels, Mary Noble, John Nixon, Jacob Nyee, Thomas Oaks, John Odle, Peter Ozias, James E. Phelps, Peter Porter, Enos Pursel, Miss Mary Phillips, Samuel Pickens in care of J. Pickens, John Parcels, Col. James Poage, John Parker, Samuel Ridgway, John Robins, George Ray, Jacob S. Rieling, William Rodgers, Thomas Remey, William Ross, Samuel Robinson, Jacob Rielin, George Rooker, Henry Rush, John Romine, Daniel Reel, Abraham Roodes, Ferdinand Rutter, William Rutledge, Nancy Riednerier, Thomas Ramley, George Ritche, William Smith, Thomas Swinney, John R. Stokes, Henry Sharp, John Stockton, Abraham Stip, Rev. Hector Sanford, James Sproll, Samuel Strane, James Summerville, William Sprigg, James Smith, Charles Steenberger, Robert Stewart, Alexander Smith, William Stockton, Joseph Sands, Hugh Scott, Thomas Sampson, Armsterd Simons, Solomon Slayback, Thomas Stothard or Asa Hankins, Thoams Smith, Michael Shavley, Abraham D. Swartz, Charles Thompson, Samuel Turner, Isaac Terboss, James Taylor, Elias Thompson, John Trimble, Richard Todhunter, Webster Thomas, Solomon Timmons, Polly True, Robert True, John Turley, Hon. Geo. Tod, John Trego, James Thompson, Thos. Thompson, Nicholas Tucker, William Tanquary, Thomas Wright, Jacob Wistenhafer, John Wosh, Miss Susan Thompson, Peter Toughman, Hugh S. Venniman, Miss Sally Wats, Jediah Wyoff, Isaac Workman, David Worley, Elliott Wilson, John Woodbridge, John Watson, Merriman White, John Webster, Obed Wyer, George Whitman, Daniel Waggoner, John Warner, Hugh Woods, Robert Wallace, Joel Waters, Thomas Wilkens, John Watt, Parker Warren, Jon. Wallace on Buckskin Creek, Jacob Zeager, sen. Entered by Joseph Tiffin.

William Ward, justice of the peace in Walnut township, regarding the murder of Reuben Cherry by John Bennett.

John Brown, living in Portsmouth, reports a runaway apprentice named Francis Baker, age about 16.

Charles M'Clung says that Robert M'Feear and William Shaw have appraised a horse found by Isaiah Driver.

James Wright, in Wayne township, Adams County, reports that Andrew Burns and William Sechrist have appraised a horse found by Eli Izzard.

John Wiley, in Chillicothe, reports that he found two promissory notes. Apply to John T. Barr & Company's store.

John Carlisle has a new shipment of goods for sale at his store.

James Moore, in Adams County, says that Wm. M'Cormick and Wm. Markland have appraised a horse found by Jane Smith.

Samuel Hardy, living about 10 miles from Chillicothe, in Ross County, Union township, has land for sale.

Volume X, Wednesday, 18 April 1810, No. 488

Marriage: Robert Robinson to Miss Sally Robinson, both of Ross County, on 17 April 1810, by Joseph Tiffin.

George Brown and John M'Cort, in Chillicothe, say that the partnership of Brown & M'Court is dissolved.

John Turner, in Pleasant township, Franklin County, reports that Thomas Chenawith and John Chenawith appraised a mare found by Abraham Vanmetre, living on Darby Creek.

Benjamin Feurt, in Union township, Scioto County, reports that Gabriel Feurt and John R. Sanderson have appraised a mare found by Samuel Smith.

Adam Kirkpatrick says that Andrew Clemmer and Aaron Kendel appraised a horse found by John Kindel, living in Wayne township, Adams County.

Volume X, Wednesday, 25 April 1810, No. 489

A note regarding William Sprigg, an ex-judge in the Supreme Court, mentions Judge Scott.

Matthew Irwin, United States Factor at Chicago, answers the charges of Capt. John Whistler, at Fort Dearborn. He includes depositions from Lieut. S. Thompson at Fort Dearborn, C. Jewett (Indian agent at Chicago), and John Kinzie and John Latime at Chicago.

Obediah Ragsdale, living in Bracken County, Kentucky, at the mouth of Big Snag Creek, reports a runaway slave, John.

Carlos A. Norton regarding a meeting of the Tammany Society.

Jacob Poisal, in Chillicothe, wants to sell his house and lot, formerly the property of Dr. Edminston, on Water Street.

Isaac Keys, in Ross County, has land for sale on the Deer Creek road.

J.W. Saxton, living in Chillicothe, reports a stray mare.

A note regarding the publication of the Fredonian and Western Intelligencer in Worthington, by Robert D. Richardson.

Volume X, Wednesday, 9 May 1810, No. 491

John Roads, in Brush Creek township, Highland County, reports that George Gall and Andrew Eater have appraised a mare found by George Criswall.

Marriage: Ferguson Fleming to Miss Susan Graham, both of Ross County, on Tuesday, 1 May 1810.

Dr. E. Tiffin is appointed clerk of Ross County Court.

An unsigned letter to the editor mentions Samuel Huntington, George Tod and William Sprigg. Another unsigned letter mentions Mr. Tod and Mr. Sprigg.

Col. William Keys is a candidate for senator from Highland County.

Carlos A. Norton regarding a meeting of the Tammany Society.

Wm. Creighton, Sen., sheriff, regarding the sale of the property of James Crain at the suit of Henry Hollar.

Henry Hall, in Pickaway County, says that his wife, Polly Hall, has left him, and he will no longer honor her debts.

Sarah Baldridge and Joseph Neilson, in Adams County, administrators of the estate of William Balbridge, dec'd, late of Adams County, about the settlement.

Peter Jackson, in Deerfield township, Ross County, reports that Barnet Downs and Ezekiel Hull have appraised a horse found by Clement Brown.

William Ashar, in Champaign County, at the head of Darby Creek, regarding the payment of his bills.

David Abbot, in Cuyahoga County, regarding the partition of land he holds by deed from Samuel Hughes of New Haven, Connecticut.

James Wright, in Wayne township, Adams County, reports that Levin Wheeler and Stephen Clark have appraised a mare found by Thomas M'Coy.

John Sale, A. Cummin and R. Dobbins regarding a camp meeting at the Bigg Bottom on the Scioto River near the Foster's place.

Jesse Spencer, Register of the Land Office in Chillicothe, has land for sale and mentions Martin and Jacob Moler, Bartmess & Hobble, Stephen Freeman, George Hoppes, Samuel Nichols, Edward Macala, Keeler & Fraser, James Neel, Jeremiah Kendale, Samuel R. Holcomb, Thomas M'Neal, John Keller, James Purl, Cornelius Neff, Joseph Shoots, Benjamin Yates, John Graham, William Stump, Isaac Coons, John Hite, Peter Drum, Isaac Snunk, Thomas Pullen, Frances and Hartley Malone, John Ratcliff, Solomon Wilkinson, Renick & Lewis, Broad Cole, Thomas Comer, Andrew Forster, William Stump, Robert Skinner, Anthony Swinehart, Abraham Doll, Joseph Babb, Joseph Vangundy, Thomas M'Naghten, jun., Asa Murphey, William Cox, John Koontz, Elizabeth Sackett, William Young.

Volume X, Wednesday, 16 May 1810, No. 492

An unsigned letter to Judge Sprigg mentions Hon. Thomas Scott, Mr. Kirker.

A note about the publication of a newspaper, the Ohio Lamp, at Lancaster, by Ebenezer F. Seaman.

David Kinkead & Company, in Chillicothe, ask those indebted to them to settle their accounts.

Peter Spurck, in Chillicothe, offers the Green Tree Tavern, formerly occupied by John Irwin, for rent. He also does clock and watch making.

Joseph S. Collins, Chillicothe, executor of the estate of Clement Brown, dec'd, late of Heller's Bottom, on Paint Creek, has corn for sale.

Jesse Wiley asks those indebted to Dr. Samuel Monett to pay their bills.

Peter Kouns, living in Greenup County, near the Sandy Salt Works, Kentucky, reports a runaway slave named Jim.

Volume X, Wednesday, 23 May 1810, No. 493

John T. Barr & Company have a new shipment of goods for sale at their store.

John Terril, on Winn Winship's farm on Scippo Creek, Pickaway County, about a stray horse. Deliver to Winship in Chillicothe.

John Roads, in Brush Creek township, Highland County, reports that James M'Glaughlin and William M'Glaughlin have appraised a horse found by Bigger Head.

James Parker, Huntington township, Adams County, says that Jonathan Rees & Matthias Pitzer appraised a mare found by James Bonner opposite Limestone.

Joseph Miller, in Chillicothe, reports a runaway apprentice to the shoe-maker's business named John Bert.

John Richhart, living one mile above the mouth of Deer Creek, eight miles from Chillicothe, Ross County, reports a stray mare.

Benj. Feurt, in Union township, Scioto County, reports that Uriah Humble and John Shewmaker appraised a mare found by Joseph Scott on Scioto Brush Creek.

Martin Landis, in Fairfield County, reports that John Sherck and Andrew Handshaw have appraised a mare found by Charles Friend.

Volume X, Wednesday, 30 May 1810, No. 494

An unsigned letter to the editor mentions Mr. Sprigg and Mr. Tod.

James & Wood, in Chillicothe, have a new shipment of goods for sale.

Martha Overdeer, Will. Brown & Jacob Grubb, in Franklinton, administrators of the estate of John Overdeer, dec'd, late of Franklin County, regarding the estate sale at his late tavern in Franklinton.

John M'Coy has a new shipment of goods for sale at his store, Chillicothe.

Carlos A. Norton regarding a meeting of the Tammany Society.

Jonathan Monroe, in Chillicothe, taylor and habitmaker, lately from Pitts-burgh, regarding his business in Chillicothe on Mulberry Street.

Stephen Horsey, in Pickaway County, has opened a tavern in the house for-merly occupied by Abraham Stipp adjoining the distillery on the road from Chil-licothe to Franklinton, about a half mile from West-fall.

John Ratcliff reports that George Rains and Laurence Rains have appraised a mare found in Jefferson township, Ross County.

James Dalgarn, in Chillicothe, on Water street, opposite John Anderson's, regarding stray horses.

Christain Benner reports that Joseph Rockhold and John Long have appraised a horse found by Joseph Heistant in Paxton township, Ross County.

Volume X, Wednesday, 6 June 1810, No. 495

An unsigned letter to the editor mentions Judge Scott, Mr. Irwin, Mr. Brown, Mr. Tod, Mr. Sprigg.

David Ridgeway, in Racoon township, Gallia County, reports that Patrick Reed and Theophilus Blake have appraised a mare found by Asariah Jinkins. Also Thos. Mathews & Jordon Manring appraised a mare found by Ebenezer Donaldson.

John W. Millar, in Seal township, Scioto County, reports that Cornelius E. Millar and Abraham Barritt have appraised a horse found by Jeremiah Cooper.

Daniel Kain reports that Oliver Lindsey and Danl. Kidd have appraised a mare found by Moses Leonard, living in Williamsburgh township, Clermont County.

Robert D. Richardson, at Worthington, about subscriptions to the Fredonian and Western Intelligencer.

Patience Wright and Richard Askren, in Adams County, administrators of the estate of Robert Wright, dec'd, regarding the estate settlement.

James Gordon reports that Cristian Chramlich and Daniel Vandmark have appraised a horse found by Abraham Vn. Courtwright.

Volume X, Wednesday, 27 June 1810, No. 498

Samuel Tagart has received a new shipment of goods at his store, Chillicothe.

Samuel Huntington, Jesup N. Couch and William Skinner, in Chillicothe, about the Ohio University at Athens, superintended by Rev. Jacob Lindsly.

John Parker, in Mifflin township, Ross County, reports that Joseph Moore and Frederick Grove have appraised a mare found by John Grove, living on Morgan's fork of Sunfish Creek.

Henry Thurman, in Union township, Fayette County, reports that Stephen Hill and Peleg Rodgers have appraised a horse found by Christopher Coffman.

Burgess Elliott, in Mifflin township, Ross County, reports that William Parker and Samuel Skowden have appraised a mare found by Isaac Margues.

Hugh Power, living at Ellis' ferry, opposite Limestone, found some cattle.

Geo. Will and Thos. Armstrong, administrators of the estate of Christian Haynes, late of Ross County, dec'd, offers his house for sale.

Geo. Frederick, in Green township, Ross County, reports that Cherry Brown and John Crouch have appraised a horse found by Joseph Ritchardson.

John Greave, in Jefferson township, Ross County, reports that Samuel Darby and Nathan Cox have appraised a horse found by William Darby. Daniel Barber and John Comer appraised a horse found by Jesse Redlick.

A note regarding an act of Congress to benefit Arthur St.Clair.

Carlos A. Norton regarding a meeting of the Tammany Society.

David Bonner, in Chillicothe, has land for sale on Main Paint Creek.

Joseph Hays reports that Thomas Crabb and Samuel Itcheson have appraised a mare found by James Davis in Pickaway County, Deer Creek township.

Joseph Jones, in Concord township, Miami County, reports a strayed horse.

Samuel Cisney & David Woolcot, Chillicothe, about notes to John M'Dougal.

James Trego about a stray horse. Deliver to Geo. Rennick near Chillicothe.

Geo. Will, in Colerain township, Ross County, reports that John Beach and David Foust have appraised a mare found by Jacob Kershner. James S. Webster and David Foust have appraised a horse found by Thomas Armstrong.

James Parker, in Huntington township, opposite Limestone, reports that Nathan Ellis and William Jacobs have appraised a mare found by James Bonner.

J.W. Campbell reports that Leonard Cole and Stephen Beach have appraised a horse found by Francis Lockhart, in Tiffin township, Adams County.

Seth Adams and Elihu Ives have Merino sheep from the flock of Col. David Humphries, of Connecticut.

Enos Prather, in Pee Pee township, Ross County, says that Arthur Chenowith and William Ward have appraised a mare found by William Acton.

Wm. Florence, Pickaway County, Darby township, says that Aaron Stevenson and Veachel Howard have appraised a mare found by David Shepherd.

Burgess Elliott, in Mifflin township, Ross County, reports that Isaac Margues and Charles O'Briant have appraised a mare found by Joshua Davis.

James Kerr, in Paint township, Fayette County, reports that Horatio Walker and David Hankins have appraised a mare found by Amos Hankins.

Moses Hewitt, living on the road from Athens to Chillicothe, in Athens County, regarding a stray mare. She was raised by James Davis, living about 5 miles from Chillicothe, near Mr. Seamore's. Also a mare from Matthew Jameson, living near Old Town on Paint Creek.

John A. Fulton, in Chillicothe, reports a strayed horse.

John T. Barr & Company have received a new shipment of books.

James Norris, living on Little Scioto, Green township, Scioto County, reports two strayed mares.

Henry Mussleman, in Springfield township, Ross County, reports that Michael Cryder, jun., and William Downs appraised a mare found by Thomas M'Collaster.

John Roads, in Brush Creek township, Highland County, reports that Jacob Ashenfelder and Felix Hufman have appraised a mare found by Samuel Clark.

John Ratcliff reports that John Wilkison and Joseph Wilkison have appraised a mare found by Solomon Cox in Jefferson township, Ross County.

Benj. Williams reports that Ambrose Grafton and Moses Jones have appraised a horse found by Enoch Cox, of Colerain township, Ross County.

Coonrod Flesher, in Fayette County, reports that Henry Flesher and John Hays have appraised a horse found by James Hays, of Paint township.

John Clark reports that John Burris and Nimrod Lister have appraised a mare found by Soloman Brittenham, living in Ross County, Deerfield township.

Volume X, Wednesday, 4 July 1810, No. 499
An unsigned letter to the editor mentions William Sprigg, George Tod, Levin Belt, William W. Irwin, Ethan A. Brown, John Thompson.

A list of letters left at the Post Office in Chillicothe includes William Askew, Catharine Anderson, William Adkins, John Arthur of Daniel, Isaac and Joseph Adamson, John Anderson, Isaac Anstill, James Adams, Jacob Armitage, Thomas Armstrong, Richard Barry, William B. Beckitt, John Bird, William Bailey, Amos Burnet, William Black, John Biarly, Henry Baker, Hugh Black, Clement Brown, Catharine Baum, William Bowdle, William Badley, George Bell or H. Countryman, David and William Baggs, John Burt, Mr. Boush, Christian Benner, Joseph Balding, James Baker, Isaac Bowen, John Berry, Francis Boldwin, Wm. Bearse, John Baker, Ephraim Bonham, John Cline, Thomas Crow, Isreal Crow, Enoch Cockrill, Daniel Crabb, Edward Crabb, sen., William Chandler, James Camel, Huton Clark, Walter Clark, George Carpenter, George Coyle, Nathaniel Cox, Abraham Claypool, William Clark, jun., Nathan Cony, Edmund Clarridge, Thomas Cochran, Benjamin Currens, Jacob Caylor, Jesse Cherry, James Curry, John Culvert, William Dixon, James Davison, John Duglass, Andrew Duglass, William Davis, John L. Dereckson, Aaron Donaldson, Spencer Dayton, George Dawson, Daniel Durt, John Devalt, Joseph Dix, Ramus Davis, James Devenport, Margert Denning and Easter Moore, George Emery, John Evans, Abram Eater, James Emmet, Samuel Edward, Adam Funk, William Florance, Gabriel Fourt, William H. Francess, jr., Isaac Flowers, Elisha Fitch, William Fleming, John Griffith, John Gilmore, Mr. Gilmore, James K. George, Jared Graham, Levi Goodwin, John Gooldsberry, Andrew Glase, John Gobb, Lewis Grove or John Crab, Mrs. Golds, Jacob Gundy, Robert Greyham, Richard Gosley, Jacob Holderman, Jacob Hotsinpiller, Mr. Hall (taylor), Samuel Harvey, John How, William Holaday or Samuel Holaday, Enock Hurley, William Hannaman, Vachel Howard, John Hunnel, Mark Hammons, Philip Hartley, John Hill, Pheildan Hubbard, Joseph Hays, Thomas Harman, Thomas Harvey, Samuel Hollida, Doctr. Geo. C. Hart, Randolph Hughes, Joseph Horn, Henry Henson, William Justis, Thomas R. Joynes, Thomas Ing, Younger Johnston, Hubbert Jones, John Jones, Ephraim Kemper, John Kow, Nancy Kendall, David Keyser, Andrew Knox, Thomas Kerney, Thomas Kearney, Robert Kennedy, Joseph Lockard, Elias Langham, William Loveless, Sally Lovett, Mr. Lamme, Jacob Lawyer, Edward Long, Doct. John Larrabee, Alexander M'Lintock, Joshua Mathews, Asa Merener, Donald M'Arthur, Thomas Millar, Wheeler Meeker, John M'Neele, John Moody, James Mines, David Meredth, James Moffett, James M'Kinney, Thomas M'Donald, Hugh Mtgomery, George Myres, Jesse Miller, Hannah Minshall, Widow M'Killip, Joseph Moore, William Mason, Alexander M'Clean, Daniel M'Ilroy, Enock M'Daniel, Robert M'Dill, Sarah Nichols, Jacob Nyce, Samuel Orr, Nimrod Owings, Richard Osborn, Levi Post, Russell E. Post, Augustus Papassion, Ruben Parris, Esqr. Patterson, Benjamin Phillips, Isaiah Pankus, Betsey Purloe, William Porter, Charles Parker, Absalom Parker, James Porter, John Prdey, Wm. Prukett or Edward Buzac, James Phillips, John Peake, Wm. Phillians, William Rogers, Mathias Ridenhour, Nathan Reeves, Edward D. Rowe, James Renick, Coonrod Ready, Thomas Romine, Garrett Rosaboom, Wm. Reede, William Rutledge, Joseph Ramey, Joseph Russel, William Rinick, Aaron Rerreck, Benjamin Rea or Thomas Nichols, Robert or Benjamin Rea on Deer Creek, Susank Roberts, Thomas Rumly, Henry Rarrdon, Henry Robinson, John Rilter, Jermiah Russell, Jno. Robins, Elizabeth Rodgers, Jacob S. Rielin, Mary Robinson, Margert Slaughter, Hector Sanford, Samuel Schouten, Jacob Snider, Samuel Shepard, Jacob Steer, William Sprigg, Samane Shepherd, Doct. Robert H. Smith, Joseph Sewell at Peepee, John R. Stokes, Benjamin Shockley, John Shackleford, Job Smith, James Shargent, Charles Snyder, Daniel Snider, James Shaphard, James Sulliven, Robert Shirley, Reuben Slaven, John Scott, Oliver Simpson, Joshua Skuttles, David Smith, Ezra Tubbs, John Tribby, Nichols Tucker, Francis Tully, Webster Thomas, Amos Taylor, George Timmons, William Thrdilkild, William Tailor, Elias Turner, William Taylor, Charles Thompson, William Townsend, Thomas Wright, Mr. Winsenheller, Thomas Ward, Col. John Watts, Wm. Wise, John Wilright, William Wilson, Moses Wright, Simeon Wayland, Daniel Woollam, Sally Warron, Charles Woodson, William Ward, James Whitesides, Humphry Warron, Benjamin Williams, William Wright, Silus Worren, John Winder, Doct. Ezra Walker, Benjamin Willias, Thomas Watkins, Robert Watson, James Watts, George Williams, James Willson, James Whitesides.

Edward Hopper, living in Franklinton, reports a stolen horse.

Henry Brush, at Chillicothe, about a meeting of the Grand Lodge of Masons.

James Kilgore reports that John Mooney and Wm. Slaughter have appraised a horse found by William How, of Jefferson township, Ross County.

Geo. Will reports that James S. Webster and David Foust have appraised a horse found by Thomas Armstrong of Colerain township, Ross County.

Volume X, Wednesday, 11 July 1810, No. 500

A note regarding Mr. Morrow in Congress.

Wm. S. Hutt is appointed clerk of the Supreme Court vice John M'Dougal.

An account of the Fourth of July celebration in Colerain township mentions Killian Ruse.

Marriage: John Cohoon married Miss Sally Cook, both of Ross County, on Sunday, 7 July 1810, by Thomas White.

Marriage: Peter Williamson, from New Jersey, to Miss Susannah Vandervort, of Ross County, on 12 June 1810, by Rev. Thomas W. Sweney.

A note regarding the Camp Meeting to be led by Rev. Solomon Langdon, the preacher in charge of the Deer Creek circuit. The meeting will be held near Gen. Worthington's house.

Carlos A. Norton regarding a meeting of the Tammany Society.

Doctor Edward Tiffin is again practicing medicine in Chillicothe.

John Richman Stokes, Chillicothe, the legal heir and representative of John Stokes, dec'd, has paid redemption money for land bought by John O'bannion, Jonathan Reeder, Jacob Wheeler, William Maxwell.

Wm. Robinson, silversmith, in Chillicothe, wants to buy clean ashes.

Nehemiah Gates reports that Hiram Bradley and N. Gates appraised a horse found by William Johnston, living on Little Darby Creek, in Jefferson township.

Henry Porter, in Twin township, Ross County, reports that Edward Keran and Alex. Monroe have appraised a horse found by Samuel Turner. Also Alex. Ramsey and Josiah Chizum have appraised a mare found by Jeffry Cox.

Wyllys Silliman, Register of the Land Office at Zanesville, has land for sale and mentions Thomas Spear, Thomas Dyson, Dennis Cassatt, Byrd Lockhart, David Harry, jun., Jacob Cooper, Frederick Young, Andrew Slinker, George Beyemer, and Jesse Oldakers.

Daniel Symmes, Register of the Land Office at Cincinnati, has land for sale and mentions John Ewing, John Couner, Enoch M'Carty, Isaac Parker, George Kister, David Hartman, Francis Patterson, Jeremiah Stansberry, Peter Parham, Amos Davis, William Pheres, Abraham Hartsell, John Swineheart, William C. Schenck, Daniel Crume, Nathan Springer, Henry Brile, John Reynolds, Alexander Stinson, John Townsend, George Gillespie, Isaac Beal, John Murphy, Martin Shuey, John Phillips, Henry Shidler, John Mote, John Ross, John Keller, John Conner.

Henry Thurman, in Union township, Fayette County, reports that Benjamin Davis and Peledge Rodgers have appraised a mare found by David Thompson.

George Hornbeck says Country Tanner and Samuel Dawson appraised a mare found by George Hornbeck, on Deer Creek, Pickaway County, Darby township.

William Lacock reports that Hutson Martin and Thomas Murphy appraised a horse found by John Glendening of Eagle township, Adams County. Also James Kindal and William Davidson appraised a horse found by Joseph Spencer.

George Creamer, in Jefferson township, Fayette County, reports that Patrick Kerans and Michael Creamer have appraised a horse found by Linhard Paret.

Jonathan Minshall reports that Walter Watson and John Warner appraised a mare found by William Jameson, living in Madison County, Union township.

John M'Donald reports that William Loveless and William Given appraised a mare found by Joseph Crouch, of Twin township, Ross County.

William Smith, in Paxton township, Ross County, reports that Benjamin M'Clure and Samuel Irvin have appraised a mare found by John Caldwell.

George Hornbeck says John Alkire & Country Tanner appraised a mare found by Benjamin Busick, living on Possum Run, Darby township, Pickaway County.

Volume X, Wednesday, 1 August 1810, No. 502

Th. S. Hinde has land for sale adjoining Massie's old Station.

Carlos A. Norton regarding a meeting of the Tammany Society.

David Kinkead gives division orders to the militia.

Jesup N. Couch about the election of a General in place of Jeremiah M'Lene.

John Perkins, in Colerain township, Ross County, reports that John Bunn and Peter Culp have appraised a mare found by Jacob Bausher.

William Robinson reports that Reuben Pursel and Thos. Brown have appraised a horse found by John M'Coy, of Union township, Ross County.

Uriah Springer reports that Joseph Long and J. Lucas have appraised a horse found by David Reynolds, of Eagle township, Adams County.

John T. Barr & Company have a new shipment of leather for sale.

A letter to Return Jonathan Meigs, jun., is printed and mentions Gen. Massie.

A letter to the public nominating Gen. Thomas Worthington for governor.

An article regarding William Blood who went to sea from Boston about eight years ago at age 18. He was made prisoner at Tripoli, but escaped. On arriving in Boston an uncle told him his family had moved to Ohio or Indiana Territory. He had 10 or 11 brothers. Jeremiah Ballard took him as far as Pittsburgh. Blood went alone from there by canoe, but fell out and was drowned.

A note regarding the election to replace Jeremiah M'Lene as general.

Christian Benner is a candidate for county commissioner.

Nominees for public office are listed: Jeremiah Morrow, James Dunlap, Edward Tiffin, Isaac Dawson, James Manary, Samuel Swearingen, Joseph Gardner, William Creighton, sen., William Rutledge, George Will.

Obituary: Mrs. Cochran, wife of Hugh Cochran, died near Chillicothe on Sunday evening last.

O.C.B. Stewart, "teacher of Latin and English school in Cincinnati", has spelling books for sale.

Zacheriah Combs, administrator of the estate of John Combs, dec'd, about the estate settlement.

James Kerr, in Paint township, Fayette County, reports that William Hays and James Hays have appraised a horse found by James Thompson.

Uriah Springer reports that Thomas Grogan and John Carbury have appraised a mare found by John Pricket of Eagle township, Adams County.

Michael Bever reports that Wm. Pemberton and Alexr. Boyd have appraised a mare found by Aaron Hibbs, of Meigs township, Adams County.

Henry Porter, in Twin township, Ross County, reports that Alexr. Ramsey and George Porter have appraised a mare found by Frederick Baker.

Wm. Harper, in Athens County, Athens township, reports that Isaac Barker and Joseph Barker have appraised a mare found by Moses Hewitt.

George Frederick, in Green township, Ross County, reports that Nicholas Bunn and Andrew Crouch have appraised a mare found by Peter Bunn.

Zechariah Welsh reports that William Welsh and John Argubright appraised a mare found by Francis Creamer, living in Springfield township, Ross County.

Henry Thurman, in Union township, Fayette County, reports that Stephen Hill and John Hoppes have appraised a mare found by William Harper, living on Paint Creek above Greenfield.

David Ridgway, in Racoon township, Gallia County, reports that Andrew Armstrong and William Nox have appraised a horse found by Thomas Farmer.

Volume X, Wednesday, 22 August 1810, No. 505

William M'Farland has a new shipment of goods for sale at his store.

David Kinkead & Co., Chillicothe, want to buy wheat at John Crouse's mill.

George Creamer, in Jefferson township, Fayette County, reports that Abner Robinson and Nicholas Robinson have appraised a mare found by Patrick Karnes.

Wm. Creighton, Sen., Sheriff, regarding a sheriff's sale of the property of James Crain at the suit of Henry Hollar.

William Young, in Chillicothe, has erected a new tan yard on Water Street. Deliver your hides to John M'Landburgh's store.

Adam Turner, in Chillicothe, has leather for sale.

Joseph Kline, living adjoining the town of New Lisbon, reports a stolen horse.

Rev. John Sale will preside over the camp meeting at White Brown's house on Deer Creek on September 1st.

Thomas Orr & Company have moved their shop to the corner of Second and Paint Streets, Chillicothe, where they have tin ware, stills and kettles for sale.

John Ratcliff says that Richard Wilkerson & John Ratcliff, jun., appraised a mare found by Charles Hobson, living on the north fork of Salt Creek, Ross County, Jefferson township.

T. Worthington says that he is a candidate for governor.

Doct. Hamm, now living in Zanesville, didn't write a letter to the editor.

An unsigned letter to the editor mentions Gen. Worthington.

R.D. Richardson, at Worthington, reports a stray horse. Deliver to Henry Brown in Franklinton, Hugh Creighton of Walnut Plains, Capt. T.H. Richardson of Jefferson on Pickaway Plains or Thomas Steel in Chillicothe.

Philip Stout, in Green township, Fayette County, reports that Thomas Ellis and Isaac Todhunter have appraised a mare found by Mordeica Ellis, living on Walnut run. Also John Todhunter and Henry Johnson appraised a horse found by Christian Barger on Lee's Creek.

Thomas Steel regarding a marshal's sale of the property of Joseph Kerr at the suits of Presly Neville and Isaac Craig.

A. Lindsay has tin ware for sale at his shop in Chillicothe.

Zur Combs, administrator of John Combs, dec'd, about the estate settlement.

John Shields, in Hillsborough, Highland County, about a runaway apprentice boy named Taply Davis, age 16, who was seen by Mr. Turner in Lancaster.

Benj. Feurt, in Union township, Scioto County, reports that Gabriel Feurt and George Feurt have appraised a horse found by John Noel.

George Hornbeck says that Country Tanner and Robert Barr appraised a mare found by Samuel Gilliland, on Possum Run, Pickaway County, Darby township.

Samuel White reports that Joseph Dickson and Wm. Domigan have appraised a horse found by Samuel White, in Franklin township, Franklin County.

John Roads reports that Martin Contryman and David Evans have appraised a mare found by James West, of Brush Creek township, Highland County.

James Moore reports that John Leech and Lewis Bible have appraised a horse found by Arthur Ellison, living in Tiffin township, Adams County.

Aaron Moore reports that John Sheppard and William Hannah have appraised a mare found by Thomas Kincade, jun., living in Adams County, Sprigg township.

Volume XI, Wednesday, 5 September 1810, No. 507

James Clark, in Jefferson township, Scioto County, reports that John Clark and Simon Conway have appraised a mare found by Henry Kirkendall.

William Lacock reports that Wm. M'Candless and Hutson Martin appraised a horse found by Stephen Davis, of Adams County, Eagle township.

John Roads reports that Job Hagigh and George Sniter have appraised a horse found by Samuel Clark, of Brush Creek township, Highland County.

Adam Kirkpatrick reports that John M'Intire and Samuel Finton appraised a horse found by William M'Intire, living in Adams County, Wayne township.

Philip Stout, in Green township, Fayette County, Rattlesnake fork of Paint, says that James Sanders and David Dutton appraised a mare found by Isaiah Row.

A note regarding the election for governor mentions Col. Meigs, Mr. Beecher, Mr. Morrow, Philemon Beecher.

An account of a quarrel at the salt-works between James Bradley and the wife and children of James Quire. Pleasant Webb tried to stop the fight and ended by fatally shooting Mr. Quire. Webb, age 45, has a wife and five or six children.

Marriage: John F. Keys, of Baltimore, to Miss Margaret Barr, of Chillicothe, on Wednesday evening last, by Rev. Mr. Wilson.

Capt. Daniel Hare's company, in Twin township, nominate the following for office: Thomas Worthington, James Dunlap, Edward Tiffin, James Manary, Joseph Gardner, Isaac Dawson. Citizens of Paxton township, meeting at Christian Platter's house with Christian Benner and William Kent presiding, nominate Thomas Worthington, Jeremiah Morrow, Joseph Kerr, Abraham Claypool, William Creighton, Jun., Henry Brush, William Sterrett, Edward Tiffin, William Creighton, sen., Christian Benner, William Rutledge. The Democratic Republican ticket mentions Thomas Worthington, Jeremiah Morrow, James Dunlap, Edward Tiffin, Isaac Dawson, William Rutledge, John Martin, James Manary, Abraham Claypool, Joseph Gardner, William Creighton, sen.

William Creighton, sheriff, regarding a sheriff's sale of the property of Hugh Bracken, on Deer Creek, at the suit of William Lamb.

Jos. S. Collins, Chillicothe, executor of the estate of Clement Brown, dec'd, regarding the estate settlement.

John Goodman and Isaac Claypool, administrators of the estate of William Dorem, dec'd, regarding the estate settlement.

John Haynes has saddles for sale at George Haynes' house in Chillicothe.

John Turner, in Pleasant township, Franklin County, reports that Samuel Kerr and John Tumbleston appraised a mare found by Thomas Strews, on Darby Creek.

Abel Larkin, in Gallia County, Salisbury township, reports that John Hysle and Saml. Arvain have appraised a mare found by Benson Jones.

William Creighton, sheriff, regarding the sheriff's sale of the property of Elias Langham to satisfy the following judgments: Joseph Beard for the use of E. Doolittle & Company; Charles M'Gowan; William Beard and Joseph Beard. The land was surveyed for Samuel Smith on Buskirk's run, waters of Deer Creek.

Robert Armstrong is a candidate for commissioner in Franklin County.

Geo. Will reports that Daniel Kershner and William Huber have appraised a mare found by George Goul, of Colerain township, Ross County.

Henry Ellis, living in Clinton County near Xenia, reports a stray horse.

John Hamm has moved to Zanesville and asks those indebted to him to settle their accounts with John Hutt.

John Bush has a horse for sale, property of John and George W. Baylor, of Ky.

Wm. Rutledge, Chillicothe, gives orders for the Militia to meet at Felix Renick's house at High Bank.

Daniel Kain reports that John Kain and James Perrine have appraised a mare found by Absolum Smith, of Williamsburgh township, Clermont County.

Volume XI, Wednesday, 26 September 1810, No. 510

Michael Cryder, Jun., has land for sale in Ross County on the Scioto River.

Jesup N. Couch, Chillicothe, has land for sale in Athens County, entered in the name of Push Davis.

Brig. Gen. Robert Lucas, at Portsmouth, reports that Maj. Joseph Campbell is appointed inspector and William Kendall, Quarter Master.

Wm. Creighton, Sen., regarding polling places in Ross County mentions Adam Stewart (living in Jefferson township where Wm. Dickson lived); Henry Toons in Deerfield township; A. Chinoweth in Pee Pee township; William Pillar in Mifflin township; Elisha Kelly in Bainbridge in Paxton township; Samuel Davis in Buckskin township; Mrs. Elliott in Twin township; John M'Neal in Concord township; David Corbett in Union township; Killian Ruse in Colerain township; George Ritchey in Green township; William Niblack in Lick township; Redman Conder in Franklin township; George Shane in Springfield township.

Obituary: James T. Crockwell, age 27, died on Monday night, 24 September 1810, in Chillicothe.

Obituary: Mrs. Trimble died last Sabbath in Ross County.

An unsigned letter to the editor mentions Mr. Worthington, Mr. Meigs.

A note regarding a meeting of the militia in Athens County mentions Capt. William Lowry, John Corey, Return J. Meigs, jun., Jeremiah Morrow, William R. Putnam, Doctor Samuel P. Hildreth, Zebulon Griffin. A similar meeting in Twin township mentions John Harness, James Dunlap, Abraham Claypool, Isaac Dawson, James Manary, Edward Tiffin, George Yoakem, Job Harness, Thomas Worthington, Joseph Gardner, Jeremiah Morrow, William Creighton, sen., Christian Benner, William Rutledge.

John Cummins, in Union township, Ross County, is a candidate for office.

Saml. Williams regarding a meeting of the Tammany Society.

Francis DeClercq, clerk of Gallia County, regarding the suit of Jeremiah Carpenter, for the use of John Forest, vs. James Schoolcraft.

John Sharp and Matt. Ferguson, administrators of the estate of William Snodgrass, dec'd, regarding the estate settlement.

William Moore, at Jefferson on Pickaway Plains, has a house for rent in Jefferson, opposite Mr. Nevill's.

Alexander Smyth, of Wythe, Virginia, reports two runaway slaves, Tom and Charlotte, heading for Ohio.

James Parker reports that Michael M'Donald and William Raines appraised a mare found by Wm. Middleton, in Huntington township.

Elisha Kelly reports that Aeneas Faulk and Robert Morrison have appraised a mare found by Robert Dill in Paxton township, Ross County.

John T. Barr & Company, in Chillicothe, want to buy hemp.

Joseph Miller, in Chillicothe, has moved his nail factory.

Stephen Barton, living on Deer Creek, Paint township, Fayette County, offers all of his livestock, farming utensils and household furniture for sale.

Ignatius Thompson and Peter Jackson, in Union township, Ross County, executors of the estate of Ozwald Thompson, dec'd, regarding the estate sale.

Geo. Frederick, in Green township, Ross County, reports that John Oruno and Henry Oruno have appraised a mare found by Samuel Arrasmith.

The tavern formerly occupied by Maj. Reynolds in Zanesville is for rent. Apply to Col. James Perry, on the premises, or William M'Farland in Chillicothe.

William Stubbs, in Chillicothe, wants to buy flax seed at John Carlisle's store or Joseph Miller's nail factory.

Andrew Clemmer, living in Wayne township, Adams County, offers a reward for the return of a stolen horse.

Jesse Spencer, Register of the Land Office in Chillicothe, has land for sale and mentions David Rees, Elnathan Scofield, Moses Dawson, J. M'Lene, Matthias Kesler, G. Hoffman, H. Fullerton, John Markle, sen., William Wilson, Samuel Edwards, Daniel VanMetre, Peter Overmire, John Crist, John Kroninger, Samuel Smith, W. Creighton, John Graham, M. Baldwin, David Shalenberger, Jun., Hugh O'Hara, Frederick Leather, Sebastian Foust, Jacob Nigh, William Entricken, Lucas Sullivant, William York, Nathaniel Willis, A. Weaver, J. Roush, Jacob Jerick, Daniel Roberts, Thomas V. Swearengen, Martin Folk, James Spencer, Jun., John Zeller, Adam Croyle, Jacob Bower, David M'Donald, Daniel Meyer, William Irwin, Christian Haynes, Hugh Poor, Benjamin Jones, John M'Dougal, Reuben Mounts, Alexander M'Intire, Augustine Friend, G. Wells, S. M'Callum, William M'Cabe, jun., Henry Huston, Asa Mounts, Benjamin Murphy, Adam Zeller, David Crull, Nicholas Bolonback, Henry Hosher, Bennett Armsworthy, Patrick Reed, John Carpenter.

John Parker, in Mifflin township, Ross County, reports that Joseph Moore and Isaac Peniston have appraised a horse found by Robert Price, living on Morgan's fork of Sunfish Creek.

Joel Woods, in Paint township, Fayette County, reports that Adam Miller and Lambert Kimble have appraised a mare found by Armstead Carder.

Benj. Feurt, in Union township, Scioto County, reports that John Vastine and John Wright, jun., have appraised a horse found by John R. Sanderson.

Levi Barber regarding the petition of Abner Lord, of Marietta, an insolvent debtor, in the court of Washington County.

Volume XI, Wednesday, 10 October 1810, No. 512

John Ellison reports that Nathl. Collins and Cyrus Sanders have appraised a mare found by John Darlinton, in Sprigg township, Adams County.

James M'Manis, Director for Clinton County, has lots for sale in Armenia.

Daniel Dresback, at the Pickaway Plains, has lots for sale in Circleville.

Joseph Darlinton and T.S. Foot (attorney) regarding the suit of Joseph Shaw vs. Samuel Latta in the Adams County Court of Common Pleas.

Philip Cherry, in Harrison township, Pickaway County, reports that Thos. Hudson and Jesse Cherry have appraised a mare found by Adam Peters.

A note regarding election returns mentions Gen. Worthington, Mr. Claypool, Mr. Tiffin, Mr. Creighton, Mr. Manary, Mr. Kerr, Mr. Brush.

A note regarding the publication of Browne's Cincinnati Almanac, by John W. Browne & Company, at the office of the Liberty Hall.

N. Beasley, Job Dinning and James Bath, commissioners, have lots for sale.

A list of letters left at the Post Office in Chillicothe includes Robert Adams, Mahlon Anderson, James Adams, John Apting, Gerdeniah Arsher, William Barnes, Stephen Butler, John Burk, Daniel Baldwin, Edward Bennett, William Baggs, Fredrick Brager, William Bull, David and William Baggs, James Blain, Richard Baily, John Boyd, Joseph Bigby, Moses Bixby, Thomas Bowin, Betsey Brown, White Brown, Christopher Bartlet, George Compton, John Carter, John H. Clarno, Hugh Cochran, sen. Uledrey Coonrod, sen., John H. Cannon, John Clark, jun., Sally Cambell, Farzay Chad, Samuel Conrad, James Caldwell, Kenner Crable, Henry Counce, William Clark, Calep Childress, Richard Douglass, Watson Douglass, Henry Davis, Benjamin Duncan, Maria Duncan, Jacob Dasher, James Dallgarl, Robert Dickey, John Downing, James

Devanport, Clarenden or Joseph Dix, Doctr. Amasa Delano, William Elwood, John Entrekin, Elener Essix, Ellas Ellis, Col. William Fontain, Isaac Funk, Hugh Flyn, Joseph Farmer, William Fielding, William Fluk, Gabriel Fourt, George Fry, Elisha Fitch, Haron Freeman, George Grayham, John Griffith, Samuel Hardy, Christian Hoffman, Johnston Hempill, Robert Hedges, George Heath, George Hann, Jonathan Hand, Joshua Hobbs, Daniel Helin, George Hays, Lucas Hawkins, John Hunnil, George Hughes, Andrew Haggerty, William Hume, Henry Hosteller, Benjamin Hutitcheson, Joseph Harton, Benjamin Hains, Anthony Hall, Henry Hester, Thomas Hardy, Jesse Huff, John Hunter, Nathaniel Hamilton, John Jean, Elijah Johnston, Jacob James, William Johnson, Ann Inglish, Cornelus Johnston, David Jones, John Jackson, Zachrs. Janes, Jesse Kimmel, James Kilgore, Mathew Kilgore, Henry Kaykendell, Peter Kear, Adam Knowls, Wm. Loveless, William Long, Elisa Loffbury, Joseph Lane, James Millar, Abraham Millar, Daniel Mussulman, James M'Chord, William M'Bride, Bethamy Moss, James M'Mahan, John W. Millar, Capt. Thomas Marshall, Alexander Morrow, John M'Hargh, Az Morgan, William Mowbray, James M'Clair, Alexander M'Clean, Capt. James M'Donnald, Benj. M'Clure, William M'Cormick, Archibald M'Lean, Isaac Margues, William Moore, John M'Million, Moses Monrow, Micheal Nicum, Thomas Nutter, William Nickls, John Nixon, C.A. Norton, William Ogdin, Henry Oldaker, Absolam Parker, Salmon Parker, Christain Platter, Elisha Porter, Russell E. Post, Anthony Potts, Isaac Pancake, Susan Pancake, Adam Peters, Henry Phillips, Elizabeth Potts, John G. Park, Agnes Park, James Peril, Jane Quality, Alexander Read, William Rodgers, Robert Rodgers, Margaret Ritchey, James Renix, Simon Robinson, Robert and Benjamin Reed, John W. Robinson, Nathan Rowings, Sary Rogard, Joseph Sands, John Stack, Robert Shirley, John Stump, Abraham Shenton, James Strong, Peter Snider, James Stewart, Wilson Stewart, Joseph Sewell, Moses Scott, John Sanders, Washington Sterret, John Culbert, William Smith, John D. Smith, Jacob Shepherd, Peter H. Storm, Euleston Smith, Ebenezar F. Seaman, Rev. Hector Sanford, Joseph Steer for Cilfred Parkins, Francis Tulley, William Thrailkild, John Terrall, jun., Ezra Tubbs, Mr. M. Turnan in care of W. Creighton, Leonard Timons, Hugh Tomlinson, Warnal Tracy, John Thompson, Henry Vanmeter, James Withrow, Moses Wilk, John Work, Isaac Warner, Thomas Wright, Elizabeth Wolf, Ben. P. and May C. Walkins, Michael Walton, Baynard White, Francis Whitlow, Landon Williams, Andrew Wilson, Thomas White, Samuel Wycoff, Frederick Zagar, Joseph Tiffin.

John Hutt regarding a runaway servant girl named Sally Hill, age 10.

Volume XI, Wednesday, 24 October 1810, No. 514

Marriage: Alexander M'Clean to Miss Maria Duncan, daughter of Benjamin Duncan, in Pickaway County, on Tuesday evening last.

Saml. Williams regarding a meeting of the Tammany Society.

Robert Stuart, in Fayette County, has lots for sale in the town of Washington.

Henry Thurman, in Union township, Fayette County, reports that Stephen Hill and John Hoppes have appraised a horse found by Jacob Young.

Geo. Will reports that Matthias Engle and Geo. Wolf have appraised a mare found by Jacob Bousher, of Colerain township, Ross County.

Henry Abrams and George Will, at Adelphi, administrators of the estate of Reuben Abrams, dec'd, regarding the estate settlement.

George Jamison and Jacob Jamison, administrators of the estate of Matthew Jamison, dec'd, regarding the estate settlement.

John M'Clean regarding the settlement of the taxes in Ross County.

John Greave, in Jefferson township, Ross County, reports that Benj. Cox and Adam Coon have appraised a mare found by Nathan Cox.

Job Dinning reports that David Duncan and John Baritt have appraised a mare found by Robert Scott, in Tiffin township, Adams County.

John Ellis reports that John Turnis and Abraham Washburn have appraised a horse found by Thomas Scott, of Sprigg township, Adams County.

Volume XI, Wednesday, 7 November 1810, No. 516

A note regarding the Chillicothe Manufacturing Society is printed.

John Martin, in Chillicothe, reports that Martin & Boyd have commenced the brewing business and have beer for sale.

William Stergeon and Beal Cullum have rented the fulling mill of John Trimble, dec'd, at Kennickenick, about seven miles from Chillicothe. Deliver cloth to E. Doolittle's store in Chillicothe.

Doctor Samuel Monett has resumed his practice of medicine in Chillicothe.

Daniel Kain reports that Stephen Smith and Thomas Foster have appraised a mare found by Samuel Maham, in Williamsburgh township, Clermont County.

Wyllys Silliman, Register of the Land Office at Zanesville, has land for sale and mentions Joseph Butler, Dennis Casset, James Johnston, Peter Weyrick, John Baird, Godfrey Weymer, Joseph Smith, William Smith, Neal M'Naughten, George Beymer, Jacob Ayres, David Finley, Increase Matthews, Joel and Silas Zane, Zacheriah Chandler, Joseph Darrah, Joseph W. Satterthwaite, Benjamin Robinson, and Joseph K. M'Cune.

Robert Stewart regarding the sale of the lots in Washington, Fayette County.

Samuel Swearingen & Company want to buy pork in Chillicothe.

Thomas Kerr, in Pee Pee township, administrator of the estate of Mary Kerr, late of Ross County, dec'd, regarding the estate settlement.

James Kilgore reports that Isaac Heaton and John Botkin have appraised a mare found by James Kilgore of Jefferson township, Ross County.

John Robins reports that Daniel Robins and Jesse Esex have appraised a horse found by Thomas Kerr, living in Ross County, Buckskin township.

Jacob Worley, in Paint township, Highland County, reports that Benjamin Bentley and William Ballard have appraised a horse found by Demcey Overman.

Joseph Kerr wants to buy hogs and wheat and to hire some coopers.

Volume XI, Wednesday, 21 November 1810, No. 518

Obituary: Mrs. Martha Irwin, age 30, wife of John Irwin and daughter of Christopher Quigley of Cumberland County, Pennsylvania, died in Chillicothe on Wednesday evening.

Rev. Robert Cloud, a minister of the Methodist Episcopal Church will preach in Chillicothe next Sabbath.

Volume XI, Wednesday, 28 November 1810, No. 519

James & Wood have a new shipment of goods for sale at their store.

Joseph Tiffin & Company have a new shipment of drugs, medicines and paints at their store in Chillicothe.

John Greave, in Jefferson township, Ross County, reports that Isaac Heaton and Isaac Greave have appraised a mare found by Samuel Logue.

H. & J. Ingham want to buy clean linen and cotton rags. Deliver to David Kinkead's store, the printing offices of Joseph S. Collins & Company and Peter Parcels and at Mr. Turney's shop in Chillicothe. Or to Aaron Dolly, Levi Warner, Joseph Gardner or White Brown in Union township. Or to John Webster or David Crouse in Green township. Or to Henry Nevell's store on Pickaway Plains. Or to David Crouse's house on Kennikenick.

John T. Barr & Company have a new shipment of goods for sale at their store.

John Daer reports that Samuel Tyler, of Hubbard township, Trumbull County, found a strayed mare.

James Parker, in Huntington township, Adams County, reports that George Shelton and Francis Smith have appraised a mare found by John Jones.

Marriage: Andrew Poe married Miss Mary Ott, both of Chillicothe, on Tuesday evening last, by John Ferguson.

Col. James Dunlap is a candidate for senator.

A note regarding a meeting of the citizens of Chillicothe mentions Gen. Joseph Kerr and Thomas James.

David Abbott is re-elected senator from Geauga, Cuyahoga, Ashtabula and Portage Counties. Peter Hitchcock and Elias Harmon are representatives.

John Woodbridge about a meeting of the Bank of Chillicothe stockholders.

Adam Kirkpatrick, in Adams County, reports that Gaven Mitchel and Joseph M'Neel have appraised a mare found by Wm. Baldridg, living in Wayne township.

Wm. S. Hutt, tax collector in Scioto township, Ross County, has lots for sale.

A note regarding books printed by John W. Browne & Company, printers, of Cincinnati, mentions Rev. Solomon Langdon, Rev. Richard Baxter, Samuel Palmer, Rev. John Jennings.

Robert Stewart regarding the sale of lots in Washington.

George Bucher, in Union township, Ross County, about a note to James Smith, sen., of Virginia.

James Renick, Sheriff of Pickaway County, regarding a special election to replace Joseph Kerr, resigned, in the Senate.

Daniel Symmes, Register of the Land Office at Cincinnati, has land for sale and mentions Blasdel & Stark, Robert Harding, Robert Renick, Jonathan Donnel, Lewis Drake, Timothy Green, Jacob Eulass, Ethel Kellogg, Richard Gray, William Powel, John Fix, Daniel Conner, Joseph Cooper, Moses Vail, Thomas Miller, Felix Rock, James Taylor, Moses Vail, Aaron Biggs, William C. Schenck, Morton Irwin, Abraham Thomas, O. Schenck, James Johnson, John Sample, James Irwin Nesbit, Stephen Jay, John Ellis, James Thompson, William Enis, Ralph French, Benjamin Ross, Joab Comstock, Jacob C. Cook, Samuel Beeler, George Moyer, Patrick Lafferty, David Fouts, David Bonta, George Gillespie, Thomas Anter, Jesse Gough, Joseph Dodds, Benj. M'Carty, Jas. Edes, Matthias Crow, William Ward, Thomas Thompson, Henry Yount, James Popenoe, Adam Dickey, Anthony Logan, Samuel Brewster, Robert M'Connell, James Willson, William Hatfield, Samuel Dillon, Charles Legg, James Harrell, William Nesbit, Ephraim Morrison, Jones Harris, John Ross, John Hawkins, Abraham Richarson, Joseph Fleming, Jacob Spiller, William Custard, John Moore, Samuel Colver, William Curry, Daniel Shryock, George Kunse, John M'Kinney, Jonathan Dayton, William Willson, Barbary Loy, Samuel Mitchell, Edward Baldwin, Alexander Kirkpatrick, Thomas M'Kinney, Cornelius Quick, John Smiley, Thomas Cowhick, Thomas Nichols, Jeremiah Symmes, Joseph Caldwell, James Coldwell, John Harrell, George Cox, Daniel Boon, Richard Stephen, Abraham Bonta, James Miller, Robert Miller, Isaac Beal, Michael Burns, William Steel, Samuel Hawkins, Adam Shuey, James Abbot, Henry Price, David Crissman, Teter Kessinger, James & G. M'Neely, William Kirkpatrick, Jacob Kunse, John Ritchey, Thomas M'Cullough, Anthony Richart.

Abraham Shane and Elizabeth Jones, administrators of the estate of Joseph Jones, dec'd, regarding the estate settlement.

Nancy Irwin and Moses Parsel, in Franklin County, administrators of the estate of Willian Irwin, dec'd, regarding the estate settlement.

Samuel Robinson reports that James Robinson and Thomas Robinson have appraised a horse found by James Ewing of Darby township, Madison County.

John Williams, in Sunberry township, Delaware County, reports that Increase Bellens and William Fancher have appraised a mare found by Henry Bennet at Dunkin's Plain.

David Yates, in Deer Creek township, Pickaway County, reports that Simon Hornback and Abraham Cade have appraised a mare found by Thomas Megath.

Volume XI, Wednesday, 12 December 1810, No. 521

Edward Tiffin, in Chillicothe, says that while he is serving in government, Doctor James Davisson will cover his medical practice. In surgical cases, he will have the aid of "the celebrated surgeon, Doctor Hinde, who intends to spend the winter, in town, on a visit to his son's".

Jeptha Beasley reports that Jacob Shephard and William Cultrough appraised a mare found by Robert M'Ferston in Adams County, Byrd township.

Benj. Feurt, in Scioto County, says that Robert Smith & Peter Nall appraised a mare found by Thomas Brown, living in Union township on Scioto Brush Creek.

Col. Dunlap is elected senator in place of Joseph Kerr, resigned.

Return J. Meigs, jun., is declared elected governor of Ohio.

A note regarding the legislature mentions E. Tiffin, R. Osborn, Adam Betz, Thomas Kirker, C.A. Norton, E. Sherlock.

Doctor John Edmeston has resumed his practice of medicine in Chillicothe in his shop on Second Street in the house lately occupied by Mr. Hough, Auditor.

John Kerr regarding a meeting of the Scioto Lodge.

Samuel Massey has opened a new store in Chillicothe.

Isaac Davis, living on Deer Creek, near Thompson's tavern, reports two stray mares and offers a reward for their return.

J.W. Peebles, agent for the Insurance Company of North America in Philadelphia, for the Chillicothe area, regarding insurance coverage.

John M'Landburgh, in Chillicothe, asks those in debt to him to pay their bills.

William Creighton, sheriff, regarding sheriff's sales of the property of Elias

Langham at the suits of E. Doolittle & Company, Joseph Beard, Charles M'Gowan, and William Beard. Also of James Crain's property at the suit of Henry Hollar.

Daniel Harris, living on Paint Creek, 3 miles from Chillicothe, in Ross County, reports a strayed mare.

David Bonner, Collector, regarding lots for sale in Chillicothe.

John Miller, in Green township of Ross County, reports that his wife, Eliza-beth Miller, has left him, and he will no longer honor her debts.

Volume XI, Wednesday, 19 December 1810, No. 522

The speech of Return J. Meigs, Jun., to the legislature is printed. Also Gov. Samuel Huntington's speech is printed and mentions Mr. Malcory, Mr. Perkins.

Gen. Thomas Worthington is elected senator in place of Col. R.J. Meigs, jun.

John Bush, in Concord township, Ross County, reports that George Gragg and Jonathan Simson have appraised a mare found by John Bryan on the North fork of Paint Creek.

Christian Benner reports that John Tully and Solomon Chalffin have appraised a mare found by Henry Benner, in Paxton township, Ross County.

John Ratcliff, in Jefferson township, Ross County, reports that Laurence Raines and Jesse Comer, sen., have appraised a mare found by George Raines.

Geo. Will reports that James S. Webster and Killian Ruse have appraised a horse found by Peter Goodman, of Colerain township, Ross County.

Abner Ewing, in Green township, says that Recompence Murphy and William Web have appraised a horse found by William Stout, in Adams County.

John Ellison reports that John Tennis and Abraham Washburn have appraised a mare found by Joseph Carl, of Sprigg township, Adams County.

INDEX

A'Dear, George 250; John 250; Peggy 250; Philip 250; Rosanah 250
Abbet, Nathaniel 154
Abbot, Aaron 17; Benjamin 161; David 101,214(2),244,302,307 Elijah 244; James 318; Mary 17
Abbott, David 84,97,209,213,317; Elijah 250; J. 187(2); James 61, 187(2); R. 187(2); Robert 298
Aberna, John 287
Abit, William 295
Abkrir, John 45
About, Eliza 250
Abraham, John 82; Mary 51
Abrahams, H. 218; John 64
Abram, Caspar 45
Abrams, Amos 250; Bazil 179,185 186,196,203,217; Henry 83,84, 186,187,201,207,209,220(2), 242,303,316; Judge 212; R. 192 193; Reben 275; Reuben 71,87, 91,165,178,186,187,188,190, 192,196,199(2),200,201,202(2), 203(3),204(2),205,207(3)208,211 217(2)220(2),223,226229,252, 265,316; Reubren 181; Rhoda 254; Ruben 184,196; Rueben 184
Academy 143,144,147,159,169,286
Achason, Samuel 247
Acheson & Duffey 15
Acheson, D. 6; David 10,26(2); Mr. 3; Thomas 15,26(3)
Ackley, Abner B. 186
Acreman, John 100
Acres, Frederick 165
Action, Richard 221
Acton, Richard 282,287,305; William 289,309
Acy, Benjamin 200
Adair, James 142,189; John 218; William 1
Adaire, James 99
Adam's mill 247
Adams 187
Adams County 32,36,38,39,45,69 70,84,87,91,111,131,164,180 181,183,185,186,190,191,192 193,198,199,200,201,203,205 210,212,213,214,216,218,224 225,226,228,229,233,237,238 239,240,243,245,250,252,253 255,259,260,263,264,265,266 267,268,269,270,271,272,273 274,276,277,278,279,280,281 283,284,285,287,288,289,290 291,293,294,297,298,299,300 301,302,303,304,305,306,307 308,309,311,312,313,315,316 317,318,319
Adams County, Penn. 304
Adams, Armstead 191; Bridget 154; David 149,151; Francis 241; George 58; Hannah 197; Isaac 250; Jacob 291; James 96,158,310,315; John 70,137 145,155; Larkins 305; Matthew 116; Mr. 57,134,152; Nancy 142; Pres. John 43; President John 41; Robert 208,267,269 275,315; Seth 279,309; Thomas 25; William 296
Adamson, Isaac 275,296,310; Joseph 287,296,310
Addison, Jacob 298; Judge 198

Adear, Benjamin 305; George 305; Peggy 305
Adelphi 220,223,234,245,265,280 285,316
Adelphia 244,255,257,264,295
Adensen, Charles 296
Adgate, A. 1; John H. 207
Adkins, William 310
Agnew, Samuel 20
Ailsworth, Josiah 16
Aiman, Peter 305
Airs, Thomas 95
Akenberry, Henry 304
Albright, Ensign J.W. 158(2); J.W. 148
Aldrige, John 171
Aleghaney township 183
Alen, George 237
Alexander & Creigh 4
Alexander township 276,280
Alexander, Agnes 144; Andrew 268,300; Elijah 263; Elizabeth 271; Francis 187,190,193,196 202(2),211; James 200,203,205 303; John 82,205,263; Joseph 270; Lieut. Francis 189; Nancy 18; Samuel 300; Thomas 15,18; Will. 216
Alexandria 39,83,178,179,185,196 199,209,218,222,228,229,231 ,239,241,258
Alexandria, Virginia 302
Alford, Jabez 269
Alfred, Jobez 265
Alger, Skilman 161
Alhine, Robert 286
Alhire, William 296
Aliail, Manna 287
Alison, Dr. 35,40; Richard 35,39
Alkier, John 267
Alkire, John 311
Allan, William 300
Allen, Charles 51; Doctor Silas 107,209; Dr. Silas 214,237; Henry 121; Jacob 66,101,128; James 165,267; John 55,90,98 107,132,237; Nathan 297; Rebecca 107; Richard 123,154; Robert 221; Samuel 187; Sergeant Benjamin 54; Washington 162
Allensworth, W. 152
Aller, Peter 296
Allger, William 127
Allin, Charles 101
Allison, Andrew 164,282; Benjamin 265; Doctor R. 40; Doctor Richard 47,66; Dr. 18; J. 174; R. 47,56; Richard 10,44 57,69,146; W. 174
Allisson, Daniel 265; Rachel 265
Alloway, Archelaus 71,177,258
Alloway, Archelus 164
Allstone, Thomas 58
Allum Creek 216
Almsbury, Peter B. 185
Alsey, S. 95
Alston, Thomas 62,78,82
Alstone, Mr. 72; Thomas 41
Alstred, Henry 212
Alt, Henry 272
Alter, Abraham 267; Frederick 139,166; Mr. 145
Altson, Thomas 18
Amanda Village 237
Amanda township 214

Amberson, William 82
American burying ground 226
Ames township 265
Ames, Sylvanus 165; Sylvester 114,229; Zenas 54
Amherstburgh 245
Amidon, Abner 109,110,132; Caleb 128,132
Amistead, Cochran 228
Ammidon, Abner 86
Amory, Alex. 216
Amsterdam 208
Anderick, John 254,257,275,282
Andericks, John 287
Anders, Micheal 254
Anderson 124
Anderson Township 58,63,73,77,93 116,119,126,141,145,150,154 160,166,169,172
Anderson's tavern 113
Anderson, Andrew 303; Bartholomew 197; Benjamin 126; Catharine 310; Charles 204; Col. 183,243; Col. Richard C. 258; Elijah 237; Gersham 287; Gershom 275; Henry 37(2),146; Hugh A. 170; I. 122; Isaac 25,27,33,41,44,50 51,52(2),53(2),57,63,72,74(5) 77,79,80(2),82,83,86,87,89,90 98(2),99,101,104,109,110,111 115,117,118(2),119,127,133 134,136,137,138,146,147,151(2) 152,153,154,159,161(2),163,164 164,171,172,199,216; James 247,250; John 37,102,180,273 308,310; Jonathan 184,254,268 273; Joseph 275; Mahlon 315; Matthew 51; Mr. 94,99,107,149 150,151(3),152,154,168; Nathaniel 287; Richard C. 102 204; Robert 37; Samuel 270; Sergeant James 20; Susana 257; T. 130; Thomas 77,227; William 230,247,267,291
Andre, Francis 64,65
Andrew, James 176; John 139; Thomas 257
Andrews, A. 4; Hugh 299; John 137; Noah 256; Thomas 263
Angel, Felty 267; Priscella 209; Prizey 254; Vallentine 287
Anght, George 251
Ankritt, John 66
Ankrom, William 291
Anno, John 24
Anshultz, George 305
Anstill, Isaac 257,310
Anter, Thomas 318
Anthony, Mekinney 34; William 127
Antram, Thomas 189
Antrim, Daniel 107; Thomas 192
Apling, John 270,282
Apothecary 102,118,140,157,172 186,211,235,237
Apple, Peter 267,297,300
Applegate, George 223; James 260; John 223; Sarah 223
Apting, John 315
Arbuckle's survey 243
Arbuckle, Lieut. 61,62; Samuel 101
Archer, Benjamin 26,91,205; Daniel 282; David 291; John 257; Judge 143; Peter 225;

320

Peter Field 193; Samuel 89; Zachariah 162
Ardery, James 35
Areery, George 297
Ares, Mr. 129
Argenbright, John 305; Philip 305
Argo, James 305
Argubright, John 285,312
Arksom, William 296
Armat, Thomas 212
Armenia 315
Armentage, Caleb 194
Armetage, Caleb 221
Armitage, Caleb 218; Calib 254; Jacob 291,310; Rebecca 257
Armsted, William 282
Armstrong's Inn 104,124
Armstrong's Mill 102,109,110 112(2),133,162
Armstrong's saw mill 115
Armstrong, Andrew 9,312; Archibald 95,96,101; Betsey 67; Capt. 7; Capt. John 2,7; Col. 90,108,138,161; Col. J. 116; Col. John 65,94,122,126, 169,174,203; Elizabeth 13; Fanny 247; Hamilton 102; J. 169,229; James 32,62,98,144 166,200,218,229,246,255,263 278,303; John 1(2),3,4(2),7,13 15(2),16,19,23,25(2),31,35,38 39,46,51,80,88,89(2),95,98 102(2),109,115,126(2),127,148 151(2),157,160(3),161,163 164(2),166,168,169,174,204,210 214,216,233,255,257; Leonard 291; Lieut. Col. John 31,35; Lieut. James 189; Maj. John 15; Martin 263,282; Miss Eliza 296; Miss Fanny 295; Mr. 57 197,224,229,240; Rachel 151; Robert 13,37,67,231,247,293 314; Samuel 47,89,104,106,107, 124,151,178; Sarah 144; Thomas 127,202,205,247,257 263,309,310,311; Thos. 302,309 William 299
Armsworthy, Bennet 275; Bennett 315
Arnall, John 127
Arnet, Samuel 137
Arnett, Jonathan 241
Arnold, Anthony 96; Mary 54; Samuel 54; Stephen 101; Thomas 288; Widow 40; Ziba 165
Arral, Thomas 26
Arrasmith, Samuel 315
Arrenote, John 231
Arreson, David 63
Arsher, Gerdeniah 315
Arthars, John 150,287
Arther, Billy 117
Arthers, Pleasent 287; Thomas 121
Arthur, John 257,267,310
Arthurs, John 61,143
Artificer's Yard 121
Artillery 82,140,157,160,201
Artillery Company 78,96,139
Arvain, Saml. 314
Arville, Thomas 137
Asa, Alathia 221; John 287
Asberry, Caleb 177
Asbury, Rev. Francis 211
Ash, Francis 14; John 14
Ashar, William 307
Ashbey, Bladin 207
Ashbough, John 288
Ashbrook, Aaron 305
Ashby, Bayless 147; Benjamin 142;

Bladen 103,126
Ashenfelder, Jacob 309
Asher, Charles 291; George 66; Jeremiah 280
Ashers' Creek 72
Ashley, Robert 183
Ashtabula County 317
Askew, John 233; Mr. 237,250; William 237,238,239,250,251 270,291,300,310; Wm. 212 236(2),237,239
Askin, John 60
Askren, Richard 308
Askue, William 227
Assembly 80,81,199,200,202,205 223,235,236,239
Atcheson, Silas 194
Atchison & Duffy 23
Atchison, George 85; Samuel 249 265,300
Ater, Abraham 300; George 260
Aterholt, George 303
Aters, Mary 270
Athens 105,182,212,223,228,229 239,256,258,289,309
Athens County 131,134,164,165 242,252,261,265,276,280,309 312,314
Athens University 152,169,193 205,206,223
Athens township 312
Atherton, David 86,121; Peter 82 86
Atkinson, James 241,264,269,274; William 272
Atres, Mary 257
Atter, Abigal 121
Attorney 3,4,13,14,18,20,23,28,40 28,40,42,43,46,48,55,56,72,73 78,80,82,88,89,91,104,109,114 118,128,129,139,147,179,183 186,188,193,195,196,197,204 206,211,219,220,224,226,227 234,235,240,241,244,246,249 250,253,254,258,259,262,264 266,267,268,269,270,271,272 273,275,288,292,294,299,304 315
Atwater, Amzi 259,261,266,276
Auctioneer 17,19,20,21,22,24,25 29,152
Audrain, J.H. 109; James H. 106 109; P. 109; Peter 46,72,73,103
Augusta 31,35
Augustas, David 287
Augustis, David 282
Augustus, Abraham 137;David 250
Augusty 16
Auld, James 95
Aurora 39,237
Aurora township 276
Austell, Isaac 282
Austen, William 178
Austin, Calvin 91,205,207,261; Isaac 215,282; Jonah 47; Mr. 32,43,44,206; William 34,37,47 63,183,186,193
Auter, Thomas 132,161
Avaicest, Joseph 121
Averson, Richard 138
Avery township 302
Avery, C. 2,34,36,61,62,77,101; Capt. Dudley 121;Charles 9, 10(2),14,17,18,24,25,27,30,35 41,42,59,63,72,73(2),77,79,80 89,92,93,97,101,107,108,144 149,151,153; Dudley 153; Joseph 95; Miss Ann 153; Mr. 22,59,64,68,76,78,89,90(2),98
Ayer, Ebenezer 101,166
Ayers, Ebenezer 161; Francis 305;

Jedediah 154; Richard 142; Thomas 60
Ayres' tavern 102
Ayres, Alexander 165; Azariah 101; Ebenezar 126; Ebenezer 170; Jackson 132; Jacob 317; Jedidiah 171; John 92,137 237; Lydia 41; Michael 41,47 70,90; Samuel 82; Thomas 77
Ayrs, Mr. 93
Babb, John 116; Joseph 292,307
Babbs, John 111
Bachelor, Samuel 161
Backen, William 284
Backman, Henry 205; John 142
Backus, Elijah 47,109,212,222,282; Matthew 168
Bacon, Edmund 149; Joel 244,250 305; Mr. 75
Bacus, John 263
Badgeley, Capt. Andrew 189
Badger, Daniel 81
Badgley, Andrew 80,197,233; James 121; Rachel 122; Robert 146
Badley, Samuel 194; William 195 270,287,310; Wm. 241
Badollet, John 109
Badot, John 222
Bagges, Mr. 93
Baggs, David 292,310,315; Mr. 85; William 310,315(2)
Bahinger, Joshua 282
Bailay, William B. 287
Bailey's Station 66
Bailey, Daniel 296; Jether 240,259 Rev. John 68; William 310
Baileys, Andrew 77; John 77
Bailiff, Daniel 172
Bails, Sarah 197
Baily, Richard 315; Robert 176; Sydnor 47
Bain, James 294
Bainbridge 260,267,291,292,294 314
Baine, John 10
Bainter, Godfrey 241; John 241
Baird, David 282,292; Elizabeth 133; James 217,230,290,315; John 182,290,317; Moses 303
Bairdstown 160
Baits, Ephraim 276
Baker, Benjamin 233,250; Chauncey 263; Christopher 267,292; Daniel 58; Elizabeth 20; Francis 306; Frederick 312; Grafton 298; Henry 292,300 310; James 286,310; John 20 215,257,261,263,267,275,290 310; Jonathan 127; Josiah 266; Lewis 137; Lieut. Dan. 75; Mahlon 124; Martin 274; Melvin 82; Melyn 107; Melyne 41; Mesheck 228,229; Purnal H. 275,296; William 283
Bakers 19,30,38,73,118,145,174 176,179,208,241,251,255,283 298
Bakery 143,262
Bakewell & Company 252
Balbridge, William 307
Balch, Hezekiah 18
Balden, Demsey 284
Balding, Joseph 310
Baldridg, Wm. 317
Baldridge, Sarah 307
Baldwin, Daniel 315; Dr. Cornelius 268; Edward 318; Eli 232; Ethan 107; Francies 267; Francis 171; John 61,127; M. 192,202,224,249,254,278,292

315; Maj. Abraham 244; Mich.
 111; Michael 71,83,84,87,90,92
 93,94(2),95(2),96(3),97(2)
 111(2),115(2),117,118(4),119
 120(3),121,123(2),124,125(3)
 126(2),127,128,179,188,194,198
 199,200(2),202,203,204,206(2)
 207,208(2),209(2),217(2),222(2)
 223(2),227,229,232,237,270,279
 302,304,305; Mr. 84,180,192
 195,199,242,250; Samuel 262
Baldy, Jacob 257
Bales, Amour 212
Baley, Richard 244; William 244
 275
Balison, Richard 279
Ball, C. 41; 41,104,105,126,139
 145,156,238; Capt. James 165;
 E. 98; Ezekial 303; Ezekiel
 97,98,99,106,109,111,150,225;
 Jacob 144; John 15; John W.
 197; Luther 41; Robert 10;
 Squire 119
Ballard, Jeremiah 312; Miss Polly
 272; William 317
Balled, Moremon 216
Ballenger, Henry 209; Joshua 202;
 Samuel 287
Ballentine, Henry 206; Mr. 200;
 Robert 95,190,197,230
Ballew, Joseph 86,199
Ballinger, Joshua 275
Ballock, Wingfield 248
Ballow, Peter 82
Balrommin, Eli 41
Baltimore 83,102,106,125,139,147
 148,157,201
Baltimore, Maryland 114
Bancraft, Ethen 297
Bancratt, John 60
Bancroft, Ethen 297; Samuel 250
Bane, Doctor 45; Doctor Evan 51;
 Evan 118; Even 123; Mr. 148
Banes, Evan 19,103; Thomas 27
Banghart, Michael 176
Banhard, David 221
Bank Lick 2,13,23,24,26,45,48,60
Bank of Chillicothe 168,169,201
 270,273,276,280,281,284,292
 295,299,301,317
Bank of Cincinnati 175
Bankard, David 184
Banker, David 227
Banks 299
Banta, Peter 122(2)
Banton, J. 71
Baptist Church 105,175
Baptist burial ground 175
Baptists 123
Bar-keeper 236
Barbary, Mary 149
Barbee, John 293; William 165(2)
Barber, Daniel 309; David 41;
 Jesse 217; John 37; Levi 136
 166,252(2),315; Uriah 178,288
Barberie, Otto V.T. 41
Barcalow, Miss Helena 160; Tobias
 162; William 107
Barcraft, Elias 284
Barcroft, Elias 275
Bardstown 67
Bare, Samuel 215
Barger, Christian 313
Baritt, John 316
Bark Stack 85
Barkeeper 252
Barker, Elias 226(3); Isaac 312;
 Joseph 167,216,227,312;
 Nathaniel 209; Robert 223;
 Sarah 123,129; Stephen Alison
 129; Stephen Allison 123;
 Thomas 156
Barkley, William 77
Barlow, Thomas 38; William 251
 254,257,262
Barnard, Anthony 279
Barnes, Alexander 70; Capt. John
 186; Charles 95; James 10,70
 99,189,209; John 189,209;
 Nathan 27,28; S. 23; Samuel
 20; William 257,315
Barnet, Abraham 133; John 133;
 Mrs. Elizabeth 173; Philip 270
Barnett, Abraham 162; John 183
Barns, Alexander 51; Capt. 208;
 Capt. John 186; John 208; Mr.
 18; Nathan 107,112; Samuel
 20; William 6,263,273
Barr, Alexander 303; Amos 237
 254,270; David 192; John 225
 236,251; John T. 288,289,295
 299,306,308,309,312,315,317;
 Miss Margaret 313; Robert 313
 Samuel 237,244,267,270; T.
 262; Thomas 178,218,222,225
 226,281,303; William 300,305
Barreck, Peter 218
Barrere, Geo. W. 259
Barret, J. 83; James 24,52,80,81
 83,89,91,199,207; John 90,226
Barrett, James 26,50,74,80,84;
 John 189,230,250
Barrick, Philip 277; William 277
Barrickman, Jacob 136
Barrill, John 288
Barrit, Thomas 292
Barritt, Abraham 308; John 253
Barron courthouse 212
Barron, Mr. 174
Barrot, James 205; Mr. 50
Barrous, Elijah P. 101
Barroussel, Thomas 18
Barrow, Henry 169
Barrus, Thomas 234
Barry, John 15; Mr. 67; Richard
 167,310
Bars, William 282
Barstler, Jacob 303
Bartell, John 15
Bartett, James 51
Bartholemew, Francis 45; Martin
 280
Bartholomy, Capt. 86
Bartilow, Amos 80
Bartle, Capt. John 1; J. 27; John
 12
Bartlet, Christopher 315; Roswell
 128; William 56
Bartlett, Dinah 305; Dumah 300;
 Elizabeth 117; Rosewell 104;
 Rosswell 127; Roswell 107,117
 153
Bartley, Alexander S. 287; Allen
 S. 291; Elijah 296; Elijah B.
 300; Isaac 275; Jacob 237,241;
 257; Thomas 292
Bartly, Christopher 270
Bartmess & Hobble 307
Barton, Joseph 220,267; Stephen
 230,285,315
Basey, Lisman 154
Baskerville, Samuel 303
Bass, William 267
Bassett, Samuel 107
Basteon, Jacob 281
Basye, Lismund 300
Bata, Mr. 282
Bateman, William 267
Bates, Clark 171; Clarke 70,88;
 Ensign Uzuel 9; Ephraim 182
 208; Frederick 74,109,156;
 Isaac 21,25,46,57,94,136,149
 152,153; John 62,185; Lieut.
 Isaac 68; Mr. 88,185; Thomas
 15; Uzal 24,146
Bathard, William 305
Baty, Thomas 18
Baum & Perry 155(2),162,163
Baum & Thompson 104
Baum, Catharine 310; Charles 47;
 Daniel 270,275; Jacob 305;
 John 287; M. 42,61,92,103;
 Martin 29,33,34,38,47,55(2),64
 68,82,88,89,94,95(3),101,110(2)
 115,118,119,138(2),139(2),144
 154,160,165,304;Mary 287,292;
 Mr. 40,57,175
Bausher, Jacob 262,312
Bawsier, Jacob 267
Baxter, E. 229; James 69,108,112
 121; Joshua 217,233,234,250
 275,292; Lieut. Joshua 189;
 Mr. 34; Reuben 187; Rev.
 Richard 317; Samuel 51,70
Baxtor, Joshua 230
Bay, David 101
Bayard, Mr. 75,77
Baylor, Col. George 216,218;
 George 293; George W. 314;
 John 314; Walker 160,216,218
Baymiller, Jacob 160; Mr. 169
Baynon, John 270
Bazadon, Laurence 53
Beach Fork 23
Beach, Capt. John 292; John 300
 309; Rossil 251; Stephen 309;
 Timothy 267
Beachamp, Risdon 209
Beadles Station 78
Beagle's Station 112
Beagles Station 82,95
Beagles' Station 74
Beakeman, John 197
Beakets, Nancy 305
Beal, Isaac 311,318; John 161;
 Maj. 43; Mr. 203; Philip 292
Beale, Ammor 250; John 62;
 Robert 33,185
Beall, Benjamin 45,169; Josiah
 299; Reasin 177,234,303
Beam, Joseph 265,302
Bean, Miss 96
Beans, William 263
Beansville 33
Bear Creek 90,94,95,105,116,126
 218,223
Bear, Mr. 88,203; Rudolph 84,109
 225
Beard, George 284; Hugh 280;
 James 170,212,279; Joseph
 227,266,280,291,314(2),319;
 Michael 295; Moses 279; Mr.
 184; Robert J. 266; Thomas
 291; William 130,133,266,314
 319
Beards Town 23
Beardstown, Kentucky 243
Bearns, John 257
Bears, William 275,300
Bearse, William 278; Wm. 310
Beasley's Mill 83,89,92
Beasley's fork 218
Beasley, Benjamin 218,279; Jeptha
 299,318; John 182(2),185,203
 204,206,245; Maj. John 245;
 Mr. 201; N. 203,315; Nathl.
 245; Sarah 245
Beasly, John 87,169; N. 88;
 Nathaniel 169,218
Beason, Jonas 170
Beatle, Everard 107
Beatty, John 212; Maj. 7; Zach. A.
 213; Zacheus A. 71(2),193

204(2)
Beaty's tavern 123
Beaty, David 61,62,82,147,162;
  Erkurious 272; Henry 263,270;
  John 41,46,58,62,97,117,144;
  Mr. 98,203,212; Robert 90,209;
  William 247,254,285; Zacheus
  A. 255
Beaubien, J.M. 191; Jean Marie
  298
Beauchamp, Risdau 196; Risdon
  199,237
Beaver Creek 29,84,86,92,101,130
  181,211,218
Beaver township 138,153,243,295
Beaver, David 244; John 214
Beavers, Thomas 260
Beazley's Mill 60,63
Beazley, J. 184; John 95,128;
  Joseph 128
Beble, Lewis 293
Beck, David 15; J. 35; James 170
  267; Jeremiah 35(2)
Becket, John 35,113,135,146,153
  155,161; William Buttler 300
Beckets, William B. 263
Beckett, John 34
Beckham & Reese 294
Beckham, Mr. 280
Beckitt, William B. 310
Beckley, John 213,216
Beckman, Gabriel 274,286;
  William 274,286
Beckwith, Basil 124
Beckworth, Benjamin 274
Bedast, Mr. 228
Bedeford, John 182
Bedford, John 72; Nathaniel 75
Bedle's Station 65(2)
Bedson, Penn. 233
Beeby, Clark 283
Beech Grove 145
Beech Spring 86
Beecher, Gen. 277; Mr. 131,280
  313; P. 166,168,262,263,278;
  Phil. 226; Philemon 95,101,150
  162,164(2),208,212,214(3),252
  253,279,280,292,313
Beedell's Station 37
Beeding, Soloman 303; Solomon
  292
Beedle's Station 84,85,96
Beedle, Francis 58
Beeler, Charles 86; Samuel 147
  169,210,269,318
Beemer, George 252; Henry 298
Beers, Philo 15
Beesley's fork 210
Beeson, Richard 213,214
Beever Creek 146
Beever, Mr. 196
Beevis, Jesse 90
Beezley, John 65
Beggart, John 194,202,247
Begget, John 254
Begles Station 82(2)
Beisseau, Benjamin 293
Bel-pre 129
Belcher, Lorenzo 45
Bele, Mr. 82
Belfield, John 293
Belie, Maj. 185
Belknap, Mr. 167
Bell & Bill 31,38
Bell Font 56
Bell, Armiger 121; Barbara 60;
  Calvin 104; Ezekiel 99; George
  310'James 31,38,90,99; John 33
  146; Joseph 275,282,287,296;
  Joshua 137; Lewis 102; Mr.
  116,175; Nancy 233,300; Peter
  35,124,135,136,174; Reason
  207
Belle Font 44
Belle-Font 47
Bellenger, Henry 192
Bellens, Increase 318
Bellepre 225
Belli, John 3,255; Maj. John 196
  290
Bellknap, Morris B. 167
Belmain, Alex. 293
Belmont 207
Belmont County 66,68,73,76,84,88
  91,92,109,111,130,131,164,192
  198,200,203,205,207,224,225
  232,239,251,252,253,264,265
  269,272,274,276,277,279,284
  303,304
Belnap, Morris B. 167
Belpre 190
Belprie 206
Belsland, William 251
Belt, Fielding 149; L. 303; Levin
  151,220,226,246,255,256(2),257
  292,303,310; Lewis 102
Belville 187
Benagh, George 282
Bender, Daniel 285; George 296;
  Jacob 154; Sidle 282
Benefiel, Col. 144; Col. John 140
  146,165; John 100,165
Benefield, Col. 129; Col. John
  126; John 92,93(2)
Bengannaw, John 32
Bengerman, Adam 268
Benham's tavern 19
Benham, Capt. 19,62; Capt.
  Robert 27,143; Mr. 37(2)
  38(2),39(2),56,181(2); R. 50;
  Richard 112; Robert 8,11,21,50
  61,62,65,77,80,97,101,103,107
  108,126,168,171,186,199
Benjamin, Dani. 234
Bennefield, John 58
Benner, Christain 308,295,299,310
  312,313(2),314,319; Henry 319
Bennet, Catharine 161; Henry 318;
  Isaac 233; James 57; John 58;
  Robert 218; Robt. 227; Samuel
  60,119,172
Bennett, Capt. John 291; Edward
  267,270,315; John 306; Joseph
  247; Joseph N. 12; Rev'd.
  Joseph 257; Rev. Joseph 282;
  Samuel 84,166; William 218;
  Wm. P. 237
Benningsen, Gen. 158
Benson, David 82
Bent, Silas 216
Bentley, Benjamin 317; George
  262; Hannah 262; House 262;
  Joseph 270; Sashbozzor 262;
  Sheshbazzan 184
Bently, Mary 39; Sergeant John
  39
Benton, Stephen 136,149,166
Bercount, John 157
Bercus, John 269
Berealow, William Francis 86
Bereman, Ele 184; Eli 187,194,197
  202,209,212; Jonathan 45,182
  297
Berkeley County, Virginia 185,187
  188,198,209
Berkley, William 79
Berkshire township 276
Bermagem, Thomas 96; William 96
Berriman, Jonathan 115
Berry's Ford 145
Berry, Alexander 247; Curtis 296;
  David 296; Francis 134; John
  275,287,300,310; Joseph 265;
  Richard 250,282; Samuel 103
  127; Washington 45(2),138;
  William C. 273; Wm. 168
Berryhill, John 257
Bert, John 308
Berthoud, James 243,248,249; Mr.
  219
Best, Mr. 145; Samuel 113,133,143
  157,158; Thomas 156,157
Beswell, John 183
Betez, John 187
Bethany 115
Bethel 54
Betherds, Ebenezer 285
Betts, William 136; Wm. 67,158
Betz's tavern 284
Betz, Adam 84,120,177,204,214
  226,240,270,286,318; John (see
  John Bates) 62,65,185,188(2)
  237; Miss Hannah 277; William
  120
Betzer, John 270; William 305
Beuel, Abner 82
Bevelin, Polly 170
Bever Creek 53
Bever town 255
Bever, Michael 312
Beviner, Geo. 304
Bevis, Anne 51; Issachar 121
Bewel, Doctor 190
Bewell, Walter 184
Beyemer, George 311
Beyerly, Jacob 248,250; Michael
  272,285; Micheal 282
Beyfield, Abraham Holmes 182
Beymer, George 233(2),317
Bezzars, John 202
Biarly, John 310
Bibb, Richard 241
Bible, Lewis 187,209,218,305,313
Bickham & Rees 229
Bickham, George 53,56,127
Bidgley, Rachel 115
Bierd, Moses 267
Bierle, Jacob 213; Nicholas 216
Big Belly 184,197,266
Big Bottom 190,217,245,257,289
Big Guiandot 234
Big Hill 16,18,21,24,27,42,45,46
  53,56,65,66,68,74,77,82,92,95
  119,125,127,175,199
Big Indian 132
Big Indian Creek 43
Big Parairi 40
Big Parara (see Prairie) 32,50,51
  82,91
Big Passing 31
Big Praiari 79
Big Praira 74,188
Big Praire 93,141
Big Prairie (see Great Prairie) 42
  68,70,71,73,110,121,125
Big Prarie 71,95,96,99
Big Priaria 40
Big Prierie 83
Big Sandy 232
Big Snag Creek 307
Big belly 257
Bigbelly 244
Bigby, Joseph 315
Bigg Bottom 307
Biggar, John 60
Biggarhead, Mr. 241
Biggart, John 82,189,293; Samuel
  52
Biggeit, John 199
Bigger, Abigail 132; Hannah 74;
  Hon. John 283,284(2); J. 278;
  John 46,80(2),83,86(3),87(2),90
  91,94,97,98(4),99,102,104

105(2),111,114,131,164,199,205 221,222,226,229,265,272; Mr. 103,105,109,164,177
Biggerhead, Mr. 205
Biggert, John 215,300
Biggs, Aaron 318; Benjamin 293; Zacheus 47,71(2),193
Bigham & Irwin 16
Bigham, Alexander 142; John 90; Sarah 132
Bilbren, Mr. 127
Bill, James 83,95,145; John 83; Mr. 31,38
Bille, John 33
Billi, John 19,186
Billings, Deacon Joseph 170; Dennis 66; Joseph 127; William 282
Billingsly, Thomas 154
Bills, James 142,147; Mr. 161; William 44
Billsland, Alexander 287
Bilsland, Abraham 263
Bilsland, Alexander 272
Bing, John 235
Bingham, Alban 186; S. 276
Bingiman, Adam 197
Binjamann, John 144
Bird township 269
Bird, Capt. 54; Charles Willing 44; John 36,121,310; Martha 121; Mr. 41,57,59
Birerly, Mr. 270
Birtcher, Jacob 276
Bishong, Valentine 179
Bishop, Abraham 147; Frederick 275,282; H. 257; James 272; John 70; Thomas 161,176
Bissell, Capt. 12; Capt. Daniel 32 75; Capt. R. 157; Capt. Russel 75; Daniel 204; John P. 235; Lieut. Daniel 18
Bitcher, Abraham 214
Bitver, William 212
Bitzer, Conrad 205
Bixbee's Settlement 293
Bixby, Moses 315
Bixley, Moses 165
Blachly, Dr. Henry W. 132
Black Horse 183
Black Horse Tavern 229,259,261 271
Black Oak Club 304
Black River 303
Black Water 232
Black's Station 9
Black, Abraham 271; David 57(3) 62,116; Hugh 300,310; Isaac 305; James 277,281; John 93 207; Joseph 103,170; Rev. Hejekiah 15; Samuel 3,9,303; Thomas 161; William 310
Blackburn, Brison 58; Bryson 106 144; Capt. 169; George 8; Hamilton 116; James 26; John 58,74,91,121,137; Robert 58,76 Win. 286
Blackford, Ephraim 60,90; Hister 78; Jeremiah 137; William 54
Blackmore, Nath. 237; William 237; William C. 215; Wm. 303
Blackney, Joseph 305
Blacksmith 4,5,7,8,14,31,33,35,38 39,48,75,111,113,135,141,173 174,206,210,212,216,221,222 228,239,240,244,245,248,276 283,289
Blacksom, William 230
Blackwater 215
Blackwell, Robert 101
Bladsoe, Moses 63

Blaer, William 244
Blagrove, Ann 45
Blain, Eliza 296; James 292,296 315
Blaine, Jas. 305
Blair, Alexander 278; Benjamin 215; Charlotte 259; Elizabeth 74; J. 187; Jacob 259; James 215; John 87,115,194,199 202(2),205,212,276,282,297; Robert 84,139,146,167,176; Rudolph 111; Thos. F. 179; Vestall 291; William 36,197
Blake, Martin 290,292; Theophilus 308
Blanchard, John 120,193
Bland, Theo. 293
Blanden, Jonathan 292
Blane, Sarah 292
Blankard, Christian 60
Blann, Moses 296
Blannerhassat, Mr. 147
Blannerhasset's island 156
Blannerhasset, Mr. 149,151,155
Blannerhassett, Herman 166,167; Mr. 166,167,168,267
Blare, John 178; Robert 209
Blasdel & Stark 318
Blasdel, Jacob 60,121
Blasdell, Jacob 94
Blasongane, Buckley 212
Blaty, John 215
Blear Creek 66
Bledsoe, Moses 187
Bleimen, Joseph 272
Blets, Cumfort 297
Blew, Frederick 121; Hannah 73; Joseph 73
Blieth, William 65,67,86
Blinco, James 259
Blincoe, James 235(3)
Bliss, Sergeant Samuel 25
Blizard, Barton 263
Blocher, Christain 282
Blocker, Christian 233
Blood, William 312
Bloom township 294,298
Bloom, John 74
Bloomfield 227
Blossom, Joseph 95,257
Bloxom, William 237
Blue dyers 34,52,105,129,201,214 223,243,252
Blue, Barnet 275,305; James 275; Joseph 82; Lambert 142; Uriah 199
Bluegrass Prairie 256
Blumer, Benjamin 272,273
Blunt, Eli 302; William 242
Boaks Creek 249
Boales, Nicholas C. 257
Boarding house 119
Boatman, Elias 274,281
Boats 155,157,177,195,204,219,241 258
Boblette, Clabourn 257
Boblit, John 301
Bobts, George 279
Bocover, John 154
Bocssean, Benjamin 282
Boden, Andrew 138,147
Boderick, Solomon 192
Boeding, Soloman 270
Bogart, Ezekiel 259,270,276; Joseph 201,209,259,270
Boggess, Robert 184,187,207
Boggs, David 288; James 288; John 224,241,244(2); Joseph 199,212,230,237,305; Miss Elizabeth 244; Moses 302; Mr. 224; Rosanah 300; Rosanna

221,233,247; Samuel 305
Bogs, Alexander 200; Ezekiel 189; John 189; Rasanah 287
Bohannon, William 43
Bohougedelass 29
Boid, William 212
Boil, Felix 234
Boisseau, Benjamin 293
Boke's Creek 231,290
Bolar, William 70
Bold Face Run 21,24
Boldwin, Francis 300,310
Bollingar, Stephen 99
Bollman, Doctor Eric 151
Bollton, James 218
Bolonback, Nicholas 315
Bolten, Joseph 132
Boltenberger, Jacob 247
Bolton, Abner 116; Joseph 74,161
Boman, Aaron 195; John 216,299; Joseph 241
Bomfill, John 32
Bomhart, Henry 165
Bomsill, John 32
Bond, Eliza 70; Joseph 305; Lewis 47,74,191; Mr. 36,37,38,39; Nathaniel 86; Shadrach 85
Bonde, John 217
Bondel, Frederick 34
Bone, Doctor 45; Jacob 78; Valentine 78
Boner, David 252,280(2); Katharine 20; Solomon 250,254 William 20
Bonham, Ep. 224
Bonham, Ephraim 288,310
Bonhorn, Warford 299
Bonnel, Calvin 110; Samuel 132
Bonner, David 184,200,261,268 282,295,298,309,319; Frederick 107; Isaac 300; James 209,266 268,293,295,298,308,309; Solomon 275; Windel 287
Bonnet, Abraham 267; Isaac 300
Bonney, Isaac 233
Bonser, Isaac 241
Bonsill, John 74
Bonta, Abraham 318; David 318; Isaac 304; Peter 304
Bonum, Benjamin 63
Bood, Reuben 26
Book binder 133,159,162,172,229 248,289,294
Booke's Creek 250
Booker, L. 293; Lewis 293
Booksellers 88,130,174
Boon County 45,74,90,95,114,122 146,149,154
Boon County, Kentucky 71,89,130 138,148,254
Boon Creek 50,89
Boon's Creek 5,203
Boon, Daniel 318
Boone County 258
Boone County, Kentucky 177
Boone, Thomas 82,95,137
Boos, John 142
Boothby, Catharine 144; Timothy 52,144
Boots, Mr. 298
Borden, Samuel 137
Border's Tavern 148
Borders, Peter 146
Bordine, Samuel 58
Borough, Joseph 53
Borris, John 287
Bosher, Peter 269
Boskirk, Peter Van 292
Boss, William 263
Both, Philip 263
Botkin, John 317

Bottelman, Christian 229
Bottleman, Christian 211
Boude, Sheriff John 100; Thomas 274,279,290
Boudinot, Elias 122(2),124(2); Mr. 38,99,122,124,129(2)
Boughman, Mr. 203
Boultinghouse, D. 261
Bouner, Frederick 101
Bourbon County, Kentucky 78,160 190,191,197,225,233,277,
Bourbon, Kentucky 208
Bourns, James 8
Bouse, Jacob 302
Boush, Mr. 310; William Walton 226
Bousher, Jacob 316
Bouton, John 221
Bouyer, John 92(2); Margaret 92(2)
Bowcock, Elijah 270
Bowdel, Joseph 270
Bowdle, Joseph 244; William 192 194,310
Bowell, Henry 282
Bowen, Alexander 190; Elizabeth 282; Isaac 300,310; Thomas 212
Bower, Daniel 275,299; Jacob 315; Phinehas 137; Solomon 211
Bowers, Adam 296; Alexander 142; George 232; Nicholas 277
Bowin, David 300; Thomas 315
Bowland, William 23
Bowler, William 209; William O. 66
Bowman & Company 194
Bowman, David 116(2); Ensign John 9; Henry 270,298; Jacob 220; John 62,65,185,187,188(2) 237; Mr. 185,279; Rev. Elisha 99
Bown, Charles 227
Bowser, Anna 126
Bowyer, Daniel 126,257; Henry 293; John 115,165
Boxlas, John 269
Boyce, John 12; Robert 273; William 187,247
Boyd, Alexr. 312; Andrew 185; Ensign 1; Francis 233; James 47,287; John 200,315; Jonathan 281; Mr. 249,316; Nancy 247; Robert 23; Samuel 47,96,252; Washington 167(2); William 304
Boyde, Widow 209
Boyer, Daniel 295; John 132; Mr. 259
Boyes, Alexander 114; Esq. 114; James 114; Robert 114
Boyiler, Joseph 254
Boyle, H. 184; Hugh 166,182,187 191,205,223,235,248,249,250 262,263,304(2); J. 184; John 182,187,191; Patrick 250; Robert 166,241; Samuel 99; William 244
Brabston, Ephraim 216; Thomas 216
Bracaw, John 34
Bracken County, Kentucky 31,307
Bracken Creek 223
Bracken, Hugh 154,313; Mr. 142
Brackenridge, Capt. 89; Mr. 35; R. 274
Breathington, Samuel 266
Brackin & Hargraves 140
Brackin 99
Brackin County 120
Brackin Creek 48
Brackin, Hugh 158(2),164; James 74,77; Jesse 103,222
Brackney, Benj. 227; Benjamin 194,197,215,218,237,257,263 292
Bradbery, David 37,60
Bradburn, Doctor John 151; John 140,151
Bradbury, Benjamin 60,176,194 202; Mr. 176
Braden, Miss Catharine 270
Bradey, James 89; John 89
Bradford & Company 257,258
Bradford, Abelard 241,250; Daniel 130; David 199,216,227,297; Dr. 114,116,117(2); Dr. John 116; H.G. 263; James M. 95; John 130,243(2),244,248,249; Joseph 70; Joshua 215; Kendel 291; Mr. 237,250,300; Qr. Master Gen. David 215; T.G. 229; Thomas G. 120,131(2),240;
Bradley, Capt. 5,6; H. 154; Hiram 311; Isaac 221,227,300; James 313; Michael 212; Moses 107; Mr. 292; William 263,267
Bradsh, Thomas 127
Bradshaw, John 254,270; William 305
Bradstreet, Daniel 37,78,86,90,107
Bradway, John 137,154
Brady, Charles 171; James 14,18 33,58,66,84,96; John 84,96; Michael 26; Mr. 256; Samuel 264; Van 264,293
Bragdon, John 60; Jonathan 101; Jotham 70
Brager, Fredrick 315
Bragley, Robert 45
Braintree, Vermont 240
Braken, Jesse 120; Major Jesse 120
Brakin, Jesse 227
Brall, Elijah 294
Bramble, James 270,296,300,305; Labin 149
Branagan, Patrick 158
Brand, William 99
Brandell, Charles 302; Polly 302
Brandy Camp 300
Brandy, Jack 219,224; John 202 220
Branin, Samuel 91
Brannon, Alexander 62; Allice 80; Andrew 80(2),110,117,136,152 153,154,171; Mr. 126
Branon, Andrew 115
Branson, Reese 269; Robert 278 284
Brant, Daniel 142; John 60
Brasher, John 77(2),158; Mr. 28,63 R. 132,171; Robert 34,51,59,78 94,118,167,175
Bratten, Jacob 268
Bratton, Jacob 289,291; John 300
Braucher, Frederick 180,222,241 278,304
Braugher, Frederick 294
Braughton, Jacob 221
Bray, Frederick 183,205,217,221, 257,275; Samuel 160; William Geo. 291
Braynard, Sol. 281
Brays, Frederick 202
Bready, William 199,202,218,263, 291; Wm. 274
Breathington, David 294
Breckinridge, Samuel 266
Breden, Robert 263,282
Breeches makers 26,42,122
Breeden, Robert 209
Breendige, Thomas 242
Breich, Adam 46
Bretney, Mr. 141
Bretney, Tobias 112
Brevoot, Henry 221
Brevort, Ensign Henry B. 78
Brewer, Amos 260,261; John 285; Joshua B. 161,292,300; Peter 139
Brewers 247,284,316
Brewery 15,143,179,194,276
Brewster, Samuel 8,66,82,318
Brian, David C. 164; Mr. 143
Brians, John 305; Joseph 305(2)
Briant, Isaiah 116
Brice, John J. 230; Rev. John 305
Brick, John 170
Bricklayers 22,166
Brickmakers 19,28,120,154,158, 251
Bridge 112,137,139,143,228
Bridge builders 109,114
Bridge, Benjamin 100; John 70; Samuel 12
Bridges, George 150; John 90,101, 121; William 70
Briel, Thos. 227
Brient, Isaiah 149
Brierly, Elizabeth 170
Briggs, John 218,304; Joseph 237, 244,261; Lieut. Charles 189; Samuel 189
Brigs, John 267
Brile, Henry 311
Brill, John 304
Brina, Daniel 196
Briney, Daniel 246; John 45,62,81, 95,103,110,247,249,296
Brining, Daniel 241
Brink, Capt. Isaac 211; Isaac 190, 209,212,233,237,250,267,300
Brinton, Thomas 17
Bristol, David 233,263
Britain, Capt. Charles 121; John 267
Briton, Charles 137
Britt, Capt. Daniel 10,40
Brittain, Charles 149,153; John 291; Mr. 159
Britten, John 184
Brittenham, Soloman 309
Britton, Catharine 178; Charles 155,157; Miss Ellenor 138; Mr. 158; Nathan 233; Thomas 230
Broadbury, David 37
Broadrick, Miss Betsy 28; Patrick 32,86; William 109
Broadstreet, Daniel 55
Broadus, James 231
Broadway, Abner 183
Broadwell, Aaron 45; J. 40; Jacob 85,108,112(2),125,126,133,136, 139,147,154,240; John 127,137; Moses 42,58,67,77; Mr. 126, 127; Nathaniel 112; Sally 101
Brocaw, John 36; Leana 36
Brock, Benjamin 305
Brockway, Titus 221
Broderick, Solomon 205; William 101
Brodley, Isaac 182
Brodrick, Mary 41; Patrick 41; Solomon 194,197; William 41
Brogan, Dennis 196
Brohers, Francis 219
Brokaw, Ferdinand 27,101(2); John 35; Leana 35; Michael 37,44,45 52,54,85,101(2)
Brombley, John 247
Brookaw, Ferdinand 13
Brookeville 173
Brookie, William 133
Brooks, Benj. 223; J. 249; James 6; Jared 131,244,249; Miss

Dolly 31; Squire 72; William 181
Brotherlin, Charles 179; Mr. 270
Brotherline, Christian 250
Brothers, Mr. 219
Brothulu, Charles 185
Brough's hall 222
Brough, Mr. 197
Brougher's tavern 236,252
Brougher, Frederick 229,235
Broughton, Job 205,215,218,230, 275,287,305
Brown & M'Cort 258,259,273,279, 293
Brown & M'Court 261,266,268,272, 286,306
Brown's Crossroads 234,235
Brown's tavern 272
Brown, Abigail 4; Absalom 300; Absolem 220; Allan 168; Andrew 51; Ann 140; Archibald 136; Ashy 142; Augustus 282; Benjamin 8,257,275; Betsey 315; Capt. 43; Capt. Benjamin 265; Capt. Henry 296; Capt. James 130; Capt. Moses 189; Carlisle 4; Casper 47; Charles 70,107,198,211; Cherry 309; Chs. 227; Clement 241,278,287 296,297,304,307,308,310,313; Clemt. 272,294; Col. 107; Col. William 109; Daniel 154,265, 274; David 132,167; Deliverance 25; Doct. Charles 20; Doct. W. 78; Doct. Wm. 302; Dr. Alex. 216; Dr. Joseph 118; Dr. Richard 302; Dr. Wm. 293; E.A. 141,143; Elizabeth 263; Ephm. 18; Ethan A. 128, 141,310; Ethan Allen 303; Ezekiel 215,276,283; Frederick 218; G. 305; Geo. 303; George 167,221,246,294,305,306; H. 275; Henry 18,20,32,41,121,136 252,261,263,270,305,313; Ignatious 51,207; Ignatius 91, 140,205,303; Israel 130; J. 204, 234; J.W. 50,83; Jack 184; Jackson 287; Jacob 26,133; James 22,149,160,199,218,233, 262,265,268,288,294,304; Jean 233; Jeremiah 282,301; John 7, 9,11,14,15(3),20,22,27,37(2), 42(2),44,45,50,57,60,85,90, 178(2),183,186,190,198,200,203 205,209,210,221,227,229,231, 232,253,254,261,265(2),288,293 303,305,306; John D. 112; John W. 30,80(2),87,98(2),99,100; Jos. 233; Joseph 47,58,74,76, 86,127,170,217; Josiah 263; Lampkin 257; Maj. 185,232; Manassah 145; Mary 282; Matthew 132; Michael 202; Miss Betsey 305; Miss Eliza 50; Montgomery 167; Moses 185, 202; Mr. 75,93,94,99,103,121, 150,151,155,172,175(2),186,233 244,247,248,253,298,308; Mrs. Elizabeth 31; Nathan A. 77,78; Nathen 275; Nual 262; Paul 112,116; Peter 282; Polly 161; Priscilla 253; Rachael 181; Rawland 14; Rebecca 218,230, 272; Rev. John W. 50; Richard 215; Robert 170; Ruth 110; S. 2661 Saml. J. 282; Samuel 204, 209(2),210,216,220,223,233,238 239,246,305; Sovereign 215; Soveren 209; T. 36,50,83; Thomas 10,37,44,58,67,73,77,

79,80,85,86,87(2),92,93,115,126 129,140,154,191,202,215,300, 305(2),318; Thos. 312; W. 50; White 218,219,230,237,241,251 252,257,261,267,279,282,287, 288,290,295,300,305,312,315, 317; Will. 308; William 19,35, 40,82,83,84,86,104,110,121,124 194,221,227,247,254(2),255,275 287; Wm. 5,215,228; Zebulon 137,161
Browne's Cincinnati Almanac 315
Browne, Adam P. 229; J.W. 105; John W. 81,84,97,100,102,103, 105(9),106,115,122,123,124, 125(2),149,159,173,199,315, 317; L. 174; Miss Mary Ann 153; Mr. 105,114,117,123,125, 135,144; Parson 135(2); Rev. John W. 111,153; Sam. 105; Sam. H. 305; Taylor 115,123
Browning, William 18
Brownlee's Mill 110
Brownlee, Elizabeth 74; Hugh 60, 76,99; James 49,99; John 69, 207; Mr. 31; T. 192;Wm. 293(2)
Brownson & M'Farland 119
Brownson, Asa 126; John 104,169, 269,304; Lieut. John W. 75
Brownsville 219
Brubaker, Abraham 231
Bruce, Charles 51,54,59,78,136, 146,147,153,168,180; James 99; William 135,168
Bruff, James 62,95
Bruharde, George 80
Bruice's Station 10,11
Brumfield, John 146
Brumley, Benjamin 274; Elizabeth 208; John 208,274
Brundee, Thomas 245
Brundige, Thomas 238
Bruner, Jacob 15,137
Brunher, Jacob 170
Brunn, Andrew 282
Brush Creek 192,197,199,200,212, 216,217,218,219,228,230,231, 237,252,257,260,263,269,282, 285
Brush Creek Settlement 239
Brush Creek township 269,278,284 291,294,301,304,307,308,309, 313
Brush creek 257
Brush, E. 46; Elijah 77,191,192, 239; H. 278; Henry 158,226(2), 240,252,255,262,263(3),264,265 277,279,284,287,291,304,311, 313; John 305; Lawyer 250; Mr. 83,166,167,283,315
Bryan's Station 22,97
Bryan, Daniel 19; David C. 159, 253; Doctor D. 32; Doctor Daniel 45; Jesse 273; John 237, 292,319; Mr. 242; Samuel 114; William 229
Bryant, Anderson 303; Benjamin 68; David 137; Isaiah 119,129, 165; James 292; Mr. 165; William 4
Bryare, David C. 252
Bryson, Patrick 165
Buchanan, Ambrose 191; James 44,62,220,232,233; Mr. 203,209 233; William 121
Buchannan, David 64; James 213; Robert 64
Buchannon's Store 215
Buchannon, Henry 304; James 227, 294; John 74; Mr. 88; William 57,294

Buchanon, Arthur 101; James 230; John 160
Bucher, George 318
Buck Creek 137
Buck, Charles 253; Elizabeth 261; John 170,197,241,250; Joseph 178,261
Buckenon, Adam 263
Buckeye Station 290
Buckhannon, Squire 134
Buckhanon, James 226; Mr. 226
Buckingham, Ebenezer 192,194, 216; Stephen 303
Buckingham, Virginia 258
Buckle makers 171
Buckles, Robert 51,221,267
Buckman, Christian 298
Bucknall, J. 90
Bucknell, J. 93; John 83
Buckner, Philip 16; William 99, 264; Wm. 254
Buckskin 202,216,219,221,233,237, 244,251,263,264,275
Buckskin Creek 178,215,218,226, 253,261,266,306
Buckskin settlement 206,219
Buckskin township 261,266,268, 277,280,281,295,303,314,317
Buckson, Enoch 122
Budd, John C. 91
Budge, Capt. James 305
Buel, J. 204; Joseph 111,143,204, 248; Mr. 177; Walter 87,192, 202
Buell, Doct. Walter 209; Doctor 186,188,209; Dr. 202; Dr. Walter 202; Joseph 115,131, 143,150,166,167,205,212,216(3) Maj. 8; Maj. Gen. 149; Maj. Gen. Joseph 215,227; Maj. John 8; Maj. John Y. 15; Timothy 168; Walter 178(2), 179,180,183,185,191,193,203, 208
Buffet, Louis 191
Buffonton, Jona 121
Buford, A. 297; Abraham 79,297
Bugh, William 127
Buits, Ephraim 254
Bull Creek 221
Bull, John 86; Thomas 227; William 220,315
Bull-Skin Creek 26
Bullett, Thomas 209
Bullock, Capt. 18; Lewis 48; Rice 6,20,41,42,43,44,45,46,48,55, 204,205,206; Robert 48; Wingfield 243(2)
Bullskin Creek 43,47,49,56,247
Bulmen, Samuel 18
Bulskin 190
Bunches, Isaac 41
Bundy, Benjamin 65,193
Bunn, Henry 292; John 285,312; Nicholas 266,276,312; Peter 212,276,295,312
Bunnel, Daniel 28; Stephen 69,78
Bunnix, George 215
Buntin, Robert 149
Bunton, Capt. 4
Buord, Abraham 293
Burbeck, Maj. 2,3
Burbridge, Mary 256
Burcaus, M. 221
Burch, Lilly 170
Burd, Captain 23
Burdge, Jonathan 142,146
Bure, Peter 303
Bureau, J.P.R. 258,259(2),260,297; John P.R. 289; John Peter Romain 230; John Peter

Romaine 222; P. 164,215,222, 230,235,240,248
Burger, John 95
Burgett, Frederick 211; Phebe 211; Widow 66
Burgher, Charles 247,254
Burk, Hannah 107,129,147,152; James 303; John 15,315; Joseph 257,263,292; Kelly 35(3); Samuel 183; Thomas 107,129,147
Burke, Hannah 256; John 249,263; Joseph 267; Mr. 185
Burlington, N.J. 1
Burne, Anthony 99
Burnell, Sergeant Zacharias 25
Burnes, James 74
Burnet, Amos 310; Capt. 77; Caroline 99; David 20,91,99, 116; Doctor William 120,124, 182; Dr. William 54,61; Geo. 34; Geo. W. 43,52; George 31, 54,65; George W. 30,42,45,48, 61,71,80,118; Hannah 99; I.G. 151; Ichabod 99; Isaac G. 91, 99,147,150,255; J. 83,156; Jac. 30; Jacob 25,31,32,34,42(2),45, 46,50,51,52,53,54,56,59,61(2), 65,69,71,72(2),73(4),80(5),81,83 89,91(2),99,105,106,109,114, 121,123(3),124,133,158,172,173 177,192,199,229; John 91(2),99; Joseph 99; Mr. 36,38(2),69,75, 122(2),124(2),129(2),147,162; Mrs. Sophia 126; Sophia 52,54, 61,71; States 99; Statis 91; Thomas 278; William 99,122, 124
Burnett, Amer 275; Jacob 244,255 Mr. 69,181,199; Thomas 74; William 250
Burney, Jacob 34
Burnham, William 229
Burns, Andrew 306; Anthony 86, 112; James 66; John 171,292; Matilah 165; Matilda 116; Michael 318
Burr's Conspiracy 152
Burr's Trial 281
Burr, A. 151,167; Aaron 167(2),249 261; Col. 151,156,160,167,253, 255,256,267; Col. Aaron 148, 152; John 250; Mr. 131,151,166 173; Peter 111,150,230,238(2), 253
Burrel, Zacheriah 18
Burris, John 309
Burrows, Eden 151; Richard 74
Burt & Dill 140
Burt & Newman 22,32,46,53,62,64, 67,82
Burt & Newmen 37
Burt, A. 53; Andrew 141,146,150 151(4),152(4); John 310; Mr. 152; Sarah 292
Burton, Charles 287; H. 254; Jacob 131,134,220,242; Joshua 288; William 116
Burtt, Jemimah 84; William 84
Burwell, Sergt. Zachariah 20; Zacharius 54
Busack, Edward 275
Busenbark, Peter 275
Bush Creek 227
Bush Mills 254
Bush, Abraham 116; Elizabeth 55; Isaac 55; Jeremiah 292; John 10,275,314,319; Michael 292; Mr. 61; Tandy 257
Bushe's settlement 257
Bushong, John 296

Busick, Benjamin 311; Edward 209
Buskirk's run 314
Buskirks, Mr. 210
Busson, Aron 257
Bustard, John 12,28,66; Mr. 12,28; William 66
Bustick, Edward 212
Butchers 4,8,13,18,23,48,63,73, 76,88,96,140,196,247,249
Butholomy, Francis 37
Butler County 91,92,93,95,96,97, 98,99,100,103,104,105,106,108 109,110,111,112,114,117,118, 119,120,123,125,126,127,128, 131,132,133,134,135,139,141, 144,145,146,147,148,149,150, 151,155,156,160,162,163,164, 167,168,169,170,172,173,175, 176,205,207,212,216,225,227, 238,242,246,253,255,280,290, 303
Butler, Amos 170; Capt. 1; Capt. Edw. 1; Capt. Edward 3,18; Capt. Ew. 3; Capt. Thomas 131; Col. Richard 131; Col. Thomas 131; Col. William 131; Daniel 247; David 297; Joseph 317; Joshua 40; Lawrence 33, 293; Lieut. Edward 131; Lieut. Pierce 131; Maj. 43; Miss Elizabeth 296; Mr. 19,175; Paul 20,34; Philip 12; Stephen 315; Tobias 119; Tobius 129; William 174,175,292
Butterfield, Jeremiah 86,161
Buttles, Joel 240; Levi 227,240; Sarah 240
Button, Jacob 202
Buxton, Edmon 109; Edmond 25,57 86,101
Buzac, Edward 310
Buzzard, John 181; Rudolf 197
Buzzy, Elizabeth 13
Byerley, Michael 217,296
Byerly, Jacob 291
Byers, Miss Betsy 234; Samuel 300; W. 289; Wm. 287
Byfield, Abraham H. 302
Byland, John 95,208
Bylery, Michael 250
Byrd township 265,266,279,281, 284,293,299,318
Byrd, C.W. 83; Charles W. 78,80, 81,83,84,85,86,199,206; Charles William 204; Charles Willing 49,62,66,76,77,78,81(2), 82(2),88,166,186,190,192,195, 199,201(2),203,204,264,290; Henry 82; Hon. Charles Willing 86; John 227; Judge 209; Martha 227; Mr. 82,84,85,233; William 113,123,132,148,153, 168,170
Byres, Abraham 176
Byrns, Joseph 161
Byxbe, Moses 277,286(2)
Cabell County, Virginia 303
Cabell, Philip 205
Cabinet makers 15,48,51,100,110, 121,129,135,191,240,248,289, 290
Cable, Michael 160; Philip 91
Cadbury, H. 90,135; Henry 51,78, 80,144,148,273; Mr. 51
Cade, Abraham 318; Charles 250, 273,278,282,285,295; Isaac 255(2),273
Cadwell, A. 52,180; Aaron 1,8,9, 12,16,27,32,35,36,37,39,42,48, 52,75,85,165,180; James 257; Josiah 51; Judge 35; Justice

11; Miss Prudence 34; Mr. 37, 38(2),39(3),40,55,122
Caedar run 218
Caesar's Creek 45,221
Caesar's Mill 219
Caesars Creek 90,99
Caey, Joel 227
Cahokia 37
Cail, David 235
Cain's Tavern 25
Cain, Abel 277,286; Asle 217; Aste 217; James 250; John 18; Miss Polly 302
Calander, John 265
Calderhead, Alexander 220
Calderwood, Capt. Adam 247
Caldun, Jacob 221
Caldwell & Jenkinson 157
Caldwell's Mill 28,54,130
Caldwell, Aaron 149; Adam 4,5, 20; Alexander 269,282; Henry 67; James 142;
Caldwell, James 17,23,51,54,56, 84,147,198(2),200(3),209,269, 315; John 10,112,137,311; Joseph 168,243,318; Lieut. James 68; Matthew 172; Miss S. 169; Mr. 117,170; Robert 56,153,163; Samuel 81,108, 112(2),209; Thomas 33; William 218,257,266,287
Caley, George 283,286,302,305
Calhoon, John 81; Mr. 283
Calken, Oliver 51
Call, Richard 184
Callahan, Elizabeth 61; Hugh 61
Calloway, John 182
Callwell, Wm. 127
Calvin, James 298
Calwell's Mill 24,29
Calwell, James 24,29,78
Cambell, Capt. Joseph 240; John 250; Joseph 250; Sally 315; Samuel 228; Will 228
Camble, Jos. 178
Cambril, Daniel 241
Camel, James 310
Cameron, Duncan 142
Camilin, Mary 275
Camlin, Mary 282,296
Cammel, Thomas 121
Cammell, Mrs. Sarah 223
Camoron, Donald 269
Camp Meeting 307,311,312
Camp, Jacob 171; Jesse 171; Peter 127
Campau, Joseph 51
Campbel, Alexander 302
Campbell & Williams 15
Campbell Co., Ky. 51
Campbell County 13,27,32,37,45, 48,74,82,137,195
Campbell County, Kentucky 26,36 37,88,95,114,115,136,145,155, 169
Campbell's mill 186,218
Campbell, Adj. Joseph 210; Alex. 282; Alexander 62,74,90,164, 238,302; Alexr. 285; Andrew 146; Archibald 25,62; Capt. Miss 7; Colin 218; Dr. 304; Dr. Alexander 299; Geo. 274; Hon. Alexander 299,302; J.W. 309; James 140,158,159,255; Jane 187; John 18,21,23,51,58,59,78, 90,142,160,261,267,287,293; John W. 212,299; Joseph 194, 199,202,204(2),205(3),209,212, 225,227,243,275,287,297,303, 305; Lieut. Joseph 18; Maj. 7,156,198; Maj. Joseph 295(2),

327

314; Math. 293; Matthew 296; Mr. 79,177,283,300; Robert 78,137,146,165,231; Samuel 165,277; Solomon 250,296; Stephen 146; Thomas 49; William 8,10,267; William F. 232,237; Wm. 98,193,204,279
Campble, John 15
Camphel, John 10
Campwell, Edward 216
Camron, Daniel 237
Canada 78,245
Canady, Peleg 283
Canby, Samuel 238
Candlish, Mr. 178,179,180,182,185 191,193,194,195,196,201(2)
Cane Run 210,249
Cane, James 51; Mr. 148
Canfield 222,232,245
Canfield, Herman 303; Noys 121
Cannon, Charles 154,161; Curtis 268,274,276; Curtiss 269,272, 277,285,287,303; James 46,144 John H. 300,305,315; Londer 241; Louder 247; Lowder 257, 268,288
Cannutt, William 167
Canton 267
Cantrell, William G. 296
Cantwell, Joseph 250
Capas, John 303
Car, John 184
Carathers, James 250
Carbeny, Henry 274,279
Carberry, Henry 290; Joseph 121; Mr. 279
Carbery, Gen. Henry 123
Carbury, Gen. 167; John 312
Card Manufactory 1
Card, Job 10
Carder, Armstead 315; Sandford 295; Sanford 241,280
Cardor, Sanford 267
Carey, A. 71; Abraham 38,74,88; Christopher 41,173; Daniel 85; M. 20; Mr. 40,88,203; Stephen 207,222
Carfort, F. 215
Carhart, Seth 8,111,229
Carhartt, Seth 189
Carico, Joseph 89
Carir, Joseph 192
Carl, David 142; Joseph 266,319
Carle, David 154
Carlen, John 132
Carlisle 6
Carlisle's store 273
Carlisle, J. 184,218,233(2),247,257 270,275,305; John 98,114,120, 182(2),184(4),185(4),186,187(3) 188,189(2),190,191(2),192, 195(2),196,197,198,202,203,204 206(2),210(2),211,214,217,218, 219,220,221,224(2),225,226,228 229(2),231(2),237,239,242,246, 253,254,255,256,258,265,270(2) 271,272,273(2),279,280,290,299 306,315; Miss Nancy 230; Mr. 182,185,204,250(2),252,287; William 271; Wm. 257,305
Carlisle, Penn. 72,188
Carmack & Smith 121
Carmack, Ephraim 144,244; Jonathan 161
Carmichael, John 164
Carmon, Joshua 99(2)
Carn, George 183
Carnahan, Col. John 189
Carneal, Thomas 45(2),55,116,217, 218,230,241,282
Carnehand, Wm. 210

Carnell, Andrew 197
Carney, D.L. 170; David L. 128, 143,149,157,163,170,172; Mr. 152
Carniel, Thomas 56
Carnohan, James 191
Carns, William 233
Carpenter & Findlay 40,41,43,47, 52,59,61,67(2),71,73,83,85,88, 92,96(2),194
Carpenter & Findley 94
Carpenter's tavern 169
Carpenter, Amos 297; Benjamin 297; Capt. 121,128,138,140,145 148,158,176; Col. Saml. 209; E. 24,187; Emanuel 83,84,115,201 209,220,243,252; Emmanuel 304; Geo. 62; George 168,310; Gilbert 300; Ira 215; J. 71,89 98,100,108,110,112,120,135, 144,146,169,170(2),174,175,176 177(2); James 11; Jeremiah 314; John 11,142,161,315; Joseph 31,38,70,86,87,90,96, 108,125(3),130,132(2),143,144, 149,150,154,157,160,168,171, 174(3),202,214; Mr. 29,34,103, 105(3),106,127; Qr. Master Gen. Sam. 215; Saml. 105; Samuel 88,121,182,183,203,205 207(2),216,223,303; Thomas 250
Carpenter 12,15,26,27,33,43,49,51 55,106,121,135,144,146,151, 158,169,175,194,205,212,213, 216,228,234,238,251,264,297
Carr's mill 262
Carr, Alexander 262; George 56; John 62; Martin 235; Mary 161; Mr. 141; Nichols P. 287; Thomas 301
Carrel, Andrew 305; Bar. 6; Robert 304; William 5
Carrell, Andrew 257; Clament 250; Sanford 164
Carriage maker 156
Carrigen, Andrew 165
Carrigue, Andrew 132,142
Carrithers, Robert 216
Carrol, Daniel 250; Michael 243
Carroll, Daniel 257
Carson, Achsha 165; David 72,175; Eli 154; Elijah 254; Enoch 161; Enock 137; Henry 62,66; Hugh 142,157(2),296; James 229; John 58; Joseph 99,268; Lieut. William 74; Miss Polly 32; Mr. 175; Robert 180,254,282; William 82,270,282,286; Wm. 175
Cartar, Richard 274,289
Carter, Daniel 169; Ephraim 145; Henry 197; James 263,267,305; John 315; Joshua 121; Lorenzo 262; Mary 101,241; Mr. 176, 248; Reuben 70,74,107,118,127 Thomas 109,112,116; W. 293; William 169; Wm. 269
Cartley, John 215
Cartmill, Nathaniel 257
Cartrow, Peter 95
Carty, William 141
Carver, Michael 90
Cary, A. 41,63; Abraham 32,37,57 68,72,73,102; Calvin 283; Christopher 116,171; Samuel 108,116; William 116; Wm. 175
Case, Christopher 88; Ebenezer 99,177; Israel P. 215; Job 297; Job W. 297; Joseph 98,142,224; Lydia 224; Mills 224

Casey, John 249; Thomas 263
Casidy, John 78
Casington, Edward 231
Caskey, James 161
Cass, L. 282; Lew. 284; Lewis 154(2),246,252(2),257,270,276, 277,280(2),284,288; Maj. Jonathan 15,187; Mr. 166,283
Cassart, Peter 75
Cassatt, Dennis 311
Cassel & Loy 130
Cassel, William 84
Casset, Dennis 317; Mr. 148
Cassidy, Henry 32; John 48,58
Cassill, H. 276,280
Cassin, Joseph 149
Castner, Michael 17
Casto, Abel 240; Able 121; Azariah 161; Hannah 66; James 92
Catelan, M. Lanise 25
Caterlin, Ephraim 128
Cates, Adam 285
Cather, Daniel 238
Catterlin, Joseph 209
Catterline, Joseph 127; Wm. 163
Causel, Peter 95
Causland, Mark 185
Cavalt, Cheniah 93
Cavanaugh, Laurance 144
Cavander, Rev. Thomas Steel 191
Cavault, Chenenigh 57
Cavenagh, Garrett 24; Nancy 24
Cavender, Rev. Thomas Steel 191; Samuel 218
Cavet, Mr. 234; Richard 282
Cayler, Adam 275
Caylor, Adam 282; Jacob 310
Cealy, Major 133
Cedar Run 225
Ceel, Abraham 73
Cellar, Thomas 205
Cellars, John 248,253,268,282; Th. 209
Cellers, John 275; Mr. 263
Census 62,186,204
Centerville 257
Centinel 17,23
Centinel of the North-western Territory 1
Cessorsville 238
Ceureer, William 15
Chabert, Francois Joncaire 191
Chad, Farzay 315
Chaffin, Soloman 305
Chair makers 16,107,110,141,155, 159,162,181
Chair manufactory 240,
Chalffin, Solomon 319
Chalmers, James 142,247
Chaman, Ezra 20
Chamberlin, William 32,86
Chambers, Alexander 103,126; B. 35,50,88,94,152; Benjamin 50, 52,58,121,165(2),167,240; Col. 130,135,177,230; Col. Benjamin 142; Doct. 67; James 66, 74,140,154,163,171,172,233; Maj. 78,80,102; Maj. B. 50; Maj. Benjamin 50,60,101,107; Mrs. Ruth 50
Champ, William 215
Champaign County 115,120,135, 163,164,166,167,177,243,249, 252,253,259,272,273,307
Champlin, Miss Lydia 187
Champline's mill 277
Chanay, James Erow 249
Chandivert, Stephen 222
Chandler, John 248; Rachel 132; Swithin 154; William 182,217,

226,275,289,292,300,310; Wm. 242; Zacheriah 317
Chandlers 24
Chanler, Daniel 274; Lt. Richard 18
Channel, John 277
Chanterlle, Michael 236
Chapell, George 282
Chapline, Col. Moses 257
Chapman, David 269; Henry 265, 279,285,298(2); John 79,289, 291,301; Mr. 218; William 270; Zachariah 172
Chapple, George 287,300
Charles, John 43,49; Joseph 88,111; Nehemiah 142,149; Nemiah 161
Charlestown 252
Charlestown, Mass. 237
Charter, James 70
Charters, James 59,82,107,127, 142; William 59
Chase, Abraham 136,156
Chatham, Conn. 230
Chebert de Joncaire, C.F. 181
Cheek, Wm. 169,269
Chenawith, John 306; Thomas 306
Chenewell, Robert 187
Chenoweth, Arthur 207,236,261; Capt. 189; Capt. John 186(2); Elijah 244,247,273; John 180, 189,205,207,261,267,287; Richard 199,201; Thomas 226, 244
Chenowith, Arthur 309
Cherokees 109
Cherrey, Big John 161
Cherry Creek 249
Cherry fork 239
Cherry, Aaron 43,99,119,178; Andrew 187; Big John 178; Jesse 310,315; John 81,95,99; Mary 43; Philip 188,233,315; Reuben 306; William 58,129
Chery, Jasper 275
Chesnut, Capt. 208,276; Charles 262; Daniel 238,263,269,274, 276,280,305; Mrs. Patrick 65, 188
Chesnutt, Charles 285; Daniel 285
Chester County, Maryland 15
Chester County, Pennsylvania 61
Chester, Pa. 1
Chesterson, George 42
Chestrester, Elias 282
Chetterson, William 269
Chew, Col. Samuel Lloyd 13; Joseph 267,282
Chewshwell, Robert 184
Chicago 307
Chickasaw Bluff 41
Chidester, William 267
Chikago 304
Childes, John 112
Childress, Calep 315
Chiles, Garland 217
Chillicothe (see Old Chillicothe) 20,28,30,33,38,39,44,47,49,60, 62,65,66,68,71,84,85,87,90,93, 94,98,103,108,112,114,125,126, 128,130,135,148,149,158,166, 167,168,169,170,172,173, and on every page from 178 to 319
Chillicothe Academy 270
Chillicothe Bluffs 219
Chillicothe Debating Society 206
Chillicothe Grammar School 266
Chillicothe Manufacturing Society 316
Chillicothe Polemic Society 252, 256,262

Chillicothe River 21
Chillicothe Town 178
Chillicothe road 206,244,248
Chineth, Thomas 300
Chinno, Samuel 183
Chinnowoth, John 275
Chinoweth, A. 280,314; Miss Betsy 124
Chinowith, Arthur 273
Chinwith, A. 294
Chipman, John 256
Chirry, John 41
Chisas, Joseph 247
Chism, Elisha 145
Chittenden, Chester 70; James 70
Chiventon, John 303
Chizem, Joseph 292
Chizum, Josiah 311
Chobert de Joncaire, C.F. 69; Charles F. 214,216
Chobert, Mr. 181
Chouteau, Augustin 37
Chovea, Thomas 89
Chramlich, Cristian 308
Chribbs, Elizabeth 44,48; William 28,48,69
Chriest, Polly 129
Chrisman & Johnson 194
Chrisman & Johnston 73
Chrisman, Coonrod 187
Christ, Abraham 146; Christian 48; Moses 66
Christian County 128,235,237
Christian, Henry A. 292,296
Christie, Andrew 16
Christy, Andrew 26,58,73; Capt. 143; Capt. David 140; D. 96; Lieut. David 82,96,139,201; Mr. 86; Nancy 132
Chritles, William 204
Chunn, J.T. 118; John T. 110,137, 138,142,160,161
Church, Sergeant Lemuel 37,60
Churchill, Armistead 13,14(2),15; John 7,14; Mrs. 13
Chy, Rev. Henry 247
Cilley, Joseph 170; Major Jonathan 145
Cilliman, John 212
Cilly, Jonathan 136; Maj. Jonathan 149
Cincinnati appears on every page from 1-178, also 180,186,218, 249,253,254,255,256,263,264, 267,273,286,291,294,304,311, 312,315,317,318
Cincinnati Academy 94
Cincinnati Congregation 43,44,65, 79
Cincinnati district 103
Cincinnati Fair 98
Cincinnati Horse Races 80,99
Cincinnati Infantry 100
Cincinnati Library 73
Cincinnati Light Infantry 61,62, 63,64,65,76,77,79,90,96,99,105, 107,116,119,121,123,126,127, 131
Cincinnati Lodge 132,140,149,156, 157,163,172
Cincinnati Lyceum 140,141,143, 148,150
Cincinnati Meeting House 66
Cincinnati Presbyterian Church 136
Cincinnati Presbyterian Congregation 137,138
Cincinnati Public Library 72
Cincinnati Republican Society 261
Cincinnati School House 53

Cincinnati Township 27,41,57,73 75,88,94,98,102,113,117,128, 133,134,141,152,153,163,164, 165,168,169,171,172
Cincinnati University 152,153, 155,156,157,158,159,160,162, 172,176,256
Circleville 315
Cisna, Robert 252; Stephen 16
Cisney, Charles 192; Samuel 309
Cisnor, Charles 203
Cissna, Charles 219,277,289; James 296; John 197,270,287; Samuel 184,241; Stephen 71, 192,296; Thomas 107,221; Thos. 228
Claiborn, Capt. 66
Claiborne, Capt. 55; Capt. F. Leigh 60; Capt. Ferdinand L. 60; Gov. 72; Gov. William C.C. 113; Mr. C.C. 183; William C.C. 215; Wm. C.C. 188
Claibourne, Capt. 66; Capt. Ferdinand L. 66
Claiburn, Capt. 50
Claimorgan, Mr. 20
Clair, John 203
Clancy, Wm. 295
Clannen, Samuel 137
Clannin, Samuel 154
Clap, John 58
Clark County 5,85,203
Clark County, Indiana 162
Clark County, Kentucky 89,148, 257,302
Clark, Ann 268; Bazil 116; Capt. 126,143,217; Capt. Edmund 282; Col. 183; D. 183; Dan. 231; Daniel 37,41,121,142; David 48,287; Dennes 161; E. 76; Edmund 83; Ezra 121; Francis 257; George 8,163,230, 287,300; George Rogers 53; Hamilton 126; Henry 242; Hezekiah 99; Houton 35; Huton 310; Israel 227,244,247,263; J. 184,280; James 45,58,90,112, 145,154,166,169(2),172,175,252 267,269,291,300,302(2),313; James Innes 152; Jeremiah 13; Jesse 116; John 19,20,45(2),55, 93,100,107,116(2),127(2),137, 161,165,167,197,202,206,209, 212,218,221,274,275,287,291, 300,309,313,315; Jonathan 137, 184,197,224,261; Joseph 170, 184,187,192,202,207,251; Joseph H. 82; Levy 296; Lieut. William 10; Maj. Gen. George R. 9; Margaret 149; Mr. 46,61 79(2),88,91,114,131,148,177; Nicholas 243; Noah 268,287; Obediah 218; Peter 300,305; Polly 165; Reuben S. 304; Richard 230; Robert 244; Rubin S. 305; Samuel 37,48,66, 82,142,189,194,226,227,254, 305,309,313; Silas 8; Stephen 127,184,276,307; Thomas 98, 120,124,135,136; Walter 310; William 85(2),91,98,102,110, 112,120,164,174,183,233,237, 300,310,315
Clarke County 121
Clarke County, Kentucky 158,234, 297
Clarke, Ambrose 18; Bazill 74; Capt. Joseph 189; Corp. James 157; Daniel 86; Ephraim 252; George 49,228; Hauton 35; Hezekiah 74; Houton 35,54; J.

20,28,31; James Innes 256;
John 16,34,40,44,86,179,216;
Jonathan 102; Joseph 236;
Lettia 244; Lieut. 5;
Mr. 72; Robert 237; Thomas
55,86; William 23
Clarkesville 16,249
Clarksburg 207
Clarno, John H. 315
Clarridge, Edmund 310
Clauson, Moses 250
Clawson, Peter 75
Clay, Green 154; James 60;
Matthew 231; Stephen 227
Claypole, Capt. 182
Claypool, Abraham 87,111,199,
200,201,202,212,237,241,248,
252,253,277(2),296,310,313(2),
314; Abram 164; Isaac 203,296,
314; Mr. 164,239,250,315
Claypoole, Abraham 178,203
Clayton, Thomas 170; William 250
Clear Creek 9,27,30,41,45,60,61,
63,65,74,75,76,78,83,86,90,91,
95,97,99,100,103,107,111,112,
115,119,191,208,211,218,219,
221,237,239,253,291
Clear Creek Island 49
Clear Creek township 245,273,284
285,287,293,294
Cleareland, Moses 227
Clearfield Creek 228
Cleaveland, Josiah 252
Cleavenger, Jesse 107; Sary 254
Cleaver, Ezekial 132; Martha 132
Cleavland, Josiah 255
Clegg, Richard 18
Clemans, Sally 241
Clemens, Christian 298; John 212,
238; Joseph 292; Mr. 200
Clements, Alexander 36; Sarah 36
Clemmans, Eleazor C. 297
Clemmer, Andrew 306,315
Clemmons, John 209
Clemons, John 204,214,231
Clendenen, John 305
Clermont 156,202
Clermont County 54,57,61,72,73,
76,79,82,84,86,88,91,96,97,98,
99,100,111,113,131,140,
150,159,160,161,163,164,167,
170,171,172,176,183,194,203,
205,210,211,212,213,217,222,
238,247,252,253,265,279,281,
285,298,303,308,314,317
Cleveland 229,262,291
Clevenger, Eden 250; Mary 254
Cleverston, Joseph 213
Clifford, James 305; Sarah 95,99,
270
Clifton, Bosman 273; Bozman 275;
Charles 296; George 267; Noah
241; Samuel 187,205
Climpson, Lieut. 47
Climson, Lieut. Eb. 109; Lieut. Eli
B. 48; Lieut. Elie B. 75
Clindenen, Robert 216
Cline, G. 257; John 310
Clingham, John 257
Clingman, John 296
Clinton 260,303
Clinton County 303,314,315
Clinton, Geo. 166; Lawyer 218;
Mr. 105(2)
Cliver, John 149
Clockmaker 108,113,120,133,140,
143,145,157,248,252,253,259,
261,268,270,307
Clopper, Nicolas 233
Close, David 116; Mr. 267
Clothier 119

Cloud, Mr. 131; Rev. Robert 317;
Robert 240,284
Clough Creek 11,43,55,90,102
Clough mill 163
Clouser, John 186,218
Clouzar, John 300
Clouzer, John 282
Clover Creek Fork 194
Clover Lick Creek 140
Clover, Henry 275,282
Clowes, Isaac 254
Clowser, John 215
Cluff Creek 47,99
Cluss Creek 25
Coachmakers 141
Coad, George 15
Coal Rain township 245
Coal, Samuel 296
Coane, Robert 187
Coar's mills 218
Cobbs, David 237
Cobler, David 241
Coburn, John 156
Cochran, Barnabus 282; George
25; Hugh 192(2),200,280,282,
292,312,315; James 288; Jean
192; John 146,233,266; Mr. 15,
30; Mrs. 312; Samuel 292;
Solomon 266; Thomas 4,28,36,
42,44,73,131,142,310; William
184,189,300; Wm. 245
Cochren, Barnaba 300
Cochron's Tavern 26
Cocke, Colin 264
Cockerill, Enoch 305
Cockran, Barnabas 250; Benjamin
F. 270,275; Hugh 296; John
275; William 202
Cockrane, Hugh 237
Cockrell, Jessee 299
Cockren, Isaac 244
Cockrian, Barnabas 267
Cockrill, Enoch 310
Cockrull, Jesse 241
Codd, George 41,61
Coder, George 255
Codinton, Benjamin 279
Coehran, Hugh 184
Coen, Edward 137; James 170
Coffee House 36,39,48
Coffee, John 247,282
Coffenberry, Elizabeth 205;
George 205; Mary 205
Coffey, John 212,275
Coffinbery, Andrew 267
Coffman, Christopher 309
Cofman, Martin 291
Cogan, Agness 137; Amsty 146;
Ansly 142; William 255
Cogle, George 257
Cogswell, Doct. 185; Dr. Joseph
190; Miss 185
Cogwill, John 112
Cohoon, John 311; Thomas 173
Cohran, Thomas 43; William 301
Coil, Gabriel 247
Coins, Andrew 192
Colbath, Sarjent 5
Colbertson, David 212,215
Colbraith, Sergeant 5
Colby, Joseph 60,92,93(2),136;
Miss Margery 165
Colderain 127
Coldrain 127,129
Coldwell, James 173,300,318
Cole, Broad 307; Edward 222;
James 70,99,116,137; Leonard
297,309; Philip 293; Shederick
287; William 285
Coleby, Joseph 102

Colem, Beel 287,292
Coleman, Henry 23; Jacob 200,203
James 137,293; John 137; Lucy
154; Mr. 172(2); William 62,73,
90; Wm. 75,83
Colerain 1,2,4,7,14,16,19,24,26,30,
32,34,37,51,62,68,74,76,78,79,
82,86,90,91,97,99,100,107,108,
112,114,121,122,126,128,132,
133,136,137,142,145,146,149,
154,161,165,227
Colerain road 89,161
Colerain township 44,58,59,73,93,
98,104,109,112,117,131,146,
161,174,175,236,241,262,263,
264,272,280,291,295,297,302,
309,311,312,314,316,319
Coles, Solomon 305
Coliher, John 62
Colleau, Joseph 199
College Township 99,102,115,122,
170,233,254
Collens, Capt. 2
Collerick, John 184
Collet, J. 278; John 182,194,217,
218,248,252,262,270; Joshua
141
Collett, John 184,187,222,223,225,
226
Collier, Daniel 212,214
Collings, William 218
Collins & Company 252
Collins, Charles 145; Doctor John
107,170; J. 275; J.S. 152,240;
John 91,205,231,241,303,305;
Jos. S. 294,313; Joseph 73,76,
263; Joseph S. 164,272,288,296
297,298,304(2),308,317; Mr.
209; Mrs. Elizabeth 179;
Nathaniel 192,278; Nathl. 266,
315; Rev. John 284,287,297,
300; Robert 58; Thomas 215;
Wm. 179
Collinsworth, John 275
Collit, John 192(2)
Collom, George 133
Collum, Wm. 136
Colnwell, James 161
Colraine township 285
Columbia 1,3,4,5,6,7,8,9,10,11,12,
13,14,15,16,19,20,21,23,24,25,
27,28,29,30,31,33,35,36,37,38,
39,41,42,43,45,47,48,49,50,51,
55,56,57,59,60,61,63,65,66,67,
68,70,71,72,73,74,76,77,78,79,
82,84,86,87,88,89,90,93,94,95,
99,100,101,102,103,104,106,
107,108,109,110,112,115,116,
118,121,122,123,124,126,127,
128,133,137,142,146,148,149,
151,154,160,161,163,164,165,
166,168,172,174,175,178,200,
202,203
Columbia County 91
Columbia Street 118,144,166,176
Columbia road 40
Columbia school house 104
Columbia town 129
Columbia township 27,57,62,69,73,
93,94,126,129,145,150,160,173,
177
Columbian Inn 174,177,294
Columbiana 109
Columbiana County 111,131,164,
205,207,213,225,232,234,238,
250,252,253,303
Columbus 44
Colven, Benjamin 221; Jacob 221;
Thomas 305
Colver, Samuel 318
Colvin, Jacle 215; James 304;

Moses 257
Colwell, Capt. James 99; James 41,161,287; Martin 130; William 300
Combess, Carvill 244
Combs, John 267,292,312,313; Widow 294; Zacheriah 312; Zur 313
Comens, John 205
Comer, Jesse 319; John 309; Thomas 300,307
Commercial Company 51
Commissioners 30,71,103,104,115, 115,119,132,134,181
Commons, Hugh 296
Compstock, Joab 88
Compton, George 315; Jacob R. 57,127; James 215,233; John 116,270; Joseph 112,170; Robert 137
Comstock's Ferry 100
Comstock, D. 292; Joab 100,318; John 215
Comton, George 245; Jacob R. 121
Con, Daniel 294; Mr. 210
Concannon, William 74
Concklin, Joseph 215
Concle, John 280
Concord 237
Concord township 165,207,211,214 226,235,236,237,245,247,256, 261,267,272,280,295,309,314, 319
Conder, Redman 314
Condon, Edward 244; Redmond 254,257
Conduke, James 305
Cone, Cephas 297; Charles 132; Mr. 164
Conger, David 255; Michael 292
Congleton, William 198
Congregation of New Hope 240
Congress 60,138,150,167,193,194 195,196,203,204,205,207,249, 250,252,254,256,286,290,304, 309,311
Conklen, John 212
Conklin, Capt. Joseph 189; David 227,233,250,257; Jos. 233; Joseph 202,227,254,267
Conkling, Joseph 144
Conly, Lemuel 257
Conn's tavern 168
Conn, Charles 25,34,51,56,110,115 127,133,166,171; Hez. 50; James 34,49,51,54,56,64,67,75, 76,103,160; John 184; Joseph 51,74,115,117,121(2),122,132, 133,136,139,141,149,150,171; Micheal 257; Mr. 61,151(3), 152; Patty 171; Thomas 29
Connecticut 48,240
Connel, James 182,194; William 282
Connell, John R. 284; Levi 270
Connelly, Elizabeth 247
Connelstown 242
Connely, Isaac 254
Conner, D. 66,143,164; Dan. 12; Daniel 36,37(2),47,54,57,60, 62(2),64,66(2),68,73,76,79,80, 81(2),84,86,94,95,101(2),102, 103,104,106(2),114,118,119(2), 127,147,155,318; Edward 270; Fisher 137; Frederick 32; Jesse 227; John 215,311; Mr. 107; Mrs. Susan 164; Samuel 189, 215,242
Connet, Benjamin 92,207,208,210, 211

Connor, Daniel 52(2); Isaac 121; Peter 302
Connover, Joseph 137
Conrad, Mr. 141; Samuel 315; Woolery 305
Conrod, Andrew 161; Cornelius 292; Daniel 156; George 300; Woollery 257
Constock, Joel 74
Contryman, Henry 278; John 278, 294; Martin 278,294,313
Convention 80,81,82,83,84,85,198, 199,200,201
Convers, James 183; Jos. 184; Mr. 183
Converse, James 88,203
Conway, Simon 313
Conwell, David 244; Fisher 244; William 305
Cony, Nathan 310
Cooch, Thomas 62,116
Cook, Arm 149; Bennett 180; Capt. 5(2); Conrod 127; Easter 215; Easther 270; Edward 56; Elizabeth 202; Isaac 44,166, 178,208,212(2),215,226,229, 237,246,255(2),256,257,267, 270(2),279,280,303(2); Jacob C. 161,318; Jesse 227,248,250; John 32,74,171; Joseph 112; Judge 250; Lieut. 200; Miss Sally 311; Moses 267; Mosses 270; Mr. 239; Thomas 75,112, 247,270; William 205
Cookes, Joseph 205; Mary 205
Cooley, Asahel 303; Ebenezer 146; Ebenezer 51; Peter 297; William 95; Wm. 297; Zadock 297
Cooly, Ebenezer 126
Coon, Adam 316; John 285; Lewis 146
Cooner, Daniel 194
Coonrod, George 227; Uledrey 315; Wooly 294
Coons, Frederick 153,161; Henry 209; Isaac 307
Coonse, Frederick 28,113
Cooper, Andrew 305; Capt. 206; Christian 105,106; D.C. 34,62 68,83,111,114,226; Daniel 216; Daniel C. 24,26,28,37,59,61,69, 78,80,82(3),84(2),87,94,111, 126,155,159,164,186,199,206; George 127; Isaac 142; Jacob 74,311; Jeremiah 308; Jesse 82; Joseph 318; Margaret 221; Rachel 105,106; Samuel 82; Thomas 300; William 147,179, 183,188,192
Coopers 2,7,10,15,33,34,38,62, 63,108,112,118,123,127,131, 136,179,180,181,301,317
Coopersmith 89
Coor, John 270
Coover, Gidion 287,292; Mary 267; Samuel 205,264
Cope, Charles 62; Samuel 157
Coppersmith 15,141,173,289
Coppinger, Michael 86
Corbat, James 210
Corbett, David 295,314
Corbley, J. 83; John 83,154
Corbly, John 58(2),81
Corbus, Godfrey 62
Corder, Sanford 250
Cordwainer 142
Core, Henry 274; John 247,257, 275
Corey, Daniel 85(2); John 314
Corier, Joseph 82

Corington, Rhoda 142
Corken, Robert 275; Robt. 227
Corkin, Robert 268
Corkrin, John 275
Corman, Dr. John 187
Corn Island 249
Corn, John 291; William 260
Cornete & Piat 132
Cornett & Pratts 107
Cornit, William 107
Corns, William 218
Cornwell, Gideon 297
Corpman, Micheal 270
Corporation of Cincinnati 154,173
Correll, Ander 250; Andrew 275, 300
Corrothers, William 158
Corry, Brother 140; William 106, 117,118,139
Corson, Eli 161
Cortrell, George 297
Corwin, George 288; Ichabod 100, 238; Mathias 111,164,238(2), 265; Matthias 138,253; Moses 298; Mr. 131,177; Phinchos 265; Samuel 74,170
Corwine, George 282,285; Samuel 291
Cory, Joseph 241; Nathan 244,247, 301; Samuel 101; Simeon 301; Thomas 37; William 164,227
Coryell, Lewis 269
Cosen, Abel 154
Coshocton County 302,303
Coss, Daniel 250
Cossart, Henry 146
Cossel, Peter 107
Cost, Daniel 175
Cotcher, John 99
Cotter, Levi 199
Cotterall, George 298
Cotton factory 175
Cotton, John 127
Cottrell, John 230
Cotts, Jacob 100
Couch, J.N. 278,279(2); Jessup N. 277(2); Jesup N. 256,259,262, 268,273,274,284,289,296,304, 309,312,314; Mr. 241,242,246; Thomas 113
Cougell, Joseph 234
Coulderwood, Adam 254
Coulter, Charles 199,237,250,263; John 54; Mr. 177
Counce, Henry 315
Councellor, John 161
Couner, John 311
Counsellor, John 142
Countryman, H. 310; John 293
Coursolle, Francis 142
Courthouse 59,65,71,83,108,115, 117,121,123,182,208,211,223
Courtnay, William 7,
Courtnay, William 7,
Courts 3,4,12,14,16,17,20,23,25,30 34,42,43,46,47,49,50,52,53,56, 57,59,61,64,69,72,73,79,80,81, 83,85,86,87,88,89,91,99,102, 104,110,113,114,115,116,118, 119,121,122,123,125,126,128, 129,130,131,133,136,139,140, 141,144,147,150,151,156,157, 158,159,161,165,166,167,171, 173,175,179,183,184,186,192, 193,196,197,200,201,204,205, 206,208,211,213,217,220,222, 224,225,226,228,229,230,233, 234,235,236,238,239,240,245, 246,248,249,250,251,252,253, 255,256,258,259,262,263,264, 267,268,269,272,273,274,277,

278,279,283,284,286,288,290, 294,297,298,299,302,304,307, 311,315
Courtwright, Abraham Vn. 308
Coutch, William 292
Couture, Jean Baptiste 298
Covalt, Bethuel 79
Cove, Calvin 164
Coven, Jacob 221; William 18
Covert, Butrun 82
Covington, Capt. Leonard 12; Edward 127,142,146
Covolt, Timothy 66
Cowan, James 109; John 109; Mary 109
Cowel, Peter 154
Cowen, Wm. 20
Cowenhoven, Elias 170
Cowgell, Eleazer 270; Elisha 230
Cowgill, Alexander 267; Elazar 267; Elisha 233
Cowhick, Thomas 318
Cowin, David 187
Cowins, Edward 146
Cowles, Isaac 230
Cowling, Aaron 15
Cowls, Thomas 78
Cownovor, Elias 161
Cox's Tavern 26,41,45
Cox's run 218
Cox, Amer 241; Andrew 69,87, 170; Benj. 316; Benjamin 10, 260,294,305; Charles 132; Christopher 292; David 65; Emmon 215; Emmor 227; Enoch 272,309; George 318; J. 148; Jacob 8,195,218,233,247, 272,282,303; James 9,10,19, 20(2),25,45,56,60,77,82,87,101; Jeffery 296,300; Jeffry 311; John 289; Joseph 48; Joshua 154; Lydia 287; Moses 305; Mr. 24,187; Nathan 309,316; Nathaniel 244,310; Nicholas 269; Samuel 241; Solomon 178, 199,201,210,309; Thomas 142, 165,230; Walter 99,142; William 107,127,246,307
Coxe, Mr. 164
Coy, Ariel 41
Coyle, George 310
Cozad, Jacob 138
Cozard, Wm. 233
Cozier, Benjamin K. 144
Crab, Edward 257; Henderson 301; John 257,310
Crabb, Daniel 275,287,310;Edward 194,263,310; Henderson 237; John 270; Thomas 309
Crabel, Jonathan 254
Crable, Kenner 315
Cradle, Ormond 209
Cradlepaugh, John 237
Crafford, Noble 254
Craft, John 149; William 247
Crag, Philip 116
Craghan, William 244,249
Craig, Abraham 267; Benjamin 38; Elijah 10,84,96; H. 107,108,113 Hugh 108; Isaac 313; Joel 132, 166; John 23,48,217,237; John H. 80,81,89; Jonathan 247,254 275,287,305; Lieut. 6; Mr. 6,66 Uriah 137; William 192,198,199 200,201,202,209,238,239; Wm. 223,235
Craige, John 163
Craigg, William 223,226
Craigmiles, John 192
Craigs, Samuel 154
Craik, Mr. 41

Crail, John 130; Wilson 73,83
Crain, Elias 146; Elihu 63; Isaac 75; James 307,312,319; John 62,275; Joseph 69,118; William 45,58
Craine, Joseph 192
Crairaft, Charles 269
Cramer, Francis 196,301; George 275
Crane, Col. John 45; Doctor 196; Elias 119,132; James 127; John 31,142; Jonas 58(2),75,146; Jonathan 85; Joseph 23,58,73, 76,128,143; Moses 66; Mr. 42, 78,90,99,105; Noah 95,101,174; Robert 194; Ruth 101; Samuel 116,137,142
Cranmer, John 115
Cranmere, John 120
Cranmore, Doctor 111
Cransar, Michael 236
Crary, John 149
Cravens, Jesse 128,132,235,237; Nathaniel 235; Nehemiah 128, 235,237
Crawfish Creek 36
Crawford's place 115
Crawford, Abel 222; Able 103; Alexander 180; Elizabeth 254; James 179,180(2),197,198,200, 201,212,218,224,225,234,243, 244; John A. 256; John H. 132, 150; N. 263(3); Noble 199, 200(2),201,208,212,233,266; Oliver 99; Robert 142; Robert Cunningham 37; Saml. S. 282, 283; William 212,214,244,250, 305
Craybell, Jonathan 285
Craycraft, Thomas 288
Crayton, Patrick 17
Creain, James 297
Creamer, Francis 312; George 305,311,312; Michael 205,250, 311
Creathers, James 233
Creaton, Edward 305
Creatures, Ezekiel 146
Creed, John 220; Mathew 246,275, 283,284
Creegar, Peter 165
Creek Indians 34
Creek, John 253
Creel, John 244
Creigan, William 197
Creigh, Ensign 9; Samuel 4,9
Creighton & Baldwin 195
Creighton, Hugh 313; Lawyer 183, 290; Mr. 239,242,250(2),283, 315; W. 193,196,197,201,208, 226,227,228,315,316; William 94,115(2),117,118(3),120,131, 134,158,166,178,180,183,186(2) 188,191,195,196(3),200,201(2), 204,207,208,212,214,216,217, 226,229,252,255(2),256,276,283 287,288,289,292,304,312,313(4) 314(2),318; Wm. 166,179(2),190 205,208,209,210(2),226,236,237 238,239(3),242,248,249,270(2), 272,278,280,284,287,290,291, 294,307,312,314
Cremer, Person 250
Cresswell, Samuel 19
Cretors, Ezekiel 140,147
Creviston, John 217; Joseph 217; Nicholas 217
Crew, Thomas 305; Walter 263
Cribbe, Wm. 15
Crichfield, Capt. 112; Philip 112
Crider, Henry 281; Jacob 224;

John 281; Michael 189; Mr. 246
Cridlebough, Rev'd. John 244
Crimm, Jacob 61
Crisman, Conrod 192
Criss, George 58
Crissman, David 318
Crist, Christian 51; Col. Henry 188; John 216,296,315; Moses 37,48
Criswall, George 307
Criswell, James 246,259
Critchfield, Philip 154
Crites, Conrad 166
Crochancy, James 250
Crocker & Kennedy 186
Crocker, Doctor 184; Doctor John 184; Dr. 184; Dr. John 185; J. 182,184,185; John 183,184(2), 185(3),186,196,208
Crocket, Andrew 305
Crocket, John 218
Crockwell, James 281; James T. 314
Croecheney, James 191
Croes, Jacob 241
Crofts, William 37
Crole, William 94
Croll, David 305; William 209
Crooked Creek 218
Crooks, James 127; William 62
Crosan, James 298; William 298
Crosby 100,114,126,137,146,149, 158,169
Crosby township 146,165
Crosby, Levi 165
Croskey, John 205
Crosley, Josiah 154,160,170; Ross 95
Cross Creek 72
Cross, Barnerd 121; Benjamin 74, 82; James 300; John 82; Miss Polly 245; Robert 250; William 188
Crossen, Collumby 146
Crossey, Josiah 154
Crossings of Hockhocking 184
Crossings of Paint Creek 181,184, 206,235,250
Crossley, Ross 34; William 72,96
Crouch, Andrew 266,276,312; John 309; Joseph 296,311; Joseph 311; William 107
Crous, David 236; John 219,239
Crouse's mill 183,218,221,237, 245(2),263
Crouse, David 189,267,317(2); J. 267; John 198,207,208,212,219, 236,255,262,264,267,277(2),280 282,295,296,312; Mr. 241
Crouze, John 200
Crow, Israel 287,310; Lieut. 211; Mathias 142; Matthias 57,146, 318; Thomas 242,245,300,310
Crows's mill 183
Crows, John 183
Crowse's mill 183,185
Crowse, Thomas 183
Croxton, Abraham 23
Croyle, Adam 315
Crull, Charles 257; David 315; Jacob 233;William 215,221,227
Crum, Abraham 132; John 104
Crumb, Abraham 78
Crume, Daniel 311
Cruw, Thomas 250
Cryder's Mill 251
Cryder, John 300; Michael 200,239 259,301,309,314; Mr. 247
Crydor, Mich. 228
Culberson, John 130
Culbert, John 316; Robert 10

Culbertson, Robert 83,87,200,201, 202,203,218(2),289; Samuel 78
Culley, Col. Matthew 161,165,170
Cullom, Francis 172; George 127; W.T. 172; Wm. T. 158,165(2)
Cullum, Beal 316; Beel 270,275; G. 29; George 7,57; Lieut. William T. 68; William T. 57, 171
Culp, Henry 286,292; Jacob 230, 297; Peter 312
Cultrough, William 318
Culver, Racheal 282
Culvert, John 310
Cumbacker, John 232
Cumberland 277,282
Cumberland County, Penn. 188, 317
Cumberland River 77
Cumings, James 300
Cummen, Alexander 296
Cummerman, Andrew 197
Cummin, A. 307; Alexander 282
Cumming, John N. 118
Cummings, Gen. 50; James 202; John 279,295,297; Lieut. John 69
Cummins, Alexander 270; Andrew 287; David 58; Gen. 124; James 134,246; John 46,57,90, 127,166,167,245,263,294,314; John N. 91; Joseph 90; William 189
Cummon, John 29
Cummons, John 275; William 192
Cungim, Henry 257
Cuningham, Patrick 277
Cuninham, Nicholas 305
Cunningham's Mill 29(2),33,34,35, 40,45,46,59,60,91,142,159
Cunningham's Station 27
Cunningham, Alexander 250; Daniel 99; Hugh 242; James 18,26,37,41,43,48,51,113,121, 155; John 292; Matthew 77; Mr. 39; Nicholas 233,244,275; Patrick 205; Rev'd. Robert M. 263; Rev. Robert 267; Richard 78; Robert 233,287; Robt. 212; Thomas 244,257,267,270,305; William 107,127
Curlet, John 254
Curran, Alex'r 179; Alexr. 282,283 David 212
Currens, Benjamin 310
Current, Hannah 19
Currey, Col. James 267
Currier, Ebenezer 261,262; William 18
Curriers 91,104,114,117,279,291
Curries, James 293
Currine, Theis 257
Currothers, George 247
Curry, Col. James 236; James 189(2),244,282,310; Rev. Hiram Miram 150,157; William 55,318
Cursevell, Rachel 267
Curtes, Mary 287
Curtis, Ely 8; Jeremiah 233
Curtiss, Lewis J. 161
Curtna, Christopher 167
Curtright, Daniel 233
Curwin, Phineas 296
Cushing, Maj. Thomas H. 3
Custard, William 318
Cuthright, John 254
Cutlar, John 245
Cutler, Capt. 281; Enos 128,149; Eph. 69; Ephraim 73,84,194; Jacob 218; Jervis 290,292;
John 256,281,291,302; Lt. Enos 173; Maj. 260,261; Major 267; Manassah 40; Mr. 38,69(2),120, 226,244,280
Cutter's Tavern 1,27
Cutter, John 17,129; Joseph 17; Mary 129(2); Miss Abigail 100; Miss Susannah 139; Mr. 52; Seth 1,5,9,12,17(2),29,33(2),42, 43,61,62,73(2),76,87,88,93, 103(2),105,113,125(2),126,127, 128,129,134,137,140,157,160, 170
Cuttraugh, Wm. 293
Cuyahoga County 303,307,317
Cuykendal, Abraham 15
Cuykindall, Mr. 18
Cynthiana 23
Cynthiana, Kentucky 233
Cyssherd, Andrew 284
Czar, Joseph 305
Dabney, Nathaniel Gardner 40
Daer, John 317
Dailey, Edward 267; John 7; John S. 107
Daily & Baxter 34
Daily, Charles 205; Elizabeth 132, 170; J. 143; James 261; John 14,31,33,38,72,90,117,127; John S. 170; Mr. 29,76; William 261
Daleny, Daniel 281
Dalgarn, James 308
Dallas, A.J. 42
Dallgarl, James 315
Dallier, Maria Josephine 192
Daly, William 211,276,278,281; Wm. 210
Daman, John 180
Dana, Edmund B. 167
Dana, Luther 20
Dancels, Benjamin 107
Dancing master 178,199
Dancing school 144,153,172,286
Danford, Enoch 112,121; Samuel 48; William 45
Daniel 310
Daniel, Enos 86; James 296; John 90,263; Peter 45; Samuel 250, 296; Thomas 263
Danly, Aaron 228
Dannel, James 275
Dannil, Samuel 299
Danston 250
Danvigan, Enock 230
Danville, Isaac 8
Dapenpower, George 12
Darah, Amus 69
Darbey's Town 16
Darby 209,211,215,221,223,241, 247,254,268,271,279,287
Darby Creek 186,188,192,200,205, 209,210,212,220,221,238,243, 244,245,247,251,254,269,273, 283,290,293,306,307,311,314
Darby Creek settlements 218
Darby township 295,309,311,313, 318
Darby's Creek 179,184,190,247
Darby, Ezra 165; Samuel 309; Sanders 241; William 289,309
Dark, William 218
Darke, William 186
Darling, Robert 280; William 51
Darlingnon, Joseph 177
Darlington's run 218
Darlington, Gen. 290; J. 70; Joseph 84,87,91,180,186,201, 253; Mr. 36(2),37(2),38(2),39,40 53,69,71,84,181,300
Darlinton, Gen. 160,262; John 315;
Jos. 240; Joseph 131,192,203, 204,205,216(2),226,239,240, 253,274,279,299,303,315; Mr. 181
Darneille, I. 10,15,16; Isaac 11,20, 85,267
Darnielle, Isaac 20
Darr, Conrad 168,169
Darrah, Joseph 317
Darrow, Amos 58; George 284
Darslinger, Thomas 292
Dart, Doctor Cyrus 74; Randolph 305
Darth, Randolph 292
Dasher, Jacob 315
Daugherty, George 137; Mr. 19; Neal 228,263; Saml. 298; Samuel 297
Daughson, William 282
Daulton, Mr. 123
Davanport, Anthony S. 255
Davenport, Anthony S. 190,255; Anthony Symmes 193; James 120,234,282; John 107; Mr. 118
Davice, David 146
David's Fork 159
David, Doctor 99
Davidson, Alexander 10; Andrew 23; Armstrong 303; Isabella 216; John 115,208,216,272,273; Joseph 269,292; Lieut. Andrew 189; Robert 23,170; Saml. 298; Samuel 267,297; Thomas 183, 197,203,230,233,267,292,296; William 304,311
Davis & Scott 281(2)
Davis boys 123
Davis' Mill 92,141
Davis, Archibald 170; Augustine 235; Ben. 20; Benjamin 30,51, 59,180,300,305,311; Capt. John 263; Capt. Samuel 186; Charles 300; D. 109; Daniel 58,65,126,242; Daniel E. 304; David 41,101,107,194,206,218; David W. 257; Doctor 269,273; Doctor David 10; Doctor Ramus 235(2),237; Dr. 276; Dr. David 75; Dr. Ramus 246,273; Eaneas 244; Elisha 51,62,66; Elizabeth 5; Enons 218; George 261,296; Hannah 197; Harman 284; Henry 112,263,315; Hezakiah 296; Hon. T.T. 183; Hugh 142,149,183; Isaac 145, 210,263,318; Jacob 218,277; James 30,42,101,107,230,273, 309(2); Jarred 236; Jerard 280; Job 90; John 26,58,103,149,154 192,260,269,300; John F. 301; Jonathan 78,154; Joseph 127, 154,274; Joshua 267,270,309; Lewis 48,233; Lieut. Samuel 261; Loes 107; Lydia 30; Mary 129; Mr. 76,109,135,183,193; Mrs. Mary 304; Nehemiah 180; Owen 211,283; Peter 5,66,95, 146; Push 314; Ramus 282,286, 310; Rev. 163; Sally 41; Samuel 18,51,74(2),107,165,189 216,218,253,314; Samuel W. 159; Stephen 58,101,107,313; Thinsey 221; Thomas 11,30,48, 58,81,123,129,215; Timothy 48; Walter 48,51; William 61,142, 208,289,291,310; Wm. 261,283
Davison, James 310; John 151; Robert C. 250; Samuel 182, 257; William 274
Daviss, David 53
Davisson, Doctor James 318; Rev.

James 296
Davoss, Daniel 292
Dawley, Aaron 206,212,218,282; Aron 275; John 282
Dawn, Charles 137
Dawson, Capt. 208,218; Capt. Isaac 185,276; Charles 112; David 180,202,292; Edward 206; George 165,267,300,310; Isaac 87,115,187,188,189,200, 202,203,211,212,270,292,293, 294,295,297,312,313(2),314; John 233; Lt. Zedekiah 189; Matthias 168; Moses 187,220, 315; Samuel 197,311; Samuel J. 78; Z. 188
Day, Abraham 142; Alva 265; Capt. Lewis 95; Edward 20(2), 21; John 95,99,116,149,169,287 Lebious 78,90; Leblue 86; Lewis 66,70,265,299; Mr. 288; Timothy 62,74
Dayne, Christopher 274
Dayton 19,20,29,34,35,43,45,47,48 48,50,54,59,64,68,72,76,79,82, 83,84,91,94,99,103,104,108,114 115,119,120,126,129,130,133, 135,139,140,141,143,144,149, 150,155,156,157,158,159,161, 162,166,167,171,172,206,214, 215,223,229,247
Dayton Academy 169
Dayton Association 77
Dayton Library Society 114,143, 229
Dayton township 58,63,73,108,167
Dayton, Gen. Jonathan 237,267; Hon. Jonathan 1; J. 163; Jonathan 27,141,151,173,244, 318; Mr. 38; Spencer 310
DeButt, Capt. 1
DeButts, Capt. 24
DeClercq, Francis 314
DeHart, William 169
DeWald, George 254
Dealy, John 2
Dean, Abm. 187; Abraham 194,226 Anna 240; Catrin 275; Ebenezer 240; James 198,270, 286; Mrs. 187; Mrs. C. 270; Samuel 280
Dear Creek 15,270
Dear, Benjamin 270; George A. 244; Susanah A. 244
Dearborn County 99,116,121,127, 131,132,142,145,173
Dearborn, Henry 82,149,201
Dearbourn, H. 213
Dearmond, John 22; King 78,121; Maj. King 149
Dearth, James 58,78,118
Death, Edward 90; John 37
Deaths, Esquire 96
Deavabaugh, Adam 220
Debating Society 111
Debee, Isaac 82
Debolt, David 165; Michael 169
Debott, Daniel 137; David 137
Decamps, David 305; Jacob 180
Decker, Josiah 153; Luke 85,292
Decoursey, John 142
Dedham 193
Dedham jail 189
Deer Creek 15,21,24,27,41,42,99, 138,143,145,149,171,184,187, 189,190,195,196,202,203,205, 206,209,210,211,215,216,217, 219,221,224,227,233,234,238, 241,244,247,254,256,257,258, 267,278,279,281,282,293,301, 308,310,311,312,313,314,315,

318
Deer Creek Praira 212
Deer Creek road 202,244,261,307
Deer Creek township 309,318
Deerfield 19,29,24,32,37,41,42,45, 49,50,51,53,55,61,62,65,67,70, 72,74,76,77,78,79,82,86,87,90, 91,95,96,97,98,99,102,113,114, 116,119,125,131,143,176,187, 219,222,262,265
Deerfield Road 49,255
Deerfield township 58,73,77,112, 146,236,237,255,256,257,259, 260,261,265,269,273,274,277, 278,280,285,289,290,291,294, 295,301,305,307,309,314
Deever, John 241
Defenbaugh, John 241
Deffabaugh's mill 262
Deffbough, Mr. 254
Deffenbaugh, Adam 221
Deford, Charles 250
DelaMater, John 15
Delahay, Nela 254
Delana, Amasa 287
Delania, Daniel 257
Delano, Amasa 188,300; Doctor 206; Doctr. 282; Doctr. Amasa 316; Dr. Amasa 194; Mrs. Mary 194
Delany, John 170
Delaplaine, J. 117,143,148; Joseph 121,142,145,159(2),171,172,173 Joshua 152; Mr. 125,130,146
Delaplane, J. 117; Joshua 30,128, 156,238
Delashmutt, Elias N. 301
Delaware 48,158
Delaware County 276,277,283,286, 297,304,318
Delaware Indians 28,52,80,121,156
Delaware Town 179
Deleplane, Joshua 37
Delong, Francis 15,18
Delse, Mr. 85
Demens, James 218
Dement, James 10,12,48; William 10
Demint, Elizabeth 21; James 21, 52,61,146,147,148,153; Mr. 2
Demler, Lieut. George F. 8
Demming, Ezekiel 115,229
Democratic Corresponding Society 89
Democratic Republicans 151,245, 255,313
Demols, Lewis 244
Demoss, John 15; Peter 132,304
Demott, Abraham 75
Demous, Marthy 20
Demsey, John 84
Denham's Town 39,47,49,54
Denham, Obed 24,35(6),36,72,281; William 35
Denison, A. 197; Alexander 195
Deniston, James 66; Wm. 66
Denman, Abner 62; Joseph 146, 170; Mathias 175; Matthias 168
Dennes, John 137
Denney, James 300
Denning, Ezekiel 166,303; James 98; Margert 310; Mr. 88,203
Dennis, Anthony 267; John 107; Philip 107
Dennison, William 163
Denny, Capt. James 255(2); David 227; George 137,278; J. 184; James 115,131,178,179,182,183 184,192,204,206,207,208(2),210 211,213(2),215,216,218(2),220,

221,226(2),231,238,239(4); Miss Jane 305; Mr. 173,221,239(2), 280; Robert S. 165; Samuel 278,296,300; William 137,257, 278
Denslaw, Chapman 287
Denslow, Chapman 257,263
Dentist 169
Depestre, Col. J. 254
Depriese, Thomas 154
Depriest, Thomas 52,127; Thomas Travis 48
Dequindre, Antoine 298
Deraoss, Lewis 257
Derby Creek 179
Dereckson, John L. 310
Derickson, John 241,267
Derrough, Amos 93,197,207
Derth, James 69
Derush, John 200,208
Desabaug, Adam 212
Deterly, Jacob 132
Detroit 30,32,37,45,46,47,48,49,51 55,56,60,61,62,63,66,68,70,72, 74,75,77,78,83,97,103,106,109, 113,121,156,191,234
Detroit River 37
Deuckson, John 233
Deured, John 212
Devall, William 187
Devalt's mill 218
Devalt, John 310; Nicholas 296
Devanport, James 292,300,316
Devaul, Nackey 11,14; Richard 11, 14
Devault, Nicholas 228,282; Nichols 287
Develine, William 200
Devenbaugh's mill 230
Devenport, Anthony S. 288; James 310
Dever, John 221,225,226,230,263
Devol, G. 204
Devolt, Nicholas 196,275
Devor, John 23,37,58
Devorse, Daniel 263
Devour, John 238
Dewese, Frederick 171
Dewit, Barney 262
Dewitt, John G. 288; Sarah 55; Zachariah P. 168
Dexter, Isaac 101,114,122,144, 148; Mr. 154; Samuel 76; Silas 192; Stephen 165; Yunice 107
Dick's Creek 53,84,85,86,87,91,93, 95,96,104,112,115,119,127,133, 137,153,195
Dick's River 14
Dick, George 170; Mr. 192; Sam. 98; Saml. 27,30; Samuel 9,37, 57,60,62,70,72,77,82(2),98(3), 99,101,106(2),118,141,214(2); Thomas 186,193,199,217(2),222 286; William 95
Dicken, Richard 130
Dickenson, William R. 90,246; Wm. R. 240
Dicker, Luke 247
Dickerson, Richard 247
Dickeson, Richard 226
Dickey's tavern 152
Dickey, Adam 85,318; Arthur 254; Capt. P. 172; Capt. Patrick 175; John M'Clelland 175; Lieut. P. 171; Lieut. Patrick 139,141; M. 291; Mr. 90; P. 86, 106; Patrick 27,57,62; Robert 164,315; William 263,273,280, 292
Dickings, Thomas 275
Dickinson, David 234; Stephen R.

131; W.R. 196,254; William R. 195,204; Wm. R. 219
Dicks, Samuel 28
Dickson, Christopher 78; John 56,58,233,282,302; Joseph 182, 255,313; Mr. 148; Sary 142; William 230,299; Wm. 314
Dicky, Patrick 97; William 270
Diddip, Archibald 19
Dieffenbach, Daniel 241
Digbey, Catharine 13; William 13
Diline, Richard 292
Dill, Capt. John 194; Capt. Thomas 252; Francis 115,197; James 127,137; John 78,90,91, 93,118,,124,125,135,140,145, 146,148,165,192,205,206,209, 218,228,230; Lieut. Andrew 189; Mary 215,230; Miss Nelly 252; Mr. 86,94,100,102(2), 105(2),106,122,140; Richard 78; Robert 315; Thomas 45
Dille, Absolom 279
Dillen, Peter 216
Dillin, David 212
Dillon, Agnes 229; Andrew 90; John 11,229; Joseph 200; Josiah 101,164,214(4),225, 243,252,265; Samuel 62,92,151, 174,318
Dillow, Elizabeth 112
Dimett, Ezekiel 102
Dimmit, Mosses 282
Dimmitt, Moses 275,292
Dimsey, Timothy 20
Dinnil, James 247
Dinning, Job 269,288,290,303(2), 305,315,316
Dinsmore, John 33,51,70
Disbrow's Inn 153
Disbrow's Tavern 140,143,147,148
Disbrow, Henry 136,139,141(2),151 152,153(2),158,166,169,255; Mr. 143,144,150,151(3)
Disebauck, George 178
Dison, John 221
Distiller 23,25,31,34,40,41,47,52, 63,66,68,72,77,92,95,97,129, 182,200,207,279
Distiller, Levy 228
Distillery 69,75,77,141,163,178, 179,231,258,278,308
District of Columbia 246
Ditchlow, Peter 244
Ditsler, Peter 221
Dittoe, Jacob 292
Ditzler, Jacob 287
Dively, John 239
Divine, William 260
Dix & Cutler 120,226
Dix & Farrar 177
Dix, Alexander 290,292; Clarend 305; Clarenden 316; John 234, 241,247; Joseph 292,305,310, 316
Dixon, Doct. Andrew 254; George 116; John 116; Mr. 34; Safford 25; William 310
Dixson, Daniel 269; John 275; William 292,296
Dlashmutt, William 8
Doane, Timothy 303
Dobbin, Rev. Mr. 241
Dobbins, Catharine 247; James 74; R. 307; Rev. Robert 247,267; Rev. Robert B. 257; Robert B. 244; Robt. B. 233
Doctors 5,8,10,15,17,18,20,21,23, 24,25,27,31,32,35,38,39,40,41, 43,45,47,51,54,55,56,57,60,61, 63,65,66,67,73,74,75,77,78,79, 82,83,86,88,91,92,94,96,97,99, 105,106,107,110,111,112,114, 115,116,117,118,119,120,121, 122,124,126,127,131,132,133, 140,141,142,143,144,146,150, 151,156,160,169,170,173,175, 182,184,185,186,187,188,189, 190,192,194,196,199,200,202, 203,206,209,210,211,212,214, 215,216,220,221,223,227,228, 229,232,235,237,241,242,244, 245,246,248,249,254,255,258, 263,264,265,267,268,269,270, 273,275,276,281,282,290,293, 295,296,299,300,302,304,307, 308,310,311,313,314,316,317, 318
Dodd, Cephas 116; James 237; Jesse 99,107,127,141,263,296, 300; John 247; William 215
Doddridge, Doct. John 254; Enock 305; John 292; Josiah 206,279
Dodds, Col. William 159; Joseph 318; W. 168; William 98(2),99, 106,214
Dodemead, Mr. 234
Dodson, John 28,43,51,74
Doerab, Joseph 244
Doherty, Mr. 17
Dold, Ensign Samuel 25
Dolehan, Hugh 267
Doll, Abraham 291,295,307
Dollon, David 221
Dolly, Aaron 317; John 267
Dolohan, John 250
Domigan, Wm. 313
Donaghy, Paul 18
Donald, John 70,101
Donaldson Creek 218
Donaldson, Aaron 250,254,310; Ebenezer 308; Israel 84,88,201, 216; Isreal 274; Moses 261; Valentine 282,287; Valintine 275
Donalley, Patrick 276
Donalson, Israel 203,204(2),302
Donaran, John 18
Donegal township 92
Donevan, Thomas 254
Donham, Henry 36; John 170; Nathaniel 36
Doniphan, Anderson 11
Donly, Patrick 263
Donnald, Jonathan 145
Donnally, Col. Andrew 20; Patrick 283
Donnan, Patrick 215; Peter 263
Donnel, James 154; Jonathan 41, 156,318; William 86
Donnis, Anthony 282
Donoughe, Precila 237; Priscilla 247,254
Donovan, Mr. 234; Thomas M. 249, 272; William 244,254
Donwooddy, William 300
Dooley, Obediah 297
Doolittle, Benjamin 234; E. 314, 317,319; Ephraim 234,249,256, 266; Epraim 302
Doraw, Isaac 165
Dorbe 200
Dorcy, Beats. 23
Dorem, William 314
Dorian, James 184
Doris, Samuel 121
Dorose, Edward 293
Dorret, Mr. 31,34,40
Dorrett, John 55
Dorsey, Bates 15; James 4,13; Joseph 251
Dosch, Edward 263
Dost, George 142
Doty, Daniel 48,121; John 106; Reuben 106; Zina 121
Doud, Conner 241; Donner 244
Dougharty, John 27
Dougherty, Francis 250; Hamilton 197,202,212; James 172; John 157,200,212,232; Michael 237; Neal 257; Samuel 221
Doughty, Ephraim 97; Mr. 146
Douglas, David 51,60,82,116
Douglass, Francis 134,240; J. 292; James 241; Joseph 269; Richard 315; Watson 315; William 241
Doulin, James 212,241
Douny, Thomas 85
Douty, Reuben 161
Dovanbergar, Jacob 276
Dovenberger, John 296,300
Dover, James 143
Dow, Alexander 197; Lorenzo 223
Dowden, Archibald 103,222; Clemmenhouse 32; Thomas C. 206
Dowlen, James 268
Dowley, Aron 257
Dowlien, James 270
Downes, Richard 56
Downing's ford 218
Downing, J. 296; John 247,315
Downs, Barnet 307; David 269; Henry 282; Mr. 184; William 309; Zepheniah 18
Dowse, Edward 293
Dowty, Reuben 165; Zachariah 13
Doxon, George 32
Doyle, John 31,53,64,66,86,215; Maj. 2,17,36,39,40,114; Maj. T. 95; Maj. Thomas 20,48,74,114, 115,116; Maj. Thos. 13; Major Thomas 123; Mr. 49; Mrs. 120; Thomas 10,15,33,41,46,47,64, 67(2),70,75,76,123
Draber, John 185(2)
Drace, Peter 241
Dragoo, Andrew 274
Dragoons 122,127,130,131,135,137 138,139,140,145,147,149,157, 159,160,168,169,170,171,252, 255,256,272
Dragoul, Belshazer 202
Drake, Daniel 174,175; Doct. Daniel 282; Enoch 59; Lewis 318; Lieut. 6; William 76,298; Wm. 57
Dralinger, Philip 89
Draper, Joseph 107
Drennan, John 292
Dresar, George 15
Dresbach, Henry 271; Miss Susannah 271
Dresback, Daniel 315
Dreshbac, Henry 238
Driver, Ezekiel 207; Francis 10,12 23; Isaiah 306; Mr. 218(2); Samuel 267
Drogoo, Belteshazer 253
Drolener, Daniel 209
Druard, George 48
Druggist 102,118,140,157,172,229
Drum, John 262; Peter 307; Philip 33
Drury, Wm. 245
Druyea, George 55
Dry Fork 81,100,106,137,140,144, 153
Dry Ridge 40,145
Dry Run 223,224,225,228,230,234, 257,261,268,278,279,285
Dryden, S. 255; Samuel 267

Dryer, George 18
DuBois, Dr. Benjamin 126
Duane, William 39
Dubois, Alexis 125; Isaac 137
Duchonquer, Francis 76
Duck Creek 27,31,34,37,43,55,63, 65,66,74,85,86,87,89,92,99,112, 117,120,121,122,123,126,127, 128,134,137,141,142,144,154, 165,173
Duck Creek Meeting House 37
Duck Creek Presbyterian Congregation 126
Duck Creek Settlement 92,106
Dudeg, Frederick 25
Due, Henry 296
Duff, Edward 276; John 48; Rev. John 37,41; Rev. Mr. 38; Thomas 183,233
Duffey, Dan. 6; Danial 13; Daniel 2,3,10,15,26(2); Daniel J. 26; Francis 263; Mr. 19; Rachel 26
Duffield, Sam. 305; Samuel 300
Duffin, Dr. 267
Duffy, Daniel 23; Francis 270; Michael 267; Rev. Daniel 146
Dufour, J.J. 83; John J. 286; John James 76,83,147
Dugan's store 168
Dugan, Mr. 127,141; T. 171; Th. 171; Tho. 170; Thomas 67,80, 89,100,102,103,104(2),112,113, 114,117,120,125(2),130,131, 132(2),133,134,136,138,141,142 143,144,145,149,150,152,154, 156,160,168,169,282,292; Thos. 267
Duggen, Tho. 209
Dugin, Thomas 218
Duglass, Andrew 310; John 310; Robert 212
Duke, Amew 247
Dulency, Daniel 269
Dulton, Jesse 250
Dumas, Silas 38
Dumegan, William 187
Dun, Parvin 24,32; Robert 82; Silas 197; Walter 279
Dunagin, Enoch 283
Dunan's salt works 195
Dunban, William 218
Dunbar, Nancy 305
Dunbarr, William 234
Duncan's Lick 182
Duncan, Abner L. 32; Amos 269; Benj. 212,228,264; Benjamin 148,194,197,230,231,247,300, 315,316; D. 179,182,187,188, 265; David 74,184,187,203,206, 288,316; Ennis 216; John 109, 225; Maria 315; Martin 244,247 Miss Maria 316; Nehemiah 260
Duncurg, Frederick 295
Dunen, Peter 230
Dungan, Jame 241; James 206,233 270,275; Jesse 287; Miss Polly 256
Dunham's Town 62,86,99,281
Dunkel, John 280
Dunken, James 191
Dunkill, John 180
Dunkin's Plain 318
Dunkin, Benjamin 219; Jesse 121; John 26
Dunkle, John 233
Dunlap's Station 34,41
Dunlap, Alexander 233; Capt. John 1; Col. 202,235,318; Col. James 185,186,198,209,224,236 291,295,317; J. 224,278; James 87,111,142,190,198,200,201, 202,203,212,213,214(4),228,230 237,238(2),250,252,253,257, 263(2),264,265,277,293,294(2), 295(2),296,297,302,305,312, 313(2),314; John 7,206,228,236; Lieut. Col. 189; Lieut. Col. James 189,208; Lt. Col. James 198; Maj. 179,180; Maj. James 181; Mary 236; Mr. 5,131; Polly 250; Samuel 213,214,302
Dunlapes Station 51
Dunlaps Station 66,70,74
Dunlavey, Francis 52
Dunlavy, F. 69,83,86,91,97,205; Frances 10,11,14,23,24,26,37, 38,70,74,80(2),81,84,86,87(2), 98,101,140,158,159,180,192, 199,202,206,303; Joseph 266; Morris 266; Mr. 35,36(2),69(2); Rev. John 199
Dunlevy, F. 50,52; Francis 50; James 282; P. 180
Dunlop, Edward 88; John 2(2),4, 19(2),27
Dunlope, John 18
Dunn, A.M. 2,6,11(2),16; Abner 21; Abner M. 3,4,6; Abner Martin 13; Asa 194,202,215; Azariah 146; Beracha 107; Capt. James 32,48; Dr. John 216; Isaac 142, 160; James 62,86,87(2),91,101, 153,202,205; John 62; Jonathan 154; Lawyer 18; Lewis 177; Mr. 129; Parvin 15,107; Samuel 42,90; Sarah 154; Thomas 78
Dunnin, Peter 190
Dunnings, Mr. 266
Dunnovan, John 26
Dunscomb, Andrew 293
Dunseth, Andrew 53,74,80,86,137, 146,154; David 67,109,169; James 44,45,154; Mr. 142,147, 157
Dunvan, Benjamin 250
Duor, William 66
Duport, Marin 259
Durkee, Silas 268
Durn, James 74
Durt, Daniel 310
Dusinbery, William 210
Duteing, Doct. 275
Dutton, David 313; William 296
Duval, Charles 167; Daniel 293; William 290
Duvall, Daniel 170
Dye, David 269,300
Dyer, John 278; William 278
Dykman, Daniel 137
Dyson, Mrs. 287; Thomas 304,311
Eagle Creek 154,191,202,213,249, 301
Eagle Tavern 252,259,269,273,281, 290,298,299
Eagle and Ball Tavern 222,232
Eagle township 274,304,311,312, 313
Eaker, Dr. Joseph 194
Eakins, John 194,285; Joseph 206, 218
Earhart, Jacob 57; Nicholas 302
Earheart, Mr. 114
Earkart, Jacob 237
Earle, Grantham 299,300,305; Thomas 194,202
Early, Peter 247
Earnest, Christopher 263
Eartost, Martin 107
East Haven 240
East Windford township 60
East, Isaac 305
Eastburn, Jesse 225
Easter, Jacob 276,303
Eastin, John 72
Easton, James 304; Moses 58
Eastwood, John 130
Eaten, William 18
Eater, Abram 310; Andrew 307
Eaton 135
Eaton township 168
Eaton, Capt. 2; David 121; Gen. 152; Isaac 179,183; Mrs. 183; Robert 86,95
Eaverson, Richard 171
Ebernon, Samuel 86
Ebinowen, Mr. 228
Echart, Mrs. 282
Echman, Jacob 300
Eckelberner, Jacob 263
Ecker, Abraham 262; Catharine 262
Eckert, Abraham 262; Catharine 262
Eckett, Jacob L. 295
Eckleberner, Jacob 245,257
Eddenfield, Thomas 275
Eddie, David 91; Mr. 88,203
Eddins, Samuel 264
Eddy, David 205,299; Hugh 286
Edes, Jas. 318
Edgar, James 41; John 25,41,252; Margaret 187; Mr. 36,37(2) 38(2),39,40,181; Robert 27; William 183
Edge, Mr. 183
Edgerton, Amos 32,55
Edgington, Jesse 305
Edinburgh College 216
Edingfield, Thomas 284
Editor 178,181,241,254
Edmanson, Thomas 296
Edmeston, Doctor John 318
Edminston, Doct. John 245; Dr. 307
Edmison, Doct. 264; Doct. John 270; Doct 275; Doctr. 282
Edministon, Doct. John 185; Doctor 200,211,295; Dr. 241,249; Dr. John 249; James 202; John 210,217,221(2),226,289; Mr. 239; William 202
Edward, Samuel 310
Edwards road 218
Edwards' Ferry 38
Edwards, Andrew 56; Doctor 170; Doctor Abraham 121; Esq. 214; Ignatious 270; James 38; Jn. 221; John 201,263,268,293; John S. 227,258,259; John Starks 197; Joseph 95,107,164; Joshua 127,147; Miss Rebecca 154; Mr. 11; Sam. 208; Samuel 251,315; Stourton 212; Thomas 42
Egal, Thomas 303
Egan, James 279
Eggleston, Mr. 193
Egleston, Joseph 225
Eidee, Samuel 11
Eigelberner, Jacob 199
Eight Mile Creek 102
Eker, Joseph 184
Elby, David 176
Elder, Eli 170,230; Ely 244; John 292; Thomas 128; William 241
Eldridge, Ebenezer 177
Election 37,42,83,85,87,88,93,94, 95,96,98,99,105,106,107,108, 109,110,111,116,119,126,128, 145,147,153,154,160,162,166, 174,175,176,177,179,180,191, 198,199,201,202,203,204,208, 209,212,213,223,224,225,226,

236,237,238,239,240,242,246,
252,262,263,264,265,272,277,
279,280,294,297,299,312,313,
315,318
Elerenman, Fred. 235
Eliot, James 127
Elizabeth Town, N.J. 54
Elizabeth township 150,160
Elizabethtown, N.J. 141
Elk Creek 90,110,125
Elkhorn Creek 56,81
Elkhorn River 159
Elkhorne Creek 49
Ellery, Elias 237; William 12,237
Elleson, John 249
Ellicott, Mr. 203
Ellies, Nathan 69
Elliot & Williams 20
Elliot, Arthur 127; Benjamin 267; Doctor 143; Fuller 227; James 15; John 214; Johnson 270; Mr. 10,20; Robert 8(2); Ruffus 81; Rufus 29; Sergt. James 20; Thomas 164,204(2),249,252,266 Thos. 282
Elliott, Ben. 250; Benjn. 254; Burgess 288,299,309(2); Dr. 43; Fuller 303; John 30,78,149,254; Joseph 236; Mary 90; Mr. 131; Mrs. 280,295,314; Rufus 73; Samuel 137; Temple 231; Thomas 55,173,177,213
Ellis' ferry 261,309
Ellis, Amos 94,99,207; Ellas 316; Ellis 216; Henry 314; James 149,199; John 316,318; M. 147; Mordeica 313; Mordica 216; Mordicah 250; Mr. 88,203; Nathan 191,198,199,207,213, 243,250,261,293,302,309; Samuel 299(2); Thomas 313; William 99,285
Ellison, Andrew 88,203,238; Arthur 260,313; John 185,187, 265,266,274,278,293,297,298, 301,302(3),315,319
Ellzey, Col. William 149,247; William 140
Elm Street 172
Elsey, William 275
Elshite, Miceal 257; Peter 257
Elsso, Joseph 282
Elstion, Eli 78
Elston, Eli 170
Elstun, Eli 121
Elsworth, Jacob 289; Oliver 227
Elwell, Josiah 170
Elwood, William 316
Ely, George 146; John 23; Joseph 86
Embree, Amos 116; Elijah 121
Emerson, Kendel 137
Emery, Ge. 235; George 180,194, 235,237,259,264,270,275,310; Mr. 236
Emmerson, Thomas 290
Emmet, James 310
Emmit, John 287,300
Emmorson, Thomas 275
Emrey, George 235,287,296
Emrick, George 187; Mr. 218
Emry, Capt. George 189
Endler, John 263
Endrick, Christian 229
Endsley, Andrew 107,116,127
Enesworth, John 1
Engart, David 146
England 12,61
England, Col. 24; John 218,244
Engle, Adam 296; Betsey 257; George 285,296; Matthias 316

English, David 197; Richard 284
Enick, John 279; Mr. 41
Enis, William 318
Enloe, David 200
Enness, Mr. 174
Ennis, Mary 154
Enoch's Mill 94,156
Enoch, Col. 94; D. 83; David 80, 183
Enock, Mr. 96
Enos, Alexander 275,287; George 142
Enox's mill 171
Enox, Abner 175
Ensley, George 23
Ensworth, Doctor Jedediah 114, 242; Dr. Jedidiah 229; John 170; Judediah 169; Lucy 227
Enterkin, John 218
Entreken, John 202
Entrekin, John 316
Entricken, William 315
Entrickin, Capt. John 218
Entriken, Capt. 208; Capt. John 189
Entsminger, John Henry 286
Enyalt, John 58
Enyard, Samuel 84
Enyart, Benjamin 137; David 107, 127,137; Samuel 90
Episcopal Church 301,303
Eredin, James 230
Erie 76
Erie Literary Society 207(2),254, 256,303
Ermsten, Benjamin 292
Ernest, Matthew 72,78
Ernhard, John 276
Ernst, George 10; Zacharias 165
Eron, Jacob 170
Ervin, Adam 217; William 226
Ervine, Samuel 282
Erwin, Andrew 273; John 241,306; Samuel 218; William 263
Esau, Capt. Alexander 68
Esex, Jesse 317
Eson, Alexander 132,146
Espy, Thomas 57,66,79,155
Esrey, Abner 296
Essery, Abner 221,267
Essex, Joseph 292
Essix, Elener 316; Joseph 282
Estel, Levi 82
Etienne, Christopher 250
Etty, John 300
Eubank, George 299
Eulass, Jacob 318
Eusry, Abner 270
Evan, Montgomery 292
Evans' settlement 218
Evans, Amos 291; Benjamin 263, 275; Capt. 81; Col. John 292, 296,300; Daniel 152,256; David 266,313; Dr. George 300; Evan 252,275,287; Gilbert 266; Isaac 257,258,259(2),272,273,281(4), 289,293,304; J. 237; James 275,287; John 36,210,212,214, 223,236,237,238,247,251,260(2) 264(2),275,282,285,288,290,310 John T. 256(2),257,270,274,287 Joseph 153,247,304,305; Lemuel 194,254,275; Richard 115; Robert 271; Sam. 208; Saml. 301,302; Samuel 74,189, 200,212,223,263,272,273,276, 282,287,303; Sarah Bloomfield 51; Thomas 265,294,298; Thomas W. 154; William 248, 258,304; Wm. 228; Wm. W. 241
Evatt, John 165

Evelet, Joseph 5
Evens, Evens 254; Richard 287
Everhart, John 46
Everits, Ambrose 206
Eversole, Abraham 165; Christian 78,137; John 218
Evilet, Joseph 5
Evins, Calib 266; Lemuel 237,287; William 12
Ewale, Bertrand 30; Jesse 30
Ewen, Charles 199
Ewin, John 107; William 252
Ewing's Tavern 104,132
Ewing, Abner 273,274,319; Capt. John 63,92; Charles 202; H. 108; Hannah 233; Henry 42,63, 91,106,108,115(2),118,132,133, 138,148,155; J. 171; James 49, 94,105,108,109,110,115(2),117, 125,128(2),136(2),137,138, 139(2),145,147,150,152,154,155 156(2),159,161,163,164,165, 171(2),173(3),175,176,206,318; John 45,58,69,70,78,86,87,91, 112,187,205,311; Joshua 215, 254; Margaret 104; Miss Eliza 139; Mr. 7,94; Mrs. Elizabeth 49; Robert 187; Samuel 104; Thomas 154; William 233
Ewings, James 282
Exenia 219
Exline, John 282,296,300
Eynon, Mr. 11,13; Zebulon 8,10,23, 36
Eyre, Catharine 228
Eyreman, Jacob 46
Eyster, Peter 250
Fagin, Abner 14; Barbery 14
Fagot, Andrew 41
Fair 98,129
Fairbanks, Jason 189,193
Fairburn, Mr. 184
Fairchield, John 249
Fairchild, John 250,262; Laura 112; Margaret 249,262; Samuel 112,146
Fairfax County, Virginia 260
Fairfield 25,26,27,63,91,131,193
Fairfield County 73,76,83,84,88,91 111,115,131,133,134,164,191, 194,201,203,204,205,206,207, 212,214,215,216,223,224,229, 234,235,239,241,242,243,245, 246,248,249,250,252,258,262, 263,273,284,285,286,287,290, 291,293,294,295,297,298,299, 301,303,304,308
Fairfield township 51,58,73,81, 162,164,167,168,170,172,177, 294
Fairlow, David 292
Fairman, Richard 149,170
Falkey, Kraft 242
Fall Muskingum 192
Falls of Ohio 92,156,157,167,185
Falls of Paint 208,210,213,216,230 233,237,238,241,242,244,245, 254
Falls of Paint Creek 114,178,179, 180,181,187,188,198,203,205, 225,228,229,238
Falls of the Ohio 113
Fallsmouth 9
Falmouth 32
Famulener, James 244
Fanchard, Richard 158
Fancher, William 318
Fanstee, Thomas 187
Faran, Charles 63,131,136
Fares, Isaac 165,167; John 167
Farguhar, Jonah 230; Mahlon 230

Faris, David 116,247; Eliphalet 74
Fariss, Charles 149
Farlin, James 83
Farmer's Academy 241
Farmer, Joseph 316; Thomas 312
Farmers' Manufacturing Company 177
Farmers' and Mechanics' Exporting Company 175
Farmington 230,240
Farnum, Hezekiah 202; Rusell 9, 15
Farquer, Virginia 301
Farran, Charles 82,118,140,151
Farrar, Mr. 177
Farrell, James 254; Moses 66; Thomas 275
Farrier 7,160
Farry, Henry 48
Faulk, Aeneas 314
Faulkner, Capt. 2; Capt. William 12
Faulks, Mr. 177
Fauquier County, Virginia 232
Favers, William 233
Fawcett, Joseph 217; Thomas 287
Fayette County 50,303,309,311, 312,313,315,316,317
Fayette County, Kentucky 9,59,68 97
Fayette County, Penn. 242
Feagans, Daniel 101,214(2)
Fearin, Mr. 181; Paul 181
Fearing, Mr. 40(2),54,56,57,60(2), 72(3),75(2),76,77,181,193(2), 198,199; P. 198; Paul 43,53,70 71,73,181,191,194,303
Featherchild, Andrew 296
Feathers, F. 214
Featherstone, William 199
Feckleton, Evans 137
Federal City 241
Fee, Elijah 167; James 171; William 47,158,159,171
Feel, Samuel 166
Feely, Michael 210,211; Timothy 210,211
Feiks, David 282
Felix, Peter 155,170; Pierre 165
Fellons, Philip 257
Felter, David 127; Erasmus 57; Jacob 48,132,143,147; William 48
Felty, I. 17; Isaac 30; John 165; Joseph 154; Mary 30; Mr. 94
Fenimore, Ebenezer 248
Fenn, Thomas 293
Fenner, James 247,282
Fenrick, Enoch 197
Fenton, George W. 173; Rosswell 146; Roswell 175
Fenwick, Enoch 202
Fenyer, Enoch 199
Ferard, J.B. 259; Margueritte Violette 260
Ferguson & M'Farland 187,191,195 203,206
Ferguson, Capt. 151,158; Capt. James 119,130,135,137,138,140 145,147(2),149,157,160,168,169 170,171,252; Col. John 305; Creighead 251; James 29,34, 107,112,115,119,127(2),135, 137,138,139,140,143,146,147, 148,149(2),151,154,157,159(2), 162,165,173,184,200,203,205, 207,208,212,213,215,218,224, 225,238,251(2),289,294; John 121,251,285,300(2),317; Maj. 241; Mathew 166; Matt. 314; Matthew 278; Miss Peggy 181;

Mr. 152,207,266; William 120, 141; Wm. 38
Fernow, John 305
Fero, Ens. David 15
Ferral, Moses 114,143,173
Ferras, Ezra 149; Isaac 57,62
Ferreal, John 263
Ferree, Joel 132
Ferrel, Daniel 58; John 261
Ferrell, James 22
Ferrill, Richard 23
Ferris, Ezra 123,144,165; Isaac 78; John 54,106; Mr. 123
Ferry 11,13,14,16,23,24,38,47,49 54,62,68,75,77,88,93,100,103, 107,120,125,133,134,137,154, 162,178,179,185,187,188,189, 194,196,197,198,203,205,223, 229,231,243,252,257,261,268, 302,304,309
Ferson, James 20
Feurt, Benj. 308,313,315,318; Benjamin 276,306; Gabriel 306, 313; George 276,313
Field, George 230; Seth 25,126; Sidney 126
Fielders, Runnel 270
Fielding, William 316
Fields, Seth 58(2)
Figgans, Daniel 212
Finamore, Ebenezer 247
Finch, Josiah R. 281,303
Findlay, Brig. Gen. James 107,117 123; Capt. James 42; Col. 51; Gen. 117,144,149,152,156(2), 157,158,159,167,168; Gen. James 155(3),158; J.S. 61,89; James 34,46,47,48(2),50(3),60, 64,66,67,73(2),74(2),82,88,91, 103,105,108,111,113,116(2),123 124,129(2),130(2),131,134,136, 142,153,162,166(2),177,199; Jonathan 105,144; Jonathan S. 40,76,80,125; Lieut. N.C. 170, 171; Mr. 5,13,16,27,28,37,38, 40(3),41,43,44,47(2),51,52,53, 54,55,59,61(2),67(3),69,71,73, 75,77,83,85,86,88,92,95,96(2), 102,105(4),122,157,181,194; Nathan C. 145; R.W. 184; Samuel 47,54,76,151
Findley, Col. 257; Col. Samuel 191; Gen. 244,292; James B. 209; Mr. 3(2),36,37,38,39(2),94; Robert 180; Samuel 206
Finely, Samuel 270
Finemore, Ebenezer 270
Fingly, Jacob 63
Finimore, L. 297; Mary 257
Finlay, Mr. 181; R.W. 194; Samuel 194
Finley, Adj. Gen. Samuel 93(2),207 208(2); Alexander 269; Col. 180,185,199,202,212; Col. Samuel 44,184,199,206; Colonel 183; David 317; Ensign 15; Gen. 229,264,300; Gen. Samuel 276; Hugh 284; James 197,239,255,303; James B. 268; John P. 237,269; Maj. 187; Miss Patty 229; Mr. 71; R.F. 188; Rev. Robt. W. 241; Robert W. 199,200(2),201,213; Sam. 178,217,219,240; Saml. 179,292,301; Samuel 33,158, 160,185,186,192(2),198(2), 199(2),200,201,202,203,205,214 216,217,232,238,242,255,256, 262,270(3),273(3),274,280(2), 281,284,286,299,304
Finly, Ensign 18; Mr. S. 181;

Robert W. 181,191; Samuel 110
Finnehon, John 13
Finnemore, E. 252; Ebenr. 238
Finney, Col. John 81;E.W. 101,150
Finnie, James 96; John 52
Finnyhon, John 8
Finton, Samuel 313
Firefighters 26
First Vine-Yard, Ky. 83
Fisher, Adam 137; Benjamin 128, 135; Brownlow 142,166; Ebenezer 100,107; F. 247; Jacob 156,221; James 11,77; John 42,77,84,277; Michael 186,209, 218,259,270,295
Fishinggut Creek 38
Fitch's tavern 288
Fitch, Andrew 235; Cook 232; Elisha 267,270,282,297,300,305 310,316; Joseph 235; Mary 235
Fitche's Inn 274
Fitchew, Perregan 235
Fithean, Lieut. 31
Fithian's Tavern 53
Fithian, G. 44,61,62; George 22,27 29,32,35,41,47,53,64,70,71, 74(2),77(2),79,80(2),97,103,110 120,128,138,144,272
Fitzgerald, Joseph 219,220
Fitzhugh, Wm. 246
Fitzpatrick, James 229,299; Robert 299; Tho. 283,284
Fitzwater, Thomas 29,142
Five Mile Creek 29
Five Mile Run 61
Five Mile Spring 84
Fix, John 318
Flat Creek 257
Flaurence, John 241
Fleckner, William 146
Fleehort, James 286
Fleming, Aggress 267; Agness 292; Alexander 254,263,296; Bartholomew 107; Capt. Tarlton 5; Daniel M. 165,170; Ferguson 307; John 233; Joseph 318; Robert 248,250, 257; William 310
Flemming, Thomas 175(2)
Flemmond, Joseph 197
Flesher, Coonrod 244,254,309; Henry 309
Fletcher, James 161; John 3; Joseph 303,305; Leve 25; William 164
Fliming, James 287; Joseph 230; William 292
Flin, Hugh 300; John 275; Mr. 3; William 33
Flinn, Agnis 41; Benjamin 51,53,81 Capt. 4; James 14,58(2); John 292; William M. 51; Wm. Miller 44
Flint, David 263; Hezekiah 10,20, 87,110,116,124,129,176
Flinte, Joseph 305
Floobur, Lanart 221
Florance, William 310
Florence, Wm. 309
Florey, George 305
Florin, Peter 18
Floro, Abijah 271
Florunce, John 230
Flournoy, Francis 84; Matthew 61
Flowers, Isaac 310
Flowlers, Aaron 141
Flowrance, William 247,263
Floyd, David 249; Davis 162,167, 244; Mr. 155,244,249
Fluk, William 316
Flush, Conrod 282

Flyn, Hugh 209,233,316
Foard, David 300
Fobes, Thomas 10
Focknor, John 23; Jonathan 23
Foley, John 247
Folk, George 153; Martin 315
Foltz, Conrod 292
Fontain, Col. William 316
Foos, Griffeth 248; Jos. 205;
  Joseph 91,212,294; Js. 301
Foose, Griffith 218
Foosythe, William 279
Foot, Andrew 293; David 154;
  Samuel 62; T.S. 315; Ziba 137,
  142,152
Forbornes, A. 293
Ford, Capt. 5,24; Capt. M. 5;
  David 23,142,161,282,292;
  Jacob 68; James 292; John
  68,275; Mordecai S. 156; Mr.
  177; Patrick 221; Peter 68;
  Polly 68; Timothy G. 221;
  William 15
Fordice, Abraham 60
Fording, Jacob 275
Fords, Patrick G. 266
Fordsman, Hugh 297
Foreman, Barnet 288
Forepaugh, Andrew 161
Foreson, Prudy 170
Forest, John 314
Forgason, James 9
Forguson, Capt. James 118,131; J.
  21; James 2,9(2),10,18,30,33,38
  39,41,49,56,59,64,66,68,71,81,
  82,88,99,104,116,129; Mr. 71
Forker, George 204
Forman, Henry 287
Forrest, George 64
Forseman, Hugh 287
Forsman, Hugh 257,282
Forst, William 287
Forster, Andrew 307
Forsyth & Smith 48
Forsyth, Dr. 216; Gideon C. 215;
  William 49
Forsythe, Andrew 11
Fort Dearborn 304,307
Fort Eustis 174
Fort Hamilton 2,4,5,6,8,10,11,14,
  16,26,27,28,30,37,45,53,61,62,
  77,90,95,96,97,99,101,108,121,
  134,141,163,280
Fort Jefferson 1,8
Fort Knox 24
Fort Lawrence 16
Fort Malden 156
Fort Massac 75
Fort Miami 24
Fort Nelson 90
Fort Recovery 6,12
Fort St. Clair 1,13
Fort Washington 5,6,7,10,11,15,20,
  21,25,27,28,34,42,43,50,54,55,
  61,64,72
Fort Wayne 14,21,26,37,39,40,48,
  51,52,60,61,62,68,70,71,73,75,
  78,82,86,91,102,107,121,141,
  177,200,262
Fortiner, Capt. 237
Forts 75
Forward, Samuel 304
Fosbiner, James 237
Foster Bottom 276
Foster's place 307
Foster's warrant 213
Foster, Aaron 305; Abner 243,284;
  Ann 237; Benjamin 228,280,295
  Chambers 170; Hepziba 129;
  Jacob 239,245; James 289,294;
  Joseph 270; Judge 108;
  Laurence 299; Lewis 212; Luke
  8,37,91,92,153(2),155,158,161,
  177,205; Mrs. Hepziba 130;
  Nathaniel 286; Peregrine 204,
  225; Perigrine 47; Richard 285,
  305; S. 171; Samual 133;
  Samuel 104,123,125,126,129(2)
  130,137,139,157,160,170(2),
  248; Seth 284; Thomas 149,289
  317; William 142,300; William
  L. 222,259; Z. 108; Zebulon 55,
  106,159,164
Fouble, Jacob 165
Foulk, Aeneas 224,291; Eneas 296
Foulke, Judah 132
Four Mile Creek 90,133,134,147,
  158,168
Fourt, Gabriel 310,316
Foust, Bastion 264; David 309(2),
  311; Sebastian 190,315
Fouts, Andrew 173; David 318
Fowble's Tavern 175
Fowble's mill 148,162,168
Fowble, J. 160; Jacob 148,154,155
  158,166(2),170,174
Fowler, Alexander 146,183; Jacob
  14,44,125; John 31,195; Mr. 79;
  Theodosius 76; William 178,231
Fox & Adams 134,152
Fox, Capt. 127; Capt. David 65;
  Charles 139,175; Claibourne
  253; David 58; John 86; Miss
  Christian 145; Mr. 121;
  Nathaniel 253; Stephen 51,66,
  121
Foy, Jacob 296
Foz, Jacob 250
Fraker, Michael 216
Frakes, Nathen 132; Robert 11,
  138,245
Fraley, Daniel 284,299; Fred. 299;
  John 287
Frally, Daniel 283
Frame, Edward 51; James 278;
  Sarah Burton 202; Thomas 19
France, John 282
Francee, John 233
Frances, James 184
Francess, William H. 310
Francis, John 215; Samuel 305
Franciscos, George 293
Frankfort, Kentucky 51,112,116,
  118,190,233,235,243,253
Frankland 86
Franklin 28,46,62,64,65,67,69,72,
  74,76,78,79,83,84,88,90,95,96,
  97,99,100,106,107,108,112,114,
  116,117,118,120,122,126,127,
  128,129,130,143,144,151,156,
  157,169,175,176,198,209,216,
  221,226,227,245,262
Franklin County 91,111,164,165,
  177,205,207,209,212,218,221,
  222,224,225,228,234,250,253,
  255,259,261,266,268,269,270,
  273,277,278,279,280,283,284,
  285,286,288,290,291,293,294,
  295,298,301,302,303,306,308,
  313,314,318
Franklin County, Kentucky 56,101
Franklin County, Pennsylvania 45
Franklin Town 219
Franklin township 38,39,44,58,73,
  103,112,198,208,269,271,280,
  282,285,288,289,291,294,295,
  299,313,314
Franklin, Anthony 180,194,218,244
  301,305; Antony 269; Charles
  282; Henry 272,303; John 121,
  305; Joseph 244; Maj. Anthony
  238; W. Owen 78
Franklington 179
Franklinton 56,179,182,183,185,
  187,190,192,194,199,200,201,
  202,203,206,207,209,211,212,
  214,215,218,219,221,223,228,
  234,255,280,285,289,294,295,
  301,302,305,308,310,313
Franklinton County 131,231
Franklintown 192
Frans, Peter 270
Fraser, Mr. 307
Frayatt, Edmund 196
Frazee's Mill 47
Frazee's Station 10
Frazee, Benjamin 54; Jacob 47,58,
  154; Jonah 141; Joseph 49;
  Samuel 82; Tho. 158; Thomas
  36; William 55
Frazer, Falvory 231; John 116,173
  Mr. 48,63; Robert 148,150;
  Thomas 43,47,49,56,61,72,74,
  110,290; Thos. 94,107
Frazes Station 14
Frazey, Samuel 104
Frazier, F. 293; Joseph 36
Frazy, Richard 112,127; Samuel
  70
Fream, Thomas 27,28,107
Frederic Co., Va. 158
Frederick County, Maryland 191
Frederick County, Virginia 263
Frederick, Geo. 309,315; George
  266,269,276,312; Lieut. George
  189; Peter 292
Fredericksburg 197
Fredin, James 244
Fredman, Aron 230
Fredonian and Western Intelli-
  gencer 307,308
Fredrick, Elizabeth 146
Free, John 292,300
Freeheart, Robert 223
Freeman & Carpenter 29
Freeman's Journal 23,29,178,180,
  181
Freeman's Lick 61
Freeman's Station 25
Freeman, A. 39,55; Aaron 247,250
  Abraham 19,25,32,41,58,61,68,
  117,132,158,169; E. 179; Edm.
  30,178; Edmond 40; dmund
  33,44,53,82,180,181(2); Emd.
  178; Ezra F. 42,44; Ezra Fitz
  16,25; Haron 316; Isra F. 8;
  James 266; John 37,82;
  Michael 293; Miss Abigail 139;
  Miss Kitty 19; Mr. 8,13,34,180;
  Phebe 74; S. 23,29; Samuel 5,
  12,15,16,24(3),25,29,30,58,181;
  Stephen 307; William 26,134;
  Wm. 24,27,28(2),29
Freemansburg 39
Freeport, Robert 223
Freize's Station 23,24
Freligh, Wm. 21
Fremore, John 178
French Tavern 138
French, James 256; Jeremiah 48,
  70,101,127,146; John 165;
  Joseph 233; Josiah 170; Lot
  23,25,161; Lott 15; Ralph 103,
  318; Samuel 101,162
Fridley, George 204(2)
Friend of Liberty 172
Friend's mill 273
Friend, Aaron 290; Augustine 315;
  Augustus 212; Charles 239,308;
  E. 302; James 302; William 302
Fries, John 31,39
Friskett, George 293
Frison, John 222

339

Front Street 1,3,12,32,64,77,106,
   113,172,174,175
Frothingham, Ensign Peter 18
Fry, Christian 300; Christly 287;
   Christopher 282; Conrod 257;
   George 244,247,270,287,296,
   305,316; Mr. 300; Nicholas 285
Fryat, Bartholomew 278
Fryatt, Bartholamew 218
Fryatt, Bartholomew 230,273;
   Barthy 263; Edmond 244
Fryback, George 229
Fryer, John 121
Fulkner, William 209
Fuller, Eli 215; Elizabeth 11;
   Jesse 212; John 137; Mr. 122;
   Peter 202,208; Seth 280;
   William 79,120; Zekiel 11
Fullers 129
Fullerton, H. 251,254,255,264,265,
   274,298,315; Humphrey 112,
   227,228,240,246,256,260,261,
   267,275,279,281,299,302,303(2)
   304; Mr. 240,276; William 252
Fulling mill 98,119,149,163,165,
   316
Fulton, Alexander 296; Charles
   63; J.A. 241,252,264; Jesse
   62,101,187,214(3),229; John
   62,218,254,270,282; John A.
   249(2),250,260(3),261,263,265,
   266,278(2),279,286,295(2),296,
   297,309; Mr. 300
Fultz, Conrod 270,278
Funk, Adam 263,310; Isaac 316
Funkhouser, Abraham 221
Furgeson, James 189,264
Furguson & M'Farland 188
Furguson, C. 288; J. 237,247(2),
   288; James 186,241,265
Furnam, Widow Hezekiah 206
Furney, Anthony 12; Elizabeth 12
Furry, Henry 62
Futhell, James 242
Gabby, Joseph 45
Gable, Daniel 46; Jacob 46; Peter
   46; Philip 91
Gabraith, John 292
Gabrell, John 254
Gabriel, John F. 247; Richard 247;
   William 197,202,209,287
Gadburg, Anthony S. 197
Gaddis, Capt. Reece 99; Reese 32
Gaforth, Aaron 256
Gahagan, William 58
Gahagen, William 7
Gailbraith, John 15
Gaines, Francis H. 101; Henry
   293; Robert B. 267
Gains, Lieut. Bnd. 4; Thomas 128,
   237
Galaway, James 209
Galbraith, John 2,11,13,19,20,21,
   178; Robert 300
Galbreath, Andrew 201,300
Gale, Nathan 257; Richard 254
Galena, Rhoda 161
Galer, Andrew 296
Gall, George 307; John Christian
   158
Gallager, Charles 219
Gallagher, Mr. 155
Gallahar, James 121
Gallaher, James 136
Gallatin 121
Gallatin, Albert 244; Mr. 46,145(2)
Gallaway, Elizabeth 143; James
   141,162
Gallia County 91,111,131,164,205
   207,222,227,229,230,235,236,
   240,248,250,252,253,258,259,

260,265,266,267,269,271,272,
   273,279,286,288,294,297,303,
   305,308,312,314
Gallia township 265
Galliapolis 215
Gallipolis 181,192,221,225,236,
   237,238,250,253,258,259,260,
   265,266,271,286,288
Gallipolis township 248,272,286,
   297
Galloway, James 46,240(2),243,
   275,287,293; John 187,263;
   Mercy 83; Samuel 185
Gamble, John 275; Robert 263,287
   Samuel 58; Thomas 199
Gamo, John 62
Ganison, Jonathan 112
Gannon, William 109,111
Gano & Company 1,3,4,6,7,17
Gano & Stanley 7,15,17,21,25,101
Gano, Col. 29,36,57,93; Col. John
   S. 51,65,94; Daniel 11,21; Gen.
   104,118,128,135,142,149,151,
   168,173,176; Gen. John S. 137;
   J.S. 61; John L. 186; John S. 1,
   7,8,9,16,17,19,21(3),29(2),31,
   42(2),44,46(2),47,48,50,51,52,
   56(2),61(2),62,64,70,72,73,79,
   80,85,87,89(3),92,96,98,101,
   103(2),104(2),106,107,108,114,
   115,117,118(2),119(2),122,
   123(3),124,126,127,128,130,132
   134,135,136,141,144(2),150(3),
   151(2),156,157,158(2),159,161,
   166,167,168,169,171,176,177,
   216(2); Lieut. Col. 33; Lieut.
   Col. John S. 32,37,42,68,80,81,
   93,97(2); Lt. Col. John S. 29;
   Maj. Gen. 114,122,123,143;
   Maj. Gen. John S. 104,105,106,
   107,109,110,125,215; Maj. John
   S. 173; Miss Sarah 151; Mr. 42,
   78,90,99,128; Rev. John 144;
   Revd. John 105
Gantz, Andrew 183; John 183
Gapen, Zechariah 21
Gaphart, Catharine 129; Peter 129
Garard, Abner 214(2)
Garch, Philip 91
Gard, Elizabeth 127; Gersham
   105,134; Gershom 57,100,124;
   Gershum 150; Job 1,10,12;
   Rev. Mr. 139; Seth 137;
   Stephen 137
Gardner's Ferry 268
Gardner, Capt. 168; Capt. John
   60,168; Corporal James 60;
   David 183; Esther 109; George
   12; James 109; John 292; Jos.
   208; Joseph 196,213,252,294(2)
   295(3),297,312,313(2),314,317;
   Squire 257; William 275
Gariet, Wm. 297(2)
Garman, Peter 304
Garmiley, Hugh 270
Garner, Thomas 133
Garnigus, Jeptha 177
Garrard's Station 22
Garrard, Abner 101,106,238; John
   142,256
Garrer, Samuel 275
Garrett, William 300
Garrison, Abraham 7,15,21,37,48,
   95; Elijah 161; Jacob 132; John
   154; Levi 70; Mr. 7; Ruben
   132; Samuel 142
Garvey, Joseph 49
Garwood, Daniel 247; James 275;
   Jonathan 90; Levi 247
Gary, Gray 116
Gaskell, James 212

Gaskill, James 197,199,299
Gaskins, J. 50; John 49; T. 231
Gass, William 88,111,203,214,299;
   Wm. 304
Gassaway, Dr. John 212
Gaston, Alexander 44,200; Hugh
   146,209; J. 108; John 20,91,129
   142; John R. 106,107,117,236;
   Joseph 300
Gatch, Philip 57,121,132,205,303;
   Phillip 161
Gates, Capt. Elijah 15; David 184;
   N. 311; Nehemiah 283,311;
   Rebecca 54,133,150,162;
   Samuel 182; Uriah 19,20,54,83
   133,150,162,174
Gath, Phillip 84
Gattin, Ignatius 118
Gatz, John 33; Joseph 33
Gaunt, Jacob 234
Gay, Jacob 161; John 194,225; Mr.
   213; William 302
Gaylord, Allen 250
Geague, Alexander 282
Geauga County 134,164,242,255,
   284,299,302,304,317
Geddis, Price 25
Gee, Edward 126
Geel, Abraham 73
Geer, John 92
Gellespie, Joseph 263
Gelston, Martha 272; Samuel 272
Genatt, Mr. 190
General Assembly 35,36,44,50,51,
   52,55,114,148,149,179,180,181,
   182,190,204,225,227,229,289
George, Capt. Parnick 189; Isaac
   245; James K. 267,269,305,310
   Jesse 233; Parnish 201;
   William 212,217,225(2); Wm.
   303
Georgetown 13,14,30,38,40,52,54,
   246,254
Georgetown road 95
Georgetown, Kentucky 14,17,55,
   84,96,100,119
Georgia 105,128,136
Geoung, Jesse 101
Gerard's Station 30
Gerard, Abner 303
Gerge, David 199
Gerke, David 218
German Virginia Eagle 268
German township 105,123,129,142,
   161,223,258
German, Caleb 85,123; Jesse 292
Germantown 139
Germany 10,11,158,169
Gernon, Richard 193
Gerrard's Station 17,26,43,68
Gerrard, A. 98; Abner 83,97,98,99;
   J. 262; John 304; Jonathan 58;
   Justus 62
Gessell, William 187
Gest, Joseph 78,86,107
Gettman, Geo. 46; Wm. 46
Gettysburgh 304
Getz, Adam 230
Geuramand, Morel 218
Guerin, Whitehead 165
Gevaltney, Josiah 90,132
Gex, Louis 137
Gharky, David 305
Gholson, Thomas 257
Ghormley, Hugh 296,305
Gibbons, Dr. William 263; J. 205;
   William 263
Gibbs, James 292; Justice 23,31,
   57; Lieut. Justice 37; Mr. 140;
   Tom 125
Gibersleeve, John 65

340

Gibler, Frederick 263; Luis 230
Gibson & Armstrong 229,240
Gibson, Capt. Alexander 10; Col. 7,12,16,29,36,51,267; Col. Thomas 31,38,80; Col. Thos. 242; David 59,174; Gen. 46, 174; George 202,281; Isaac 58; James 94; John 89,91,98,109; Mr. 51,128(3); T. 60; Th. 73, 229; Tho. 205; Thomas 2,9,13, 18,24(2),27,30(2),33,35,36,43, 46,52,59,66,68,90,101,124,127, 134(2),135,138,184,206(2),207, 240,242,257; Thos. 2,149; William 2,240,247,250,257; Wm. 231
Giffin, James 21; Robert 200,280
Gifford, Joseph 187,247
Gilbert, Augustus 303; Jonah 78
Gildersleeve, John 70
Gildersleve, I. 109; Isaac 74,124, 286; John 88,113; Mrs. Nelly 88
Giles, Hon. W.B. 72; James 84; Mr. 72,75,77; William 178
Gilkeson, Thomas 270
Gilkison, Elizabeth 266; James 254,266; John 15,25
Gilkisson, Mr. 133
Gill, Andrew 121,127
Gillaspe, Alexander 300
Gillaspey, Robert 177
Gillaspie, Alexander 301; Alexr. 265,294; George 15,26,142; James 34,83; Joseph 270; Zacheriah 259,277
Gillaspy, Joseph 267
Gillespie, Alexander 247; George 118,173,311,318; James 15; Joseph 257; Robert 176
Gillet, Stephen 25
Gillfillan, John 283; Thomas 275
Gilliland, James 116; Samuel 313
Gillisbie, John 282
Gillispie, George 74; Joseph 149
Gillman, Benjamin I. 104; Benjamin Ives 40,87(2); Daniel 121, 154; John 66,86,107,116; Mr. 109
Gillolian, Adam 221
Gillum, John 206
Gilly, Jonathan 136,140
Gilman, B.I. 85,87; Benj. I. 175; Benjamin I. 198; Benjamin Ives 43,84,181(2),183,186,203,226; Daniel 169; Elias 297; Elizabeth 116,127; Hon. Joseph 181, 186; John 60,87,92,187; Joseph 54,139,181,182; Judge 188; Judge Joseph 65; Mr. 155; Pierre 110
Gilmore, Andrew 263; John 310; Mr. 310
Gilpin, George 293; Mr. 67
Gilson, R. 265
Gincon, Alexander 237
Ginkins, Alexander 247
Ginnans, George 161
Ginnis, John M. 219
Girton, Christopher 154,165
Giskin, Gudrich 275
Gissert, Timothy 233
Gitts, Andrew 274
Givans, George 232
Given, William 311
Givens, George 197,250; John 241
Givins, George 189,206
Givylin, William 90
Glancy, William 300
Glann, William 265
Glase, Andrew 310

Glasgow, William 268
Glass, Andrew 100
Glaze, Adam 263; Andrew 254,263 266,267,282; Richard 244,257; Thomas 247
Gledwell, William 142
Gleen, David 122
Glen, Allice 80
Glendening, John 265,284,311
Glenn, Allice 82; David 122; James 18,24,25
Glidwell, William 170
Glinn, James 13
Globs, James 300
Glosson, John 263
Glove makers 122
Glover, E. 152; Elias 141,147,150, 151(5),152(5),153,167(4),168, 170,171,173,177,255,257; Elijah 279,288; James 244,249; Mr. 147
Gobb, John 310
Goble, Daniel 35; Henry 25; Isaac 149,170; John 134,146; Margaret 35; Stephen 82
Goddard, Daniel 297; Moses 297; Mr. 75,77
Godfrey, John 170; Robert 278; Thomas 173
Godwin, Levi 292
Goff, J. 215; Samuel 250; William 142,149
Goforth, A. 135,242; Aaron 70,74, 75,77(3),79(3),80,84,108,113, 115,116(2),117,118,120(2),121, 126,127,138(2),139,143(2),145, 147,158,171,174,175(2),242, 303; Doctor 82,91,156; Doctor William 77,144,146; Dr. 63, 175; Dr. William 51,65,85; Judge 19,90; Maj. 43,105; Maj. William 63,77; Mr. 37(2),38(2), 39(3),40(2),54,84(2),105,106, 109,122,175,181(2),198; W. 50, 61,80,81,83,204; William 11,13, 16,23,28,29,47,50,61,67(2),69, 71,80,83,84(2),88,92,93(3),94(2) 96,97,102,103(2),106,108,110, 120(2),158,199,206,207(2),208, 209(2),223,225(2),226(2); Wm. 81
Gohren, Susannah 116
Goings, John 263
Golden, Stephen 78; William 137
Golding, Mr. 175
Golds, Mr. 296; Mrs. 310; Priscilla 305
Goldsberry, Edward 305; Thomas 275,292; William 275; Wm. 249
Goldsmith 79,207
Goldsmith, Vincent 169
Goldtrap, John 149
Goldwell, Wm. 302
Gollahar, James 18
Golle, George 305
Goloher, Samuel 37
Gomber, Jacob 303
Gone, John 267
Goodal, Lincoln 255
Goodhouse, Christian 45
Goodin, Benjamin 279
Gooding, Benjamin 192; Samuel 170
Goodman, John 257,302,314; Peter 254,295,319
Goodrich, C. 46; E. 57
Goodwin, Levi 270,310; Lewis 275; Samuel 146; Thomas 110; William 75; William G. 136
Gooldsberry, John 310
Goose Island 249

Goose Pond Bottom 22
Gootee, Whaland 247
Gorden, Alben 229; Alexander 235; Basset 269; Daniel 60; Elizabeth 267; George 169; Joanna 56; William 300
Gordin, John 142
Gordon's Hotel 13
Gordon, Ambrose 264; Capt. 8; Capt. George 71; Charles H. 132; Geo. 25,186; George 4(2) 11,16,17,19,20,21,28,31,39,141, 145,154,165,201,226; James 209,215,221,228,308; John 117, 149,165(2); Mr. 5,6; Philip 107, 138; Robert 296; William 296, 305
Gordy, John 296
Gore, Reubin 287
Gorrel, John 194
Goslee, Richard 300
Gosley, Richard 310
Goss, Solomon 15
Gossard, Mary 189
Gossert, Mrs. Marean 187
Gossett, John 80,197
Gosslee, Elizabeth 305
Gossom, John 241,270,287,292
Gosson, John 244
Gossurre, John 236
Gotsholkson, Solomon 66
Gottshalkson, Mrs. Eliza 71; Solomon 56,78
Gottsholkson, Solomon 68
Goudy's Mill 31,36,37,42,45,47(2), 48(2),49(2),,50,51,53,54,55,64, 65
Goudy, Capt. 33,36,37,42,81; Capt. Thomas 68; Delila 112; Elizabeth 94; James 27,103; Mr. 7,24; Robert 112,127; Samuel 94; T. 9,17,50,135; Thomas 1,3,4,7,12,16,23,24,31, 32,35,41,44,47,49,50(2),52,53, 61,66,101,103,145; William 28; Wm. 102
Gough, Jesse 318
Goul, George 314
Gould, Dr. William B. 300; Elizabeth 227; James 227; Joseph 82,99,300; William B. 290
Gowble, John 74
Gowdy, Thomas 28; Wm. 28
Goyer, Alexander 250
Graeff, John 75
Grafton, Ambrose 309
Gragg, George 319
Graham's Station 16
Graham, George 17; James 254; Jared 310; John 192,209,224, 231,246,257,296,302,307,315; John K. 142; Miss Susan 307; Mr. 49; Patrick 21,24,70,151; Robert 282; Samuel 236; Thomas 300
Grail, Wilson 73,83
Grainger, Gideon 119
Granby, Conn. 227
Grand Jury 4,8,46,59,60,69,135
Grand Lodge 311
Granger, Gideon 149,195,299
Grant's Creek 142
Grant's Lick 107
Grant's Lick, Kentucky 143
Grant's salt works 114
Grant, Alexander 103; Col. 143; David 305; Hugh 255; Jesse 101; John 45,114; Mr. 66; Sqr. 36; Squire 21; William 86,112, 134,137,142,170
Granville 238,245,250,256

Granville Library Society 152
Granville township 297
Grass, John 67
Grassey Creek 32
Grasson, Lieut. Peter 21
Grassy Praira 200
Grassy Prairie 244,250
Grave Creek 215,216
Grave, Issaac 232; John 289
Graves, Enoch 297; Franky 68; John 298; Rosewell 297; Thomas 232; William 267
Graveyard 115,168,175,193,226
Gray, Absolom 116; Absolum 112; Benjamin 84; Capt. 169; Col. John 95; David 227; Jacob 119; James 70,116,153,194,273; James G. 295,296; John 62,233 John M. 165,171; Mr. 87; Richard 318; Samuel 146; Thomas 154,244,282; William 244; Wm. 233
Grayham, George 316; John 279; Robert 291; Thomas 291
Grayson, Ens. Peter 15
Grayton, Capt. Richard 15
Greagry, Jonathan 172
Great Miami River 2,4
Great Miami Village 95
Great Praira 200
Great Prairia 42
Great Prairie 76
Great Road 18
Greatan, Capt. 26
Greaton, Capt. 5; Capt. R.H. 74, 75; Capt. Richard H. 60
Greave, Alexander 261,269; Isaac 272,302,317; John 260,261,269, 272,274,289,294,309,316,317; William 274
Greaves, John 285
Green County 91,93,97,98,107,110 111,113,129,130,134,138,153, 173,205,207,211,216,220,221, 233,240,241,243,244,249,253, 299,303
Green River 27
Green Tree 230,281,289,305
Green Tree Tavern 290,302,307
Green township 207,213,217,218, 227,230,232,236,241,244,251, 255,259,262,266,268,269,270, 273,274,276,277,279,285,287, 290,295,302,309,312,313,314, 315,317,319
Green's steam mill 175
Green, Abner 89; Benjamin 97; C. 204; Charles 263; Daniel 267, 292; G. 276; George 254,270; Griffin 205,223; J. 215; Jacob 104,244; James 121; John 52, 84,91,92,154,229,294; Mr. 154; Mrs. Clander 282; Peter 24,52, 61; Philip 109,223; Rev. Isaac 92; Robert 293; Thomas 228, 247,250,301,302(2); Timothy 146,189,207,215,218,318; William 116,154,214,221,254; Wm. 175
Greene County 119,164,211,252
Greene township 280
Greene, G. 198; Miss Sophia 31
Greenfield 147,197,212,250,282, 312
Greenfield town 219
Greenlee, Robert 206; Thomas 265
Greensburg 212
Greensburgh, Pennsylvania 126
Greenup County 308
Greenup, Christo. 243
Greenville 2,3,4,5,8,12,14,15,16,18 20,21,80,96,170,243,250,262
Greenwell, Barney 165
Greer & Baymiller 160,169
Greer, Dixon 133,134,160,169; James 144; John 25,41,45,75, 114,120,160,205,282; Mr. 165; Robert 41,184
Greere, John 284
Greg, Capt. 212
Grege, George 37
Gregery, James 270
Gregg's tavern 192
Gregg, Aaron 18; Capt. Thomas 180,183,185,186(2),187,189(2), 193,197,199,211; Daniel 191; George 75; Isaac 90; Jacob 263; John 261; Lieut. A. 12; Lieut. Aaron 21; Mr. 197,204, 219,221,223; N. 181,201,212, 221,224,258(2); Nathan 180,187 212,222,226,256,291,294; R. 181,201,221,224,258(2); Rev. Jacob 139; Robert 187,189,192 196,219,222,226,246,294; Smith 48,74; T. 189,198(2); Thomas 33,68,178,180,184, 185(2),186,187,189(2),192,195, 196,197(3),200,201,204,209,214 217,218,226,242,271; William 123,136,139
Greggery, Zekiel 252
Greghon, Robert 305
Gregorie's Creek 46
Gregories, Widow 107
Gregories Creek 63,70,76,86
Gregory Creek 74
Gregory's Creek 65,124,127,199
Gregory, David 180; Jehiel 69,112, 114(2),115,216,223,229(2),299; Levi 74,86; Maj. Jehiel 223; Mr. 239; Richard 254; Samuel 76
Gregorys Creek 90
Gressy Prairie 254
Greton, Capt. 5
Grewel, Lawrence 304
Grey, Jacob 120,121; Mr. 123
Greyham, Robert 310
Gribe, Daniel 90
Grier, Capt. 9; John 1; Rev. Mr. 210,211
Griffee, Francis 121
Griffen, Daniel 69
Griffeth, Elizabeth 266; Joseph 257; Paris 244; Philip 260,266
Griffey, Zacheriah 292
Griffin & Hatfield 110
Griffin, Alexander 233; Daniel 87, 103,110,156; David 87; Ebenezer 106; James M. 170; John 118,183; Joseph 66; Samuel 161; William 70,71; Zebulon 314
Griffing's Mill 118
Griffing, Daniel 85(2),113,115
Griffis, David 71; Jacob 89; Zachariah 254
Griffith, Alexander 241; B. 95; Benjamin 18; D. 25; David 107, 116; Dr. Elias 15; Elias 8; Faris 254; John 170,310,316; Maurice 112; Philip 258,287,305
Grigg, Moses H. 237,241
Grim, Jacob 287
Grimes, James 234; John 292; Mary 265; Noble 88,189,203, 204(2); Samuel 137,146,149,154 Thomas 265; William 265
Grimm, Jacob 61
Griner, Charles 149
Grist mills 155,166,190,278

Griswold, E. 222; Ezra 301; Isaac 254,256; Mr. 76,77,293,299,303 Ruth 256; Stanley 290,291,298, 299(2),300; William 186
Grogan, Thomas 312
Groh, Jacob 161
Gromin's Mill 30
Gromin, Mr. 30
Grommon, Mr. 86
Groniger, Jacob 295
Groninger, Jacob 206
Groom, John 78,121
Grose, Jacob 166
Grosvenor, Oliver 227
Grove, Frederick 286,309; George 266,286(2); John 309; Lewis 310; Michael 89,286; William 269
Groves, William 289
Grovner, John 209
Grow, Jacob 157
Grubb, Daniel 187; Jacob 212,214, 218,261,308; James 83,84,87, 194,198,199,200(2),202,203,211 212,215,226,228,230,242,249; John 142,249
Grummen, David 34
Grummon's Mill 29,33,37,38(2),39, 40,46,47(2),48(2),49,51(2),53(2) 54,55,60,69,72,75,77,81(2),87, 89,96,97,98
Grummon's Tavern 88
Grummon's stable 89
Grummon, D. 81,92(2); David 29, 30,33,36,37,38,47,53,68,69,74 77,80,82,87(2),89(3),90(2),93, 107,108(2),128,150; Mr. 29,89, 90
Grummons, David 106,107
Grunby, Robert 202
Gryder, John 291
Gubanks, George 254
Guerdiner, James 37
Guernsey County 302,303
Guess, Mr. 212,224; Solomon 48
Guest, Garret 132
Guiandot 270
Guion, Capt. J. 2,3
Gumb, William 226
Gunchel, Philip 253
Gunckle, Philip 255
Gunday, John 287
Gunde, Jacob 263
Gundey, S. 263
Gundy's mill 209,211
Gundy, Jacob 189,267,292,305,310 John 212,292
Gunkle's Mills 118,123
Gunkle, Squire 123
Gunnel, William 260
Gunsmith 31,53,78,80,149,172, 219,233,281
Gunter, Charles 229
Gurley, Daniel 230
Gustin, Benajah 55; Jeremiah 208; John 48
Gutbery, John 254
Gutery, John 234; Moses 275
Guthery, Arch. 260; Archd. 289; Archibald 284; Aron 284; Geo. 260; John 201,260,261(2),267, 279,284,289; Joseph 284,290; Moses 284; Wm. 260
Guthrey, John 208; William 183
Guthridge, Col. 293
Guthrie, Col. John 199; John 142, 154,189,200,247,297; Joseph 303; Robert 74; William 189
Guthry, Col. 186; John 282(2)
Gutman, John 197,202
Gutry, James 170

Guttrey, Daniel 37
Guttridge, John 225
Guyan 202
Gwaltney, Josiah 137,169
Gwathmey, Samuel 121
Gwathney, Mr. 249; Samuel 244, 249
Gwatney, Josiah 154
Gwillin, Morgan 45
Gwillym, Morgan 48; William 48
Habit makers 144,159,172,173,175 176,253,294,298,308
Hacket, Geo. 15; Peter 282; Sergt. George 21
Haden, Anthony 137; John 161
Hafer, Henry 145,176
Haff, Benjamin 247
Haffley, Charles 165
Hagan, Hugh 59; Huhey 101; Samuel 162
Hagarman, Adrian 70
Hageman, Christian 96
Hager, Peter 46
Hagerman's mill 134
Hagerman, A. 98; Adrian 97,98, 99,124(2),125,165; John 101, 134; Margaret 101; Mr. 128
Haggard, Daniel 305
Haggerty, Andrew 316
Hagigh, Job 313
Haifleigh, Frederick 155
Haifligh, Frederic 132; Frederick 139
Haighut, Israel 272
Hailey, Jether 259
Haily, Timothy 16
Haine's mill 147
Haine, John 147
Haines, Andrew 292; Benjamin 228,257,275,300; George 180, 182,217,228; Jesse 215; John 292,293
Hains, Benjamin 316; Christian 302; Henry 287,300; James 287; Jesse 219; Jonathan 244; Joseph 176; Robert 112
Hair, John 269(2),273; Joseph 58; Lieut. Jacob 189
Hairdressers 4,139,147
Hales, Henry 218
Halfield, Joseph 98
Halfpenny, John 84
Halin, Paul 241
Hall's mill 243
Hall, Anthony 287,316; Capt. 276; Capt. John T. 127; Doctor 39; Edward 279; Ezekiel 155,159, 171(2),172,174,175,176,177; Henry 89,307; James 14,74,154 219,250; Jeremiah 101; John 45,51,89,254,263,287,300,305; John T. 32,41,51,53,82,107; Joseph 304; Joshua 255,257; Mr. 56,57,64,175,236,242,310; Mrs. 187,188; Nicholas 197,209 Pheby 3; Polly 307; R. 14; Richard 3; Robert 10; Samuel 132,292; Samuel A. 226; Samuel S. 215; Stephen 51,70; Widow Mary 187; William 132, 154,214,264,275,305
Haller, Henry 257
Halley, Allen 150; Capt. Samuel 150; J. 153,163,166; Josiah 166,172,173; Maj. 174; S. 163; Samuel 153,166(2),172,173
Halloway, Samuel 276
Hally, Josiah 165
Halsey, Ichabod 32; Ichabod B. 207; Ichabod Benten 86
Halso, John 276

Halstead, John 137
Hamble, John 209
Hambleton, John 14
Hamel, Thomas 131
Hamer, Jacob 233; William 21
Hamill, Doct. John 254; Robert 146; Samuel 182
Hamilton 24,25,28,29,30,34,39,42, 46,47,51,52,55,57,60,62,63,64, 66,67,68,70,71,72,75,77,78,79, 80,82,86,92,93,97,99,100,103, 104,109,110,114,116,117,119, 120,124,126,128,134,135,136, 141,142,143,144,146,150,152, 155,158,160,162,163,166,167, 170,171,172,173,175,180,212, 272,303
Hamilton Artillery Company 201
Hamilton County appears on every page from page 1-177; also on 180,181,186,191,193,194,196, 198,199,205,207,221,227,236, 240,253,303
Hamilton County Commissioners 156,157,176,177
Hamilton Militia 97
Hamilton Prison 15
Hamilton Road 26,31,34,43,44,48, 54,66,82,92,103,122,137
Hamilton horse races 167
Hamilton prison 16
Hamilton township 302
Hamilton, Alexander 45,58,63,90, 101,107,212,215,233,300; Andrew 83; Capt. 32,34,77; Capt. John 81,104,105; Cumberland 25; Cumland 21; Daniel 192,197,206,209,213, 223; David 200; George 163, 305; James 147,151,156,228, 250,257,275,282; John 73,82 84,139,163,287; Maj. Gen. 43; Mr. 174,202; Nathaniel 316; Samuel 228,229; Sheriff James 131; Thomas 163; William 237, 241,250,253,254
Hamlet, James 221
Hamm, Doct. 313; Dr. 296; Dr. John 290; John 291,314
Hammil, Doctor John 112
Hammill, Doctor John 107
Hammit, Daniel 101,110; W. 78; William 54,73
Hammitt, Daniel 87,104
Hammon's Creek 101
Hammond, C. 200,284,304; Charles 167,198,206; Mr. 140
Hammons, Mark 310
Hamon, William 216
Hamphell, Johnston 184
Hampsher, John 206
Hampshire County, Virginia 256
Hampson, James 303; John 300
Hampstard, Mr. 148
Hampton, Dr. 232; John 277; William 292,300,305
Hamson, John 292
Hamstead, Hallam 131
Hamtramack, John F. 289
Hamtramck, Col. 2,33; Col. John F. 74,75,78; Lieut. Col. 24
Hamtramick, John Francis 169
Hamtramock, Col. 234
Hanagan, Edward B. 132; Mr. 133
Hanaman, William 292,296
Hanby, Wm. 149
Hanchet, Hiram 161; Nathan 300
Hancock, John 121; Joseph 66
Hand, George 132; Holland 293; John 116,137,244; Jonathan 267,305,316; Jonathand 257;

William 137,154; Wm. 165
Handerson, Daniel 275
Handford, Thadeus 101,121
Handrix, David 82
Handsbrough, James 10
Handshaw, Andrew 308
Hane, Daniel 257; Ronemas 170
Hanes, Frederick 264; George 248; John 275; Robert 104; Sally 116
Hanford, Thaddeus 110,118
Hanger, Charles 275
Hangerer, Charles 305
Hanick, Romenous 161
Hanies, James 292
Hanke, Michael 250
Hankens, Richard 29
Hankins, Amos 309; Asa 306; David 309; Richard 137,149
Hanks, Sarah 275; Thomas 247
Hann, George 316
Hanna, Joseph 99; Mary 121; Robert 78,116,127; Thomas 305
Hannah's Town 45
Hannah, J. 95; William 218,313
Hannaman, Christopher 170; John 279; William 300,310
Hannegan, Edward B. 128,136(2), 139,141; Mr. 138,139,142
Hannen, Richd. 70
Hanover township 277
Hansel, David 202; Rachael 202
Hanshaw, George 215
Hanson, John 277; Samuel 280
Haragan, Daniel 82
Harbaugh, Daniel 232; Wm. 168
Harbert, Asher 209
Harckless, Miss Jane 96
Harden township 167
Harden, Christopher 142; H. 248; Harry 58; Jacob 171; Jacob Weston 292; James 98; John 17,57; Mr. 129
Hardesty, Robert 264
Hardford, Thaddeus 166
Hardie, James 192
Hardin's Creek 281
Hardin, Jacob 154; John 227; M.D. 244,249; Mark 27; Thomas 41
Harding, Elanear 142; Jacob 112; James 126,146; John 117; Robert 318; Samuel 163
Hardisty, Levi 132; Levy 142
Hardon's Creek 178
Hardon, Christopher 147
Hardy County, Virginia 234
Hardy, David 67,291; Mr. 192; Sally 296; Samuel 296,306,316; Thomas 202,220,281,296,316
Hare, Capt. Daniel 313; Jane 161
Hargis, Mrs. 237
Hargrave, Samuel 275
Hargraves, Mr. 140
Hargus, Catharine 259; John 259
Harison, John 282
Harlan, Aaron 51,55; George 63, 156,164,167,238,303
Harlen, George 265
Harley, Cornelius 127
Harlin, George 252; Mr. 183
Harlow, Giles 142
Harman, Jacob 229;Thomas 305(2) 310
Harmer's trace 7
Harmer, Gen. 3
Harmin, Fredirick 299
Harmon, Elias 317; Isabella 230; Middleton 230
Harn, James 142
Harness & Penick 275

343

Harness, Jacob 236(2); Job 314;
  John 314; Joseph 202,231,257;
  Michael 99,142,165; Mr. 126
Harper, Alexander 184; Jacob 191;
  James 275,276,281; James A.
  224; John 48,54,241; John A.
  224; Mr. 41; Peter 296;
  Richard 292; Robert 32;
  Thomas 95,142,165; William
  61,247,267,281,300,305,312;
  Wm. 312
Harpole, William 267
Harr, Daniel 251,260; Evared 270;
  Everard 183,193,215,282;
  Evorard 182
Harred, Samuel 71
Harrell, James 318; John 318;
  Martin 137
Harrey, John 66; Samuel 282
Harrigan, Daniel 21
Harriman, John 99; Leonard 60
Harris, Abner 89; Amos 77; Daniel
  200,319; David 121,127,132,
  137,142,146; Edward 266,267;
  Edwin L. 72; Ezra 154; Isaac
  244,251; Isreal 99; James 55;
  John 32,127,146,200; Jones
  121,137,146,154,165,318;
  Joseph 165; Judge 211; Maj.
  Joseph 161; Miss Abby 163;
  Richard 60,120,127; William
  15,50,72,132,154
Harrison & Striker 159
Harrison County 107
Harrison County, Kentucky 23,230
Harrison township 231,259,288,315
Harrison, Capt. 30,39,59; Charles
  252; Dr. P. 221; Eli 270; Elisha
  270,282; Gov. 83,105,136,174,
  208,223,234; Gov. W.H. 229;
  Gov. William H. 240; Gov.
  William Henry 31,98; Hon.
  Henry 181; James 170; John 37
  161; John Peyton 140; Lieut.
  William 8; Mr. 44,45,46(3),
  55(2),56; Obed 305; Peachy
  186; Richard 202,206,219;
  Sophia 270; W.H. 47,53,181;
  William 72,74,107,200,247;
  William H. 28,38,39,41,44,123;
  William Henry 33,37,46,53,89,
  91(2),110,156,181,289; Wm. H.
  25,29
Harriss, Ephraim 277
Harrod, John 275
Harrover, Alexander 304
Harrow, Frances 228
Harrs, John 284
Harry, Abraham 116; David 311
Harryman, John 92,93(2)
Harsey, Doct. Thomas 184
Hart's tavern 163
Hart, David 272; Doct. 186;
  Doctr. Geo. C. 310; Edward 6;
  Elias Evelin 230; Elijah 260;
  Heth 273,282; John 107,127,
  136,146,147,161,174,175,273;
  Joseph 121,142; Noah 132,137;
  Thomas 142,178,273,287
Harter, Andrew 305
Hartes, Christian 296
Hartford County, Conn. 230
Hartley, John 23; Philip 310
Hartman, Christopher 164; David
  311; Isaac 164,305; William
  164
Harton, Joseph 316
Hartsell, Abraham 311
Hartshorn, Capt. 6; Doct. 186;
  Lieut. 7; Mr. 6
Harvey, Asa 34,58,82,108(2),119,
  121; D. 232; David 216,222,242
  Elizabeth 250; Ezra 51; J. 222;
  James 149; Philimon 149;
  Robert 219; Samuel 257,263,
  270,310; Thomas 310; William
  250
Harvie, John 204
Haskell, Maj. J. 15
Haskins, Richard 107
Haslip, Elizabeth 206
Hason, Wm. 275
Hassley, Charles 165
Hastings, Mr. 75
Haston, Robert 66
Hatch & Barns 18,20
Hatch, Doct. John 23; Elijah 111,
  165,252; John 23; Mr. 131;
Hatcher, Joshua 200; Josiah 203
Hatchinson, Simpson 267
Hatfield, George 110; Jonas 304;
  Mr. 110; Nathan 154,170;
  William 74,318
Hathaway's Tavern 100
Hathaway, Ephraim 100,117,130,
  233,238(2); Mr. 92,97; William
  213
Hatters 3,32,45,63,64,77,76,78,97,
  119,132,136,137,138,158,160,
  200,212,239,242,251,254,258,
  260,270,291
Hauer, John 244
Haugh, Benjamin 238
Haugham, Aaron 56
Haughton, R. 40; Richard 52,178
Hauk, Frederick 257
Hause, Mrs. 124
Havans, Thomas 132
Havens, Thomas 142
Haver, Mr. C. Westen 192
Havner, John 112,114,223,229
Haw, Samuel 293
Hawke, Andrew 211
Hawkins, Capt. 208; Capt. James
  189; Capt. Lucas 189; John
  206,215,219,318; Joseph 166;
  Lucas 187,192,205,215,217,233
  250,316; Martin 66(2); Nicholas
  8; Samuel 318; Widow 102;
  William 126
Hawley, Joseph 60
Hawthorn, Alexander 195
Hay Run 256,275
Hay, Ann 153; John 121; Mr. 167;
  William 153
Haydon, Christopher 149
Hayens, George 275
Hayes, D. 233; David 158,260;
  Nathan 233; Samuel 233,250
Hayman, James 270
Hayne, Thomas 251
Hayner, George 233; John 69
Haynes, Christian 309,315; Colial
  212,219; Daniel 107; George
  190,281,314; Jacob 301; John
  238,314; Philip 301
Hays, Andrew 62; Caleb 34,58;
  Capt. William 95; Charles 305;
  David 200,249,259; George 247
  265,268,275,278,292,316;
  James 184,200,244,257,309,312
  John 275,309; Joseph 131,282,
  305,309,310; Levay 267; Levi
  240,292,296,297; Lieut.
  Michael C. 292; Maj. John 212;
  Nathan 247; Rev. Joseph 267;
  Samuel 233; Seth 297; Thomas
  16; William 312
Hayway, Daniel 180
Hazel, Elizabeth 82
Head, Archibald 191; Bigger 217,
  233,269,278,284,291,301,308;
William 278,291
Headly, Sarah 300
Headon, Robert 154
Heady, Thomas 200
Heald, Lieut. N. 218; Lieut.
  Nathan 75,209,212
Hear, Daniel 305
Hearh, Capt. John 18
Hearley, Doctor Thomas 37
Hearne, James 170
Hearsey, Doctor Thomas 37
Heart, Heath 267; Joseph
Heartsough, Christopher
Heat, Thomas 90
Heath, Ashel 282,287; Ge
  George 316; James 1
  Nancy 245; Peter 22
  265,270
Heaton, Ebenezer 99; Isa
  280,317(2); James 112,1
  254; Margrate 170; Mr. 1
Heaverlo, Andrew 254
Heaverlom, Andrew 247
Hedge, Aaron 187
Hedger, John 94
Hedges, Elias 267; James 278,296,
  305; Jesse 284; Joshua 231;
  Josiah 109,225; Mary 231;
  Matthew 41; Mr. 33; Philip
  305; Robert 316
Heffer, Velentine 250
Heffernan, James 220
Hegeman, Adrian 125,127(2),128,
  144; Mr. 128
Hegerman, Adrian 128
Heggerman, Adrian 240
Heighway, John 155; Samuel 59,79
  90,119,120,143
Heigley, Bruster 205
Heines, Enos 74
Heintz, Hoss 241
Heir, Jacob 231
Heirs, Richard 101
Heistand, Joseph 291
Heistant, Joseph 308
Helin, Daniel 316
Hellard's Bottom 275
Heller's Bottom 186,298,308
Helm, Frederick 264
Helm, Jacob 263,284
Helmich, Isaac 92
Helmick, Isaac 205
Helms, William 88
Helpenstine, Peter 257
Helphinstine, Peter 250,254
Helsler, Jacob 62
Helvinstin, Sarah 248
Hempehill's road 218
Hemphell, Johnston 237,250
Hemphill, Edward 294; James 285;
  John 226; Johnston 189,200,
  212; Margaret 187
Hempill, Johnston 316
Hempstead, Hallam 256; Robert
  55,74
Hempsted, Robert 76
Henderson, Alexander 129;
  Brother 149; Capt. 208; Capt.
  David 189; D. 250; Daniel 270;
  David 244,254,263; James 263,
  287; John 17; Jonathan 270;
  Mary 131; Matthew 220;
  Mosses 270; Mr. 151,283; Mrs.
  144,169; Rev. M. 15; Rev. Mr.
  18; Robert 90; Thomas 144,
  158(2),159(2),162(2)
Hendison, John 170
Hendric, Samuel 183
Hendrick, Elizabeth 305
Hendricks, Elizabeth 287; Eliza-
  beth 267,275; Joseph 267,269,

273,274,287; William 165; Wm. 176
Hendrix, James 296
Henley, Martha 137
Henly, James B. 300
Hennen, Henry 127
Henrie, Arthur 137
Henry, Burton 241; Capt. James 2; D. 194; Elizabeth 78; James 64 74,78,118,186,239,298; John T. 217; Joseph 70,141,150; Mr. 45; Samuel 187,206,212,231, 274,278,289,291; Thomas C. 296
Henson, Henry 310; Heny 287
Hent, Isaac 274
Henthom, John 203
Henthorn, Adam 82,165
Hentor, Thomas 270
Her, Jacob 305
Hercules, Wm. 28
Hereman, John 120
Herey, Thomas 180
Herick, Samuel 304
Herod, Capt. 94,96,103,207(2), 208(2),222(2)
Herold, Martin 142
Heron, Francis 206; J. 231(2); James 242,279; John 297
Herran, Francis 202; Jesse 143
Herrel, Isaac 166
Herrell, Isaac 137
Herren, Doctor William B. 220
Herrick, Edward 284,297; S. 288; Samuel 268,273,285,293,303
Herrin, Jesse 159
Herrod, Capt. 222; Capt. Thomas 189
Herron, Francis 212,218; Frencas 231; James 135,242,250; James G. 9
Hersy, Thomas 187
Hesher, Henry 300
Hess, Beltze 187
Hessley, Charles 270
Hestend, Jacob 257
Hester, Caleb 250; Henry 282,292, 300,316
Heter, Peter 301
Heth, Capt. Andrew 16; Eleanor 16; Mr. 287
Hethe, George 293
Hetler, Mr. 213
Heulings, Jose 121
Heuston, Matthew 94
Heuthorn, Jacob 95
Hewes, Mary 270
Hewit, Philip 300,305; Robert 146; Rubert 121
Hewitt, Moses 258,309,312; William 193,228
Hewling, Joseph 78
Hewlings, Margaret 78
Hews, Henry 242
Hewvitt, William 250
Heyfin, Marcus 300
Heylin, Marcus 296
Hibbs, Aaron 312
Hick, John 171
Hickcox, Eleazer 241
Hickle, Jacob 305; Tevault 257, 291
Hickman, John 201; Richard 302; William 201,211,216,263
Hickox, Eleazer 299
Hicks, Drury 302; Thomas 166,209 230,255,260,268,287,303; William 142
Hickston, Thomas 303
Hiderd, Joseph 172
Hiett, William 296

Hiette, Stephen 217
Higans, James 275
Higgans, John 209,212
Higgin, Robert 77
Higgins, Capt. Robert 202; Col. 72; Francis 70; John 237; Mary 187; Mr. 82,241; Robert 55,57 79,111; Thomas 57,70,113,170
High Bank 184,191,194,201,221, 232,233,234,237,238,241,252, 258,259,267,271,314
High Bank Prairie 242
Highday, Jacob 101
Highfield, Philip 116
Highfill, Philip 174
Highful, Philip 56
Highland County 115,131,164,229, 230,233,252,253,255,258,259, 261,262,265,266,268,269,272, 273,274,276,278,281,282,283, 284,286,291,293,294,297,299, 301,302,303,304,307,308,309, 313,317
Highland, William 292
Highlands, Anthony 116,170; John 90
Highsil, Philip 56
Highway, Mr. 67; Samuel 19,62, 139
Hiks, Moses 298
Hildebrand, Michael 86
Hilderbrand, Christian 121; Elizabeth 61; Laurence 61
Hilditch, Hannah 177; Mr. 73,86, 153; S. 63; Samuel 77,79,88,94 101,104,109,124,146,172,175, 177
Hildreth, Doctor Samuel P. 314
Hildritch, Samuel 30
Hiley, Abraham 26
Hill's fork 218
Hill, Alexander 285,298; Andrew 18,58,76,92; Baylor 254; Benjamin 267,270,292; Daniel 1; Elizabeth 292; George 189; James 18,21,43,89,132; Jared 241,287,233; John 14,310; Joseph 241; Lucy 81; Manerieffe 15; Nathaniel 237; Philip 116; Robert 137(2); Sally 316; Samuel 202,255,270; Stephen 309,312,316; Thomas 51,62,63,86,112,116,149,197, 199,204,237; William 215,270, 296; Zenas 81,100,137; Zenis 121
Hillard, Charles 172
Hillhouse, William 227
Hillier, John 75
Hillman, James 135,256,270,302, 303
Hillmane, William 146
Hills, Dr. James H. 276
Hillsborough 158,260,265,269,293, 297,301,313
Hillyer, Justin 297
Hilmam, James 231
Hilman, James 242
Hiltzaroad, Francis 137
Hinckley, Nathaniel 82
Hind, Th. S. 281
Hinde, Doctor 318; T.S. 252,254, 262,306; Th. S. 263,293,302, 311; Thomas 257; Thomas S. 250,282
Hindman, Samuel 101,261,268,269, 273,286
Hinds, James 123,136,137,139
Hindsey, Cornelius 170; William 170
Hine, Homer 111,216; Mr. 131

Hineman, Mr. 118
Hines, Henry 260; Jacobas 227,256 James 146; John 301,302
Hinkle, Jacob 237
Hinksman, Samuel 275
Hinkson, George 170; Samuel 267; Thomas 122,142
Hinkston, Mr. 123
Hinsey, Sarah 127
Hinshaw, Henry 268
Hinton, Thomas 187,296; William 149,187
Hiram township 259,261
Hister, Henry 241
Hitchcock, Caleb 266,288,296; Jesse 266; Mr. 177,303; Peter 317
Hitchens, George 250
Hite & Robertson 102
Hite, John 307
Hittle, Mr. 170
Hixson, John 209,228,270
Hoback, Philip 200
Hobaugh, Andrew 212; Philip 212
Hobble, Mr. 307
Hobbs' tavern 258
Hobbs, Edward 305;Joshua 247,316
Hobough, Philip 200
Hobson, Charles 313; George 275
Hobsons Choice 37
Hocken 182,184
Hockhocking (see Crossings of Hockhocking) 69,102,186,193, 194,211,214,305
Hockhocking River 112,178,181, 183,223
Hockhocking road 196
Hocking 238
Hockings, Samuel 55
Hockins, Lucas 244
Hoddy's mill 186
Hoddy, John 208,229,247; Robert 272,275; William 190(2),241, 246,248,256
Hodes, Joshua 265
Hodge, Andrew 272
Hodges, Daniel 269,270; Levi 274, 276,305; Pertheney 250; Thomas 250,263
Hoff, Abraham 15; Isaac 95; John 244
Hoffman, Christian 275,316; Daniel 282; G. 211(2),315; Geo. 214; George 65,109,210,226, 298(2); John 300; Joseph 184
Hofner, Henry 10
Hogaland, Richard 142
Hogan, Elijah 38; George 42
Hoge, David 47,243,251,265; J. 267,275; James 267(2); Moses 227; Rev. James 282; William 74
Hoggatt, Stephanas 107; Stephen 244
Hogland, Wm. 15,18
Hoglin, Miss Mary 189
Hohns, Mr. 244
Hoine, Lu 23
Holaday, Samuel 310; William 275, 310
Holanes, Alexander 146
Holcomb, Ezra 297; Samuel R. 260,265,269,307; Stephen 260, 269
Holden, John 142
Holdenby, William 202
Holderman, Abraham 237,244,257, 270; Jacob 275,292,310
Holdin, Alex. 277
Hole's Creek 41,115
Hole's Station 38,45

345

Hole, Baroti 91; Dr. John 41;
  James 173; John 4,15,58,64,69,
  78; Walter 173; Zacha. 87;
  Zachariah 69
Holerder, Jesse 255
Holes Creek 62
Holes Station 143
Holes' Station 122
Holinsworth, Thomas 132
Hollada, Jesse 252
Holladay, Robert 287; Thomas 270
Holland, George 26,40; James 12;
  John 21,22,27,51,70; Katharine
  22; Mrs. 26; Sarah M. 206;
  Thomas 146,165,170; William
  225,226,235; Zachariah 125,
  130,162,165
Hollar, Adam 208,220,255,262;
  Henry 307,312,319
Holleday, Robert 219
Hollers, Vincent 207
Holley, William 279
Hollida, Samuel 310
Holliday, Elijah 263(2); Robert
  215; William 263(2); Wm. 216
Hollinback, Thomas 231
Hollinger, Daniel 247,257,289
Hollingsworth, Isaac 275
Hollinshead, Daniel 250; Francis
  182
Hollis, Daniel 108
Hollond, Elizabeth 165
Holloway, Elizabeth 292; George
  228; John 270; Thomas 257;
  William 292,296
Holly's Mills 112
Holly, Josiah 116
Holmes' mill road 218
Holmes' old mill 218
Holmes, Alexander 284; Edward
  218,224; Jas. M. 136; Jna. 215;
  Jno. 293; John 296; Jonathan
  284; Lieut. Jonathan 189
Holms, Robert 300
Holner, Nicholas 101
Holstead, John 111
Holt, Capt. 143; James 231;
  Jerom 82,157; Noker 197;
  Thomas 226
Holton, Benj. 263; Lieut. Benjamin
  189; Samuel 220,235
Holyergrass, John 292
Homer, Dr. 38
Homes, Dr. 38
Honducks, Joseph 282
Honey Creek 82,139,150
Hood, Archibald 127,146
Hoofman, Philip 285,290
Hoofnougle, Matthias 274
Hook, John 277; Lieut. 60; Lieut.
  Moses 75; William 258
Hooker, Noadiah 230
Hoop, John 199
Hoover, Christian 296; David 165,
  256,Jacob 291,300,304;
  Lowrence 99; Mary 292
Hopkins & D. Henry 194
Hopkins & Henry 45
Hopkins, Benjamin K. 174; Capt.
  276; Elisha 121; John 186,192,
  199,200,201,272; Joseph 180,
  191,237,256,261(2),267,272,293
  300; Lieut. Henry 75; Moses
  267; Noah P. 21; Samuel 206,
  231,237,255,275; Thos. 107;
  William 296
Hopkinson, Mr. 46
Hopper, Edward 310
Hoppes, George 307; John 312,316
Hoptkins, Samuel 234
Horey, George 305

Hormell, John 43
Hormston, George 247
Horn, Joseph 231(2),287,310; Mr.
  237
Hornback, Simon 295,318
Hornbeck, George 301,311(3),313
Hornblower, Mary 99
Horner, John 116,278; Joseph 287;
  Mr. 171; Nancy 278; Nicholas
  133
Hornet, Elisha 280
Horse Races 67,99,107,126,128,
  129,141,145,147,160,62,167,
  200,201,212,213,223,239,251,
  252,295,296
Horse mill 191,
Horsey, Stephen 247,249,271,308
Horsington, Harzava 187
Horsley, Ann 95
Horsly, Ann 74
Horsman, Jacob 290,291
Horton, Daniel 146
Hortwell, Oliver 219
Hos, John 149
Hosack, Adam 212,228,266
Hosbrook, Daniel 161
Hosebrook, Daniel 170
Hosey, Outy 275
Hoshaw, Mr. 298
Hoshawe, G. 197
Hoshawr, Henry 275
Hosher, Henry 315
Hosier, Abraham 94; Polly 94
Hoskins, Richard 228
Hosletter, Henry 292
Hosteller, Henry 316
Hostler 195
Hosuck, Adam 178
Hot, Mr. 251
Hotchison, Wilas 221
Hotels 13,30,87,90.150,162,190,
  214
Hotsenpillen, Jacob 270
Hotsinpiller, Jacob 310
Houch, Frederick 305; Jacob 137,
  241
Houck, Frederick 281,282
Hough, Benj. 304; Benjamin 131,
  164,168,172,216,249,272,302;
  Jacob 232; Joseph 170; Justice
  283(2); Mr. 148,283,318;
  Thomas 142
Hougham, Aaron 74
Houghland, Mr. 208
Houghn, Nicholas 285
Houler, William 38
Houlet, William 38
House joiner 231
House of Representatives 30,37,
  38,39,40,47,53,54,70,71,87,91,
  111,123,131,282
House of entertainment 27,31,39,
  61,71,77,90,91,94,204,206,210,
  214,231,241,243,255,294
House's Tavern 162
House, Henry 57; Mr. 148,156;
  Robert 230
Householder, John 218
Housejoiners 144
Housewright, Thomas 209
Houston, John 6; Robert 60
Hover, Lawrence 215
Hovey, Benjamin 240,244; Gen.
  Benj. 244; Gen. Benjamin 249
How, James 228,301; Jesse 274;
  John 296,310; Joseph 228,296;
  Mr. 122,201; Thomas 146;
  William 282,311
Howard, Barbary 121; Benjamin
  97; George 116; Hannah 234;
  Horton 237; James 51,300,305;

John 101,146,251,275; Joseph
  234; Mr. 48; Samuel 178,234;
  Solomon 82; Vachel 310;
  Veachel 309; Wm. W. 165
Howe, David 95; Perley 40;
  Thomas 58
Howel, Silas 23
Howell, Capt. Silas 41; Miss Ann
  Lewis 163
Howey, Gen. Benjamin 300
Hown, George 282
Howsman, Wm. 305
Howthorn, William 10
Hoxie, Christopher 169
Hoy, Adam 43
Hoyde, Jacob 74
Hubbard township 317
Hubbard, Asenath 92; Elizabeth
  224,250; Fielding 207,220;
  Jacob 188(2),196,224,254; John
  92,183,187,190,196,219,224,
  225,288; Mary 288; Mr. 187,
  195; Pheildan 310; Pheilden
  197,196(2),206,207,230(2),300;
  Phielding 184(2)
Hubbart, Jacob 215
Hubbell, Hezekiah 298; Sampson
  154; Thomas 154; W. 56
Hubbert, John 137; Kirby 142
Hubble, Isaac 55,153
Huber, Jacob 159; John 46;
  William 314
Hudson 284
Hudson township 266,284
Hudson, Daniel 244,249; David
  210; Francis 18; Luke 32;
  Robert 116,137,270,296; Thos.
  315; William 282; Wm. 292
Hueston, M. 63; Matthew 27; Mr.
  72; Paul 70; Thomas 172
Huet, John 202
Huey, Samuel 203
Huff, Caleb 244,257,263,290;
  Doctor 186; Jacob 232; Jesse
  316; John 247
Huffman, Geo. 217; Henry 292;
  John 300
Hufman, Felix 301,309; Joseph
  305
Hughes, E. 66; Ezekial 99; Ezekiel
  23,30,32,51,154,162; George
  121,316; Henry 247; James
  116,237; Jesse 244; Lieut.
  Daniel 75; Mr. 299; Randolph
  254,270,310; Robert 303;
  Samuel 307
Hughey, Alexander 138; Charles
  245; Isaac 266,279; James 233,
  237,263,282,300
Hughs, Ezekiel 175; George 131;
  James 254,270,305; Jesse 303;
  Mrs. Joanna 305; Sarrah 275
Hughy, Isaac 299; James 250
Hulic, Barnet 169,269
Hull, David 298; Eliakim 5;
  Ezekiel 307; General 116; Gov.
  164,239(2),299; Gov. William
  239,298; William 156,226
Huller, John 257
Humane Society 44,262
Humble, Uriah 308
Hume, Robert 194,249,256;
  William 316
Humes, Dr. 38; John 16,58,67,85,
  115,117,132(2),153; Mr. 39;
  Mrs. Margaret 132; Robert
  199,212; William 170
Humphrey, Mr. 88,203,207
Humphreys, Charles 112; Edward
  112,132; George 84,204(2);
  Isaac 166; James 122

Humphries, Col. David 309; Isaac 167
Humpson, John 194
Hunbolt, Thadeus 55
Hungerford, Lemuel R. 78
Hunis, William 267
Hunnel, John 310
Hunnil, John 316
Hunt & Sedam 101
Hunt's tanyard 41,108,125,162, 171
Hunt, A. 2(2),3,6(2),10,15,18(2), 21,22,29,35,40,45,46,73,95,114, 145; Aaron 63; Abijah 14,29,46 56,64,81,98,167; Caleb 143; Col. Thomas 121; Edward 149, 177; J. 15,18(2),21,22,35,40,45, 46,73,95,114,145,269; Jer. 73; Jeremiah 21,29,50,61,121,146, 169(2); Jesse 14,29,44,46,55, 57(2),61,80,88,89,91,92,93,94, 95(2),101,103,112,118,119,134, 139,152,154,160,171; Jessey 263; John 206,228,231; John W. 48; Maj. Thomas 60,74; Miss Ruth 121; Mr. 28,169; N. 63, 122,124,171; Nathaniel 237; Nehemiah 8,47,74,81,116,117, 172; Phineas 233; Ralph 119; Ralph W. 28,29,48,51,57,60, 137,144,158; Robert 143; Thomas 74,127; William 11
Hunter, Charles 48,192; James 243(2),248; John 14,18,30,52,71 73,149,163,172,194,263,295, 298,316; Joseph 116,117,162, 184,215; Lieut. Robert 21; Mr. 183,213,253; Narsworthy 183; Nasworthy 72; Thomas 37,45, 82,91,107,172,243; William 41,57,66,74,82,99,107,127,130, 131,164; Wm. 164(2),233
Huntingdon, Jonathan 55; Samuel 84
Huntington County, Penn. 295
Huntington township 266,269,270, 279,293,298,299,301,308,309, 314,317
Huntington, Col. 207; Gov. 290, 293,298,299(2),300; Gov. Samuel 298,299,302,319; Governor Samuel 177; Hon. S. 131; Hon. Samuel 125,263,280; Judge 116,162,261,262,263,277 280,298; Mr. 177(2),280; S. 262,277; Sam. 96,97; Samuel 91,205,206(2),228,262(2),263, 278,285,291,307,309
Huntinton, Samuel 280
Huntsberger, R. 46
Huntsman, Jesse 251
Hupp, George 274
Hurd, Mr. 105
Hurdus, Adam 138,152,161
Hurford, Samuel 287; Thomas 146
Hurin, Enos 42,94,117,127,136; Enox 116; Silas 36,43,100,117
Hurlbunt, Zehial 254
Hurlem, Geo. 202
Hurley, Enock 310; John 267
Hurst, Levi 194,215; Levy 228; Thomas 282
Hurt, Clem 265
Husam, Joseph 182
Huse, Henery 261
Husey, Christopher 270
Hush, Peter 292
Husk, Hugh 237
Husler, Isaac 215
Husong, Christian 43; Daniel 172
Husser, Isaac 221

Hust, Nancy 305; Thomas 300
Huston, Andrew 189; David 303; Henry 183,205,315; Hugh 237, 241,300; James 55,78,296; John 107,124,150,159; M. 172; Mary 124; Matthew 95,101,103 Mrs. 300; Mrs. Sally 303; Paul 90,190,192,221; Robert 180, 305; Samuel 292; William 250, 275,288
Hut, John 199
Hutchin, William 169
Hutchings, Gabriel 15; Moses 275; Thomas 77
Hutchins, Moses 98
Hutchinson's Inn 119
Hutchinson's fulling mill 174
Hutchinson's mill 163
Hutchinson's tavern 129
Hutchinson, Ann 60; Charles 154; E. 94,144,149,163,174; Ezekiel 66,70,115,119,122(2),127,144, 153(2),154,155,164,165(2),168, 170,177; Isaac 137; Jacob 55; James 154; Mr. 93,163; Samuel 187; Thomas 154
Hutchison's Tavern 107
Hutchison, Amos 148; Ezekiel 107
Huthison, Ezekiel 104
Hutitcheson, Benjamin 316
Hutson, Sergt. 15
Hutt, John 194,217(2),226,236,238, 246,258,262,265,269,271(2),272 273(2),291,295,297,314,316; Mrs. 194; W.S. 202; William 217,249,287; William S. 202, 210,253,266,274,278,280,288; Wm. S. 194(2),311,317
Hutton, James 217; John 287,300; Thomas 32
Huy, James 300
Hyde, Charles 5; Ensign Charles 5; John 300; Lieut. Charles 10,15;
Hyer, Samuel 182
Hyle, Samuel 303
Hymer, John B. 132
Hynamon, John M. 15
Hynd, John 149
Hyndman, Samuel 86
Hyne, Michael 267
Hysle, John 314
Iams, John 252; Polly 191
Ibiff, Richard 302
Idding, Benjamin 172
Igeming, George 161
Illinois Grant 15,74
Illinois country 46
Illinois grant 39
Imble, John 180
Imlay, Mr. 177; Peter 151
Imley, Mr. 57
Immel, John 205,215
Independent Church 241
Independent Republican 299,304
Indian Creek 33,91,137,141,179, 187,209,218,224,225,226,232, 250,254,263,269,274,285
Indian Hill 43
Indian King 158
Indian King Tavern 159,286
Indian Trace 178
Indian Wheeling Creek 220
Indian agent 141,177,307
Indian attack 140,141,157,161,207
Indian trader 192
Indiana 156
Indiana Canal Company 240,244, 249
Indiana Territory 46,53,85,89,91, 98,103,104,105,109,114,116, 117,121,124,126,131,135,161,

162,183,195,204,219,223,225, 226,240,289,312
Indians 1,2,3,4,5,6,7,8,10,11,12,15, 29,31,32,33,34,35,46,52,62,68, 75,78,80,93,94,96,103,109,112, 120,121,135,156,162,174,176, 179,208,211,214,222,229,234, 242,243,245,247,259,262,303
Infantry (see Cincinnati Light Infantry, Light Infantry) 93,96 100,105,114,116,119,121,122, 123,126,127,131,134,138,139, 141,142,144,156,157,158,159, 160,161,171,172,194,196,240, 243
Ing, Thomas 310
Ingersall, Lieut. 5(2)
Ingersol, Daniel 90
Ingersoll, Daniel 55,147
Ingersul, Enock 137
Ingersull, Enoch 120
Ingham, H. 317; J. 317
Ingle, Capt. 276; Mathias 275
Inglish, Ann 316; Mr. 195; William 104
Ingman, Edmund 284
Inlow, Abraham 91
Inman, Elijah 121; Elisha 116
Innes, Joseph 23
Innis & Grant 66
Innis, Francis 56; Rachel 56,62; Widow 68
Innkeepers (see taverns) 4,5,14,76, 77,79,93,106,192,198,209,220, 286
Inns 82,
Inskeep, Abraham 292; James 250, 292; Job 300; Joshua 292
Inskep, Joshua 244
Inskip, Daniel 282
Instone, John 93
Insurance Company 73,318
Inyard, David 149
Iost, Abraham 80
Ireland 1,5,10,11,12,33,49,54,59 64,157,158,172,211
Ireland, Aaron 29; Aron 137; George 216; John 283; Mary 289
Irish Land 222
Irish, John Clark 112
Iron Ridge township 191
Irons, David 233,237,244,291
Irvin, James 60,254; Samuel 311; Thomas 12,51; W.W. 250,304; William 10,127,133,134,205; William W. 252(2); Wm. W. 304
Irvine, Doctor 187; Doctor James 189; William 131,211(2); Wm. W. 235
Irwin Creek 305
Irwin's tavern 281
Irwin, Alexander 282,306; David 243; Doctor James 188; Edward 292; Isaac 224; J. 299; James 257(2),276; Jared 296; Jarnied 223; John 67,116, 134,168,297,307,317; Matthew 304,307; Morton 318; Mr. 16,65 166,276,308; Mrs. Martha 317; Nancy 318; Samuel 69,146; Thomas 66,115,254,287; W.W. 249,262; William 88,115,131, 182,203(2),204,229,240,299, 315; William W. 164,303,310; Willian 318; Wm. 131,224,241, 276; Wm. W. 168,272
Irwine, James 132
Isaac's Creek 211,263
Isgrig, Daniel 161; Joshua 154; Michael 154

347

Isguig, Joshua 149
Ish, George 292
Isham, George 90
Itcheson, Samuel 309
Ives, Elihu 309
Izzard, Eli 306
Jackman, Edward 74,116
Jacks, Gardner 264,282,306; Garner 270; Nicholas 250,270
Jackson, Andrew 77; David 191; Edward 90; Flora 137; George 273(2),285; Jacob 167,263, 281(2); John 55,95,135,181,185, 191,221,264,287,300,316; Joseph 60; Lieut. 167; Mr. 46; Peter 237,259,260(2),261,265, 267,274,277,278,289(2),290,291 294,301,307,315; Rev. Mr. 179; Robert 137; Samuel 185,191, 203; Samuel D. 192; Thomas 137; W. 204; William 114,204, 212,214,229,276; Wm. 136,230
Jacob, Hester 241; John 161
Jacobs, Joseph 60; Robert C. 231; Samuel 262; William 309
Jacson, Samuel 270
Jaens, Zacariah 270
Jail 107,116,120
James & M'Coy 188,191,197,201, 202(2),204(3),207,258,259,265, 266,272,281
James & Wood 298,308,317
James, Henry 134; Jacob 316; John 206,214,296,306; Lawrence 282; Lemuel 202,207 223,228,237,240(2),247,268; Mathias 300; Mr. 139,195; Samuel 110,111,117,119,120, 151,156,158; Sarah 153; Thomas 11,218,228,238,240(2), 246,247,253,256,258,264,265, 268,280,298,299,317; Thos. 240,241,289; W. 83; William 80(2),81(2),83,86,87(2),91(2), 96,202,205(2),216; Wm. 86
Jameson, Alexander 107; David 205; Dr. David 194; George 277; Hugh 103; James 264; Matthew 309; Samuel 107; William 311
Jamison, Capt 127; Charles 30; David 91; Elizabeth 215; George 295,316; Jacob 316; Matthew 316; William 250
Janes, Zachrs. 316
Janis, Thomas I. 200
Jannings, Simeon 74
January, J. 184; James 191,201, 213(2),214; Mr. 38
Jaquess, Jonathan 183,
Jardon, John 107
Jarnison, George 86
Jassoft, Jonathan 251
Jaudin, Charle 12; Elizabeth 12
Jay, Stephen 318; Wm. 110
Jean, John 316
Jeanes, Zachariah 287
Jefferies, Joseph 288
Jeffers, Capt. 7; Catharine 236; Joab 146; Joseph 236
Jefferson 109,213,232,256,260,272 274,279,286,295,298,313,314
Jefferson Co., Ky. 90
Jefferson County 34,66,69,84,88, 91,111,131,164,177,181,186, 203,205,207,213,216,221,232, 236,240,252,264,303
Jefferson County, Kentucky 28,48 68,124,160,284
Jefferson County, Va. 227
Jefferson Town 75

Jefferson township 207,217,231, 232,236,248,251,252,260,261, 263,268,269,270,272,273,274, 277,278,279,280,283,285,289, 291,294,295,298,301,308,309, 311,312,313,314,316,317,319
Jefferson, John 303; Mr. 59; Pres. Th. 169,210; Pres. Tho. 97,215; Pres. Thomas 168; Th. 149,166; Thomas 105(2)
Jeffersonville 249
Jelly, Andrew 142
Jemison, Thomas 63
Jenkenson, John 165
Jenkins, A. 192,215; Aaron 97,99; Alexander 71,194; Baldwin 107 Henry 79; James 241,293; John 264,300; Mr. 291; William 275
Jenkinson, Henry 135; John 44; Joseph 90,101,116,127,137,175, 176; Mr. 157,175
Jenning, Henry 87
Jennings, Benjamin 28; Effy 82; Henry 43,47,99,101; Levi 27,42 62; Lieut. 174; O. 264; Obediah 249; Oliver 134,240; Rev. John 317; Wm. 13
Jerick, Jacob 315
Jesemon township 233
Jessamine County, Kentucky 83, 90,112
Jessop, John 276
Jessup, Daniel 161; Mr. 31
Jewel, Thomas 119
Jewelers 13,140,145,157,235,248, 252,253,261,268
Jewett, C. 307; Doct. 280; Doctor Leonard 206; Leonard 164,168, 252,261,262; Mr. 164,166
Jewit, Mr. 148
Jice, Henry 95
Jimison, Samuel 170
Jinens, Charles 301
Jinings, Capt. Daniel 18
Jinkins, Alexander 206; Ann 253; Asariah 308; Josiah 253; Samuel 190
Jinkinson, John 58(3)
Jinnin, William 265
Jinnius, Mr. 86
Joabe, John 282
Joans, Robin 237
Jobe, John 264,292
Jobin, Joseph 298
John, Elizabeth 90; George 291; Isaac 90; James 111,113; John Petit 248; Lemuel 296; Mary 101,138; Moses 11; Richard 263; Thomas 13,86,101,138,275 William Petet 248
Johns, George 258; Thomas 154, 161
Johnson, Abner 174; Capt. James 254; Cave 147; Col. Robert 18; Corn. 154; Cornelius 37,121, 136; Daniel 66; Henny 158,313; J.R. 286; James 112,163,238, 318; James W. 235; Jeremiah 214; John 1,3,146,261,294; Levi 280; Michael 277; Michael H. 42; Mr. 194; Nathaniel 195, 209; Patrick 301; Perry 158; Polly 277; Rachal 101; Robert 151,176,200; Samuel 170,180; Sterling 200; Thos. M. 221; Wider 275; William 55,291,316
Johnston, Alexander 12; Andrew 187,189; Archibald 232; Charles 287; Cornelius 71,184, 282,306; Cornelus 316; Daniel 242,248; Dr. 210; E. 178;

Edward 41,90,170,270; Elijah 274(2),316; Ephraim 210; Gary 146; Gaven 267; Gavin 244,247 254; George 189,231,244,287, 289; Henry 217; Isaac 19,270, 282,300; Ja. 212; Jacob 283, 300; James 10,51,60,76,182, 209,215(2),219(2),226,228,231, 246,258,267,282,290,293,294(2) 317; James L. 287; Jeremiah 86,132; John 10(2),107,177,192, 206,208,215,219,231,244,257, 267,269,270,275,282,283,289, 292,296,297,299,300,306; Jonathan 300; Levi 250; Margaret 267; Micajah 287; Miss Polly 302; Mr. 73; Nathaniel 271; Nicholas 70,78; Nicholas 78; Pressley 271; Rebecca 32; Rev'd. William 264; Robert 21,226; Robert H. 274; Samuel 51,90,275,296; Thomas 270,272,295; Thomas B. 270; Walter 121; William 131,182,189,214,222,228,257, 271,275(3),282,287,311; Younger 310
Joice, D. 33; E. 33; James 107; Mrs. 74
Jolly, Alexander 265,279; Andrew 112,116; David 266
Jonas, Benjamin 248
Jonathan's Creek 210,230
Joncaire, C. 239; C.F. Chebert de 181; C.F. Chobert de 69
Jones & Silvers 33
Jones, Abraham 146,209,212,241, 244,282; Abram 231; Amos 244,269,270; Aramus 237; Benj. 228; Benjamin 262,287, 315; Benson 314; Cadwallader 231; Casner 137; Col. 160; Col. John 124,125(2),143,161; Colonel 126; Daniel 82,170; David 142,149,154,209,215(2), 231,316; Elisha 268; Elizabeth 72,163,257,318; Enoch 165; Ensign John 261; Erasmus 225; Evangelist 190; F. 10; Francis 8; George 291; Henry 200,306; Hubbard 248; Hubbert 310; Isaac 244,247,257,264,306; Isabella 190; Isabelle 212; James 74,75,90,132,161,279; Jared 205; Jesse 161,175; John 30,126,128(2),145,147,160(2), 164,174,175,253,264,310,317; John Rice 41,121; Jonathan 137,146,165,170; Joseph 99, 117,146,170,254,292,309,318; Kastner 132,165; Lydia 170; M. 30,32,33,34,38(3),49,54,65,72; Marshal S. 258; Michael 32,80, 83,86(2),87(3),91,92(2),109,202 205; Miss Elizabeth 241; Moses 60,254,275,296,309; Mr. 5,131, 148,155,175,199,231; Mrs. Abram 215; Mrs. Margaret 88; Nicholas 45; Peter 243,267,270 306; Philip 89; Rev. David 25; Rev. Wm. 175; Richard 36,38, 46(2),267; Robert 194,206,250, 275; Samuel 154,251,257,277, 300,306; Samuel G. 226; Sarah 165; Thomas 149,232,264,282; Thomas K. 76; W. 30,33,38,49, 65; William 6,9,14,26,45,51,70, 72,87,92,142,297; Wm. 19,31, 32(2),34,38(2),54,72,88,291
Jonston, J. 252; James 248; William R. 244

348

Jordan, James 142; John 40,243, 244,249; Samuel 206,212,221; William 288
Jordon, John 248
Jourdon, John 143
Jowder, Mr. 15
Joyce, Mr. 119
Joynes, Thomas R. 310
Joyns, Levin 293
Juder, John 270
Judge 8,12,13,14,16,19,20,21,57, 85,91,92,96,102,110,113,114, 115,116,125,134,205,211,216, 220,226,229,240,241,242,246, 265
Judy, John 260
Juette, Leonard 252
Julien, John 293,294; Rene 294; Stephen 141,293
Julin, John 287
Julow, Ezekiel 55
Jump, William S. 122
Jumulear, Jacob 247
Justice, Robert 180; William 221, 255
Justices, John 287; William 271
Justis, William 310
Kain, Daniel 97,100,159,303,308, 314,317; James 44,72; John 314; Mr. 183
Kamper, E.Y. 158; James 9,44,47; John F. 138; Mr. 121; Mrs. Judeth 161; Parson 158; Peter 154; Rev. James 163; Rev. Mr. 112
Kan, Thomas 244
Kanedy, Mr. 268
Kanhawa County 232
Karm, Stuffel 149
Karnes, Patrick 312
Karns, William 296
Karr, Alexander 250,287; F. 171; John 63,279; Jos. 212
Kase, Henry 154
Kaskaskia 41,109,282
Kaskaskias 75,105
Kating, Cornelius 300
Kaufman, William 290
Kautz, Jacob 158
Kauz, Mr. 149
Kavanah, Mr. 48
Kavenagh, James 7,14,15,17,18, 20(2),24
Kaykendell, Henry 316
Kean, James 47; John 39,293; Mrs. Rhoda 39; Peter 58; Robert 8, 18
Keana, Joseph 276
Kear, Peter 244,247,316; W. 271
Kearney, Thomas 310; Thos. 300
Kearns, Benjamin 230
Keasbey, D. 76,90,97,106
Keasby, D. 113; Delzil 64,116(2), 138
Keefer, Jacob 292
Keeler & Fraser 307
Keeler, James 269
Keelin, Davis 122
Keen's Station 18
Keen, Hoffman 146; Peter 74,82
Keene, Peter 99
Keener, John 247,267
Keens, John 182
Keer, Henry 134; Thomas L. 294
Kees, John 287
Keffer, Valentine 287
Kehr, David 215
Kelgore, James 178
Keller, Geo. 190; John 307,311
Kelley, Capt. Nathan 117; Ezekiel 284; N. 16; Nathan 58;
Nicholas 200
Kellin's town 218
Kellogg, Ethel 318
Kellor, John 254
Kelly's Tavern 12,25
Kelly, Capt. 25; Daniel 306(2); David 21,55,58; Elisha\194,299, 305,314(2); Elizha 178; Ezekel 292; Ezekiel 275,278; George 48,110,121,166; Gorden 41; Hugh 297; Jaen 146; James 107,182; Jane 26; Joseph 13, 107; Mathew 266; Matthew 266 Mr. 24,113,160; Nathan 45,57, 99,119; Sheriff 28; Thomas 197; William 2,12,26,28
Kelough, Parker 278
Kelsey, Isaac 4
Kelso, William 282,284
Kemberly, Mr. 109
Kemper, Ephraim 310; James 131, 163; Parson 101; Peter 41(2),42 51,57,61; Reuben 32; Rev. 33, 42; Rev. James 151,153; Rev. Mr. 54,96; Rev. Mr. James 130 Samuel 76; Thomas 51
Kemplin, Thomas 215
Kempton, Robert 154
Kenady's Ferry 125
Kendal, James 304
Kendale, Jeremiah 307
Kendall, Aaron 237,267; Joel 296; Nancy 310; Stephen 192; William 314; Zabud 298
Kendel, Aaron 306; Henry 142
Kendrick, Ben. 292
Keneday, David 132
Kenedy, James 74; Samuel 62; Thomas 37,82(2); William 154, 278
Kenhawa County, Virginia 270
Kennady, Mr. 11
Kennard, John 165
Kenneady, John 84
Kenneday, Mr. 183
Kennedy's Ferry 13,23
Kennedy, David 237; Doctor 184; Dr. 185; Dr. N. 185; Dr. Nathan 184(2); Francis 23; James 45,78; John 165,304; Joseph 58,79,130; Miss Mary 156; Miss Nancy 237; Mr. 26, 133,186; Mrs. Nancy 79; N. 182,184,185(2),186,199; Nathan 183,184,185,196,200,208(2); Rebecca 14,23(2); Rev. John 188; Robert 310; Samuel 98; Thomas 13,14,45,54,61,165,261 Widow 26; William 241
Kennekanic 183
Kennel, William 284
Kenney, Capt. Robert 156; D.M. 291; John 257
Kennickenick 317
Kennikenick 317
Kennon, Richard 293
Kenny, Lewis 115,216; Thomas 91
Kent, James 220; John 269,275; William 229,234,275,282,287, 313
Kenton, Gen. 243; Gen. Simon 233; John 239; S. 231; Simon 6,45,109,115,206,216,225
Kentucky 3,4,5,6,11,20,37,42,43, 46,56,61,66,68,70,74,81,89,91, 92,94,102,105,107,112,118,128, 130,140,156,159,160,161,164, 169,173,174,176,183,187,191, 195,205,207,210,220,231,235, 236,237,251,264,301,308
Kentucky Herald 24
Kentucky River 10,54,66,160
Kentucky Volunteers 8
Kenyon, John 177
Keppy, Joseph 60
Ker, Henry 51,95,96
Keran, Edward 311; William 198, 257,306
Kerans, Patrick 311
Kerkendall, John 215,236; Rebecca 236
Kerker, Thomas 148
Kerney, Thomas 292,300,310
Kerns, Abner 300,306; Benjamin 194,240,259,268
Kerr's farm 254
Kerr's mill 268
Kerr, Alexander 183,263; Gen. 295; Gen. Joseph 317; General 298; Henry 134,154,170; J. 233,237; Jacob 27; James 254, 309,312; John 176(2),201,213, 221,224,226,237,252,255,256(2) 260,270,273,275(2),280,290,293 302,318; Jos. 212,242,301; Joseph 53,83,111,117,123(2), 126,127,128,131,178,191,192, 193,198,199,200,201,205,213, 214,223,224,229,235,236,237, 239,242,243,244,247,254(2),257 258,260,261,262(3),270,271,274 275,282,283,290,291,295(2), 296(3),297,299,313(2),317, 318(2); Lewis 73,75,79,83,88; Mary 317; Mr. 82,271,315; Robert 190,275,283; Samuel 254,290,292,293,300,314; Thomas 170,317(2); Thomas L. 281; William 271,275; Wm. 265
Kerrh, Mrs. 251
Kerron, John 217
Kershner, Daniel 314; Jacob 309; Mr. 153
Kerst, William 228
Kerswell, Rachel 250
Kesler, Matthias 315
Kesser, Valentine 244
Kessinger, Teter 318
Ketchel, Moses 86
Ketchen, Thomas 161
Ketchum, Andrew 172
Ketrow, Charles 140; Peter 140
Kettro, Peter 99
Key's tavern 219
Keyes, Samuel 247; William 240, 264
Keys' tavern 228
Keys, Col. William 307; Isaac 307; John F. 313; Mr. 180,187(2), 192,204,208,283; William 183(2),184,185(2),189,197(2), 198,202(2),205,209,213,217(2), 223(2),224(2),269; Wm. 181,183 190(2),211,231,283
Keyser, David 310
Keyt, John 269
Kibbey's Tavern 29,38
Kibbey, Capt. 4,5; Capt. Ephream 19; Ephm. 29; Ephraim 86,101, 214; Maj. Ephraim 120; Timothy 38
Kibby, Adjutant Timothy 31; Capt. 10,14; Capt. E. 23,29,36, 61; Capt. Ephraim 4; Capt. Timothy 91; Col. Timothy 160; E. 83,98; Ephraim 32,41,58(2), 61,80,87(2),97,98(3),99,106(2) 108,115,116,119,130,152,202, 214; Joseph 114; Lieut. Timothy 35; Maj. 143; Maj. Ephraim 167; Rachel 140; Timothy 29,39,115,135,140

Kid, Mr. 65
Kidd, Danl. 308; John 15,38,45,70; Mr. 62,64
Kiddy, William 250
Kiene, Joseph 247
Kiernan, John 154
Kiger township 273
Kight, Caty 241; James 237; John 228,244,264,275,306
Kilbourn, James 222,249; Josiah 292; Lemuel 212; Lieut. Col. J. 293; Maj. James 276; Mrs. Lucy 257; Rev'd. James 257; Rev. James 256,258
Kilburn, James 218; John 250; L. 257; Rev. James 223
Kilburne, Lemuel 254
Kile, George 226; Robert 10
Kiler, George 117
Kilgore, Capt. 276; Capt. Mathew 189; Charles 32,90,103,218,267 George 251; James 190,212, 253,263,268,269,270,273,274(2) 290,311,316,317(2); Maj. James 290; Mathew 316; Mr. 70; Samuel 253,263; William 281, 303
Killbuck, Peter 52
Killen, William 121
Killgore, C. 31,51,61,118,157,158, 159,160; Charles 37,41,44,84, 103,105,107,109,111,119,125, 137,139,147,152,161,162(2); David 110; James 206,247; Maj. 144; Mr. 66,69,72; Samuel 244
Killman, James 242
Killogh, Allan 269
Kilpatrick, Saml. 212
Kilworth, James 216
Kimberley, Mr. 181
Kimberly & Company 15,20,21
Kimberly, Mr. 53,69(2),71,181; Z. 69; Zenas 90,203,213,225
Kimble, Elijah 265; Lambert 315
Kimmel, Jesse 316; William 194
Kimmell, William 194
Kinan, Wm. 287
Kincade, Thomas 313
Kincaid, Samuel 268
Kincart, Samuel B. 273,282
Kindal, Aron 275; James 311
Kindel, John 306
Kindle, James 274
Kine, Thomas 109,225
Kinesly, John 257
King's Creek 110,129
King, A. 121,133; Alex. 75; Alexander 74,89,102,113(2),115 116(2),117,128,129,130,131, 134(2),136(2),143,145(2),147, 148,153; Christian 101,235,303 David 259; Ebenezer 259; Elisha 81; Elizabeth 275; Fidelio 259; George 219; Jacob 219; John 136,254,257; Jotas 12; Miles 293; Mr. 163; Nehemiah 299,303; Phebe 136; Robert 235; Samuel 192; Thomas 41,146; Thomas B. 257; William 215,231(2),237, 254,306
Kingary, Michael 277
Kingery, John 221
Kingorre, John 228
Kingrey, Micheal 282
Kingsberry, Capt. 26
Kingsbury, Mr. 131(2)
Kingsman, John 134,242
Kingston, Paul 275
Kinickinic 251,252

Kinikinick 277
Kinkade, John 192; William 142
Kinkead, David 266,280,281,290, 297,299,307,311,312,317; Mr. 276
Kinnan, David 112; Edward 117
Kinner, Thoams 146
Kinney, Abraham 91,122; Capt. Thomas 124; Hannah 91,99
Kinniar, Andrew 300
Kinnicinic 202
Kinnickanic 183,185,219
Kinnickanick 191
Kinnickinic 208,221,245,258
Kinnickinic Creek 218
Kinnickonic 239
Kinny, John 121
Kinser, Jacob 165
Kinslair, James 230; John 230
Kinsman, John 259
Kinton, Simeon 34
Kinzer, George 165
Kinzie, John 307
Kirby, Ephraim 109; James 176; Jonathan 165; Richard 95
Kirk, Mr. 262; Wm. 165
Kirkbridge, Joseph 149
Kirkendall, Henry 292,313
Kirker, Gov. 162,164; Gov. Thomas 173; Mr. 156,166,177, 307; Philip 149; Tho. 158; Thomas 84,88,111(2),131,149, 156(2),158,160,164(3),166(2), 173,177,191,201,203,212,222, 238,255,256,262,277,285,318; Thos. 280
Kirkindall, Henry 187; Jeremiah 275
Kirkpartrick, David 209
Kirkpatrick, Absolam 267; Adam 280,283,306,313,317; Alex. 264; Alexander 121,127,318; Benjamin 233; David 198; Joseph 265,280; Mary 51; Mr. 217; Samuel 55,172,257; Tho. B. 303; William 318
Kirkwood, William 161
Kirns, Benjamin 264
Kirtland, Jurhard 225; Mr. 109; Turhand 134,242; Tushland 230
Kirtz, Jacob 191
Kiser, John 119
Kishler, Jacob 275
Kisling, John 154; Peter 154
Kisser, Vallentine 241
Kissinger, Andrew 306
Kister, George 311
Kitchel, Asa 41,78,80,82; Calvin 145; John 21,80,81,84,87,91, 199,205,207; Joseph 117,125, 126,160; Luther 145; Moses 95; Mr. 84
Kitchell, Asa 36,55,60,83,132; Benajah 127; Calvin 132; J. 83; John 58(2),216; Joseph 143,145 151,161,162,174,175(2); Judge 114; Moses 132; Mr. 160,175
Kitterle, David 275
Kittsenfiller, William 304
Kizinger, George 302
Klein, Daniel 46; Jacob 46; John 46
Klimper, Ephraim 287
Kline, Joseph 312
Klowser, John 209
Knap, Moses 146
Knigh, John 296
Knight, Bob 277; Enos 285; Fielding 271; James 32,86; John 282,300; Valentine 275
Kniseley, David 282

Knoles, Adam 282,306; Ephraim 306; Ephrim 300
Knott, Francis 107
Knotts, Nathaniel 74,99
Knowles, Adam 228,281; Ezekiel 281,287; Thomas 277
Knowls, Adam 316
Knowlton, Joshua 127
Knox County 14,16,34,36,55,85, 121,294,299,304
Knox, Andrew 306,310; Hudson Titus 250; Joseph 276,302; Samuel 184
Koil, George 254
Kolly, Daniel 282
Komer, Mr. 180
Kompton, Thomas 55
Kook, Isaac 192
Koons, George 126
Koontz, John 307; Joseph 275
Kore, John 254
Kotts, Miss Pheby 118
Kouns, Peter 308
Kow, John 310
Krafft, Michael 73
Kraizer, Mr. 204
Krantz, Frderick 244
Krasst, Michael 73
Kratser, Samuel 88,203
Kratzar, Samuel 252
Kratzer, Sam. 205; Samuel 205, 206,213,242,244
Kreble, David 272
Kreddlebough, John 228
Kreysure, John 264
Krider, Capt. 276; Sergt. 8
Kroninger, John 315
Krozer, William 70
Krum, Christian 275
Krumbaugh, Peter 171
Kuchell, Calvin 57
Kuder, John 264; Valentine 46
Kue, Benj. 282; Ths. 282
Kunch, Mr. 42
Kunse, George 318; Jacob 318
Kuntz, John 183
Kurkereck township 301
Kuter, John 244,254,257
Kyle, Gabriel 282; Gabril 287; Samuel B. 163
Kyler, George 15
Kylor, George 107
LaCroix & Dubois 125
LaCroix, Joseph F. 125
LaFayette, Mr. 59
Lacassagne, Michael 15
Lacey, William 264,300
Lackie, Richard 120
Lacky, Andrew 160; Hans 160
Lacock, William 274,304,311,313
Ladd, Benjamin W. 287; Elison 296; Jacob 292; Joseph 275; Milton 267
Lafferty, Cornelius 253; Jane 306; Lydia 253; Neal 226,299; Patrick 28,318; Samuel 232; Widow 287,300
Lafontaine, Francois 298
Lahaw, David 84
Laing, Lewis 14,142
Lake, Asa 211
Lakes, Abraham 70
Lakin, Benjamin 146,257; Benjamin V. 233; John 158
Lalance, Peter 259
Lamar, Mark 16
Lamb's Tavern 148,192,196,202, 235
Lamb, Capt. 33,196,208(2),219,224 235,236,237,248(2); Capt. Joseph 74; Capt. William 128,

186(2),196(2),198,201; Capt.
  Wm. 207,220,224,237,243; Col.
  Joseph 137; J. 202; Joseph 82;
  Mr. 187,232; Sally 82; W. 230,
  233,234,244,250,254(2);
  William 87,182,189,201,202,
  217,218(2),220,221,228,238,242
  245,246,259,271,313; Wm. 182,
  185,209(2),242
Lambant, Daniel 180
Lamberson, Phillip 82
Lambert, Barnabas 209,218;
  Barnard 221; Benjamin 144;
  Daniel 19,42,57,66,121; James
  209; John 144; Mary 144
Lamen, Andrew 176
Lamison, Thomas 187
Lamme, Capt. Nathan 93; Elizabeth 69,78; Mr. 310; Nathan
  69,87,97,123; Robert 69,78;
  William 69,78,115
Lammer, Nathan 217,230
Lampher, David 91
Lampier, David 70
Lampkin, Lieut. Peter 74
Lampson, Amos 132
Lamson, Amos 132; Eleazer 132
Lamun, Joseph 265,266
Lanaway, Thomas 149
Lancaster 42,49,62,191,193,194,
  197,205,213,214,220,223,231,
  239,240,246,248,249,252,262,
  263,265,280,285,286,304,305,
  307,313
Lancaster County, Penn. 227
Lancaster County, Va. 285
Lancaster Road 281
Lancaster, William 230
Landers, Samuel 235
Landes, Martin 191,252,273;
  Samuel 284
Landis, Martin 308
Landon, Daniel 102; Elisha 101,
  117,136; William 137
Landy, Nathan 272
Lane, Aaron 48,51,66,78; Denis
  250; Doct. Josleph 142; Garret
  144,153; John 264,287; Joseph
  146,200,209,225,264,296,298,
  316; Samuel 63; Shadrack 63
Lanester, Charles 216
Lang, Jacob 74; Lewis 118
Langdale, Samuel 197,254,261,267
  300
Langdon, John W. 174; Rev.
  Solomon 311,317
Langham's Trace 149,293
Langham, Angus L. 256; Col. 189,
  196,220,242,261; Col. E. 248;
  Col. Elias 93,185(2),186(2),
  187,199; E. 33,43,49,70,179(2),
  181,182(2),183,188,190,192,194
  198(2),199(2),211(2),225,228,
  250,256,264; Elias 33,69(2),73
  94(3),95,96,97,101,103,104,
  105(2),106(4),109(3),164,185(2),
  188,191,194,199(3),200,201,206
  208(3),209(2),212(2),214(3),
  216(2),217,219(3),220,221,223,
  224(2),225(2),226,231,233,238,
  252(2),260(2),261,262(2),263,
  265,284,287,310,314,319; John
  S. 292; Lieut. Col. E. 189; Lt.
  Col. E. 198,210; Maj. 57,59,
  178; Maj. Elias 180; Mr. 36,
  37(2),38,(2),39(3),40(2),53,69,71
  108,109,122,131,181(2),198,226
Langley, Thomas 158
Langloir, M. 78
Langlois, Francis 73
Lanier, Doctor 142; Dr. James W.
  160; Maj. James 48
Lannel, Joseph 264
Lanpher, David 61
Lape, Henry 165
Laramore, Catherine 281; Samuel
  281
Larance's Mill 92
Lard, Col. 155; Mr. 155
Laremer, Mr. 178
Larew, John 60
Larimer, Ebenezar 252,292; Isaac
  301
Larimore, Samuel 278(2),289
Larison, George 122; Thomas 81,
  142
Larkin, Abel 314
Larkins, James 250,287
Larned, Ezekiel 45
Larrabee, Doct. John 310
Larrick, Jacob 280
Larrison, George 115(2),132,146;
  Thomas 170
Larsh, Charles 293,298
Larue, Abraham 78; John 146
Larwell, W.C. 234
Larwill, Joseph 154; Joseph H.
  278,296
Lash, Jacob 200
Lashmutt, E.N. 306
Lasselle, Francois 298
Lasserly, Neal 202
Lata, Moses 200
Latime, John 307
Latimore, Samuel 78
Latin, David 203,209
Laton, Joseph 55
Latta, Alexander 182; Moses 192,
  199,241,255; Mosses 282;
  Samuel 315
Lauders, Martin 287
Laughlin, William 178,197
Laughrey's Creek 80
Laughridge, William 302
Lauman, Barnet 300
Laurance, John 146
Laurel Creek 216
Laurence, John 250
Laverly, Alexander 178
Lavett, Capt. 276
Law, Stephen 141
Lawler, David 90
Lawnes, Betsey E. 282
Lawranceburgh 144
Lawrel, John 278
Lawrence, Calvin 137; Charity
  154; Frances 292; Francis 271;
  Francis E. 250; Frank 153;
  William 25
Lawrenceburgh 75,99,177,230
Lawrenceburgh 72,107,111,118,
  124,131,132,135,137,138,142,
  143,145,151,159,160,167,173,
  175
Laws, Robert 165
Lawsin, William 261
Lawson, James 253,278; Mr. 249;
  William 250
Lawwell, David 281
Lawyer, Jacob 310
Layman, David 51
Layton, Asher 283,302; Elias 241,
  283,302; Joseph 66
LeClerg, Francis 225
Leach, John 191
Leading Creek 267
Leamon, David 41
Leard, William 41
Leasner, Henry 137
Leath, John 267
Leather, Frederick 252,292,315;
  William 228

Leathers, Capt. John 170; John 23
Leavel, Benjamin 148
Leavell, John 264
Leavells, John 241
Leavitt, John 207,261
Lebanon 100,111,117,120,126,
  127,130,135,138,139,141,143,
  144,146,150,151,156,158,164,
  168,171,173,174,228,233,247,
  254,270,301,303
Lebanon township 135
Lebergar, Andrew 281
Lebey, John 267
Ledwick, Mr. 88,203
Lee's Creek 209,228,233,313
Lee, Allen 265; Charles 24; David
  70; Doct. Samuel H.P. 258;
  Doctor 249; Dunn 37; Ensign 5;
  Gerhana 161; John 9,42,112,
  201; Joseph 45; Lieut. 5; Mr.
  142; Peter 240; Samuel 41,66;
  Thomas 237; William 233,262
Leech, John 313
Leedham, William 269
Leeper, Allen 154
Leer, Miss Catharine 275
Lees, George 287; Samuel 170
Leesen, James 66
Leet, Abraham 141
Leeth, John 182
Lefever, Peter 141; Rachel 141
Lefiuvr, Francis 241
Legg, Charles 318; William 95,107
  112,117(2)
Leggett, Sarah 163
Legislature (see General Assembly, Assembly) 9,10,12,13,14,
  15,16,38,41,43,53,54,66,69,71,
  89,90,92,93,97,98,101,111,112,
  114,115,121,131,148,149,150,
  151,152,164,166,167,168,169,
  177,181,182,191,193,201,202,
  203,204,205,206,207,211,214,
  215,216,217,223,227,228,229,
  236,239,240,241,242,254,256,
  277,299,300,301,302,303,318,
  319
Lehman, Lyon 76
Lehre, Jacob E. 264
Leibert, Joseph B. 131,143,144,
  149; Sidney 144
Leiby, John 271
Leininger, Frederick 254
Leist, Andrew 296
Leitch, David 10
Leith, George 103
Leith, Jameson & Company 103
Leiven, William 243
Lelman, John 204
Leman, William 146
Lemasters, Isaac 142,161
Lemming, Thomas 293
Lemmon & Wilson 79
Lemmon Township 95,98,100
Lemmon, James 100; John 91;
  William 87
Lemmons, Samuel 257
Lemon Township 112,132,150
Lemon, John 119
Lemond, Martha 16,20; William
  20,67; Wm. 14,16
Lemun, Joseph 229,253
Lenard, Mary 260
Lend, William 146
Lennan, Francis 32
Lennell, Elkanah 297; Joseph 297
Lenton, William 190,192
Leonard, Abraham 212; B. 35;
  Barton 39,56,64,82; Charles
  221,228; Chs. 212; Mary 56,64;
  Moses 30,213,308; Nathaniel

273

Leppenneott, Samuel 228
Lerbert, Joseph B. 82
Leslie, George 173
Lesslie, Jonathan 264
Letart's Falls 229
Letart's township 235,259
Lether, Frederick 219
Letler, Elisha 287
Lettleton, Thomas 257
Levadoux, Rev. M. 74
Levenworth, Seth M. 175
Leves, Hugh 267
Levey, Christian 262
Leviney, Thomas 205
Levingston 251
Levingston, Miss Jane Ann 145; William 145
Levit, John 207
Lewell, John 275
Lewis and Clark expedition 148
Lewis, Abel 166,226,233(2),246, 248,268,273,274,279,288,294; Amous 4; Andrew 101,141; Benjamin 107; Caleb 289; Capt. 208,243; Capt. Merriwether 75; Capt. Thomas 5,8; Chas. 231; Col. Thomas 15; Daniel 136; David 101,203,283, 286,303; Frederick 190,192; Jacob 84; James 64,86,97,118; Jedediah H. 262,268,297; John 43,306; Joseph 56; Lieut. Col. P. 227; Mary 188; Mr. 131,146, 224,239,307; P. 166,279,283; Paul 127,146,203; Phil. 88; Philip 111,164,225,227,238,253 279; Sabra 268,297; Sarah 254; Stephen 287; Thomas 274,276; Tilgman 237; Tilman 188,221, 275; Warner 183,194; William 164,207,209,218,231,236,237, 238,247,261,262,263(2),264,273 279
Lewistown, Pennsylvania 222
Lewkins, Lieut. Jesse 15
Lewvell, John 257
Lexington 88,93,105,168,233,234, 277
Lexington Valley, Pa. 97
Lexington, Kentucky 14,22,48,73, 104,111,167,171,179,184,209, 210,216,235,254,297
Leybourne, Lieut. 60
Leyrand, Thomas 292
Libargar, Andrew 274,277
Liberty 238
Liberty Hall 105,114,122,123,125, 135,144,145,150,162,233,315
Liberty Town 237
Liberty township 155,238,240,247, 253,255,265,266,272,273,274, 282,283,284,291,301,302
Libey, John 265
Library 72,73,114,135,143,152,169 229,303
Library Society 256
Lice, Philip 49
Lick Run 20,268
Lick fork 237
Lick township 207,236,243,248,277 280,290,295,297,314
Licking 9,13,20,21,216,219
Licking County 272,277,284,297, 305
Licking Creek 188,190,218,247
Licking River 1,11,20,27,32,54,74, 130,139,193
Lieby, John 269
Liganier, Ruth Ann 155
Ligget, Alexander 86; William 275

Light Infantry 77,114
Light Infantry Company 49,50,51, 52,94
Light, Jacob 86,117; Mr. 43; Peter 35,57; Sheriff P. 72; Sheriff Peter 79; Squire 142
Lightfoot, Joseph 282
Lightner, Lucy 155
Lights, Jacob 77
Ligner, George 209
Lile, John 185
Lilly, Thos. 306
Lilver, Adam 60
Limestone 38,55,123,126,133,164, 178,181,185,186,190,193,219, 222,232,243,252,261,290,293, 308,309
Limestone Road 197,236,237,244, 277,294
Limestone, Kentucky 61
Liming, Gabriel 154; Joseph 247
Limpus, Enock 221
Limthecome, J. 11
Lin, John 169
Linch, Mrs. Jane 306
Lincoln County, Kentucky 4,14,89
Lindlay, Abraham 117; Isaac 117
Lindley, Abraham 42,77
Lindsay, A. 313; Andrew 271; Elisha 228; Thomas 23
Lindsey, Andrew 306; Francis 296; John 190; Oliver 303,308; Theophilus 16
Lindsly, Rev. Jacob 309
Line, Benjamin 58; David 164; John 30; Sarah 30; Solomon 142,170,253
Lineninger, Frederick 264,284
Lingard, Maj. 244
Lininger, Frederick 292
Linley, Jacob 115; Rev. Jacob 289
Linn, Alexander 271
Linnel, Joseph 154,257
Linsay, Stephen 99
Linsey, John 212; Stephen 66
Linton, Samuel 212; William 254, 285; Zachariah 275,285(2),295, 296
Linzee, Capt. Robert 223
Linzes, Andrew 282
Linzy, Stephen 78
Lion Tavern 243,271
Lionbuger, Peter 211
Lipscom, John 21
List, David 247; John 149
Lister, Nimrod 274,309
Litle, Hugh 221; Mr. 4,16
Littell, David 84,85; Samuel 154
Little Miami 1,140
Little Prairie 62
Little, Andrew 287; Benjamin 163; Cornelius 78; David 89; Doctor Squire 112; Ephraim 146; Grizel 146; James 233,267; John 121; Martha 233,237,306; O. 236; Samuel 306; Sarah 89, 132; Squire 97; Stephen 41
Littlejohn, William 257
Littler, Elisha 244,257
Livingood, Catharine 274; Jacob 274
Livingston 238,246,253,261,270, 273,276
Livingston County 124
Livingston, Andrew 303; Capt. John W. 75; Edward C. 244; Mr. 44,105,300
Lloyd, John 49; Joseph W. 139; Thomas 294,298
Loar, Henry 80
Lochery Creek 132

Lock, Andrew 29,76,88; Sally 88; Sarah 29; Thomas 237
Lockard, Elijah 206; Joseph 310; William 248; Wm. 221
Lockart, Robert 142
Lockhart, Byrd 311; Francis 309
Lockwood, David 205; Lieut. 15; Lieut. Ben. 21; Lieut. Benj. 10
Locus Creek 26
Loder, Benjamin 146
Lodor, Edward 70
Lodwick, John 225,289
Loffbury, Elisa 316
Logan's Gap 218
Logan, Anthony 112,318; David 18 127; James 161,272,278; John 272; Martha 233; William 44, 132,142,161,243
Logsdon, Joseph 43,56
Logue, Samuel 248,258,317; Sarah 248,258
Logwood, Thomas 221
Loller, David 41; Phebe 41
London 253
London, David 267
Londonderry 114
Long & Bretney 141
Long & Carr 141
Long & Conrad 141
Long & Mears 173
Long & Price 108,140
Long, Abigail 117; Andrew 300; Charles 78; Daniel 63; David 146,286; Edward 233,270,282, 310; Harman 108,140; Harmon 176; Harmong 146; Henry 128, 292; James 66,97,238,275, 292; Jockey John 124; John 254,300,308; Joseph 137,312; Long John 124,130; Miss Nancy 176; Mr. 119; Peter 273; Robert 192,292,300; Thomas 231; William 270,275,316
Longbrake, George 291
Longfelt, Israel 146
Longly, Miss Patty 164
Longshore, James 282; Mahlon 250
Longsvite, Samuel 261
Longworth, Nicholas 147,158,164; Robert 247
Looborough, David 192
Loofbourow, David 165
Loofbourrow, J.W. 221
Looker, Mr. 175,283; Othaniel 143; Othniel 125,147,159,160, 161,164,174,175
Loosberry, John W. 231
Loosborough, Doctor 122
Lootborough 99
Lord, Abner 315; Col. 156,157, 258; Joseph 165; Thomas 303
Lords, Col. 4
Loree, Solomon 132
Loremiers 32
Lorey, John 117
Loring, I. 61; Israel 147; John 166
Losey, Jacob 122
Lot, William 264; Wm. 247
Lott, Charles 275; William 250, 275
Lottery 152,153,155,156,157,159 160,255,256,260,270,273,274, 276,280,283,294
Louden County, Virginia 140
Loudon, David 91
Louisiana 96,117,118,124,166
Louisiana Purchase 213,220
Louisiana Territory 129,156,160
Louisiana Treaty 213
Louisiana expedition 213
Louisville 15,20,29,51,72,79,93,

352

195,227,243,244
Louisville, Kentucky 227,302
Loukes, Abraham 151
Lounsdil, James 217
Lourens, John C. 170
Loury, Fielding 150
Love, Abraham 244; George 34; John 275; Joseph 176; Peter 120,129,145(2),149,158,161,165 175; William 119
Lovelace, Barton 119
Loveland, Joseph 252; Mr. 230
Loveless, John 187,197,276; Joseph 257; William 276,310, 311; Wm. 316
Lovete, Elias 287,254,271,282; Sally 310
Low, Jacob 78; Jacob D. 86,303; Judge 143
Lowe, Jacob 11,58; Jacob D. 56,57 60,91,205; James 37; Judge 118
Lower Blue Licks 231
Lower, Henry 170
Lowery, Archibald 58; Thomas 69; William 81,83
Lowes, C. 135; James 37,38,58, 63,74,146,177
Lowler, David 132
Lowman, Barnet 306; John 8,239
Lownes, Hyatt 249; Mr. 236(2)
Lowrey, Archibald 152; Elizabeth 135,152; John 25; Mrs. Margaret 88; Nathaniel 105; Thomas 135; William 88(2),105
Lowrie, Lieut. 1
Lowry, Capt. William 314; David 21,163; Elizabeth 163; John 102; Mr. 93; Thomas 41; Wm. 89
Lowther, Uriah 244,292
Loy, Barbary 318; Mr. 130
Loyal Stock Creek 211
Loyd, Wood 292
Loyns, Morris 306
Lucas' ferry 231
Lucas, Abraham 306; Bosel 281; Brig. Gen. Robert 314; Capt. William 231; Col. Robert 305; Elizabeth 239,298; Gen. Wm. 126,236; J. 312; Jesse 281,293; Jessee 303; John B.C. 118; Joseph 87,91,203,205,207,239, 267; Joshua 293; Robert 194, 196,231,233,241,263; Samuel 285; William 19,213,239,292, 298
Luce, John 103; Robert 107
Lucket, Mr. 141; Samuel N. 267
Luckett, Dr. John M. 227
Luckins, Lieut. Jesse 25
Lucy's River 247
Ludlam, Smith 72
Ludlow & Company 134
Ludlow's Farms 25,42
Ludlow's Mill 81,89,90,96,97,98, 100,101,103,104(2),109,110,112 113,115,117,125
Ludlow's Station 2,7,9,12,18,24(2), 152
Ludlow's line 104
Ludlow's settlement 19
Ludlow's survey 77
Ludlow, Capt. Isreal 8,19; Charlotte 134; Charlotte C. 124, 156; Col. 78(2),93,129; Col. Israel 103; Cornet Stephen 118; Henry 99; Israel 12,16(2), 18,33,40,47,48,59,60(2),63(2), 75,79,80,88(2),94,95,101,102, 112,118,124,125,134,153,214;

Isreal 18,32; J. 52,180; John 1, 2(2),25,36,39,42,50,55,57,58,59 63,66,69,80(3),81,83,98(3),99, 100,115(2),124,126,127,134,137 149,153,180,199(2); Maj. 32,33, 34(3),35,51,199; Maj. Israel 190; Major 31,32; Maxfield 104,130,134,161,163,165; Miss Agnes 36; Mr. 1,13,37,38(2), 39(2),41,47,53,55,56,57,69,71, 181(2); Sheriff John 4; Stephen 70,137; W. 50; William 37,39, 41,48,55,58(2),98,99,106,119, 135,138,139,141(2),144,146,151 152(2),161,162,165(2),170,172; Wm. 98,216
Ludon, William 58
Ludwig, Daniel 253(2),257(2),270; George 257; John 214,258,264, 298
Lues, Nicholas 250
Luke, Asa 212; Francis 100; Samuel 157
Lukens, Capt. 60
Lukes, Abraham 48
Lukis, Samuel 206; William 206
Lull, Lieut. Jesse 75
Lum, John 142
Lumber Yard 143,153
Lummis, Joseph 19,21; Mr. 36
Lunbeck, Margret 275
Lund, John 180
Lundbeck, Henry 250
Lundy, Lathan 221
Lupton, Rachel 219; Solomon 228
Luse, Robert 101
Lusk, John 187,237; Patrick 212; Sally 121
Luthers, John 41
Luttrell, Lewis 219,306
Lutz, Jacob 231,262; John 245
Lyassert, Philip 237
Lybrand, Samuel 237,250,304,305
Lydle, Robert 107
Lyle, Andrew 32; William 32
Lyman, Capt. Cornelius 76; Capt. Cors. 75
Lynch, Charles 68; Edward 82; Jon. 248; Jonathan 252; Mr. 88,203
Lyndon, Mr. 15
Lynes, Rev. William 156; William 106; Wm. 142,165
Lyon & M'Ginnis 48
Lyon Tavern 44,224
Lyon's mill 51,55
Lyon, James 94,115,136,165; John 31,44,49,50,51(2),66,70,97,117, 124,135(2),137,150,152,156; Jonathan 112; Jonathan W. 143 Lieut. James 9; Mary 142; Mr. 39; Nathaniel 154; Sally 165; Samuel 135,137,161; Solomon 58; Stephen 25
Lyons, Bogardus 151; James 5,132; John 53,54,265; Mr. 168; Sally 112; Solomon 106; Thomas 300; Timothy 165
Lytle, Andrew 58,70,78,86,238(2); Col. 107,143; Col. William 144; Col. Wm. 241; Edward 168; Gen. 171; Genl. W. 282; John 211; Mr. 181(2); Robert 137, 303; W. 50,52; William 43,49, 78,80,94,95(2),96,140,150,180, 190,194,197,200,213,225; Wm. 133,168,180
Lyttle, John 98; Robert 132; William 165
M'Adams, John 129(2); Mr. 73; Thomas 78

M'Adow, Doct. 275; Doctor 184; Dr. Samuel 186,192; Samuel 71,192,193,241
M'Afferty, John 206
M'Allester, John 121
M'Allister, Daniel 73,194; James 293; John 293
M'Alpine, George 234
M'Ance, David 137
M'Ansay, Dan. 10
M'Apherson, Robert 275
M'Arther, Daniel 209; Mr. 148
M'Arthers, Peter 154
M'Arthur, Col. 261(2); Col. D. 275; Col. Duncan 253(2),270; D. 131,199,224,231,254; Donald 300,310; Duncan 94,111,162, 164,168,,183(2),188,192,194, 196,198(2),201,202,203,204,208 213(2),215,225(4),226(2),228, 237(3),238,239(2),240,250,255, 256,258,260(2),262(3),263(2), 264,265,270,274,278,280,282, 288,292,293(2),294(3),295(2), 297; Gen. 295,298; Gen. Duncan 281,291,295(2),299; Maj. 111,194,208,209,226,235, 239,243,249; Maj. D. 210; Maj. Duncan 185,186,208,224,225, 236; Maj. Gen. Duncan 270,285 Mr. 164,182,239,240,262(2); Peter 297
M'Atthur, John 247
M'Aully, Henry 228
M'Axter, Daniel 206
M'Ay, Alex. 228
M'Beath, Andrew 275; Joseph 170
M'Beth, Alexander 177
M'Bride, Andr. 286; Richard 229, 286; William 212,275,292,296, 305,316
M'Cabe, Archibald 22; James 70; John 9,69,78,87; William 194, 229,315
M'Cafferty, James 285; John 187, 244,255
M'Cain, William 99
M'Cale, John 195
M'Call, Capt. 82; Capt. Hugh 63; James 285; Rebecca 121
M'Calla, James 297; William 297
M'Callester, Alexander 164
M'Callum, S. 315
M'Calmont, Isaac 55
M'Cammon, Isaac 175
M'Can, George 275; John G. 266; Robert 277; William 12
M'Cance, David 76,117,152
M'Candless, Wm. 313
M'Candlish, John 184
M'Cane, John 102
M'Cann, William 101; William 35
M'Cannon, John 15
M'Cardell, Thomas 5
M'Carran, Barney 30,91
M'Cart, Andrew 250; John 249
M'Cartney, Alexander 196; James 237,296
M'Carty, Benj. 318; Capt. Jonathan 121; Enoch 311; Jonathan 99; Joseph 302; Patrick 55,95, 107,142
M'Cary, John 170
M'Cash, David 140,151
M'Cashen, James 22,65,69,87,103, 115,163; John 79(2); Maj. John 144; Mr. 193
M'Cashin, John 162
M'Cashing, John 113
M'Casland, Henry 200
M'Causlin, Thomas 265

353

M'Caw, David 95
M'Certney, James 300
M'Chesney, John 51,137
M'Chord, James 306,316
M'Cish, Jas. 228
M'Ckaaihn, Daniel 281
M'Claen, John 265
M'Clain, Archibald 300; Forgus 58,301; Frank 15; Hugh 70,200; John 78,87,89,212; Joseph 300; Levi 31
M'Clair, James 316
M'Clanburgh, John 245
M'Clane, Alexander 251; Allen 78; John 22,78; Peter 150
M'Clarin, William 268
M'Clary, Capt. 74(2); Capt. Jn. 109; Capt. John 75; Isaac 294; John 215
M'Clasky, Lettice 74; William 215
M'Clave, William 165
M'Clean, Alexander 292,310,316(2) Allin 70; Archibald 306; Catharine 97,100; Hugh 234; Jno. 123; John 70,154,213,217, 239,243,246,248,253,256,265, 266,316; Levi 46,73,97,100,106 152,153,162
M'Cleary, John 206
M'Cleland, Wm. 46,48
M'Clellan, David 267; Doctor 119; Robert 160; W. 83; William 28, 103,119; Wm. 151
M'Clelland, Frances 184; H. 136; Hugh 134,162; James 45,70,86, 89,91,99,139,294; John 216; Joseph 184; Mr. 136(2),138,144 147,148,153; Robert 61,64,190; Thomas 32,45; William 50,52, 58,64,98,120,126,128,148,156, 173,207,238; Wm. 80,82,100
M'Clellon, Hugh R. 297
M'Clenaugh, John 184
M'Clene, Jeremiah 280
M'Clenehan, John 187
M'Clennan, Joseph 200
M'Clentock, Alexander 237
M'Clernand, Dr. J. 216; John 215, 216
M'Clerry, Robert 251
M'Cleve, George 58
M'Climmons, John 182
M'Clintick, Alexander 226,254; Martha 292
M'Clintock, Alex'r. 247; Alexander 244,251; John 63; Joseph 282; Thomas 254; William 197
M'Clish, Thomas 189
M'Closkey, Elizabeth 82; James 82,298
M'Cloud, Mr. 138,245
M'Cluchy, Isaac 141
M'Cluer, James 251,291
M'Cluney, William 182
M'Clung, Charles 301,306; Charter 234; Hon. Judge 69; William 140
M'Cluny, Wm. 19
M'Clure, Benj. 212,316; Benjamin 58,203,311; Capt. 276; D.R. 33; Daniel 62,69; David 74,119; Doctor 17(2),24,27; Doctor Robert 41,45,55,60,74; Dr. 8; Dr. Robert 66,88; Hugh 17; J. 29; James 15,23,48,70,80,81, 83,107,118,159,164,215,216, 221,265; Jonathan 264,285(2); Miss Margarat 247; Mr. 131; R. 4,6(2); Richard 121; Robert 8, 10,28,37(2),46,50(2),52,53,68, 77,86,87(2),92,95,100,202;

William 86,98(2),99,101,106, 175,214(2); Wm. 98
M'Clury, Michael 37
M'Coll, Solomon 289
M'Collaster, Thomas 309
M'Collister, Mr. 184
M'Colloch, Samuel 281
M'Collock, Andrew 232; Sam. 94, 208
M'Collom's Inn 92,130
M'Collom, Hugh 38,90,91,92,94(2) 130; Mr. 59; R. 61
M'Collough, Mr. 230
M'Collum, Hugh 51; Thomas 289
M'Comas, James 260
M'Conall, James 192
M'Conico, Christopher 219
M'Conkle, William 291
M'Connel, Dennis 287; James 192; John 109,206,225,231,238,241, 253; Polly 247; Robert 214; Samuel 296
M'Connell, James 200,254; John 164,187,215,243,287; Mr. 131; Robert 318
M'Connico, Christopher 221
M'Cord, David 91,162; Samuel 250
M'Cormac, Francis 99
M'Cormack, Effe 212; Esse 212; F. 30; Francis 29,48; George 267, 300; James 100,142,170; John 58,108; Samuel 160,244; Thomas 70; William 212
M'Cormic, Francis 175; Mr. 177
M'Cormick, George 271,295,306; James 48,191; John 20,37,146; Samuel 138,263,292; Thomas 32; William 316; Wm. 306
M'Cort, John 306; Mr. 258,259,273 279,293
M'Coskry, Doct. William 23; Doctor William 55
M'Court, Mr. 261,266,268,272,286, 306
M'Coy's mill 209
M'Coy, Angus 21; Capt. 92,208, 214; Capt. Joseph 189,199; I. 200; J. 305; John 180,183, 186(2),189,193,198,209,219,222 226,232,239,246,251,253,255, 258(2),278,289,298,308,312; John 298,308,312; Jos. 286; Joseph 181,200(2),218,230,287, 292; Mr. 8,188,191,197,201, 202(2),204(3),207,258,259,265, 266,272,276,281; Thomas 193, 250,255,276,287,291,307; William 201,219,230,237,247
M'Crackin, Miss Jane 278; Thomas 275
M'Crary, Archibald 142
M'Craw, Samuel 222
M'Cray, Archibald 112; Martin 40; Samuel 74,82,102
M'Crea, Gilbert 78; Robt. 2
M'Creary, James 250,251; Robert 249
M'Cuiel, John 241
M'Cullagh, John 26,29,34(2),44,50 53,55,85,87,92,101; Thomas 24, 26,28; Thos. 29
M'Cullah, Robert 102
M'Cullaugh & Son 107
M'Cullaugh, Jno. 61; John 63,67,76 86,91; Mrs. 113; Sampson 63,91 Thomas 67
M'Cullick, William 193
M'Culloch, Wm. 280
M'Cullock, George 253; James 230; Judge 135; Mr. 190; Samuel 217,230

M'Cullok, Robert 251
M'Cullom, Hugh 79,100,161,175; John 154; Mr. 78,135; Mr. H. 31
M'Cullough's Mill 128
M'Cullough, John 13,19,27,37(2),42 55,60,146,153,217,257,287,296; Lawson 286; Miss Patty 163; Mr. 115,124; Mrs. 144; Pat. 104; Sampson 127,154; Samuel 115,132,156,266,282; Tho. 170; Thomas 72,101,128,136,145, 156,294,318; William 57
M'Cullum, Hugh 38,39,183
M'Cune, David 264; John 55; Joseph 225,269; Joseph K. 317; Margaret 225; Miss Kezea 237; Mr. 69,88,203,207; Mrs. M. 264; Thomas 69,111,164,191, 204(2),277; William 264
M'Curdey, Andrew 285
M'Curdy, Daniel 45; John 45
M'Curr, James 238
M'Cutchan, John 291
M'Cutchen, Alexander 269; John 247,251; Robert 235
M'Cutcheon, Capt. Samuel 93; S. 219
M'Daniel, Enock 310; George 301, 302; Rowland T. 150
M'Dannel, George 273; Henry 212
M'Deed, Edward 221
M'Dermett, William 161
M'Dill, J. 267; Jacob 206; Joseph 250; Robert 272,310
M'Donald's Mill 118
M'Donald, Archibald 14,171,178, 200,237,264,292; Capt. 261(2); Capt. J. 275; Capt. James 278, 279; Capt. John 261; Col. John 295; David 315; James 166,190 192,197,200,216,264,288; John 8,182,188,190,199,200,209,210, 213,237,241,249,278,288,292, 297,305,311; Lemuel 51,52,67; Michael 314; Mr. 147,252; Thomas 178,192(2),209,237,250 253,300,310; William 188,215, 256; Wm. 300
M'Donnald, Daniel 100
M'Donnald, Capt. James 316; Rhodah 14; Thomas 183; William 183; Wm. 269
M'Donnel, John 146
M'Donough, Edward Hart 282; Edward Hunt 284
M'Dougal, George 216; J. 184;202; James 215,256(2),282; John 167,178(3),179(7),180(3),181(3), 182(3),183,185,186,188(2), 189(2),190(2),195(3),197(2),199, 201(2),202,203,204(2),205,206, 207,210,211(2),212,222,223,224 226(5),227,228,231,233(2),234, 237,245,248,256(3),259(2),262, 269,282(2),285,288,289(3),293, 298,301,309,311,315; Mr. 166, 239,250; Stephen 262,272,284, 297
M'Dougall, G. 69; Geo. 239; George 69,191(2),214,298; John 178(2),187,191,193(2),195,198, 207,208; Mr. 192
M'Dougle, John 83
M'Dowe, Dr. 215
M'Dowel, James 241; John S. 16
M'Dowell, Dr. John 92; Easter 211; Esther 92(2),210; James 233; Joshua 121; Matthew 91; Miss 208; Miss Esther 207; W. 257,266; William 263,299; Wm.

253,276
M'Dowll, Samuel 209
M'Dugal, John 111,147; Joseph 142
M'Elhany, Robert 121
M'Elhenny, Robert 113
M'Elheny, Robert 24
M'Elheran, Daniel 203
M'Elhiney, Sam. 15
M'Elvey, Daniel 131
M'Elwain, David 244
M'Entire, William 191
M'Ewin, John 107
M'Faddon, Daniel 264,283; Mr. 283
M'Fadon, Alexander 46
M'Fall, John 138
M'Farlan, William 79
M'Farland, Capt. 96(2),100; Capt. Robert 287; Capt. William 78, 82,96,102,201; Daniel 178,187, 231,244,251; James 63,228,231 Jean 163; John 142,259; Mr. 119,123,148,187,188,191,195, 203; Robert 296; S. 122; Samuel 182,215,271; Sheriff William 128; Stephen 151, 152(2),157,160,162; T. 108; Th. 171; Thomas 42(2),73,74,77,79, 86,87,106,107,112,117,124,147, 154,161,163,171,172,202; Thos. 87; W. 172; William 36,56,74, 76,79(2),80,83(2),84(2),87(4),88 90(3),94,96,99,101,103,106,108, 109,111,121,124(2),126,127, 133(2),134,135(4),136,138,139, 143(2),145(2),147,149,151,152, 159,165,184,206,217,221,223, 224,251,253,255,257,259,270, 286,294,303,312,315; Wm. 39, 77,103,124(2),128,134,138,145, 146,177,181,230,239(2),242,243 244,245,247,249,270,276,278 291
M'Farlane, Henley 12
M'Farlin, Maj. John 35
M'Farling, Jashua 219; Joshua 212, 282
M'Farran, Andrew 138
M'Feear, Robert 306
M'Ferson, Robert 267
M'Ferston, Robert 318
M'Gance, David 76
M'Garrah, William 210
M'Garvin, James 48; Sergt. 8
M'Geary, Henry 297
M'Gee, Col. Thomas 45; Joseph 57; William 154
M'Gehan, Barney 65; Tempy 65
M'Gennis, Robert 33
M'Gibben, William 300
M'Gibbons, Richard 200
M'Gill, Arthur 15; Christopher 117,167; James 203,206; Rebecca 167
M'Gilliard, John 63
M'Gines, James 268
M'Ginnes, Barnard Robert 27; Edward 74; James 95,107,135, 154; Mary 102; Mr.227; Robert 292; Robert 74; James 91,162, 200,212; John 209,212; Mr. 48, 110; Robert 66,99,300; William 66
M'Glaughlin, James 308; William 308
M'Gowan, Charles 266,314,319; Elizabeth 266
M'Gowen, William 194
M'Gowin, Wm. 7
M'Graw, Dominicus 41
M'Greary, Henry 265
M'Grew, John 69,78,89

M'Grig, William 250
M'Guffin & Hittle 170
M'Guire, Jonathan 154; Robert 231
M'Hargh, John 316
M'Harry, Alexander 184
M'Hary, Robert 184
M'Hatton, James 66; John 66,132
M'Hendrick, Alexander 59
M'Hendry, James 75; Joseph 72,75 83
M'Henrey, Mr. 50
M'Henry, Francis 245,256,259,275, 292; Joseph 22,57,70,71,73,74 145,146; Mr. 79,175; Samuel 162,174,175; Widow 160
M'Hory, Daniel 306
M'Illeree, Jenny 306
M'Ilroy, Daniel 310
M'Ilvain, David 282; James 288; Mr. 243; William 292
M'Intire, Alexander 202,315; Andrew 283; John 69,84,103, 242,276,313; Mr. 157,183; Nathaniel 142,161; Thomas 12, 58; William 96,209,313
M'Intosh, Mr. 234; William 48,112, 282
M'Intyre, Wm. 235
M'Kane, James 107
M'Kay, Robert 74,102,217
M'Kean, Daniel 20; James 60; Joseph 32; Mr. 42
M'Kee, Alexander 73; Andrew 285; Hon. Samuel 282; James 57; Joseph 213,216,303; Mary 146; Ruthy 60; Samuel 75,165,271; Sarah 176; Wm. 176
M'Keen, John 264
M'Keene, James 63
M'Keever, Capt. James 93; James 219
M'Kefferty, John 237
M'Kelvy, James 190
M'Kenney, D. 262,272; Daniel 238, 260; Ephraim 200; John 244
M'Kennie, Josiah 180
M'Kenny, John 200; Josiah 231
M'Kentire, Alexander 253; Benjamin 253; John 253
M'Kernan, Patrick 15,18
M'Kibbon, Mr. 293
M'Killip, Widow 310
M'Kim, Jane 271; John 257,267, 271; Margaret 251; Polly 267
M'Kiman, Miss Jane 275
M'Kiney, Cain 285
M'Kingle, Pesse 275
M'Kinley, Joseph 284; William 265; Wm. 235
M'Kinness, George 306
M'Kinney, Danl. 284; James 310; John 191,318; Mr. 303; Thomas 318
M'Kinnie, Josias 219
M'Kinnis, William 100
M'Kinnor, Daniel 170
M'Kinsey, Duncan 303; James 170; Jesse 282
M'Kinzey, John 251
M'Klewer, Samuel 300
M'Knight, John 98; Robert 294
M'Konkey, Mr. 293
M'Kown, Alexander 296; James 296
M'Lain, John 190,206,254,275,287; Joseph 306
M'Lanburg, Lieut. John 189
M'Lanburgh, John 228,229,240,280
M'Landburg & Candlish 179,182, 191,193,195,196,201

M'Landburg, Mr. 273
M'Landburgh & Candlish 178,180, 185,194,201
M'Landburgh, John 215,220,224, 227,253,259,266,272,290,299, 300,312,318; Mr. 268
M'Landish, William 206
M'Lane, Capt. Daniel 124; Jer. 223(2); John 180,260(2),261,262 263(3),264,305
M'Laren, William 290
M'Laughlin, A. 190; Alex. 212; Alexander 50,71,73,182,187, 192,193,194(2),201,204,211; John 164,212,244,252; Mr. 131; William 41,278
M'Lean, Allen 69; Allin 87;
M'Lean, Archibald 316; Charles 243; Jer. 178,183; John 69,87, 203,228,251,290,303; Levi 29, 32,33,38,39,56,68,73,173; Mrs. 38
M'Leise, James 271
M'Lene , Gen. Jer. 276; Gen. 160, 242,262; Gen. J. 262; Gen. Jeremiah 245,270,273,290; J. 192,228,278,315; Jer. 179,184, 189,198,210,211,217,221,244, 245,253,277,278; Jeremiah 71, 73,87,164,185,188,191,192,193, 194,199,201,202(2),203,207, 224(2),225,226,236(2),239,246, 261,262(2),263(2),265,266,279, 286,302,304,312(2); John 187, 194,213,236(2),238(2),239,249, 250,262; Lieut. John 189; Maj. 208; Maj. Jeremiah 185,186, 235; Mr. 177; Patrick 256
M'Leod, John 5
M'Lernand, John 219
M'Lernard, John 228
M'Lintock, Alexander 310
M'Lone, Samuel 228,254
M'Loughlin, Alexander 21; James 21
M'Luaghlin, John 111
M'Machan, Maj. 6(2); William 292
M'Mahan, Francis 89; James 271, 316; John 110,187; Joseph 29, 51,63,82,110; Rbt. 212; Robert 267,275,296
M'Mahen, James 300; Robert 184; William 247,
M'Mahon, Robert 203,210,221,306; Simon Cray 199
M'Maken, John 304; Joseph 86
M'Manis, James 315
M'Manus, Patrick 247
M'Meal, John 231
M'Mechan, John 114
M'Meead, Dan 15
M'Meeker, Benjamin 228
M'Meerice, William 228
M'Mehan, Robert 187
M'Meker, Patrick 129
M'Mellon, Mr. 181; William 181
M'Micael, Dan. 21
M'Micheal, Mr. 18
M'Michel, James 192
M'Mickle, James 194; Peter 282
M'Millan, Constance 106; Mr. 37, 38(2),39(2),55(4),56(2),57(4), 59(4),60(2),93,122,181,198; Robert 142,154; Samuel 132; W. 83; William 3,5,7,8,44,46,48 50(3),53,60,61,64,74,80(2),81, 91,93(2),94(2),95,96,97,106, 117(2),123,181,182,188,209, 209(2); Wm. 50,78,80,81,83
M'Millen, Mr. 37; William 2,199; Wm. 208

M'Millin, Thomas 257
M'Million, John 316
M'Mullan, William 96,97
M'Mullen, Alexander 206,269; John 296; Joseph 298; Mrs. 174; Rev. Samuel 174; Robert 107,112,128,135
M'Mullin, Alexander 197; Edward 273; French 269; Hugh 302; John 228,251,298,302; Mrs. Maria 269
M'Mullon, John 185
M'Mum, William 219
M'Munn, Samuel 244,264,275,280, 282; William 233,237,254,280
M'Murdie, Adam 178
M'Murtry, Samuel 265
M'Mustrie, Robert 221; Simon 221
M'Nabb, John 157
M'Naghten, Thomas 307
M'Naman, John 197
M'Namar, Philip 233
M'Naughten, Neal 317
M'Naughton, Pat 8
M'Neal, John 233,251,269,271,314; Rees 287; Thomas 287,307; Thos. 302
M'Neale, Benjamin 285
M'Nealy, James 127
M'Near, Lewis 271
M'Neel, John 280; Joseph 317
M'Neele, John 310
M'Neely, G. 318; James 147(2),154 318; Robert 132; Sarah 147
M'Neil, John 292
M'Neill, Reese 306; Robert 251
M'Neille, John 306
M'Nemair, Michael 82; Rev. Richard 82
M'Nemar, John 209
M'Nenar, Philip 247
M'Neonar, Elizabeth 250
M'Nicoll, Mr. 110; Peter 158
M'Night, Mary 56
M'Nut, James 281
M'Nutt, Alex. 175,244,245; Alexander 127,136,161,175,284; James 224,254; John 175(2)
M'Nuttey, William 275
M'Onnell, James 261
M'Pherson, Capt. 243; James 94, 208; Jas. 103,222
M'Quady, John 127
M'Quality, Jane 283; Owen 283
M'Quilkin, Samuel 283
M'Quitty, Samuel 259
M'Rea, Lieut. William 10
M'Roberts, John 92
M'Vay, Benj. 215
M'Vicker, Duncan 77
M'Whorter, Doctor R. 106; James 173
M'Whorton, John 300
M'Williams, John 200,207; William 200
M'Worter, John 228
Mabee, Barthotlomew 219
MacKenzie, William 254
Macala, Edward 307
Macan, J.G. 185,238; John G. 180(2),184,189(2),198,199,200, 201,207,208(2),211,212,217,223 224,231,233,242,257,273,282, 295(2),296; Mr. 185,199
Macbean & Poyzer 104
Macbean, William 73
Macbin, Jno. 36
Maccgee, John 306
Macconnel, James 2,4(2),6,7,9
Macdoniel, William 231
Mace, Edward 251; Jacob 271

Machesney, John 121
Machey, Andrew 267
Machin, Jno. 36
Machir & Eynon 11
Machir, John 11,211,263
Mackelwaine, William 6
Mackey, Alexander 161; George 200; Robert 282,306
Mackhenry, Isaac 306
Mackin, Charles 183
Macklain, Gen. John 257
Macklin, Jacob 299
Macky, James 21
Macomb, Lieut. Alexander 75; Lt. Alexander 70
Macon, Mr. 77; Nathl. 166
Macy, Obid 206
Mad River 15,18,21,27,37,39,41,45 48,51,55,70,74,78,81,83,85,86, 91,93,94,95,99,111,113,115,120 132,137,146,164,181,187,190, 195,197,200,206,207,208,210, 215,219,220,221,223,229,230, 240,246,248,273
Mad River Road 27,46,62,65,95, 103,112,116,139,144,199
Mad River settlement 53,245
Mad River township 106
Madden, Susannah 287
Maddison, John 306
Maddus, David 296
Madearys, Benjamin 151
Madison County 8,303,311,318
Madison County, Kentucky 154
Madison township 280,290,291,295 302
Madison, James 85(3)
Mages, Mary 37
Magill, Arthur 227
Magovney, James 214
Magrew, John 112
Magruder, Allan B. 124
Maham, Samuel 317
Mahan, Patrick C. 62
Mahany, John 25
Mahard, John 66,68,94,100,108, 115,116(3),118,120,136,156,159 160,163(2),168(2),171; Judge 173
Mahin, James 231; John 251
Maholam, Sally 197
Mahon, William 70,102
Mahoney, Mr. 47,54
Mahony, John 35
Main Eagle Creek 52
Main Street 38,67,79,101,113,120 122,125,130,133,140,142,155, 158,159,162,165,166,172,173, 174,176,209,292
Maine, Sergeant Thomas 55
Maise, John 221
Major, William 86
Malcory, Mr. 319
Mallon, Adam 267; Francis 209; Samuel 215
Mallory's survey 293
Mallott, Daniel 222
Malon, Mr. 251
Malone, Frances 307; Francis 206; Hartley 307; James 251; Richard 200; Samuel 206
Malony, Polly 94,207
Malson, Jacob 149
Maltbie, Benjamin 92
Man's Lick 29,39,47,86,143,147, 254,264
Man's Lick, Kentucky 15,72
Manara, Maj. 208
Manary, Gen. James 291; James 213,312,313(2),314; Maj. 213; Maj. James 185,214; Mr. 315

Manchester 39,178,183,185,187, 192,200,206,210,212,218,238, 245,247,249,274
Manchester, Virginia 235
Maning, Elisha 282
Maniville, Patrick 122
Manly, John 306
Mann's Lick 67,168
Mann, Jesse 306; John 69; Miss Eliza 185; Miss Nancy 253
Mannan, Cornelius 271,282
Manneg, Reuben 187
Manring, Jordon 308
Mansefild, John 41
Mansfield 278,296
Mansfield, Gen. 136,159; Jared 244,249; John 97,172; John F. 147,172,277; John L. 306; Mr. 165
Manson, Capt. John 107; John 149; Thomas 137
Mantle, John 196,200(2),209,212, 215,240,269; Mr. 201; Polly 212
Mantua maker 144,163
Manvil, Eli 297
Many, Lieut. James B. 64
Mapes, James 98; Mary 68,82
Maracle, Capt. 276
Maranda, James 98,106,115,130
Marandy, James 108
Marandy, James 60
Marcell, Mr. 141,162
Marcus, William 200
Mare, Edmund 275; Henry 285
Margues, Isaac 309(2),316
Marietta 4,9,31,40,47,53,56,61,93, 109,110,135,139,147,149,152, 154,155,156,169,175,181,182, 183,190,193,197,204,217,218, 222,223,225,226,228,229,240, 241,242,243,256,258,263,278, 280,300,315
Mark, Peter 306
Markan, William 74
Markel, John 232
Markelin, George 168
Market House 62,66,103,110,117, 122,124,141,143,196,197,266, 293
Market Street 158
Markham, George 244
Markland, Garah 161; John 305; Jonathan 32,51; Wm. 306
Markle, George 82; John 315
Marks, Capt. Peter 238; Conrad 46(2); Jacob 284,285; James 241,244,264,267; Jno. 284; John 285,293; Lieut. Hasten 5; Lieut. Hastings 5; Mr. 135,243; Peter 251,287
Marple, Mr. 177
Marquis' mill 220
Marquis, Christopher 288
Marschalk, Capt. Andrew 15
Marsh, Chauncey 117; Daniel 124, 183; Darius 37,134; Israel 97; Jeffery 50; John 63,86; John Squire 32,37,41,60,66; Judge 124; Mary 63; Mr. 38; Samuel 144; Sarah 97; Serren 121; Serring 86; William 192
Marshal, Henry 132; John 124,129; Libius 54; Mr. 125
Marshall, A. 235; A.K. 270; Andrew 198,200,203,214(2); Archibald 14; Capt. Thomas 316; Ellis 187; Henry 152; Ichabad 187; Ichabod 91,237; Ichabud 187; James 294(2); John 41,147,166,293; Lebeus

38; Libius 56; Mary 255; Miss Jane 176; Rev. Robert 102; Samuel 294; Sergeant John 37; William 166,218,222,237,255
Marster, Andrew 21
Marsters, Sarah 117
Marston, James 91
Martain, Capt. 81
Marthau, Ichabod 206
Martin & Boyd 316
Martin, Abia 29; Abiah 37,81; Absalon 23; Adam 174; Alexander 58,86,94,99,159,207; Ann 78,176; Capt. 197; Capt. Samuel 68,153; Catharine 88; David 234; Doctor 187; Dr. James 221; Elijah 198,200; Evi 161; Fielden 279; Francis 170; Hugh 269; Hugh R. 298; Hutson 311,313; I. 50; Isaac 2,3,15,36 37,38,41,48,58,81,88,117,137; Jacob 205; James 82(2),91,112, 127,176,186,228,237,254,269, 284; James T. 148; Jere. 216; Jeremiah 200; John 93,139,147 148,158,201,241,252,273,275, 283,288(2),298,313,316; Joseph 95,192,274; Joseph J. 261; Joseph John 292; Luther 167; Maj. Thomas 74,168; Mary 99; Moses 74; Mr. 36,38,56,95,100, 101,120,181(2),193; Reuben 23; Richard 82,95,102; Robert 141, 161,170,287; Roger 84; Samuel 32,57,99,102,136; Samuel G. 96 107; Thomas 253,293(2),296; William 13,209,300,304; Wm. 234
Martindale, Moses 146; William 99
Martins, Samuel 296
Martinsburg, Va. 248
Martion, Robert 107
Marts, Capt. Wm. 14,21; Lieut. William 5,12; Lieut. Wm. 12
Marvin, Seckel 111
Masapotamia 197
Mash, Aaron 71; Sirran 117
Mason County, Kentucky 7,8,11, 13,16,108,133,142,212,217,223, 232,233,238,239,273,277
Mason's Mill 49,51,52
Mason, Armistead Thompson 106; Benjamin 145,158,170; Capt. 52; Dorsey 264; Dossie 237; E. 264; Enoch 267; James 57,101, 214; John 228; Sam 92; Stephen 265; Thomas 55,161; William 18,23,60,64,82,244,247 292,310; Wm. 300
Masonic Society 105
Masons (see Cincinnati Lodge) (see stonemasons) 1,22,26,32, 132,140,142,155,157,166,253, 266,299,311
Massac 204
Masses Creek 173
Massete, John 282
Massey, Henry 59; Lieut. 5(2); Samuel 318
Massie & Sterret 271
Massie Creek 246
Massie's Creek 96,100,220
Massie's mills 114
Massie's old Station 311
Massie, Abraham 264; Ann 211; Betsey 211; Col. 196,199,204, 206,216; Col. N. 36; Col. Nathaniel 59,180,200; Doct. Thomas 282; Gen. 164,175, 229(2),246,250,254,261(2),262, 263,290,295(2),312; Gen. John

45; Gen. Nath. 221; Gen. Nathaniel 225; General 114; H. 219,247(2),275; Henery 249; Henry 65,71,178,183,186,189, 192,198,199(2),204,205,207,209 217,218,219,223(2),236,241,251 252,272,278(2),279,290,293,304 John 211; Maj. Gen. Nath. 215, 218,221; Maj. Gen. Nathl. 234; Miss Charlotte 241; Mr. 37(2), 38(2),39(3),40(2),54,56,84,103, 109,122,160,162,181,182,186, 198,265; N. 70,262(2),278; Nath. 92,93,94,95,96,101,103, 104,105(2),106(2),192,199,206, 214,216,217,219,229,231; Nathaniel 45,69,84,86,87,89, 103,106(2),108,110,120,160(2), 164,166(3),167,181,199,200,202 203,206,214,216(2),223,225(2), 226(2),229,250,252,253,255(2), 256,260(2),261,262(3),263(2), 264,265,270,272,277,280,294, 295,296,297,302,303(2); Nathl. 244,292; Thomas 287; William 211
Mast, John 169,269
Masters, Andrew 18,25; Benjamin 200; James 251
Mastin, Charles F. 303; Elizabeth 282
Mates, Stephen 194
Mather, Joseph 263
Mathers, William 200,201
Mathew's survey 266
Mathews, Gen. George 215,256; J. 278; James 163; John 186,220, 222,225,227,236,238(3),239, 248,267,269,271,275,277,281, 289; Joshua 310; R. Lott 262; Revd. John 251; Thomas 305; Thos. 308
Mathies, John 216
Matson, J. 134; James 177; Jane 134; John 58(4),119,124,125, 126,128(2),134,139,159
Matt, James 254
Matten, Elias 234
Matthew, George 221; William 13
Matthews & Scofield 220
Matthews, Dr. 186; Gen. Geo. 297; George 56; Increase 317; James 56,90,102,104,154, 265; John 12,57,154,164,187, 216,293,294,297; Thomas 99, 153; Tom 157; Wm. 26
Matthias, Henry 284
Mawthews, David 282
Maxon, James 297
Maxville, William 87
Maxwell, Charles 242(2); Hamilton 192; J. 205; John 95,173,194; Mr. 91; Robert 69,78,247; Thomas 277,281; W. 1,2,4,7,12, 13(2),14,16,20(2),21(2),23,24; William 1,16,28,39,58(2),78(2), 86,87,91(2),202,205,216,311; Wm. 16
May's Lick 238
May, Andrew 60; Elizabeth 70; Henry 112,268,300,306; James 69,186,191(2),215,220,247,254, 298,300; John 206; Mr. 234
Maybee, Bartle 200
Mayberry, Richard 78
Mayer, Mebeker 244; P. 15
Mayes, James 241
Maynard, Doctor Stephen 293; Dr. Stephen 276; Stephen 268,297
Mayo, D. 118; Daniel 16,24,25(2), 37,45,61(2),88,89,94,95(3),101,

103,119,139; Mr. 93; Nathan 37
Mays, John 182
Mayson, Dorsey 294
Maysville 200,233
Mcafee, Joseph 264
Mead, E. 293; Miss Betsy 236; Richard E. 292
Meade, David Suth 203; Edward 225; Richard E. 167,256; Richard K. 231
Meaden, Alfred 306
Mealman, Andrew 227
Meann, G. 231
Means, Philip 167; Robert 219,221 231,257,279
Mears, John 86; Mr. 173
Meason, Isaac 298
Mechanics 143,163,167
Mecutchen, John 244
Mede, Everard 193
Medearies, William 142
Medford, Charles 264,267; John 237
Medical Springs 107,219
Medill, James 244
Medsker, George 80,197,304; Jacob 180
Meed, John 84
Meek, Alex. A. 143; Alexander 112; Hugh 23,78,135,147; John 238; Robert 299; Silvester 15
Meeker's Hall 286
Meeker's tavern 158,232,264
Meeker, Cochran & Company 30
Meeker, Abner 182,194,196,232, 233,251,298; E. 261; Elizabeth 3; F. 254,263; Forrest 158,243, 246,251,254,272,290; John 3,5, 137; Joseph 103,275; Mr. 231, 236; Samuel 280; Wheeler 310
Meeks, Alex. A. 174; Alexander A. 163; Capt. Edward 184;Edward 65,87,104,124,150,166,173,174; Isaac 213; John 248; Mr. 88, 203; Samuel 235
Meesty's Mill 49
Meeting House 76,79,98,126,152, 183,240
Mefford, Mr. 72
Mefseck, Nathan 244
Megate, John 210
Megath, Thomas 318
Meggitts, John 281
Meggs, Col. 140
Megie, Benjamin 60,63,66; Joseph 66
Megs, R.J. 65
Mehony, John 13
Meiggs township 228
Meiggs, Return Jna. 91,205
Meigs township 260,268,269,272 274,276,277,285,287,289,291, 301,303,312
Meigs, Col. 160,164,175,313; Col. Jonathan 192; Col. R.J. 181, 319; Col. Return J. 21; Gov. Return Jonathan 177; Hon. Judge 60; Hon. Return J. 280; Hon. Return Jonathan 186; J. 219,258; John 221; Judge 59, 140,147,149,187,188,197,204, 262,263; Mr. 38,39(2),40,53,122 162,175,176(2),181(2),265,314 R.J. 53,172,213,261,265(2),278; Return J. 109,159,166,167(2), 174,177,198,206,215,216,249, 256,261,262,263,281,314,318, 319; Return Jonathan 53,54,87, 102,143,159(2),164,166(3),167, 175,177,181(2),182,203,206,217 248,261,312

Meldrum, G. 239; Geo. 78; George 74
Melick, John 121
Meliorn, Henry 254
Mellheny, John 161
Melligan, John 69
Mellott, Elizabeth 91
Melone, James 285; Richard 291
Melony, Patrick 12
Melvin, Jonathan 154; Noble 266
Memberger, G. 46; H. 46
Memminger, Capt. 64
Menard, Pierre 121
Menary, Gen. James 301; James 210,246,255,288; Maj. James 245
Meniceir, Francis 48
Menissier, Brother 155
Mennefee, Jarret 181
Mennesier, F. 39; Mr. 39,40,161
Mennesiers, Francis 31; Mr. 32
Mennessier's Hotel 59
Mennessier, F. 92; Francis 115; Mr. 59,103,157,171
Mennessiere, Mr. 65
Mennessieres, Mr. 84
Mennessiers, F. 53; Francis 36,48; M. 78
Menshal, Jonathan 284
Menshall, Ellis 238
Mercer County 107
Mercer's Inn 158
Mercer, Capt. 21,36; Capt. John 148; Go. 225; John 8,50,65,73 75,87,111,112,153,171,172,227; John F. 79; Jonathan 95,99; Mrs. 158,165,171(2); Mrs. S. 170; Susan 171,172; Susanah 153
Merchant 3,6,20,21,55,85,88,110 112,114,120,124,130,135,143, 145,148,153,156,164,175,184, 185,193,194,203,205,219,234, 241,249,251,253,278,285,289, 302
Merchant, Ad. 233; Nathan 291
Merchants 1,2,4,9,10,16,20,28,31, 33,38,56,79,103,178,226
Mercier, John 138
Meredth, David 306,310
Merener, Asa 310
Merewether, James 293
Meritt, Moses 200
Mermaid 231
Merret, Hezekiah 279
Merrie & M'Nicoll 110
Merrietta 223
Merrill, James 93; Samuel 255
Merrit, Daniel 200; Jesse 70
Merry, Ebenezer 303; Pullyman 18 William 150
Mershal, Henry 8
Mershon, Benjamin 277; Solomon 277,303; Timothy 234,277
Merwin, E.B. 266
Meryman, Joshua 117
Messack, George 267; Nathan 267
Messenger, David 297
Messick, Lewis 294,301; Sergt. Jacob 46
Messicks, George 271; Nathan 271
Mesteck, Nathan 244
Mestine, John 188
Methodist Church 252
Methodist Episcopal Church 211, 317
Metholgy, Chief 34
Meyer, Daniel 315
Meyers, Nelchor 209
Mezzura 183
Miami 10,16,21,25,55,95,99,107, 112,126,129,165,170,171,177, 192,195,196,216,226,229,230, 243,280
Miami Baptist Association 123
Miami County 159,160,164,165, 170,172,309
Miami Exporting Company 89,92, 93,94,95,101,103,108,118,119, 136,139,143,146,148,153,158, 159,164,171,172,207,291
Miami Military Lands 1
Miami Mill 163
Miami Purchase 9,10,24,29,35,102, 124,129,175
Miami River 14,16,20,21,22,23,25, 26,28,29,30,31,32,34,35,36,37, 38,39,40,41,42,43,44,45,46,47, 48,49,51,52,53,55,56,59,60,61, 62,63,64,65,66,67,68,70,71,72, 74,75,77,78,79,81,82,83,84,86, 87,88,89,90,91,92,93,94,95,96, 97,99,100,101,102,104,106,108, 109,112,113,114,115,116,117, 118,119,120,121,122,123,124, 125,126,127,128,129,130,132, 133,134,135,136,141,142,143, 146,147,148,153,154,155,158, 159,161,162,163,164,165,171, 187,198,206,218,232,240,243, 246,247,249,251,252,254,258, 262
Miami Township 30,57,73,93,119, 146,161,173,176
Miami University 302,303
Micheal, Lieut. John 18
Michel, Joseph 134; Kisiah 134; Martha 292; Peter 228; Robert 254
Michigan 156
Michigan Territory 114,116,125, 156,164,239,291,298
Mickel, Peter 63
Micker, Abner 231
Mickey, Andrew 275; Daniel 226
Mickinson, Andrew 230; Thomas 230
Mickle, Peter 195,244
Mickles, Daniel 251; Peter 250
Mickneal, John 251
Micks, Isaac 231
Middle-Town 83
Middlefield 224
Middlesex County 60
Middleton, E. 282; Eleanor 296; John 234; Mrs. Eleanor 295; William 74,190; Wm. 314
Middletown 9,27,84,101,106,107, 135,141,144,162,169,223
Mielimans, John 287
Miers, Andrew 142; George 275, 306
Miexer, Ezekiel 154
Mifflin township 261,266,274,280, 283,286,289,294,299,301,302, 309,314,315
Migic, Joseph 91
Milbury 240
Miler, Michael 287
Miles Ferry 107
Miles, Colin 146; John W. 118,129, 130,170,171; Joseph 170;
Micheal 257
Milford 134,247,257
Milford township 162,173,176,246
Miligan, James 197
Milikin, Daniel 164,303
Milin, Joshua 264
Milis, Hope 65
Military 1,2,3,8
Military school 159
Militia (see Dragoons, Light Infan-try, artillery) 4,7,29,31,32,33, 35,36,37,42,46,68,77,78,80,81, 82,93,94,96,97,98,100,102,104, 105,106,107,109,110,114,116, 117,119,120,121,122,123,125, 126,127,128,131,137,138,139, 140,145,148,156,158,160,169, 170,173,177,186,190,198,206, 207,210,213,215,216,218,221, 227,234,235,244,255,260,261, 262,263,268,270,273,274,276, 278,285,290,291,292,305,311, 314
Militia school 157
Mill Creek 9,19,20,21,22,24,26,27, 29,30,32,33,34,35,36,37,38,39, 40,42,43,44,45,48,51,53,54,55, 59,60,63,65,67,68,69,70,71,74, 75,77,78,81,84,85,86,88,89,90, 91,95,99,100,101,102,104,107, 108,110,112,113,116,117,121, 122,125,127,132,133,134,137, 139,141,142,143,144,145,146, 147,148,149,151,152,153,154, 155,157,159,161,162,163,164, 165,166,168,171,172,173,174, 176,177,184,249,
Mill Creek Farm 44
Mill Creek township 174,176
Mill wright 109,114,248,251
Millar, Abraham 254,271,301,316; Barbara 282; Cornelius E. 308; Elizabeth 254,295; Ichabod B. 126; Jacob 247; James 300, 302(2),303,316; Jn. W. 299; Jno. W. 295; John 257,295,300, 306; John W. 251,308,316; Justice 294; Moses 67; Phelix 257; Thomas 310; William 212, 292; Wm. 221
Millbank, Charles 251,254
Millbanks, Charles 275
Millcreek 78
Millcreek Farm 31
Milleasey, Henry 300
Millegan, Hugh 300
Millenee, Dudley 287
Miller's Bank 186,224
Miller's Bottom 228
Miller, Abel 242; Abraham 130, 134,254,269,279,286,287; Adam 315; Alexander 69; Anthony 287; Benj. 196,199; Benjamin 197,221,272,276,277; Bill 209; Capt. 5(2),23,42(2),43; Capt. Edward 33,51,55,66,149; Capt. James 15; Charles 296; Christian 286; Conklin 78; Conkling 121; Cornelius 299; Daniel 129(2),275; Ed. 102; Edward 63,102,124,272,294; Edward W. 127; Eli 161; Elias 117; Elizabeth 319; Ensign 196; Ezra 121,132; Frederic 177; Frederick 7,304; George 53,54; George F. 133; Henry W. 107, 127; I.B. 3,6,25,32,50,59,98(2) 108,126,128,147;Icha. B. 106(2) Ichabad B. 51; Ichabod 25; Ichabod B. 35,98,106,115,214; Isaac 210; J. 238; J.B. 64,101, 214; Jacob 102,117,132,146, 170(2),221,226,244,272,279, 301; James 10,18(2),102,142, 145(2),239,269,297,318; Jesse 296,306,310; John 4,8,10,23,41, 58,107,121,139,155,159,161, 173,187,219,228,235,244,245, 250,251,260,267,274,275,285, 293,297,319; John W. 219; Joseph 231,260,271,272(2),279,

280,288,298,299,304,308,315(2)
Justice 223,228; Justis 231; M.
52,180; Marama 241; Martin
176; Matthias 170; Micheal 264
Moses 50(3),66,69,78,80,180,
199; Mr. 25,69,99,183,196,250,
294; Nancy 107; Oveler 10;
Polly 228; Robert 265(2),291,
318; Samuel 251(2); Samuel B.
127; Sarah 70,159,173; Stephen
132; Thomas 58,117,285,318;
West 24,280,295; William 52,
228,272; William M. 217; Wm.
24; Wm. M. 272; Worrick 274
Millers 1
Millersburg 225,233
Millford township 168,290
Milligan, George 275; James 99,
206,221,271,275; John 69,84,
111,191,203,213,222,238
Milligen, Hugh 271; Samuel 280
Millikan, Jesse 296; John 285
Millington, Peter 219,237
Millone, John 287
Mills & Dunn 129
Mills 21,24,28,29,30,31,33,34,35,
36,37,38,39,40,42,43,45,46,47,
48,49,50,51,52,53,54,55,56,57,
59,60,61,62,63,64,65,66,67,68,
69,71,72,75,76,77,79,81,82,83,
84,86,87,89,90,91,92,93,94,95,
96,97,98,100,101,102,103,104,
107,108,109,110,111,112,113,
114,115,117,118,119,120,123,
124,125,126,128,129,130,131,
132,133,134,138,140,141,142,
144,145,146,147,148,149,151,
154,155,156,159,162,163,164,
165,166,168,171,173,174,175,
176,177,183,185,186,190,191,
193,194,196,197,202,204,207,
209,210,211,216,217,218,219,
220,221,223,225,227,228,229,
230,237,238,239,240,243,244,
245,247,250,251,252,253,254,
261,262,263,264,265,268,273,
277,278,280,285,289,305,312,
316
Mills, Benj. 269; Capt. Wm. 21;
Charles 212,214,253; Col. 156;
Delaun 261; Hope 30; Isaac 10,
21,58(2),72,73,75,79,143,147,
149,177,261; James 206; John
55,154; John R. 29,30,40,47,50,
62,66,69,80,81,82,87,88,89,94,
107,116,120,123,126,132,165;
Lieut. Isaac 118; Lieut. John
R. 32; Maj. 24; Maj. John 3,21;
Major John 23; Peter 112,164,
176,244,267,288; Pritchett 271
Richard 190; Sally 69,71,120,
193; William 154(2),264; Wm.
24,172
Millwright 60,69,209,212
Milton 153
Milton, Joshua 267,271
Minack, Frederick 271
Mineos, Elizabeth 282
Miner, John 224
Mines, James 310
Mingo Village 243
Mingo nation 94
Minguy, Henry 236; J.P. 236
Ministers 15,18,21,25,31,33,34,37
38,39,40,41,43,44,45,50,51,53,
54,55,60,63,64,65,66,68,70,71,
74,76,77,79,81,82,86,90,92,94,
96,99,101,102,105,110,111,113,
115,122,130,135,136,137,139,
142,143,145,146,150,151,152,
153,154,156,157,160,163,164,

169,170,174,175,176,179,181,
183,188,191,192,195,197,199,
200,205,210,211,221,222,223,
228,229,241,243,244,245,247,
248,250,251,252,256,257,258,
259,263,264,267,270,275,278,
282,284,286,287,289,295,296,
297,300,305,306,309,311,312,
313,316,317
Minner, Richard 137
Minnis, C. 231
Minor, Gideon 293; Isaac 303;
Stephen 132
Minshal, Hannah 296
Minshall, Hannah 310; Jonathan
311
Minthon, Jacob 112
Minton, Jacob 107
Minturn, Jacob 230,231
Miranda, James 140,166; Phebe
140
Mirega, John 271
Mires, Henry F. 293
Misneer, Henry 107
Misner, Henry 117; John 112,132,
161
Mississippi River 73,95
Mississippi Territory 72,109,183,
188
Misslenburgh 6
Missouri 183
Mitchel, Charles 285; D. 278;
Daniel 161,278,282,295,303;
Gaven 317; James 203; John
246; Martha 259; Mathew 244,
251; Robert 5,20,21; Samuel
209,278,295; Sylvenus 297;
Thomas 263,292; Wm. 180
Mitchell, Daniel 161; David 269,
287(2); Edward 304; F. 63;
Graney 194; James 183,184,
197,212,259; Jane 230; John
187,221,238; Judge Wm. 272;
Martha 306; Mr. 7,73; Robert
10,17,18,20,233; Samuel 318;
Susanna 180; Sylvanus 297;
Thomas 200; William 37,163;
Wm. 30
Mitchson, Jane 120
Mitten, Joshua 292
Mitzker, Lieut. George 189
Mixer, Ezekiel 170; Isaac 241
Mixwell, Valentine 86
Mobray, William 251,275
Moffet, Solaman 272
Moffett, James 310
Moffit's mills 261,264,289
Moffitt's Mills 285
Moffitt, John 228; Joseph 294;
Soloman 264
Mofford, Thomas 301
Mogan, Jacob 126
Moier, Christian 111; Elizabeth
111; Henry 111
Moler, Jacob 307; Martin 307
Molston, Francis 127; Nicholas
127
Mone, Joseph 200
Monett, Doctor 254; Doctor Samuel 295,317; Dr. Samuel 308;
Mr. 283; Rev. William 286; S.
278; Samuel 277,279,283,288,
293,294(2),295(2),297
Mongommery, William 63
Monnett, Abraham 237
Monroe, Alex. 311; Dr. Geo. 293;
Jonathan 308
Monrow, Moses 316
Montanye, Abraham 45,65,69,136;
Montayne, Abraham 74; Abrm. 75
Montfort, Henry 123

Montgomery 92,93
Montgomery County 91,97,98,99,
103,105,111,119,123,129,130,
131,132,133,135,137,140,142,
148,153,157,159,161,164,167,
168,205,207,215,223,233,239,
243,253,258,298,303
Montgomery County, Kentucky 63
256,257
Montgomery township 295
Montgomery, Col. William 89;
Hugh 206,233; Humphrey 187,
197; Humphry 187,212; James
55,56(2),61,70,82,117,164; John
183,185,275; Robert 103;
William 244
Montony, Isaac 264
Montreal, Canada 103
Mood, Coonrod 241
Moody, John 310
Moois, Conrod 196
Moomaw, Philip 231
Moon, James 110
Mooney, James 250,267,303; John
182,311; Mary 18; Samuel 18
Moor & Kanedy 268
Moor's mill 145
Moor, Charles 104; Elizabeth 243;
Furgu 183; Henry 269; James
101; John 289; Levi 78; Mrs.
280
Moore & M'Clelland 134,136(2),
138,144,147,148,153
Moore's Mill 141,163,164
Moore, Aaron 218,313; Abner 112;
Adam 173,174,175; Adeline
174; Alexander 142; Andrew
240; Benjamin 82; Bustard 138;
Capt. 243; Charles 55,115,138,
170,206; Cornelius 137; Daniel
91; Easter 310; Enos 299;
Fergus 199,201,207,218,236,
260; Furgus 265; G. 82; Hannah
100; Henry 10,251,254,302;
Hosea 91,205; Hugh 110,124,
125(2),129,130(2),132,134,135,
137,141(2),142,143,144,152,
153(2),154,156(2),158(2),160(2),
162,163,164,172; James 66,110
170,237,240,260,264,272,275,
284,292,293,294,305,306,313;
James F. 48; Jane 154; John
107,243,289,318; Joseph 244,
250,254,257,274,286(2),289,292
301,302,309,310,315; Lawrence
137; Levi 68; Lydie 132; Maj.
135,242,243,245; Major 262;
Margaret 295; Michael 277;
Miss Martha 36; Mr. 63,65,67,
122,257; Mrs. 295; Mrs.
Eleanor 146; Nancy 228;
Nathaniel 82; Nicholas 291;
Patrick 11,19,27,28,29,129,138
141; Peter 241,247,284,296;
Phillis 305; Robert 18,23,171,
240,269; Samuel 51,57,62,100,
121,138,141,298; Thomas 46,47
48,50,125,169,219,259,269,282;
W. 202; William 12,102,103,222
265,271,295,296,300,306,314,
316
Moorefield 234
Moorehead, Moses 95; Robert 99
Moorhead, Moses 203; Robert 132
Moots, John 184
Moran, James 103
Moravian Indians 303
Mordock, James 161
More, Henry 293,294; William 264
Morean, John 251
Moreford, Cornelous 257

Morehead, Moses 198
Morelan, William 276
Moren, Mandwelle 282
Morfoot, Catherine 17; George 8, 17,20; Katherine 20
Morford, John 217; Thomas 297
Morgan Settlement 92
Morgan fork 283
Morgan township 294
Morgan's fork 257,274,286,289,309 315
Morgan, Az 316; Capt. Richard 170; Charles 14,45,82; David 246; Gen. 210,293; Jacob 129, 146; John 243,244,296; John E. 282,296; Jonathan 110,285; Moses 11; Pallace 221; Richard 154; Thomas 247,251; William 190,296
Morgantown 195
Morgon, Charles 63
Morhouse, Reuben 78
Morial, William 257
Morin, Roadham 50
Moringo, Mary 306
Morison, Alexander 303; Ephraim 34
Morral, Wm. 306
Morrass, Richard 231
Morrel, Calvin 3,8,30,58,73; Doctor Calvin 74,96
Morres, Fanny 248; Ralph 248
Morril, Doctor 117
Morris Town 39
Morris, Benjamin 127; Cavliea 132; David 30,116; Dr. David 117; Ezekial 292; Ezekiel 218, 271; Fraze 89; Frazer 78; George 244; Isaac 48; James 212,221,244; John 23,142,154, 172,254,284,289,291; Joseph 292; Joseph F. 242; L.R. 75,76; Mark 195,227; Mr. 57,75,85, 177,283; Preslay 288; Richard 251,252,257; Robert 81,132, 218; Thomas 30,44,53,57,159, 177,179,203,212,219,244,252, 303
Morrison, A. 222; David 165; Duncan 200,216,276; Ephraim 37,318; Hans 102; Isaac 154; J. 146; James 4,33,48,74,140,146, 203,233; John 300,306; Joseph 233; Robert 296,314; Samuel 78; William 37,233,305
Morrow, Alexander 316; Elizabeth 19; J. 50,52,69,81,83,180; James 19,172; Jer. 79,80,277; Jeremiah 23,41,52,70,74,78,80, 84,86(2),87(2),90,93,94(2),95,96 97,98,103,106,107,109(4),142, 143,145(3),147,151,155,168,173 174,175,180,192,199,202,207, 208(2),209(2),225,226,252(4), 279(2),280,312,313(2),314(2); John 132; Mr. 69,84,93,108,136 137,138,175,177,224,246(2),248 249(2),250(2),272,280(2),300, 311,313; Richard 25
Morse, Chancy 137,142; Chauncy 107; Joseph 66
Morsman, Susanna 258,259; William W. 258,259
Morton, John 267; Joseph A. 292
Morvin, Pecket 228
Mosbey, Mrs. 37
Moseley, Benjamin 134; Thomas 161
Mosley, Samuel 267
Moss, Bethamy 316; Chancy 132; Samuel 149; William 158,163

Mosser, Abraham 279,290
Mostker, Jacob 221
Mote, John 311
Mott, Josiah 10,24,27(2)
Moudy, Peter 161
Moules, Walter 135
Mouney, Joseph 91
Mounot, Stephen 192
Mount Pleasant 2,101,136,145
Mount Sterling 256
Mount Sterling, Kentucky 187
Mount Vernon 135,136
Mount, Samuel 154; Widow 65
Mountain, James 223
Mountjoy, Col. John 37; John 139; Wm. 293
Mounts, Asa 214,220(2),222(2),315; Jesse 219,282; Joseph 271; Reuben 315; Rev. Jesse 200; Thomas 142; William 81
Mountz, Jesie 257
Moura, Christian 209
Mouser, James 228,231,244; Peter 231; Thomas 244,257
Moutfort, John 32
Mow, Samuel 146,149
Mowbray, William 300,316
Moyer, George 318; Henry 126; Jacob 192
Moyers, Samuel 203
Mtgomery, Hugh 310
Muchmore, Samuel 83,92,93,126, 129,145
Muddy Creek 32,41,65,67,110
Muddy Praira 191,195,201
Muddy Praire 207
Muddy Priari 197
Muhlenberg, Frederick Augustus 62
Muhum, Issachar 112
Muin, James 171
Muir, William 10
Mulberry Street 231,258,289,308
Mulenburgh, Peter 293
Mulford, Benjamin 112; Caleb 65(2); Daniel 102
Mull, George 258
Mullen, George M. 267; Isaac 241; Michael 187
Mullin, Alexander 221; Charles 198(2); Dan. 212; Isaac 86,121; Jane 198; John 102
Mumford, Charles 78,197
Mun, James 215
Mundel, Jonathan 51
Munen, Samuel 58
Munger's Settlement 92
Munger, Capt. Edmund 41,60; Edmund 41; Jonathan 37
Munn, David 212,268; James 208, 212; Maj. James 221
Munro, Robert 234
Munroe, Amos 33; Charles 33; Col. J. 177; Mr. 23
Munrow, Amos 38; Charles 38; Soloman 192
Munsell, Levi 2,8,21,26; Mr. 5(2)
Munson, Augustus 297; Ephraim 23 Ephram 18; Jeremiah A. 255; Jeremiah R. 297(2); Jesse 297(2); Sergt. Ephraim 15
Murdach, James 25
Murday, John 253
Murdock, John 154
Murfey, William 7
Murfy, Levina 169; Samuel 169
Murphey, Asa 307; David 279,306; James 251; John 155,193,252
Murphy, Benjamin 213,315; David 269,295; Dennis 193,295; Gabriel 247; Isaac 170; James 244,257,264; John 219,311; Joseph 161; Recompence 319; Thomas 311; William 273,274
Murrander, James 231
Murray, A. 293; Andrew 25; D. 98; Miss Jeny 275; Mr. 300; William 304
Murry, Charles 71
Musard, Ami 161
Muselman, Henry 271
Musgrave, Moses 142
Musgrove, John 162; Miss Nancy S. 273; Moses 163,167; Nancy 163
Muskingum 183,187,188,190,192, 210
Muskingum Academy 197,222
Muskingum County 111,131,164, 216,222,224,226,227,232,233, 241,245,246,248,252,260,268, 269,272,273,274,277,279,280, 281,285,286,288,290,291,294
Muskingum River 193,277
Muskingum Salt Works 216,303
Mussard, Arnie 253
Musselman's mill 228,229
Musselman, Daniel 221,234,237; Henry 205,211,212,215,229,281 286,291
Mussleman, Henry 301,309
Mussulman, Daniel 316
Mustard, William 200,274,278,289
Mutes, Conrod 250
Muzzy, Anna 220; Nathan 220
Myer, Christian 105,223; Joseph 232; William 244,254
Myers, David 102; George 306; Henry 55; Jacob 1,210; John 165,170,192; Jonathan 161; Joseph 271; Martin 218; Nancy 232; Samuel 200,285,287; Widow 116
Myles, John 290
Myns, Samuel 285
Myres, George 310; Henry 245
Nabb, Charles 29
Nagle, Jacob 200
Nail factory 87,104,260,271,315
Nail makers 139
Nail manufactory 141,195,243,245
Nailer, John 12
Nailers 304
Nain, John 126
Nall, Martin 128; Peter 318
Nanary, James 244
Nancarrow, Eliza 56; John 29,30, 102,114,115; Miss Polly 135; Mr. 102
Nanhook, Samuel 262
Nap, Moses 154
Napp, Thomas 254
Nash, John 142,146; Letty 146
Nashee & Denny 173,280
Nashee, George 278
Natches 41
Natches, Henry 142
Natchez 32,35,37,39,49,59,62,72, 76,78,89,93,100,124,141,155, 176,193,234
Natten, Simon 169
Nawles, John 264
Naylor, John 51
Neal, John P. 238,287; Levi 132; Patrick 247; Ruth 172; Thomas 121; William 172
Nealy, John 81
Neave, Jeremiah 167
Nebecker, Lucas 251
Nebeker, George 244; Lucas 271; Lukes 244
Nebergal, Jacob 271,292

Necker, John 41
Need, George 90
Needham, Mr. 232,240,242;
    Thomas 224(2),227,238,243,246
    294,302
Neel, James 73,78,307; John 217,
    248
Neff, Adam 234; Christian 244;
    Cornelius 307; Henry 234;
    Leonard 241,247
Negro (see slaves) 4,5,7,13,264,
    297
Neilson, Joseph 307; Thomas 233
Nellson, Abraham 227; James 227
Nelly, Benjamin 48
Nelson 248
Nelson County 216
Nelson County, Kentucky 72,188
Nelson's Station 5
Nelson, David 215; George 200;
    Jane 89; Joel 74,121,161,170;
    John 102,290,293;John Garrett
    244; Joseph 86,117,134,170;
    Miss 202; Mr. 5; Ross 247,295;
    Samuel 54; Thomas 120;
    William 54
Nelzle, Henry 287
Nesbit, David 15; J.E. 243; James
    Irwin 152,318; William 123,318
Nesbitt, David 40
Ness, Harmond 209
Nest, Neal 270
Nettleville 29,30,117
Nevel, Mr. 232
Nevell, Benjamin 197; Henry 213,
    317
Nevil & Nancarrow 102
Nevil, Henry 272; Jethr. 213;
    William 102
Nevill, Henry 232,256,260; Jetho
    244; Jethro 137,201; Mr. 249,
    314
Neville, H. 305; Henry 298; Presly
    313
Nevious, Sergeant Peter 48
New Ark 216,230,242,277
New Lancaster 188,192,194,195,
    198,205,206,210,214,215,217,
    227,239,294
New Lisbon 232,312
New Lisbon Academy 303
New Madrid 92
New Market 41,45,47,194,198,199,
    200,201,202,205,206,207,209,
    212,213,218,223,241,247,249,
    251,254,258,260,286
New Market township 80,197,222,
    261,268,269,273,283,286,302
New Orleans 180,207,241,256
New Port 11,27,116,218
New Port, Kentucky 253,281
New Station 2
New Town 37,40,42,45,85
New-Market 199,297
New-Port 1,16
New-Town 26,133,150
NewTown 92
Newark 205
Newby, Pollard 132
Newcom, Elijah 294; George 168;
    Maj. Mathew 130
Newcomb, George 239
Newcome, George 72,79(2),83,130
Newcomer, Peter 132
Newcommer, Peter 112
Newcumber, Peter 95
Newel's town 216
Newel, John 142; Wm. 241
Newell's Town 215
Newell, Benjamin 206,218; John
    150; Leazen 150; Samuel 170

Newhum, George 206; Mathew 206
Newkirk, Barnabas 150; Henry 252
    Reuben 252; Tunis 290,292
Newland, Jacob 272; Joel 103,222
Newman, George 62,64,67,70,144;
    J. 53; Jacob 278,292,296; John
    282,287; Joseph 31,62(2),64,67,
    70,75; Mr. 22,32,46,53,65,79,82
    William 2
Newmarket 158,170
Newmarket road 217
Newmen, Mr. 37
Newport 11,14,22,24,25,26,27,28,
    29,44,45,48,55,61,87,90,93,95,
    111,136,158,167,168,187,195,
    215
Newport Academy 45,104
Newport Horse Races 162
Newport, Kentucky 79,134,145,
    148,151,154,155,156,157,167,
    174
Newport, Thomas 91
Newsome, George 73
Newspapers 180,202,252,266,268,
    278,307
Newton township 274,305
Newton, Sina 227
Newtown 24,25,32,44,47,59,75,79
    82,129,137,140,165,169
Newtown Library company 169
Niagara 74
Niblack, Col. 250,260; Lieut. 196;
    Lieut. Col. Wm. 227; Samuel
    241,290,297; W. 230; William
    182,197,214,217(2),218,225(2)
    226,236,241,252,268,280,295,
    314; Wm. 182,211,220(2),222,
    223,224,226,229,232,248
Niblick, William 195
Nibuchar, Lucas 223
Niceleson, Henry 287
Niceley, Abraham 225
Nicels, Baly 306; Daniel 306
Nicewanges, Peter 199
Nichelson, Charles 161
Nichlas, Daniel 244
Nicholas County, Kentucky 180
Nicholas, Andrew 247; Christain
    282; Doctor John 241; Francis
    262; John 262; Mr. 45; Nathan
    148; Nathaniel 146; Samuel
    247,276
Nicholl, Austin 142; John 86
Nichols, Balace 241,248; Bolace
    238; Daniel 234; David 42; Eli
    275; Francis 294; John 102,272
    279; Nathan 68; Nathaniel 234;
    Peter 296; Samuel 307; Sarah
    310; Thomas 310,318;Tounsand
    271; William 282
Nicholson, Henry 254; James
    165(2),172; Joseph 252; Mr.
    193; Robert 256; Simon 161;
    William 187; Wm. 244
Nickans, John 292
Nickels, James 117
Nickelson, Henry 271,296
Nickins, Moses 259
Nickls, William 316
Nickols, John 189
Nicol, Matthew 142,170; William
    267,275,300
Nicols, Samuel 243
Nicum, Micheal 316
Nief, John 146
Nigh, Jacob 315
Nihell, Daniel 132
Nile township 260,262,272,287,291
Nimmo, Gen. 149; J. 98,100,101,
    109,113(2); John 94,97,104,105
    108,111,120,122,123,124(3),125

126,128,141,146,148,151,152(2)
    153,155; Judge 151,167,168; M.
    63,65,67,85,98,100,101,105,
    109(2),113(2),152; Mathew 128
    Matthew 69(3),75,78,83,84,87,
    89,94,96,97,103,104(2),105,
    108(2),110,111(3),113,115,116,
    117,119,120,122,124(2),125,126
    130,132,136,137,148,149(2),
    151(3),152,165,167,173,229,233
    Mr. 113,152,153,168; Mrs. John
    142
Nine Mile Creek 61,113
Nisbet, James 117; Thomas 280,
    290,291
Nisbett, Hugh 161
Nisewonger, John 253
Nivergall, Jacob 287
Nixon, Allen 112; John 306,316;
    William 302
Noble, Elizabeth 41; Henry 19;
    James 162; Jonathan 254,256;
    Mary 306; Seth 280; Thomas
    41,48; William 128
Noe, Andrew 170
Noel, Jacob 277; John 313; Peter
    218,292
Noels, Thomas 277
Noggle, Isaac 271
Noills, Peter 298
Noker, Richard 191
Nolan, Mr. 143; Philip 162,167
Noland, James 274; John 223;
    Thomas 184,275
Nolelon, Jese 146
Nolin, Lt. John 189; Richard 186,
    204; Thomas 289(2); William
    186,260
Nolind, John 185,187
Noll, Martin 103
Norfolk County 189
Norfolk, Virginia 83
Norrell, James 193
Norris, Bethuel 45; James 74,309
Norriss, Otho 292
North Bend 9,10,11,13,14,20,29,39
    41,42,48,51,62,68,74,78,79,82,
    83,86,89,91,93,98,108,110,121,
    122,127,129,132,142,156,163,
    199,200
North Bend township 67
North Fork 184,190,193
North Liberty 218
North, Thomas 285,300
North-Bend 1,4,6,16,17,19,24,25,
    26,54
North-Bend township 65
Northampton, Mass. 249
Northbend 10,32,33,37,38,86,147
Northumberland 247
Northumberland County, Pa. 1
Northup, Henry 212,231
Northwest Territory (see Terri-
    tory) 2,4,6,7,8,9,14,22,25,34,36
    41,43,44,45,46,47,48,49,53,54,
    55,56,57,61,73,75,76,77,83,85,
    88,100,139,178,182,193,194,
    196
Norton & Gibbs 147
Norton, C.A. 316,318; Carlos A.
    177,275,299,305,307(2),308,309
    311(2); Joab 300; Moses 234;
    Mr. 250
Nosteller, Christopher 132
Notary Public 285
Noteman, Andrew 179,214; Catha-
    rine 179,214
Notoway County, Virginia 128
Nott, Ezekiel 265; Simeon 15
Nourse, Charles J. 132,242;
    Robert 293

Noutman, Andrew 200; William 200
Nova Caesaria Harmony Lodge 42
Nova Caesaria Lodge 41,43,47,54, 55,69,76,77,85,94,101,111,112, 120
Nowland, John 267,300
Nowlin, Thomas 234
Nox, William 312
Noyes, J. 259
Null, Christian 58; Martin 110
Nunnamacker, Micheal 275
Nursery 88
Nuts, Elizabeth 67; Frederick 67
Nutt, Aaron 99; Adam 86,154,165;
Nutter, Thomas 316; Thomas C. 296
Nutts, Aaron 92,125; Frederick 132; Fredrick 100; S. 5; T. 5
Nyce, Jacob 310
Nye, Ebenezer 226; Ichabod 227
Nyee, Jacob 306
Nyel, Jacob 257,
O'Brian, John 54; Thomas 137; William 33
O'Briant, Charles 309
O'Connar, Charles 266
O'Donnall, Hugh 48
O'Faukne, Miss Isabella 296
O'Ferral, John 144
O'Ferrall, J. 173; Jno. 141,173; John 145,148,149(2),152,153, 154,157,162,163,164,165,168, 169(2),174,291
O'Hara, Col. James 192; Hugh 11, 315; James 11,41; Patrick 11
O'Hare, Patrick 1
O'Harra, Arthur 285; Hugh 19
O'Harrow, Arthur 215
O'Lackey, Dennis 264
O'Neal, Abijah 107; Joseph 158; Mr. 225; Patrick 150; Petrick 154
O'Neil, Abijah 66
O'bannion, John 311
Oaks, Thomas 306
Oaky, Levin 216
Obanion 157
Obanion Creek 89
Obannon 176
Obannon's Creek 130
Obannon, John 14,49,294
Oblinger, John 70,91,127
Ocheltree, Michael 41
Odel, Mordecai 296
Odell, James 276; Nathan 277
Oden, Elizabeth 151; Richard A. 115,151
Odle, John 189,196,208,213,214, 217,231,244,245,246,264,289, 306; Lott 257; Thomas 88,203; William 254,275,289
Ogden, David 276; Gen. 124; William 264,296
Ogdin, William 316
Ogg, Loyd 74
Ogglaze 2
Ogle, Alexander 162; Jean 107; Robert 162,168(2); Thomas 274; William 168
Oharra, A. 218; Arthur 288; Hugh 218
Ohio Almanack 126,144,148
Ohio Canal Company 113,131,243, 244,248,249
Ohio Company 54,256
Ohio County 155
Ohio County, Va. 249
Ohio District 11
Ohio Exporting Company 175
Ohio Gazette 147,198

Ohio Herald 236,243,250
Ohio Lamp 307
Ohio River 1,8,11,16,23,28,30,32, 35,37,38,43,47,49,51,54,60,65, 67,72,75,77,78,79,80,86,87,92, 95,101,102,103,110,115,122, 125,134,135,141,151,154,164, 167,169,175,178,186,189,199, 205,209,230,234,241,249,252, 258,277,289,290,302,305
Ohio Township 58,79,113
Ohio University 115,219,239,289, 299,309
Ohio Valley 112
Ohio bottom 152
Ohio township 34,35,36,52,73,172, 272,286
Oil mill 238
Oiler, Joseph 305
Okey, Levin 215,272
Old Chelicotha 37
Old Chillicothe 46,121,182,188, 190,196,197,202,207,209,211, 212,227,244,247,250,251
Old Garrison 156
Old Station 238
Old Town 200,217,230,245,254,257 261,309
Old, Jacob 37
Oldaker, Henry 316; John 267
Oldakers, Jesse 311
Oldfield, William 244,255,267,287
Oldkre, John 257
Oldwine, Barnabas 10; Barney 10
Olinger, George 280; John 244,257
Olivar, Mr. 181
Oliver & Buchanan 209,220,233
Oliver & Buchannan 213
Oliver & Buckhanon 226
Oliver, Allen 67; Col. 199; Col. Robert 54,181; David 227; Ezekial 121; Gisley 227; Jacob 66; John 233; Miss Electa 112; Miss Elizabeth 21; Mr. 39,69; Richard 158; Robert 34,53(2), 59(3),71,73,76(4),181(2),182(2), 186,193,230; Thomas 107; William 182
Ollim, Jacob 264
Olliver, Thomas 17
Olmsted, Francis 254,256
Olner, Henry 218
Olney, Maj. Coggershel 226; Sarah 226; Sylvenus 8
Olny, Silvenius 21
Ondrian, Mr. 234
Oneal, Abijah 86
Oneel, Mary 264; Sarah 264
Onondago Lake 268
Oram, Samuel H. 271
Orbison, John 91,120
Orcott, Darius C. 58(2),163
Orcutt, Capt. D.C. 14; D.C. 1,4,19 Darius C. 5,33; Darius Curtis 16; Lieut. Darius C. 9
Orears, Jacob 267
Oren, John 216
Orleans 68,85,130
Orleans Territory 242
Orleans boat 204
Ormsbey & Wilson 80
Ormsby & Bustard 12,28
Ormsby & Stanley 155,157,164
Ormsby, O. 118,119,127,133; Oliver 9(3),12,28,50,57,101, 102,118,143,155; Peter B. 243, 248
Orphans' Court 47,50,52,61,64,70, 118,131,192
Orr, Isaiah 97,117; James 187; Miss Peggy 35; Mr. 183;

Robert 53,154; Robert 53; Samuel 310; Sebulon 257; Thomas 289,303,312; Watson 117; William 118; Wm. 138,245
Orsborn, Caleb 154; Jeremiah 127; Joseph 137; Richard 219
Orsborne, Ebenezer 74
Orsburn, Margaret 13; Samuel 13
Orsea, Jonathan 257
Oruno, Henry 315; John 315
Osborn, Barcella 35; Barzella 35; Bazele 86; Caleb 117; Cyrus 25,58; R. 318; Ralph 177; Richard 241,275,310; Usual 95
Osborne, Abner 128; Mar. 41
Osbourn, Ralph 264
Osburn, Caleb 173; Samuel 25
Osenall, John 51
Osstill, Willi 264
Oston, Jonathan 165
Otis, Mr. 59; Samuel A. 244,249
Ott, Jacob 271,282; Miss Mary 317; Philip 249
Overdear, John 294,305
Overdeer, John 308; Martha 308
Overly, Eve 288; Frederick 227, 271,288,301; Martin 227,267
Overman, Demcey 317
Overmire, Peter 315
Overstreet, James H. 297
Overter, Andrew 132
Owen, Amsa 51; Brackett 28; Capt. 14; David 228; William 51
Owens, Lieut. Simon 75; Thomas 167; William 23; Zibbin 258
Owings, Nimrod 310
Owins, Isaac 244
Owl Creek 216,260
Owns, Peter 13
Owry, Thomas 95
Oxford township 293
Oxfored, John 286
Oyston, Isaac 282
Ozias, Peter 306
Ozier, Stephen 271
P. Plains 215
Pacier, John 170
Pack, William 132,163,164,165
Padget, John 170
Page, Aaron C. 117; John 170, 236(2),285(2); William 25
Pain, Mr. 69; Sela 267
Paine, Aurel 228; Edward 69,228, 255,302; Edward 69; Eleazer 228; George 125; Mr. 71; Sela 275
Painsville 284
Paint 283,293,313
Paint Creek (see Crossings of Paint and Falls of Paint Creek) 103,147,178,180,184,185,187, 188,190,192,193,194,196,197, 199,200,203,205,209,210,211, 212,216,217,218,219,220,221, 226,228,230,231,233,234,235, 237,238,240,241,242,244,245, 246,247,248,250,251,253,256, 257,261,262,263,264,265,266, 267,270,271,272,273,278,281, 282,283,284,293,298,299,302, 308,309,312,319
Paint Street 230,252,258,290,297, 312
Paint township 276,280,281,293, 295,303,309,312,315,317
Painter, Maj. George 284,288; Matthias 112
Painters 148,240,260,274
Paisals, Jacob 295
Palladium 112

Palmer, Corporal Seth 60; Joseph 164; Mrs. Cloe 262; Samuel 317; Thomas 262
Pancake, Isaac 287,316; John 209, 268; Lieut. John 189; Mr. 186; Susan 316
Pancoast, J. 171
Pandine, Isaac 91
Pane, Margaret 262
Pankus, Isaiah 310
Panton, John 68
Papassion, Augustus 310
Paper mills 84,96,305
Paperhangers 143
Papermakers 14,158
Parara 49
Parash, Zachariah 161
Parce, Carman 123
Parceil, Reuben 287
Parcel, James 161; John 101
Parcell, Richard 51
Parcels, John 285,306; Peter 195, 266,281,299(2),304,317; William 296
Parci, John 149
Paret, Linhard 311
Parham, Peter 311
Parine, Daniel 78
Paris 78
Paris, Kentucky 185,197
Paris, William 274
Parish, James 50,179; Joseph 200; Joshua 200,208; Robert 247
Park, Agnes 316; Andrew 43; Benjamin 126; Culbertson 43, 64; John G. 316; Joseph 133; Prentes 251,265,283; Prentis 260,292; Robert 32,89; William 269
Parker, Aaron 300; Absalom 310; Absalom 316; Absalom 283; Alexander 33,196,243,248,269; Alexr. 244,249; Alxr. 243; Charles 300,310; Col. 43; George S. 296; Isaac 125,311; James 183,266,269,270,279,298 299,304,308,309,314,317; John 132,171,257,266,274,286,289, 301,302,306,309,315; Jourdan 275; Mr. 88,203,251; Nancy 132,142; Nathaniel 287; Peter 279; Salmon 316; Samuel 82; Stephen 29; Thomas 33,196(2); Timothy W. 108,114; William 182,264,267,271,299,309
Parkeson, William 58
Parkhill, John 79
Parkins, Andrew 275; Cilfred 316
Parkinson, George 200; Maxwell 163
Parkison, William 91
Parks, Andrew 74; Culberson 154; Culbertson 90,106; David 273; Doctor Printes 296; John 251, 267,284; Joseph 53,58(2),79, 115,119,137,223; Mr. 242; Ro. 215; Robert 66,70,234,244; William 275
Parkson, Isaac 55
Parler, Joshua 215
Parmer, Purnel 251
Parnish, Joshua 209
Parr, John 302
Parrell, James 247; Maj. John 261
Parress, John 264
Parret, Capt. 293; Capt. Joseph 293
Parrill, John 275
Parris, Ruben 310; Samuel 183
Parrish, Joshua 221
Parrit, Joseph 264

Parse, Michael 127
Parsel, Moses 318; Richard 99
Parson, Harmon 35; Mathias 15; Sam. 15; Wm. 293
Parsonet, James 170
Parsons, Chatfield 150; Geo. 259; George 255,258(2),259(2); Harris 169; Judge 183; Samuel H. 222; Samuel Holden 227,230 William 204,241
Partimore, John 284
Parvin, Enoch 146
Pashen, George 209
Pasteur, Capt. T. 24; Capt. Tho. 75
Pasture, Capt. 4; Capt. Thomas 55 82
Paterson, John 164,261; Mr. 33; N.J. 144
Patrick, Levee 209; Levi 195,206; Robert 180,
Patrick, Robert 195,206,207,209, 215,221; Robt. 219
Patriotic Farmer 135,144
Patten, Isaac S. 200; James 195; Mark 146
Patters, Joseph 57
Patterson's Creek 256
Patterson, Charles 101; Col. R. 243; Dr. 216; Elizabeth 243; Esqr. 310; Francis 311; Gen. John 244,249; James 37,60, 70(2),78,112,146,149,150,170, 174; John 265,271,275,276,303; Joseph 18; Margret 121; Moses 259,283; Mr. 93,162; Peter 221; R. 103; Robert 174,293; Robt. 286; Saml. 47; Samuel 54,63,115,117,136,145,154,171; Thomas 112; William 117,142, 161; Wm. Ewing 215
Pattin, William 287
Patton's run 186,218
Patton, Catharine 239,249,255,283 Hon. William 130; Hon. Wm. 239; Isaac 102; John 99,102, 215,222; M. 217; Maj. William 185; Mary 222,262; Mr. 237, 239; Mrs. Catharine 249; Robert 206,247,257; Robt. 184; Samuel 275; Sergeant William 60; Thomas 229,271,303; Thos. 241; W. 199,244; Widow 244; William 37,51,82,83,86,87,91, 111,112,156,157,180,192,199, 200,201,202(2),203,205,207(2), 217,222,224,226,234,238(3), 239(3),249,255; Wm. 199,224, 235,237,239(5)
Paturr, Samuel 212
Paugh, Peter 203
Paul, James 271; John 17,80(2),81, 83,84,86(2),87(2),98,139,143, 144,196,199,202,211,212,219
Pauling, Lieut. Uriah 189
Paullen, Uriah 247
Paullin, Uriah 299
Paully, John 145
Pavey, Isaac 286
Pawlin, Uriah 275
Pawling, Uriah 195
Paxon, William 55
Paxton township 199,201,207,218, 223,228,229(2),236,250,254,255 266,280,294,295,299,305,308, 311,313,314,315,319
Paxton's Settlement 92
Paxton, Col. 91; Col. Thomas 47, 161; Thomas 48,86
Payn, Daken 64; Margret 64
Payne, Col. 256; Daken 178;

Daniel 173; John 140; William 101,140; Wm. 293
Payton township 195
Payton, Col. Francues 238
Pe Pee 186,195,197,200,203,206, 209,212,219,227,228,233,234, 250,251,259,270,271
Pe Pee Creek 189,242
Pe Pee settlement 214
Pe Pee township 199,201,207,260, 273,283,303
PePee 191
Pea Pee Road 218
Peairs, Isaac 201; James 201
Peak, John 161
Peake, John 310
Pearce, Isaac 238; Joseph 303; Levi 157; Michael 244; Phillip 165
Pears, Benjamin 142
Pearson, Abraham 142; Harman 35; Harmon 35; Isaac 276; Sineas 90,124(2)
Pease, C. 91,205,303; Calvin 186, 195,206,222,281,284; Judge 283,287; Seth 150
Peck, Col. Wm. 129; George 161; Mr. 122; Pascal Paoli 129; Wm. 165
Peddycord, Nathan 212
Pee Pee 187,209,223,237,244,250, 254,255,275,300,305
Pee Pee Creek 266,282
Pee Pee road 254
Pee Pee township 236,261,280, 286,288,289,294,301,309,314, 317
PeePee 184,310
PeePee Scioto 178
Peeble, John 271
Peebles, J.W. 318; Thomas 235
Peet, Truman 268
Peeters, Mary Ann 299
Peirce, Joseph 143
Peirson, Capt. William 255; David 264; Mathias 69; William 271, 300
Pellers, Mr. 203
Pelly, Solomon 161
Pelmira 215
Peltier, Charles 74; James 48
Pemberson, William 274(2)
Pemberton, William 301; Wm. 312
Pemturton, Wm. 276
Pence, Henry 302
Pendergrass, Patrick 261
Pendleton County 40
Pendleton County, Kentucky 84, 139,169
Pendleton, Nathaniel 241
Peneston, George 266; Isaac 266
Penick, Mr. 275
Penisten, Isaac 274
Penister, George 228
Peniston, George 289; Isaac 257, 286,289,315
Pennell, Richard 244
Penneston, Isaac 264
Pennisten, Geo. 301; Isaac 301
Penniston, Isaac 203
Pennsylvania 48
Pennywitt, Adam 218
Pensacola 32
Pentland, E. 252
Penwell, John 170
Peoples, Samuel 23
Peper, Jesse 217
Peppers, John 206,219,221,241,283 287; William 244
Perce, Stephen 8
Percival, Calvin 175; Doctor 175;

Jabez 79
Peril, James 316
Perine, Daniel 10,82,121; James 82,99
Perkins, Achilles 293; Doctor 105, 223; Elijah 233; Elisha 215; Isaac 99; John 238,291,295,312 Mr. 319; N. 109; Nicholas 112; Phineas 276; Reuben 233,297; Samuel 21,74; Thomas 112
Perlee, Benjamin 12; Peter 74; Rebecca 107
Perley, Abraham 82
Perlieu, Lieut. Benjamin 69
Perlu, Benjamin 41
Perrell, John 292; Jon 212
Perret, Joseph 261
Perrety, Joseph 261
Perrin, Joseph 161
Perrine, James 314
Perrineence, William 300
Perrins, William 264
Perry, Col. James 315; John 228, 229,270; Maj. William 77,142; Mr. 155(2),162,163; Nathan 303; Needham 216,303; Samuel 60,63; Sheriff William 57; William 73,79(2),89,148,160, 228,229; Wm. 173,176
Person, Willis 57
Personett, Joseph 150
Peshon, John 267
Petecrow, James 44
Peters, Abm. 284; Abraham 234; Adam 315,316; Alex. 293; Daniel 234; Maj. W. 148; Maj. William 164; Maj. Wm. 82; Polly 137; Wm. 82
Petersburgh, Virginia 128
Peterson, Ruliff 135; William 137
Petet, Lucy 54,182
Petit, Lucy 120,182
Petlers, Mr. 254
Petro, Leonard 70
Petters, Gersham M. 300
Pettet, Doctor John Gilbert 32
Petticrew, James 58(2)
Pettie's run 231
Pettigrew, James 247
Petty, Capt. 208; Capt. Ebenezer 186(2); Ebenezer 189,221,292; Joseph 219(2),292
Peyster, Philip D. 212
Peyton, John 293; Timothy 279
Phares, Johnston 249,275
Phebus, George 264; Sam. 228
Phelix, Mr. 139
Phellips, John 251
Phelps, Col. 149; Edward 146,254, 256,300; Geo. 245,252; George 222,245,249; Hezekiah 127; Hon. Jesse 284; James E. 252, 306; Jesse 134,242; Mr. 131; Thomas 228
Pheres, William 311
Phibus, John 189
Philadelphia 3,7,28,49,64,80,83, 88,100,110,118,119,125,131, 141,159,174,193,195,210,211, 222,259,260,281
Philbee, John 273
Philips, H.G. 157; Horatio G. 167; Jabish 58; James 237,292; John 184,279,280; Joseph 70; Miss Elizabeth 265; Nehemiah 271; Ralph 300; Thomas 121; William 190
Philipson, Jacob 146,156; Mr. 145
Phillians, Wm. 310
Phillip, Nehemiah 296
Phillips, Benjamin 310; Elizabeth 221; Henry 218,316; Jabish 102; James 73,181,185,194,222 244,282,300,310; John 82,178, 311; Major 251; Miss Mary 306; Nehemiah 287; Ralph 57,158, 170; Richard 170; Thomas 117, 161,165; William 256; William R. 29
Philps, John 297
Phiplips, James 241
Phleming, Thomas 146
Piat, Mr. 132
Piatt, Abraham 168; B. 161; Benjamin 111,118,132,142,160; Daniel 122; J. 161; Jacob 78; John 107,111,118,132,154; John H. 149,153,160(2),165,168 170,174; Lindsay 107; Robert 78,127,132
Picaway Plains 194
Pickaway 179,218,219,224,229,237 241,244,247,248,249,253
Pickaway County 225,302,303,304, 307,308,309,311,313,315,316, 318
Pickaway Plains (see Plains) 183, 195,196,200,202,206,209,210, 213,214,216,218,219,225,231, 232,233,234,238,246,251,255, 256,257,260,261,265,266,268, 270,271,272,274,279,286,295, 296,298,302,305,313,314,315, 317
Pickaway Planes 244
Pickaway races 225
Pickaway road 196
Pickaway township 183,207,218, 236,241,251,254,255,260,265, 268,270,278,280,285,290,291, 295
Pickel, Henry 16
Picken, John 275
Pickens, J. 306; John 230; Samuel 306; William 142
Pickerell, Wm. 221
Pickering, Col. 46
Picket, John 137
Pickett, John 277
Pickings, William 264
Pickle, Henry 13; Jacob 302
Pickrell, Wm. 221
Pickway 237
Picuway Plain 178
Pierce, Capt. John 6(2),7,10(2),11, 15; Daniel 146,150; Isaac 186, 232; Josleph 142; Michael 107; Mr. 195; Sarah 232; Susanna 86; Thomas 274
Pierse, Isaac 190
Pierson, Daniel 117; David 127, 137; Isaac 82; Luddow 173; Ludlow 165; Mathias 9; Matthias 45,78,89,112; Senias 134; Sineas 113; Sineus 132,165 William 247,283; Willys 251; Wyllis 48,161; Willys 31,69
Pigeon Creek 20
Pigg, Levi 153
Pigget, Rebecca 137
Piggot, Rebecca 142
Pigman, Jesse 296; Joshua 137; Mr. 161
Pike, Capt. Z.M. 165; Capt. Zebu. 5; Capt. Zebulon 21; Isabel 99; Isabela 102; Issabella 132; Lieut. 160; Lieut. Z.M. 46,162; Lieut. Zebulon M. 55,75; Maj. Zebulon 75; Zebulon 147
Pikens, John 283
Pilars, William 218
Pillar, William 280,314
Pillars, William 231; Wm. 294
Pillips, Ralph 231
Pilman, Thomas 209
Pilsworth, William 5
Pinckney 49
Pinckney, Mr. 57
Pindar, Peter 28
Pinder, Mrs. 4; Peter 4,6
Pindle, William 276
Pinkney, Lieut. N. 106,109; Lieut. Ninian 109; N. 109
Pinney, Abner 231; Azariah 231; Capt. Abner P. 276; Ensign P. 222; Lieut. Levi 293
Piper, James 146; Mr. 169; Philip 226
Pipper, Philip 234
Pitcher, Abraham 305(2); R. 257; Rudolph 305(2)
Pitman's Tavern 97,124,125
Pitman, Jacob 264; John 11; Jonathan 54,73,79(2),80,81, 92(2),93,116,126,129,145,147, 159,199
Pitmans, Jonathan 45
Pitsby, Abigail 129
Pitt, Robert 275
Pittenger, William 287
Pittinger, William 209
Pittman's Tavern 125,141
Pittman, Jonathan 58,106,125,141, 143(2),161,168; Mr. 145,160(2)
Pitts, Josiah 14
Pittsburg 1,3,4,6,16,25,46,49,50,56 64,109,258
Pittsburgh 139,147,157,174,192, 246,252,255,308
Pitzer, Matthias 308; Mr. 205
Piyley, Casper 287
Plainfield 72
Plains 202,250
Plater, Christian 280
Plato, Christian 207
Platte, Christian 199
Platter, C. 181,228; Christain 316; Christian 213,218,234,236,295, 313; Mr. 228,261; Peter 287, 301
Platto, Christian 201
Pleasant Farm 214
Pleasant Point 210
Pleasant Run 61,66,70,71,123,169
Pleasant township 97,204,207,229, 234,273,279,285,286,290,291, 293,298,299,301,306,314
Pleasants, William H. 264
Pleasent Valley Station 8
Plesant township 265
Plough and Harrow 219
Plowman, Mechee 277
Poage, Col. James 306; James 238
Poats, David 269
Poe, Andrew 317; Miss Eliza 300
Pogue, Conrad 10; Samuel 173
Point Coupe 85
Point Coupes 92
Point Peter 34
Point Pleasant 3
Points, Sally 282; William 279
Poisal, Jacob 307
Poland 230
Poland Library Society 303
Poland, Richard 281(2)
Polen, William 296
Polhemes, Lieut. John 23
Polke, Isaac 91
Pollard, Mr. 196
Pollock's Mill 113
Pollock, Capt. John 150; David 263; James 18,57; John 164; Mr. 177

364

Pollox's Mill 92,115
Ponshes, Andrew 215
Ponta, Petrus 31
Pontious, Andrew 197,300
Pontus, Frederick 302
Pool, John 59,62; Simeon 167; Simon 187; William 247,300
Poole, John 66
Poolley, John 221
Poor & Kershner 153
Poor & Washburn 37
Poor, David 39; David J. 48,52,56, 63,71,74,76,85,96,105,111(2), 128,167; Hugh 315; Mr. 83; Rachel 71
Poore, David J. 170,171; Hugh 283
Poorkins, William 247
Pooterpaugh, David 142
Pope, Alexander 6; Capt. Piercy 35; Lieut. Piercy 21; N. 234, 275; Nathaniel 218,257,262,275 Wm. 228; Worden 243,248
Popejoy, Ann 244; John 280,295; Mary 244; Nathan 283
Popenoe, James 318
Port William, Kentucky 66
Port, James 283; John 244,247,255 283; William 180(2),186
Portage County 276,284,299,304, 317
Porter, Alexr. 43; Capt. 5(2); Charlotte 161; Elias 86; Elisha 316; George 180,188,193,221, 281,282,312; Henry 273,284, 296,311,312; James 127,310; John 208; Joseph 146,216,217, 228,234,296; Miss Nancy 284; Miss Polly 287; Mr. 148; Nathaniel 132; Peter 193,247, 255,276,281,282,306; Philip 86; W. 184; William 280,310
Portsmouth 229,248,256,266,268, 288,305,306,314
Posey, Thomas 40,198,243,293
Possom Run 286
Possum Run 311,313
Post, Joseph 52; Josiah 51,70,116, 131; Levi 310; Mary 131; Nancy 116; R.E. 266; Russell E. 310,316
Poston, Tom 260
Posy, Thomas 40
Potomack River 232
Pottenger, Samuel 64
Potter, Bethier 127; Daniel 107; Joseph 91,99,107,183,184, 186(2),197,199,201; Moses 58; Mr. 192; Peleg 231
Potters 15,39,56,177,305
Pottinger, Dennis 291
Pottman, Jane 127
Potts, Anthony 264,303,316; David 251; Doc. Anthony 228; Doct. Anthony 209,255,257; Elizabeth 316; James 263,264,287, 296; John 64; Mrs. 267; Robert 248
Poullen, Uriah 267
Poullin, Uriah 221
Pounds, Samuel 27
Powel, Barr 140; James 244; Joseph 286,301; Robert 231; Seymore 290; William 8,318
Powell, Leven 231; Payton 231; Seymore 204; Seymour 293; William 167
Powels, James 234
Power, Hugh 261,293,299,309; Thomas 167
Powers, Aaron 117; Avery 212; Esq. 212; Jacob 41,74,184;

Thomas 151; William 15,241
Powhatan County, Virginia 86
Powner, John 150
Poydras, J. 113
Poyzer, Mr. 104
Prairie (see Grassy Prairie, Muddy Prairie, Great Prairie, Big Prairie) 95,203,241
Prather, Enos 273,286,288,289,301 303,309; John 298; Thomas 243(2),248
Prathers, Enos 283
Pratt's company 4
Pratt, Christopher 70; David 300; Worthy 297
Pratter, Henry 271
Pratts, Mr. 107
Prdey, John 310
Preble County 177
Prentes, Russel 165
Prentice, Cournel 74
Prentiss, Thomas G. 300
Presbyterian Church 38,39,287
Presbyterian Meeting House 120, 174,280,284
Presbyterian Society 157,169,256, 303
Presbyterian burial ground 168, 175
Presbyterian church yard 163
Presbyterians 126,136,137,138
Presquelisle 233
Preston 17
Preston, Joseph 74; Mr. 196
Price, Capt. 1; Capt. Benjamin 10; Daniel 45; Easter 200; Evan 164; George 170; H. 108; Henry 318; Hez. 111; Hezekiah 106,124,125,128(2),143,145,147 159,164,170,175,253; John 74; Joseph 219; Joseph P. 48; Miss Sally 270; Mr. 108,131,157,160, 164; Philip 145; Philip P. 174; Phillip 140(2); Robert 315; Stephen 296; William 270,283, 290,293,296
Prichard, James 131,223
Prick, Hezekiah 50
Pricker, John 292
Pricket, John 312
Priddy, John 296
Pride, John 293
Prier, Andrew 121; Elizabeth 5; Moses 5; Mrs. 3
Priest, Obediah 172
Prince, Capt. 43; Dr. 73; John 17(2),19,20(2),21,22,24(2),25(2); Joseph 3,10,21,50,59(2),69,72, 73,74,80,90,93,94,100,104,109, 110,111,115,122,133,148,160; Mrs. Sarah 171
Prine, Daniel 18,165
Pringle, William 161
Printer 2,12,14,21,23,31,33,34,40, 53,88,73,88,120,130,160,178, 180,181,184,187,188,191,194, 206,210,213,222,231,237,240, 241,247,252,258,264,281,290, 299,317
Printing office 9
Prior, Andrew 37,57; Capt. Abner 60; Silas 292
Pritchard, Col. James 249,303; E. 273; James 88,103,106,108,109 110,111,115,118,120,121,126(2) 131(2),145,147,203,205,221, 225(3),226(2),240(2),245,246, 248,252; Mr. 37,38(2),103,109, 145,177(3),181(2),246,249(2), 250,252,283; Rees 112
Pritchett, Winget 48

Prodis, Alexander 155
Proud, James 296; John 231,238
Proviance, Thomas 192
Prukett, Wm. 310
Pryer, Andrew 53,150; John 45,63
Pryor, Andrew 51; Col. John 15; John 70
Ptts, Dr. 267
Pugh, Dav. 78; David 114; Joseph 165,168; Squire 105(2)
Pullen, James 231; Thomas 307
Puntany, George H. 290
Purcell, Jonathan 264
Purdie, Capt. 89
Purdy, Ensign Robert 8
Purl, James 307; Seth 200
Purloe, Betsey 310
Pursel, Enos 306; Reuben 257,312; Zadock 288
Pursell, John 212; Rewben 251; William 264
Purtee, John 297
Pusley, John 180
Puthuff's tavern 279
Puthuff, Col. W.H. 273; Col. Wm. H. 290; Maj. 300; W. 267; W.H. 268,269,274,279,295; William H. 252(2),259(2); Wm. H. 271
Puthuffs, William H. 238
Putman, Philip 292
Putnam, David 242; Edwin 40; G.W. 205; Gen. Rufus 181; Hon. Rufus 8; Israel 114,229; J.W. 91; Mr. 69,71,84,177; Rufus 53,54,63,84,105,181(2), 223,289; W.R. 69,204; William R. 198,314; Wm. Rufus 225
Pyatt, Benjamin 218
Pye, Thomas 257
Quaker settlement 293
Quakers 128,131,191,287
Quality, Jane 316; Owen 251; Owin 244
Quarles, Wm. 293
Queen Anne's County, Maryland 15
Queen, John 288
Queens Rangers 74
Quick, Amos 146; Cornelius 318; John 38
Quigley, Christopher 317; John 45,230
Quigly, Mr. 33
Quimby, Ephraim 109,213,214,225, 303; J. 90
Quinby, Archelus 63; Ephraim 244, 261,288; Samuel 288
Quinn, James 303; Rev. James 247; Thomas 280
Quire, James 313
Rabb, Elizabeth 130; John 130; Samuel 203
Raccoon township 260
Race, Moses 304
Rachford, Alexander 278
Rackoon township 265
Racoon Waters 290
Racoon township 308,312
Radcliff, Daniel 287,292
Radiliff, John 277
Radlay, John 127
Radley, John 107,170
Radliff, Benjamin 283
Radner township 304
Rafe, Sergt. Thomas 23
Rager, John 187
Ragon, Eli 282; Yose 289
Ragsdale, Obediah 307
Raidliff, Capt. 276
Raines, George 319; Laurence 319; William 300,314

365

Rainey, William 209
Rains, George 308; James 151; Laurence 308; Thomas 288
Rairy, Charles 302
Raldiff, John 255
Ralston, Edward 103,110; Robert 273,274; Silvester 160
Ramblers retreat 275
Rambo, Jackson 170
Ramey, Joseph 310
Ramley, Thomas 306
Ramsay, Capt. 161; Mr. 161; Thomas 151,154; William 52, 136,139,154
Ramsey, Alex. 311; Alexr. 312; Elizabeth 170; Geo. 212; George 283; James 215; John 86,286; Joseph 264; Larence 284; Mr. 37,62,102,116; Samuel 215,286; Tho. 158; Thomas 49, 90,97,98,111,115,135,141,144, 151,152(2),158; W. 55; William 15,50,57(2),70,72,73,75,76,81, 83,90,115; Wm. 37
Ramy, Polly 275
Randal, Ananis 212
Randel, Benjamin 163
Randle, Zabul 271
Randolph 247
Randolph County 17,36,41,121
Randolph, Benjamin F. 61; John 168; Lewis F. 161; Mr. 87(2)
Rankin, Hugh 216; Thomas 283; William 216,257; Wm. 221
Rankins, Hugh 182; William 287
Ransom, John P. 257
Ransome, Ambrose 74; John P. 247
Ranson, Ambrose 37,91,205
Ransone, Ambrose 159; John P. 255
Raper, Leonard 78
Rarrdon, Henry 310
Rase, Sergt. Thomas 23
Rashblean, Philip 41
Rastone, Ambrose 60
Ratcliff, John 264,307,308,309, 312(2),319
Rattle Snake Fork 178,212,242, 313
Rattlesnake Creek 279
Ravencraft, Samuel 264
Ravenna 195,259
Ravenore 197
Ravenscraft, Samuel 251
Rawle, Abraham 117
Rawling, Nathan 206
Rawlins, Mr. 147,151; Tho. 166; Thomas 108,111,115,122,128, 140,151,156,157,173,176(2),177 233; Thos. 177
Ray & Schillenger 120
Ray, George 306; Richard W. 155
Rayburn, John 70
Raynel, Abbe 77
Raynold, Mary 267
Raynolds, W. 241,259; William 286
Rea, Benjamin 271,310(2); John 51
Read, Alexander 316; John 267; Will. 234; William 295; Wm. 303
Reader, Daniel 180; Jacob 9; Joseph 19; Nathaniel 5; Stephen 9
Reading 149,176
Reading township 298
Reading, Samuel 165
Readman, James 296
Ready, Coonrod 310; William 12
Really, Thomas 293
Reams, Elizabeth 292; Jordon 146

Reasner, Leonard 219
Reaves, Cyrus 255
Record's mill 229
Records, William 287
Recton, William 255
Rector, E. 292; Elias 188,210,238; Frederick 282; John 69,241,242 Mr. 239; Naomi 282; Whorton 255; William 146,184,238,251, 256,257; Wm. 142
Red Bank 52
Red Bank Station 11,30,127
Red Lion 26,187,190,213,219,227 249,259,290,301
Red Lion Tavern 246,248,252,253, 254,256,257,261,266
Red Lyon 224
Red Oak 86
Red Oak Creek 169,279
Redden, John 295; Reve. 170
Reddick, David 227; James 110; Jonathan 228; Thomas 32; Thomas F. 200,219; Ths. F. 228
Redding 38,104,112,125,133,142, 155
Redding town 109
Redding, Rev. Joseph 90
Reddingburgh, Mr. 29
Redenbauch, John 142
Redenbough, Mr. 171
Redenour, Mathias 300
Redfeam, John 272
Redfearn, John 285,289
Redick, Jesse 289; Jonathan 210
Reding 165,171
Reding township 286
Redlick, Jesse 309
Redlon, Abraham 63
Redman, Elijah 265,281; Isaac 255; James 271,295; John 301; Nevill 265; Rezin 221
Redstone 207
Reece, David 216; John 66
Reed makers 94,146,183
Reed's tavern 236
Reed, A. 98; Abraham 106,271; Alexander 238,264; Andrew 98, 99; Archibald H. 54; Benjamin 271,292,316; Capt. 78; Capt. John 21; David 184,221,241, 286; Elizabeth 102; George 165,238,245,271,292; Hamilton 148; Henry 3(2);Isaac78,98,142, 147,156; J. 183,194; Jacob 251; James 39,142,170,191,209,219, 221,228; Jane 271,296; Jas. 234; Jean 292; Job 231,241,247 Jobe 264; John 17,41,60,61,63, 64,66,70,184,238,271; Joseph 210,221; Leonard 254; Lieut. 1; Mary 7,81,98,101; Mr. 200,245; Mrs. Sarah 219; Nathaniel 60, 283; Nehemiah 219; Patrick 308,315; Reuben 165; Richard 257,275; Robert 32,60,316; Samuel 216,229; Sergt. James 144; Thomas 195,197,206,207, 212,215,219,220,223,226,229, 231,234,236(2),239,256; Thos. 208,240; William 7,15,51,197, 203,206,215,219,228,231,238, 264,275
Reede, James 192; Wm. 310
Reeder & Marcell 141
Reeder's tavern 143
Reeder, Amos 271; Capt. 81,199; Capt. D.F. 143; Capt. Stephen 68,81; Charles 305; D. 52,83, 180; Daniel 50,52,62,63,69,75, 80,86,87,117,120,126,167,199; Daniel F. 127,139; David 18;

Doctor 63,143; Dr. 83,117,127, 199; E. 114,117; Jacob 27,80, 100,209; Jesse 65,92,126,144, 156,158,162,167,172; Jonathan 311; Joseph 57,95,141; Mr. 29, 69(2),96,116,133,155,199; Mr. E. 116; Mrs. 114,117; Mrs. Mary 167; Mrs. Phebe 92; Nath. 95; Nathan 136; Nathaniel 56,64,79,90,107,116, 155(2); Stephen 29,55,57,80, 104,112,136,137,154; William 78
Reeker, John 292
Reel, Daniel 306
Rees, D. 257; David 88,111,203, 286,315; Emanuel Felter 102; Jonathan 200,269,298,308; Lewis 150; Mr. 224,229; Thomas 252; William 216
Reese, Caleb 294; David 273; Henry 122,142,165; Jacob 53, 56; Mr. 280,294; Samuel 91
Reety, Conrod 296
Reeve, Nathaniel 63,161; Richard 293; Samuel 78; Susanna 78; William 154
Reeves' Crossing 302
Reeves, Capt. Nathan 33; Eli 265, 266,269,281,293; Gust. 71; Gustavus 145; N. 254; Nathan 197,206,238,271,310; Nathaniel 281; Samuel 283
Reid, David 161,298; George 221, 278,291; Wm. 22
Reide, John S. 303
Reider, Daniel 45
Reiley, John 73,144,251,296; Mr. 90
Reily, Benjamin 190; Charles 170; Isaac 200; Isaac M. 249; John 5,12,37,41,52,53,57,61,67(2), 69(2),71(3),72,73(3),75,76,80(2) 81(2),82,83,84,86,87(3),88,89, 90,94,104,106(2),111,128,124,139, 141,143,150,156,163,181,191, 192,194,199,226,227; Mr. 84,85 109
Reling, Joseph 154
Remey, Thomas 306; Wm. 152
Reneck, Felix 283
Renick & Lewis 307
Renick, Ann 270; Felix 224,255, 264(2),292,296,314; G. 244,247, 254,258,265,268,270,272; George 120,217,234,255,256(2) 270,275,280,287,297,299,304; James 297,304,310,318; Jonathan 224,243; Mr. 257; Polly 255; Robert 103,152,166, 190,222,233,318; Thomas 224; W. 270; William 241
Renicks, Felix 226; James 238; John 238
Renix, Felix 205,207(2); James 316
Rennick, Geo. 309; Mr. 221
Rennix, Mr. 91
Reno, George 127
Renssalar, Capt. Van 7
Repblogel, Daniel 132
Republican Association 175
Republican Blues 281,293
Republican Corresponding Society 77,79,80,84,85,97,103,105,139, 140,141,143,159,160,166,172, 173,175,176
Republican Delegates 174
Republican Mechanics 166
Republican Society 120,123,124, 125,143,160,204,244,245

Republican Society of Cincinnati 141
Republican Society of Columbia 203
Republicans 83,222,223,224,246, 261
Republicans of Chillicothe 246
Republicans of Cincinnati 96,97, 124
Republicans of Washington County 248
Rerreck, Aaron 310
Restine, Barney 182
Retton, Silas 114
Reuck, Aaron 300
Rever, Peter 194
Revolutionary War 40,105,123,124 131,148,172,210,284
Revolutionary War soldier 23
Reyley, Jacob 257; John 257
Reynolds, David 312; Doctor Edward Gantle 74; Edward 75; Isaac 298; John 25,115,247,311 Joseph 203,292; Maj. 315; Maj. William 293; Mary 257; Reuben 17; Silvanus 39,51; Thomas 292; William 166,231,272; Wm. 231
Rhawle, Lidia 37
Rhea, Lieut. James 75; Matthew 293
Rhinehart, Daniel 117
Rhoad, John 294
Rhodes, Abraham 245; Sarah 221
Rhods, John 203
Rice, A. 267; Adam 184,190,192; Andrew 293; O. 204; Oliver 69(2); Rev. David 115,137; Shadrick 67; William 23
Rich, George 103
Richand township 249,250
Richard, Christian 221
Richards, Augustus 219,226,275; Christian 241; Dudley E. 264; George 266,269,274,278,284, 301; John 238; Thomas 200
Richardson, Aaron 18,27; Asa 37, 58,73,106,134; Asa S. 109, 114(2),122(2),133(2),137,138; Assa 146; Capt. T.H. 313; Elijah 154; James 119,154,164; John 45,48,95,122,172,184; Mathew 109,111,212,225; Matthew 82,86,128,176(2),238; Matthias 290; Mr. 24,109,115, 213; R.D. 313; Robert 171; Robert D. 307,308; Samuel 134; William 82,95,226; Wm. 167
Richarson, Abraham 318
Richart, Anthony 318; Jacob 204, 209
Richcreek, Casper 5
Richeson, Jacob 100
Richey, Adam 117; G. 257; George 245,287; James 105,139,163, 164; John 70; Mat. 215; Mathew 197; Robert 95,122; Samuel 269; Stuart 9
Richfield 224,248
Richhart, John 308
Richharts, Christian 217
Richland County 278,303
Richmond, Capt. James 75;109; Lieut. 25
Richmond, Virginia 235,254,257
Richy, Stuart 17
Rickabough, Anna 204,205(2); Peter 204
Ricker, Samuel 107
Ridale, John 73

Riddick, Thomas F. 221
Riddle & Woodson 28
Riddle's Mill 191
Riddle, Capt. 81; Capt. John 68; Capt. Wm. 220; David 122; James 28,32,39,82,132; Jas. 37; John 6,9,57,74,86,103,119, 124,136,139,141,153,154,155, 159,244,245; John R. 176; Maj. 136(2); Maj. John 129,174; Mr. 153; Mrs. Nancy 174; Widow 195; William 163
Rideles, William 142
Ridenhour, Mathias 310
Ridenour, Anthony 292,300; Joseph 165; Mathew 251; Mathias 296
Rider, Adam 245
Ridgeway, David 308; Samuel 286
Ridgley, T. 133
Ridgway, David 312; Samuel 306
Ridingout, Matthias 230
Riednerier, Nancy 306
Rielin, Jacob 306; Jacob S. 310
Rieling, Jacob S. 306
Riely, Joel 287; John 120,173
Rife, Joseph 273
Riffle, David 167
Rigel, Mathias 142
Riggle, George 78,170
Riggs, Abigail J. 99; Elizabeth 60; George 107; Rev. B. 169
Right, James 216; John 221,244; Thomas 25
Riker, Samuel 102
Riley, Jacob 267; Jeremiah 271; John 181,224,225
Riller, Catea 292
Rilter, John 310
Rim, John 171
Riner, David 142
Rinick, Felix 305; William 310
Rinicks, Jonathan 182
Rinker, Abijah 209; Elijah 200,219
Rion, Joseph 296
Rippey, Doctor John 41
Rissle, David 167
Ritchards, Mr. 253
Ritchardson, Joseph 309
Ritche, George 306
Ritchey, George 241,259,262,314; James 295; John 318; Margaret 241,283,296,316; Matthew 187, 295; Robert 241,263; William 275
Ritchie, John 293
Ritenour, Mathias 292
Ritler, Henry 264; John 264
Rittenhouse, Adam 161; Garret 82; Geo. 121; Samuel 241,251, 267,271,284,287; William 15,48 55,58(2),82
Ritzer, John 250
River, Miami 99
Roach, George 122
Roades, Anthony 200
Roads 20
Roads, Abraham 146; John 292, 295,296,307,308,309,313(2)
Roas, David 20; Peggy 20
Roback, George 275
Robarts, John 15
Robb, Alexander 146; Andrew 107; John 146; Robert 211; S. 107; Samuel 67,99,101; William 163
Robbins, John 178,294; Jonathan 159
Roberson, Daniel 120(2); John 66; Joseph 81
Robert, Rea, 310
Roberts, Asa 120(2); Capt. 211,

276; Capt. William 208(2); Charles 69,296; Daniel 315; James 287; Job 251; John 32, 74,275,293; Mr. 48; Mrs. 206; Susank 310; Thomas 142,241, 264,292; William 271
Robertson's store 9
Robertson, Alex. 212; Alexander 303; Daniel 103,222; David 58; Ezra 55; Jacob 234; John 9,15, 18,63; Littleton 14; Mr. 66, 102; Patty 124; Thomas 67; Walter L. 124; William 103,202 266
Robeson, William 176
Robins, Daniel 189,266,317; Jno. 310; John 208,255,266,280(2), 296,306,317
Robinson, Abner 312; Alexander 215,292,296; Barey 292; Benjamin 273,317; Capt. John 189; Edward 101; George 162; Henry 310; J. 262; James 209, 226,231,295,296,300,318; Job 273; John 95,107,112,252,257, 273,288; John F. 161; John W. 316; Joseph 112,255; Mary 209, 212,287,310; Michael 285; Miss Sally 306; Mr. 131; Nicholas 312; Rev. James 292; Richard 272; Robert 133,190,212,226, 306; Samuel 7,18,295,306,318; Simon 316; Stephen 122; Thomas 272,318; W. 208; William 8,87,130,150,190,198, 203(2),217,230,239,255,260,264 267,278,288,290,291(2),300, 301(2),303,312; Wm. 261,311; Wolsey 209; Woolsey 318
Robison, Charles 170; Jacob 102; James 7; John 48; Joseph 13; Robert 99,119; Samuel 78,95; William 51,187,275
Robitaile, James 94
Robitaille, James 220; Jas. 208
Rochenfield, Aaron 130
Rock Farm 153,164
Rock's farm 115
Rock, Felix 91,318; George 61,63; Patrick 106,223
Rockbridge County, Va. 97
Rockenfeller, John 132; Samuel 132
Rockhold, Joseph 264,308
Rockingham County, Virginia 184
Rocksold, Joseph 245
Rockwell, Henry 60,132
Rocky Fork 217,235,246,273,281, 293,299
Rocky Spring 107
Rodgers, Benjamin 303; Capt. John 270; Elizabeth 271;310; George 285; Hamilton 215; John 182,268,287,288,292; Jos. 12; Levi 238; Lewis 197,252; Lieut. Joshua S. 78; Mary 102; Peledge 311; Peleg 309; Robert 316; Thomas 255,266, 269; William 198,212,255,292, 300,301,306,316
Rodman, Mrs. Elizabeth 33
Rodney, Isabella 59; Patrick 59
Rodrique, Lieut. Phillip 75
Roe, Daniel 134,139,143(2),149, 164
Rogard, Sary 316
Rogers, Andrew 95,99,107; Ann 194; Edward 28; Elizabeth 300; Hamilton 184; Henry 86; James 194,296,300; John 216; Joseph 22; Levi 159; Lewis R.

367

283,300; Lieut. Joshua S. 60, 74; Mary 107,127,228,255; Philip 123,151; Robert 165; Simeon 107; Thomas 221,287; Trypheny 123; William 183,184 194,209,218,230,283,288,296, 310; Wm. 231
Rolins, Samuel 154
Roll, Abraham C. 146,161; Edward 122; Jacob 132; John 59,110, 117,170,172(2); Matthias 111, 172; Sally 122
Rollans, John 264
Rollins, John 182,192; Jonathan 160
Rolston, Andrew 206; Benjamin 237; Ezekiel 190; Mr. 155; Robert 190,237; Robt. 184
Roman, Jacob 137,161,170; John 164
Romane, Jacob 168
Romans, Thomas 273,288
Romine, John 306; Thomas 310
Romney 232
Ronck, Joseph 170
Roney, Jno. 109
Rood, Huldah 227; Reuben 26,227
Roodes, Abraham 306
Roog, Lieut. Joshua S. 55
Rook, Nancy 24
Rooker, George 306
Root, Martin 297
Roots town 251
Rope makers 5,14,20,120,129,145, 158,161,165,175
Rope-walk 93
Rore, Micheal 283
Ros, John 149
Rosaboom, Garrett 310
Rose, Hiram 297; Lemuel 297; Levi 297; Timothy 284,297; William 219
Roseboom, Andrew 245
Rosebrough, Charles 192
Roseman, James 146
Rosian Society 231,232
Ross & Green 154
Ross County 28,30,36,39,41,45,51 69,70,73,80,83,84,87,91,94,102 111,131,148,164,165,178,179, 181,182,183,184,185,186,187, 188,189,191,193,195,196,197, 198,199,200,201,202,203,204, 205,206,207,208,210,211,212, 213,214,215,217,218,219,220, 221,222,223,224,226,227,228, 229,230,231,232,233,234,235, 236,238,239,241,242,243,245, 246,247,248,249,251,252,253, 255,256,257,258,259,260,261, 262,263,264,265,266,267,268, 269,270,271,272,273,274,276, 277,278,280,281,282,283,284, 285,286,288,289,290,291,294, 295,297,298,299,301,302,303, 305,306,307,308,309,311,312, 313,314,315,316,317,318,319
Ross County Commissioners 190, 250,265,266
Ross township 163,247
Ross, Aaron 154; Augus 107; Benjamin 105,127,318; Daniel 137, 209,219,257,283; Ezekiel 146; George 268; Hugh 14,17; Ignatius 5,58,130,146; Isaiah 302; Jacob 137; James 198,247 248,251,255; James T. 264,267; John 105,146,219,234,267,280, 234,293,298,311,318; Magdalain 296; Matthias 95,117,161; Miss Jane 300; Mr. 46,82,89;

Nathaniel 55,82,127; Ogden 104,125; Ogdon 112; Oliver 192,199,201,203,207,218; Philip 271; Robert 69,78,105, 192,200; Stephen 247,257,264, 271; Talmage 291; Thomas 248 255,296; William 126,257,271, 296,306; Wm. 286
Rossville 137,141,157,158
Rotenhouse, Lieut. William 8
Rothrauf, Jonathan 286
Roudebush, Daniel 89
Rough Creek 155
Round Bottom 29,32,38,48,69,74, 79,81,82,86,93,95,99,108,120, 131,136,171,240
Round Bottom Mill 57,81,112,133
Round Bottom Station 9
Round Praire 227
Round Prairie 256
Roush, J. 315
Rousz, Kilcan 221
Row, Isaiah 313; John 210
Rowan township 269
Rowan, Alexander 150,161,238; John 243,244,249; Mr. 67; Philip 102; Robert 77
Rowbuck, Aaron 256; Benjamin 256; Elizabeth 256
Rowe, Edward D. 310; Jesse 300; John 94,97,207; Richard 292; Sandrige 267; Thomas 94
Rowen, Alexander 159,234
Rowings, Nathan 316
Rowland, Jane 154; John 209; Joshua 38,167
Rowletter, George 12
Rowley, Alpheus 292,296
Rowlson, Silvester 161
Royr, Nehemiah 241
Ruble, George 209
Ruby, Isaac 192
Ruck, James 287; John 287
Rucub, John 197; Joseph 197
Ruddell, Stephen 162
Ruddenbough, Phillip 165
Rude, Abner 99,132,142; Elizabeth 99
Rudisyll, Jacob 232
Ruff, Samuel 284
Ruffin's ferry 154
Ruffin's tavern 154
Ruffin, Adjutant Wm. 80; Lieut. William 68,81,93,97(2); Maj. 122,168; Major 126; Mr. 77(2), 94,129; W. 66; William 32,37, 41,45,50,51(2),55,57,59(2),60, 63,64(2),68,71,72,73,74(2),75, 76,78,79,81,82,83,87,89(2), 90(2),91,95,99,100,102(2),103, 104,106,108,109,110,112,114, 116,117,121,122(2),123,125,127 133(2),136,138,139,147,160,161 168,170,173,177,230; Wm. 48, 66,89,126,135,142,149,150,160, 162,165,170,172,273
Ruffner, Tobias 305
Ruggles, Benjamin 303
Ruland, Israel 46
Ruling, Israel 55
Rumery, Moses 86
Rumly, Thomas 310
Rumney, Moses 95
Rumsey, Nathan 99
Runckle, Catherine 262; Jacob 262
Rundle, Zabud 187
Runion, Henry 112
Runix, James 283
Runkle, John 257
Runnian, Thomas 165

Runyan, Absolom 135; John 115; Mr. 137,231; Samuel 151
Runyon, Henry 91(2); John 102
Ruse, Gillian 245,260,280; Killian 311,314,319
Rusell, Larry 280
Rush, Andrew 264,267; Henry 195, 213,306; John 206,212,219,231, 255(2),257,296; Peter 257; Philip 46
Rusher, Peter 218
Rusk, Thomas 86
Russel, George 53,59; J. 279; James 170,293; Jno. 290; John 268,273,274,280,285,286; Joseph 310; Martin 177; Shelea 231; Stephen 18; William 87, 192,228,274,287,291,302(2); Wm. 279
Russell, Caleb 200; George 170; J.W. 83; James 78,103,158; Jermiah 310; Joseph 292; R. 305; Robert 92,298,302; Shelah 234; Stephen 15; Thomas 251; William 203(2),231,300; Wm. 303
Ruth, George 274
Rutherford's ferry 188
Rutherford, Benjamin 264,283; John 178,180,189(2),195; Mr. 283
Rutledge, Mr. 46; William 71,73, 192,194,202(2),226,287,306,310 312,313(2),314; Wm. 276,305, 314
Rutten, Lanson 165
Rutter, Ferdinand 306; Mr. 49
Rybolt, Michael 173
Ryland, John 15
Ryley, Joel 292; John 296
Ryon, William 101
Sacket, Aaron 112,117
Sackett, Aaron 133,150,165; Cyrus 33; Elizabeth 307
Saddle tree maker 130,279
Saddler, William 288; Wm. 284
Saddlers 14,18,22,32,33,49,54,64, 67,75,79,81,83,89,90,93,118, 122,124,144,145,146,148,151, 155,161,168,190,263,272,285, 294
Sadler, Jacob 243
Safford, R. 90,204; Robert 192, 204,205,207,303
Safrington, James 209
Sage, Capt. Joseph 276,293
Sager, Christian 278
Sagersa, Jacob 159
Sagerson, Robert 41,82
Sailor, W. 112
Sainders, James 267
Saldmon, Benjamin 248
Sale, John 307; Rev'd. John 245; Rev. John 312
Salem 248,278
Salem township 167,264,274,301
Salem, New Hampshire 114
Salem, Young 193
Saline township 305
Salisbury township 314
Salivan, Jerimiah 10
Sallady, Jacob 107
Saljmon, Christopher 40
Salman, Benjamin 248
Salmon, Dr. 199; Mr. 51
Salor, Jacob 142
Salt Creek 116,197,202,206,212, 227,237,241,244,245,247,250, 251,255,261,262,263,264,280, 313
Salt Lick 182,202,212,215,218,219,

221,223,227,228,231,252,264, 269
Salt Lick Creek 178,185,199,201, 210,218,220,246
Salt Lick Road 214,245,246
Salt Lick settlement 214
Salt Spring Tract 222
Salt Works 114,116,146,195,200, 202,203,205,207,209,212,215, 216,219,220,221,225,227,231, 242,253,297,299,303,313
Salt fork 238
Salt's Ferry 49
Salter, Thomas 254,256; William 48,117
Salters, John 257
Salterthwaite, William 232
Saltgarver, Jacob 234
Saltonstall, Gurdeon F. 161
Saltors, William 112
Salts, Edward 275
Saltzgarver, Jacob 264
Salyear, John 133
Salyers, John 296
Sample, Jacob 93,279,293; John 162,318
Samplers, Mr. 217
Sampson, Thomas 306
Sams, James 266; Stephen 266
Samsel, Abrm. 46
Sanders, Benjamin 292; Cyrus 315; James 313; Joel 146; John 146, 316; Paul 165,170; Simeon 95; William 60; Wm. 51
Sanderson, James 298; John R. 306,315
Sandeson, James 293
Sandford, Rev. Hector 300; Thomas 47
Sands, Joseph 306,316
Sandusky 91
Sandusky Bay 179
Sandwich 234
Sandy Island 155
Sandy Salt Works 308
Sanford, Col. Thomas 122; Gen. Thomas 264; Hector 240,310; Lawrence 117; Rev. Hector 306,316; Thomas 45,88
Sankey, Thomas 51,63,168
Santee, George 284; Samuel 274, 302
Santer, George 296
Sapington, James 219
Saratoga County, N.Y. 65
Sargeant, James 293; Mr. 33,38, 148; William 22; Winthrop 134
Sargent, Col. 35; Eli 245,275,283, 288; George 273,283,288; Gov. Winthrop 6; Hon. Winthrop 11, 21; James 84,86,111,131,212, 222,238; John 190,292; Rev. Mr. 79; Samuel 74; Silas 158; Snowden 218,245,289; William 283; Winthrop 2,6,7(3),8,9(4),22 24,25,26,27,40,41,72(2),183,206 207(2)
Sarjent, Rev. Mr. 65
Sarky, Thomas 70
Satterthwaite, Joseph W. 317
Satts, Mary 271
Saum, Frederick 302(2)
Saunders, Col. Robert 190; Nathaniel 141; Paul 176; Simeon 86; Thos. 28
Savary, J. 225; John 234
Saw mills 29,155,166,186,190,278
Sawyers 81,289
Sawyer, Joseph 112; William 111
Sawyers, Capt. 143; Joseph 103; William 108

Saxon, Andrew 300
Saxton, J.W. 307
Sayer, John 19
Sayers, David 241,272; Lemuel 206,207,218,264,287
Saylor, Elizabeth 231; Jacob 179; John 209; Jonathan 234
Sayman, Isaac 209
Sayre, Benjamin 117; Daniel 271; Ezekial 16; Ezekiel 18; Levi 16,18
Sayres, Mary 153; Noah 154
Sayrs, Calvin 122; David 287; Sarah 37
Scannel, Timothy 10
Scannell, Timothy 10
Scantlin, Alex'r. 277
Scenk, William C. 28
Schaag, Michael 233
Schenck, Brig. Gen. W.C. 120,126, 139,156; Brig. Gen. William C. 145; Daniel 120,126,142; Gen. 117,129,130,143; Gen. W.C. 143; Gen. Wm. C. 231; General 114; John 139,227; John N.C. 103,119,209,219; Mr. 38,69,71 181; Mr. W.C. 181; O. 318; Obadiah 139,234; Obediah 304; Peter T. 161; Ralph 41; W.C. 24,29,35,41,50(3),53,61(2),66, 68,69,72,80(2),83,85,90,97,98, 99,114,117(2),156,181,199,216, 222; William 98; William C. 34,66,80(2),87(2),91,94,99,108 109,205,227,258,300,311,318; Wm. C. 81,86,88,89,90,98, 118(2),304
Schenk, Gen. 262; Mr. 37; W.C. 34
Schetler, John 117
Schieffelin, John 214; Jonathan 191,195,216; Mr. 69(2),192
Schiefflin, J. 69
Schillenger, Mr. 120
Schmelzer, Valentine 268
Schnebly, Jacob 57
Schofield, John 228; Jonathan 95
Schoolcraft, James 314
Schooley, Capt. 81; John 48
Schoolmaster 235,251
Schools 9,17,27,38,40,51,52,53,54, 55,59,62,68,73,74,77,79,81,82, 84,86,87,92,93,94,97,99,104, 105,110,113,115,124,126,128, 129,132,133,136,138,139,140, 141,142,143,144,146,148,150, 151,153,157,158,159,166,169, 172,176,178,193,194,195,197, 199,207,211,213,222,241,250, 259,266,270,286,303
Schooly, John 9,133; Wm. 7
Schoonhover, John 250
Schouten, Samuel 310
Schovley, John 117
Scioto 178,184,185,187,189,190, 192,194,195,200,201,202,203, 209,212,215,218,219,221,223, 229,231,238,239,244,254,260, 263,309
Scioto Bank Lottery 256,260,270, 273,274,276,280,283,294
Scioto Brush Creek 221,279,283, 308,318
Scioto County 91,111,126,131,164, 205,207,208,213,216,218,222, 225,226,227,230,236,238,239, 241,243,253,260,261,262,263, 266,267,272,274,276,277,278, 279,282,283,285,287,288,289, 290,291,294,295,298,299,301, 303,305,306,308,309,313,315, 318

Scioto Gazette 89,94,152,180,185, 195,202,213,219,225,235,240, 241,255,266,281,290
Scioto Lick 165
Scioto Lodge 253,266,273,280,290, 299,318
Scioto River 3,44,48,112,177,178, 179,181,182,185,186,187,189, 193,196,197,199,203,204,205, 206,207,209,211,213,215,223, 224,225,228,232,233,238,241, 242,250,255,288,289,307,314
Scioto Salt Lick 225,232,258
Scioto Salt Works 146,202,205,216 225,243,253,297,299,303
Scioto branch 228
Scioto salt lick 209,219,232
Scioto township 186,207,209,218, 253,265,266,269,272,273,274, 276,277,280,281,289,317
Scipo Creek 254
Scippo 232,266
Scippo Creek 218,237,308
Scissna, Charles 248
Scoffield, Jared 41; Joseph 82
Scofield, Elnathan 164,220,223, 252(2),281,296,315; Jared 51, 91; Mr. 164,220,304
Scogan, Aaron 142,161
Scogin, Aaron 112
Scot, George 300; John 63
Scott County, Kentucky 18,38,147 254,264
Scott, Alex. 188; Alexander 53, 147; Andrew 58,147; Capt. E. 281,293; Capt. Obediah 48; D. 262; Doct. John M. 21; Doctor 186,194,269,273; Doctor Wm. B. 78; Dr. 276,281(2); Dr. Joseph 203,229; E. 253; Edward 274; Elihu 215; Gen. 1, 4; Gen. Charles 6; George 300; Hon. Thomas 304,307; Hugh 296,306; James 87,133,137, 199(2)200,201(2),202,203,219, 253,266,269,274; John 63,66,74 206,246,257,260,265,268(2),271 275,292,296,310; Jonathan 154; Joseph 282,286(2),308; Judge 298,307,308; Maj. Gen. 1,8; Mary 275; Mathew T. 258; Michael 137,142; Miss Ann 300; Miss Jane 128; Moses 316; Mr. 46,88,203; Mrs. Sarah 223; Nehemiah 265; Obadiah 23; Obediah 2; Rev. Thomas 286; Robert 316; Samuel 238; T. 166; Thomas 84(2),87,90,101, 111,131(2),135,148,149,164,186 194,195,204,205,208(2),214(2), 223,226(2),232,236,238,240(2), 242(2),246,249,250,253,259,263 266,267,298,303,316; Thos. 241; William 70,257,271,275; William C. 283,284; William M.D. 298
Scrager, Jacob 234
Screggs, Alexander 212
Scribner, John 277
Scrogg, Ebenezer 231
Scroggs, Alexander 206,228
Scudder, Aaron 151,154,158; Henry 161; Joseph 142,150,154
Scuder, Joseph 146
Seagrove, James 34
Seal Township 261,266,267,274, 278,279,289,291,295,299,308
Sealls, James 248
Seaman, Ebenezer F. 316; Ebenezer F. 307; John 99,161,168; Jonas 99; Jonathan 168; Mr. 94

Seamans, Benjamin 64; Jonas 40; Sergt. B. 65; Sergt. Benjamin 62,64
Seamer, John 158
Seamers, Sergeant John 37
Seamon, John 173; Jonathan 173
Seamons, Benjamin 61; Mr. 66
Seamore, Henry 270; Mr. 309; William 245
Searle, John 209
Searles, Daniel 108,149,163,172
Sears, Benjamin 74; David 283; Gideon 108; Simeon 148; Thomas 231
Sebree, William 137
Sebring, Robert 238
Sechrist, William 306
Second Street 89,180,220,229,268, 284,312,318
Sedam, C.R. 50(2),73,74,75,113, 117,137,168; Capt. Cornelious R. 62; Col. 86,145; Col. C.R. 102; Col. Cornelius R. 108; Cor. R. 50,100; Cornelius R 37,40,42,46,57(2),81,98,127,134 136,139,154; Cornl. R. 165; Lieut. Col. Cors. R. 93; Mr. 101
Sedwell, Levi 215
Seeds, James 296
Seeley, John W. 164
Seelize, David 206
Seels, Catharine 209
Seeman, James 111
Segler, George 283
Seightes, Hendrick 70
Seinnes, Jessee 201
Selby, George M. 214; George W. 206; Lloyd 287; Thomas 221
Selden, Roger 203,221,243
Selder, D. 50
Seldon, Saml. 290; Samuel 293
Select Council 72,93,194
Sellars, Thomas 219
Sellers, John 275; Miss Nancy 195
Sellman & Hall 56,57,62,64
Sellman, Doctor 31,39(2),73,140, 141,144,169; Doctor John 150, 151; Dr. 43,111,133; J. 50; John 33,39,50,52,56,57,64,82, 90,100,113,151,152(3),166,171
Sells, Abraham 285,298; Benjamin 192,223,255; John 177; Peter 177
Selman, Adam 284; Doctor 106; John 50
Seman, Hannah 37
Seminary 144,158
Semple, Lieut. Robert 37
Senate 101,111,116,127,130,131, 168
Senators 91,205
Senff, Micheal 283
Senss, Michaell 241
Sentz, Peter 248
Sergent, John 275
Serjeant, Winthrop 24
Serreau, Madame 18
Serring, Mr. 3; Samuel 58
Sessor's-vill 283
Settle, Francis 95,108
Seven Mile Creek 95,96,99,104, 120,137,173,212
Seventeen Stars 213
Severen, Benjamin 287
Seward, Abigail 102; Isaac 91,102; James 8,77; John 112; Mr. 113; Revd. John 275; Samuel 6,9, 1C3,165
Sewell, David 187; John 95; Joseph 310,316

Sexton, Elijah 176; Zadock 175
Seymore, William 230
Seymores, W. 237
Seymour, William 212,255; Wm. 303
Shackleford, Henry 231; John 310
Shackley, Michael 297
Shadd, David 188,190
Shadden, Isaac 188
Shade River 108,247
Shadons, Edward 182
Shaefer, Adam 302; Andrew 305
Shaffer, Jacob 299
Shagley, Michael 231
Shain, Abraham 250
Shaker settlement 174
Shalenberger, David 302,315
Shalley, John 166
Shamburgh, Capt. 37
Shamrock, James 150
Shane, Abraham 273,318; Geo. 273; George 304,314
Shaner, Peter 292
Shanklin, John 63; Lieut. Andrew 15
Shannon, Hugh 74; John 21,181; Mr. 251; Robert 303; Samuel 154; Thomas 56; William 102, 283
Shanton, Abraham 218,260
Shantz, Abrm. 46
Shaphard, James 310
Sharer, Ludiwick 165; Michael 165
Shargent, James 300,310
Sharon 254,256
Sharp, Benjamin 265; Esquire 275; Henry 275,306; J. 186; Job 221,223,234,241; John 134,164, 182,205,265,284,287,296,314; Joseph 88,130,131,200,203,220, 239; Mr. 148,164; Robert 275; Samuel 277; Squire 192; William 247
Shattrick, William 169(2)
Shautz, Michael 161
Shavley, Michael 306
Shaw & Hathaway 92
Shaw, Alban 58; Albin 58,227; Alexander 251; Capt. John 14, 16,99; Hezekiah 150,154; J.J. 255; James 215; John 58,75, 97,141,150,156,227; Joseph 315; Knoles 58; Knowles 73,74, 227; Sally 227; Samuel 183,185 215; Sarah 97; William 257,271 275,300,301,306
Shawnee 208
Shawnee Indians 34,112
Shawney Indians 94,245
Shaylor, Joseph 36,99,102; Maj. Joseph 42; Mary 36
Sheaner, Peter 275
Shearer, Christian 258; John 236, 296
Shearwook, Stephen 146
Sheeley, Henry 228,229; Jacob 219
Sheely, Henry 203
Sheerer, Joseph 184(2)
Sheerman, John 161
Shees, Henry 203
Sheets, Casper 2
Shelby County 89,96
Shelby County, Kentucky 68,161, 162
Shelby, Capt. 111,225,226; Capt. David 186(2),236; Charity 255; David 83,87,189,200,201,202, 203,207,208,212,215,225,237, 238(2),250,251,252,253,260,265

290,297; Jacob 215; Mr. 131, 226
Shelbyville 61,96
Shelbyville, Kentucky 148
Shelcut, Samuel 141
Sheldon, Ebenezer 276; Thomas 60
Sheley, Henry 189
Shelkey, Kraft 239
Shelldon, Thomas 55
Shellenberger, David 243,252; Henry 243,252; Samuel 295
Shelley, Henry 258
Shelpman, Cornelius 221
Shelton, George 317; James D. 294; Thomas 293
Shenadoah County, Virginia 231
Shenar, Samual S. 218
Shenton, Abraham 316
Shepard, Samuel 310
Shephard, Dickey 238; Jacob 318
Shepherd's Town, Va. 1
Shepherd, Abraham 111,211,214, 225,231,238,253,255,284,302; Benjamin 274; D. 260; David 198,206,223,248,252,258,259, 264,266,276(2),277,278,299, 309; George 103; Jacob 204, 226,292,296,316; John 274; Johnathan 154; Joseph 133, 170; Maj. 277; Martha 257; Mr. 131,212,224,250,300; Nathan 251; Samane 310; Samuel 102, 133,208; Stephen 149; Thomas 89,106,108,198;William103,169
Shepherds-Town 198
Shepherdsville 124
Sheppard, John 313
Sherar, John 267
Sherck, John 308
Sheren, John 271
Sherer, John 205,213,219,232,245, 246,253,259,266,273,281,288, 292
Sheridan, Abraham 255
Sherlock, E. 318; Edward 120,177, 240
Sherluck, Edward 131
Sherly, Robert 290
Sherman, John 157
Sherradan, John 231
Sherraden, John 264
Sherrer, John 242,283
Sherry, Montgomery 206
Sherwood, Thomas 161
Shettrick, William 159
Shetz, Jacob 264
Shever, John 300
Shevrin, John 255
Shew, William 296
Shewmaker, Adam 261; John 308
Shibeler, George 25
Shidler, Henry 311
Shieffelin, Jonathan 191
Shields, Archibald 112; James 21, 108,253; John 180,200,238,313; Robert 287
Shiepy, George 251
Shiffelin, Jonathan 69
Shilpman, Cornelius 274
Shimer, Jesse 269
Shingles, Philip John 35
Shinn, Vincen 146
Ship yard 234
Shipman, A. 5
Shippard, John 275
Ships 258
Shipwright 161
Shiras, Lieut. 60; Lieut. Peter 54
Shireck, Jacob 267
Shirick, Jacob 300

Shirk, Andrew 61,146
Shirley, Lawrence 283,296; Robert 296,310,316
Shob, Jacob 245
Shobe, David 103; Jacob 293; Mr. 235
Shock, Michael 86
Shockley, Archibald 257; Benjamin 292,310; Charles 289(2)
Shoemaker, Capt. 60,63; Elias 85, 158,176; Jacob 258,284,285, 303; John 219
Shoemakers 7,8,24,29,37,49,59,61 104,117,134,155,158,159,167, 171,176,207,281,283,291,295, 298,299,308
Sholly, John 155
Shomaker, Capt. 55; Elias 99
Shook, George 63
Shoots, Joseph 228,307
Shoppel, Michael 255
Shoppell, Michael 237
Short, Capt. 24; James 190; John 195; Maj. Peyton 101; Payton 91; Peyton 20,39,59,74,118, 152(2),156; Stephen 247
Shots, Michael 102
Shotwell, Jasper 57
Shoub, John 296
Shoup, Jacob 284
Shoutts, Joseph 203
Shover, Simon 296
Shreave, George C. 74
Shreaves, Jonas 293
Shreve, Israel 56
Shreves, Israel 29
Shrewsbury 90,93
Shrieve, Col. Israel 70
Shroder, Otho 160
Shrom, Joseph 295
Shry, Jacob 280
Shryock, Daniel 318
Shuey, Adam 318; Martin 311
Shultate, Nicholas 283
Shultz, Jacob 266; Peter 268,297; Samuel Andrew 156
Shumar, Samuel 127
Shunkwiler, Adam 294; Daniel 294
Shuppert, Jacob 112; John 112
Shurly, Robert 288(2)
Shute, Andrew 49
Shyreigh, John 267
Sibbet, James 183
Sibbley, Solomon 60
Siberell, Nichols 292
Sibley, Mr. 30,38(2),39(3),54,69(2), 83,181(2),198,199,254; Solomon 32,37,54,56,72,78
Sibrael, Nicholas 271; Wm. 271
Sickels, Daniel 48
Sickle, George 122
Sidenbender, George 265,278,287
Sidener, William 192
Sidenor, Philip 219,291
Sidim, Moses 276
Sidwell, Levi 241,256
Siegmond, John 168
Siftin, Henry 133
Sigler, George 271
Signer, George 251
Silley, Major Jonathan 108
Sillick, John 292
Sillik, John 212; Thomas 275
Silliman (see Williman) Mr. 198; W. 91,177,204(2),205,211,220, 224,249,294,298; Wyllis 102, 207,214,218,220,303,304,311, 317
Sillman, Wm. 228
Sillyman, W. 268
Silver Creek 53,249

Silver, James 3,10,19,102,205; Jas. 17; Joseph 102
Silvers, Hon. James 158; James 33,48,61,86,87(2),91,92,186, 190,303; Jas. 29; John 207; Jos. 212; Joseph 76; Judge 108, 156; Miss Elizabeth 200; Patience 82
Silversmith 46,67,113,133,145, 157,207,219,235,248,252,253, 261,268,311
Silvester, Miss Sally 171
Simeons, Sergt. 200
Simerl, Jesse 274
Simermon, Andrew 283
Simmerman, Andrew 234; Nichols 292
Simmermon, Andrew 188; Catharine 163
Simmison, Robert 205,207
Simmons, Andrew 70; Edward 294; George 301; James 167; Michael 78; Stephen 283
Simonds, M'Kegah 102; William 48; Wm. 21
Simone, Miss Hannah 34
Simons, Armsterd 306; David 197; Miss 34
Simonton, Benjamin 163; Samuel 148,156
Simors, Abraham 267
Simpson, Abraham 137; Alban 58; Alexander 106; Allen 54; Isaac 290; Jesse 82,86,99,102; John 96,219,238; Jonathan 238,264, 277,284; Mr. 42; Oliver 310; Patrick 14; Rebecca 106; Robert 91,188
Simson, Jonathan 319
Sinclair, John 55,245
Sinet, James 297
Singelves, Wm. 191
Singer, Jacob 203; Miss Nancy 36; Thomas 272
Singing Spring 230
Singing school 250
Single, John 161
Sinkey, John 109
Sinking Spring 214,222,247,250, 263,304
Sinks, Andrew 158
Sipes, Charles 137
Sipperel, Nicholas 275
Sish, James 257
Sisk, James 221,241
Sisson, James 152
Sittle, William 63
Sittler, Isaac 109
Skeating, Mr. 12
Skeed, William 258
Skellman, Jacob 122
Skelton, Phebe 142
Skemmelpenick, Dr. John Van Grout 277
Skevington, William 171
Skidmore, Alexander 134; George 189
Skigenes, James 275
Skillinger, Daniel S. 170
Skillman, Benjamin 165; Jacob 125 146; Mary 161
Skin dressers 26,38,42,54,63,76, 122
Skinner, Abraham 55,228; Daniel 86,115,154,165; Robert 307; Thomas 127,154,161; W. 204; William 74,135,166,242(2),304, 309; Wm. 256
Skipwith, Fulwar 76
Skowden, Samuel 309
Skuttles, Joshua 310

Slaget, William 99
Slat Creek 218
Slaughter, Margert 310; Mr. 224; Philip 293; Robert 225,226; Robert F. 88,150,151,203,229, 249,250,252,278; William 300; Wm. 311
Slaven, Reuben 310
Slavery 198,199
Slaves (see Negro) 5,7,8,9,11,12,13 14,22,23,27,28,36,37,38,44,45, 48,50,52,55,56,62,63,65,67,68, 71,72,77,78,81,84,86,89,90,93, 96,97,99,101,108,116,118,121, 125,126,127,130,138,139,147, 154,158,159,160,161,162,164, 167,169,179,181,185,187,188, 189,193,194,196,197,202,203, 210,215,232,234,235,238,239, 243,254,256,257,258,260,263, 264,270,277,297,301,302,303, 307,308,314
Slayback, Solomon 306
Sled, Joshua 145; Winny 145
Slegge, Micheal 264
Slinker, Andrew 311
Slipp, Abraham 192
Slith, Henry 255
Sloan, J.W. 163; James 22,52,61, 158,300; James W. 144,158,169 John 111,131,164; Mr. 269
Sloane, John 121,131,213,214, 240(2),267,286
Slone, Bryant 89; John 127,128; William 30
Slough, Capt. 7
Slown, Mrs. Margaret 20
Sluke's Warehouse 10
Sly, George 127; Jacob 39,303
Small pox 44,111,116
Small, Andrew 65,100; Col. John 32; John 85,167; Mr. 36,37(2), 38(2),39(2)
Smalley, Andrew 276; John 127
Smallwood, Permenius 292; Walter 231
Smathy, David 260
Smawly, Andrew 248
Smiley, James 146,268,271; John 137,154,318; Thomas 275
Smith & Findlay 5,13,16,27,28, 40(2),44,47,51,53,54,55,61,67 69,75,77,86,95,102
Smith & Findley 3
Smith & Loveland's mill 230
Smith County, Tennessee 125
Smith's Mill 46,51,55,64,79,81(2), 84,86,93,98,100,104,110,140, 148
Smith's section 133
Smith, Maj. Ballard 3; A.D. 151, 167; Able 192; Abner 154; Abraham 122,216; Absolum 314; Alexander 118,144,306; Ambrose 151,255; Ambrose D. 168; Ambrose Dudley 167; Amos 43; Anthony 120,255; Archibald 269; Ballard 231; Bartholomew 27; Benjamin 193 285; Burrowes 147,159,254; Burrows 132,134,155; Capt. 33,63,77,81,86,103,114,122; Capt. James 50,51,52(4),61,68, 76,77,90,94,96,98,100,105,107, 116,119,121,123,126,127,131, 138,141; Capt. John 102; Capt. Thomas 75,91,140; Charles 42, 57,102,170,247; Christopher 144; Col. James 63,174; Constantine 161; Curtis 275, 287; Daniel 109,255; David

163,173,300,310; Doct. Robert H. 310; Eacy 107; Edward 157, 161; Elder John 99; Eliza 234; Enoch 189,216,228; Enoch B. 282,284,301,302; Euleston 316; Francis 245,317; George 86, 206,215,231(2),246,248,264,287 289; George W. 139; Henry 46, 49,180,191,277,292; Hezekiah 182,252; Hon. John 55,57, 168(2); Isaac N. 10; Israel 23, 25,117,146,166,234; Isreal 82; J. 52,81,156,180,207,215; J. Pennington 1; Jacob 87,128, 131,161,179,180,184,198,200, 201,202(2),203,206,208,234, 238(2),244,255; James 26,27(2), 28,31(3),32(2),34,35(2),38(3),39 40,41(2),42(2),43,44,47(2),48(2), 49,50(2),52(3),54,56,57,59,61, 62(3),66(3),67,69,70,72,73(3),74 75,77,86(2),87(2),92,94,97,100, 101,104,106,107,108,115,118, 119,120,122,123(2),128,130,131 136,138,142,145,146,147(2),148 153,155,163,194,203,214(3),219 225,231,238,239,242,255,289(2) 306,318; James E. 32; Jane 306; Jean 191; Jeremiah 142, 170,248; Job 238,247,310; Joel 237,238,297; John 22,23,24,26, 35(2),36(2),38,40,50(3),51,52,54 55(3),56(2),57,59(4),60(2),61, 67(2),68,69(2),79(2),80(2),81(6), 83,84,88,89,91,93(2),95,98,104, 107,108(2),117,122,125,126(2), 127,128,131,133,134,136,139, 142,145,147,149,150,151(3), 152(2),164,166,167(3),168, 171(2),172(2),180,188,199,205, 219,244,254,255,256,264,268, 273(2),275,280,281,286,301; John D. 316; John Horner 99; Joseph 150,317; Joseph T. 127; Lieut. Campbell 7; Lieut. Robert 261; Litishi 122; Lydia 165; Mahlon 122; Maj. Ballard 3,4,7; Margret 190; Martha 286; Martin 109,225; Mary 142, 258,275; Miss Sally Watkins 86; Mr. 18,37(2),38(2),39(3),40(3), 48,53,56(2),57(2),84(2),103,121, 122(2),123,126,127,136,138,150 173,181(2),190,198; Mrs. 122; Mrs. Ann 161; Mrs. Mary Ann 286; Nathan 122; Nicholas 221; Obediah 293; Oliver 209,212; Peter 48,63,70,99,300; Rev. James 86; Rev. John 19,60,76, 81,92; Rev. Mr. John 55; Rev. Peter 41,45,60,86,122; Richard 45,74; Robert 120,182,192,217, 261,267,274,286,292,318; Robert R. 271; S. 240; S.H. 161; Sampson 175; Samuel 102, 117,154,180,185,195,196,202, 203,206,209,212,216,225(2),228 234,238,245,257,292,293,296, 301,304,306,314,315; Samuel Arrow 238; Samuel H. 242,260, 272; Sandy 289; Sen. John 167, 173; Senator 167; Senator John 168; Serice 287; Seth 216,250; Sheriff 103; Sheriff James 28, 33,56,59,61,64,72,73,75,76(2), 78,80,81(2),85,87,88,91,93, 98(2),101,102,103,107,108,110, 113; Solomon 142,154,245; Squire 237; Stephen 96,112, 117,155,203,227,234,236(2),242 249,305,317; Tho. R. 152;

Thoams 306; Thomas 38,68, 80(2),82(2),83,98,100,102,110, 122,151,186,199,206,219,221, 234(2),255,271,296; Thompson 203,219,255,275; Thomson 238; Walter 146; White B. 292; William 8,10,24,55,63,74,91, 104,108,133,154,172,205,212, 225,228,234,245,248,306,311, 316,317; Wm. 303
Smithfield 257
Smyer, Michael 46
Smyth, Alexander 314; Anthony 4,7,18,19,23; George 63; Richard 298
Snake, Capt. 243
Snap, John 292
Snapp, George 267,271; John 267, 271,283
Snaveley, Micheal 264
Snead, John S. 281(2); Smith 293
Snider, Abraham 246,272; Archibald 300; Charles 296; Conrod 74; Cornelious 60; Cornelius 57,80,106,111,159,207; Daniel 310; David 146; George 144; Henry 212,283; Jacob 296,310; John 264; Peter 264,316; Richard 302
Snidner, Nicholas 245
Snieder, Cornelius 131; James 114; Mr. 108
Sniff, Michael 287
Sniter, George 313
Snodgrass & Doyle 49
Snodgrass, David 31,51,55; Mr. 48; W. 58; William 31,37,45,98,283 314; Wm. 24,33
Snoock, William 133
Snook, John 255; William 248
Snowden, Jacob 55; James 33,97, 98,99,106,303; Mr. 98
Snunk, Isaac 307
Snyder, Charles 275,310; Coonrod 66; Cornelius 228; George 292; Isaac 287; Mr. 62; Peter 292; Peter D. 15
Society of Cincinnati 75,77
Society of the Cincinnati 53,181
Solander, Francis 6,11
Solauder, Monsieur Francis 5
Solavan, Derbey 298
Soldier's run 218
Sollers, Lieut. Ignatious 189
Solomonson, Gottshalk 71
Somerville, James 300
Somes, John 237
Sommers, Mr. 170
Soney Creek 243
Songe, Peter 267
Sorden, Ellender 228
Sorency, Jacob 28
Sortridge, Col. 232,233
Sotherland, John 275
Souglar, Christian 293
South Bend 24,27,29,31,36,62,63, 121,133,144,163
South Bend Township 28,32,57,73
South, James 35(2)
Southard, Abraham 32,91; Hudson 299; Robert 301
Southgate, Richard 45
Southward, Joseph 174
Southwourth, Edward 200
Sox, Christ. 46
Spafford, Amos 111,228,262
Spain, Mr. 293
Spanglar, Michael 294
Spangle, Henry 277
Spangler, Christian 288; David 302; Mr. 222; Samuel 234

Sparhawk, Jonathan H. 91; Doctor Hubbard 86
Sparks' tavern 264
Sparks, Capt. Richard 21; Elijah 60,122; Isaac 57,102,108,112, 127,146,154; Selathel 218
Sparrow, Richard 209
Speak, Joshua 296
Spear, Rev. Mr. 188; Rev. William 53,197; Robert 260; Thomas 304,311
Spears, David 234
Speed, James 287; John 29,51
Speer, Mrs. Sally 192; Rev. William 44,181,183,192,195, 205; Richard 212; Robert 303; William 182
Speers, Richard 235
Speese, Mathias 251
Spelman, Spencer 297; Timothy 238,297
Spence, Collin 108
Spencer, Gano, Crane & Company 42,78,99
Spencer, Benjamin 12; Col. 43, 122,132; Col. Oliver 122; Col. Oliver 51,77,94; Collin 91; Ezra 94(2),101,114,131,161; Gustavus 262,268; James 315; Jesse 204,219,221,238,241,247, 252,256,258,262,268,271,276, 278,281,284,292,296,302(2), 304,307,315; Joel 133; Joseph 43,311; Mr. 198; Mr. E. 115; O.H. 40(2); O.M. 41,59,158,159 164,170,171; Oliver 8,65,78,94, 99,100,112,134; Oliver M. 78; Samuel 18,21; Samuel S. 207(2) 216,219,236,243,264; Thomas 70; William 127,286,298
Spenser, Gano, Crane & Company 90
Spenser, Jesse 242; John 304; Oliver 90
Sponsor, Anderson 162
Spicker, Nicholas 246
Spiller, Jacob 318
Spilman, Thomas 212
Spinney, Isaac 238
Spinning wheel maker 16,191,229
Spinning, Capt. Isaac 77; Ichabod 141,143(2),176; Isaac 80,83,91 143,205,303; Jonathan 137; Judge 141; Mathias 21; Matthias 85; Newton 161,176
Spotswood, William 251
Spread Eagle 238
Sprig, Sergeant 15; William 219
Sprigg township 265,274,278,284, 293,297,298,301,302,313,315, 316,319
Sprigg, Hon. William 209; Hon. Wm. 125; Judge 295,298,307; Mr. 292,307,308(2); Sergt. 18; W. 303; William 150,206,221, 228(2),234,242(2),243,264,267, 278,287,306,307(2),310(2); Wm. 213,246
Spriggs, Robert 23; William 91,205 296
Spring Farm 130,137,151
Spring Hill town 198
Spring Prairie Survey 258
Spring township 266
Spring, Nahum 151
Springer's camp 240
Springer, Capt. Uriah 2; Levi 243; Maj. Uriah 206; Nathan 311; Richard 263; Sally 211,212; Uriah 211,219,222,226(3),238, 243,312(2)

Springers' Camp 243
Springfield 25,55,62,63,66,70,74,
  82,86,90,91,95,97,100,112,115,
  116,117,121,122,125,126,127,
  129,137,138,142,144,146,148,
  149,150,152,154,156,161,165,
  218,219,222,228,229,232,241,
  246,248,273
Springfield Meeting House 80,95,
  143,145
Springfield Township 28,42,48,58,
  66,73,76,77,79,80,93,110,122,
  130,132,133,136,141,146,147,
  156,166,170,174,176,177,272,
  280,281,285,286,291,295,301,
  309,312,314
Sproat, Col. 207; E. 11,23,280;
  Earl 69(2); Ebenezer 204
Sproll, James 306
Sprong, David 117
Sproul, Robert 22
Sprowl, Hugh 146
Spugg, Samuel 300
Spurck, Peter 253,259,261,271,276
  279,290,307
Spurgeon, Elijah 294; James 200;
  Samuel 294
Spurrier, Thomas 57,137
Spyker, Jonathan 296,300
Squire, David 130;William 144,165
Squires, George 292; William 146
St. Clair County 17,36,85,121
St. Clair Township 44,58,73,77,81,
  98,110,141,163,176
St. Clair's Ville 201,214
St. Clairsville 214,220,224,256,264
  272,277,285
St. Clairville 197,198
St. Clarville 235
St. Genevieve 129
St. John's Church 152,256
St. Louis 32,119,125,140
St. Mary's River 34
St. Vincents 46
St.Clair 22
St.Clair's road 18
St.Clair, A. 39,108; Ar. 9,38,41,
  43(2),44(2),45(2),46,48,54,59(2)
  61,65,71(2),76(4),85(2),89,99,
  181(2),182(3),193,201,211;
  Arthur 2,6,11,25,59,69,73,82,
  84,87(2),88,91(2),108,147,
  162(2),191,194,199,201(2),202,
  203,309; Gen. 7,142; General
  Arthur 137; Gov. 9(3),13(3),14,
  15(2),16(5),17,19,24,28,32(2),
  36(2),43(2),45,46,50,53(3),55(2)
  56,59,61,63(2),71,74,78,79,
  85(2),94,181,182,183,190,192,
  198(2),200,261; Gov. A. 192;
  Gov. Ar. 36,38,49,54,59,69,71,
  73,84,189,190,193; Gov. Arthur
  8,12(2),13,14,15,17,30,54,55,59
  61,66(2),68,70,77,82,84,181(2),
  183,189,190,191(2),201,203;
  Mr. 59,147
St.Clear, James 291
St.John, John 43
Stable 7,12,40,46,48,65,89,90,110,
  132,149,152,169,173,183,184,
  188,190,193,194,217,224,229,
  230,233,243,244,245,255,270,
  271,281,288
Stack, John 316
Stacker, Elizabeth 224
Stackhouse, Thomas 106
Stacy, Thomas 154; Warkam 170
Stadden, Isaac 190
Stafford, Amos 109,225; John 258;
  Jonas 294
Stag Spring 45

Stage coach 124,251
Stahler, Anthony 46
Stake, William 120,157,173; Wm.
  161,165,174
Stalcup, Capt. 276; Edward 214,
  220(2),222
Stalda, John 284
Staler, William 238
Stall, Adjutant 168; Doctor 142;
  Dr. Edward H. 150; Edward
  210,219; Edward H. 102,118,
  140,151,157,172; George W.
  169; John 102,115,116(2),118,
  122,124,132,190; Lieut. G.W.
  53,60; Lieut. George W. 75;
  Mr. 152
Stallcup, Edward 222
Stalnaker, William 247
Stanberry, Elias 272; Jonas 224,
  246,273
Stanbery, Jonas 254,256
Stanbury, Solomon 120
Standfield, Jonah 216; Samuel 216
Standiford, James 28
Stanes, James 108
Stanley, Capt. 121,128,138,140,
  145,148,158,163; Capt. William
  170; Elizabeth 232; Isaac 108,
  117,163,164,167,168,170,172,
  232; James 275; Lieut. William
  68; Mr. 15,17,25,101; Peter 65;
  W. 69,75,146,148; William 7,9,
  19,21(2),42,46,47,54,61,65,70,
  72,73,74,81,82(2),88,94,95(2),
  101,108,115,118(2),119,131,
  143(2),148,155,157,164,219;
  Wm. 85,101,103,127,135,142,
  155,170; Zachariah 167
Stanly, James 262
Stansberry, Jeremiah 311
Stansbury, Silas 14; Tho. 169;
  Thomas 143; William 134
Stanton 157,303
Stanton, Richard 8,291
Stapleton, Mr. 93
Star, John 188; Peter 177; Samuel
  278
Stark, Mr. 318; Mrs. Sarah 88
Starkey, James 161; Mary 16
Starks, Samuel 292
Starling, Lyne 166
Starr, Ephraim 259; Ph. Martimer
  261
Starrett, Isaac 226
Stars, Capt. Philip Mortemer 292;
  John 257
Statehood 182,194,195,196,197,
  198
Stations 10,11,12,14,16,17,18,19,
  20,21,22,23,24,25,26,27,29,30,
  34,37,38,41,42,43,44,45,51,53,
  63,65,66,68,69,70,71,74,78,82,
  84,85,87,95,96,97,112,114,122,
  127,143,152,238,258,290,311
Staton, Reuben 127; Willaughby
  142
Staunton 139,160,165,170,235,262,
  268
Stauton 154
Stealy, Gabrial 278
Steaurt, Matthew 110
Steauthus, John 235
Stebbins, Elijah 60
Stebbons, Asaph 286
Stedgar, John 238
Stedman, Alex. 242; Alexander
  261,262
Steedman, Wm. 15
Steel, Archibald 84; George 186;
  James 161; John 66,267; Lieut.
  John 32; Mary 51; Mathias 154;

Mr. 199; Rev. John 228;
  Richard 264; Robert 86,127,
  258,271,287; Sergt. Thomas
  256; Thomas 217,256,265,274,
  278,290,294,313(2); Thos. 292;
  William 32,162,318
Steele, Adam 243(2),244,248,249;
  Archabald 52; James 211;
  Lieut. John 10; Mathew 232;
  Mrs. Eliza. 211; Richard 148;
  Robert 120,245; T. 278;
  Thomas 120,246,279
Steely, Jacob 271
Steen, Edward 150; Frederick 275
Steenbergen, Charles 231
Steenberger, Charles 260,306
Steenburgan, Charles 241
Steer, Jacob 310; Joseph 316;
  Thomas 170
Steily, John 257
Stein, Miss Jane 265; Miss Sally
  271
Steley, Gabriel 238
Stemble, Henry 8
Stenson, Thomas 170
Stephans, Jacob 150
Stephen, John 82; Richard 318
Stephens, Blackall 294; Dr. 244;
  John 266; Joseph 249; Joshua
  197; Josiah 240,244; Zachariah
  212,249
Stephenson, Aaron 180; Hugh
  211(2); James 154; John 211;
  Joseph 161; Lemuel 150;
  Marcus 211; Mills 301; William
  267; Zadock 154
Sterete, John 221
Sterfar, James 212
Stergeon, William 316
Steritt, John 252
Sterling, Ensign Henry P. 15;
  Henry P. 25; Lyne 271
Sterrat, Washington 271
Sterret, John 98,102,106; Lieut.
  James 21; Mr. 271; Thomas
  271; Washington 316; William
  253; Wm. 235
Sterrett, John 98,99; Mr. 131;
  William 276,313
Sterritt, John 97,111
Steubenville 47,135,149,229,236,
  243,265,283,302,303
Steubenville township 232
Stevens, Dr. 244; Hannah 150;
  Widow 42
Stevenson, Aaron 309; Asaah 292;
  James 122
Steveson, Capt. 15; Robert 56,57
Steward & Butler 19
Steward, Bernard 41; Hugh 271,
  275; Jacob 6,19,78,117; James
  197; Thomas 258,275; Zadoc
  112
Stewart, A. 178; Abraham 249,251
  Adam 83,127,170,275,314;
  Allen 200; Andrew 66,74,102;
  Arthur 154,190,195(2);
  Benjamin 137; Bernard 37;
  Charles A. 158,254,274; Daniel
  169; David 235; E. 224; Eliza-
  beth 300; Hugh 300; Isaac 245;
  J. 33; Jacob 19,23,70,115,127,
  136,154,171; James 255,316;
  James H. 24; John 1,51,96,109,
  111,130,225,239,252; Joseph
  41,43; Miss Margaret 300; Mrs.
  49; Nathaniel 163; O.C.B. 312;
  Pallas P. 167; Pollus P. 153;
  Robert 306,317(2); Samuel 99;
  Sargent 74; Thomas 269;
  William 11,49,60,64,267;

Wilson 316; Zadock 161; Zedoc 154
Stewer, Henry 78
Stewyer, Henry 82
Stibbins, Capt. Ziba 99; Zibe 58
Stibbons, Elijah 91
Stibings, Samuel 150
Stickell, Nicholas 292
Stickle, Nicholas 283
Stidger, John 206
Stiles, Benjamin 207
Still Water 79,153
Still house 95
Still, Oliver 283
Stille, David 165
Stilley, Peter 238
Stillwagon, William 146
Stinchcomb, David 107
Stineman, Daniel 154
Stingley, Jacob 188,251,267,280, 295
Stinson, Alexander 123,311; Elizabeth 235; James 269,276,285; Robert 235
Stip, Abraham 306
Stipp, Abraham 231,249,256,257, 258,260,308; John 264; Mr. 256
Stites, B. 50; Benjamin 20,23,25, 37,45,56,58,61,82,89,103(2),104 106,108,115,118,123,124,130, 138,140(2),166; Capt. B. 24,29; Capt. Benjamin 15; Doctor 94; Hannah 25; Hezekiah 43; John 87; Maj. 5,133,135; Maj. B. 23, 29; Maj. Benjamin 23,37,41,63, 110; Mary 25; Rachel 23,25; Richard 140; Samuel 95
Stits, Hezekiah 15
Stitt, John 153; Samuel 69,74,78, 116(2),123,134,139,153; William 69,78
Stitts, Mr. 66
Stittwell, Sarah 165
Stiver, John 161
Stockdan, Mrs. Jane 192
Stockdell's tavern 167,171(2),172
Stockdell, Simon 117; Simon M. 157,166(2),190
Stockdon, Capt. Thomas 206; David 189,192; Thomas 87,203
Stockhouse, James 146
Stockman, David 190
Stockmorton, William 192
Stockton, Anne 275; Capt. Caleb 188; David 188,198,263; John 127,225,248,292,296,300,306; Miss Ann 191; Mr. 248; Mrs. Mary 224; Rev. Philip 50; Thomas 202,217,224,225(2),250 287; William 306
Stockwell, Joseph 146,170; Michael 267; Simon 55; William 267
Stocton, Ensign William 261; John 264
Stccum, Cornelius 297
Stodard, John 249
Stoddard, George 154; James 15; James 18
Stoddart, Capt. Amos 151
Stode, Jeremiah 255
Stokely, James J. 300
Stoker, Jonathan 36
Stokes, Ann 221; Benjamin 12(2); Benjamin M. 34; John 293,311; John R. 306,310;John Richman 311; Mathew 221; Nathaniel 10,12,21
Stokesbury, John 180
Stone cutter 241,295
Stone ware manufacturer 193
Stone, Augustus 150,154; Benjamin F. 150; Christopher C. 154,161; E. 109; Ethan 116(2), 145,147,153,160(2),166,168, 176(2),209,253; Israel 188; James 248; Jonathan 181(2); Lawyer 162; Marshall 258; Mr. 81,153,160,162; Thomas 37,63, 102,170; William 86
Stone-mason 246
Stoner, Benedic 177; Phillip 91
Stony Creek 243
Stookey, Daniel 180
Stooky, Abraham 261,296
Stoops, Esquire 182
Storck, George 161
Storee, Marshal 267
Stores appear on every page of this book
Storm, Peter H. 316
Storms, Daniel 221
Story, Daniel 228; Rev. Daniel 222,229
Stothard, George 112; Thomas 283,306
Stout, Aaron 127,146,170; Abel 70; Abraham 142,154; Daniel 91,112; Hezekiah 133; John 99; Josiah 274,290; Mary 108; Philip 267,313(2); Reuben 127; Samuel D. 170; William 319
Stover, Samuel 231
Stow, Aleander 296; John 296
Strain, John 268
Strane, Elizabeth 271; John Rippy 292; Samuel 275,306; Thomas 257,271
Stratten, William 143; Wm. 153, 155
Stratton, Elias 163; Mr. 153; William 157
Straughter, Samuel 12
Strawster, Henry 257
Strayer, Adam 251
Streby, Paul 232
Streeby, Paul 208
Street, Aaron 112; Jean 161; John 112; Zadock 251
Stretchbery, John 234
Streve, Jacob 245
Strews, Thomas 314
Strickberry, John 192
Strickler, John 251
Striker, Mr. 159
Strong, Aaron 219; Areal 238; Ariel 271; Augustus 60; Capt. 78; Col. 1,2,68; Col. David 47,75,190; Daniel 209,304; David 1; Doctor 5; Elijah 75; Gilbert 242; Horatio 209; James 316; Jerod 231; Lieut. Aug't. 86; Lieut. Col. D. 5,50, 60; Lieut. Col. David 47,54,55, 67; Lt. Col. D. 26; Nestern 41; Noah 86,133,228,238; Oliver 206,209,212; Orasha 186,219; Reuben 215,219; Ruben 228, 231,238,283
Strother, George 227; Mr. 219; Robert 221; W.S.T. 219
Stroud, Jesse 245
Stroup, Jacob 43; Michael 251
Strouse, Jacob 200,284,292
Strouser, Henry 264
Strout, Anthony 206
Struthers, Alex. 224
Stuart's Crossings 271
Stuart, Arthur 193; Bernard 45; C.A. 240; Ch. A. 281; Jacob 24,117; James 195; Jean 122; P.P. 61,66; Pallas P. 111;
Pallus P. 128,168; Robert 316; Samuel 108; William 33; Wm. 52
Stubbs, Miss Ann 295; Mr. 79; Mr. 87; Nathan 150; Rev. Robert 45,86,154,160; Robert 45,84, 87,92,104,115,126,144,155; William 260,315
Stubeley, Isaac 55
Stubenville 242
Studdert, George 173
Studeybaker, Mr. 220
Stull, Daniel 222; Martin 233
Stumb, Mr. 245
Stump, Abraham 300; John 285, 316; William 128,245,307(2)
Stunbergin, Charles 228
Sturgeon, Peter 180; Robert 290; Thomas 198; William 203,252
Sturgon, Thomas 194
Sturgus, Isaac 150
Sturm, Peter 296
Stuthard, John 300
Stutson, Oliver 122,127
Stutzman, Nicholas 221
Suck, John 285
Suel, Timothy 122
Sugar Creek 33,66,74,82,107
Suggett, Rev. James 264
Sukey, Andrew 209
Sulavan, Patrick 10
Sulivan, Henry 137
Sulivance, James 257
Sulivin, Darby 290
Sullavan, Aaron 264
Sullavent, Henry 215
Sullivan, Aaron 228,255; Amelia 99; Daniel 13; Darby 274; David 258; Henry 117; William 37,60
Sullivant, Henry 127,165; Lucas 56,179(2),180,183,184,188,192, 194,197,200,212,219,224,228, 231,234,280,288,293,297,315
Sulliven, James 310
Summer, Bowten 293
Summers, Harden 255; Lewis 275, 300; Mr. 170; Salem Harden 251
Summerville, James 306
Sumner County, Tennessee 121, 215
Sumner, Boawter 245
Sumners, Simeon 226
Sump, William 108
Sumption, C. 267
Sun fish 234
Sun-fish Creek 218,291
Sunberry township 297,318
Sunbury township 283
Sunderland, John 23; Peter 201
Sunfish 203,223,244,250,257,267, 274,283,286,289
Sunfish Creek 218,231,239,241,286 299,309,315
Suppan, Joseph 221
Supporter 173,278,280,283
Supreme Court 139,140,213,246, 248,249,253,258,259,262,263, 304,307,311
Surry County, Virginia 187
Surveyor 1,4,9,18,19,136,159, 166,191,206,221,222,225,231, 299
Sutherland & Brown 75,93,94,99, 103,155,172,175
Sutherland, John 168; Mr. 150; William 251
Sutlers 4
Sutton, Benjamin 218; David 50,58 72,73,79(2),87,134,140(2),141,

374

144(2),150,207; Isaiah 25; James 28,42; Maj. David 37,51 102; Stephen 58; William 147
Swadner, Adam 117
Swain, John 241
Swaine, Ensign Thomas 21; Lieut. William 75
Swallow, Erreminah 161; Isaac 150
Swan, Caleb 10,18,23; Gen. J. 190; James 32; John 219,251,264, 299; Robert 170
Swanger, Isaac 247
Swarts, Abraham 275,296
Swartwout, Mr. 151
Swartz, Abraham D. 306
Swatselby, Abraham 150
Swayne, Joseph 219,231,234
Swearengen, Thomas V. 315
Swearingan, Samuel 275
Swearingen's mill 197,207
Swearingen, Isaac 8,102; Joseph 152,206,256; Lieut. James 117; Samuel 299,312,317; T.V. 194, 198,201; Thomas 202; Thomas Van 218; Thos. V. 179
Swearingin, Isaac 37,98,99; Isaac S. 97; Mr. 98
Swearringame, Joseph 248
Sweat, John 169
Sweeney, Thomas 91
Sweet, Mr. 165
Swelt, Stephen 66
Sweney, James 51; Mr. 224; Rev. Thomas W. 311; William 46
Sweringen, Joseph 296
Swift, John 46
Swigard, Daniel 190,191
Swim, Leazelyear 305
Swinehart, Adam 111,304; Anthony 209,307; Gabriel 111; Peter 304; Sally 111
Swineheart, Anthony 248; John 311
Swing, Mr. 172; S. 171; Samuel 170,173
Swingle, George 122
Swinney, Thomas 306
Swisher, William 167; Wm. 166
Swiss Settlement 137
Sycamore 71,108,112,124,126,129, 132,146,149,150,161,165
Sycamore Creek 29,30,44,62,63
Sycamore Street 1,47,89,129,144, 145,152,157,176
Sycamore township 167
Symes, Daniel 19,273
Symme, Judge 20,29
Symmes' patent 118
Symmes' purchase 143,233
Symmes, Capt. 81,96; Capt. Daniel 68,98; Celadon 58,134, 190,207,213; Celedon 242; Charles 293; D. 37; Dan. 11,61; Daniel 7(2),11,14,16,17,21,22, 25(2),26,27,28,40(2),41,44,51, 53(2),56,61(2),70,77,86(2),87(2) 88,89,94,95(2),97,98(2),99,100, 103,104,106,110,111,113,114, 115,117,118(3),120(2),121, 123(3),124,125(3),127,128,150, 151(2),153,155,166(2),168,169, 171(2),173(3),177,183,186(2), 193,213,214,216,222,227,229(3) 267,269,286,291,304,311,318; Ensign Celadon 9; Gen. Daniel 217; Hon. Daniel 242,255; Hon. J.C. 59; Hon. John C. 33; Hon. John Cleves 9,19,61,186,190(2) J.C. 76,80,90(2),233; Jeremiah 318; John C. 10,17(2),40,42,50, 51(2),55,57,60,63,67(2),70,71,

72(2),74,75,77,79,80,81(3),83, 90,100(2),101,122,145,159, 160(2),161,168,193; John Cleve 50; John Cleves 9,14(2),19,24, 26,32,34,35(2),36(2),38(3),39(2) 43,44(3),45,48,49,51(2),52,57(2) 59,62(2),63,67(4),69(3),70(2), 76(2),77(3),78,81,82,86,87(4),88 89(2),91,94(2),97,98,99,101,102 103,104,113,115,117,122(4), 123(2),124(2),129(2),134,152, 156,159,168,191,204(2),213(2), 242; Judge 12,13,15,16(4),17,19 28(2),29,31,37,39,40,44,46,47, 48,50,51,55(3),56(2),57(2),59(2), 60(2),63,69,79,84,89,93,102,110 122,123,151(2),152,160(2),164, 168,183; Judge Daniel 141,150, 152; Judge John C. 60; Judge John Cleves 47; Lieut. Celadon 11; Lieut. Daniel 31,32,35,36; Miss 9; Miss Polly 130; Mr. 121,123,148,151,153; Mrs. 9; Qr. Master Gen. Daniel 215; Selidon 93; Sheriff Daniel 15, 16(2),23; Sheriff Danl. 17; Susan 159; Timothy 8; William 58,190; Wm. 156
Symms, Daniel 13,202; J.C. 193
Tabb, Capt. John L. 272; John L. 240,248,277,289
Tabor, Elisha 138
Tagart, John 252; Samuel 302,308
Taggart, Samuel 298
Tague, Conrad 10,73
Tailor, William 310
Tailors (see taylors) 6,63,82,151, 175,200,215,226,298
Tait, Robert 2,3,4; William 6; Wm. 2,4
Talbert, Jonathan 237
Talbot, Isham 243; John 301; N. 152; Nathan 58; Tobias 51
Talbott, Archibald 137
Taleman, Ann 23; Harmanus 15
Taliaferro, Richard 159
Talmon, Harmonious 29
Talor, Jacob 142
Tammany Society 305,307,308,309 311,314,316
Tamset, Samuel 108
Tamsett, John 120; Samuel 120
Tannahill, Adamson 183
Tanner's Creek 124
Tanner's Station 38,71,114,258
Tanner, Cotency 273; Coteney 301; Country 311(2),313; Edward 273; Tryal 232
Tanner 2,3,51,63,87,89,104,114, 117,133,162,171,203,213,215, 217,256,279,284,291
Tanners Creek 48
Tanquary, Abraham 247; William 306
Tanyards 10,11,13,36,41,45,46,73, 104,108,125,162,171,200,215, 240,312
Taply Davis 313
Tappan, Ben. 303; Benjamin 109, 195,197,213,222,225,303
Tappin, Benjamin 186
Tapscott, James 212,221
Tarascon, Brothers, Berthoud & Company 219
Tarlton 305
Tarrants, Samuel 98
Tate township 247,281
Tate, Robt. 228
Tatman, Joseph 134,164,216,241, 252,253
Tatmen, James 47; Joseph 135

Tatum, Z. 241
Taulman, John 108
Tavernkeeper 237,255
Taverns (see innkeepers, house of entertainment) 1,4,9,12,14,15, 16,17,19,25,26,27,28,29,30,32, 33,38,41,42,43,44,45,47,48,49, 52,53,54,60,62,65,66,68,71,76, 77,79,82,87,88,92,93,97,100, 102,103,104,106,107,108,111, 113,118,119,123,124,125,129, 130,132,136,138,140,141,143, 147,148,152,153,154,157,158, 159,162,163,167,168,169,171, 172,173,174,175,177,178,179, 182,183,187,188,190,192,194, 196,197,198,199,201,202,204, 206,208,209,210,213,214,219, 220,222,224,226,227,228,229, 230,231,232,233,234,235,236, 237,238,239,240,241,243,245, 246,248,249,251,252,253,254, 256,257,258,259,261,262,264, 266,269,271,272,273,274,279, 281,284,286,288,289,290,294, 297,298,299,301,302,305,307, 308,315,318
Tayler, Hubbard 203; Joseph 208
Taylor's Creek 92,99,161
Taylor's Creek Station 21
Taylor's Mill 31,43,45,46,47,65,76, 193
Taylor's Station 74,78
Taylor, Amos 310; Benjamin 15; Capt. 6,276; Capt. James 12, 280,295; Col. 167,173; Col. James 167; Edmund H. 90; Geo. G. 5; George 258; H. 14; Henry 47,58,133,135,162,296; Hubbard 89; Isaac 296; Jacob 127,137; James 11,14,22,24,43, 45,88,95,134,192,195,219,231, 245,264,267,275,284,306,318; John 78,287; Jonathan 8,101, 212,214(2),232,238,245,248; Joseph 287; Louther 231; Lowther 234; Mathew 197; Matthew 206,229; Nathan 137; Peter 167(2); R. 245; Reuben 217; Rev. John 70; Revd. John 21; Robert 21,140; Sally 137; Samuel 225,287; Stephen 275; Teagle 154; Teakle 147; Tekel 150; Thomas 133; Townsand 287; William 234,310; Zachariah 238
Taylor (see Tailor) 6,11,42,62,86, 89,95,97,105,106,108,120,144, 155,157,158,159,165,172,173, 174,176,177,203,205,206,210, 217,220,245,248,253,258,294, 308,310
Taylors Mill 82,95
Taylors' Creek 76
Teabolt, Henry 67
Teachers (see schoolmaster) 30,36 43,44,52,62,67,68,70,73,74,77, 81,82,97,105,144,174,183,235, 284
Teagle, Severn 275
Teague, Conrad 65
Teal, Jacob 102,209
Teas, Moses 7; Samuel 251
Teats, Christopher 262
Tebbals, Capt. Saml. 108
Tecumseh 174
Teditner, George 301
Teeter, Samuel 208
Teeters, George 271
Tegarden, Isaac 150
Teirnan, Michael 71

Telford, David 14
Tell, Henry 228
Telliaferro, Benjamin 293
Templain, Solomon 195
Templane, John 204,226
Temple, John 17; Sarah 17
Templen, James 200
Templeton, Capt. John 91; John 70,78,86,99,112,133; Robert 182
Templin, Isaac 276; J. 215; James 221; Salmon 200; Solomon 197; Terah 266
Tench, John 293
Tennery, George F. 87,133
Tennis, John 319
Terboss, Isaac 306
Terlton 218
Terman, Benjamin 221
Terrall, John 316
Terrel, Alexander 12; John 206
Terril, John 308
Territory 55,56,59,62,71,72,76,182 183,186,188,192,193,194,195, 196,201
Terry, Robert 57,154,171; Stephen 258; William 113; Wm. 29
Terwillager, Ann 45
Terwilleger, Ann 37; Mr. 62
Teter, Daniel 289; George 289
Teters, Samuel 283
Tetrick, Joseph 147; Mary 108
Tevebaugh, John 278
Tewillegar, Anne 29
Thacher, Elisha 15
Thald, Simon 301
Tharp, Andrew 122; Capt. John 45; John 37,66(2),82,91,150; Robert 26
Tharpe, Andrew 142
Thatcher, Daniel 107; Elisha 25, 27
Theall, H. 168; Hachalia 170
Theater 66,67,69,70,72,122,128, 130,132,133,145,148,151,231, 232,271
Thespian Society 130
Theu, Daniel 32
Thevenin, Hannah Mion 230; Nicholas 230
Thew, Eliza 99
Thomas, Abraham 318; Alexander 170; Benjamin 217; Capt. 276; Charles 212; David 283; Heth 275; Isaac 102,234,274; Jacob 271,292,296; James 127; Jeremiah 271; Jesse B. 173,240 289; John 63,86,202,212,238, 248,251,253(2),275,287; Mary 301; Michael 197,203,234,292, 303; Micheal 283; Mr. 148,164, 166; Nathan G. 254; Nicholas 285; Orms 287; Philemon 212, 217,225,231; Philomon 13; Richard 128,233,235,237; Richard S. 128,133,135,141,150 164,238(3),252,253,258,303; Samuel 184,202,206,209; Thomas 285; Webster 306,310; William 82,91,94,170,207;
Thompson's tavern 318
Thompson, A. 14; Andrew 184,271; Arch'd. 251; Benjamin 219; Capt. 5(2),41; Capt. Samuel 293; Catharine 104; Charles 210,258,277,281,306,310; David 116,292,299,301,311; Edmond 117; Elias 306; Enoch 37,45,63; Ensign David 32; Henry 136; Ignatius 315; Isaac 302; Israel 256,283; J. 87,287;
James 43,69,70,91,97,98(2),99, 106,108,223,259,286,292,301, 306,312,318; Jobe 267; John 34,112,141,151,180,188,198, 200(2),212,255,271,275(2),278, 283,294,295(4),297,301,302,303 304,310,316; Jos. 212; Joseph 63,82,146,206,212,213; Judge 293; Lieut. S. 307; Miss Ann 300; Miss Susan 306; Moses 206; Mr. 104,111,217; Mrs. 116; Mrs. Fanny 283; Nimrod 258,264,271,273; Oswald 196; Oswell 212,264; Ozwald 315; Ozwell 260; Price 45,48,70; Rev. John 102,142; S. 235,248, 258; Sally 131; Samuel 1,3,9, 104; Seth 219,252,271,283; Smith 45,117,131,154; Tho. 138; Thomas 33,42,55,64,67,68, 83,110,115,116,134,135,143, 144,203,220,275,276,318; Thos. 306; Timothy 66,78; William 70,133,137(2),147,195,222,228, 295; Wm. 304
Thomson's tavern 234
Thomson, Matthew 238; Mr. 226, 236; O. 212; Price 18; Thomas 195
Thopson, Jonathan 301
Thorn township 298
Thorn, Azarres 82
Thornsburgh, Wm. 283
Thornton, Joseph 147; William 206
Thorp, William D. 239
Thrailkild, William 316
Thrall, Samuel 297
Thrdilkild, William 310
Three Islands 184
Three Mile Creek 279
Throckmorton, Ariss 232; James 99; Richard 56,64
Thruston, James 101; Mordaica 124,147; Mr. 125
Thunn, Daniel 242
Thurman, Henry 294,301,309,311, 312,316
Thursbey, Thomas 6
Thurston, Mr. 129
Thuston, Mordecai 129
Tibbals, Samuel 99
Tibbs & Graham 49
Tibbs, John 142
Tice, Henry 86; John 109
Tichnor, Jonathan 25
Tiffin Township 229,260,265,266, 268,269,288,293,294,297,303, 305,309,313,316
Tiffin's tavern 192
Tiffin, Doctor 206; Doctor E. 169; Doctor Edward 295,311; Dr. 57,172,186; Dr. E. 307; Dr. Edward 287,299; E. 69,197,209, 299,318; Edward 30,36,37,41(2) 43(3),44(2),45(2),53,54(2),56, 59(3),69,70,71,73(2),76(4),83(2) 84,85,86,87(5),88(2),89,90,94, 101,125,128(3),131(2),149,158, 168,177,178,180,181(2),182(2), 184,186,191,192,193,194(2),195 196,198(2),199,200(3),202(3), 203(3),204(4),205(2),207,213, 237,238(2),239,240,245,256,273 285,291,293,294(2),295(2),297, 302,312,313(3),314,318; Gov. 88,93,97,150,168,213,222,236, 239(2),247,250; Gov. Edward 88,94,96(2),110,131,134,148, 149(2),150,204(2),206,208(3), 209,210(2),213,214,215(2),216, 222,225,226,227(2),228,240;
Governor 122; Hon. Edward 166,268,271,286,290,299,302; J. 184,218,228,233(2),234,237, 242,258,275; Jos. 230,233; Joseph 178,180,182(2),183, 184(2),186,187,188(3),190(2), 192,193,194(2),195,196,197,200 201(3),202(2),203,206,209,210, 212,213(2),214,215,217,218,219 221,225,228,230,231,234,237, 238,242,245,255,256,262(2),264 268,271,273,276,283,288,289, 292,295,296,299,301,306(2),316 317; Mr. 36,56,167,181,198,199 280,281,315; Mrs. 93; Mrs. Mary 201
Tiley, Walter 212
Tilson, Luther 95
Timberlake, John 287
Timmans, Stephen 212
Timmens, John 260
Timmins, Baslitt 221
Timmons, Abraham 301; Elizabeth 275; George 310; James 275; John 168,242,258,260,261,271, 273,274,275(2),278,283,287; Joseph 274,290; Solomon 306; Stephen 201,203,238,259,261, 274,283,287
Timons, Leonard 316; Stephen 236
Tin manufactory 226
Tin-plate worker 251
Tinbrook, Francis 78
Tindle, Isaac 283
Ting, Thomas 255
Tingle, Jedidiah 18
Tingly, Jacob 66
Tinsmith 83,89,108,120,272,289
Tipton, Joseph 231,238
Tisdale, Elijah 15
Tittle, Jacob 288
Titus, Philip 108
Titus, Timothy 117
Tivebough, Solomon 269
Toby-town 209,214
Tod, George 109,131,150,194,225 246,256,278,283(2),303,307, 310; Hon. Geo. 306; Judge 267, 283(2),284(4),298; Judge George 282; Mr. 307,308(2); Samuel 292,301
Todd's Fork 98,106,140,187
Todd, Gen. 6; Geo. 78; George 73,177; Hon. Thomas 264; James 133; John 63,275; Judge 268,296; Margarat 91; Miss Margaret 86; Mr. 71,131,177; Owen 57,78; Robert 80,140; Samuel 272,296; Thomas 166, 283
Todds Fork 95
Todhunter, Isaac 313; John 234, 313; Richard 306
Tolbert, John 296
Tomason, James 267
Tomb, Mathew 304
Tomling, Capt. 276
Tomlinson, Hugh 316; James 242; Jesse 231; Mibeah 245; Richard 301; Thomas 264
Tompkins, Bennet 84; William 45
Tompson, John 283; Joseph 255
Tomson, Samuel 7
Toner, Edward 24; James 200
Tong, George 190
Toomy, John 99
Toons, Henry 314
Toot, David 108
Tootle, John 301
Tootte, John 221; Thoams 200
Toph, William 36,128

Tophand, Ezekiel 233
Topping, John 301; Zophan 301
Torbet, John 305
Torence, John 120
Torn, Henry 296
Tornapseed, Jacob 299
Torrence, Emmy 168,171,172;
    John 47,55,58,60,66,72,73,
    79(2),82,109,110,117,120,134,
    136,142,146,162,164,167,168,
    171; Mrs. 171; Samuel 175(2)
Torrey, Lieut. 6
Torry, Mr. 6
Tortle Creek 197
Totton, Joseph 101
Toughman, Peter 306
Toulman, Har. 110; Joseph 112
Toulmin, Harry 112,116;Judge 155
Tousard, Louis 76
Tousey, Moses 137
Tower, Abigail 137
Towles, Lieut. Henry B. 7
Townesley, John 100
Towns, Ann 288; John 288
Townsand, William 287
Townsend, Abraham 41,55; John
    311;John B. 79;William 296,310
Townsley, John 249; Robert 127,
    209; Thomas 149
Towsey, Moses 108; Thomas 108
Towsley, Robert 159
Toxell, Henry 156
Tracy, Mr. 182; Warnal 316;
    Warnel 275; William 264,275
Trant, Lawrence 294
Traughmon, John 291
Trautner, George 206
Traverse, Mercy 23; Scott 3
Travis, Amos 91; Ezra 228; Silas
    56,64; William 56,64
Traxler, E. 262
Tray, Christopher 108
Treaty of Greenville 96
Trebar, John 237
Treber, John 250
Trege, James 245
Trego, James 287,309; John 287,
    306
Tremble, William 88,178
Trenton, N.J. 73
Trexler,Emanuel 209,255;Peter 48
Tribby, John 310
Tribel, James 274; Thomas 274
Trigg, William 244,249
Trigo, John 301
Trim, John 122
Trimble, Isaac 117; James 152,256
    John 248,258,301,306,316; Maj.
    A. 297; Mrs. 314; William 203,
    290,291
Trimbly, Daniel 137
Troop of Horse 118
Troop of Light Dragoons 119,122,
    135
Trousdale, Samuel 95
Trout, John 164
Trowsdale, Nathan 74
Troxell, Joseph 78
Troy 303
Troy, Christopher 99,127
True, Martin 287; Polly 306;
    Robert 306
Truelark, Thomas 32
Truerdale, Asa 301
Truesdall, Nathan 63
Truesdell, Asa 248; Job 168
Truitt, Thomas 190
Trulock, Thomas 25
Trumbull County 48,69,84,91,109,
    131,134,164,186,195,204,205,
    207,210,213,222,224,225,227,
    228,229,230,232,235,242,245,
    246,249,252,255,258,259,261,
    265,266,278,299,303,317
Tryon, Noah 74,82,91,108,112,122
Tubbs, Asa 227; Ezra 248,255,258,
    275,287,292,310,316
Tuckahoe Indian 176
Tuckaw, Kenawa 222
Tucker's Station 11,19,20,21,22,63
    66
Tucker, Benjamin 41(2),70; Corp.
    William 1; Ephraim 70,137,150,
    161,165; George W. 108; Henry
    58,108,153,161; James 41,54;
    John 25,116,247,255,258; Miss
    Eliza 136; Nicholas 306;
    Nichols 310; Thomas Tudor 151
    William 261
Tuff, John 137
Tught, Lenard 245
Tullas, Michael 162
Tulley, Francis 316; John 12
Tullis, Aaron 99; Amos 108
Tully, Francis 310; John 319
Tumbleston, John 314
Tump, William S. 122
Tuppan, Benjamin 259
Tupper, Anselm 183; Benjamin
    115,218,286,289; Edward 66;
    Edward W. 93,143,248,297
Turk, Samuel 15
Turkey Bottom 138
Turley, John 306
Turnan, M. 316
Turner, Wadsworth & Gilkisson
    133
Turner, A. 306; Adam 203,206,225
    235,255,289,312; B. 296; Capt.
    12,74; Capt. D.E. 8; Capt. E.D.
    63; Elias 242,310; G. 3,4,5,14,
    15,17,61,83,85,87,111,113(2),
    146,148,175; Geo. 70; George
    12,14,51,56,72(2),76,78,82,83,
    95,117,146,182,193,195,203,
    209; Hon. George 4(4),12;
    James 114,122,161; John 200,
    290,293,306,314; Judge 4,13,
    15(2),16(4),21,22,122; Judge
    George 12,16; Lieut. 5(2); Mr.
    313; Samuel 294,306,311; Wal-
    ter 247; Will 8;William 188,296
Turnerville 21
Turney, Daniel 256; Henry 228,292
    Mr. 317
Turnis, John 316
Turpin, Philip 101
Turtle Creek 31,43,46,47,48,54,63,
    65,74,75,77,84,85,92,97,99,107,
    121,156,174,193
Turwan, Benjamin 200
Tuscarawa Creek 216
Tuscarawas County 293,301,303
Tuscarawas township 274,277,280,
    281,286
Tuskarawa 194,294
Tuskerora 192
Tustin, Charles 117
Tuthill, James 295
Tuttle, Arthanial 228; Ebenezar
    264; Ebenezer 242,275; Francis
    75; Soloman 228
Tway, John 70,144
Twelve Mile Creek 50,86
Twin Creek 100,106,123,130,137,
    145,161,171,197,215,218,231,
    234,238,242,251,257,258,275
Twin Township 177,236,249,255,
    263,269,271,274,276,280,284,
    295,305,311,312,313,314
Twiney, Henry 248
Twinn Creek 208
Twinney, Thomas W. 193
Two Mile Creek 234
Twrney, Henry 245
Twyman, Ruben 65
Tyger's Valley 235
Tygoard, Isaac 200
Tylee, Samuel 227
Tyler, Comfort 149; Mr. 151,167,
    168; Samuel 317; Walker 225
Tyson, Gideon 251
Ulm, Edward 277
Uncel, Frederick 150
Underwood, Alexander 287; John
    197,213; William 206
Union Inn 175
Union Township 172,193,207,210,
    217,221,222,225,236,244,255,
    258,260,261,263,268,269,276,
    277,278,279,280,281,284,286,
    288,291,294,295,298,299,301,
    303,305,306,308,309,311,312,
    313,314,315,316,317,318
Union town 248
United Brethren 301,302,303
University 115,152,153,155,156,
    157,158,159,160,162,169,172,
    176,205,206,219,223,228,239,
    256,289,299,302,303,309
Unseht, George 271
Unsel, Frederick 195
Unsell, Frederick 209
Updegrast, Nathan 84
Updigraff, Nathan 251
Urbana 249
Urbanna 272,293
Urmston, B. 194,197,233(2),234,
    270,275; Benj. 179,213,224,281
    295; Benjamin 33,87,180,183(2)
    184,185,192,194,195,198,202,
    203,217,221,224(4),226,227,
    229(2),239,241,244,251,253,
    258(2),259,270,277,279,288,
    299; Lieut. Benjamin 189; Maj.
    226,249,253,260;Maj. Benj. 227
    Major 229; Mr. 186,190,226
Urmstone, David 78
Usard, Lewis 147
Uselton, William 231
Utt, Henry 234
Utter, Samuel 146,147,148,153
Vail's Mill 112
Vail, Abraham 70,78; Benjamin
    234; David 122,
Vail, David 86,95,150,173; George
    154,173; Moses 74,318(2); Mr.
    230; Samuel 141,168; Shobal 45
    Shobal 71; Stephen 48,66,83,
    135,150(2); Steven 84
Valentine, Amos 51,82,127;
    Benjamin 41; Clark 127; Henry
    258; John 258
Valintine, Henry 270
Valton, Francis 235
Vameyes, Cornelius 32
Van-Eaton, John 47
Van-Hook, Benjamin 112
Van-Horn's Mill 112,132
Van-Horn, Mr. 148,153
Van-Horne, Rev. William 113
Van-Ness, James 122
Van-Sickle, Abraham 112
VanBlaricum, Garret 42
VanBlarracom, David 142
VanCleve, B. 77,133(2),139;
    Benjamin 130,144(2),191
VanCounty, Jacob 219
VanCourtright, Abraham 298
VanDyke, Dominieus 154
VanGrundy, Joseph 189
VanGundy, Christian 252;John 283
VanHook, B. 20; Benj. 12,93; Ben-

jamin 70,100,103; Samuel 291
VanHorn's Mill 108,112,132
VanHorn, Col. Isaac 293; Ezekiel 304; Gerret 305; Isaac 288; Joseph 137,138,153,154,158
VanHorne's mill 104,110
VanHorne, Jos. 157; Joseph 136, 157,159(2)
VanKamp, John 13
VanMatre, Joseph 228
VanMetre, Daniel 315
VanNest, Garut 171
VanNice, John 75
VanNuise, Isaac 73
VanNuiss, Isaac 194
VanNuys & Best 145
VanNuys, Cornelius 57,70; Isaac 31,74,75(2),85,113,120,124,157; John 33,34,173,286
VanNyees & Smith 18
VanRenssalar, Capt. 7
VanSwearingen, Thomas 218
VanWinkel, Moses 288
VanWinkle, Moses 273; William 95
Vanasdol, John 152
Vanblaricum, Garret 78
Vanblarigan, John 32
Vance & Dill 86,94,100,102(2),105, 106
Vance's Settlement 33,92
Vance, Alexander 238; Capt. 49,52 53,55,60(2),66,142(2),143; Capt. S. 159; Capt. Samuel C. 61; Col. 199; Col. David 197; Dav. 251; David 34,91,166,192, 200,205,255; George 216,296; John 51,58,74; Joseph 35,207, 223,250; Joseph C. 98,108,211, 249; Mr. 10,36,37,39,69,181; Robert 184; S.C. 269; Sam. C. 147; Saml. C. 116; Samuel 169; Samuel C. 72,75,80,89,94,95, 103,119,124(3),131,132,135,139 254,270,276,277,280,288; William 88,111,164,203,265, 299; Wm. 168,222
Vancent, Anthony 18
Vanclerveer, Andrew 108
Vancleve, B. 80,83; Benjamin 58, 156
Vandeburg, Henry 34
Vandement, John 271,283
VanderBurg, H. 41
VanderBurgh, H. 36,41,43(2),44(2), 45(2),46,198,298; Henry 54,56, 181,183
VanderVeer, Arthur 86
Vanderberg, Mr. 36
Vanderburgh, H. 89; Judge Henry 14; Maj. 199
Vanderford, Eli 271
Vandermont, John 296
Vanderveere, Arthur 91
Vandervort, Jonah 166; Miss Susannah 311
Vandevert, Jonah 158,163
Vandivert, Jonah 168
Vandivont, Jonah 173
Vandmark, Daniel 308
Vandyke, T.J. 15
Vanest, Garet 102
Vangelder, David 147
Vangilder, David 142,150,161
Vangundy, Joseph 307
Vanhook, B. 9; Isaac 10; Samuel 272
Vanhorn's Mill 108,109,126
Vanhorn, John 182; Joseph 117, 126(2),150,155,157,158,187
Vanhorne's mill 109
Vanhorne, Isaac 166

Vankerk, Barnet 242
Vankirk, Barnet 245,287
Vanlard, Joseph 232
Vanmater, Isaac 271; Joseph 82
Vanmatre, Absolem 228; Elizabeth 228; Isaac 42; John 258,271; Joseph 78
Vanmeter, Dan. 199; Daniel 205, 207; Henry 204,221,245,316; Isaac 127,188,229,251,286; John 221; Joseph 192
Vanmeters, Jos. 249
Vanmetre, Abraham 306; Henry 206; Isaac 32; John 183,267; Morgan 301
Vanness, Garret 175; Mr. 169
Vannest, George 51; Mr. 96
Vannice, Ensign Garret 9
Vanorsdall, Cornelius 122
Vanpelt, Benjamin 276
Vanse, Isaac 28
Vanseyte, Aaron 167
Vansickle, Abraham 91,127,162
Vansicle, Aram 184
Vansont, Garret 161
Vantilburg, John 108
Vantner, Daniel 61
Vantreece, Manuel 51
Vantrees' mill 107
Vantrees, Amanuel 55; Emanuel 60(2);Emmanuel 129;Henry 147
Vantreese, E. 80,83; Emanuel 123, 163
Vantresse, Conrod 58; Hartman 59
Vanvoorhis, Daniel 48
Vanwinkle, David 301; William 127,154
Vanwy, Burris 264
Varner, Martin 80; Samuel 277
Varnum, Judge 183; Mr. 57
Vartner, Daniel 64
Vasbender, James 242
Vashen, George 209
Vass, Canaley 291; Hannally 292
Vastine, John 315
Vattier, C. 61,85,158; Charles 56, 64,73,76,77,103(2),114(2),120, 122,128,133(3),135,138,153, 155(3),156(3),157(2),158,159, 160(2),162,172; Mr. 68,157; Mrs. 156; Pamela 156
Vaughan, John 74,78,154; Thomas 41
Vazy, William 206
Veal's Mill 92
Veal, Moses 58,127
Vellee, Cornelius 251
Velvin, George 77
Venable, Dr. Sam. M. 232
Venniman, Hugh S. 306
Verdue, Isaac 251
Verner, Martin 130
Vernon, Edward 271,275
Vernor, Alexander 302; John 147; Martin 3
Vertner, D. 164; Daniel 88,238; Mr. 178
Vesser, Samuel 226
Vestal, John 110
Vezey, William 264
Viana 250
Viers, Brice 216; Qr. Master Gen. Brice 215
Villars, Joseph 78
Vince, James 245
Vincenheller, G. 208; Jacob 240
Vincennes (see St. Vincents) 14,20, 32,36,46,75,83,85,109,110,136, 225,226,289
Vincent, Jesse 291
Vincenthiller, George 232

Vinconhaler, Jacob 301
Viner, Emanuel 205,217
Vineyard, William 120
Vining, Elam 286
Vinson, Cuthbert 267
Vinsonhaler, George 271
Vinsonhaylor, George 212
Vinsonhealter, George 258
Virdin, Isaac 292
Virgin, Brice 58(2),65
Virginia Army Lands 59,98,114, 198,210,229,242
Virginia Continental line 243
Virginia Military District 60,65, 71,183,189,191,192,240,254, 256,278,286,303
Virginia Military Tract 59,114
Visgar, Jacob 69,191,298; Mr. 39, 181
Visger, Jacob 191; Mr. 39,181
Vitiar, Charles 12
Volzetine, Amos 74
Voorhees Town 165
Voorhees, Abraham 248; Miny 30
Voorheese, Abm. 70,135; Abraham 82,99,135,147,176(2); Cornelius 82,104,124,130,131,141,150(2); Jacob 131; Minne 70; Miny 135
Voorheise, Cornelieus 110
Voorhese, Garret 57
Voorhis, Isaac 133
Vore, Isaac 27
Vorheas, Abraham 34
Vorhees, Abraham 39; Miny 39; Stephen 127
Vorheese, Abraham 38,49; Cornelius 101(2); Miney 49; Minny 101
Vorhese, Abraham 33; Garret 33
Vorris, Curtis 60; Garret 174
Vouht, John 301
Wachop, Thompson 63
Wackatomaka Creek 279
Waddle, Benjamin 292; John 189, 236,237,246,251,253,258,263, 275,276(2),281,290(2),297,300, 301; Mr. 276,281; Thomas 284; William 212
Wade, D.E. 50,108,118; David 140; David E. 10,37(2),50,59,64,72, 73,80(2),83,87,103,106,107(4), 108(4),115,117,119,129,136, 139(2),172; Jotham 140; Mary 140; Mr. 158; Thomas 161; Thomas C. 57,106
Wadsworth, E. 281; Elijah 216,222; Gen. 272,278; Jesse 216; Maj. Gen. Elijah 215,227; Mr. 133; William 230
Waggoner, Daniel 271,306; Martin 172; Philip 86; Phillip 82
Wagner, Jacob 271,292
Wagon makers 65,153,162
Wagoner, Aaron 150; Jacob 166; Maj. 271
Wainsville 104,110,212
Wait, Mr. 7
Waits, Reuben 281
Wakefield, Andrew 102,147
Wakely, Samuel 215
Walace, James 267; William 280
Waldo, Phipps 242
Waldon, Cornelius 272; Elizabeth 272
Waldren, Philip 285,301
Waldron, Francis 5
Waldsmith's Mill 52,64,65,66,81 86,89,92,94,96,98,100,103,104, 109,110,112,123,124,129,130, 146,171
Waldsmith, C. 69,79; Christian 57,

378

94,95(2),98,100,101,103,113, 119(2),130,132,139,165; Mr. 79
Wale's Man 218
Wales 194
Walgmot, David 293
Walker's mill 176
Walker's tavern 174
Walker, Benj. 34; Benjamin 143; Christopher 174,177; David 97, 110,112,122; Doct. Ezra 310; Doctor Joseph 99; Ezra 296; Horatio 309; James 86,108,133 137,248; Jno. 212; Joel 248,255 John 58,203,206,221,228,283; Joseph 32,44,58; Margaret 195; Mr. 148,271;Peter 274; Samuel 95; Thomas 287; William 96, 125,206,264; Wm. 271
Walkins, Ben. P. 316; May C. 316
Wall, Daniel 93; George 150; James 255; John 144,155,168, 169
Wallace & Ross 89
Wallace's Mill 62,63
Wallace, A. 97; Andrew 117; Ann 110; Benjamin 161; Cadwallader 279,299; Capt. 9; Col. 107; Col. John 147;David C.167,229 Dr. John C. 66; G. 3; George 51,108,125; J. 108; James 90, 206,264(2),291,292; John 37,45, 49,66,74,78,82,91,98(3),99,101, 106(2),107,126,160,188,214(2), 258,261,266(2),268,277,280; John S. 160; Jon. 251,306; Jonathan 133; Lieut. Col. John 107; Maj. John 69,81; Matthew G. 68,86,87,99,147; Mr. 160, 225; Nelly 238; Rev. Matthew G. 82,136(3),139,143,145(2), 152,164; Rev. Mr. 43(2),77,102, 135; Revd. Dr. 110; Revd. Matthew 94; Robert 167,231, 251,264,277,306; Samuel 166, 238,264,276(2); William 89,110, 189,206,217,252,265,285; William B. 134; Wm. 110,254, 290; Wm. B. 293
Wallas, James 296
Wallen, Elias 16,103,119(2),136(2); Mary 119(2)
Waller, Ashbel 127; John 228,233; Thomas 111,218,225,238
Wallere, John 9
Wallice's Mill 40
Walling, Joseph 123; William 301
Wallis & Ross 82
Wallis, James 200; John 200
Wallsmith's mill 57
Wallsmith, Christian 38
Wallsworth, William 170
Wallworth, John 91
Walnut Creek 182,212,213,217,218 233,244,248,257,267,275,280, 294,302,305
Walnut Grove 179,180,194,198
Walnut Hills 9,37,41
Walnut Plains 313
Walnut run 313
Walnut street 255
Walnut township 261,297,306
Walrond, Keziah 238
Walsmith's mill 247
Walsmith, Christian 60
Waltars, Major 127
Walten, Mr. 192
Walter, John 209,228; Thomas 10
Walters, John 274; Mr. 123; Nicholas 119
Walton, Boaz 301; Michael 316; William 151

Walworth, John 205,262
Wanesville 86
Waps, Mr. 158
Ward, Col. 222; Col. William 137; Col. William 91; Colonel 80; Corporal John 66; David 25; David L. 254,264; Isaac 63,112; James 7,230; Joel 264; John 4(2),27,122,186,236,251(2); Joseph 32; Lewis 147,161; Mary 178; Nehemiah 108; Talbott 295; Thomas 292,303, 310; Tully 242; Uzal 43; W. 83,231; William 34,80(2),82,83, 86,87(2),98(3),99,103,128,132, 217,222,230,238(2),240,252,288 306,309,310,318; Wm. 222
Wardell, T. 143; Thomas 143
Warden, John 219
Wards, John S. 261
Ware, Andrew 1; John 150; Leonard 48; Thompson 5
Wared, Corneous 21
Warehouse 229
Warfield, W. 59
Waring, Jonathan 82;R.W. 140,159
Warlick, Henry 203
Warman, Thomas J. 141
Warmsley, Isaac 251
Warner, Isaac 188,192,197,203,206 212,245,257,283,292,316; J. 270; John 301,306,311; Jude 133; L. 275; Leve 258; Levi 317; William 276
Warnstorf, Henry 264
Waron, Samuel 264
Warran, John 71
Warren 135,242,258
Warren County 91,96,97,98,99,100 103,104,105,107,108,110,111, 112,113,116,117,119,123,126, 130,131,135,136,138,139,140, 141,144,145,146,150,151,161, 164,169,174,205,207,208,216, 222,227,238,247,253,259,261, 270,303
Warren township 284
Warren, Isaac 190; John 91,278; Levi 301; Lieut. Stephen 189; Parker 251,271,296,306; Rodger 88,203; Roger 223; Samuel 267; Stephen 192; Thomas 277; William 184; Wm. 52
Warring, Jonathan 161
Warrington, Abraham 248
Warron, Humphry 310; Sally 310
Warth, John 303
Warum, Stephen 251
Warwick, Jacob 150,154,170; Rev'd. Robert 264; Rev. John 45; Rev. M. 137; Rev. Mr. 142, 170; Rev. Robert 55,63; Robert 122,150
Washbourne, Lewis 74
Washburn, Abraham 316,319; Isaac 225; Lieut. Tabor 82,201; Mr. 37,60,68,88,95,203; Perminus 302; T. 96,113,117; Tabor 39, 90,96(2),97,128,133,135
Washington 11,13,54,59,60,72,85, 108,166,185,218,219,232,245, 256,271,285,302,305,316,317
Washington City 74,132,151,186, 194,213,216,242
Washington County 23,34,40,43,69 71,84,91,111,131,143,150,164, 168,181,183,186,187,203,204, 205,212,214,216,225,227,230, 248,252,282,303,315
Washington County, Kentucky 27
Washington County, Md. 1,57,89

Washington County,Pa. 92,184,227
Washington Social Library Company 303
Washington township 54,160,167, 171,269,280,284,294,295,298
Washington, Bailey 188; Gen. George 42(2),43(2),44; George 10,20;William 264,299;Wm. 293
Washington, Kentucky 46,53,88,93 97,122,164,211,238,240,242, 253,267,270
Wasington Presbytery 174
Wason, Henry 80,145
Wasser, Abraham 274
Wasson, Henry 140; Robert 267
Wast, John 276
Watchmakers 79,108,113,120,133, 140,143,145,157,207,219,235, 248,252,253,259,261,268,270, 307
Water Street 94,172,183,201,205, 208,209,215,217,223,224,230, 231,232,235,236,240,241,245, 247,251,253,255,258,264,269, 271,288,289,290,291,293,295, 307,308,312
Waterford 187,230
Waters, Corp. James 5; Joel 306; Josephus 110; R.C. 193; Rich. C. 225; Richard Jones 72; Samuel 297; Wm. 293
Watkins, James 133; Jonathan 296; Robert 128; Thomas 310
Watrs, Sergeant William 51
Wats, Miss Sally 306
Watson, Abraham 293; Alex. 274; David 178,251; James 66,82, 301; Jesse 245,251; John 45,58, 63,74,82,148,150,231,269,283, 287,306; Robert 310; Thomas 63; Walter 287,311; William 63 171,292; William P. 276
Watsonburgh 210
Watt, James 296; John 306; Samuel 271,287,292
Watton, John 108
Watts, Col. John 245,310; James 310; John 182; Sally 292; Sergeant W. 70
Waugh, Capt. James 206; George 286; Henry 286; Jos. 221; Joseph 248,275
Wayland, Simeon 310
Wayne County 37,46,49,69,72,103, 131,181,186,191
Wayne Township 170,183,196,199, 201,207,231,236,260,264,265, 268,269,271,274,276,277,280, 281,283,285,286,288,290,295, 306,307,313,315,317
Wayne's-ville 206
Wayne, Anthony 7,23; Gen. 6; Gen. Anthony 5
Waynesville 45,48,51,66,74,78,79 95,96,98,99,100,105,107,114, 118,120,143,147,225,247
Waynesville township 171
Weacamp, David 269
Weakland, Charles 138
Weatherington, Thomas 217
Weatherinton, Jesse 221
Weathers, William 18; Wm. 15
Weaver & Martin 95,100,101,120
Weaver, A. 315; Anthony 212,292, 298; Capt. 276; Frederick 82; H. 61; Henry 11,45,58,66,70,76 87,99,110,114,115,127,133(2), 135,144(3),150,152,153,156,162 199; Littleberry 242; Peter 91, 102; Susan R. 45; Valentine 267; William 76

379

Weavers 1,64,114,183,214,252,288
Web, William 319
Webb, Aden 234; Adin 211; Benjamin 142; Clayton 127,174; Conrad 128; George 15,23; Harden C. 203; Isaac 293; John 36,58; Pleasant 313; William 154,285; Winney 277
Webster, Capt. Resin 70; Capt. Rezin 66; Hannah 211; James 197,251,283; James S. 223,236, 264,272,280,297,309,311,319; John 170,211,258,306,317; Lieut. 60; Lieut. R. 54; Resin 60; Taylor 195
Webstor, John 231
Weby, John Davis 195
Wedener, Jacob 239
Wedner, Jacob 238
Week, Moses 212
Weekly Messenger 88
Weeks, Benjamin 147
Weewn, Thomas 271
Weider, Jacob 217,219
Weight, George W. 296
Weill, Peter 147
Weimar, Daniel 245
Weir, Alexander 88; James 147
Weirick, George 51,55
Weker, William 251
Welch, Abraham 252; Benjamin 186,268; Ebenezer 286; James 292; John 138,148,149,212,233; Lieut. Aaron 212; Rev. Dr. J. 243; Rev. Samuel 252; Samuel 32,52; Valentine 228; Zachariah 285; Zecheriah 257
Well's Creek 169,238
Weller, Lodewick 122; Loudewick 127
Wells, Aaron 158; Baz. 224; Bazaleel 84,97,104,209,225,226 Bazaliel 203(2); Bazella 106(2); Bezaliel 88(2); Caleb 200;Capt. Francis 235; Capt. William 71; Ezekiel 297; G. 315; Gen. Samuel 68; Israel 297; James 207; John 301; Losen 147; Major W. 102; Mr. 2(2),109,113 162; W. 37,62,204; William 14,27,31,41,48,60,61,78,82,121, 141,166,184,203,216,222,262, 279,288; Wm. 68,256
Wellsworth, John 134
Welsh, Benjamin 252; David 276; Doctor I. 143; Doctor James 120; Dr. James 115; Drussella 283; Jacob 251; James 171,286 John 279; Mary 70; Mr. 217; Mrs. Drusilla 200; Peter 4; Samuel 63; William 312; Z. 251; Zachariah 280,295; Zacheriah 280; Zechariah 291, 301,312
Welshaunce, Abraham 301; John 301
Welshmen 112
Welton, Uni 182; Ure 301
Wentworth, Levi 233
Wentzell, William 154
Werden, Issac 238
Were, Obed 234
Wert, Asal 276; John 133
Wesson, Aaron 127
West Lancaster 190
West Union 218,235,237,286,290, 297
West, Cato 183; George 238,258; James 313; John 260,292; Peter 276; Robert 270; Thomas 138; William 184

West-fall 308
Westbrook, Joseph 279
WestenHaver, Mr. C. 192
Westend, Mary 133
Westerberger, Adam 242
Westerfield, Samuel 35(3)
Western Library Association 303
Western Oracle 266
Western Reserve 48
Western Spy 40,47,48,51,55,57,59, 62,64,66,67,72,78,79,81,85,86, 88,91,96,97,98,102,105,114,123 124,125,129,131,135,143,147, 148,149,150,156,160,163,168, 169,171,173,174,175,176,177
Western Star 154,174,222
Western Telegraphe 184
Westfall 202,203,211,212,221,223, 224,225,228,231,233,237,242, 248,249,254,255,256,257,258, 260,267
Westfall road 202,217,218,254,265
Westfall, Abel 224,286; Andrew 46 Cornelius 102,245,251; Job 133; Moses 82; Susannah 46; Thomas 82; William 58
Westhing, Moses Christ 32
Westmoreland County, Pa. 45
Weston, Stephen 174
Wetherby, Danforth 176
Wetmore, William 299; Wm. 304
Wetzel, Isaac 219
Wever, Christopher 234
Weyer, Daniel 273,283; Jacob 251
Weymer, Godfrey 317
Weyrick, Peter 317
Whaley, John 258,283
Whallan, James 74
Whallon, James 122
Whalon, James 112
Whealen, R. 14
Whealing, Robert 8
Wheat fan makers 49
Wheaton, Mr. 98; Uriah 217,260
Wheatstone 212
Wheaver, Anthony 215
Wheelen, Robert 10
Wheeler, A. 122; Aaron 91,204,205 242; Abraham 134; Aquila 147, 148,149,150,153(2),159; Aquilla 115,116,133,136; Capt. A. 160; George N. 40; I.G. 40; Jacob 86(2),97,118,151,162,173,294, 311; Levin 307; Lieut. Aquila 96,157; Miss Harriet 156; Mr. 70,155; Rhoda 151; Samuel 137 Stephen 92,117,136,151; Thomas 264
Wheeling 33,93,148,186,193,200, 201,210,243,252
Wheeling Road 194,205,211,251, 261
Wheeling, Virginia 305
Wheelwright 66,265,268
Whelan, Robert 57
Whelen 201
Wheler, Aquila 130
Wherley, Mr. 187
Whetnow, James 301
Whetsail, Isaac 301
Whetston, John 125,163
Whetstone 212,234
Whetstone Creek 216
Whetstone River 44,45,179,244
Whetstone, George 197; James George 209; John 86,101,122, 154,161,176; Rheuben 11
Whig 128,129
Whipple, Commodore 61; Elijah 142,161; John 298; Levi 166, 227; Lieut. John 55,60,75

Whisler & Wells 113
Whisler, J. 10; Jacob 113; Lieut. John 10,12
Whistler, Capt. J. 304; Capt. John 33,70,307; Lieut. John 5; Lieut. Wm. 75
Whitacre, Robert 140; William 147
Whitaker, Isaac 154; Nathaniel 127,142,147,149; William 63
Whitcomb, John 154
White & Delaplaine 121,125,130
White Oak 63
White Oak Creek 119,231,247
White River 82
White Water 34,42,44,51,52,54,70, 74,75,76,78,81,82,86,91,95,99, 100,106,112,116,117,121,122, 126,127,129,132,137,140,142, 144,153,215
White Water township 93,120,146, 161
White Woman Creek 16,277
White's Mill 55,56,57,64,65,66, 67(2),68,69,72,77,81,84,87,96, 98,100,104,110,112,145,154
White's Station 1,3,5(2),6,23,29,30, 38,42,43,44,51,53,68,69,87
White, A. 51,188; Alex. 49; Alexander 44,182,209,223,292; Baynard 266,294,316; Benjamin 131,200,224,225; Capt. 29,57, 67,81,92,104; Capt. Jacob 29(2),30,32,68,69,78; Fanny 256; Francis 78,89,134; Isaac 296; Isaiah 180; Ithamar 25; J. 50,52,180; Jacob 39,41(2),50(2) 51,52,56,57,63(2),65(2),66,67, 68,69(3),79,80,81,83,87(2),88, 93,100,106(2),108,119,121,138, 142,150,153,180,199,233,304; James 27,38,66,82,101,102,134 215,228; Jemmy 63; Jeremiah 251; John 58(2),163,170,245, 263,287,292,301; Joseph 93; Mary 45,63; Massey 55; Merriman 306; Mr. 36,69(2),108,233; Nancy 63(2); Pelatial 115; Peter 41,45,55,63,203; Providence 153; Samuel 313(2); Tarpley 264; Thomas 45,62,78, 142,154,169,190,199,203,206, 215,234,238,242,245,251,258, 271,276,278(2),279,286,292,301 311,316; Thos. 212,291; Timothy L. 72; William 71,279
Whitecomb, Anthony 165; John 165
Whitecotton, James 221
Whiteman, Benjamin 8,205,240; Brig. Gen. 243; Col. Benjamin 126; Gen. 160,262; Matthias 235
Whitenger, Frances 55
Whiteoak settlement 258
Whiteside, R. 252; Robert 270,284
Whitesides, James 264,310(2); Robert 296; William 85
Whitesmith 149
Whitestone, George 219
Whitewater 86,122,137
Whitewater River 151
Whitworth, John 114
Whiting, Elisha 265; Thomas 217, 238
Whitinger, Francis 45,91
Whitlecey, Duvern 154
Whitley, Henry 276; Lieut. William 66
Whitlock, A. 28,34,36,50,60; Ambrose 73,76; Lieut. Ambrose 75

Whitlow, Francis 316; Hugh 243; Susan 243
Whitman, Benjamin 91; George 306; Lemuel 230
Whitoath, John 234
Whitser, Isaac 277
Whitstone, John 13
Whitten, William 274,277,281,286, 294
Whitthor, William 228
Whittinger, Francis 86
Whittington, Benjamin 15
Whitton, William 280
Whitworth, J. 30,79; John 122,140; Maj. 143; Maj. John 143
Whorter, Doctor W. 150
Wiandot chiefs 94
Wiandot nation 208
Wickerham, Peter 218,301
Wickliff, Charles 23
Wickton, Jacob 242; Joseph 245
Widar, Jacob 251
Wider, Jacob 217
Widner, Jacob 206,231,292; James 283,292
Widnor, James 273
Wier, John 23
Wiger, Jacob 269
Wiggins, Thomas 292
Wilbourn, George 265
Wilcock, David 221
Wilcocks, Edward 203
Wilcox, Doctor 248,265; Peter 102; Robert 247
Wildbahn, George 245,270
Wildbrand, George 242
Wilds, Francis 161; G. 233
Wiley, Jaret 266; Jesse 266,308; John 303,306; John D. 212,282, 297; Thomas 286
Wilie, Lewis 122
Wilk, Moses 296,316
Wilkens, James 64; Thomas 306
Wilkerson, Richard 312
Wilkins, Charles 5,10,48; John 5, 10,15,33,48,178; Michael 58,66 68,142,154; Rachael 209; Richard 302; Stewart 1; Thomas 25,200,206,251,271, 301; Tolomin 137
Wilkinson, Abner 26,42,63; Brig. Gen. 1,64; Brig. Gen. James 75; Capt. 276; Doctor Joseph 60; Gen. 7(2),33,49,70,85,119, 183; Gen. James 32,117,118, 125,160,167,168; General 24; J.B. 37; James 117,244(2),249; James B. 147; Jas. 6,11; John 23,82,137; Joseph 147; Robert 272,294; Solomon 307; Thomas 41
Wilkinsonville 67,68,70,74,190
Wilkison, John 309; Joseph 309; Thomas 250
Will's Creek 71
Will, Geo. 297,302,309(2),311,314, 316,319; George 285,312,316
Willard, Luthar 238; Mr. 225; Samuel 8
Willaughbay, Leven 287
Willbourn, Mary 256
Willcocks, Edward 221; John 242
Willcox, Edward 296; Mary 263; Nancy 7; P.L. 3,7; Robert 263, 268
Willenmyre, Jacob 279
Willer, Ludwick 161
Willermy, Stephen 230
Willes, Eli 245
Willett, Maj. John 291; Samuel 182

Willey, Charles 119; Israel 51,133; J. 108; John 150,170,192; Judah 97,106,111,145,147,170, 174,175; Maj. Isreal 161; Noah 206
William & Biggerhead 205
William, Jonathan 146; Joseph 283
Williams & Moore 122
Williams' Mill 55,72,100,110,128, 131
Williams' Tavern 103,108,157
Williams, A.J. 238(2),252,253, 304(2); Abm. J. 229; Abraham 237; Abraham J. 236,256,259, 271,272,273,288; Abram J. 223; Anthoney 52; Anthony 63, 82,96,99,122,276; Anthy. 235; Benj. 309; Benjamin 119,267, 271,287,292,301,310; Capt. Joshua 136; Charity 41; Charles 274,281,286,294; Col. Thomas 267; David 9,32,41,51, 85,162; Edward 231,245,251; Eli 178; Elie 20,282; Elmer 33; Elmor 87,122,124,138; Elmore 34,43,44,92,105,106(2),108,113, 115(2),117(2),120,127,128, 136(2),143,154,163,166(2),170; Enos 135; G. 208; Gammage 301; George 74,91,108,188,190, 197,209,212,220,242,276,310; George W. 271; Hatfield 147; Henry 202,228,251; Isaac 11, 160,188,203,206,228; J. 174; Jacob 33,64,104(2),106,109, 113(2),117,126,127,128,131,135 139,141,142,157,163,171,172(2) James 142,197,200,221,279,293 298; Jesse 278; Joel 12,14,16, 27,29(2),32(2),33,35,38,41,45, 61,63,66,73,74,78(2),81,93,94, 100,103,110,119,125,128,129, 131,137(2),145,162,168,172; John 108,212,221,230,276,283, 288,298,318; John H. 62,74,75; John Logan 197; Jonathan 32, 41,60,68,73,74,75,120,126,133; Jonethan 138; Joseph 218,296; Joshua 115,117,157,158,171; Landon 316; Lawyer 250; Lieut. Elmor 122; Lieut. Elmore 118; Magdalene 85; Mars 120; Marsh 57,126; Mash 49; Mathew 301; Morgan 197; Mr. 10,13,15,131,172,175,207; Mrs. 49; Nathaniel 32,108; Obadiah 104; Obediah 197(2); R. 76; Robt. 96; Sam. 276; Saml. 291, 314,316; Samuel 24,27,41(2), 269,296; Sarah 301; T. 122(2); Thomas 8(2),14,19,26,27,38,42, 48,54(2),57,63,84,85,90,97,104, 113,116(2),117,120,123,124,135 140,158,170,271,296; William 195,260,268,302; Wm. 305; Yewel 268; Youell 182
Williamsburg 43,44,47,49,53,57,70, 78,170,176,183,194,197,207, 213,222,223,225
Williamsburgh 72,79,94,95,96,98, 100,143,144,150,155,170,171, 179,200,201,210,211,241,247
Williamsburgh township 164,303, 308,314,317
Williamson County 287
Williamson, Cornelius 271; Geo. 133,168,169,177; George 83(2) 89,90,136(2),145(2),154,159,162 173; John 150; Joseph 43,304; Miss Elizabeth 245; Mr. 79,172 Mrs. 113; Peter 311; Rev.

William 248; Samuel 276; Thomas 268,269; William 189, 242,245,271,278,285
Willian, David 228
Willias, Benjamin 310
Williby, Richard 251
Willihn, George 276
Williman, Wyllys 206
Willington, Joshua 228
Willis' Inn 172
Willis, Benjamin 18; Hannah 99, 173,216(2); Isaac 41,99,117; Mary 91; Miss Susan 164; Mr. 73,94,180(2),181(2),187(2),192, 193,194,199,204,231; Mrs. 115, 144,153,162,172; Mrs. H. 153; Mrs. Hannah 119; N. 130,131, 184,185(2),188,192,195(2),196, 205,207(2),210(2),216,217,218, 219,224,226,229,235,236,241, 251,255; Nathaniel 73,120,131, 194,205,213,214,240,255,256, 270,280,294,315; Robt. 60; Widow Lois 161; William 79
Willits, Isaac 188; Richard 292
Willkin, Phillip 305
Willman, Samuel 258
Willouby, Mrs. 240
Willoughby, Mary 230; William 251
Willow Bottom 190
Willred, Judah 51
Wills' Creek 242,277,286
Wills' Creek crossing 205
Wills, A. 49; Capt. 196; Capt. John S. 208; J.J. 49; J.S. 25; Jno. S. 226; John S. 21,23,30, 46,95,183(2),188(3),189,195, 198(2),200,201(2),206,208, 211(3),215,216,221,224,226,234 238,242,245,248,256,258,264, 294; Maj. William 200; Mr. 199; William 108
Willson's Settlement 92
Willson, Andrew 292; James 304, 310,318; Joseph 188; Peter 46; Rev. Robert 278; Robert 291; William 188,318
Willy, Judah 108,128
Wilright, John 310
Wilmington, Del. 1
Wilson's Inn 167
Wilson's Mill 218
Wilson's Settlement 81
Wilson's Tavern 236
Wilson, Abner 162; Alexander 91, 108; Andrew 55,74,108,127,128 145,283,296,316; Archibald 277; Benjamin 161,170; Brown 86,102,163; Daniel 294; David 276; Eblet 271; Elizabeth 248; Elliott 306; Francinah 127; Francis 6,8,18,19,25(2),56,111, 163; Francis H. 170; Geo. 243; George 81,221,243,248,291; Hon. William 284; Isaac 43,57, 102,113,142,144,147,165; J. 61,83,215,266; Jacob 122,149; James 66(2),76,86,91,95,145, 152,190,203,233,234,235,242, 248(2),251,268,294,304; Jane 71,193; Jas. 235; Jean 69,192; Jesse 112; John 21,51,58,71,78, 80,81,83,84,87,89,98,99,150, 154,176,199,206,209,248,291; Joseph 53,66,74,99,102,180,183 187,192,267,269,288; Joshua 138; Josiah 86,102,209; Judge 131; Lieut. John 66,74; Maj. George 72; Mary 163; Mr. 79, 80,287; Nancy 66; Nathaniel 195; Rev'd. 250; Rev. Joshua

381

176; Rev. Mr. 31,39,295,313;
Rev. Peter 33,34,40,44,50,64,
70; Rev. R. 259; Rev. Robert
234,248,270; Rev. Robt. 267;
Robert 2,5,37,101,102,108,118,
165,267; Sam. 208; Samuel 93,
96,122,133,170,191,200,212,
217,231,234,238,258,267,292;
Sarah 165,187; Spence 245;
Spencer 248; Stephen R. 87,
129; Thomas 95,109,111,163,
170,176,225,258,276; Thomas
A. 160; W. 102,191; William
3,7,10,69,74(2),144,192,206,221
255,258,260,267(2),273,274,275
283,287,301,310,315; Willian
234; Wm. 17,122
Wimp, James 291
Winans, Carman 41,63; Doctor
John C. 63; Dr. John C. 66;
Isaac 110; John 142; John C.
54,56,96,146,173; Mary 142
Winchel, Silas 297
Winchester 211
Winchester, Virginia 279
Winchil, Silas 297
Winder, James 225,250; John 223,
310
Windmills 98
Wingate, Benjamin 22; John 117,
168,171,172; Joseph 112,117,
122,142,143; Ziba 165
Winlock, Joseph 249
Winn, William S. 301
Winsenheller, Mr. 310
Winship & Willis 73,180(2),181(2),
193,194
Winship, Mr. 192,268; W. 185,271;
Winn 83,184,188,192,198,199
200,201,203,207,217,225,226,
230,234,238,249,256,270(2),277
296,301,308
Winslow, Robert 89
Winston, Maj. 5; Maj. William 61;
Maj. Wm. 21
Winters, Elisha 14,100; John 48,71
91; Miss Debby 118; Mr. 162
Winton's Mill 104,120(2)
Winton, M. 12; Mary 133; Mathew
2; Matthew 9,17,19,48,59,73,78
135,153
Wiple, L. 222
Wise, Michael 78; Sergt. John 8;
Wm. 310
Wiseman, Samuel 297
Wisenhaver, Christian 302
Wisler & Wells 111
Wisler, Henry 251,271
Wistenhafer, Jacob 306
Witham, Elder Maries 60; James
57; Morris 66,74
Witherall, James 298
Witherow, James 135
Withgott, Thomas 291
Withrow, James 258,264,292,316
Witsel, Isaac 234
Witteker & Willard 225
Wodsworth, Daniel 297
Wohrley, Henry 209
Wolcomb, Sireno 245
Wolcot, John 191; Johnson 191
Wolcott, David 197,231; Oliver 25
Woldon, James 221
Wolf Creek 115,120,139,157
Wolf, Adam 235; David 214; Elizabeth 235,316; Geo. 316; John
236,264; Lenhort 209; Peter
235; Philip 196,201,252
Wolfe, Gen. 59; David 197,248;
Leonard 94,95
Wolff, Mr. 194(2),207; Philip 197,
209,233; Rebecca 221
Wolffe, Philip 183
Wolfley, Geo. 258; Ludwick 304
Woller, Truster 262
Wolrick, Peter 142
Wolverton, John 57
Wolworth, John 242
Womsley, William 283
Wood County, Virginia 87,129,214
Wood Courthouse 199
Wood's mill 81,110
Wood, Benjamin 213(2),218,254;
Day 148,153,163; Dr. 79,110,
131; Dr. Stephen 25,124,173;
Eli 133; Elijah 84; George 195,
288; Hugh 236; J. Noble 85;
James 21,23; John 91(2),205,
261,283,298; Joseph 142,164,
204; Miss Mary 258; Mr. 148,
153,160,164,308,317; Mrs.
Mary 258; Rev. William 45,51,
71,74; Revd. Wm. 66; S. 83;
Stephen 14,16(2),19,32,80,81,
91,97,98(2),99,106(2),108,111,
117,125,126,128(2),131,152,153
155,159,164,173,174,199,214,
277,303; Titus 251,255;William
49,56,73,75(2),102,214(2); Wm.
83,91; Zachariah 258
Woodard, Wm. 171
Woodbride, Wm. 284
Woodbridge, D. 184,204; Ducley
205; Dudley 193,216,289; J.
252,256,301; John 255,256,259,
273,280,281,290,299,306,317;
Mr. 276,280; Ruffas 63; W. 282
Woodford County 183
Woodford County, Kentucky 9,52
55,65,81,96,127,133,194
Woodford Courthouse, Ky. 67
Woodland Farms 40,42,165,168
Woodrow, Andrew 269; Joseph 283
Woodruff, Demas 154,161,170;
Dennas 95; Dennes 117; Dennis
86; Elihu 127; Isaac 122; Joel
83; John 258; Mahala 170;
Matthias 154,170; Stephen 161
Woods' Mills 119
Woods' grist mill 61
Woods, Adam 99; E. 251,264,269,
279(2); Elijah 88,200,203; Hugh
180,192,242,271,306; Isaac 63;
Joel 315; John 150; Matthew
192; Micah 265,266,299; Moses
301; Mr. 61,177; Stephen 8;
William 42
Woodson, Charles 310; Mr. 28;
Samuel 112
Woodstock town 231
Woodstown 241
Woodward & Reeder 29
Woodward, Abigail 129; Augustus
B. 298; Capt. Levi 9; Daniel
55,142; Enos 25; John 150;
Joshua 133; Levi 1,5,31,32,38,
42,47,67,104,118,180; Maj.
122; Maj. Levi 82; Mrs. Jane
32; William 32,67,73,74,100,
101,125,126,129,137,143,145,
147; Wm. 174,175(2)
Woodworth, W. 78
Wool carders 140
Woolcot, David 309; Sally 204,
205(2)
Woolcott, David 272; John 204
Woolcutt, Miss Elizabeth 248
Woolf, Philip 182(2),199,271
Woollam, Daniel 310
Woolley, Anthony 143
Woolsey, Jos. 215
Wooly, John 150
Word, William 289
Work, John 188,292,316
Workman, Isaac 306; Richard 16
Worley, David 207,301,306; Henry
212; Jacob 317; Jno. 212;
Malcom 99; Sarah 207
Wormuch, Mr. 142
Worren, Silus 310
Worth, John 256; Richard 23
Worthington 152,177,222,228,231,
240,249,256,257,258,262,268,
276,293,297,301,307,308,313
Worthington Academy 169
Worthington's Mill 196,228,250,
254
Worthington's road 239
Worthington's survey 270,300
Worthington, Ann 242,292; Col.
131,150,180,192,194,196,197,
199(2),202,207(2),220,240,242,
245,251,254,262; Col. Robert
82; Col. Thomas 156,180(2),200
210,235,237,242; Gen. 261(3),
262,276,277,280,291,296,311,
313,315; Gen. T. 278,285; Gen.
Th. 287; Gen. Thomas 285,291,
312,319; Hon. Thomas 219;
Jesse 185,231; Mr. 36,37(2),
38(2),39(3),40,54,69,84(2),92,
166,176(2),177,181(2),198,314;
R. 217; Robert 182,184; Robt.
212; T. 69,70,73,76,83,90,131,
158,162,179,185,192,196,198,
204,205,218,230,234,247,250,
256,261,262,313; Thomas 47,73
84,86,87(2),91,131,138,145,
164(2),175,177,178,180,182,186
194,200,202,203(2),204(2),
205(2),240,241,249,260(2),
262(2),263(2),264,265,277,279,
293,300,304,313(3),314; Thos.
199,280; William 283
Wosh, John 306
Woulsey, Capt. William 60
Wright, Daniel 249; Eias 251; Elias
264; J. 221; Jabez 271; James
268,271,274,276(2),277,281,292
306,307; John 175,176,190,214,
269,276(2),301,315; Jonathan
247; Levin 271; Malcom 228,
264; Moses 209,310; Mr. 212,
249; Patience 308; Rev. John
221; Robert 276,308; Samuel
276; Sarah 247; Spencer 297;
Squire 239; Thomas 267,292,
306,310,316; Tubman 264;
William 281,310
Wrigley, John 122
Write, Jonathan 228
Writtenhouse, Samuel 264
Wroughtor, Leven 296
Wyalt, Nathaniel 238
Wyandott nation 208
Wyatt, Joseph 274; Nath. 302;
Nathaniel 189,242,245; William
125
Wyche, James 234
Wyckoff, Samuel 215
Wycoff, Samuel 316
Wyer, Obed 228,306
Wyeth, Joshua 174; Prentis 174
Wyly, Robert 21
Wynn, Wm. 301
Wyoff, Jediah 306
Wyokoff, Samuel 283
Wyre, Jacob 303
Wyrick, Peter 200
Wyrin, William 264
Wythe, Virginia 314
Xenia 98,108,143,144,211,294,314
Yarnall, Mordecai 251

Yarnell, Samuel 248
Yates, Benjamin 261,307; Capt. David 261,263; David 200,206, 261,295,318; Joseph 195
Yats, Benjamin 251
Yatts, David 209
Yawger, Peter 146
Yazou River 85
Yeakey, John 255; Peter 288
Yearian, Adam 219,268; Barbary 268
Yeatman's Hotel 150
Yeatman's Inn 169
Yeatman's Tavern 29,32,33,49(2), 52(2),66,71,111,118,124
Yeatman's house 126
Yeatman, G. 59,62,66,103,119,141 142,151; Griffin 17,19,26(3),27, 29,31,32,37,43,44,52,57,59,60, 61,62(2),73,75,82(3),95,100,101 111,116,118,119,120(2),121,122 129(2),130,131,135,136,137,139 142(2),144,150,154,217; Mr. 19,42,50(2),51,53,55,59,61,63, 67,68,71,72,73,93,98,119,138, 142,150,151(2),172,255
Yeats, Benjamin 258; David 258
Yellott, Geo. 238
Yellow Bud 233,237
Yellow Bud Creek 218,250,255
Yellow Medical Springs 94
Yellow Springs 124,125
Yengundy's mill 193
Yengundy, Caristian 193
Yering, David 18
Yerion, Adam 233,261
Yerkia, David 228
Yoakam, George 271
Yoakem, George 314
Yoakum, George 264
Yocas, George 251
Yocken, George 213
Yoghigany River 242
Yokum, George 268
York 160
York township 272,274
York, Abraham 127; William 315
Youart, Samuel 169
Younds, Alexander 268
Young's-Town 195
Young, Adam 268; Andrew 74,176, 195; Charles 56,72,76,83(2); David 218; Frederick 311; George 200; Harry 171; Henry 217; Jacob 316; James 161; John 89,190; Lieut. Husband 8; Morgan 286; Moses B. 108; Mr. 33,192; Patrick 221; Rev. Jacob 296; Robert 192; Samuel 269,297; Sarah 74; Stephen 5; Thomas 138,283; William 17, 276,290,307,312
Younghusband, Lieut. 8; Lieut. Isaac Pleasent 8
Youngstown 235
Youngstown township 235
Yount, Henry 318
Youtsey, Peter 140,142
Youtzer, Peter 122
Zagar, Frederick 316
Zane's Road 184,185,232,238
Zane's tract 219
Zane, E. 181; Isaac 76,94,193,208; J. 181; Joel 317; John 221,298; Jonathan 71,193(2); Mr. 237; N. 181; Noah 189,209,252; Silas 317
Zanes, Ebenezer 221
Zanesville 166,177,183,186,205, 218,220,222,227,228,232,241, 242,249,250,254,259,272,277, 280,284,285,286,288,293,298, 302,303,304,311,313,314,315, 317
Zeager, Jacob 306
Zean, Jonathan 69; Noah 69
Zehring, John 284
Zeiglar, David 157,159
Zeigler, D. 151; David 3,12,13,16, 21,28,37,50(2),52,54,61(2),71, 72,73,74,79(4),80,83,87,89, 90(2),119,121,124,134,136,150, 204,232,255; Maj. 43,48,49(3) 51,81,92,106,114,117,123,127, 136; Maj. David 4,94,156,166
Zeller, Adam 315; Andrew 258; Jacob 102; John 315(2)
Zellor, Polly 142
Zemmer, George 231
Zenia township 173
Zent, John 296(2)
Zerkins, Reuben 285(2)
Ziglar, George 288(2)
Zimmer, George 203,206
Zimmerman, Andrew 231; Frederick 296(2); Martin 209; Michael 231,271; Nicholas 268
Zimmers, George 238
Zineaurman, Micheal 251
Zorder, Isaac 301(2)
Zorder, Isaac 301
Zugler, D. 217
Zyph, William 173